Women's Lives

Multicultural Perspectives

Third Edition

Gwyn Kirk

Margo Okazawa-Rey

Boston   Burr Ridge, IL   Dubuque, IA   Madison, WI   New York   San Francisco   St. Louis
Bangkok   Bogotá   Caracas   Kuala Lumpur   Lisbon   London   Madrid   Mexico City
Milan   Montreal   New Delhi   Santiago   Seoul   Singapore   Sydney   Taipei   Toronto

Higher Education

WOMEN'S LIVES: MULTICULTURAL PERSPECTIVES, THIRD EDITION
Published by McGraw-Hill, a business unit of The McGraw-Hill Companies, Inc., 1221
Avenue of the Americas, New York, NY, 10020. Copyright © 2004 by The McGraw-Hill
Companies, Inc. All rights reserved. Previous editions © 2001, 1998 by Mayfield Publishing
Company. No part of this publication may be reproduced or distributed in any form or by
any means, or stored in a database or retrieval system, without the prior written consent
of The McGraw-Hill Companies, Inc., including, but not limited to, any network or other
electronic storage or transmission, or broadcast for distance learning.

Some ancillaries, including electronic and print components, may not be available to
customers outside the United States.

1 2 3 4 5 6 7 8 9 0 FGR/FGR 0 9 8 7 6 5 4 3

Vice president and editor-in-chief: *Thalia Dorwick*
Publisher: *Phil Butcher*
Sponsoring editor: *Sherith Pankratz*
Development editor: *Beth Kaufman*
Editorial coordinator: *Amy Shaffer*
Marketing manager: *Dan Loch*
Production services manager: *Jennifer Mills*
Production service: *Fairplay Publishing Service*
Manuscript editor: *Margaret Moore*
Art director: *Jeanne M. Schreiber*
Design coordinator: *Jean Mailander*
Cover designer: *Susan Breitbard*
Interior designer: *Carolyn Deacy*
Art manager: *Robin Mouat*
Photo researchers: *Judy Mason, Gwyn Kirk, and Margo Okazawa-Rey*
Illustrators: *Joan Carol and ColorType*
Production supervisor: *Tandra Jorgensen*

The text was set in 9/11 Palatino by ColorType and printed on acid-free 45# New Era Matte
by Quebecor World, Fairfield.

Cover image: © Jacob P. Halaska/Index Stock Imagery

The credits for this book begin on page C-1, a continuation of the copyright page.

Library of Congress Cataloging-in-Publication Data
Kirk, Gwyn.
    Women's lives : multicultural perspectives / Gwyn Kirk, Margo Okazawa-Rey.—3rd ed.
      p. cm.
    Includes bibliographical references and index.
    ISBN 0-07-282244-9
    1. Women—United States—Social conditions. 2. Women—United States—Economic
    conditions. 3. Feminism—United States. I. Okazawa-Rey, Margo. II. Title.

HQ1421.K573 2003
305.42'0973—dc21

2003046364

www.mhhe.com

To those who connect us to the past,
our mothers,
who birthed us, raised us,
taught us, inspired us, and took no nonsense from us
Edwina Davies, Kazuko Okazawa, Willa Mae Wells
and to those who connect us to the future
Charlotte Elizabeth Andrews-Briscoe
Gabrielle Raya Clancy-Humphrey
Jesse Simon Cool
Akani Kazuo Ai-Lee James
Ayize Kimani Ming Lee James
Hansoo Lim
Uma Talpade Mohanty
Camille Celestina Stovall-Ceja
Aya Sato Venet

Brief Contents

Contents

CHAPTER TWO

◆◆◆

Identities and Social Locations: Who Am I? Who Are My People?   59

READINGS

◆ **PART TWO** ◆

OUR BODIES, OURSELVES

CHAPTER THREE

Women's Bodies 111

Body Image and the Beauty Ideal 111

Resisting Beauty Stereotypes 116

Feminist Theorizing about Body Image and Beauty Ideals 118

Body Politics 119

READINGS

CHAPTER FOUR

◆◆◆

Women's Sexuality 143

CHAPTER FIVE

◆◆◆

Women's Health 173

CHAPTER SIX

◆◆◆

Violence Against Women   225

◆ PART THREE ◆

MAKING A HOME, MAKING A LIVING

CHAPTER SEVEN

◆◆◆

Relationships, Families, and Households   273

CHAPTER EIGHT

◆◆◆

Work, Wages, and Welfare   317

CHAPTER NINE

◆◆◆

Living in a Global Economy   371

The Global Factory   372

The Profit Motive   375

Consumerism, Expansionism, and Waste   375

The Myth of Progress   376

Emphasis on Immediate Costs   376

◆ PART FOUR ◆

SECURITY AND SUSTAINABILITY

CHAPTER TEN

◆◆◆

Women, Crime, and Criminalization 413

CHAPTER ELEVEN

◆◆◆

Women and the Military, War, and Peace   453

CHAPTER TWELVE

◆◆◆

Women and the Environment   491

READINGS

◆ **PART FIVE** ◆

ACTIVISM AND CHANGE

CHAPTER THIRTEEN

Creating Change: Theory, Vision, and Action 521

READINGS

Preface

An introductory course is perhaps the most challenging women's studies course to conceptualize and teach. Depending on their overall goals for the course, instructors must make difficult choices about what to include and what to leave out. Students come into the course for a variety of reasons and with a range of expectations and prior knowledge, and most will not major in women's studies. The course may fulfill a distribution requirement for them, or it may be a way of taking one women's studies course during their undergraduate education out of a personal interest to broaden their knowledge of women's lives. For women's studies majors, the course plays a very different role, offering a foundation for their area of study.

Several factors related to the wider university setting and societal context also shape women's studies. Women's studies programs continue to build their reputations in terms of academic rigor and scholarly standards. Nowadays there is increasing awareness of the difficulties of what it means for mainly White instructors to teach about the broad diversity of women's experiences in the United States. Outside the academy, a range of economic changes and government policies have made many women's lives more difficult in the United States—a loss of factory and office work as jobs continue to be moved overseas or become automated; government failure to introduce a health care system that will benefit everyone or to introduce an adequate system of child care; cuts in welfare programs; greater restriction of government support to immigrants and their families; and a dramatic increase in the number of women now incarcerated compared with fifteen years ago.

This text started out as two separate readers that we used in our classes at Antioch College (Gwyn Kirk) and San Francisco State University (Margo Okazawa-

Rey) from 1993 to 1995. Serendipitously, as it seemed at the time, we were introduced to each other by a mutual friend. We talked about our teaching and discovered many similarities in approach despite our very different institutional settings. We decided to take what we thought were the best parts of our readers and combine them into a book that would work for an introductory course.

What We Want in an Introductory Women's Studies Book

Several key issues concern us as teachers. We want to present a broad range of women's experiences to our students in terms of class, race, culture, nation, disability, age, and sexual orientation. We assume that hierarchies based on these factors create systems of disadvantage as well as systems of privilege and that women's multiple positions along these dimensions shape our life experiences in important and unique ways. Although the national discourse on race, for example, continues to be presented in Black/White terms, we want teaching materials that do justice to the diversity and complexity of race and ethnicity in this country. We also want materials that address the location of the United States in the global economic and political system. Students need to understand the economic forces that affect the availability of jobs in this country and elsewhere. They also need to understand the significance of U.S. dominance abroad in terms of language and popular culture, the power of the dollar and U.S.-based corporations, and the prevalence of the U.S. military.

In our introductory courses, we both included some discussion of theory because a basic understanding of various theoretical frameworks is a powerful tool not only for women's studies courses but also for other courses students take. Another shared concern we have is women's activism. As women's studies has become more established and professionalized, it has tended to grow away from its roots in the women's liberation movement, a trend that troubles us. As we talked about our own lives, it was clear that we both value our involvements in political movements. This activism teaches us a great deal and provides us with vital communities of like-minded people. Currently, there are many women's activist and advocacy projects across the country, but many students do not know about them. In our teaching, we make it a point to include examples of women's activism and urge students to think of themselves as people who can make a difference in their own lives and in the world around them. Much of the information that students learn in women's studies concerning the difficulties and oppression of women's lives can be discouraging. Knowing about women's activism can be empowering, even in the face of daunting realities. This knowledge reinforces the idea that current inequalities and problems are not fixed but have the potential to be changed.

Linking Individual Experiences to National and International Trends and Issues

We are both trained in sociology. We have noticed that students coming into our classes are much more familiar with psychological explanations for behavior and experience than they are with structural explanations. They invariably enjoy first-person accounts of women's experiences, but a series of stories, even wonderfully insightful stories, leaves us unsatisfied. In class, we provide a context for the various issues students study. Taking a story about a woman with cancer, for example, we add details about how many women in the United States have cancer, possible explanations for this, the effects of age, race, and class on treatment and likelihood of recovery. The overview essay for each chapter provides some broader context for the personal accounts. We've included readings that reflect the complexity of women's identities, where the authors wrote, for example, about being African American and bisexual in an integrated way. We added a section on crime and criminalization in response to the great increase in women caught up in the criminal justice system in the past fifteen years, and added a chapter on women and the environment.

Challenges for the Twenty-First Century: Security and Sustainability

We are concerned about the challenges facing women and men in the twenty-first century: challenges regarding work and livelihood, personal and family relationships, violence on many levels, and the fragile physical environment. These issues pose major questions concerning the distribution of resources, personal and social values, and the definition of security. How is our society going to provide for its people in the years to come? What are the effects of the increasing polarization between rich and poor in the United States and between rich and poor countries of the world? Genuine security—at personal, community-wide, national, and planetary levels—is a key issue for the future, and, similarly, sustainability. These themes of security and sustainability provide a wider framework for the book.

As teachers, we are concerned with students' knowledge and understanding, and beyond that, with their aspirations, hopes, and values. One of our goals for this book is to provide a series of lenses that will help students understand their own lives and the lives of others, especially women. The second goal is that, through this understanding, they will be able to participate in some way in the creation of a secure and sustainable future.

New to the Third Edition

In the second edition we added two new chapters, one on sexuality and another on violence against women. We paid more attention to the role of women in politics, in both feminist movements and electoral politics. And we made explicit acknowledgment of the fact that women's studies students include a growing number of men.

This third edition relies on the analyses, principles, and style of the first two editions, with the following important additions and changes:

- Updated statistics throughout, and new readings on marriage, parenting, women and work, welfare, AIDS, women and political activism, militarism, and ecofeminism

- Reference to Bush administration policies and legislation, the erosion of *Roe v. Wade,* Title IX, affirmative action policies, and the worsening economy

- Explicit attention to the role of media representations and popular culture in the creation of knowledge

- A new section at the end of each overview essay, titled "Finding Out More on the Web," which encourages students to explore various questions on the Internet

- Photos, cartoons, and diagrams throughout

- More poetry

- A more solid pedagogical structure for each chapter

- A new comprehensive Instructor's Resource Manual, authored by Gwyn Kirk

A number of considerations—sometimes competing and contradictory—influenced these decisions. We are committed to including established writers and lesser-known writers, and writers from a range of racial and ethnic backgrounds and with differences in ability, age, class, culture, nation of birth, and sexuality. As before, we have looked for writers who, implicitly or explicitly, integrate several levels of analysis (micro, meso, macro, and global) in their work. Teachers invariably want more theory, more history, and more research-based pieces. The students we talked with, including our own, love first-person pieces as this kind of writing helps to draw them into the more theoretical discussions. In the second edition we included more articles that give historical or theoretical accounts as a complement to the first-person writings in each chapter, recognizing that if teachers do not assign the book, students will never see it. As we searched for materials, however, we found much more theoretical work by White women than by women of color. We assume this is because there are far fewer women of color in the academy, because White women

scholars and writers have greater access to publishers, and because prevailing ideas about what theory is and what form it should take tend to exclude work by women of color. This can give the misleading impression that, aside from a few notable exceptions, women of color are not theorists. This raises the whole issue of what theory is and who can theorize, questions we take up in the first chapter. We have tried hard not to reproduce this bias in our selection, but we note this problem here to make this aspect of our process visible.

This new edition represents our best effort to balance these considerations, as we sought to provide information, analysis, and inspiration concerning the myriad daily experiences, opportunities, limitations, oppressions, hopes, joys, and satisfactions that make up U.S. women's lives.

Acknowledgments

Many people—especially our students, teachers, and friends—made it possible for us to complete the first edition of this book, and we listed them in detail there. We are grateful to everyone at Mayfield who so thoughtfully worked to put our manuscript between covers: Franklin Graham, our editor, whose confidence in our ideas never wavered and whose light hand on the steering wheel and clear sense of direction got us to this place; Julianna Scott Fein, production editor; the production team; and Jamie Fuller, copyeditor extraordinaire.

For the second edition, we were fortunate to have the support of Hamilton College as Jane Watson Irwin Co-Chairs in Women's Studies (1999–2000). Women's studies colleagues and other faculty members welcomed and supported us. Again, we recognize the Mayfield team: Serina Beauparlant, our editor; Julianna Scott Fein, production editor; the production team; and Margaret Moore, a wonderful copyeditor.

This third edition has benefited from the accumulated work, help, and support of many people who continue to sustain us. Particular thanks this time go to Sarah Wunsch and Kathy Ferguson for providing leads to new material; to Christina Leaño and Shirley Royster, who wrote specifically for this edition; and for research support provided by DataCenter, an Oakland-based nonprofit, providing research and training to grassroots social justice organizations across the country. We also appreciate the support of the Women's Leadership Institute at Mills College. We thank the feminist scholars and activists whose work we have reprinted and all those whose research and writing not only have informed our work but have shaped the field of women's studies. We appreciate the independent bookstores and small presses that keep going due to dedicated staff and loyal readers, despite the difficulties of staying afloat, especially our "local"—Modern Times in San Francisco. We also rely on other feminist publishing "institutions": *The Women's Review of Books, Ms.* and (until 2002) *Sojourner,* as well as scholarly journals, and WMST-L, ably "mastered" by Joan Korenman.

During our preparation of this edition, the world lost the talents and commitment of four remarkable public figures: June Jordan, a poet activist scholar who bridged community and academy with insight and grace; Yayori Matsui, a Japanese feminist who worked tirelessly to hold her government accountable for the atrocities against "comfort women" in World War II; Representative Patsy Mink, perhaps best known for her key role in getting Title IX into the 1972 Education Act; and Senator Paul Wellstone, who worked consistently for feminist, labor, and environmental issues. Their passing leaves enormous holes in the progressive landscape of this country and internationally. We are among the many people who found inspiration in the way they sought to live their lives according to their principles, values, and visions.

This is our first edition with McGraw-Hill. We greatly appreciate the encouragement, enthusiasm, and skills of our editor, Beth Kaufman, and the work of the entire book team: Amy Shaffer, Sherith Pankratz, Katherine Bates, Karyn Morrison, Jen Mills, Jean Mailander, and April Wells-Hayes. Once again we benefited from the insights and advice of outside reviewers:

Christina G. Bobel, University of Massachusetts, Boston
Piya Chatterjee, University of California, Riverside
Wendy A. Ho, University of California, Davis
Elizabeth Kamarck Minnich, The Union Institute and University
Molly Kerby, Western Kentucky University
Chana Kai Lee, University of Georgia
Stephanie Rodriguez, Texas Women's University
Susan Sánchez-Casal, Hamilton College
Mab Segrest, Connecticut College

Lastly, we acknowledge the importance of our friendship, deepening over these past ten years, that provides a firm foundation for our shared understandings and our work together. We continue to be inspired by the cultural work of Sweet Honey in the Rock, a national living treasure now in their thirteenth year, whose blend of music and politics touches the head, heart, and hands, and also by the "sociological imagination"—C. Wright Mills' concept—that draws on the need for complex social analysis in order to make change.

To everyone, very many thanks.

We have chosen each other
and the edge of each other's battles
the war is the same
if we lose
someday women's blood will congeal
upon a dead planet
if we win
there is no telling
we seek beyond history
for a new and more possible meeting.

—AUDRE LORDE

The Framework of This Book

To study alongside men, to have access to the same curriculum, and to be admitted to male professions were goals that dominated women's education in the United States for several generations, from the early nineteenth century on. In the late 1960s and early 1970s, however, the gendered nature of knowledge itself—with its focus on White, male, and middle-class perspectives that are assumed to be universal—was called into question by feminists.

The Focus of Women's Studies

The early 1970s saw the start of many women's studies programs across the country, building on the insights and energies of the women's liberation movement. Early courses had titles like "Women's Liberation," "The Power of Patriarchy," or "Sexist Oppression and Women's Empowerment." Texts often included mimeographed articles from feminist newsletters and pamphlets, as there was so little appropriate material in books. By contrast, women's studies is now an established field of study with an extensive body of literature and more than seven hundred programs nationwide in universities and colleges, including master's and Ph.D. programs. Women's studies gradu-

ates are employed in many fields, including law, business, publishing, health, social and human services, and education and library work (Luebke and Reilly 1995). Students report that women's studies courses are informative and empowering; they provide a perspective on one's own life and on other college courses in ways that are often life changing (Luebke and Reilly 1995; Musil 1992).

Women's studies seeks new ways of understanding—more comprehensive than those offered by traditional academic disciplines that so often view women in stereotypical ways, if at all. In addition, women's studies goes beyond description and analysis to focus on the consequences and applications of knowledge. In a women's studies class, you are encouraged to share your own experiences and to relate the readings and discussions to your own life. Women's studies courses provide data that are often absent in the rest of the curriculum. You may be challenged by this and pushed to rethink some of your assumptions about gender, your own experiences of schooling, family, and relationships, and your positions on a number of complex issues. This kind of study often evokes strong emotional reactions, as your own life may be deeply affected by issues under discussion. These aspects of women's studies have

1

given rise to criticisms that it is too "touchy-feely," more like therapy than serious study, or that it is an extended gripe session against men. We discuss these criticisms later in this introduction. Women's studies also often generates anger in students at the many forms of women's oppression, at other students' ignorance or lack of concern for this, at being female in a male-dominated world, and at the daunting nature of the issues and problems faced by women (Boxer 1998; Howe 2000).

The Framework for This Book: Collective Action for a Sustainable Future

This book is concerned with women in the United States and the rich diversity of their life experiences. We have selected readings that reflect this diversity. Each chapter also includes an overview essay to give some historical and contemporary context for the specific readings. As writers and editors, a big challenge for us has been to choose effective writings and salient facts from the vast wealth of materials available. There has been a groundswell of women's writing and publishing in the past thirty-five years, as well as a proliferation of popular and scholarly books and journals on issues of interest to women's studies students. When opinion polls, academic studies, government data, public debates, and grassroots research, available in print and through electronic media, are added to this, it is easy to be swamped with information and opposing viewpoints.

In making our selections, we have filtered this wealth of material according to a number of principles—our particular road map.

An Activist Approach

We argue that women and men in the United States face a range of serious problems in the years ahead if we are to sustain our lives, the lives of our children, and the lives of our children's children. Although some women have benefited from greater opportunities for education and wage earning, many are now working harder, or working longer hours, than their mothers did, under pressure to keep a job and to juggle their work lives with family responsibilities. In the 1980s and 1990s, a range of economic changes and government policies made many women's lives more difficult. Examples include a loss of factory and office work as jobs were moved

overseas or became automated; government failure to introduce an adequate system of child care or a health-care system that would benefit everyone; cuts in welfare; greater restriction of government support to immigrants and their families; and a dramatic increase in the number of women now incarcerated compared with the number from fifteen years ago. While the U.S. military budget consumes a massive 46 percent of federal income tax (for the fiscal year 2003), according to the War Resisters League (2002), and some states spend more public money on new jails and prisons than on higher education, countless thousands of people are homeless, inner-city schools lack basic resources, and funding for Head Start and other preschool programs is cut back. Individual women and men are personally affected by these changes and policies as they negotiate intimate relationships and family life.

We see collective action for progressive social change as a major goal of scholarly work, and thus, in the face of these economic and political trends, we take a deliberately activist approach in this book. We mention many practical projects and organizations to give students a sense of how much activist work is going on that is often not visible in the mainstream media. Throughout our discussion we emphasize the diversity of women's experiences. These differences have often divided women. We assume no easy "sisterhood" across lines of race, class, nation, age, or sexual orientation, for example, but we do believe that alliances built firmly on the recognition and understanding of such differences make collective action possible.

A Sustainable and Secure Future

We see sustainability and security as central issues for the twenty-first century. These involve questions about the distribution of wealth, both within the United States and between the rich and poor countries of the world, and about the direction of future economic development. Another concern is the rapid deterioration of the physical environment on our overburdened planet. In many chapters, security is an underlying theme. This includes the individual security of knowing who we are; having secure family relationships; living in freedom from threats, violence, or coercion; having adequate income or livelihood; and enjoying health and well-being. It also involves security for the community, the nation, and the planet, and includes issues like crime, the role of the military, and the crucial importance of the physical environment. Throughout the book we emphasize severe structural inequalities between people: women and men, White people and people of color, older people and young people, for example. We see these inequalities as a major threat to long-term security because they create literal and metaphorical walls, gates, and fences that separate people and maintain hierarchies among us. We also argue that a more sustainable future means rethinking materialism and consumerism and finding new ways to distribute wealth so that everyone has the basics of life. These issues affect not only women, of course, and are not solely the responsibility of women, but women are actively involved in community organizing and movements for economic and environmental justice in the United States and many other countries, often in greater numbers than men.

The United States in a Global Context

This is not a book about global feminism. Its focus is on the United States, but we also comment on the wider global context within which the United States operates. We recognize the racial and ethnic diversity of this country; many people in the United States were not born here and come with hopes for a better future, but they also have no illusions about inequalities in the United States. We argue that people in the United States need to understand the significance of this country's preeminence in the world, manifested culturally, through the dominance of the English language and in widespread distribution of U.S. movies, pop music, books, and magazines; economically, through the power of the dollar as an international currency and the impact of U.S.-based corporations abroad; and militarily, through the global reach of U.S. foreign policy, troops, bases, and weapons. We need to understand the significance of the globalization of the economy for people in the United States as well as throughout the world. We must understand the connections between domestic policy issues like health care, child care, and welfare, and foreign policy issues such as military expenditures and foreign aid.

Linking the Personal and the Global

Throughout the book we use the terms **micro level** (personal or individual), **meso level** (community, neighborhood, or school, for example), **macro level** (national), and **global level.** To understand people's experiences or the complexity of a particular issue, it is necessary to look at all of these levels and how they interconnect. For instance, a personal relationship between two people might be thought to operate on a micro level. However, both partners bring all of themselves to the relationship. Thus, in addition to micro-level factors such as appearance, generosity, or their determination not to repeat the mistakes of their parents' relationships, there are meso-level factors—such as their connections to people of other faiths or races—and macro-level factors—such as the obvious or hidden ways in which men or White people are privileged in this society. As editors we have made these connections in our overview essays and looked for writings that make these links between levels of analysis.

A Matrix of Oppression and Resistance

Underlying our analysis throughout the book is the concept of oppression, which we see as a group phenomenon, regardless of whether individuals in a group think they are oppressed or want to be in dominant positions. Men, as a group, are advantaged by sexism, for example, whereas women, as a group, are disadvantaged. Every form of oppression—for instance, **sexism, racism, classism, heterosexism, anti-Semitism, able-bodyism**—is rooted in our **social institutions,** such as the family, education, religion, and the media. Oppression, then, is systemic, and it is systematic. It is used consistently by one group of people—those who are dominant in this society—to rule, control, and exploit (to varying degrees) another group—those who are subordinate—for the benefit of the dominant group.

Oppression works through systems of inequality, as well as the dominance of certain values, beliefs, and assumptions about people and how society should be organized. These are institutional and ideological controls. Members of dominant groups generally have built-in economic, political, and cultural benefits and power, regardless of whether they are aware of, or even want, these benefits. This process of accruing benefits and power from institutional inequalities is often referred to as **privilege.** Those most privileged are often those least likely to be aware of it or to recognize it (McIntosh 1988). Oppression works on personal (micro), community (meso), national (macro), and global levels.

Oppression involves **prejudice,** which we define as unreasonable, unfair, and hostile attitudes toward people, and **discrimination,** differential treatment favoring those who are in positions of dominance. But oppression reaches beyond individual bigotry or good intentions: It is promoted by the **ideologies** and practices of every institution we encounter and are part of and cannot be fully changed without fundamental changes in these institutions. Our definition of oppression assumes that everyone is socialized to participate in oppressive practices, thereby helping to maintain them. People may be involved as direct perpetrators or passive beneficiaries, or they may direct **internalized oppression** at members of their own group. Oppression results in appropriation—the loss—both voluntary and involuntary—of voice, identity, and agency of oppressed peoples.

It is important to think about oppression as an intricate system, at times blatantly obvious and at others subtly nuanced, rather than an either/or dichotomy of privileged/disadvantaged or oppressor/oppressed. We use the term **matrix of oppression and resistance** to describe the interconnection and interrelatedness of various forms of oppression. People can be privileged in some respects (race or gender, for example) and disadvantaged in others (class or sexual orientation, for example). Even negative ascriptions may be the source of people's resistance based on shared identity.

Feminisms:
Tangling with the "F" Word

Whether or not you consider yourself a feminist as a matter of personal identity, in women's studies you will study feminist perspectives and theories because these seek to understand and explain gender. In a nutshell, *feminism* concerns the liberation of women and girls from discrimination based on gender. The goal of feminist theory and practice is women's self-determination. For some feminists this means securing equal rights for women within existing institutions—from marriage and the family to government policy and law. For others it means fundamentally changing these institutions. We focus on feminist theories in Chapter 1 and discuss a range

of feminist perspectives throughout the book. Brief summaries for reference are provided in the glossary. Gender subordination is linked to discrimination based on other systems of inequality such as race, class, sexuality, and national origin, and we emphasize these links through selected readings and in our introduction to each chapter.

Feminism is a term with a great deal of baggage. For some it is positive and empowering. For others it conjures up negative images of "ugly" women in overalls and flannel shirts, women who do not wear makeup or shave their legs or underarms and who are said to be lesbians, man-haters, or "ball-busters." Many women do not want to be associated with the label "feminist." They may agree that women deserve higher pay, sexual freedom, or greater opportunity, but they are careful to start their comments with a disclaimer: "I'm not a feminist, but . . ."

In the past decade, virtually every major U.S. publication published a "feminism has gone too far" or "feminism is dead" piece. Some lamented the difficulties of being White and male; others blamed women's dissatisfactions on "too much equality"; and still others equated feminism with a "victim" mentality. A number of women have been highly visible in this discourse, courted by talk-show hosts and interviewed in the Sunday newspapers. Writer Naomi Wolf (1993), for example, promoted "power feminism"—the idea that real feminists are go-getting, smart, and equal contenders for power with men. Writer Karen Lehrman (1993) attempted to discredit women's studies as unacademic, inappropriately personal, providing easy credits, and selling women short in terms of education. Historian Elizabeth Fox-Genovese (1994) criticized "the new Puritanism" of feminism. Writer Katie Roiphe (1993) attacked "rape crisis feminism." Humanities professor Camille Paglia (1990) commented that women who go to frat houses on campus deserve to be raped. An *Esquire* magazine article talked approvingly of "do me feminism" and quoted a woman academic who claimed that there are a lot of "homely girls" in women's studies (Quindlen 1994). According to Erica Jong (1998), *Time* magazine has published "no less than 119 articles" criticizing feminism during the last twenty-five years. Its June 29, 1998, cover story, "Is Feminism Dead?" argued that feminism has become "a whole lot of stylish fluff"(p. 56). To make this point, black-and-white cover photos of three women

Girls display their banner at a demonstration protesting war against Iraq, San Francisco, February 16, 2003.

activists—Susan B. Anthony, Betty Friedan, and Gloria Steinem—were juxtaposed with a full-color photo of TV character Ally McBeal, as if to mark this alleged downward progression.

When women talk of violence—battering, incest, rape, sexual abuse, and harassment—or racism, or living in poverty, or aging without health insurance, they are said to be "victim" feminists or, perhaps worse, "feminazis"—antisex, no fun, whining critics who are out to destroy men and the male establishment. This is part of what Pulitzer Prize–winning writer Susan Faludi (1991) meant when she wrote of a backlash against feminism and women's rights and an erosion of the gains made for and by women in the past thirty-five years or so. In our society, women are socialized to care for men and to spare their feelings, but recognizing and discussing institutional inequalities between women as a group and men as a group are very different from "man-bashing." This garbled, trivializing media framework contributes to the many myths and misunderstandings about women's studies on the part of students and scholars in other fields. We consider three of these myths here.

Myth 1: Women's Studies Is Ideological

Some people assume that women's studies is not "real" scholarship but, instead, is feminist propaganda. Yet feminist inquiry, analysis, and activism have arisen from real problems experienced by real women, from well-documented inequalities and discrimination. For instance, data on women's wages recorded for more than one hundred years in the United States show that women's wages, on average, have never risen above 75 percent of what men earn on average—that is, on average, women earn seventy-five cents for every dollar earned by men. And

THE INCREDIBLE SHRINKING WOMAN

women of color fare much worse in this respect than White women. As we mentioned earlier, women's studies arose out of feminist organizing, and it values scholarly work that is relevant to activist concerns. Women's studies courses and projects seek to link intellectual, experiential, and emotional forms of connected knowing with the goal of improving women's lives. Women's studies is a rigorous endeavor, but its conception of rigor differs from that of much traditional scholarship, which values abstract, in-depth knowledge, narrowly defined. By contrast, women's studies scholarship places a high value on breadth and connectiveness; this kind of rigor requires broad understandings grounded in a range of experiences and the ability to make connections between knowledge and insights from different fields of study. Knowledge is never neutral, and in women's studies this is made explicit.

To some students and scholars, feminism is something to believe in because it provides a perspective that makes sense of the world and is personally empowering. But students who blithely blame everything on "rich White men" or "the patriarchy" without taking the trouble to read and think critically are anti-intellectual and inadvertently reinforce the notion that women's studies is anti-intellectual.

Myth 2: Women's Studies Is a White, Middle-Class Thing

Some White middle-class feminists have made, and still make, untenable claims about all women based on their own, necessarily partial, experience. Since the writings of Aphra Behn in the early 1600s, however, there have been White women who have thought about race and class as well as gender. Some White feminists worked against slavery in the nineteenth century, organized against the Ku Klux Klan, and participated in the civil rights movement of the 1950s and 1960s. Indeed, the 1970s revitalization of feminism in the United States came out of civil rights organizing. In the past thirty years or so, some White feminists have linked race and gender in their teaching, research, and activism (e.g., Frankenberg 1993; McIntosh 1988; Pratt 1984; Rich 1986c; Segrest 1994). Many notable scholars, writers, and activists of color also identify as feminists, among them the Combahee River Collective, Sandra Cisneros, Audre Lorde,

Elizabeth Martínez, Chandra Talpade Mohanty, and Barbara Omolade included in this anthology. Recent scholarship on the diverse beginnings of "second wave" U.S. women's movements (late 1960s and early 1970s) also explodes this myth (Becky Thompson, Reading 78; Baxandall 2001; Baxandall and Gordon 2000). African American writer bell hooks (2000) argues that "there should be billboards; ads in magazines; ads on buses, subways, trains; television commercials spreading the word, letting the world know more about feminism," because "feminism is for everybody" (p. x).

Myth 3: Women's Studies Is Narrowly Concerned with Women's Issues

Although women's studies aims to focus on women's experiences—in all their diversity—we do not see this as catering to narrow "special interests." On the contrary, feminist analyses provide a series of lenses to examine many topics and academic disciplines, including psychology, sociology, anthropology, political science, law, international relations, economic development, national income accounting, human biology, philosophies of science, and physics. Feminist scholarship is on the cutting edge of many academic fields, especially literature, history, philosophy, and film and media studies. It also raises crucial questions about teaching and learning, research design and methodologies, and theories of knowledge. Far from narrow, women's studies is concerned with thinking critically about the world in all its complexity.

It is important to acknowledge that women's studies students include a growing number of men. Although most of the readings in this book are by women, we have included several articles by men. We are mindful that our readership includes male students, and in places we pose questions and give specific suggestions to them. There are many ways that men can contribute to and support wider opportunities for women—as sons, brothers, fathers, partners, friends, coworkers, supervisors, labor organizers, spiritual leaders, teachers, doctors, lawyers, police officers, judges, legislators. Kimmel (1998) calls for pro-feminist men to be cheerleaders, allies, and foot soldiers; "and we must be so in front of other men, risking our own fears of rejection, our own membership in the club of masculinity, confronting our own fears of other men" (p. 68). The questions at the end of each chapter and suggestions for taking action provide pointers in this direction. There is a long history of men's support for women's equality in the United States (see, for example, Digby 1998; Kimmel and Mosmiller 1992; and Movement for a New Society 1983), and a training in women's studies can provide a powerful impetus for this. Clearly, the changes we discuss in this book cannot be achieved by women alone without male allies. But we also assume that there is something for men in this whole project, beyond being allies to women (Johnson 1997). We believe that those in dominant positions (on any social dimension, be it gender, race, class, age, ability, and so forth) are also limited by oppressive structures, that masculinity is socially constructed and highly constrained in our society. Despite the obvious benefits, privilege separates people and makes us ignorant of important truths. To be able to look others in the eye openly and completely, to join together to create a secure and sustainable future for everyone, we have to work to end systems of inequality. This repudiation of privilege, we believe, is not a sacrifice but rather the possibility of entering into genuine community, where we can all be more truly human.

Scope of the Book

This book is concerned with the project of theorizing about the oppressive conditions facing women today and the long-term work of transforming those conditions. In Part 1 (Chapters 1 and 2), we discuss the creation of knowledge and the significance of identity and social location for understanding ourselves, our communities, and the world we live in. Part 2 (Chapters 3–6) explores women's experiences of self in terms of our bodies, sexuality, health, and gender violence. In Part 3 (Chapters 7–9), we look at what is involved in making a home and making a living, and the significance of living in a global economy. In Part 4 (Chapters 10–12), we discuss women's experiences of crime and criminalization, the military, and the environment. We end, in Part 5 (Chapter 13), with a discussion of social change and focus on the importance of theories, visions, and action for creating change. Our overall argument is that to improve the lives of women in the United States also means redefining security and directing ourselves, our communities, this society, and the wider world toward a more sustainable future.

1

$$\blacklozenge\blacklozenge\blacklozenge$$

Theories and Theorizing: Integrative Frameworks for Understanding

Why are girls in the United States generally better at creative writing than at math? Has this always been so? Is this difference inevitable? Is rape about sexuality? Power? Both? Or neither? What is pornography? Is it the same as erotica? Do lesbians really want to be men? Why do so many marriages end in divorce? Why are so many children in the United States brought up in poverty? Why are more women going to jail than ever before?

People often say that facts speak for themselves. On the contrary, we argue that facts are always open to interpretation. They are "made to speak" according to your particular point of view. This is why we open this book about U.S. women's lives with a chapter on theory and theory making. How you think about women's situations and experiences affects what you see and what you understand by what you see. This chapter may seem abstract in the beginning, and you may want to return to it as you work with the material in the book. It would also be a good idea to review it at the end of your course. In

this chapter we look at theory and theory making in general terms and give a brief account of feminist theoretical perspectives in preparation for understanding and interpreting women's experiences and issues presented in the rest of the book. In this discussion we will consider these questions: What is a theory? Who creates theory, and how is it created? What is the purpose of theory?

Definition of a Theory

Consider the following assertion about poverty that many people in our society make: Poor people are poor because they are lazy. Think about the following questions:

1. What is the purpose of this statement?

2. What are the underlying assumptions on which it is based?

3. If the statement were true, what would it imply about action that should be taken?
4. Who came up with this idea, under what circumstances, and when?
5. How did this idea become popular?
6. What would you need to know to decide whether this statement is really true?

The statement above is a theory. It is one explanation of poverty, of why people are poor. It is built on a set of assumptions, or certain factors taken for granted. For example, this theory assumes there are well-paying jobs for all who want to work and that everyone meets the necessary requirements for those jobs, such as education, skills, or a means of providing for child care. These factors are proposed as facts or truths. This explanation of poverty takes a moral perspective. A psychological explanation of poverty may argue that people are poor because they have low self-esteem, lack self-confidence, and take on self-defeating behaviors. A sociological explanation might conclude that structures in our society, such as the educational and economic systems, are organized to exclude certain groups from being able to live above the poverty line. Each theory explicitly or implicitly suggests how to address the problem, which could then lead to appropriate action. If the problem is defined in terms of laziness, a step to ending poverty might be to punish people who are poor; if it is defined in psychological terms, assertiveness training or counseling might be suggested; and if it is defined in terms of structural inequality, ending discrimination would be the answer.

Theories, Theorizing, and Ways of Knowing

Every human being participates in theorizing, the activity of creating theory. For instance, we analyze the causes of poverty in our communities, the impact of immigration on the state we live in, or the experience of date rape. Theories generated by ordinary people, however, are not regarded as worthy of consideration beyond their own spheres of influence, among friends or coworkers, for example. Historically, Western, university-educated men from the upper classes—most often academics—and their theories, which are supported by societal institutions such as education and government, have had the greatest impact on how human beings and social phenomena are explained and understood. Their considerable influence, indeed, has even compelled many people simply to accept what is presented to them as conventional wisdom. For instance, a proposition that most people apparently agree with is "There will always be poverty," though this is not necessarily true. In the following sections, we discuss how only certain kinds of theories have been legitimized in this society and suggest another way of theorizing and developing knowledge that engages ordinary people.

The Dominant Perspective

From the perspective of the **dominant culture**—the values, symbols, means of expression, language, and interests of the people in power in this society—only certain types of theories have authority. Generally, the authoritativeness of a theory about human beings and society is evaluated primarily along two dimensions. One is its degree of formality, which is determined according to how closely its development followed a particular way of theorizing, the so-called scientific method, the basics of which most of us learned in high school science classes. The second is the scope and generality of the theory (Smelser 1994).

Although in practice there are several variations of the scientific method, key elements must be present for a theory to fit in this category. The scientific method, originally devised by natural scientists, rests on the presumption of **objectivity,** "an attitude, philosophy, or claim . . . independent of the individual mind [through emotional detachment and social distance] . . . verified by a socially agreed-upon procedure such as those developed in science, mathematics, or history" (Kohl 1992, p. 84). Objectivity is seen as both a place to begin the process of theorizing and the outcome of that process. It has been long argued that "if done properly, [science] is the epitome of objectivity" (Tuana 1989, p. xi). Therefore, theories developed correctly using the scientific method are held out as value-free and neutral. The method is also empirical. That is, for something to be a fact, it must be physically observable and countable or measurable. This proposition is extended to include the notion that something is either true or not true, fact or not fact. Last, the experimental method, commonly used in science, "attempts to understand a whole by examining its parts, asking how something works rather than why it works, and derives abstract formulas to predict future results" (Duff 1993, p. 51). In summary, these elements add up to research methods that

> generally require a distancing of the researcher from her or his subjects of study; . . . absence of emotions from the research process; ethics and values are deemed inappropriate in the research process, either as the reason for scientific inquiry or as part of the research process itself; . . . adversarial debates, whether written or oral, become the preferred method of ascertaining truth: the arguments that can withstand the greatest assault and survive intact become the strongest truth.
>
> *(Collins 1990, p. 205)*

The scientific method was adopted by theorists in the social sciences as a way to validate and legitimate social scientific knowledge beginning in the late nineteenth century, as disciplines such as psychology and sociology were being developed. Since that time, academic disciplines like education, nursing, and social work have also adopted it as the primary method with which to develop new knowledge in their fields.

The second dimension for evaluating and judging theory is concerned with its scope and generality. The range is from the most specific explanation with the narrowest scope and most limited generality to the other end of the continuum, the general theory, which is the most abstract and is assumed to have the most general application (Smelser 1994). Many general theories have been promoted and accepted as being universally applicable. One of them, **biological determinism,** holds that a group's biological or genetic makeup shapes its social, political, and economic destiny. In mainstream society, biology is often assumed to be the basis of women's and men's different roles, especially women's ability to bear children. Most social scientists and feminist theorists see behavior as socially constructed and learned through childhood socialization, educa-

tion, and the media, as argued by sociologist Judith Lorber (Reading 1). They explain differences in women's and men's roles in these terms and argue that variations in gender roles from one society to another provide strong evidence for a **social constructionist** view.

Alternative Perspectives

Evaluating and judging theories according to the scientific method has come under heavy criticism from theorists who typically have been viewed as outsiders to traditional academic circles, such as scholars in women's studies, ethnic studies, gay/lesbian studies, and some mainstream academics (e.g., Bleier 1984; Collins 1990; Duran 1998; and Shiva 1988). These theorists have seen the fallacies, biases, and harmful outcomes of that way of creating knowledge. The primary criticisms are that knowledge created by the scientific method is not value-free, neutral, or generalizable to the extent it is claimed to be. Science, as with other academic disciplines, is "a cultural institution and as such is structured by the political, social, and economic values of the culture within which it is practiced" (Tuana 1989, p. xi). As biologist Ruth Hubbard (1989) argues:

> To be believed, scientific facts must fit the worldview of the times. Therefore, at times of tension and upheaval, such as during the [1970s and 1980s], some researchers always try to prove that differences in the social, political, and economic status of women and men, blacks and whites, poor people and rich people, are inevitable because they are the results of people's inborn qualities and traits. Such scientists have tried to "prove" that blacks are innately less intelligent than whites, or that women are innately weaker, more nurturing, less good at math than men. *(p. 121)*

Rather than being neutral, all knowledge is socially constructed, value-laden, and biased and reflects and serves the interests of the culture that produced it, in this case the dominant culture.

The problem is not that theories are value-laden or biased, but that the values and biases of many theories are hidden under the cloak of "scientific objectivity." Moreover, there is the assumption that "if the science is 'good,' in a professional sense [following closely the rules of scientific method], it will also be good for society" (Hubbard 1989, p. 121). Many theories are applied by mainstream scholars not only to the United States but also to the rest of the world, often without acknowledgment that they primarily serve the interests of the dominant group in the United States. They use these theories to justify the inequalities in our society as well as differences and inequalities between the United States and other societies. Despite claims to the contrary, general theories created by mainstream scholars serve a political purpose in addition to whatever other purpose they are intended to serve. And, as sociologist Patricia Hill Collins (1990) asserts, "Because elite white men and their representatives control structures of knowledge validation, white male interests pervade thematic content of traditional scholarship" (p. 201).

We further argue that theorizing is a political project, regardless of whether this is acknowledged. Social theories—explaining the behavior of human beings and society—serve to support the existing social order or can be used to challenge it. For women and men of color, White women, poor people, members of oppressed groups, and people with privilege who are interested in progressive social change, the political work of theorizing is to generate knowledge that challenges conventional wisdom and those formal theories that do not explain their real lived experiences, provide satisfactory solutions to their difficulties, or lead to their liberation. Director of the Center for Women's Global Leadership, Rutgers University, Charlotte Bunch (1987) has recommended an effective way to think about theory: describing what exists, analyzing why that reality exists, determining what should exist, and hypothe-sizing how to change what is to what should be.

The Role of Values

"Determining what should exist," the third part of Charlotte Bunch's model, is clearly a matter of values and beliefs. It involves being able to envision a world free from discrimination and oppression, if only vaguely. Feminism is concerned with values by definition: the liberation of women and girls from discrimination based on gender. Values do not come from facts or from the analysis of a situation but rather from people's beliefs in principles like fairness, equality, or justice. We may learn such principles from our families and communities, or through organized religion or a more personal sense of spirituality. We may think of them in terms of fundamental human rights (e.g., Bunch and Carillo 1991; Bunch and Reilly 1994; and Kerr 1993). Whatever the source, feminist work invariably involves values whether stated explicitly or implied. In Reading 6, JeeYeun Lee describes a woman's studies class she took as an undergraduate: "For the first time I found people who articulated those murky half-formed feelings that I could previously only express . . . as 'But that's not fair!'" Notice the value positions in all the readings in this chapter and throughout this book. Christina Leaño (Reading 76) writes from an explicitly faith-based perspective that informs her view of the world, her sense of life purpose, and the life decisions she makes.

Theoretical Frameworks for Understanding Women's Lives

As an interdisciplinary field of study, women's studies incorporates theoretical insights from several academic disciplines, including anthropology, cultural studies, economics, history, literature, philosophy, politics, psychology, and sociology. In turn, feminist scholarship has made significant contributions to these disciplines.

Women's studies also draws on feminist theories that primarily seek to understand and explain women's experiences. Many of these theories were developed in the context of women's organizing for change—for the abolition of slavery, for women's suffrage, for labor rights, the civil rights of people of color, women's rights, and gay/lesbian/bisexual/transgender rights. Feminist theories have been concerned with fundamental questions: Why are women in a subordinate position in our society and, indeed, worldwide? What are the origins of this subordination, and how is it perpetuated?

We argue for a theoretical framework that allows us to see the diversity of women's lives and the fundamental structures of inequality and opportunity that shape our experiences. The readings we have selected for this chapter all contribute to this understanding. Judith Lorber (Reading 1) argues that gender is not natural but learned from infancy. Gender differences are maintained by key social institutions such as education, marriage, popular culture, news media, government, and law. The implication of her argument is that our society's gender arrangements are not fixed or "god-given," but can be changed.

Sociologist Jackie Stacey (1993) notes that the concept of **patriarchy,** meaning "the systematic organization of male supremacy" (p. 53), is one that many feminist theorists have found useful. Sociologist Allan Johnson discusses this concept in Reading 2, arguing that patriarchy is not just a collection of individuals but a system as well—a set of relationships and shared understandings. Its core value is control and domination. Everyone is involved and implicated in this system, but we can choose *how* we participate. This emphasis on a wider system is crucial for understanding the world in which we live. Without it, as Johnson shows, our thinking and discussion get reduced to the personal level and bogged down in accusations, defensiveness, and hurt feelings.

An important strand in feminist thinking—**liberal feminism**—grew out of one of the most significant strands of U.S. political thought, liberalism, a theory about individual rights, freedom, choice, and privacy with roots in seventeenth-century European political thought (e.g., the writings of John Locke). Liberalism has been a significant strand in U.S. political discourse since the inception of the nation, although political and legal rights were originally limited to White men who owned land and property. Liberal feminists explain the oppression of women in terms of unequal access to existing political, economic, and social institutions (see Eisenstein 1981; Friedan 1963; and Steinem 1983). They are concerned with women's rights being equal to those of men and that women have equal access to opportunities within existing economic and social structures. From the mid-nineteenth century onward, much feminist organizing—for example, for the vote, equal pay, and women's access to education and the professions—is based on this view. Many people hold liberal feminist opinions though they may not realize it. Despite the disclaimer "I'm not a feminist . . . ," the comment "but I *do* believe in equal pay" is a liberal feminist position. Women's right to legal abortion in the United States, established in 1973, is grounded in this tradition, as a right to privacy. Liberal feminism can be criticized because it

accepts existing institutions as they are, only seeking equal access for women within them. This objective should not be underestimated, however, given the strength of patriarchy as a system. Many gains for women over the past thirty years are increasingly under attack. The right to abortion, for example, has been steadily whittled away, and is increasingly contested (see Chapter 5).

In Reading 3, the Combahee River Collective, a group of Black feminists in the Boston area, provide an integrated analysis of interlocking systems of oppression based on race, class, gender, sexuality, and so forth. They note that "Black, other Third World, and working women have been involved in the feminist movement from its start," but that their participation has been obscured by external forces like the media, and internal racism and elitism (also see readings by Barbara Omolade and Becky Thompson in Chapter 13 on this point). "What we believe"— the values part of their thinking—is explicit: Black women have inherent value; "our liberation is a necessity not as an adjunct to somebody else's but because of our need as human persons for autonomy." This statement comes out of a three-year process (1974–77) of meeting, thinking, sharing perspectives, working in various social movements and organizations, reflecting on this activism, clarifying a shared analysis over time. Starting with an emphasis on race and gender, the group went on to critique **capitalism** and **imperialism** as well as patriarchy in the essay reprinted here.

The Combahee River Collective identified themselves as **socialists** who believed that "work must be organized for the collective benefit of those who do the work and create the products, and not for the profit of the bosses." This links to another significant strand of feminist thought, **socialist feminism,** that grew out of Marxist theories of the economy and concern for the emancipation of workers as a class from economic exploitation and drudgery. Feminist activists and writers who draw from this Marxist tradition see the oppression of women in terms of two interconnected systems, patriarchy and capitalism, and they are particularly concerned with the economic-class aspects of women's lives (Eisenstein 1979; Ferguson 1989; Hartmann 1981; Hennessy and Ingraham 1997; Roberts and Mizuta 1993). Zillah Eisenstein (1998) notes that "the language of socialism" seems foreign nowadays in the United States, due to the collapse of the former Soviet Union and the discrediting of the political philosophy of socialism along with it. She argues that an anticapitalist, feminist politics is currently of great relevance given the increasing integration of the world economic system, though "whether those politics are named socialist feminism remains to be seen" (p. 219). The Combahee River Collective's "Black Feminist Statement" also includes an anti-imperialist strand, reflecting the fact that, in the 1960s, '70s, and '80s, many U.S. feminists of color, as well as White feminists, supported liberation movements in Africa, Asia, and Central America.

The thinking of Collective members also overlapped with a third key strand of feminist theory, **radical feminism,** that provided a major contribution to what is sometimes called **second-wave feminism** in the United States (late 1960s to late 1980s). On this view, male domination manifests itself in women's sexuality, gender roles, and family relationships, and it is carried over into the male-dominated world of work, government, religion, and law (Bell and Klein 1996; Daly 1976; Echols 1989; Harne and Miller 1996; Koedt, Levine, and Rapone 1973). For radical feminists, women's liberation requires the eradication of patriarchy and the creation of alternative ways of living. Lesbians were particularly influential in developing this strand of feminist thought and creating alternative women's institutions, including women's health projects, publishing companies, bookstores, coffeehouses, recording studios, and music festivals (Shugar 1995). The Combahee River Collective found White radical feminism too focused on male domination at the expense of oppressions based on race and class. Lesbian **separatism,** advocated by some White lesbians, was also found by the Collective to be too limiting theoretically and in practice. These writers argued that the most profound politics "come directly out of our own identity." Their emphasis on **identity politics** meant that they saw no role for White heterosexual men in the transformation they envisioned, though they did challenge White women to work on their racism.

In the late 1960s and 1970s, many prominent U.S. feminist activists and writers were White, middle-class, heterosexual women who generalized from their own experiences or those of women like them. They focused on their subordination as women with-

out paying attention to their privilege on other dimensions, notably race, class, and sexual orientation. These limitations have been roundly criticized by women of color (hooks 1984a; Moraga and Anzaldua 1983; Smith 1983; Trujillo 1998), working-class women (Kadi 1996; Steedman 1986), women from outside the United States (Mohanty, Russo, and Torres 1991), women with disabilities (Fiduccia and Saxton 1997), and lesbians and bisexual women (Harne and Miller 1996; Lorde 1984; Pharr 1988; Rich 1986a).

We have discussed the Combahee River Collective's "Black Feminist Statement" in some detail because of its significance as an early example of writing about the **intersectionality** of race, class, gender, sexuality, and nation. In Reading 4, antiracist, feminist educator and scholar Chandra Talpade Mohanty writes about this intersection in tracing her experiences as a South Asian woman studying and working in the United States. She notes that "racism and sexism became the analytic and political lenses through which I was able to anchor myself here." She made a very significant shift in her sense of self when she began to think of herself as a student of color rather than a foreign student. This new set of understandings also challenged her to rethink her place in Indian society. Mohanty is explicit in her values: opposing social injustice, opposing Hindu fundamentalism, and opposing the role of the World Bank and International Monetary Fund in "restructuring" the Indian economy—all the time holding a vision of radical transformation. She describes her genealogy—this tracing of her complex identity as a South Asian immigrant in the United States and an expatriate Indian citizen in India—as "interested, partial, and deliberate." This suggests perspectives of **postcolonial** and **postmodern feminisms.** These theoretical strands, developed by academic feminists in the 1980s and '90s, emphasize the particularity of women's experiences in specific cultural and historical contexts (Ferguson and Wicke 1992; Nicholson 1990). An integrative perspective that emphasizes intersectionality is not only the prerogative of women of color, though White women have been much slower to develop this kind of analysis (e.g., Frankenberg 1993; Segrest 1994; and Spelman 1988). Writer, organizer, and educator Minnie Bruce Pratt explores what this means for her, as a White woman, "raised small-town middle-class, Christian, in the Deep South" (Reading 5).

Some feminists have asked whether it is meaningful to talk of women as a group, when there are so many differences among women (Weedon 1987). Denise Riley (1988) argues that the category "woman" has not meant the same thing throughout history and that its specific meaning should be investigated in different historical contexts, not assumed. An emphasis on difference also raises the question as to whether women can engage in collective action, something which 1970s feminists usually took for granted. Jackie Stacey (1993) argues that postmodern theorists have also emphasized the ways people's **subjectivity**—our thoughts, feelings, and actions—are produced and limited by external constraints. This has been useful in thinking about why women "accept" their subordinate position. Previous explanations of power and subordination, Stacey notes, emphasized coercion, or social conditioning through childhood socialization, schooling, and media representations. Both the Combahee River Collective and Chandra Talpade Mohanty commit themselves to activist projects arising out of their reflection and theoretical analysis.

Theoretical perspectives are developed in response to particular circumstances and with reference to previous theories. They are refined and adapted as understanding grows and as events shed new light on issues or problems. Theory is never finished but is continuously evolving. In the 1990s, the mainstream media consistently depicted facile stereotypes of feminism and feminists that have deterred many younger women from using the term, even though they often support feminist ideas. Young women may think of themselves as **third-wave feminists,** challenging the second-wave feminism of their mothers' generation as no longer relevant and emphasizing personal voice, ambiguity, contradiction, and multiple identities (Baumgardner and Richards 2000; Findlen 1995; Heywood and Drake 1997; Walker 1995; Zita 1997). JeeYeun Lee (Reading 6) exemplifies this approach and advocates genuinely inclusive feminisms. She calls for "recognition of the constructed racial nature of *all* experiences of gender"; that "heterosexual norms do not oppress solely lesbians, bisexuals and gay men, but affect all of our choices and non-choices"; that "issues posed by differently abled women question our basic assumptions about body image, health care, sexuality and work"; and so forth.

The wave metaphor suggests both continuity and discontinuity with the past as women shape theoretical understandings for their generation and historical period. Second-wave feminism was specific to its time and also built on the work of suffragists and women's rights advocates active toward the end of the nineteenth century and into the twentieth century (**first-wave feminism**). Note that these shorthand labels make complex, powerful transformative movements, with their divergent and overlapping strands, seem much neater, more unitary, and more static than they are in reality.

In seeking to understand U.S. women's lives, we are also concerned with the deterioration of the physical environment, which leads us to consider **ecofeminism.** JeeYeun Lee comments that ecofeminists "challenge our fundamental ideas about living on and with the earth, about our interactions with animals, plants, food, agriculture, and industry." Ecofeminist writer Ynestra King (1998) notes that for ecofeminists, "Modern Western science and technology . . . capitalism and Eurocentric masculinist culture together pose a threat to the continuation of life on earth" (p. 207). A core point in ecofeminist analysis involves the concept of dualism, where various attributes are thought of in oppositional terms: culture/nature, mind/body, male/female, civilized/ primitive, self/other, and so on. Philosopher Val Plumwood (1993) argues that these dualisms are mutually reinforcing and should be thought of as an interlocking set. In each pair, one side is valued over the other. Culture, mind, male, civilized, for example, are valued over nature, body, female, primitive, which are thought of as "other" and inferior.

"Socially Lived" Theorizing

As discussed earlier, traditional scholarship primarily validates knowledge that is produced using some form of the scientific method, by White men and others who form an elite group of scholars or subscribe to their views and approaches. We argue that theorizing is not the sole domain of elites. Feminist legal scholar Catharine MacKinnon (1991) talks about "articulating the theory of women's practice—resistance, visions, consciousness, injuries, notions of community, experiences of inequality. By practic[e], I mean socially lived" (p. 20). The writings included in this chapter all exemplify socially lived theorizing. A notable example is provided by Abra Fortune Chernik (Reading 15), who discusses her personal struggle with an eating disorder and the process of understanding and overcoming it. Our framework for theory-making is based on the following assumptions:

- All knowledge is socially constructed; there is no value-free or neutral knowledge.

- Everyone has the capacity to be a creator of knowledge.

- What one knows comes out of a specific historical and cultural context, whether one is an insider or an outsider to that context.

- It is the responsibility of everyone to reflect on, evaluate, and judge the world around us, and our places in that world, as an essential element of theorizing.

- Knowledge should be used for the purposes of helping to liberate oppressed people and to transform the current social and economic structures of inequality into a sustainable world for all people.

As Catharine MacKinnon (1991) remarks, "It is common to say that something is good in theory but not in practice. I always want to say, then it is not such a good theory, is it?" (p. 1).

In writing about the Holocaust—the mass murder primarily of Jewish people but also of Roma people, people with disabilities, and gay people in Europe during World War II—philosopher Alan Rosenberg (1988) makes a profound distinction between knowing and understanding something. According to Rosenberg, knowing is having the facts about a particular event or condition. We know the Holocaust happened: Eight million people were murdered, and countless others were tortured, raped, and otherwise devastated; the Nazis, under the leadership of Adolf Hitler, were the perpetrators; others, both inside and outside Germany, including the United States initially, were unable or refused to help; the result was the slaughter of six million Jewish people. Traditional educational practices, epitomized by the scientific method, teach us primarily

to know. For Rosenberg, knowing is the first step to understanding, a much deeper process that, in the case of the Holocaust, involves not only comprehending its significance and longer-term effects but also trying to discover how to prevent similar injustices in the future.

> Knowing . . . refers to factual information or the process by which it is gathered. Understanding refers to systematically grasping the significance of an event in such a way that it becomes integrated into one's moral and intellectual life. Facts can be absorbed without their having any impact on the way we understand ourselves or the world we live in; facts in themselves do not make a difference. It is the understanding of them that makes a difference.   *(Rosenberg 1988, p. 382)*

Recognizing theory-making as a political project helps us understand, in the way Rosenberg describes it, the conditions facing women in particular, as well as others in subordinate positions. So, how do we begin to understand?

Early in the U.S. women's liberation movement of the sixties and seventies, the slogan "The personal is political" was popularized to validate individual women's personal experiences as a starting point for recognizing and understanding discrimination against women as a group. This promoted the practice of "starting from one's own experiences" as a legitimate way to theorize and create new knowledge. This practice was also useful in countering the dominant view of theorizing that personal experience, along with emotions and values, contaminates the "purity" of the scientific method. As a first step, starting from what we know the most about—our experiences, our subjectivity—is helpful, but it also contains obvious problems. On the one hand, there is self-centeredness, as reflected in comments such as "I can know only my experience," "I can speak only for myself," and "What does all this have to do with me?" On the other hand, a naive generalization like "As a woman, I assume that all women have experienced the same things I have" also limits the extent to which we can understand diverse women's experiences.

As mentioned earlier in our brief discussion of feminist theories, different social and historical situations give rise to very different experiences and theories about those experiences, hence the importance of **situated knowledge** (Belenky, Clinchy, Goldberger, and Tarnle 1986; Collins 1990) or **standpoint theory** (Hartsock 1983). What we know is the direct result of our experience, is understood in a specific historical and cultural context, and cannot be generalized. For instance, the experience of being a single mother as a poor teenager in a rural community in the 1990s would be very different from that of being a single mother as an established professional in a big city in the twenty-first century. One could not apply her experience to the other, and neither could speak authoritatively about being a single mother in the 1960s.

Our task of socially lived theorizing involves several important challenges. We are faced with the self-centeredness of pure subjectivity, "in which knowledge and meaning [are] lodged in oneself and one's own experiences" (Maher and Tetreault 1994, p. 94). We must also negotiate the problem of the **cultural relativism** of situated knowledge, in which the authenticity of subjective knowledge is not challenged because it is seen as someone's, or some group's, "real experience," and consequently, others do not have the authority to question it. Thus, the White supremacist views of Ku Klux Klan members might be considered equally as valid as those held by antiracist activists, or a New York judge could sentence a Chinese immigrant man to a mere five years' probation for killing his wife on the argument that the murder was the result of "cultural differences" (Yen 1989).

Given these major challenges arising out of pure subjectivity and cultural relativism, how can we generate knowledge that reflects the perspectives and interests of a broad range of people, communities, and life circumstances, that is visionary, not just reactive, and that could lead to social change? Socially lived theorizing requires a methodology that includes collective dialogue and **praxis**—reflection and action on the world to transform it. Paulo Freire (1989), Brazilian founder of the popular education movement, calls this methodology **conscientization,** or gaining a "critical consciousness," and describes it as "learning to perceive social, political, and economic contradictions, [the effects of the push and pull of opposing forces], and to take action against the oppressive elements of this reality" (p. 19).

"Learning to perceive social, political, and economic contradictions" is a tall order for many of us who have been formally educated by what Freire calls the "banking method," whereby teachers deposit knowledge—dates, historical facts, formulas for problem solving, for example—into the minds of students and expect them to be able to withdraw this information at a given time, such as during exams, quizzes, and class presentations. During our schooling most of us are not often asked such questions as, What are the assumptions in the statement you are making? How do you know what you know? Why do you think so? What are the implications of your position? Many of us may have sat in class listening to a teacher or other students and have kept quiet when we knew what was being said did not match our experience. When we put forward our ideas and observations, they might have been shot down as silly, naive, or too idealistic. We were expected to back up our experience with facts. We were encouraged to accept facts and ideas as they were given to us and to accept social conditions as they are. Indeed, we may often have accepted things as they are without thinking about them, or simply not noticed injustices happening around us. Most likely, too, we have had little opportunity to engage in honest dialogue with others—both people like ourselves and those from differentbackgrounds—about important issues.

Having honest dialogues and asking critical questions move us beyond excessive subjectivity because we are compelled to see and understand many different sides of the same subject. Creating theory for social change—something that will advance human development and create a better world for all—gives us a basis for making critical judgments of facts and experiences. This in turn provides a framework for deciding where to draw the line on cultural relativism. Through ongoing, detailed discussion and conscientious listening to others, we can generate a carefully thought-out set of principles that lead to greater understanding of issues and of acceptable actions in a given situation.

Many assume that the scientific method involves authoritativeness and rigor. We believe this alternative way of theorizing redefines rigor by demanding the engagement of our intellectual, emotional, and spiritual selves. It compels us to think systematically and critically, requires us to face the challenges of

talking about our differences, and obligates us to consider the real implications and consequences of our theories. Knowledge created in this way helps us "to systematically grasp . . . the significance of an event in such a way that it becomes integrated into [our] moral and intellectual life," also a form of rigor (Rosenberg 1988, p. 382).

Media Representations and the Creation of Knowledge

As we have suggested, a major source of our understanding of our own lives is our ability to reflect on our experiences. We learn about people from other groups through our, often limited, interactions with them and through many kinds of media representations. It is a truism to say that we live in a media-saturated culture with constant access to the Internet, TV and radio stations broadcasting 24 hours a day, daily newspapers, weekly magazines, new movies coming out all the time, and so on. This list shows the plurality of media sources (singular: medium). From opinion polls to academic research, media studies evaluate the role of media in creating opinions, attitudes, and knowledge. The line between information and entertainment is blurred as TV shows take up serious issues and news reporting focuses on the flip, titillating, and controversial. The

repetition of images on television also shapes our view of history (Morrow 1999). The mainstream media are owned and controlled by mega-corporations like Disney/ABC and Time Warner/Turner. One of the media's main functions is to round up an audience for advertisers, and advertisers exert considerable influence concerning media content, especially in television. From time to time they threaten to pull advertising if they think the content of a show will "turn off" their intended audience, and editors and directors are usually forced to tow the line.

As consumers of media, we develop sophisticated skills in "reading" media texts, whether they are ads or documentaries. Media audiences bring their experiences, values, and beliefs to what they watch, read, and hear, just as students bring their experiences, beliefs, and ideas into the classroom. The more we know about particular people, the more we are able to judge the accuracy of media portrayals and to notice whether they reproduce myths and stereotypes, and romanticize or exoticize people.

Women have been marginalized in media portrayals, as have people of color and working-class people. "Blatantly stereotypical images dominated the earlier years of mass media" (Croteau and Hoynes 1997, p. 147). More recently, there has been "a wider diversity of images and roles for women" (p. 147), though still with serious distortions. Women on television, for example, are still mainly shown in the context of entertainment, sport, home, and family.

How to Watch TV News

1. **In encountering a news show, you must come with a firm idea of what is important.** TV news is highly selective. Your values and beliefs are essential in judging what it is that really matters in the reporting of an event.

2. **In preparing to watch a TV news show, keep in mind that it is called a "show."** A TV news show is a successful business enterprise as well as a form of entertainment and a public service.

3. **Never underestimate the power of commercials.** They tell a great deal about our society. Note contradictory messages as you compare commercials and the news.

4. **Learn something about the economic and political interests of those who run TV stations.** This is relevant to judging what they say and don't say.

5. **Pay special attention to the language of newscasts.** Film footage and visual imagery claims our attention on TV news shows, but it is what newscasters *say* that frames the pictures and tells us how to interpret them.

(Adapted from Postman and Powers 1992, pp. 160–68.)

Sports coverage is still male-dominated, but with some significant changes due to the marked increase in women's athleticism over the past twenty years. In Reading 7, Angharad Valdivia discusses the stereotypical portrayal of Latina women in the films of Rosie Perez. Writer and radio reporter Laura Flanders (1997) notes that in the news media, women and girls are usually represented in "human interest" stories. Media representations serve to reinforce ideological notions of women's roles, women's bodies, and sexuality, while also giving complex and sometimes contradictory messages. David Croteau and William Hoynes discuss the role of films and television shows in the normalization of stereotypical gender roles (Reading 69). Cynthia Enloe notes the increasing militarization of U.S. culture (Reading 68).

To summarize, in this chapter we argue that facts are always open to interpretation and that everyone makes theory in trying to understand their experiences. Feminist theories that seek to explain women's lives involve clear value positions and constitute a critique of the dominant view that sees theory as "objective" or "value-free." Socially lived theorizing is essential for women's studies. It creates knowledge that reflects the points of view and interests of a broad range of people. It is visionary and can lead to social change. Socially lived theorizing requires collective dialogue, careful listening to other people's theories, and sophisticated skills in "reading" media texts so that we do not draw stereotypical notions of others into our theory-making.

◆◆◆

Questions for Reflection

In attempting to understand any theoretical perspective, we find the following questions helpful:

1. What does the theory aim to explain?
2. How does it do this? What are the basic arguments and assumptions?
3. What does the theory focus on? What does it ignore?
4. What is the cultural and historical context giving rise to the theory?
5. Do you find this perspective useful? If so, why?
6. Are you convinced by the arguments? Why or why not?
7. What kinds of research questions does this perspective generate?
8. What kinds of actions and projects follow from this perspective?

As you read and discuss the readings in this chapter, think about these questions:

1. How do you explain poverty?

2. How do you explain inequality between women and men in this country? Between White people and people of color in this country?

3. How do you think change happens? How is knowledge related to social change?

4. How do people with privilege contribute to eliminating the systems of privilege that benefit them?

5. Think about people and events that have affected the development of your thinking. How did this happen?

Finding Out More on the Web

1. In the Combahee River Collective's "Black Feminist Statement," the writers mention Dr. Kenneth Edelin, Joan Little, and Inéz García. Who were these people? Why were they significant?

2. Explore the Web site of a women's organization. What can you learn about the organization's theoretical framework? How does this perspective inform its activities? Here are a few examples to get you started:

   Center for Women's Global Leadership: **www.cwgl.rutgers.edu**

   Global Women's Strike: **http://womenstrike8m.server101.com**

   National Organization for Women: **www.now.org**

   Third Wave Foundation: **www.thirdwavefoundation.org**

   Women of Color Resource Center: **www.coloredgirls.org**

Taking Action

1. Analyze what happens when you get into an argument with a friend, classmate, or teacher about an issue that matters to you. Are you both using the same assumptions? Do you have compatible understandings of the issue? If not, how can you explain your position more clearly? Are facts enough to convince someone who is skeptical of your views?

2. Pay attention to the theoretical ideas incorporated into TV news reports. When the presenter says, "Now for the stories behind the headlines," whose stories are these? Who is telling them? What, if anything, is missing from these accounts? What else do you need to know in order to have a full explanation?

3. Look critically at media representations of people in your group and other groups. How are they portrayed? What is left out of these representations? What stereotypes do they reinforce?

4. Read a novel like Gerd Brantenberg's *Egalia's Daughters* or Marge Piercy's *Woman on the Edge of Time* that redefines gender roles and stereotypes.

ONE

The Social Construction of Gender

Judith Lorber

Talking about gender for most people is the equivalent of fish talking about water. Gender is so much the routine ground of everyday activities that questioning its taken-for-granted assumptions and presuppositions is like thinking about whether the sun will come up. Gender is so pervasive that in our society we assume it is bred into our genes. Most people find it hard to believe that gender is constantly created and recreated out of human interaction, out of social life, and is the texture and order of that social life. Yet gender, like culture, is a human production that depends on everyone constantly "doing gender" (West and Zimmerman 1987).

And everyone "does gender" without thinking about it. Today, on the subway, I saw a well-dressed man with a year-old child in a stroller. Yesterday, on a bus, I saw a man with a tiny baby in a carrier on his chest. Seeing men taking care of small children in public is increasingly common—at least in New York City. But both men were quite obviously stared at—and smiled at, approvingly. Everyone was doing gender—the men who were changing the role of fathers and the other passengers, who were applauding them silently. But there was more gendering going on that probably fewer people noticed. The baby was wearing a white crocheted cap and white clothes. You couldn't tell if it was a boy or a girl. The child in the stroller was wearing a dark blue T-shirt and dark print pants. As they started to leave the train, the father put a Yankee baseball cap on the child's head. Ah, a boy, I thought. Then I noticed the gleam of tiny earrings in the child's ears, and as they got off, I saw the little flowered sneakers and lace-trimmed socks. Not a boy after all. Gender done.

Gender is such a familiar part of daily life that it usually takes a deliberate disruption of our expectations of how women and men are supposed to act to pay attention to how it is produced. Gender signs and signals are so ubiquitous that we usually fail to note them—unless they are missing or ambiguous. Then we are uncomfortable until we have successfully placed the other person in a gender status; otherwise, we feel socially dislocated. In our society, in addition to man and woman, the status can be *transvestite* (a person who dresses in opposite-gender clothes) and *transsexual* (a person who has had sex-change surgery). Transvestites and transsexuals construct their gender status by dressing, speaking, walking, gesturing in the ways prescribed for women or men—whichever they want to be taken for—and so does any "normal" person.

For the individual, gender construction starts with assignment to a sex category on the basis of what the genitalia look like at birth. Then babies are dressed or adorned in a way that displays the category because parents don't want to be constantly asked whether their baby is a girl or a boy. A sex category becomes a gender status through naming, dress, and the use of other gender markers. Once a child's gender is evident, others treat those in one gender differently from those in the other, and the children respond to the different treatment by feeling different and behaving differently. As soon as they can talk, they start to refer to themselves as members of their gender. Sex doesn't come into play again until puberty, but by that time, sexual feelings and desires and practices have been shaped by gendered norms and expectations. Adolescent boys and girls approach and avoid each other in an elaborately scripted and gendered mating dance. Parenting is gendered, with different expectations for mothers and for fathers, and people of different genders work at different kinds of jobs. The work adults do as mothers and fathers and as low-level workers and high-level bosses, shapes women's and men's life experiences, and these experiences produce different feelings, consciousness, relationships, skills—ways of being that we call feminine or masculine. All of these processes constitute the social construction of gender.

Gendered roles change—today fathers are taking care of little children, girls and boys are wearing unisex clothing and getting the same education, women and men are working at the same jobs. Although many traditional social groups are quite strict about maintaining gender differences, in other social groups they seem to be blurring. Then why the one-year-old's earrings? Why is it still so important to mark a child as a girl or a boy, to make sure she is not taken for a boy or he for a girl? What would happen if they were? They would, quite literally, have changed places in their social world.

To explain why gendering is done from birth, constantly and by everyone, we have to look not only at the way individuals experience gender but at gender as a social institution. As a social institution, gender is one of the major ways that human beings organize their lives. Human society depends on a predictable division of labor, a designated allocation of scarce goods, assigned responsibility for children and others who cannot care for themselves, common values and their systematic transmission to new members, legitimate leadership, music, art, stories, games, and other symbolic productions. One way of choosing people for the different tasks of society is on the basis of their talents, motivations, and competence—their demonstrated achievements. The other way is on the basis of gender, race, ethnicity—ascribed membership in a category of people. Although societies vary in the extent to which they use one or the other of these ways of allocating people to work and to carry out other responsibilities, every society uses gender and age grades. Every society classifies people as "girl and boy children," "girls and boys ready to be married," and "fully adult women and men," constructs similarities among them and differences between them, and assigns them to different roles and responsibilities. Personality characteristics, feelings, motivations, and ambitions flow from these different life experiences so that the members of these different groups become different kinds of people. The process of gendering and its outcome are legitimated by religion, law, science, and the society's entire set of values.

Gender as Process, Stratification, and Structure

As a social institution, gender is a process of creating distinguishable social statuses for the assignment of rights and responsibilities. As part of a stratification system that ranks these statuses unequally, gender is a major building block in the social structures built on these unequal statuses.

As a *process*, gender creates the social differences that define "woman" and "man." In social interaction throughout their lives, individuals learn what is expected, see what is expected, act and react in expected ways, and thus simultaneously construct and maintain the gender order: "The very injunction to be given gender takes place through discursive routes: to be a good mother, to be a heterosexually desirable object, to be a fit worker, in sum, to signify a multiplicity of guarantees in response to a variety of different demands all at once" (J. Butler 1990, 145). Members of a social group neither make up gender as they go along nor exactly replicate in rote fashion what was done before. In almost every encounter, human beings produce gender, behaving in the ways they learned were appropriate for their gender status, or resisting or rebelling against these norms. Resistance and rebellion have altered gender norms, but so far they have rarely eroded the statuses.

Gendered patterns of interaction acquire additional layers of gendered sexuality, parenting, and work behaviors in childhood, adolescence, and adulthood. Gendered norms and expectations are enforced through informal sanctions of gender-inappropriate behavior by peers and by formal punishment or threat of punishment by those in authority should behavior deviate too far from socially imposed standards for women and men.

Everyday gendered interactions build gender into the family, the work process, and other organizations and institutions, which in turn reinforce gender expectations for individuals. Because gender is a process, there is room not only for modification and variation by individuals and small groups but also for institutionalized change (J. W. Scott 1988, p. 7).

As part of a *stratification* system, gender ranks men above women of the same race and class. Women and men could be different but equal. In practice, the process of creating difference depends to a great extent on differential evaluation. As Nancy Jay (1981) says: "That which is defined, separated out, isolated from all else is A and pure. Not-A is necessarily impure, a random catchall, to which nothing is external except A and the principle of order that separates it from Not-A" (45). From the individual's point of view, whichever gender is A, the other is Not-A; gender boundaries tell the individual who is like him or her, and all the rest are unlike. From society's point of view, however, one gender is usually the touchstone, the normal, the dominant, and the other is different, deviant, and subordinate. In Western society, "man" is A, "wo-man" is Not-A.

(Consider what a society would be like where woman was A and man Not-A.)

The further dichotomization by race and class constructs the gradations of a heterogeneous society's stratification scheme. Thus, in the United States, white is A, African American is Not-A; middle class is A, working class is Not-A, and "African-American women occupy a position whereby the inferior half of a series of these dichotomies converge" (P. H. Collins 1989, 70). The dominant categories are the hegemonic ideals, taken so for granted as the way things should be that white is not ordinarily thought of as a race, middle class as a class, or men as a gender. The characteristics of these categories define the Other as that which lacks the valuable qualities the dominants exhibit.

In a gender-stratified society, what men do is usually valued more highly than what women do because men do it, even when their activities are very similar or the same. In different regions of southern India, for example, harvesting rice is men's work, shared work, or women's work: "Wherever a task is done by women it is considered easy, and where it is done by [men] it is considered difficult" (Mencher 1988, 104). A gathering and hunting society's survival usually depends on the nuts, grubs, and small animals brought in by the women's foraging trips, but when the men's hunt is successful, it is the occasion for a celebration. Conversely, because they are the superior group, white men do not have to do the "dirty work," such as housework; the most inferior group does it, usually poor women of color (Palmer 1989). . . .

Societies vary in the extent of the inequality in social status of their women and men members, but where there is inequality, the status "woman" (and its attendant behavior and role allocations) is usually held in lesser esteem than the status "man." Since gender is also intertwined with a society's other constructed statuses of differential evaluation— race, religion, occupation, class, country of origin, and so on—men and women members of the favored groups command more power, more prestige, and more property than the members of the disfavored groups. Within many social groups, however, men are advantaged over women. The more economic resources, such as education and job opportunities, are available to a group, the more they tend to be monopolized by men. In poorer groups that have few resources (such as working-class African Amer-

icans in the United States), women and men are more nearly equal, and the women may even outstrip the men in education and occupational status (Almquist 1987).

As a *structure*, gender divides work in the home and in economic production, legitimates those in authority, and organizes sexuality and emotional life (Connell 1987, pp. 91–142). As primary parents, women significantly influence children's psychological development and emotional attachments, in the process reproducing gender. Emergent sexuality is shaped by heterosexual, homosexual, bisexual, and sadomasochistic patterns that are gendered—different for girls and boys, and for women and men—so that sexual statuses reflect gender statuses.

When gender is a major component of structured inequality, the devalued genders have less power, prestige, and economic rewards than the valued genders. In countries that discourage gender discrimination, many major roles are still gendered; women still do most of the domestic labor and child rearing, even while doing full-time paid work; women and men are segregated on the job and each does work considered "appropriate"; women's work is usually paid less than men's work. Men dominate the positions of authority and leadership in government, the military, and the law; cultural productions, religions, and sports reflect men's interests. . . .

Gender inequality—the devaluation of "women" and the social domination of "men"—has social functions and social history. It is not the result of sex, procreation, physiology, anatomy, hormones, or genetic predispositions. It is produced and maintained by identifiable social processes and built into the general social structure and individual identities deliberately and purposefully. The social order as we know it in Western societies is organized around racial, ethnic, class, and gender inequality. I contend, therefore, that the continuing purpose of gender as a modern social institution is to construct women as a group to be the subordinates of men as a group.

The Paradox of Human Nature

To say that sex, sexuality, and gender are all socially constructed is not to minimize their social power. These categorical imperatives govern our lives in the most profound and pervasive ways, through the social experiences and social practices of what Dorothy

Smith calls the "everday/evernight world" (1990, 31–57). The paradox of human nature is that it is *always* a manifestation of cultural meanings, social relationships, and power politics; "not biology, but culture, becomes destiny" (J. Butler 1990, 8). Gendered people emerge not from physiology or sexual orientation but from the exigencies of the social order, mostly, from the need for a reliable division of the work of food production and the social (not physical) reproduction of new members. The moral imperatives of religion and cultural representations guard the boundary lines among genders and ensure that what is demanded, what is permitted, and what is tabooed for the people in each gender is well known and followed by most (C. Davies 1982). Political power, control of scarce resources, and, if necessary, violence uphold the gendered social order in the face of resistance and rebellion. Most people, however, voluntarily go along with their society's prescriptions for those of their gender status, because the norms and expectations get built into their sense of worth and identity as [the way we] think, the way we see and hear and speak, the way we fantasy, and the way we feel.

There is no core or bedrock in human nature below these endlessly looping processes of the social production of sex and gender, self and other, identity and psyche, each of which is a "complex cultural construction" (J. Butler 1990, 36). *For humans, the social is the natural.* Therefore, "in its feminist senses, gender cannot mean simply the cultural appropriation of biological sexual difference. Sexual difference is itself a fundamental—and scientifically contested—construction. Both 'sex' and 'gender' are woven of multiple, asymmetrical strands of difference, charged with multifaceted dramatic narratives of domination and struggle" (Haraway 1990, 140).

REFERENCES

Almquist, Elizabeth M. 1987. "Labor market gendered inequality in minority groups," *Gender & Society* 1:400–14.

Butler, Judith. 1990. *Gender Trouble: Feminism and the Subversion of Identity.* New York and London: Routledge.

Collins, Patricia Hill. 1989. "The social construction of black feminist thought," *Signs* 14:745–73.

Connell, R. [Robert] W. 1987. *Gender and Power: Society, the Person, and Sexual Politics.* Stanford, Calif.: Stanford University Press.

Davies, Christie. 1982. "Sexual taboos and social boundaries," *American Journal of Sociology* 87:1032–63.

Dwyer, Daisy, and Judith Bruce (eds.). 1988. *A Home Divided: Women and Income in the Third World.* Stanford, Calif.: Stanford University Press.

Haraway, Donna. 1990. "Investment strategies for the evolving portfolio of primate females," in Jacobus, Keller, and Shuttleworth. *Body/politics: Women and the Discourse of Science.*

Jacobus, Mary, Evelyn Fox Keller, and Sally Shuttleworth (eds.). 1990. *Body/politics: Women and the Discourse of Science.* New York and London: Routledge.

Jay, Nancy. 1981. "Gender and dichotomy," *Feminist Studies* 7:38–56.

Mencher, Joan. 1988. "Women's work and poverty: Women's contribution to household maintenance in South India," in Dwyer and Bruce. *A Home Divided: Women and Income in the Third World.*

Palmer, Phyllis. 1989. *Domesticity and Dirt: Housewives and Domestic Servants in the United States, 1920–1945.* Philadelphia: Temple University Press.

Scott, Joan Wallach. 1988. *Gender and the Politics of History.* New York: Columbia University Press.

——. 1990. *The Conceptual Practices of Power: A Feminist Sociology of Knowledge.* Toronto: University of Toronto Press.

West, Candace, and Don Zimmerman. 1987. "Doing gender," *Gender & Society* 1:125–51.

◆◆◆

Patriarchy, the System

An It, Not a He, a Them, or an Us

Allan G. Johnson

"When you say patriarchy," a man complained from the rear of the audience, "I know what you *really* mean—me!" A lot of people hear "men" whenever someone says "patriarchy," so that criticism of gender oppression is taken to mean that all men—each and every one of them—are oppressive people. Not surprisingly, many men take it personally if someone merely mentions patriarchy or the oppression of women, bristling at what they often see as a way to make them feel guilty. And some women feel free to blame individual men for patriarchy simply because they're men. Some of the time, men feel defensive because they identify with patriarchy and its values and don't want to face the consequences these produce or the prospect of giving up male privilege. But defensiveness more often reflects a common confusion about the difference between patriarchy as a kind of society and the people who participate in it. If we're ever going to work toward real change, it's a confusion we'll have to clear up.

To do this, we have to realize that we're stuck in a model of social life that views everything as beginning and ending with individuals. Looking at things in this way, we tend to think that if evil exists in the world, it's only because there are evil people who have entered into an evil conspiracy. Racism exists, for example, simply because white people are racist bigots who hate members of racial and ethnic minorities and want to do them harm. There is gender oppression because men want and like to dominate women and act out hostility toward them. There is poverty and class oppression because people in the upper classes are greedy, heartless, and cruel. The flip side of this individualistic model of guilt and blame is that race, gender, and class oppression are actually not oppression at all, but merely the sum of individual failings on the part of blacks, women, and the poor, who lack the right stuff to compete successfully with whites, men, and others who know how to make something of themselves.

What this kind of thinking ignores is that we are all participating in something larger than ourselves or any collection of us. On some level, most people are familiar with the idea that social life involves us in something larger than ourselves, but few seem to know what to do with that idea. When Sam Keen laments that "THE SYSTEM is running us all,"[1] he strikes a deep chord in many people. But he also touches on a basic misunderstanding of social life, because having blamed "the system" (presumably society) for our problems, he doesn't take the next step to understand what that might mean. What exactly *is* a system, for example, and how could it run us? Do *we* have anything to do with shaping *it*, and if so, how? How, for example, do we participate in patriarchy, and how does that link us to the consequences it produces? How is what we think of as "normal" life related to male dominance, women's oppression, and the hierarchical, control-obsessed world in which they, and our lives, are embedded? . . .

. . . If we see patriarchy as nothing more than men's and women's individual personalities, motivations, and behavior, for example, then it probably won't even occur to us to ask about larger contexts—such as institutions like the family, religion, and the economy—and how people's lives are shaped in relation to them. From this kind of individualistic perspective, we might ask why a particular man raped, harassed, or beat a woman. We wouldn't ask, however, what kind of society would promote persistent *patterns* of such behavior in everyday life, from wife-beating jokes to the routine inclusion of sexual coercion and violence in mainstream movies. We are quick to explain rape and battery as the acts of sick or angry men; but we rarely take seriously the question of what kind of society would produce so much male anger and pathology or direct it toward sexual violence rather than something else. We rarely ask how gender violence might serve other more "normalized" ends such as male control and domination. . . .

. . . If the goal is to change the world, this won't help us. We need to see and deal with the social roots that generate and nurture the social problems that are reflected in the behavior of individuals. We can't do this without realizing that we all participate in something larger than ourselves, something we didn't create but that we have the power to affect through the choices we make about *how* to participate.

That something larger is patriarchy, which is more than a collection of individuals (such as "men"). It is a system, which means it can't be reduced to the people who participate in it. If you go to work in a corporation, for example, you know the minute you walk in the door that you've entered "something" that shapes your experience and behavior, something that isn't just you and the other people you work with. You can feel yourself stepping into a set of relationships and shared understandings about who's who and what's supposed to happen and why, and all of this limits you in many ways. And when you leave at the end of the day you can feel yourself released from the constraints imposed by your participation in that system; you can feel the expectations drop away and your focus shift to other systems such as family or a neighborhood bar that shape your experience in different ways. To understand a system like a corporation, we have to look at more than people like you, because all of you aren't the corporation, even though you make it run. If the corporation were just a collection of people, then whatever happened to the corporation would by definition also happen to them, and vice versa; but this clearly isn't so. A corporation can go bankrupt, for example, or cease to exist altogether without any of the people who work there going bankrupt or disappearing. Conversely, everyone who works for the corporation could quit, but that wouldn't necessarily mean the end of the corporation, only the arrival of a new set of participants. We can't understand a corporation, then, just by looking at the people who participate in it, for it is something larger and has to be understood as such.

So, too, with patriarchy, a kind of society that is more than a collection of women and men and can't be understood simply by understanding them. *We are not patriarchy,* no more than people who believe in Allah *are* Islam or Canadians *are* Canada. Patriarchy is a kind of society organized around certain kinds of social relationships and ideas. As individuals, we participate in it. Paradoxically, our participation both shapes our lives and gives us the opportunity to be part of changing or perpetuating it.[2] But *we are not it,* which means that patriarchy can exist without men having "oppressive personalities" or actively conspiring with one another to defend male privilege. To demonstrate that gender oppression exists, we don't have to show that men are villains, that women are good-hearted victims, that women don't participate in their own oppression, or that men never oppose it. If a society is oppressive, then people who grow up and live in it will tend to accept, identify with, and participate in it as "normal" and unremarkable life. That's the path of least resistance in any system. It's hard not to follow it, given how we depend on society and its rewards and punishments that hinge on going along with the status quo. When oppression is woven into the fabric of everyday life, we don't need to go out of our way to be overly oppressive in order for an oppressive system to produce oppressive consequences. As the saying goes, what evil requires is simply that ordinary people do nothing.

"The System"

In general, a system is any collection of interrelated parts or elements that we can think of as a whole. A car engine, for example, is a collection of parts that fit together in certain ways to produce a "whole" that is identifiable in many cultures as serving a particular purpose. A language is also a collection of parts—letters of the alphabet, words, punctuation marks, and rules of grammar and syntax—that fit together in certain ways to form something we can identify as a whole. And societies include a variety of interrelated parts that we can think of as a whole. All of these are systems that differ in the kinds of parts they include and how those parts are related to one another.

The crucial thing to understand about patriarchy or any other kind of social system is that it's something people participate in. It's an arrangement of shared understandings and relationships that connect people to one another and something larger than themselves. In some ways, we're like players who participate in a game. Monopoly, for example, consists of a set of shared understandings about things such as the meaning of property and rent, the value of competition and accumulating wealth, and various rules about rolling dice, moving around a board, buying, selling, and developing property, collecting rents, winning, and losing. It has positions—player, banker, and so on—that people occupy. It has material elements such as the board, houses and hotels, dice, property deeds, money, and "pieces" that represent each player's movements on the board. As such, the game is something we can think of as a social system whose diverse elements cohere with a unity and wholeness that distinguish it from other games and from nongames.[3] Most important, we can describe it as a system without ever talking about the personal characteristics or motivations of the individual people who actually play it at any given moment.

If we watch people play Monopoly, we notice certain routine patterns of feeling and behavior that reflect paths of least resistance that are inherent in the game itself. If someone lands on a property I own, for example, I collect the rent (if I happen to notice), and if they can't pay, I take their assets and force them from the game. The game encourages me to feel good about this, not necessarily because *I'm* greedy and merciless, but because the game is about winning, and this is what winning consists of in Monopoly. Since everyone else is also trying to win by driving me out of the game, each step I take toward winning protects me and alleviates some anxiety about landing on a property whose rent *I* can't pay.

Since these patterns are shaped by the game far more than by the individual players, we can find ourselves behaving in ways that might seem disturbing in other situations. When I'm not playing Monopoly, I behave quite differently, even though I'm still the same person. This is why I don't play Monopoly anymore—I don't like the way it encourages me to feel and behave in the name of "fun," especially toward people I care about. The reason we behave differently outside the game doesn't lie in our personalities but in the *game's* paths of least resistance, which define certain behavior and values as appropriate and expected. When we see ourselves as Monopoly players, we feel limited by the rules and goals the game defines, and experience it as something external to us and beyond our control. It's important to note how rarely it ever occurs to people to simply change the rules. The relationships, terms, and goals that organize the game aren't presented to us as ours to judge or alter. The more attached we feel to the game and the more closely we identify ourselves as players, the more likely we are

to feel helpless in relation to it. If you're about to drive someone into bankruptcy, you can excuse yourself by saying "I've got to take your money, those are the rules," but only if you ignore the fact that you could choose not to play or could suggest a change in the rules. Then again, if you can't imagine life without the game, you won't see many alternatives to doing what's expected of you.

If we try to explain patterns of social behavior only in terms of individual people's personalities and motives—people do greedy things, for example, because they *are* greedy—then we ignore how behavior is shaped by paths of least resistance found in the systems people participate in. The "profit motive" associated with capitalism, for example, is typically seen as a psychological motive of individuals that explains capitalism as a system: capitalism exists because there are individuals who want to make a profit. But this puts the cart before the horse by avoiding the question of where wanting to make a profit comes from in the first place. We need to ask what kind of world makes such wants possible and encourages people to organize their lives around them, for although we may pursue profit as we play Monopoly or participate in real-world capitalism, the psychological profit motive doesn't originate with us. We aren't born with it. It doesn't exist in many cultures and was unknown for most of human history. The profit motive is a historically developed aspect of market systems in general and capitalism in particular that shapes the values, behavior, and personal motives of those who participate in it. To argue that managers lay off workers, for example, simply because managers are heartless or cruel ignores the fact that success under capitalism often depends on this kind of competitive, profit-maximizing "heartless" behavior. Most managers probably know in their hearts that the practice of routinely discarding people in the name of profit and expedience is hurtful and unfair. This is why they feel so bad about having to be the ones to carry it out, and protect their feelings by inventing euphemisms such as "downsizing" and "outplacement." And yet they participate in a system that produces these cruel results anyway, not because of cruel personalities or malice toward workers, but because a capitalist system makes this a path of least resistance and exacts real costs from those who stray from it.

To use the game analogy, it's a mistake to assume that we can understand the players without paying attention to the game they're playing. We create even more trouble by thinking we can understand the *game* without ever looking at it as something more than what goes on inside individuals. One way to see this is to realize that systems often work in ways that don't reflect the experience and motivations of the people who participate in them. . . .

In spite of all the good reasons not to use individual models to explain social life, they are a path of least resistance because individual experience and motivation are what we know best. As a result, we tend to see something like sexism as the result of poor socialization through which men learn to act dominant and masculine and women to act subordinate and feminine. While there is certainly some truth to this, it doesn't work as an explanation of patterns like gender oppression. It's no better than trying to explain war as simply the result of training men to be warlike, without looking at economic systems that equip armies at huge profits and political systems that organize and hurl armies at one another. . . .

Since focusing just on individual women and men won't tell us much about patriarchy, simply trying to understand people's attitudes or behavior won't get us very far so long as patriarchy goes unexamined and unchallenged as the only gender game in town. And if we don't look beyond individuals, whatever change we accomplish won't have much more than a superficial, temporary effect. Systemic paths of least resistance provide powerful reasons for people to go along with the status quo. This is why individual change is often restricted to people who either have little to lose or who are secure and protected enough to choose a different path. So change typically gets limited to the most oppressed, who have the least to lose and are in the weakest position to challenge the system as a whole, and the most privileged, who can afford to attend workshops or enter therapy or who can hire someone (typically a woman) to take care of their children. In this latter group in particular, it's easy for men to fool themselves into thinking they can find nicer, less oppressive ways to participate in an oppressive system without challenging it, and therefore without disturbing the basis for male privilege. It's like the myth of a kinder, gentler capitalism in which managers still overwork and lay off employees in order to bolster the bottom line and protect shareholders' interests; but now they do it with

greater interpersonal sensitivity. The result is pretty much the same as it was before, but now they can feel better about it. After all, if changing the system isn't a goal, then it makes sense to accommodate to it while maintaining the appearance of regretting its oppressive consequences. And an individualistic approach is perfectly suited to those ends, for the privileged can feel bad about the people who suffer even as they shield from scrutiny the system that makes both suffering and privilege inevitable. . . .

Either way, the individualistic model offers little hope of changing patriarchy because patriarchy is more than how people think, feel, and behave. As such, patriarchy isn't simply about the psychic wounding of sons by their fathers, or the dangers and failures of heterosexual intimacy, or boys' feelings about their mothers, or how men treat women and one another. It *includes* all of these by producing them as symptoms that help perpetuate the system; but these aren't what patriarchy *is*. It is a way of organizing social life through which such wounding, failure, and mistreatment can occur. If fathers neglect their sons, it is because fathers move in a world that makes pursuit of goals other than deeply committed fatherhood a path of least resistance.[4] If heterosexual intimacy is prone to fail, it is because patriarchy is organized in ways that set women and men fundamentally at odds with one another in spite of all the good reasons they otherwise have to get along and thrive together. And if men's use of coercion and violence against women is a pervasive pattern—and it is—it is because force and violence are supported in patriarchal society; it is because women are designated as desirable and legitimate objects of male control, and because in a society organized around control, force and violence *work*.

We can't find a way out of patriarchy or imagine something different without a clear sense of what patriarchy is and what that's got to do with us. Thus far, the alternative has been to reduce our understanding of gender to an intellectual gumbo of personal problems, tendencies, and motivations. Presumably, these will be solved through education, better communication skills, consciousness raising, "heroic journeys," and other forms of individual transformation. Since this isn't how social systems actually change, the result is widespread frustration and cycles of blame and denial. . . .

We need to see more clearly what patriarchy is about as a system. This includes cultural ideas about men and women, the web of relationships that structure social life, and the unequal distribution of rewards and resources that underlies oppression. We need to see new ways to participate by forging alternative paths of least resistance, for the system doesn't simply "run us" like hapless puppets. It may be larger than us, it may not *be* us, but it doesn't exist except *through* us. Without us, patriarchy doesn't *happen*. And that's where we have power to do something about it and about ourselves *in* it.

Patriarchy

The key to understanding any system is to identify its various parts and how they're arranged to form a whole. To understand a language, for example, we have to learn its alphabet, vocabulary, and rules for combining words into meaningful phrases and sentences. With a social system such as patriarchy, it's more complicated because there are many different kinds of parts, and it is often difficult to see just how they're connected. Patriarchy's defining elements are its male-dominated, male-identified, and male-centered character, but this is just the beginning. At its core, patriarchy is a set of symbols and ideas that make up a culture embodied by everything from the content of everyday conversation to literature and film. Patriarchal culture includes ideas about the nature of things, including men, women, and humanity, with manhood and masculinity most closely associated with being human and womanhood and femininity relegated to the marginal position of "other." It's about how social life is and how it's supposed to be; about what's expected of people and about how they feel. It's about standards of feminine beauty and masculine toughness, images of feminine vulnerability and masculine protectiveness, of older men coupled with young women, of elderly women alone. It's about defining women and men as opposites, about the "naturalness" of male aggression, competition, and dominance and of female caring, cooperation, and subordination. It's about the valuing of masculinity and maleness and the devaluing of femininity and femaleness. It's about the primary importance of a husband's career and the secondary status of a wife's, about child care as a priority in women's lives and its secondary importance in men's. It's about the social acceptability of anger, rage, and toughness in men but not in women, and

of caring, tenderness, and vulnerability in women but not in men.

Above all, patriarchal culture is about the core value of control and domination in almost every area of human existence. From the expression of emotion to economics to the natural environment, gaining and exercising control is a continuing goal of great importance. Because of this, the concept of power takes on a narrow definition in terms of "power over"—the ability to control others, events, resources, or oneself in spite of resistance—rather than alternatives such as the ability to cooperate with others, to give freely of oneself, or to feel and act in harmony with nature.[5] To have power over and to be prepared to use it are defined culturally as good and desirable (and characteristically "masculine"), and to lack such power or to be reluctant to use it is seen as weak if not contemptible (and characteristically "feminine").

The main use of any culture is to provide symbols and ideas out of which people construct their sense of what is real. As such, language mirrors social reality in sometimes startling ways. In contemporary usage, for example, the words "crone," "witch," "bitch," and "virgin" describe women as threatening, evil, or heterosexually inexperienced and thus incomplete. In prepatriarchal times, however, these words evoked far different images.[6] The crone was the old woman whose life experience gave her insight, wisdom, respect, and the power to enrich people's lives. The witch was the wise-woman healer, the knower of herbs, the midwife, the link joining body, spirit, and Earth. The bitch was Artemis-Diana, goddess of the hunt, most often associated with the dogs who accompanied her. And the virgin was merely a woman who was unattached, unclaimed, and unowned by any man and therefore independent and autonomous. Notice how each word has been transformed from a positive cultural image of female power, independence, and dignity to an insult or a shadow of its former self so that few words remain to identify women in ways both positive and powerful.

Going deeper into patriarchal culture, we find a complex web of ideas that define reality and what's considered good and desirable. To see the world through patriarchal eyes is to believe that women and men are profoundly different in their basic natures, that hierarchy is the only alternative to chaos, and that men were made in the image of a masculine

God with whom they enjoy a special relationship. It is to take as obvious the idea that there are two and only two distinct genders; that patriarchal hetero-sexuality is "natural" and same-sex attraction is not; that because men neither bear nor breast-feed children, they cannot feel a compelling bodily connection to them; that on some level every woman, whether heterosexual or lesbian, wants a "real man" who knows how to "take charge of things," including her; that females can't be trusted, especially when they're menstruating or accusing men of sexual misconduct. To embrace patriarchy is to believe that mothers should stay home and that fathers should work out of the home, regardless of men's and women's actual abilities or needs.[7] It is to buy into the notion that women are weak and men are strong, that women and children need men to support and protect them, all in spite of the fact that in many ways men are not the physically stronger sex, that women perform a huge share of hard physical labor in many societies (often larger than men's), that women's physical endurance tends to be greater than men's over the long haul, that women tend to be more capable of enduring pain and emotional stress.[8] And yet such evidence means little in the face of a patriarchal culture that dictates how things *ought* to be and, like all cultural mythology,

> will not be argued down by facts. It may seem to be making straightforward statements, but actually these conceal another mood, the imperative. Myth exists in a state of tension. It is not really describing a situation, but trying by means of this description *to bring about* what it declares to exist.[9]

To live in a patriarchal culture is to learn what's expected of us as men and women, the rules that regulate punishment and reward based on how we behave and appear. These rules range from laws that require men to fight in wars not of their own choosing to customary expectations that mothers will provide child care, or that when a woman shows sexual interest in a man or merely smiles or acts friendly, she gives up her right to say no and control her own body. And to live under patriarchy is to take into ourselves shared ways of feeling—the hostile contempt for femaleness that forms the core of misogyny and presumptions of male superiority, the ridicule men direct at other men who show signs of vulnerability or weakness, or the fear and insecurity that

every woman must deal with when she exercises the right to move freely in the world, especially at night and by herself. . . .

The prominent place of misogyny in patriarchal culture, for example, doesn't mean that every man and woman consciously hates all things female. But it does mean that to the extent that we don't feel such hatred, it's *in spite of* paths of least resistance contained in our culture. Complete freedom from such feelings and judgments is all but impossible. It is certainly possible for heterosexual men to love women without mentally fragmenting them into breasts, buttocks, genitals, and other variously desirable parts. It is possible for women to feel good about their bodies, to not judge themselves as being too fat, to not abuse themselves to one degree or another in pursuit of impossible male-identified standards of beauty and sexual attractiveness. All of this is possible; but to live in patriarchy is to breathe in misogynist images of women as objectified sexual property valued primarily for their usefulness to men. This finds its way into everyone who grows up breathing and swimming in it, and once inside us it remains, however unaware of it we may be. So, when we hear or express sexist jokes and other forms of misogyny we may not recognize it, and even if we do, say nothing rather than risk other people thinking we're "too sensitive" or, especially in the case of men, "not one of the guys." In either case, we are involved, if only by our silence. . . .

To understand patriarchy, we have to identify its cultural elements and see how they are related to the structure of social life. We must see, for example, how cultural ideas that identify women primarily as mothers and men primarily as breadwinners support patterns in which women do most domestic work at home and are discriminated against in hiring, pay, and promotions at work. But to do anything with such an understanding, we also must see what patriarchy has to do with us as individuals—how it shapes us and how we, in choosing how to participate, shape *it*.

The System in Us in the System

One of the most difficult things to accept about patriarchy is that we're involved in it, which means we're also involved in its consequences. This is especially hard for men who refuse to believe they benefit from women's oppression, because they can't see how this could happen without their being personally oppressive in their intentions, feelings, and behavior. For many men, being told they're *involved* in oppression can only mean they *are* oppressive. . . .

. . . Societies don't exist without people participating in them, which means that we can't understand patriarchy unless we also ask how people are connected to it and how this connection varies, depending on social characteristics such as race, gender, ethnicity, age, and class. Capitalism, for example, didn't just happen on its own but emerged as an economic system in a patriarchal world dominated by men and their interests, especially white European men of the newly emerging merchant class. The same can be said of industrialization, which was bound up with the development of capitalism in eighteenth- and nineteenth-century Europe. This line of thinking might seem to undermine the argument I've made about including systems in our thinking—"It really comes down to individuals after all"—but it's more complicated than that. The problem isn't society and it isn't us. It's the relationship between the two that we have to understand, the nature of the thing we participate in and how we choose to participate in it and how both are shaped in the process. In this sense, it's a mistake to equate patriarchy with men; but it's also wrong to act as though systems like patriarchy or capitalism have nothing to do with gender and differences in power and interests that distinguish and separate men and women. It's equally wrong to act as though all men or all women are the same, as though dynamics such as racism and class oppression don't affect how patriarchy operates and affects people's lives in different ways.

One way to see how people connect with systems is to think of us as occupying social positions that locate us in relation to people in other positions. We connect to families, for example, through positions such as "mother," "daughter," and "cousin"; to economic systems through positions such as "vice president," "secretary," or "unemployed"; to political systems through positions such as "citizen," "registered voter," and "mayor"; to religious systems through positions such as "believer" and "clergy." How we perceive the people who occupy such positions and what we expect of them depend on cultural ideas—such as the belief that mothers are naturally better than fathers at child care or the ex-

pectation that fathers will be the primary breadwinners. Such ideas are powerful because we use them to construct a sense of who we and other people are. When a woman marries, for example, how people (including her) perceive and think about her changes as cultural ideas about what it means to be a wife come into play—ideas about how wives feel about their husbands, for example, what's most important to wives, what's expected of them, and what they may expect of others. . . .

We can think of a society as a network of interconnected systems within systems, each made up of social positions and their relations to one another. To say, then, that I'm white, male, college educated, and a writer, sociologist, U.S. citizen, heterosexual, middle-aged, husband, father, brother, and son identifies me in relation to positions which are themselves related to positions in various social systems, from the entire world to the family of my birth. In another sense, the day-to-day reality of a society only exists through what people actually do as they participate in it. Patriarchal culture, for example, places a high value on control and maleness. By themselves, these are just abstractions. But when men and women actually talk and men interrupt women more than women interrupt men, or men ignore topics introduced by women in favor of their own or in other ways control conversation,[10] or when men use their authority to sexually harass women in the workplace, then the reality of patriarchy as a kind of society and people's sense of themselves as female and male within it actually happen in a concrete way.

In this sense, like all social systems, patriarchy exists only through people's lives. Through this, patriarchy's various aspects are there for us to see over and over again. This has two important implications for how we understand patriarchy. First, to some extent people experience patriarchy as external to them; but this doesn't mean that it's a distinct and separate thing, like a house in which we live. Instead, by participating in patriarchy we are of patriarchy and it is *of* us. Both exist *through* the other and neither can exist without the other. Second, patriarchy isn't static; it's an ongoing *process* that's continuously shaped and reshaped. Since the thing we're participating in is patriarchal, we tend to behave in ways that create a patriarchal world from one moment to the next. But we have some freedom to break the rules and construct everyday life in different ways, which means that the paths we choose to follow can do as much to change patriarchy as they can to perpetuate it.

We're involved in patriarchy and its consequences because we occupy social positions in it, which is all it takes. Since gender oppression is, by definition, a system of inequality organized around gender categories, we can no more avoid being involved in it than we can avoid being female or male. *All* men and *all* women are therefore involved in this oppressive system, and none of us can control *whether* we participate, only *how*. . . .

NOTES

1. Sam Keen, *Fire in the Belly: On Being a Man* (New York: Bantam, 1991), 207.

2. This is one of the major differences between organisms like the human body and social systems. Cells and nerves cannot "rebel" against the body and try to change it into something else.

3. Although the game analogy is useful, social systems are quite unlike a game in important ways. The rules and other understandings on which social life is based are far more complex, ambiguous, and contradictory than those of a typical game and much more open to negotiation and "making it up" as we go along.

4. For a history of American fatherhood, see Robert L. Griswold, *Fatherhood in America: A History* (New York: Basic Books, 1993).

5. For a thorough discussion of this distinction, see Marilyn French, *Beyond Power: On Men, Women, and Morals* (New York: Summit Books, 1985).

6. For discussions of language and gender, see Jane Caputi, *Gossips, Gorgons, and Crones* (Santa Fe: Bear and Company, 1993); Mary Daly, *Gyn/Ecology: The Metaethics of Radical Feminism* (Boston: Beacon Press, 1978); Dale Spender, *Man Made Language* (London: Pandora, 1980); Barbara G. Walker, *The Woman's Encyclopedia of Myths and Secrets* (San Francisco: Harper and Row, 1983); idem, *The Woman's Dictionary of Symbols and Sacred Objects* (San Francisco: Harper and Row, 1988). For a very different slant on gender and language, see Mary Daly (in cahoots with Jane Caputi), *Webster's First New Intergalactic Wickedary of the English Language* (Boston: Beacon Press, 1987).

7. See Arlie Hochschild (with Anne Machung), *The Second Shift* (New York: Avon Books, 1989).

8. See, for example, Rosalyn Baxandall, Linda Gordon, and Susan Reverby, eds., *America's Working Women: A Documentary History—1600 to the Present* (New York: Vintage Press, 1976); Ashley Montagu, *The Natural Superiority of Women* (New York: Collier, 1974); Robin Morgan, ed., *Sisterhood Is Global* (New York: Anchor, 1990); and Marilyn Waring, *If Women Counted: A New Feminist Economics* (San Francisco: HarperCollins, 1988).

9. Elizabeth Janeway, *Man's World, Woman's Place: A Study in Social Mythology* (New York: Dell, 1971), 37.

10. See, for example, P. Kollock, P. Blumstein, and P. Schwartz, "Sex and Power in Interaction," *American Sociological Review* 50, no. 1 (1985): 34–46; N. Henley, M. Hamilton, and B. Thorne, "Womanspeak and Manspeak: Sex Differences and Sexism in Communication," in *Beyond Sex Roles*, ed. A. G. Sargent (New York: West, 1985), 168–185; and L. Smith-Lovin and C. Brody, "Interruptions in Group Discussions: The Effect of Gender and Group Composition," *American Sociological Review* 51, no. 3 (1989): 424–435.

THREE

A Black Feminist Statement

*Combahee River Collective**

We are a collective of Black feminists who have been meeting together since 1974.[1] During that time we have been involved in the process of defining and clarifying our politics, while at the same time doing political work within our own group and in coalition with other progressive organizations and movements. The most general statement of our politics at the present time would be that we are actively committed to struggling against racial, sexual, heterosexual, and class oppression and see as our particular task the development of integrated analysis and practice based upon the fact that the major systems of oppression are interlocking. The synthesis of these oppressions creates the conditions of our lives. As Black women we see Black feminism as the logical political movement to combat the manifold and simultaneous oppressions that all women of color face.

We will discuss four major topics in the paper that follows: (1) the genesis of contemporary Black feminism; (2) what we believe, i.e., the specific province of our politics; (3) the problems in organizing Black feminists, including a brief herstory of our collective; and (4) Black feminist issues and practice.

1. The Genesis of Contemporary Black Feminism

Before looking at the recent development of Black feminism we would like to affirm that we find our origins in the historical reality of Afro-American

women's continuous life-and-death struggle for survival and liberation. Black women's extremely negative relationship to the American political system (a system of white male rule) has always been determined by our membership in two oppressed racial and sexual castes. As Angela Davis points out in "Reflections on the Black Woman's Role in the Community of Slaves," Black women have always embodied, if only in their physical manifestation, an adversary stance to white male rule and have actively resisted its inroads upon them and their communities in both dramatic and subtle ways. There have always been Black women activists— some known, like Sojourner Truth, Harriet Tubman, Frances E. W. Harper, Ida B. Wells Barnett, and Mary Church Terrell, and thousands upon thousands unknown—who had a shared awareness of how their sexual identity combined with their racial identity to make their whole life situation and the focus of their political struggles unique. Contemporary Black feminism is the outgrowth of countless generations of personal sacrifice, militancy, and work by our mothers and sisters.

A Black feminist presence has evolved most obviously in connection with the second wave of the American women's movement beginning in the late 1960s. Black, other Third World, and working women have been involved in the feminist movement from its start, but both outside reactionary forces and racism and elitism within the movement itself have served to obscure our participation. In 1973 Black feminists, primarily located in New York, felt the necessity of forming a separate Black feminist group. This became the National Black Feminist Organization (NBFO).

Black feminist politics also have an obvious connection to movements for Black liberation, particularly those of the 1960s and 1970s. Many of us were active in those movements (civil rights, Black nationalism, the Black Panthers), and all of our lives were greatly affected and changed by their ideology, their goals, and the tactics used to achieve their goals. It was our experience and disillusionment within

---

*The Combahee River Collective was a Black feminist group in Boston whose name came from the guerrilla action conceptualized and led by Harriet Tubman on June 2, 1863, in the Port Royal region of South Carolina. This action freed more than 750 slaves and is the only military campaign in American history planned and led by a woman. The Combahee River Collective was most active from 1976 to 1980.

these liberation movements, as well as experience on the periphery of the white male left, that led to the need to develop a politics that was antiracist, unlike those of white women, and antisexist, unlike those of Black and white men.

There is also undeniably a personal genesis for Black feminism, that is, the political realization that comes from the seemingly personal experiences of individual Black women's lives. Black feminists and many more Black women who do not define themselves as feminists have all experienced sexual oppression as a constant factor in our day-to-day existence. As children we realized that we were different from boys and that we were treated differently. For example, we were told in the same breath to be quiet both for the sake of being "ladylike" and to make us less objectionable in the eyes of white people. As we grew older we became aware of the threat of physical and sexual abuse by men. However, we had no way of conceptualizing what was so apparent to us, what we *knew* was really happening.

Black feminists often talk about their feelings of craziness before becoming conscious of the concepts of sexual politics, patriarchal rule, and most importantly, feminism, the political analysis and practice that we women use to struggle against our oppression. The fact that racial politics and indeed racism are pervasive factors in our lives did not allow us, and still does not allow most Black women, to look more deeply into our own experiences and, from that sharing and growing consciousness, to build a politics that will change our lives and inevitably end our oppression. Our development must also be tied to the contemporary economic and political position of Black people. The post–World War II generation of Black youth was the first to be able to minimally partake of certain educational and employment options, previously closed completely to Black people. Although our economic position is still at the very bottom of the American capitalistic economy, a handful of us have been able to gain certain tools as a result of tokenism in education and employment which potentially enable us to more effectively fight our oppression.

A combined antiracist and antisexist position drew us together initially, and as we developed politically we addressed ourselves to heterosexism and economic oppression under capitalism.

2. What We Believe

Above all else, our politics initially sprang from the shared belief that Black women are inherently valuable, that our liberation is a necessity not as an adjunct to somebody else's but because of our need as human persons for autonomy. This may seem so obvious as to sound simplistic, but it is apparent that no other ostensibly progressive movement has ever considered our specific oppression as a priority or worked seriously for the ending of that oppression. Merely naming the pejorative stereotypes attributed to Black women (e.g. mammy, matriarch, Sapphire, whore, bulldagger), let alone cataloguing the cruel, often murderous, treatment we receive, indicates how little value has been placed upon our lives during four centuries of bondage in the Western Hemisphere. We realize that the only people who care enough about us to work consistently for our liberation are us. Our politics evolve from a healthy love for ourselves, our sisters and our community which allows us to continue our struggle and work.

This focusing upon our own oppression is embodied in the concept of identity politics. We believe that the most profound and potentially the most radical politics come directly out of our own identity, as opposed to working to end somebody else's oppression. In the case of Black women this is a particularly repugnant, dangerous, threatening, and therefore revolutionary concept because it is obvious from looking at all the political movements that have preceded us that anyone is more worthy of liberation than ourselves. We reject pedestals, queenhood, and walking ten paces behind. To be recognized as human, levelly human, is enough.

We believe that sexual politics under patriarchy is as pervasive in Black women's lives as are the politics of class and race. We also often find it difficult to separate race from class from sex oppression because in our lives they are most often experienced simultaneously. We know that there is such a thing as racial-sexual oppression which is neither solely racial nor solely sexual, e.g., the history of rape of Black women by white men as a weapon of political repression.

Although we are feminists and lesbians, we feel solidarity with progressive Black men and do not advocate the fractionalization that white women who are separatists demand. Our situation as Black people necessitates that we have solidarity around the fact of race, which white women of course do not need to have with white men, unless it is their negative solidarity as racial oppressors. We struggle together with Black men against racism, while we also struggle with Black men about sexism.

We realize that the liberation of all oppressed peoples necessitates the destruction of the political-economic systems of capitalism and imperialism as well as patriarchy. We are socialists because we believe the work must be organized for the collective benefit of those who do the work and create the products, and not for the profit of the bosses. Material resources must be equally distributed among those who create these resources. We are not convinced, however, that a socialist revolution that is not also a feminist and antiracist revolution will guarantee our liberation. We have arrived at the necessity for developing an understanding of class relationships that takes into account the specific class position of Black women who are generally marginal in the labor force, while at this particular time some of us are temporarily viewed as doubly desirable tokens at white-collar and professional levels. We need to articulate the real class situation of persons who are not merely raceless, sexless workers, but for whom racial and sexual oppression are significant determinants in their working/economic lives. Although we are in essential agreement with Marx's theory as it applied to the very specific economic relationships he analyzed, we know that his analysis must be extended further in order for us to understand our specific economic situation as Black women.

A political contribution which we feel we have already made is the expansion of the feminist principle that the personal is political. In our consciousness-raising sessions, for example, we have in many ways gone beyond white women's revelations because we are dealing with the implications of race and class as well as sex. Even our Black women's style of talking/testifying in Black language about what we have experienced has a resonance that is both cultural and political. We have spent a great deal of energy delving into the cultural and experiential nature of our oppression out of necessity because none of these matters has ever been looked at before. No one before has ever examined the multilayered texture of Black women's lives. An example of this

kind of revelation/conceptualization occurred at a meeting as we discussed the ways in which our early intellectual interests had been attacked by our peers, particularly Black males. We discovered that all of us, because we were "smart" had also been considered "ugly," i.e., "smart-ugly." "Smart-ugly" crystallized the way in which most of us had been forced to develop our intellects at great cost to our "social" lives. The sanctions in the Black and white communities against Black women thinkers are comparatively much higher than for white women, particularly ones from the educated middle and upper classes.

As we have already stated, we reject the stance of lesbian separatism because it is not a viable political analysis or strategy for us. It leaves out far too much and far too many people, particularly Black men, women, and children. We have a great deal of criticism and loathing for what men have been socialized to be in this society: what they support, how they act, and how they oppress. But we do not have the misguided notion that it is their maleness, per se—i.e., their biological maleness—that makes them what they are. As Black women we find any type of biological determinism a particularly dangerous and reactionary basis upon which to build a politic. We must also question whether lesbian separatism is an adequate and progressive political analysis and strategy, even for those who practice it, since it so completely denies any but the sexual sources of women's oppression, negating the facts of class and race.

3. Problems in Organizing Black Feminists

During our years together as a Black feminist collective we have experienced success and defeat, joy and pain, victory and failure. We have found that it is very difficult to organize around Black feminist issues, difficult even to announce in certain contexts that we *are* Black feminists. We have tried to think about the reasons for our difficulties, particularly since the white women's movement continues to be strong and to grow in many directions. In this section we will discuss some of the general reasons for the organizing problems we face and also talk specifically about the stages in organizing our own collective.

The major source of difficulty in our political work is that we are not just trying to fight oppression on one front or even two, but instead to address a whole range of oppressions. We do not have racial, sexual, heterosexual, or class privilege to rely upon, nor do we have even the minimal access to resources and power that groups who possess any one of these types of privilege have.

The psychological toll of being a Black woman and the difficulties this presents in reaching political consciousness and doing political work can never be underestimated. There is a very low value placed upon Black women's psyches in this society, which is both racist and sexist. As an early group member once said, "We are all damaged people merely by virtue of being Black women." We are dispossessed psychologically and on every other level, and yet we feel the necessity to struggle to change the condition of all Black women. In "A Black Feminist's Search for Sisterhood," Michele Wallace arrives at this conclusion:

> We exist as women who are Black who are feminists, each stranded for the moment, working independently because there is not yet an environment in this society remotely congenial to our struggle—because, being on the bottom, we would have to do what no one else has done: we would have to fight the world.[2]

Wallace is pessimistic but realistic in her assessment of Black feminists' position, particularly in her allusion to the nearly classic isolation most of us face. We might use our position at the bottom, however, to make a clear leap into revolutionary action. If Black women were free, it would mean that everyone else would have to be free since our freedom would necessitate the destruction of all the systems of oppression.

Feminism is, nevertheless, very threatening to the majority of Black people because it calls into question some of the most basic assumptions about our existence, i.e., that sex should be a determinant of power relationships. Here is the way male and female voices were defined in a Black nationalist pamphlet from the early 1970s.

> We understand that it is and has been traditional that the man is the head of the house. He is the leader of the house/nation because his

knowledge of the world is broader, his awareness is greater, his understanding is fuller and his application of this information is wiser . . . After all, it is only reasonable that the man be the head of the house because he is able to defend and protect the development of his home . . . Women cannot do the same things as men—they are made by nature to function differently. Equality of men and women is something that cannot happen even in the abstract world. Men are not equal to other men, i.e. ability, experience or even understanding. The value of men and women can be seen as in the value of gold and silver—they are not equal but both have great value. We must realize that men and women are a complement to each other because there is no house/family without a man and his wife. Both are essential to the development of any life.[3]

The material conditions of most Black women would hardly lead them to upset both economic and sexual arrangements that seem to represent some stability in their lives. Many Black women have a good understanding of both sexism and racism, but because of the everyday constrictions of their lives cannot risk struggling against them both.

The reaction of Black men to feminism has been notoriously negative. They are, of course, even more threatened than Black women by the possibility that Black feminists might organize around our own needs. They realize that they might not only lose valuable and hard-working allies in their struggles but that they might also be forced to change their habitually sexist ways of interacting with and oppressing Black women. Accusations that Black feminism divides the Black struggle are powerful deterrents to the growth of an autonomous Black women's movement.

Still, hundreds of women have been active at different times during the three-year existence of our group. And every Black woman who came, came out of a strongly-felt need for some level of possibility that did not previously exist in her life.

When we first started meeting early in 1974 after the NBFO first eastern regional conference, we did not have a strategy for organizing, or even a focus. We just wanted to see what we had. After a period of months of not meeting, we began to meet again late in the year and started doing an intense variety of consciousness-raising. The overwhelming feeling that we had is that after years and years we had finally found each other. Although we were not doing political work as a group, individuals continued their involvement in Lesbian politics, sterilization abuse and abortion rights work, Third World Women's International Women's Day activities, and support activity for the trials of Dr. Kenneth Edelin, Joan Little, and Inéz García. During our first summer, when membership had dropped off considerably, those of us remaining devoted serious discussion to the possibility of opening a refuge for battered women in a Black community. (There was no refuge in Boston at that time.) We also decided around that time to become an independent collective since we had serious disagreements with NBFO's bourgeois-feminist stance and their lack of a clear political focus.

We also were contacted at that time by socialist feminists, with whom we had worked on abortion rights activities, who wanted to encourage us to attend the National Socialist Feminist Conference in Yellow Springs. One of our members did attend and despite the narrowness of the ideology that was promoted at that particular conference, we became more aware of the need for us to understand our own economic situation and to make our own economic analysis.

In the fall, when some members returned, we experienced several months of comparative inactivity and internal disagreements which were first conceptualized as a Lesbian-straight split but which were also the result of class and political differences. During the summer those of us who were still meeting had determined the need to do political work and to move beyond consciousness-raising and serving exclusively as an emotional support group. At the beginning of 1976, when some of the women who had not wanted to do political work and who also had voiced disagreements stopped attending of their own accord, we again looked for a focus. We decided at that time, with the addition of new members, to become a study group. We had always shared our reading with each other, and some of us had written papers on Black feminism for group discussion a few months before this decision was made. We began functioning as a study group and also began discussing the possibility of starting a

Black feminist publication. We had a retreat in the late spring which provided a time for both political discussion and working out interpersonal issues. Currently we are planning to gather together a collection of Black feminist writing. We feel that it is absolutely essential to demonstrate the reality of our politics to other Black women and believe that we can do this through writing and distributing our work. The fact that individual Black feminists are living in isolation all over the country, that our own numbers are small, and that we have some skills in writing, printing, and publishing makes us want to carry out these kinds of projects as a means of organizing Black feminists as we continue to do political work in coalition with other groups.

4. Black Feminist Issues and Projects

During our time together we have identified and worked on many issues of particular relevance to Black women. The inclusiveness of our politics makes us concerned with any situation that impinges upon the lives of women, Third World and working people. We are of course particularly committed to working on those struggles in which race, sex and class are simultaneously factors in oppression. We might, for example, become involved in workplace organizing at a factory that employs Third World women or picket a hospital that is cutting back on already inadequate health care to a Third World community, or set up a rape crisis center in a Black neighborhood. Organizing around welfare and daycare concerns might also be a focus. The work to be done and the countless issues that this work represents merely reflect the pervasiveness of our oppression.

Issues and projects that collective members have already worked on are sterilization abuse, abortion rights, battered women, rape and health care. We have also done many workshops and educationals on Black feminism on college campuses, at women's conferences, and most recently for high school women.

One issue that is of major concern to us and that we have begun to publicly address is racism in the white women's movement. As Black feminists we are made constantly and painfully aware of how little effort white women have made to understand and combat their racism, which requires among other things that they have a more than superficial comprehension of race, color, and Black history and culture. Eliminating racism in the white women's movement is by definition work for white women to do, but we will continue to speak to and demand accountability on this issue.

In the practice of our politics we do not believe that the end always justifies the means. Many reactionary and destructive acts have been done in the name of achieving "correct" political goals. As feminists we do not want to mess over people in the name of politics. We believe in collective process and a nonhierarchical distribution of power within our own group and in our vision of a revolutionary society. We are committed to a continual examination of our politics as they develop through criticism and self-criticism as an essential aspect of our practice. In her introduction to *Sisterhood Is Powerful,* Robin Morgan writes:

I haven't the faintest notion what possible revolutionary role white heterosexual men could fulfill, since they are the very embodiment of reactionary-vested-interest-power.

As Black feminists and Lesbians we know that we have a very definite revolutionary task to perform and we are ready for the lifetime of work and struggle before us.

NOTES

1. This statement is dated April 1977.
2. Michele Wallace, "A Black Feminist's Search for Sisterhood," *The Village Voice,* 28 July 1975, pp. 6–7.
3. Mumininas of Committee for Unified Newark, Mwanamke Mwananchi (The Nationalist Woman), Newark, N.J., © 1971, pp. 4–5.

FOUR

◆◆◆

Defining Genealogies

Feminist Reflections on Being South Asian in North America

Chandra Talpade Mohanty

My local newspaper tells me that worldwide migration is at an all-time high in the early 1990s. Folks are moving from rural to urban areas in all parts of the Third World, and from Asia, Africa, the Caribbean and Latin America to Europe, North America and selected countries in the Middle East. Apparently two percent of the world's population no longer lives in the country in which they were born. Of course, the newspaper story primarily identifies the "problems" (for Europe and the USA) associated with these transnational migration trends. One such "problem" is taking jobs away from "citizens." I am reminded of a placard carried by Black and Third World people at an anti-racism rally in London: We Are Here Because You Were There. My location in the USA then, is symptomatic of large numbers of migrants, nomads, immigrants, workers across the globe for whom notions of home, identity, geography and history are infinitely complicated in the late twentieth century. Questions of nation(ality), and of

"belonging" (witness the situation of South Asians in Africa) are constitutive of the Indian diaspora. This essay is a personal, anecdotal meditation on the politics of gender and race in the construction of South Asian identity in North America.

On a TWA flight on my way back to the U.S. from a conference in the Netherlands, the professional white man sitting next to me asks: (a) which school do I go to? and (b) when do I plan to go home?—all in the same breath. I put on my most professional demeanor (somewhat hard in crumpled blue jeans and cotton T-shirt—this uniform only works for white male professors, who of course could command authority even in swimwear!) and inform him that I teach at a small liberal arts college in upstate New York, and that I have lived in the U.S. for fifteen years. At this point, my work is in the U.S., not in India. This is no longer entirely true—my work is also with feminists and grassroots activists in India, but he doesn't need to know this. Being "mistaken" for a graduate student seems endemic to my existence in this country—few Third World women are granted professional (i.e. adult) and/or permanent (one is always a student!) status in the U.S., even if we exhibit clear characteristics of adulthood, like grey hair and facial lines. He ventures a further question: what do you teach? On hearing "women's studies," he becomes quiet and we spend the next eight hours in polite silence. He has decided that I do not fit into any of his categories, but what can you expect from a *Feminist* (an *Asian* one!) anyway? I feel vindicated and a little superior—even though I know he doesn't really feel "put in his place." Why should he? He has a number of advantages in this situation: white skin, maleness and citizenship privileges. From his enthusiasm about expensive "ethnic food" in Amsterdam, and his J. Crew clothes, I figured class difference (economic or cultural) wasn't exactly an issue in our interaction. We both appeared to have similar social access as "professionals."

I have been asked the "home" question (When are you going home?) periodically for fifteen years now. Leaving aside the subtly racist implications of the question (go home—you don't belong), I am still not satisfied with my response. What is home? The place I was born? Where I grew up? Where my parents live? Where I live and work as an adult? Where I locate my community—my people? Who are "my people"? Is home a geographical space, a historical space, an emotional, sensory space? Home is always so crucial to immigrants and migrants—I even write about it in scholarly texts, perhaps to avoid addressing it as an issue that is also very personal. Does two percent of the world's population think about these questions pertaining to home? This is not to imply that the other ninety-eight percent does not think about home. What interests me is the meaning of home for immigrants and migrants. I am convinced that this question—how one understands and defines home—is a profoundly political one.

Since settled notions of territory, community, geography, and history don't work for us, what does it really mean to be "South Asian" in the USA? Obviously I was not South Asian in India—I was Indian. What else could one be but "Indian" at a time when a successful national independence struggle had given birth to a socialist democratic nation-state? This was the beginning of the decolonization of the Third World. Regional geographies (South Asia) appeared less relevant as a mark of identifica-

tion than citizenship in a post-colonial independent nation on the cusp of economic and political autonomy. However, in North America, identification as South Asian (in addition to Indian, in my case) takes on its own logic. "South Asian" refers to folks of Indian, Pakistani, Sri Lankan, Bangladeshi, Kashmiri, and Burmese origin. Identifying as South Asian rather than Indian adds numbers and hence power within the U.S. State. Besides, regional differences among those from different South Asian countries are often less relevant than the commonalities based on our experiences and histories of immigration, treatment and location in the U.S.

Let me reflect a bit on the way I identify myself, and the way the U.S. State and its institutions categorize me. Perhaps thinking through the various labels will lead me back to the question of home and identity. In 1977, I arrived in the USA on an F1 visa—a student visa. At that time, my definition of myself—a graduate student in Education at the University of Illinois, and the "official" definition of me (a student allowed into the country on an F1 visa) obviously coincided. Then I was called a "foreign student," and expected to go "home" (to India—even though my parents were in Nigeria at the time) after getting my Ph.D. Let's face it, this is the assumed trajectory for a number of Indians, especially the post-independence (my) generation, who come to the U.S. for graduate study.

However, this was not to be my trajectory. I quickly discovered that being a foreign student, and a woman at that, meant being either dismissed as irrelevant (the quiet Asian woman stereotype), treated in racist ways (my teachers asked if I understood English and if they should speak slower and louder so that I could keep up—this in spite of my inheritance of the Queen's English and British colonialism!), or celebrated and exoticized (you are so smart! your accent is even better than that of Americans—a little Anglophilia at work here, even though all my Indian colleagues insist we speak English the Indian way!).

The most significant transition I made at that time was the one from "foreign student" to "student of color." Once I was able to "read" my experiences in terms of race, and to read race and racism as it is written into the social and political fabric of the U.S., practices of racism and sexism became the analytic and political lenses through which I was able to anchor myself here. Of course, none of this happened in isolation—friends, colleagues, comrades, classes, books, films, arguments, and dialogues were constitutive of my political education as a woman of color in the U.S.

In the late 1970s and early 1980s feminism was gaining momentum on American campuses—it was in the air, in the classrooms, on the streets. However, what attracted me wasn't feminism as the mainstream media and white Women's Studies departments defined it. Instead, it was a very specific kind of feminism, the feminism of U.S. women of color and Third World women, that spoke to me. In thinking through the links between gender, race and class in their U.S. manifestations, I was for the first time enabled to think through my own gendered, classed post-colonial history. In the early 1980s, reading Audre Lorde, Nawal el Sadaawi, Cherríe Moraga, bell hooks, Gloria Joseph, Paula Gunn Allen, Barbara Smith, Merle Woo, and Mitsuye Yamada, among others, generated a sort of recognition that was intangible but very inspiring. A number of actions, decisions, and organizing efforts at that time led me to a sense of home and community in relation to women of color in the U.S. Home not as a comfortable, stable, inherited, and familiar space, but instead as an imaginative, politically charged space where the familiarity and sense of affection and commitment lay in shared collective analysis of social injustice, as well as a vision of radical transformation. Political solidarity and a sense of family could be melded together imaginatively to create a strategic space I could call "home." Politically, intellectually, and emotionally I owe an enormous debt to feminists of color—and especially to the sisters who have sustained me over the years. Even though our attempt to start the Women of Color Institute for Radical Research and Action fell through, the spirit of this vision, and the friendships it generated, still continue to nurture me. A number of us, including Barbara Smith, Papusa Molina, Jacqui Alexander, Gloria Joseph, Mitsuye Yamada, Kesho Scott, and myself, among others, met in 1984 to discuss the possibility of such an Institute. The Institute never really happened, but I still hope we will pull it off one day.

For me, engagement as a feminist of color in the U.S. made possible an intellectual and political genealogy of being Indian that was radically challenging as well as profoundly activist. Notions of home and community began to be located within a deeply political space where racialization and gender and class relations and histories became the prism through which I understood, however partially, what it could mean to be South Asian in North America. Interestingly, this recognition also forced me to re-examine the meanings attached to home and community in India.

What I chose to claim, and continue to claim, is a history of anti-colonialist, feminist struggle in India. The stories I recall, the ones that I retell and claim as my own, determine the choices and decisions I make in the present and the future. I did not want to accept a history of Hindu chauvinist (bourgeois) upward mobility (even though this characterizes a section of my extended family). We all choose partial, interested stories/histories—perhaps not as deliberately as I am making it sound here. But consciously, or unconsciously, these choices about our past(s) often determine the logic of our present.

Having always kept my distance from conservative, upwardly mobile Indian immigrants for whom the South Asian world was divided into green-card holders and non-green-card holders, the only South Asian links I allowed and cultivated were with Indians with whom I shared a political vision. This considerably limited my community. Racist and sexist experiences in graduate school and after made it imperative that I understand the U.S. in terms of its history of racism, imperialism and patriarchal relations, specifically in relation to Third World immigrants. After all, we were into the Reagan-Bush years, when the neo-conservative backlash made it impossible to ignore the rise of racist, anti-feminist, and homophobic attitudes, practices, and institutions. Any purely culturalist or nostalgic/sentimental definition of being "Indian" or "South Asian" was inadequate. Such a definition fueled the "model minority" myth. And this subsequently constituted us as "outsiders/foreigners" or as interest groups who sought or had obtained the American dream.

In the mid-1980s, the labels changed: I went from being a "foreign student" to being a "resident alien." I have always thought that this designation was a stroke of inspiration on the part of the U.S. State, since it accurately names the experience and status of immigrants—especially immigrants of color. The flip side of "resident alien" is "illegal alien," another inspired designation. One can be either a resident or an illegal immigrant, but one is always an alien. There is no confusion here—no melting-pot ideology or narratives of assimilation—one's status as an "alien" is primary. Being legal requires identity papers. (It is useful to recall that the "passport"and by extension the concept of nation-states and the sanctity of their borders—came into being after World War I.)

One must be stamped as legitimate (that is, not-gay-or-lesbian and not-communist!) by the Immigration and Naturalization Service (INS). The INS is one of the central disciplinary arms of the U.S. State. It polices the borders and controls all border crossings—especially those into the U.S. In fact, the INS is also one of the primary forces which institutionalizes race differences in the public arena, thus regulating notions of home, legitimacy, and economic access to the "American dream" for many of us. For instance, carrying a green card documenting resident alien status in the U.S. is clearly very different from carrying an American passport, which is proof of U.S. citizenship. The former allows one to enter the U.S. with few hassles; the latter often allows one to breeze through the borders and ports of entry of other countries, especially countries which happen to be trading partners (much of Western Europe and Japan, among others) or in an unequal relationship with the U.S. (much of the noncommunist Third World). At a time when notions of a capitalist free-market economy seem (falsely) synonymous with the values attached to democracy, an American passport can open many doors. However, just carrying an American passport is no insurance against racism and unequal and unjust treatment within the U.S. It would be important to compare the racialization of first-generation immigrants from South Asia to the racialization of second-generation South Asian Americans. For example, one significant difference between these two generations would be between experiencing racism as a phenomenon specific to the U.S., versus growing up in the ever-present shadow of racism in the case of South Asians born in the U.S. This suggests that the psychic effects of racism would be different for these two constituencies. In addition, questions of home, identity and history take on very different meanings for South Asians born in North America. But to be fair, this comparison requires a whole other reflection that is beyond the scope of this essay.

Rather obstinately, I have refused to give up my Indian passport and have chosen to remain as a resident alien in the U.S. for the last decade or so. Which

leads me to reflect on the complicated meanings attached to holding Indian citizenship while making a life for myself in the USA. In India, what does it mean to have a green card—to be an expatriate? What does it mean to visit Bombay every two to four years, and still call it home? Why does speaking in Marathi (my mother tongue) become a measure and confirmation of home? What are the politics of being a part of the majority and the "absent elite" in India, while being a minority and a racialized "other" in the U.S.? And does feminist politics, or advocating feminism, have the same meanings and urgencies in these different geographical and political contexts?

Some of these questions hit me smack in the face during my last visit to India, in December 1992—post-Ayodhya (the infamous destruction of the Babri Masjid in Ayodhya by Hindu fundamentalists on 6 December 1992). In earlier, rather infrequent visits (once every four or five years was all I could afford), my green card designated me as an object of envy, privilege, and status within my extended family. Of course the same green card has always been viewed with suspicion by left and feminist friends who (quite understandably) demand evidence of my ongoing commitment to a socialist and democratic India. During this visit, however, with emotions running high within my family, my green card marked me as an outsider who couldn't possibly understand the "Muslim problem" in India. I was made aware of being an "outsider" in two profoundly troubling shouting matches with my uncles, who voiced the most incredibly hostile sentiments against Muslims. Arguing that India was created as a secular state and that democracy had everything to do with equality for all groups (majority and minority) got me no where. The very fundamentals of democratic citizenship in India were/are being undermined and redefined as "Hindu."

Bombay was one of the cities hardest hit with waves of communal violence following the events in Ayodhya. The mobilization of Hindu fundamentalists, even paramilitary organizations, over the last half century and especially since the mid-1980s had brought Bombay to a juncture where the most violently racist discourse about Muslims seemed to be woven into the fabric of acceptable daily life. Racism was normalized in the popular imagination such that it became almost impossible to publicly raise questions about the ethics or injustice of racial/ethnic/

religious discrimination. I could not assume a distanced posture towards religion any more. Too many injustices were being done in my name.

Although born a Hindu, I have always considered myself a non-practicing one—religion had always felt rather repressive when I was growing up. I enjoyed the rituals but resisted the authoritarian hierarchies of organized Hinduism. However, the Hinduism touted by fundamentalist organizations like the RSS (Rashtriya Swayamsevak Sangh, a paramilitary Hindu fundamentalist organization founded in the 1930s) and the Shiv Sena (a Maharashtrian chauvinist, fundamentalist, fascist political organization that has amassed a significant voice in Bombay politics and government) was one that even I, in my ignorance, recognized as reactionary and distorted. But this discourse was real—hate-filled rhetoric against Muslims appeared to be the mark of a "loyal Hindu." It was unbelievably heart-wrenching to see my hometown become a war zone with whole streets set on fire, and a daily death count to rival any major territorial border war. The smells and textures of Bombay, of home, which had always comforted and nurtured me, were violently disrupted. The scent of fish drying on the lines at the fishing village in Danda was submerged in the smell of burning straw and grass as whole bastis (chawls) were burned to the ground. The very topography, language and relationships that constituted "home" were quietly but surely exploding. What does community mean in this context? December 1992 both clarified as well as complicated for me the meanings attached to being an Indian citizen, a Hindu, an educated woman/feminist, and a permanent resident in the U.S. in ways that I have yet to resolve. After all, it is often moments of crisis that make us pay careful attention to questions of identity. Sharp polarizations force one to make choices (not in order to take sides, but in order to accept responsibility) and to clarify our own analytic, political and emotional topographies.

I learned that combating the rise of Hindu fundamentalism was a necessary ethical imperative for all socialists, feminists and Hindus of conscience. Secularism, if it meant absence of religion, was no longer a viable position. From a feminist perspective, it became clear that the battle for women's minds and hearts was very much center-stage in the Hindu fundamentalist strategy. Feminists in India

have written extensively about the appeal of fundamentalist rhetoric and social position to women. (The journals *The Economic and Political Weekly of India* and *Manushi* are good sources for this work.)

Religious fundamentalist constructions of women embody the nexus of morality, sexuality, and Nation—a nexus of great importance for feminists. Similar to Christian, Islamic, and Jewish fundamentalist discourses, the construction of femininity and masculinity, especially in relation to the idea of the Nation, are central to Hindu fundamentalist rhetoric and mobilizations. Women are not only mobilized in the "service" of the Nation, but they also become the ground on which discourses of morality and nationalism are written. For instance, the RSS mobilizes primarily middle-class women in the name of a family-oriented, Hindu nation, much like the Christian Right does in the U.S. But discourses of morality and nation are also embodied in the normative policing of women's sexuality (witness the surveillance and policing of women's dress in the name of morality by the contemporary Iranian State). Thus, one of the central challenges Indian feminists face at this time is how to rethink the relationship of nationalism and feminism in the context of religious identities. In addition to the fundamentalist mobilizations tearing the country apart, the recent incursions of the International Monetary Fund and the World Bank with their structural adjustment programs which are supposed to "discipline" the Indian economy, are redefining the meaning of postcoloniality and of democracy in India. Categories like gender, race, caste/class are profoundly and visibly unstable at such times of crisis. These categories must thus be analyzed in relation to contemporary reconstructions of womanhood and manhood in a *global* arena increasingly dominated by religious fundamentalist movements, the IMF and the World Bank, and the relentless economic and ideological colonization of much of the world by multinationals based in the U.S., Japan and Europe. In all these global economic and cultural/ideological processes, women occupy a crucial position.

In India, unlike most countries, the sex ratio has declined since the early 1900s. According to the 1991 census, the ratio is now 929 women to 1000 men, one of the lowest (if not *the* lowest) sex ratios in the world. Women produce seventy to eighty percent of all the food in India, and have always been the hardest hit by environmental degradation and poverty. The contradictions between civil law and Hindu and Muslim personal laws affect women—rarely men. Horrific stories about the deliberate genocide of female infants as a result of sex determination procedures like amniocentesis, and recent incidents of sati (self-immolation by women on the funeral pyres of their husbands) have even hit the mainstream American media. Gender and religious (racial) discrimination are thus urgent, life-threatening issues for women in India. In 1993, politically-conscious Indian citizenship necessitates taking such fundamentally feminist issues seriously. In fact, these are the very same issues South Asian feminists in the U.S. need to address. My responsibility to combat and organize against the regressive and violent repercussions of Hindu fundamentalist mobilizations in India extends to my life in North America. After all, much of the money which sustains the fundamentalist movement is raised and funneled through organizations in the U.S.

Let me now circle back to the place I began: the meanings I have come to give to home, community and identity. By exploring the relationship between being a South Asian immigrant in America and an expatriate Indian citizen in India, I have tried, however partially and anecdotally, to clarify the complexities of home and community for this particular feminist of color/South Asian in North America. The genealogy I have created for myself here is partial, interested and deliberate. It is a genealogy that I find emotionally and politically enabling—it is part of the genealogy that underlies my self-identification as an educator involved in a pedagogy of liberation. Of course, my history and experiences are far messier and not at all as linear as this narrative makes them sound. But then the very process of constructing a narrative for oneself—of telling a story—imposes a certain linearity and coherence that is never entirely there. But that is the lesson, perhaps, especially for us immigrants and migrants: i.e., that home, community and identity all fall somewhere between the histories and experiences we inherit and the political choices we make through alliances, solidarities and friendships.

One very concrete effect of my creating this particular space for myself has been my recent involvement in two grassroots organizations, one in India and the other in the U.S. The former, an organization called *Awareness,* is based in Orissa and works to empower the rural poor. Their focus is political education (similar to Paolo Freire's notion of "conscientization"), and they have recently begun to very consciously organize rural women. *Grassroots Leadership of North Carolina* is the U.S. organization I work with. It is a multiracial group of organizers (largely African American and White) working to build a poor and working peoples movement in the American South. While the geographical, historical and political contexts are different in the case of these two organizations, my involvement in them is very similar, as is my sense that there are clear connections to be made between the work of the two organizations. In addition, I think that the issues, analyses, and strategies for organizing for social justice are also quite similar. This particular commitment to work with grassroots organizers in the two places I call home is not accidental. It is very much the result of the genealogy I have traced here. After all, it has taken me over a decade to make these commitments to grassroots work in both spaces. In part, I have defined what it means to be South Asian by educating myself about, and reflecting on, the histories and experiences of African American, Latina, West Indian, African, European American, and other constituencies in North America. Such definitions and understandings do provide a genealogy, but a genealogy that is always relational and fluid as well as urgent and necessary.

───────

This essay is dedicated to the memory of Lanubai and Gauribai Vijaykar, maternal grandaunts, who were single, educated, financially independent, and tall (over six feet) at a time when it was against the grain to be any one of these things; and to Audre Lorde, teacher, sister, friend, whose words and presence continue to challenge, inspire, and nurture me.

FIVE

"Who Am I If I'm Not My Father's Daughter?"

Minnie Bruce Pratt

As a white woman, raised small-town middle-class, Christian, in the Deep South, I was taught to be a *judge,* of moral responsibility and punishment only in relation to *my* ethical system; was taught to be a *preacher,* to point out wrongs and tell others what to do; was taught to be a *martyr,* to take all the responsibility for change and the glory, to expect others to do nothing; was taught to be a *peacemaker,* to mediate, negotiate between opposing sides because *I* knew the right way. When I speak, or speak up, about anti-Semitism and racism, I struggle not to speak with intonations, the gestures, the assumption of these roles, and not to speak out of any role of ought-to; I ask that you try not to place me in that role. I am trying to speak today to women like myself, out of need: as a woman who loves other women passionately and wants us to be able to be together as friends in this unjust world.

But where does the need come from, if by skin color, ethnicity, birth culture, we are women who are in a position of material advantage, where we gain at the expense of others, of other women? A place where *we* can have a degree of safety, comfort, familiarity, just by staying put. Where is our *need* to change what we were born into? What do we have to gain?

When I try to think of this, I think of my father, of how, when I was about eight years old, he took me up the front marble steps of the courthouse in my town. He took me inside, up the worn wooden steps, stooped under the feet of the folks who had gone up and down to be judged, or to gawk at others being judged, up past the courtroom where my grandfather had leaned back in his chair and judged for more than 40 years, up to the attic, to some narrow steps that went to the roof, to the clock tower with a walled ledge.

What I would have seen at the top: on the streets around the courthouse square: the Methodist church, the limestone building with the county health department, board of education, welfare department (my mother worked there), the yellow brick Baptist church, the Gulf station, the pool hall (no women allowed), Cleveland's grocery, Ward's shoe store; then all in a line, connected: the bank, the post office, Dr. Nicholson's office, one door for whites, one for blacks, then separate: the Presbyterian church, the newspaper office, the yellow brick jail, same brick as the Baptist church, and as the courthouse.

What I could not have seen from the top: the sawmill, or Four Points where the white mill folks lived, or the houses of blacks in Veneer Mill quarters.

This is what I would and would not have seen, or so I think, for I never got to the top. When he told me to go up the steps in front of him, I tried to, crawling on hands and knees, but I was terribly afraid. I couldn't—or wouldn't—do it. He let me crawl down: he was disgusted with me, I thought. I think now that he wanted to show me a place he had climbed to as a boy, a view that had been his father's, and his, and would be mine. But I was *not* him. I had not learned to take that height, that being set apart as my own: a white girl, not a boy.

And yet I know I have been shaped by my relation to those buildings, and to the people in the buildings, by ideas of who should be working in the board of education, of who should be in the bank handling money, of who should have the guns and the keys to the jail, of who should be *in* the jail; I have been shaped by what I didn't see, or didn't notice, on those streets.

Each of us carries around with us those growing-up places, the institutions, a sort of backdrop, a stage-set. So often we act out the present against a backdrop of the past, within a frame of perception that is so familiar, so safe that it is terrifying to risk changing it even when we know our perceptions are distorted, limited, constricted by that old view.

So this is one gain for me as I change: I learn a way of looking at the world that is more accurate, complex, multilayered, multidimensioned, more truthful: to see the world of overlapping circles, like movement on the millpond after a fish has jumped, instead of the courthouse square with me in the middle. I feel the *need* to look differently because I've learned that what is presented to me as an accurate view of the world is frequently a lie: so that to look through an anthology of women's studies that has little or no work by women of color is to be up on that ledge above the town and be thinking that I see the town, without realizing how many lives have been pushed out of sight, beside unpaved roads. I'm learning that what I think that I *know* is an accurate view of the world is frequently a lie: as when I was in a discussion about the Women's Pentagon Action with several women, four of us Christian-raised, one Jewish. In describing the march through Arlington Cemetery, one of the four mentioned the rows of crosses. I had marched for a long time through that cemetery; I nodded to myself, visualized rows of crosses. No, said the Jewish woman, they were headstones, with crosses or Stars of David engraved above the names. We four objected; we had all seen crosses. The Jewish woman had some photographs of the march through the cemetery, laid them on the table. We saw rows and rows of rectangular gravestones, and in the foreground, clearly visible, one inscribed with a name and a Star of David.

So I gain truth when I expand my constricted eye, an eye that has only let in what I have been taught to see. But there have been other constrictions: the fear around my heart when I must deal with the *fact* of folk who exist, with their own lives, in other places besides the narrow circle I was raised in. I have learned that my fear of these folks is kin to a terror that has been in my birth culture for years, for centuries, the terror of people who have set themselves apart and *above,* who have wronged others and feel they are about to be found out and punished. It is the terror that in my culture has been expressed in lies about dirty Jews who kill for blood, sly Arab hordes who murder, brutal Indians who massacre, animal blacks who rise in rebellion in the middle of the night and slaughter. It is the terror that has *caused* the slaughter of all these peoples. It is the terror that was my father with his stack of John Birch newspapers, his belief in a Communist-Jewish-Black conspiracy. It is the desperate terror, the knowledge that something is *wrong,* and tries to end fear by attack.

I get afraid when I am trying to understand myself in relation to folks different from me, when there are discussions, conflicts about anti-Semitism and racism among women, criticisms, criticisms of *me;* when, for instance, in a group discussion about race

and class, I say I feel we have talked too much about race, not enough about class, and a woman of color asks me in anger and pain if I don't think her skin has something to do with class; when, for instance, I say carelessly to a Jewish friend that there were no Jews where I grew up, she begins to ask me: How do I know? Do I hear what I'm saying? and I get afraid; when I feel my racing heart, breath, the tightening of my skin around me, literally defenses to protect my narrow circle, I try to say to myself: yes, that fear is there, but I will try to be at the edge between my fear and the outside, on the edge at my skin, listening, asking what new thing will I hear, will I see, will I let myself feel, beyond the fear. I try to say to myself: that to acknowledge the complexity of another's existence is not to deny my own. I try to say: when I acknowledge what my people, what those who are like me, have done to people with less power and less safety in the world, I can make a place for things to be different, a place where I can feel grief, sorrow, not to be sorry *for* the others, but to mourn, to expand my circle of self, follow my need to loosen the constrictions of fear, be a break in the cycle of fear and attack.

To be caught within the narrow circle of the self is not just a fearful thing, it is a *lonely* thing. When I could not climb the steps that day with my father, maybe I knew on some level that my place was with women, not with men, that I did not want his view of the world. Certainly, I have felt this more and more strongly since my coming out as a lesbian. Yet so much has separated me from other women, ways in which my culture set me apart by race, by ethnicity, by class. I understood abruptly one day how lonely this made me when a friend, a black woman, spoke to me casually in our shared office: and I heard how she said my name: the lingering accent, so much like how my name is said at home. Yet I knew enough of her history and mine to know how much separated us: the chasm of murders, rapes, lynchings, the years of daily humiliations done by my people to hers. I went and stood in the hallway and cried, thinking of how she said my name like home, and how divided our lives were.

It is a pain I come to over and over again when, for instance, I realize how *habitually* I think of my culture, my ethics, my morality, as the culmination of history, as the logical extension of what has gone before; the kind of thinking represented by my use, in the past, of the word *Judeo-Christian,* as if Jewish history and lives have existed only to culminate in Christian culture, the kind of thinking that the U.S. government is using now to promote Armageddon in the Middle East; the kind of thinking that I did until recently about Indian lives and culture in my region, as if Indian peoples have existed only in museums since white folks came in the 1500s; the kind of thinking that separates me from women in cultures different from mine, makes their experience less central, less important than mine. It is painful to keep understanding this separation, within myself and in the world. Yet I have felt that the need to be with other women can be the breaking through the shell around me, painful, but a coming through into a new place, where with understanding and change, the loneliness won't be necessary.

If we have these things to gain, and more, by struggling against racism and anti-Semitism in ourselves, what keeps us from doing so, at any one moment, what keeps us from action? In part, I know I hesitate because I have struggled painfully, for years, to make this new place for myself with other women, and I hesitate to disrupt it.

In part I hesitate because the process of uncovering my complicity is so painful: it is the stripping down, layer after layer, of my identity: skin, blood, heart: to find out how much of what I am has been shaped by my skin and family, to find out which of my thoughts and actions I need to change, which I need to keep as my own. Sometimes I fear that stripping away the layers will bring me to nothing, that the only values that I and my culture have are based on negativity, exclusion, fear.

Often I have thought: *what* of who I am is worth saving? worth taking into the future? But I have learned that as the process of shaping identity was long, so the process of change is long. I know that change speeds up the more able I am to put into material shape what I have learned from struggling with anti-Semitism and racism, to begin to act for change can widen perception, loosen fear, ease loneliness. I know that we can choose to act in ways that get us closer to the longed-for but unrealized world, a world where we each are able to live, but not by trying to make someone less than us, not by someone else's blood or pain.

S I X

◆◆◆

Beyond Bean Counting

JeeYeun Lee

I came out as a woman, an Asian American and a bisexual within a relatively short span of time, and ever since then I have been guilty of the crime of bean counting, as Bill Clinton oh-so-eloquently phrased it. Every time I am in a room of people gathered for any reason, I automatically count those whom I can identify as women, men, people of color, Asian Americans, mixed-race people, whites, gays and lesbians, bisexuals, heterosexuals, people with disabilities. So when I received the call for submissions . . . I imagined opening up the finished book to the table of contents and counting beans; I then sent the call for submissions to as many queer Asian/Pacific American women writers as I knew.

Such is the nature of feminism in the 1990s: an uneasy balancing act between the imperatives of outreach and inclusion on the one hand, and the risk of tokenism and further marginalization on the other. This dynamic has indelibly shaped my personal experiences with feminism, starting from my very first encounter with organized feminism. This encounter happened to be, literally, Feminist Studies 101 at the university I attended. The content of the class was divided into topics such as family, work, sexuality and so forth, and for each topic we studied what various feminist paradigms said about it: "liberal feminism," "socialist feminism," "radical feminism" and "feminism and women of color."

Taking this class was an exhilarating, empowering and very uneasy experience. For the first time, I found people who articulated those murky half-formed feelings that I could previously only express incoherently as "But that's not fair!" People who agreed, sympathized, related their own experiences, theorized, helped me form what I had always known. In seventh grade, a teacher made us do a mock debate, and I ended up arguing with Neil Coleman about whether women or men were better cooks. He said more men were professional chefs, therefore men were better. I responded that more women cooked in daily life, therefore women were better. He said it was quality that mattered, not quantity, and left me standing there with nothing to say. I knew there was something wrong with his argument, something wrong with the whole issue as it was framed, and felt extremely betrayed at being made to consent to the inferiority of my gender, losing in front of the whole class. I could never defend myself when arguments like this came up, invariably with boys who were good at debates and used to winning. They left me seething with resentment at their manipulations and frustrated at my speechlessness. So to come to a class that addressed these issues directly and gave me the words for all those pent-up feelings and frustrations was a tremendously affirming and empowering experience.

At the same time, it was an intensely uncomfortable experience. I knew "women of color" was supposed to include Asian American women, but I could not find any in the class readings. Were there no Asian American feminists? Were there none who could write in English? Did there even exist older Asian American women who were second or third generation? Were we Asian American students in the class the first to think about feminism? A class about women, I thought, was a class about me, so I looked for myself everywhere and found nothing. Nothing about Asian American families, immigrant women's work patterns, issues of sexuality and body image for Asian women, violence against Asian American women, Asian American women in the seventies feminist movement, nothing anywhere. I wasn't fully conscious then that I was searching for this, but this absence came out in certain feelings. First of all, I felt jealous of African American and Chicana feminists. Their work was present at least to some degree in the readings: They had research and theories, they were eloquent and they *existed.* Black and Chicana women in the class could claim them as role models, voices, communities—I had no one to claim as my own. My emerging identification as a woman of color was displaced through the writings of black and Chicana women, and I had to read myself, create my politics, through theirs; even now, to a certain extent, I feel more familiar with their issues than those of Asian American women. Second, I felt guilty. Although it was never expressed outright, I felt that there was some pressure on me to represent Asian American issues, and I could not. I felt

estranged from the Asian American groups on campus and Asian American politics and activism in general, and guilty about this ignorance and alienation.

Now mind you, I'm still grateful for this class. Feminism was my avenue to politics: It politicized me; it raised my consciousness about issues of oppression, power and resistance in general. I learned a language with which I could start to explain my experiences and link them to larger societal structures of oppression and complicity. It also gave me ways that I could resist and actively fight back. I became interested in Asian American politics, people of color politics, gay/lesbian/bisexual politics and other struggles because of this exposure to feminism. But there is no excuse for this nearly complete exclusion of Asian/Pacific American women from the class. Marginalization is not simply a politically correct buzzword, it is a material reality that affects people's lives—in this case, my own. I would have been turned off from feminism altogether had it not been for later classes that dealt specifically with women of color. And I would like to name names here: I went to Stanford University, a bastion of privilege that pretends to be on the cutting edge of "multiculturalism." Just under twenty-five percent of the undergraduate population is Asian/Pacific American, but there was no mention of Asian/Pacific American women in Feminist Studies 101. All the classes I took on women of color were taught by graduate students and visiting professors. There was, at that time, only one woman of color on the feminist studies faculty. I regret that I realized the political import of these facts only after I left Stanford.

I understand that feminists in academia are caught between a rock and a hard place—not too many of us hold positions of decision-making power in universities. And I must acknowledge my gratitude for their struggles in helping to establish feminist studies programs and produce theories and research about women, all of which create vital opportunities and affirmation. But other women's organizations that are not constrained by such explicit forces are also lily-white. This obviously differs from group to group, and I think many of them are very conscientious about outreach to historically marginalized women. But, for instance, in 1992 and 1993, at the meetings I attended of the Women's Action Coalition (WAC) in New York City, out of approximately two hundred women usually fewer than twenty women of color were present.

But this is not a diatribe against feminism in general. I want to emphasize that the feminism that I and other young women come to today is one that is at least sensitive to issues of exclusion. If perhaps twenty years ago charges of racism, classism and homophobia were not taken seriously, today they are the cause of extreme anguish and soul-searching. I am profoundly grateful to older feminists of color and their white allies who struggled to bring U.S. feminist movements to this point. At the same time, I think that this current sensitivity often breeds tokenism, guilt, suspicion and self-righteousness that have very material repercussions on women's groups. I have found these uneasy dynamics in all the women's groups I've come across, addressed to varying degrees. At one extreme, I have seen groups that deny the marginalizing affects of their practices, believing that issues of inclusion really have nothing to do with their specific agendas. At the other extreme, I have seen groups ripped apart by accusations of political correctness, immobilized by guilt, knowing they should address a certain issue but not knowing how to begin, and still wondering why "women of color just don't come to our meetings." And tokenism is alive and well in the nineties. Those of us who have been aware of our tokenization often become suspicious and tired of educating others, wondering if we are invested enough to continue to do so, wondering if the overall goal is worth it.

In this age when "political correctness" has been appropriated by conservative forces as a derogatory term, it is extremely difficult to honestly discuss and confront any ideas and practices that perpetuate dominant norms—and none of us is innocent of such collusion. Many times, our response is to become defensive, shutting down to constructive critiques and actions, or to individualize our collusion as solely a personal fault, as if working on our individual racist or classist attitudes would somehow make things better. It appears that we all have a lot of work to do still.

And I mean *all.* Issues of exclusion are not the sole province of white feminists. I learned this very vividly at a 1993 retreat organized by the Asian Pacifica Lesbian Network. It has become somewhat common lately to speak of "Asian and Pacific Islanders" or "Asian/Pacific Americans" or, as in this case, "Asian Pacifica." This is meant to be inclusive, to recognize some issues held in common by people from Asia and people from the Pacific Islands. Two women of Native Hawaiian descent and some Asian American allies confronted the group at this retreat to ask for more than lip service in the organization's name: If the group was seriously committed to being an inclusive coalition, we needed to educate ourselves about and actively advocate Pacific Islander issues. And because I don't want to relegate them to a footnote, I will mention here a few of these issues: the demand for sovereignty for Native Hawaiians, whose government was illegally overthrown by the U.S. in 1893; fighting stereotypes of women and men that are different from those Asian people; decrying U.S. imperialist possession and occupation of the islands of Guam, the Virgin Islands, American Samoa, the Marshall Islands, Micronesia, the Northern Mariana Islands and several others.

This was a retreat where one would suppose everyone had so much in common—after all, we were all queer API women, right? Any such myth was effectively destroyed by the realities of our experiences and issues: We were women of different ethnic backgrounds, with very different issues among East Asians, South Asians, Southeast Asians and Pacific Islanders; women of mixed race and heritage; women who identified as lesbians and those who identified as bisexuals; women who were immigrants, refugees, illegal aliens or second generation or more; older women, physically challenged women, women adopted by white families, women from the Midwest. Such tangible differences brought home the fact that no simplistic identity politics is *ever* possible, that we had to conceive of ourselves as a coalition first and foremost; as one woman on a panel said, our identity as queer API women must be a *coalitional* identity. Initially, I thought that I had finally found a home where I could relax and let down my guard. This was true to a certain degree, but I discovered that this was the home where I would have to work the hardest because I cared the most. I would have to be committed to push myself and push others to deal with all of our differences, so that we *could* be safe for each other. And in this difficult work of coalition, one positive action was taken at the retreat: We changed the name of the organization to include "bisexual," thus becoming the Asian Pacifica Lesbian and Bisexual Network, a name that people started using immediately.

All this is to say that I and other young women have found most feminist movements today to be at this point, where there is at least a stated emphasis on inclusion and outreach with the accompanying risk of tokenism. I firmly believe that it is always the margins that push us further in our politics. Women of color do not struggle in feminist movements simply to add cultural diversity, to add the viewpoints of different kinds of women. Women of color feminist theories challenge the fundamental premises of feminism, such as the very definition of "women," and call for recognition of the constructed racial nature of *all* experiences of gender. In the same way, heterosexist norms do not oppress solely lesbians, bisexuals and gay men, but affect all of our choices and non-choices; issues posed by differently abled women question our basic assumptions about body image, health care, sexuality and work; eco-feminists challenge our fundamental ideas about living on and with the earth, about our interactions with animals, plants, food, agriculture and industry. Many feminists seem to find the issues of class the most difficult to address; we are always faced with the fundamental inequalities inherent to late-twentieth-century multinational capitalism and our unavoidable implication in its structures. Such an overwhelming array of problems can numb and immobilize us, or make us concentrate our energies too narrowly. I don't think that we have to address everything fully at the same time, but we *must* be fully aware of the limitations of our specific agendas. Progressive activists cannot afford to do the masters' work for them by continuing to carry out oppressive assumptions and exclusions.

These days, whenever someone says the word "women" to me, my mind goes blank. What "women"? What is this "women" thing you're talking about? Does that mean me? Does that mean my mother, my roommates, the white woman next door, the checkout clerk at the supermarket, my aunts in Korea, half of the world's population? I ask people to specify and specify, until I can figure out exactly what they're talking about, and I try to remember to apply the same standards to myself, to deny myself the slightest possibility of romanticization. Sisterhood may be global, but who is in that sisterhood? None of us can afford to assume anything about anybody else. This thing called "feminism" takes a great deal of hard work, and I think this is one of the primary hallmarks of young feminists' activism today: We realize that coming together and working together are by no means natural or easy.

SEVEN

✦✦✦

A Latina in the Land of Hollywood
Transgressive Possibilities
Angharad N. Valdivia

Representation remains an important theoretical and political component of any strategy that seeks to redress issues of cultural and material inequality. As such, it occupies a nearly unassailable place in debates about multiculturalism. In a rather intuitive manner from the early days of the second wave of the women's movement, scholars and activists (not mutually exclusive categories) have surmised that we need a greater representation of women in popular culture. . . . Furthermore, Latina women have insisted on a broader operationalization of the "women of color" category, expanding it beyond the binary opposition of white and black into a spectrum of ethnicities that spans any number of variations, including the many Latina possibilities (Valdivia 1995). Additionally, critical scholars underscore the need to consider class issues simultaneously with those of gender and race. . . .

Enter Rosie Perez, who presents us with an ideal case study of the politics of representation. At issue is not just whether minorities are present on the Hollywood screen, for Rosie demonstrates that some Latina women can get there. It is also important to underscore that Hollywood is not opening its arms to very many Latina actresses; Rosie seems to be one of the few to have achieved significant crossover success, though others have appeared in the very occasional Latino movie (Amador 1988; Chua-Eoan 1988; Corliss 1988; Lacayo 1988; Zoglin 1988). She may have, in fact, opened the way for other Latina actresses to enter the select group of Hollywood film stars. More recently, Salma Hayek and Jennifer

Rosie Perez in *Somebody to Love*

Lopez have appeared in a number of Latina and non-Latina roles, and it remains to be seen whether their presence will be a long tenure or a short appearance like Rosie's seems to have been. . . .

Theoretical Background

To understand the phenomenon of Rosie Perez, we must examine the theoretical traditions whose disparate roots meet in Rosie's body, as it were. From traditional, mainstream feminist scholarship, we get the notion of symbolic annihilation (Tuchman, Daniels, and Benet 1978), whose two components are that women are underrepresented in media content, and that when represented, they are marginalized, trivialized, or victimized. Though this finding was originally applied to white, middle-class women, we get additional insight from the women of color perspective. First, research suggests that women of color are less represented than white women—that is, they appear in a less proportionate manner. Second, when people of color do appear, they are generally men. Furthermore, we find that when women of color appear, they are more likely to be African American, with Latina, Native American, and Asian women appearing less often. . . .

Portrayal, as we have learned from three decades of research and activism, is necessary but not sufficient. First, increasing frequency of portrayal is not enough, although even that minimal level of progress has been difficult to achieve for Latinos in the United States. Second, one of the ways in which Hollywood represents people of color is through Anglo protagonists (Hadley-García 1990). We have the extreme version of this phenomenon with the blackfaced Al Jolson, but the tradition continues to this day. It is especially easy to have brunettes portray Latinas, and in fact, Marisa Tomei, one of Rosie's contemporaries, has played such a role several times, as has Anjelica Huston. The latest version of Zorro has a Welsh woman playing the leading female role. Third, there appears to be a peculiar tendency to cast a particular type of Latina actress. For example, two of the most successful Latinas in Hollywood history, Carmen Miranda and Sonia Braga, have been Brazilian, suggesting either that all of the other American countries, including the United States, are unable to yield acceptable talent or that Brazil occupies a feeder role with regards to crossover talent. A fourth issue within representational politics is the repetition of stereotypical portrayals that ignore the multiplicity of experiences and contributions by the heterogenous Latina/Latino population in the United States. The fact is that Latinos come from a variety of backgrounds. Even those of the same country of origin may not share class, racial, ethnic, religious, or language characteristics. Thus, the stereotypical portrayal of the inner-city, Mexican or Puerto Rican, violent, inept, and/or drug-addicted Latino tokenizes and effaces a diverse group of people (Amador 1988; Siegel 1995).

Latinas, then, are portrayed in a limited number of roles. Some, such as the maid and the welfare mother, overlap with African American female images. We also get the binary virgin-whore opposition that representations of women in general project in the popular culture of patriarchal societies. Thus, in contrast to the rosary-praying maids or devoted mothers, we get the sexually out of control and utterly colorful spitfire, an image quite specific to Latinas. A large component of this image is sexually suggestive dancing. Additionally, Latina women in Hollywood film almost always have thick, unshakable, often humorous, and self-depreciating accents, most extremely portrayed by Charo, though dating back to Carmen Miranda[1] and others, despite the fact that many Latina women in the United States speak "accentless" English as their first language. In large part, the endurance of the accent in the stereotype stems from the mistaken and recurrent characterization of all Latinos as recent and quite often illegal immigrants (Saldívar 1997). Many Latinos have many generations of living in this country, and as Renato Rosaldo (1993) so eloquently puts it, they have not crossed a border; the border has crossed them.

From another tradition in media studies, we pose questions about individual agency within organizations that have deeply embedded rules and conventions and that are in turn part of institutions with historically rooted norms and values (Cantor 1989; McQuail 1987; van Zoonen 1994). Without precluding individual initiative and creativity (the individual level of analysis), media workers face a number of limits and constraints in the workplace (the organizational level of analysis), which are also influenced by societal norms and values (the institutional level of analysis). This process is directly related to issues of representation in that though individual actors may be of a particular ethnic or racial background, they may not necessarily be powerful enough to demand a sensitive portrayal, whatever it may be. Quite often, actors are told that they are not black or Latino enough—that is, according to stereotypes that have become paradigmatic in producers' minds. Also, not all actors of a particular ethnic or racial background will necessarily want to deviate from stereotype or to acknowledge that there are stereotypes!

. . . Regarding underrepresentation, we have the issue that a limited number of images bear the burden of representing all of that group. The burden of underrepresentation results in major demands placed upon that one or those few images. Witness the large literature and debate concerning *The Cosby Show* precisely because there had been so few well-adjusted, affluent, and nuclear African American families on U.S. television. The democratization strategy should therefore focus on text and representations produced by a broad spectrum of sources, what Shohat and Stam (1994) call "cultural polyphony." . . .

So far, I have foregrounded the production of media or what Hall (1980) would call the "encoding" component of a signification process. I wish to turn now to "decoding"—that is, when meaning is made at the site of reception. At the site of production, Latinas are encoded with preferred meanings that do not guarantee they will be interpreted in the intended manner. In particular, given that we bring to the process of signification a knowledge that checks or contradicts the stereotype, we would expect women of color in general and Latinas in particular to resist or reject the dominant representation on the screen. . . .

In sum, based on the past thirty years of activism inspired by both the Civil Rights and women's movements, we have learned that textual strategies or increased representations by themselves have to be supplemented and complemented by production strategies—an increased playing field of producers who speak for an expanded spectrum of participants in our multicultural reality—and by an understanding of the different interpretive positions of members of the audience. . . .

Textual Musings

Rosie Perez made her video debut as a dancer and choreographer in *Soul Train* and later as one of the Fly Girls in the Fox show *In Living Color*. From there, she appeared in Spike Lee's *Do the Right Thing* (1989) after he reportedly saw her dancing atop a speaker in an L.A. club. Her other movies include *White Men Can't Jump* (1992), *Untamed Heart* (1993), *Fearless* (1993), and *It Could Happen to You* (1994).[2] She was nominated for an Oscar for *Fearless*, though she did not win. However, this nomination remains a notable and noted accomplishment, especially in Latina/Latino circles. Since then, she has not had a major role in a widely released Hollywood movie, though she's made a few cameo appearances.

From a preferred position, one that "decodes the message in terms of its reference code" (Hall 1980, 136), Rosie could be said to play more or less positive roles.[3] For example, she brings a subtle, gentle sensuality to her part opposite Mookie in *Do the Right Thing*. In *White Men Can't Jump*, her character forces the Woody Harrelson character to grow up or be alone rather than succumbing to his frequent pleas for forgiveness. Also, she makes the most of her limited educational resources by showing a wonderful mastery of middle-class popular culture when succeeding at *Jeopardy*. In *Fearless*, she explores the melodramatic genre in a professional sense, and her character brings Jeff Bridges out of his stupor and depression, inadvertently accomplishing what neither his wife nor therapist nor support group could. In *Untamed Heart*, she proves to be a loyal girlfriend and tolerant coworker. In *It Could Happen to You*, she plays a shrew quite well so that reviewers praise her for such a role. From a hegemonic perspective, . . . Rosie is indeed a representational improvement of and a success for Latinas in Hollywood.

However, from an oppositional perspective,[4] one that understands the literal connotations and uses an alternative framework of reference (Hall 1980, 137–138), Rosie's roles become less charming and downright annoying. To begin with, Rosie Perez plays a supporting role in all of the analyzed movies. In *Do the Right Thing*, Spike Lee foregrounds the interracial struggles between an Italian family and the African American community within which the Italian restaurant resides. There are also Latinos in this community. Rosie plays Mookie's (Spike Lee) girlfriend Tina, the mother of their child. The opening scene features her body gyrating to the tune of Public Enemy's "Fight the Power." In fact, much of the portrayal of Latinas/Latinos in this film revolves around music and music struggles—the lengthiest one being a streetside standoff between loud rap and salsa. One could say that Latinos provide a background of cultural contestation over musical and cultural terrain, whereas the Italian and African American struggle is over the material and physical terrain of the ghetto. Nevertheless, the struggle is primarily in the masculine domain of the public sphere of work in the restaurant and in the streets. Rosie stays at home as the mother in the private sphere. Most of her interactions and appearances take place in the bedroom or elsewhere in the home. In substance, these scenes concern issues of relationship and parenting, classic female-gendered issues in feminine spaces.

In both *It Could Happen to You* and *Untamed Heart*, Rosie plays a supporting role as well. In *It Could Happen to You*, she is the wife (and then ex-wife) of the Nicholas Cage character, secondary to his budding romance with leading lady Bridget Fonda. In *Untamed Heart*, she is the girlfriend-coworker of Marisa Tomei's leading lady. In *White Men Can't Jump*, she is Woody Harrelson's girlfriend. The movie is a classic buddy film with a biracial twist: Woody's buddy, Wesley Snipes, is African American. However, Rosie plays the woman who eventually skates out of the picture as Woody and Wesley demonstrate their loyalty to each other and remain hustling the urban bas-

ketball courts of Los Angeles. Finally, in *Fearless*, Rosie plays the catatonic crash survivor who is rescued from despair by Jeff Bridges. In both *White Men Can't Jump* and *Fearless*, she does not enter the dialogue until the movie has foregrounded the male character's quest for self for nearly twenty minutes!

In addition to being typecast as a supporting actress, Rosie plays a working-class woman in all of these films. As such, she is engaged in a representative range of working-class occupations, including waitress, hairdresser, housewife, and wannabe *Jeopardy* contestant. The latter role, though unusual, is typical in that it highlights more of a working-class version of success. For example, Rosie is not studying for the MCATS, the medical school examination. Though she never possesses degrees of higher education in any of her roles, she is very street savvy, especially when it comes to romance and men, the exception being *Fearless*, where Jeff Bridges saves her from despair.

Her Latina/Puerto Rican ethnicity is collapsed with her working-class status in an inextricable manner. She is at once Latina because she is working class and working class because she is Latina. One codetermines the other in a classic case of piggybacking undervalued positions of dominant binary explanatory frameworks. Her class and ethnic status are illustrated by her dress, demeanor, and juxtaposition with the leading or the white ladies. . . .

In terms of dress, the operative style begins with hoop earrings and is complemented by big hair. In *White Men Can't Jump*, the hoops come in all different colors, but they are always big. In *Fearless*, she begins with little hearts, but as she recovers, she is back to large gold or silver hoops. The earrings have not gone unnoticed by the reviewers. One reviewer describes her *Fearless* performance as "her first non-big-earring role" (Udovitch 1993, 66). Even as a waitress in *Untamed Heart*, she wears hoops, sporting a pair of black ones for the funeral scene. Hair is also an important indicator of class and ethnicity.[5] Big hair goes with the big hoops. Rosie's curls are coiffed up, and her bangs are tall, especially when compared to the hair of the other women in the films, including the blonde and straight pageboy cut of Bridget Fonda or the stylishly short brunette look of Isabella Rosellini or the short ponytail of Marisa Tomei. Though African American, even Wesley Snipe's wife in *White Men Can't Jump* has straighter and smaller hair than Rosie. In effect, Rosie sports what our students call "mall chick hair," a slang term that captures the essence of working-class femininity and is more often than not deployed on the bodies of Latina women.

Thus, even when juxtaposed to white working-class women, Rosie's style sets her apart as different. However, the juxtaposition is all the more salient when she plays opposite an upper-middle-class white woman, such as the character played by Isabella Rosellini in *Fearless.* Toward the end of the film when Isabella tells Rosie to lay off her man, we have a classic juxtaposition: the upper-middle-class white, European woman at home in her upscale surroundings, wearing an expensive ensemble in rich but subdued green, with small yet expensive jewelry, the natural look in makeup, and, of course, small hair opposite Rosie's big, curly hair, large hoop earrings, low-cut turquoise leotard, short tight skirt, and colorful ethnic-style cloth bomber jacket. To top it off, Isabella is smoking some sort of dark and thin European-looking cigarette, which she lights with an equally expensive-looking lighter. We have already been shown that Isabella is a classical ballet teacher with a hobby in small porcelain figurines, whereas we can only deduce that Rosie does not work and has no hobbies or activities other than her wifely duties, which have nearly ceased since the death of her child and her separation from her husband. Isabella is in her domain, and clearly Rosie is physically and symbolically class trespassing as she is told to retreat from Isabella's other property, her man. In fact, other than the initial scene of Rosie crying in her bed, we often meet her on the street outside of her house, whereas we encounter Isabella in her house or her place of work. Portrayals of middle-class women appear to be partly accomplished through position in inside spaces, whereas working-class women appear outdoors.

With regard to demeanor, Rosie also usually portrays a lively person. One of the stereotypes of Latinos in general, whether male or female, is their ability to dance, a stereotype reinforced for Rosie by the fact that she was a dancer first and an actress second. So it is only appropriate that she dances during the opening credits for *Do the Right Thing* though she does not dance for the rest of the movie. In *Untamed Heart,* she is shown dancing, even though her role in that movie is that of a waitress. We, in fact, get to see her dancing at work, as she conveniently plays the jukebox when cleaning up, and at a disco, where she drags the nondancing leading lady Marisa Tomei.

We might say that another component to whiteness, in addition to the implication that they can't jump, is that they can't dance either. The director, however, claims that Rosie's dancing at the jukebox was her own improvisation (Millea 1993). Finally, in *It Could Happen to You,* she partly seduces the older tycoon by dancing. In all three movies, she dances alone, which codes the dancing as something other than the classy pairings portrayed by the likes of Ginger Rogers and Fred Astaire. Her dancing is seductive and "other," not socially sanctioned for white people.

In accordance to the tradition of both working-class women and women of color, Rosie is no fly on the wall in her relationships. In fact, her demeanor could be described as ranging from assertive to loud. Other than her catatonic role in *Fearless,* she is a vocal partner. In *Do the Right Thing,* she demands that Mookie come home more often, stay longer, and ask for higher wages and better working conditions. In *It Could Happen to You,* she wants the full share of her husband's lottery winnings. Additionally, in this particular movie, her character is demanding to the point of being extreme about it so that we as the audience are almost inevitably positioned to dislike her greedy posture, which of course is all the more salient when compared to that of her husband, angelically played by Nicholas Cage, or of the good other woman, played by Bridget Fonda. This particular character is very frustrating from an oppositional perspective, for Rosie plays it so well that one can almost not help hating her while simultaneously hating oneself for allowing the hegemonic meaning to be so seductive. Finally, in *White Men Can't Jump,* though unemployed and devoted to the questionable quest of preparing for a highly unlikely appearance on *Jeopardy* (she studies in categories, such as "foods beginning with the letter Q"), she still makes demands on her hustler partner and leaves him twice, the second time for good.

As well, Rosie plays sexually active women, demonstrating what Shohat (1991) has documented as Hollywood's tendency to transfer sexuality onto the bodies of women of color so that white women can remain pure. Rosie is loud; Rosie is pushy; Rosie gets left behind for quieter, whiter, more subdued, less colorful women or men.

This point brings us to Rosie as a woman and partner. Her romantic liaisons are both eventually unsuccessful and biracial. In *Do the Right Thing,* she is paired off with Spike Lee; in *It Could Happen to*

You, she is paired off with Nicholas Cage and leaves him for an older and presumably richer but still white man, but at the movie's end she is left without money and without a man because it turns out she was just being used for the money. Meanwhile, Cage ends up happy and paired off with Bridget Fonda. Similarly, in *White Men Can't Jump,* she begins as Woody Harrelson's girlfriend and eventually leaves him, but only after he repeatedly hustles their money away, even after all his debts are paid. Though Woody Harrelson is left pining after Rosie, he still seems pretty happy as he walks off into the sunset with his buddy Wesley Snipes while Rosie skates out of the picture alone. In *Untamed Heart,* she is peripheral enough to the main plot that we can't really tell if she has one steady boyfriend, but she does seem pretty intimate with her date in the one scene where we get to see her outside of the diner. Even in *Fearless,* she breaks up with her husband, yet also walks away from Jeff Bridges after her short talk with his wife, the ever so proper, upper-middle-class Isabella Rosellini. In these roles, Rosie functions as a bridge between white and African American people (*Do the Right Thing*); as a facilitator in the eventual happiness of white men with white women (*It Could Happen to You, Untamed Heart,* and *Fearless*); or as a link between two male buddies (*White Men Can't Jump*). In Hollywood film, Rosie provides a touristic detour into the lives of otherwise upstanding citizens and monoracial or monogender couples.

However, this reading is not the only possible oppositional reading of the Rosie phenomenon. Drawing on a public/private sphere analysis based on Nancy Fraser's groundbreaking work, Fregoso (1995) suggests another interpretation. Positioning *pachucas* and *cholas,* different versions of Latina homegirls, as transgressive individuals, she suggests that the production of this particular urban identity "defies, provokes, and challenges the traditional basis of our representation and formulation of the Chicano nation" (327). Pachucas and cholas, Fregoso adds, blur the boundaries between the domestic (read "the home") and the public (read "the street"), all the while asserting a strong female voice based on camaraderie with other women and an ability to survive in difficult situations. One can thus see Rosie as a version of the chola who maintains agency and celebrates a sensuality that may be transgressive in a hegemonic version of white middle-class aesthet-

ics yet who remains true to her own cultural roots, as disparate as these may be.

What the two latter readings suggest is that representations can be decoded in different ways even within an oppositional framework. My general reading is far more pessimistic than Fregoso's validating possibility. At the very least, Rosie opens up a space for a conversation among Latina feminists about the possibilities of representations of strong and seemingly stereotypical Latina women.

Two Thumbs Up?
Reviewers Look at Rosie

Movie reviewers offer another possible source of representation analysis and therefore decoding of meaning that spans a broad range of positions and competencies. For example, in terms of degree of sensitivity to multicultural issues and interventions, mainstream reviewers—including both critical reviewers and those who seem to be promoting movies—seldom consider issues of race, class, and gender. Even the left of the Latino press might not necessarily be expected to provide a nuanced critique that takes into account the intersecting vectors of class, gender, and ethnicity as Bobo (1988) shows in regards to *The Color Purple* and the black press.

Many reviews and articles about Rosie open with comments about her accent. For example, in an article entitled "Distinctive Voice," Patrick Z. McGavin (1994) begins by focusing on, what else, her voice: "for a reception in her honor . . . [she lets] out one of her trademark cries. Pausing in midsentence, she screamed, 'My Gawd, they're like alcoholics here'" (8). . . . He continues: "With her staccato, stream-of-consciousness speaking patterns, stylized body rhythms and distinctive New York intonations, Perez capably balances the verbal and the physical" (8). Another reviewer comments on her "cartoon soprano . . . peppered with slang and expletives" (Handelman 1993, 206). Still another complains that Perez, "with a whine like a high-speed drill, quickly wears out her welcome" (Ames 1994, 56). Even the mostly promotional *Vibe* interviewer Mim Udovitch (1993) tells us her "vocal range . . . starts at Betty Boop and ends somewhere around car alarm" (65). Reviews of *Fearless,* a film that was supposed to break the streak of loud Puerto Rican portrayals, also mention her voice. . . .

Reviewers also comment on her "tenacity, guts and innate sense of how to play to the camera" (McGavin 1994, 8). As a point of reference, nearly all mention that she is from "Little Puerto Rico," the Bushwick sector of New York. Also mentioned is her large family. Reviewers such as McGavin delve into her poor and troubled past and her rags-to-riches story, and Udovitch (1993) provides a synopsis of her childhood, all the while acknowledging that neither Rosie nor her manager like to talk about these things: "She was born very poor in Bushwick, Brooklyn, to Lydia Perez, who was not married to Rosie's father, Ismael Serrano, a merchant marine who lived primarily in Puerto Rico. She has ten brothers and sisters, some full, some half. She grew up partly in a convent home called St. Joseph's in Peekskill, New York, where her mother placed her as a toddler, and this is the root cause of their estrangement" (66). In one small segment, Udovitch manages to highlight many of the stereotypes about Latinas/os in the United States. We are poor. We reproduce out of wedlock and with different partners. We reproduce too much as evidenced by huge families. Our men are not around. Our own mothers place us away from home. And, of course, we are all Catholic.

Characterizations of her personality contain a weird mixture of sexuality and problematic accounts of her intelligence. For example, in one essay, the author focuses both on her sexiness and her street savvy: "Rosie Perez even hails a taxi like a fly girl—not only holding out an arm but also extending one sexy leg into Houston Street until a very impressed cab driver politely pulls over. . . . While much has been made of her street savvy, Perez is more book-smart than most people give her credit for. Before she was 'large and in charge,' she says she studied biochemistry at several L.A.-area colleges" (Chambers 1993, 86). "Fly girl" seems to be one of the ways she is commonly described—as, for example, in a short article in *Essence* (Gregory 1993). It is easy to do because the term combines the slang for street savvy, the name of the dancing ensemble in *In Living Color,* and her role in the flight-crash movie *Fearless.*

In terms of particular films, reviewers most often discuss *It Could Happen to You,* but they have mixed feelings about it. Some tout the movie as a forties romance blooming in the nineties (see Ames 1994) or an "urban fairy tale" (Rafferty 1994, 74; Rozen 1994, 15). Others object to the script, especially Rosie's "grating cliche" performance (Travers 1994, 63). Though others praise Rosie's performance despite the bad script: "There's nothing subtle, as usual, about Perez as she flashes her manicure and screeches her lines, but that doesn't keep her from stealing scenes" (Rozen 1994, 15). . . . Nevertheless, this particular movie garnered Rosie the most attention. . . .

Rosie Speaks about Rosie: Testimonies of Agency

Rosie Perez was not interviewed that often during the period in which these movies were made, perhaps because of her perennial casting as a supporting actress and/or her unmistakable Latinaness. Topics of interest were the expected ones. For example, "Does she really talk like that?" Rosie's accent is her trademark, and one wonders whether it is slightly affected in order to fit her stereotypical Puerto Rican roles or it's actually how she talks. Apparently, the latter. She tells of how Peter Weir, the director of *Fearless,* sent her to a voice coach to reduce her voice level an octave, yet after frustrating weeks had to admit, "I guess that's just you" (McGavin 1994, 8). Even so, Perez acknowledges that attacks and negative comments about her usually center on her voice: "Most of the time the attacks are personal because it's my voice; it has nothing to do with my acting or my ability to perform. Now if somebody says, 'I don't like her because I don't like her voice,' I just can say, 'Oh, OK'" (McGavin 1994, 8).

Similarly, when told she had to lose her big behind despite a whittled down 103-pound frame, she responded, "The butt stays, so get used to it" (Gregory 1993, 48). This is as close as Perez comes to confronting issues of racism or stereotyping. On an ABC news website, she is quoted saying, "The racism, the sexism, I never let it be my problem, it's their problem. If I see a door comin' my way, I'm knockin' it down. And if I can't knock down the door, I'm sliding through the window. I'll never let it stop me from what I wanna do" (available: www.umhl.com/video/xx-01l.avi). Otherwise, her approach to these difficult and potentially alienating subjects is very indirect. In another article, as she and the interviewer discuss her casting in *Fearless* for a role that was originally written for a white actress, the tension between the stereotyped framework and her attempts to break from it are barely beneath the surface. When the interviewer begins with "Fly girl–actress Rosie Perez doesn't wait for Latin-specified movie roles to cha-cha to her door" (Gregory 1993, 48), Rosie adds, "Honey, I can give drama. I'm from Brooklyn!" Yet quickly the article informs us that the director had to rewrite the role for "Perez' look and accent," including, by her insistence, "Cafe Bustelo in the kitchen and a shrine" as well as a "Catholic Church with a Spanish-speaking priest." Thus, culturally if not politically Rosie exercises some degree of agency.

Rosie also complains about the quantity and quality of coverage she receives. People, it seems to her, make many assumptions—for example, that she is never acting, rather just playing herself, despite the fact, she says, that in each consecutive movie she plays a different role (McGavin 1994). Nevertheless, she also claims that she is not into overanalyzing her roles: "I'm not a deep actress. I do what the director tells me to and I find truth in what he wants me to deliver. I don't overanalyze things" (Chambers 1993, 86). She even goes so far as to admit that she's never had an acting lesson. . . . And even though she danced on *Soul Train* and *In Living Color,* she reminds us that she never took dance lessons either. In short, she picked up all of her skills as she went along, which fits rather nicely with her construction as "street savvy."

In fact, Rosie is particularly guarded about her past and about ascribing past traumas into her current acting, despite the fact that or perhaps because most reviewers at least bring up her humble origins, her large family, and quite often imply a difficult life, especially her experience in remedial speech classes. She does not seem equally shy about sexual matters. For example, in one article (Udovitch 1993), she freely discusses masturbation and lovemaking with Puerto Rican men (she says they're the best). Her focus is most decidedly on the present and on her sensuality. Although a number of articles describe her other ventures into recording, directing, and so on, she does not appear eager to discuss these ventures herself.

As in the movies, interviews or focus articles sometimes pair Rosie in "real life" with other actresses who happen to be white and upper middle class. For example, in the article entitled "Women in Waiting" (Handelman 1993), Rosie juxtaposes herself through dress, customs, and religion to leading lady Marisa Tomei: "I didn't know I had second-hand clothes; I just thought my mother had bad taste" (206). As usual, Rosie Perez combines a self-deprecating type of humor to describe herself, her background, and her experiences with an in-your-face attitude that reminds you that although she may be a "'fly girl,' she is no fly on the wall" (206).

Conclusion

Rosie Perez presents us with a . . . case study into the politics of representation. As is usually the case, we have more information on the level of textual documents—that is, the films—than about her motives, her struggles, her agency and degrees of freedom within the Hollywood machinery, and the casting practices and pressures that result in her films. Hollywood film has a language of its own. Part of the success of the film industry rests precisely on the fact that we learn its language so early that it appears natural or transparent. As many media scholars have noted, one possible site of intervention into a cycle of representation is the occasional negotiated or oppositional reading of a mainstream cultural product. Part of what enables such a reading is an alternative subjectivity, which is produced out of complex material, historical, and intellectual components—in sum, an oppositional or negotiated ideological position.

The seduction of Hollywood film is greatly mitigated by this process of decoding. Although it is quite possible, from a preferred hegemonic perspective, to see Rosie and the characters she plays as an improvement of previous Latina roles in Hollywood, matters look quite different and far more complicated from an oppositional perspective. Perhaps because of her voice, she is almost always typecast as a loud Puerto Rican. Hollywood's inability to envision a Latina with an accent as other than a working-class person means Rosie is always working class, even when she is not loud. Class and ethnicity are inextricable in this case. This connection can be seen as problematic or empowering in a transgressive manner. Furthermore, reviewers like her precisely because she conforms to the stereotypical portrayal of a loud, working-class, Latina woman. In fact, many claim she has saved otherwise insipid scripts by her over-the-top performances! In terms of her own agency, whether it's because she realizes that she could do little to change her type-casting or because she is not fully aware of the typecasting or not bothered or concerned by it, she is not explicitly forceful about changes in the stereo-types. However, her roles and the resulting opposi-tional readings suggest she thickens, complicates, and deconstructs her own stereotypical representa-tion, thereby undermining the very parts she is brought in to play, at least for some members of the audience.

NOTES

1. In classic overdetermined casting, though Miranda spoke English fluently and flawlessly, she was made to have a thick accent on screen to fit the U.S. audience's ex-pectation of Latinas.

2. In fact, it was as a result of viewing *It Could Happen to You* that this project began. I went to see the movie with a Latina friend, and we were astonished and greatly both-ered by the role played by Rosie Perez.

3. I owe Norm Denzin credit for suggesting this avenue of analysis prior to the more oppositional one, as well as for his very helpful comments, which I incorporate nearly verbatim into the conclusion.

4. I might add that this is one possible oppositional perspective, one derived from my own and my sisters' (both figuratively in the sense of fellow feminist Latina scholars and literally in the sense of my female siblings) in-terpretations and frustrations with Rosie. . . . I have found that a significant number of my Latino colleagues and friends . . . find Rosie quite sexy, a fact documented by the many available websites that show a nude Rosie, and see her as upstaging any other Anglo or African American ac-tresses with her sensuality and sass.

5. Hair is highlighted in two very different movies such as *Hairpiece* and *School Daze*. Hair is *the site* of strug-gle over issues of class and ethnicity within the dominant construction of femininity.

REFERENCES

Amador, O. G. 1988. Galanes latinos, lita y "La Bamba." *Americas*, 40, 2–9.

Ames, K. 1994. Psst! Want a good tip? *Newsweek*. 1 Aug., 56.

Cantor, M. G. 1989. Writing fiction as women's work. In R. R. Rush and D. Allen (eds.), *Communications at the crossroads: The gender gap connection*. Norwood, NJ: Ablex.

Chambers, V. 1993. Learning to fly. *Premiere*. Nov., 86–87.

Chua-Eoan, H. G. 1988. People: Up, up, and . . . ole. *Time*. 11 July, 72–74.

Corliss, R. 1988. Born in East L.A. *Time*. 11 July, 66–67.

Fregoso, R. 1995. Homegirls, cholas, and pachucas in cin-ema: Taking on the public sphere. *California History*. Fall. 317–27.

Gregory, D. 1993. People. Rosie Perez: This actress is turn-ing Hollywood out! *Essence*. Oct., 48.

Hadley-García, G. 1990. Hispanic Hollywood: The Latins in motion pictures. New York: Citadel Press.

Hall, S. 1980. Encoding/decoding. In S. Hall, D. Hobson, A. Lowe, and R. Willis (eds.), *Culture, media, language*. London: Hutchinson.

Handelman, D. 1993. Women in waiting. *Vogue*. March, 183, 206.

Lacayo, R. 1988. A surging new spirit. *Time*. 11 July, 46–49.

McGavin, P. Z. 1994. Distinctive voice. *Chicago Tribune*. 6 Nov., 8.

McQuail, D. 1987. *Mass communication theory: An Introduc-tion*. Second edition. Newbury Park, Calif.: Sage.

Millea, H. 1993. Behind the scenes: Wild at heart. *Premiere*. 6 March, 35.

Rafferty, T. 1994. The current cinema: "After the Crash." *New Yorker*, 70. 1 Aug., 74–76.

Rosaldo, R. 1993. *Culture and truth: The remaking of social analysis*. Boston: Beacon Press.

Rozen, L. 1994. Picks and pans. Screen: "It Could Happen to You." *People Weekly*. 1 Aug., 15.

Saldívar, J. D. 1997. *Border matters: Remapping American cul-tural studies*. Berkeley: University of California Press.

Siegel, G. 1995. Familia values. *Los Angeles*. May, 21.

Shohat, E. 1991. Gender and culture of empire: Toward a feminist ethnography of the cinema. *Quarterly Review of Film and Video*, 13 (1–3), 45–84.

Shohat, E. and R. Stam. 1994. *Unthinking Eurocentrism: Mul-ticulturalism and the media*. New York: Routledge.

Travers, P. 1994. Review: "It Could Happen to You." *Rolling Stone*. 11 Aug. 62–63.

Tuchman, G., A. K. Daniels, and J. Benet (eds.). 1978. *Hearth and home: Images of women in the mass media*. New York: Oxford University Press.

Udovitch, M. 1993. I Latina, *Vibe*, 1 (4), Dec. 1993/Jan. 1994, 64–68.

Valdivia, A. N. 1995. Feminist media studies in a global setting: Beyond binary contradictions and into multi-cultural spectrums. In A. N. Valdivia (ed.), *Feminism, multiculturalism and the media: Global diversities*. Thou-sand Oaks, Calif.: Sage.

van Zoonen, L. 1994. *Feminist media studies*. Thousand Oaks, Calif.: Sage.

Zoglin, R. 1988. Awaiting a gringo crumb. *Time*. 11 July, 76.

2

$\blacklozenge\blacklozenge\blacklozenge$

Identities and Social Locations:
Who Am I? Who Are My People?

Our identity is a specific marker of how we define ourselves at any particular moment in life. Discovering and claiming our unique identity is a process of growth, change, and renewal throughout our lifetime. As a specific marker, identity may seem tangible and fixed at any given point. Over the life span, however, identity is more fluid. For example, an able-bodied woman who suddenly finds herself confined to a wheelchair after an automobile accident, an assimilated Jewish woman who begins the journey of recovering her Jewish heritage, an immigrant woman from a traditional Guatemalan family "coming out" as a lesbian in the United States, or a young, middle-class college student, away from her sheltered home environment for the first time and becoming politicized by an environmental justice organization on campus, will probably find herself redefining who she is, what she values, and what "home" and "community" are. Many of the authors in this chapter write about the cultural contexts they grew up in and how their lives were shaped by these contexts as well as by particular events. Looking back, they are able to see how their sense of identity has changed over time.

Identity formation is the result of a complex interplay among a range of factors: individual decisions and choices, particular life events, community recognition and expectations, societal categorization, classification and socialization, and key national or international events. It is an ongoing process that involves several key questions:

Who am I? Who do I want to be?

Who do others think I am and want me to be?

Who and what do societal and community institutions, such as schools, religious institutions, the media, and the law, say I am?

Where/what/who are my "home" and "community"?

Which social group(s) do I want to affiliate with?

Who decides the answers to these questions, and on what basis?

Answers to these questions form the core of our existence. In this chapter, we examine the complex issue of identity and its importance in women's lives.

The *American Heritage Dictionary* (1993) defines *identity* as

> the collective aspect of the set of characteristics by which a thing is definitely known or recognizable;
>
> a set of behavioral or personal characteristics by which an individual is recognizable as a member of a group;
>
> the distinct personality of an individual regarded as a persisting entity;
>
> individuality.

The same dictionary defines *to identify* as "to associate or affiliate (oneself) closely with a person or group; to establish an identification with another or others."

These definitions point to the connections between us as individuals and how we are perceived by other people and classified by societal institutions. They also involve a sense of individual agency and choice regarding affiliations with others. Gender, race, ethnicity, class, nationality, sexual orientation, age, religion, disability, and language are all significant social categories by which people are recognized by others. Indeed, on the basis of these categories alone, others often think they know who we are and how we should behave. Personal decisions about our affiliations and loyalties to specific groups are also shaped by these categories. For example, in many communities of color, women struggle over the question of race versus gender. Is race a more important factor than gender in shaping their lives? If a Latina speaks out publicly about sexism within the Latino community, is she betraying her people? This separation of categories, mirrored by our segregated social lives, tends to set up false dichotomies in which people often feel that they have to choose one aspect of their identity over another. It also presents difficulties for mixed-race or bisexual people, who do not fit neatly into such narrow categories.

In order to understand the complexity and richness of women's experiences, we must examine them from the micro, meso, macro, and global levels of social relations. In the selections included in this chapter, several writers make connections between these levels of analysis. Each level involves the standards—beliefs, behaviors, customs, and worldview—that people value. But it is important to emphasize that in a society marked by serious social and economic inequality, such as the United States,

oppressed peoples rarely see their values reflected in the dominant culture. Indeed, this absence is an important aspect of their oppression. For example, writing about her family, whom she describes as "the ungrateful poor," Dorothy Allison (Reading 9) states: "My family's lives were not on television, not in books, not even comic books. There was a myth of the poor in this country; but it did not include us, no matter how hard I tried to squeeze us in."

Critically analyzing the issue of identity at all of these levels of analysis will allow us to see that identity is much more than an individual decision or choice about who we are in the world. Rather, it is a set of complex and often contradictory and conflicting psychological, physical, geographical, political, cultural, historical, and spiritual factors, as shown in the readings that follow.

Being Myself: The Micro Level

At the micro level, individuals usually feel the most comfortable as themselves. Here one can say, for example, "I am a woman, heterosexual, middle class, with a movement disability; but I am also much more than those categories." At this level we define ourselves and structure our daily activities according to our own preferences. At the micro level we can best feel and experience the process of identity formation, which includes naming specific forces and events that shape our identities. At this level we also seem to have more control of the process, although there are always interconnections between events and experiences at this level and the other levels.

Critical life events, such as entering kindergarten, losing a parent through death, separation, or divorce, or the onset of puberty, may all serve as catalysts for a shift in how we think about ourselves. A five-year-old Vietnamese American child from a traditional home and community may experience the first challenge to her sense of identity when her kindergarten teacher admonishes her to speak only in English. A White, middle-class professional woman who thinks of herself as "a person" and a "competent attorney" may begin to see the significance of gender and "the glass ceiling" for women when she witnesses younger, less experienced male colleagues in her law office passing her by for promotions. A woman who has been raped who attends her first meeting of a campus group organizing against date rape feels the power of connection with other rape survivors and their allies. An eighty-year-old woman, whose partner of fifty years has just died, must face the reality of having lost her life-time companion, friend, and lover. Such experiences shape each person's ongoing formulation of self, whether or not the process is conscious, deliberate, reflective, or even voluntary.

Identity formation is a lifelong endeavor that includes discovery of the new; recovery of the old, forgotten, or appropriated; and synthesis of the new and old, as illustrated by several writers in this chapter who reflect on how their sense of identity has developed over the course of their lives. At especially important junctures during the process, individuals mark an identity change in tangible ways. An African American woman may change her name from the anglicized Susan to Aisha, with roots in African culture. A Chinese Vietnamese immigrant woman, on the other hand, may adopt an anglicized name, exchanging Nu Lu for Yvonne Lu as part of becoming a U.S. citizen. Another way of marking and effecting a shift in identity is by altering your physical appearance: changing your wardrobe or makeup; cutting your hair very short, wearing it natural rather than permed or pressed, dyeing it purple, or letting the gray show after years of using hair coloring. More permanent changes might include having a tattoo, having your body pierced, having a face lift or tummy tuck, or, for Asian American women, having eye surgery to "Europeanize" their eyes. Transsexuals—female to male and male to female—have surgery to make their physical appearance congruent with their internal sense of self. Other markers of a change in identity include redecorating your home, setting up home for the first time, or physically relocating to another neighborhood, another city, or another part of the country in search of a new home.

For many people, home is where we grow up until we become independent, by going to college, for example, or getting married; where our parents, siblings, and maybe grandparents are; where our needs for safety, security, and material comfort are met. In reality, what we think of as home is often a complicated and contradictory place where some things we need are present and others are not. Some people's homes are comfortable and secure in a material sense but are also places of emotional or physical violence and cruelty. Some children grow up in homes that provide emotional comfort and a sense of belonging, but as they grow older and their values diverge from those of their parents, home becomes a source of discomfort and alienation.

Regardless of such experiences—perhaps because of them—most people continue to seek places of comfort and solace and others with whom they feel they belong and with whom they share common values and interests. Home may be a geographic, social, emotional, and spiritual space where we hope to find safety, security, familiarity, continuity, acceptance, and understanding, and where we can feel and be our best, whole selves. Home may be in several places at once or in different places at different times of our lives. Some women may have a difficult time finding a home, a place that feels comfortable and familiar, even if they know what it is. Finally, this search may involve not only searching outside ourselves but also piecing together in some coherent way the scattered parts of our identities—an inward as well as an outward journey.

Community Recognition, Expectations, and Interactions: The Meso Level

It is at the meso level—at school, in the workplace, or on the street—that people most frequently ask "Who are you?" or "Where are you from?" in an attempt to categorize us and determine their relationship to us. Moreover, it is here that people experience the complexities, conflicts, and contradictions of multiple identities, which we consider later.

The single most visible signifier of identity is physical appearance. How we look to others affects their perceptions, judgments, and treatment of us. Questions such as "Where do you come from?" and questioning behaviors, such as feeling the texture of your hair or asking if you speak a particular language, are commonly used to interrogate people whose physical appearances especially, but also behaviors, do not match the characteristics designated as belonging to established categories. At root, we are being asked, "Are you one of us or not?" These questioners usually expect singular and simplistic answers, assuming that everyone will fit existing social categories, which are conceived of as undifferentiated and unambiguous. Among people with disabilities, for example, people wanting to identify each other may expect to hear details of another's disability rather than the fact that the person being questioned also identifies equally strongly as, say, a woman who is White, working class, and bisexual.

Community, like home, may be geographic and emotional, or both, and provides a way for people to express group affiliations. "Where are you from?" is a commonplace question in the United States among strangers, a way to break the ice and start a conversation, expecting answers like "I'm from Tallahassee, Florida," or "I'm from the Bronx." Community might also be an organized group like Alcoholics Anonymous, a religious group, or a political organization like the African American civil rights organization, the National Association for the Advancement of Colored People (NAACP). Community may be something much more abstract, as in "the women's community" or "the queer community," where there is presumed to be an identifiable group. In these examples there is an assumption of shared values, interests, culture, or language sometimes thought of as essential qualities that define group membership and belonging. This can lead to **essentialism,** where complex identities get reduced to specific qualities deemed to be essential for membership of a particular group: being Jewish or gay, for example.

At the community level, individual identities and needs meet group standards, expectations, obligations, responsibilities, and demands. You compare yourself with others and are subtly compared. Others size up your clothing, accent, personal style, and knowledge of the group's history and culture. You may be challenged directly, "You say you're Latina. How come you don't speak Spanish?" "You say you're working class. What are you doing in a professional job?" These experiences may both affirm our identities and create or highlight inconsistencies, incongruities, and contradictions in who we believe we are, how we are viewed by others, our role and status in the community, and our sense of belonging.

Some individuals experience **marginality** if they can move in two or more worlds and, in part, be accepted as insiders (Stonequist 1961). Examples include bisexuals, mixed-race people, and immigrants, who all live in at least two cultures. Margaret, a White, working-class woman, for instance, leaves her friends behind after high school graduation as she goes off to an elite university. Though excited and eager to be in a new setting, she often feels alienated at college because her culture, upbringing, and level

of economic security differ from those of the many upper-middle-class and upper-class students. During the winter break she returns to her hometown, where she discovers a gulf between herself and her old friends who remained at home and took full-time jobs. She notices that she is now speaking a slightly different language from them and that her interests and preoccupations are different from theirs. Margaret has a foot in both worlds. She has become sufficiently acculturated at college to begin to know that community as an insider, and she has retained her old community of friends, but she is not entirely at ease or wholly accepted by either community. Her identity is complex, composed of several parts.

Dorothy Allison (Reading 9) describes her experience of marginality in high school and in college. First-generation immigrants invariably experience marginality, as described by Chandra Talpade Mohanty (Reading 4) and Shailja Patel (Reading 11). The positive effect of marginality—also mentioned by several writers in this chapter—is the ability to see both cultures more clearly than people who are embedded in any one context. This gives bicultural people a broader range of vision and allows them to see the complexity and contradictions of both cultural settings. It also helps them to be cultural interpreters and bridge builders, especially at the micro and meso levels (Kich 1992; Okazawa-Rey 1994; Root 1996; Walker 2001).

Social Categories, Classifications, and Structural Inequality: Macro and Global Levels

Classifying and labeling human beings, often according to real or assumed physical, biological, or genetic differences, is a way to distinguish who is included and who is excluded from a group, to ascribe particular characteristics, to prescribe social roles, and to assign status, power, and privilege. People are to know their places. Thus social categories such as gender, race, and class are used to establish and maintain a particular kind of social order. The classifications and their specific features, meanings, and significance are socially constructed through history, politics, and culture. The specific meanings and significance were often imputed to justify the conquest, colonization, domination, and exploitation of entire groups of people, and although the specifics may have changed over time, this system of categorizing and classifying remains intact. For example, Native American people were described as brutal, uncivilized, and ungovernable savages in the writings of early colonizers on this continent. This justified the near-genocide of Native Americans by White settlers and the U.S. military and public officials, as well as the breaking of treaties between the U.S. government and Native American tribes (Zinn 1995). Today, Native Americans are no longer called savages but are often thought of as a vanishing species, or a nonexistent people, already wiped out, thereby rationalizing their neglect by the dominant culture and erasing their long-standing and continuing resistance. Frederica Y. Daly speaks to the oppression of Native American people, as well as their success in retaining traditional values and the cultural revival they have undertaken (Reading 8).

These social categories are at the foundation of the structural inequalities present in our society. In each category there is one group of people deemed superior, legitimate, dominant, and privileged while others are relegated—whether explicitly or implicitly—to the position of inferior, illegitimate, subordinate, and disadvantaged.

Category	Dominant	Subordinate
Gender	Men	Women, transgender people
Race	White	Peoples of color
Class	Middle and upper class	Poor, working class
Nation	U.S./global North	Global South
Ethnicity	European	All other ethnicities
Sexual orientation	Heterosexual	Lesbian, gay, bisexual, transgender
Religion	Christian	All other religions
Physical ability	Able-bodied	Persons with disabilities
Age	Youth	Elderly persons
Language	English	All other languages

In people's lived experience these categories are not binaries. Many people are privileged on one or more dimensions, and at the same time subordinated on other dimensions. Self-awareness involves recognizing and understanding the significance of our identities, which are often complex and contradictory. For White people descended from European immigrants to this country, the advantages of being White are not always fully recognized or acknowledged. In Reading 13, Mary C. Waters describes how, at the macro level, this country's racial hierarchy benefits European Americans who can choose to claim an ethnic identity as, for example, Irish Americans or Italian Americans. These symbolic identities are individualistic, she argues, and do not have serious social costs for the individual compared with racial and ethnic identities of people of color in the United States. As a result, White people in the United States tend to think of all identities as equal: "I'm Italian American, you're Polish American. I'm Irish American, you're African American." This assumed equivalence ignores the very big differences between an individualist symbolic identity and a socially enforced and imposed racial identity. In Reading 14, Melanie Kaye/Kantrowitz writes about the complex social location of Jews in the United States, and her conviction that privilege can and should be deployed to bring about equality and justice. In Reading 5, Minnie Bruce Pratt writes about becoming more aware of her advantaged position and describes her fear of losing her familiar place as she becomes conscious of how her White privilege affects people of color. She sees the positive side of this process—"I gain truth when I expand my constricted eye"—and asks what White women have to gain by changing systems of inequality.

Maintaining Systems of Structural Inequality

Maintaining systems of inequality requires the objectification and dehumanization of subordinated peoples. Appropriating their identities is a particularly effective method of doing this, for it defines who the subordinated group/person is or ought to be. This happens in several ways:

Using the values, characteristics, features of the dominant group as the supposedly neutral standard against which all others should be evaluated. For example, men are generally physically larger and stronger than women.

Many of the clinical trials for new pharmaceutical drugs are conducted using men's bodies and activities as the standard. The results, however, are applied equally to both men and women. Women are often prescribed the same dosage of a medication as men are even though their physical makeup is not the same. Thus women, as a distinct group, do not exist in this research.

Using terms that distinguish the subordinate from the dominant group. Terms such as "non-White" and "minority" connote a relationship to another group, White in the former case and majority in the latter. A non-White person is the negative of the White person; a minority person is less than a majority person. Neither has an identity on her or his own terms.

Stereotyping. Stereotyping involves making a simple generalization about a group and claiming that all members of the group conform to this generalization, as discussed by Angharad Valdivia (Reading 7). Stereotypes are behavioral and psychological attributes; they are commonly held beliefs about groups rather than individual beliefs about individuals; and they persist in spite of contradictory evidence. Lesbians hate men. Latinas are dominated by macho Latinos. Women with physical disabilities are asexual. Fat women are good-humored but not healthy. As philosopher Judith Andre (1988) asserts, "A 'stereotype' is pejorative; there is always something objectionable in the beliefs and images to which the word refers" (p. 260).

Exoticizing and romanticizing. These two forms of appropriation are particularly insidious because on the surface there is an appearance of appreciation, as described by Joanna Kadi in Reading 12. For example, Asian American women are described as personifying the "mysterious orient," Native American women as "earth mothers" and the epitome of spirituality, and Black women as perpetual towers of strength. In all three cases, seemingly positive traits and cultural practices are identified and exalted. This "positive" stereotyping prevents people from seeing the truth and complexity of who these women are. Joanna Kadi (Reading 12) makes a crucial point about **cultural appropriation.** She is furious that outsiders, especially White people,

> use derbekes perceiving them as generic, no-name drums unencumbered by hard political/ historical/cultural realities, never asking themselves the questions that would uncover these

realities, such as: whose music is this? What has imperialism and racism done to the people who created this music? Do I have a right to play this instrument? What kind of beliefs do I hold about Arabs? Ignoring these questions and ignoring Arab musical traditions translates into cultural appropriation.

Similar questions should be asked about White people's use of "exotic" clothing; wearing cowrie shells, beaded hairstyles, cornrows and dreadlocks; and claiming to have been Native American in a former life (Smith 1991). Kadi argues for *"authentic* multiculturalism" but against cultural appropriation that "feeds and reinforces imperialist attitudes" and is a form of "cultural genocide."

Another way to think about the appropriation of identity concerns representation—the images that are circulated and popularized about a group of people. How are various groups of women typically depicted in this society? The fundamental problem with the representation of women, as with all oppressed peoples, is that "they do not have central control over the production of images about themselves" (McCarthy and Crichlow 1993, p. xvii). The four processes of identity appropriation described earlier are used to project images of women that generally demean, dehumanize, denigrate, and otherwise violate their basic humanity, a point elaborated by Angharad Vildivia in connection with Latinas in film (Reading 7).

In the face of structural inequalities, the issue of identity and representation can literally and metaphorically be a matter of life and death for members of subordinated groups for several reasons. They are reduced to the position of the "other"—that is, fundamentally unlike "us"—made invisible, misunderstood, misrepresented, and often feared. Equally significant, designating a group as "other" justifies its exploitation, its exclusion from whatever benefits the society may offer, and the violence and, in extreme cases, genocide committed against it. Therefore, at the macro and global levels, identity is a matter of collective well-being and survival. Individual members of subordinate groups tend to be judged by those in dominant positions according to negative stereotypes. If any young African American women, for example, are poor single mothers, they merely reinforce the stereotype the dominant group holds about them. When young African American women hold advanced degrees and are economically well off, they are regarded as exceptional by those in the dominant group, who rarely let disconfirming evidence push them to rethink their stereotypes.

Given the significance of identity appropriation as an aspect of oppression, it is not surprising that many liberation struggles have included projects and efforts aimed at changing identities and taking control of the process of positive identity formation and representation. Before liberation struggles, oppressed people often use the same terminology to name themselves as the dominant group uses to label them. One crucial aspect of liberation struggles is to get rid of pejorative labels and use names that express, in their own terms, who people are in all their humanity. Thus the name a group uses for itself gradually takes on more of an insider perspective that fits the evolving consciousness growing out of the political movement.

As with individual identity, naming ourselves collectively is an important act of empowerment. One example of this is the evolution of the names African Americans have used to identify themselves, moving from Colored, to Negro, to Black, to Afro-American, and African American. Similarly, Chinese Americans gradually rejected the derogatory label "Chink," preferring to be called Orientals and now Chinese Americans or Asian Americans. These terms are used unevenly, sometimes according to the age and political orientation of the person or the geographic region, where one usage may be more popular than another. Among the very diverse group of people connected historically, culturally, and linguistically to Spain, Portugal, and their former colonies (parts of the United States, Mexico, the Caribbean, and Central and South America), some use more inclusive terms such as Latino or Hispanic; others prefer more specific names such as Chicano, Puerto Rican, Nicaraguan, Cuban, and so on. Elizabeth Martínez discusses this terminology in Reading 10.

Colonization, Immigration, and the U.S. Landscape of Race and Class

Global-level factors affecting people's identities include colonization and immigration. Popular folklore would have us believe that the United States has welcomed "the tired, huddled masses yearning to breathe free" (Young 1997). This ideology that the United States is "a land of immigrants" obscures several important issues excluded from much mainstream debate about immigration: Not all Americans came to this country voluntarily. Native American peoples and Mexicans were already here on this continent, but the former experienced near-genocide and the latter were made foreigners in their own land. African peoples were captured, enslaved, and forcibly imported to this country to be laborers. All were brutally exploited and violated—physically, psychologically, culturally, and spiritually—to serve the interests of those in power. The relationships between these groups and this nation and their experiences in the United States are fundamentally different from the experiences of those who chose to immigrate here, though this is not to negate the hardships the latter may have faced. These differences profoundly shaped the social, cultural, political, and economic realities faced by these groups throughout history and continue to do so today.

Robert Blauner (1972) makes a useful analytical distinction between colonized minorities, whose original presence in this nation was involuntary, and all of whom are people of color, and immigrant minorities, whose presence was voluntary. According to Blauner, colonized minorities faced insurmountable structural inequalities, based primarily on race, that have prevented their full participation in social, economic, political, and cultural arenas of U.S. life. Early in the history of this country, for example, the Naturalization Law of 1790 (which was repealed as recently as 1952) prohibited peoples of color from becoming U.S. citizens, and the Slave Codes restricted every aspect of life for enslaved African peoples. These laws made race into an indelible line that separated "insiders" from "outsiders." White people were designated insiders and granted many privileges while all others were confined to systematic disadvantage. As Mary C. Waters points out in Reading 13, the stories that White Americans learn of how their grandparents and great-grandparents triumphed in the United States "are usually told in terms of their individual efforts." The role of labor unions, community organizations, and political parties, as well as the crucial importance of racism, is usually left out of these accounts, which emphasize individual effort and hard work.

Studies of U.S. immigration "reveal discrimination and unequal positioning of different ethnic groups" (Yans-McLaughlin 1990, p. 6), challenging

A Timeline of U.S. Immigration Law and Policy*

Throughout U.S. history, tens of millions of newcomers have made their way to the United States, sometimes at the express invitation of the government and sometimes not. The United States has resettled on a permanent basis more refugees fleeing persecution than any other industrialized nation. By contrast with other countries, it is relatively easy to qualify for and obtain U.S. citizenship. These newcomers have transformed and invigorated their adopted country; the United States would not be what it is today without them. At the same time, U.S. immigration law and policy have not always been fairly or evenly applied. Particularly in times of economic stress or when there is a perceived threat to national security, the United States has quickly turned inward and raised legal barriers to the admission of individuals from other countries.

1790   The first immigration law, the Naturalization Law of 1790, which was not repealed until 1952, limited naturalization to "free white persons" who had resided in the United States for at least two years. Slave Codes restricted every aspect of life for enslaved African peoples.

1875   The Immigration Act of 1875 denied admission to individuals considered "undesirable," including revolutionaries, prostitutes, and those carrying "loathsome or dangerous contagious diseases."

1882   The Chinese Exclusion Act, one of the most racist immigration laws in U.S. history, was adopted and subsequently upheld by the U.S. Supreme Court; variations were enforced until 1943. The act was a response to fear of the large numbers of Chinese laborers brought to the United States to lay railroads and work in mines.

1917   Congress designated Asia (with the exception of Japan and the Philippines) as a barred zone from which no immigrants were to be admitted.

1921   The Immigration Act of 1921 set an overall cap on the number of immigrants admitted each year and established a nationalities quota system that strongly favored northern Europeans at the expense of immigrants from southern and eastern Europe and Asia.

1924   The Immigration Act of 1924 (the Johnson-Reed Act) based immigration quotas on the ethnic composition of the U.S. population in 1920; it also prohibited Japanese immigration.

1945   President Harry Truman issued a directive after World War II allowing for the admission of 40,000 refugees.

1946   The War Brides Act permitted 120,000 foreign wives and children to join their husbands in the United States.

1948   The Displaced Persons Act of 1948 permitted entry to an additional 400,000 refugees and displaced persons as a result of World War II.

1952   The Immigration and Nationality Act of 1952 (the McCarren-Walter Act) was a response to U.S. fear of communism and barred the admission of anyone who might engage in acts "prejudicial to the public interest, or that endanger the welfare or safety of the United States." It allowed immigration for all nationalities, however, and established family connections as a criterion for immigrant eligibility.

1953   The Refugee Relief Act of 1953 admitted 200,000 people, including Hungarians fleeing communism and Chinese emigrating after the Chinese revolution.

1965   The Immigration Act of 1965 established an annual quota of 120,000 immigrants from the Eastern Hemisphere, which increased the number of Asian immigrants, especially middle-class and upper-middle-class people.

1980   The Refugee Act of 1980 codified into U.S. law the 1951 United Nations Convention Relating to the Status of Refugees and its 1967 Protocol; it defines a

*Thanks to Wendy A. Young for the material.

refugee as a person outside her or his country of nationality who has a well-founded fear of persecution on account of race, religion, nationality, political opinion, or membership in a particular social group.

1986   The Immigration Reform and Control Act of 1986 was introduced to control the growth of illegal immigrants through an "amnesty" program to legalize undocumented people resident in the United States before January 1, 1982, and imposing sanctions against employers who knowingly employ undocumented workers.

1990   The Immigration Act of 1990 affirmed family reunification as the basis for most immigration cases; redefined employment-based immigration; created a new system to diversify the nationalities immigrating to the United States, ostensibly to compensate for the domination of Asian and Latin American immigration since 1965; and created new mechanisms to provide refuge to those fleeing civil strife, environmental disasters, or political upheaval in their homelands.

1996   The Illegal Immigration Reform and Immigrant Responsibility Act was the first legislation in recent years to target both legal and illegal immigration. It provided for increased border controls and penalties for document fraud; changes in employer sanctions; restrictions on immigrant eligibility for public benefits, including benefits for those lawfully in the United States; and drastic streamlining of the asylum system.

The Personal Responsibility and Work Opportunity Reconciliation Act mainly dealt with changes in the welfare system and made legal immigrants ineligible for various kinds of federal assistance. In 1997, Congress restored benefits for some immigrants already in the country when this law took effect. There is a five-year waiting period before noncitizens can receive Medicaid or Temporary Assistance for Needy Families.

2000   The Immigration and Naturalization Service Data Management and Improvement Act requires the development of an integrated entry and exit data system.

2001   Uniting and Strengthening America by Providing Appropriate Tools Required to Obstruct Terrorism Act (known as the USA Patriot Act) was signed into law on October 26, 2001, following the attacks on the World Trade Center and the Pentagon on September 11. It significantly enhances the government's powers of detention, search, and surveillance, and cuts back on individual rights. It permits the detention of noncitizens if the attorney general has "reasonable grounds to believe" that they endanger national security. It permits the definition of domestic groups as terrorist organizations; authorizes the interception of "wire, oral, and electronic communication relating to terrorism"; makes it easier for the FBI to get access to records about a person that are maintained by a business; and expands the use of secret searches. It requires financial institutions to monitor daily financial transactions and academic institutions to share information about students.

The "pull" factors drawing immigrants to the United States include the possibility of better-paying jobs, better education—especially for children—and greater personal freedom. "Push" factors include poverty, the dire effects of wars, political upheaval, authoritarian regimes, and fewer personal freedoms in the countries they have left. Immigration will continue to be a thorny issue in the United States as the goals of global economic restructuring, filling the country's need for workers, and providing opportunities for family members to live together are set against the fears of those who see continued immigration as a threat to the country's prosperity and security and to the dominance of European Americans.

the myth of equal opportunity for all. According to political scientist Lawrence Fuchs (1990), "Freedom and opportunity for poor immigrant Whites in the seventeenth and eighteenth centuries were connected fundamentally with the spread of slavery" (p. 294). It was then that European immigrants, such as Irish, Polish, and Italian people began to learn to be White (Roediger 1991). Thus the common belief among descendants of European immigrants that the successful assimilation of their foremothers and forefathers against great odds is evidence that everyone can pull themselves up by the bootstraps if they work hard enough does not take into account the racialization of immigration that favored White people.

On coming to the United States, immigrants are drawn into the racial landscape of this country. In media debates and official statistics, this is still dominated by a Black/White polarization in which everyone is assumed to fit into one of these two groups. Demographically, the situation is much more complex and diverse, but people of color, who comprise the more inclusive group, are still set off against White people, the dominant group. Immigrants identify themselves according to nationality—for example, as Cambodian or Guatemalan. Once in the United States they learn the significance of racial divisions in this country and may adopt the term *people of color* as an aspect of their identity here. Chandra Talpade Mohanty notes her transition from "foreign student" to "student of color" in the United States. "Racist and sexist experiences in graduate school and after made it imperative that I understand the U.S. in terms of its history of racism, imperialism and patriarchal relations, specifically in relation to Third World immigrants" (Reading 4).

This emphasis on race tends to mask differences based on class, another important distinction among immigrant groups. For example, the Chinese and Japanese people who came in the nineteenth century and early twentieth century to work on plantations in Hawai'i, as loggers in Oregon, or building roads and railroads in several western states were poor and from rural areas of China and Japan. The 1965 immigration law made way for "the second wave" of Asian immigration (Takaki 1987). It set preferences for professionals, highly skilled workers, and members of the middle and upper-middle classes, making this group "the most highly skilled of any immigrant group our country has ever had" (quoted in Takaki 1987, p. 420). The first wave of Vietnamese

refugees who immigrated between the mid-1970s and 1980 were from the middle and upper classes, and many were professionals; by contrast, the second wave of immigrants from Vietnam was composed of poor and rural people. The class backgrounds of immigrants affect not only their sense of themselves and their expectations but also how they can succeed as strangers in a foreign land. For example, a poor woman who arrives with no literacy skills in her own language will have a more difficult time learning to become literate in English than one who has formal schooling in her country of origin that may have included basic English.

Multiple Identities, Social Location, and Contradictions

The social features of one's identity incorporate individual, community, societal, and global factors, as discussed in the readings that follow. **Social location** is a way of expressing the core of a person's existence in the social and political world. It places us in particular relationships to others, to the dominant culture of the United States, and to the rest of the world. It determines the kinds of power and privilege we have access to and can exercise, as well as situations in which we have less power and privilege.

Because social location is where all the aspects of one's identity meet, our experience of our own complex identities is sometimes contradictory, conflictual, and paradoxical. We live with multiple identities that can be both enriching and contradictory and that push us to confront questions of loyalty to individuals and groups. This is discussed by Dorothy Allison, Shailja Patel, Melanie Kaye/Kantrowitz, and Chandra Talpade Mohanty (Readings 9, 11, 14, and 4).

It is also through the complexity of social location that we are forced to differentiate our inclinations, behaviors, self-definition, and politics from how we are classified by larger societal institutions. An inclination toward bisexuality, for example, does not mean that one will necessarily act on that inclination. Defining oneself as working class does not necessarily lead to activity in progressive politics based on a class consciousness.

Social location is also where we meet others socially and politically. Who are we in relation to people who are both like us and different from us? How do we negotiate the inequalities in power and privilege? How do we both accept and appreciate who we and others are, and grow and change to meet the challenges of a multicultural world? In the readings that follow, the writers note significant changes in the way they think about themselves over time. Some mention difficulties in coming to terms with who they are, describing things that have happened to them and the complexities of their contradictory positions. They also write about the empowerment that comes from a deepening understanding of identity, enabling them to claim their place in the world.

Questions for Reflection

As you read and discuss the readings in this chapter, think about these questions:

1. Where do you come from? Who are you? How has your identity changed? How do you figure out your identity?
2. Which parts of your identity do you emphasize? Which do you underplay? Why?
3. Who are your "people"? Where or what are your "home" and "community"?
4. How many generations have your family members been in the United States? What was their first relationship to it? Under what conditions did they become a part of the United States?
5. What do you know of your family's culture and history before it became a part of the United States?
6. What is your social location?
7. Which of the social dimensions of your identity provide power and privilege? Which provide less power and disadvantage?

Finding Out More on the Web

1. Find out about women who are very different from you (in terms of culture, class, race/ethnicity, nationality, or religion) and how they think about their identities.
2. Research identity-based organizations. Why did they form? Who are their members? What are their purposes and goals? Did/do they have a vision of justice and equality?

♦♦♦

Taking Action

1. Think about all aspects of your own identity. How do you identify yourself?
2. Talk to your parents or grandparents about your family history. How have they constructed their cultural and racial/ethnic identities?

EIGHT

Perspectives of Native American Women on Race and Gender

Frederica Y. Daly

... Native Americans constitute well over five hundred recognized tribes, which speak more than two hundred (mostly living) languages. Their variety and vital cultures notwithstanding, the official U.S. policy unreflectively, and simply, transforms them from Indians to "Americans" (Wilkinson 1987). Some consideration will be given to their unifying traditions, not the least of which are their common history of surviving genocide and their strong, shared commitment to their heritage.

Any discussion of Indian people requires a brief review of the history of the violent decimation of their populations as well as the massive expropriation of their land and water holdings, accomplished with rare exception with the approval of American governments at every level. To ignore these experiences prevents us from understanding the basis for their radical and profound desire for self-determination, a condition they enjoyed fully before the European incursions began. . . .

Historical Overview

Indian history, since the European invasion in the early sixteenth century, is replete with incidents of exploitation, land swindle, enslavement, and murder by the European settlers. The narration includes well-documented, government-initiated, biological warfare, which included giving Indians clothing infected with smallpox, diphtheria, and other diseases to which Indians were vulnerable. Starvation strategies were employed, with forced removal from their lands and the consequent loss of access to basic natural resources, example, the Cherokee and Choctaw experiences in the famous "trail of tears."

Wilkinson as well as Deloria and Lytle (1983) assert that Indian history is best understood when presented within a historical framework established by four major, somewhat overlapping, periods. The events dominate federal policy about Indians, subsequent Indian law, and many of the formational forces described in Indian sociology, anthropology, and culture.

Period 1: 1532–1828

This period is described by Europeans as one of "discovery" and is characterized by the conquest of Indians and the making of treaties. The early settlers did not have laws or policies governing their relationships with the indigenous tribes until the sixteenth-century theologian Francisco de Vitorio advised the king of Spain in 1532 that the tribes should be recognized "as legitimate entities capable of dealing with the European nations by treaty." As a result, writes Deloria, treaty making became a "feasible method of gaining a foothold on the continent without alarming the natives" (1970, 3). Deloria explains further that inherent in this decision was the fact that it encouraged respect for the tribes as societies of people and, thus, became the workable tool for defining intergroup relationships. By 1778 the U.S. government entered into its first treaty, with the Delaware Indians, at which point the tribe became, and remains, the basic unit in federal Indian law. . . .

Period 2: 1828–87

The second period, beginning little more than a few decades before the Civil War, witnessed massive removal of Indians from their ancestral lands and subsequent relocation, primarily because of their resistance to mainstream assimilation and the "missionary efforts" of the various Christian sects.

Early in his presidency Andrew Jackson proposed voluntary removal of the Indians. When none of the tribes responded, the Indian Removal Act of 1830 was passed. The act resulted in the removal of the tribes from the Ohio and Mississippi valleys to the plains of the West. "Nearly sixteen thousand Cherokees walked from Georgia to Eastern Oklahoma . . . the Choctaws surrendered more than ten million acres and moved west" (Deloria and Lytle 1983, 7). Soldiers, teachers, and missionaries were sent to reservations for policing and proselytizing purposes, activities by no means mutually exclusive and which represented the full benefit of the act as far as the tribes were concerned. Meanwhile, discovery of gold (especially "strikes" on or near Indian land) in the West, coupled with the extension of the railroad, once again raised the "Indian Problem." But at this point, with nowhere else to be moved, Indian tribes were even more in jeopardy, setting the basis for the third significant period.

Period 3: 1887–1928

During the final years of the nineteenth century, offering land allotments seemed to provide a workable technique for assimilating Indian families into the mainstream. The Dawes Act of 1887 proposed the formula for allotment. "A period of twenty-five years was established during which the Indian owner [of a specified, allotted piece of reservation property] was expected to learn proper methods of self-sufficiency, e.g., business or farming. At the end of that period, the land, free of restrictions against sale, was to be delivered to the allottee" (Deloria and Lytle 1983, 9). At the same time, the Indian received title to the land and citizenship in the state.

The Dawes Act and its aftermath constitute one of the most sordid narratives in American history involving tribal peoples. Through assimilation, swindling, and other forms of exploitation, more than ninety million acres of allotted land were transferred to non-Indian owners. Furthermore, much of the original land that remained for the Indians was in the "Great American Desert," unsuitable for farming and unattractive for any other kind of development. During this same period, off-reservation boarding schools began to be instituted, some in former army barracks, to assist in the overall program of assimilation, and the Dawes Act also made parcels of reservation land available to whites for settlement. The plan to assimilate the Indian and thereby eradicate the internal tribal nations caused immense misery and enormous economic loss. But as we know, it failed. Phyllis Old Dog Cross, a nurse of the North Dakota Mandan Tribe, mordantly puts it, "We are not vanishing" (1987, 29).

Period 4: 1928–Present

The fourth period is identified by Wilkinson especially as beginning just before the Depression in 1928. It is characterized by reestablishment of tribes as separate "sovereignties" involving moves toward formalized self-government and self-determination, and cessation, during World War II, of federal assistance to the tribes.

Prucha (1985) reminds us that, with the increased belief in the sciences in the 1920s and the accompanying beliefs that the sciences could solve human problems, attitudes toward Indians hardened. At this point the professional anthropologist began to be sent and be seen on the reservations to study and live with the people, alongside the missionaries. The changing attitudes continued into the 1930s with the Roosevelt administration. It was during this period that John Collier became commissioner of Indian Affairs, and the reforms of the Indian Reorganization Act of 1934 invalidated the land allotment policies of the Dawes Act, effectively halting the transfer of Indian land to non-Indians. As Deloria indicates, the Reorganization Act provided immense benefits, including the establishment and reorganization of tribal councils and tribal courts.

After about a decade of progress, the budgetary demands of World War II resulted in deep reductions in domestic programs, including assistance to the tribes. John Collier resigned in 1945 under attack from critics and amid growing demands in Washington to cancel federal support for Indians. . . .

Deloria writes that Senator Watkins of Utah was "firmly convinced that if the Indians were freed from federal restrictions, they would soon prosper by learning in the school of life those lessons that a cynical federal bureaucracy had not been able to instill in them" (1970, 18). He was able to implement his convictions during the Eisenhower administration into the infamous Termination Act of 1953, in consequence of which several tribes in at least five states were eliminated. In effect, as far as the government was concerned, the tribes no longer existed and could make no claims on the government. Contrary to its original intent as a means of releasing the tribes from their status as federal wards under BIA [Bureau of Indian Affairs] control, the Termination Act did just the opposite, causing more loss of land, further erosion of tribal power, and literally terrorizing most of the tribes with intimidation, uncertainty, and, worst of all, fear of the loss of tribal standing.

Deloria quotes HR Doc. 363 in which, in 1970, President Nixon asserted, "Because termination is morally and legally unacceptable, because it produces bad practical results, and because the mere threat of termination tends to discourage greater self-sufficiency among Indian groups, I am asking the Congress to pass a new concurrent resolution which would expressly renounce, repudiate, and repeal the termination policy" (1970, 20). This firm repudiation by Nixon of the termination policy earned him the esteem of many Indian people, in much the same way that presidents Kennedy and Johnson are esteemed by many African Americans for establishing programs designed to improve their socioeconomic conditions.

From the Nixon administration through the Carter administration, tribal affairs were marked by strong federal support and a variety of programs aimed at encouraging tribal self-determination. The Indian Child Welfare Act of 1978, which gave preference to Indians in adoptions involving Indian children and authorized establishment of social services on and near reservations, was one of the major accomplishments of this period.

Prucha believes that the tribes' continued need for federal programs is an obstacle to their sovereignty. He asserts that dependency persists but that no one knows how to eliminate it (1985, 97). Deloria insists that Indians are citizens and residents of the United States and of the individual states in which they live and, as such, "are entitled to the full benefits and privileges that are offered to all citizens" (246). . . .

Contemporary Native American Women and Sexism

I have just presented a very abbreviated statement of the general, post-European influx historical experiences of Indians in America, drawing from the research and insights of lawyers and social scientists. Without this introduction it would be difficult to understand Native American women and their contemporary experiences of sexism and racism.

Although many tribes were matrilineal, Indian women were seldom mentioned prominently in the personal journals or formal records of the early settlers or in the narratives of the westward movement. They were excluded from treaty-making sessions with federal government agents, and later ethnologists and anthropologists who reported on Indian women frequently presented distorted accounts of their lives, usually based on interviews with Chris-

tianized women, who said what they believed would be compatible with the European worldview. Helen Carr, in her essay in Brodzki and Schenck's *Life-Lines: Theorizing Women's Autobiographies,* offers some caveats about the authenticity of contemporary autobiographies of Indian women, when they are written in the Euro-American autobiographical tradition. She cautions that, in reading the autobiographies collected by early anthropologists, we need to be "aware that they have been structured, consciously or unconsciously, to serve particular 'white' purposes and to give credence to particular white views" (1988, 132).

Ruby Leavitt, writing in Gornick and Moran's *Women in Sexist Society,* states: "Certainly the status of women is higher in the matrilineal than the patrilineal societies. Where women own property and pass it on to their daughters or sisters, they are far more influential and secure. Where their economic role is important and well defined . . . they are not nearly so subject to male domination, and they have much more freedom of movement and action" (1972, 397).

We do not learn from social scientists observing Indian communities that women also were the traders in many tribes. With this history of matrilinealism and economic responsibilities, it is not surprising that some Indian women deny the existence of an oppressed, nonparticipatory tribal female role. Yet just as other North American women, they are concerned with child-care needs, access to abortion, violence against women, and the effects of alcoholism on the family, all symptomatic of sexism experiences. They are also aware of these symptoms as prevalent throughout our society in the United States; they do not view them as specifically Indian related.

Bea Medicine, Lakota activist, anthropologist, and poet *as quoted* in the preface of *American Indian Women—Telling Their Lives,* states "Indian women do not need liberation, they have always been liberated within their tribal structure" (1984, viii). Her view is the more common one I have encountered in my readings and in conversations with Native American women. In the middle 1970s, Native American women who were in New York City to protest a U.S. treaty violation, in a meeting to which they had invited non-Indian women, were adamant that they did not need the "luxury of feminism." Their focus, along with that of Indian men, concerned the more primary needs of survival.

The poet Carol Sanchez writes in *A Gathering of Spirit*, "We still have Women's societies, and there are at least thirty active woman-centered Mother rite cultures existing and practicing their everyday life in that manner on this continent" (1984, 164). These groups are characterized by their "keeping of the culture" activities.

Medicine and Sanchez concur about the de-emphasis of the importance of gender roles in some tribes as reflected in the "Gia" concept. *Gia* is the word in the Pueblo Tewa language which signifies the earth. It is also used to connote nurturance and biological motherhood. The tribal core welfare role, which can be assumed by a male or a female, is defined by the tribe in this Gia context. To be a nurturing male is to be the object of much respect and esteem, although one does not act nurturing to gain group approval. Swentzell and Naranjo, educational consultant and sociologist, respectively, and coauthors, write, "The male in the gia role is a person who guides, advises, cares, and universally loves and encompasses all." The authors describe the role, saying, "The core gia was a strong, stable individual who served as the central focus for a large number of the pueblo's members . . . [for example], 'she' coordinated large group activities such as marriages, feast days, gathering and preparing of food products, even house building and plastering" (1986, 37). With increasing tribal governmental concerns the role of core group Gia has lessened, "so that children are no longer raised by the core group members" (39). Interestingly, the Gia concept is being used currently by social ecologists. For them it parallels the notion of Mother Earth and corresponds with the increasingly widespread understanding of the earth as a living organism.

Charles Lange, in *Cochiti—A New Mexico Pueblo, Past and Present*, says: "Among the Cochiti, the woman is boss; the high offices are held by men, but in the households and in the councils of the clans, woman is supreme. . . . She has been arbiter of destinies of the tribe for centuries" (1959, 367). The important role performed by the "Women's Society," Lange continues, includes "the ceremonial grinding of corn to make prayer meal" (283). Compatible with women's having spiritual role assignments is the fact that in some tribes the gods are women—for example, in the matrifocal Cherokee and Pueblo nations, Corn Mother is a sacred figure.

A Cheyenne saying reflects the tribe's profound regard for women: "A nation is not conquered until the hearts of its women are on the ground. Then it is done, no matter how brave its warriors, nor how strong its weapons" (Kutz 1988, 143–58). Historically, in some tribes women were warriors and participated in raiding parties. The Apache medicine woman and warrior Lozen lived such a role and was the last of the women warriors (Kutz 1988, 143–58). Paula Gunn Allen, in *The Sacred Hoop* (1986), notes that "traditional tribal lifestyles are more often gynocratic . . . women are not merely doomed victims of Western progress; they are also the carriers of the dream. . . . Since the first attempts at colonization . . . the invaders have exerted every effort to remove Indian women from every position of authority, to obliterate all records pertaining to gynocratic social systems and to ensure that no Americans . . . would remember that gynocracy was the primary social order of Indian America" (2–3). Later she alludes to the regeneration of these earlier roles: "Women migrating to the cities are regaining self-sufficiency and positions of influence they had held in earlier centuries" (31). "Women's traditions," she says, "are about continuity and men's are about change, life maintenance/risk, death and transformation" (82).

When Indian women deny having experienced sexism they seem mainly to be referring to their continuing historical roles within their tribes, in which they are seen as *the keepers of the culture*. There exists a general consensus that the powerful role of tribal women, both traditionally and contemporarily, is not paralleled in the non-Indian society. Additionally, they allude to the women serving in various tribes as council members, and they point to such prominent, well-known leaders as Wilma Mankiller, chief of the Oklahoma Cherokee Nation; Verna Williamson, former governor of Isleta Pueblo; and Virginia Klinekole, former president of the Mescalero Apache Tribal Council.

Contemporary Native American Women and Racism

The relentless system of racism, in both its overt and covert manifestations, impacts the lives of Indian women; most are very clear about their experiences of it, and they recognize it for what it is. Although many are reticent about discussing these experiences, a growing number of Native American women writers are giving voice to their encounters with racism.

Elizabeth Cook-Lynn, a poet and teacher with combined Crow, Creek, and Sioux heritage, writes about an editor who questioned her about why Native American poetry is so incredibly sad. Cook-Lynn describes her reaction . . . : "Now I recognize it as a tactless question asked out of astonishing ignorance. It reflects the general attitude that American Indians should have been happy to have been robbed of their land and murdered" (1987, 60–61).

In the same anthology Linda Hogan, from the Chickasaw Tribe in Oklahoma, writes with concern about the absence of information about Native American people throughout the curricula in our educational systems: "The closest I came to learning what I needed was a course in Labor Literature, and the lesson there was in knowing there were writers who lived similar lives to ours. . . . This is one of the ways that higher education perpetuates racism and classism. By ignoring our lives and work, by creating standards for only their own work" (1987, 243). Earlier she had written that "the significance of intermarriage between Indian and white or between Indian and black [has not] been explored . . . but the fact remains that great numbers of apparently white or black Americans carry notable degrees of Indian blood" (216). And in Brant's *A Gathering of Spirit* Carol Sanchez says, "To be Indian is to be considered 'colorful,' spiritual, connected to the earth, simplistic, and disappointing if not dressed in buckskin and feathers" (1984, 163).

These Indian women talk openly about symptoms of these social pathologies, example, experiencing academic elitism or the demeaning attitudes of employees in federal and private, nonprofit Indian agencies. Or they tell of being accepted in U.S. society in proportion to the lightness of skin color. The few who deny having had experiences with racism mention the equality bestowed upon them through the tribal sovereignty of the Indian nations. In reality the tribes are not sovereign. They are controlled nearly completely by the U.S. Department of Interior, the federal agency that, ironically, also oversees animal life on public lands.

Rayna Green, a member of the Cherokee nation, in her book *That's What She Said* (1984), makes a strong, clear statement about racism and sexism: "The desperate lives of Indian women are worn by poverty, the abuse of men, the silence and blindness of whites. . . . The root of their problem appears attributable to the callousness and sexism of the Indian men and white

society equally. They are tightly bound indeed in the double bind of race and gender. Wasted lives and battered women are part of the Indian turf" (10). It is not surprising to find some Indian men reflecting the attitudes of the white majority in relating to Indian women. This is the psychological phenomenon found in oppressed people, labeled as identification with the oppressor.

Mary Tallmountain, the Native Alaskan poet, writes in *I Tell You Now* (1987) that she refused to attend school in Oregon because her schoolmates mocked her "Indianness": "But, I know who I am. Marginal person, misfit, mutant; nevertheless, I am of this country, these people" (12). Linda Hogan describes the same experience, saying, "Those who are privileged would like for us to believe that we are in some way defective, that we are not smart enough, not good enough" (237). She recalls an experience with her former employer, an orthodontist, whom she says, "believed I was inferior because I worked for less than his wife's clothing budget or their liquor bill . . . and who, when I received money to attend night school and was proud, accused me of being a welfare leech and said I should be ashamed" (242). In her poem "Those Who Thunder," Linda translated the experience into verse:

> *Those who are timid are sagging in the soul,*
> *And those poor who will inherit the earth*
> *already work it*
> *So take shelter you*
> *because we are thundering and beating on floors*
> *And this is how walls have fallen in other cities.*
> (242)

In the United States we do not know one another, except from the stereotypes presented in the media. As a result, there is the tendency to view people of a differing group vicariously, through the eyes of media interpreters.

Louise Erdrich and Michael Dorris, both Indian and both university professors and eminent writers, reported in Bill Moyers's *World of Ideas* (1989): "We had one guy come to dinner, and we cleaned our house and made a nice dinner, and he looks and says, kind of depressed, 'Do you always eat on the table?'" (465). They used the example to demonstrate how people "imagine" (as distinguished from "know") Indians on the basis of movie portrayals, usually as figures partially dressed or dressed in the fashion of the nineteenth century and typically eating while seated on the ground. It is difficult to form accurate perceptions of the people and worldview of another group. Carol Sanchez seems to challenge us to do just that when she asks us not to dismiss Native Americans and then asks, "How many Indians do you know?" (163). . . .

Sanchez charges non-Indians with the wish to have Indians act like whites, so they will be more acceptable to whites, another example of accommodation, assimilation. She is describing the attitude cited by the young child-care worker who said to me, "They like our food, our drum music, our jewelry, why don't they like us!?" Activist Winona La Duke, of the Ojibwa Tribe and by profession an economist, asserts in her offering in *A Gathering of Spirit:* "As far as the crises of water contamination, radiation, and death to the natural world and her children are concerned, respectable racism is as alive today as it was a century ago . . . a certain level of racism and ignorance has gained acceptance . . . in fact respectability . . . we either pick your bananas or act as a mascot for your football team . . . in this way, enlightened people are racist. They are arrogant toward all of nature, arrogant toward the children of nature, and ultimately arrogant toward all of life" (65–66). . . .

Continuing Tensions

That since the sixteenth century the history of Native Americans is one of racist oppression has become an integral part of contemporary historical understanding. Indian women are speaking with increasing frequency and force about their experiences of the double jeopardy of racism and sexism. I wish now to consider three factors that continue to contribute to serious tensions within the tribes and between the tribes and the so-called dominant culture. . . .

Tensions within the Indian Community

Indian People who wish to retain their identity and culture by continuing reservation life have constantly to struggle with choices regarding adaptation to the dominant culture. They realize that extremism in either direction will result in destruction of their ways of life. Those who resist any adaptation will be made to do so involuntarily, and those who accept "white men's ways" completely and without modification

by that very fact forgo their heritage. For well over a century, governmental policy favored assimilation and the concomitant dissolution of Indian tribal existence. Real estate value and greed for precious natural resources were crucial motivating factors throughout the period. Indians simply were in the way of the invaders' efforts to amass money. . . .

At the Flathead reservation in Montana, attempts are under way to "revive the traditional Salish culture and preserve the rugged land from development" (Shaffer 1990, 54). Attempts to protect the Indian land for future generations are buttressed by the traditional, nearly universal Indian belief that we do not own the land, that we are simply caretakers of it and will pass it on to future generations. Thus, how the land is used can become an issue of deep tension between strict traditionalists and those who want to assimilate contemporary economic development thinking into tribal life and institutions. Likewise, nearly universally held precepts include the prevailing rights of the tribe over individual rights and the discouragement of aggression and competitiveness, which are seen as threats to tribal harmony and survival. Phyllis Old Dog Cross, a Sioux and a nurse, speaking at a health conference in Denver in 1987, stated: "The need not to appear aggressive and competitive within the group is still seen among contemporary Indians . . . even quite acculturated Indians tend to be very unobtrusive. . . . [If not,] they receive strong criticism . . . also anything that would seem to precipitate anger, resentment, jealousy was . . . discouraged, for it is believed that tribal group harmony is threatened" (1987, 20).

Acknowledging their need for self-sufficiency as reductions in federal funding continue, the tribes are searching intensively for economic solutions. Some have introduced organized gambling onto the reservations and the leasing of land to business corporations; others are considering storage on reservation land of toxic wastes from federal facilities. Many of these measures are resisted, especially by traditionalists within the tribes, who see them as culturally destructive.

Erosion of Tribal Life: Cultural Marginality

Cultural marginality is increasingly experienced by Indian people because of the confusion resulting from ambiguities about what defines Indian identity, individually and tribally. The questions "Who is an

Indian?" and "What is a tribe?" no longer permit neat unequivocal answers.

Different tribes have different attitudes toward people of mixed heritage. In some a person with white blood may be accepted, while a person with some African-American blood may or may not be identified as Indian. Indian women, if they marry non-Indians, may or may not be identified within their tribes as Indians. To be a member of a tribe, a person must meet that tribe's requirements. Many tribes require proof of a person's being one-sixteenth or one-quarter or more of Indian descent to receive tribal affiliation. . . .

A group or an individual may qualify as an Indian for some federal purposes but not for others. A June 1977 statement by the U.S. Department of Labor on American Indian Women reads: "For their 1970 Census, the Bureau included in their questionnaire the category 'American Indian,' persons who indicated their race as Indian. . . . In the Eastern U.S., there are certain groups with mixed white, Negro, and Indian ancestry. In U.S. censuses prior to 1950, these groups had been variously classified by the enumerators, sometimes as Negro and sometimes as Indian, regardless of the respondent's preferred racial identity." LeAnne Howe, writing in Paula Gunn Allen's *Spider Woman's Granddaughters*, says, "Half-breeds live on the edge of both races . . . you're torn between wanting to kill everyone in the room or buying them all another round of drinks" (1989, 220).

Paula Gunn Allen, of the Laguna Pueblo tribe and a professor of literature, in her essay in *I Tell You Now*, writes: "Of course I always knew I was an Indian. I was told over and over, 'Never forget that you're an Indian.' My mother said it. Nor did she say, 'Remember you're part Indian'" (1987, 144).

Conflicts between Tribal and Other Governmental Laws

The Bureau of Indian Affairs, which has specific oversight responsibilities for the reservations, has played, at best, an ambivalent role, according to its very numerous critics. There have been many rumors of mishandled funds, especially of failure of funds to reach the reservations. It is the source of endless satire by Indian humorists, who, at their kindest, refer to it as the "Boss the Indian Around" department. By federal mandate the BIA is charged with coordinating the federal programs for the reservations. Originally, it was a section of the War Department, but for the last century and a half it has operated as part of the Department of the Interior.

Continuing skirmishes occur over violations of reservation land and water rights. Consequently, the tribes continue to appeal to the Supreme Court and to the United Nations for assistance in redressing federal treaty violations. When these cases are made public, they become fodder for those who continue to push for the assimilation of Indians into the dominant society as well as for the ever-present cadre of racial bigots.

Federal law and policy have too often been paternalistic, detrimental, and contrary to the best interests of the Indian people. Further, the federal dollar dominance of the tribes has a controlling interest on Indian life. Levitan and Johnston conclude that "for Indians, far more than for any other group, socioeconomic status is a federal responsibility, and the success or failure of federal programs determines the quality of Indian lives" (1975, 10).

To receive eligibility for government services requires that the person live on or near a reservation, trust, or restricted land or be a member of a tribe recognized by the federal government. To be an Indian in America can mean living under tribal laws and traditions, under state law, and under federal laws. The situation can become extremely complex and irksome, for example, when taxes are considered. The maze and snarl of legalese over such questions as whether the Navajo tribe can tax reservation mineral developments without losing its "trust status" and accompanying federal benefits would defeat, and does, the most ardent experts of jurisprudence. And the whole question of income tax for the Indian person living on a reservation and working in a nearby community requires expertise that borders on the ridiculous.

University of New Mexico law professor Fred Ragsdale, describing the relationship of reservation Indians with the federal government, compares it to playing blackjack: "Indians play with their own money. They can't get up and walk away. And the house gets to change the rules any time it wants" (1985, 1).

The outlawing of certain Indian religious practices occurred without challenge until the 1920s, when the laws and policies prohibiting dancing and ceremonies were viewed as cultural attacks. With the passage of the Indian Civil Rights Act in 1964, Indians have been able to present court challenges to discrimination based on their religious practices. Members of the North American Church use peyote, a psychoactive drug, in their ceremonies. Many consider their religion threatened by the . . . Supreme Court ruling that removes First Amendment protection of traditional worship practiced by Native Americans.

The negative impact of the 1966 Bennett freeze, a federally attempted solution to the bitter Navajo-Hopi land dispute, continues to cause pain to the Hopi, who use this 1.5-million-acre land mass for grazing, and to the Navajo, many of whom have resided on this land for generations. Sue Ann Presley, a *Washington Post* reporter, describes the area as being among the poorest in the nation and notes that the people living there are prohibited by law from participating in federal antipoverty programs. She reports that 90 percent of the homes have neither electricity nor indoor plumbing, and home repairs are not permitted. She quotes Navajo chair, Peterson Zah: "There are many Navajos who want to live in what we call the traditional way. But that does not mean they want to live with inadequate sewers, unpaved roads, no running water or electricity and under the watchful eye of the Hopi Tribe" (1993, B1). The forced removal of some of the Navajos from this area to border town housing caused a tremendous increase in the number of people who sought mental health treatment for depression and other disorders, according to the clinical observations of Tuba City, Arizona, psychologist Martin Topper. . . .

Conclusions

This closing decade of the twentieth century, as a promise for continuing scientific discovery and almost geometric progress, offers a special framework as a time for healing. The healing should be aligned with bias-free hope, and it should be as universally inclusive as possible. I think it a modest suggestion to say that it could well start with sharper identification and diagnosis by the scientific community of Native American women's experience of sexism and racism. Studies showing the impact of the privileged culture and dominant race on the development of Native Americans deserve continued exposure and extended development. We need medical research

that investigates the health conditions and illnesses of minorities, including Native American women, whose general health status has to be among the worst in America. . . .

The development of new theories must include appropriate, representative definitions of the total population, free of gender bias and not derived disproportionately from the observation of middle-class white men and women. Curriculum offerings with accurate and comprehensive historical data about gender-specific Native American experiences are needed. . . .

As a country, we have failed to acknowledge our despicable treatment of the Indians. . . . It is hoped that the Indian quest for self-determination and proper respect will be realized, and with it will come our healing as a nation as well. There exists a tremendous need to help the U.S. public begin to understand the real significance of Indian history. . . .

REFERENCES

Allen, P. G. 1986. *The Sacred Hoop.* Boston: Beacon Press.
——. 1987. "The Autobiography of a Confluence." In *I Tell You Now,* ed. B. Swann and A. Krupat. Lincoln: University of Nebraska Press, 141–54.
——. ed. 1989. *Spider Woman's Granddaughters.* Boston: Beacon Press.
Bataille, G., and K. Sands. 1984. *American Indian Women—Telling Their Lives.* Lincoln: University of Nebraska Press.
Bergman, R. 1971. "Navajo Peyote Use: Its Apparent Safety." *American Journal of Psychiatry* 128:6.
Canby, W. C. 1981. *American Indian Law.* St. Paul, Minn.: West Publishing.
Carr, H. 1988. "In Other Words: Native American Women's Autobiography." In *Life-Lines: Theorizing Women's Autobiographies,* ed. Bella Brodzki and Celeste Schenck. Ithaca, N.Y.: Cornell University Press, 131–53.
Cook-Lynn, E. 1987. "You May Consider Speaking about Your Art." In *I Tell You Now,* ed. B. Swann and A. Krupat. Lincoln: University of Nebraska Press, 55–63.
Deloria, V. 1970. *We Talk, You Listen.* New York: Dell Publishing.
Deloria, V., and C. Lytle. 1983. *American Indians, American Justice.* Austin: University of Texas Press.
Erdrich, L., and M. Dorris. 1989. "Interview." In *Bill Moyers: A World of Ideas,* ed. B. S. Flowers. New York: Doubleday, 460–69.
Gornick, V., and B. Moran, eds. 1972. *Women in Sexist Society.* New York: Signet.
Green, R. 1984. *That's What She Said.* Bloomington: University of Indiana Press.

Hogan, L. 1987. "The Two Lives." In *I Tell You Now,* ed. B. Swann and A. Krupat. Lincoln: University of Nebraska Press, 231–49.

Howe, L. 1989. "An American in New York." In *Spider Woman's Granddaughters,* ed. P. G. Allen. Boston: Beacon Press, 212–20.

Kutz, J. 1988. *Mysteries and Miracles of New Mexico.* Corrales, N.M.: Rhombus Publishing.

La Duke, W. 1988. "They Always Come Back." In *A Gathering of Spirit,* ed. B. Brant. Ithaca, N.Y.: Firebrand Books, 62–67.

Lange, C. 1959. *Cochiti—A New Mexico Pueblo, Past and Present.* Austin: University of Texas Press.

Levitan, S., and W. Johnston. 1975. *Indian Giving.* Baltimore: Johns Hopkins University Press.

Old Dog Cross, P. 1987. "What Would You Want a Caregiver to Know about You?" *The Value of Many Voices Conference Proceedings,* 29–32.

Presley, S. 18 July 1993. "Restrictions Force Deprivations on Navajos." *The Washington Post,* G1–G2.

Prucha, F. 1985. *The Indians in American Society.* Berkeley: University of California Press.

Ragsdale, F. 1985. Quoted in Sherry Robinson's "Indian Laws Complicate Development." *Albuquerque Journal,* 1.

Sanchez, Carol. 1984. "Sex, Class and Race Intersections: Visions of Women of Color." In *A Gathering of Spirit,* ed. B. Brant. Ithaca, N.Y.: Firebrand Books.

Shaffer, P. January/February 1990. "A Tree Grows in Montana." *Utne Reader,* 54–63.

Swentzell, R., and T. Naranjo. 1986. "Nurturing the Gia." *El Palacio* (Summer–Fall): 35–39.

Tallmountain, M. 1987. "You Can Go Home Again: A Sequence." In *I Tell You Now,* ed. B. Swann and A. Krupat. Lincoln: University of Nebraska Press, 1–13.

Wilkinson, C. 1987. *American Indians, Time, and the Law.* New Haven, Conn.: Yale University Press.

N I N E

◆◆◆

A Question of Class

Dorothy Allison

. . . My people were not remarkable. We were ordinary, but even so we were mythical. We were the *they* everyone talks about, the ungrateful poor. I grew up trying to run away from the fate that destroyed so many of the people I loved, and having learned the habit of hiding, I found that I also had learned to hide from myself. I did not know who I was, only that I did not want to be *they,* the ones who are destroyed or dismissed to make the real people, the important people, feel safer. By the time I understood that I was queer, that habit of hiding was deeply set in me, so deeply that it was not a choice but an instinct. Hide, hide to survive, I thought, knowing that if I told the truth about my life, my family, my sexual desire, my real history, then I would move over into that unknown territory, the land of *they,* would never have the chance to name my own life, to understand it or claim it.

Why are you so afraid? my lovers and friends have asked me the many times when I have suddenly seemed to become a stranger, someone who would not speak to them, would not do the things they believed I should do, simple things like applying for a job, or a grant, or some award they were sure I could acquire easily. Entitlement, I have told

them, is a matter of feeling like *we,* not *they.* But it has been hard for me to explain, to make them understand. You think you have a right to things, a place in the world, I try to say. You have a sense of entitlement I don't have, a sense of your own importance. I have explained what I know over and over again, in every possible way I can, but I have never been able to make clear the degree of my fear, the extent to which I feel myself denied, not only that I am queer in a world that hates queers but that I was born poor into a world that despises the poor. The need to explain is part of why I write fiction. I know that some things must be felt to be understood, that despair can never be adequately analyzed; it must be lived. . . .

I have known I was a lesbian since I was a teenager, and I have spent a good twenty years making peace with the effects of incest and physical abuse. But what may be the central fact of my life is that I was born in 1949 in Greenville, South Carolina, the bastard daughter of a poor white woman from a desperately poor family, a girl who had left the seventh grade the year before, who worked as a waitress and was just a month past fifteen when she had me. That fact, the inescapable impact of being born in a condition of poverty that this society finds shameful, contemptible, and somehow deserved, has dominated me to such an extent that I have spent my life trying to overcome or deny it. I have learned with great difficulty that the vast majority of people pretend that poverty is a voluntary condition, that the poor are different, less than fully human, or at least less sensitive to hopelessness, despair, and suffering.

The first time I read Melanie Kaye Kantrowitz's poems, I experienced a frisson of recognition. It was not that my people had been "burned off the map" or murdered as hers had. No, we had been erased, encouraged to destroy ourselves, made invisible because we did not fit the myths of the middle class. Even now, past forty and stubbornly proud of my family, I feel the draw of that mythology, that romanticized, edited version of the poor. I find myself looking back and wondering what was real, what true. Within my family, so much was lied about, joked about, denied or told with deliberate indirection, an undercurrent of humiliation, or a brief pursed grimace that belies everything that has been said—everything, the very nature of truth and lies, reality and myth. What was real? The poverty depicted in books and movies was romantic, a kind of backdrop for the story of how it was escaped. The reality of self-hatred and violence was either absent or caricatured. The poverty I knew was dreary, deadening, shameful. My family was ashamed of being poor, of feeling hopeless. What was there to work for, to save money for, to fight for or struggle against? We had generations before us to teach us that nothing ever changed, and that those who did try to escape failed.

My mama had eleven brothers and sisters, of whom I can name only six. No one is left alive to tell me the names of the others. It was my grandmother who told me about my real daddy, a shiftless pretty man who was supposed to have married, had six children, and sold cut-rate life insurance to colored people out in the country. My mama married when I was a year old, but her husband died just after my little sister was born a year later. When I was five, Mama married the man she lived with until she died. Within the first year of their marriage Mama miscarried, and while we waited out in the hospital parking lot, my stepfather molested me for the first time, something he continued to do until I was past thirteen. When I was eight or so, Mama took us away to a motel after my stepfather beat me so badly

it caused a family scandal, but we returned after two weeks. Mama told me that she really had no choice; she could not support us alone. When I was eleven I told one of my cousins that my stepfather was molesting me. Mama packed up my sisters and me and took us away for a few days, but again, my stepfather swore he would stop, and again we went back after a few weeks. I stopped talking for a while, and I have only vague memories of the next two years.

My stepfather worked as a route salesman, my mama as a waitress, laundry worker, cook, or fruit packer. I could never understand how, since they both worked so hard and such long hours, we never had enough money, but it was a fact that was true also of my mama's brothers and sisters, who worked in the mills or the furnace industry. In fact, my parents did better than anyone else in the family, but eventually my stepfather was fired and we hit bottom—nightmarish months of marshals at the door, repossessed furniture, and rubber checks. My parents worked out a scheme so that it appeared my stepfather had abandoned us, but instead he went down to Florida, got a new job, and rented us a house. In the dead of night, he returned with a U-Haul trailer, packed us up, and moved us south.

The night we left South Carolina for Florida, my mama leaned over the back seat of her old Pontiac and promised us girls, "It'll be better there." I don't know if we believed her, but I remember crossing Georgia in the early morning, watching the red clay hills and swaying gray blankets of moss recede through the back window. I kept looking back at the trailer behind us, ridiculously small to contain everything we owned. Mama had, after all, packed nothing that wasn't fully paid off, which meant she had only two things of worth, her washing and sewing machines, both of them tied securely to the trailer walls. Through the whole trip, I fantasized an accident that would burst that trailer, scattering old clothes and cracked dishes on the tarmac.

I was only thirteen. I wanted us to start over completely, to begin again as new people with nothing of the past left over. I wanted to run away completely from who we had been seen to be, who we had been. That desire is one I have seen in other members of my family, to run away. It is the first thing I think of when trouble comes, the geographic solution. Change your name, leave town, disappear, and make yourself over. What hides behind that solution is the conviction that the life you have lived, the person you are, are valueless, better off abandoned, that running away is easier than trying to change anything, that change itself is not possible, that death is easier than this life. Sometimes I think it is that conviction—more seductive than alcoholism or violence and more subtle than sexual hatred or gender injustice—that has dominated my life, and made real change so painful and difficult.

Moving to central Florida did not fix our lives. It did not stop my stepfather's violence, heal my shame, or make my mother happy. Once there our lives became dominated by my mother's illness and medical bills. She had a hysterectomy when I was about eight and endured a series of hospitalizations for ulcers and a chronic back problem. Through most of my adolescence she superstitiously refused to allow anyone to mention the word cancer. (Years later when she called me to tell me that she was recovering from an emergency mastectomy, there was bitter fatalism in her voice. The second mastectomy followed five years after the first, and five years after that there was a brief bout with cancer of the lymph system which went into remission after prolonged chemotherapy. She died at the age of fifty-six with liver, lung, and brain cancer.) When she was not sick, Mama, and my stepfather, went on working, struggling to pay off what seemed an insurmountable load of debts.

By the time I was fourteen, my sisters and I had found ways to discourage most of our stepfather's sexual advances. We were not close but we united against our stepfather. Our efforts were helped along when he was referred to a psychotherapist after losing his temper at work, and was prescribed psychotropic drugs that made him sullen but less violent. We were growing up quickly, my sisters moving toward dropping out of school, while I got good grades and took every scholarship exam I could find. I was the first person in my family to graduate from high school, and the fact that I went on to college was nothing short of astonishing.

Everyone imagines her life is normal, and I did not know my life was not everyone's. It was not until I was an adolescent in central Florida that I began to realize just how different we were. The people we met there had not been shaped by the rigid class structure that dominated the South Carolina Piedmont. The first time I looked around my junior high classroom and realized that I did not know who those people were—not only as individuals but as categories, who their people were and how they saw themselves—I realized also that they did not know me. In Greenville, everyone knew my family, knew we were trash, and that meant we were supposed to be poor, supposed to have grim low-paid jobs, have babies in our teens, and never finish school. But central Florida in the 1960s was full of runaways and immigrants, and our mostly white working-class suburban school sorted us out, not by income and family background, but by intelligence and aptitude tests. Suddenly I was boosted into the college-bound track, and while there was plenty of contempt for my inept social skills, pitiful wardrobe, and slow drawling accent, there was also something I had never experienced before, a protective anonymity, and a kind of grudging respect and curiosity about who I might become. Because they did not see poverty and hopelessness as a foregone conclusion for my life, I could begin to imagine other futures for myself.

Moving into that new world and meeting those new people meant that I began to see my family from a new vantage point. I also experienced a new level of fear, a fear of losing what before had never been imaginable. My family's lives were not on television, not in books, not even comic books. There was a myth of the poor in this country, but it did not include us, no matter how hard I tried to squeeze us in. There was an idea of the good poor—hardworking, ragged but clean, and intrinsically noble. I understood that we were the bad poor, the ungrateful: men who drank and couldn't keep a job; women, invariably pregnant before marriage, who quickly became worn, fat, and old from working too many hours and bearing too many children; and children with runny noses, watery eyes, and bad attitudes. My cousins quit school, stole cars, used drugs, and took dead-end jobs pumping gas or waiting tables. We were not noble, not grateful, not even hopeful. We knew ourselves despised.

But in that new country, we were unknown. The myth settled over us and glamorized us. I saw it in the eyes of my teachers, the Lions' Club representative who paid for my new glasses, and the lady from the Junior League who told me about the scholarship I had won. Better, far better, to be one of the mythical poor than to be part of the *they* I had known before. *Don't let me lose this chance*, I prayed, and lived in fear that I might suddenly be seen again as what I knew I really was.

As an adolescent, I thought that the way my family escaped South Carolina was like a bad movie. We fled like runaway serfs and the sheriff who would have arrested my stepfather seemed like a border guard. Even now, I am certain that if we had remained in South Carolina, I would have been trapped by my family's heritage of poverty, jail, and illegitimate children—that even being smart, stubborn, and a lesbian would have made no difference. My grandmother died when I was twenty and after Mama went home for the funeral, I had a series of dreams in which we still lived up in Greenville, just down the road from where Granny had died. In the dreams I had two children and only one eye, lived in a trailer, and worked at the textile mill. Most of my time was taken up with deciding when I would finally kill my children and myself. The dreams were so vivid, I became convinced they were about the life I was meant to have had, and I began to work even harder to put as much distance as I could between my family and me. I copied the dress, mannerisms, attitudes, and ambitions of the girls I met in college, changing or hiding my own tastes, interests, and desires. I kept my lesbianism a secret, forming a relationship with an effeminate male friend that served to shelter and disguise us both. I explained to friends that I went home so rarely because my stepfather and I fought too much for me to be comfortable in his house. But that was only part of the reason I avoided home, the easiest reason. The truth was that I feared the person I might become in my mama's house.

It is hard to explain how deliberately and thoroughly I ran away from my own life. I did not forget where I came from, but I gritted my teeth and hid it. When I could not get enough scholarship money to pay for graduate school, I spent a year of blind rage working as a salad girl, substitute teacher, and maid. I finally managed to get a job by agreeing to take any city assignment where the Social Security Administration needed a clerk. Once I had a job and my own place far away from anyone in my family, I became sexually and politically active, joining the Women's Center support staff and falling in love with a series of middle-class women who thought my accent and stories thoroughly charming. The stories I told about my family, about South Carolina, about being poor itself, were all lies, carefully edited to seem droll or funny. I knew damn well that no one would want to hear the truth about poverty, the hopelessness and fear, the feeling that nothing you do will make any difference, and the raging resentment that burns beneath the jokes. Even when my lovers and I formed an alternative lesbian family, sharing all our resources, I kept the truth about my background and who I knew myself to be a carefully obscured mystery. I worked as hard as I could to make myself a new person, an emotionally healthy radical lesbian activist, and I believed completely that by remaking myself I was helping to remake the world.

For a decade, I did not go home for more than a few days at a time.

It is sometimes hard to make clear how much I have loved my family, that every impulse to hold them in contempt has sparked in me a counter-surge of stubborn pride. (What is equally hard to make clear is how much that impulse toward love and pride is complicated by an urge to fit us into the acceptable myths and theories of both mainstream society—Steven Spielberg movies or Taylor Caldwell novels, the one valorizing and the other caricaturing—and a lesbian feminist reinterpretation—the patriarchy as the villain and the trivialization of the choices the men and women of my family have made.) I have had to fight broad generalizations from every possible theoretical viewpoint. Traditional feminist theory has had a limited understanding of class differences or of how sexuality and self are shaped by both desire and denial. The ideology implies that we are all sisters who should turn our anger and suspicion only on the world outside the lesbian community. It is so simple to say the patriarchy did it, that poverty and social contempt are products of the world of the fathers. How often I felt a need to collapse my sexual history into what I was willing to share of my class background, to pretend that both my life as a lesbian and my life as a working-class escapee were constructed by the patriarchy. The difficulty is that I can't ascribe everything that has been problematic or difficult about my life simply and easily to the patriarchy, or even to the invisible and much-denied class structure of our society. . . .

One of the things I am trying to understand is how we internalize the myths of our society even as we hate and resist them. Perhaps this will be more understandable if I discuss specifically how some of these myths have shaped my life and how I have been able to talk about and change my own understanding of my family. I have felt a powerful temptation to write about my family as a kind of moral tale with us as the heroes and the middle and upper classes as the villains. It would be within the romantic myth, for example, to pretend that we were the kind of noble Southern whites portrayed in the movies, mill workers for generations until driven out of the mills by alcoholism and a family propensity to rebellion and union talk. But that would be a lie. The truth is that no one in my family ever joined a union. Taken as far as it can go, the myth of the poor would make my family over into union organizers or people broken by the failure of the unions. The reality of my family is far more complicated and lacks the cardboard nobility of the myth.

As far as my family was concerned, union organizers, like preachers, were of a different class, suspect and hated as much as they might be admired for what they were supposed to be trying to achieve. Serious belief in anything—any political ideology, any religious system, or any theory of life's meaning and purpose—was seen as unrealistic. It was an attitude that bothered me a lot when I started reading the socially conscious novels I found in the paperback racks when I was eleven or so. I particularly loved Sinclair Lewis's novels and wanted to imagine my own family as part of the working man's struggle. But it didn't seem to be that simple.

"We were not joiners," my Aunt Dot told me with a grin when I asked her about the union. My cousin Butch laughed at that, told me the union charged dues and said, "Hell, we can't even be persuaded to toss money in the collection plate. An't gonna give it to no fat union man." It shamed me that the only thing my family wholeheartedly believed in was luck, and the waywardness of fate. They held the dogged conviction that the admirable and wise thing to do was to try and keep a sense of humor, not to whine or cower, and to trust that luck might someday turn as good as it had been bad—and with just as much reason. Becoming a political activist with an almost religious fervor was the thing I did that most outraged my family and the Southern working-class community they were part of.

Similarly, it was not my sexuality, my lesbianism, that was seen by my family as most rebellious; for most of my life, no one but my mama took my sexual preference very seriously. It was the way I thought about work, ambition, and self-respect that

seemed incomprehensible to my aunts and cousins. They were waitresses, laundry workers, and counter girls. I was the one who went to work as a maid, something I never told any of them. They would have been angry if they had known, though the fact that some work was contemptible was itself a difficult notion. They believed that work was just work, necessary, that you did what you had to do to survive. They did not believe so much in taking pride in doing your job as they did in stubbornly enduring hard work and hard times when you really didn't have much choice about what work you did. But at the same time they did believe that there were some forms of work, including maid's work, that were only for black people, not white, and while I did not share that belief, I knew how intrinsic it was to how my family saw the world. Sometimes I felt as if I straddled cultures and belonged on neither side. I would grind my teeth at what I knew was my family's unquestioning racism but still take pride in their pragmatic endurance, but more and more as I grew older what I truly felt was a deep estrangement from the way they saw the world, and gradually a sense of shame that would have been completely incomprehensible to them.

"Long as there's lunch counters, you can always find work," I was told by both my mother and my aunts, and they'd add, "I can always get me a little extra with a smile." It was obvious that there was supposed to be nothing shameful about it, that needy smile across a lunch counter, that rueful grin when you didn't have rent, or the half-provocative, half-begging way my mama could cajole the man at the store to give her a little credit. But I hated it, hated the need for it and the shame that would follow every time I did it myself. It was begging as far as I was concerned, a quasi-prostitution that I despised even while I continued to use it (after all, I needed the money). But my mother, aunts, and cousins had not been ashamed, and my shame and resentment pushed me even further away from them.

"Just use that smile," my girl cousins used to joke, and I hated what I knew they meant. After college, when I began to support myself and study feminist theory, I did not become more understanding of the women of my family but more contemptuous. I told myself that prostitution is a skilled profession and my cousins were never more than amateurs. There was a certain truth in this, though like all cruel judgments made from the outside, it ignored the conditions that made it true. The women in my family, my mother included, had sugar daddies, not johns, men who slipped them money because they needed it so badly. From their point of view they were nice to those men because the men were nice to them, and it was never so direct or crass an arrangement that they would set a price on their favors. They would never have described what they did as prostitution, and nothing made them angrier than the suggestion that the men who helped them out did it just for their favors. They worked for a living, they swore, but this was different.

I always wondered if my mother had hated her sugar daddy, or if not *him* then her need for what he offered her, but it did not seem to me in memory that she had. Her sugar daddy had been an old man, half-crippled, hesitant and needy, and he treated my mama with enormous consideration and, yes, respect. The relationship between them was painful because it was based on the fact that she and my stepfather could not make enough money to support the family. Mama could not refuse her sugar daddy's money, but at the same time he made no assumptions about that money buying anything she was not already offering. The truth was, I think, that she genuinely liked him, and only partly because he treated her so well.

Even now, I am not sure whether or not there was a sexual exchange between them. Mama was a pretty woman and she was kind to him, a kindness he obviously did not get from anyone else in his life, and he took extreme care not to cause her any problems with my stepfather. As a teenager with an adolescent's contempt for moral failings and sexual complexity of any kind, I had been convinced that Mama's relationship with that old man was contemptible and also that I would never do such a thing. The first time a lover of mine gave me money, and I took it, everything in my head shifted. The amount she gave me was not much to her, but it was a lot to me and I needed it. I could not refuse it, but I hated myself for taking it and I hated her for giving it to me. Worse, she had much less grace about my need than my mama's sugar daddy had displayed toward her. All that bitter contempt I had felt for my needy cousins and aunts raged through me and burned out the love I had felt. I ended the relationship quickly, unable to forgive myself for *selling* what I believed should only be offered freely—not sex but love itself.

When the women in my family talked about how hard they worked, the men would spit to the side and shake their heads. Men took real jobs—hard, dangerous, physically daunting work. They went to jail, not just the hard-eyed, careless boys who scared me with their brutal hands and cold eyes, but their gentler, softer brothers. It was another family thing, what people expected of my mama's family, my people. "His daddy's that one was sent off to jail in Georgia, and his uncle's another. Like as not, he's just the same," you'd hear people say of boys so young they still had their milk teeth. We were always driving down to the county farm to see somebody, some uncle, cousin, or nameless male relation. Shaven-headed, sullen and stunned, they wept on Mama's shoulder or begged my aunts to help. "I didn't do nothing, Mama," they'd say and it might have been true, but if even we didn't believe them, who would? No one told the truth, not even about how their lives were destroyed. . . .

By 1975, I was earning a meager living as a photographer's assistant in Tallahassee, Florida, but the real work of my life was my lesbian feminist activism, the work I did with the local Women's Center and the committee to found a Feminist Studies Department at Florida State University. Part of my role as I saw it was to be a kind of evangelical lesbian feminist, and to help develop a political analysis of this woman-hating society. I did not talk about class, more than by giving lip service to how we all needed to think about it, the same way I thought we all needed to think about racism. I was a serious and determined person, living in a lesbian collective, studying each new book that purported to address feminist issues and completely driven by what I saw as a need to revolutionize the world. . . .

The idea of writing fiction or essays seemed frivolous when there was so much work to be done, but everything changed when I found myself confronting emotions and ideas that could not be explained away or postponed for a feminist holiday. The way it happened was simple and completely unexpected. One week I was asked to speak to two completely divergent groups: an Episcopalian Sunday School class and a juvenile detention center. The Episcopalians were all white, well-dressed, highly articulate, nominally polite, and obsessed with getting me to tell them (without their having to ask directly) just what it was that two women did together in bed. The delinquents were all women, eighty percent black and Hispanic, dressed in green uniform dresses or blue jeans and workshirts, profane, rude, fearless, witty, and just as determined to get me to talk about what it was that two women did together in bed.

I tried to have fun with the Episcopalians, teasing them about their fears and insecurities, and being as bluntly honest as I could about my sexual practices. The Sunday School teacher, a man who had assured me of his liberal inclinations, kept blushing and stammering as the questions about my growing up and coming out became more detailed. When the meeting was over, I stepped out into the sunshine angry at the contemptuous attitude implied by all their questions, and though I did not know why, also so deeply depressed that I couldn't even cry. The delinquents were different. Shameless, they had me blushing within the first few minutes, yelling out questions that were partly curious and partly a way of boasting about what they already knew.

"You butch or femme?" "You ever fuck boys?" "You ever want to?" "You want to have children?" "What's your girlfriend like?" I finally broke up when one very tall confident girl leaned way over and called out, "Hey girlfriend! I'm getting out of here next weekend. What you doing that night?" I laughed so hard I almost choked. I laughed until we were all howling and giggling together. Even getting frisked as I left didn't ruin my mood. I was still grinning when I climbed into the waterbed with my lover that night, grinning right up to the moment when she wrapped her arms around me and I burst into tears.

It is hard to describe the way I felt that night, the shock of recognition and the painful way my thoughts turned. That night I understood suddenly everything that happened to my cousins and me, understood it from a wholly new and agonizing perspective, one that made clear how brutal I had been to both my family and myself. I understood all over again how we had been robbed and dismissed, and why I had worked so hard not to think about it. I had learned as a child that what could not be changed had to go unspoken, and worse, that those who cannot change their own lives have every reason to be ashamed of that fact and to hide it. I had accepted that shame and believed in it, but why? What had I or my cousins really done to deserve the contempt directed at us? Why had I always believed

us contemptible by nature? I wanted to talk to someone about all the things I was thinking that night, but I could not. Among the women I knew there was no one who would have understood what I was thinking, no other working-class women in the women's collective where I was living. I began to suspect that we shared no common language to speak those bitter truths.

In the days after that I found myself . . . thrown back into my childhood, into all the fears and convictions I had tried to escape. Once again I felt myself at the mercy of the important people who knew how to dress and talk, and would always be given the benefit of the doubt while I and my family would not.

I felt as if I was at the mercy of an outrage so old I could not have traced all the ways it shaped my life. I understood again that some are given no quarter, no chance, that all their courage, humor, and love for each other is just a joke to the ones who make the rules, and I hated the rule makers. Finally I also realized that part of my grief came from the fact that I no longer knew who I was or where I belonged. I had run away from my family, refused to go home to visit, and tried in every way to make myself a new person. How could I be working-class with a college degree? As a lesbian activist? I thought about the guards at the detention center, and the way they had looked at me. They had not stared at me with the same picture-window emptiness they turned on the girls who came to hear me, girls who were closer to the life I had been meant to live than I could bear to examine. The contempt in their eyes was contempt for me as a lesbian, different and the same, but still contempt. . . .

In the late 1970s, the compartmentalized life I had created burst open. It began when I started to write and work out what I really thought about my family. . . . I went home again. I went home to my mother and my sisters, to visit, talk, argue, and begin to understand.

Once home I saw that, as far as my family was concerned, lesbians were lesbians whether they wore suitcoats or leather jackets. Moreover, in all that time when I had not made peace with myself, my family had managed to make a kind of peace with me. My girlfriends were treated like slightly odd versions of my sisters' husbands, while I was simply the daughter who had always been difficult but was still a part of their lives. The result was that I started trying to confront what had made me unable to really talk to my sisters for so many years. I discovered that they no longer knew who I was either, and it took time and lots of listening to each other to rediscover my sense of family, and my love for them.

It is only as the child of my class and my unique family background that I have been able to put together what is for me a meaningful politics, gained a sense of why I believe in activism, why self-revelation is so important for lesbians, reexamining the way we are seen and the way we see ourselves. There is no all-purpose feminist analysis that explains away all the complicated ways our sexuality and core identity are shaped, the way we see ourselves as parts of both our birth families and the extended family of friends and lovers we invariably create within the lesbian community. For me the bottom line has simply become the need to resist that omnipresent fear, that urge to hide and disappear, to disguise my life, my desires, and the truth about how little any of us understand—even as we try to make the world a more just and human place for us all. Most of all I have tried to understand the politics of *they*, why human beings fear and stigmatize the different while secretly dreading that they might be one of the different themselves. Class, race, sexuality, gender, all the categories by which we categorize and dismiss each other need to be examined from the inside.

The horror of class stratification, racism, and prejudice is that some people begin to believe that the security of their families and community depends on the oppression of others, that for some to have good lives others must have lives that are mean and horrible. It is a belief that dominates this culture; it is what made the poor whites of the South so determinedly racist and the middle class so contemptuous of the poor. It is a myth that allows some to imagine that they build their lives on the ruin of others, a secret core of shame for the middle class, a goad and a spur to the marginal working class, and cause enough for the homeless and poor to feel no constraints on hatred or violence. The power of the myth is made even more apparent when we examine how within the lesbian and feminist communities, where so much attention has been paid to the politics of marginalization, there is still so much exclusion and fear, so many of us who do not feel safe even within our chosen communities.

I grew up poor, hated, the victim of physical, emotional, and sexual violence, and I know that suffering does not ennoble. It destroys. To resist destruction, self-hatred, or lifelong hopelessness, we have to throw off the conditioning of being despised, the fear of becoming that *they* that is talked about so dismissively, to refuse lying myths and easy moralities, to see ourselves as human, flawed and extraordinary. All of us—extraordinary.

T E N

A Word about the Great Terminology Question

Elizabeth Martínez

When you have a name like Martínez, sooner or later someone will ask the Great Terminology Question. Say that you prefer to be called a Chicana, not Mexican American, and you'll have to explain it at some length. Say that you prefer to be called Latina rather than Hispanic, and prepare for an even longer discussion. Say you are indigenous, and you'd better make another pot of coffee for a long night's debate. So it goes in this land of many identities, with new ones emerging all the time.

On one hand, there are real grounds for confusion. The term "Chicano" or "Chicana" eludes simple definition because it stands for a mix that is both racial and cultural. It refers to a people who are neither strictly Mexican nor strictly Yankee—as well as both. Go to Mexico and you will quickly realize that most people there do not see Chicanos as Mexican. You may even hear the term "brown gringo." Live in the United States, and you will quickly discover that the dominant population doesn't see Chicanos as real Americans.

Confusion, ignorance and impassioned controversy about terminology make it necessary, then, to begin . . . with such basic questions as: what is a Chicana or Chicano? (And remember, Spanish is a gendered language, hence Chicana/Chicano.)

For starters, we combine at least three roots: indigenous (from pre-Columbian times), European (from the Spanish and Portuguese invasions) and African (from the many slaves brought to the Americas, including some 200,000 to Mexico alone). A smattering of Chinese should be added, which goes back to the sixteenth century; Mexico City had a Chinatown by the mid-1500s, some historians say. Another *mestizaje,* or mixing took place—this time with Native Americans of various nations, pueblos and tribes living in what is now the Southwest—when Spanish and Mexican colonizers moved north. Later our Chicano ancestors acquired yet another dimension through intermarriage with Anglos.

The question arises: is the term "Chicano" the same as "Mexican American" or "Mexican-American"? Yes, except in the sense of political self-definition. "Chicano/a" once implied lower-class status and was at times derogatory. During the 1960s and 1970s, in an era of strong pressure for progressive change, the term became an outcry of pride in one's peoplehood and rejection of assimilation as one's goal. Today the term "Chicano/a" refuses to go away, especially among youth, and you will still hear jokes like "A Chicano is a Mexican American who doesn't want to have blue eyes" or "who doesn't eat white bread"

or whatever. (Some believe the word itself, by the way, comes from "Mexica"—pronounced "Meshica"—which was the early name for the Aztecs.)

People ask: are Chicanos different from Latinos?

At the risk of impassioned debate, let me say: we are one type of Latino. In the United States today, Latinos and Latinas include men and women whose background links them to some 20 countries, including Mexico. Many of us prefer "Latino" to "Hispanic," which obliterates our indigenous and African heritage, and recognizes only the European, the colonizer. (Brazilians, of course, reject "Hispanic" strongly because *their* European heritage is Portuguese, not Spanish.) "Hispanic" also carries the disadvantage of being a term that did not emerge from the community itself but was imposed by the dominant society through its census bureau and other bureaucracies, during the Nixon administration of the 1970s.

Today most of the people who say "Hispanic" do so without realizing its racist implications, simply because they see and hear it everywhere. Some who insist on using the term point out that "Latino" is no better than "Hispanic" because it also implies Eurocentricity. Many of us ultimately prefer to call ourselves "La Raza" or simply "Raza," meaning "The People," which dates back many years in the community. (Again we find complications in actual usage: some feel that Raza refers to people of Mexican and perhaps also Central American origin, and doesn't include Latinos from other areas.)

We are thus left with no all-embracing term acceptable to everyone. In the end, the most common, popular identification is by specific nationality: Puerto Rican, Mexican, Guatemalan, Colombian and so forth. But those of us who seek to build continental unity stubbornly cling to some broadly inclusive way of defining ourselves. In my own case, that means embracing both "Chicana" and "Latina."

At the heart of the terminology debate is the historical experience of Raza. Invasion, military occupation and racist control mechanisms all influence the evolution of words describing people who have lived through such trauma. The collective memory of every Latino people includes direct or indirect (neo-)colonialism, primarily by Spain or Portugal and later by the United States.

Among Latinos, Mexicans in what we now call the Southwest have experienced U.S. colonialism the longest and most directly, with Puerto Ricans not far behind. Almost one-third of today's United States was the home of Mexicans as early as the 1500s, until Anglos seized it militarily in 1848 and treated its population as conquered subjects. (The Mexicans, of course, themselves occupied lands that had been seized from Native Americans.) Such oppression totally violated the Treaty of Guadalupe Hidalgo, which ended the 1846–48 war and promised respect for the civil and property rights of Mexicans remaining in the Southwest. The imposition of U.S. rule involved taking over millions of acres of Mexican-held land by trickery and violence. Colonization also brought the imposition of Anglo values and institutions at the expense of Mexican culture, including language. Hundreds of Mexicans were lynched as a form of control.

In the early 1900s, while colonization continued, the original Mexican population of the Southwest was greatly increased by an immigration that continues today. This combination of centuries-old roots with relatively recent ones gives the Mexican-American people a rich and varied cultural heritage. It means that Chicanos are not by origin an immigrant people in the United States (except compared with the Native Americans); their roots go back four centuries. Yet they also include immigrants. Too many Americans see only the recent arrivals, remaining blind to those earlier roots and what they signify.

We cannot understand all that history simply in terms of victimization: popular resistance is its other face. Raza resistance, which took the form of organized armed struggle in the Southwest during the last century, continues today in many forms. These include rejecting the colonized mentality, that pernicious, destructive process of internalizing a belief in the master's superiority and our inferiority.

The intensity of the terminology debate comes as no surprise, then, for it echoes people's struggles for non-racist—indeed, anti-racist—ways of defining themselves. Identity continues to be a major concern of youth in particular, with reason. But an obsession with self-definition can become a trap if that is all we think about, all we debate. If liberatory terminology becomes an end in itself and our only end, it ceases to be a tool of liberation. Terms can be useful, even vital tools, but the house of La Raza that is waiting to be built needs many kinds.

E L E V E N

Shilling Love

Shailja Patel

One

They never said / they loved us

Those words were not / in any language / spoken by my parents

I love you honey was the dribbled caramel / of Hollywood movies / Dallas / Dynasty / where hot water gushed / at the touch of gleaming taps / electricity surged / 24 hours aday / through skyscrapers banquets obscene as pornography / were

mere backdrops / where emotions had no consequences words / cost nothing meant nothing would
never / have to be redeemed

My parents / didn't speak / that / language

1975 / 15 Kenyan shillings to the British pound /
my mother speaks battle

Storms the bastions of Nairobi's / most exclusive
prep schools / shoots our cowering / six-year-old
bodies like cannonballs / into the all-white classrooms / scales the ramparts of class distinction /
around Loreto convent / where the president /
sends his daughter / the government ministers,
foreign diplomats / send their daughters / because
my mother's daughters / will / have world-class
educations

She falls / regroups / falls and re-groups / in endless assaults on visa officials / who sneer behind
their bulletproof windows / at US and British con-
sulates / my mother the general / arms her daughters / to take on every citadel

1977 / 20 Kenyan shillings to the British pound /
my father speaks / stoic endurance / he began at
16 the brutal apprenticeship / of a man who takes
care of his own /relinquished dreams of / fighter
pilot rally driver for the daily crucifixion / of
wringing profit from a small business / my father
the foot soldier, bound to an honour / deeper than
any currency / *you must / finish what you start you
must / march until you drop you must / give your life
for those / you bring into the world*

I try to explain love / in shillings / to those who've
never gauged / who gets to leave who has to stay /
who breaks free and what they pay / those who've
never measured love / byevery rung of the ladder /
from survival / to choice

A force as grim and determined / as a boot up
the backside / a spur that draws blood / a moun-
taineer's rope / that yanks / relentlessly / up

My parents never say / they love us / they save
and count / count and save / the shilling falls
against the pound / college fees for overseas students / rise like flood tides / love is a luxury /
priced in hard currency / ringed by tariffs / and
we devour prospectuses / of ivied buildings
smooth lawns vast / libraries the way Jehovah's

witnesses / gobble visions of paradise / because
we know we'll have to be / twice as good three
times as fast four times as driven / with angels
powers and principalities on our side just / to
get / on / the / plane

Thirty shillings to the pound forty shillings to the
pound / my parents fight over money late in
the night / my father pounds the walls and yells /
I can't—it's impossible—what do you think I am? /
My mother propels us through school tuition exams
applications / locks us into rooms to study / keeps
an iron grip on the bank books

1982 / gunfire / in the streets of Nairobi / military
coup leaders / thunder over the radio / Asian
businesses wrecked and looted Asian women
raped / after / the government / regains control /
we whisper what the coup leaders planned

Round up all the Asians at gunpoint / in the
national stadium / strip them of whatever / they
carry / march them 30 miles / elders in wheelchairs / babies in arms / march them 30 miles to
the airport / pack them onto any planes / of any
foreign airline / tell the pilots / down the rifle bar-
rels / *leave / we don't care where you take them / leave*

I learn like a stone in my gut that / third-generation
Asian Kenyan will never / be Kenyan enough /
all my patriotic fervor / will never turn my skin
black / as yet another western country / drops a
portcullis / of immigration spikes / my mother
straps my shoulders back with a belt / to teach
me / to stand up straight

50 Kenyan shillings to the pound / we cry from
meltdown pressure / of exam after exam where
second place is never good enough / they snap /
faces taut with fear / *you can't be soft / you have to
fight / or the world will eat you up*

75 Kenyan shillings to the pound / they hug us /
tearless stoic at airports / as we board planes for
icy alien England / cram instructions into our
pockets like talismans / *Eat proper meals so you don't
get sick / cover your ears against the cold / avoid those
muffathias / the students without purpose or values /
learn and study / succeed / learn and study / suceed /
remember remember remember the cost of your life*

they never say / they love us

Two

I watch how I love / I admonish exhort / like a
Himalayan guide I / rope my chosen ones / yank
them remorselessly up / when they don't even
want to be / on the frigging mountain

like a vigilante squad I / scan dark streets for
threats I / strategize for war and famine I / slide
steel down spines

I watch heat / steam off my skin / when Westerners
drop / *I love you*'s into conversation / like blue-
berries hitting / soft / muffin / dough / I convert
it to shillings / and I wince

December 2000 / 120 shillings to the British pound /
90 Kenyan shillings to the US dollar / my sister
Sneha and I / wait for our parents / at SFO's
international terminal /

Four hours after / their plane landed / they have
not emerged

And we know with the hopeless rage / of third-
world citizens / African passport holders / that
the sum of their lives and labour / dreams and
sacrifice / was measured sifted weighted found /
wanting / by the INS

Somewhere deep in the airport's underbelly / in
a room rank with fear and despair / my parents /
who have travelled / 27 hours / across three continents / to see their children / are interrogated /
by immigration officials

My father the footsoldier / numb with exhaustion /
is throwing away / all the years / with reckless
resolve / telling them / *take the passports / take them /
stamp them / no readmission EVER / just let me out
to see my daughters*

My mother the general / dizzy with desperation /
cuts him off shouts him down / demands *listen to
me I'm the one / who filled in the visa forms* / in her
mind her lip curls she thinks / *these Americans / call*

*themselves so advanced so / modern but still / in the
year 2000 / they think it must be the husband in charge /
they won't let the wife speak*

On her face a lifetime / of battle-honed skill and
charm / turns like a heat lamp / onto the INS man
until he / stretches / yawns / relents / he's tired /
it's late / he wants his dinner / and my parents /
trained from birth / to offer Indian / hospitality /
open their bags and give their sandwiches / to this
man / who would have sent them back / without
a thought

Sneha and I / in the darkened lobby / watch the
empty exit way / our whole American / dream-
bought-with-their-lives / hisses mockery around
our rigid bodies / we swallow sobs because / they
raised us to be tough / they raised us to be fighters
and into that / clenched haze / of not / crying

here they come

hunched / over their luggage carts our tiny /
fierce / fragile / dogged / indomitable parents

Hugged tight they stink / of 31 hours in transit /
hugged tighter we all stink / with the bravado of
all the years / pain bitten down on gargantuan
hopes / holding on throug near-disasters / never
ever / giving in / to softness

The stench rises off us / unbearable / of what /
was never said

Something / is bursting the walls of my arteries
something / is pounding its way up my throat like
a volcano / rising / finally / I understand / why
I'm a poet

Because I was born to a law / that states / before
you claim a word you steep it / in terror and shit /
in hope and joy and grief / in labour endurance
vision costed out / in decades of your life / you
have to sweat and curse it / pray and keen it /
crawl and bleed it / with the very marrow / of
your bones / you have to earn / its / meaning

TWELVE

◆◆◆

Moving from Cultural Appropriation toward Ethical Cultural Connections[1]

Joanna Kadi

My grandmother trudged from the hills of rural Lebanon to the shores of the Mediterranean, carrying clothes and a derbeke.[2] She and the drum survived several weeks in the steerage compartment of a large boat. No small feat. And now she's dead, and the derbeke sits on a shelf far away from me. But I ended up with my sittee's determination, which I've needed to navigate through the stormy waters of drumming.

After experiencing so much anti-Arab hatred growing up, I cut myself off from my culture as soon as I could. I tried hard to assimilate, with the attendant craziness and confusion; but thankfully, my journey into political awareness and action brought me back to my racial/cultural heritage, and in particular to its music. Hearing familiar rhythms, I found myself thinking about—and wanting—a brass derbeke with a chrome finish and intricate engraving. Just like the one my grandmother brought from Lebanon.

So my lover and I embarked on a grand search to ferret out my derbeke. It took a long time, partly because I didn't know where to look, partly because white people's interest in drumming hadn't fully impacted the market. In January 1991, a year after the search began, Jan and I marched in Washington, D.C., to protest the slaughter of Arabs in the vicious outbreak of U.S. imperialism known as the Gulf War. During that weekend, alternating between grief and numbness, we chanced upon a store specializing in musical instruments from around the world. I found my derbeke.

The end of my search? No. Just the beginning. Now I needed a teacher and a community that would offer technical assistance and political respect. I attended drumming workshops, but each proved as problem-laden as my first, where I found an overwhelmingly white group of women who apparently hadn't given much thought to the issue of playing congas or derbekes. I'm using the word "play" loosely, because even as an unskilled beginner I could tell these women didn't know the traditional Arabic

techniques and rhythms I knew simply from listening to Arabic music. Further dismay resulted when I questioned two women and discovered they didn't know the name of their drums; they had just been drawn to the derbeke for some unknown reason and made a purchase. They spent the workshop banging happily on their drums in ways bearing no resemblance to proper derbeke-playing style.

I sat through this drumming workshop, and subsequent ones, with a familiar mix of anger and fear. Anger at the casual (mis)use by white people of important aspects of culture from various communities of color, fear that such groups would prove the only resource available and I would simply have to put up with crap in order to learn. These disheartening experiences led to another year of my derbeke gathering dust as I grew more certain I'd never find what I needed.

But after much searching, I found a wonderful teacher, Mick Labriola, as well as drumming friends/acquaintances I connect with politically and musically. Because of this, and because of my deep determination to forge ahead in spite of obstacles, drumming has proved an incredible positive experience. I've re-connected with my roots. Experiencing how much beauty and importance Arabs have given the world has helped me feel pride, as opposed to shame, about being Arab.

Then there's anger and grief. My initial experiences at drumming workshops proved common. I continually see derbekes in white people's homes, played by white musicians, banged on at drumming circles. Many players don't even know the name of the instrument, or where it comes from. They don't play properly, and they don't know traditional Arabic rhythms.

But none of this seems to raise any concern, as more and more white people jump on the drumming bandwagon. Why drumming? Why so popular? Because it's a powerful activity? Because it's a wonderfully communal instrument? Because it allows people to learn about other cultures through music? Most days I think these explanations provide a more positive interpretation than the situation warrants, especially when I notice the apolitical spirituality of the New Age movement embracing the concept of "getting in touch with inner rhythms" via the drums of people of color; white people dredding their hair and buying African drums; people "playing" an instrument without knowing its name.

Within these actions, I sense an imperialist attitude in which privileged people want to own segments of other people's cultures. To me, it's cultural appropriation, a subject I'm confused about and infuriated by. I have many questions and ideas, but few answers. The complexity of the subject lends itself more to books (*not* written by white people) than single essays, so be forewarned; I can't tackle everything. I've tried to streamline this by focusing it around drumming, and in particular derbekes, since issues and questions relating to drumming carry over to other types of cultural appropriation.

I've thought long and hard about defining cultural appropriation. Culture includes any and all aspects of a community that provide its life force, including art, music, spirituality, food, philosophy, and history. To "appropriate" means to take possession of. "Cultural" appropriation means taking possession of specific aspects of someone else's culture in unethical, oppressive ways.

While helpful, this basic definition simplifies rather than deepens. It doesn't examine various aspects of cultural appropriation. To do that, I'll analyze what happens when white people play derbekes incorrectly.

It seems to me those white people use derbekes perceiving them as generic, no-name drums unencumbered by hard political/historical/cultural realities, never asking themselves the questions that would uncover these realities, such as: whose music is this? What has imperialism and racism done to the people who created this music? Do I have a right to play this instrument? What kind of beliefs do I hold about Arabs? Ignoring these questions and ignoring Arab musical traditions translates into cultural appropriation—white people taking possession of Arabic culture by commandeering an important instrument and the music it produces. The derbeke and its playing style are important pieces of Arab

culture, with thousands of years of history attached. To disregard that and play however one chooses whitewashes the drum, and by implication Arab culture. When stripped of its historical legacy, the drum is placed outside Arab culture, suggesting that Arab culture and history aren't worth taking seriously; even though Arabs have created something valuable and life-enhancing in our music, that doesn't matter. White people can and will choose to perceive the drum as ahistorical and culturally empty—a plaything that can be given whatever meaning the player chooses.

To perceive a derbeke as a plaything is to carry the privileged attitude that has wrought devastation all over our planet: "Everything is here for me to play with and use." Whether peoples, lands, our cultures, it's there for the grabbing. This take-take-take attitude pushed white colonizers through whole peoples and lands on the Asian, African, and American continents. Although brown, black, and yellow people filled those continents, white people perceived them as empty.

That kind of colonization continues, and new forms have evolved. The colonialist attitude has affixed itself to our music, clothing, religions, languages, philosophies and art. I overheard a white shopper in a music store examining a derbeke. "Cool drum. I'll take a couple." He perceived the derbeke as an empty vessel waiting to have meaning infused into it, as opposed to an important cultural symbol/reality embodying centuries of meaning.

I don't believe every white person who buys a derbeke holds that attitude, or that no other issues or desires are mixed in. But I do believe large and small vestiges of colonialist ideas live in many places, and it frightens and angers me. These ideas and their practice have already destroyed so many of our people and may well destroy more. Many white people don't know they possess such a mindset, and unthinking, unexamined ignorance can cause irreparable harm.

These political questions must be raised, along with the psychological effects of cultural appropriation. Many times people of color gloss over these, possibly because we don't want to admit the extent of our pain. I want to try.

Cultural appropriation causes me anger and grief. Anger about flagrant disregard and disrespect for me and my community, about unexamined privilege and power, about cavalier white people who use important cultural symbols/realities and turn them into no-name items. And grief, which stems from a hopeless, powerless feeling that I/my community will never get the respect and consideration we deserve, that no matter how hard we struggle, no one hears our words or heeds our demands.

Along with those responses is one that so far hasn't been examined in our thinking and writing about cultural appropriation; for me this causes deep pain. Cultural appropriation cuts away at and undermines my basic racial identity.

It's been hard for me to create a clear, strong identity as Arab-American. It's been hard for me to believe I really exist as such a person, when dominant society categorically trivializes, diminishes, and whitewashes Arabs. I've struggled with this for years, and recently my identity has been strengthened, thanks in part to my derbekes. They help me realize I come from somewhere, my community exists, and we've created wonderful cultural expressions over the centuries.

When, as happens frequently, I come across the attitude that clearly says the derbeke is an empty vessel, I begin doubting myself and my community, doubting our very existence. I fight constantly against internalizing the message—if the derbeke means nothing, if it comes from nowhere, I don't exist.

It's impossible to examine increased derbeke sales or the increased numbers of white "shamans" without discussing multiculturalism. Strange things are happening under the guise of "honoring diversity," because multiculturalism, as defined and practiced by white people, is partly responsible for the increase in cultural appropriation. While I'm not opposed to *authentic* multiculturalism, I do believe unauthentic or artificial or perverse multi-culturalism simply feeds and reinforces imperialist attitudes. Examples of this abound. Young white schoolchildren aren't taught to connect ethically with other cultures; they're taught to take whatever they want from other cultures and use it. White adult consumers snatch our various arts, wanting the stuff but not caring if its creators are systematically destroyed.

Given the brutal racism endemic to our society, it makes sense that much of what passes for multiculturalism is actually covert and overt cultural appropriation, actually a form of cultural genocide. As

dominant white society casually buys and sells our symbols/realities, their cultural meaning is watered down and their integrity diminished. Today items from various communities of color are all the rage, but I'm not happy to see the walls of white people's homes adorned with African masks, Asian paintings, and Native ceremonial objects. Behind the rhetoric and hype about multiculturalism and honoring diversity lurk the same attitudes of entitlement and privilege that form part of structural racism. For the most part, these white people haven't done the work necessary to become allies to people of color. They know little or nothing about current global struggles of people of color, as we define and articulate them. They don't engage in acts of solidarity around specific issues such as Native self-determination or Palestinian liberation. They don't read books by radical authors of color.

Further, these white people haven't analyzed a monster related to racism, that is, classism and the global capitalist system. All of us need to be clear about how and where and why the capitalist system fits into the picture. We need to ask critical questions. Is "multiculturalism" the latest capitalist fad? Who's in control? Who's benefiting? And who's making money, now that it's popular to hang Native dream webs on bedroom walls? Could it be people of color? Hardly. As more and more people of color are forced to live on the streets, white entrepreneurs are getting rich selling our art, music, and spirituality. Watching them profit as they exploit and appropriate our cultures, when for years we experienced hostility and scorn trying to preserve them in a racist society, is truly galling. I grew up with white people belittling and "joking" about my family's choice of music and dancing; now I can watch those same people rush to sign up for "real" belly-dancing lessons. Taught by a white woman, of course.

Economics impact culture, as the belly dance example shows. The particular combination of racism and classism that has popularized belly dancing taught by white people has several implications for Arab-American culture. Arab dancers who can't make a living teaching may be eventually forced to give up their serious studies of traditional dance altogether; this is one factor that eventually leads to cultural genocide. If a certain type of belly dancing becomes popular and another particular strain never catches on with white teachers, the latter could slowly disappear. Again, this factors into cultural genocide. For every cultural form happily adopted by the dominant culture's racist and classist system, another falls by the wayside. Some expressions discarded by dominant society will continue to thrive among marginalized communities, some will be lost forever.

Further, class exploitation crosses over with racism in certain ways, and thus many people of color are working-class or working-poor. Consequently, we can't afford to buy the now-available music, paintings, instruments, and books from our cultures. We can't afford travel to our countries of origin. Observing white, middle-class people engaging in these activities adds yet another layer of anguish and complexity to these issues.

Recently I talked over the phone with a white, middle-class man who has traveled extensively in various Arab countries, attended Arabic language schools, and now speaks Arabic fluently. Upon discovering I was Arab-American, he began speaking Arabic to me.

As is all too usual, I got so choked up with rage I couldn't think clearly. I said curtly, "I don't speak Arabic," and hung up. Next time, I have a response all planned out: "Gee, if only my grandparents hadn't experienced so much racism and been so isolated! Then they wouldn't have tried to assimilate. Then they would have taught us to speak Arabic. Which would be so helpful these days, now that multiculturalism is in. For those who can afford it, which of course precludes most people of color. Oh well, I hope you're having a splendid time with it all."

The discussion of cultural appropriation between white people and people of color is critically important, but I want to push further. If we keep the focus on relationships between colored and white, we come up with an overly simplistic analysis that ignores the fact that many people of color are just as inattentive to these issues and thus act inappropriately toward each other. It implies the only groups worth discussing are *the* white people and *the* people of color, two broad categories which are sometimes helpful but also present problems in terms of understanding the complexities of race. These simplistic categories feed into the myth that people of color constitute a monolithic group unscathed by differences of skin color, immigrant status, gender, ability, sexuality, language, class, and religion. Further, reductionist categories support the lie that we can only be discussed in relation to white people, that our only important relationships exist with white people.

A simplistic analysis of cultural appropriation minimalizes and trivializes what we as people of color from different communities do to each other, glossing over the fact that we can and do commit acts of cultural appropriation, and thus hurt each other badly. I've had the painful experience of watching other people of color using derbekes as no-name drums. Our racial identity doesn't rule out unjust acts toward each other. If I were drawn to an African mask in a store and bought it without knowing where it came from, what it represents, and who made it, would that be acceptable? Of course not. I'd be committing an act of cultural appropriation as surely as any white person who did the same thing.

Our existence as people of color doesn't mean we know much—if anything—about other communities of color. It doesn't mean we've done the hard work of freeing ourselves from stereotypes and lies about other racial/ethnic groups. I've heard, time and again, the same kind of anti-Arab racism out of the mouths of people of color that I've heard from white people. Unless people of color do the same anti-racist work we want white people to do, we can't become true allies and friends.

However, I don't equate the actions of people of color with those of white people. There's a difference between a white person and a person of color playing derbekes incorrectly. The white person's actions feed into structural racism; they're part and parcel of the systemic oppression by white people of people of color. The person of color's actions stem, I think, from a mix of structural racism and horizontal violence in which the dominant white power structure keeps us carefully divided from each other, duplicating their mistreatment, and ignorant about the many ways our lives connect.

Even with this understanding, it still hurts when a Latino uses a derbeke as a generic drum. In some ways, because I so badly want and need solidarity from other people of color, these actions hurt more. I don't expect as much from white people, so I'm not as shocked and hurt by their actions. But betrayal from other people of color cuts deeply.

Betrayal appears in varied forms, and I briefly want to mention sexism. Many men of color bring a problematic and divisive note to discussions of drumming and culture by insisting women can't drum because it's not "traditional." I have two responses to this. First, there's historical documentation from many cultures, including Arabic ones, of women drumming in earlier times. Second, even in relation to preserving our cultures, I find the label "traditional" almost irrelevant. If women didn't drum in the past, why would we want to carry on with that aspect of our culture? Are the men who propose this anxious to continue every traditional cultural practice, from the most inane to the most misogynist?[3] Plenty of manifestations of sexism and misogyny in Arab cultures need to be kissed goodbye.

As a person of color, I want to do more than react to oppression by white people. It's important that, as a subject and moral agent with power in the world, I state what I want and what I consider acceptable. For starters, do I want to share cultural traditions?

There are several reasons I do. First, when healthy cultural connections occur, it's personally and communally affirming. Someone has taken the time and energy to understand and appreciate the derbeke. She's taken me and my community/culture seriously, and shown respect. This affirms me and helps strengthen racial identity.

Second, I'm enriched by participating in an authentic multiculturalism that involves having friends, listening to the music, learning the histories, and being allies in struggle with people from various cultures. This type of multiculturalism has, at its root, respect, thoughtfulness, a political analysis, and openness.

Third, in practical terms, I don't know how to separate. I was born of an interracial marriage. I live in a racially mixed community and belong to organizations and groups that cut across cultures. I've read and listened to and integrated perspectives of people from different racial/ethnic communities. How to undo this mixing? Forget the books, the stories, the poems, the music that have become part of me? Give up friends? Return to my places of origin—which isn't physically possible, and where I may not feel at home for other reasons? It seems foolhardy to consider this.

I support the idea of sharing across cultures, but I also believe some things should never be shared. For starters, sacred instruments, rhythms, and rituals. Yet, unbelievably, this has happened, continues to happen. Several years ago I attended a music festival where two white women planned to perform with a sacred instrument from a community of Australian indigenous people. Although an Australian aboriginal woman was present and voiced objections, it didn't matter to the musicians. At the last minute, outcries from a larger group prevented the show. I don't know if these two musicians used the instrument other times, but given the depth of their resistance to restriction of their "artistic freedom," I wouldn't be surprised if they did.

Of course, I question whether those women should have been performing at all, since their show consisted of playing instruments from various communities of color. I'm tired of seeing white people get the praise, money, and publicity from public performance. However, I can't deal with these questions and issues here. The topic needs an essay of its own and quite possibly its own book.

Back to making and preserving connections across communities. How to make such links? And what to call them? Words carry critical weight in liberation struggles. Naming ourselves and our desires is vital. The term "ethical cultural connection" embodies my ideas. It focuses clearly on culture, on the lifeforce of a community. "Connection" speaks to a freely-chosen bonding experience between two people or two groups. The adjective "ethical" clarifies the type of connection—one based on respect, justice, and integrity.

Ethical cultural connections are comprised of respect for the community involved, a desire to learn and take action, an openness to being challenged and criticized, a willingness to think critically about personal behavior, and a commitment to actively fighting racism. These cornerstones remain the same whether I'm getting to know one Native person or buying a carving from a Native museum. They apply to people of color and white people.

I've come to the conclusion that I'm not opposed to non-Arabs playing derbekes if it's done with respect, knowledge, and seriousness, and if these attitudes manifest themselves in concrete action. I want drummers to learn the derbeke's culture and history, and the proper way to play. And to take this knowledge a step further by actively countering the imperialism, racism, and genocide Arabs experience today. It's not enough to celebrate cultural difference by learning language, music, or history, when people's whole worlds are at risk.

Of course, this raises a critical question. How do I know if someone's doing those things? By watching? Maybe the person plays the derbeke correctly, maybe he knows Arab rhythms. But that doesn't tell me how much he knows and cares about my people.

I can only know for sure if I talk to the drummer. That's the only way any of us will know. Typing out guidelines or policing cultural events won't do it. We need to talk—across cultures and classes. I've spent days and days and days writing this essay, and months pondering it, and I've been unable to think of any other way to know where a person stands. My analysis doesn't help in isolation. It helps as we communicate across all racial groups—Asian (including Arabs), Latino, Native, African, and white.

And talking to one person won't cut it. I'm sure any white person interested in assuaging her conscience could find enough white-identified Arabs to assure her whatever she does with the derbeke is okay. There are many such people in all communities—people who for whatever reasons have become so alienated from their roots and their communities that they casually approve of the worst kinds of cultural appropriation. At the music festival I mentioned earlier, participants discussed cultural appropriation several times, and it appeared the women of color shared a clear and unified response. That is, until a well-known woman of color, a superb drummer, announced from the stage that anyone who wanted a drum from whatever culture should buy it and play it. So much for solidarity.

I don't want white people seeking out white-identified people of color to give them the stamp of approval. I want white people to talk to many people, including political activists. I want discussion around power and privilege, about who benefits from cultural appropriation and in what ways, about who will decide how cultural connections happen and what makes them ethical. I want discussion about actions and the meanings they carry.

In these discussions, participants need to take emotional reactions into account without letting them dictate the whole discussion. If I'm so sick and tired of watching non-Arabs thoughtlessly pound away on derbekes, I might not notice when someone's doing it right. I might not even care. I'm entitled to my anger, but one person's emotions can't set the tone and agenda for these discussions.

I believe politicized people of color and our white allies must start framing discussions with helpful guidelines that make sense to us. Discussions must be cross-cultural and focused on tough questions about racism, classism, unauthentic multiculturalism, power, and privilege. And I suggest we include the ways in which personal experience can help frame critical thinking on cultural appropriation.

Looking at the five derbekes that now grace this home, I'm struck by the connection between my drumming and my political thinking. The deeper I go with one, the deeper I go with the other. The political analysis I push myself to do translates into more meaningful drumming. Playing the derbeke helps deal with the pain I experience around vivid examples of cultural appropriation. I offer this personal example not as a "feel-good," quick, on-the-surface remedy for oppression and cultural genocide, but rather as a somber statement of possibility. We can plumb the depths of the worst in our society while participating in meaningful cultural activities that ground us and keep hope alive.

NOTES

1. Many thanks to Jan Binder for her help with this article.

2. A derbeke (pronounced der-beck-ee) is a traditional Arabic hand drum. I've seen several different spellings, but this is the one I prefer. The drum is also known as a *dumbek* (pronounced doom-beck)—there are varied spellings for that word as well.

3. Another problem with this attitude is that it feeds into the dangerous lie/myth that cultures are static and unchanging entities.

THIRTEEN

Optional Ethnicities

For Whites Only?

Mary C. Waters

This paper reviews the current meaning of ethnicity for the descendants of nineteenth- and early twentieth-century European immigrants to the United States and contrasts that experience with the identities of people with non-European origins—the descendants of earlier forced immigrants and conquered peoples and the growing number of voluntary immigrants from non-European countries. . . .

Ethnic Identity for Whites in the 1990s

What does it mean to talk about ethnicity as an option for an individual? To argue that an individual has some degree of choice in their ethnic identity flies in the face of the commonsense notion of ethnicity many of us believe in–that one's ethnic identity is a fixed characteristic, reflective of blood ties and given at birth. However, social scientists who study ethnicity have long concluded that while ethnicity is based in a *belief* in a common ancestry, ethnicity is primarily a *social* phenomenon, not a biological one (Alba 1985, 1990; Barth 1969; Weber [1921] 1968, p. 389). The belief that members of an ethnic group have that they share a common ancestry may not be a fact. There is a great deal of change in ethnic identities across generations through intermarriage, changing allegiances, and changing social categories. There is also a much larger amount of change in the identities of individuals over their life than is commonly believed. While most people are aware of the phenomenon known as "passing"— people raised as one race who change at some point and claim a different race as their identity—there are similar life course changes in ethnicity that happen all the time and are not given the same degree of attention as "racial passing."

White Americans of European ancestry can be described as having a great deal of choice in terms of their ethnic identities. The two major types of options White Americans can exercise are (1) the op-

tion of whether to claim any specific ancestry, or to just be "White" or American (Lieberson [1985] called these people "unhyphenated Whites"), and (2) the choice of which of their European ancestries to choose to include in their description of their own identities. In both cases, the option of choosing how to present yourself on surveys and in everyday social interactions exists for Whites because of social changes and societal conditions that have created a great deal of social mobility, immigrant assimilation, and political and economic power for Whites in the United States. Specifically, the option of being able to not claim any ethnic identity exists for Whites of European background in the United States because they are the majority group—in terms of holding political and social power, as well as being a numerical majority. The option of choosing among different ethnicities in their family backgrounds exists because the degree of discrimination and social distance attached to specific European backgrounds has diminished over time.

The Ethnic Miracle

When European immigration to the United States was sharply curtailed in the late 1920s, a process was set in motion whereby the European ethnic groups already in the United States were for all intents and purposes cut off from any new arrivals. As a result, the composition of the ethnic groups began to age generationally. The proportion of each ethnic group made up of immigrants or the first generation began to gradually decline, and the proportion made up of the children, grandchildren, and eventually great-grandchildren began to increase. Consequently, by 1990 most European-origin ethnic groups in the United States were composed of a very small number of immigrants, and a very large proportion of people whose link to their ethnic origins in Europe was increasingly remote.

This generational change was accompanied by unprecedented social and economic changes. The very success of the assimilation process these groups experienced makes it difficult to imagine how much the question of the immigrants' eventual assimilation was an open one at the turn of the century. At the peak of immigration from southern and central Europe, there was widespread discrimination and hostility against the newcomers by established Americans. Italians, Poles, Greeks, and Jews were called derogatory names, attacked by nativist mobs, and derided in the press. Intermarriage across ethnic lines was very uncommon—castelike in the words of some sociologists (Pagnini and Morgan 1990). The immigrants and their children were residentially segregated, occupationally specialized, and generally poor.

After several generations in the United States, the situation has changed a great deal. The success and social mobility of the grandchildren and great-grandchildren of that massive wave of immigrants from Europe has been called "The Ethnic Miracle" (Greeley 1976). These Whites have moved away from the inner-city ethnic ghettos to White middle-class suburban homes. They are doctors, lawyers, entertainers, academics, governors, and Supreme Court justices. But contrary to what some social science theorists and some politicians predicted or hoped for, these middle-class Americans have not completely given up ethnic identity. Instead, they have maintained some connection with their immigrant ancestors' identities—becoming Irish American doctors, Italian American Supreme Court justices, and Greek American presidential candidates. In the tradition of cultural pluralism, successful middle-class Americans in the late twentieth century maintain some degree of identity with their ethnic backgrounds. They have remained "hyphenated Americans." So, while social mobility and declining discrimination have created the option of not identifying with any European ancestry, most White Americans continue to report some ethnic background.

With the growth in intermarriage among people of European ethnic origins, increasingly these people are of mixed ethnic ancestry. This gives them the option of which ethnicity to identify with. The U.S. census has asked a question on ethnic ancestry in the 1980 and 1990 censuses. In 1980, 52 percent of the American public responded with a single ethnic ancestry, 31 percent gave multiple ethnic origins (up to three were coded, but some individuals wrote in more than three), and only 6 percent said they were

American only, while the remaining 11 percent gave no response. In 1990 about 90 percent of the population gave some response to the ancestry question, with only 5 percent giving American as a response and only 1.4 percent reporting an uncodeable response such as "don't know" (McKenney and Cresce 1992; U.S. Bureau of the Census 1992).

Several researchers have examined the pattern of responses of people to the census ancestry question. These analyses have shown a pattern of flux and inconsistency in ethnic ancestry reporting. For instance, Lieberson and Waters (1986, 1988, p. 93) have found that parents simplify children's ancestries when reporting them to the census. For instance, among the offspring in situations where one parent reports a specific single White ethnic origin and the other parent reports a different single White origin, about 40 percent of the children are not described as the logical combination of the parents' ancestries. For example, only about 60 percent of the children of English-German marriages are labeled as English-German or German-English. About 15 percent of the children of these parents are simplified to just English, and another 15 percent are reported as just German. The remainder of the children are either not given an ancestry or are described as American (Lieberson and Waters 1986, 1993).

In addition to these intergenerational changes, researchers have found changes in reporting ancestry that occur at the time of marriage or upon leaving home. At the ages of eighteen to twenty-two, when many young Americans leave home for the first time, the number of people reporting a single as opposed to a multiple ancestry goes up. Thus while parents simplify children's ancestries when they leave home, children themselves tend to report less complexity in their ancestries when they leave their parents' homes and begin reporting their ancestries themselves (Lieberson and Waters 1986, 1988; Waters 1990).

These individual changes are reflected in variability over time in the aggregate numbers of groups determined by the census and surveys. Farley (1991) compared the consistency of the overall counts of different ancestry groups in the 1979 Current Population Survey, the 1980 census, and the 1986 National Content Test (a pretest for the 1990 census). He found much less consistency in the numbers for northern European ancestry groups whose immigration peaks were early in the nineteenth century—the

English, Dutch, Germans, and other northern European groups. In other words, each of these different surveys and the census yielded a different estimate of the number of people having this ancestry. The 1990 census also showed a great deal of flux and inconsistency in some ancestry groups. The number of people reporting English as an ancestry went down considerably from 1980, while the number reporting German ancestry went up. The number of Cajuns grew dramatically. This has led officials at the Census Bureau to assume that the examples used in the instructions strongly influence the responses people give. (Cajun was one of the examples of an ancestry given in 1990 but not in 1980, and German was the first example given. English was an example in the 1980 instructions, but not in 1990.)

All of these studies point to the socially variable nature of ethnic identity—and the lack of equivalence between ethnic ancestry and identity. If merely adding a category to the instructions to the question increases the number of people claiming that ancestry, what does that mean about the level of importance of that identity for people answering the census? Clearly, identity and ancestry for Whites in the United States, who increasingly are from mixed backgrounds, involve some change and choice.

Symbolic Ethnicities for White Americans

What do these ethnic identities mean to people, and why do they cling to them rather than just abandoning the tie and calling themselves American? My own field research with suburban Whites in California and Pennsylvania found that later-generation descendants of European origin maintain what are called "symbolic ethnicities." Symbolic ethnicity is a term coined by Herbert Gans (1979) to refer to ethnicity that is individualistic in nature and without real social cost for the individual. These symbolic identifications are essentially leisure-time activities, rooted in nuclear family traditions and reinforced by the voluntary enjoyable aspects of being ethnic (Waters 1990). Richard Alba (1990) also found later-generation Whites in Albany, New York, who chose to keep a tie with an ethnic identity because of the enjoyable and voluntary aspects to those identities, along with the feelings of specialness they entailed. An example of symbolic ethnicity is individuals who identify as Irish, for example, on occasions such as Saint Patrick's Day, on family holidays, or for vaca-

tions. They do not usually belong to Irish American organizations, live in Irish neighborhoods, work in Irish jobs, or marry other Irish people. The symbolic meaning of being Irish American can be constructed by individuals from mass media images, family traditions, or other intermittent social activities. In other words, for later-generation White ethnics, ethnicity is not something that influences their lives unless they want it to. In the world of work and school and neighborhood, individuals do not have to admit to being ethnic unless they choose to. And for an increasing number of European-origin individuals whose parents and grandparents have intermarried, the ethnicity they claim is largely a matter of personal choice as they sort through all of the possible combinations of groups in their genealogies.

Individuals can choose those aspects of being Italian, for instance, that appeal to them, and discard those that do not. Or a person whose father is Italian, and mother part Polish and part French, might choose among the three ethnicities and present herself as a Polish American. For instance, a nineteen-year-old college student, interviewed in California in 1986, told me he would have answered Irish on the 1980 census form that asked about ethnic ancestry. These are his reasons:

Q: Why would you have answered that?

A: Well, my Dad's name is Kerrigan and my mom's name is O'Leary, and I do have some German in me, but if you figure it out, I am about 75 percent Irish, so I usually say I am Irish.

Q: You usually don't say German when people ask?

A: No, no, I never say I am German. My dad just likes being Irish. . . . I don't know I just never think of myself as being German.

Q: So your dad's father is the one who immigrated?

A: Yes. On his side is Irish for generations. And then my grandmother's name is Dubois, which is French, partly German, partly French, and then the rest of the family is all Irish. So it is only the maternal grandmother who messes up the line.
(Waters 1990, p. 10)

Thus in the course of a few questions, this man labeled himself Irish, admitted to being part German but not identifying with it, and then as an afterthought added that he was also part French. This is not an unusual case. With just a little probing, many people will describe a variety of ancestries in their family background, but do not consider these ancestries to be a salient part of their own identities. Thus the 1990 census ancestry question, which estimated that 30 percent of the population is of mixed ancestry, most surely underestimates the degree of mixing among the population. My research, and the research of Richard Alba (1990), shows that many people have already sorted through what they know of their ethnic ancestries and simplified their responses before they ever answer a census or survey question (Waters 1990).

But note that this freedom to include or exclude ancestries in your identification to yourself and others would not be the same for those defined racially in our society. They are constrained to identify with the part of their ancestry that has been socially defined as the "essential" part. African Americans, for example, have been highly socially constrained to identify as Blacks, without other options available to them, even when they know that their forebears included many people of American Indian or European background. Up until the mid-twentieth century, many state governments had specific laws defining one as Black if as little as one-thirty-second of one's ancestors were defined as Black (Davis 1991; Dominguez 1986; Spickard 1989). Even now when the one drop rule has been dropped from our legal codes, there are still strong societal pressures on African Americans to identify in a particular way. Certain ancestries take precedence over others in the societal rules on descent and ancestry reckoning. If one believes one is part English and part German and identifies in a survey as German, one is not in danger of being accused of trying to "pass" as non-English and of being "redefined" English by the interviewer. But if one were part African and part German, one's self identification as German would be highly suspect and probably not accepted if one "looked" Black according to the prevailing social norms.

This is reflected in the ways the census collects race and ethnic identity. While the ethnic ancestry question used in 1980 and 1990 is given to all Americans in the sample regardless of race and allows multiple responses that combine races, the primary source of information on people defined racially in the United States is the census race question or the Hispanic question. Both of these questions require a person to make a choice about an identity. Individuals are not allowed to respond that they are both Black and White, or Japanese and Asian Indian on

the race question even if they know that is their background. In fact, people who disobey the instructions to the census race question and check off two races are assigned to the first checked race in the list by the Census Bureau.

In responding to the ancestry question, the comparative latitude that White respondents have does not mean that Whites pick and choose ethnicities out of thin air. For the most part, people choose an identity that corresponds with some element of their family tree. However, there are many anecdotal instances of people adopting ethnicities when they marry or move to a strongly identified neighborhood or community. For instance, Micaela di Leonardo (1984) reported instances of non-Italian women who married into Italian American families and "became Italian." Karen Leonard (1992) describes a community of Mexican American women who married Punjabi immigrants in California. Some of the Punjabi immigrants and their descendants were said to have "become Mexican" when they joined their wives' kin group and social worlds. Alternatively she describes the community acknowledging that Mexican women made the best curry, as they adapted to life with Indian-origin men.

But what do these identities mean to individuals? Surely an identity that is optional in a number of ways—not legally defined on a passport or birth certificate, not socially consequential in terms of societal discrimination in terms of housing or job access, and not economically limiting in terms of blocking opportunities for social mobility—cannot be the same as an identity that results from and is nurtured by societal exclusion and rejection. The choice to have a symbolic ethnicity is an attractive and widespread one despite its lack of demonstrable content, because having a symbolic ethnicity combines individuality with feelings of community. People reported to me that they liked having an ethnic identity because it gave them a uniqueness and feeling of being special. They often contrasted their own specialness by virtue of their ethnic identities with "bland" Americanness. Being ethnic makes people feel unique and special and not just "vanilla" as one of my respondents put it. For instance, one woman describes the benefits she feels from being Czech American:

> I work in an office and a lot of people in there always talk about their background. It's weird

because it is a big office and people are of all different backgrounds. People are this or that. It is interesting I think to find out. Especially when it is something you do not hear a lot about. Something that is not common like Lithuania or something. That's the good part about being Czech. People think it is something different.   (Waters 1990, p. 154)

Because "American" is largely understood by Americans to be a political identity and allegiance, and not an ethnic one, the idea of being "American" does not give people the same sense of belonging that their hyphenated American identity does. When I asked people about their dual identities—American and Irish or Italian or whatever—they usually responded in a way that showed how they conceived of the relationship between the two identities. Being an American was their primary identity; but it was so primary that they rarely, if ever, thought about it—most commonly only when they left the country. Being Irish American, on the other hand, was a way they had of differentiating themselves from others whom they interacted with from day to day—in many cases from spouses or in-laws. Certain of their traits—being emotional, having a sense of humor, talking with their hands—were understood as stemming from their ethnicity. Yet when asked about their identity as Americans, that identity was both removed from their day-to-day consciousness and understood in terms of loyalty and patriotism. Although they may not think they behave or think in a certain way because they are American, being American is something they are both proud of and committed to.

Symbolic ethnicity is the best of all worlds for these respondents. These White ethnics can claim to be unique and special, while simultaneously finding the community and conformity with others that they also crave. But that "community" is of a type that will not interfere with a person's individuality. It is not as if these people belong to ethnic voluntary organizations or gather as a group in churches or neighborhoods or union halls. They work and reside within the mainstream of American middle-class life, yet they retain the interesting benefits—the "specialness"—of ethnic allegiance, without any of its drawbacks.

It has been suggested by several researchers that this positive value attached to ethnic ancestry, which became popular in the ethnic revival of the 1970s, is the result of assimilation having proceeded to an advanced stage for descendants of White Europeans (Alba 1985; Crispino 1980; Steinberg 1981). Ironically, people celebrate and embrace their ethnic backgrounds precisely because assimilation has proceeded to the point where such identification does not have that much influence on their day-to-day life. Rather than choosing the "least ethnic" and most bland ethnicities, Whites desire the "most ethnic" ones, like the once-stigmatized "Italian," because it is perceived as bringing the most psychic benefits. For instance, when an Italian father is married to an English or a Scottish or a German mother, the likelihood is that the child will be reported to the census with the father's Italian ancestry, rather than the northern European ancestries, which would have been predicted to have a higher social status. Italian is a good ancestry to have, people told me, because they have good food and a warm family life. This change in the social meaning of being Italian American is quite dramatic, given that Italians were subject to discrimination, exclusion, and extreme negative stereotyping in the early part of the twentieth century.

Race Relations and Symbolic Ethnicity

However much symbolic ethnicity is without cost for the individual, there is a cost associated with symbolic ethnicity for the society. That is because symbolic ethnicities of the type described here are confined to White Americans of European origin. Black Americans, Hispanic Americans, Asian Americans, and American Indians do not have the option of a symbolic ethnicity at present in the United States. For all of the ways in which ethnicity does not matter for White Americans, it does matter for non-Whites. Who your ancestors are does affect your choice of spouse, where you live, what job you have, who your friends are, and what your chances are for success in American society, if those ancestors happen not to be from Europe. The reality is that White ethnics have a lot more choice and room to maneuver than they themselves think they do. The situation is very different for members of racial minorities, whose lives are strongly influenced by their race or national origin regardless of how much they may choose not to identify themselves in terms of their ancestries.

When White Americans learn the stories of how their grandparents and great-grandparents triumphed in the United States over adversity, they are usually told in terms of their individual efforts and triumphs. The important role of labor unions and other organized political and economic actors in their social and economic successes are left out of the story in favor of a generational story of individual Americans rising up against communitarian, Old World intolerance and New World resistance. As a result, the "individualized" voluntary, cultural view of ethnicity for Whites is what is remembered.

One important implication of these identities is that they tend to be very individualistic. There is a tendency to view valuing diversity in a pluralist environment as equating all groups. The symbolic ethnic tends to think that all groups are equal; everyone has a background that is their right to celebrate and pass on to their children. This leads to the conclusion that all identities are equal and all identities in some sense are interchangeable—"I'm Italian American, you're Polish American. I'm Irish American, you're African American." The important thing is to treat people as individuals and all equally. However, this assumption ignores the very big difference between an individualistic symbolic ethnic identity and a socially enforced and imposed racial identity.

My favorite example of how this type of thinking can lead to some severe misunderstandings between people of different backgrounds is from the *Dear Abby* advice column. A few years back a person wrote in who had asked an acquaintance of Asian background where his family was from. His acquaintance answered that this was a rude question and he would not reply. The bewildered White asked Abby why it was rude, since he thought it was a sign of respect to wonder where people were from, and he certainly would not mind anyone asking HIM about where his family was from. Abby asked her readers to write in to say whether it was rude to ask about a person's ethnic background. She reported that she got a large response, that most non-Whites thought it was a sign of disrespect, and Whites thought it was flattering:

Dear Abby,
I am 100 percent American and because I am of Asian ancestry I am often asked "What are

you?" It's not the personal nature of this question that bothers me, it's the question itself. This query seems to question my very humanity. "What am I? Why I am a person like everyone else!"

Signed, A REAL AMERICAN

Dear Abby,
Why do people resent being asked what they are? The Irish are so proud of being Irish, they tell you before you even ask. Tip O'Neill has never tried to hide his Irish ancestry.

Signed, JIMMY

In this exchange, JIMMY cannot understand why Asians are not as happy to be asked about their ethnicity as he is, because he understands his ethnicity and theirs to be separate but equal. Everyone has to come from somewhere—his family from Ireland, another's family from Asia—each has a history and each should be proud of it. But the reason he cannot understand the perspective of the Asian American is that all ethnicities are not equal; all are not symbolic, costless, and voluntary. When White Americans equate their own symbolic ethnicities with the socially enforced identities of non-White Americans, they obscure the fact that the experiences of Whites and non-Whites have been qualitatively different in the United States and that the current identities of individuals partly reflect that unequal history. . . .

Institutional Responses

Our society asks a lot of young people [on college campuses]. We ask young people to do something that no one else does as successfully on such a wide scale—that is to live together with people from very different backgrounds, to respect one another, to appreciate one another, and to enjoy and learn from one another. The successes that occur every day in this endeavor are many, and they are too often overlooked. However, the problems and tensions are also real, and they will not vanish on their own. We tend to see pluralism working in the United States in much the same way some people expect capitalism to work. If you put together people with various interests and abilities and resources, the "invisible hand" of capitalism is supposed to make all the parts work together in an economy for the common good.

. . . There is a lot to be said for the idea that bringing people who belong to different ethnic or racial groups together in institutions with no interference will have good consequences. Students from different backgrounds will make friends if they share a dorm room or corridor, and there is no need for the institution to do any more than provide the locale. But like capitalism, the invisible hand of pluralism does not do well when power relations and externalities are ignored. When you bring together individuals from groups that are differently valued in the wider society and provide no guidance, there will be problems. In these cases the "invisible hand" of pluralist relations does not work, and tensions and disagreements can arise without any particular individual or group of individuals being "to blame." On college campuses in the 1990s some of the tensions between students are of this sort. They arise from honest misunderstandings, lack of a common background, and very different experiences of what race and ethnicity mean to the individual.

The implications of symbolic ethnicities for thinking about race relations are subtle but consequential. If your understanding of your own ethnicity and its relationship to society and politics is one of individual choice, it becomes harder to understand the need for programs like affirmative action, which recognize the ongoing need for group struggle and group recognition, in order to bring about social change. It also is hard for a White college student to understand the need that minority students feel to band together against discrimination. It also is easy, on the individual level, to expect everyone else to be able to turn their ethnicity on and off at will, the way you are able to, without understanding that ongoing discrimination and societal attention to minority status makes that impossible for individuals from minority groups to do. The paradox of symbolic ethnicity is that it depends upon the ultimate goal of a pluralist society, and at the same time makes it more difficult to achieve that ultimate goal. It is dependent upon the concept that all ethnicities mean the same thing, that enjoying the traditions of one's heritage is an option available to a group or an individual, but that such a heritage should not have any social costs associated with it.

As the Asian Americans who wrote to *Dear Abby* make clear, there are many societal issues and involuntary ascriptions associated with non-White identities. The developments necessary for this to change are not individual but societal in nature. Social mobility and declining racial and ethnic sensitivity are closely associated. The legacy and the present reality of discrimination on the basis of race or ethnicity must be overcome before the ideal of the pluralist society, where all heritages are treated equally and are equally available for individuals to choose or discard at will, is realized.

REFERENCES

Alba, Richard D. 1985. *Italian Americans: Into the Twilight of Ethnicity.* Englewood Cliffs, NJ: Prentice-Hall.

——. 1990. *Ethnic Identity: The Transformation of White America.* New Haven, CT: Yale University Press.

Barth, Frederik. 1969. *Ethnic Groups and Boundaries.* Boston: Little, Brown.

Crispino, James. 1980. *The Assimilation of Ethnic Groups: The Italian Case.* Staten Island, NY: Center for Migration Studies.

Davis, Floyd James. 1991. *Who Is Black? One Nation's Definition.* University Park: Pennsylvania State University Press.

di Leonardo, Micaela. 1984. *The Varieties of Ethnic Experience: Kinship, Class and Gender among Italian Americans.* Ithaca, NY: Cornell University Press.

Dominguez, Virginia. 1986. *White by Definition: Social Classification in Creole Louisiana.* New Brunswick, NJ: Rutgers University Press.

Farley, Reynolds. 1991. "The New Census Question about Ancestry: What Did It Tell Us?" *Demography* 28:411–29.

Gans, Herbert. 1979. "Symbolic Ethnicity: The Future of Ethnic Groups and Cultures in America." *Ethnic and Racial Studies* 2:1–20.

Greeley, Andrew M. 1976. "The Ethnic Miracle." *Public Interest* 45 (Fall): 20–36.

Leonard, Karen. 1992. *Making Ethnic Choices: California's Punjabi Mexican Americans.* Philadelphia: Temple University Press.

Lieberson, Stanley. 1985. "Unhyphenated Whites in the United States." *Ethnic and Racial Studies* 8:159–80.

Lieberson, Stanley, and Mary Waters. 1986. "Ethnic Groups in Flux: The Changing Ethnic Responses of American Whites." *Annals of the American Academy of Political and Social Science* 487:79–91.

——. 1988. *From Many Strands: Ethnic and Racial Groups in Contemporary America.* New York: Russell Sage.

——. 1993. "The Ethnic Responses of Whites: What Causes Their Instability, Simplification, and Inconsistency?" *Social Forces* 72(2): 421–50.

McKenney, Nampeo R., and Arthur R. Cresce. 1992. "Measurement of Ethnicity in the United States: Experiences of the U.S. Census Bureau." Paper presented at the Joint Canada–United States Conference on the Measurement of Ethnicity, Ottawa, Canada, April 1–3.

Pagnini, Deanna L., and S. Philip Morgan. 1990. "Intermarriage and Social Distance among U.S. Immigrants at the Turn of the Century." *American Journal of Sociology* 96(2): 405–32.

Spickard, Paul R. 1989. *Mixed Blood*. Madison: University of Wisconsin Press.

Steinberg, Stephen. 1981. *The Ethnic Myth: Race, Ethnicity, and Class in America*. Boston: Beacon Press.

U.S. Bureau of the Census. 1992. *Census of Population and Housing, 1990: Detailed Ancestry Groups for States*. Supplementary Reports CP-S-1–2. Washington, DC: U.S. Government Printing Office.

Waters, Mary C. 1990. *Ethnic Options: Choosing Identities in America*. Berkeley and Los Angeles: University of California Press.

Weber, Max. 1921. *Economy and Society: An Outline of Interpretive Sociology*, edited by Guenther Roth and Claus Wittich, translated by Ephraim Fischoff. New York: Bedminster Press.

FOURTEEN

♦♦♦

Jews, Class, Color, and the Cost of Whiteness

Melanie Kaye/Kantrowitz

asleep: dream. i walk down the street wearing shorts and a t-shirt and the new earrings my ex-lover just gave me for my birthday. i pass two young hip-looking women.

she's all japped out, they say. about me. i cringe, self-conscious.

then i look down at my shorts & t-shirt. i'm not even dressed up, except for the earrings. suddenly i understand that no matter what i wear i will be perceived as "all japped out."

When I wake I realize I've never heard the expression. But I know exactly what it means.

Awake: vision. I walk down 106th street, a big wide street, in the mostly Puerto Rican and Dominican neighborhood where I live, after 25 years away from New York. I spot a man I've seen before on Broadway, asking for money. He's out in the street, shaking his fist at cars, gesturing as if in a silent movie—he looks like he's shouting and no words come out, or at least I can't hear them. He moves in jerky, violent spurts so that when he veers toward the sidewalk, people scatter, afraid. I watch him for a bit, afraid he'll hurt himself, wondering if I should do something. I walk into the copy shop I sometimes use. Everyone's speaking Spanish. I don't, and so I ask, "Do you speak English?" Yes. I discuss the problem with the man behind the counter. We go out into the street and watch. We decide to phone 9-1-1, the emergency number.

First question they ask: *is he white black or hispanic?* Like the new baby question: *boy or girl?* Asian doesn't even exist.

White, I say, knowing it's only because he's white that I can phone cops on his behalf. If he were Black or Latino, I'd be afraid of how they'd treat him. I keep walking towards Broadway. So does the silently cursing man. He miraculously crosses Broadway to the traffic island without incident and plunks down on a park bench, one of two white men on the Upper West Side asking for money. I watch for a while. No police car arrives.

Awake: more vision. Last night on Broadway I saw the man who had asked me and Helena for money, and I ran across the street against the light and dangerously close to traffic to get away. He scares me. A couple of weeks ago we were walking home, we were almost on my block, 106th between Amsterdam and Columbus, where no one ever asks for money because no one assumes anyone east of Amsterdam has any money. We told him, sorry, not today. I had just given money to two different people, and Helena had three dollars to her name.

By the time we reached the end of the block he'd circled back, stood in front of us, asking again. *You know, I don't want to rob or anything but I just might have to,* he says.

I'm not about to respond, but he keeps talking. *I don't want to be like this, asking for money on the street, but you know I need money, and I don't want to rob or anything.* . . . Finally, Helena gives him a dollar.

It seems that he came back to us, rather than the dozen other people on the street, because he (a black man) assumes we have money (we're white) and will be afraid (we're women). The truth is, we are neither moneyed nor afraid, and we give (Helena) or not (me) for our own reasons. The truth also is, he's desperate and we're not.

The next night I'm walking home by myself, late, and there he is, practically in front of my building. He approaches, extends his hand. *I'm sorry about last night,* he says. We shake hands, smile. Then he says, *but I need some money again, could you give me some?*

Late and dark. I don't want to stand there going through my pockets and especially taking out my wallet. Most of all I'm disturbed that he knows me. I am afraid of him becoming mine: *my beggar.* I don't want to be responsible for him. I don't want him to expect anything from me. Half the movies I've ever seen rise up in me, and I know if this were a movie I'd run into him every day for a week and at the end of the week he'd stab me. Everyone watching would recognize the heavy symbolism.

I shove aside the racist movie images. I say, *I can't give you money today*—and now I am stuck with my lie. I could give something. But I want to keep moving, get home.

He demands, *I need money.*

I can't . . .

I need . . .

I can't . . .

I need . . .

until finally I say, *hey man, I dig it but do you hear me?*

He nods. We both know I'm lying, that I'm the one who gets to say yes or no. We say goodnight, smile.

Let me walk you around my neighborhood. On 106th street at Broadway, people of all colors and ages shopping, walking, sitting at street cafes, waiting for buses, heading for the subway, wheeling children in strollers. But notice the people, and there are many, stretched out asleep on the benches and even on the sidewalks—winter is harsh here and still they're in the street, sometimes without shoes— the people shaking cups, asking, *can you spare some change,* saying, *I'm very hungry, can you give me something, even a quarter.* They're almost all African American men, a few women, also African Ameri-

can. Look at the taxi drivers. Step into one of the hundreds of small shops, restaurants, groceries, stationery shops that line Broadway. I see owners and often their families, and hired clerks: Asian, Indian, Arab, Latino, Greek, Jewish, sometimes Caribbean Black. Rarely are they African American. Practically all of them speak English wrapped in the vowels and consonants of their mother tongue, which is not English; except their kids, teenagers who help out after school and Saturdays, as I used to help out in my parents' store, are fluently bilingual, perfect English, as well as rapid-fire Chinese, Korean, Spanish. . . . They will go to college, their kids will probably lose their language, their culture. This is the American dream.

South of 96th street the balance of color shifts from brown to white, Latino to yuppie. Gentrified, white graduates of elite colleges live in buildings with swimming pools and elaborate doormen, views of the George Washington bridge—men and women in their twenties whose parents, or trust funds, bought them apartments costing maybe a million dollars.

There are lots of old Jews, surviving still in their rent-controlled apartments that will probably turn co-op when they die. Lots of harried thirty-somethings and forty-something Jewish women and men, their Jewishness visible only to those familiar with the intricacies and codes of New York Jews. They had their kids late, they split economically between upper middle and middle, and politically between liberals and radicals. Some are insistent about sending their kids to public schools, and some have given up on the public schools, refusing, in their words, to sacrifice their kids to a principle. They are professionals who live on schedules so tight that any unforeseen disruption is a minor disaster. To cope with the stress of life by the clock, and because they were raised to, or have taught themselves to, expect some joy and fulfillment in life, they see therapists, acupuncturists, chiropractors, and belong to health clubs where they work out and stay in shape. On the Upper West Side (and all over New York City), class shows in well-developed calves and trim forms. Fat is sloppy. Fat is poor. I am sure that the average weight in my immediate neighborhood among the women is 15 pounds higher than 15 blocks south.

One more thing: in my immediate neighborhood, when you see women with children, they tend to be the same color, brown to black. A few blocks west or south, when I see a woman and child of the same color, I'm almost surprised; the norm is women of color caring for white children, what I've come to think of as the underbelly of feminism. Most of the women are immigrants. Some of the children are Jews.

Let me adjust the lens, for accuracy. Not all Jews are professionals (45% are working class or poor); not all African Americans are homeless or poor, generation after generation (though a full third live below the poverty line). Not all whites are yuppies, New York is not the nation, and the Upper West Side is not even all of New York. . . .

But whatever is coming apart in the nation is doing so to some extent in New York first. When the public schools are essentially abandoned; when thousands upon thousands of people have no place to live, and everyone who does carries key rings heavy with metal, for the two to five locks required to simply get in one's apartment; when the threat of rape and other street violence against women controls our every decision about where to go, how long to stay, how much it will cost, and how much anxiety we can tolerate; when hate crimes of all kinds are on the rise, this is the future of our nation if something doesn't change. . . . This is the human cost of our nation's priorities.

In the early and mid-eighties, I was working out some thoughts on racism and anti-Semitism. . . . The way the debate was being framed as Black-Jewish or even Black-white obscured, I felt, the issue of class and the complexity of race. I wrote about the ways racism played out very differently against the various peoples of color—Chinese, Japanese, Arab, Native American. . . . I wrote about why I saw anti-Semitism as a form of racism, meaning racist ideology. This last seemed like a truism to me; the camps of Europe were revealed three months before I was born. . . . And I said then, the difficulty some people have in grasping anti-Semitism as a serious concern and as a form of racism is that it hasn't kept Jews poor. (In fact, anti-Semitism often claims that all Jews are rich.) I also saw what was getting called Black-Jewish conflict as a mutual scapegoating— Jews were getting blamed for white racism and Blacks for christian anti-Semitism—as well as obscured class conflict.

But I have come to believe that this analysis needs to be pushed further. I am troubled, for example, by analogies between Asians and Jews, be-

tween Arabs and Jews, not because these analogies are not valid—with the difference that Asians almost always look Asian, while Jews and Arabs may often pass. What troubles me is this: while class and general principles of race-hate are illuminated by these analogies, something else gets obscured: the intransigence and virulence of oppression of African Americans . . . and something else.

The structure of apartheid is useful to contemplate here, not because things in the U.S. are so fixed and clear; they're not. But let me pursue the analogy. South Africa has not two racial categories, but three: white, black and colored. It's the particular buffer zone of colored that I want to examine. Colored are those who will never be white but at least aren't black. Colored are those who have more access to higher status and all that implies—better housing, jobs, education, health, leisure, safety, respect. I want to suggest that in many places in the U.S., Japanese, Korean, and some Chinese, Indians and Pakistanis, Arabs and lighter-skinned or wealthier Latinos get to be colored. Sometimes Caribbean Blacks, by virtue of their accent, their education, the strength of growing up as the majority, also get to be colored. And African Americans, I want to suggest, are not the only "blacks," though they are the most visible. Many Latinos are black—dark in color—and also those most Indian of Chicanos, tracked in the lowest social and economic status. Immigrants from Southeast Asia hold some of the hardest, worst-paying jobs in the nation. And in the Southwest and sometimes Northwest, where there are few African Americans, native Americans are kept the lowest of the low, and every cruel stereotype of inferiority shows up in local racist culture.

As I've said, these categories are not totally fixed. There is a certain permeability that characterizes the class-race system in the U.S., a certain amount of passing—literally, for those with skin light enough, who shed their accents, language, culture; and approximately, for those who, laboring under the heavy burden of racism, through luck and extraordinary heroism and sometimes through hardness against their own people, still squeak through. Clarence Thomas rises up from poverty to hobnob with the white male club called the Senate precisely by abandoning his people's concerns.

The point of this white/colored/black classification is not to violate the hope of solidarity among people of color by dividing them, but to recognize divisions that exist and must be named in order to bridge them. The Iraqi-Black conflicts in Detroit; Korean-Black in Flatbush and L.A.; Cuban-Black in Miami. Conflicts which a generation ago often were Jewish-Black because they are in part the inevitable result of who owns what in whose community, and who is poor, and who is accessible.

You could say, as my sister did when I was sharing these thoughts with her, aren't you talking about class? Yes and no. . . .

Let me meander for a moment in the swamp of class. Top down, billionaires, millionaires: control and power; wealth so beyond the needs of one person, one family, it staggers the mind; here we find unlimited access to health care, comfort, resources; mostly WASP. Seventy percent of Congress comes from this class. While most white people aren't in it, most people in it are white, some Jews.

Middle class includes low-level managers, social workers, small shopkeepers, and teachers—K–12, secondary school, junior college, university—as well as business people, doctors, lawyers, and other professionals with incomes of $200,000 a year and more. . . . When a class category includes both those piling up assets and those applying for food stamps, we should recognize an obsolete term and come up with something else. Here is where we find over half the Jews in the U.S., spread throughout the category, and a fair number of people of color, mostly represented at the lower end of the class.

Working class is also problematic as an economic category. The nonunionized women in the chicken factories, Black in the South, white in Maine; Asians and Latinas in the endlessly transforming, infinitely stable New York City sweatshops once worked by Italian and Jewish women: these are working-class, and, as we see, part of the problem with the category is gender. Working class also includes the racially diverse members of the UAW, the men whose sons used to be guaranteed the best-paid laboring jobs in the U.S.—but today Michigan, heart of the auto industry, endures 35 percent unemployment. Working class excludes the endemic poor, the poor without a prayer of breaking out of it, not those who perform backbreaking work of past generations of immigrants but those who can find no work at all, or can only find work that pays so badly that, for example, women with children can't afford to give up welfare to earn money that will all get swallowed by

child-care costs. They are African American, Latino, Native American, Asian. As for the rural white poor, because there are no jobs, their children leave for the cities, become essentially immigrants, and in the cities their white skin serves them in finding work—but, like other immigrants, they lose their culture. Working class spans well-paid unionized fields, many of which are now threatened because of automation, and because successful unionization has challenged owners' greed and sent manufacturing jobs abroad to pay workers less and maximize profits. Whole industries abandon communities of workers who have served them for generations; even keypunch work which requires English is shipped to Ireland (lest we miss the dominance of class/poverty as theme, and mistake it entirely for race/color), because Irish women are so poor as to demand so little. The two fields of labor still growing in the U.S., the hardest to organize and the worst paid, are office work and the service industry, including maids and restaurant workers.

Who does this office and service work? Women. People of color, especially immigrants, a replenishing, flexible pool of cheap labor, thankful to work hideously long hours for little money, because it is more than they had, and because they came here, often, not for their own betterment but for their children's. And so they groom their kids to escape the parents' lives, to assimilate, much as I, raised passionately pro-union, was groomed to escape the working class, and even the lower-middle-class shopkeeping existence at which my parents had succeeded.

It is precisely this access to better-paid working-class jobs or lower-middle-class small business opportunities, along with access to education for the next generation, that characterizes the experience of "colored" in the U.S. It is precisely this lack of better working-class jobs and small-business opportunities along with systematic disadvantaging and exclusion by the educational system, that characterizes the experience of "blacks" in the U.S. Sherry Gorelick's *City College and the Jewish Poor* describes how City College was created as a path to upward mobility to distract the radical Jewish poor from the revolutionary class struggle predicted by Marx; the path of higher education was taken by thousands and thousands of poor and working-class Jews. But college was free for us, and there was room, if not at the top, then certainly in the middle. Where are the free colleges now? Private colleges cost more than $20,000 a year. And where is room in the middle, when even the middle is suffering?

This shared economic disaster could and should unite most people across lines of color. But the illusory protection of "whiteness" offers a partial escape route toward which anyone who can scrambles. This desire to identify with whiteness, as well as bigotry and fear, blocks solidarity.

In this white-colored-black scheme, where are the Jews?

Of the groups I've named as targeted by a general hate I'll call race-hate, Jews are the closest to white. Many would say we are white, and indeed a common-sense visual response suggests that many of us are.

But listen to the prophet James Baldwin: "No one was white before he/she came to America," Baldwin wrote in the mid-eighties.* "It took generations, and a vast amount of coercion, before this became a white country. . . ."

It is probable that it is the Jewish community— or more accurately, perhaps, its remnants— that in America has paid the highest and most extraordinary price for becoming white. For the Jews came here from countries where they were not white, and they came here in part because they were not white; and incontestably— in the eyes of the Black American (and not only in those eyes) American Jews have opted to become white. . . .

Now, the point is not for us, Jews, to escape the category "white," to evade confronting our own racism, nor is it to insert ourselves artificially into a category of oppression, as sometimes happens in our movements where oppression in some puny paradoxical way confers privilege. It is to recognize a continuum where we are the closest of the coloreds to white, or the closest of the whites to colored.

This is hardest to see in New York City, where Jews can hardly be called a minority. If there is the diaspora and Eretz Yisroel, I have come to think of

New York as a third category, somewhere between the two. "I'm in exile from Brooklyn," I used to joke, but it's no joke. Jews in New York City, except for select neighborhoods, experience the luxury of normality. To assume christianity in New York is to be hopelessly provincial. In New York one finds Jewish culture on a broad spectrum: orthodox, secular, lesbian and gay, Sephardic, Yiddishist, feminist. . . . The paradoxical result is a majority of Jews who operate without consciousness of their Jewishness. It's not an issue. Anti-Semitism is occasional, focused, and historical, and in recent years, for New Yorkers, has been associated mostly with African Americans. Quite the opposite from what's going on in the farm belt, the Northwest, and the South, where alliances between Jews and people of color are obvious to everyone.

Yet I'm suggesting that progressive Jews recognize our position in between colored and white, a source of tension but also of possibility. . . . The challenge is to build progressive coalitions not only among the coloreds but between the coloreds and the blacks, and between these and the economically struggling whites—and then to expand still further. The issue of hate crimes, for example, can unite Jews with people of color, and with lesbians and gays; and we should insist on the legal—and moral— classification of violence against women as a hate crime. That will be a powerful coalition indeed.

What I want to focus on is this: in James Baldwin's phrase, "the extraordinary price of becoming white."

Many of us chose, or had chosen for us, a white path. A path of assimilation, of passing, often accompanied by extreme cultural loss. How many of us speak or read Yiddish or Ladino or Judeo-Arabic? What do we know of our own histories, our literature, our music, our cultural diversity, our rich traditions? What do we know beyond or besides the now-usual sources of American Jewish identity, which are, in a nutshell, religion, Israel, and the Holocaust. Nothing wrong with these sources—but as the sum total of Jewish identity, this is limited. Where does this restricted focus leave secularists or confirmed diasporists? What happens when we disagree, as we do, about solutions to the Israeli-Palestinian conflict? How does this restricted focus help us create and strengthen an authentic Jewish American identity? How does it enable us to see the Holocaust in a context of Jewish history, the tragedy of which

---

*James Baldwin, "On Being 'White' and Other Lies," *Essence* (April, 1984).

was not only the destruction of millions of lives—as though that were not tragedy enough—but also the destruction of a rich and varied culture.

It's called assimilation. We, like others who pass or partly pass, can choose where to direct our allegiance: upward and whitening, restricting our Jewishness to that which assimilation increasingly demands, *a Jew at home, a "man" in the streets,** white people who go to Jewish church, i.e., synagogue; or we can deepen both our identity and our affiliation, with the other "others," the outsiders: the coloreds and the blacks.

Think about shedding whiteness. I don't mean to pretend that Jews who are white endure the same visual vulnerability as people of color; though we should recognize that many Jews, especially outside the U.S., simply *are* people of color, that the definition of Jews as automatically "European" is incorrect. In addition, many Sephardi and also many Ashkenazi Jews are sufficiently dark to be readily perceived, at least in the South and in the heartland, as people of color. Think also about the Hasids; think about wearing a Jewish star, or other item that identifies you as a Jew; think about never taking it off. Think about driving through Mississippi.

So: is fighting anti-Semitism a diversion from fighting racism? Do we think we can fight anti-Semitism without fighting racism? Do we think Jews can be safe within a white supremacist society?

I do not. I believe, along with a great many other Jews, that a color/class barrier means injustice, and our culture teaches us to pursue justice. I also believe that a color/class barrier threatens Jews, in two ways:

1. Because race hate will never exclude us. As long as the world is divided into us and them, minorities are vulnerable. Fascism is on the rise. In our century, can we be naive about the danger?

2. Because the particular nature of anti-Semitism, which defines Jews as money, as powermongers—especially marks us as scapegoats for the abuses of capitalism, and we are living through a time of rampant abuse. . . .

The rich get richer. And who does the dominant culture blame? Jews; Asians, especially Japanese; Arabs; foreigners; let's face it, "the colored" get blamed for various contributions to economic disaster; for controlling the economy, or making money on the backs of the poor; for raising the price of oil; for stealing or eliminating jobs (by importing goods or exporting production); for taking the jobs. African Americans, Latinos, Native Americans, "the blacks," get blamed for urban violence and chaos, for drugs, for the skyrocketing costs and failures of social programs. That is, coloreds get blamed for capitalism's crimes; blacks for capitalism's fallout. Do I need to point out who escapes all blame?

When we are scapegoated we are most conscious of how we feel humiliated, alienated, and endangered. But the other function of scapegoating is at least as pernicious. Scapegoating protects the source of the problem we are being scapegoated for, the vicious system of profit and exploitation, of plenty and scarcity existing side by side. . . .

I want to make one last point about Jews and class, and this is about privilege and power. Hatred, chauvinism, oppression always function to keep people from their power, to mute their strength. Because they're laboring under heavier odds. Because they're taught to feel bad about themselves.

Anti-Semitism has a peculiar edge because the myth is that we're too powerful, too rich, and much too pushy. I began with my dream, where displaying a simple gift of earrings, walking down the street daring to feel okay, means: *she's all japped out.* Any particle of this that we absorb makes us afraid of our strength, loath to use our power, embarrassed by the relative economic and social success of Jews as a people, afraid it will be used against us (and it will).

Jewish progressives often buy into this scheme of contempt for "most Jews," assumed to be uniformly well off, or they experience a nostalgic longing for the time when Jews were authentically the right class, that is, poor and working-class.

I think we need to look critically at this attitude. First, because it erases working-class Jews and poor Jews. Second, because it writes off the political energy and concerns that exist sometimes apart from class, the ripe possibilities for coalition of feminist Jews, of lesbian and gay Jews, of Jewish educators and cultural workers, of Jewish seniors, and on and on, not to mention Jews who see anti-Semitism for what it is, a form of race hate which must be fought along with other forms of race hate, and those who are simply hungry for economic and social justice.

---

*The phrase was used to characterize the "modern" Jew of the European Enlightenment.

Who do not wish to spend our lives deciding whether or not to give quarters or dollars to other human beings who need more than we can possibly give; who do not wish to abandon the cities with their fabulous human variety because of the stresses of economic inequality, alienation, and violence; who still believe a better way is possible.

Third, because this attitude of contempt for Jews who are not poor, which is, after all, a form of internalized anti-Semitism, ignores the fact that education, choice, comfort are all valuable. One cannot walk the streets of any of our cities, see people living in cardboard boxes or wrapped in torn blankets, and not appreciate the material basis for human existence. The problem is not relative Jewish success. The problem is a severe class system that distributes success so unequally.

Used well, education, choice, even comfort, can strengthen people, individually and collectively. As for money—let me say the dirty word—nothing gets done without it. The question is, what do we do with our education, our choice, privilege, skills, experience, passion for justice: our power. Don't racism and anti-Semitism make you sick? Doesn't hatred scare you? Don't you feel at least a little desperate about the way things are going unless something intervenes?

I think Jews need to gather our power, make it visible, and use it right. I'm sick of the more conservative wing of the Jewish community speaking for all of us. Everyone knows that Jews are all over progressive movements, what I've come to think of as the political diaspora. Maybe our task is to ingather the Jews, just a little, into a new civil and human rights coalition, in which we are present and visible as Jews. It means being proud of our collective strength, confident that we can use it right. Someone will always call us pushy. Isn't it time to really push?

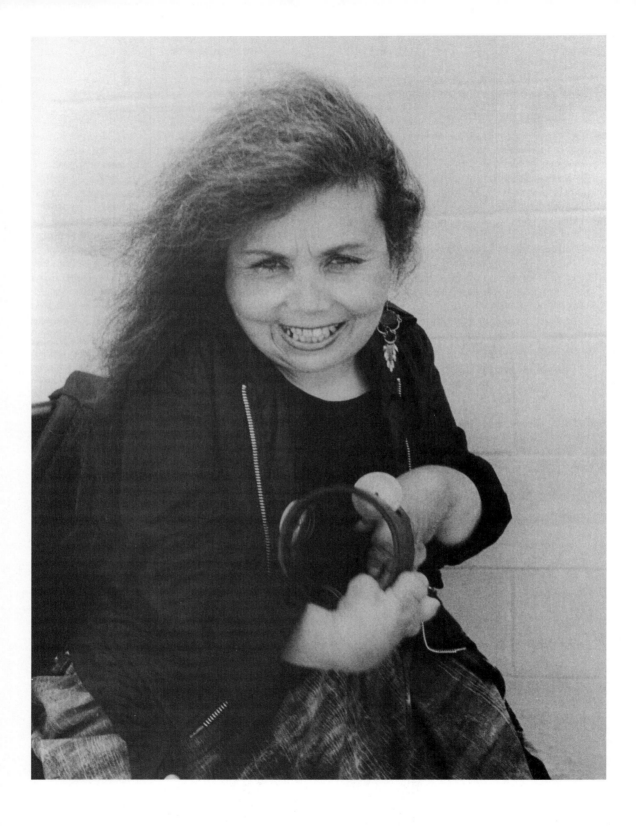

3

◆◆◆

Women's Bodies

Our bodies grow and develop from the first moments of life. They provide us with a living, physical basis for our identity where all aspects of our selves are literally embodied. The life cycle—from birth to youth to aging to dying—plays itself out through our bodies, minds, and emotions as we experience these life stages.

Body Image and the Beauty Ideal

Through our bodies we feel pain, and we experience sexuality, healing, and the complex physical, hormonal, neurological, and emotional changes that come with menstruation and menopause, pregnancy, and aging. Many of us develop and experience physical strength, agility, concentration, and coordination through exercise, dance, sports, martial arts, and outdoor activities. We show our dexterity in such things as handling tools, from kitchen knives to hammers and saws, or in fixing cars. We experience our bodies' suppleness through yoga. Pregnancy and childbirth provide intense understanding of our elasticity, strength, and stamina and the wonder of being able to sustain another body develop-

ing inside us. We have an awareness of our bodily rhythms throughout the day or through the menstrual cycle—the ups and downs of mental and physical energy, tiredness, stiffness, and cramps—and of bodily changes that are part of growing older.

The dominant culture often reduces women to bodies, valuing us only as sex objects or as bearers of children. Postmenopausal women, for example, are sometimes thought of as no longer "real" women, their lifework over. This chapter is concerned with how women think and feel about our bodies, the impact of idealized images of beauty, and the ways gender and sexuality are both grounded in our bodies and socially constructed. Something as intimate and personal as how we feel about our bodies is thus also profoundly cultural and political.

Although there are physiological, financial, and technological limits to how much we can shape them, up to a point our bodies are malleable and we can change how we look, who we are, or who we appear to be. We make choices about clothing, hair, makeup, tattoos or piercing, as well as gestures and mannerisms. We may diet or exercise, use skin-lightening creams or tanning salons, have a nose job or tummy tuck, and consciously adopt particular postures and body language. We may have corrective surgeries for disabilities; our bodies may be altered by mastectomy due to breast cancer; we may need to use reading glasses, wheelchairs, or hearing aids. Transsexual people may choose to have surgery to make their physical appearance congruent with their internal sense of self. Others may deliberately defy cultural boundaries by looking as androgynous as possible or by changing their appearance in **gender-bending** ways. As in the previous chapter, the four levels of analysis—micro, meso, macro, and global—are helpful in understanding the range of factors that shape women's bodies. Thus, individual, micro-level choices about our bodies should also be seen within the context of a system that is White-supremacist, patriarchal, and capitalist.

The Beauty Ideal

Starting in childhood with dolls like Barbie, women and girls in the United States are bombarded with images showing what they should look like and how to achieve this look. Movies, TV programs, posters, billboards, magazine articles, and ads all portray images of the "ideal" woman. She is young and tall, with long legs, small breasts and hips, smooth skin, and well-groomed hair. Her body is trim, toned, and very lean. In some years, cleavage is the desired trait; in others, it may be fuller lips; but the basic formula holds. Thus, Naomi Wolf (1991) comments that "450 full-time American fashion models who constitute the elite corps [are] deployed in a way that keeps 150 million women in line" (p. 41). In most of these images, the women are White. Where women of color are used, they are often light-skinned and conform to this same body type.

By contrast, in real life, women come in all shapes, sizes, and skin tones. Many of us have rounded—even sagging—breasts and stomachs. We may have varicose veins, scars, stretch marks, warts, wrinkles, or blemishes, and definitely body hair. Our bodies reflect our lives, as Lani Ka'ahumanu writes in her poem "My Body Is a Map of My Life" (Reading 18). Many women are short and stocky and will never look tall and willowy no matter how many diets and exercise routines they follow. The ideal standard of beauty is one that even the models themselves cannot achieve. Magazine ads and feature photos are airbrushed and enhanced photographically using

computer-based image processing to get rid of imperfections and promote the illusion of flawlessness (Dziemianowicz 1992). Not only do these images show no blemishes; they rarely even show pores. Because this ideal of beauty is all around us, it is not surprising that many women and girls—including models and film stars—think there is something wrong with their bodies and work hard, even obsessively, to eliminate, or at least reduce, their "flaws" (Edut 2000; Lakoff and Scherr 1984; Naidus 1993).

As girls and teenagers, many of us learn to inspect our bodies critically and to loathe ourselves. Young children pick up the idea that fat is bad; girls aged eight or nine are on self-imposed diets; many teenage girls think they are overweight; and by college age one in eight young women in the United States is bulimic, imagining herself to be much fatter than she actually is (Bordo 1993; Fraser 1997; Russell 1995; Thompson 1994). In a study for *Psychology Today,* psychologist D. M. Garner (1997) found that body dissatisfaction in the United States is increasing at a faster rate than ever before, especially among younger women. He reports that 89 percent of the 3,452 female respondents wanted to lose weight. Liz Dittrich (1997) found no ethnic differences in body-image dissatisfaction levels among her diverse sample of 234 women attending a junior college. Myers et al. (1998) argue that heterosexual-beauty mandates also affect lesbians to the extent that they continue to worry about their weight. These negative attitudes are increasingly common at a global level as U.S. images of women are distributed worldwide. In Korea and Japan, for example, dieting has increased due to changes in beauty standards linked to an influx of foreign (read Western, especially U.S.) TV programs and advertising (Efon 1997).

In *The Body Project,* social historian Joan Brumberg (1997) argues that U.S. girls' self-scrutiny and anxiety about their bodies has intensified during the course of the last hundred years. Her analysis is based on the diaries of girls aged thirteen to eighteen, from the mid-nineteenth century to the 1990s. She notes a range of "body projects" including hair care and styling, skin care, external constraints on body shape (like corsets and now "bodyshapers"), internal constrains (diets and exercise), orthodontia, and shaving. Greater personal freedom, earlier menarche, and earlier sexual activity, as well as the availability of running water, mirrors, bathroom scales, contact lenses, women's razors, and a myriad "beauty products," have all contributed to many U.S. girls thinking of their bodies as their primary project.

The Beauty Business

Ideal standards of beauty are reinforced by, and a necessary part of, the multi-billion-dollar beauty industry that sees women's bodies only in terms of a series of problems in need of correction. These notions of ideal beauty are very effective ways for men—as well as women—to compare and judge women and to keep them on the treadmill of "body management." Allan Johnson (1997) comments: "To live in patriarchy is to breathe in misogynist images of women as objectified sexual property valued primarily for their usefulness to men" (p. 87).

The beauty business creates needs by playing on our insecurities about our bodies and selling us creams, lotions, sprays, and handy roll-ons to improve our complexions, deodorize body scents, curl, color, condition, and straighten hair, or get rid of unwanted body hair altogether. Americans spend more than $10 billion a year on diet drugs, exercise tapes, diet books, diet meals, weight-loss classes, diet doctors, diet surgery, and "fat farms" even though research reveals that most diets don't work (Fraser 1997). We buy exercise equipment and pay for fitness classes or join a gym. We buy magazines that continually urge us to improve ourselves:

> Bored with your looks? Create a new you
>
> Work off those extra pounds! Be a successful eater
>
> Do you have lazy skin? The over-40 look is over
>
> Do you dress to hide your body? Shape up for summer
>
> Learn to dress thin

Women's magazines suggest that anyone who is comfortable with her body must be lazy or undisciplined, "letting herself go" rather than "making the best of herself."

Despite the fact that genes, metabolism, shape, and size set limits on the possibilities for drastic bodily changes, surgery and hormone therapies are pushing back the boundaries of what once was possible, defying natural processes. Liposuction, for example, described in ads as body "sculpting," is designed to remove unwanted body fat from people of normal weight and is one of the fastest-growing operations in the country. It is the most common cosmetic surgery procedure. The average surgeon's fee for liposuction is $2,000, not including anesthesia, operating-room facilities, or other related expenses (American Society of Plastic Surgeons 2002). Ads emphasize the benefits of slimmer knees and thighs or smoother hips, but like any surgery, liposuction has risks: the chance of injuries to capillaries, nerves, and skin or the possibility of infection. Despite "problems ranging from pulmonary embolisms (which killed about a dozen patients during the early 1980s) to uneven skin tone and texture, it has been judged hugely successful by doctors and patients alike" (Haiken 1997, p. 290). Such risks, taken together with greater public awareness and discussion of the dangers of silicon breast implants, for example, have not stopped women—and some men—from wanting surgical procedures to achieve their desired body profiles. Indeed, the number of such surgeries has tripled since 1992. Women are 87 percent of those who undergo plastic surgery, mainly between the ages of 35 and 50 (American Society of Plastic Surgeons 2002).

Commodification and Co-option

Striving to achieve and then maintain a perfect body is an ongoing project that takes time, energy, money, and determination. Laura Fraser (1997) describes women's attempts to be thin as a third job, in addition to being a desirable woman, wife, and mother and to working for a living. Our bodies become objects, commodities, somehow separate from ourselves, something to deplore and strive to change. Nancy Mairs (1990) emphasizes the separation of body and mind as a fundamental element of Western thought, where the body is considered inferior to the mind. "I *have* a body, you are likely to say if you talk about embodiment at all; you don't say, I *am* a body" (p. 84). Further, we learn to see ourselves as disconnected parts: ankles, thighs, hips, bottoms, breasts, upper arms, noses, and chins, all in need of improvement; and this **objectification** and **commodification** of women by the advertising media paves the way for women's dismemberment (literal and figurative) in pornography. While women's

Italian fashion designer Valentino and two supermodels who helped make his collection a success.

bodies are used in ads to sell "beauty" products, they are also used to sell virtually everything else— soft drinks, beer, tires, cars, fax machines, chain saws, or gun holsters. The underlying message in a Diet Coke ad is: If someone as beautiful as this drinks Diet Coke, you should, too. You can look like this if you drink Diet Coke. The smiling women draped over cars or caressing fax machines in ads have nothing to do with the product; they are merely tools to draw men's attention and increase sales.

Ads are costly to produce and carefully thought out, with great attention to every detail: the style of the product, its name, color, the shape of the packaging, and the text and layout of the ads (Kilbourne 1999, 2000). Ad designers make it their business to know women's interests and worries, which they use, co-opt, and undermine. The Nike slogan "Just Do It!" appeals to women's sense of independence and self-directedness while co-opting it for the consumption of products. Another slogan, "Running Like a Girl," takes the commonplace put-down and

turns it into a compliment. Over twenty-five years ago, Virginia Slims pioneered this kind of co-option with "You've Come a Long Way, Baby," to advertise a new brand of cigarettes designed specifically for women. The use of the word "Slims" is no accident, as many women smoke to control their weight. The smoking rate of girls is now higher than that of boys, with weight control as a key motivation. Wendy Chapkis (1986) notes that 1970s feminists' insistence that a woman is beautiful just as she naturally appears has also been co-opted by the cosmetics industry and "re-written in a commercial translation as the Natural Look. The horrible irony of this is, of course, that only a handful of women have the Natural Look naturally" (p. 8).

Whites Only? Forever Young? Always Able?

These ideal notions of beauty are racist, ageist, and ableist. Even though White women are held to unreasonable beauty standards, they see beauty all around them defined as White. Women of color, by contrast, rarely see themselves reflected in mainstream images of beauty. Veronica Chambers (1995) criticizes White women who do not acknowledge or understand that this may make women of color hate their looks. "To say simply, 'I don't look like Cindy Crawford either,' or 'I think Whitney Houston is really beautiful,' doesn't address the real pain that many black women have experienced. We are still acculturated to hate our dark skin, our kinky hair, our full figures" (p. 26). For example, Naomi Wolf (1991) discusses how expectations of beauty affect women in the paid workforce but does not refer to African American women. Chambers criticizes Wolf for

> failing to give voice to the many ways that black women are instructed to look as "white" as possible, especially with regard to their hair. She doesn't mention the African American flight attendant who brought a famous suit against her employers, who had fired her because she wore braids. She doesn't mention how often braids, dreads and even Afros are strictly prohibited in many workplaces, forcing black women to straighten their hair and wear styles that are more "mainstream."   (p. 27)

More recent research and writing focuses on how African American women think about their bodies and dominant beauty standards (e.g., Bennett and Dickerson 2001; Harris and Johnson 2001; Lovejoy 2001; Rooks 1996).

Indeed, White standards of beauty together with internalized racism are responsible for a hierarchy of value based on skin color among some people of color in the United States. Reading 16, "The Coming of Maureen Peal," an excerpt from Nobel laureate Toni Morrison's novel *The Bluest Eye,* shows the affirmation and validation given to a light-skinned African American girl by her teachers, other adults, and her peers. Judith Ortiz Cofer describes how her light skin, which she describes as *leche con café,* was praised in her Puerto Rican community, but that White people in the United States saw her as dark (Reading 17).

The ideal standard of beauty emphasizes youth and associates youth with sexuality, especially for women. Gray-haired men are often thought distinguished or wise. Women are urged to look young and are thought old at least a decade before men of the same age. The phrase "old woman" is used neg-

atively in mainstream culture. Many middle-aged women do not like others to know their age or are flattered to be told that they look younger than they are. A combination of beauty products, diet, exercise, surgery, and wealth has made movie stars in their fifties and sixties, like Raquel Welch, Sophia Loren, and Jane Fonda, look much younger than their years. These women reinforce ageist standards of beauty as well as selling thousands of copies of their exercise videos and other products. Oprah Winfrey's accounts of her struggles with diet, exercise, and weight losses and gains have also become best-sellers.

Books, tapes, and magazine articles advise women in their sixties and seventies about fitness, nutrition, and sexuality, with an emphasis on "successful aging," new interests, productive lives, and personal growth. Although these images are positive, they assume that older women have the money for dancing lessons, vacations, and retirement financial planning, for example, and give no suggestion that many older women live in poverty and poor health. Eleanor Palo Stoller and Rose Campbell Gibson (1994) note that U.S. culture reflects mixed images of older people—as wise, understanding, generous, happy, knowledgeable, and patriotic, but also as forgetful, lonely, dependent, demanding, complaining, senile, selfish, and inflexible. Not all middle-aged or older women mourn the passing of their youth. Many in their fifties, sixties, or older feel that they have really come into themselves, into their own voice, with newfound confidence and purpose (Bird 1995). They find that these years may be a time of self-definition and autonomy when they can resist earlier pressures to conform to dominant beauty standards or to set a good example. At the same time, older women must come to terms with their changing looks, physical limitations, and loss of independence and loved ones, as described by Lillian Rubin (Reading 21; also see Furman 1997; Jacobs 1993; Macdonald 1983; Walker 1999). Writer Meridel Le Sueur (1982) used the word "ripening" to describe the growth of her work over five decades, and her satisfaction with her fulfilling life—a positive way of thinking about aging with an emphasis on "generativity, rather than decline" (Browne 1998, p. 68). Elders are highly respected among many cultural groups including Native Americans, African Americans, Asian Americans, and Latinos, by contrast with White U.S. society. In these cultures gray hair, for example, is a mark of honor associated with experience and wisdom, which, if they are lucky, young people may be able to share. Annette Dula's description of "Miss Mildred," an elderly African American woman (Reading 31) is relevant here.

In addition to being racist and ageist, this ideal standard of beauty is profoundly ableist. Even if one is not born with a disability, everyone ages and dies. Aging is a fact of life that cannot be prevented, despite face creams, hair dyes, or hormone treatments. Most people have less physical energy, poorer eyesight and hearing, or weaker immune systems as they age. Philosopher Susan Wendell (1992) writes that "aging is disabling. Recognizing this helps us to see that disabled people are not 'other,' but that they are really 'us.' Unless we die suddenly, we are all disabled eventually" (p. 66). Ynestra King (1993a) notes:

> The common ground for the person—the human body—is a place of shifting sand that can fail us at any time. It can change shape and properties without warning; this is an essential truth of embodied existence. Of all the ways of becoming "other" in our society, disability is the only one that can happen to anyone, in an instant, transforming that person's life and identity forever.   *(p. 75)*

In *Aché: A Journal for Lesbians of African Descent*, Aisha (1991) writes:

> I personally feel that we all have challenges, some are visible and some are hidden, mine just happens to be physical but yours is still there! . . . Get in touch with the ways in which you are challenged by being able to share openly my challenge . . . and not become frightened by FEAR (False Evidence Appearing Real) superiority and bigotry.   *(p. 28)*

Thanks to untiring campaigning on the part of people with disabilities and their nondisabled allies, the U.S. government passed the Americans with Disabilities Act (ADA) in 1990, the only piece of legislation quite like it in the world, though its provisions are not consistently observed or enforced. Under this act, a person with a disability is defined as having "a physical or mental impairment that substantially limits one or more . . . major life activities." About 53 million people (roughly 19 percent of the U.S. population) have some form of disability, in-

cluding movement and orthopedic problems, poor physical or mental health that is disabling in some way, blindness, deafness, and learning disabilities (U.S. Department of Labor 2002). Despite their numbers, people with disabilities are largely absent from the mainstream media, or they are portrayed as pitiful victims—helpless and passive—or as freaks. In the readings that follow, Cheryl Marie Wade (her photo is on page 110) and Donna Walton break these stereotypes (Readings 19 and 20). Walton argues that she is handicapped by the mental limitations of nondisabled people, not by being an amputee.

Resisting Beauty Stereotypes

Many women flout dominant beauty standards: by not using makeup, for example, by wearing sensible shoes and practical clothes, or by showing hairy legs and underarms. Some breast cancer survivors who have had one or both breasts removed have chosen to go without artificial breasts or have had their mastectomy scars tattooed. Some women challenge conventional standards by gender-bending, pushing a boyish look beyond the dictates of current mainstream fashion into a more genuinely androgynous area. Others do not buy into this ideal but may need to make concessions at times, such as wearing appropriate clothes and makeup for work or family gatherings.

Beauty standards are always cultural constructions and vary among different groups, hence the importance of a meso-level analysis. For instance, in African American communities, very thin, boyish-looking women are not necessarily thought beautiful. Queen T'isha notes:

> Racism and sexism as practiced in America includes body hostilities. I didn't grow up with the belief that fat women were to be despised. The women in my family were fat, smart, sexy, employed, wanted, married, and the rulers of their households.
> *(Quoted in Edison and Notkin 1994, p. 106)*

Extreme thinness may be associated with poverty, malnutrition, and illnesses such as cancer or AIDS, which eat the body away from the inside. Women who are large, fleshy, and rounded embody strength, sexiness, comfort, and nurturance. American Jewish culture has the word *zaftig,* a positive term for voluptuous women (St. Paige 1999).

Large women challenge many stereotypes and taken-for-granted assumptions: that they are undisciplined, depressed, sexless, unwanted, or unhealthy; and that they have only themselves to blame for letting themselves go. Elise Matthesen argues,

> We have a right to take up space. We have a right to stretch out, to be big, bold, to be "too much to handle." To challenge the rest of the world to grow up, get on with it, and become big enough themselves to "handle" us. . . .
> *(Quoted in Edison and Notkin 1994, p. 107)*

And Dora Dewey-McCracken confounds common assumptions about fatness with regard to health:

> I've been diabetic since I was nineteen. . . . All my life I gained and lost at least sixty pounds each year. . . . I tried all diets, eating disorders, and fasts, only to gain the fat back, and more each time. I'm the fattest I've ever been, and yet my diabetic blood work is the best it's ever been. My doctor once told me, "As long as your disease is controlled and your blood chemistry is good, your fat is just a social issue." I'm extremely lucky to have this doctor; with most doctors, fat-phobia is the rule, not the exception. They see the fat and their brains turn off.
> *(Quoted in Edison and Notkin 1994, p. 104)*

There are many ways to be a woman—a spectrum of looks and behaviors, ranging from the conventionally feminine at one end to being able to pass for a man at the other, with various femme/butch combinations in between. Lesbians in the 1950s and '60s who identified as butch or femme adopted dress and hairstyles accordingly. Joan Nestle (1992) argues that this was not a replication of heterosexual gender polarization but rather "a lesbian-specific way of deconstructing gender that radically reclaims women's erotic energy" (p. 14). Many 1970s lesbian feminists saw idealized notions of beauty as oppressive to women and also critiqued butch-femme roles as inherently patriarchal. They adopted flannel shirts, overalls, and short hair, as a rejection of conventional womanly looks. Silva Tenenbein (1998) comments that in mainstream culture women have power in their physical beauty. "I want to reverse

the beauty-is-power equation. For dykes it's not beauty which makes us powerful but power that makes us beautiful . . . our passion, our strength, and our courage to choose to be 'other' . . . our adamant refusal to be deflected from what we want" (pp. 159, 160). Current fashion includes practical boots and shoes and leather jackets for women, and fashion ads portray androgynous women, suggesting bisexuality or lesbianism. Lesbian and gay characters are turning up in films and TV shows, and magazines, including *Vanity Fair,* have done issues on "lesbian chic." As women, and men too, push the boundaries of gender and sexual categories, this is represented in the media and also co-opted (Hamer and Budge 1994).

Numerous women's organizations and projects across the country are working on these issues. Self-help books (e.g., Erdman 1995; Newman 1991) and publications like *Radiance: The Magazine for Large Women* are a source of information and positive attitudes. Organizations that challenge sexist media images include the Body Image Task Force (Santa Cruz, Calif.), Challenging Media Images of Women (Framingham, Mass.), and Media Watch and Media Action Alliance (Circle Pines, Minn.). Those challenging fat oppression include the Boston Area Fat Liberation (Cambridge, Mass.), the Council on Size and Weight Discrimination (Mount Marion, N.Y.), Largess—the Network for Size Esteem (New Haven, Conn.), and the National Association to Advance Fat Acceptance (Sacramento, Calif.). The Gray Panthers (Washington, D.C.) and the Older Women's League (Washington, D.C.) both have many local chapters that advocate for older women around a range of issues, including prejudice and discrimination based on age and looks. Senior Action in a Gay Environment (New York) and the National Pacific/Asian Resource Center on Aging (Seattle, Wash.) support particular groups. Centers for independent living in many cities work with women with disabilities, as do projects like the Disabled Women's Theater Project (New York) and dance groups for women with disabilities.

Social historian Joan Jacobs Brumberg (1997) argues that girls should be encouraged to be physically active and taught from an early age that their power is in other things than their appearance. They need to be informed, to know what they want, and to be able to articulate it. She comments that it is an important political/personal mental-health decision not to let a preoccupation with the perfect body rule one's life.

Feminist Theorizing about Body Image and Beauty Ideals

Explanations of women's dissatisfaction with their bodies are often linked to psychological factors like low self-esteem; depression; childhood teasing, disappointment, and trauma; and family structure and dynamics (Bloom, Chesney-Lind, and Owen 1994; Chernin 1985). Women who diet obsessively, for example, may do it as a way of maintaining control over their bodies, in contrast to the many pressures they experience in other areas of their lives from parents, teachers, and peers. Abra Fortune Chernik (Reading 15) confirms this: "I felt powerful as an anorexic. Controlling my body yielded an illusion of control over my life." Part of her recovery was to face the many ways she had denied herself contact with family and friends, and the social and educational opportunities of college life, so as to avoid eating or to maintain her exercise regime. She comments that she needed to go beyond psychological explanations "to understand why society would reward my starvation and encourage my vanishing," and concludes: "Gaining weight and getting my head out of the toilet bowl was the most political act I have ever committed." Chernik reflects on her experience of anorexia and also theorizes about it. This is an excellent example of how women develop theory from our lived experience by raising broader questions—analyzing our micro-level experiences and also seeking to understand the meso- and macro-level contexts that affect us.

The constant promotion of an ideal body image is a very effective way of oppressing women and girls, taking up time, money, and attention that could be devoted to other aspects of life, like education or self-development, or to wider issues such as the need for affordable health care, child care, elder care, and jobs with decent pay and benefits. Striving for a better body keeps us in check. Although ideals of beauty—and fashions in clothes, makeup, hairstyles, and body shape—are not new, sociologist Sharlene Hesse-Biber (1996) notes that they have become increasingly stringent and elusive. Over the past thirty years or so, women in the United States have made significant gains toward greater equality with men in education and admission to professions and manual trades with higher pay scales. But, as Faludi (1991) notes in her analysis of backlash against women's progress, as women have gained more independence socially and economically, body standards have become harder to achieve.

Anthropologist Mary Douglas (1966) advanced the insight that the body is a symbolic medium of culture and that one can "see the powers and dangers credited to social structure reproduced in small on the human body" (p. 115). Philosopher Susan Bordo (1993) discusses the contradictory ideals and directives girls and women receive about femininity from contemporary culture that may affect their attitudes to food and eating. She argues that the **gendered division of labor,** under which women have the main responsibility for home and nurturing and men are mainly active in the public sphere, has barely changed despite women's entry into jobs and professions once closed to them. Women are supposed to nurture and care for men—their fathers, brothers, boyfriends, husbands, lovers, bosses, colleagues, and sons. Thus women learn to feed others—emotionally and literally—rather than themselves.

Bordo (1993) notes that women who aspire to be successful professionally "must also learn to embody the 'masculine' language and values of that arena—self control, determination, cool, emotional discipline, mastery, and so on" (p. 171). The boyish body ideals of current fashion ads suggest a new freedom from the limitations of reproductive femininity, but when placed next to solid, muscular male models, these ultra-slim women look fragile and powerless. Part of their allure, it seems, is in this relative powerlessness, in their image as little girls who will never grow up to be true equals. Bordo (1993) analyzes the prevalence of hysteria among middle-class, U.S. women in the nineteenth century, agoraphobia in the 1950s and '60s, and anorexia in the 1980s and '90s. She shows that women may attempt to resist assigned gender roles "paradoxically, by pursuing conventional feminine behavior . . . to excess" (p. 179). She suggests that a conception of power as a "network of practices, institutions, and technologies that sustain positions of dominance and subordination" (p. 167) is helpful in understanding why women would willingly accept norms and practices that limit them.

Much research into body image and eating disorders in the 1980s and '90s involved White middle-class women. Becky Thompson (1994) broke new ground in her qualitative research with a small, but diverse, group of women. She argues that struggles with food and appetite for women of color, White lesbians, and working-class women may not be about wanting to be thin. Her respondents' compulsive eating, she argues, is a response to the stress of living with physical and psychic atrocities such as sexism, racism, classism, heterosexism, and physical, emotional, and sexual abuse. Food can be a significant source of comfort and pleasure, numbing bad feelings, anxiety, and anger. Food is available, inexpensive, and socially acceptable, and it is a safer way to buffer pain than drugs or alcohol. Thompson sees the women she interviewed as courageous survivors dealing with trauma. She argues that freedom from eating problems depends on long-term psychological work at a personal level as well as macro-level political change to transform systems of oppression.

Meg Lovejoy (2001) discusses significant differences between African American women and White women in terms of body image and apparent satisfaction with their weight and looks. She suggests that African American women's more positive body image "may stem from a number of healthy sources, such as their resistance to negative societal images of Black women, the supports they receive from within the Black community, and a feminine gender role that affords greater agency" (p. 255). She quotes a study of Black and White high school girls (Parker et al. 1995), which found that the Black girls were

> more flexible and fluid than their white counterparts in their concepts of beauty, and they expressed far greater satisfaction with their body shape. The white girls described their ideal girl in terms of a set of uniform and fixed physical attributes (e.g., tall, thin, blonde hair, high cheekbones) encapsulated by the word *perfect*. By contrast, the African American girls de-emphasized external beauty, instead describing their ideal girl in terms of various personality traits, style, attitude, and ability to project a sense of pride and confidence. *(p. 250)*

Lovejoy notes that African American women are "typically raised to be strong, independent, and self-reliant" (p. 254) compared with middle-class White women. She argues that African American women do have eating problems—compulsive eating and obesity—that "exact a serious toll on Black women's physical and psychological well-being" (p. 249). Lovejoy (2001) follows Thompson (1994) and earlier work by African American health advocates and theorists (e.g., Avery 1900; hooks 1993; White 1991) in emphasizing Black women's eating problems as a way of coping with multiple oppressions.

Compared with men, most women in the United States have little structural power in terms of money, professional status, inherited wealth, or political influence. Women who are considered beautiful, though, have this personal power, which may help them "catch" a man but is no guarantee that he will stay. Robin Lakoff and Raquel Scherr (1984) argue that this power is more illusory than real when compared with material wealth and political clout. Moreover, beauty, as conventionally defined, does not last. To the extent that beautiful women have personal power, they will probably lose it as they age. Colette Browne (1998) argues that many feminist theorists do not focus on older women and the process of aging. She urges "a feminist age analysis that can document t he strengths of older women, who . . . are trivialized and ignored by patriarchal society" (p. 109).

Body Politics

The body is central to patriarchal oppression of women and is a crucial site of resistance, as mentioned here. We develop this discussion in the next three chapters: with a focus on sexuality (Chapter 4), on health (Chapter 5), and on violence against women (Chapter 6). In Chapter 2, we noted the significance of marking and effecting shifts in identity by changing physical appearance.

The body is where everything is played out: our choices and desires, as well as the societal forces that shape our lives. Institutions such as the mass media, technology, law, government, and religion all have a profound influence on who we are, who we become, and how we imagine ourselves. Retaining control of our bodily lives is an important aspect of women's autonomy and liberation.

Questions for Reflection

As you read and discuss the readings that follow, consider these questions:

1. How do you feel about your own body?
2. Do you think that makeup, piercing, tattooing, dieting, and body building make women look beautiful? Sexy? Are looking beautiful and looking sexy the same thing?
3. What makes you feel good about your body? About yourself? Are they different?
4. What images of women do you consider positive? Where do you find them?
5. What are positive images of aging? How can aging be celebrated in women's lives?
6. Why is there currently no significant political movement against the ideal of bodily perfection?
7. How would you organize activities among your peers, on your campus, or in your home community to draw attention to the issue of body image for women and to challenge common stereotypes?
8. How can women with disabilities and nondisabled women work together on the issue of body image?
9. How can young women and older women work together on this issue?
10. How much did you eat while reading this section? How much exercise did you do?

Finding Out More on the Web

1. Research the work of organizations cited in this chapter. How are they working to challenge sexist media images of women, fat oppression, or negative images of older women?
2. Mobility International USA is involved with disability rights activists internationally (www.miusa.org). How are women organizing for disability rights? What are they learning from each other? What strategies are they using to improve the lives of women with disabilities?
3. Cheryl Marie Wade mentions Sharon Kowalski and Karen Thompson in her dedication (Reading 19). Who were they and why are they significant?

Taking Action

1. Make it your daily practice to affirm your body. What do/can you do to feel good about your body?
2. Write a letter to a TV station or magazine that shows positive (or negative) images of women and let them know what you think.
3. Find out more about how your body works, for example, by reading *Our Bodies, Ourselves for the New Century.*
4. Learn about the body concerns of women from a different group than your own.
5. Attend a meeting of an organization concerned with body issues.

◆◆◆

FIFTEEN

The Body Politic

Abra Fortune Chernik

My body possesses solidness and curve, like the ocean. My weight mingles with Earth's pull, drawing me onto the sand. I have not always sent waves into the world. I flew off once, for five years, and swirled madly like a cracking brown leaf in the salty autumn wind. I wafted, dried out, apathetic.

I had no weight in the world during my years of anorexia. Curled up inside my thinness, a refugee in a cocoon of hunger, I lost the capacity to care about myself or others. I starved my body and twitched in place as those around me danced in the energy of shared existence and progressed in their lives. When I graduated from college crowned with academic honors, professors praised my potential. I wanted only to vanish.

It took three months of hospitalization and two years of outpatient psychotherapy for me to learn to nourish myself and to live in a body that expresses strength and honesty in its shape. I accepted my right and my obligation to take up room with my figure, voice and spirit. I remembered how to tumble forward and touch the world that holds me. I chose the ocean as my guide.

Who disputes the ocean's fullness?

Growing up in New York City, I did not care about the feminist movement. Although I attended an all-girls high school, we read mostly male authors and studied the history of men. Embracing mainstream culture without question, I learned about womanhood from fashion magazines, Madison Avenue and Hollywood. I dismissed feminist alternatives as foreign and offensive, swathed as they were in stereotypes that threatened my adolescent need for conformity.

Puberty hit late; I did not complain. I enjoyed living in the lanky body of a tall child and insisted on the title of "girl." If anyone referred to me as a "young woman," I would cry out, horrified, "Do not call me the W word!" But at sixteen years old, I could no longer deny my fate. My stomach and breasts rounded. Curly black hair sprouted in the most embarrassing places. Hips swelled from a once-flat plane. Interpreting maturation as an unacceptable lapse into fleshiness, I resolved to eradicate the physical symptoms of my impending womanhood.

Magazine articles, television commercials, lunchroom conversation, gymnastics coaches and write-ups on models had saturated me with diet savvy. Once I decided to lose weight, I quickly turned expert. I dropped hot chocolate from my regular breakfast order at the Skyline Diner. I replaced lunches of peanut butter and Marshmallow Fluff sandwiches with small platters of cottage cheese and cantaloupe. I eliminated dinner altogether and blunted my appetite with Tab, Camel Lights, and Carefree bubble gum. When furious craving overwhelmed my resolve and I swallowed an extra something, I would flee to the nearest bathroom to purge my mistake.

Within three months, I had returned my body to its preadolescent proportions and had manipulated my monthly period into drying up. Over the next five years, I devoted my life to losing my weight. I came to resent the body in which I lived, the body that threatened to develop, the body whose hunger I despised but could not extinguish. If I neglected a workout or added a pound or ate a bite too many, I would stare in the mirror and drown myself in a tidal wave of criticism. Hatred of my body generalized to hatred of myself as a person, and self-referential labels such as "pig," "failure" and "glutton" allowed me to believe that I deserved punishment. My self-hatred became fuel for the self-mutilating behaviors of the eating disorder.

As my body shrank, so did my world. I starved away my power and vision, my energy and inclinations. Obsessed with dieting, I allowed relationships, passions and identity to wither. I pulled back from the world, off of the beach, out of the sand. The waves of my existence ceased to roll beyond the inside of my skin.

And society applauded my shrinking. Pound after pound the applause continued, like the pounding ocean outside the door of my beach house.

The word "anorexia" literally means "loss of appetite." But as an anorexic, I felt hunger thrashing inside my body. I denied my appetite, ignored it, but never lost it. Sometimes the pangs twisted so sharply, I feared they would consume the meat of my heart. On desperate nights I rose in a flannel nightgown and allowed myself to eat an unplanned something.

No matter how much I ate, I could not soothe the pangs. Standing in the kitchen at midnight, spotlighted by the blue-white light of the open refrigerator, I would frantically feed my neglected appetite: the Chinese food I had not touched at dinner; ice cream and whipped cream; microwaved bread; cereal and chocolate milk; doughnuts and bananas. Then, solid sadness inside my gut, swelling agitation, a too-big meal I would not digest. In the bathroom I would rip off my shirt, tie up my hair, and prepare to execute the desperate ritual, again. I would ram the back of my throat with a toothbrush handle, crying, impatient, until the food rushed up. I would vomit until the toilet filled and I emptied, until I forgave myself, until I felt ready to try my life again. Standing up from my position over the toilet, wiping my mouth, I would believe that I was safe. Looking in the mirror through puffy eyes in a tumescent face, I would promise to take care of myself. Kept awake by the fast, confused beating of my heart and the ache in my chest, I would swear I did not miss the world outside. Lost within myself, I almost died.

By the time I entered the hospital, a mess of protruding bones defined my body, and the bones of my emaciated life rattled me crazy. I carried a pillow around because it hurt to sit down, and I shivered with cold in sultry July. Clumps of brittle hair clogged the drain when I showered, and blackened eyes appeared to sink into my head. My vision of reality wrinkled and my disposition turned mercurial as I slipped into starvation psychosis, a condition associated with severe malnutrition. People told me that I resembled a concentration camp prisoner, a chemotherapy patient, a famine victim or a fashion model.

In the hospital, I examined my eating disorder under the lenses of various therapies. I dissected my childhood, my family structure, my intimate relationships, my belief systems. I participated in experiential therapies of movement, art and psychodrama. I learned to use words instead of eating patterns to communicate my feelings. And still I refused to gain more than a minimal amount of weight.

I felt powerful as an anorexic. Controlling my body yielded an illusion of control over my life; I received incessant praise for my figure despite my sickly mien, and my frailty manipulated family and friends into protecting me from conflict. I had reduced my world to a plate of steamed carrots, and over this tiny kingdom I proudly crowned myself queen.

I sat cross-legged on my hospital bed for nearly two months before I earned an afternoon pass to go to the mall with my mother. The privilege came just in time; I felt unbearably large and desperately wanted a new outfit under which to hide gained weight. At the mall, I searched for two hours before finally discovering, in the maternity section at Macy's, a shirt large enough to cover what I perceived as my enormous body.

With an hour left on my pass, I spotted a sign on a shop window: "Body Fat Testing, $3.00." I suggested to my mother that we split up for ten minutes; she headed to Barnes & Noble, and I snuck into the fitness store.

I sat down in front of a machine hooked up to a computer, and a burly young body builder fired questions at me:

"Age?"

"Twenty-one."

"Height?"

"Five nine."

"Weight?"

"Ninety-nine."

The young man punched my statistics into his keyboard and pinched my arm with clippers wired to the testing machine. In a moment, the computer spit out my results. "Only ten percent body fat! Unbelievably healthy. The average for a woman your age is twenty-five percent. Fantastic! You're this week's blue ribbon winner."

I stared at him in disbelief. *Winner? Healthy? Fantastic?* I glanced around at the other customers in the store, some of whom had congregated to watch my testing, and I felt embarrassed by his praise. And then I felt furious. Furious at this man and at the society that programmed him for their ignorant approbation of my illness and my suffering.

"I am dying of anorexia," I whispered. "Don't congratulate me."

I spent my remaining month in the hospital supplementing psychotherapy with an independent examination of eating disorders from a social and political point of view. I needed to understand why society would reward my starvation and encourage my vanishing. In the bathroom, a mirror on the open door behind me reflected my backside in a mirror over the sink. Vertebrae poked at my skin, ribs hung like wings over chiseled hip bones, the two sides of my buttocks did not touch. I had not seen this view of myself before.

In writing, I recorded instances in which my eating disorder had tangled the progress of my life and thwarted my relationships. I filled three and a half Mead marble notebooks. Five years' worth of: *I wouldn't sit with Daddy when he was alone in the hospital because I needed to go jogging; I told Derek not to visit me because I couldn't throw up when he was there; I almost failed my comprehensive exams because I was so hungry; I spent my year at Oxford with my head in the toilet bowl; I wouldn't eat the dinner my friends cooked me for my nineteenth birthday because I knew they had used oil in the recipe; I told my family not to come to my college graduation because I didn't want to miss a day at the gym or have to eat a restaurant meal.* And on and on for hundreds of pages.

This honest account of my life dissolved the illusion of anorexic power. I saw myself naked in the truth of my pain, my loneliness, my obsessions, my craziness, my selfishness, my defeat. I also recognized the social and political implications of consuming myself with the trivialities of calories and weight. At college, I had watched as classmates involved themselves in extracurricular clubs, volunteer work, politics and applications for jobs and graduate schools. Obsessed with exercising and exhausted by starvation, I did not even consider joining in such pursuits. Despite my love of writing and painting and literature, despite ranking at the top of my class, I wanted only to teach aerobics. Despite my adolescent days as a loud-mouthed, rambunctious class leader, I had grown into a silent, hungry young woman.

And society preferred me this way: hungry, fragile, crazy. *Winner! Healthy! Fantastic!* I began reading feminist literature to further understand the disempowerment of women in our culture. I digested the connection between a nation of starving, self-obsessed women and the continued success of the patriarchy. I also cultivated an awareness of alternative models of womanhood. In the stillness of the hospital library, new voices in my life rose from printed pages to echo my rage and provide the conception of my feminist consciousness.

I had been willing to accept self-sabotage, but now I refused to sacrifice myself to a society that profited from my pain. I finally understood that my eating disorder symbolized more than "personal psychodynamic trauma." Gazing in the mirror at my emaciated body, I observed a woman held up by her culture as the physical ideal because she was starving, self-obsessed and powerless, a woman called beautiful because she threatened no one except herself. Despite my intelligence, my education, and my supposed Manhattan sophistication, I had believed all of the lies; I had almost given my life in order to achieve the sickly impotence that this culture aggressively links with female happiness, love and success. And everything I had to offer to the world, every tumbling wave, every thought and every passion, nearly died inside me.

As long as society resists female power, fashion will call healthy women physically flawed. As long as society accepts the physical, sexual and economic abuse of women, popular culture will prefer women who resemble little girls. Sitting in the hospital the summer after my college graduation, I grasped the absurdity of a nation of adult women dying to grow small.

Armed with this insight, I loosened the grip of the starvation disease on my body. I determined to re-create myself based on an image of a woman warrior. I remembered my ocean, and I took my first bite.

Gaining weight and getting my head out of the toilet bowl was the most political act I have ever committed.

I left the hospital and returned home to Fire Island. Living at the shore in those wintry days of my new life, I wrapped myself in feminism as I hunted seashells and role models. I wanted to feel proud of my womanhood. I longed to accept and honor my body's fullness.

During the process of my healing, I had hoped that I would be able to skip the memory of anorexia like a cold pebble into the dark winter sea. I had dreamed that in relinquishing my obsessive chase after a smaller body, I would be able to come home to rejoin those whom I had left in order to starve, rejoin them to live together as healthy, powerful women. But as my body has grown full, I have sensed a hollowness in the lives of women all around me that I had not noticed when I myself stood hollow. I have made it home only to find myself alone.

Out in the world again, I hear the furious thumping dance of body hatred echoing every place I go. Friends who once appeared wonderfully carefree in ordering late-night french fries turn out not to eat breakfast or lunch. Smart, talented, creative women talk about dieting and overeating and hating the beach because they look terrible in bathing suits. Famous women give interviews insulting their bodies and bragging about bicycling twenty-four miles the day they gave birth.

I had looked forward to rejoining society after my years of anorexic exile. Ironically, in order to preserve my health, my recovery has included the development of a consciousness that actively challenges the images and ideas that define this culture. Walking down Madison Avenue and passing emaciated women, I say to myself, *those women are sick.* When smacked with a diet commercial, I remind myself, *I don't do that anymore.* I decline invitations to movies that feature anorexic actors, I will not participate in discussions about dieting, and I refuse to shop in stores that cater to women with eating-disordered figures.

Though I am critical of diet culture, I find it nearly impossible to escape. Eating disorders have woven their way into the fabric of my society. On television, in print, on food packaging, in casual conversation and in windows of clothing stores populated by ridiculously gaunt mannequins, messages to lose my weight and control my appetite challenge my recovered fullness. Finally at home in my body, I recognize myself as an island in a sea of eating disorder, a sea populated predominantly by young women.

A perversion of nature by society has resulted in a phenomenon whereby women feel safer when starving than when eating. Losing our weight boosts self-esteem, while nourishing our bodies evokes feelings of self-doubt and self-loathing.

When our bodies take up more space than a size eight (as most of our bodies do), we say, *too big.* When our appetites demand more than a Lean Cuisine, we say, *too much.* When we want a piece of a friend's birthday cake, we say, *too bad.* Don't eat too much, don't talk too loudly, don't take up too much space, don't take from the world. Be pleasant or crazy, but don't seem hungry. Remember, a new study shows that men prefer women who eat salad for dinner over women who eat burgers and fries.

So we keep on shrinking, starving away our wildness, our power, our truth.

Hiding our curves under long T-shirts at the beach, sitting silently and fidgeting while others eat dessert, sneaking back into the kitchen late at night to binge and hating ourselves the next day, skipping breakfast, existing on diet soda and cigarettes, adding up calories and subtracting everything else. We accept what is horribly wrong in our lives and fight what is beautiful and right.

Over the past three years, feminism has taught me to honor the fullness of my womanhood and the solidness of the body that hosts my life. In feminist circles I have found mentors, strong women who live with power, passion and purpose. And yet, even in groups of feminists, my love and acceptance of my body remains unusual.

Eating disorders affect us all on both a personal and a political level. The majority of my peers—including my feminist peers—still measure their beauty against anorexic ideals. Even among feminists, body hatred and chronic dieting continue to consume lives. Friends of anorexics beg them to please start eating; then these friends go home and continue their own diets. Who can deny that the millions of young women caught in the net of disordered eating will frustrate the potential of the next wave of feminism?

Sometimes my empathy dissolves into frustration and rage at our situation. For the first time in history, young women have the opportunity to create a world in our image. But many of us concentrate instead on re-creating the shape of our thighs.

As young feminists, we must place unconditional acceptance of our bodies at the top of our political agenda. We must claim our bodies as our own to love and honor in their infinite shapes and sizes. Fat, thin, soft, hard, puckered, smooth, our bodies are our homes. By nourishing our bodies, we care for and love ourselves on the most basic level. When we deny ourselves physical food, we go hungry emotionally, psychologically, spiritually and politically. We must challenge ourselves to eat and digest, and allow society to call us too big. We will understand their message to mean too powerful.

Time goes by quickly. One day we will blink and open our eyes as old women. If we spend all our energy keeping our bodies small, what will we have to show for our lives when we reach the end? I hope we have more than a group of fashionably skinny figures.

The Coming of Maureen Peal

Toni Morrison

Winter tightened our heads with a band of cold and melted our eyes. We put pepper in the feet of our stockings, Vaseline on our faces, and stared through dark icebox mornings at four stewed prunes, slippery lumps of oatmeal, and cocoa with a roof of skin.

But mostly we waited for spring, when there could be gardens.

By the time this winter had stiffened itself into a hateful knot that nothing could loosen, something did loosen it, or rather someone. A someone who splintered the knot into silver threads that tangled us, netted us, made us long for the dull chafe of the previous boredom.

This disrupter of seasons was a new girl in school named Maureen Peal. A high-yellow dream child with long brown hair braided into two lynch ropes that hung down her back. She was rich, at least by our standards, as rich as the richest of the white girls, swaddled in comfort and care. The quality of her clothes threatened to derange Frieda and me. Patent-leather shoes with buckles, a cheaper version of which we got only at Easter and which had disintegrated by the end of May. Fluffy sweaters the color of lemon drops tucked into skirts with pleats so orderly they astounded us. Brightly colored knee socks with white borders, a brown velvet coat trimmed in white rabbit fur, and a matching muff. There was a hint of spring in her sloe green eyes, something summery in her complexion, and a rich autumn ripeness in her walk.

She enchanted the entire school. When teachers called on her, they smiled encouragingly. Black boys didn't trip her in the halls; white boys didn't stone her, white girls didn't suck their teeth when she was assigned to be their work partners; black girls stepped aside when she wanted to use the sink in the girls' toilet, and their eyes genuflected under sliding lids. She never had to search for anybody to eat with in the cafeteria—they flocked to the table of her choice, where she opened fastidious lunches, shaming our jelly-stained bread with egg-salad sandwiches cut into four dainty squares, pink-frosted cupcakes, sticks of celery and carrots, proud, dark apples. She even bought and liked white milk.

Frieda and I were bemused, irritated, and fascinated by her. We looked hard for flaws to restore our equilibrium, but had to be content at first with uglying up her name, changing Maureen Peal to Meringue Pie. Later a minor epiphany was ours when we discovered that she had a dog tooth—a charming one to be sure—but a dog tooth nonetheless. And when we found out that she had been born with six fingers on each hand and that there was a little bump where each extra one had been removed, we smiled. They were small triumphs, but we took what we could get—snickering behind her back and calling her Six-finger-dog-tooth-meringue-pie. But we had to do it alone, for none of the other girls would cooperate with our hostility. They adored her.

When she was assigned a locker next to mine, I could indulge my jealousy four times a day. My sister and I both suspected that we were secretly prepared to be her friend, if she would let us, but I knew it would be a dangerous friendship, for when my eye traced the white border patterns of those Kelly-green knee socks, and felt the pull and slack of my brown stockings, I wanted to kick her. And when I thought of the unearned haughtiness in her eyes, I plotted accidental slammings of locker doors on her hand.

As locker friends, however, we got to know each other a little, and I was even able to hold a sensible conversation with her without visualizing her fall

off a cliff, or giggling my way into what I thought
was a clever insult.

One day, while I waited at the locker for Frieda,
she joined me.

"Hi."

"Hi."

"Waiting for your sister?"

"Uh-huh."

"Which way do you go home?"

"Down Twenty-first Street to Broadway."

"Why don't you go down Twenty-second Street?"

" 'Cause I live on Twenty-first Street."

"Oh. I can walk that way, I guess. Partly, anyway."

"Free country."

Frieda came toward us, her brown stockings
straining at the knees because she had tucked the toe
under to hide a hole in the foot.

"Maureen's gonna walk part way with us."

Frieda and I exchanged glances, her eyes begging my restraint, mine promising nothing.

It was a false spring day, which, like Maureen,
had pierced the shell of a deadening winter. There
were puddles, mud, and an inviting warmth that
deluded us. The kind of day on which we draped
our coats over our heads, left our galoshes in school,
and came down with croup the following day. We
always responded to the slightest change in weather,
the most minute shifts in time of day. Long before
seeds were stirring, Frieda and I were scruffing
and poking at the earth, swallowing air, drinking
rain. . . .

As we emerged from the school with Maureen,
we began to molt immediately. We put our head
scarves in our coat pockets, and our coats on our
heads. I was wondering how to maneuver Maureen's fur muff into a gutter when a commotion
in the playground distracted us. A group of boys
was circling and holding at bay a victim, Pecola
Breedlove.

Bay Boy, Woodrow Cain, Buddy Wilson, Junie
Bug—like a necklace of semiprecious stones they
surrounded her. Heady with the smell of their own
musk, thrilled by the easy power of a majority, they
gaily harassed her.

"Black e mo. Black e mo. Yadaddsleepsnekked.
Black e mo black e moya dadd sleeps nekked. Black
e mo . . ."

They had extemporized a verse made up of two
insults about matters over which the victim had no
control: the color of her skin and speculations on the

sleeping habits of an adult, wildly fitting in its inco-
herence. That they themselves were black, or that
their own father had similarly relaxed habits, was irrelevant. It was their contempt for their own black-
ness that gave the first insult its teeth. They seemed
to have taken all of their smoothly cultivated ignorance, their exquisitely learned self-hatred, their
elaborately designed hopelessness and sucked it all
up into a fiery cone of scorn that had burned for ages
in the hollows of their minds—cooled—and spilled
over lips of outrage, consuming whatever was in its
path. They danced a macabre ballet around the victim, whom, for their own sake, they were prepared
to sacrifice to the flaming pit.

Black e mo Black e mo Ya daddy sleeps nekked.
Stch ta ta stch ta ta
stach ta ta ta ta ta

Pecola edged around the circle crying. She had
dropped her notebook, and covered her eyes with
her hands.

We watched, afraid they might notice us and
turn their energies our way. Then Frieda, with set
lips and Mama's eyes, snatched her coat from her
head and threw it on the ground. She ran toward
them and brought her books down on Woodrow
Cain's head. The circle broke. Woodrow Cain grabbed
his head.

"Hey, girl!"

"You cut that out, you hear?" I had never heard
Frieda's voice so loud and clear.

Maybe because Frieda was taller than he was,
maybe because he saw her eyes, maybe because he
had lost interest in the game, or maybe because he had
a crush on Frieda, in any case Woodrow looked frightened just long enough to give her more courage.

"Leave her 'lone, or I'm gone tell everybody
what you did!"

Woodrow did not answer; he just walled his eyes.

Bay Boy piped up, "Go on, gal. Ain't nobody
bothering you."

"You shut up, Bullet Head." I had found my
tongue.

"Who you calling Bullet Head?"

"I'm calling you Bullet Head, Bullet Head."

Frieda took Pecola's hand. "Come on."

"You want a fat lip?" Bay Boy drew back his fist
at me.

"Yeah. Gimme one of yours."

"You gone get one."

Maureen appeared at my elbow, and the boys seemed reluctant to continue under her springtime eyes so wide with interest. They buckled in confusion, not willing to beat up three girls under her watchful gaze: So they listened to a budding male instinct that told them to pretend we were unworthy of their attention.

"Come on, man."

"Yeah. Come on. We ain't got time to fool with them."

Grumbling a few disinterested epithets, they moved away.

I picked up Pecola's notebook and Frieda's coat, and the four of us left the playground.

"Old Bullet Head, he's always picking on girls."

Frieda agreed with me. "Miss Forrester said he was incorrigival."

"Really?" I didn't know what that meant, but it had enough of a doom sound in it to be true of Bay Boy.

While Frieda and I clucked on about the near fight, Maureen, suddenly animated, put her velvet-sleeved arm through Pecola's and began to behave as though they were the closest of friends.

"I just moved here. My name is Maureen Peal. What's yours?"

"Pecola."

"Pecola? Wasn't that the name of the girl in *Imitation of Life?*"

"I don't know. What is that?"

"The picture show, you know. Where this mulatto girl hates her mother 'cause she is black and ugly but then cries at the funeral. It was real sad. Everybody cries in it. Claudette Colbert too."

"Oh." Pecola's voice was no more than a sigh.

"Anyway, her name was Pecola too. She was so pretty. When it comes back, I'm going to see it again. My mother has seen it four times."

Frieda and I walked behind them, surprised at Maureen's friendliness to Pecola, but pleased. Maybe she wasn't so bad, after all. Frieda had put her coat back on her head, and the two of us, so draped, trotted along enjoying the warm breeze and Frieda's heroics.

"You're in my gym class, aren't you?" Maureen asked Pecola.

"Yes."

"Miss Erkmeister's legs sure are bow. I bet she thinks they're cute. How come she gets to wear real shorts, and we have to wear those old bloomers? I want to die every time I put them on."

Pecola smiled but did not look at Maureen.

"Hey." Maureen stopped short. "There's an Isaley's. Want some ice cream? I have money."

She unzipped a hidden pocket in her muff and pulled out a multifolded dollar bill. I forgave her those knee socks.

"My uncle sued Isaley's," Maureen said to the three of us. "He sued the Isaley's in Akron. They said he was disorderly and that that was why they wouldn't serve him, but a friend of his, a policeman, came in and beared the witness, so the suit went through."

"What's a suit?"

"It's when you can beat them up if you want to and won't anybody do nothing. Our family does it all the time. We believe in suits."

At the entrance to Isaley's, Maureen turned to Frieda and me, asking, "You all going to buy some ice cream?"

We looked at each other. "No," Frieda said.

Maureen disappeared into the store with Pecola.

Frieda looked placidly down the street; I opened my mouth, but quickly closed it. It was extremely important that the world not know that I fully expected Maureen to buy us some ice cream, that for the past 120 seconds I had been selecting the flavor, that I had begun to like Maureen, and that neither of us had a penny.

We supposed Maureen was being nice to Pecola because of the boys, and were embarrassed to be caught—even by each other—thinking that she would treat us, or that we deserved it as much as Pecola did.

The girls came out. Pecola with two dips of orange-pineapple, Maureen with black raspberry.

"You should have got some," she said. "They had all kinds. Don't eat down to the tip of the cone," she advised Pecola.

"Why?"

"Because there's a fly in there."

"How you know?"

"Oh, not really. A girl told me she found one in the bottom of hers once, and ever since then she throws that part away."

"Oh."

We passed the Dreamland Theatre, and Betty Grable smiled down at us.

"Don't you just love her?" Maureen asked.

"Uh-huh," said Pecola.

I differed. "Hedy Lamarr is better."

Maureen agreed. "Ooooo yes. My mother told me that a girl named Audrey, she went to the beauty parlor where we lived before, and asked the lady to fix her hair like Hedy Lamarr's, and the lady said, 'Yeah, when you grow some hair like Hedy Lamarr's.'" She laughed long and sweet.

"Sounds crazy," said Frieda.

"She sure is. Do you know she doesn't even menstrate yet, and she's sixteen. Do you, yet?"

"Yes." Pecola glanced at us.

"So do I." Maureen made no attempt to disguise her pride. "Two months ago I started. My girl friend in Toledo, where we lived before, said when she started she was scared to death. Thought she had killed herself."

"Do you know what it's for?" Pecola asked the question as though hoping to provide the answer herself.

"For babies." Maureen raised two pencil-stroke eyebrows at the obviousness of the question. "Babies need blood when they are inside you, and if you are having a baby, then you don't menstrate. But when you're not having a baby, then you don't have to save the blood, so it comes out."

"How do babies get the blood?" asked Pecola.

"Through the like-line. You know. Where your belly button is. That is where the like-line grows from and pumps the blood to the baby."

"Well, if the belly buttons are to grow like-lines to give the baby blood, and only girls have babies, how come boys have belly buttons?"

Maureen hesitated. "I don't know," she admitted. "But boys have all sorts of things they don't need." Her tinkling laughter was somehow stronger than our nervous ones. She curled her tongue around the edge of the cone, scooping up a dollop of purple that made my eyes water. We were waiting for a stop light to change. Maureen kept scooping the ice cream from around the cone's edge with her tongue; she didn't bite the edge as I would have done. Her tongue circled the cone. Pecola had finished hers; Maureen evidently liked her things to last. While I was thinking about her ice cream, she must have been thinking about her last remark, for she said to Pecola, "Did you ever see a naked man?"

Pecola blinked, then looked away. "No. Where would I see a naked man?"

"I don't know. I just asked."

"I wouldn't even look at him, even if I did see him. That's dirty. Who wants to see a naked man?" Pecola was agitated. "Nobody's father would be naked in front of his own daughter. Not unless he was dirty too."

"I didn't say 'father.' I just said 'a naked man.'"

"Well . . ."

"How come you said 'father'?" Maureen wanted to know.

"Who else would she see, dog tooth?" I was glad to have a chance to show anger. Not only because of the ice cream, but because we had seen our own father naked and didn't care to be reminded of it and feel the shame brought on by the absence of shame. He had been walking down the hall from the bathroom into his bedroom and passed the open door of our room. We had lain there wide-eyed. He stopped and looked in, trying to see in the dark room whether we were really asleep—or was it his imagination that opened eyes were looking at him? Apparently he convinced himself that we were sleeping. He moved away, confident that his little girls would not lie open-eyed like that, staring, staring. When he had moved on, the dark took only him away, not his nakedness. That stayed in the room with us. Friendly-like.

"I'm not talking to you," said Maureen. "Besides, I don't care if she sees her father naked. She can look at him all day if she wants to. Who cares?"

"You do," said Frieda. "That's all you talk about."

"It is not."

"It is so. Boys, babies, and somebody's naked daddy. You must be boy-crazy."

"You better be quiet."

"Who's gonna make me?" Frieda put her hand on her hip and jutted her face toward Maureen.

"You all ready made. Mammy made."

"You stop talking about my mama."

"Well, you stop talking about my daddy."

"Who said anything about your old daddy?"

"You did."

"Well, you started it."

"I wasn't even talking to you. I was talking to Pecola."

"Yeah. About seeing her naked daddy."

"So what if she did see him?"

Pecola shouted, "I never saw my daddy naked. Never."

"You did too," Maureen snapped. "Bay Boy said so."

"I did not."

"You did."

"I did not."

"Did. Your own daddy, too!"

Pecola tucked her head in—a funny, sad, helpless movement. A kind of hunching of the shoulders, pulling in of the neck, as though she wanted to cover her ears.

"You stop talking about her daddy," I said.

"What do I care about her old black daddy?" asked Maureen.

"Black? Who you calling black?"

"You!"

"You think you so cute!" I swung at her and missed, hitting Pecola in the face. Furious at my clumsiness, I threw my notebook at her, but it caught her in the small of her velvet back, for she had turned and was flying across the street against traffic.

Safe on the other side, she screamed at us, "I *am* cute! And you ugly! Black and ugly black e mos. I *am* cute!"

She ran down the street, the green knee socks making her legs look like wild dandelion stems that had somehow lost their heads. The weight of her remark stunned us, and it was a second or two before Frieda and I collected ourselves enough to shout, "Six-finger-dog-tooth-meringue-pie!" We chanted this most powerful of our arsenal of insults as long as we could see the green stems and rabbit fur.

Grown people frowned at the three girls on the curbside, two with their coats draped over their heads, the collars framing the eyebrows like nuns' habits, black garters showing where they bit the tops of brown stockings that barely covered the knees, angry faces knotted like dark cauliflowers.

Pecola stood a little apart from us, her eyes hinged in the direction in which Maureen had fled. She seemed to fold into herself, like a pleated wing. Her pain antagonized me. I wanted to open her up, crisp her edges, ram a stick down that hunched and curving spine, force her to stand erect and spit the misery out on the streets. But she held it in where it could lap up into her eyes.

Frieda snatched her coat from her head. "Come on, Claudia. 'Bye, Pecola."

We walked quickly at first, and then slower, pausing every now and then to fasten garters, tie shoelaces, scratch, or examine old scars. We were sinking under the wisdom, accuracy, and relevance of Maureen's last words. If she was cute—and if anything could be believed, she *was*—then we were not. And what did that mean? We were lesser. Nicer, brighter, but still lesser. Dolls we could destroy, but we could not destroy the honey voices of parents and aunts, the obedience in the eyes of our peers, the slippery light in the eyes of our teachers when they encountered the Maureen Peals of the world. What was the secret? What did we lack? Why was it important? And so what? Guileless and without vanity, we were still in love with ourselves then. We felt comfortable in our skins, enjoyed the news that our senses released to us, admired our dirt, cultivated our scars, and could not comprehend this unworthiness. Jealousy we understood and thought natural—a desire to have what somebody else had; but envy was a strange, new feeling for us. And all the time we knew that Maureen Peal was not the Enemy and not worthy of such intense hatred. The *Thing* to fear was the *Thing* that made *her* beautiful, and not us.

◆◆◆

The Story of My Body

Judith Ortiz Cofer

Migration is the story of my body.

—Victor Hernandez Cruz

1. Skin

I was born a white girl in Puerto Rico, but became a brown girl when I came to live in the United States. My Puerto Rican relatives called me tall; at the American school, some of my rougher classmates called me "skinny-bones" and "the shrimp," because I was the smallest member of my classes all through grammar school until high school, when the midget Gladys was given the honorary post of front-row center for class pictures and scorekeeper, bench warmer in P.E. I reached my full stature of five feet even in sixth grade.

I started out life as a pretty baby and learned to be a pretty girl from a pretty mother. Then at ten years of age I suffered one of the worst cases of chicken pox I have ever heard of. My entire body, including the inside of my ears and in between my toes, was covered with pustules that, in a fit of panic at my appearance, I scratched off of my face, leaving permanent scars. A cruel school nurse told me I would always have them—tiny cuts that looked as if a mad cat had plunged its claws deep into my skin. I grew my hair long and hid behind it for the first years of my adolescence. This was when I learned to be invisible.

2. Color

In the animal world it indicates danger: The most colorful creatures are often the most poisonous. Color is also a way to attract and seduce a mate. In the human world, color triggers many more complex and often deadly reactions. As a Puerto Rican girl born of "white" parents, I spent the first years of my life hearing people refer to me as *blanca*, white. My mother insisted that I protect myself from the intense island sun because I was more prone to sun-burn than some of my darker, *triqueno* playmates. People were always commenting within my hearing about how my black hair contrasted so nicely with my "pale" skin. I did not think of the color of my skin consciously, except when I heard the adults talking about complexion. It seems to me that the subject is much more common in the conversation of mixed-race peoples than in mainstream U.S. society, where it is a touchy and sometimes even embarrassing topic to discuss, except in a political context. In Puerto Rico I heard many conversations about skin color. A pregnant woman could say, "I hope my baby doesn't turn out *prieto* (slang for dark or black) like my husband's grandmother, although she was a good-looking *negra* in her time." I am a combination of both, being olive-skinned—lighter than my mother yet darker than my fair-skinned father. In America, I am a person of color, obviously a Latina. On the island I have been called everything from a *paloma blanca*, after the song (by a black suitor), to *la gringa*.

My first experience of color prejudice occurred in a supermarket in Paterson, New Jersey. It was Christmastime and I was eight or nine years old. There was a display of toys in the store where I went two or three times a day to buy things for my mother who never made lists but sent for milk, cigarettes, a can of this or that, as she remembered from hour to hour. I enjoyed being trusted with money and walking half a city block to the new, modern grocery store. It was owned by three good-looking Italian brothers. I liked the younger one with the crew-cut blond hair. The two older ones watched me and the other Puerto Rican kids as if they thought we were going to steal something. The oldest one would sometimes even try to hurry me with my purchases, although part of my pleasure in these expeditions came from looking at everything in the well-stocked aisles. I was also teaching myself to read English by sounding out the labels in packages: L&M cigarettes, Borden's homogenized milk, Red Devil potted ham, Nestlé's chocolate mix, Quaker oats, and Bustelo coffee, Wonder bread, Colgate toothpaste, Ivory soap, and Goya (makers of products used in Puerto Rican dishes) everything—these are some of the brand names that taught me nouns. Several times this man had come up to me wearing his bloodstained butcher's apron and, towering over me, had asked in a harsh voice whether there was something he could help me find. On the way out I would glance at the younger brother who ran one of the registers and he would often smile and wink at me.

It was the mean brother who first referred to me as "colored." It was a few days before Christmas and my parents had already told my brother and me that since we were in *los estados* now, we would get our presents on December twenty-fifth instead of *Los Reyes, Three Kings Day,* when gifts are exchanged in Puerto Rico. We were to give them a wish list that they would take to Santa Claus, who apparently lived in the Macy's store downtown—at least that's where we had caught a glimpse of him when we went shopping. Since my parents were timid about entering the fancy store, we did not approach the huge man in the red suit. I was not interested in sitting on a stranger's lap anyway. But I did covet Susie, the talking schoolteacher doll that was displayed in the center aisle of the Italian brothers' supermarket. She talked when you pulled a string on her back. Susie had a limited repertoire of three sentences: I think she could say: "Hello, I'm Susie Schoolteacher; two plus two is four," and one other thing I cannot remember. The day the older brother chased me away, I was reaching to touch Susie's blond curls. I had been told many times, as most children have, not to touch anything in a store that I was not buying. But I had been looking at Susie for weeks. In my mind, she was my doll. After all, I had put her on my Christmas wish list. The moment is frozen in my mind as if there were a photograph of it on file. It was not a turning point, a disaster, or an earthshaking revelation. It was simply the first time I considered—if naively—the meaning of skin color in human relations.

I reached to touch Susie's hair. It seems to me that I had to get on tiptoe since the toys were stacked on a table and she sat like a princess on top of the fancy box she came in. Then I heard the booming "Hey, kid, what do you think you're doing!" spoken very loudly from the meat counter. I felt caught although I knew I was not doing anything criminal. I remember not looking at the man, but standing there feeling humiliated because I knew everyone in the store must have heard him yell at me. I felt him approach and when I knew he was behind me, I turned around to face the bloody butcher's apron. His large chest was at my eye level. He blocked my way. I started to run out of the place, but even as I reached the door I heard him shout after me: "Don't come in here unless you gonna buy something. You PR kids put your dirty hands on stuff. You always look dirty. But maybe dirty brown is your natural color." I heard him laugh and someone else too in the back. Outside in the sunlight I looked at my hands. My nails needed a little cleaning as they always did since I liked to paint with watercolors, but I took a bath every night. I thought the man was dirtier than I was in his stained apron. He was also always sweaty—it showed in big yellow circles under his shirt sleeves. I sat on the front steps of the apartment building where we lived and looked closely at my hands, which showed the only skin I could see, since it was bitter cold and I was wearing my quilted play coat, dungarees, and a knitted navy cap of my father's. I was not pink like my friend Charlene and her sister Kathy who had blue eyes and light-brown hair. My skin is the color of the coffee my grandmother made, which was half milk, *leche con café* rather than *café con leche.* My mother is the opposite mix. She has a lot of café in her color. I could not understand how my skin looked like dirt to the supermarket man.

I went in and washed my hands thoroughly with soap and hot water, and, borrowing my mother's nail file, I cleaned the crusted watercolors from underneath my nails. I was pleased with the results. My skin was the same color as before, but I knew I was clean. Clean enough to run my fingers through Susie's fine gold hair when she came home to me.

3. Size

My mother is barely four feet eleven inches in height, which is average for women in her family. When I grew to five feet by age twelve, she was amazed and began to use the word tall to describe me, as in: "Since you are tall, this dress will look good on you." As with the color of my skin, I didn't consciously think about my height or size until other people made an issue of it. It is around the pre-adolescent years that in America the games children play for fun become fierce competitions where everyone is out to "prove" they are better than others. It was in the playground and sports fields that my size-related problems began. No matter how familiar the story is, every child who is the last chosen for a team knows the torment of waiting to be called up. At the Paterson, New Jersey, public schools that I attended, the volleyball or softball game was the metaphor for the battlefield of life to the inner city kids—the black kids vs. the Puerto Rican kids, the whites vs. the blacks vs. the Puerto Rican kids; and I was 4F, skinny, short, bespectacled, and apparently impervious to the blood thirst that drove many of my classmates to play ball as if their lives depended on it. Perhaps they did. I would rather be reading a book than sweating, grunting, and running the risk of pain and injury. I simply did not see the point in competitive sports. My main form of exercise then was walking to the library, many city blocks away from my barrio.

Still, I wanted to be wanted. I wanted to be chosen for the teams. Physical education was compulsory, a class where you were actually given a grade. On my mainly all-A report card, the C for compassion I always received from the P.E. teachers shamed me the same as a bad grade in a real class. Invariably, my father would say: "How can you make a low grade *for playing games?*" He did not understand. Even if I had managed to make a hit (it never happened), or get the ball over that ridiculously high net, I already had a reputation as a "shrimp," a hopeless nonathlete. It was an area where the girls who didn't like me for one reason or another—mainly because I did better than they on academic subjects—could lord it over me; the playing field was the place where even the smallest girl could make me feel powerless and inferior. I instinctively understood the politics even then; how the *not* choosing me until the teacher forced one of the team captains to call my name was a coup of sorts—there you little show-off, tomorrow you can beat us in spelling and geography, but this afternoon you are the loser. Or perhaps those were only my own bitter thoughts as I sat or stood in the sidelines while the big girls were grabbed like fish and I, the little brown tadpole, was ignored until Teacher looked over in my general direction and shouted, "Call Ortiz," or worse, "Somebody's *got* to take her."

No wonder I read Wonder Woman comics and had Legion of Super Heroes daydreams. Although I wanted to think of myself as "intellectual," my body

was demanding that I notice it. I saw the little swelling around my once-flat nipples; the fine hairs growing in secret places; but my knees were still bigger than my thighs and I always wore long or half-sleeve blouses to hide my bony upper arms. I wanted flesh on my bones—a thick layer of it. I saw a new product advertised on TV. Wate-On. They showed skinny men and women before and after taking the stuff, and it was a transformation like the 97-pound weakling turned into Charles Atlas ads that I saw on the back cover of my comic books. The Wate-On was very expensive. I tried to explain my need for it in Spanish to my mother, but it didn't translate very well, even to my ears—and she said with a tone of finality, eat more of my good food and you'll get fat—anybody can get fat. Right. Except me. I was going to have to join a circus someday as "Skinny Bones," the woman without flesh.

Wonder Woman was stacked. She had a cleavage framed by the spread wings of a golden eagle and a muscular body that has become fashionable with women only recently. But since I wanted a body that would serve me in P.E., hers was my ideal. The breasts were an indulgence I allowed myself. Perhaps the daydreams of bigger girls were more glamorous, since our ambitions are filtered through our needs, but I wanted first a powerful body. I daydreamed of leaping up above the gray landscape of the city to where the sky was clear and blue, and in anger and self-pity I fantasized about scooping my enemies up by their hair from the playing fields and dumping them on a barren asteroid. I would put the P.E. teachers each on their own rock in space too where they would be the loneliest people in the universe since I knew they had no "inner resources," no imagination, and in outer space, there would be no air for them to fill their deflated volleyballs with. In my mind all P.E. teachers have blended into one large spiky-haired woman with a whistle on a string around her neck and a volleyball under one arm. My Wonder Woman fantasies of revenge were a source of comfort to me in my early career as a shrimp.

I was saved from more years of P.E. torment by the fact that in my sophomore year of high school I transferred to a school where the midget, Gladys, was the focal point of interest for the people who must rank according to size. Because her height was considered a handicap, there was an unspoken rule about mentioning size around Gladys, but of course there was no need to say anything. Gladys knew her place: front-row center in class photographs. I gladly moved to the left or to the right of her, as far as I could without leaving the picture completely.

4. Looks

Many photographs were taken of me as a baby by my mother to send to my father who was stationed overseas during the first two years of my life. With the army in Panama when I was born, he later joined the navy and traveled often on tours of duty. I was a healthy, pretty baby. Recently I read that people are drawn to big-eyed round-faced creatures, like puppies, kittens, and certain other mammals and marsupials, koalas for example, and, of course, infants. I was all eyes, since my head and body, even as I grew older, remained thin and small-boned. As a young child I got a lot of attention from my relatives and many other people we met in our barrio. My mother's beauty may have had something to do with how much attention we got from strangers in stores and on the street. I can imagine it. In the pictures I have seen of us together, she is a stunning young woman by Latino standards: long, curly black hair and round curves in a compact frame. From her I learned how to move, smile, and talk like an attractive woman. I remember going into a bodega for our groceries and being given candy by the proprietor as a reward for being *bonita,* pretty.

I can see in the photographs and I also remember that I was dressed in the pretty clothes, the stiff, frilly dresses, with layers of crinolines underneath, the glossy patent leather shoes, and, on special occasions, the skull-hugging little hats and the white gloves that were popular in the late fifties and early sixties. My mother was proud of my looks, although I was a bit too thin. She could dress me up like a doll and take me by the hand to visit relatives, or go to the Spanish mass at the Catholic church, and show me off. How was I to know that she and the others who called me pretty were representatives of an aesthetic that would not apply when I went out into the mainstream world of school?

In my Paterson, New Jersey, public schools there were still quite a few white children, although the demographics of the city were changing rapidly. The original waves of Italian and Irish immigrants, silk-mill workers and laborers in the cloth industries, had been "assimilated." Their children were now the middle-class parents of my peers. Many of them moved their children to the Catholic schools that proliferated enough to have leagues of basketball teams. The names I recall hearing still ring in my ears: Don Bosco High vs. St. Mary's High, St. Joseph's vs. St. John's. Later I too would be transferred to the safer environment of a Catholic school. But I started school at Public School Number 11. I came there from Puerto Rico, thinking myself a pretty girl, and found that the hierarchy for popularity was as follows: pretty white girl, pretty Jewish girl, pretty Puerto Rican girl, pretty black girl. Drop the last two categories; teachers were too busy to have more than one favorite per class, and it was simply understood that if there was a big part in the school play, or any competition where the main qualification was "presentability" (such as escorting a school visitor to or from the principal's office), the classroom's public address speaker would be requesting the pretty and/or nice-looking white boy or girl. By the time I was in the sixth grade, I was sometimes called by the principal to represent my class because I dressed neatly (I knew this from a progress report sent to my mother, which I translated for her), and because all the "presentable" white girls had moved to the Catholic schools (I later surmised this part). But I was still not one of the popular girls with the boys. I remember one incident where I stepped out into the playground in my baggy gym shorts and one Puerto Rican boy said to the other: "What do you think?" The other one answered: "Her face is okay, but look at the toothpick legs." The next best thing to a compliment I got was when my favorite male teacher, while handing out the class pictures, commented that with my long neck and delicate features I resembled the movie star Audrey Hepburn. But the Puerto Rican boys had learned to respond to a fuller figure: long necks and a perfect little nose were not what they looked for in a girl. That is when I decided I was a "brain." I did not settle into the role easily. I was nearly devastated by what the chicken-pox episode had done to my self-image. But I looked into the mirror less often after I was told that I would always have scars on my face, and I hid behind my long black hair and my books.

After the problems at the public school got to the point where even nonconfrontational little me got beaten up several times, my parents enrolled me at St. Joseph's High School. I was then a minority of one among the Italian and Irish kids. But I found several good friends there—other girls who took their studies seriously. We did our homework together and talked about the Jackies. The Jackies were two popular girls, one blonde and the other red-haired, who had women's bodies. Their curves showed even in the blue jumper uniforms with straps that we all wore. The blond Jackie would often let one of the straps fall off her shoulder, and although she, like all of us, wore a white blouse underneath, all the boys stared at her arm. My friends and I talked about this and practiced letting our straps fall off our shoulders. But it wasn't the same without breasts or hips.

My final two and a half years of high school were spent in Augusta, Georgia, where my parents moved our family in search of a more peaceful environment. There we became part of a little community of our army-connected relatives and friends. School was yet another matter. I was enrolled in a huge school of nearly two thousand students that had just that year been forced to integrate. There were two black girls and there was me. I did extremely well academically. As to my social life, it was, for the most part, uneventful—yet it is in my memory blighted by one incident. In my junior year, I became wildly infatuated with a pretty white boy. I'll call him Ted. Oh, he was pretty: yellow hair that fell over his forehead, a smile to die for, and he was a great dancer. I watched him at Teen Town, the youth center at the base where all the military brats gathered on Saturday nights. My father had retired from the military and we had all our base privileges—one other reason we had moved to Augusta. Ted looked like an angel to me. I worked on him for a year before he asked me out. This meant maneuvering to be within the periphery of his vision at every possible occasion. I took the long way to my classes in school just to pass by his locker, I went to football games that I detested, and I danced (I too was a good dancer) in front of him at Teen Town—this took some fancy footwork since it involved subtly moving my partner toward the right spot on the dance floor. When Ted finally approached me, "A Million to One" was playing on the jukebox, and when he took me into his arms, the odds suddenly turned in my favor. He asked me to go to a school dance the following Saturday. I said yes, breathlessly, I said yes but there were obstacles to surmount at home. My father did not allow me to date casually. I was allowed to go to major events like a prom or a concert with a boy who had been properly screened. There was such a boy in my life, a neighbor who wanted to be a Baptist missionary and was practicing his anthropological skills on my family. If I was desperate to go somewhere and needed a date, I'd resort to Gary. This is the type of religious nut that Gary was: When the school bus did not show up one day, he put his hands over his face and prayed to Christ to get us a way to get to school. Within ten minutes a mother in a station wagon on her way to town stopped to ask why we weren't in school. Gary informed her that the Lord had sent her just in time to get us there for roll call. He assumed that I was impressed. Gary was even good-looking in a bland sort of way, but he kissed me with his lips tightly pressed together. I think Gary probably ended up marrying a native woman from wherever he may have gone to preach the Gospel according to Paul. She probably believes that all white men pray to God for transportation and kiss with their mouths closed. But it was Ted's mouth, his whole beautiful self that concerned me in those days. I knew my father would say no to our date, but I planned to run away from home if necessary. I told my mother how important this date was. I cajoled and pleaded with her from Sunday to Wednesday. She listened to my arguments, and must have heard the note of desperation in my voice. She said very gently to me: "You better be ready for disappointment." I did not ask what she meant. I did not want her fears for me to taint my happiness. I asked her to tell my father about my date. Thursday at breakfast my father looked at me across the table with his eyebrows together. My mother looked at him with her mouth set in a straight line. I looked down at my bowl of cereal. Nobody said anything. Friday I tried on every dress in my closet. Ted would be picking me up at six on Saturday: dinner and then the sock hop at school. Friday night I was in my room doing my nails or something else in preparation for Saturday (I know I groomed myself nonstop all week) when the telephone rang. I ran to get it. It was Ted. His voiced sounded funny when he said my name, so funny that I felt compelled to ask: "Is something wrong?" Ted blurted it all out without a preamble. His father had asked who he was going out with. Ted had told him my name. "Ortiz?

That's Spanish, isn't it?" the father had asked. Ted had told him yes, then shown him my picture in the yearbook. Ted's father had shaken his head. No. Ted would not be taking me out. Ted's father had known Puerto Ricans in the army. He had lived in New York City while studying architecture and had seen how the *spics* lived. Like rats. Ted repeated his father's words to me as if I should understand *his predicament* when I heard why he was breaking our date. I don't remember what I said before hanging up. I do recall the darkness of my room that sleepless night, and the heaviness of my blanket in which I wrapped myself like a shroud. And I remember my parents' respect for my pain and their gentleness toward me that weekend. My mother did not say "I warned you," and I was grateful for her understanding silence.

In college, I suddenly became an "exotic" woman to the men who had survived the popularity wars in high school, who were now practicing to be worldly: They had to act liberal in their politics, in their lifestyles, and in the women they went out with. I dated heavily for a while, then married young. I had discovered that I needed stability more than social life. I had brains for sure, and some talent in writing. These facts were a constant in my life. My skin color, my size, and my appearance were variables—things that were judged according to my current self-image, the aesthetic values of the times, the places I was in, and the people I met. My studies, later my writing, the respect of people who saw me as an individual person they cared about, these were the criteria for my sense of self-worth that I would concentrate on in my adult life.

◆◆◆

EIGHTEEN

My Body Is a Map of My Life

Lani Ka'ahumanu

There is a ritual I do when I remove my clothes with someone whether it's to sunbathe, sauna, massage, or to make love.

I tell the stories of my scars.

Besides the pearly stretch marks that texture my arms, legs, breasts and belly from two pregnancies and a weight gain there are scars: a flat wide 7 inch gall bladder scar running along my right rib line, a thin peniculectomy scar line from hip to hip and one around my belly button.

MY BODY IS A MAP OF MY LIFE
A PATCHWORK QUILT
THAT IS WARM AND SOFT AND STRONG.

I didn't always appreciate my body. I used to be ashamed and embarrassed. I had a difficult time baring myself with or even without other people around. I would avoid looking at myself, I mean really looking beyond the self-hate, beyond the media image that I should be, that

I could be if only . . . There was no real sense other than I wasn't good enough. I was constantly comparing myself with others. The more I denied this closet character the more control it had over my life. It was a drag. I wanted to be free; so I practiced. I practiced being nude dancing, walking, sitting, laying, playing all while looking in the mirror at myself from every possible angle.

It wasn't easy but as the months and years passed I became more comfortable and accepting. You could even say I developed a nonchalant attitude when in the nude. I began to feel at home in my body and in the growing sense of well-being SCAR WOMAN emerged from the closet. All imperfections exposed, I claimed the unique, distinctive markings, making them perfect in the showing.

MY BODY IS A MAP OF MY LIFE
A PATCHWORK QUILT
THAT IS WARM AND SOFT AND STRONG.

◆◆◆

NINETEEN

I Am Not One of the*

Cheryl Marie Wade

I am not one of the physically challenged—

I'm a sock in the eye with gnarled fist
I'm a French kiss with cleft tongue
I'm orthopedic shoes sewn on a last of your fears

I am not one of the differently abled—

I'm an epitaph for a million imperfect babies left
    untreated
I'm an ikon carved from bones in a mass grave at
    Tiergarten, Germany
I'm withered legs hidden with a blanket

I am not one of the able disabled—

I'm a black panther with green eyes and scars like
    a picket fence
I'm pink lace panties teasing a stub of milk white
    thigh
I'm the Evil Eye

I'm the first cell divided
I'm mud that talks
I'm Eve   I'm Kali
I'm The Mountain That Never Moves
I've been forever   I'll be here forever
I'm the Gimp
I'm the Cripple
I'm the Crazy Lady

I'm The Woman With Juice

---

*This poem is dedicated "to all my disabled sisters, to the activists in the streets and on the stages, to the millions of Sharon Kowalskis without a Karen Thompson, to all my sisters and brothers in the pits, closets, and institutions of enlightened societies everywhere."

◆◆◆

What's a Leg Got to Do with It?

Donna Walton

What's a leg got to do with it? Exactly what I thought when, during a heated conversation, a female rival told me I was less than a woman because I have one leg.

Excuse me. Perhaps I missed something. How could she make such an insensitive comment about something she had no experience with? Was she some expert on disabilities or something? Was she, too, disabled? Had she—like me—fought a battle with cancer that cost her a limb? For a split second, my thoughts were paralyzed by her insensitivity. But, like a defeated fighter who returns to the ring to regain victory, I bounced back for a verbal round with Ms. Thang.

I am woman first, an amputee second and physically challenged last. And it is in that order that I set out to educate and testify to people like Ms. Thang who are unable to discern who I am—feisty, unequivocally attractive African-American woman with a gimpy gait who can strut proudly into any room and engage in intelligent conversation with folks anxious to feed off my sincere aura.

It is rather comical and equally disturbing how folks—both men and women—view me as a disabled woman, particularly when it comes to sexuality. They have so many misconceptions. Straight women, for example, want to know how I catch a man, while most men are entertained with the idea that because I have one leg sex with me must be a blast.

I have even been confronted by folks who give me the impression that they think having sex is a painful experience for me. Again, I say, What's a leg got to do with it?

For all of those who want to inquire about my sexual prowess but dare not to, or for those who are curious about how I maintain such positive self-esteem when life dealt me the proverbial "bad hand," this story is for you. But those who have a tough time dealing with reality probably should skip the next paragraph because what I am about to confess is the gospel truth.

I like sex! I am very sexual!! I even consider myself sexy, residual limb and all. You see, I was a sexual being before my leg was amputated 19 years ago. My attitude didn't change about sex. I just had to adjust to the attitudes of others.

For example, I remember a brother who I dated in high school—before my leg was amputated—then dated again five years later. The dating ended abruptly because I realized that the brother could not fathom the one-leg thing. When he and I were home alone, he was cool as long as we got hot and bothered with my prosthesis on. However, whenever I tried to take off my artificial leg for comfort purposes, he immediately panicked. He could not fathom seeing me with one leg.

I tried to put him at ease by telling him Eva's story from Toni Morrison's novel *Sula*—that "my leg just got tired and walked off one day." But this brother just could not deal. He booked.

On the other hand, my experiences with lesbians have varied; they don't all book right away, but some have booked. Not all are upfront with their feelings 'cuz women are socialized to be courteous, emotional, and indirect, sparing one's feelings. Instead, some tend to communicate their discomfort with my missing limb in more subtle ways. For example, one lesbian I dated did not want to take me out to bars, clubs and other social settings. My lopsided gait was an embarrassment, and the fact that I use a cane garnered unwanted attention for her. Behind closed doors, she did not have any problems with it. How we would be perceived by trendy lesbians was her main concern.

Conversely, I have had positive experiences with lesbians as well. For instance, I have dated and been in love with women who have been affirming and supportive while respecting my difference. My wholeness has been shaped by all of these experiences. Without hesitation, I can now take off my prosthesis, be comfortable hopping around on one-leg and the sex . . . . is still a blast.

How does a woman with one leg maintain such a positive self-esteem in a society where people with disabilities are not valued? Simply by believing in myself. I know you're saying, "That sounds much too hokey." But as I said earlier, this is the gospel truth.

I was 19 years old when my leg was amputated. I was diagnosed with osteogenic sarcoma, bone cancer. During the first five years after my surgery, concentrating on other folks' perceptions of me was the least of my concerns. I was too focused on beating the odds against dying. You see, I was given only a 15% chance of survival—with spiritual guidance and support from my family—I had made the very difficult decision to stop taking my chemotherapy treatments. Doctors predicted that, by halting the dreadful chemotherapy, I was writing my own death certificate. However, through what I believe was divine healing, my cancer was eradicated.

Before this cancerous ordeal, I was not strong spiritually, and my faith was rocked when my leg was amputated because I thought I was to keep my leg. At the time, I could not see past the physical. After my amputation, I was preoccupied with the kinds of crippling thoughts that all the Ms. Thangs of the world are socialized to believe: that I was not going to be able to wear shorts, bathing suits or lingerie; that my womanness was somehow compromised by the loss of a limb.

If you have a disability and are in need of some fuel for your spirit, check out any novel by Toni Morrison (*Sula* is my favorite because of the one-legged grandmother, Eva) or Khalil Gibran's "The Prophet." These resources helped me build self-esteem and deal with my reality.

Ultimately, building positive esteem is an ongoing process. To that end, I am currently producing a motivational video that will outline coping strategies for female amputees.

No matter what your disability or circumstance, you cannot give in to a defeatist attitude. When you do, your battle is lost. There is a way of fighting back. It is called self-esteem.

Believe in yourself, and you will survive—and thrive.

◆◆◆

TWENTY-ONE

Tangled Lives
Daughters, Mothers, and the Crucible of Aging*

Lillian B. Rubin

I feel as if the last two years have been a rehearsal, as if all the anticipatory angst was necessary to, as we say in the trade, work through my mother's death and my ascent to the head of the generational line. After seventy-five years of living and thirty as a therapist, I'm still awed by the inner workings of the mind, by the way our unconscious can lead the way, if we'll only listen. I know, of course, that those same unconscious forces can send us down the path of pain and despair, which is why it's so important to get on speaking terms with them.

It's two weeks since my birthday party, and I'm surprised that, as seventy-five settles in on me, I find myself largely untroubled by it. It's as if the years of wrestling with my fears and feelings, of chewing on them, spitting them out, and swallowing them again, allowed me to digest the reality without the emotional bellyache it gave me before. The old crone of my dreams, her transformation from a witch to a woman I can recognize and relate to, remains a recurrent image, a companion in my day life who is also an eloquent reminder of both my fears and their resolution. . . .

I worry sometimes that this calm inside me is little more than the afterglow of feeling so loved and affirmed by friends and family, that I'll wake up tomorrow or the next day and be back in the struggle. But I don't really think so. It isn't that I believe that this is the end of my contest with getting old. But however that conflict makes itself felt from here on, it will be different because something has shifted inside me and, in some fundamental way, I'm actually glad to be where I am.

Glad to be old? Images of my mother in the last few years of her life rise unbidden to my mind. That's old age, not this—not me with my vibrant,

energetic life, with my body that shows the results of years of pushing weights around, with work I love and another lifetime of experiences yet to be lived. It saddens me when I compare my old age to my mother's. Long before she reached seventy-five, she not only looked old, she was old, and her life had been emptied of meaning. She had nothing to do, nowhere to go, no one to count on, not even her children in whom she felt little but the bitter taste of disappointment. She spent the next twenty years waiting for death—wanting it, fearing it, calling upon God to take her to him, while also resisting it with every fiber of her being. . . .

I know the downside of aging very well—too well some might say, since that knowledge has, perhaps, made these last years harder than they had to be. Still, it's not just the private angst but the public stigma that makes getting old in America so hard. A fifty-five-year-old man I know, who recently lost his executive job in one of those corporate mergers that are so common today, was smarting over his inability to find an equivalent one. "I sometimes wonder if there's any place in this society for wisdom. I'm a lot smarter today than I was twenty years ago, and I think I'm better at my job now than I was then. But these yo-yo kids who are in charge don't even see me and what I can do; they only see my age, and that's the end of it." A plight common enough to warrant a *New Yorker* cartoon featuring a cigar-smoking, bewildered-looking sixtyish man saying ruefully, "I think I've acquired some wisdom over the years, but there doesn't seem to be much demand for it."

I think about the meaning of those words, about what it will mean in my life when this book is published and I've announced to the world that I'm an old woman. Will my patients see me differently? Will I suddenly become irrelevant, relegated to the nether world of the aged where, like the man in the *New Yorker* cartoon, there will be no demand for my words, my thoughts, my lifetime of accumulated experience and wisdom?

---

*This excerpt is from the last chapter of Lillian Rubin's book with this title.

I talk with my friend Riese about my anxieties. "If I publish this book, I'm afraid people who respected me, even sought me out before, will suddenly see me as just another old woman."

She's silent, her dark eyes fixed intently on my face. I can almost hear her internal struggle as she looks for the words to reply honestly. Before she can speak, my anger takes over. "It's an outrage that I should even have to worry about this; that's just the point of the whole drama of aging in this culture, isn't it?"

"That's just what I was thinking," she says. "It is an outrage, and it's also true that you have to be prepared for a range of reactions. This business of aging and the vulnerability that goes with it doesn't lie easily with us, and I expect what you say and how you say it will make some people very uncomfortable. And you know very well that when you puncture their denial, people tend to want to kill the messenger."

"So maybe I shouldn't publish the damn book. Maybe I don't need to open that door and take whatever I'll find on the other side."

She smiles. "That's a lot of maybes, but we both know you'll do it because that's who you are, young or old."

I'm reminded of this conversation a few days later when I'm . . . listening to a National Public Radio (NPR) interview with the author of a book about the aged in America entitled *Another Country*—a title that suggests the depth of isolation, alienation, and fear that afflicts the old of our nation. It's an interesting book, moving and eloquent in its examination of the dilemmas of old age, not just for the old but for the younger generations as well. But when she talks on the air about the social stigma of aging, the best the author can offer is to say that "we need a new language of aging" and suggests, as an example, that we replace words like *old, aged,* and *elderly* with the world *elder.*

I understand her point. *Elder* in some cultures is a term of respect, an honorific, an implicit bow to the wisdom embodied in years of living. But among those people, it's not the word alone that confers this special status. It's the cultural context within which the word is spoken, the meaning it carries in the society, which, in turn, is related to the role and function the elders fulfill in group life. Among other things, the old in these societies are the carriers of culture and the bearers of their social history. Without them, group life would be immeasurably impoverished and the past would fade out of human memory.

Can we say anything comparable about the elders of our nation? The problem, it seems to me, is not the language but the reality that we live in a society where the old, like the very young, have no social role, no function that adds value to the life of the group. But the young are our future; whatever burden they present carries within it a promise. The old, however, are our past. And in a society that changes as fast as ours does, where the commonplace of twenty years ago now seems like ancient history, where real historical memory hardly exists, we have little use for the past and those who lived it.

In such a society, changing the word *aged* to *elder* would have as much meaning as it did when we changed *old* to *senior*—a change in the language that has done nothing to ameliorate the stigma of old age. Indeed, nothing will until we are ready to change our deep-seated cultural abhorrence for the aged, which means, among other things, coming to accept our own aging and with it the old people who live among us.

Given the reciprocal and reinforcing interactions between my internal struggles and our national aversion to the aged, it's not a surprise that I've never before been able to glimpse the upside of this stage of life—the sense of accomplishment; the realization that I have nothing more to prove, that I can live as I please and see whom I like; the belief that, in some important ways, I've gained some wisdom; the triumph I feel sometimes when I can stand back and see who I am and what I look like to the world outside; and not least, the inner peace that comes from knowing that I've earned my place in the world and with it, freedom from pressure I've never known before—not just the external pressures but the internal ones that, in the final analysis, are more oppressive and compelling than anything from the outside.

The limitations of time that I confront almost daily remain hard. It's still not the finiteness of my own time that occupies me but the knowledge that there's so little of it left with Hank, or at least with the man I've known and loved for so many wonderful and important years. Not that I think he's going to die soon, but I see the slight mental slippages that I fear signal the beginning of cognitive disarray, which pains me deeply and, in some ways, is worse than contemplating his death. So when friends ask whether we'd like to join them in some plan for next year—whether season tickets to the ballet, a concert series, or a trip abroad—my mind immediately goes to *if*: *if* we're still healthy, *if* we're still around, *if* . . .

It helps that we can talk about all of this, sometimes seriously, often with the kind of ironic, tragicomic humor that's so central to our way of managing the difficulties of living through this stage of our lives. But there's also genuine mirth and joy as we revel in each other and contemplate the sometimes absurd comedy we call *life.*

I know the vision I've presented of getting old is at odds with the sugary one that has become popular in the literature lately. The stories about the seventy-five-year-old woman who runs the Boston marathon in respectable time, the eighty-four-year-old man who plays a hard game of tennis every day, the seventy-year-old woman who's learning to ski, the eighty-one-year-old man who climbs the sheer face of El Capitan in Yosemite, the hundred-and-two-year-old woman who graduates from high school with a 4.0 grade point, the ninety-year-old man who still has an eye for the women and the wherewithal to do something about it—all these are wonderfully inspiring. But how many of us can aspire to such achievements? How many of us want to?

This isn't to say that these remarkable feats aren't an important part of the modern aging narrative. As we continue to live longer, healthier lives more of us will find physical and mental capacities unknown in the elders of earlier times. Meanwhile, just knowing such people exist is helpful, since they provide models of the possible, not just for those of us who are already old but, more important, for our children who are not far behind.

The other side of these rah-rah efforts to cheer ourselves up, however, is that they set us up for false expectations that can leave us more depressed than facing the truth in all its complexity. Betty Friedan's insistence in *The Fountain of Age* that getting old is just a state of mind—that the seventies and eighties are a breeze so long as we find the secret to what she calls *vital aging*—is a lovely but unreal fantasy. And William Regelson's *The Superhormone Promise*, which declares that aging is "not a normal life event but a disease," is surely the ultimate denial.

Certainly, if we can find the key to living vital, engaged, and productive lives into old age these years will be easier. But until this life stage, that engagement has been found in the expectations and institutions by which our lives were bound—family, school, work. When our schooling is done, our families no longer need us, and the world of work closes its doors, whether at our instigation or theirs, then what? Without the institutions to give shape and meaning to our daily lives, we're set adrift into uncharted territory. True, some people find their way. They go to school, they climb mountains, they volunteer for much needed public service. But this, by and large, is a gift of the privileged—those of us who have the good health and the financial resources to make such a life possible.

For all of us, however—whether rich or poor, healthy or infirm—getting old is fraught with inescapable irony. At the very moment when we have time, we're intensely aware of how little of it is left. At the very time when we feel wise, few want to hear what we have to say. At the very season when we're ready to fly, we're hobbled by a body that keeps us grounded.

Faced with these contradictory realities, we're forced to reorder our image of ourselves, a redefinition of self and life that infuses these years with the sadness that comes with loss. And that's another inalienable fact: Old age, whatever else we may say about its positives and negatives, inescapably confronts us with a keen sense of loss—the loss of roles, of friends and loved ones, of the structure and clarity of our lives until now, of the physical capabilities that just yesterday we took for granted.

It may be momentarily comforting to some people to read that the lumps, bumps, thinning hair, waning strength, and memory lapses that come with age don't count, that the assault to the self that accompanies these changes is just vanity, an unnecessary product of our narcissism. But the reassurance is fleeting, and the comfort slips away quickly when we come up against our waning powers. Not just the serious ones, but the small daily reminders that we can no longer count on our bodies to do what we ask of them.

Personally, when I hear the cheery platitudes about the joys of getting old I want to shout: "Oh yeah! Tell it to my brain when it has trouble getting perfectly ordinary words to my tongue. Or to my body when it huffs and puffs up a hill it climbed easily just a couple of years ago. Or to my drooping belly that no longer responds to the crunches that used to keep it in shape."

When I stare these truths in the face, it's hard sometimes not to think, "Okay, so even if seventy-five is fine, seventy-six is coming, and seventy-seven, and seventy-eight, and . . . As inevitably as the sun will rise, the day will come when there's nothing but decline and death left."

That's true, of course, but it's not the whole truth.

Then I remember that this is what I thought when seventy-five was still on the horizon and that now that I'm actually living it the fears have faded before the reality of a life that's no different than it was before, except that each day seems more precious to me now. Which may mean only that this is the central dilemma of this time of life—an intense appreciation of the moment that lives side by side with the knowledge that it's fleeting, a paradox that brings a sharp poignancy to the beauty and pain in every experience, along with a wish to hold on, while knowing we have no choice but to let go. It's not an easy lesson to learn, but it's the one we need if we're to make our way relatively peacefully through the tangle of sorrow and joy that old age brings.

4

◆◆◆

Women's Sexuality

The body is the place where biological sex, socially constructed gender, and sexuality come together. Sexual attitudes and behaviors vary considerably from society to society and across historical time periods (Caplan 1987; Lancaster and di Leonardo 1997). Sexuality is not instinctive but learned from our families, our peers, sex education in school, popular culture, negotiations with partners, and listening to our own bodies. Much is learned from what is not said as well as what is made explicit. In this society, sexuality is a source of intimacy and pleasure, vulnerability and danger. Over the course of our lives, women's sexuality may take different forms and take on different degrees of significance. There is a heavy emphasis on sexuality in advertising, news reporting, and popular culture. At the same time, there is a dearth of accurate information about women's sexuality, and there are many constraints on it. To explore your sexuality, ideally you need a comfortable, safe place and freedom from worries about being attractive, getting pregnant, or getting sexually transmitted infections. You also need time, self-awareness, and a cooperative partner to discover what you want sex to be for you.

This chapter focuses on women's experiences of sexuality, the meso- and macro-level forces that shape these experiences, and the ways that women are defining sexuality for themselves. As you read this chapter, think also about the social construction of male sexuality.

Stereotypes, Contradictions, and Double Standards

In advertising images and popular culture, sexuality is the prerogative of the young, slender, and able-bodied. Many of these images portray White women. Melba Wilson (1993) notes that racism and sexism converge in mainstream stereotypes of women of color as "exotic creatures of passion" and "oversexed" (p. 66). Contemporary "pornographic images of black women show us as picturesque, removed from self and deserving of—even asking for—enslavement." She argues that this imagery is based in the historical abuse of Black women by White slave masters (p. 76). Asian and Asian American women are stereotyped as "Suzie Wong" or as "exotic flowers," passive, accommodating, and focused on serving men. The film *Slaying the Dragon* (1988; distributed by Women Make Movies) provides an excellent critique of this stereotype. In reality, older women, large women, and women with disabilities are also sexually active, as noted in the previous chapter (Doress and Siegal 1987). According to the late Barbara Waxman Fiduccia, an advocate for reproductive rights for people with disabilities, and Marsha Saxton, a teacher of disability studies, women with disabilities have been kept socially isolated and discouraged from expressing their sexuality. In their "Disability Feminism: A Manifesto" (1997), they write: "We want our sexuality accepted and supported with accurate information" (p. 60). Lillian Gonzales Brown, of the Institute on Disability Culture (Honolulu, Hawaii), notes the influence of the disability rights movement on changing attitudes for people with disabilities. There has been a shift from feeling shame, wanting to assimilate, to disability pride. In workshops on sexuality for women with disabilities, she urges participants to explore their sexuality and to see themselves as sexual beings (L. G. Brown, personal communication, October 1996).

Ads that use women's bodies to sell products also sell an idea of women's sexuality as passive and accommodating. As sex objects, women are commonly portrayed as child-like or doll-like playthings. These images flow from and reinforce macro-level patriarchal constructions of sexuality and gender based on the following assumptions: Heterosexuality is prescribed or natural for women and men, men are the initiators in heterosexual encounters, and men's sexuality is assumed to be assertive and in need of regular release. Women are expected to be modest and virtuous, to look beautiful, and, simultaneously, to lure men and to fend them off. Traditionally, a woman has been expected to remain a virgin until marriage, untouched except by her husband, and this attitude is still strong in many communities in the United States and around the world. Men's sexual activity is assumed and accepted; after all, "Boys will be boys." Sexually active women and girls are likely to be condemned as "sluts."

This fundamental contradiction between encouraging men's sexuality and expecting women to be chaste results in the construction of two categories of women: "good" women and "bad" women, virgins and whores—the women men marry and the women they fool around with. This double standard controls women's sexuality and autonomy, and serves to divide women from each other. This is significant at the micro, meso, and macro levels. Growing up in a Mexican American community, Sandra Cisneros (Reading 22) writes that *la Virgen de Guadalupe* was the model held up to girls. The boys "were fornicating like rabbits while the Church ignored them and pointed us women towards our destiny—marriage and motherhood. The other alternative was *puta*hood," being defined a whore. Writer and literature professor Gloria Wade-Gayles (1993) learned the same double standard, but women in her Memphis neighborhood also divided men into two categories: good men who care for their wives and families, and "dogs" who "only want one thing." This latter category included White men who cruised through the neighborhood "in search of black women who, they assumed, were naturally sensuous, sexually superior, and easy" (p. 84).

It is important to note that many girls and women experience sexual coercion and abuse—in childhood, as adults, or both. Some struggle for many years with the devastating effects of sexual abuse on their confidence, trust, sexuality, and sense of themselves in the world. In Reading 24, Aurora Levins Morales refers to her childhood experience of sexual abuse and her path toward reclaiming "the wounded erotic." At the core of that process, she writes, is "blazing and untarnished aliveness."

What Is Women's Autonomous Sexuality?

In the 1960s there was much talk of a sexual revolution in the United States, partly made possible by the availability of contraceptive pills for the first time. Women "on the pill" could be sexually active with men without the same fear of pregnancy as in the past. In practice, many feminists argued that this "revolution" was very much on men's terms (Segal 1994), although, since that time, there has been increasing discussion of women's own sexual needs and preferences (Boston Women's Health Book Collective 1998; Cox 1999; Drill, McDonald, and Odes 1999; Ehrenreich, Hess, and Jacobs 1986; Ensler 1998; hooks 1993; Muscio 1999). Women's health advocate Rebecca Chalker (1995) describes this process as a "real woman-friendly sexual revolution in progress" (p. 52). Women's magazines have provided one forum for this discourse, as well as women's erotica (Blank 2001; Bright 2000; Bruce 2001; Slugocki and Wilson 2000) and images of pop stars like Madonna, who revels in her sexuality in public. Eve Ensler, a playwright and screenwriter, has performed her Obie-winning show, *The Vagina Monologues,* in many parts of the country. She notes that, for many women, the word *vagina* is associated with shame, embarrassment, and silencing, even violation.

> And as more women say the word, saying it becomes less of a big deal; it becomes part of our language, part of our lives. Our vaginas become integrated and respected and sacred. They become part of our bodies, connected to our minds, fueling our spirits. And the shame leaves and the violation stops.
> *(Ensler 1998, p. xxiv)*

Starting in 1998, students, staff, and faculty from hundreds of U.S. colleges and universities have performed Ensler's script as part of the V-Day College Initiative, a nationwide project to celebrate women and to oppose sexual violence.

Women's sexual autonomy still has organized opponents. In 1998, for example, the state of Alabama passed a law that included a ban on the sale or distribution of vibrators and other "devices designed or marketed as primarily useful for the stimulation of human genital organs." In 1999, six women—two of them married—challenged it by filing suit (*Williams v. Pryor*). The court argued that Alabama does have "a legitimate interest in banning 'the commerce of sexual stimulation and auto-eroticism, for its own sake, unrelated to marriage, procreation, or familial relationships'" (Kaminer 2000). But the court ruled that the ban was "arbitrary and irrational, partly because it interfered with 'sexual stimulation and eroticism' in the approved context of marital relationships" (Kaminer 2000). This decision was overturned on appeal, and the ban upheld.

Traditional cultural limitations on women's sexuality and sexual expression can divide women in immigrant communities in the United States, as described by human rights activist Surina A. Khan (Reading 26) and by psychologist Shamita das Dasgupta and pediatrician Sayantani DasGupta (1996). Das Dasgupta and DasGupta write,

> As Asian women of two different generations, we attest to the politically divisive and psycho-logically unbearable situation in which we have been placed. As daughters, we are faced with the choice of rejecting our community and culture or destroying our sexual selves. As mothers, we can be exiled as destroyers of community culture or be our daughters' prison guards. *(p. 240)*

They understand the Asian Indian community's control of women's sexuality as an attempt to resist cultural erasure in the United States and as a response to the racism of this society, as well as a result of patriarchal control within their own community. They endorse Indian women's activism (against violence against women, and for gay, lesbian, and bisexual rights) as a way of creating a progressive South Asian space to "define our private selves as public and discover our collective power" (p. 241).

Shere Hite is one of the few popular U.S. researchers to conduct extensive surveys of men's and women's sexual experiences and preferences. The following questions, from one of her surveys, were written for women, but they are also relevant for men:

> Is sex important to you? What part does it play in your life?
>
> Who sets the pace and style of sex—you or your partner or both? Who decides when it's over?
>
> Do you think your genital area and vagina are ugly or beautiful!?
>
> If you are sexually active, do you ever fake orgasms? Why?
>
> What are your best sex experiences? What would you like to try that you never have?
>
> What is it about sex that gives you the greatest pleasure? Displeasure?
>
> Have you chosen to be celibate at any point? What was/is that like for you?
>
> In the best of all possible worlds, what would sexuality be like?
>
> Do you know as much as you'd like to know, about your own body? Orgasm? Conception and pregnancy? Safe sex?
>
> Do your partners know about your sexual desires and your body? If not, do you ask for it or act yourself to get it?
>
> *(Hite 1994, pp. 17–22)*

In the 1980s and '90s, feminists engaged in heated argument about women's sexuality and the possibility of genuine sexual agency (Jaggar 1994; Snitow, Stansell, and Thompson 1983; Vance 1984). Philosopher Marilyn Frye (1992) notes that "the word 'virgin' did not originally mean a woman whose vagina was untouched by any penis, but a free woman, one not betrothed, not married, not bound to, not possessed by any man. It meant a female who is sexually and hence socially her own person" (p. 133)—virtually an impossibility under patriarchy. Frye argues that radical feminist lesbians have created ways of living out this kind of virginity. Is this also possible for heterosexual women? As Frye puts it: "Can you fuck without losing your virginity?" (p. 136). She concludes that this is unlikely, but concedes it may be possible if women are willing to be wild and undomesticated—sexually, socially, and politically.

In Reading 23, Naomi Wolf notes that "all over the country, millions of feminists have a secret indulgence. By day they fight gender injustice; by night they sleep with men. . . . Is sleeping with a man, 'sleeping with the enemy'?" She resolves this question by advocating what she calls "radical heterosexuality." To achieve this, women would need financial independence, marriage would have to be very different, and both women and men would have to give up their "gender benefits." Psychologist Lynne Segal (1994) and sociologist Pepper Schwartz (1994) describe how some heterosexual couples are negotiating sex to make it more egalitarian. Schwartz notes that in U.S. culture there is a commonly held feeling that "male leadership and control is inherently erotic," that role differences between women and men and "the mystery of not knowing each other" make for a more exciting sex life (p. 70). Against this, she argues:

> Reducing difference can be sexy. Equitable treatment and role innovation can be exciting. . . . Hierarchy and domination are not essential for arousal. The natural ebb and flow of power in a relationship and the gulf between any two human beings that continually needs bridging gives enough natural tension and interest for peer sexuality to include passion.
>
> *(pp. 77–78)*

But only some men, Schwartz writes, "perhaps those with strong mothers, or with a great respect for competence and intelligence, find equality compelling and sexy" (p. 78). And not all women "refuse to be an instrument in male orchestration" (p. 78). She comments that passion is a Western ideal for marriage, although research shows that passion decreases over the length of a relationship. A long-term **peer marriage,** which is intentionally egalitarian, she notes, may be better at providing romance and respect than providing passion—unless, presumably, the notion of passion is reconstructed.

Challenging Binaries

Our society constructs sex in strictly binary terms: female or male. Geneticist and professor of biology Anne Fausto-Sterling (1993) shows how intersexual people challenge these categories in a fundamental way. Their social, surgical, and hormonal treatment—which makes them a specific gender and pressures them to stick with it—shows how important this dichotomy is. Sexuality, too, has been defined in binary terms. According to Jonathan Katz (1995), a historian of sexuality, the concept of heterosexuality developed in parallel with the concept of homosexuality, and both date from the end of the nineteenth century. The word *heterosexuality* was first used in the 1890s, an obscure medical term applied to non-procreative sex—that is, sex for pleasure. At the time, this was considered a deviant idea, showing "abnormal or perverted appetite toward the opposite sex" (p. 86). Webster's dictionary did not include the word *heterosexuality* until 1934, and it gradually came into common usage in the United States as a "stable sign of normal sex" (p. 40).

Lesbians and gay men have long challenged the legitimacy and "normalcy" of heterosexuality (Allen 1986; Boswell 1994; Cavin 1985; Duberman, Vicinus, and Chauncey 1989; Faderman 1981; Grahn 1984; History Project 1998). Bisexual people have argued for greater fluidity in sexual desire and behaviors, what Kathleen Bennett (1992) calls "a both/and option for an either/or world" (see also Hutchins and Kaahumanu 1991; Storr 1999; Weise 1992). Lisa Orlando (1991) notes that stereotypes about bisexuality have grown out of the fact that bisexuals are poised between what "appear as two mutually exclusive sexual cultures" and from a common assumption "that homosexual and heterosexual desires exclude each other." Eridani (1992) argues that many women are probably bisexual and do not fit into a gay/straight categorization. She suggests that sexual orientation, meaning a "deeply rooted sense . . . that serious relationships are possible only with persons of the opposite sex or the same sex" (p. 174), is itself a masculinist perspective. In Reading 25, the late June Jordan writes "bisexuality invalidates either/or formulation," and urges bisexuality and sexual freedom as part of a wider struggle for freedom and justice. Riki Anne Wilchins (1997) notes the limited notion of the erotic entailed in hetero-homo dualism: "an entire Geography of the Absent—body parts that aren't named, acts one mustn't do, genders one can't perform—because they are outside the binary box" (p. 167).

Those who refuse to tailor their looks and actions to conventional categories—for example, butch lesbians, cross-dressers, drag queens, and queers, described by socialist activist Leslie Feinberg (1996) as "transgender warriors"—are involved in something

profoundly challenging and transgressive. Drag, for example, has a long history in Euro-American culture (Bullough and Bullough 1993; Ekins 1997; Garber 1992; Lorber 1994). It plays with the idea of appearance as an illusion; mimics and parodies conventions; and raises questions as to who the person really is in terms of both outside appearance and inner identity. During the 1980s and '90s, younger people reclaimed the word *queer,* which for many older lesbians and gay men was a hateful and oppressive term (Bernstein and Silberman 1996). This is a broader definition of queerness, with an emphasis on experimentation and playfulness, and includes all who challenge heteronormativity (Gage, Richards, and Wilmot 2002).

Writing about transgender politics, Leslie Feinberg describes herself:

> I am a human being who unnerves some people. As they look at me, they see a kaleidoscope of characteristics they associate with both males and females. I appear to be a tangled knot of gender contradictions. . . . I'm a female who is more masculine than those prominently portrayed in mass culture . . . . My life only comes into focus when the word *transgender* is added to the equation.
>
> *(Reading 27)*

Leslie Feinberg (1998) and Kate Bornstein (1995, 1998) point out that transgender people are creating a broader space for everyone to express their gender and their sexuality. Philosopher and queer theorist Judith Butler (1990) considers "the binary framework for both sex and gender" to be "regulatory fictions" that consolidate and naturalize the power of masculine and heterosexist oppression (p. 33). Her conception of gender as performative allows and requires us to think of gender and sexuality more fluidly than rigid categories permit. It also opens the possibility that, under less repressive circumstances, people would have a much wider repertoire of behaviors than most currently do. At the same time, Butler notes that people "who fail to do their gender right" by standards held to be appropriate in specific contexts and at particular times, may be punished for it, through name calling, discrimination, hate, and outright violence (p. 140).

Writer Phyllis Burke (1996) argues that transsexuals who choose sexual reassignment surgery both challenge binary gender categories and reinforce them. Sociologist Judith Lorber (1994) notes that "it is Western culture's preoccupation with genitalia as the markers of both sexuality and gender and the concept of these social statuses as fixed for life that produces the problem and the surgical solution for those who cannot tolerate the personal ambiguities Western cultures deny" (p. 86). Transsexuals do not change their sex completely. Their chromosomes remain the same, and they rely on hormone treatments to alter their body shape, hair distribution, and the development of secondary sex characteristics like breasts or beards. Women-to-men transsexuals, for example, do not produce sperm. Lorber argues that they change *gender,* and have to construct a new gender identity, but that they do not disrupt "the deep genderedness of the modern Western world" (p. 96). Whether transgenderism as a movement can deal with structural inequalities of power between men and women raises the question of how personal freedoms, played out through the construction of sexuality and the body, are connected to other political issues and other progressive groups in society, as discussed by June Jordan (Reading 25). Two spokespeople for this movement, Leslie Feinberg (1998) and Riki Anne Wilchins (1997), are making those connections.

Theorizing Sexuality

In *The Second Sex,* Simone de Beauvoir (1973) argued that gender is neither biological nor natural but learned. She concluded that one is not born a woman, but, rather, becomes one. In dominant ideology, woman is the Other to the male Self. De Beauvoir's work has been highly influential in shaping later feminist formulations of gender and sexuality. In addition, "Four linked political and intellectual movements—the sexual revolution, feminism, gay liberation, and the civil rights/race-minority power—have altered common perceptions of proper women's and men's lives, of sexual behavior" (Lancaster and di Leonardo 1997, p. 1). Feminists were critical of the so-called 1960s sexual revolution, mainly on male terms as mentioned earlier, and began to "discuss sexual and bodily matters with a new, unladylike frankness" (p. 2). Medical anthropologist Carole Vance (1984) sums up the contradictions of sexuality for women:

> Sexuality is simultaneously a domain of restriction, repression, and danger as well as a domain of exploration, pleasure, and agency. To focus only on pleasure and gratification ignores the patriarchal structure in which women act, yet to speak only of sexual violence and oppression ignores women's experience with sexual agency and choice and unwittingly increases the sexual terror and despair in which women live. *(p. 1)*

In her now classic essay, award-winning poet and writer Adrienne Rich (1986a) discusses how social institutions like law, religion, philosophy, official kinship, and popular culture support what she terms compulsory heterosexuality. She argues that patriarchy *demands* heterosexuality to keep women serving masculinist interests. For Rich, what needs to be explained is not why women identify as lesbians, but how and why so many women are heterosexual, since, typically, we first experience the intimacy of emotional caring and physical nurture with women—our mothers. In many cultural settings, women and girls spend time together, care for and depend on one another, and enjoy each other's friendship—often passionately. Why would women ever redirect that search? Rich asks. As you read this chapter, consider Rich's question: What are "the societal forces which wrench women's emotional and erotic energies away from themselves and other women and from human-identified values" (p. 35), which teach us systematically to see men as appropriate partners?

Many feminists have focused on sexual violence—both theoretically and through active participation in rape crisis centers and shelters for battered women—and understand that sexuality can be a source of profound vulnerability for women. Anti-rape activist writer Andrea Dworkin (1987), for example, argues that intercourse is inherently repressive for women, partly for anatomical reasons, but more because of unequal power relations between women and men. As a way of repudiating the eroticization of inequality, some feminists have argued that women's sexuality should be based on sexual acts that are safe, loving, and intimate, in the context of a caring, monogamous relationship. Others have seen this as a new—feminist—restriction on women's freedom of expression (Duggan and Hunter 1995; Jaggar 1994; Leidholdt and Raymond 1990).

Sociologist Steven Seidman (1992) characterizes this polarization in terms of sexual romanticism on the one hand and sexual **libertarianism** on the other. Carole Vance (1984) compiled papers presented at the Scholar and the Feminist IX Conference, "Towards a Politics of Sexuality," which was held in New York City, April 1982, and intended to advance feminist understandings of sexuality. Gayle Rubin (1984) noted two strains of feminist thought concerning sexuality: one criticizing "restrictions on women's sexual behavior," denouncing "the high costs imposed on women for being sexually active," and calling for "a sexual liberation that would work for women as well as for men"; the other considering "sexual liberation to be inherently a mere extension of male privilege" and full of "conservative, anti-sexual discourse" (p. 301). Critics of the conference argued that some of the presenters were antifeminist and should not have been invited to participate, and that prostitution and other forms of sex work, pornography, and **S/M** are inherently violent to women, never to be accepted by feminists.

After the Stonewall Riots (New York) in 1969, a gay rights movement flourished, drawing on feminist ideas as well as "strands of sex research that did not treat homosexuality as pathological, and on an urban gay subculture that had been expanding since the end of World War II" (Lancaster and di Leonardo 1997, p. 3).

> With varying degrees of success and through struggles that continue today, gay and lesbian activists have publicly championed all that is positive, pleasurable and creative in same-sex desire while opposing the obvious sources of antigay oppression: police harassment, social stigma, religious bigotry, psychiatric persecution, and sodomy laws. In the process, these concrete struggles have revealed the less obvious heteronormative premises deeply embedded in law, science, philosophy, official kinship, and vernacular culture.
>
> *(Lancaster and di Leonardo 1997, p. 3).*

This gay and lesbian activism, together with gay men's theorizing and feminist theorizing about sexuality as exemplified in Rubin's approach, mentioned earlier, led to the development of queer theory and queer studies (Alcoff 1988; Fuss 1991; Stein 1997), which take sexuality as the main category of analysis. Queer theorist Eve Sedgwick's (1990) Axiom #2 states: "The study of sexuality is not coextensive with the study of gender; correspondingly, antihomophobic inquiry is not coextensive with feminist inquiry" (p. 27). Though not identical, feminism and antihomophobic work often overlap, as exemplified in writer and activist Suzanne Pharr's (1988) analysis of homophobia as a weapon of sexism and her comment that "as long as the word lesbian can strike fear in any woman's heart, then work on behalf of women can be stopped; the only successful work against sexism must include work against homophobia" (p. 26). Note the unfortunate use of the term *homophobia*, meaning fear of homosexuals, rather than *heterosexism*. This latter term refers to the system of heterosexuality as a place of institutional privilege, parallel to systems of inequality based on race (racism) or gender (sexism).

Lisa Orlando (1991) comments: "I don't think anyone knows what desire is, where it comes from, or why it takes the general and specific form it does." She hypothesizes that it involves "some kind of interaction between a more or less shapeless biological 'drive' and a combination of individual experiences and larger social forces." She notes that the very notion of sexual identity is specific to our culture and time in history.

Economic changes such as industrialization, the development of the factory system, and the spread of wage labor had a profound impact on family life. Gradually, families stopped producing the goods they needed and supported themselves through wage labor. Children, who had been an economic advantage to their families by contributing to household production, became a liability and an expense. The U.S. birthrate dropped dramatically during the twentieth century as a result. Further, developments like the contraceptive pill, alternative insemination, in vitro fertilization, and other reproductive technologies have made possible the separation of intercourse and procreation. Heterosexual women can be sexually active without becoming pregnant, and lesbians as well as heterosexual women can become pregnant without having intercourse. Historian John D'Emilio (1984) argues that these trends create conditions "that allow some men and women to organize a personal life around their erotic/emotional attraction to their own sex" (p. 104). They have "made possible the formation of urban communities of lesbians and gay men, and more recently, of a politics based on a sexual identity" (p. 104). On this

analysis, sexual identity has a basis in macro-level circumstances rather than personal factors (D'Emilio and Freedman 1997), although cultural acceptance of lesbians and gay men does not always follow economic possibilities, in White communities or communities of color (Anzaldúa 1987; Eng and Hom 1998; Smith 1998; Trujillo 1991). D'Emilio (1984) accepts that there have been same-sex partnerships for generations, as claimed by Adrienne Rich (1986a) and many other authors and researchers cited above. He complicates this claim, however, by differentiating homosexual *behavior* from homosexual *identity*, and argues that only under certain economic conditions are homosexual identity and community possible. Clare Hemmings (2002) notes that such communities both generate and require supportive locations to survive and flourish, in her discussion of Northampton (Mass.) and San Francisco as cities that support gay, lesbian, and bisexual communities.

This links to the experience of Surina A. Khan (Reading 26), a Pakistani American woman who struggled to reconcile the various parts of her iden-

tity. Despite the fact that images of same-sex couples have been part of the history of South Asia for hundreds of years, she notes that most people from South Asia do not have words for homosexuality and regard it as a Western phenomenon. This apparent paradox is exactly what D'Emilio's distinction between behavior and identity helps to explain. Further, it may be useful to think of four distinctive categories: inclination, behavior, identity, and politics. One may have sexual inclinations but may decide not to act on them. One may engage in certain sexual behaviors but not adopt a bisexual or gay identity, for example. One may identify as a lesbian or transgendered woman but not act on that identity in a political way.

Several recent publications on sexuality focus on the complexities and contradictions of pleasure and desire (e.g., Johnson 2002; Phillips 2000). In *Jane Sexes It Up: True Confessions of Feminist Desire* (Johnson 2002), for example, twenty third-wave feminists reopen debates about sexual autonomy in their discussions of sexual experiences that include sex work, self-mutilation, masturbation, and using porn. Writer and activist Eli Clare's memoir (1999) brings together her experiences as a queer, feminist, and disability rights activist, and theorizes intersections among these perspectives.

The Erotic as Power

The issue of sexuality is part of our wider concern with security in the sense that sexuality can be a source of restriction and vulnerability—hence insecurity—for women. This is true for women whose sexual activities and identities fit patriarchal norms and expectations, and also for those who challenge or repudiate them. Like beauty—however it is defined—sexuality can be a source of power, affirmation, and self-definition for women. Many women are exploring their sexuality, claiming the right to sexual pleasure on their own terms, and challenging the limitations of conventional expressions of sexuality. Sexuality is a key element in personal relationships, of course, and we explore this in Chapter 7, focused on relationships and families.

Black lesbian poet and activist Audre Lorde discusses the power of the erotic in the broadest way (Reading 28). She sees the erotic as "our most profoundly creative source." She notes that women have been "taught to separate the erotic . . . from most vital areas of our lives other than sex." By contrast, she writes: "When I speak of the erotic . . . I speak of it as an assertion of the life-force of women: of that creative energy empowered, the knowledge and use of which we are now reclaiming in our language, our history, our dancing, our loving, our work, our lives." Lorde sees the distortion and suppression of the erotic as one of the ways that women are oppressed, and concludes: "Recognizing the power of the erotic in our lives can give us the energy to pursue genuine change within our world."

Activism and Sexuality

Many informal networks, local groups, and national organizations support and advocate for lesbians, bisexual and transgendered women, and gay men, especially in urban areas. Some are primarily social groupings; others are support groups that provide information, encouragement, and social connections. Still others focus on particular issues like women's health, HIV/AIDS, parenting, community or police violence, religious bigotry, or the situation of gays in the military. Others run journals, magazines, newsletters, bookstores, presses, churches, bars, coffeehouses, bands, sports teams, and theater companies; support political candidates for local, state, or national office; oppose city and state ordinances designed to limit lesbian, gay, bisexual, and transgender (LGBT) rights; or raise funds for LGBT organizations. These various networks and organizations span a broad political spectrum. Some are overtly feminist; others are more closely aligned with queer politics. Examples include Queer Nation, and Lesbian Avengers—national networks with local participating groups, the Boston Bisexual Women's Network, the Detroit Women's Coffeehouse, Older Lesbians Organizing for Change (Houston, Texas), New York Association for Gender Rights Advocacy, the National Gay and Lesbian Taskforce (Washington, D.C.), the National Latino/a LGBT Organization (Washington, D.C.), Gender Education and Advocacy (www.gender.org), and the International Gay and Lesbian Human Rights Commission (San Francisco). In addition, lesbians and bisexual women are active in antiracist organizing, rape crisis centers, shelters for battered women, labor unions, antimilitarist organizations, and women's studies programs where they link their knowledge and experiences of oppression based on sexuality with other oppressions.

Questions for Reflection

As you read and discuss the readings that follow, consider the questions raised by Shere Hite, listed on page 145.

Finding Out More on the Web

1. Research an organization mentioned in this chapter. What are its goals, strategies, and activities?

2. The World Wide Web is a significant new tool in the commodification of women. Type "Philippine women" or "Asian women" into your search engine and see what comes up. Also look at www.asianwomenonline.com—where Asian women are reclaiming cyberspace and breaking stereotypical portrayals.

Taking Action

1. Write in your journal or have a candid conversation with a friend about your ideas about sexuality. How do you recognize the power of the erotic as Aurora Levins Morales and Audre Lorde describe it?

2. Analyze the way women's magazines and men's magazines discuss women's sexuality.

3. Look critically at the way women's sexuality is portrayed in movies, on TV, and in ads.

4. However you define your sexuality, participate in campus or community events to commemorate National Coming-Out Day (usually in October) or Gay Pride (usually in June).

T W E N T Y - T W O

Guadalupe the Sex Goddess

Sandra Cisneros

In high school I marveled at how white women strutted around the locker room, nude as pearls, as unashamed of their brilliant bodies as the Nike of Samothrace. Maybe they were hiding terrible secrets like bulimia or anorexia, but, to my naive eye then, I thought of them as women comfortable in their skin.

You could always tell us Latinas. We hid when we undressed, modestly facing a wall, or, in my case, dressing in a bathroom stall. We were the ones who still used bulky sanitary pads instead of tampons, thinking ourselves morally superior to our white classmates. *My mama said you can't use tampons till after you're married.* All Latina mamas said this, yet how come none of us thought to ask our mothers why they didn't use tampons *after* getting married?

Womanhood was full of mysteries. I was as ignorant about my own body as any female ancestor who hid behind a sheet with a hole in the center when husband or doctor called. Religion and our culture, our culture and religion, helped to create that blur, a vagueness about what went on "down there." So ashamed was I about my own "down there" that until I was an adult I had no idea I had another orifice called the vagina; I thought my period would arrive via the urethra or perhaps through the walls of my skin.

No wonder, then, it was too terrible to think about a doctor—a man!—looking at you down there when you could never bring yourself to look yourself. *¡Ay, nunca!* How could I acknowledge my sexuality, let alone enjoy sex, with so much guilt? In the guise of modesty my culture locked me in a double chastity belt of ignorance and *vergüenza*, shame.

I had never seen my mother nude. I had never taken a good look at myself either. Privacy for self-exploration belonged to the wealthy. In my home a private space was practically impossible; aside from the doors that opened to the street, the only room with a lock was the bathroom, and how could anyone who shared a bathroom with eight other people stay in there for more than a few minutes? Before college, no one in my family had a room of their own except me, a narrow closet just big enough for my twin bed and an oversized blond dresser we'd bought in the bargain basement of *el Sears.* The dresser was as long as a coffin and blocked the door from shutting completely. I had my own room, but I never had the luxury of shutting the door.

I didn't even see my own sex until a nurse at the Emma Goldman Clinic showed it to me—*Would you like to see your cervix? Your os is dilating. You must be ovulating. Here's a mirror; take a look.* When had anyone ever suggested I take a look or allowed me a speculum to take home and investigate myself at leisure!

I'd only been to one other birth control facility prior to the Emma Goldman Clinic, the university medical center in grad school. I was 21 in a strange town far from home for the first time. I was afraid and I was ashamed to seek out a gynecologist, but I was more afraid of becoming pregnant. Still, I agonized about going for weeks. Perhaps the anonymity and distance from my family allowed me finally to take control of my life. I remember wanting to be fearless like the white women around me, to be able to have sex when I wanted, but I was too afraid to explain to a would-be lover how I'd only had one other man in my life and we'd practiced withdrawal. Would he laugh at me? How could I look anyone in the face and explain why I couldn't go see a gynecologist?

One night, a classmate I liked too much took me home with him. I meant all along to say something about how I wasn't on anything, but I never quite found my voice, never the right moment to cry out— *Stop, this is dangerous to my brilliant career!* Too afraid to sound stupid, afraid to ask him to take responsibility too, I said nothing, and I let him take me like that with nothing protecting me from motherhood but luck. The days that followed were torture, but fortunately on Mother's Day my period arrived, and I celebrated my nonmaternity by making an appointment with the family planning center.

When I see pregnant teens, I can't help but think that could've been me. In high school I would've

thrown myself into love the way some warriors throw themselves into fighting. I was ready to sacrifice everything in the name of love, to do anything, even risk my own life, but thankfully there were no takers. I was enrolled at an all-girls' school. I think if I had met a boy who would have me, I would've had sex in a minute, convinced this was love. I have always had enough imagination to fall in love all by myself, then and now.

I tell you this story because I am overwhelmed by the silence regarding Latinas and our bodies. If I, as a graduate student, was shy about talking to anyone about my body and sex, imagine how difficult it must be for a young girl in middle school or high school living in a home with no lock on the bedroom door, perhaps with no door, or maybe with no bedroom, no information other than misinformation from the girlfriends and the boyfriend. So much guilt, so much silence, and such a yearning to be loved; no wonder young women find themselves having sex while they are still children, having sex without sexual protection, too ashamed to confide their feelings and fears to anyone.

What a culture of denial. Don't get pregnant! But no one tells you how not to. This is why I was angry for so many years every time I saw a *la Virgen de Guadalupe,* my culture's role model for brown women like me. She was damn dangerous, an ideal so lofty and unrealistic it was laughable. Did boys have to aspire to be Jesus? I never saw any evidence of it. They were fornicating like rabbits while the Church ignored them and pointed us women toward our destiny—marriage and motherhood. The other alternative was *puta*hood.

In my neighborhood I knew only real women, neither saints nor whores, naive and vulnerable *huerquitas* like me who wanted desperately to fall in love, with the heart and soul. And yes, with the *panocha* too.

As far as I could see, *la Lupe* was nothing but a Goody Two-shoes meant to doom me to a life of unhappiness. Thanks, but no thanks. Motherhood and/or marriage were anathema to my career. But being a bad girl, that was something I could use as a writer, a Molotov cocktail to toss at my papa and *el Papa,* who had their own plans for me.

Discovering sex was like discovering writing. It was powerful in a way I couldn't explain. Like writing, you had to go beyond the guilt and shame to get to anything good. Like writing, it could take you to deep and mysterious subterranean levels. With each new depth I found out things about myself I didn't know I knew. And, like writing, for a slip of a moment it could be spiritual, the cosmos pivoting on a pin, could empty and fill you all at once like a Ganges, a Piazzolla tango, a tulip bending in the wind. I was no one, I was nothing, and I was everything in the universe little and large—twig, cloud, sky. How had this incredible energy been denied me!

When I look at *la Virgen de Guadalupe* now, she is not the Lupe of my childhood, no longer the one in my grandparents' house in Tepeyac, nor is she the one of the Roman Catholic Church, the one I bolted the door against in my teens and twenties. Like every woman who matters to me, I have had to search for her in the rubble of history. And I have found her. She is Guadalupe the sex goddess, a goddess who makes me feel good about my sexual power, my sexual energy, who reminds me that I must, as Clarissa Pinkola Estés so aptly put it, "[speak] from the vulva . . . speak the most basic, honest truth," and write from my *panocha*.

In my research of Guadalupe's pre-Columbian antecedents, the she before the Church desexed her, I found Tonantzin, and inside Tonantzin a pantheon of other mother goddesses. I discovered Tlazolteotl, the goddess of fertility and sex, also referred to as Totzin. Our Beginnings, or Tzinteotl, goddess of the rump. *Putas*, nymphos, and other loose women were known as "women of the sex goddess." Tlazolteotl was the patron of sexual passion, and though she had the power to stir you to sin, she could also forgive you and cleanse you of your sexual transgressions via her priests who heard confession. In this aspect of confessor Tlazolteotl was known as Tlaelcuani, the filth eater. Maybe you've seen her; she's the one whose image is sold in the tourist markets even now, a statue of a woman squatting in childbirth, her face grimacing in pain. Tlazolteotl, then, is a duality of maternity *and* sexuality. In other words, she is a sexy mama.

To me, *la Virgen de Guadalupe* is also Coatlicue, the creative/destructive goddess. When I think of the Coatlicue statue in the National Museum of Anthropology in Mexico City, so terrible it was unearthed and then reburied because it was too frightening to look at, I think of a woman enraged, a woman as tempest, a woman *bien berrinchuda*, and I like that.

La Lupe as *cabrona*. Not silent and passive, but silently gathering force.

Most days, I too feel like the creative/destructive goddess Coatlicue, especially the days I'm writing, capable of fabricating pretty tales with pretty words, as well as doing demolition work with a volley of *palabrotas* if I want to. I am the Coatlicue-Lupe whose square column of a body I see in so many Indian women, in my mother, and in myself each time I check out my thick-waisted, flat-assed torso in the mirror.

Coatlicue, Tlazolteotl, Tonantzin, *la Virgen de Guadalupe*. They are each telescoped one into the other, into who I am. And this is where *la Lupe* intrigues me—not the Lupe of 1531 who appeared to Juan Diego, but the one of the 1990s who has shaped who we are as Chicanas/*mexicanas* today, the one inside each Chicana and *mexicana*. Perhaps it's the Tlazolteotl-Lupe in me whose *malcriada* spirit inspires me to leap into the swimming pool naked or dance on a table with a skirt on my head. Maybe it's my Coatlicue-Lupe attitude that makes it possible for my mother to tell me, "No wonder men can't stand you." Who knows? What I do know is this: I am obsessed with becoming a woman comfortable in her skin.

I can't attribute my religious conversion to a flash of lightning on the road to Laredo or anything like that. Instead, there have been several lessons learned subtly over a period of time. A grave depression and near suicide in my thirty-third year and its subsequent retrospection. Vietnamese Buddhist monk Thich Nhat Hanh's writing that has brought out the Buddha-Lupe in me. My weekly peace vigil for my friend Jasna in Sarajevo. The writings of Gloria Anzaldúa. A crucial trip back to Tepeyac in 1985 with Cherríe Moraga and Norma Alarcón. Drives across Texas, talking with other Chicanas. And research for stories that would force me back inside the Church from where I'd fled.

My *Virgin de Guadalupe* is not the mother of God. She is God. She is a face for a god without a face, an *indigena* for a god without ethnicity, a female deity for a god who is genderless, but I also understand that for her to approach me, for me to finally open the door and accept her, she had to be a woman like me.

Once watching a porn film, I saw a sight that terrified me. It was the film star's *panocha*—a tidy, elliptical opening, pink and shiny like a rabbit's ear. To make matters worse, it was shaved and looked especially childlike and unsexual. I think what startled me most was the realization that my own sex has no resemblance to this woman's. My sex, dark as an orchid, rubbery and blue-purple as *pulpo*, an octopus, does not look nice and tidy, but otherworldly. I do not have little rosette nipples. My nipples are big and brown like the Mexican coins of my childhood.

When I see *la Virgen de Guadalupe* I want to lift her dress as I did my dolls, and look to see if she comes with *chones* and does her *panocha* look like mine, and does she have dark nipples too? Yes, I am certain she does. She is not neuter like Barbie. She gave birth. She has a womb. *Blessed art thou and blessed is the fruit of thy womb. . . .* Blessed art thou, Lupe, and, therefore, blessed am I.

◆◆◆

Radical Heterosexuality

Naomi Wolf

All over the country, millions of feminists have a secret indulgence. By day they fight gender injustice; by night they sleep with men. Is this a dual life? A core contradiction? Is sleeping with a man "sleeping with the enemy"? And is razor burn from kissing inherently oppressive?

It's time to say you *can* hate sexism and love men. As the feminist movement grows more mature and our understanding of our enemies more nuanced, three terms assumed to be in contradiction—radical feminist heterosexuality—can and must be brought together.

Rules of the Relationship

But how? Andrea Dworkin and Catharine MacKinnon have pointed out that sexism limits women to such a degree that it's questionable whether the decision to live with a man can ever truly be free. If you want to use their sound, if depressing, reasoning to a brighter end, turn the thesis around: radical heterosexuality demands substituting choice for dependency.

Radical heterosexuality requires that the woman be able to support herself. This is not to belittle women who must depend financially on men; it is to recognize that when our daughters are raised with the skills that would let them leave abusers, they need not call financial dependence love.

Radical heterosexuality needs alternative institutions. As the child of a good lifetime union, I believe in them. But when I think of pledging my heart and body to a man—even the best and kind-

est man—within the existing institution of marriage, I feel faint. The more you learn about its legal structure, the less likely you are to call the caterers.

In the nineteenth century, when a judge ruled that a husband could not imprison and rape his wife, the London *Times* bemoaned, "One fine morning last month, marriage in England was suddenly abolished." The phrase "rule of thumb" descends from English common law that said a man could legally beat his wife with a switch "no thicker than his thumb."

If these nightmarish echoes were confined to history, I might feel more nuptial; but look at our own time. Do I want the blessing of an institution that doesn't provide adequate protection from marital rape? That gives a woman less protection from assault by her husband than by a stranger? That assigns men 70 percent of contested child custodies?

Of course I do not fear any such brutality from the man I want to marry (no bride does). But marriage means that his respectful treatment of me and our children becomes, despite our intentions, a kindness rather than a legally grounded right.

We need a heterosexual version of the marriages that gay and lesbian activists are seeking: a commitment untainted by centuries of inequality; a ritual that invites the community to rejoice in the making of a new freely chosen family.

The radical heterosexual man must yield the automatic benefits conferred by gender. I had a lover once who did not want to give up playing sports in a club that had a separate door for women. It must be tempting to imagine you can have both—great squash courts *and* the bed of a liberated woman—but in the mess hall of gender relations, there is *no such thing as a free lunch.*

Radical heterosexual women too must give up gender benefits (such as they are). I know scores of women—independent, autonomous—who avoid assuming any of the risk for a romantic or sexual approach.

I have watched myself stand complacently by while my partner wrestles with a stuck window, an intractable computer printer, maps, or locks. Sisters, I am not proud of this, and I'm working on it. But people are lazy—or at least I am—and it's easy to rationalize that the person with the penis is the one who should get out of a warm bed to fix the snow on the TV screen. After all, it's the very least owed to me *personally* in compensation for centuries of virtual enslavement.

Radical heterosexuals must try to stay conscious—at all times, I'm afraid—of their gender imprinting, and how it plays out in their erotic melodramas. My own psyche is a flagrant *son et lumière* of political incorrectness. Three of my boyfriends had motorcycles; I am easy pickings for the silent and dysfunctional. My roving eye is so taken by the oil-stained persona of the labor organizer that myopic intellectuals have gained access to my favors merely by sporting a Trotsky button.

We feminists are hard on each other for admitting to weakness. Gloria Steinem caught flak from her left-wing sisters for acknowledging in *Revolution from Within* that she was drawn to a man because he could do the things with money and power that we are taught men must do. And some were appalled when Simone de Beauvoir's letters revealed how she coddled Sartre.

But the antifeminist erotic template is *in* us. We would not be citizens of this culture if swooning damsels and abandoned vixens had not been beamed at us from our first solid food to our first vote. We can't fight it until we admit to it. And we can't identify it until we drag it, its taffeta billowing and its bosom heaving, into the light of day.

I have done embarrassing, reactionary, abject deeds out of love and sexual passion. So, no doubt, has Norman Schwarzkopf. Only when we reveal our conditioning can we tell how much of our self-abasement is neurotic femininity, and how much is the flawed but impressive human apparatus of love.

In the Bedroom

Those are the conditions for the radical heterosexual couple. What might this new creation look like in bed? It will look like something we have no words or images for—the eroticization of consent, the equal primacy of female and male desire.

We will need to tell some secrets—to map our desire for the male body and admit to our fascination with the rhythms and forces of male arousal, its uncanny counterintuitive spell.

We will also need to face our creature qualities. Animality has for so long been used against us—bitch, fox, *Penthouse* pet—that we struggle for the merit badges of higher rationality, ambivalent about our animal nature.

The truth is that heterosexual women believe that men, on some level, are animals; as they believe that we are animals. But what does "animal" mean?

Racism and sexism have long used animal metaphors to distance and degrade the Other. Let us redefine "animal" to make room for that otherness between the genders, an otherness fierce and worthy of respect. Let us define animal as an inchoate kinship, a comradeship, that finds a language beyond our species.

I want the love of two unlikes: the look of astonishment a woman has at the sight of a male back bending. These manifestations of difference confirm in heterosexuals the beauty that similarity confirms in the lesbian or gay imagination. Difference and animality do not have to mean hierarchy.

Men We Love

What must the men be like? Obviously, they're not going to be just anyone. *Esquire* runs infantile disquisitions on "Women We Love" (suggesting, Lucky Girls!). Well, I think that the men who are loved by feminists are lucky. Here's how they qualify to join this fortunate club.

Men We Love understand that, no matter how similar our backgrounds, we are engaged in a cross-cultural (if not practically biracial) relationship. They know that we know much about their world and they but little of ours. They accept what white people must accept in relationships with people of other ethnicities: to know that they do not know.

Men We Love don't hold a baby as if it is a still-squirming, unidentifiable catch from the sea.

Men We Love don't tell women what to feel about sexism. (There's a postcard that shows a dashing young fellow, drawn Love-comix-style, saying to a woman, "Let me explicate to you the nature of your oppression.") They do not presume that there is a line in the sand called "enlightened male," and that all they need is a paperback copy of Djuna Barnes and good digital technique. They understand that unlearning gender oppressiveness means untying the very core of how we become female and male. They know this pursuit takes a lifetime at the minimum.

Sadly, men in our lives sometimes come through on personal feminism but balk at it intellectually. A year ago, I had a bruising debate with my father and brother about the patriarchal nature of traditional religious and literary canons. I almost seized them by their collars, howling "Read Mary Daly! Read Toni Morrison! Take Feminism 101. *No, I can't* explain it to you between the entrée and dessert!"

By spring, my dad, bless his heart, had asked for a bibliography, and last week my brother sent me *Standing Again at Sinai,* a Jewish-feminist classic. Men We Love are willing, sooner or later, to read the Books We Love.

Men We Love accept that successful training in manhood makes them blind to phenomena that are fact to women. Recently, I walked down a New York City avenue with a woman friend, X, and a man friend, Y. I pointed out to Y the leers, hisses, and invitations to sit on faces. Each woman saw clearly what the other woman saw, but Y was baffled. Sexual harassers have superb timing. A passerby makes kissy-noises with his tongue while Y is scrutinizing the menu of the nearest bistro. "There, there! Look! Listen!" we cried. "What? Where? Who?" wailed poor Y, valiantly, uselessly spinning.

What if, hard as they try to see, they cannot hear? Once I was at lunch with a renowned male crusader for the First Amendment. Another Alpha male was present, and the venue was the Supreme Court lunchroom—two power factors that automatically press the "mute" button on the male ability to detect a female voice on the audioscope. The two men began to rev their motors; soon they were off and racing in a policy-wonk grand prix. I tried, once or twice, to ask questions. But the free-speech champions couldn't hear me over the testosterone roar.

Men We Love undertake half the care and cost of contraception. They realize that it's not fair to wallow in the fun without sharing the responsibility. When stocking up for long weekends, they brave the amused glances when they ask, "Do you have this in unscented?"

Men We Love know that just because we can be irrational doesn't mean we're insane. When we burst into premenstrual tears—having just realized the cosmic fragility of creation—they comfort us. Not until we feel better do they dare remind us gently that we had this same revelation exactly 28 days ago.

Men We Love must make a leap of imagination to believe in the female experience. They do not call women nags or paranoid when we embark on the arduous, often boring, nonnegotiable daily chore of drawing attention to sexism. They treat it like adults taking driving lessons: if irked in the short term at being treated like babies, they're grateful in the long term that someone is willing to teach them patiently how to move through the world without harming the pedestrians. Men We Love don't drive without their gender glasses on.

A Place for Them

It's not simple gender that pits Us against Them. In the fight against sexism, it's those who are for us versus those who are against us—of either gender.

When I was 16, my boyfriend came with me to hear Andrea Dworkin speak. While hearing great feminist oratory in a sea of furious women changed my life, it nearly ended my boyfriend's: he barely escaped being drawn and quartered.

It is time to direct our anger more acutely at the Men We Hate—like George Bush—and give the Men We Love something useful to do. Not to take over meetings, or to set agendas; not to whine, "Why can't feminists teach us how to be free?" but to add their bodies, their hearts, and their numbers, to support us.

I meet many young men who are brought to feminism by love for a woman who has been raped, or by watching their single mothers struggle against great odds, or by simple common sense. Their most frequent question is "What can I do to help?"

Imagine a rear battalion of committed "Men Against Violence Against Women" (or Men for Choice, or what have you)—of all races, ages, and classes. Wouldn't that be a fine sight to fix in the eyes of a five-year-old boy?

Finally, the place to make room for radical feminist heterosexuality is within our heads. If the movement that I dearly love has a flaw, it is a tendency toward orthodoxies about other women's pleasures and needs. This impulse is historically understandable: in the past, we needed to define ourselves against men if we were to define ourselves at all. But today, the most revolutionary choice we can make is to affirm other women's choices, whether lesbian or straight, bisexual or celibate.

NOW President Patricia Ireland speaks for me even though our sexual lives are not identical. Simone de Beauvoir speaks for me even though our sexual lives are not identical. Audre Lorde speaks for me even though our sexual lives are not identical. Is it the chromosomes of your lovers that establish you as a feminist? Or is it the life you make out of the love you make?

TWENTY-FOUR

Radical Pleasure

Sex and the End of Victimhood

Aurora Levins Morales

1

I am a person who was sexually abused and tortured as a child. I no longer define myself in terms of my survival of this experience, but what I learned from surviving it is central to my political and spiritual practice. The people who abused me consciously and deliberately manipulated me in an attempt to break down my sense of integrity so they could make me into an accomplice to my own torture and that of others. They deliberately and consciously interfered with my sexuality as one method of accomplishing this. We are so vulnerable in our pleasures and desires. The fact they could induce physical pleasure in me against my will allowed them to shame me. It allowed them to persuade me that my sexuality was untrustworthy and belonged to others. It allowed them to persuade me that my desires were dangerous and were one of the causes of my having been abused. My sexuality has stuttered ever since, flaring and subsiding in ways I have not known how to manage, ricocheting from intense excitement to absolute numbness, from reckless trust to impenetrable guardedness. This place of wounded eroticism is one that is honored in survivor culture, evidence of blows inflicted and then denied by our abusers. When the skeptical ask us "Where are your scars?" we can point to the unsteady rhythms of fascination and disgust, obsession and revulsion through which we experience sex as evidence of what we know to be true.

2

"So why choose to reclaim sex?" This is the final question in a five-hour interview of me by my friend Staci Haines. We have been talking about the seductiveness of the victim role; about the thin satisfactions that come from a permanent attitude of outrage. About how having to resist too much, too young, locks us into rigid stances of resistance that interfere with intimacy, which ultimately requires vulnerability and surrender. About the seductiveness of an identity built on righteous indignation, and how close that stance actually lies to rampant self-pity. So when she asks me "Why reclaim sex?" I answer in layers.

Of course because it is part of aliveness. But among the many topics we've ranged over in our hours of conversation, the one that grabs me now is the need and obligation to leave victimhood behind. Staci and I share a somewhat taboo belief that as survivors we have an obligation to think about the healing of the perpetrators who are, after all, our kin—victims who survived in body but were unable to remain spiritually intact. So what comes to mind is the high price we pay when we settle for being wronged. Victimhood absolves us from having to decide to have good lives. It allows us to stay small and wounded instead of spacious, powerful and whole. We don't have to face up to our own responsibility for taking charge of things, for changing the world and ourselves. We can place our choices about being vulnerable and intimate and effective in the hands of our abusers. We can stay powerless and send them the bill.

But deciding not to heal fully, not to reclaim that place of intimate harm and make it flourish, is also unjust. By making the damage done to us permanent and irreversible, we lock both ourselves and the perpetrators away from any hope of healing. We saddle them with an even bigger spiritual debt than they have already incurred, and sometimes the reason is revenge, as if our full recovery would let them off the hook and we must punish them by seeing to it that our victimhood is never diminished or challenged. But when we refuse healing for the sake of that rage, we are remaking ourselves in the image of those who hurt us, becoming the embodiment of the wound, forsaking both ourselves and the abandoned children who grew up to torment us.

3

The path of reclaiming the wounded erotic is neither placid nor boring. It is full of dizzying precipices, heady moments of release, crushing assaults of shame. But at its core is the real fire we are all after, that blazing and untarnished aliveness that lies within everything of value and spirit that we do. Right here in our bodies, in our defense of our right to experience joy, in the refusal to abandon the place where we have been most completely invaded and colonized, in our determination to make the bombed and defoliated lands flower again and bear fruit, here where we have been most shamed is one of the most radical and sacred places from which to transform the world. To shamelessly insist that our bodies are for our own delight and connection with others clearly defies the predatory appropriations of incestuous relatives and rapists; but it also defies the poisoning of our food and water and air with chemicals that give us cancer and enrich the already obscenely wealthy, the theft of our lives in harsh labor, our bodies used up to fill bank accounts already bloated, the massive abduction of our young people to be hurled at each other as weapons for the defense and expansion of those bank accounts—all the ways in which our deep pleasure in living has been cut off so as not to interfere with the profitability of our bodies. Because the closer I come to that bright, hot center of pleasure and trust, the less I can tolerate its captivity, and the less afraid I am to be powerful, in a world that is in desperate need of unrepentant joy.

TWENTY-FIVE

◆◆◆

A New Politics of Sexuality

June Jordan

As a young worried mother, I remember turning to Dr. Benjamin Spock's *Common Sense Book of Baby and Child Care* just about as often as I'd pick up the telephone. He was God. I was ignorant but striving to be good: a good Mother. And so it was there, in that best-seller pocketbook of do's and don't's, that I came upon this doozie of a guideline: Do not wear miniskirts or other provocative clothing because that will upset your child, especially if your child happens to be a boy. If you give your offspring "cause" to think of you as a sexual being, he will, at the least, become disturbed; you will derail the equilibrium of his notions about your possible identity and meaning in the world.

It had never occurred to me that anyone, especially my son, might look upon me as an asexual being. I had never supposed that "asexual" was some kind of positive designation I should, so to speak, lust after, I was pretty surprised by Dr. Spock. However, I was also, by habit, a creature of obedience. For a couple of weeks I actually experimented with lusterless colors and dowdy tops and bottoms, self-consciously hoping thereby to prove myself as a lusterless and dowdy and, therefore, excellent female parent.

Years would have to pass before I could recognize the familiar, by then, absurdity of a man setting himself up as the expert on a subject that presupposed women as the primary objects for his patriarchal discourse—on motherhood, no less! Years passed before I came to perceive the perversity of dominant power assumed by men, and the perversity of self-determining power ceded to men by women.

A lot of years went by before I understood the dynamics of what anyone could summarize as the Politics of Sexuality.

I believe the Politics of Sexuality is the most ancient and probably the most profound arena for human conflict. Increasingly, it seems clear to me that deeper and more pervasive than any other oppression, than any other bitterly contested human domain, is the oppression of sexuality, the exploitation of the human domain of sexuality for power.

When I say sexuality, I mean gender: I mean male subjugation of human beings because they are female. When I say sexuality, I mean heterosexual institutionalization of rights and privileges denied to homosexual men and women. When I say sexuality I mean gay or lesbian contempt for bisexual modes of human relationship.

The Politics of Sexuality therefore subsumes all of the different ways in which some of us seek to dictate to others of us what we should do, what we should desire, what we should dream about, and how we should behave ourselves, generally. From China to Iran, from Nigeria to Czechoslovakia, from Chile to California, the politics of sexuality—enforced by traditions of state-sanctioned violence plus religion and the law—reduces to male domination of women, heterosexist tyranny, and, among those of us who are in any case deemed despicable or deviant by the powerful, we find intolerance for those who choose a different, a more complicated—for example, an interracial or bisexual—mode of rebellion and freedom.

We must move out from the shadows of our collective subjugation—as people of color/as women/as gay/as lesbian/as bisexual human beings.

I can voice my ideas without hesitation or fear because I am speaking, finally, about myself. I am Black and I am female and I am a mother and I am bisexual and I am a nationalist and I am an anti-nationalist. And I mean to be fully and freely all that I am!

Conversely, I do not accept that any white or Black or Chinese man—I do not accept that, for instance, Dr. Spock—should presume to tell me, or

any other woman, how to mother a child. He has no right. He is not a mother. My child is not his child. And, likewise, I do not accept that anyone—any woman or any man who is not inextricably part of the subject he or she dares to address—should attempt to tell any of us, the objects of her or his presumptuous discourse, what we should do or what we should not do.

Recently, I have come upon gratuitous and appalling pseudoliberal pronouncements on sexuality. Too often, these utterances fall out of the mouths of men and women who first disclaim any sentiment remotely related to homophobia, but who then proceed to issue outrageous opinions like the following:

- That it is blasphemous to compare the oppression of gay, lesbian, or bisexual people to the oppression, say, of black people, or of the Palestinians.

- That the bottom line about gay or lesbian or bisexual identity is that you can conceal it whenever necessary and, so, therefore, why don't you do just that? Why don't you keep your deviant sexuality in the closet and let the rest of us—we who suffer oppression for reasons of our ineradicable and always visible components of our personhood such as race or gender—get on with our more necessary, our more beleaguered struggle to survive?

Well, number one: I believe I have worked as hard as I could, and then harder than that, on behalf of equality and justice—for African-Americans, for the Palestinian people, and for people of color everywhere.

And no, I do not believe it is blasphemous to compare oppressions of sexuality to oppressions of race and ethnicity: Freedom is indivisible or it is nothing at all besides sloganeering and temporary, short-sighted, and short-lived advancement for a few. Freedom is indivisible, and either we are working for freedom or you are working for the sake of your self-interests and I am working for mine.

If you can finally go to the bathroom wherever you find one, if you can finally order a cup of coffee and drink it wherever coffee is available, but you cannot follow your heart—you cannot respect the response of your own honest body in the world—

then how much of what kind of freedom does any one of us possess?

Or, conversely, if your heart and your honest body can be controlled by the state, or controlled by community taboo, are you not then, and in that case, no more than a slave ruled by outside force?

What tyranny could exceed a tyranny that dictates to the human heart, and that attempts to dictate the public career of an honest human body?

Freedom is indivisible; the Politics of Sexuality is not some optional "special-interest" concern for serious, progressive folk.

And, on another level, let me assure you: if every single gay or lesbian or bisexual man or woman active on the Left of American politics decided to stay home, there would be *no* Left left.

One of the things I want to propose is that we act on that reality: that we insistently demand reciprocal respect and concern from those who cheerfully depend upon our brains and our energies for their, and our, effective impact on the political landscape.

Last spring, at Berkeley, some students asked me to speak at a rally against racism. And I did. There were four or five hundred people massed on Sproul Plaza, standing together against that evil. And, on the next day, on that same plaza, there was a rally for bisexual and gay and lesbian rights, and students asked me to speak at that rally. And I did. There were fewer than seventy-five people stranded, pitiful, on that public space. And I said then what I say today: That was disgraceful! There should have been just one rally. One rally: freedom is indivisible.

As for the second, nefarious pronouncement on sexuality that now enjoys mass-media currency: the idiot notion of keeping yourself in the closet—that is very much the same thing as the suggestion that black folks and Asian-Americans and Mexican-Americans should assimilate and become as "white" as possible—in our walk/talk/music/food/values—or else. Or else? Or else we should, deservedly, perish.

Sure enough, we have plenty of exposure to white everything, so why would we opt to remain our African/Asian/Mexican selves? The answer is that suicide is absolute, and if you think you will survive by hiding who you really are, you are sadly misled: there is no such thing as partial or intermittent suicide. You can only survive if you—who you really are—do survive.

Likewise, we who are not men and we who are not heterosexist—we, sure enough, have plenty of exposure to male-dominated/heterosexist this and that.

But a struggle to survive cannot lead to suicide: suicide is the opposite of survival. And so we must not conceal/assimilate/integrate into the would-be dominant culture and political system that despises us. Our survival requires that we alter our environment so that we can live and so that we can hold each other's hands and so that we can kiss each other on the streets, and in the daylight of our existence, without terror and without violent and sometimes fatal reactions from the busybodies of America.

Finally, I need to speak on bisexuality. I do believe that the analogy is interracial or multiracial identity. I do believe that the analogy for bisexuality is a multicultural, multi-ethnic, multiracial world view. Bisexuality follows from such a perspective and leads to it, as well.

Just as there are many men and women in the United States whose parents have given them more than one racial, more than one ethnic identity and cultural heritage to honor; and just as these men and women must deny no given part of themselves except at the risk of self-deception and the insanities that must issue from that; and just as these men and women embody the principle of equality among races and ethnic communities; and just as these men and women falter and anguish and choose and then falter again and then anguish and then choose yet again how they will honor the irreducible complexity of their God-given human being—even so, there are many men and women, especially young men and women, who seek to embrace the complexity of their total, always changing social and political circumstance.

They seek to embrace our increasing global complexity on the basis of the heart and on the basis of an honest human body. Not according to ideology. Not according to group pressure. Not according to anybody's concept of "correct."

This is a New Politics of Sexuality. And even as I despair of identity politics—because identity is given and principles of justice/equality/freedom cut across given gender and given racial definitions of being, and because I will call you my brother, I will call you my sister, on the basis of what you *do* for justice, what you *do* for equality and what you *do* for freedom and *not* on the basis of who you are, even so I look with admiration and respect upon the new, bisexual politics of sexuality.

This emerging movement politicizes the so-called middle ground: Bisexuality invalidates either/or formulation, either/or analysis. Bisexuality means I am free and I am as likely to want and to love a woman as I am likely to want and to love a man, and what about that? Isn't that what freedom implies?

If you are free, you are not predictable and you are not controllable. To my mind, that is the keenly positive, politicizing significance of bisexual affirmation:

To insist upon complexity, to insist upon the validity of all of the components of social/sexual complexity, to insist upon the equal validity of all of the components of social/sexual complexity.

This seems to me a unifying, 1990s mandate for revolutionary Americans planning to make it into the twenty-first century on the basis of the heart, on the basis of an honest human body, consecrated to every struggle for justice, every struggle for equality, every struggle for freedom.

T W E N T Y - S I X

◆◆◆

The All-American Queer Pakistani Girl

Surina A. Khan

I don't know if my grandmother is dead or alive. I can't remember the last time I saw her—it must have been at least ten years ago, when I was in Pakistan for a visit. She was my only living grandparent, and her health was beginning to fail. Every once in a while, I think she's probably dead and no one bothered to tell me.

I'm completely out of touch with my Pakistani life. I can hardly speak Urdu, my first language; I certainly can't read or write it. I have no idea how many cousins I have. I know my father comes from a large family—eleven brothers and sisters—but I don't know all their names. I've never read the Koran, and I don't have faith in Islam.

As a kid, I remember being constantly reminded that I was different—by my accent, my brown skin color, my mother's traditional clothing, and the smell of the food we ate. And so I consciously Americanized myself. I spent my early childhood perfecting my American accent, my adolescence affirming my American identity to others, and my late teens rejecting my Pakistani heritage. Now, at the age of twenty-seven, I'm feeling the void I created for myself.

Sometimes I think of what my life would be like if my parents hadn't moved to Connecticut in 1973, when I was five. Most of my family has since moved back to Pakistan, and up until seven years ago, when I came out, I went back somewhat regularly. But I never liked going back. It made me feel stifled, constrained. People were always talking about getting married. First it was, "You're almost old enough to start thinking about finding a nice husband," then, "When are you getting married?" Now I imagine they'd say, with disappointment, "You'll be an old maid."

My family is more liberal than most of Pakistani society. By American standards that translates into conservative (my mother raised money for George Bush). But I was brought up in a family that valued education, independence, integrity, and love. I never had to worry about getting pressured into an arranged marriage, even though several of my first cousins were—sometimes to each other. Once I went to a wedding in which the bride and groom saw each other for the first time when someone passed them a mirror after their wedding ceremony and they both looked into it at once. That's when I started thinking my family was "modern."

Unfortunately they live in a fundamentalist culture that won't tolerate me. I can't even bring myself to visit Pakistan. The last time I went back was seven years ago, for my father's funeral, and sometimes I wonder if the next time will be for my mother's funeral. She asks me to come visit every time I talk to her. I used to tell her I was too busy, that I couldn't get away. But three years ago I finally answered her truthfully. I told her that I didn't like the idea of traveling to a country that lashed lesbians one hundred times in public. More important, I didn't feel comfortable visiting when she and I had not talked about anything important in my life since I had come out to her.

Pakistan has always been my parents' answer to everything. When they found out my sisters were smoking pot in the late 1970s, they shipped all of us back. "You need to get in touch with the Pakistani culture," my mother would say. When my oldest sister got hooked on transcendental meditation and started walking around the house in a trance, my father packed her up and put her on a plane back to the homeland. She's been there ever since. Being the youngest of six, I wised up quickly. I waited to drop my bomb until after I had moved out of the house and was financially independent. If I had come out while I was still living in my parents' home, you can bet I'd have been on the next flight to Islamabad.

When I came out to my mother, she suggested I go back to Pakistan for a few months. "Just get away from it all," she begged. "You need some time. Clear your head." But I knew better. And when I insisted that I was queer and was going to move to Washington, D.C., to live with my girlfriend, Robin (now my ex-girlfriend, much to my mother's delight), she tried another scare tactic: "You and your lover better watch out. There's a large Pakistani community in D.C., and they'll find out about you. They'll break your legs, mutilate your face." That pretty much did it for me. My mother had just validated all my fears associated with Pakistan. I cut all ties with the community, including my family. *Pakistan* became synonymous with *homophobia*.

My mother disowned me when I didn't heed her advice. But a year later, when Robin and I broke up, my mother came back into my life. It was partly motivated by wishful thinking on her part. I do give her credit, though, not only for nurturing the strength in me to live by my convictions with integrity and honesty but also for eventually trying to understand me. I'll never forget the day I took her to see a lawyer friend of mine. She was on the verge of settling a lawsuit started by my father before he died and was unhappy with her lawyer. I took her to see Maggie Cassella, a lawyer/comedian based in Hartford, Connecticut, where I was again living. "I presume this woman's a lesbian," my mother said in the car on the way to Maggie's office. "Yes, she is," I replied, thinking, *Oh, no, here it comes again.* But my mother took me by surprise. "Well, the men aren't helping me; I might as well go to the dykes." I didn't think she even knew the word *dyke*. Now, *that* was a moment.

Her changing attitude about my lesbian identity was instilling in me a desire to reclaim my Pakistani identity. The best way to do this, I decided, would be to seek out other Pakistani lesbians. I barely knew any Pakistanis aside from my family, and I sure as hell didn't know, or even know of, any Pakistani lesbians. I was just naive enough to think I was the only one.

It wasn't easy for me even to arrive at the concept of a Pakistani lesbian. Having rejected my culture from a young age, I identified only as a lesbian when I came out, and in my zeal to be all-American, I threw myself into the American queer liberation movement. I did not realize that there is an active South Asian gay and lesbian community in the United States—and that many of us are here precisely because we're able to be queer and out in the Western world.

South Asian culture is rampant with homophobia—so much so that most people in South Asia literally don't have words for homosexuality, which is viewed as a Western phenomenon despite the fact that images of gays and lesbians have been a part of the subcontinent's history for thousands of years. In the temples of Khajuraho and Konarak in India, there are images of same-gender couples—male and female—in intimate positions. One temple carving depicts two women caressing each other, while another shows four women engaged in sexual play. There are also references to homosexuality in the *Kāma-sūtra*, the ancient Indian text on the diversities of sex. Babar, the founder of the Mughal dynasty in India, is said to have been gay, as was Abu Nawas, a famous Islamic poet. The fact is that homosexuality is as native to South Asia as is hetero-sexuality. But since the culture pressures South Asian women to reject our sexual identity, many South Asian queers living in the United States reject South Asian culture in turn. As a result, we are often isolated from one another.

Despite the odds, I started my search for queer people from South Asia—and I found them, all across America, Canada, and England. Connecting with this network and talking with other queer South Asians has begun to fill the void I've been feeling. But just as it took me years to reject my Pakistani heritage, it will likely take me as long, if not longer, to reintegrate my culture into my life as it is now.

I'm not ready to go back to Pakistan. But I am ready to start examining the hostility I feel toward a part of myself I thought I had discarded long ago.

◆◆◆

TWENTY-SEVEN

We Are All Works in Progress

Leslie Feinberg

The sight of pink-blue gender-coded infant outfits may grate on your nerves. Or you may be a woman or a man who feels at home in those categories. Trans liberation defends you both.

Each person should have the right to *choose* between pink or blue tinted gender categories, as well as all the other hues of the palette. At this moment in time, that right is denied to us. But together, we could make it a reality. . . .

I am a human being who would rather not be addressed as Ms. or Mr., ma'am or sir. I prefer to use gender-neutral pronouns like *sie* (pronounced like *"see"*) and *hir* (pronounced like *"here"*) to describe myself. I am a person who faces almost insurmountable difficulty when instructed to check off an "F" or an "M" box on identification papers.

I'm not at odds with the fact that I was born female-bodied. Nor do I identify as an intermediate sex. I simply do not fit the prevalent Western concepts of what a woman or man "should" look like. And that reality has dramatically directed the course of my life.

I'll give you a graphic example. From December 1995 to December 1996, I was dying of endocarditis—a bacterial infection that lodges and proliferates in the valves of the heart. A simple blood culture would have immediately exposed the root cause of my raging fevers. Eight weeks of 'round-the-clock intravenous antibiotic drips would have eradicated every last seedling of bacterium in the canals of my heart. Yet I experienced such hatred from some health practitioners that I very nearly died.

I remember late one night in December my lover and I arrived at a hospital emergency room during a snowstorm. My fever was 104 degrees and rising. My blood pressure was pounding dangerously high. The staff immediately hooked me up to monitors and worked to bring down my fever. The doctor in charge began physically examining me. When he determined that my anatomy was female, he flashed me a mean-spirited smirk. While keeping his eyes fixed on me, he approached one of the nurses, seated at a desk, and began rubbing her neck and shoulders. He talked to her about sex for a few minutes. After his pointed demonstration of "normal sexuality," he told me to get dressed and then he stormed out of the room. Still delirious, I struggled to put on my clothes and make sense of what was happening.

The doctor returned after I was dressed. He ordered me to leave the hospital and never return. I refused. I told him I wouldn't leave until he could tell me why my fever was so high. He said, "You have a fever because you are a very troubled person."

This doctor's prejudices, directed at me during a moment of catastrophic illness, could have killed me. The death certificate would have read: Endocarditis. By all rights it should have read: Bigotry.

As my partner and I sat bundled up in a cold car outside the emergency room, still reverberating from the doctor's hatred, I thought about how many people have been turned away from medical care when they were desperately ill—some because an apartheid "whites only" sign hung over the emergency room entrance, or some because their visible Kaposi's sarcoma lesions kept personnel far from their beds. I remembered how a blemish that wouldn't heal drove my mother to visit her doctor repeatedly during the 1950s. I recalled the doctor finally wrote a prescription for Valium because he decided she was a hysterical woman. When my mother finally got to specialists, they told her the cancer had already reached her brain.

Bigotry exacts its toll in flesh and blood. And left unchecked and unchallenged, prejudices create a poisonous climate for us all. Each of us has a stake in the demand that every human being has a right to a job, to shelter, to health care, to dignity, to respect.

I am very grateful to have this chance to open up a conversation with you about why it is so vital to also defend the right of individuals to express and define their sex and gender, and to control their own bodies. For me, it's a life-and-death question. But I also believe that this discussion will have great meaning for you. All your life you've heard such dogma about what it means to be a "real" woman or a "real" man. And chances are you've choked on some of it. You've balked at the idea that being a woman means having to be thin as a rail, emotionally nurturing, and an airhead when it comes to balancing her checkbook. You know in your guts that being a man has nothing to do with rippling muscles, innate courage, or knowing how to handle a chain saw. These are really caricatures. Yet these images have been drilled into us through popular culture and education over the years. And subtler, equally insidious messages lurk in the interstices of these grosser concepts. These ideas of what a "real" woman or man should be straightjacket the freedom of individual self-expression. These gender messages play on and on in a continuous loop in our brains, like commercials that can't be muted.

But in my lifetime I've also seen social upheavals challenge this sex and gender doctrine. As a child who grew up during the McCarthyite, Father-Knows-Best 1950s, and who came of age during the second wave of women's liberation in the United States, I've seen transformations in the ways people think and talk about what it means to be a woman or a man.

Today the gains of the 1970s women's liberation movement are under siege by right-wing propagandists. But many today who are too young to remember what life was like before the women's movement need to know that this was a tremendously progressive development that won significant economic and social reforms. And this struggle by women and their allies swung human consciousness forward like a pendulum.

The movement replaced the common usage of vulgar and diminutive words to describe females with the word *woman* and infused that word with strength and pride. Women, many of them formerly isolated, were drawn together into consciousness-raising groups. Their discussions—about the root of women's oppression and how to eradicate it—resonated far beyond the rooms in which they took place. The women's liberation movement sparked a mass conversation about the systematic degradation, violence, and discrimination that women faced in this society. And this consciousness raising changed many of the ways women and men thought about themselves and their relation to each other. In retrospect, however, we must not forget that these widespread discussions were not just organized to

talk about oppression. They were a giant dialogue about how to take action to fight institutionalized anti-woman attitudes, rape and battering, the illegality of abortion, employment and education discrimination, and other ways women were socially and economically devalued.

This was a big step forward for humanity. And even the period of political reaction that followed has not been able to overturn all the gains made by that important social movement.

Now another movement is sweeping onto the stage of history: Trans liberation. We are again raising questions about the societal treatment of people based on their sex and gender expression. This discussion will make new contributions to human consciousness. And trans communities, like the women's movement, are carrying out these mass conversations with the goal of creating a movement capable of fighting for justice—of righting the wrongs.

We are a movement of masculine females and feminine males, cross-dressers, transsexual men and women, intersexuals born on the anatomical sweep between female and male, gender-blenders, many other sex and gender-variant people, and our significant others. All told, we expand understanding of how many ways there are to be a human being.

Our lives are proof that sex and gender are much more complex than a delivery room doctor's glance at genitals can determine, more variegated than pink or blue birth caps. We are oppressed for not fitting those narrow social norms. We are fighting back.

Our struggle will also help expose some of the harmful myths about what it means to be a woman or a man that have compartmentalized and distorted your life, as well as mine. Trans liberation has meaning for you—no matter how you define or express your sex or your gender.

If you are a trans person, you face horrendous social punishments—from institutionalization to gang rape, from beatings to denial of child visitation. This oppression is faced, in varying degrees, by all who march under the banner of trans liberation. This brutalization and degradation strips us of what we could achieve with our individual lifetimes.

And if you do not identify as transgender or transsexual or intersexual, your life is diminished by our oppression as well. Your own choices as a man or a woman are sharply curtailed. Your individual journey to express yourself is shunted into one of two deeply carved ruts, and the social baggage you are handed is already packed.

So the defense of each individual's right to control their own body, and to explore the path of self-expression, enhances your own freedom to discover more about yourself and your potentialities. This movement will give you more room to breathe—to be yourself. To discover on a deeper level what it means to be your self.

Together, I believe we can forge a coalition that can fight on behalf of your oppression as well as mine. Together, we can raise each other's grievances and win the kind of significant change we all long for. But the foundation of unity is understanding. So let me begin by telling you a little bit about myself.

I am a human being who unnerves some people. As they look at me, they see a kaleidoscope of characteristics they associate with both males and females. I appear to be a tangled knot of gender contradictions. So they feverishly press the question on me: woman or man? Those are the only two words most people have as tools to shape their question.

"Which sex are you?" I understand their question. It sounds so simple. And I'd like to offer them a simple resolution. But merely answering woman or man will not bring relief to the questioner. As long as people try to bring me into focus using only those two lenses, I will always appear to be an enigma.

The truth is I'm no mystery. I'm a female who is more masculine than those prominently portrayed in mass culture. Millions of females and millions of males in this country do not fit the cramped compartments of gender that we have been taught are "natural" and "normal." For many of us, the words *woman* or *man, ma'am* or *sir, she* or *he*—in and of themselves—do not total up the sum of our identities or of our oppressions. Speaking for myself, my life only comes into focus when the word *transgender* is added to the equation.

Simply answering whether I was born female or male will not solve the conundrum. Before I can even begin to respond to the question of my own birth sex, I feel it's important to challenge the assumptions that the answer is always as simple as either-or. I believe we need to take a critical look at the assumption that is built into the seemingly innocent question: "What a beautiful baby—is it a boy or a girl?"

The human anatomical spectrum can't be understood, let alone appreciated, as long as female or male are considered to be all that exists. "Is it a boy or a girl?" Those are the only two categories allowed on birth certificates.

But this either-or leaves no room for intersexual people, born between the poles of female and male. Human anatomy continues to burst the confines of the contemporary concept that nature delivers all babies on two unrelated conveyor belts. So, are the birth certificates changed to reflect human anatomy? No, the U.S. medical establishment hormonally molds and shapes and surgically hacks away at the exquisite complexities of intersexual infants until they neatly fit one category or the other.

A surgeon decides whether a clitoris is "too large" or a penis is "too small." That's a highly subjective decision for anyone to make about another person's body. Especially when the person making the arbitrary decision is scrubbed up for surgery! And what is the criterion for a penis being "too small"? Too small for successful heterosexual intercourse. Intersexual infants are already being tailored for their sexuality, as well as their sex. The infants have no say over what happens to their bodies. Clearly the struggle against genital mutilation must begin here, within the borders of the United States.

But the question asked of all new parents: "Is it a boy or a girl?" is not such a simple question when transsexuality is taken into account, either. Legions of out-and-proud transsexual men and women demonstrate that individuals have a deep, developed, and valid sense of their own sex that does not always correspond to the cursory decision made by a delivery-room obstetrician. Nor is transsexuality a recent phenomenon. People have undergone social sex reassignment and surgical and hormonal sex changes throughout the breadth of oral and recorded human history.

Having offered this view of the complexities and limitations of birth classification, I have no hesitancy in saying I was born female. But that answer doesn't clear up the confusion that drives some people to ask me, "Are you a man or a woman?" The problem is that they are trying to understand my gender expression by determining my sex—and therein lies the rub! Just as most of us grew up with only the concepts of *woman* and *man,* the terms *feminine* and *masculine* are the only two tools most people have to talk about the complexities of gender expression.

That pink-blue dogma assumes that biology steers our social destiny. We have been taught that being born female or male will determine how we will dress and walk, whether we will prefer our hair shortly cropped or long and flowing, whether we will be emotionally nurturing or repressed. According to this way of thinking, masculine females are trying to look "like men," and feminine males are trying to act "like women."

But those of us who transgress those gender assumptions also shatter their inflexibility.

So, why do I sometimes describe myself as a masculine female? Isn't each of those concepts very limiting? Yes. But placing the two words together is incendiary, exploding the belief that gender expression is linked to birth sex like horse and carriage. It is the social contradiction missing from Dick-and-Jane textbook education.

I actually chafe at describing myself as masculine. For one thing, masculinity is such an expansive territory, encompassing boundaries of nationality, race, and class. Most importantly, individuals blaze their own trails across this landscape.

And it's hard for me to label the intricate matrix of my gender as simply masculine. To me, branding individual self-expression as simply feminine or masculine is like asking poets: Do you write in English or Spanish? The question leaves out the possibilities that the poetry is woven in Cantonese or Ladino, Swahili or Arabic. The question deals only with the system of language that the poet has been taught. It ignores the words each writer hauls up, hand over hand, from a common well. The music words make when finding themselves next to each other for the first time. The silences echoing in the space between ideas. The powerful winds of passion and belief that move the poet to write.

That is why I do not hold the view that gender is simply a social construct—one of two languages that we learn by rote from early age. To me, gender is the poetry each of us makes out of the language we are taught. When I walk through the anthology of the world, I see individuals express their gender in exquisitely complex and ever-changing ways, despite the laws of pentameter.

So how can gender expression be mandated by edict and enforced by law? Isn't that like trying to handcuff a pool of mercury? It's true that human self-expression is diverse and is often expressed in ambiguous or contradictory ways. And what degree of gender expression is considered "acceptable" can depend on your social situation, your race and national, your class, and whether you live in an urban or rural environment.

But no one can deny that rigid gender education begins early on in life—from pink and blue color-coding of infant outfits to gender-labeling toys and games. And those who overstep these arbitrary borders are punished. Severely. When the steel handcuffs tighten, it is human bones that crack. No one knows how many trans lives have been lost to police brutality and street-corner bashing. The lives of trans people are so depreciated in this society that many murders go unreported. And those of us who have survived are deeply scarred by daily run-ins with hate, discrimination, and violence.

Trans people are still literally social outlaws. And that's why I am willing at times, publicly, to reduce the totality of my self-expression to descriptions like masculine female, butch, bulldagger, drag king, cross-dresser. These terms describe outlaw status. And I hold my head up proudly in that police lineup. The word *outlaw* is not hyperbolic. I have been locked up in jail by cops because I was wearing a suit and tie. Was my clothing really a crime? Is it a "man's" suit if I am wearing it? At what point—from field to rack—is fiber assigned a sex?

The reality of why I was arrested was as cold as the cell's cement floor: I am considered a masculine female. That's a *gender* violation. My feminine drag queen sisters were in nearby cells, busted for wearing "women's" clothing. The cells that we were thrown into had the same design of bars and concrete. But when we—gay drag kings and drag queens—were thrown into them, the cops referred to the cells as bull's tanks and queen's tanks. The cells were named after our crimes: gender transgression. Actual statutes against cross-dressing and cross-gendered behavior still exist in written laws today. But even where the laws are not written down, police, judges, and prison guards are empowered to carry out merciless punishment for sex and gender "difference."

I believe we need to sharpen our view of how repression by the police, courts, and prisons, as well as all forms of racism and bigotry, operates as gears in the machinery of the economic and social system that governs our lives. As all those who have the least to lose from changing this system get together and examine these social questions, we can separate the wheat of truths from the chaff of old lies. Historic tasks are revealed that beckon us to take a stand and to take action.

That moment is now. And so this conversation with you takes place with the momentum of struggle behind it.

What will it take to put a halt to "legal" and extralegal violence against trans people? How can we strike the unjust and absurd laws mandating dress and behavior for females and males from the books? How can we weed out all the forms of trans-phobic and gender-phobic discrimination?

Where does the struggle for sex and gender liberation fit in relation to other movements for economic and social equality? How can we reach a point where we appreciate each other's differences, not just tolerate them? How can we tear down the electrified barbed wire that has been placed between us to keep us separated, fearful and pitted against each other? How can we forge a movement that can bring about profound and lasting change—a movement capable of transforming society?

These questions can only be answered when we begin to organize together, ready to struggle on each other's behalf. Understanding each other will compel us as honest, caring people to fight each other's oppression as though it was our own.

T W E N T Y - E I G H T

◆◆◆

Uses of the Erotic

The Erotic as Power

Audre Lorde

There are many kinds of power, used and unused, acknowledged or otherwise. The erotic is a resource within each of us that lies in a deeply female and spiritual plane, firmly rooted in the power of our unexpressed or unrecognized feeling. In order to perpetuate itself, every oppression must corrupt or distort those various sources of power within the culture of the oppressed that can provide energy for change. For women, this has meant a suppression of the erotic as a considered source of power and information within our lives.

We have been taught to suspect this resource, vilified, abused, and devalued within western society. On the one hand, the superficially erotic has been encouraged as a sign of female inferiority; on the other hand, women have been made to suffer and to feel both contemptible and suspect by virtue of its existence.

It is a short step from there to the false belief that only by the suppression of the erotic within our lives and consciousness can women be truly strong. But that strength is illusory, for it is fashioned within the context of male models of power.

As women, we have come to distrust that power which rises from our deepest and nonrational knowledge. We have been warned against it all our lives by the male world, which values this depth of feeling enough to keep women around in order to exercise it in the service of men, but which fears this same depth too much to examine the possibilities of it within themselves. So women are maintained at a distant/inferior position to be psychically milked, much the same way ants maintain colonies of aphids to provide a life-giving substance for their masters.

But the erotic offers a well of replenishing and provocative force to the woman who does not fear its revelation, nor succumb to the belief that sensation is enough.

The erotic has often been misnamed by men and used against women. It has been made into the confused, the trivial, the psychotic, the plasticized sensation. For this reason, we have often turned away from the exploration and consideration of the erotic as a source of power and information, confusing it with its opposite, the pornographic. But pornography is a direct denial of the power of the erotic, for it represents the suppression of true feeling. Pornography emphasizes sensation without feeling.

The erotic is a measure between the beginnings of our sense of self and the chaos of our strongest feelings. It is an internal sense of satisfaction to which, once we have experienced it, we know we can aspire. For having experienced the fullness of this depth of feeling and recognizing its power, in honor and self-respect we can require no less of ourselves.

It is never easy to demand the most from ourselves, from our lives, from our work. To encourage excellence is to go beyond the encouraged mediocrity of our society. To go beyond the encouraged mediocrity of our society is to encourage excellence. But giving in to the fear of feeling and working to capacity is a luxury only the unintentional can afford, and the unintentional are those who do not wish to guide their own destinies.

This internal requirement toward excellence which we learn from the erotic must not be misconstrued as demanding the impossible from ourselves nor from others. Such a demand incapacitates everyone in the process. For the erotic is not a question only of what we do; it is a question of how acutely and fully we can feel in the doing. Once we know the extent to which we are capable of feeling that sense of satisfaction and completion, we can then observe which of our various life endeavors bring us closest to that fullness.

The aim of each thing which we do is to make our lives and the lives of our children richer and more possible. Within the celebration of the erotic in all our endeavors, my work becomes a conscious decision—a longed-for bed which I enter gratefully and from which I rise up empowered.

Of course, women so empowered are dangerous. So we are taught to separate the erotic demand from most vital areas of our lives other than sex. And the lack of concern for the erotic root and satisfactions of our work is felt in our disaffection from so much of what we do. For instance, how often do we truly love our work even at its most difficult?

The principal horror of any system which defines the good in terms of profit rather than in terms of human need, or which defines human need to the exclusion of the psychic and emotional components of that need—the principal horror of such a system is that it robs our work of its erotic value, its erotic power and life appeal and fulfillment. Such a system reduces work to a travesty of necessities, a duty by which we earn bread or oblivion for ourselves and those we love. But this is tantamount to blinding a painter and then telling her to improve her work, and to enjoy the act of painting. It is not only next to impossible, it is also profoundly cruel.

As women, we need to examine the ways in which our world can be truly different. I am speaking here of the necessity for reassessing the quality of all the aspects of our lives and of our work, and of how we move toward and through them.

The very word *erotic* comes from the Greek word *eros*, the personification of love in all its aspects—born of Chaos, and personifying creative power and harmony. When I speak of the erotic, then, I speak of it as an assertion of the lifeforce of women; of that creative energy empowered, the knowledgeand use of which we are now reclaiming in our language, our history, our dancing, our loving, our work, our lives.

There are frequent attempts to equate pornography and eroticism, two diametrically opposed uses of the sexual. Because of these attempts, it has become fashionable to separate the spiritual (psychic and emotional) from the political, to see them as contradictory or antithetical. "What do you mean, a poetic revolutionary, a meditating gunrunner?" In the same way, we have attempted to separate the spiritual and the erotic, thereby reducing the spiritual to a world of flattened affect, a world of the ascetic who aspires to feel nothing. But nothing is farther from the truth. For the ascetic position is one of the highest fear, the gravest immobility. The severe abstinence of the ascetic becomes the ruling obsession. And it is one not of self-discipline but of self-abnegation.

The dichotomy between the spiritual and the political is also false, resulting from an incomplete attention to our erotic knowledge. For the bridge which connects them is formed by the erotic—the sensual—those physical, emotional, and psychic expressions of what is deepest and strongest and richest within each of us, being shared: the passions of love, in its deepest meanings.

Beyond the superficial, the considered phrase, "It feels right to me," acknowledges the strength of the erotic into a true knowledge, for what that means is the first and most powerful guiding light toward any understanding. And understanding is a handmaiden which can only wait upon, or clarify, that knowledge, deeply born. The erotic is the nurturer or nursemaid of all our deepest knowledge.

The erotic functions for me in several ways, and the first is in providing the power which comes from sharing deeply any pursuit with another person. The sharing of joy, whether physical, emotional, psychic, or intellectual, forms a bridge between the sharers which can be the basis for understanding much of what is not shared between them, and lessens the threat of their difference.

Another important way in which the erotic connection functions is the open and fearless underlining of my capacity for joy. In the way my body stretches to music and opens into response, hearkening to its deepest rhythms, so every level upon which I sense also opens to the erotically satisfying experience, whether it is dancing, building a bookcase, writing a poem, examining an idea.

That self-connection shared is a measure of the joy which I know myself to be capable of feeling, a reminder of my capacity for feeling. And that deep and irreplaceable knowledge of my capacity for joy comes to demand from all of my life that it be lived within the knowledge that such satisfaction is possible, and does not have to be called *marriage*, nor *god*, nor *an afterlife*.

This is one reason why the erotic is so feared, and so often relegated to the bedroom alone, when it is recognized at all. For once we begin to feel deeply all the aspects of our lives, we begin to demand from ourselves and from our life-pursuits that they feel in accordance with that joy which we know ourselves to be capable of. Our erotic knowledge empowers us, becomes a lens through which we scrutinize all aspects of our existence, forcing us to evaluate those aspects honestly in terms of their relative meaning within our lives. And this is a grave responsibility, projected from within each of us, not to settle for the convenient, the shoddy, the conventionally expected, nor the merely safe.

During World War II, we bought sealed plastic packets of white, uncolored margarine, with a tiny, intense pellet of yellow coloring perched like a topaz just inside the clear skin of the bag. We would leave the margarine out for a while to soften, and then we would pinch the little pellet to break it inside the bag, releasing the rich yellowness into the soft pale mass of margarine. Then taking it carefully between our fingers, we would knead it gently back and forth, over and over, until the color had spread throughout the whole pound bag of margarine, thoroughly coloring it.

I find the erotic such a kernel within myself. When released from its intense and constrained pellet, it flows through and colors my life with a kind of energy that heightens and sensitizes and strengthens all my experience.

We have been raised to fear the *yes* within ourselves, our deepest cravings. But, once recognized, those which do not enhance our future lose their power and can be altered. The fear of our desires keeps them suspect and indiscriminately powerful, for to suppress any truth is to give it strength beyond endurance. The fear that we cannot grow beyond whatever distortions we may find within ourselves keeps us docile and loyal and obedient, externally defined, and leads us to accept many facets of our oppression as women.

When we live outside ourselves, and by that I mean on external directives only rather than from our internal knowledge and needs, when we live away from those erotic guides from within ourselves, then our lives are limited by external and alien forms, and we conform to the needs of a structure that is not based on human need, let alone an individual's. But when we begin to live from within outward, in touch with the power of the erotic within ourselves, and allowing that power to inform and illuminate our actions upon the world around us, then we begin to be responsible to ourselves in the deepest sense. For as we begin to recognize our deepest feelings, we begin to give up, of necessity, being satisfied with suffering and self-negation, and with the numbness which so often seems like their only alternative in our society. Our acts against oppression become integral with self, motivated and empowered from within.

In touch with the erotic, I become less willing to accept powerlessness, or those other supplied states of being which are not native to me, such as resignation, despair, self-effacement, depression, self-denial.

And yes, there is a hierarchy. There is a difference between painting a back fence and writing a poem, but only one of quantity. And there is, for me, no difference between writing a good poem and moving into sunlight against the body of a woman I love.

This brings me to the last consideration of the erotic. To share the power of each other's feelings is different from using another's feelings as we would use a kleenex. When we look the other way from our experience, erotic or otherwise, we use rather than share the feelings of those others who participate in the experience with us. And use without consent of the used is abuse.

In order to be utilized, our erotic feelings must be recognized. The need for sharing deep feeling is a human need. But within the european-american tradition, this need is satisfied by certain proscribed erotic comings-together. These occasions are almost always characterized by a simultaneous looking away, a pretense of calling them something else, whether a religion, a fit, mob violence, or even playing doctor. And this misnaming of the need and the deed give rise to that distortion which results in pornography and obscenity—the abuse of feeling.

When we look away from the importance of the erotic in the development and sustenance of our power, or when we look away from ourselves as we satisfy our erotic needs in concert with others, we use each other as objects of satisfaction rather than share our joy in the satisfying, rather than make connection with our similarities and our differences. To refuse to be conscious of what we are feeling at any time, however comfortable that might seem, is to deny a large part of the experience, and to allow ourselves to be reduced to the pornographic, the abused, and the absurd.

The erotic cannot be felt secondhand. As a Black lesbian feminist, I have a particular feeling, knowledge, and understanding for those sisters with whom I have danced hard, played, or even fought. This deep participation has often been the forerunner for joint concerted actions not possible before.

But this erotic charge is not easily shared by women who continue to operate under an exclusively european-american male tradition. I know it was not available to me when I was trying to adapt my consciousness to this mode of living and sensation.

Only now, I find more and more women-identified women brave enough to risk sharing the erotic's electrical charge without having to look away, and without distorting the enormously powerful and creative nature of that exchange. Recognizing the power of the erotic within our lives can give us the energy to pursue genuine change within our world, rather than merely settling for a shift of characters in the same weary drama.

For not only do we touch our most profoundly creative source, but we do that which is female and self-affirming in the face of a racist, patriarchal, and anti-erotic society.

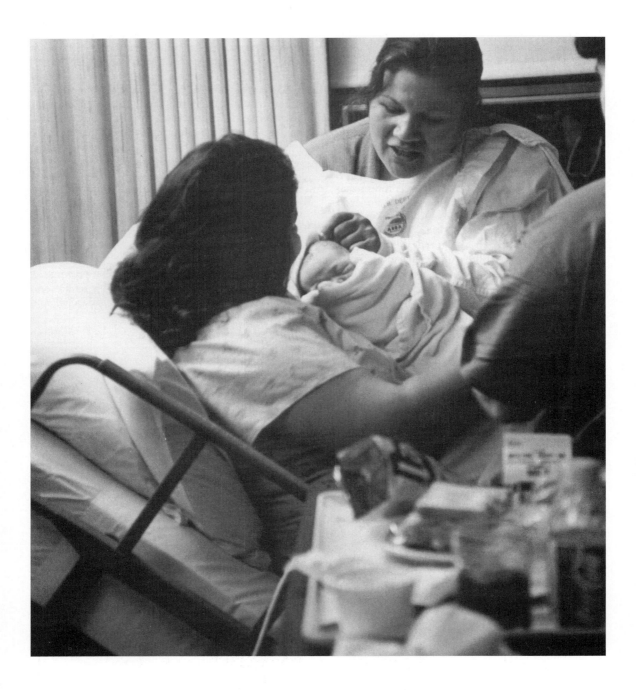

5

◆◆◆

Women's Health

Health, healing, and learning about our bodies are all issues of major concern to women, helping us to take care of ourselves and others. In times gone by, women made teas, tinctures, oils, and salves and gave baths and massages to heal sickness and alleviate pain. Some women still study the medicinal properties of plants and treat many complaints with herbal remedies (Gladstar 1993; Perrone, Stockel, and Krueger 1989; Potts 1988). Healthy processes like pregnancy, childbirth, and menopause have become increasingly medicalized from the mid-nineteenth century onward. Many women come into contact with the medical system, not through illness, but through pregnancy, or because we want to control our fertility. Health is a complex mix of physical, mental, emotional, and spiritual states of well-being, but Western medicine separates these connected aspects into different specialisms with different practitioners. The professionalization of health care over many decades has given doctors—mostly White men trained in university-based medical schools—authority in medical matters. Our subjective experiences of health and illness are negotiated with medical experts and, increasingly, mediated through technologies like mammograms or ultrasound. Women's health varies greatly depend-ing on individual factors like diet, exercise, smoking, stress, or violence, as well as macro-level factors such as race and class. This chapter discusses reproductive health, illness, the U.S. medical industry, and ways to move away from an overreliance on drugs and surgery to a more balanced conception of health care.

Reproductive Health, Reproductive Rights

The ability to become pregnant and have a baby is one of the most fundamental aspects of women's lives. Having a child is a profound experience, usually with far-reaching consequences for the mother. A woman becomes pregnant for many reasons: she wants to have a child; she wants to experience pregnancy and childbirth; she believes it will make her a "real" woman; she hopes it will keep her relationship together or make her partner happy. Some women plan to be pregnant; others get pregnant by accident, still others as a result of being raped. This deeply personal experience is also a public issue. The government has an interest in the numbers of children born, who their parents are, and whether they are married, whether they are teens, poor, or recent immigrants. This interest is reinforced by, and also influences, dominant notions of what kinds of women should be mothers. For some women—especially teenagers, lesbians, and mothers receiving welfare—there may be a serious tension between the personal event of pregnancy and societal attitudes to it. African American women have consistently tried to be self-determining in their reproductive lives despite having been used as breeders by slaveholders and despite subsequent systematic state interventions to control their fertility (Darling 1999; Dula 1996; Roberts 1997; Taylor 1999). These include state-sponsored sterilization programs, chemical contraceptives like Depo-Provera and Norplant, and now the chemical sterilizing agent, Quinacrine. Law professor and legal scholar Dorothy Roberts (1997) refers to this phenomenon as nothing less than "killing the black body."

An important indicator of infant and maternal health comes from data on infant mortality, the number of infants who die before their first birthday. Infant mortality is commonly a result of low birth weight, poor nutrition, inadequate prenatal care, the mother's level of education, and her overall health, whether affected by poor diet, stress, smoking, drinking and drug use, or HIV/AIDS.

Infant mortality for babies born in 1997, for example, showed the typical pattern in the United States. Asian and Pacific Islanders have the lowest rate (5 deaths per 1,000 live births), White infants (6.0), Puerto Rican (7.9), and African American (13.7) (Ventura et al. 2000).* Infant mortality rates have steadily decreased over the past sixty years, but

---

*Official statistics are a key source of information but are limited for discussion of diversity, as they are usually analyzed according to three main categories only: White, Black, and Hispanic. "Hispanic" includes Puerto Ricans, Cubans, Mexican Americans, and people from Central and South America. Some reports give a separate category for Native Americans and Native Alaskans, or for Asians and Pacific Islanders, another very heterogeneous group for whom there are few data at a national level. Data on many social issues are not usually analyzed by class, another serious limitation. We have tried to be as inclusive as possible; sometimes this is limited by the availability of adequate data.

Black infants continue to die at twice the rate of White infants (National Center for Health Statistics 2002b, Table 34). They are four times as likely to die from causes related to low birthweight, resembling infant mortality rates of developing countries. Mortality rates were higher for infants whose mothers did not have prenatal care in the first trimester, did not complete high school, were unmarried, were teenagers or older than forty, or smoked during pregnancy. Rates of first-trimester care are low for Native American, Mexican American, and African American women, compared with White women and Asian American women.

Controlling Fertility

Women's reproductive years span roughly half our lifetimes, from our teens to our forties. But, typically, women want only two children. Many women in the United States want to control their fertility—to limit the number of children they have, to avoid pregnancy with a particular partner, to postpone pregnancy until they are older, or to avoid it altogether—or to have the freedom to bear children. To do this we need sex education that is accurate and culturally appropriate; affordable and reliable birth control; safe, legal, affordable abortion; prenatal care and care through childbirth; health care for infants and children; and alternative insemination. In addition we need an adequate income, good general health care, and widespread cultural acceptance that we have a right to control our lives in this way.

Once a woman learns that she is pregnant, the decision to have a child or to have an abortion depends on a broad range of factors, including her age, personal circumstances, economic situation, whether or not she already has children, her level of overall health, cultural attitude to abortion, and the circumstances that led her to become pregnant (Arcana 1994; Lunneborg 1992; Townsend and Perkins 1992). As argued by Marsha Saxton in Reading 30, women with disabilities must also fight for the right to have children in the face of a dominant view that they are nonsexual beings who could not cope with being mothers (see also Finger 1990). Women of color are, disproportionately, victims of sterilization abuse, as discussed below.

Birth Control   Barrier methods like condoms and diaphragms have been used for many years. In the

1960s the intrauterine device (IUD), often called the coil, was introduced despite severe unwanted side effects for some women, such as heavy bleeding, pain, and cramps. The pill, introduced around the same time—and the most popular form of contraception today for women under 30—was the first chemical contraceptive to be taken every day. It affects the whole body continuously, as do newer methods like Depo-Provera (an injectable contraceptive that is effective for three months) and Norplant (implanted under the skin and effective for up to five years). Poor African American and Native American women and Latinas are much more likely than White women to be encouraged to use these long-acting contraceptives. Official policy seeks to limit their pregnancies and assumes that these women would be unreliable using other methods, thereby continuing the long connection between birth control and eugenics (Roberts 1997; Smith 2002). The Black Women's Health Network, the National Latina Health Organization, and other women's health advocates have called for the withdrawal of Depo-Provera as unsafe and also called attention to the fact that many women using Norplant had difficulty finding anyone to remove it. These methods compound many of the health problems suffered by poor women of color, including hypertension, diabetes, and stress. By the mid-1990s, doctors were taking out many more implants than they put in, as many women had experienced severe side effects. In 1999 American Home Products Corporation, which sells Norplant, agreed to offer cash settlements to 36,000 women who filed suit claiming that they had not been adequately warned about possible negative effects of using Norplant (Morrow 1999a). These included excessive menstrual bleeding, headaches, nausea, dizziness, and depression.

Other birth-control methods include the female condom, a loosely fitting, polyurethane (not latex) pouch with a semiflexible plastic ring at each end that lines the vagina. It also fits over the vulva. According to Planned Parenthood, it is not as effective as the male condom, but has the advantage of protecting against sexually transmitted infections (STIs) as well as unwanted pregnancy. Emergency contraception, a chemical method, involves taking multiple doses or oral contraceptives within 72 hours of unprotected sex, the sooner the better. These pills must be prescribed by a doctor, which is a great disadvantage if one has unprotected sex on Friday night

and cannot get to the doctor's office before Monday. They have been used by very few women to date, and "only one in five gynecologists tells patients about them in advance of any need" (Brody 2001).

Pharmaceutical companies have all but abandoned the field of contraceptive research in this country. Of the nine major companies that were involved in the 1960s and '70s, only two remain. This is due to a decline in funding from the government, international sources, and private foundations, as well as political opposition.

Abortion   Attitudes toward abortion have varied greatly from one society to another. Historically, the Catholic Church, for example, held the view that the soul did not enter the fetus for at least forty days after conception and allowed abortion up to that point. In 1869, however, Pope Pius IX declared that life begins at conception, and thus all abortion became murder in the eyes of the Church. In the United States up until the mid-nineteenth century, women were allowed to seek an abortion in the early part of pregnancy before they felt the fetus moving, a subjectively determined time, referred to as the quickening. After the Civil War more restrictive abortion laws were passed, partly to increase population and partly to shift authority over women's reproductive lives to the medical profession. By 1900 the only legal ground for an abortion was to save the life of the mother. Many women were forced to bring unwanted pregnancies to term in poverty, illness, or appalling personal circumstances. Thousands died trying to abort themselves or at the hands of "backstreet" abortionists. Some upper- and middle-class women found doctors to perform safe abortions for a high price, though they and the doctors risked prosecution if they were found out, as described by Grace Paley (1998) in her short article, "The Illegal Days" (also see Jaffe 1995; Miller 1993; Solinger 1994). Women with knowledge of herbs or medicine tried to help other women. The Jane Collective organized a clandestine feminist abortion service in the Chicago area in the early 1970s (Kaplan 1995).

In 1973 the landmark case *Roe v. Wade* made abortion legal. It defined freedom of choice as a right to privacy, protected by the U.S. Constitution. It recognized that no one except the woman herself has the right to decide whether to have an abortion. Ever since this legislation was enacted, it has been contested. This began in 1977 with the

Hyde Amendment that withdrew state funding for abortion for poor women. Subsequent measures included rules requiring waiting periods and parental consent for teens. Throughout the 1990s, anti-choice organizations staged violent protests at abortion clinics, bombed clinics, harassed patients, and killed doctors known to perform abortions as part of their practice (Baird-Windle and Bader 2001; Jaggar 1994). Women's health advocates have struggled to keep clinics open and lobbied for the Freedom of Access to Clinic Entrances Act (1994), which reduced harassment outside clinics. These legal restrictions, together with severe harassment, have reduced the number of abortion providers, and, in 2002, 86 percent of U.S. counties had no abortion provider. Fewer doctors are being trained to carry out the procedure, and many have stopped performing abortions because of the risks to themselves and their families.

In 1998, 17 of every 1,000 women of reproductive age (15 to 44) had abortions, the lowest rate since 1975 (National Center for Chronic Disease Prevention and Health Promotion 2002). Factors assumed to be responsible for this decline include reduced access to abortion, an increased willingness to use contraception, and negative attitudes toward abortion. Most women who had an abortion in 1998 were 25 or younger, White, and unmarried; and 56 percent of the procedures were done in the first two months of pregnancy and 88 percent before thirteen weeks. Women's feelings about having an abortion were downplayed initially by some pro-choice activists. Negative reactions have been exploited ruthlessly by anti-choice activists. Writer and activist Krista Jacob (2002) includes "unapologetic writings on abortion."

During the 1990s, the National Organization for Women, the Fund for a Feminist Majority, the National Abortion Rights Action League, and others campaigned for RU-486 (the "abortion pill," also called Mifepristone) to be made available in this country. In September 2000, the U.S. Food and Drug Administration approved this drug for use under very specific conditions. It can only be dispensed by physicians who are able to provide a surgical abortion or to refer a woman to such a provider in the small number of cases (estimated at 5 percent) where it does not work (Ginty 2001).

White feminists made abortion the centerpiece of reproductive rights activism in the 1980s and '90s.

According to the Black Women's Health Project (1995), when faced with an unintended pregnancy, the percentage of Black women who choose abortion is about equal to that of White women. Because Black women experience unintended pregnancies twice as often as White women, they are twice as likely to have abortions. Women of color have generally seen abortion as only one piece in a wider reproductive-health agenda that includes health care for women and children and the freedom to have children. This broader view has been endorsed by established feminist organizations, but much of their work is still focused on keeping abortion legal. January 2003 marked the thirtieth anniversary of *Roe v. Wade*. A whole generation of women has grown up, taking abortion rights for granted despite the growing gap between legality and access (Fried 2002). Opinion polls show that the majority of people in this country (65 percent) oppose a constitutional amendment prohibiting abortion (*Los Angeles Times* 2000). Yet, for the last thirty years, well-funded right-wing groups have worked strategically to undermine and overturn the right to abortion, and have financed anti-choice candidates at city, state, and congressional levels. According to the National Abortion Rights Action League (2002), "Since 1995, Congress voted 139 times to restrict reproductive rights and health options. Pro-choice forces lost all but 24." In 2001 the House passed bills that further restrict access to abortion: the Unborn Victims of Violence Act, which would give legal status or "personhood" to a fetus hurt or killed when a federal crime is committed; and the Child Custody Protection Act, which would criminalize an adult who accompanies a young woman seeking an abortion out-of-state if the home state's rules for parental consent have not been met. These bills await Senate consideration and approval. In November 2002, incoming Senate majority leader, Trent Lott (R-Miss.), vowed that the Senate will pass and the President will sign legislation to end legal abortion.

Sterilization   Sterilization abuse, rather than the right to abortion, has been a concern of poor women, especially women of color, for many years (Davis 1983a; Roberts 1997). Sterilization, without women's full knowledge or under duress, has been a common practice in the United States for poor Latina, African American, and Native American women. Dorothy Roberts (1997) notes that sterilization was a key tool in repressing the fertility of women of color in the 1930s, '40s, and '50s. Discussing sterilization of women of color in the 1960s, she comments:

> It is amazing how effective governments— especially our own—are at making sterilization and contraceptives available to women of color, despite their inability to reach these women with prenatal care, drug treatment, and other health services.   *(p. 95)*

By 1982, 24 percent of African American women, 35 percent of Puerto Rican women, and 42 percent of Native American women had been sterilized, compared with 15 percent of White women (Black Women's Health Project 1995; also see Jaimes and Halsey 1986; Lopez 1995; Smith 2002). Currently, sterilization is federally funded under the Medicaid program and is free on demand to poor women. Quinacrine, a chemical sterilizing agent, is the newest method and has dangerous side effects.

Teen Pregnancy   U.S. teenagers are having sex at younger ages, despite the risk of contracting sexually transmitted infections and HIV. Unintended teenage pregnancies have declined from an all-time high in 1991 to a record low (5 births for every 1,000 women aged 15 to 19) in 2000 (National Center for Health Statistics 2000). This is apparently because of increased condom use, the adoption of injectable and implant contraceptives (Depo-Provera and Norplant), and a leveling off of teenage sexual activity. Analyzed by race and ethnicity, teen birthrates were highest for Mexican American, African American, Native American, and Puerto Rican teenagers. In many cases the fathers of these babies are considerably older than the young women (Males 1999). Babies born to teens present a tremendous responsibility for young women and their families. Many community programs seek to prevent teen pregnancy, although sex education in schools and programs to distribute condoms, to prevent the spread of HIV/AIDS as much as pregnancy, have run into opposition from some parents, school boards, and conservative religious groups.

Sexually Transmitted Infections (STIs)   Sexually transmitted infections affect some 15 million people each year (Centers for Disease Control and Prevention 2000), but women and infants disproportion-

ately bear their long-term effects. The term STI refers to more than twenty-five diseases, including herpes, genital warts, pubic lice ("crabs"), chlamydia, gonorrhea, syphilis, and HIV. With the exception of syphilis, all STIs are increasing at an alarming rate. One reason for this is that women often do not have any symptoms or, if they do, the symptoms are mistaken for something else. Sexually transmitted infection can affect how a woman feels about her body and her partner and can lead to pelvic inflammatory disease or infertility. Knowing about safer sexual practices is important in reducing the risk of sexually transmitted infections, including HIV/AIDS. But knowing is not enough. Reading 33 reports women's attitudes to condom use and their ability to influence sexual partners to use condoms. The researchers conclude that power dynamics between men and women, women's assumptions about assertiveness and what it means to be a "good lover," together with their ideals of giving and sharing, may be in conflict with their desire for safer sex. It is important to note that condoms (male or female) are the only form of birth control that also give some protection against sexually transmitted infections.

Toxic Hazards   Working in toxic workplaces is a serious health hazard for many poor women and disproportionately for women of color. Some companies have kept women out of the most hazardous work—often the highest paid among blue-collar jobs—or required that they be sterilized first, to avoid being sued if these workers later give birth to babies with disabilities (Daniels 1993).

Medicalization of Reproductive Life

Childbirth   Before there were male gynecologists, midwives helped women through pregnancy and childbirth (Ehrenreich and English 1978). As medicine became professionalized in the nineteenth century, gynecology and obstetrics developed as an area of medical specialization. Doctors eroded the position of midwives and ignored or scorned their knowledge as "old wives' tales." Largely for the convenience of the doctor, women began to give birth lying on their backs, perhaps the hardest position in which to deliver a child. Forceps and various pain-killing medications were widely used. From the 1950s onward cesarean sections (C-sections) became more common, often for the doctors' convenience or from fear of malpractice suits. In 2000, 22.9 percent of births in the United States were C-sections, the highest rate in the world (Martin et al. 2002). The past twenty-five years have seen a further extension of this medicalization process as doctors monitor pregnancy from the earliest stages with a battery of new techniques such as amniocentesis, sonograms, and ultrasound. Although this technology allows medical practitioners, and through them, pregnant women, to know details about the health and condition of the fetus, as well as its sex, it also changes women's experiences of pregnancy and childbirth and can erode their knowledge of and confidence in their bodily processes. In Reading 29, Joy Harjo describes changes in Native American women's experiences of childbirth over three generations.

Menopause   This natural life process is increasingly treated as a disease rather than as a series of complex bodily and emotional changes. Many middle-aged women are advised to take hormone-replacement therapy (HRT) to control the symptoms of menopause such as hot flashes, insomnia, and vaginal dryness (Klein and Dumble 1994; Komesaroff, Rothfield, and Daly 1997). A major study of 46,355 women conducted by the National Cancer Institute confirmed that long-term use of hormone replacement after menopause can increase the risk of breast cancer (Grady 2000).

Reproductive Technologies   Technologies such as in vitro fertilization (IVF), in which a woman's eggs are fertilized by sperm outside her body and the fertilized embryo is then implanted into her womb, are an important development. They push the medicalization of pregnancy and childbirth one step further and hold out the hope that infertile couples or post-menopausal women will be able to have children. Bearing a child as a surrogate mother under contract to an infertile couple is one way a relatively poor young woman, usually White, can earn $10,000 or so, plus medical expenses, for nine months' work. Fertility clinics also need ovum donors and seek to harvest the eggs of young, college-educated women from a range of specified racial and ethnic groups. Infertility treatments so far have had a spectacularly low success rate and are very expensive. They are aimed at middle- and upper-middle-class women as a way of widening individual choice. Infertility may stem from a range of causes such as sexually transmitted infections, the effects of IUDs, delayed child-

bearing, and occupational and environmental factors. Infertility rates were lower in the 1990s than in previous decades, but this issue has a higher profile nowadays because of technological developments.

These reproductive technologies open up an array of economic, legal, and moral questions (Donchin and Purdy 1999; Hubbard 1990; Teays and Purdy 2001). Are they liberating for women? for which women? and at what costs? Some feminists have argued that women's biology and the ability to reproduce have been used to justify their social and economic subordination. In her now classic radical feminist text, Shulamith Firestone (1970), for example, was convinced that women's liberation requires freedom from biological reproduction and looked forward to developments in reproductive technology that would make it possible for a fetus to develop outside the womb. This is in stark contrast to sociologist Barbara Katz Rothman (1986) and the myriad women who believe that, if women lose their ability to reproduce, we lose a "quintessential female experience" (p. 111). Other feminist critics of reproductive technologies have focused on their invasiveness and consumers' lack of power over and knowledge about these methods, as compared with that of medical experts or "medocrats" (Arditti, Klein, and Minden 1984; Corea 1985, 1987; Lublin 1998; Petchesky 1997; Stanworth 1987).

Women and Illness

There is a rich and growing literature on women's experiences of illness, healing, and recovery, particularly in relation to breast cancer, chronic fatigue immune deficiency syndrome (CFIDS), and multiple sclerosis (e.g., Duff 1993; Griffin 1999; Lorde 1996; Mairs 1996; Rosenblum 1997; Sigler, Love, and Yood 1999). Counselor and writer Kat Duff (1993) notes that our society's "concepts of physical and psychological health have become one-sidedly identified with the heroic qualities most valued in our culture: youth, activity, productivity, independence, strength, confidence, and optimism" (p. 37). Illness challenges us to rethink our definition of self, our value and worth, in this ablist society, as these authors attest.

In general, women in the United States live longer than men. Women's average life expectancy is 80 years, compared to 74 years for men. On average, African American women die younger than White women (at age 75) but live longer than African American men, who have a life expectancy of 68 years (National Center for Health Statistics 2002a, Table 12). Asian Americans of both sexes live longer than White people. Like men, women in the United States are most likely to die from heart disease or cancer, followed by strokes, diabetes, respiratory diseases, pneumonia, and accidents. Older women suffer higher rates of disabling diseases such as arthritis, Alzheimer's, diabetes, cataracts, deafness, broken bones, digestive conditions, and osteoporosis than do men (Doyal 1995). Women under 45 mostly use reproductive health services. Women over 45 use hospitals less than men do, reflecting a basic health difference between the sexes: Men are more likely to have fatal diseases, whereas women have chronic conditions that worsen with age.

Effects of Gender, Race, and Class on Health and Illness

Taken as a whole, the health of African American women, Native American women, and Latinas is significantly worse than that of White women and Asian American women (Ross et al. 2002). A number of macro-level factors affect women's health, the treatments that doctors prescribe, and our ability to pay. White, middle-class, educated women, for example, are more likely to know about mammograms as a screening procedure for the early detection of breast cancer and that they are recommended for women over 40. They are more likely to have insurance to cover mammograms and to be registered with a doctor who encourages having them. Late diagnosis of breast cancer is directly related to higher mortality rates. Among cancer patients, White women also get what the literature refers to as "more aggressive treatment" compared to African American women, who are generally not told about all relevant treatment options, not given the full range of tests, and not always prescribed the most effective medications. The incidence of breast cancer increases with age, though African American women are more likely than White women to get it at younger ages. Fewer African American women get cancer, but their mortality rate is 28 percent higher. Breast cancer affects one woman in nine nationwide, though there are much higher incidences in certain geographic areas. Rita Arditti and Tatiana Schreiber (Reading 32) argue that environmental factors are significant in ex-

The World's Deadliest Disease Is Poverty

- In 1998, roughly six million children worldwide died before their fifth birthday, mainly from malnutrition, malaria, acute respiratory infections, measles, and diarrhea.

- Most of these conditions can be prevented or cured with improvements in sanitation, clean water supply, better housing, an adequate food supply, and general hygiene. The majority of deaths from infectious diseases can be prevented with existing, cost-effective measures including childhood vaccinations, bed nets and other malaria-prevention treatments, oral rehydration therapy, and antibiotics.

- Underweight causes the highest number of premature deaths, worldwide. By itself, underweight accounts for over three million childhood deaths a year in "developing countries."

- Diarrhea is responsible for about 1.7 million deaths a year, worldwide, caused by unsafe water, sanitation, and hygiene. Nine out of ten such deaths are children and virtually all are in "developing countries."

- Diseases linked to high blood pressure, cholesterol, tobacco, alcohol, and obesity have been most common in industrialized countries. They are now becoming more prevalent in developing countries, reflecting changes in living patterns, including diet, physical activity, the availability of tobacco and alcohol, and cultural upheavals.

Source: World Health Organization 2002.

plaining this discrepancy. The higher incidence is linked to race and class, as poor women, especially women of color, often live in areas with poor physical environment.

Among the top ten causes of death for African American women and Latinas aged 20 to 34 are

conditions connected to pregnancy and childbirth, not found in the top ten causes of death for White women in the same age range (National Center for Health Statistics 2002b, Table 1). More African American women die in their twenties as a result of HIV/AIDS, maternal mortality, drug use, and homicide compared to White women. Tuberculosis, an infectious disease associated with poverty and poor living conditions, was prevalent in the late nineteenth century and all but eradicated in the United States during the twentieth century. Compared with the general population, Native Americans are four times as likely to have tuberculosis. Twice as many Native American women die young (age 15 to 24) compared to White women the same age. Frederica Daly (Reading 8) gives detailed historical, legal, and economic background for her brief discussion of Native American health, which is among the worst in the country. Hypertension, a major risk factor for heart disease and stroke, is much more prevalent among African American women than it is among White women. Public health researchers Nancy Krieger and Stephen Sidney (1996) attribute this difference, in part, to stress related to racism. Obesity is a risk factor for heart disease, diabetes, and strokes, and it particularly affects African American women (Avery 1990; hooks 1993; Lovejoy 2001; White 1991).

Gender has also been a significant factor in diagnosing women with HIV/AIDS (Goldstein and Manlowe 1997). In 1993, for the first time, U.S. women's deaths from HIV/AIDS rose more than men's, and there were more African American women and Latinas than White women in this group (Hammonds 1995). Women have not been diagnosed as early as men because their symptoms are not so clear-cut and doctors were less likely to look for symptoms of HIV/AIDS in women. Also, because there were fewer women in clinical research trials, they did not receive the better treatment that men received. Primary care internist Barbara Ogur (1996) has pointed out that negative stereotypes of HIV-positive women (as drug users and women with multiple sex partners) have affected their visibility and care. In the late 1990s, women comprised half the reported HIV cases for young people (aged 13 to 24), and 77 percent of women with AIDS were African Americans and Latinas (Centers for Disease Control and Prevention 1999). Shirley Royster describes the life circumstances that led to her HIV-positive status and the work she has done subsequently as an HIV/AIDS activist and educator (Reading 34).

Women of all race and class groups who are beaten by their partners or suffer emotional violence or sexual abuse are subject to a significant health hazard (see Chapter 6).

Mental and Emotional Health

Many more women have some sort of mental illness compared to men, especially depression. Men are most likely to be diagnosed with alcohol- and drug-related conditions. There are many problems with diagnostic categories, however, and a great deal of room for interpretation based on individual and cultural factors. For example, the American Psychological Association did not drop homosexuality from its list of mental disorders until 1973. Lesbianism was thought to be caused by dominant mothers and weak fathers or, conversely, by girls' having exclusively male role models. Those who "came out" in the 1950s and '60s risked being sent to psychotherapists or mental institutions for a "cure." Since the 1980s, young women who do not conform to traditional gender roles may be diagnosed with "gender identity disorder" (Scholinski 1997).

Hopelessness and anger at one's life circumstances—which may include childhood sexual abuse, rape, domestic violence, poverty, homelessness, or simply dull routines—are not irrational reactions. Women's symptoms can seem vague to doctors, who may not really try to find out what is troubling them. Even when understood by doctors, women's traumas and difficulties are not easy to cure. More women than men attempt suicide, but men are more likely to use guns and to be successful, whereas women tend to use drug overdoses and are often found before their attempts are fatal. Patients in mental hospitals represent a relatively small proportion of those who are suffering mentally and emotionally. In general, women are admitted to mental hospitals as inpatients in roughly the same numbers as men. Women aged 25 to 44 are more likely than women in other age groups to be admitted to a psychiatric hospital.

One reason why more women are classified as having mental illness may be that the proportion of women seeking help for personal or emotional problems is twice as high as it is for men. It increases with educational attainment for both men and women. For both men and women, more persons who were formerly married seek help than do those currently married or never married (Dargan 1995). However, one cannot infer from these data that everyone who "seeks help" is doing so voluntarily; sometimes seeing a counselor or therapist is required by a social service agency or is a condition of probation. Voluntarily seeking help for emotional problems is linked to one's ability to pay, finding a suitable therapist, and cultural attitudes toward this kind of treatment.

Many people of all classes and racial groups attempt to deal with the pain and difficulty of their lives through drugs and alcohol. Frederica Daly (1994) notes that rates of alcoholism, homicide, and suicide among Native Americans are significantly higher than the national rates. In the United States, drug addiction is generally thought of as a crime rather than as a health issue. We discuss it further under the topic of crime and criminalization in Chapter 10, but we also see it as a symptom of stress brought on by the pres-

sures of life, often caused by social and economic inequality. There are far fewer drug-treatment programs than required, and fewer for women than for men.

A number of feminist writers have argued that contemporary approaches to mental distress, as illness, can be harmful to women (Chesler 1972; Ehrenreich and English 1978; Lerman 1996; Russell 1995; Showalter 1987; Ussher 1991). Philosopher Denise Russell (1995) briefly traces the history of definitions of madness from medieval Europe, where it was thought of as a combination of error and sin. During the seventeenth century, economic crises and rising unemployment in Europe prompted local officials to build houses of confinement for beggars, drunks, vagabonds, and other poor people and petty criminals, as well as for those who were thought mad. Through the eighteenth and nineteenth centuries, psychiatry gradually developed as a new medical specialty and asylums in Europe and the United States were headed by doctors, who theorized that much mental distress experienced by women was due to their reproductive capacities and sexuality. Hysteria, thought to be due to a disturbance of the womb, became a catchall category to describe women's mental illness. (The English word *hysterical* comes from the Greek word *husterikos*, meaning "of the womb.") Writer/literary critic Elaine Showalter (1987) and psychologist/psychotherapist Phyllis Chesler (1972) show how definitions of madness have been used to suppress women's creativity, education, and political involvement. Nineteenth-century White upper- and middle-class women who wanted to write, paint, travel, or speak out in public on issues of the day were assumed by their husbands—and by psychiatrists—to be insane. Charlotte Perkins Gilman's powerful fictional work *The Yellow Wallpaper,* for example, describes this experience and was written as a result of having lived through it. In the twentieth century, depression and premenstrual syndrome (PMS) replaced "hysteria" as stock phrases used in describing mental illness in women.

Feminist writers offer scathing critiques of the alleged objectivity of much contemporary mental health theorizing and of the value judgments and blatant sexism involved in many diagnostic categories like depression, behavioral disorders, and personality disorders that affect women more than men. Symptoms for these disorders are often very general, vague, and overlapping, and, according to Russell (1995), there is little agreement among practitioners as to what conditions are indicated by the symptoms. She questions the assumption that there is a biological or neurological basis for mental distress and argues that drug therapies based on this assumption have very mixed results in practice. Rather, she points to many external factors affecting women's mental equilibrium, including childhood sexual abuse, domestic violence, restricted educational or economic opportunities, and pressure to look beautiful, to be thin, to be compliant wives and long-suffering mothers, any of which could reasonably make women depressed or "crazy." Women have written powerful fiction and autobiographical accounts of mental illness and medical treatments (e.g., Danquah 1998; Kaysen 1994; Millet 1990; Plath 1971; Slater 1998).

Health and Aging

The health of women in middle age and later life is partly linked to how healthy they were when they were younger. The effects of stress, poor nutrition, smoking, or not getting enough exercise build up over time. Exposure to toxic chemicals, the physical and emotional toll of pregnancies, accidents, injuries, and caring for others all affect our health as we grow older. A lifetime of poverty often translates into poor health later in life.

Older women often have to accept the fact that they need support and care. They have to face their changed looks, physical limitations, and the loss of independence and loved ones, which calls on their emotional and spiritual resources, including patience, forbearance, optimism, and religious faith (see, for example, Doress-Worters and Siegal 1994). Older women's health is also adversely affected by caring for their sick partners when they themselves are old and sick. Shevy Healey (1997) argues that confronting ageism in society, as well as individual women's negative feelings about aging, is a must for women's mental health.

Over three million women in the United States provide personal assistance to family members who are sick or disabled, and over ten million women provide care to people outside their own households, usually their elderly parents and their husbands' elderly parents. This caretaking of elders may go on for as much as fifteen years and often overlaps with the women's other responsibilities—holding jobs, taking care of growing children, and managing homes. This regimen can be very trying; it involves physical and emotional stress and added expense and can seriously affect the quality of life and health for women in their middle years, who may have to give up opportunities for education, social life, or leisure-time activities. These women may be reluctant and resentful at times but accept their situation as part of what it means to be a good wife or daughter. It is important to recognize that women who care for others need support and respite themselves.

The Medical Industry

Since the seventeenth century, Western thought has consistently viewed organic, bodily processes as separate from those of the mind. The Western medical model separates physical, mental, emotional, and spiritual states of well-being and focuses on illness and disease rather than on the wholeness of people's lives, often treating symptoms rather than causes (Candib 1995). For example, though stressors generated by racism are a strong influence in the hypertension that disproportionately affects African Americans, the medical response is to treat the symptoms with medication, rather than to involve doctors, patients, and the wider society in combating racism. Similarly, many women are prescribed antidepressants rather than being empowered and supported in changing their life circumstances. This Western medical model also contributes to fantasies of immortality to be achieved by life-prolonging surgeries and drug treatments, as well as expensive cosmetic surgeries.

Because medical care is provided on a fee-paying basis in the United States, the medical industry has many of the characteristics of any business venture (see the discussion of the global economy in Chapter 9). Hospitals, nursing homes, and clinics that cannot balance their books are forced to lower their standards of treatment or are taken over by more profitable companies. The emphasis is on high-tech treatments, particularly drug therapies and surgery, as these are the most profitable for drug companies and manufacturers of medical equipment. Most people have benefited from vaccines and antibiotics, and the use of drugs and surgery may improve the lives of cancer patients, give relief from constant arthritic pain, or restore good vision to elderly people with cataracts. However, this overall emphasis has severely skewed the range of treatments available. It has led to an overproduction of intensive-care equipment, for example, while many people, especially the poor, have little access to the most rudimentary medical services. This emphasis has also shaped public policy through the testing and use of new drugs, the routine use of mammograms in breast cancer screening, sonograms and amniocentesis in pregnancy, and the prevalence of hysterectomies and births by cesarean section.

Paying for Medical Care

How we pay for medical care as a nation and who can afford it are questions much discussed in recent years, especially in connection with proposals for a national health plan put forward by President Clinton (1992–96). This plan was successfully opposed by medical insurers, some doctors, and the American Medical Association, who convinced enough voters, editorial writers, and members of Congress that standards of care would inevitably decline under a nationalized health system. The United States is the only industrialized country in the world, except South Africa, that does not have such a system.

Although 70 percent of people in the United States do have some kind of private medical insurance (Campbell 1999), this often covers only emergencies and hospitalization. Only 7 to 8 percent of participants in group plans are fully covered for hospital maternity charges. Fewer African American women and Latinas initiate prenatal care in the first trimester of pregnancy, at least in part because they lack insurance coverage; by contrast, 80 percent of White women seek early prenatal care. Women's Wellness programs are currently a profitable screening service provided by hospitals, though many insurance policies do not cover them, and they are not always culturally sensitive for all women's needs, especially women of color, women with disabilities, and lesbians. Many large-group insurance plans do not routinely cover any kind of contraception.

For most people who have private medical insurance (62 percent), this is employment-related. The figures for men and women with private coverage are very similar. Twenty-three percent of the population receive coverage through Medicaid or Medi-

care. More women than men are covered this way, reflecting Medicaid eligibility criteria that focus on mothers and children, and the greater numbers of women among the elderly who rely on Medicare. Cuts in Medicaid and Medicare during the 1990s meant that some people lost medical coverage altogether or in part. In 2001, 18 percent of the U.S. population (aged 18 to 64) was uninsured (National Center for Health Statistics 2002c, Table 1). Those without health insurance for the entire year are more likely to be young (18 to 34 years), people of color—especially Latino/as—or immigrants. Access to health insurance is also directly related to income, educational attainment, and employment. People without health insurance tend to be concentrated in small businesses with low rates of unionization or are working part-time or on a temporary basis.

Recent immigrants are often employed in low-paying jobs without benefits. It is not surprising that states with large immigrant populations have the highest proportion of uninsured people: Arizona, California, Louisiana, New Mexico, and Texas (Mills 2000). Since the mid-1990s, changes in government policy have sought to bar undocumented people and some legal immigrants from public health-care services, including emergency care. Undocumented women may risk jeopardizing their work and residence in the United States if they seek medical care for themselves or their children (Calvo 1996). There is sufficient confusion about eligibility to deter some eligible immigrant women from seeking services.

Hospitals, health maintenance organizations (HMOs), and nursing homes increasingly use a managed-care approach. It works on a prepayment system: If the care provided costs more than the prepayment, the HMO loses money. Although the managed-care approach started out with an emphasis on prevention and coordination among providers, there is always pressure to lower costs in order to increase profits. Treatment tends to be parceled out according to preset formulas that may not meet individual needs. As childbirth became medicalized, for example, women used to be hospitalized for a week or more. This was gradually cut back by insurers to the point where many women had to go home after only one night (increased to two in 1996). In Reading 31, Annette Dula has created the character of Miss Mildred, an elderly African American woman, to make the point that people are not

standardized machines and that we need medical care that is affordable and appropriate physically, emotionally, and culturally.

Other Barriers and Biases in Medical Services and Research

Other barriers to people's use of medical services, include fear of treatment, transportation difficulties, long waiting times, not being able to take time off work or losing pay for doing so, child-care responsibilities, language and cultural differences, and residential segregation, which may mean that there are few medical facilities in some communities of color or rural communities. Most inner cities have large teaching hospitals that treat local people, predominantly people of color, in their emergency rooms, but this treatment may be slanted toward the educational needs of the hospital's medical students rather than to the health needs of the patients. African Americans tend to be diagnosed or seek treatment later than Whites for many diseases, which may reduce the effectiveness of treatment and their ability to survive. Once under medical treatment, they receive what official reports describe as "less aggressive" treatment than White people, as mentioned earlier.

Women visit doctors and other health practitioners more often than men do. Despite this, there is a clear male bias in medical knowledge (Candib 1995). Most doctors in the United States are White, upper-middle-class men, and a meager 13 percent of government research funds was spent on women's health

in the early 1990s (Doyal 1995). Federal law now requires that women and men of color be included in research, but it will take time before this makes a big difference to the state of medical knowledge. Heart disease, which affects both men and women, was thought of as a man's disease for many years. As a result, it was studied much more than breast cancer (Dickersin and Schnaper 1996). Preliminary testing of antidepressant medications—prescribed mainly to women—was done only on men, despite evidence suggesting a difference in the drugs' effects between men and women. Research into health problems that men and women share was done on men and made to seem universal, not accounting for specific factors that might affect women differently. For example, the NIH-sponsored five-year Physicians Health Study concerning the effects of aspirin on heart disease used a sample of 22,071 men and no women, even though heart disease is also the number-one killer of women (Nechas and Foley 1994). Recommended drug treatments are also tested on men and then prescribed for women on the assumption that they will be equally effective, though whether this is so is not known (Nechas and Foley 1994). In 2001, a sixteen-member panel of the National Academy of Sciences recommended that, in experiments and drug trials, medical researchers should pay much more attention to the different effects of disease and medical treatments on women and men. They also noted that "editors of scientific journals should encourage researchers to analyze their results by sex whenever possible" (Pear 2001, p. A14; also Lerner 2001). There has been very little research concerning women and

AIDS, the long-term effects of birth control pills, or new safe, reliable forms of contraception. Too little is known about the health needs of women of color, older women, and women with disabilities (Gill 1996; Krieger and Fee 1996).

Health as Wellness

Requirements for Good Health

Health is not just the absence of illness, as implied by the medical model described earlier. Feeling well involves a complex mix of physical, mental, and emotional factors. Many aspects of life are not under our control. For example, living in damp housing or near a busy freeway or polluted industrial area, working in hazardous factories and mines, being exposed to toxic pesticides in agricultural work, doing repetitive tasks all day, and sitting in the same position for long periods of time are all aspects of daily life that can compromise one's health. The many newspaper and magazine articles that focus on individual lifestyle factors—diet, cigarette smoking, weight, exercise, and a positive attitude to coping with stress—urge us to take more personal responsibility for our health. Although this is valuable advice, lifestyle is only part of the story. Rita Arditti and Tatiana Schreiber present data on links between breast cancer and environmental contamination in Reading 32. Cancer research efforts that focus on individual neurological or genetic factors miss this crucial environmental connection.

Health requires clean water, air, and food, adequate housing, safety, healthy working conditions, and emotional and material supports. Thus, seemingly unconnected issues like poverty, racism, and sexism are also health issues.

Feminist Approaches to Wellness

Women's health has been a central issue for activists for the past thirty years or more (Avery 1990; Morgen 2002; Norsigian 1996; Nowrojee and Silliman 1997; Ross et al. 2002; White 1990). Activist and political commentator Loretta Ross et al. (2002) describe the formation of the SisterSong Women of Color Reproductive Health Project in the late 1990s. This is a collaboration of sixteen women of color organizations (Native American, African American, Latina, and Asian American/Pacific Islander) working together to share information on the health of women of color and to provide and advocate for better services, as a matter of human rights. Because many women's health needs are not currently met under the current system, especially those of women of color, feminist health practitioners and advocates urge a fundamental shift in emphasis toward a more holistic system of health care that recognizes that physical, emotional, and mental health are intimately connected and which emphasizes self-education, prevention, self-help, alternative therapies, a restructuring of medical financing, and a wider provision of basic facilities and appropriate services. For many feminist health workers, reproductive freedom is an essential part of women's health, as mentioned earlier.

Self-Education and Preventive Care   Preventing illness through self-education has low priority in the United States, and beyond basic immunization for infants and some minimal sex education for teens, it has generally been left to interested practitioners, organizations like the American Cancer Society, or self-help health-care projects. It involves learning to listen to our bodies and becoming more conscious of what they can tell us; learning to eat well and to heal common ailments with home remedies; taking regular exercise; quitting smoking; doing breast self-exams; and practicing safer sex. Self-education and preventive care also include various types of self-help, such as programs dealing with substance abuse or codependence. Many of these, like Alcoholics Anonymous, Al-Anon, Narcotics Anonymous, and other twelve-step programs, have been successful in helping people change negative habits and attitudes, though they usually do not address macro-level factors like institutionalized racism, sexism, and heterosexism. A self-help approach also means taking a greater degree of personal responsibility for one's health and being able to make informed decisions about possible remedies and treatments, rather than simply consuming services. Finally, preventive care encompasses all the creative activities and projects, like dancing, music, poetry, sports, and homemaking, that give us joy and make us feel alive.

Alternative Therapies   Therapies such as acupuncture, homeopathy, deep tissue massage, and chiropractic care that do not rely on drug treatments and surgery may be highly beneficial for a range of complaints. Although they have been scorned as quackery by many mainstream medical practitioners, they are being used more widely, sometimes in conjunction with Western medicine. At present, most alternative therapies are not financially accessible even for people with medical insurance, and they are usually available only in larger cities.

Reform of Health-Care Financing   Many advocates for women's health argue for a fundamental change in the way health care is paid for. In May 1993, for example, the Women's Convergence for National Health Care, attended by over five hundred women from twenty states, called for a universal health-care plan to provide equal access, comprehensive benefits, freedom to choose doctors and other caregivers, health education and prevention, reproductive health, public accountability, and progressive, fair financing (Baker 1993). Participants argued that universal health care is a major component of a social justice agenda. Currently, proposals for a national "single-payer" system incorporate these points (e.g., Physicians for a National Health Program 2002).

Feminist Health Projects   Such projects have been active since the early 1970s. Examples include courses in women's health; informal self-health groups like the Bloomington Women's Health Collective (Bloomington, Ind.); women's health centers (e.g., in Concord, N.H., and Burlington, Vt.); campaigns for reproductive rights (e.g., National Abortion Rights Action League and regional affiliates) or public funding for breast cancer research and treatment (e.g., Women's Community Cancer Project, Cambridge, Mass.); community health campaigns (e.g., Boston Health Access Project); and national organizations like the Black Women's Health Project (Atlanta), the National Asian Women's Health Organization (San Francisco), the National Latina Health Organization (Oakland, Calif.), the National Women's Health Network (Washington, D.C.), and the Native American Women's Health and Education Resource Center (Lake Andes, S. Dak.). The Boston Women's Health Book Collective's groundbreaking book *Our Bodies, Ourselves* first started as mimeographed notes for a course in women's health and was later developed for publication. It has become an essential resource on women's health and sexuality for women of all ages.

Questions for Reflection

As you read and discuss this chapter, consider these questions:

1. How do you know when you're healthy? Sick?
2. How can you learn more about your own body and your health?
3. What is a health crisis? For an individual person? At the national level?
4. Who should pay for health care? How? Why do you think this?
5. How does an individual, a family, or a society construct definitions of illness?
6. How do you define reproductive health? Reproductive rights? Reproductive freedom?

Finding Out More on the Web

1. Find out about the history of *Roe v. Wade.* How and why did this piece of legislation gain support? What was the cultural and historical context? Who were some of the key players who helped to make it happen? What is its status now?
2. Find out more about the positions, arguments, and activities of anti-choice organizations (e.g., the Army of God, the Christian Coalition, Focus on the Family, Operation

Rescue) and pro-choice organizations (e.g., Choice USA, Fund for a Feminist Majority, Planned Parenthood, National Abortion Rights Action League). What do you think about what you learned here? Do you have any concerns that are not included?

3. Research one of the women's health organizations mentioned in this chapter. What are its goals, strategies, and activities?

◆◆◆

Taking Action

1. List all the steps you take to care for yourself and any additional ones you could take.

2. Find out more about what your family and community consider effective self-care practices.

3. Find out where women can go to keep healthy or get quality health care in your community.

TWENTY-NINE

◆◆◆

Three Generations of Native American Women's Birth Experience

Joy Harjo

It was still dark when I awakened in the stuffed back room of my mother-in-law's small rented house with what felt like hard cramps. At 17 years of age I had read everything I could from the Tahlequah Public Library about pregnancy and giving birth. But nothing prepared me for what was coming. I awakened my child's father and then ironed him a shirt before we walked the four blocks to the Indian hospital because we had no car and no money for a taxi. He had been working with another Cherokee artist silk-screening signs for specials at the supermarket and making $5 a day, and had to leave me alone at the hospital because he had to go to work. We didn't awaken his mother. She had to get up soon enough to fix breakfast for her daughter and granddaughter before leaving for her job at the nursing home. I knew my life was balanced at the edge of great, precarious change and I felt alone and cheated. Where was the circle of women to acknowledge and honor this birth?

It was still dark as we walked through the cold morning, under oaks that symbolized the stubbornness and endurance of the Cherokee people who had made Tahlequah their capital in the new lands.

I looked for handholds in the misty gray sky, for a voice announcing this impending miracle. I wanted to change everything; I wanted to go back to a place before childhood, before our tribe's removal to Oklahoma. What kind of life was I bringing this child into? I was a poor, mixed-blood woman heavy with a child who would suffer the struggle of poverty, the legacy of loss. For the second time in my life I felt the sharp tug of my own birth cord, still connected to my mother. I believe it never pulls away, until death, and even then it becomes a streak in the sky symbolizing that most important warrior road. In my teens I had fought my mother's weaknesses with all my might, and here I was at 17, becoming as my mother, who was in Tulsa, cooking breakfasts and preparing for the lunch shift at a factory cafeteria as I walked to the hospital to give birth. I should be with her; instead, I was far from her house, in the house of a mother-in-law who later would try to use witchcraft to destroy me.

After my son's father left me I was prepped for birth. This meant my pubic area was shaved completely and then I endured the humiliation of an enema, all at the hands of strangers. I was left alone in a room painted government green. An overwhelming antiseptic smell emphasized the sterility of the hospital, a hospital built because of the U.S. government's treaty and responsibility to provide health care to Indian people.

I intellectually understood the stages of labor, the place of transition, of birth—but it was difficult to bear the actuality of it, and to bear it alone. Yet in some ways I wasn't alone, for history surrounded me. It is with the birth of children that history is given form and voice. Birth is one of the most sacred acts we take part in and witness in our lives. But sacredness seemed to be far from my lonely labor room in the Indian hospital. I heard a woman screaming in the next room with her pain, and I wanted to comfort her. The nurse used her as a bad example to the rest of us who were struggling to keep our suffering silent.

The doctor was a military man who had signed on this watch not for the love of healing or out of awe at the miracle of birth, but to fulfill a contract for medical school payments. I was another statistic to him; he touched me as if he were moving equipment from one place to another. During my last visit I was given the option of being sterilized. He explained to me that the moment of birth was the best time to do it. I was handed the form but chose not to sign it, and am amazed now that I didn't think too much of it at the time. Later I would learn that many Indian women who weren't fluent in English signed, thinking it was a form giving consent for the doctor to deliver their babies. Others were sterilized without even the formality of signing. My light skin had probably saved me from such a fate. It wouldn't be the first time in my life.

When my son was finally born I had been deadened with a needle in my spine. He was shown to me—the incredible miracle nothing prepared me for—then taken from me in the name of medical progress. I fell asleep with the weight of chemicals and awoke yearning for the child I had suffered for, had anticipated in the months proceeding from his unexpected genesis when I was still 16 and a student at Indian school. I was not allowed to sit up or walk because of the possibility of paralysis (one of the drug's side effects), and when I finally got to hold him, the nurse stood guard as if I would hurt him. I felt enmeshed in a system in which the wisdom that had carried my people from generation to generation was ignored. In that place I felt ashamed I

was an Indian woman. But I was also proud of what my body had accomplished despite the rape by the bureaucracy's machinery, and I got us out of there as soon as possible. My son would flourish on beans and fry bread, and on the dreams and stories we fed him.

My daughter was born four years later, while I was an art student at the University of New Mexico. Since my son's birth I had waitressed, cleaned hospital rooms, filled cars with gas (while wearing a mini-skirt), worked as a nursing assistant, and led dance classes at a health spa. I knew I didn't want to cook and waitress all my life, as my mother had done. I had watched the varicose veins grow branches on her legs, and as they grew, her zest for dancing and sports dissolved into utter tiredness. She had been born with a caul over her face, the sign of a gifted visionary.

My earliest memories are of my mother writing songs on an ancient Underwood typewriter after she had washed and waxed the kitchen floor on her hands and knees. She too had wanted something different for her life. She had left an impoverished existence at age 17, bound for the big city of Tulsa. She was shamed in a time in which to be even part Indian was to be an outcast in the great U.S. system. Half her relatives were Cherokee full-bloods from near Jay, Oklahoma, who for the most part had nothing to do with white people. The other half were musically inclined "white trash" addicted to country-western music and Holy Roller fervor. She thought she could disappear in the city; no one would know her family, where she came from. She had dreams of singing and had once been offered a job singing on the radio but turned it down because she was shy. Later one of her songs would be stolen before she could copyright it and would make someone else rich. She would quit writing songs. She and my father would divorce, and she would be forced to work for money to feed and clothe four children, all born within two years of each other.

As a child growing up in Oklahoma, I liked to be told the story of my birth. I would beg for it while my mother cleaned and ironed. "You almost killed me," she would say. "We almost died." That I could kill my mother filled me with remorse and shame. And I imagined the push-pull of my life, which is a legacy I deal with even now when I am twice as old as my mother was at my birth. I loved to hear the story of my warrior fight for my breath. The way it was told, it had been my decision to live. When I got older, I realized we were both nearly casualties of the system, the same system flourishing in the Indian hospital where later my son Phil would be born.

My parents felt lucky to have insurance, to be able to have their children in the hospital. My father came from a fairly prominent Muscogee Creek family. *His* mother was a full-blood who in the early 1920s got her degree in art. She was a painter. She gave birth to him in a private hospital in Oklahoma City; at least that's what I think he told me before he died at age 53. It was something of which they were proud.

This experience was much different from my mother's own birth. She and five of her six brothers were born at home, with no medical assistance. The only time a doctor was called was when someone was dying. When she was born her mother named her Wynema, a Cherokee name my mother says means beautiful woman, and Jewell, for a can of shortening stored in the room where she was born.

I wanted something different for my life, for my son, and for my daughter, who later was born in a university hospital in Albuquerque. It was a bright summer morning when she was ready to begin her journey. I still had no car, but I had enough money saved for a taxi for a ride to the hospital. She was born "naturally," without drugs. I could look out of the hospital window while I was in labor at the bluest sky in the world. I had support. Her father was present in the delivery room—though after her birth he disappeared on a drinking binge. I understood his despair, but did not agree with the painful means to describe it. A few days later Rainy Dawn was presented to the sun at her father's pueblo and given a name so that she will always be recognized as a part of the people, as a child of the sun.

That's not to say that my experience in the hospital reached perfection. The clang of metal against metal in the delivery room had the effect of a tuning fork reverberating fear in my pelvis. After giving birth I held my daughter, but they took her from me for "processing." I refused to lie down to be wheeled to my room after giving birth; I wanted to walk out of there to find my daughter. We reached a compromise and I rode in a wheelchair. When we reached the room I stood up and walked to the nursery and demanded my daughter. I knew she needed me. That began my war with the nursery staff, who

deemed me unknowledgeable because I was Indian and poor. Once again I felt the brushfire of shame, but I'd learned to put it out much more quickly, and I demanded early release so I could take care of my baby without the judgment of strangers.

I wanted something different for Rainy, and as she grew up I worked hard to prove that I could make "something" of my life. I obtained two degrees as a single mother. I wrote poetry, screenplays, became a professor, and tried to live a life that would be a positive influence for both of my children. My work in this life has to do with reclaiming the memory stolen from our peoples when we were dispossessed from our lands east of the Mississippi; it has to do with restoring us. I am proud of our history, a history so powerful that it both destroyed my father and guarded him. It's a history that claims my mother as she lives not far from the place her mother was born, names her as she cooks in the cafeteria of a small college in Oklahoma.

When my daughter told me she was pregnant, I wasn't surprised. I had known it before she did, or at least before she would admit it to me. I felt despair, as if nothing had changed or ever would. She had run away from Indian school with her boyfriend and they had been living in the streets of Gallup, a border town notorious for the suicides and deaths of Indian peoples. I brought her and her boyfriend with me because it was the only way I could bring her home. At age 16, she was fighting me just as I had so fiercely fought my mother. She was making the same mistakes. I felt as if everything I had accomplished had been in vain. Yet I felt strangely empowered, too, at this repetition of history, this continuance, by a new possibility of life and love, and I steadfastly stood by my daughter.

I had a university job, so I had insurance that covered my daughter. She saw an obstetrician in town who was reputed to be one of the best. She had the choice of a birthing room. She had the finest care. Despite this, I once again battled with a system in which physicians are taught the art of healing by dissecting cadavers. My daughter went into labor a month early. We both knew intuitively the baby was ready, but how to explain that to a system in which numbers and statistics provide the base of understanding? My daughter would have her labor interrupted; her blood pressure would rise because of the drug given to her to stop the labor. She would be given an unneeded amniocentesis and would have her labor induced—after having it artificially stopped! I was warned that if I took her out of the hospital so her labor could occur naturally my insurance would cover nothing.

My daughter's induced labor was unnatural and difficult, monitored by machines, not by touch. I was shocked. I felt as if I'd come full circle, as if I were watching my mother's labor and the struggle of my own birth. But I was there in the hospital room with her, as neither my mother had been for me, nor her mother for her. My daughter and I went through the labor and birth together.

And when Krista Rae was born she was born to her family. Her father was there for her, as were both her grandmothers and my friend who had flown in to be with us. Her paternal great-grandparents and aunts and uncles had also arrived from the Navajo Reservation to honor her. Something *had* changed.

Four days later, I took my granddaughter to the Saguaro forest before dawn and gave her the name I had dreamed for her just before her birth. Her name looks like clouds of mist settling around a sacred mountain as it begins to speak. A female ancestor approaches on a horse. We are all together.

THIRTY

◆◆◆

Reproductive Rights
A Disability Rights Issue

Marsha Saxton

In recent years, the women's movement has broadened its definition of "reproductive rights" to include not only abortion, but all aspects of sexuality, procreation, and parenthood. . . .

Some women may take for granted birth control, reproductive health care, and sex education, forgetting that people with different life experiences based on class, race, or physical or mental ability may not have access to these fundamental aspects of reproductive freedom. But for people with disabilities, *all* the reproductive rights are still at stake.

For centuries, the oppression of people with disabilities has denied us "choice": choice about who should be regarded as "a sexual being," who should have babies, which babies should be born, which babies should be allowed to live after they're born, who should raise these babies into adulthood. These choices were made, for the most part, by others. People with disabilities are beginning to demand a say in these decisions now that the Americans with Disabilities Act (ADA) has forced the public to perceive our issues as civil rights issues. In the decades to come, we hope to see a transformation in the public's perception of disability and of people with disabilities. The issue of reproductive rights can serve as a catalyst for this transformation.

The stereotype of asexuality is slowly lifting. There are now a few disabled characters in the popular literature and media who are portrayed as sexual beings participating in intimate activities. (Some of these movie personalities, such as actress Marlee Maitlin, themselves are deaf or have physical disabilities. However, most disabled characters on TV or in the movies are still played by non-disabled actors.)

New and complex issues are emerging in regard to disability and procreation. Many relate to new developments in reproductive technologies. Others reflect changing social values. What follows is a discussion of how these new issues affect people with disabilities.

Reproductive Health Care

Because of patronizing attitudes about disabled people, many medical practitioners and health care facilities do not consider offering reproductive health care services to their patients who have disabilities. Many people with disabilities or with chronic illness, because of the "preexisting condition" exclusion in most health insurance, have been denied access to *any* health care, not only reproductive health care.

There are few medical or nursing schools that offer any training on the reproductive health of people with disabilities. Only in the last five years has there been any research on the effects of various birth control methods for people with different kinds of disabilities or chronic illness, and these studies are limited, often focusing only on spinal cord injury. Even people with the more common disabling conditions like diabetes, arthritis, or multiple sclerosis have little or no information about whether they should or shouldn't use particular methods of birth control.

In Chicago, a group of disabled women have created a "disability accessible" gynecological clinic through the Chicago Rehabilitation Institute and the Prentice Women's Hospital, staffed with practitioners who have been trained to serve disabled women. The Health Resource Center for Women with Disabilities is unique. One day a week, it offers accessible core gyn services for women with disabilities and now serves more than 200 women. The staff includes nurse practitioners and midwives; and a nurse who has a disability has been hired. The clinic program plans to expand its resources to include a project director to monitor clinic services and to oversee a library with health-related videos and publications. It will also add an 800 telephone number staffed by a woman with a disability to respond to questions about accessible health care services. The center has initiated research directed at documenting the medical experiences of women with disabilities and improving services for traditionally underserved populations, including developmentally disabled, learning disabled, and mentally retarded women.

Sex Education

Disabled children and adults need information about dating, sex, menstruation, pregnancy, birth control, AIDS, and other sexually transmitted diseases. Attitudes have changed, and increasingly, parents and educators are recognizing that disabled children need sex education. But this is not the norm. Disabled children are still often overprotected by adults who don't know how to teach them about "the facts of life." Questions such as the following tend to provoke confusion: how can blind children be given information about gender anatomy? How should re-

tarded children be told about AIDS? How can deaf children, children who use wheelchairs, or any child who may have felt the stigma of disability be encouraged to interact positively with non-disabled and disabled peers and to learn positive sexual self-esteem? Many disabled adults never received important information about sex. They are vulnerable to confusing or dangerous misinformation and serious difficulties with their own sexuality, difficulties that result not from actual physical limitations but simply from exclusion from information and experience.

Marriage Disincentives

In the United States, people with disabilities who receive certain kinds of Social Security or Medicaid benefits are discouraged from getting married by threat of reduced or eliminated benefits. These "marriage disincentives" (like "employment disincentives," which discourage disabled people from employment by threat of reduced medical coverage) reveal the serious disability discrimination fundamentally built into our disability policies. If an SSI (Supplemental Security Income) recipient marries, his or her spouse's earnings are considered income, thus reducing the recipient's benefits, jeopardizing essential medical and personal care attendant services, and often placing enormous financial burden on the couple to finance prohibitively expensive services or equipment. The current law has the effect of forcing people with disabilities to accept "living together" as temporary sweethearts rather than an adult, community-sanctioned marriage. . . . While the outward rationale for the law is to save taxpayer money on people who could be supported by a spouse (based on the assumption that two can live as cheaply as one), social scientists and disability rights activists suspect that drafters of these marriage disincentive laws were also intending to thwart marriage and potential procreation for disabled people.

"Reproducing Ourselves"

The very idea of disabled persons as parents scares some people and exposes discriminatory attitudes that might otherwise remain hidden. Acceptance of disabled people as parents simply requires the larger community's acceptance of us as human beings. By denying our rights to be mothers and fathers, it is not only our competence to care for our young, but our very existence, our desire to "reproduce ourselves," that is forbidden.

In late 1991, TV news anchor Bree Walker, who has a genetic disability and who was pregnant, became the brunt of a call-in radio talk show when the host Jane Norris asked listeners, "Should disabled people have children?" Callers aired their opinions about whether Walker should have her baby or, as Norris posed the question, "Is it 'fair' to bring a child with a disability into the world?" The incident became the focal point of the disabled women's community's challenge to the idea that people with disabilities should not be born.

Qualifications for Parenthood

The Earls are a married Michigan couple, both severely disabled with cerebral palsy. They had a baby, Natalie, and sought assistance from the Michigan Home Help Program in providing physical care for the infant. Their desire to raise their own child and to demonstrate their competence as loving parents was thwarted by state regulations that bar the personal care assistant (PCA) of a disabled client from touching the client's child during paid work hours. One result of this regulation seems to be that disabled people who rely on the PCA program for help in daily living cannot have children.

Of course, people with disabilities must take seriously the responsibilities of adult sexuality and the potential for pregnancy and parenthood. We must also educate ourselves, the disability community, and our families and friends about what it means to be a parent and be disabled. And we must be prepared to take on the discriminatory policies of a variety of institutions: medical, social services, legal, and media. But we must also do battle within ourselves. We must overcome the voices we've internalized that say, "You can't possibly do this, you can't be good parents, and you don't deserve the benefits or the assistance required to raise your own children."

In Berkeley, California, an agency called Through the Looking Glass offers the first program specifically designed to assist parents with disabilities in skills development, community resources, and peer support. [Through the Looking Glass also publishes a newsletter, which can be ordered at 2198 Sixth St., Suite 100, Berkeley, CA 94710.]

Custody Struggles

Tiffany Callo is a young woman who wanted to raise her newborn son. Because of her cerebral palsy, the California Department of Social Services challenged her ability to care for the child. Armed with lawyers and court orders, the department refused to allow her to demonstrate her parenting skills in an appropriate environment that would enable her to show the creative approaches she had developed to handle the baby. *Newsweek* reporter Jay Mathews picked up her story, and Callo became a spokesperson for the cause of mothers with disabilities who fight for the right to raise their own children. Social service and child protection agency professionals need training and awareness to allow them to perceive the *abilities* of disabled parents, not only the stereotyped limitations.

Adoption

A large number of children adopted or waiting for adoption are disabled. Many disabled adults were adopted or placed in foster homes. It is still largely the case that adoption agencies do not consider disabled people as prospective parents for either disabled or non-disabled children. We need to challenge this stereotype that people with disabilities cannot be good adoptive parents. A few adoption agencies are changing policies, allowing disabled people to adopt, and in some cases even encouraging disabled adults to adopt children with disabilities. For example, Adoption Resource Associates in Watertown, Massachusetts, has taken a special interest in prospective disabled parents and makes specific mention in their brochure that they do not discriminate on the basis of disability in their placement services.

Sterilization Abuse

Consider this story of a woman with a psychiatric disability: "When I was twenty, I got pregnant by my boyfriend at the state mental school. Of course, there was no birth control for patients. We weren't allowed to have sex, but it went on all the time, even between patients and attendants. A doctor forced my mother to sign a paper giving me an abortion, even though I wanted to give up the baby for adoption. When I woke up, I found out I had had a hysterectomy. Maybe I couldn't take care of the baby then, but nobody even asked me what I wanted to do, or what I hoped for when I got older."

When a guardian or medical professional decides that people labeled retarded, mentally ill, or with other disabilities should not be parents, sterilization without consent may occur. Often, guardians or other decision makers who intervene on behalf of these disabled people have little exposure to the Independent Living Movement, or other community disability resources. As disabled people, we need to be empowered to make our own decisions regarding sexuality and procreation.

Abortion

Women with disabilities have reported significant difficulties with regard to abortion. These include being pressured to undergo an abortion because it is assumed that a disabled woman could not be a good parent, or, conversely, being denied access to abortion because a guardian decides the woman was incapable of making her own reproductive choices. Sometimes, after birth, a disabled woman's child is taken away from her. Women with disabilities experience the same kinds of abortion access difficulties as non-disabled women, but these difficulties are often magnified by disability discrimination.

Prenatal Screening

Scientific advances in the field of genetics have created technologies that can detect an increasing number of genetic conditions in the womb. While the general public seems to regard this medical technology as a wonderful advance and a way to reduce the incidence of disability and improve the quality of life, people with disabilities often have a very different view. As revealed in the Bree Walker case mentioned above, the unchallenged assumption often accompanying the use of these screening tests is that the lives of people with genetically related disabilities (such as muscular dystrophy, Down syndrome, cystic fibrosis, sickle cell anemia, and spina bifida) are simply not worth living and are a burden that families and society would rather not endure. The options to abort a fetus who might die early in life, or to abort in order to preclude the birth of a child with severe disabilities, are framed as "reproductive options." But in this era of health care cost containment, the notion of controlling costs by eliminating births of disabled babies may become a requirement, rather than an option. Then it ceases to be reproductive freedom and becomes quality control of babies—eugenics. The availability of these tests reinforces these notions, and the tests are actually marketed to women and to health care providers on this basis. Women are increasingly pressured to abort a fetus identified as disabled. Real choice must include the right to bear children with disabilities.

We in the disabled community must voice our ideas about selective abortion and attest to the true value of our lives. Only when a valid picture of the quality of our lives is available can prospective parents make choices about the use of tests for genetic disabilities in fetuses.

The Reproductive Rights Movement

The women's movement has begun to reach out to women with disabilities as a group. Women's organizations have begun to understand and challenge their own discriminatory attitudes and behaviors. More and more events in the women's movement are beginning to be wheelchair accessible and interpreted for the hearing impaired. But we have a long way to go to make the women's community fully welcoming of disabled people. This is a good time to get involved and share our thinking and energies. To be fully integrated into society, we must get involved and take leadership in all movements, and the movement for reproductive health care and real choice is an especially important one for people with disabilities to take on.

As disabled people, we have unique perspectives to share. Our views can enlighten everyone about the fundamental issues of sexuality and reproduction. We have gained much knowledge and experience with medical intervention, asking for and effectively managing help, dealing with bureaucracy, and fighting for access and power. Other controversial issues to which we can contribute our thinking include surrogate motherhood, population concerns, birthing technologies, artificial insemination, and *in vitro* fertilization.

The movement for reproductive rights needs to include people with disabilities as much as disabled people need to be included in the movement.

◆◆◆

The Life and Death of Miss Mildred
An Elderly Black Woman

Annette Dula

Who is the elderly black woman? What do health care workers need to know about her life when they treat her for her numerous chronic ailments? . . .

. . . Miss Mildred is a composite of elderly black women in the rural southern community where I grew up: They are my mothers, grandmothers, aunts, great aunts, and cousins. They are blood and non-blood relatives. . . .

I have chosen to present a life story because many health care workers do not know the elderly black woman outside the private office, the emergency room, or the clinic. Because what they know about elderly blacks comes from the experts, this paper attempts to let Miss Mildred speak for herself. After all, she is the expert on her life. If one listens carefully, it is clear what she thinks* about her illnesses, her folk health beliefs, her health care providers, life-sustaining therapies, and her approaching death. . . .

In the black community, traditionally, the elderly black woman sits on a throne of grace, emanating an aura of dignity that permeates her being. She is respected for her wisdom, admired for her strength, and honored for her contributions to the health and well-being of both the black family and its community. She is tapped as a valuable resource and a knowledgeable advisor because of her life experiences. Her presence provides a "certain steadiness, a calming effect on younger adults and young middle-aged adults as they are moving through the critical periods of adult development." She is an upright, upstanding member of the community; her very presence has served as a buttress against racism and discrimination. She plays a critical role in imparting values on work, education, religion, and family and community responsibility.

She is never referred to by her first name; she is Miss Mildred[†] to non-family members, Sister Mildred to her age peers and church ladies, and Aint Mildred to her dozens of younger relatives. She is called Big Mama by her grandchildren, her great grandchildren, and all the other blood and non-blood relatives that she has raised and cared for over the years. Almost never is she called just "Mildred."

Her beautiful flower garden with the snapdragons, zinnias, and azaleas is the talk of the neighborhood. She still cans, or "puts up," apples, blackberries, peaches, and tomatoes— all harvested from her own garden with her own hands. At church fetes, members line up to make sure they get some of Sister Mildred's famous fried chicken and deep-dish peach cobbler.

She is somewhat overweight, but *no one* in the community would have the nerve to call her fat. One of her church Sisters might dare to

---

*In Miss Mildred's story, references are included to substantiate Miss Mildred's reflections.

[†]Regardless of marital status, adult or elderly black women in the south are called "Miss." Hence, throughout this narrative, "Miss Mildred" rather than "Mrs. Mildred" is used. Also, "Aint" is a synonym for "Aunt" used extensively in some southern communities.

say, "You looking right healthy, Sister Mildred. Life must be treating you pretty good."

Sister Mildred might piously, yet playfully, reply, "Yes Sister, the Lord's been right good to me. I can't complain. If he calls me tomorra, I'm ready to go. And Sister, I hope you can say the same thing, too." And under her breath, she might be heard to mumble indignantly, "Don't you be getting all se-ditty and uppity on me, Tillie Mae. I knowed you before you became a Christian—when you wasn't nothing but a old fast gal, giving your life to the devil."

Elderly black women have a very strong faith; they believe in the Lord with all their hearts. They may show it inside or outside the church. As active church participants, they sing in the choir, teach Sunday School, or head a missionary group. Indeed, they are more active than elderly black males. Elderly black women occupy a most respected role as elders of the church and loudly extol the glory and the grace of God through shouting. They have given to the church all their lives, and when they become sick, the church gives back to them. The church provides some material sustenance, particularly in hard economic times or in sickness. Most of all, however, it provides spiritual sustenance.

Indeed, the older they get, the more religious elderly black women often become. A friend of mine recently said to me, "Chile, every time I go home, Mama done got more religious than she was the last time I was home. One of these days, she's going to fly right off to heaven."

There is another group of elderly black women who do not spend so much time in the church, perhaps because of poor health, employment requirements, or lack of transportation. But their faith is just as strong. They pray and read the bible frequently, listen to religious radio, and watch religious TV. They have been faithful supporters of evangelical ministers like Oral Roberts, Jimmy Swaggart, Jim Bakker, and Billy Graham for a good number of years. Even if they cannot attend church services regularly, they do manage to attend the bigger and more famous of the traveling church revivals and camp meetings. Elderly black women contribute financially to the church, even though their income is meager.

Although Sister Mildred may have little, she will share her food and visit with the infirm and others doing less well than she. As she puts it, "I ain't got much, but the Good Lord done said that we got to help them that needs help. We got to give food to the hungry, visit the old folks and the lonely folks, and minister to the sick. Don't matter what color they is neither. We're all God's children."

Outside the black community, there is a different portrait of the elderly black woman. There, she is often seen just as a poor old black auntie or as an uneducated, domineering matriarch. Her main interactions in the white community are as a patient in the health care system and as a domestic in private or public service.

A number of surveys reveal that she thinks that her health is poor. If she is not doing too poorly, she may still be working in a private white household; some studies show that 72 percent of employed blacks over the age of 55 work as service workers in private homes and businesses. Although her health care provider and employers may recognize her strength, they do not often see her dignity, her nobility, her beauty, or her importance to her family and the black community.

She may not speak standard English very well, and most likely she has not received formal education beyond the eighth grade. Public school education in the pre-war South revolved around the picking of cotton, the cutting of sugarcane, the harvesting of tobacco, and the explicit and purposeful exclusion of blacks from equal education.

Miss Mildred cooks for the white folks and does a bit of light cleaning. She does not work nearly as hard as she did when she first started working for the Braehills. (She's been working for them off and on for the past four decades.) Over the years, she has worked as hard as any man or woman: She has picked cotton and tobacco; she has nursed white children; she has worked as a domestic worker for several white families; she has washed and ironed white folks' laundry in her own home. (Of all her jobs, she preferred taking in laundry, because working at home meant that she could be her own boss.)

"I even worked in a textile mill and in a furniture factory back in the '60s, when they first began letting us women work the shifts. That was the time I said I wasn't going to be no maid for white folks no more. But I had to quit both them jobs. Those chemicals and dust made me dizzy and sick to the stomach. So I had to go back to work for Miss Braehill."

Things have changed a lot since she first started working for Miss Braehill. In fact, Miss Mildred's white folks treat her pretty decently now, except at holidays. On Thanksgiving and Christmas, they expect her to bake ten cakes and ten pies and cook enough food for all Miss Braehill's relatives who come in for the holidays.

"It ain't so easy for me to do all that cooking nowadays. My bunions hurt me sometimes. I sure get mighty tired when I have to stand up for a long time. But Miss Braehill is pretty good to me. Since I got old she hired somebody else to do most of the cleaning. Now she even lets me leave early on holidays with hardly no fuss a'tall. After all these years, it finally come to her mind that I've got to spend some time with my own family and my own children on holidays. I remember in the old days, I used to hate it real bad when Christmas would fall on a Sunday. That meant I couldn't go to church. And that pained me a heap."

Sister Mildred started her own Thanksgiving dinner this year about a week before the holiday, so all the food was prepared by Thanksgiving day. She cooked candied yams, a 20-pound turkey, two sweet potato pies, 20 pounds of chitlins cooked with hot peppers, potato salad, a pork roast, some buttermilk biscuits, and collard greens seasoned with ham hocks and fat back.

"I know I ain't supposed to be eating these foods. And I done cut back on them some. These is the foods that make your blood hot, and rich, and thick. That's when you get 'high blood.' High blood is a disease that done killed lots o' us black folks. Now, you can cool down and thin the blood if you take a little bit of garlic water, or lemon juice, or vinegar. That's what my herb doctor told me to do. And I believe it works. But you've got to stop eating pork and grease. That's the hard part, 'cause that's what us old folks was raised on. The chitlins, and the ears, and the tails was the parts o' the pig that the white folks didn't want."

Miss Mildred invited all of her family to Thanksgiving dinner. They include her two remaining blood sisters and five middle-aged children. Only ten of the grandchildren came

to dinner, but 20 great grandchildren showed up at Big Mama's. Uncle Boy was there too. He has no blood family, but the ladies in the community look out for him and make sure he has at least one good hot meal every day.

All the grandchildren and great grandchildren call Sister Mildred "Big Mama." Big Mama and Daddy Joe raised their nine children, two grandchildren, and the two Jones kids. The Jones kids lost their parents in the big fire of 1945. They didn't have anyplace to go, so Big Mama took them in. Aint Hominy still lives with Big Mama. Nobody knows where she came from—she just showed up one day and started living with the family. Now she is family. Thirty years later, Miss Hominy and Sister Mildred have the big house to themselves, except when somebody needs a place to stay.

Although the black family structure is showing signs of stress, it has traditionally been the strongest African American institution. One function of the black family has been to act as a buffer against the stress of living in a racist society. The African American family includes nuclear, extended, and augmented family forms. Strong kinship bonds in which relatives and friends support and reinforce one another are based on African heritage and the slavery experience. Often, a multigenerational family lives under the same roof. It is likely that our composite elderly woman lives in a multigenerational family. Some of those members are relatives, and some are not, but it doesn't matter. They are all considered family.

Sister Mildred has been feeling poorly lately. In fact, she hasn't felt too good ever since she had that operation two years ago. They took out her gallbladder. If she had had her druthers, she would not go back to Miss Braehill's. Lord knows she hasn't felt like it. She likes Miss Braehill; she is a nice white lady. The other day, Sister Mildred told Miss Hominy, "I'm so tired. I been cleaning up after white folks nigh on 60 years now. But I needs to take care of my burial. So I needs to keep working."

Miss Mildred had thought about retiring but decided, "Us poor colored women can't retire; that's what white folks do. We just keep on working and getting sicker and sicker. And then we die.

"Sister Hominy, at my funeral, I want you to make sure they put some gladiolas on top o' the hearse that carries m' body. I get a little bit o' money from the government, but honey, you know it ain't much. But one thing's for sure. I ain't got to ask nobody for nothing. I been paying two dollars a week for my burial ever since I turned 50. Soon's I die, Ebony Funeral Home's going to put up two thousand dollars for my burial. I done picked out and paid for my tombstone and a little plot o' land over in Freedman cemetery. Don't want none of the kin folks to have to put me away.

"I been planning for my death a long time. I know the Lord is coming after me soon. And I'm gonna be ready to go. I want to be buried in that pretty white dress my baby grand-daughter give me two years ago. I ain't never wore it but twice. I want little Donna—how old is she now? 'Bout 30, I reckon—I want her to sing 'I Am Climbing Jacob's Ladder.' That sure is a pretty song."

No matter how poor they may be, many elderly black folks have a little burial insurance on the side.

"I still has to pay for some of my medicine and I have to pay for it out o' that little bit o' money that I get from the government and from Miss Braehill. I also set a little money aside each month for the herb doctor. But if I don't have the money, she doctors me just the same."

Although Miss Mildred has been working since she was 11 years old, for the most part, none of her employers have contributed to her Social Security fund. She does receive Supple-mental Security Income (SSI), which is pretty meager but keeps the wolf from the door. She doesn't quite understand that Medicare and Medicaid business. Medicaid is supposed to be for poor folks and Medicare for old folks. But even with Medicaid and Medicare help, it is still hard for Miss Mildred to pay for all of her health care needs. Still, she thinks, "Things is much better for us elderly since Mama died. Didn't have no Medicare and Medicaid to help the elderly then. But even if things is better for us than they used to be, I don't believe colored folks get the same care that white folks get."

Yes, Sister Mildred *has* been feeling poorly lately. It is all she can do to drag herself out of bed every day and do her housework and put in a few hours at Miss Braehill's. But she isn't quite ready to tell the family how lowly she's been feeling lately. Black elderly describe ill-ness according to their ability to perform the activities of daily living: cooking their meals, cleaning their homes, doing their laundry, shopping, and going to the bathroom without aid. Although they may consider themselves in poor health, they do not regard themselves as really ill until they are no longer able to func-tion on their own.

Sister Mildred will go see Dr. McBee. She doesn't think that Doc McBee is helping her much but since Dr. McBee likes her, Sister Mildred humors the doctor a little bit. "Dr. McBee treats me real good. But she ain't so good at explaining things. She uses these big words, and I don't know a bit more what she's talking about. She told me I had a tumor in my lung that was going to kill me. I didn't know she was talking about cancer until one of my grandchildren asked me if it was malignant. (I didn't know what that word meant either.) I don't know why them doctors can't just come on out and use plain language. Sometimes *she* don't understand things too good neither. One time my hip was hurting me real bad, and she wanted me to tell her what the pain was like. Now the only thing I could think of was that time I fell off the old mule and got kicked in the side. I told the doctor it had hurt so much that I liked to uh' died.

"And that fool doctor, much as I like her, thought I was saying I wanted to kill myself. That's when she asked me if I knew what eu-thanasia is. First I thought it had something to do with young people—youthanasia. When she told me what euthanasia is, I looked at her like she was crazy. I was kind of surprised that she even brought it up, since sometimes black folks can be mighty touchy about white folks trying to get rid of us. Maybe she went to one of them conferences that she's always going to and they told her to talk to her patients about these things. They sure didn't teach her how to talk to me about it though.

"But you know what? Ever since we talked about it, looks like every time I turn on the TV, somebody's talking about euthanasia, and doctors helping kill off old and sick folks. Well, I ain't seen them ask nary a elderly black on none of them TV shows and news programs what they thought about euthanasia. I believe the Lord will take me away when it's time to go. Ain't nobody going to hurry me along. You got to be careful what you tell these doctors. Even the good ones.

"Now, McBee's been talking about a living will. I'm kinda confused. I thought about signing that thing. But I didn't know whether they was going to try to kill me by not giving me good doctoring, or keep me alive on them machines, or keep me doped up on them medicines. I just ain't sure about this living will thing. I don't want to be kept alive on no machines. To tell you the truth, I wouldn't put it past them doctors to kill me off anyhow. Well, I don't really think McBee would kill me off, but she ain't the only doctor that tends me. So I ain't about to make it easy for them. I done told Sister Hominy what I want done if I get to the place that I can't talk for myself. That way the doctors can't play God and decide that I done lived long enough. Them doctors think a pore old colored lady ain't got no sense a'tall. Well, I'm here to tell'em different.

"Chile, they had Sister Johnny doped up so bad that she did not know nothing. Lordy, it was pitiful to see her. She couldn't do nothing for herself. If the family hadn't come in and combed her hair and greased her skin, why, she'da looked like nobody cared nothing about her. The nurses tried to do right, but they don't know how to take care of colored people's skin and hair. Sister Johnny woulda just died of pure dee shame if she coulda knowed that she was messing all over herself. And them nurses, honey. If they was busy, they'd just let her lay in her own mess. I do declare, I don't want to be no burden to nobody. But I don't want them to kill me off, neither. I'm afraid if I sign that living will thing, them doctors will use that piece of paper to kill me off.

"My blood has been real high, and the medicine that Dr. McBee give me just ain't working. So I been goin' to the herb doctor over in West-End and she's been treating my high blood. She told me to take some garlic for my high blood. And I been rubbing my side in alcohol and

camphor for that pain that I been having for so long. My sugar's been high, too. My eyesight is bad because of the diabetes; I don't read nothing but the Bible and the newspaper these days. McBee is worried that I am going to get glaucoma and go blind. Well, I'm a bit worried about that, too. Even if I ain't got long for this world, I want to see it while I'm here.

"She didn't help me none, neither, when she told me twice as many black people die each year from sugar diabetes than white people. I don't know why she's telling me all this stuff, 'cause I ain't going nowhere till the Lord calls me. She just caused me to have an attack of 'high-pertension.' I don't care what them doctors say, there ain't nothing you can do for high-pertension except to stop worrying and try to get your nerves under control."

Miss Mildred has also been "bleeding from down below." She told her granddaughter that it was like having a period again. It sure is a nuisance, particularly since she had thought that her bleeding was all done with. Now Sister Mildred thinks that if she can just get through Christmas dinner, she will go see Dr. McBee the next day. She has decided that as a last resort, once it became clear that the herb doctor's medications weren't working either. She knows that Dr. McBee will find time to see her. She always does.

Miss Mildred has made it through Christmas dinner, but just barely. It was obvious to other members of the family that Sister Mildred was not herself. She seemed to be in a lot of pain. And she had to take to the bed a couple of times to rest a bit.

"I'm just tired," she told the family when they all tried to make her go to the emergency room of the hospital. "I ain't going to no doctor tonight. I just needs me some rest. Besides, the doctor can't do me no good. But I'll go tomorrow if ya'll will quit pestering me. All this aggregation is sure to kill me off. There won't be no need to worry about the doctors doing it."

After a family discussion, they have decided that 16-year-old BettyeLou will stay with her great-grandmother and Miss Hominy that night, in case Big Mama has to go to the hospital.

In her heart of hearts, Miss Mildred does not want to go to the doctor this time. She is afraid that she will be hospitalized, and for Miss Mildred, the hospital is a place for old people to go and die. She'd rather die at home. She is getting along in age; she'll be 85 years old come Valentine's Day. That is already longer than most black folks live. She knows her time is coming soon, and she has no regrets. All in all, she has had a good life. And she is ready. Most of her friends have already "gone home." She is tired, too, and about ready to go and see her husband Daddy Joe and her own Mama and Papa.

She thinks to herself, "Daddy Joe sure was a good man. He worked real hard for me and the young'uns. But they beat him to death back in 1959. I always told Daddy Joe that his big mouth was going to get him kilt. Them policemen said he had a heart attack in the jail house. Humph! I knows they beat him to death. And there weren't nothing I could do about it. Yes, I'm tired and I'm ready to move on where there ain't no more sickness, and meanness, and racial hatred."

Miss Mildred goes back and forth to and from the hospital several times over the next few months. Although her condition has noticeably deteriorated, collapses in cognition have not occurred. She has been approached on several occasions by her physician, who has requested that she "legalize" her treatment preferences through an advance directive. Dr. McBee understands that Miss Hominy is an informal proxy and that informal directives may be just "as ethically compelling as any formal document." But since Miss Mildred had so many relatives, her provider is afraid there will be some difficulties and lack of family consensus in carrying out Miss Mildred's wishes. Miss Mildred—after careful consultation with Miss Hominy, her siblings, her youngest daughter, and her pastor—finally agrees to document her preferences. She formally designates Miss Hominy as her proxy. She particularly lets it be known that food and water—whether artificially administered or ingested through the mouth—are to be provided under all conditions.

"Food and water ain't medication. I don't care how they give it to you. If you take away food and water from a person, you might as well kill 'em. I ain't saying that they have to do every blessed thing. I just want them to respect me and give me good care. Why, you'd give even a thirsty dog some water, wouldn't you? I just want the doctors and the nurses and all these young people learning how to be doctors to treat me just as good as they do the white patients. Like the Good Book say, 'Give comfort to all the sick, not just to some o' them.'"

It has been a couple of weeks since Miss Mildred signed the advance directive. She is certainly getting weaker and weaker each day, but her mind is still clear. She has spent some time in the intensive care unit, but now she is back on the floor. She wonders whether she has been returned to the floor because they have given up on her. She's heard that they do that sometimes—to make room for white patients. But to be fair, she doesn't really think Doc McBee would let them abandon her, just like that. After all, wasn't it Doc McBee who got the hospice people to come over every day when she was home?

Miss Mildred doesn't feel too good within herself about how she is being treated. Since she has come back from intensive care, she feels that the nurses and doctors are just waiting for her to die. They are kind enough; it just seems that they have already disengaged themselves from her, they don't seem to care anymore whether she is comfortable or not. When she signed that living will, they'd been oh so careful to promise her that she would get good care and comfort.

Miss Mildred has her good days and her bad days. Yesterday, she choked on her phlegm. BettyeLou cleared the phlegm from Big Mama's mouth and kept her lips and tongue moistened with a wet cloth. The worst part, though, was when she had to go to the toilet. Usually someone in the family is around to help her. But every now and then she has to depend on the staff. She does not mind using the bedpan if she only has to make water, but it is a matter of self-respect and pride to get up and go to the toilet for a bowel movement. Thank God she can still get to the bathroom, even though she needs a little help. That morning, though, she'd rung and rung, but no one had come to see about her. That was the straw that broke the camel's back. That was when she decided that she would just tear up that darn advance directive.

One of the nurses finally showed up, cheerily inquiring, "Hi there, Hon. How are we doing this morning?"

Big Mama, with all the dignity and iciness that she could muster, answered, "I don't know how *we* are doing, Nurse, but I want you to go and get me that living will that I signed and bring it here to me so that I can tear it up. Maybe then I can get some attention. Ain't nobody paid no attention to me since I signed that thing."

Miss Mildred decides that she wants to spend as much of her remaining time as possible in her own home among friends and family, who are honored and happy to take care of her. Dr. McBee makes arrangements for her to be as comfortable as possible. Different hospice workers spend a couple of hours with her every day. Dr. McBee also manages to find time to drop in each day or so, just to check up on her state and to chat with her. (After all, Mildred has been her patient for 25 years.)

The community will prepare itself and the family for her death; they will talk about all the good Miss Mildred has done, the people she has helped, the wise counsel she has given. They will joke about how she loved to go fishing almost as much as she loved to go to church. The few old friends who are still living will bring her food (which she will pretend to eat) and sit with her for a spell. Neighbors, friends, or family will clean her house; others will make sure she has clean sheets every day. And the younger ones will comb, brush, and braid her hair daily. Friends and family will come in and sit up with Miss Mildred—all night if it seems necessary. She will never be left alone. When she dies, someone in the community will most likely be with her to help her cross over into the other land.

Conclusion

Miss Mildred should not be regarded as a stereotype of the elderly black woman. Although a great many elderly black women are religious, live in southern states, and are surrounded by family and friends, a sizable portion do not fit that mold. Many do bask in the warmth and love of family, friends, church, and community, but some live alone in dangerous and poor urban neighborhoods—without either kin or social, psychological, and spiritual support.

Nor should the elderly black woman be romanticized. There is nothing romantic about having a nutritionally deficient diet or living in unhealthy and substandard housing with the constant threat of utility shutoffs or even evictions and homelessness, as is the case for many elderly black women and men. Whatever lens one uses to try to understand their life situations, it is clear that elderly blacks, as a group, are sicker and poorer than any other adult group in this country.

I have presented the life story of an elderly black woman because her biography is insufficiently appreciated, and because she is more likely than the black man to live long enough to be considered elderly. Although there may be other portraits, I have tried to present one picture of an elderly black woman's life—one that is embedded in a matrix of family, religion, and community. It is a profile in which health disparities in access, inequalities in health status, and end-of-life discussions cannot be considered apart from historical, social, and economic aspects of life. We have seen that Miss Mildred is an example of an important and respected member of a multigenerational extended family that includes both blood relatives and members who are not related. When decisions about life and death are being made, various family members will be involved. For the health care practitioner who is unfamiliar with black culture, it may be difficult to sort out who is who. She may not know that "Mamma Sis," "Aunt Tubby," "Aint Sister," and "Elizabeth" are all the same person.

After the family, religion is the most important institution in the biographies of many elderly black women and is intricately tied to family life. Religious involvement provides not only spiritual succor, but also social life, practical information, and political consciousness.[*]

If an elderly black woman is 75 years old, she has probably been working for at least 60 of those years, yet has not accumulated wealth or assets. Furthermore, she is unlikely to be enrolled in supplementary

---

[*]Langston Hughes, highly acclaimed African American author, pointed out that many of the old Negro spirituals were really calls for political action. For example, "Swing Low, Sweet Chariot," is a song about a "chariot of freedom from slavery," not about a "chariot of death."

medical insurance or to receive Social Security benefits, and she may have only a vague understanding of the intricacies of Medicare and Medicaid. Small SSI payments do little to ameliorate her poverty. Therefore, she may still be employed part-time as a service worker, not because she wants to work but because she needs to supplement her income. If she is among the few elderly blacks enrolled in supplementary medical insurance, some of her small earned income will go to pay for that coverage.

The elderly black woman understands white middle-class people because she has been the recipient of intimacies that the white mistress would not even tell her best friend. Because of race, class, and ethnicity barriers, however, health care practitioners do not know the elderly poor black outside the clinical setting. To morally intervene in the lives of their patients, providers need to understand those patients' culture, including family and community norms. They need to be familiar with the life stories of their patients, for it is through stories that we get to walk in other people's shoes. Stories open our eyes to other people's ethical dilemmas and dramas surrounding life and death. In a health care system in which the providers are mostly white and the sickest people are elderly African Americans, a larger sense of each patient's story will improve the quality of the everyday practice of medicine as well as the quality of communication with the person who is ill or approaching death. . . .

T H I R T Y - T W O

Breast Cancer: The Environmental Connection—a 1998 Update

Rita Arditti and Tatiana Schreiber

Today in the United States we live in the midst of a cancer epidemic. Cancer is currently the second leading cause of death; one out of every three people will get some kind of cancer, and one out of four will die from it. [Over thirty] years have gone by since the National Cancer Act was signed, yet the treatments offered to cancer patients are the same ones as those offered fifty years ago: surgery, radiation, and chemotherapy (or slash, burn, and poison, as they are called bitterly by both patients and increasingly disappointed professionals). And in spite of sporadic pronouncements from the cancer establishment, survival rates for the three main cancer killers—lung, breast, and colorectal cancer—have remained virtually unchanged and depressingly low.

In the 1960s and 1970s environmental activists and a few scientists emphasized that cancer was linked to environmental contamination, and their concerns began to make an impact on the public awareness of the disease.[1] In the 1980s and early 1990s, however, with an increasingly conservative political climate and concerted efforts on the part of industry to play down the importance of chemicals in causing cancer, we were presented with a new image of the disease. It was portrayed as an individual problem that could be overcome only with the help of experts and then only if one had the money and the know-how to recruit them for one's personal survival efforts. The emphasis on personal responsibility, lifestyle, and genetic factors has reached absurd proportions. People with cancer are asked "why they brought this disease on themselves" and why they don't work harder at "getting well." Testing for "cancer genes" is presented as one of the most important new developments in cancer research, with little or no evidence of the usefulness of this testing for the vast majority of the population.

While people with cancer should be encouraged not to fall into victim roles and to do everything they can to strengthen their immune systems (our primary line of defense against cancer), the sociopolitical and economic dimensions of cancer have been pushed almost completely out of the picture by the conservative backlash of our times. "Blaming the victim" is a convenient a way to avoid looking at the larger environmental and social issues that frame individual experiences. This retrenchment has happened in spite of the fact that many lines of evidence indicate that cancer *is* an environmental disease. Even the most conservative scientists[2] agree that approximately 80 percent of all cancers are avoidable and in some way related to environmental factors (this includes smoking). Support for this view relies on four lines of evidence: (1) the dramatic differences in the incidence of cancer between communities (the incidence of cancer among people of a given age in different parts of the world can vary by a factor of 10 to 100); (2) changes in the incidence of cancer (either lower or higher rates) in groups that migrate to a new country; (3) changes in the incidence of particular types of cancer over time; and (4) the actual identification of specific causes of certain cancers (such as beta-naphthylamine, responsible for an epidemic of bladder cancer among dye workers employed at DuPont factories in the 1930s).[3] Other well-known environmentally linked cancers are lung cancer (linked to asbestos, arsenic, chromium, several other chemicals, and, of course, smoking); endometrial cancer, linked to estrogen use; thyroid cancer, often the result of childhood exposure to irradiation; and liver cancer, linked to exposure to vinyl chloride.

The inescapable conclusion is that if cancer is largely environmental in origin, it is largely preventable. "Environment" as we use it here includes not only air, water, and soil, but also our diets, medical procedures, and living and working conditions. This means that the food we eat, the water we drink, the air we breathe, the radiation to which we are exposed, where we live, what kind of work we do, and the stress that we suffer are responsible for up to 80 percent of all cancers. In this article we discuss some of the recent research on possible environmental links to breast cancer, the controversies that surround it, and the need for prevention-oriented research and political organization around cancer and the environment.

Breast Cancer and Chemicals

In the United States, breast cancer has reached epidemic proportions: in 1998, estimates are that 178,700 women will develop breast cancer and 43,900 will die from it.[4] In other words, in 1998 nearly as many women will die from breast cancer as the number of American lives lost in the entire Vietnam War. Cancer is the leading cause of death among women of ages thirty-five to fifty-four, and approximately one-third of these deaths are due to breast cancer. African American women occupy a special place in this picture: in spite of the fact that their breast cancer incidence rate is lower than white women's, African American women have a higher breast cancer mortality rate and are more likely to get breast cancer at

an earlier age.[5] Evidence indicates that breast cancer fulfills three of the four lines of reasoning regarding its nature as an environmental disease: (1) the rates of incidence of breast cancer between communities can vary by a factor of 7, (2) the rate for breast cancer among populations that have migrated conforms to that of their new residence within one generation, and (3) the lifetime incidence of breast cancer in the United States has increased from one in twenty in 1950 to one in eight in the 1990s.

A number of factors have been linked to breast cancer: age (the risk of breast cancer increases with age), a first blood relative (parent, sibling, or child) with the disease, early onset of menstruation, late menopause, no childbearing or late age at first full-term pregnancy, and higher education and socioeconomic status. However, for the overwhelming majority of breast cancer patients (70 to 80 percent), their illness is not clearly linked to any of these factors. Furthermore, only 5 to 7 percent of breast cancer is hereditary, making the discovery of the so-called breast cancer genes, BRCA1 and BRCA2, irrelevant to the vast majority of breast cancer patients. As for those women who may carry one of these genes, Kay Dickerson, an epidemiologist who has had breast cancer and is herself a likely carrier of the gene, has put it clearly: "We have nothing to offer women who test positive."[6]

In the early 1990s work began to appear focusing on the chemical–breast cancer connection. Elihu Richter and Jerry Westin reported that Israel had seen a real drop in breast cancer mortality in the decade of 1976–1986, despite a worsening of all known risk factors.[7] Westin and Richter could not account for the drop solely in terms of demographic changes or improved medical intervention. Instead, they suspected that the change may have been related to the 1978 ban on three carcinogenic pesticides (benzene hexachloride, lindane, and DDT) that heavily contaminated milk and milk products in Israel. These pesticides are known as inducers of a superfamily of enzymes called the cytochrome P450 system. These enzymes can promote cancer growth, can weaken the immune system, and are capable of destroying anticancer drugs. The researchers suspected that these induced enzymes could have increased the virulence of breast cancer in women and thereby increased the mortality rates. They speculated that the removal of the pesticides from the diet resulted in much less virulent cancer and reduced mortality from breast cancer. Other researchers then began to directly measure chemical residues in women who had breast cancer and compare them with those who didn't. Mary Wolff and Frank Falk did a case-controlled study of fifty women in which a number of chemical residues, including DDE (a DDT metabolite) and PCBs, were measured, and they found that these were significantly elevated in cases of malignant disease as compared with nonmalignant cases.[8] A follow-up study by Wolff, Paolo Toniolo, and colleagues examined DDE and PCB residues in stored blood samples of women enrolled in the New York University Women's Health Study between 1985 and 1991. The study matched 58 women who developed breast cancer with 171 similar women who did not. After controlling for confounding factors (such as first-degree family history of breast cancer, lifetime lactation, and age at first full-term pregnancy), the data showed a fourfold increase in the risk of developing breast cancer for women who had a higher level of DDE in their blood sera.[9] Another study compared data among women in different racial groups[10] and looked at the level of DDE and PCBs in the stored blood of white, Asian American, and African American women who developed breast cancer, as compared with matched controls. At first glance, this study did not reveal statistically significant differences. However, reanalysis of the data showed that the white and African American subjects with the highest level of exposure to the chemicals were two to three times more likely to acquire breast cancer than those with lower levels.[11]

A critical point to bear in mind in assessing these studies is that DDE and PCBs in our bodies may be associated with other chemicals that have not yet been identified. Also, in the real world we are exposed to dozens of chemicals, many of which have effects on our metabolism and may potentiate each other. So although these studies are important, they hardly reflect the conditions in which we live.

Additional research has implicated plastics in breast cancer development because of their ability to leach substances that have estrogenic effects. Ana Soto and Carlos Sonneschein discovered this effect unexpectedly while studying the role of estrogen on the development of breast cancer cells in the lab. Using methods they had long successfully employed to remove all estrogen from their blood samples, they were surprised to find one day that their samples continued to show estrogenic activity. The reason turned out to be that a new type of centrifuge tube they were using was leaching *p*-nonyl-phenol into the cultures, causing the estrogenic effect. Nonyl-phenols are part of a group of compounds, alkyl-phenols, that are widely used in plastics, as lubricants in condoms, and in spermicides and vaginal foams. While many of these chemicals are individually present in the environment at levels too low to produce an effect of their own, Soto reports that "when you take the 10 estrogenic chemicals and combine each of them at one-tenth of their effective dose, you now have an effective dose."[12]

Out of these (and other) studies a hypothesis started to emerge. It is a generally accepted fact that estrogen, a hormone produced by the ovaries, is a risk factor for breast cancer. The hormone influences cell growth by binding to an intracellular protein known as the estrogen receptor. Complexes of the hormone and receptor can bind to DNA in the nucleus and activate the genes that direct cell division, increasing the likelihood that a carcinogenic mutation will take place. The new hypothesis suggested that certain substances that are introduced into the body from the environment mimic the action of estrogen produced in cells or alter the hormone's activity. These substances were named xenoestrogens (foreign estrogens), and some of them, found in pesticides, drugs, fuel, and plastics, could amplify the effects of estrogen and promote breast cancer. However, other xenoestrogens (phytoestrogens), found in plant foods such as soy, cauliflower, and broccoli, could alter the hormone's activity and protect against breast cancer. This helps to explain the lower breast cancer incidence of Asian women whose diets are rich in phytoestrogens.[13] Timing of exposure may also be an important factor in breast cancer development. According to Devra Lee Davis and Leon Bradlow, "Various investigations suggest that unusually high exposure to estrogen during prenatal development, adolescence, or the decade or so before menopause primes breast cells to become malignant. At those times, the estrogen presumably programs the cells to respond strongly to stimulation later in life."[14]

The work on xenoestrogens and other endocrine-disrupting materials suggests that they may also be contributing to abnormal development in animals and to a range of reproductive disorders in men worldwide, such as testicular cancer, undescended testis, urinary tract defects, and lowered sperm counts. For some researchers, the disruption of the hormonal balance of many species and the transgenerational effects are, in the long run, even more frightening than their carcinogenic effects. Carlos Sonneschein believes that "the effect of these pollutants can wipe out the whole species. . . . It's not that one species disappears and that's it; the disappearance of one species affects others, for example, when we don't have bees, fruits and vegetables are affected. . . . One has to have a strategy that concerns both the short-term and the long-term effects of these compounds."[15]

Breast Cancer and Radiation

Another area that demands urgent investigation is the role of radiation in breast cancer development. It is widely accepted that high doses of ionizing radiation cause breast cancer, whereas low doses are generally regarded as safe. Questions remain, however, regarding the shape of the dose-response curve, the length of the latency period, and the significance of age at time of exposure. These questions are of great importance to women because of the emphasis on mammography for early detection. Few voices dare challenge mammography screening. One of them is Rosalie Bertell, who criticized the breast cancer screening program of the Ontario Health Minister in Canada in 1989. Bertell argued that the program would "increase breast cancer death by increasing breast cancer incidence" and presented a risk-benefit assessment of the program to support her criticism.[16]

According to Bertell, the present breast cancer epidemic is a direct result of "above ground weapons testing" carried out in Nevada between 1951 and 1963, when two hundred nuclear bombs were set off and the fallout dispersed across the country. Because the latency period for breast cancer peaks at about 40 years, this is an entirely reasonable hypothesis. Chris Busby in the United Kingdom has recently come up with results that support Bertell's hypotheses. In the UK the increases in cancer incidence began in areas of high rainfall, such as Wales, Scotland, and the west country; cancer incidence did not increase in the dry areas. A good explanation for this is that the cancers were the result of atmospheric nuclear bomb testing in the period 1955 to 1963 by the nuclear superpowers in Kazakhstan, Nevada, and the South Pacific. The explosions drove "large quantities of radioactive material into the stratosphere, and this was circulated globally, falling to Earth everywhere, but particularly in high rainfall areas." At the peak of the testing (1961–1963), infant mortality began to rise and there was concern that strontium-90, accumulating in the milk, might be affecting babies. At the World Conference on Breast Cancer in 1997, in Ontario, Canada, Busby reported that this cohort of women, the nursing mothers exposed at the peak of testing, have shown the largest increase in breast cancer.[17]

Questions have also been raised about the possible effect of electromagnetic fields (EMFs). Studies on telephone company and electrical workers have raised the possibility of a connection between EMF exposure and breast cancer in *males*. Genevieve Matanoski of Johns Hopkins University studied breast cancer rates on male New York Telephone employees from 1976 to 1980 and observed a dose-response relationship to cancer and two cases of male breast cancer.[18] Another study, by Paul Demers of the Hutchinson Cancer Research Institute in Seattle, Washington, also found a strong correlation between breast cancer risk for men and jobs that involved exposure to EMFs.[19] Finally, in 1994, a study appeared on *female* electrical workers in the United States. It showed excessive breast cancer mortality relative to other women workers.[20] While this study has limitations because it is based on mortality statistics, which do not include information on other known risk factors, its results are consistent with the work of David Blask and others concerning melatonin. This work has shown that exposure to low-frequency electromagnetic fields, as well as exposure to light at night, reduces the pineal gland's production of its main hormone, melatonin. Melatonin, when given in normal physiological doses, is able to inhibit the growth of breast cancer cells in culture and in animals; it does so by decreasing the production of the cell's estrogen receptors.[21] Clearly, further investigation is strongly warranted in this area.

The Precautionary Principle

The importance of environmental factors to the current breast cancer epidemic is often dismissed; their contribution is considered too small to worry about. But as Rachel Carson succinctly explained in her groundbreaking work in 1962, repeated small doses of a carcinogen can be more dangerous than a single large dose. She wrote, "The latter may kill cells outright, whereas the small doses allow some to survive, though in a damaged condition. These survivors may then develop into cancer cells. This is why there is no 'safe' dose of a carcinogen."[22]

In November 1996, the Harvard Center for Cancer Prevention released a report claiming to summarize the current knowledge about the causes of human cancer. Shockingly, the report claimed that only 2 percent of U.S. cancer deaths can be attributed to environmental pollution. However, the definition of "environmental pollution" used in the report was extremely limited ("air pollution and hormonally active aromatic organochlorines") and has been sharply criticized by other scientists and environmental activists. All other environmental hazards were covered under separate categories. For example, adding the percentage of risk that the report attributed to factors we would consider "environmental," such as occupational factors, radiation, and food additives and contaminants, brings the figure to 10 percent, and since a half million deaths are caused by cancer in the United States each year, that means that 50,000 deaths are due to environmental factors. The report suggests that an additional 30 percent of cancer mortality is due to diet and obesity, but it does not discuss the issue of environmental carcinogens in food, particularly those stored in fat. Water contamination (a significant source of pesticide residues in the diet) was not included in the environmental pollution section. The report also discusses socio-economic status as a risk factor without clarifying that money or education does not *cause* cancer and that socioeconomics is always a surrogate for something else. Minimizing environmental factors through this kind of manipulation of statistics, while emphasizing "lifestyle" factors instead, obstructs real progress in the struggle against cancer.

"It's a blame-the-victim perspective," said Peter Montague, the editor of *Rachel's Environment and Health Weekly.* "You can make a choice about eating spinach or not. It's more difficult to choose not to eat pesticides, or to control what's in your water or what's in your food. The choice just isn't available to most people to pick clean or contaminated food."[23] Cancer activists saw the report as a backlash against the small inroads being made on the topic of cancer and the environment, and pointed out that the Harvard School of Public Health, which sponsored the report, lists in its 1996 annual report dozens of major chemical manufacturers among its large donors.

These include ARCO Chemical Company; Asarco, Inc.; Chevron; CIBA-GEIGY, Ltd.; Dow Chemical; DuPont; Eastman Chemical Company; General Electric; Monsanto; Shell Oil; Texaco; Union Carbide; and Procter & Gamble. DuPont and Asarco were among the companies reporting the highest release of toxic substances in 1994, according to an Environmental Protection Agency report. CIBA-GEIGY is the brains behind Atrazine and Simazine (widely used herbicides that have been classified as possible human carcinogens), and Monsanto is the maker of bovine somatropin (also called BGH), the growth hormone given to cows to increase milk production.[24] Clearly, it is not in the interest of chemical manufacturers to support a major report that would accurately name environmental pollution as a significant causal factor in cancer risk.

The question that screams to be addressed is, what should be considered sufficient proof to take action to eliminate potentially harmful substances from the environment? Or, as the Ontario Task Force on the Primary Prevention of Cancer put it in their March 1995 report,

> The central issue facing those involved in the primary prevention of cancer attributable to environmental sources is how much evidence is required and how strong the evidence must be before remedial action is taken to reduce or eliminate exposures.[25]

The Precautionary Principle is a public health guideline requiring that we act to prevent illness and death. Framing an issue from a public health perspective means that we recognize the existence of other factors apart from personal habits—such as economic, political, and cultural factors—that determine the parameters of the problem. We do not need to wait for absolute proof of harm. The Precautionary Principle emphasizes prevention and puts the burden of proof on those who risk the public health by introducing potentially harmful chemicals into the environment. As a public health principle, it has an honorable history and has been incorporated into several international agreements. The case of the Great Lakes is a good example of its application in North America. For more than forty years the Great Lakes have been a dumping ground for toxic chemicals produced by industry. More than eight hundred chemicals have been identified in the Great Lakes, many of them implicated in cancer, birth defects, and damage to the nervous and immune systems. An outpouring of concern forced the United States and Canada to sign a sweeping document requiring an end to the discharge of toxic substances. A binational commission responsible for monitoring and assessing the progress made after the agreement took a responsible view and came down clearly on the side of the Precautionary Principle. They wrote, "It is first necessary to shift the burden of responsibility for demonstrating whether substances should be allowed in commerce. The concept of reverse onus, or requiring proof that a substance is not toxic or persistent before use, should be the guiding philosophy of environmental management agencies, in both countries."[26] The Precautionary Principle takes a "weight of evidence" approach to assessing environmental health risks. It synthesizes the evidence gathered from epidemiological and biochemical research, wildlife observation, and other approaches, taking into account the cumulative weight of the studies that focus on the question of injury (or the likelihood of injury) to life, instead of narrowly focusing on one type of study alone. It brings an interdisciplinary and much needed holistic perspective to the sciences, and it introduces an important value: prudence. If there is not enough evidence, let's err on the side of caution!

The Precautionary Principle is necessary in order to protect public health and the environment, since the regulation of toxic chemicals in the United States is ineffective and out of date. The Toxic Substances Control Act (TSCA) was established in 1976 to determine which chemicals are dangerous and how the public can be protected from them. There are some 70,000 chemicals now in use, and every year about 1000 new chemicals enter the commercial market. During a typical year, the National Toxicology Program—a consortium of eight federal agencies—studies the cancer effects of one or two dozen chemicals. It is impossible, given the resources allocated to the program, to evaluate the dangers of all the chemicals now in circulation. A corporate self-regulation provision of the law proved completely ineffective, with chemical corporations failing to report scientific data on adverse health effects from chemicals. The overall outcome of twenty-one years of work under the TSCA has been to remove nine chemicals from the market.[27]

In her [1998] book *Living Downstream,* ecologist Sandra Steingraber writes that we all live downstream from toxic wastes dumped into the environment, and that to end cancer we need to go upstream and stop the pollution that is poisoning our lives.[28] In practice, however, national cancer policies emphasize early diagnosis and treatment, with minimal attention directed toward prevention. The recent highly publicized Breast Cancer Prevention Trial using tamoxifen (an antiestrogen synthetic hormone) on healthy volunteers considered to be at high risk for breast cancer raises troubling questions about what prevention really means for the medical establishment. In this study, although breast cancer incidence decreased among those taking tamoxifen, the number of deaths was the same between the treated and untreated groups because of other life-threatening conditions that developed among the group taking tamoxifen.[29] It is estimated that 29 million healthy women would be "potentially eligible" for preventive treatment with tamoxifen. At a cost of $80 to $100 for a month's supply, this is truly a "big deal" for Zeneca, the company that manufactures the drug under the name Nolvadex.

Biochemist Ross Hume Hall's analysis of the reasons we are making so little progress on cancer is compelling.[30] In discussing who directs cancer policy, he takes a look at a coalition of shared interests, which he calls the "medical industrial complex," that conducts research, develops drugs and medical equipment, and provides treatment. The medical part of the complex controls a vast number of cancer institutes, all focusing on diagnosis, treatment, and the search for a cure; the industrial part of the complex, on the other hand, has no interest in prevention because healthy people do not need their products or services. The hugely powerful chemical industry fights every initiative that would reduce the number of pollutants in the environment and funds much of cancer research. A striking example of this conflict of interest is offered by the case of Zeneca, the company mentioned previously. Zeneca owns and manages eleven cancer treatment centers in the United States; it is also the primary sponsor of October as Breast Cancer Awareness Month and has veto power over any materials produced in connection with this month of activities. Not surprisingly, the literature of Breast Cancer Awareness Month never mentions the word carcinogen, and it relentlessly emphasizes mammography as the "best protection" for women. Given the results of the Breast Cancer Prevention Trial, it is likely that tamoxifen will be included in their list of recommendations for breast cancer prevention. Zeneca is also the producer of a carcinogenic herbicide, acetochlor, and has been involved in litigation stemming from environmental damage to California harbors. Thus, Breast Cancer Awareness Month reveals the close connection between the chemical industry and the cancer research establishment.

Women's cancer groups at both the local and international levels have been at the forefront of criticism of the medical-industrial complex and have asked for the development of a true prevention approach, summarized by the phrase "Stop cancer before it starts." At the 1997 World Conference on Breast Cancer, delegates from fifty-four countries emphasized that breast cancer not only is a medical issue, but is also a social problem that needs to be addressed by international activism. Environmental factors were discussed in depth. Nancy Evans, a delegate from California, was clear about the need for environmental activism: "We are losing the war on cancer because we are fighting the wrong enemies," she said. "The cancer establishment has taught us to look for the enemy within—within our genes, our unwise reproductive choices or our stressful lifestyle. Although these factors may contribute to breast cancer and other cancers, our real enemies are faceless transnational corporations that spread their poisons around the globe in the name of free trade. . . . Prevention activism means understanding who these enemies are."[31]

Indeed, if we want to stop not just breast cancer but all cancers, we need to think in global terms and link across nations and disciplines, building a perspective that incorporates the knowledge gained from public health science, grassroots environmental groups, and people living with cancer. Only then will we be able to reverse the trend that has resulted in the present epidemic, and set the basis for a healthy future for ourselves and the following generations.

NOTES

1. See, for instance, Epstein, Samuel. *The Politics of Cancer*. Garden City, NY: Anchor Press/Doubleday, 1979; and Agran, Larry. *The Cancer Connection*. New York: St. Martin's Press, 1977.

2. Doll, Richard, and Richard Peto. *The Causes of Cancer: Quantitative Estimates of Avoidable Risks of Cancer in the United States Today*. New York: Oxford University Press, 1981.

3. Proctor, Robert N. *Cancer Wars: How Politics Shapes What We Know and Don't Know about Cancer*. New York:

Basic Books, 1995, p. 38. See also Clayson, D. B., "Occupational Bladder Cancer," *Preventive Medicine*, Vol. 5, 1976, pp. 228–244.

4. American Cancer Society. *Cancer Facts & Figures—1998*. Atlanta, GA: American Cancer Society, 1998.

5. Moormeier, Jill. "Breast Cancer in Black Women," *Annals of Internal Medicine*, Vol. 124, No. 10, May 15, 1996, pp. 897–905.

6. Quoted in Batt, Sharon. *Patient No More*. Charlottetown, PEI, Canada: Gynergy Books, 1994, p. 169.

7. Westin, Jerome B., and Elihu Richter. "The Israeli Breast-Cancer Anomaly," *Annals of the New York Academy of Science*, "Trends in Cancer Mortality in Industrial Countries," edited by Devra Davis and David Hoel. 1990, pp. 269–279.

8. Falk, Frank, Andrew Ricci, Mary S. Wolff, James Gobold, and Peter Deckers. "Pesticides and Polychlorinated Biphenyl Residues in Human Breast Lipids and Their Relation to Breast Cancer," *Archives of Environmental Health*, Vol. 47, No. 2, March/April 1992, pp. 143–146.

9. Wolff, Mary S., Paolo G. Toniolo, Eric W. Lee, Marilyn Rivera, and Neil Dubin. "Blood Levels of Organochlorine Residues and Risk of Breast Cancer," *Journal of the National Cancer Institute*, Vol. 85, No. 8, April 21, 1993, pp. 648–652.

10. Krieger, Nancy, Mary S. Wolff, Robert A. Hiatt, Marilyn Rivera, Joseph Vogelman, and Norman Orentreich. "Breast Cancer and Serum Organochlorines: A Prospective Study Among White, Black, and Asian Women," *Journal of the National Cancer Institute*, Vol. 86, No. 8, April 20, 1994, pp. 589–599.

11. Davis, Devra Lee, and H. Leon Bradlow. "Can Environmental Estrogens Cause Breast Cancer?" *Scientific American*, October 1995, pp. 166–172.

12. Soto, Ana M., Honorato Justiia, Jonathan W. Wray, and Carlos Sonneschein, "*p*-Nonyl-Phenol: An Estrogenic Xenobiotic Released from 'Modified' Polysterene," *Environmental Health Perspectives*, Vol. 92, 1991, pp. 167–173; and personal communication with Ana Soto and Carlos Sonneschein, October 1994.

13. See note 11, p. 170.

14. See note 11, p. 168. See also vom Saal, Frederick. "Getting to the Truth: What We Know and Don't Know about the Hazards of Endocrine Disrupting Chemicals," *Pesticides and You*, Vol. 17, No. 3, 1997, pp. 9–16.

15. Arditti, Rita, and Tatiana Schreiber. "Breast Cancer: Organizing for Prevention," *Resist*, Vol. 3, No. 9, November 1994, p. 4. See also Colborn, Theo, Dianne Dumanoski, and John Peterson Myers. *Our Stolen Future*. New York: Dutton, 1996.

16. The paper can be obtained by writing to Dr. Rosalie Bertell, President, International Institute of Concern for Public Health, 830 Bathurst Street, Toronto, Ontario, Canada, M5R 3G1. See also Bertell, Rosalie. "Breast Cancer and Mammography," *Mothering*, Summer 1992, pp. 949–957.

17. Busby, Chris. "Cancer and the 'Risk-Free' Radiation," *The Ecologist*, March/April 1998, Vol. 28, No. 2, pp. 54–56.

18. Matanoski, G. M., P. N. Breysse, and E. A. Elliott. "Electromagnetic Field Exposure and Male Breast Cancer," *Lancet,* No. 337, 1991, p. 737.

19. Demers, P. A., D. B. Thomas, K. A. Rosenblatt, et al. "Occupational Exposure to Electromagnetic Fields and Breast Cancer in Men." *American Journal of Epidemiology,* Vol. 134, 1991, pp. 340–347.

20. Loomis, Dana P., David A. Savitz, and Cande V. Ananth. "Breast Cancer Mortality among Female Electrical Workers in the United States," *Journal of the National Cancer Institute,* Vol. 86, No. 12, June 15, 1994, pp. 921–925.

21. Personal communication with Dr. David E. Blask, September 1994. See also Hill, Steven M., and David E. Blask. "Effects on the Pineal Hormone Melatonin on the Proliferation and Morphological Characteristics of Human Breast Cancer Cells (MCF-7) in Culture," *Cancer Research,* No. 48, November 1, 1988, pp. 6121–6126.

22. Carson, Rachel. *Silent Spring.* Boston: Houghton Mifflin, 1962, p. 232.

23. Schreiber, Tatiana. "Misleading and Irresponsible: Cancer Activists Decry Harvard Report," *Resist,* Vol. 6, No. 3, April 1997, p. 5.

24. See note 23.

25. *Recommendations for the Primary Prevention of Cancer.* Report of the Ontario Task Force on the Primary Prevention of Cancer, Ministry of Health, March 1995, p. 33. See also Arditti, Rita. "The Precautionary Principle: What It Is and Why We Should Embrace It," *Women's Community Cancer Project Newsletter,* Summer 1997, pp. 1–2.

26. *Seventh Biennial Annual Report on Great Lakes Water Quality.* International Joint Commission, Windsor, Ontario, 1994, pp. 1–2.

27. Montague, Peter. "Is Regulation Possible?" *Ecologist,* Vol. 28, No. 2, March/April 1998, pp. 59–61.

28. Steingraber, Sandra. *Living Downstream: An Ecologist Looks at Cancer and the Environment.* Reading, MA: Addison-Wesley, 1997.

29. Arditti, Rita. "Tamoxifen: Breast Cancer Prevention That Is Hard to Swallow," *Sojourner,* July 1998, p. 32.

30. Hume Hall, Ross. "The Medical-Industrial Complex," *Ecologist,* Vol. 28, No. 2, March/April 1998, pp. 62–68.

31. John, Lauren. "World Conference Calls for Global Action Plan," *Breast Cancer Action Newsletter,* No. 44, October/November 1997, p. 9.

THIRTY-THREE

◆◆◆

"If It's Not On, It's Not On"—Or Is It?

Discursive Constraints on Women's Condom Use

Nicola Gavey, Kathryn McPhillips, and Marion Doherty

"If it's not on, it's not on!" Slogans such as these exhort women not to have sexual intercourse with a man unless a condom is used. Health campaigns targeting heterosexuals with this approach imply that it is women who should act assertively to control the course of their sexual encounters to prevent the spread of HIV/AIDS and other sexually transmitted infections (STIs). Researchers and commentators, too, have sometimes explicitly concluded that it is women in particular who should be targeted for condom promotions on the basis of assumptions such as "the disadvantages of condom use are fewer for girls" (Barling and Moore 1990). . . .

Aside from the obvious question of whether women *should* be expected to take greater responsibility for sexual safety, this approach relies on various assumptions that deserve critical attention. For example, what constraints on women's abilities to unilaterally control condom use are overlooked in these messages? What assumptions about women's sexuality are embedded in the claim that the disadvantages of condoms are fewer for women? That is, is safer sex simply a matter of women deciding to use condoms at all times and assertively making this happen, or do the discursive

Author's note: We gratefully acknowledge the women we interviewed for this study. We thank members of the University of Auckland Psychology Discourse Research Unit (Alison Towns, Fiona Cram, Kate Paulin, Peter Adams, Ray Nairn, and Tim McCreanor) for critical feedback on an earlier draft of this article, Maree Burns for research assistance support, and our friend (nameless, to protect participants' anonymity) for help with recruiting participants. We also thank Christine Bose and two anonymous reviewers for helpful comments on the article. This research was supported, in part, by grants from the Health Research Council of New Zealand, the University of Auckland Research Committee, and by the Department of Psychology Summer Research Assistantship Programme.

parameters of heterosex work to subtly constrain and contravene this message? Moreover, are condoms as unproblematic for women's experiences of sex as the logic offered for targeting women implies? These questions demand further investigation given that research has repeatedly shown the reluctance of heterosexuals to consistently use condoms despite clear health messages about their importance.

There is now a strong body of feminist research suggesting that condom promotion in Western societies must compete against cultural significations of condom-*less* sexual intercourse as associated with commitment, trust, and "true love" in relationships (e.g., Holland et al. 1991; Kippax et al. 1990; Willig 1995; Worth 1989; see also Hollway 1989). Here, we contribute to this body of work, which collectively highlights how women's condom use needs to be understood in relation to some of the complex gender dynamics that saturate heterosexual encounters. In particular, we critically examine (1) the concept of women's control over condom use that is tacitly assumed in campaigns designed to promote safer sex and condoms to women and (2) the foundational assumption of such campaigns that condoms are relatively unproblematic for women's sexual experiences. . . .

The Study

In-depth interviews were conducted by the first author with 14 predominantly Pakeha women (two women had mixed ethnic backgrounds but primarily identified as Pakeha). Pakeha are non-Maori New Zealanders of European descent, who form approximately 80 percent of the New Zealand population (Statistics New Zealand 2001). Our group of participants does not, therefore, represent the cultural and ethnic diversity of New Zealand. The women's ages ranged from 22 to 43 years, and 12 of the women were between 27 and 37 years old. They came from diverse work situations and educational backgrounds but could be described as generally middle class. They all had experience of heterosexual relationships and at least some experience with condoms. The women were recruited through word of mouth. . . . All participants either chose or were given pseudonyms to protect their anonymity.

Interviews were semistructured to the extent that all women were questioned about the same broad range of topics, including their past and current experiences with condoms, their heterosexual relationships and practices more generally where relevant, their personal views of condoms, and how they thought others regarded condoms. We were interested in women's condom use or intended use for both contraceptive purposes and the prevention of sexually transmitted infections. An interview schedule was used as a guide, although the style of the interviews was more conversational than a question-answer format. . . .

Assertion, Identity, and Control

Either your partner uses a condom or you don't have sex. If a women doesn't look out for herself, who will? We must learn how to say no to a partner who won't use condoms. It's either that or abstinence.   (Sack 1992, 118)

Public sexual health education fervently promotes the rights of women to demand condom use by male partners. Against a backdrop of implied male aversion to condoms, both the Planned Parenthood Federation of America (1988–2001) and the Family Planning Association (2000) in New Zealand offer mock scripts that despite an air of gender neutrality suggest ways women can assert their right to insist on a condom being used for sexual intercourse. In this section, we consider what these kinds of hard-line "calls to assertiveness" might look like in practice. The excerpt below is taken from the interview with Rose, a young woman in her early 20s. At the very beginning of the interview, in response to a question about her "current situation, in terms of your relationships," she said, "My last experience was fairly unpleasant and so I thought I'll really try and um devote myself to singledom for a while before I rush into anything." In this one-night stand, approximately three weeks prior to the interview, Rose did manage to successfully insist that her partner use a condom. Her account of this experience is particularly interesting for the ways in which it graphically demonstrates the kinds of interactional barriers that a woman might have to overcome to be assertive about using a condom; moreover, it demonstrates how even embodiments of the male sex drive discourse that are not perceived to be coercive can act out levels of sexual urgency that provide a momentum that is difficult to stop. Although the following quote is unusually long, we prefer to present it intact to convey more about the flavor of the interaction she describes. We will refer back to it throughout this article and want to keep the story intact.

Nicola: So were condoms involved at all in that—

Rose: Yeah um, actually that's quite an interesting one because we were both very drunk, but I still had enough sense to make it a priority, you know, and I started to realize that things were getting to the point where he seemed to be going ahead with it, without a condom, and I was— had to really push him off at one point and— 'cause I kept saying sort of under my breath, are you going to get a condom now, and— and he didn't seem to be taking much notice, and um—

Nicola: So you were actually saying that?

Rose: Yeah. I was—

Nicola: In a way that was audible for him to—

Rose: Yeah. (Nicola: Yeah) And um— at least I think so. (Nicola: Yeah) And— and it got to the point where [laughing] I had to push him off, and I think I actually called him an arsehole and— I just said, look fuck, you know, and— and so he did get one then but it seemed—

Nicola: He had some of his own that he got?

Rose: Yeah. (Nicola: Yeah) Yeah it was at his flat and he had them. In fact that was something I'd never asked beforehand. I presumed he would have some. And um he did get one and then you know— and that was okay, but it was sort of like you know if I hadn't demanded it, he might've gone ahead without it. And I am fairly sure that he's pretty, um— you know he has had a pretty dubious past, and so that worried me a bit, I know he was very drunk and out of control and, um— otherwise the whole situation would never have occurred I'm sure, but still I had it together enough, thank God, to demand it.

Nicola: And you actually had to push him off?

Rose: Yeah, I think— I'm pretty sure that I did, you know it's— it's all quite in a bit of a haze, [laughing] (Nicola: laughing) but um, it wasn't that pleasant, the whole experience. It was— he was pretty selfish about the whole thing. And um— yeah.

Nicola: How much old— how— You said that he was a bit older than you.

Rose: Ohh, he's only twenty-eight or nine, but that's quite a big difference for me. I usually see people that are very much in my own age-group. Mmm.

Nicola: And um, you said that it was kind of disappointing sexually and otherwise and he was quite selfish, (Rose: laughter) like at the point where you know you were saying, do you want to get— are you going to get a condom, at that point were you actually wanting to have sexual intercourse?

Rose: Um, mmm, that's a good question. I can't remember the whole thing that clearly. And I seem to remember that I was getting um— I was just getting sick of it, or— [laughing] or— I might have been, but my general impression was that it was quite a sort of fumble bumbled thing, and— and it was quite— he just didn't— he didn't have it together. He wasn't— he possibly would've been better if he was less drunk, but he was just sort of all over the place and um— and I was just thinking, you know, I want to get this over and done with. Which is not the [laughing] best way to go into— into that sort of thing and um— yeah I— I remember at points— just at points getting into it and then at other points it just being a real mess. Like he couldn't— he wasn't being very stimulating, he was trying to be and bungling it 'cause he was drunk. And being too rough and just too brutish, just yeah. And um—

Nicola: When you say he was trying to [laughing] be, what do you—

Rose: Ohh, he was just like you know, trying to use his hands and stuff and just it— it was just like a big fumble in the dark (Nicola: Right) type thing. I mean I'm sure h— I hope he's not usually that bad it was just like— I was in— sometimes— most of the time in fact I was just saying, look don't even bother. [laughing] You obviously haven't got it together to make it pleasurable. So in some ways—

Nicola: You— you said you were thinking that or you said that?

Rose: I just sort of— I did push his hand away and just say, look don't bother. Because— and I thought at that point that probably penetration would be, um more pleasurable, yeah. But— and then— yeah. And I think I was actually wanting to just go to sleep and I kept— I think I um mentioned that to him as well and said, you know why don't we— we're not that capable at the moment, why don't we leave it. But he wasn't keen on [laughing] that idea.

Nicola: What did he— is that from what he said, or just the fact that he didn't—

Rose: I think he just said, ohh no, no, no we can't do that. It was kind of like we had to put on this big passionate spurt but um it just seemed quite farcical, considering the state we were both in. And um, so I— yeah I thought if— yeah I thought it would probably be the best idea to [laughing] just get into it and like as I— as I presumed— ohh, actually I don't know what I expected, but he didn't last very long at all, which was quite a relief and he was quite— he was sort of a bit apologetic and like ohh you know, I shouldn't have come so soon. And I was just thinking, oh, now I can go to sleep. [laughing] Yes, so I just um— since then I've just been thinking, um one-night stands ahh don't seem to be the way to go. They don't seem to be much fun and [laughing] I'm not that keen on the idea of a relationship either at the moment. So I don't know. Who— I— it's hard to predict what's going to happen but— mmmm.

This unflattering picture of male heterosexual practice painted by Rose's account classically illustrates two of the dominant organizing principles of heterosexual sex—a male sex drive discourse and a coital imperative. The male sex drive discourse (see Hollway 1984, 1989) holds that men are perpetually interested in sex and that once they are sexually stimulated, they need to be satisfied by orgasm. Within the terms of this discourse, it would thus not be right or fair for a woman to stop sex before male orgasm (normatively through intercourse). This discursive construction of male sexuality thus privileges men's sexual needs above women's; the absence of a corresponding discourse of female desire (see Fine 1988) or drive serves to indirectly reinforce these dominant perceptions of male sexuality.

The extent to which male behavior, as patterned by the male sex drive discourse, can constrain a woman's attempts to insist on condom use are graphically demonstrated in Rose's account. The man she was with behaved with such a sense of sexual urgency and unstoppability that although she was able to successfully ensure a condom was used, it was only as a result of particularly determined and persistent ef-

forts. He was unresponsive to her verbal requests and did not stop proceeding with intercourse until Rose became more directly confrontational—calling him "an arsehole" and physically pushing him off. At this point, he eventually did agree to wear a condom and did not use his physical strength to resist and overcome her actions to retain or take control of the situation. We will come back to analysis of Rose's account later in this article.

Another participant, Anita, who was in her mid-20s, described a very similar experience:

Anita: This one friend and I— I mean I got quite drunk, I have to say, and we had penetrative sex without a condom but then— no I think we— I— think we had sex without a condom and then I stopped, and 'cause I was like, no no no, you have to use a condom.

Nicola: What you mean after he'd ejaculated you stopped, or—

Anita: No no no, it was just— (Nicola: You stopped) we did— and like he did put his penis inside me, (Nicola: Right) we were just sort of having sex and I suddenly thought he hasn't got a condom on, (Nicola: Right) [laughing] 'cause I was really pissed. So was he. And I made him stop, and he said, "Ohh no, it's all right, I trust you." And I was [laughing] just floored. Fuck you arrogant— what a nerve, and stopped, at that point.

Nicola: What you mean you— you sort of physically stopped him?

Anita: Yeah, I pushed him off (Nicola: Yeah yeah yeah) and said, "That's not— that's you know— that's not okay, I can't believe you said that." And, um, I think he had sex with a condom after that.

Rose and Anita did indeed act in "Trojan woman fashion" (Chapman and Hodgson 1988, 104), but their accounts demonstrate how this can be anything but straightforward to do. For both, acting assertively necessitated strong physical resistance and verbal censure. The literature on women's heterosexual experiences (e.g., Holland et al. 1998), as well as our own interviews for this study, strongly suggests that this will not be an attractive or possible option for many, or even most, women. Indeed, we would argue that advice to women that simply encourages them to be assertive is deeply problematic, not because it is undesirable for women to act with strength and experience real choices in their sexual relationships with men but because these kinds of mottos deny the complex interpersonal and subjective constraints on achieving this. As we will see in later sections, the kind of assertiveness shown by Rose and Anita requires enacting attributes and an identity not compatible with traditional embodiments of female sexuality and thus not readily accessible to some women. Moreover, these kinds of assertive actions not only could expose women to danger (such as physical retaliation from the man) but also may jeopardize her chances of continuing with that particular heterosexual encounter (and, possibly, relationship)—a choice that may be undesirable if not impossible for many women to make. Indeed, Rosenthal, Gifford, and Moore (1998) have argued that some women and men regard "casual sex as a strategy for obtaining the possibility of 'love'" and that the use of condoms at such times may be seen to risk romance and the promise of love.

Pleasing a Man

The male sex drive discourse constructs masculinity in ways that directly affect women's heterosexual experiences as evidenced in the above descriptions of Rose's and Anita's experiences. However, as we alluded to above, this discursive framework can also constitute women's sexual subjectivity in complex and more indirect ways. For example, for some women situated within this discursive framework, their ability to "please a man" may be a positive aspect of their identity. In this sense, a woman can be recruited into anticipating and meeting a man's "sexual needs" (as they are constituted in this discursive framework) as part of her ongoing construction of a particular kind of identity as a woman.

Sarah reported not liking condoms. She said she did not like the taste of them; she did not like the "hassle" of putting them on, taking them off, and disposing of them; and that they interfered with her sexual pleasure. However, it seemed that her reluctance to use them was also related to her sexual identity and her taken-for-granted assumptions about men's needs, desires, and expectations of her during sex. Sarah traced some of her attitudes toward sex to her upbringing and her mother's attitudes in which the male sex drive discourse was strongly ingrained.[1] She directly connected the fact that "when I've started, I never stop" to her difficulty in imagining asking a man to use a condom. As she said in an ironic tone,

If a man gets a hard-on, you've gotta take care of it because he gets sick. You know these are the mores I was brought up with. So you can't upset his little precious little ego by asking to use a condom, or telling if he's not a good lover.

Sarah explained her own ambivalence toward this male sex drive discourse by drawing on a psychoanalytic distinction between the conscious and unconscious mind:

I mean I've hopefully done enough therapy to have moved away from that, but it's still in your bones. You know there's my conscious mind can say, that's a load of bullshit, but my unconscious mind is still powerful enough to drive me in some of these moments, I would imagine.

Thus, despite having a rational position from which she rejected the male sex drive discourse, Sarah found that when faced with a man who wanted to have sex with her, her embodied response would be to acquiesce irrespective of her own desire for sex. Her reference to this tendency being "in [her] bones" graphically illustrates how she regarded this as a fundamental influence. It is evocative of Judith Butler's suggestion "that discourses do actually live in bodies. They lodge in bodies, bodies in fact carry discourses as part of their own lifeblood" (Meijer and Prins 1998, 282). Sarah recalled an incident where her own desire for sex ceased immediately on seeing the man she was with undress, but she explained that she would not be prepared to stop things there:

Sarah: He's the hairiest guy I ever came across. I mean— but no way I would stop. I mean, as soon as he took his shirt off I just kind of about puked [laughing], but I ain't gonna say— I mean having gone to all these convolutions to get this thing to happen there's no way I'm gonna back down at that stage.
Nicola: So when he takes his shirt off he's just about the most hairiest guy you've ever met, which you find really unappealing.
Sarah: Terribly.
Nicola: Um, but you'd rather go through with it?
Sarah: Well I wouldn't say rather, but I do it.

Sarah also described another occasion where she met a man at a party who said, "Do you want to get together?" and I said, "Well, you know, I just want to cuddle," and he said, "Well, that's fine, okay." She explained that it was very important to her to make her position clear before doing anything. However, they ended up having sexual intercourse, because as she said,

Sarah: I was the one. I mean we cuddled, and then I was the one that carried it further.
Nicola: And what was the reason for that?
Sarah: As I said, partly 'cause I want to and partly 'cause if ohh he's got a hard-on you have to.

For women like Sarah, it seemed that an important part of their identity involved being a "good lover." This required having sexual intercourse to please a man whenever he wanted it and, in Sarah's case, to the point of anticipating this desire on the basis of an erect penis. She implied that among people who know her, she would have a reputation as a woman who had enjoyed sex with a lot of men, and thus she would subconsciously expect a man to think she was silly if she suggested using a condom—"Why make the fuss, you know." Given these expectations, and her belief that most men do not like condoms, it is not surprising that she had developed an almost fatalistic attitude toward her own risk of contracting HIV, such that she could say, "There's a part of me that also says, as long as I'm clear and not passing it on, I'm not gonna worry. You know, and if I get it, hey, it was meant to be."

For understanding the actions of Sarah and women like her, the assertiveness model is not at all helpful. In these kinds of sexual encounters, Sarah's lack or possession of assertiveness skills is beyond the point. What stops her from acting assertively to avoid undesired sex are deeply inscribed features of her own identity—characteristics that are not related to fear of assertion so much as the production of a particular kind of self. Well before she gets to the point of acting or not acting assertively, she is motivated by other (not sexual) desires, about what kind of woman she wants to *be*.

In a similar way to Sarah, an important part of Sally's identity was having "integrity about sexuality." She explained her position in relation to not "leading somebody on" in terms of a desire for honesty:

And so— and I— that really was clinched somehow that you didn't lead somebody on and so that's part of— that's one of the sort

of ways in which I understand that contract notion, really. And so maybe that had something to do with how I see myself about being a person with a reasonable— with integrity about sexuality. I won't go into something with false promises kind of thing.

Prior to these comments, Sally talked about the origins of her beliefs about this kind of contractual notion where it was not possible to be physically intimate with someone unless you were prepared to have intercourse. She remembered feeling awful about touching a man's penis when she was younger:

I had been unfair because of the— I suppose the feeling of sort of cultural value of— of the belief that men somehow you know it's tormenting to them to leave a cock unappeased (N: [laughter]) [laughing] basically or something like that.

Like Sarah, Sally too reflected on her experiences in a way that highlights the limitations of attempting to influence sexual behavior based on understandings of people as unitary rational actors. Sally discussed a six-month relationship with a past lover in which she had not used condoms. She said that she had made the decision not to use condoms because she already had an intrauterine device (IUD) and because they were seen to connote a more temporary rather than long-lasting relationship (a view ironically reinforced by the advice of a nurse at the Family Planning Clinic):

Sally: It's like condoms are about more casual kinds of encounters or I mean— I mean, I'm kind of— um they are kind of anti-intimacy at some level.
Nicola: And so, if you'd used condoms with him, that would've meant—
Sally: Maybe it would have underscored its temporariness or its— yeah, its lack of permanence. I don't understand that. What I've just said really particularly. It doesn't [seem] very rational to me. [laughter]
Nicola: [laughter] No it's very rational and I—
Sally: [indistinguishable] it seems to be coming out of you know, somewhere quite deeper about um— I think it goes back to that business about ideals stuff. And I think that's one of the things about not saying no, you know. And that the ideal woman and lover— the ideal woman is a

good lover and doesn't say no. Something like that. And it is incredibly counterproductive [softly] at my present time in life. [sigh/laugh]

Sally's reference to the ideal woman who is a good lover (because) she does not say no implicitly recognizes the strength of male sex drive discourse and its effect on her sexual experiences. In a construction that is similar to Sarah's, Sally refers to this kind of influence as "deeper" than her "rational" views. She presents an appreciation of this kind of cultural ideal as internalized in some way that is capable of having some control over her behavior despite her assessment of this as "counterproductive."

Engaging in Unwanted Sex

Many of the women in this study recounted experiences of having sex with men when they did not really want to, for a variety of reasons. This now common finding (e.g., Gavey 1992) underscores the extent to which women's control of sex with men is limited by various discursive constraints in addition to direct male pressure, force, or violence. As Bronwyn said, it is part of "the job":

Nicola: You said that you enjoy intercourse up to a point. Um, beyond that point, um, what are your reasons for continuing, given that you're not enjoying it?

Bronwyn: Ohh I just think it's part of my function if you like [laughter] that sounds terribly cold-blooded, but it is, [laughing] you know, it's part of the job.

Nicola: The job of—

Bronwyn: Being a wife. A partner or whatever.

Rose's account of her confrontational one-night stand, discussed previously, can be seen to be influenced in complex and subtle ways by the discursive construction of normative heterosexuality in which male sexuality and desire are supreme. She described the encounter as being quite unpleasant and disappointing, both sexually and in the way that he treated her—with respect to condoms and more generally throughout the experience. She described his actions during the encounter as clumsy and not the least bit sexually arousing ("He wasn't being very stimulating, he was trying to be and bungling it because he was drunk. And being too rough and just too brutish"), and at one stage she suggested that they give up and go to sleep but he rejected this

idea very strongly. Despite the extremely unsatisfactory nature of the sexual interaction and despite Rose's demonstrated skills of acting assertively, she did continue with the encounter until this man had had an orgasm through vaginal intercourse. It is difficult to understand why she would have done this without appreciating the power of the male sex drive discourse and the coital imperative in determining the nature of heterosexual encounters.

Although she did not define herself as a victim of the experience, Rose's account also makes clear that somehow she did not feel it was an option to end sex unless he gave the okay:

> It was sort of like— and I guess in that case he didn't have my utmost respect by that point. But it was sort of like, um, you know, he'd— he seemed to be just going for it, and I really really — I was drunk and sort of dishevelled and— and pretty resigned to having a bit of loose un— and unsatisfactory time which I didn't have a lot of control over.

She partially attributed this lack of control over the situation to the fact that the encounter took place at his flat, but this seems to be reinforced by underlying assumptions about sexuality and the primacy of his desires:

> Um, but it was kind of like he had his idea of what was going to happen and um I sort of realized after a while that he was so intent on it and the best thing to do was to just comply I guess, and make it as pleasurable as possible. Try and get into the same frame of mind that he was in. And— and yeah. Mmm, get it over with. It sounds really horrible in retrospect, it wasn't that bad it was just lousy, you know. It was just sort of a poor display of [laughing] everything. I suppose. Of intelligence and— and good manners. [laughter]

Part of the reason for the ambivalent nature of her account (swinging from describing what happened in very negative terms to playing down the experience as a poor display of manners) can be argued to originate from her positioning within a kind of liberal feminist discourse about sex. She had made a point of saying that she did not think things went in stages and defining herself in opposition to a model of female sexuality as fragile and in need of protection. The result of the connection between this liberal discourse of sexuality and that of the male sex drive is that she is left with no middle ground from which to negotiate within a situation of this kind. The absence of an alternative discourse of active female sexuality leaves her in a position of no return once she has consented to heterosexual relations and when certain minimal conditions are fulfilled (for her, this was the use of condoms). If heterosexuality were instead discursively constructed in such a way that women's sexual pleasure was central rather than optional, it makes sense that Rose may have felt able to call an end to this sex—which was, after all, so unpleasant that it led to her resolve to "devote [herself] to singledom for a while."

The Question of Pleasure

"I'm probably atypical from what I read of women in the fact that I personally don't like condoms." Sarah made this comment in the first minutes of the interview, and then much later she shared her assumption about how men regard using condoms: "Most men hate it. I've never asked them, but . . . that's the feeling I have from what I've read or heard." Sarah's generalized views about how women and men regard condoms echo dominant commonsense stories in Western culture. That is, most men do not like condoms—a view shared by 80.5 percent of women in one large U.S. sample (Valdiserri et al. 1989), while women do not mind them. To explain her own dislike of condoms, Sarah was forced to regard herself as atypical. In the following section, we will discuss evidence that challenges the tacit assumption that condoms are relatively unproblematic for women.

Enforcers of the Coital Imperative: Condoms as Prescriptions for Penetration

Research on how men and women define what constitutes "real sex" has repeatedly found that a coital imperative exists that places penis-vagina intercourse at the center of (hetero)sex (Gavey, McPhillips, and Braun 1999; Holland et al. 1998; McPhillips, Braun, and Gavey 2001). The strength of this imperative was also reflected in the current research—as one woman explained, "I don't think I worked out a model of being with someone like naked intimate touching which doesn't have sex at the end of it" (Sally defined sex as penis-vagina intercourse during the interview). Although this coital imperative

could be viewed as forming part of the male sex drive discourse examined above, it is addressed separately here as it has particular consequences for safer sex possibilities.

Condoms seem to reinforce the coital imperative in two interconnected ways, both in terms of their symbolic reinforcement of the discursive construction of sex as *coitus* and through their material characteristics that contribute at a more practical level to rendering sex as finished after coitus. In the analyses that follow, we will be attending to the material characteristics of condoms as women describe them. As discussed earlier, we adopt a realist reading of women's accounts here. What the women told us about the ways in which condoms help to structure the material practice of heterosex casts a shadow over the assumption that condoms are unproblematic for women's sexual experience. These accounts illuminate how the male sexual drive discourse can shape not only the ways people speak about and experience heterosex, but also the ways in which a research lens is focused on heterosexual practice to produce particular ways of seeing that perpetuate commonsense priorities and silences (which, in this case, privilege men's pleasure above women's). That is, the ways in which condoms can interfere with a woman's sexual pleasure are relatively invisible in the literature, which tends, at least implicitly, to equate "loss of sexual pleasure" with reduced sensation in the penis, or disruption of desire and pleasure caused by the act of putting a condom on. As the following excerpts show, the material qualities of condoms have other particular effects on the course of sex. These effects are especially relevant both to the question of a woman's pleasure and to the way in which the coital imperative remains unchallenged as the definitive aspect of heterosex.

While many of the women said they like (sometimes or always) and/or expect sexual intercourse (i.e., penis-vagina penetration) when having sex with a man, many of the women noted how condoms operated to enforce intercourse as the finale of sex. Several women found this to be a disadvantage of condoms, in that they tend to limit what is possible sexually, making sex more predictable, less spontaneous, playful, and varied. That is, once the condom is on, it is there for a reason and one reason only—penile penetration. It signals the beginning of "the end." Women who identified this disadvantage tended to be using condoms for contraceptive purposes and so were comparing sex that involved condoms unfavorably to intercourse with some less obtrusive form of contraception such as the pill or an IUD, or with no contraception during a "safe" time of the month.

For example, Julie found that condoms prescribed penetration at a point where she could be more flexible if no condom was involved:

> That's what I mean about the condom thing. It's like this is *the act* you know, and you have to go through the whole thing. Whereas if you don't use condoms, you know, like he could put it in me and then we could stop and then put it in again, you know, you can just be a bit more flexible about the whole thing.

The interconnection between the material characteristics of condoms (its semen-containing properties require "proper use") and the discursive construction of the encounter (coitus is spoken about as *"the act"*) has the effect of constraining a woman's sexual choices and leaving this generally unspoken coital imperative unchallenged. The discursive centrality of coitus within heterosex is materially reinforced by the practical difficulties associated with condoms, as Deborah said,

> Once you've put on the condom . . . that limits you. Once you've got to the stage in sex that you put a condom on, you then— it's not that you can't change plans, but it's a hassle if you then decided that you might like to move to do um— you might like to introduce oral sex at this stage, as opposed to that stage, then you have to take it off, or you don't, or—

Similarly, Rose said,

> Well that's the one problem, I suppose with condoms, is that you've already had penetrative sex with one and you either decide to um stop that and go onto something else, or you've finished and maybe you want to start again later, is that, you know, it's got that— you can't have oral sex because of that horrible taste. Or you can, but it really— it really does taste quite yucky.

And Suzanne, commenting about the unpleasant smell and taste of condoms, said, "And so like once it's on you're sort of committed to penetration, in a way. Um, as you sex."

Thus, condoms not only signaled when penetration would take place, but their use served to reinforce the taken-for-granted axiom of heterosexual practice, that coitus is the main sexual act. Furthermore, one woman (Sally) described how the need for a man to withdraw his penis soon after ejaculation when using a condom disrupted the postcoital "close feeling" she enjoyed. These excerpts can be seen to represent a form of resistance to the teleological assumptions of the coital imperative; women's accounts of desiring different forms of sexual pleasure (including, but by no means limited to, emotional pleasures) may provide rich ground for exploring safer sex options. This potentially productive area has yet to be fully exploited by traditional health campaigns, which perhaps reflects the lack of acknowledgment given to discourses of female sexual desire and pleasure in Western culture in general (see also Fine 1988).

Some women also talked about the effect using condoms had on their sexual pleasure by using the language of interruption and "passion killing" more commonly associated with men. Sarah, who rarely used condoms, said that "it breaks the flow":

> I have a lot of trouble reaching an orgasm anyway, and it's probably one of the reasons I don't like something that's interrupting, because I do go off the boil very quickly. Um, once it's on and it's sort of decided that penetration tends to be what happens. I don't suppose it's a gold rule, but it seems to be the way it is. So you know there's no more warm-up.

Unlike health campaigns directed at the gay community, which have emphasized the range of possible sex acts carrying far less risk of HIV infection than penile penetration, campaigns aimed at heterosexuals have done little to challenge the dominant coital imperative. Health campaigns that promote condoms as the only route to safer sex implicitly reinforce this constitution of heterosexuality and the dominance of the male sex drive discourse. As the responses of the women in this study demonstrate, this reluctance to explore other safer sex possibilities may be a missed opportunity for increasing erotic possibilities for women at the same time as increasing opportunities for safer sex. The fact that all of these women spent some time talking about the ways in which condoms can operate to enforce the coital imperative or reduce their desire indicates the importance of taking women's pleasure into account when designing effective safer sex programs. That is, it may simply not be valid to assume that "the disadvantages of condom use are fewer for girls" (Barling and Moore 1990) if we expect women's sexual desires and pleasures to be taken as seriously as men's. Special effort may be required to ask different questions to understand women's experiences in a way that doesn't uncritically accept a vision of heterosex as inherently constrained through the lens of the coital imperative and male sex drive discourses.

Discussion

Research on sexual coercion has shown that women may have limited control over the outcome of (hetero)sex even in the absence of direct force or violence from their male partners (Gavey 1992). Discourses of normative heterosexuality, such as those discussed in this article, play an important role in maintaining power dynamics between men and women. In the context of safer sex, the same cultural scripts that serve to legitimize various levels of coercion also limit the ways in which women may control the course and outcomes of heterosexual encounters. As the accounts of the women in this research show, power is infused in discursive constructions of normative heterosexuality, organized around a male sex drive discourse and a coital imperative, in ways that limit women's control and safer sex options. Anecdotal reports suggest that some women have been beaten and raped because they have tried to negotiate safer sex (Read 1990). In the absence of direct force, however, identities can be discursively produced in ways that render us particular kinds of subjects (e.g., "good lovers"), for whom desires associated with being this kind of person can override any desire for condom use (where that would be incompatible with this particular type of personhood). The question of a woman being assertive, then, to ensure that her partner wears a condom, will not even arise if her own desire for a condom to be worn is exceeded by these other kinds of desires. More simply, the strong ethic of individualism that is reified within the concept of assertiveness (Crawford 1995) arguably runs counter to dominant constructions of femininity. Moreover, contemporary ideals of reciprocity (see Gilfoyle, Wilson, and Brown 1992), mutuality, sharing, and giving arguably render the whole notion of assertiveness a delicate achievement

within the context of sexual relatedness (especially without recourse to an analysis of gendered power).

Achieving condom use is not a challenge of immense proportions for all women, however. Some of the women in this study demonstrated that they had embraced sentiments like the "If it's not on, it's not on" slogan as their own in ways that were strong and positive. Both Rose and Anita, for example, recalled situations in which they described themselves as being very "drunk," but it was nevertheless a high priority for them not to have sexual intercourse in such circumstances without a condom. These two women were seemingly able to act in these ways with relative ease; they were clear that they wanted the men to use condoms, they were clear about their rights to insist on this, they were clear they did not like what was happening, and they were apparently unafraid of acting physically and verbally to change this. The ability of these women to act from a position of strength and determination is perhaps cause for optimism about the discursive possibilities available to women. However, for a range of complex reasons, this sort of action is not easy for all women in all circumstances (Gavey 1992; Holland et al. 1998). Rose's and Anita's accounts also highlight both the limits and the possible consequences of enacting resistance to dominant constructions of heterosexuality. On one hand, their physical responses toward the men placed them in a position outside traditional notions of femininity, and their actions may have jeopardized future relations with their male partners. On the other hand, while the men they were with acted in ways that dramatically reduced their appeal, neither woman at that stage extricated herself from the ongoing sexual encounter. Less optimistically, then, it is perhaps only when casual sex is characterized by neither emotional nor physical pleasures that the conditions lend themselves to women asserting condom use. It is striking, for example, that the specter of romance is not particularly evident in the alcohol-facilitated one-night stands Rose and Anita described. As Warr (2001) and others have argued, romance can provide a context in which "even the self-interest of physical pleasure is often irrelevant" (243) to the attainment of other kinds of pleasures associated with love or "emotional intimacy and warmth" (243) and where "sex is figurative for an exchange of self" (242) in ways that contradict thinking about sex in terms of health risk (see also Rosenthal, Gifford, and Moore 1998).

Holland et al. (1998) have argued that heterosexual relations as they stand are premised on a construction of femininity that endangers women. Evidence for this position can be drawn from the current study as the interaction of discourses determining normative heterosexuality produces situations in which women are unable to always ensure their safety during sexual encounters. Holland et al. (1998) have argued that a refiguring of femininity is needed to ensure that women have a greater chance of safer heterosexual encounters. One of the prerequisites for change of this kind would be acknowledgment of the discourses of active female desire, which have traditionally been repressed (Fine 1988). Indeed, our research here suggests that the claim that condoms are "relatively unproblematic" for women is based on a continued relegation of the importance of women's sexual pleasure, relative to men's. Without challenging the gendered nature of dominant representations of desire, and more critically examining the coital imperative, condom promotion to women is likely to remain a double-edged practice. As both a manifestation and a reinforcement of normative forms of heterosex, it may be of limited efficacy in promoting safer heterosex.

NOTE

1. It should be emphasized that Sarah's mother's attitudes would have been in line with contemporary thought at the time. Take, for example, the advice of "A Famous Doctor's Frank, New, Step-by-Step Guide to Sexual Joy and Fulfilment for Married Couples" (on front cover of Eichenlaub 1961, 36), published when Sarah was nearly an adolescent:

> *Availability:* If you want good sex adjustment as a couple, you must have sexual relations approximately as often as the man requires. This does not mean that you have to jump into bed if he gets the urge in the middle of supper or when you are dressing for a big party. But it does mean that a woman should never turn down her husband on appropriate occasions simply because she has no yearning of her own for sex or because she is tired or sleepy, or indeed for any reason short of a genuine disability. (Eichenlaub 1961, 36)

REFERENCES

Barling, N. R., and S. A. Moore. 1990. Adolescents' attitudes towards AIDS precautions and intention to use condoms. *Psychological Reports* 67:883–90.

Chapman, S., and J. Hodgson. 1998. Showers in raincoats: Attitudinal barriers to condom-use in high-risk heterosexuals. *Community Health Studies* 12:97–105.

Crawford, M. 1995. *Talking difference: On gender and language.* London: Sage.

Eichenlaub, J. E. 1961. *The marriage art.* London: Mayflower.

Family Planning Association. 2000. *Condoms* [Pamphlet]. Auckland, New Zealand: Family Planning Association. (Written and produced in 1999. Updated 2000.)

Fine, M. 1988. Sexuality, schooling, and adolescent families: The missing discourse of desire. *Harvard Educational Review* 58:29–53.

Gavey, N. 1992. Technologies and effects of heterosexual coercion. *Feminism & Psychology* 2:325–51.

Gavey, N., K. McPhillips, and V. Braun. 1999. Interruptus coitus: Heterosexuals accounting for intercourse. *Sexualities* 2:37–71.

Gilfoyle, J., J. Wilson, and Brown. 1992. Sex, organs, and audiotape: A discourse analytic approach to talking about heterosexual sex and relationships. *Feminism & Psychology* 2:209–30.

Holland, J., C. Ramazonaglu, S. Scott, S. Sharpe, and R. Thomson. 1991. Between embarrassment and trust: Young women and the diversity of condom use. In *AIDS: Responses, interventions, and care,* edited by P. Aggleton, G. Hart, and P. Davies. London: Falmer.

Holland, J., C. Ramazonaglu, S. Sharpe, and R. Thomson. 1998. *The male in the head: Young people, heterosexuality and power.* London: TheTufnell.

Hollway, W. 1984. Gender difference and the production of subjectivity. In *Changing the subject: Psychology, social regulation and subjectivity,* edited by J. Henriques, W. Hollway, C. Urwin, and V. Walkerdine. London: Methuen.

———. 1989. *Subjectivity and method in psychology: Gender, meaning, and science.* London: Sage.

Kippax, S., J. Crawford, C. Waldby, and P. Benton. 1990. Women negotiating heterosex: Implications for AIDS prevention. *Women's Studies International Forum* 13:533–42.

McPhillips, K., V. Braun, and N. Gavey. 2001. Defining heterosex: How imperative is the "coital imperative"? *Women's Studies International Forum* 24:229–40.

Meijer, I. C., and B. Prins. 1998. How bodies come to matter: An interview with Judith Butler. *Signs: Journal of Women in Culture and Society* 23:275–86.

Planned Parenthood Federation of America, Inc. 1998–2001. *Condoms.* Retrieved 18 June 2001 from the World Wide Web: http//www.plannedparenthood.org.

Read, V. 1990. Women and AIDS. *Australian Nurses Journal* 20:22–24.

Rosenthal, D., S. Gifford, and S. Moore. 1998. Safe sex or safe love: Competing discourses? *AIDS Care* 10:35–47.

Sack, F. 1992. *Romance to die for: The startling truth about women, sex and AIDS.* Deerfield Beach, FL: Health Communications.

Statistics New Zealand. 2001. *Statistics and information about New Zealand.* Retrieved 4 July 2001 from the World Wide Web: http://www.stats.govt.nz/default.htm.

Valdiserri, R. O., V. C. Arena, D. Proctor, and F. A. Bonati. 1989. The relationship between women's attitudes about condoms and their use: Implications for condom promotion programs. *American Journal of Public Health* 79:499–501.

Warr, D. J. 2001. The importance of love and understanding: Speculation on romance in safe sex health promotion. *Women's Studies International Forum* 24:241–52.

Willig, D. 1995. "I wouldn't have married the guy if I'd have to do that." Heterosexual adults' accounts of condom use and their implications for sexual practice. *Journal of Community and Applied Social Psychology* 5:75–87.

Worth, D. 1989. Sexual decision-making and AIDS: Why condom promotion among vulnerable women is likely to fail. *Studies in Family Planning* 20:297–307.

THIRTY-FOUR

◆◆◆

"I Am a Beautiful, Multifaceted Black Woman"

Interview with Shirley Royster, HIV/AIDS Educator and Activist[1]

MOR: We met back in 1981 at WEAVE.[2] I was an adult basic education teacher. You were one of about 12 Black, Latina, and White women who came to our tiny school that winter. Most of you were completing drug rehab treatment and you brought a deep desire to learn. I remember you going through some very difficult times back then, but underneath, you consistently projected a sense of being on a mission, a quest. In that way, you were a beacon of hope. After WEAVE, you entered Roxbury Community College, earned your Associate of Arts degree, got off welfare. Later you became a professional advocate, first in the Domestic Violence movement and subsequently in the HIV/AIDS movement. You now live in a house you own with your partner of almost 20 years, Catherine Joseph, and members of your loving extended family. You have raised two grown daughters, Tina and Sherita, and you belong to a long-enduring friendship network. So, how would you describe who you are now?

SR: I am a beautiful, multifaceted Black woman: I am a mother, lover, sister, friend, lesbian, feminist, AIDS educator and activist. I am loyal, generous, smart, committed. I really love people, and I believe we can create a better world for ourselves, our children, our grandchildren, and our grandchildren's children.

MOR: What were your early years like?

SR: I was born and grew up in Richmond, Virginia. Up until the time I was 14 I lived in a, I guess, a happy home—my mother, my father, my sisters, and my brothers. I was the oldest girl, so lots of stuff—chores and stuff—was done by my mother and me. That summer, I remember it was in the sixties, must have been around '66, I came home from my babysitting job and when I got to the door, my oldest brother told me that my mother had died. It seems like she went shopping, then laid on the couch, and she had died. Needless to say, that changed my whole life. I say that because if I'd had support and guidance at the age of 14, maybe my life would have been different. Maybe I wouldn't be sitting here now, telling my story. But it so happens that my mother did die when I was 14. She left me with a year-old baby and the other kids. At that time, I didn't have any support to help me become the mother of the house. All my younger siblings were taken into foster care by the state of Virginia. I didn't see them until they were in their late teens and early 20s. I didn't have support to help me go through my teenage years either. As a result, I got pregnant at the age of 17 and had a baby when I was 18. Got pregnant again when I was 18 and had another baby when I was 19. So I had two kids, still trying to be a kid myself and still no regular support. I ran

Shirley Royster, HIV/AIDS educator and activist

away. I just took the kids to DSS [Department of Social Services] one day and said, "I can't do it any more!" and hit the street. I never saw those two kids again.

I guess that was my growing-up period. My unstructured education—street education. I learned that there was nobody there to help you. Everything was on you. But I didn't really learn that because I kept trying to lean on people, kept trying to find my home, kept trying to find support. And I have to say that I did have this one family I went to and this lady. She was into structured religion and persuaded me that I should be baptized. I guess I was about 19 then, and I did. I went and got baptized because I thought that was what was missing from my life and some kind of way, that would save me from whatever was gonna happen to me.

During that time in the '60s, the Civil Rights Movement was big. There were meetings and marches going on around Richmond and all over the country. I wasn't directly involved in it, but the messages about Black people being entitled to have all the rights White people had, about Black people being somebody, about Black people's contributions to this country's de-

velopment were all around me. Even though I wasn't paying that much attention to them, somewhere in the back of my mind, those ideas stuck. Those teachings came back to me later, as I tried to understand myself, this country called America.

MOR: How did you get addicted to drugs?

SR: I finally came to Boston. I got here when I was 21. I came here on my birthday. That was 1970. I was pregnant and the guy that I came with left me here, seven months pregnant, and still looking, still trying to find something. I don't know what it was, but I was still trying to find it. Actually I also "came out" at that time. I found a lady who was great support to me. She knew I had gone through a whole domestic violence issue with my daughter's father, and so she took me to this club and I got introduced to my first lover who I was with for eight years. Her name was Rodney. Rodney was wonderful to me. But I didn't know when I first met Rodney that she was sneaking around for drugs. I'd been introduced to drugs in Virginia, although I wasn't doing them on a regular level when I first came here. But to make a long story short, I did go into drugs. I guess I did drugs for about seven years until I found Women Inc.[3]

MOR: What made you decide to get clean, and how did you do it?

SR: When I found Women Inc. I was desperate. I was about a minute away from permanently losing custody of my daughters, Tina and Sherita, who I birthed in Boston. The DSS social worker was practically signing the papers. I wanted to keep my children.

Women Inc. was one of those programs that was unique. It didn't treat my drug issue so much as it treated *me*. They wanted to know what made me tick, what made me react, my feelings. Why was I doing the things I was doing? Who was this person that I was? I had never had that before. I guess it gave me me time-out to think about who I wanted to be. Where I had come from. Where I was going. I had no structure. I didn't really have any limits for myself or for anybody else. I was just existing. I tried to hide out when I was going through this whole process with Women Inc. I tried to hide out in my room. I wore a wig on my head. I didn't know who I was; I didn't look in the mirror. My shades were down in my room. I couldn't see out and no one could see in.

That time was when I met you. You were a big influence in my life simply because you cared. I was going through Women Inc., I had a lot of support from my peers, from people who were drug treatment counselors. The feeling I got from you was that it wasn't about the drugs but it was about who's that person inside, who did I want to be, as I go through this life. You helped me in those kinds of ways. I just thought that you were sincere and honest. That's the bottom line. In my world, there weren't too many honest and sincere people at that time.

I began to realize that I also loved to learn. I wanted to learn. I loved to read. I was always a reader, an avid mystery reader, which I still am today. I wanted to find things to read. I wanted to learn about history. I wanted to learn about what made other people go through problems and come out on the other side and not use drugs to escape the pain they were in. I wanted that more than anything. I wanted to emulate you, and Barbara, and Mercedes.[4] I just wanted what you had. I started out in my mind to get that. I changed how I dressed, how I looked, how I talked. I changed all the people I was with. Basically, I took you all with me, because I wasn't strong enough to stand on my own at that time. Because I did take you with me, I began to feel better. I began to feel like there was something else more to me than just . . . I guess they [the staff at WEAVE] were saying to me, "Fake it 'til you can make it." That's what happened to me. I was faking it 'til I was making it. I began to have strength and I didn't really recognize what it was, except that I began to want to give away what was being given to me. I wanted to help other people. I wanted to find people who needed help, and to give them what I had. I think that was the biggest change in my life. Before I was just selfish and trying to find out who I was. But after a while my strength came in trying to help other people.

MOR: What was your experience of learning that you were HIV-positive?

SR: I tested positive for HIV in September 1986. I only got tested because of Catherine. I was very much in love with Catherine. I knew I'd done risky behaviors. I'd just found out that Rodney had died of AIDS. She'd been sick with AIDS. She had even come to live with me and hadn't told me. When I went to the hospital, they were asking me all kinds of questions about her mental capabilities and . . . she was actually having dementia. She didn't remember a lot of the people we were talking about and a lot of things— a lot of common experiences we had. The nurses were questioning me about that and that's when they let me know she had AIDS.

When I met Catherine, I decided to go get tested. Lo and behold . . . I have to tell you that, even though I thought I was HIV-positive, and thought I would be able to accept it, it was a traumatic experience for me. It was just so heartbreaking. I didn't want to have this virus. I didn't want to have it; I didn't want to die. I didn't want to live in an uncertain time in which I didn't know what was going to happen to my kids. I didn't want to be known as someone who had AIDS because at that time, as it is now, the stigma of AIDS was something you didn't want to have. There was no telling what my family would have thought if I had told them. But I did have some support systems in place. I had my lesbian mothers group; I had you and Mercedes. I was able to tell you because I needed to have that guidance because I didn't know what I was going to do. I just didn't know what I was going to do.

I took my daughters through a terrible period during that time. I wanted Tina [the eldest] to grow up because, like me, I thought, she wasn't going to grow up without a mother so she had to be prepared to be able to take care of her sister—mother her sister. That's what I thought. So I put a lot of stress on her and I really regret that. I should have seen that was an unfair thing to do to her. But at the time, I didn't know any better.

I found peer support groups also at that time, which helped me start trying to live just one day at a time. Living one day at a time actually helped more than anything else. Just getting up in the morning, going to work and coming home in the afternoon, and taking care of myself and my kids. I also told Catherine right away because I wanted to release her from any obligations she thought she might have toward me. I actually said to her that she needed to leave because I couldn't tell her how long I had to live. She didn't leave. She's still here.

I think what helps is that I have never been ill, in the hospital. I am in a lot of pain, though. Sometimes, I just lay in bed all morning because my body hurts, so I do need some care-taking. But the care-taking I need is more emotional than physical. I think that helps a lot because we both lean on each other for emotional support. I've taught her a lot about giving up some of her inhibitions. Catherine helped me not to be so reactive and how to control impulsive behaviors. That's where we are. I love her. I love her so much.

MOR: How did you become involved in the education and advocacy work you do?

SR: The advocacy work I do stems directly from my time with Women Inc. and wanting to give back what I'd gotten. I appreciate it so much, it's part of my make-up. I never relapsed to going back to drugs again because I never wanted to close my eyes again. The pain I'd experienced and all the pain I've experienced since then help me keep my eyes open. Sometimes it's been very painful and I've felt isolated, but I've always tried to deal with it. When I talk to women now, and speak to people about this virus, I let them know that this is something you can live with. The power of positive thinking and having a spiritual base is something that's greater than all the medications in the world. With your spirituality and being true to yourself and others, you can accomplish anything. I truly, truly, believe that. It's not that it doesn't hurt to go through the pain. The fear sometimes is so great, it's like walking through a dark could, but at some point that cloud will be removed and you will be able to go through it.

Now I say to people, "I'm not afraid to die anymore because I have lived, I have truly lived." I've had some of the worst experiences and I've had the best experiences. Years ago when I was on drugs, I would do anything to get high. I was very sleazy. Since I turned my life around, I've experienced the best. One thing is attending the International AIDS Conference in Durban, South Africa, in 2000. I've also had many opportunities to visit homeless shelters, transitional living programs, detox programs, and school, as a peer educator. Right now, if something were to happen

to me, I'd have no regrets. I have wonderful kids; I have wonderful friends. I have a wonderful life I've been able to make for myself with the help of others. Truly, I feel as though I've been blessed.

Sometimes I think where I would be if I didn't have this virus. I don't know where I would be. I think it helped mold my character. I know it has helped me to talk to other people about being diagnosed and the uncertain times they have to go through. It only takes one thing, one thing to remember: do not be alone. It takes strength to raise a child. I also think it takes that same strength to give one person support. It really does. And again you have to be honest with yourself to be able to ask for that support. Right now there's nowhere to hide; I can look in the mirror with my fat self and be very proud of who I am. Last year, I educated over 1,700 people about basic HIV and AIDS education. I facilitated support groups and workshops. I spoke at conferences and schools, and visited shelters. And I enjoy that. It keeps me in touch with who I am and where I came from; I never ever forget that. I never forget living in the projects. I never forget being that scared little girl who felt useless and who didn't know how to ask for help. I never ever forget that. I never forget the people who reached out to me. I try not to do anybody wrong. I am not perfect by any means. I am opinionated. I am judgmental. I can be stubborn. And I even lie [said with a little chuckle]. Yep, believe it or not, I lie, but I try not to make it a habit. And I ask for forgiveness because I am not perfect. I ask for strength to keep going on, to keep trying to be who I am. I ask for strength for my daughters, that they can be happy, and that my loving them and my education for them will make them strong enough to go through this life without too many trials and tribulations.

MOR: What advice do you have for younger people, especially women?

SR: Women have to find ways to forgive their mothers. I think many times we are disappointed because we didn't get from them what we needed or wanted. Many of our mothers have done the best they knew how to do. We also have to learn to love and forgive ourselves. And we have to learn that getting men's approval is not the most important thing in the world. Many of us have put ourselves through terrible experiences in order to get their approval, so we can say, "I have a man." We use drugs to please them and shape our bodies to suite their desires. We suppress our emotions, creativity, strength, our intelligence and deeply held values. We are even sexual when we don't want to be.

MOR: You said earlier that you learned a lot about this country. What can you say about this country's priorities and how they affect the lives of poor women of color, people with AIDS, children, and others who are on the margins of this society?

SR: This country was built on the back of Native Americans, enslaved Africans, poor Europeans, Chinese, Filipino, other Asian and Mexican workers, and women of all those groups. Instead of recognizing a profound debt owed to them, many of the people who run the government and corporations demand more. They put the responsibility of this country's financial problems on people who can't help themselves. They spend billions for wars and only a dime for poor women and children. So we have come to realize that we can't depend on our government to care for its people. That's why I think we should learn to support each others' causes. What I mean is, for example, people with AIDS should fight for homeless people. Advocates for health care should support people with AIDS. Advocates for quality, affordable housing should help workers struggling for livable wages. We have to band together to support each other to make a difference.

MOR: What important principles guide your life now?

SR: Sometimes I feel like I don't know enough, but I don't get hung up on whether or not I have to please anybody right now. It's not that I'm selfish. It's just that I can only do what I can do. And if I'm accepted for that, that's good. If not, then I am not willing to put on falsehoods or spend a lot of time trying to make myself somebody I'm not. People think I love people. But it's not just that I love people. I love the differences that come in the package of the person. I love the way

people's eyes are open. I just did a workshop for third-year residents at Boston University Dental School. There were a lot of student nurses, a lot of doctors, and some advocates there. You know, getting up and telling who I am helps me relive it and that helps me. When the program is over, people come up to me and thank me for sharing my story. And so I hope that as I'm doing this work I'm also giving back. I guess that's my mission—to give back what I got. I'm not dwelling on what's going to happen to me as the virus eats away at my immune system. That's not really my concern. I don't have any way of controlling that. My focus is to be the person I can be, and to give support to anyone who's ready to accept it. And to help them come out of that dark place, like I've had help.

MOR: Thank you for giving me your words to share with others. I also want to thank you so much for what you've given me personally—the way you saved my life when I was in a very dark place. I think the greatest gift for a teacher is mutual learning with students, each giving and receiving.

NOTES

1. Interview conducted by Margo Okazawa-Rey, November 2002.

2. WEAVE (Women's Vocational and Education Program) of Women Inc., was an adult basic education program for women completing substance-abuse treatment. Some women studied for a high school diploma, others wanted to learn how to read, write, and do arithmetic. The youngest woman was about 20 years old, the oldest in her late 50s.

3. In 1974, Women Inc. became one of four residential drug rehabilitation program nationwide, which recognized that, in order for addicted women to complete rehabilitation successfully, their children had to be included in the process. Along with three other programs, Women Inc. became a demonstration project funded by the National Institute on Drug Abuse that allowed women to bring their children to treatment and to address the entire family's needs.

4. Barbara Neumann and Mercedes Tompkins also were staff members of WEAVE.

6

◆◆◆

Violence Against Women

Gender violence affects women in all societies, all socioeconomic classes, all racial/ethnic groups, and it can occur throughout the life cycle (Heise, Pitanguy, and Germain 1994). Lori Heise (1989) comments: "This is not random violence; the risk factor is being female" (p. 13). In the United States, this includes the interpersonal violence of battering, rape, child sexual abuse, stalking, hassles on the street, obscene phone calls, sexual harassment at school or workplace. Underlying these incidents and experiences are systemic inequalities, also a kind of violence, that maintain women's second-class status—culturally, economically, and politically. The fact that Native Americans were dispossessed of their land and enslaved African people forced to work for slave masters was a profound violation, in addition to sexualized violence against women of these groups (Reading 39; also see Trask 1999). This chapter focuses on violence against women in this country and the many efforts to stop it. This is a key issue and we refer to it in other chapters also: with regard to relationships and family (Chapter 7), as a workplace issue (Chapter 8), regarding women in prison (Chapter 10), and in connection with the military (Chapter 11).

Since the 1970s, women in many communities have broken the silence about sexual violence, the limits it places on all our lives, ways to heal from it, and how to stop it (e.g., Bart and O'Brien 1993; Bass and Davis 1988; Brownmiller 1975; Koppelman 1996; NiCarthy 1986, 1987; White 1985; and Zambrano 1985). Women have written fiction, such as Dorothy Allison's *Bastard Out of Carolina* (1992), also filmed for HBO. They continue to organize "Take Back the Night" marches and rallies, where women still dare to speak out for the first time about their experiences. In Reading 35, Grace Caroline Bridges writes about a girl's experience of sexual abuse. Barbara Harman (1996) describes how a woman in an abusive relationship is always second-guessing and responding to an abusive partner in her attempts to avoid further violence:

Don't raise your voice. Don't talk back. Don't say no to sex. Like whatever he does. Don't ask him to do anything he has not already done. Get up when he gets up. Go to bed when he goes to bed. Wait. Do what he wants to do. Never contradict him. Laugh at what he thinks is funny. Never ask for his time, attention, his money. Have your own money, but give it to him if he wants it. Never go out alone but do not expect him to go with you. If he is angry in the car, walk home. Be his friend except when he needs an enemy. Defend his family except when he hates them. Understand everything.

(p. 287)

What Counts as Violence Against Women?

Most women tolerate a certain amount of what could be defined as sexual violence as part of daily life. We experience hassles on the street, in parks, or in cafés and bars. We put up with sexist comments from bosses or coworkers. We sometimes make compromises as part of maintaining intimate relationships, including going along with sex when we do not really want it, or tolerating put-downs, threats, and inconsiderate behavior. We may define some of these experiences as violence, and others not.

Researchers and writers do not use terms like *sexual assault, sexual abuse, battering,* or *domestic violence* in a standardized way. Differences of definition and terminology have led to marked discrepancies in reporting and have contributed to considerable confusion about these issues, which should be borne in mind throughout this chapter.

The United Nations Declaration on Violence Against Women (General Assembly resolution 48/104) of December 20, 1993, defines such violence as "any act of gender-based violence that results in, or is likely to result in, physical, sexual or psychological harm or suffering to women, including threats of such acts, coercion or arbitrary deprivation of liberty whether occurring in public or private life" (Heise, Pitanguy, and Germaine 1994, p. 46). This includes physical acts like battering, rape, child sexual abuse, stalking, and inappropriate touching in the case of sexual harassment in the workplace. It includes verbal and psychological violence against intimate partners like yelling, intimidation, and humiliation; inappropriate personal remarks made to coworkers or students; and offensive sexist "jokes." It also includes forced isolation, denial of support, and threats of violence or injury to women in the family. This broad definition implicitly recognizes that men as a group have power over women—the women they are close to and those they encounter in public places.

Women may be physically smaller or weaker, they may be economically dependent on their partner, or they may need their boss's support to keep their jobs or to get a promotion or a pay raise. Thus, macro-level inequalities are present in violence at the micro level. An important element of this male power is that it is sexualized. This is a given in interactions between intimate partners. It is also often true of interactions that are violent or that border on violence between men and women who are not intimate but who are friends, coworkers, teachers and students, or complete strangers (see Figure 6.1).

Many researchers and commentators do not use such a broad definition of violence against women. They focus on specific physical acts that can be measured. Emotional violence and the fear of threats are impossible to quantify precisely. It is much easier to bring charges of violence if one can show clear evidence of physical coercion or harm. Indeed, the legal system demands demonstrable damage or there is nothing to claim. The problem with this kind of quantification is that one cannot see the wider social and political context within which violence occurs.

The definition of violence against women can also be expanded beyond the United Nations definition quoted earlier. Psychologist Hussein Bulhan (1985), for example, proposes the following:

Violence is any relation, process, or condition by which an individual or a group violates the physical, social, and/or psychological integrity of another person or group. From this perspective, violence inhibits human growth, negates inherent potential, limits productive living, and causes death. (p. 135)

This would include colonization, poverty, racism, lack of access to education, health care and medical insurance, negative media representations, as well as environmental catastrophes. These factors can affect men as well as women. But women as a group are poorer than men; women's rights may be limited with regard to reproductive freedom; and women are systematically objectified and commodified in the media. We argue that these macro-level factors jeopardize women's security and should be part of this discussion of violence even though they may not always have an explicitly sexual dimension. Some activists and writers use the word *rape*—for example, rape by the economic or legal system—to refer to macro-level violence. We caution against this

Figure 6.1 The Dynamics of Domestic Violence: Power and Control Wheel. *Source:* Asian Women's Shelter, adapted from Domestic Abuse Intervention Project, Duluth, MN. Used with permission.

as it reduces the power of the term to refer to sexual violation.

At micro and meso levels, women as well as men can be violent. Women may abuse children, other family members, their peers, and people who work for them. Writer and cultural critic bell hooks (1984b) notes that women "may employ abusive measures to maintain authority in interactions with groups

over whom they exercise power" (p. 119). Research shows that, in general, women hit children more than men do, but they also spend much more time with children. Women may contribute to the dynamic of a violent relationship. They may hit their partner first. Occasionally women kill abusive partners in self-defense, seemingly the only way out of situations in which they believe they would be killed

Gender Violence Worldwide, Throughout the Life Cycle

PHASE	TYPE OF VIOLENCE
Prebirth	Sex-selective abortion (e.g., in China, India, Republic of Korea); battering during pregnancy (emotional and physical effects on the woman; effects on birth outcome); coerced pregnancy (for example, mass rape in war).
Infancy	Female infanticide; emotional and physical abuse; differential access to food and medical care for girl infants.
Girlhood	Child marriage; genital mutilation; sexual abuse by family members and strangers; differential access to food and medical care; child prostitution.
Adolescence	Dating and courtship violence (for example, acid throwing in Bangladesh, date rape in the United States); economically coerced sex (African secondary school girls having to take up with "sugar daddies" to afford school fees); sexual abuse in the workplace; rape; sexual harassment; forced prostitution; trafficking in women.
Reproductive age	Abuse of women by intimate male partners; marital rape; dowry abuse and murders; partner homicide; psychological abuse; sexual abuse in the workplace; sexual harassment; rape; abuse of women with disabilities.
Elderly	Abuse of widows; elder abuse (in the United States, the only country where data are now available, elder abuse affects mostly women).

Source: Heise, Pitanguy, and Germain (1994), p. 5.

if they did not defend themselves (Jones 1980; Richie 1996). In 1999, 4 percent of all male murder victims were killed by their wives or girlfriends compared to 32 percent of all female murder victims who were killed by their husbands or boyfriends (Rennison 2001). Indeed, the vast majority of gender violence is violence against women. The chance of being victimized by an intimate is significantly greater for a woman (85 percent) than for a man (15 percent) (Rennison 2001). We prefer the term "violence against women" over "gender violence" because it makes this inequality explicit.

The Incidence of Violence Against Women

Domestic violence, rape, sexual abuse, and child sexual abuse are all illegal in the United States. The incidence of such violence is difficult to estimate accurately because of discrepancies in definition and terminology, limited research, and underreporting.

According to the Family Violence Prevention Fund (1998), "Every year, as many as 4 million American women are physically abused by men who promised to love them" (p. 1). The U.S. Department of Justice (1994) reported that women are more often victims of domestic violence—meaning violence by intimate partners—than victims of burglary, muggings, or other physical crimes combined. The U.S. Department of Justice (1997) reported that 37 percent of all women who sought care in hospital emergency rooms for violence-related injuries in 1997 were injured by a current or former spouse, boyfriend, or girlfriend. Abuse-related injuries include bruises, cuts, burns and scalds, concussion, broken bones, penetrating injuries from knives, miscarriages, permanent injuries such as damage to joints, partial loss of hearing or vision, and physical disfigurement. There are also serious mental health effects of isolation, humiliation, and ongoing threats of violence. As mentioned earlier, many writers and researchers do not take account of psychological and emotional dimensions of domestic violence because

they are difficult to measure. They define it as physical assault only, which gives the impression that quantifiable acts of violence—kicking, punching, or using a weapon—tell the whole story.

One in five high school girls surveyed reported that she had been physically or sexually abused; the majority of these incidents occurred at home and happened more than once (Commonwealth Fund 1997). Girls aged 16 to 19 experience one of the highest rates of violence by an intimate partner (Greenfeld et al. 1998; Rennison 2001). In 1999, 18 percent of public high school girls in Massachusetts reported having ever been physically or sexually assaulted by someone they were dating (Goode 2001). June Larkin and Katherine Popaleni's (1997) interviews with young women reveal how young men use criticism, intimidation, surveillance, threats, and force to establish and maintain control over their girlfriends. Laura O'Toole and Jessica Schiffman (1997) note that young women are vulnerable to abuse because they may feel that involvement in a personal relationship is necessary to fit in; they may be flattered by a dating partner who demands time and attention; and they lack experience negotiating affection and sexual behavior.

The legal definition of rape turns on force and nonconsent. Consent to sexual intercourse is not meaningful if given under the influence of alcohol, drugs, or prescription medication. Like domestic violence, rape is not always reported, and the true scope of the problem is difficult to estimate. Between 1992 and 2000, 63 percent of completed rapes and 65 percent of attempted rapes were not reported to the police (Rennison 2002). Rape is defined as forced sexual intercourse—vaginal, anal, or oral penetration. Sexual assault includes attacks involving unwanted sexual contact; it may involve force and include grabbing or fondling, also verbal threats. The groups most at risk for sexual assault are 16- to 19-year-olds, then 20- to 24-year-olds. In contrast to popular ideas about rape committed by a stranger in a dark alley, 76 percent of women who reported that they had been raped or physically assaulted since the age of 18 said that their partner or date committed the assault (National Institute of Justice and Centers for Disease Control and Prevention 1998). An early-1990s survey found that 13 percent of adult women are victims of forcible rape: one woman in seven (National Victim Center 1992). A 1998 survey reported that 18 percent of women had experienced a completed rape or attempted rape at some time in their lives (National Institute of Justice and Centers for Disease Control and Prevention 1998).

A study of date rape on campuses in the mid-1980s found that one in nine college women had been raped and that eight out of ten victims knew their attacker, although as few as 5 percent reported the crime (Koss 1988). One in twelve college men responding to the same survey admitted that they had committed acts that met legal definitions of rape (Koss, Dinero, and Seibel 1988). The FBI's Uniform Crime Report (compiled from over 16,000 law enforcement agencies covering 96 percent of the nation's population) estimated that one in four U.S. college women is a victim of rape or attempted rape, and this estimate is still widely used by academics, activists, and journalists. Skeptics counter that such figures are highly inflated and that many women who claim to have been raped blame their dates for their own poor judgement in having sex (Paglia 1990; Roiphe 1993). Female students are most at risk of date rape in the first few weeks of college. They often do not report a rape because of confusion, guilt, or fear, or because they feel betrayed; they may be ashamed to tell parents or college counselors; and they may not identify the experience as rape. However, the reporting of date rape increased significantly on U.S. college campuses during the 1990s. The psychological effects of rape can be devastating, traumatic, and long-lasting. They include feelings of humiliation, helplessness, anger, self-doubt, self-hate, and fear; and a student may become depressed and withdrawn and do poorly in school.

Effects of Race, Class, Nation, Sexuality, and Disability

Although these forms of violence occur across the board, women's experiences are complicated by race, class, sexual orientation, and disability.

Research   The Bureau of Justice Statistics (1995) notes that domestic violence is consistent across racial and ethnic lines. Jody Raphael and Richard Tolman (1997) found that past and current victims of domestic violence were overrepresented among women on welfare and families with extremely low incomes. Callie Marie Rennison (2002) found that, in 1999, African American women aged 20 to 24 experienced more intimate violence than White women of the same age. Estimates that are based on official reports of violence are limited by the fact that many cases are not reported. Those that rely on research are limited by the scope of studies undertaken. Children and adolescents, prostituted women, homeless women, women with mental disabilities, institutionalized women, very poor women, and women in neighborhoods with high crime rates are rarely included in surveys. Women and girls with physical and mental disabilities are particularly vulnerable to physical, emotional, and sexual abuse from partners, caregivers, and service providers (Abramson et al. 2000; Young et al. 1997). The few studies that exist suggest that women with disabilities are between four and ten times as likely to be sexually assaulted as other women.

Reporting   Violence between intimate partners is illegal in this country, but it is seriously underreported because of confusion, shame, self-blame, loyalty to the abuser, lack of information, or fear of repercussions, including loss of his income. Women may not believe that reporting violence to the police will do any good. Women of color, poor women, and prostituted women often have very negative experiences with the police. Women of color may decide not to report domestic violence or rape to avoid bringing more trouble on husbands, partners, friends, and acquaintances who already suffer discrimination based on race, as mentioned by Fernando Mederos (Reading 36) and Andy Smith (Reading 38). In many communities of color the police are perceived not as helpful but, rather, as abusive, harassing, and violent. Women as well as men "bear the brunt of police indifference and abuse" and "men are frequently targeted for false arrest" (M. Smith 1997). Their community may expect women of color to maintain silence about sexual assault, to protect "family honor and community integrity" (Crenshaw 1993, p. 5). Melba Wilson (1993) discusses the conflicting pressures operating here and urges Black women to hold men accountable for sexual abuse of children. Older women may not report acts of violence committed by spouses, adult children, caregivers, relatives, and neighbors, because they fear being rejected, losing their caregiver, being placed in a nursing home, or losing their property—particularly their home or independent access to money. Immigrant women who are dependent on an abusive partner for their legal status may fear repercussions from the INS if they report violence, as discussed by Lora Jo Foo in Reading 37. Some women have been reluctant to speak about abuse in lesbian relationships, perhaps assuming that domestic violence happens only between women and men or not wanting to feed negative stereotypes of lesbians in the wider society.

Responses of the Police, Support Services, Medical and Legal Systems   The response to reports of violence against women and the provision of services have greatly expanded over the last thirty years as this issue has become recognized publicly. Police officers, judges, doctors, nurses, and emergency-room staff may undergo professional training, although much more still needs to be done in this regard. During slavery times, the rape of Black women in the United States was legal and commonplace. They were chattel, the property of their masters, and available for anything and everything. Currently, negative stereotypes about women of color, poor White women, prostituted women, and lesbians all perpetuate the idea, in the wider society, that these women are not worthy of respect. They are less likely to be taken seriously when they report acts of violence. Law professor Kimberlé Crenshaw (1993) notes an early-1990s study of sentences given to convicted rapists in Dallas: "The average sentence given to the rapist of a Black woman was two years . . . to the rapist of a Latina . . . five years, and . . . to the rapist of a white woman . . . ten years. Interviews with jurors reveal that the low conviction rate of men accused of raping Black women is based on ongoing sexual stereotypes about Black women" (p. 4).

Explanations of Violence Against Women

Most explanations of violence against women are social theories. Before discussing some of these, we note the resurfacing of a biological explanation of rape. Randy Thornhill and Craig Palmer (2000) argue that rape evolved historically as a form of male reproductive behavior. These authors base their claims on studies of animal species from the scorpion fly to primates. As with other sociobiological theories, they make huge leaps between animal behavior and human life, they are not grounded in an analysis of

social systems, and their claims are not borne out by the experience of women who have suffered acts of violence.

As in other chapters, we focus on social theories and separate micro- and macro-level explanations.

Micro-level Explanations

Whatever form it takes, violence against women is always experienced at the personal or micro level. Family violence, rape, and child sexual abuse are often explained in terms of an individual mental health problem, innate sexual craving, or personal dysfunction on the part of perpetrators. By contrast, Jean Grossholtz (1983), a professor of political science and women's studies, argues that research on rapists and batterers shows them to be "ordinary men, indistinguishable from nonrapists and nonbatterers" (p. 59). Another micro-level explanation for domestic violence is that the partners have an "unhealthy" relationship.

Three psychological syndromes have been advanced to explain violence against women: battered woman syndrome, rape trauma syndrome, and false memory syndrome.

Battered Woman Syndrome   Psychologist Lenore Walker (1979, 1984) put forward the notion of a "battered woman syndrome." She noted a pattern of behavior that she termed "learned helplessness," whereby women who are repeatedly battered "learn" it is impossible to escape. After an episode of violence, they are seduced back by the batterer with declarations of love and promises that he will change. These calm, loving episodes alternate with periods of accelerating violence, isolating the woman further and tying her closer to him. Attorneys have used a "battered woman syndrome" defense for women who kill violent partners by arguing that their clients' judgment was affected "in such a way as to make them honestly believe that they were in imminent danger and that the use of force was their only means of escape" (Gordon 1997, p. 25).

Rape Trauma Syndrome   This term is used by mental health and legal professionals to refer to women's coping strategies following rape. The focus is on women's reactions and responses rather than on the actions of the perpetrators or the prevalence of sexual violence in our society. Rape trauma syndrome has been used to explain women's apparently "counterintuitive" reactions—such as not reporting a rape for days or even months, not remembering parts of the assault, appearing too calm, or expressing anger at their treatment by police, hospital staff, or the legal system—in terms of pathology (Stefan 1994, p. 1274). Women diagnosed with rape trauma syndrome—who are generally White and middle class—are given psychiatric treatment with the goal of recovery and resolution. Expert testimony concerning rape trauma syndrome in rape trials improves the chances that a perpetrator will be convicted but at the cost of representing the woman as a pathetic victim. Susan Stefan (1994), an attorney and law professor, argues that the creation of this syndrome has depoliticized the issue of rape.

False Memory Syndrome   Childhood sexual abuse by parents, older siblings, stepparents, and other family members, exemplified in Dorothy Allison's novel *Bastard Out of Carolina* (1992), is another aspect of family life that has gradually become a public issue through the efforts of survivors, counselors, and feminist advocates (Reading 35). Many abused children block out memories of what happened to them, and these may not surface again until their adult years, perhaps through flashbacks, nightmares, panic attacks, or pain (Petersen 1991; White 1988). They then gradually piece together fragments of their experience that have been suppressed. Those who have been abused as children often experience confusion, shame, fear, or fear of being crazy. They may spend years thinking they were to blame. They may have feelings of not being worth much, or conversely, they may feel special. The child is invariably told that this special secret must never be spoken about. Healing from the effects of childhood sexual abuse takes time, courage, and support (Bass and Davis 1988; Herman 1992; Petersen 1991; E. C. White 1985; L. White 1988; Wilson 1993), and many families do not want to open up this can of worms. False memory syndrome (FMS) has been invoked by parents who believe they "have been falsely accused [of incest] as a result of their adult children discovering 'memories' in the course of therapy" (Wasserman 1992, p. 18) and by lawyers acting on their behalf. According to FMS, the incest survivor is someone with impaired cognitive functioning. Memory is complex cognitively, and there are well-regarded psychologists on both sides of this issue.

These syndromes were developed for legal or therapeutic purposes. As explanations of violence against women, they are all inadequate. They pathologize women who suffer acts of violence as helpless victims. As legal defenses in cases involving acts of violence, they are also highly problematic. A battered-woman-syndrome defense for women who have killed abusive partners represents battered women as impaired, rather than as "rational actors responding to perceived danger" (Gordon 1997, p. 25). Attorneys have tried to get courts to accept that the law of self-defense applies to battered women, but without much success. These syndromes all blame the victim for her situation. The advice that police departments often give to women for their safety also assumes that we bring assaults on ourselves: Do not go out alone late at night; do not wear "provocative" clothing; always walk purposefully; do not make eye contact with men on the street; park your car in a lighted area; have your keys ready in your hand before you leave the building; look into the back seat before getting in your car, and so on. This advice is well intentioned and may be helpful. However, it assumes that women are responsible for acts of violence against them, either directly "asking for it" by their dress or behavior or indirectly encouraging it by not being sufficiently cautious.

Macro-level Explanations

Micro-level explanations of violence against women can be compelling if one focuses on specific personal interactions, but by themselves they cannot explain such a universal and systemic phenomenon. It is essential to analyze this issue at the meso and macro levels to understand it fully and to generate effective strategies to stop it.

Macro-level explanations focus on the cultural legitimation of male violence and the economic, political, and legal systems that marginalize, discriminate against, and disempower women.

Hussein Bulhan (1985) uses a very broad definition of violence that emphasizes the structural nature of violence. It rests on several assumptions:

> Violence is not an isolated physical act or a discrete random event. It is a relation, process, and condition undermining, exploiting, and curtailing the well-being of the victim. These violations are not just moral or ethical, but also physical, social, and/or psychological. They

involve demonstrable assault on or injury of and damage to the victim. Violence in any of the three domains—physical, social, or psychological—has significant repercussions in the other two domains. Violence occurs not only between individuals, but also between groups and societies. Intention is less important than consequence in most forms of violence. Any relation, process, or condition imposed by someone that injures the health and well-being of others is by definition violent.   *(p. 135)*

Applying these ideas to violence against women may make it easier to see this violence in terms of inequalities of power under patriarchy, as argued by Allan Johnson (Reading 2, Chapter 1). In Reading 38, Andy Smith shows the links between patriarchy and White supremacy in her discussion of sexual violence and American Indian genocide. Macro-level factors such as sexism, heterosexism, racism, economic opportunities, working conditions, unemployment, poverty, or loss of status and cultural roots that may accompany immigration also affect personal and family relationships from the outside. This is not to excuse men and women who abuse their partners or children but, rather, to provide a wider context for understanding violence. Indeed, family violence is embedded in institutional roles and relationships, supported by cultural standards and expectations—meso- and macro-level factors.

The Cultural Legitimation of Male Violence   This includes cultural beliefs in male superiority and male control of women's behavior and of the family, which are supported by social institutions such as education, law, religion, and popular culture. The old idea that a wife is the property of her husband still lingers in custom and in law (see Naomi Wolf, Reading 23, Chapter 4, and Jaclyn Geller, Reading 42, Chapter 7). Wives are supposed to agree to sex, for example, as part of their wifely duty. Rape in marriage was made a crime in the United States as recently as 1993, but in thirty-three states there are varying exemptions from prosecuting husbands for rape, which indicates that rape in marriage is still treated as a lesser crime than other forms of rape (National Clearinghouse on Marital and Date Rape 1998). Examples of exemptions are when a wife is mentally or physically impaired, unconscious, or asleep (Bergen 1996, 1999). Another example of male control is street harassment, where women may be "touched, harassed,

commented upon in a stream of constant small-scale assaults" (Benard and Schlaffer 1997, p. 395). The public street is defined as male space where women without male escorts are considered "fair game." Cheryl Benard and Edith Schlaffer note that women need to "plan our routes and our timing as if we are passing through a mine field" (p. 395).

The cultural legitimation of male superiority involves patterns of male and female socialization in the family and in schools, and the social construction of masculinity and of male sexuality (see Kimmel 1993; 2000, chap. 11; Kimmel and Messner 1995; Lefkowitz 1997; Messner 1992). In a White-supremacist society, men of color may be attracted to a construction of masculinity that derives from White patriarchal attitudes and behavior. Discussing violence against women in African American communities, bell hooks (1994) writes:

> Black males, utterly disenfranchised in almost every arena of life in the United States, often find that the assertion of sexist domination is their only expressive access to the patriarchal power they are told all men should possess as their gendered birthright.   *(p. 110)*

Haki Madhubuti takes up this issue in Reading 39.

We live in a society where war toys, competitive games, violent and aggressive sports, video games, and violence on TV and in movies are integral to children's socialization, especially that of boys. Popular culture, news media, and advertising all reinforce these cultural attitudes and contribute to the objectification and commodification of women. Rape, beating, and verbal abuse of women are commonplace in feature films and TV shows. At the meso level too, in various communities, cultural attitudes and religious beliefs support domestic violence as a husband's prerogative to "discipline" his wife. Some psychological explanations invoke a culture of violence that violent families perpetuate.

Economic Systems That Disempower Women   Women as a group earn less than men as a group. It may be difficult for a woman to leave a violent marriage or relationship if she is financially dependent on her partner. In the workplace, women may find it difficult to speak up about sexual harassment. Sociologist Michael Kimmel (1993) notes that sexual harassment "fuses two levels of power: the power of employers over employees and the power of men over women. Thus what may be said or intended as a man to a woman is also experienced in the context of superior and subordinate" (p. 130). We return to this issue in Chapter 8.

Legal Systems That Discriminate Against Women
This includes inadequate laws and practices concerning violence against women, and insensitive treatment of women by police and the courts. Martha Mahoney (1994) emphasizes the narrowness of legal categories and procedures in dealing with violence against women. For instance, the "statute of limitations," a limit on the time period allowed for bringing a lawsuit for damages or criminal charges against a perpetrator, stops some women from using the law for redress in cases of rape or childhood sexual abuse. In the latter case, they may be in their twenties, and years past the time limit, before they recognize that they were abused as children and gain the personal strength to confront the perpetrator publicly. Jean Grossholtz (1983) argues that violence against women has not "simply been overlooked by the criminal justice system" (p. 67), but that this is part of the way patriarchal power compels women "through fear and endangerment, to submit to self-depreciation, heterosexuality, and male dominance in all spheres of life" (pp. 67–68).

Political Systems That Marginalize Women's Concerns   Women are still a small minority in elected office in the United States, especially at the congressional level. Violence against women is often not taken seriously by policy makers or legislators. Compared to male voters, more women are concerned about violence against women. More women also favor meaningful gun control, an end to the international trade in arms, reductions in military spending, and disarmament, believing that such changes would greatly increase their security and the well-being of their communities (Abzug 1984; Gallagher 1993; Smeal 1984). We take up the issue of women in electoral politics in Chapter 13.

The levels of violence mentioned earlier are interconnected and reinforce each other. Debra Borkovitz (1995) argues that it is necessary to transform prevailing ideas of *domination,* whether of racism, imperialism, male violence against women, or same-sex battering. Similarly, bell hooks (1984b) argues that violence against women should be seen as part of a general pattern of violence between the powerful and the powerless stemming from the "philosophical notion of hierarchical rule and coercive authority that is the root cause of violence against women, of adult violence against children, of all violence between those who dominate and those who are dominated" (p. 118). She argues that feminists should oppose all forms of coercive domination rather than concentrating solely on male violence against women. Kimberlé Crenshaw (1993) points out that the anti-violence movement must be an anti-oppression movement. This theme was emphasized by speakers at The Color of Violence Conference (University of California/Santa Cruz, April 2000), and we return to it below.

Ending Violence Against Women

Violence against women has engaged the attention, anger, and activist efforts of scholars, policy makers, and organizers around the world. Historian Linda Gordon (1988, 1997) notes that U.S. feminists challenged wife-beating as part of antidrinking campaigns in the late nineteenth century, then again in the 1930s in campaigns for child custody and welfare for single mothers so that they could leave abusive men. Extremely important feminist work in the 1960s and '70s broke through the prevailing silence on this subject, as mentioned in Chapter 1 (Brownmiller 1975; Griffin 1971; Russell 1975). Feminists reframed and politicized the issue of rape, exposing the myth that rape is about sex—a crime of "frustrated attraction, victim provocation, or uncontrollable biological urges, perpetrated only by an aberrant fringe" (Caputi and Russell 1990, p. 34). Rather, rape is about power and control—a "direct expression of sexual politics and an assertion of masculinist norms that reinforce and preserve the gender status quo" (Caputi and Russell 1990, p. 34). Feminist writers and organizers insisted that no woman deserves to be abused, or brings it on herself, or "asks for it."

The Importance of a Political Movement

Educator and organizer Judith Herman, M.D. (1992) argues that changing public consciousness about a traumatic issue like violence against women takes a concerted political movement. In her study of trauma and recovery connected to violence, she writes that perpetrators of violence "ask bystanders to do nothing, simply to ignore the atrocity"; whereas "victims demand action, engagement, and remembering" (pp. 7–8). Feminist writers and workers in shelters and rape crisis projects often use the term *survivor* to refer to women who are coping with acts of violence, rather than calling them victims. Herman's use of the term *victim* in the following discussion is unfortunate, but her comments on the processes of denial and silencing that often surround violence against women are very insightful.

> In order to escape accountability for his crimes, the perpetrator does everything in his power to promote forgetting. Secrecy and silence are the perpetrator's first line of defense. If secrecy fails, the perpetrator attacks the credibility of his victim. If he cannot silence her absolutely, he tries to make sure that no one listens. To this end, he marshals an impressive array of arguments, from the most blatant denial to the most sophisticated . . . rationalization. After every atrocity one can expect to hear the same predictable apologies: it never happened; the victim lies; the victim exaggerates; the victim brought it upon herself; and in any case it is time to forget the past and move on. The more powerful the perpetrator, the greater is his prerogative to name and define reality, and the more completely his arguments prevail.
>
> *(p. 8)*

Herman argues that to cut through the power of the perpetrators' arguments "requires a social context that affirms and protects the victim and that joins victim and witness in a common alliance" (p. 9). For the individual victim of violence, relationships with family, friends, and lovers create this context. For the wider society, "the social context is created by political movements that give voice to the disempowered," (p. 9), a key example being feminist movements.

Philosopher Nadya Burton (1998) criticizes second-wave feminists for using oversimplistic rhetoric in their attempts to get the issue of violence on the public agenda. They also emphasized fear, passivity, and victimhood in discussing violence against women. While acknowledging the damage suffered as a result of violence, it is also important to see women as resistors and survivors, people who cope with violation, who are not defined by it, and who thrive despite it. As Martha Mahoney (1994) comments, it is easy to see this issue in terms of victimization and, hence, to obliterate women's agency.

Feminist theorizing about the systemic nature of violence against women under patriarchy led to concerted efforts to provide supports for women who experienced such violence, to educate the wider society on the issue, and to change public policy.

Providing Support for Victims/Survivors

The first shelter for battered women in the United States opened in 1974. Now there are over 2,500 shelters and service programs nationwide, stretched to capacity. More shelters are needed, and those that exist need to be more accessible—physically and culturally—to women with disabilities, women of color, immigrant women, and lesbians. Shelters that emphasize culturally relevant perspectives and services include the Asian Women's Shelter (San Francisco); Baitul Salaam (a Muslim organization in Atlanta); Black, Indian, Hispanic and Asian Women in Action—BIHA (Minneapolis); Casa Myrna Vasquez (Boston); the Farmworker Women's Leadership Project (Pomona, Calif.); Hermanas Unidas (Washington, D.C.); the Korean American Family Service Center (New York); Sakhi, a South Asian project (New York); and Uzuri (Minneapolis). They include an analysis and understanding of cultural factors, religious beliefs, economic issues, and language barriers facing their clients, in a way that many shelters organized by White women have not done (Bhattacharjee 1997; Tan 1997) as discussed in Readings 36 and 38. Domestic violence is not restricted to heterosexual relationships; it occurs between lesbians, bisexual, and transgender women (Girshick 2002; Lobel 1984; Renzetti 1992; Wingspan Domestic Violence Project 1998).

Similarly, rape crisis centers operate in many cities throughout the country. Volunteers and paid staff answer emergency calls to crisis hotlines, give information, and refer women who have been raped to counseling, medical, and legal services. They may accompany a woman to the police or a doctor or advocate for her in court proceedings. Rape crisis centers often conduct public education and self-defense training for women, and many have peer counselors who are rape survivors. Over the years, some rape crisis projects that mainly served White women have become multicultural by broadening their perspectives to include antiracist work. Other organizations focus their efforts on the needs of women of color, lesbians, bisexual women, and transgender women.

College women reporting rapes have often been blamed for putting themselves in compromising situations, especially if they have been drinking. Generally, the men involved have been protected and punished lightly if at all, especially if they are university athletes. Some administrators have been concerned about the effects of alcohol and drug use and the role of fraternity parties in campus rapes (Sanday 1990). Others seem more concerned to protect their college's reputation. Campus materials and workshops on date rape for incoming students emphasize girls' and boys' different socialization and attitudes toward dating. Notable among the efforts to deal with this issue is Antioch College's sexual offense policy, which expects students to talk through a sexual encounter step by step, giving verbal consent at each step (Gold and Villari 2000), and the work of Students Active for Ending Rape (New York).

Men's projects that work on violence against women are making a crucial contribution to creating change on this issue. Examples include the National Organization for Men Against Sexism (Louisville, Colo.), Emerge (Cambridge, Mass.), Men Can Stop Rape (Washington, D.C.), and MOVE (Men Overcoming Violence; San Francisco). Haki Madhubuti discusses this issue from a male perspective (Reading 39), arguing that men must acknowledge and deal with their sexist socialization and work with other men to stop violence against women.

Public and Professional Education

Compared with a generation ago, there is now considerable public information and awareness about violence against women, including public service announcements, bumper stickers, and ads on billboards, buses, and TV. Increasingly, employers and labor unions recognize that domestic violence can interfere with a woman's ability to get, perform, or keep a job. In a 1994 survey of Fortune 1000 companies, nearly half (49 percent) said that domestic violence had a harmful effect on their company's productivity, 44 percent said it had a harmful effect on health-care costs, and 66 percent agreed that a company's financial performance would benefit from addressing the issue among employees (U.S. Department of Labor, Women's Bureau, 1996, p. 3). Some corporations and labor unions have developed education and training

programs on domestic violence for managers and workers. Others contribute financially to shelters.

There is a growing body of research as well as much theoretical, therapeutic, and political writing on this subject (Bart and O'Brien 1993; Bass and Davis 1988; Bohmer and Parrot 1993; Buchwald, Fletcher, and Roth 1993; Fineman and Mykitiuk 1994; Herman 1992; Jones 1994b; Koppelman 1996; Koss et al. 1994; NiCarthy 1986, 1987; Russell 1990; White 1985; Zambrano 1985). Public exhibitions like The Clothesline Project (East Dennis, Mass.) also make powerful statements. Another development has been the growth of professional education on violence against women for doctors, nurses, emergency-room staff, and other health-care providers, as well as social workers and teachers. Greater knowledge and understanding are also imperative for police officers, judges, and legislators. National-level organizations like the Family Violence Prevention Fund (Washington, D.C.; San Francisco), INCITE! Women of Color Against Violence, the National Clearinghouse on Marital Rape and Date Rape (Berkeley, Calif.), the National Coalition Against Domestic Violence (Denver, Colo.), the National Resource Center on Domestic Violence (Harrisburg, Pa.), the Network for Battered Lesbians (Boston), and V-Day (New York) provide visibility, public education, research, and expertise to local organizations, the news media, and policy makers at state and federal levels. The work of the National Latino Alliance for the Elimination of Domestic Violence (Arlington, Va.) is included in Reading 36.

Policy and Legislative Initiatives

Thirty years ago there were no laws concerning domestic violence. Now there is a growing, if uneven, body of law, mainly at the state level, including protection orders that prohibit the abuser from coming near or contacting the woman and her children. The rape laws have also been reformed because of pressure from feminists and rape survivors. This has been a piecemeal process and also varies from state to state. Nowadays, rape laws no longer require the corroboration of a victim's testimony; women are no longer required to have resisted their attackers; and the sexual histories of rape victims are no longer subject for cross-examination, unless shown to be relevant.

On the federal level, the Violence Against Women Act (VAWA) was signed into law as part of the Violent Crime and Law Enforcement Act of 1994. It authorized $1.6 billion to be spent over six years to address and prevent violence against women. In 2000, VAWA was reauthorized with funds for the National Domestic Violence Hotline, battered women's shelters and community initiatives, training for judges and court personnel, improvements in arrest policies, and legal advocacy programs for victims. It also included additional provisions to deal with violence against women with disabilities and for elder abuse, neglect, and exploitation.

Contradictions in Seeking State Support to End Violence Against Women

An increase in government funding and increasing professionalization of work involving violence against women may be seen as major successes. A negative aspect of this development is the fact that shelters and rape crisis centers have come under closer official scrutiny, especially regarding workers' qualifications. Although there is still a vital role for volunteers, many leadership positions require a master's degree in social work (MSW) or a counseling qualification. This is linked to the current emphasis on individual services and therapeutic remedies compared to the more political approach of the 1970s and '80s. Yet, as hard as women work to help particular individuals, there are always many more— seemingly an endless stream of women needing help. This can lead to burnout among workers who well understand the continuing strength of meso- and macro-level factors that support violence against women.

There is an inherent contradiction in looking to the government—the State—to solve this problem. The State is involved in the oppression of women. For example, it supports and requires the maintenance of the nuclear family and the gendered division of labor. As Jean Grossholtz noted twenty years ago, "Shelters are radical forces in the midst of social service agencies and radical threats to the ongoing political economy of violence. . . . A battered women's shelter cannot take the maintenance of the nuclear family or sex-role stereotypes as its goal" (1983, p. 67). The State condones and legitimizes violence against women through laws, judges' decisions, and police treatment that discriminate against victims of violence, despite some improvements in the ways courts and the police deal with violence

against women and despite federal funding for their education and training under VAWA.

In their capacity as government employees, U.S. prison guards rape and abuse women, as mentioned by Nancy Kurshan (Reading 59, Chapter 10). Border patrols along the U.S.-Mexico border have assaulted undocumented women entering the United States (Light 1996; Martinez 1998), and INS guards have abused women at an immigrant detention center near Miami (Sachs 2000).

Military personnel also commit acts of violence against women (Guenter-Schlesinger 1999; Morris 1999). They are socialized into a highly masculinist military culture and are trained to dehumanize "the enemy" to be able to kill in time of war (Reardon 1985). Rape in war is a violation against women of the enemy group or country and, through them, an act of aggression, hostility, and humiliation against their husbands, sons, fathers, and brothers.

Examples include the rape of American Indian women by U.S. troops in the nineteenth century (Reading 38), the rape of Vietnamese women by U.S. troops during the Vietnam War (Enloe 1988), and the mass rape and forced impregnation of Muslim and Croatian women by Serbian soldiers in Bosnia-Herzegovina in the early 1990s (Eve Ensler, Reading 40; also MacKinnon 1993, 1998; Pitter and Stilmayer 1993; Tax 1993). In April 2000, participants at The Color of Violence conference, held at the University of California, Santa Cruz, called for a re-politicization of work regarding violence against women and set up a new organization, INCITE! Women of Color Against Violence. In the opening keynote, activist, writer, and scholar Angela Davis (2001) expressed a core contradiction in current anti-violence work that looks to the state for solutions:

> Given the racist and patriarchal patterns of the state, it is difficult to envision the state as the holder of solutions to the problem of violence against women. However, as the anti-violence movement has been institutionalized and professionalized, the state plays an increasingly dominant role in the way we conceptualize and create strategies to minimize violence against women. One of the major tasks of this conference, and of the anti-violence movement as a whole, is to address this contradiction, especially as it presents itself to poor communities of color. *(p. 13)*

Reporting on the conference, Andrea Smith (2001) argues for the need to address personal violence and state violence at the same time: to ensure safety for women affected by violence, but without strengthening the criminal justice system that is "brutally oppressive toward communities of color" (p. 66). The conference endorsed a very broad definition of violence against women, echoing Hussein Bulhan (1985), that includes colonization, indigenous people's land rights, and the criminalization of communities of color. In Reading 38, Andy Smith gives examples of alternative approaches currently being pursued in Native American communities in contrast to mainstream anti-violence organizations that are calling for longer prison sentences for batterers and rapists.

Women's Rights as Human Rights

In December 1979, the United Nations adopted the Convention on the Elimination of All Forms of Discrimination Against Women (CEDAW), which includes violence against women. One hundred sixty-five countries have ratified CEDAW and adopted it as national policy, though often with many reservations so that implementation has been much more limited. Nearly twenty-five years later, U.S. women's organizations are still lobbying for the United States to ratify CEDAW.

Lori Heise (1989) notes that "sex-specific violence has not been treated with the same seriousness as other human rights abuses" (p. 13). Defining violence against women as a human rights issue has been a successful strategy to get this issue onto the international agenda (Beasley and Thomas 1994; Bunch and Carillo 1991; Kerr 1993). In June 1993, women from many countries organized the Global Tribunal

on Violations of Women's Human Rights to coincide with the Non-Governmental Organization (NGO) Forum of the U.N. World Conference on Human Rights, held in Vienna (Bunch and Reilly 1994). In 1994 the U.N. Commission on Human Rights created a new position—the Special Rapporteur on Violence Against Women, Its Causes and Consequences—based in Geneva, Switzerland. The Center for Women's Global Leadership (Rutgers University) sponsors an annual 16 Days of Activism Against Gender Violence (Nov. 25 to Dec. 10). V-Day and Communities Against Violence Network (Washington, D.C.) are other U.S.-based organizations working on an international level.

As this chapter makes clear, there is an urgent need for many changes at micro, meso, macro, and global levels for women to be secure from violence including:

- the socialization and education of all children to respect and value each other;

- changes in the social construction of femininity and masculinity, and the abolition of cultural attitudes and systems of inequality that support male superiority;

- an end to the objectification and commodification of women;

- changes in women's work and wages, and support for community-based economic development to give women economic security and independence;

- changes in the law, court decisions, police practices, and the political system so that women's human rights are central; and

- continued collaboration among all who are working to end violence, and challenges to those who are not.

◆◆◆

Questions for Reflection

In reading and discussing this chapter, consider these questions:

1. What beliefs about rape are really myths? How would your life be different if rape and the threat of rape did not exist?

2. How does the intersectionality of gender, race, class, nation, sexuality, and so forth, affect violence against women?

3. How do boys in your community learn to respect women? To disrespect women?

4. How has abuse or violence affected your life? Your family? Your community?

5. What kinds of masculinity would help to create personal security for women?

6. What are men's roles in ending violence against women?

Finding Out More on the Web

1. Research how the Web is used to support and reinforce beliefs about violence against women.

2. Research U.S. and international organizations working to end violence against women. What are their goals, strategies, and activities? What theoretical frameworks shape their work? Try to find culturally diverse women's organizations, student organizations, and organizations of men against rape.

3. Eve Ensler wrote "My Vagina Was My Village" based on an interview with one woman among thousands who were raped as a systematic tactic of war in Bosnia in 1993. Find out more about this—and about other examples of rape in war.

Taking Action

1. Talk about this issue with your peers, and initiate public discussion on your campus or in your community. Find out about your college's policy on sexual assault and how it is enforced (or not). Find out about rape crisis centers, shelters, and support groups in your area so that you can support someone who is coping with sexual assault.

2. Volunteer with a rape crisis project on campus or at a shelter for victims of domestic violence. Men students: Work with other men on this issue.

3. Support or participate in a campus production of *The Vagina Monologues*, Eve Ensler's play.

THIRTY-FIVE

◆◆

Lisa's Ritual, Age 10

Grace Caroline Bridges

Afterwards when he has finished
lots of mouthwash helps
to get rid of her father's cigarette taste.
She runs a hot bath
    to soak away the pain
        like red dye leaking from her
           school dress in the washtub.

She doesn't cry.

When the bathwater cools she adds more hot.
She brushes her teeth for a long time.

Then she finds the corner of her room,
curls against it. There the wall is
hard and smooth
as teacher's new chalk, white
as a clean bedsheet. Smells
fresh. Isn't sweaty, hairy, doesn't stick

to skin. Doesn't hurt much
when she presses her small backbone
into it. The wall is steady
while she falls   away:
    first the hands   lost
arms dissolving   feet gone
    the legs   dis-   jointed
        body cracking down
            the center like a fault
                she falls inside
                    slides down like
    dust   like kitchen dirt
                slips off
    the dustpan into
                    noplace

a place where
nothing happens,
nothing ever happened.

When she feels the cool
wall against her cheek
she doesn't want to
come back. Doesn't want to
think about it.
The wall is quiet, waiting.
It is tall like a promise
only better.

◆◆◆

National Symposium on La Violéncia Doméstica

An Emerging Dialogue Among Latinos (excerpt)

Fernando Mederos

Forty Latinos and Latinas—domestic violence activists, clinicians, researchers, lawyers and survivors of violence from the United States and Puerto Rico—met on November 6 and 7, 1997, in Washington, D.C., for the National Symposium on La Violéncia Doméstica: An Emerging Dialogue Among Latinos. Our purpose was to begin a national dialogue about domestic violence, to acknowledge its impact on our children and on our communities, to make recommendations for action, and to increase the allocation of federal resources to eliminate domestic violence in our neighborhoods. The Steering Committee that organized and led this meeting was composed of six women and two men who have provided leadership in domestic violence work in Latino communities. The Symposium was sponsored by the U.S. Department of Health and Human Services (DHHS), which is the lead federal agency in the implementation of the Family Violence Prevention and Services Act. DHHS recognizes the need to bring in the voices of Latino researchers, practitioners, and activists into policy discussions.

This Symposium operated on two levels. First, it was a policy forum with plenary presentations and

in-depth discussions with participants. This was not a hierarchical, experts dictating to the people event, but rather a gathering of people with extensive experience in the field who were selected for their expertise. They came to listen and learn from each other and to contribute to a thoughtful dialogue. . . .

At another level, the Symposium was a force for unity, strength and connection for a very diverse group. Participants came from many parts of the United States. While many were long-term immigrants from Mexico, Central and South America, and the Caribbean, most were born in the United States or Puerto Rico, not unlike the U.S. Latino population. . . .

Accordingly, the Symposium began with a Ceremony of Connection with our past and with our spirituality. This celebrated the solemnity and sacredness of the Symposium's purpose, helping the group to recognize the bonds of tradition and belief that link the participants. This was followed by a *Conocimiento,* which is a gathering of acknowledgement and interconnectedness during which participants are encouraged to share their stories. Many persons told their stories, often speaking on behalf of the communities they represented. This broke down many barriers and allowed the participants to recognize the experiences they have in common.

This account will begin with a summary of these exchanges, though it is impossible to convey the passion and intensity of the occasion. At best, it is like using words to describe music.

Building a Vision: Ceremony

In setting the stage for the Ceremony, Steering Committee member Jerry Tello reminded us that as a people, spirituality has always been a part of the Latino people's ethos. He explained the role of the altar in the center of the room. It was to be a place where every person, regardless of faith, could put something that represented themselves and their family. The altar was a centering place that became the focus of our interconnectedness.[1]

Concha Saucedo began the Ceremony with a prayer for healing and balance. She explained that the altar is a *mesa*, a table of spiritual nourishment. She asked us to stand and join hands around the table. In joining together, she reminded us that we all have energy, which is embodied in our words, and that our words can heal. A prayer was said in the four directions (north, south, east and west), representing also the man, the woman, the child, and the elder. She invoked the energy of the east, embodying the sun, the direction of *guerreros* and *guerreras*, male and female warriors and defenders, and the energy of the north, the place of our ancestors, the old ones, the teachers, to strengthen us in our purpose.

Representing the voice of the elders, Isaac Cardenas of San Antonio, Texas, offered this prayer:

Great-grandfather, holy spirit, great spirit, watch over all of these Latinos and Latinas. Give them strength, give them your love, take care of them, help them to reach their destination, both in their personal life, and in the goals we seek here.

Griselda Tapia, representing the voice of the child, expressed her hope that through education we can overcome the secret of domestic violence that has stayed within families. She offered her prayer on behalf "of all the children who have to live in families where domestic violence is present."

Another participant, representing the voice of men, said:

Creator, we first want to thank you, and ask for permission, for those first keepers of this land here, that we are on today. . . . And we also give thanks, and ask your blessing for all these people, for all the nations gathered here . . . and open all the barriers that we need, that this organization needs [opened] to complete its goal.

The last prayer, representing the voice of women, was that of Concha Saucedo (translated):

The seed is one, it comes from the Creator. Our hearts beat together. Yours, mine, with the same seed, seeds from the Creator, the seed of a universe. And thus you and I are one, we are of the universe. You are my other self, *tu eres mi otro yo*, woman, man, children, elders, ancestors, teachers, grandparents. Thanks, Mother Earth. For those who are part of this movement, thank you. You are my other self.

The Conocimiento: A Gathering of Acknowledgement and Interconnectedness

Continuing the link with the altar, Jerry Tello passed around a basket of polished stones and asked that each person take two, one for themselves and one for those they represent. All were then asked to introduce themselves and those they represent to the group. After receiving our energy, these stones would go on the altar, stay there during our meeting and, at the end of the Symposium, be taken by each person as a continuing connection with the gathering.

Everyone spoke during the next two hours. These shared thoughts, feelings and histories slowly converged throughout the Symposium into a common vision. It is impossible to reproduce each person's account, as valuable as they all were. Instead, here is an edited cross-section of our words, with names omitted to protect participants' privacy:

Man from New Orleans: If I had to say who I represent, gosh, too many people, I feel. I am a person who was born in Cuba.... I feel that any kind of violence is connected one with another, and that the violence that we may find inside of a home or a house, has to do too much with the violence that is outside of the house.... The thing that impresses me the most, are the children. And I'm so impressed to see how much, not only are they suffering from the violence they see between their parents, but the violence they feel from their parents to them. Not only physical violence, but emotional violence.

Woman from New York: I bring my New Yorkrican self, and that transplants to California.... And I think more than anything else I bring truth in the sense that I think we have the ability, within ourselves, to end domestic violence, but we have to do it our way. We can't do it the way that other people want us to do it; we have to do it our way.... And the other thing I bring, I think, is a challenge to us to work together on this issue as men and women. So stepping out of the box, the traditional box of defining domestic violence as a woman's issue, and really embracing that this is a community issue that when one family, or one child, or one individual is devastated by domestic violence, we are all devastated by it. So, you know, let's be together in every sense of the way, and that is my challenge, and that is my hope.

Woman from California: I'm also a survivor of domestic violence. I survived 23 years ago, and for the past 10 years I've been working with the men, running a Latino batterers' program. And the reason I'm doing that is because when I was living with violence, I had always hoped that there was some help, and particularly some help for my spouse. So I'm here to represent the batterers, who are also in a lot of pain. These are men who have been victims themselves, who are living in a lot of pain.

Man from California: But let me tell you, *yo soy un Chicano de East L.A.* ... (I'm a Chicano from East L.A. ...) I'm born, raised, continue to live, work, and I'm probably going to die there.... I don't take drugs anymore.... I come from a background of violence; I know it well. *Yo era lo que se dice bato loco. Era pandillero.* ... (I used to be what they call a wise guy. I was a gangster. ...) But my blessing has been [a woman I met as] a 15-year-old *chicanita con el nombre de Angelina* (called Angelina).... We have been married 45 years, we have five children, eight grandchildren, three great-grandchildren, and an-

other one that we hope to see when we get back. And, in fact, my children have quit having babies, and my grandchildren are having babies, if you get the picture. So that is who I am, in terms of me as a person. In my professional life, I'm a licensed psychotherapist.... I work with batterers, with men who like to kick women's ass, okay? And in that area I think I'm very good because of my violent background. *A mi no me van a madrear. Que me provocó?* (They can't fool me. She provoked me?) Give me a break, man. Do you know what *provocar* means? She provoked me? It is a classic excuse.

Man from New York: ... I am a black Puerto Rican. I think that is very important to stress.... I represent the races in the Latino community.... As we talk about the reality of what confronts us as people, we need to understand that the brutality and racism in this world, in this country, have affected us in this community, as well.... I want us to appreciate the culture, but we need to recognize both its strengths and also its limitations. Because part of the limitations is what is contributing to the violence, and to the harm to the children.... I represent East Harlem.... I am, indeed, honored to be here with all of you.

Woman from California (all translated): I arrived three years ago from Puerto Rico.... I bring the strength of women who, with fewer resources, I think, than all of us here survive in this country ... and not only domestic violence, which is perhaps what brings them to our programs, but also all of the other oppressions that we suffer as Latinos.... I want to leave with the hope that as Latinos and Latinas we can do the work in a different way, even though we are oppressed by institutions that make us do things in certain ways in order to get the money we need to do this work. But I think that having this altar in the center is a symbol that our culture has many ways of doing things, and that we have to rescue those ways if we want to reach our communities.

Woman from Chicago: ... In order to stop domestic violence, I feel we have to face the problem. I mean, I heard over, and over again, my mom and my grandmother say: *pero que va a decir la gente, yo no quiero que se den cuenta de lo que pasa* (but what will people say, I don't want them to know what's going on). You know, I'm sick and tired of hearing that. I mean, to tell you the truth, I feel that everyone knew about it, but they didn't do anything. . . . Well, I think we have to stop thinking about other people and think about ourselves, especially our families, and our children. We need to unite as a community, and help those families who are in need. Finally, I would like to leave you with a quote that reads: "We did then what we knew then, now that we know better, we do better." And I truly hope we do better for our children.

Conclusion of the Conocimiento

Todas las Relaciones Son Sagradas: All Relationships Are Sacred

At the end of the Conocimiento, Jerry Tello, a Steering Committee member, articulated the collective vision of the eight women and men who had met to plan the Symposium: that in the Latino community men, women, elders, and children will work together against domestic violence, recognizing that doing this will require tremendous trust and a leap of faith and healing among participants. Faith, trust, and healing are not "policy issues"; they are a form of knowledge and conviction that each person has gained from life and from the heart. Jerry was chosen to convey this vision by telling participants the story about the lessons his father and his culture have offered him. In a sense, this is the Steering Committee's collective Conocimiento. It is also a story of marginalization and of struggling for honorable manhood. The following is a summary of his remarks:

> I remember as a little boy, going with my dad to the store to buy milk for my little sister. And he would want to pay and the men who were running the store were sitting in the back playing cards and they wouldn't come to collect the money. My dad would say, "Hey, *quiero pagar,* I want to pay" and they would say, "It's a stupid wetback, make him wait." I would look at my dad and he would begin getting mad. They made him wait a long time and called him ugly names and I would wonder why doesn't he do something—hit them, knock something over, or rip off the milk, but he couldn't because then he would go to jail. Then he wouldn't be able to work and we wouldn't

eat. He just got more angry and when I asked him why he didn't do anything, he slapped me on the head and said, "Shut up, you don't understand." He then put on his hat and put the rest of the anger under it. Sometimes that anger would slip out from under the hat and I didn't know why.

> When my brother got busted for being on the wrong side of the tracks, my dad would get angry and tell us that my brother was not a good example to follow—so my dad would be angry and my brother would get angry too. At the same time, society was telling us that Mexican men were wetbacks, gang bangers, drunks and womanizers and as a little boy this is what I thought *Macho* was—I thought this was what a Latino man was supposed to be and how he was supposed to act. What I didn't understand was that this was society's way of breaking us down, reinforcing false teachings, and hiding our true knowledge. But the old writings of the *HueHues* (Elders) told us what it meant to be a true *hombre* and *mujer* (man and woman). That in order to be an *Hombre Noble* (Noble Man) you must respect women—that the first lesson in crossing the bridge to manhood is respect for *"El Otro Yo"* (your other self), woman. If you didn't learn that lesson, then you didn't go on. It is our responsibility to reteach these old lessons and to bring harmony and balance to our relationships.

> So, struggling with working in this field, I'm a father, I'm a son, I also represent your fathers and your sons, and your partners. I also represent the men that have abused, that have been the perpetrators. And so, for them, and especially to you [women in the audience], I apologize for those of us that have been irresponsible, for those of us that couldn't keep it under our hat, for those of us that made excuses, and for those of us that were violent to any of you, for any of the women you represent, I take responsibility and apologize.

> Because the first aspect of anything is *mujer,* creation, you; without you, we would not be. And so in looking back, I begin to understand that *de veras un macho es un hombre* (really a male is a man who is) honorable, dignified, respectful, sensitive, supportive, accountable,

all of those things. . . . And I just want to thank the women here, all of you, that have taught us, that have accepted us, and maybe somehow can forgive us, and to allow us an opportunity to learn and grow, so that maybe your sons, when they grow up, people will not be afraid of them. . . . So I think the task is interconnected, it is about grandparents, it is about children, it is about *mujeres* and about *hombres* (about women and men), and I just feel blessed to be in this room, to be able to be present where there are so many strong *mujeres* with a lot of experience; elders and people with stories, *jóvenes* (young people), and all of that.

And I think we represent each other, and whether we think we are ready or not, whether we think we are experienced, got degrees or not, *ni modo* (it doesn't matter), we have to do it, because we are the voice for many, many people that are hurting, and many more that we can actually make a better way for.

The interconnectedness between Latinos and Latinas and our desire to work together was voiced again and again by participants throughout the gathering, and the Steering Committee provided leadership in this respect through their example, as women and men working together on the Steering Committee.

Plenary I

Hablando del Sistema: Talking About the System

The first plenary, *Hablando del Sistema,* addressed current policy crises at the national and local levels and explored strategies that we can use to promote helpful policies. It was chosen as the first theme because recent policy initiatives, such as limits on welfare benefits, and restrictions on health care coverage and disability benefits for residents, have further exacerbated long-term problems such as colonialism, racism, poverty, and police brutality. Other legislation that is troubling includes deportation provisions for legal residents, English-only laws, and Proposition 187 (which denies public education in California to children whose parents are undocumented). Finally, there is the challenge of our own internalized oppression that divides us. . . .

Plenary II

Entre Familia: Among Family

The next plenary, *Entre Familia,* shifted the emphasis to the most intimate arena: our families, how our history has affected us, and how we can use our own resources and our culture to heal our wounds.

Steering Committee member Sonia Davila Williams of the School of Social Work at the University of Minnesota moderated this session. She noted that the extended family is the norm in Latino culture. Family includes uncles, aunts, grandparents, first, second and third cousins, relatives by marriage and their relatives, even *compadres* and *comadres,* who may be godparents or long-term intimate friends not related by blood. In a sense, even the community is part of *la familia* since it is made up of families.

She introduced Dr. Concepción Saucedo Martinez, otherwise known in this text as Concha Saucedo. Dr. Saucedo is a clinical psychologist and a Yaqui elder and healer. Currently, she is Executive Director of the Family Institute of La Raza in San Francisco.

Dr. Saucedo was asked to speak about (a) the legacy and impact of colonization, immigration, and acculturation on family values, (b) the ensuing dynamics between child and parent and between child and child, both intergenerational and intergender, that are part of domestic violence in our community, and (c) the strengths (the healing resources within our community), the negatives, and what can we do to promote healing. An attempt has been made to remain faithful to her voice by rendering the essence of her remarks in the first person. . . .

To understand ourselves, we have to go back 500 years to the Spanish invasion. Since then, we have survived and there are things that we carry from that survival, both gifts and burdens. In the struggle to survive, we lost awareness of this legacy of gifts and burdens. And having lost that awareness, we carry and transmit the burdens onto our families, our marriages, and our children. Violence is part of that burden, but we do not recognize it as violence. We see it as endemic and inherent in the culture, and it survives. We also forget our gifts.

In order to change this we must empower ourselves to rename things and to recapture our gifts for healing and growth. For example, we should not accept the limitations and the labels that the federal government places on us. Currently, there is an international movement for everybody to be "documented." This has created certain divisions in our own communities, between the documented and the undocumented. "You are not a person unless you have a *tarjeta* [green card], right?"

So what will we name ourselves? . . . Do we name ourselves Hispanics, do we name ourselves *raza* (the race, the people), do we name ourselves Chicano, do we name ourselves *Indios* (Indians), do we name ourselves *Centroamericanos* (Central Americans), do we name ourselves *immigrantes* (immigrants), do we name ourselves *migrantes* (migrants)? . . . And I say . . . papers for no one, no one needs a paper to be who they are. And I begin looking at myself, and everyone else in this room, as a migrant on this continent, and on these islands, right? And a migrant can move anyplace, that is our right. We did that before the invader came. People in Puerto Rico did business with people on the coast of Mexico. They were entrepreneurs; they traded. People crossed what is now *La Frontera* (the U.S.-Mexico frontier), freely, for years. We've done that for a millennium. . . .

We are not interlopers or outsiders. Our interventions and our work with our communities should acknowledge this.

We must also rename family. The federal definition of family is limited to mother and father and children. For us, family includes not only blood and marriage relations, but also relations based on *compadrazgo* (relationships created through godparenting or long-term intimate friendships). We often use ceremonies to create relationships and sometimes these relationships take the place of blood relations, when they are not able to function in a healthy way. This capacity to create relationships and to be bound by them is one of the gifts of survival and this is a resource that must be used and encouraged in interventions within our community. It is a source of strength, help, and healing.

Renaming family also means accepting gay and lesbian relationships as families. These men and women are part of our circle; they are part of us. They are not a separate circle. Accepting our oneness is a source of strength and healing.

Las pandillas, the gangs, are also families that have gone a little crazy. They are trying to provide sustenance to each other that they did not get in their families. We failed in some way. We did not provide

certain directions, and now we have to rectify that. So when working with young people, it is important to include other young people, because that is who they listen to. They can move out of violence if one treats them with respect and responds to them as *familia*.

As we continue renaming, we must remember *respeto* (respect). In our culture, people may have different roles and functions, but they are recognized for their innate value, their essence. In a sense, we are all sacred. This is the core of our understanding of respect. We still have a lot of this in our culture. It is something positive that we can use and teach. If a man says that he wants to be respected, that he was not being respected and that is why he beat his wife up, then he is not talking about *respeto*. We can redefine *respeto* for individuals. Is *respeto* hitting someone or being a provider? Redefining *respeto* is the cornerstone of change.

Respeto also implies acceptance of diversity within our culture. Some of us, like me, have more indigenous background. Others appear more European, but we are all Latinos even though our values may differ somewhat. We share a feeling that family is what is most important—this is a unifying force for us.

We need to redefine and rename our diversity even further. My mother was a full-blood Yaquì and her people were massacred again and again by the Mexican government. I have certain feelings about the Mexicanness that is in me, so I identify more on the native side, and with northern natives here as well, and have learned much from them. Do those issues also appear in Cuban Americans, in Puerto Ricans? You have Africa and Spain and what is left of the native Tainos. What does all that variation and color mean in a family? How does it get played out in violence issues? How does that get played out in our own communities? Exploring these legacies should be a part of our healing practice.

Another element that we need to rename and recover is traditional medicine, which may use herbs, ceremonies, or words. This may provide a better treatment in many situations, and these traditions need to be recognized and fostered.

We have to make changes with or without the money. Sometimes government assistance has hampered us, because we end up forgetting "that we can do it ourselves, and we can do it well, and we can do it as a group." For example, in San Francisco, people try to do things together. Seven years ago 55 deaths of young people were counted over a short period of time. There was no response to this crisis. Finally, the community declared a violence prevention initiative and brought people together without money. They partnered with different sectors: public health, recreation, economic and community development, and arts and culture. This initiative now has a name: the *Comunidad Unida Para La Salud* (the Community United for Health): A Blueprint for a Healthy Mission Community.

Through education, information and the use of community campaigns, cultural norms regarding family, domestic violence, use of alcohol and other drugs can be shifted. If young men get drunk on weekends because it is a way of feeling closeness and brotherhood, then we have to find something that gives them that sense of closeness—a way that they can bond with other men.

The prevention and promotion strategies promote alternatives to violence, drug abuse, and other ills. They present affirming alternatives that center on balance and harmony. Whenever a problem is addressed and described, it is accompanied by other possibilities, or positive ways of living, to help people visualize alternatives to change. Thus, a continuum of strategies that support and promote behaviors that are positive and strengthening is always available. Next, the initiative needs to have a commitment to spiritual healing as a core value to connect with and affirm non-material internal values.

A promotional strategy or campaign is an initiative to create a healthy community. It must respect cultural values of diverse populations of the community, understand differing levels of biculturation, and use a culturally-based filter in program design that is adaptable and flexible. It needs to bring together separate professions, agencies, categories, disciplines, and create a marriage between traditional and conventional approaches. Public and private sectors need to work together, under the leadership of the community. And such a campaign needs to adapt segmented funding, such as substance abuse treatment monies, to family-centered approaches.

Finally, these campaigns must be based on the belief that change is slow and incremental, that it happens in small pieces, and that outcome research has to be done with the indices that the community says are the indices of health. If we save one woman, we save one child. If one child goes on and does whatever they want, whatever dream they had, whether it was to be a television star, or to sing a song, that is a success.

Success with abusive men is a difficult issue with respect to criteria or indices of success. Abusers need accountability and consequences. They have to develop a sense of responsibility. But, if our response is to simply put them in jail, they go into another battering system, and we have lost other souls. In the old, old days, in the village, if certain people did certain things, they were vanished from the village, a *palizas, verdad?* (with a beating, right?) We need community mechanisms for men who batter that are more effective and that react more rapidly than the judicial system. . . .

In the ensuing commentaries, four main themes were discussed at length. . . .

1. How do consequences for offenders, such as involving the police and incarceration, fit into community responses to domestic violence?

- A participant stated that, on the one hand, there is a profound reluctance to send men to jail, since this amounts to sending them into institutions that brutalize them. On the other hand, some people are so damaged that if they are not restrained (sent to jail), they will hurt someone badly.

- A participant revealed that he had had his son arrested because he was extremely dangerous and out of control. There was no other option in that acute situation. Some participants acknowledged that this is a painful reality. This led to a suggestion that laws should not be categorical, that interventions should fit the offenders' level of dangerousness and that there ought to be provisions for community intervention in the process of holding offenders accountable. There was no consensus about these issues, but a realization that a deeper dialogue needs to take place about offenders and that the Latino community must be a full partner in that discussion.

- In another series of commentaries, . . . practitioners with extensive experience working with abusive Latinos shared their perspective on their work.

One said that physically abusive men should be considered lost spirits—people who need rebalancing, which involves intense work in the physical, emotional, psychological, and spiritual spheres. This is where the community should have a significant role.

Another stated that these men have a very narrow, insecure, and distorted image of what manhood is: "They bought the lie. . . . They live in the lie (associating manhood with dominance and violence), but they are insecure inside. . . . And if you begin stripping the defenses, they run from any kind of treatment. So we know that what works is building a greater value system that is greater than that very narrow, distorted image of manhood and violence, and you do find that in our *cultura* (culture)."...

2. How can one incorporate our spiritual beliefs and our family orientation into domestic violence work?

- One participant reminded the group that the *Ceremonia* (Ceremony) started with acknowledging the four directions, representing men, women, elders, and children. He urged the group to always keep in mind this framework in developing responses to domestic violence: "They all have to be considered, and if we consider them together always, we will not come up with solutions that just see men as perpetrators, but as men who need help being with women, elders and children."

- Another participant shared her experience of developing domestic violence services for Latinos in an isolated community. There was an "organic" growth process as new services were developed to respond to the requests of community members. The first step was to offer women's support groups in Spanish. Participants requested baby-sitting and, once the children were present, an educational and support group was developed for them. The children became very strong and committed participants. Eventually the women said, "Why are you not talking to the men?" This led to a decision to start a men's group and, after a long process, a male facilitator was trained. Now, the agency has groups for Latino men. Currently many men are court-referred, but many are coming voluntarily and many stay after the 24-week standard men's program. Participation in women's groups is vol-

untary, but there is an enthusiastic response. "We did not know that we were not supposed to do that (have groups for men and women). We were oriented to working with families, so that is what we did." Feedback from women indicates that there have been good results with respect to stopping violent behavior, but less impact on verbal and emotional abuse. Very high levels of sexual abuse have also been reported, both by women and by men (as perpetrators). The staff is thinking about responding to this information as they continue program development.

3. Are we giving enough attention to rape and sexual violence in our work on domestic violence?

- Participants repeatedly mentioned that many Latinas have experienced rape and other forms of sexual violence in relationships and in other settings.

- There was a strong feeling that this issue needs more attention in men's programming, in public education campaigns about violence, and in research with Latinas about violence.

4. Participants strongly acclaimed Dr. Saucedo's affirmation of diversity within diversity—the fact that Latinos are not one group, but many nationalities and histories who share many basic values, but are not all the same. In other words, we are many identities with a common tradition and spiritual base. . . .

Entre Familia ended with two spontaneous and somewhat parallel accounts, by a man and a woman, regarding the importance of working together and of learning from each other as men and women.

The man is a Mexican American, a grandfather and a psychotherapist who works with violent Latinos. He stated that he had begun to wonder where the spirituality he uses in his work with men comes from:

Yo soy terapista (I am a therapist), as you all know. And I think I'm a good therapist, I think I have a direct connection to the male ego, in all its beauty and in all its ugliness. I think a great part of my treatment is based on spirituality. And in assessing my life, my career, and my development. . . . I try to look for where my spiritual talent came from in treating these men. *Lo busqué en mi jefe, en mis carnales, en mis home boys, en mis tíos* (I looked for it in my boss, in my male relatives, in my home boys, in my uncles), in all the males that I have been exposed to, and I couldn't find one that gave me any real spiritual food, you could say. They taught me about a lot of other things, and I learned how to be a male in the male world, but nothing in terms of the spiritual aspects.

He went on to state that as he thought about his life, he remembered various women: first, his blind grandmother, who had taken care of him when he was between the ages of three and five, and spent much time telling him entrancing stories. Then he thought of his mother, who established herself as a supportive and compassionate presence when he was nine years old. She became his adviser and his confidante. After that, his wife took that place in his life. She touched, and still touches, his heart; he has a powerful connection with her. Later on, he had a daughter who had cerebral palsy and died at the age of eight, but she was yet another powerful source of connection and a motivator for change. He recounted the following:

> I had already made changes, but I think she was the icing on the cake, which is the source of my life, and she was the one that brought it all together. This has been 15, 20 years now. I guess what I'm trying to say is that I want to publicly thank all you women that are here, because without you, I wouldn't know the way, I wouldn't know that the Creator is very important to me. I'm not a very spiritual person in terms of standing up and saying prayers, but He is in my heart, and I feel Him all the time. So, *otra vez* (again), I love you all, and thank you and thanks to all the women. They are the spiritual seed and the spiritual force in the world. And I believe all that is true and that we have somehow or other kept them down, to keep them from touching us.

The woman who gave a parallel account spoke about the special men in her life. Her grandfather, with whom she lived for a few years in Puerto Rico, was special and unique, someone who made her feel understood and loved. As she came back to the United States to work in the battered women's movement, she confronted again and again the reality of what men do to women. In addition, she resented and distrusted men's lack of involvement in the movement: "I said, but we have to do something, men have to get involved; they have to do something. And I always would criticize that constantly, about how we had men who had survived, who are not living violent lives, but yet weren't coming back to the community and doing anything about it."

The participant explained that she had had two sons, but was reluctant to have a daughter, fearing what kind of world she would bring her into. When she met her partner, her sense of trust grew: "But then I met a man in my life, my *compañero* (my partner) today. He is *casi un santo* (almost a saint) my *compañeras* (my friends) tell me, because of how supportive he is with my work. I would like for him to be a little more involved, but *él no es de las personas que tiene coraje como muchos de nosotros aquí* (but he is not one of those people who carries the same level of passion for this issue as many of us here). But he understands the issues, and believes in them. And then I had my daughter. I decided I wanted a daughter; I couldn't be complete without a daughter. So I had my daughter Margarita, who is four now."

> I'm sharing all of this because for a long, long time, until very recently, I thought and was made to believe by others that this was a woman's issue, and that we have the responsibility . . . to re-educate our sons, our brothers, our compañeros, so that this would stop, this cycle would end. And there is truth in that, lots of it.

However, she went on to explain that in the last few years she also had met and worked with two Latinos from New York, deeply committed men who counsel physically abusive Latinos, and felt understanding, support and partnership. She stated that these men were both at the Symposium and that their presence was important to her. She also felt the presence and commitment of other men in the room, and a sense of trust was in her words and expression:

> And today to sit here, and I really would like for us to look around, one, two, three, four . . . fourteen, fifteen, sixteen [men]. This is the first time, in the fifteen years that I have been doing

this work, that I have been among so many men. So I want to thank you, men, for being here.

Perhaps it is not a coincidence that *Entre Familia—Among Family*—ended with these accounts. They acknowledge how we can help each other to grow and to complete our work in this difficult field. . . .

NOTE

1. In pre-Columbian times, Mesoamerican teachings about relationships were couched in ceremony. These were taught at home, in schools, and in various aspects of society. These ceremonies were documented in the codices and, more importantly, were also shared through oral traditions.

T H I R T Y - S E V E N

Domestic Violence and Asian American Women

Lora Jo Foo

Prevalence of Domestic Violence Against Asian American Women

A woman is physically battered every nine seconds in the United States. One out of three women reports physical abuse at the hands of an intimate partner at least once in their lives. Every year, an estimated 1.5 to 3.9 million women are physically abused by their partners. In all intimate relationships, both heterosexual and lesbian, domestic violence occurs 20–25% of the time. Domestic violence occurs in every community regardless of race, ethnicity, class, or sexual orientation. Yet, domestic violence is an underreported crime.

For Asian American communities, the paucity of data makes it even more difficult to estimate the prevalence of partner abuse. This report extrapolates from the few specific studies that do exist. The studies indicate that domestic violence is at least as prevalent in the Asian American population as the general American population[1] and may be higher in certain Asian subgroups.[2] For example, in Chicago, a survey of 150 Korean women found that 60% reported physical abuse. The data also suggests that Asian American women may be at higher risk for fatalities related to domestic violence than women in the general population. For example, Santa Clara County in California is comprised of 17.5% Asians. However, between 1994 and 1997, almost one-third of the 51 deaths related to domestic violence occurred among Asian women, the highest of any ethnic group. In Massachusetts, Asians constituted 3% of the population. However, in 1997, 18% of Massa-

chusetts residents killed as a result of domestic violence were Asian.

Safety Needs Neglected

What accounts for the higher fatality rates related to domestic violence for Asian American women? Why are the safety needs of Asian American women not being met by the systems that exist? To date, there has been no research to answer these questions. We do know that Asian American women in abusive relationships face different challenges than white women who speak English and are American citizens, for whom most shelter and outreach programs are designed. Asian American women, the majority of whom are foreign-born immigrants with different languages and cultures, experience numerous institutional barriers to seeking safety. The categories of safety-related challenges particular to Asian American women—ill-equipped shelter programs, language barriers, laws that discriminate against immigrants, cultural values that lead to violent behavior, and barriers to safety for Asian American lesbians—are described below.

Lack of Culturally and Linguistically Accessible Services

1. Limited and Inadequate Shelter Space Shelter space in general is limited, but those with the capacity to serve Asian women's language needs and who make their facilities culturally supportive for immigrant women are in extremely short supply. In Massachusetts, out of 35 women's shelters, only two have Asians on staff. Some shelters do not accept non-English-speaking women at all. The Asian Women's Shelter (AWS) in San Francisco has the capacity to help non-English-speakers but is forced to turn away 600 individuals each year. This number represents 75% of the women who contact the clinic. Moreover, mainstream women's shelters are not designed for women with more than one or two kids.[3] Hmong women in the St. Paul/Minneapolis area who have larger than average families were not able to make use of most shelters until Asian Women United designed a shelter to accommodate larger families. Asian Health Services, an Oakland community health clinic, believes that these institutional barriers are so formidable that only 2 out of 10 Asian American women patients who experience abuse actually find refuge in a shelter. This ratio is low compared to the mainstream population.

2. Lack of Accurate Interpretation   Police who respond to domestic violence calls are seldom bilingual and often do not bring interpreters with them. They seek to communicate with someone who speaks English and that is often the husband. As a result, in many cases the Asian woman's story goes unheard. In some instances, children, family, and friends have inappropriately been asked to interpret. When those close to the situation have judgmental attitudes and/or fear retaliation by the abuser, they often engage in victim-blaming and are unable to accurately or completely convey the woman's perspective. An example of the tragic results of inadequate translation occurred in the state of Washington. A battered woman's estranged husband threatened her with a gun, with the intention to kill her. Because of the lack of adequate translation, the abuser was never prosecuted because the police did not obtain statements from the victim and two witnesses with sufficient detail for the prosecutor to proceed. A year after the incident, the abuser killed his wife.

In addition, many Asian women come from countries where police and other institutions do not respond to domestic disputes, which contributes to the lack of reporting. Moreover, the U.S. criminal justice system is viewed as discriminatory toward immigrants, people of color, and other minorities, and this also creates negative perceptions that prevent women from seeking police protection when necessary.

3. Lack of Services for Batterers   In most parts of the U.S., linguistically and culturally accessible intervention programs for batterers from the Asian community do not exist. Court sentences for batterers that require mandatory participation in such programs are rendered meaningless if no such program exists in the batterer's native tongue.[4]

Laws That Trap Asian Women in Violent Domestic Situations

1. Anti-Immigrant Legislation   Anti-immigration legislation poses the most difficult barrier to Asian immigrant women seeking safety. Prior to 1986, a U.S.-citizen husband could petition for and obtain lawful permanent residence status (a green card) for his immigrant wife immediately after marriage. However, in 1986 Congress enacted the Immigration Marriage Fraud Amendments (IMFA) that created a new conditional residence status requiring that an immigrant spouse must stay married to a citizen spouse for two years. At the end of two years, the partners must file a joint application to adjust the conditional status to permanent status. As a result, some immigrant women were trapped in violent domestic situations, unable to leave out of fear that their husbands would become unwilling to cooperate in jointly filing the application, thereby rendering them undocumented and thus subject to deportation at the end of the two years.

In 1990, Congress enacted the Battered Spouse Waiver to remedy the unintended consequences of the 1986 law after powerful documentation of the physical, emotional, and economic abuses suffered by battered immigrant women was brought to light. The Battered Spouse Waiver allowed a battered immigrant woman to leave her U.S.-citizen husband and "self-petition" for lawful permanent residence without the cooperation of her husband. In 1994, Congress enacted the Violence Against Women Act (VAWA) to provide broader protections to immigrant women, allowing any woman, documented or undocumented, married to a citizen or green-card-holder to self-petition if she is a victim of domestic violence. When VAWA was reauthorized by Congress in 2000, other barriers to the self-petition process were removed. These included allowing divorced spouses to self-petition, allowing abused wives living abroad to self-petition if married to employees of the government or U.S. military, and eliminating the requirement to show extreme hardship to her or her children if deported to her home country.[5]

2. Limitations of the Battered Spouse Waiver and VAWA The Battered Spouse Waiver and VAWA have been on the books for twelve and eight years, respectively. However, because of lack of education and outreach, many monolingual women are unaware of these legal protections. Many women are under the impression that their batterers have complete control over their immigration status and continue to live in dangerous and violent domestic situations. In addition, there are not enough attorneys trained in immigration law, family law, and domestic violence law to deal with the most complicated VAWA cases, especially those involving undocumented women. Even when a woman self-petitions, she may not get the relief she seeks.

An attorney from the Asian Law Caucus in San Francisco found that Asian immigrant women have difficulty meeting the documentation requirements for self-petitioning. For example, in order to self-petition for permanent residence status after leaving an abusive husband, immigrant women must document the abuse through either police reports or protective orders, record of time spent at a shelter, or affidavits from friends. The extreme isolation of many Asian immigrant women, their lack of awareness of the availability of shelter programs or police protection, and the language barriers to obtaining assistance from them, make it difficult for them to use these channels to document the abuse. In addition, because the crime of domestic violence is a deportable offense, some Asian immigrant women hesitate to report their batterers to law enforcement. These women often must use only their own declarations and rely on the discretion of INS officers. But an advocate who tracks VAWA cases nationally notes that the INS has a great deal of discretion in hearing a case, and even if the woman's declaration is legally sufficient, many INS officers in local district offices are not sympathetic to the plight of battered immigrant women.

3. Restrictions Created by Welfare Reform Welfare reform has resulted in serious financial barriers to Asian immigrant women seeking safety. Recognizing that welfare programs serve as an essential bridge to safety for women fleeing domestic abuse, Congress created exceptions for battered immigrant women. For example, a battered immigrant woman, even if she is undocumented, is eligible for public benefits when she has a pending VAWA or family-sponsored petition. Battered women are also exempted from the "sponsor deeming" requirements. Congress also created the Family Violence Option (FVO), which allows states to exempt a battered woman from TANF [Temporary Assistance for Needy Families] work requirements if meeting these requirements would make it more difficult for the woman to escape an abusive situation. FVO also permits the clock on the five-year lifetime cap to stop running until the woman is safe. Under FVO, a state can waive the paternity establishment and child support requirements. However, the widespread, erroneous impressions among both caseworkers and battered women themselves that "immigrants aren't entitled to any benefits anymore" have kept battered women from applying and caseworkers from accepting applications. There is anecdotal evidence that caseworkers ignorant of FVO provisions have sanctioned battered women for not complying with job search and work requirements, and thus reducing or terminating their benefits. In addition, fear of mandatory reporting to INS and fear of becoming a deportable public charge[6] has also kept eligible Asian immigrants from applying for public benefits.

Without a safety net to keep them from falling into dire circumstances if they leave the batterer, women remain in dangerous and violent situations. In a report by the Family Violence Prevention Fund that chronicles the effects of welfare reform, an advocate from Massachusetts relays:

> Many women are afraid to apply for benefits because of the public charge issue. We've heard of cases where someone received benefits only briefly—just for the time it took to leave a dangerous relationship—and was denied legal permanent residency by the INS and put into deportation proceedings. To many women, it just doesn't seem worth it.[7]

Welfare reform has also resulted in shelters mistakenly believing that it is unlawful to provide services to undocumented women and thus increasingly denying services to battered immigrant women. In fact, emergency medical care and shelters continue to be available to everyone, regardless of immigration status. Some shelters also believe that their funding streams preclude them from serving immigrant women when in fact federal domestic violence funding carries no such restrictions. Given the limited number of beds, some shelters have chosen to provide services only where there is a guarantee of public benefits reimbursement and to deny these services to immigrant women whose eligibility for public benefits is in doubt. One Asian women's shelter director suspects that instead of fund-raising to increase language capacity and transitional programs specifically needed by immigrant women, these shelters justify discriminating against Asian immigrant women by simply stating that their programs cannot serve their needs.

Cultural Norms and Values That Lead to Violent Behavior

1. Acceptance of Violence Against Women

A survey conducted by the Boston Asian Task Force revealed that 20–25% of the respondents from the Cambodian, Chinese, Korean, South Asian, and Vietnamese communities surveyed thought that violence against a woman was justifiable in certain domestic disputes. The report also found that a higher number of Asian men than women condone family violence. Among Korean respondents, 29% (the highest percentage among the five ethnic groups surveyed) felt that a battered woman should not tell anyone. In general, Cambodian and Vietnamese respondents believe that a battered woman should not leave or divorce her husband. South Asian respondents felt that the woman in marriage becomes her husband's property and thus she cannot turn to her family and/or parents to ask them to intervene. Older Chinese respondents were more tolerant of the use of violence in certain situations, and younger Chinese were less likely to see leaving and divorce as viable options for battered women. Response patterns were similar between the foreign-born and U.S.-born. Moreover, these attitudes permeate all sectors of a community, including those who are supposed to protect battered women. One legal advocate who represents battered women in Hawai'i was dismayed to hear female interpreters at an immigrant social service agency siding with a particularly violent batterer on the grounds that his estranged wife was pregnant by another man.

In the home countries of many Asian women, extended families often exert collective pressure to prevent abuse of wives. However, migration to the U.S. broke up extended families and changed social practices to the detriment of women who often rank lowest in the family structure. In some communities this has resulted in the perversion of extended families from protector to perpetrator. NARIKA, a South Asian domestic violence resource center in Berkeley, has reported that there are cases where entire families, extended and joint, get involved in abusing a woman, with some members holding her down while others do the hitting. Therefore, conventional legal restraints, such as protective orders against the lone male abuser, are of limited use when there are multiple perpetrators including in-laws and other women in the family.

2. Cultural Emphasis on Preserving Family

The notion of having to preserve the family and "save face" often makes Asian women more hesitant to leave and break up the family. Women in abusive marriages are frequently blamed for not behaving or told to tolerate the abuse in order to save face for the entire family or clan. Because certain Asian communities are small and close-knit, victim advocates from the communities often face harassment and threats from the abuser and the family for helping women leave the relationship and upsetting the social order. Also, this pronounced belief in the sanctity of the family even in the face of violent victimization, combined with a cultural antipathy toward divorce, makes it more difficult for white shelter workers and advocates to provide support and understanding to Asian women. As the Boston-based Asian Task Force against Domestic Violence notes, "One of the biggest and most important challenges to addressing family violence within Asian communities is reconciling the differences between Western ideals of independence and individualism with Asian ideals of interdependence and group harmony."

In addition, the traditional Asian gender roles of male providers and female homemakers are often disrupted by the American economy that requires both partners to work outside the home. While this has been liberating for some Asian women, women's economic independence is seen as a threat to social orders that privilege men and has, in some communities, contributed to a rise in domestic violence.

3. Transforming Culture

Culture is not static, fixed, and unchangeable. Norms, values, and beliefs are constructed in the interchanges between and among people within cultural groups and are constantly evolving. As Asian immigrants, it can be threatening in light of changes forced by relocating to the United States, to think that cultures must also be changed from within. Who will we be then? Will we disappear as a distinct social group? There are aspects of Asian cultures that are worthy of saving and passing on. There are others that must be transformed in order to honor basic human rights—in this case, the right of women to be free from domestic violence.[8] In Asian American communities, for example, the emphasis on preservation of the family is worthy but must be transformed so that it is achieved not by pressuring women into staying in violent situations, but by changing the cultural and social cues that sanction men's use of violence to control women. Thus, a number of Asian women's shelters and outreach groups frame their organizing work as "work to perpetuate the core values of each Asian community that are positive and to eliminate those parts that are no longer useful or healthy."

Battered Queer Asian American Women[9]

Domestic violence is equally prevalent in queer Asian women's relationships. However, there is little research and data on same-gender relationship violence[10] and what does exist tends to underreport the incidents involving queer Asian women.[11] There are several causes for this underreporting. In 1998 national and local focus groups held by the Family Violence Prevention Fund and the San Francisco-based Asian Women's Shelter, queer Asian women divulged that they did not feel safe reporting relationship violence to the police or authorities. They feared that disclosing oneself as a lesbian being abused by another lesbian may subject them to further abuse at hands of the police. Many were hesitant to access service providers due to sexism, racism, homophobia, language and cultural barriers, and fear of disbelief among service providers. Queer Asian women often do not feel safe even speaking to friends. They may also hesitate to report their abusive partner because they do not want to further isolate a woman who is already marginalized by society or subject her to a homophobic, racist legal system and its consequences.

Even when abused queer Asian women seek help, they find that the vast majority of domestic violence agencies are not able to meet their needs. One factor is that the domestic violence movement does not acknowledge same-gender relationship violence. The mainstream domestic violence movement understands violence as a patriarchal phenomenon, deriving from sexism, with men using violence to control women. Within the queer women's community, it is not always the more masculine, or butch, woman that is the abuser. Women can be survivors and batterers. The typical response of mainstream domestic violence agencies is to ostracize the batterer. But banishing the abuser from a small, marginalized queer Asian community is akin to cutting her off from her only family members. Agencies do not have programs that assist both the batterer and survivor. The San Francisco shelter is the only program with a Queer Asian Women Services project.

The Organizations

The Shelter Programs

Since the first shelter program for Asian American women and children started in Los Angeles in 1981, six other Asian women's shelters have emerged across the country[12] along with over a dozen outreach, education and hotline programs for Asian women. The majority of these were started by and for South Asian women. These include organizations such as Apna Ghar ("our home" in Hindi-Urdu), Manavi ("primal women" in Sanskrit), the Nav Nirmaan Foundation, Inc., the New York Asian Women's Center, Raksha ("protection" in several languages), Pragati ("progress"), and Sakhi ("women's friend").

The handful of shelters that are available cannot meet the need of Asian American women, especially limited-English-speaking women, in their regions, let alone the country. All these groups and shelters conduct some form of community education and outreach as part of their prevention activities to address the root causes of domestic violence. Shelters have conducted local advocacy, such as pressuring police departments to hire interpreters or working with them on protocols on handling domestic violence calls in Asian communities. Not until 1997 was the first large national pan-Asian conference convened in California that brought together 400 service providers and activists from across the country. Since then, other conferences have been held, such as one for Koreans in Los Angeles, South Asians in New York, and a pan-Asian conference in Ohio. With such limited capacity, locally based shelters and programs have relied on coalitions such as the National Network on Behalf of Battered Immigrant Women to conduct the statewide and national advocacy needed to address the unique challenges Asian women face, when and if those challenges dovetail with the agenda of these broader coalitions.[13]

Coalition Work

In 2000, as a means to address the lack of a national Asian American battered women's advocacy organization, the San Francisco-based Asian Women's Shelter, the Asian & Pacific Islander American Health Forum, the Family Violence Prevention Fund, and the National Resource Center on Domestic Violence, launched the *Asian and Pacific Islander Domestic Violence Institute (APIDVI)*. The mission of APIDVI is to advocate for policy changes and increased ethnicity specific data collection, facilitate the sharing of service models for battered Asian women and children, and promote national discussions on differing Asian community perceptions of domestic violence, community responses to the problem and the intersecting cultural values. Since the formation of APIDVI, all the various Asian women's shelters and domestic violence programs have become members. Based on evidence of higher fatality rates among battered Asian women, its first research project is a fatality review of deaths of Asian and Pacific Islander women in major urban centers like Chicago, Santa Clara, San Francisco, and Boston. Its first advocacy project will focus on getting police departments to disaggregate fatality data by ethnicity because most departments simply put Asians under the "Other" category after "White," "Black," and "Hispanic." The APIDVI advocacy will focus on two areas: Welfare Reform and Cultural Competency as they relate to domestic violence. This work will be conducted by working groups consisting of its member organizations and coordinated by APIDVI staff. Initial funding came from the U.S. Department of Health and Human Services.

Transformative Initiatives

An example of work to transform local community attitudes on domestic violence in the Korean community is the SHIMTUH project—a joint project between the Asian Women's Shelter in San Francisco and the Korean Community Center of the East Bay. SHIMTUH has direct service, outreach, and organizing components. It reaches out to the social networks, structures, and institutions in the Korean community to transform cultural norms. Through cultural events, drumming, singing, working with the Korean press, and outreach to indigenous Korean religious institutions, SHIMTUH engages in public dialogue with religious leaders and others to influence more and more spheres in the community. Another example is the Family Violence Prevention Fund's reframing of the concept of "hiya" or shame in the Filipino community. In a poster campaign, the FVPF introduced the concept of "nakakahiya"—a woman should not feel ashamed for having bruises and being beaten, and the community should be ashamed for not helping her.

One example of work among immigrant men is the Tapestri Men's Group, a project of the Refugee's Women's Network, Inc., in Atlanta, Georgia. Tapestri's philosophy is twofold. First, it believes that cultural norms are not immutable and can evolve. Second, it views the violence of men not as an individual pathology amenable to counseling or therapeutic intervention in one-on-one sessions, but rather as a social malaise where a man has leaned through modeling at home and in society that the use of violence against women is an accepted way of resolving differences. Thus, Tapestri does not provide anger management because it views men's violence against women not as an angry man out of control, but as a man who chooses to be violent to control his partner.

In the men's groups where Asian, Latino, Caribbean, African, and East European men have participated, the transformative and re-education work takes place not by experts imparting information top down to batterers, but through a process where men themselves critically explore, in an atmosphere of mutual respect and horizontal relationships, the antecedents, dynamics, and effects of their violent behaviors, values, and expectations. In the process, men's views of themselves and their roles as partners and fathers are transformed, gender identities are de-constructed and re-constructed, and the men become agents of change in their communities. The Tapestri Men's Group and others like it were created when domestic violence survivors, who did not want to leave their marriages, requested intervention programs for their husbands. As the men participate in the 24-week program, women advocates from Tapestri work with their wives to provide support, ensure that they are not in danger, and monitor the progress being made by the men.

Recommendations for Action

- Address racism, homophobia, and xenophobia within social service and law enforcement agencies that deal with battered Asian American women.

- Increase language access to all services needed by battered women through hiring of interpreters and bilingual staff and creating culturally competent services in police departments, shelters, and counseling and court intervention programs for men.

- Eliminate barriers to public benefits such as the chilling effects of mandatory reporting to the INS, fear of being designated a public charge, and hostile caseworkers.

- Train eligibility caseworkers on the exceptions for battered women, the Family Violence Option in TANF, and the myriad categories of immigrants to correct the widespread erroneous perception that immigrants are no longer eligible for benefits.

- Educate both government agencies and social service providers and immigrant women to understand and utilize the protective provisions in VAWA.

- Repeal the conditional residence status that has trapped women in violent homes and which the passage of VAWA simply will not fix.

- Address and transform cultural norms that accept violence against women as a means of discipline or control. This includes creating programs for both female and male Asian American batterers.

- Conduct studies on relationship violence in queer Asian women communities. Redefine domestic violence theories to include same-gender relationship violence.

NOTES

1. In Boston, a survey of men and women from the Cambodian, Chinese, Korean, South Asian, and Vietnamese communities found that 38% of respondents reported knowing a woman who had been physically abused or injured by her partner. A focus group with Southeast Asian Chinese estimated that 20–30% of Chinese husbands hit their wives. A Northern California survey found that 25% of Filipinas had experienced domestic violence in the Philippines, the U.S., or both.

2. Research indicates a higher incidence of domestic violence among military families. Advocates in Hawai'i, which has a large military base population, have noticed that Asian immigrant women married to U.S. servicemen have fewer financial and social resources, suffer from prejudices against interracial marriages, and are especially vulnerable to abuse.

3. Mainstream shelters are designed in dormitory styles with congregated dining that is alienating to Asian women used to cooking their own foods, feeding their own children, and keeping their children with them most of the time. Additionally, Asian women have a difficult time following mainstream shelters' programs and procedures, such as participating in shelter chores selection, because of their inability to communicate with staff and other residents. They also report feeling very lost when they were forbidden to have any contacts with their mothers, who have traditionally been their source of support.

4. Court sentences that involve serving time and mandatory participation in intervention programs are often insufficient to convey the gravity of the crime to the batterer. In addition, there needs to be culturally relevant sentencing. For example, in the Hmong community, when clan elders resolve domestic violence cases through the mediation process, they may order the husband to hire a shaman for a soul-calling ceremony to heal the wife. When a wife has been abused, the soul leaves her body because it has been mistreated. When the soul is not well, the body is not well. In a soul-calling ceremony, a shaman calls the soul back to the body.

5. VAWA 2000's other provisions allow self-petitioning by women whose abuser husbands die or lose their immigration status or whose husbands have committed bigamy. In addition, VAWA 2000 also created a new visa, the U visa, for women not covered by VAWA, such as battered wives of men holding temporary worker visas or student visas

and victims of sexual and other crimes, such as rape and torture. However, it is more difficult to obtain relief through the U visa than through VAWA's self-petitioning process because the woman must show substantial physical or emotional abuse.

6. INS's May 1999 guidelines state that use of non-cash benefits such as Medicaid and food stamps does not make one a public charge. VAWA 2000 barred the INS from finding a woman a public charge based on her use of non-cash benefits that she is legally qualified to use.

7. Family Violence Prevention Fund, "Caught at the Public Policy Crossroads: The Impact of Welfare Reform on Battered Immigrant Women," January 1999.

8. See Julia L. Perilla, "Domestic Violence as a Human Rights Issue: The Case of Immigrant Latinos," reprinted from *Hispanic Journal of Behavioral Sciences,* Vol. 21, No. 2, May 1999, pp. 107–133.

9. The term "queer" is controversial within the lesbian/gay/bisexual/transgender (LGBT) community. However, many LGBTs have reclaimed "queer" as a positive term. This report uses it to encompass the diversity of the LGBT community.

10. In both national and local focus groups of queer Asian women held by the Family Violence Prevention Fund and the San Francisco-based Asian Women's Shelter, survivors expressed discomfort with the label of domestic violence and preferred the term "relationship violence" to describe violence in queer relationships.

11. In October 2000, the National Coalition of Anti-Violence Programs issued a report that there were over 3,000 cases of LGBT domestic violence (47% female, 50% male survivors) throughout the U.S., with 1,356 cases in Los Angeles, 741 in San Francisco, and 510 in New York. For San Francisco, 75% of the cases involved whites and 25% people of color, including Asian Americans.

12. The seven shelters are the Asian Women's Home in San Jose, the Asian Women's Shelter in San Francisco, the Asian Women United in Minneapolis/St. Paul, the Center for Pacific Asian Families in Los Angeles, the New Moon Shelter in Boston, Apna Ghar in Chicago, and the New York Asian Women's Center. There are also programs within larger shelter programs like the Asian Unit of Interval House in Long Beach/Orange County, CA. In Atlanta, Georgia, the International Women's House serves women who do not speak English, including Asian immigrant women.

13. The National Network is made up of three groups, the Family Violence Prevention Fund, the Immigrant Women Program of NOW Legal Defense Fund (formerly housed at AYUDA, Inc.), and the National Immigration Project of the National Lawyer's Guild.

REFERENCES

Chan, Sue, M.D., "Domestic Violence in Asian and Pacific Islander (API) Communities," compilation of studies, statistics, and data on domestic violence and API's, Asian Health Services.

Family Violence Prevention Fund, January 1999, "Caught at the Public Policy Crossroads: The Impact of Welfare Reform on Battered Immigrant Women."

Perilla, Julia L., "Domestic Violence as a Human Rights Issue: The Case of Immigrant Latinos," reprinted from *Hispanic Journal of Behavioral Sciences,* Vol. 21, No. 2, May 1999, pp. 107–133.

Santa Clara County Death Review Sub-Committee for the Domestic Violence Council, Final Report, 1997.

Warrier, Sujata, Ph.D, "(Un)heard Voices: Domestic Violence in the Asian American Community," Family Violence Prevention Fund, produced with a grant from the Violence Against Women Office, Office of Justice Programs, U.S. Department of Justice.

Yoshioka, Marianne, Ph.D., M.S.W.,"Asian Family Violence Report: A Study of the Cambodian, Chinese, Korean, South Asian and Vietnamese Communities in Massachusetts," Nov. 2000, Boston, MA.

THIRTY-EIGHT

◆◆◆

Sexual Violence and American Indian Genocide

Andy Smith

I once attended a conference where a speaker stressed the importance of addressing sexual violence within Native communities. When I returned home, I told a friend of mine, who was a rape survivor, about the talk. She replied, "You mean other Indian women have been raped?" When I said yes, she asked, "Well, why don't we ever talk about it?" Indeed, the silence surrounding sexual violence in Native communities—particularly the sexual assault of adult women—is overwhelming. Under Janet Reno, the Department of Justice poured millions of dollars into tribally-based sexual and domestic violence programs. Although domestic violence programs are proliferating, virtually no tribes have developed comprehensive sexual assault programs.

Native survivors of sexual violence often find no support when they seek healing and justice. When they seek help from non-Indian agencies, they are often told to disassociate themselves from their communities, where their abusers are. The underlying philosophy of the white-dominated anti-rape movement is implicit in Susan Brownmiller's statement: "[Rape] is nothing more or less than a conscious process of intimidation by which all men keep all women in a state of fear."[1] The notion that rape is "nothing more or less" than a tool of patriarchal control fails to consider how rape also serves as a tool of racism and colonialism. At the same time, when Native survivors of sexual violence seek healing within their communities, other community members accuse them of undermining Native sovereignty and being divisive by making their abuse public. According to the Mending the Hoop Technical Assistance Project in Minnesota, tribally-based sexual assault advocates believe that a major difficulty in developing comprehensive programs to address sexual assault in tribal communities, particularly sexual violence against adult women, is that many community members believe that sexual violence is "traditional." Historical evidence suggests, however, that sexual violence was rare in Native communities prior to colonization, and that it has served as a primary weapon in the U.S. war against Native nations ever since. . . . Far from being traditional, sexual violence is an attack on Native sovereignty itself. As one elder stated at a conference I attended: "As long as we destroy ourselves from inside, we don't have to worry about anyone on the outside."

The Colonial Context of Sexual Violence

Ann Stoler argues that racism is a permanent part of the social fabric: "[R]acism is not an effect but a tactic in the internal fission of society into binary opposition, a means of creating 'biologized' internal enemies, against whom society must defend itself."[2] She notes that in the modern state, it is the constant purification and elimination of racialized enemies that ensures the growth of the national body.

"Racism does not merely arise in moments of crisis, in sporadic cleansings. It is internal to the biopolitical state, woven into the web of the social body, threaded through its fabric."[3] Similarly, Kate Shanley notes that Native peoples are a permanent "present absence" in the U.S. colonial imagination, an "absence" that reinforces the conviction that Native peoples are vanishing and that the conquest of native lands is justified.[4] Ella Shoat and Robert Stam describe this absence as "an ambivalently repressive mechanism [which] dispels the anxiety in the face of the Indian, whose very presence is a reminder of the initially precarious grounding of the American nation-state itself. . . . In a temporal paradox, living Indians were induced to 'play dead,' as it were, in order to perform a narrative of manifest destiny in which their role, ultimately, was to disappear."[5] This "absence" is effected through the metaphorical transformation of Native bodies into a pollution from which the colonial body must purify itself. In the 1860s, white Californians described Native people as "the dirtiest lot of human beings on earth." They wear "filthy rags, with their persons unwashed, hair uncombed and swarming with vermin."[6] An 1885 Proctor & Gamble ad for Ivory Soap also illustrates this equation between Indian bodies and dirt:

> We were once factious, fierce and wild,
> In peaceful arts unreconciled
> Our blankets smeared with grease and stains
> From buffalo meat and settlers' veins.
> Through summer's dust and heat content
> From moon to moon unwashed we went.
> But IVORY SOAP came like a ray
> Of light across our darkened way
> And now we're civil, kind and good
> And keep the laws as people should.
> We wear our linen, lawn and lace
> As well as folks with paler face
> And now I take, where'er we go
> This cake of IVORY SOAP to show
> What civilized my squaw and me
> And made us clean and fair to see.[7]

In the colonial imagination, Native bodies are also polluted with sexual sin. . . . In 1613, Alexander Whitaker, a minister in Virginia, wrote: "They live naked in bodie, as if their shame of their sinne deserved no covering: Their names are as naked as their bodie: They esteem it a virtue to lie, deceive and steale as their master the divell teacheth them."[8] Furthermore, according to Bernardino de Minaya: "Their [the Indians'] marriages are not a sacrament but a sacrilege. They are idolatrous, libidinous, and commit sodomy. Their chief desire is to eat, drink, worship heathen idols, and commit bestial obscenities."[9]

This understanding of Native peoples as dirty whose sexuality threatens U.S. security was echoed in the comments of one doctor in his attempt to rationalize the mass sterilization of Native women in the 1970s:

> People pollute, and too many people crowded too close together cause many of our social and economic problems. These in turn are aggravated by involuntary and irresponsible parenthood. . . . We also have obligations to the society of which we are part. The welfare mess, as it has been called, cries out for solutions, one of which is fertility control.[10]
>
> . . .

Because Indian bodies are considered "dirty," they are sexually violable and "rapable." In patriarchal thinking, only a "pure" body can really be violated. The rape of bodies that are considered inherently impure simply does not count. For instance, women in prostitution have an almost impossible time if they are raped because the dominant society considers a prostituted woman as lacking bodily integrity and violable at all times. Similarly, the history of mutilation of Indian bodies, both living and dead, makes it clear to Indian people that they are not considered to have bodily integrity. President Andrew Jackson, for instance, ordered the mutilation of approximately 800 Muscogee Indian corpses, cutting off their noses and slicing long strips of flesh from their bodies to make bridle reins.[11] Tecumseh's skin was flayed and made into razor-straps.[12] A soldier cut off the testicles of White Antelope to make a tobacco pouch. Colonel John Chivington led an attack against the Cheyenne and Arapahoe in which nearly all the victims were scalped, their fingers, arms, and ears amputated to obtain rings, necklaces, and other jewelry, and their private parts were cut out to be exhibited before the public in Denver.[13] Throughout the history of massacres against Indian people, colonizers attempted not only to defeat Indian people but to eradicate their very identity and humanity. They attempted to transform Indian people from human beings into tobacco pouches, bridle reins, or souvenirs—objects for white people's consumption.

As Stoler explains this process of racialized colonization, "[T]he more 'degenerates' and 'abnormals' [in this case, Native peoples] are eliminated, the lives of those who speak will be stronger, more vigorous, and improved. The enemies are not political adversaries, but those identified as external and internal threats to the population. Racism is the condition that makes it acceptable to put [certain people] to death in a society of normalization."[14] She further notes that "the imperial discourses on sexuality cast white women as the bearers of a racist imperial order."[15] By extension, as bearers of a counter-imperial order, Native women pose a supreme threat to the imperial order. Symbolic and literal control over their bodies is important in the war against Native people, as these examples attest:

> When I was in the boat I captured a beautiful Carib woman. . . . I conceived desire to take pleasure. . . . I took a rope and thrashed her well, for which she raised such unheard screams that you would not have believed your ears. Finally we came to an agreement in such a manner that I can tell you that she seemed to have been brought up in a school of harlots.[16]

> Two of the best looking of the squaws were lying in such a position, and from the appearance of the genital organs and of their wounds, there can be no doubt that they were first ravished and then shot dead. Nearly all of the dead were mutilated.[17]

> One woman, big with child, rushed into the church, clasping the altar and crying for mercy for herself and unborn babe. She was followed, and fell pierced with a dozen lances . . . the child was torn alive from the yet palpitating body of its mother, first plunged into the holy water to be baptized, and immediately its brains were dashed out against a wall.[18]

> The Christians attacked them with buffets and beatings. . . . Then they behaved with such temerity and shamelessness that the most powerful ruler of the island had to see his own wife raped by a Christian officer.[19]

> I heard one man say that he had cut a woman's private parts out, and had them for exhibition

on a stick. I heard another man say that he had cut the fingers off of an Indian, to get the rings off his hand. I also heard of numerous instances in which men had cut out the private parts of females, and stretched them over their saddle-bows and some of them over their hats.[20]

Although the era of deliberate, explicit Indian massacres in North America is over, in Latin America the wholesale rape and mutilation of indigenous women's bodies has continued. . . . Many white feminists are correctly outraged by mass rapes in Bosnia, and have organized to instigate a war crimes tribunal against the Serbs. Yet one wonders why the mass rapes of indigenous women in Guatemala, Chiapas, or elsewhere in Latin America have not sparked the same outrage. Feminist legal scholar Catherine MacKinnon argues that in Bosnia, "the world has *never* seen sex used this consciously, this cynically, this elaborately, this openly, this systematically . . . as a means of destroying a whole people."[21] She seems to forget that she only lives on this land because millions of Native people were raped, sexually mutilated and murdered. Is mass rape of European women 'genocide,' while mass rape of indigenous women is business as usual? Even in the white feminist imagination, are native women's bodies more rapable than white women's bodies?

The colonization of Native women's bodies continues today. In the 1980s, when I served as a nonviolent witness for the Chippewa spearfishers who were being harassed by white racist mobs, one white harasser carried a sign saying "Save a fish; spear a pregnant squaw." During the 1990 Mohawk crisis in Oka [Quebec], a white mob surrounded an ambulance taking a Native woman off the reservation because she was hemorrhaging after giving birth. She was forced to "spread her legs" to prove it. The police at the scene refused to intervene. An Indian man was arrested for "wearing a disguise" (he was wearing jeans), and was brutally beaten, with his testicles crushed. Two women from Chicago WARN (Women of All Red Nations, the organization I belong to) went to Oka to videotape the crisis. They were arrested and held in custody for eleven hours without being charged, and were told that they could not go to the bathroom unless the male police officers could watch. The place they were held was covered with pornographic magazines.

In 1982, this colonial desire to subjugate Indian women's bodies was quite apparent when Stuart Kasten marketed a new video, "Custer's Revenge," in which players get points each time they, in the character of Custer, rape an Indian woman. The slogan of the game is "When you score, you score." He describes the game as "a fun sequence where the woman is enjoying a sexual act willingly." According to the promotional material:

You are General Custer. Your dander's up, your pistol's wavin'. You've hog-tied a ravishing Indian maiden and have a chance to rewrite history and even up an old score. Now, the Indian maiden's hands may be tied, but she's not about to take it lying down, by George! Help is on the way. If you're to get revenge you'll have to rise to the challenge, dodge a tribe of flying arrows and protect your flanks against some downright mean and prickly cactus. But if you can stand pat and last past the strings and arrows—You can stand last. Remember? Revenge is sweet.[22]

Ironically, while enslaving women's bodies, colonizers argued that they were actually freeing Native women from the "oppression" they supposedly faced in Native nations. Thomas Jefferson, for example, argued that Native women "are submitted to unjust drudgery. This I believe is the case with every barbarous people. It is civilization alone which replaces women in the enjoyment of their equality."[23] The *Mariposa Gazette* similarly noted that when Indian women were safely under the control of white men, they "are neat, and tidy, and industrious, and soon learn to discharge domestic duties properly and creditably."[24] In 1862, a Native man in Conrow Valley was killed and scalped with his head twisted off; his killers said, "You will not kill any more women and children."[25] Apparently, Native women can only be free while under the dominion of white men, and both Native and white women have to be protected from Indian men, rather than from white men. . . .

. . . Although stereotypes of Native women as beasts of burden for their men prevail, prior to colonization Indian societies were not male-dominated for the most part. Women served as spiritual, political, and military leaders. Many societies were matrilineal and matrilocal. Although there was a division of labor between women and men, women's and men's labor was accorded similar status.[26] Thus, the historical record would suggest, as Paula Gunn Allen argues, that the real roots of feminism should be found in Native societies. . . .

Just as, historically, white colonizers who raped Indian women claimed that Indian men were the real rapists, white men who rape and murder Indian women often make this same claim today. In Minneapolis, a white man, Jesse Coulter, raped, murdered and mutilated several Indian women. He claimed to be Indian, adopting the name Jesse Sittingcrow, and emblazoning an AIM tattoo on his arm.[27] Similarly, Roy Martin, a full-blooded Native man, was charged with sexual assault. The survivor identified the rapist as white, about 25 years old, with a shag haircut. Martin was 35 with hair past his shoulders.[28] Although this case was eventually dismissed, the fact that it even made it to trial indicates the extent to which Native men are seen as the rapists of white women.

Of course, Indian men do commit acts of sexual violence. After years of colonialism and boarding-school experiences, violence has been internalized in Indian communities. However, this view of the Indian man as the "true" rapist serves to obscure who has real power in this racist and patriarchal society. The U.S. is indeed engaged in a "permanent social war" against Native bodies, particularly Native women's bodies, which threaten its legitimacy.[29] Colonizers evidently recognize the wisdom of the Cheyenne saying, "A Nation is not conquered until the hearts of the women [and their bodies as well] are on the ground."

Through this colonization and abuse of their bodies, Indian people have learned to internalize self-hatred. Body image is integrally related to self-esteem. When one's body is not respected, one begins to hate oneself.[30] For example, Anne, a Native boarding-school student, reflects on this process:

> You better not touch yourself. . . . If I looked at somebody . . . lust, sex, and I got scared of those sexual feelings. And I did not know how to handle them. . . . What really confused me was if intercourse was sin, why are people born? . . . It took me a really long time to get over the fact that . . . I've sinned: I had a child.[31]

As her words indicate, when the bodies of Indian people are inherently sinful and dirty, it becomes a sin just to be Indian. Thus, it is not a surprise that Indian people who have survived sexual abuse often say that they no longer wish to be Indian. The Menominee poet Chrystos writes in such a voice in her poem "Old Indian Granny."

> *You told me about all the Indian women you counsel*
> *who say they don't want to be Indian anymore*
> *because a white man or an Indian one raped them*
> *or killed their brother*
> *or somebody tried to run them over in the street*
> *or insulted them or all of it*
> *our daily bread of hate*
> *Sometimes I don't want to be Indian either*
> *But I've never said so out loud before*
> *Since I'm so proud and political*
> *I have to deny it now*
> *Far more than being hungry*
> *having no place to live or dance*
> *no decent job no home to offer a Granny*
> *It's knowing with each invisible breath*
> *that if you don't make something pretty*
> *they can hang on their walls or wear around their necks*
> *you might as well be dead.*[32]

The fact that many Native peoples will argue that sexual violence is "traditional" indicates the extent to which our communities have internalized self-hatred. . . . Then, as Michael Taussig notes, Native peoples are portrayed by the dominant culture as inherently violent, self-destructive and dysfunctional. For example, in 1990, Mike Whelan made the following statement at a zoning hearing in South Dakota, calling for the denial of a permit for a shelter to serve Indian women who have been battered:

> Indian Culture as I view it, is presently so mongrelized as to be a mix of dependency on the Federal Government and a primitive society wholly on the outside of the mainstream of western civilization and thought. The Native American Culture as we know it now, not as it formerly existed, is a culture of hopelessness, godlessness, of joblessness, and lawlessness. . . . Alcoholism, social disease, child abuse, and poverty are the hallmarks of this so-called culture that you seek to promote, and I would suggest to you that the brave men of the ghost dance would hang their heads in shame at what you now pass off as that culture. . . . I think that the Indian way of

life as you call it, to me means cigarette burns in arms of children, double-checking the locks on my cars, keeping a loaded shotgun by my door, and car bodies and beer cans on the front lawn. . . . This is not a matter of race, it is a matter of keeping our community and neighborhood away from that evil that you and your ideas promote.[33]

Taussig comments on the irony of this logic: "Men are conquered not by invasion but by themselves. It is a strange sentiment, is it not, when faced with so much brutal evidence of invasion."[34]

Completing the destruction of a people involves the destruction of the integrity of their culture and spirituality that forms the matrix of Native women's resistance to sexual colonization. Native counselors generally agree that a strong cultural and spiritual identity is essential if Native people are to heal from abuse. This is because Native women's healing entails healing not only from any personal abuse she has suffered, but also from the patterned history of abuse against her family, her nation, and the environment in which she lives.[35] Because Indian spiritual traditions are holistic, they have the ability to restore survivors of abuse to the community, and to restore their bodies to wholeness. That is why the most effective programs for healing revolve around reviving indigenous spiritual traditions.

In the colonial discourse, however, Native spiritual traditions become yet another site for the commodification of Indian women's bodies. As part of the genocidal process, Indian cultures lose the means to restore wholeness and become objects of consumerism for the dominant culture. Haunani Kay Trask, a Native Hawai'ian activist, describes this process as "cultural prostitution." "Prostitution, in this context, refers to the entire institution which defines a woman (and by extension the 'female') as an object of degraded and victimized sexual value for use and exchange through the medium of money. . . . My purpose is not to exact detail or fashion a model but to convey the utter degradation of our culture and our people under corporate tourism by employing 'prostitution' as an analytical category. . . . The point, of course, is that everything in Hawai'i can be yours, that is, you the tourist, the non-tourist, the visitor. The place, the people, the culture, even our identity as a 'Native' people is for sale. Thus, Hawai'i, like a lovely woman, is there for the taking."[36]

Thus, this "New Age" appropriation of Indian spiritualities represents yet another form of sexual abuse for Indian women, and hinders their ability to help women heal from abuse. Columnist Andy Rooney . . . argues that Native spiritual traditions "involving ritualistic dances with strong sexual overtones [are] demeaning to Indian women and degrading to Indian children."[37] Along similar lines, Mark and Dan Jury's film, *Dances: Sacred and Profane* (August 1994), was advertised with a claim that it "climaxes with the first-ever filming of the Indian Sundance ceremony." This so-called ceremony consisted of a white man, hanging from meat hooks from a tree, praying to the "Great White Spirit." This was followed by C. C. Sadist, a group that performs sadomasochistic acts for entertainment.[38] Similarly, "plastic medicine [men]" are notorious for sexually abusing their clients in fake Indian ceremonies. Jeffrey Wall, for example, was recently sentenced for sexually abusing three girls while claiming this was part of American Indian spiritual rituals that he was conducting as a supposed Indian medicine man.[39] David "Two Wolves" Smith and Alan "Spotted Wolf" Champney were also charged for sexually abusing girls during supposed "cleansing" ceremonies.[40] In response to such abusive acts, legitimate spiritual leaders have been forced to issue statements such as "no ceremony requires anyone to be naked or fondled,"[41] which signifies the extent to which colonial practices attempt to shift the meaning of Indian spirituality from something healing to something abusive.

Meanwhile, the colonizing religion [of Native peoples], Christianity, which is supposed to "save" Native women from allegedly sexually exploitative traditional practices, has only made them more vulnerable to sexual violence. The large-scale introduction of sexual violence in Native communities is largely a result of the Christian boarding-school system, which began in the 1600s under Jesuit priests along the St. Lawrence River. The system was more formalized in 1870 when Congress set aside funds to erect school facilities to be run by churches and missionary societies.[42] Attendance was mandatory and children were forcibly taken from their homes for the majority of the year. They were forced to practice Christianity (native traditions were prohibited) and speak English only.[43] Children were subjected to constant physical and sexual abuse. Irene Mack

Pyawasit, a former boarding-school resident from the Menominee reservation, testifies to her experience, which is typical of many:

> The government employees that they put into the schools had families, but still there were an awful lot of Indian girls turning up pregnant. Because the employees were having a lot of fun, and they would force a girl into a situation, and the girl wouldn't always be believed. Then, because she came up pregnant, she would be sent home in disgrace. Some boy would be blamed for it, never the government employee. He was always scot-free. And no matter what the girl said, she was never believed.[44]

Even when teachers were charged with abuse, boarding schools refused to investigate. In the case of just one teacher, John Boone, at the Hopi school, FBI investigations found that he had sexually abused over 142 children, but the school principal had not investigated any allegations of abuse.[45] Despite the epidemic of sexual abuse in boarding schools, the Bureau of Indian Affairs did not issue a policy on reporting sexual abuse until 1987, and did not issue a policy to strengthen the background checks of potential teachers until 1989.[46]

Although all Native people did not view their boarding-school experiences as negative, it appears that abuse became endemic in Indian families after the establishment of boarding schools in Native communities. Randy Fred, a former boarding-school student, says that children in his school began to mimic the abuse they were experiencing.[47] After Father Harold McIntee from St. Joseph's residential school on the Alkali Lake reserve was convicted of sexual abuse, two of his victims were later convicted of sexual abuse charges.[48]

Anti-Colonial Responses to Sexual Violence

The struggle for Native sovereignty and the struggle against sexual violence cannot be separated. Conceptualizing sexual violence as a tool of genocide and colonialism leads to specific strategies for combatting it. Currently, the rape crisis movement has called for strengthening the criminal justice system

as the primary means to end sexual violence. Rape crisis centers receive much state funding, and, consequently, their strategies tend to be state-friendly: hire more police, give longer sentences to rapists, etc. There is a contradiction, however, in relying upon the state to solve the problems it is responsible for creating. Native people *per capita* are the most arrested, most incarcerated, and most victimized by police brutality of any ethnic group in the country.[49] Given the oppression Native people face within the criminal justice system, many communities are developing their own programs for addressing criminal behavior based on traditional ways of regulating their societies. However, as James and Elsie B. Zion note, Native domestic violence advocates are often reluctant to pursue traditional alternatives to incarceration for addressing violence against women.[50] Survivors of domestic and sexual violence programs are often pressured to "forgive and forget" in tribal mediation programs that focus more on maintaining family and tribal unity than on providing justice and safety for women. In his study of traditional approaches for addressing sexual/domestic violence on First Nations reserves in Canada, Rupert Ross notes that these approaches are often very successful in addressing child sexual abuse where communities are less likely to blame the victim for the assault. In such cases, the community makes a proactive effort in holding perpetrators accountable so that incarceration is often unnecessary. When a crime is reported, the working team that deals with sexual violence talks to the perpetrator and gives him the option of participating in the program. The perpetrator must first confess his guilt and then follow a healing contract, or go to jail. The perpetrator can decline to participate in the program and go through the normal routes in the criminal justice system. Everyone affected by the crime (victim, perpetrator, family, friends, and the working team) is involved in developing the healing contract. Everyone also holds the perpetrator to his contract. One Tlingit man noted that this approach was often more difficult than going to jail.

> First one must deal with the shock and then the dismay on your neighbors' faces. One must live with the daily humiliation, and at the same time seek forgiveness not just from victims, but from the community as a whole. . . . [A prison sentence] removes the offender from the daily

accountability, and may not do anything towards rehabilitation, and for many may actually be an easier disposition than staying in the community.[51]

Along similar lines, Elizabeth Barker notes that the problem with the criminal justice system is that it diverts accountability from the community to players in the criminal justice system. Perpetrators are taken away from their community and are further limited from developing ethical relationships within a community context.[52] Ross notes: "In reality, rather than making the community a safer place, the threat of jail places the community more at risk."[53] Since the Hollow Lake reserve adopted this approach, 48 offenders have been identified. Only five chose to go to jail, and only two who entered the program have repeated crimes (one of the re-offenders went through the program again and has not re-offended since). However, Ross notes, these approaches often break down in cases where the victim is an adult woman because community members are more likely to blame her instead of the perpetrator for the assault.[54]

Many Native domestic violence advocates I have interviewed note similar problems in applying traditional methods of justice to cases of sexual assault and domestic violence. One advocate from a tribally-based program in the Plains area contends that traditional approaches are important for addressing violence against women, but they are insufficient. To be effective they must be backed up by the threat of incarceration. She notes that medicine men have come to her program saying, "We have worked with this offender and we have not been successful in changing him. He needs to join your batterers' program." Traditional approaches to justice presume that the community will hold a perpetrator accountable for his crime. However, in cases of violence against adult women, community members often do not regard this violence as a crime and will not hold the offender accountable. Before such approaches can be effective, we must implement community education programs that will change community attitudes about these issues.

Another advocate from a reservation in the Midwest argues that traditional alternatives to incarceration might be more harsh than incarceration. Many Native people presume that traditional modes of justice focused on conflict resolution. In fact, she argues, penalties for societal infractions were not lenient. They included banishment, shaming, reparations, and sometimes death. This advocate was involved in an attempt to revise tribal codes by reincorporating traditional practices, but she found that it was difficult to determine what these practices were and how they could be made useful today. For example, some practices, such as banishment, would not have the same impact today. Prior to colonization, Native communities were so close-knit and interdependent that banishment was often the equivalent of a death sentence. Today, however, Native peoples can simply leave home and join the dominant society. In addition, the elders with whom she consulted admitted that their memories of traditional penal systems were tainted with the experience of being in boarding school. Since incarceration is understood as punishment, this advocate believes that it is the most appropriate way to address sexual violence. She argues that if a Native man rapes someone, he subscribes to white values rather than Native values because rape is not an Indian tradition. If he follows white values, then he should suffer the white way of punishment.

However, there are a number of difficulties in pursuing incarceration as the solution for addressing sexual assault. First, so few rapes are reported that the criminal justice system rarely has the opportunity to address the problem. Among tribal programs I have investigated, an average of about two cases of rape are reported each year. Because rape is a major crime, rape cases are generally handed to the State's Attorney, who then declines the vast majority of cases. By the time tribal law-enforcement programs even see rape cases, a year might have passed since the assault, making it difficult for them to prosecute. Also, because rape is covered by the Major Crimes Act, many tribes have not developed codes to address it as they have for domestic violence. One advocate who conducted a training for southwestern tribes on sexual assault says that the participants said they did not need to develop codes because the "Feds will take care of rape cases." She asked how many rape cases had been federally prosecuted, and the participants discovered that not one case of rape had ever reached the federal courts. In addition, there is inadequate jail space in many tribal communities. When the tribal jail is full, the tribe has to pay the surrounding county to house its prisoners. Given financial constraints, tribes are reluctant to house prisoners for any length of time.

But perhaps most importantly, as sociologist Luana Ross (Salish) notes, incarceration has been largely ineffective in reducing crime rates in the dominant society, much less Native communities. "The white criminal justice system does not work for white people; what makes us think it's going go work for us?" she asks.

> The criminal justice system in the United States needs a new approach. Of all the countries in the world, we are the leader in incarceration rates. . . . Society would profit if the criminal justice system employed restorative justice. . . . Most prisons in the United States are, by design, what a former prisoner termed "the devil's house." Social environments of this sort can only produce dehumanizing conditions.[55]

As a number of studies have demonstrated, more prisons and more police do not lead to lower crime rates.[56] For instance, the Rand Corporation found that California's three-strikes legislation, which requires life sentences for three-time convicted felons, did not reduce the rate of "murders, rapes, and robberies that many people believe to be the law's principal targets."[57] Changes in crime rate often have more to do with fluctuations in employment rates than with increased police surveillance or increased incarceration rates.[58] Steven Walker concludes: "Because no clear link exists between incarceration and crime rates, and because gross incapacitation locks up many low-rate offenders at a great dollar cost to society, we conclude as follows: gross incapacitation is not an effective policy for reducing serious crime."[59] Similarly, criminologist Elliot Currie found that "the *best* face put on the impact of massive prison increases, in a study routinely used by prison supporters to prove that 'prison works,' shows that prison growth seems not to have 'worked' at all for homicide or assault, barely if at all for rape. . . ."[60]

The premise of the justice system is that most people are law-abiding except for "deviants" who do not follow the law. However, given the epidemic rates of sexual and domestic violence in which 50 percent of women will be battered and 47 percent will be raped in their lifetime, it is clear that most men are implicated in our rape culture. It is not likely that we can send all of these men to jail. As Fay Koop argues, addressing rape through the justice system simply furthers the myth that rape/domestic violence is caused by a few bad men, rather than seeing most men implicated in such violence.[61] Thus, relying upon the criminal justice system to end violence against women may strengthen the colonial apparatus in tribal communities that furthers violence while providing nothing more than the illusion of safety to survivors of sexual and domestic violence. . . .

Sexual violence is a fundamental attack on Indian sovereignty, and both Native and non-Native communities are challenged to develop programs that address sexual violence from an anti-colonial, anti-racist framework so that we don't attempt to eradicate acts of personal violence by strengthening the apparatus of state violence. Nothing less than a holistic approach towards eradicating sexual violence can be successful. As Ines Hernandez-Avila states:

> We must imagine a world without rape. But I cannot imagine a world without rape, a world without misogyny, without imagining a world without racism, classism, sexism, homophobia, ageism, historical amnesia and other forms and manifestations of violence directed against those communities that are seen to be 'asking for it.' Even the Earth is presumably 'asking for it.'. . . What do I imagine then? From my own Native American perspective, I see a world where sovereign indigenous peoples continue to plunge our memories to come back to our originality, to live in dignity and carry on our resuscitated and ever-transforming cultures and traditions with liberty. . . . I see a world where native women find strength and continuance in the remembrance of who we really were and are . . . a world where more and more native men find the courage to recognize and honor—that they and the women of their families and communities have the capacity to be profoundly vital and creative human beings.[62]

NOTES

1. Susan Brownmiller, *Against our will* (Toronto: Bantam Books, 1986), p. 5.

2. Ann Stoler, *Race and the education of desire* (Durham, N.C.: Duke University Press, 1997), p. 59.

3. Ibid., p. 59.

4. Lecture, Indigenous Intellectual Sovereignties Conference. UC Davis, April 1998.

5. Ella Shohat and Robert Stam, *Unthinking Eurocentrism: Multiculturalism and the media* (London: Routledge, 1994), pp 118–119.

6. James Rawls, *Indians of California: The changing image* (Norman: University of Oklahoma Press, 1984), p. 195.

7. Andre Lopez, *Pagans in our midst* (Mohawk Nation: *Akwesasne Notes*), p. 119.

8. Robert Berkhofer, *The White Man's Indian* (New York: Vintage, 1978), p. 19.

9. David Stannard, *American Holocaust: Columbus and the conquest of the New World* (New York: Oxford University Press, 1992), p. 211.

10. Oklahoma: Sterilization of native women charged to I.H.S., in *Akwesasne Notes*, mid Winter, p. 30.

11. Stannard, *American Holocaust*, p.121.

12. David Wrone and Russell Nelson (eds.), *Who's the savage? A documentary history of the mistreatment of the Native North Americans* (Malabar: Robert Krieger Publishing, 1982), p. 82. Quote William James, *A full and correct account of the military occurrences of the late war between Great Britain and the United States of America* (2 vols., London: printed by the author, 1818), vol. 1, pp. 293–296.

13. John Terrell, *Land grab: The truth about the 'winning of the West'* (New York: Doubleday, 1972), p. 13.

14. Stoler, p. 85.

15. Ibid., p. 35.

16. From Cuneo, an Italian nobleman, quoted in Kirkpatrick Sale, *The conquest of paradise: Christopher Columbus and the Columbian legacy* (New York: Knopf, 1990), p. 140.

17. Wrone and Nelson, *Who's the savage?* p. 123. Cite U.S. Commissioner of Indian Affairs, *Annual Report for 1871* (Washington, D.C.: Government Printing Office, 1871), pp. 487–488.

18. Ibid., p. 97. Cite LeRoy R. Haven (ed.), *Ruxton of the Rockies* (Norman: University of Oklahoma Press, 1950), pp. 46–149.

19. Las Casas, p. 33.

20. *The Sand Creek Massacre: A documentary history,* pp. 129–130. Quotes Lieutenant James D. Cannon from "Report of the Secretary of War," 39th Congress, Second Session, Senate Executive Document 26, Washington, D.C., 1867. New York: Sol Lewis, 1973.

21. Catherine MacKinnon, Turning rape into pornography: Postmodern genocide, in *Ms. Magazine,* 4, no.1, p. 27 (emphasis added).

22. Undated promotional material from Public Relations: Mahoney/Wasserman and Associates, Los Angeles, Calif.

23. Quoted in Roy Harvey Pearce, *Savagism and civilization* (Baltimore: Johns Hopkins Press, 1965), p. 93.

24. Robert Heizer (ed.), *The destruction of California Indians* (Lincoln: University of Nebraska Press, 1993), p. 284.

25. James Rawls, *Indians of California,* p. 182.

26. See Annette Jaimes and Theresa Halsey, American Indian women: At the center of indigenous resistance in North America, in Annette Jaimes (ed.), *The state of Native America: Genocide, colonization, and resistance* (Boston: South End Press, 1992), pp. 311–344.

27. Mark Brunswick and Paul Klauda, Possible suspect in serial killings jailed in N. Mexico, in *Minneapolis Star and Tribune,* May 28, 1987, p. 1A.

28. Indian man being tried for rape with no evidence, in *Fargo Forum,* January 9, 1995.

29. Stoler, p. 69.

30. For further discussion on the relationship between bodily abuse and self-esteem, see *The courage to heal: A guide for women survivors of child sexual abuse,* edited by Ellen Bass and Laura Davis (New York: Harper & Row, 1988), esp. pp. 207–222; and Bonnie Burstow, *Radical feminist therapy* (London: Sage, 1992), esp. pp. 187–234.

31. Quoted in Celia Haig-Brown, *Resistance and renewal* (Vancouver: Tilacum, 1988), p. 108.

32. Chrystos, *Fugitive Colors* (Vancouver: Press Gang, 1995), p. 41.

33. Native American Women's Health and Education Resource Center, *Discrimination and the double whammy* (Lake Andes, S.Dak.: Native American Women's Health and Education Resource Center, 1990), pp. 2–3.

34. Michael Taussig, *Shamanism, colonialism and the wild man.* (Chicago: University of Chicago Press, 1987), p. 20.

35. Justine Smith (Cherokee), personal conversation, February 17, 1994.

36. Haunani Kay Trask, *From a native daughter: Colonialism and sovereignty in Hawai'i* (Monroe, Maine: Common Courage Press, 1993) pp. 185–194.

37. Andy Rooney, Indians have worse problems, *Chicago Tribune,* March 4, 1992.

38. Jim Lockhart, AIM protests film's spiritual misrepresentation, *News from Indian Country,* late September 1994, p. 10.

39. Shaman sentenced for sex abuse, *News from Indian Country,* mid-June 1996, p. 2A.

40. David Melmer, Sexual assault, *Indian Country Today,* April 30–May 7, 1996, p. 1.

41. Michael Pace in ibid.

42. Jorge Noriega, American Indian education in the United States: Indoctrination for subordination to colonialism, in *State of Native America,* p. 380.

43. Frederick Binder and David M. Reimers (eds.), *The way we lived* (Lexington, Mass.: D. C. Heath, 1982), p. 59. Quotes U.S. Bureau of Indian Affairs, "Rules for Schools," Annual Report of the Commissioner of Indian Affairs, 1890, Washington, D.C., pp. cxlvi, cl–clii.

44. Fran Leeper Buss, *Dignity: Lower income women tell of their lives and struggles* (Ann Arbor: University of Michigan Press, 1985), p. 156. For further accounts of the widespread nature of sexual and other abuse in boarding schools, see Native Horizons Treatment Center, *Sexual abuse handbook* (Hagersville, Ont.), pp. 61–68; The end of silence, *Maclean's,* vol. 105, no. 37, September 14, 1992, pp. 14, 16;

Jim deNomie, American Indian boarding schools: Elders remember, in *Aging News,* Winter 1990–91, pp. 2–6; David Wrone and Russell Nelson, *Who's the savage?* pp. 152–154, cite U.S. Congress, Senate, Subcommittee on Indian Affairs, *Survey of the conditions of the Indians in the United States,* Hearings before a subcommittee of the Committee on Indian Affairs, Senate, SR 79, 70th Congress, 2d session, 1929, pp. 428–429, 1021–1023, 2833–2835.

45. Goodbye BIA, Hello New Federalism, in *American Eagle,* vol. 2, no. 6, December 1994, p. 19. After the allegations of abuse became public, the BIA merely provided a counselor for the abused children who used his sessions with them to write a book.

46. Child sexual abuse in federal schools, in *The Ojibwe News,* January 17, 1990, p. 8.

47. Celia Haig-Brown, *Resistance and renewal,* pp. 14–15.

48. Native Horizons Treatment Center, *Sexual abuse handbook,* p. 66. Quotes *The Province,* July 19, 1989, and *Vancouver Sun,* March 17, 1990.

49. Troy Armstrong, Michael Guilfoyle, and Ada Pecos Melton, Native American delinquency: An overview of prevalence, causes, and correlates, in Marianne O. Nielsen and Robert A. Silverman (eds.), *Native Americans, crime, and justice* (Boulder, Colo.: Westview Press, 1996), p. 81.

50. James Zion and Elsie Zion, Hazho's Sokee'—Stay together nicely: Domestic violence under Navajo common law, in Nielsen and Silverman (eds.), *Native Americans, crime, and justice,* p. 106.

51. Rupert Ross, *Return to the teachings* (London: Penguin Books, 1997), p. 18.

52. Elizabeth Barker, The paradox of punishment in light of the anticipatory role of abolitionism, in Herman Bianchi and Rene van Swaaningern (eds.), *Abolitionism* (Amsterdam: Free University Press, 1986), p. 91.

53. Ross, *Return to the teachings,* p.38.

54. Rupert Ross, Leaving our white eyes behind: The sentencing of native accused, in Nielsen and Silverman (eds.), *Native Americans, crime, and justice,* p. 168.

55. Luana Ross, *Inventing the savage: The social construction of Native American criminality* (Austin: University of Texas Press, 1998).

56. Steven Donziger, *The real war on crime* (New York: HarperCollins, 1996), p. 42, 162; Samuel Walker, *Sense and nonsense about crime and drugs* (Belmont, Calif.: Wadsworth, 1998); Elliott Currie, *Crime and punishment in America* (New York: Metropolitan Books, 1998).

57. Quoted in Walker, *Sense and nonsense about crime and drugs,* p. 139.

58. Steve Box and Chris Hale, Economic crisis and the rising prisoner population in England and Wales, in *Crime and social justice,* 1982, vol. 17, pp. 20–35. Mark Colvin, Controlling the surplus population: The latent functions of imprisonment and welfare in late U.S. capitalism, in B. D. MacLean (ed), *The political economy of crime* (Scarborough: Prentice-Hall Canada, 1986). Ivan Jankovic, Labour market and imprisonment, in *Crime and social justice,* 1977, vol. 8 pp. 17–31.

59. Walker, *Sense and nonsense about crime and drugs,* p. 130.

60. Currie, *Crime and punishment in America,* p. 59.

61. Fay Honey Koop, On radical feminism and abolition, in *We who would take no prisoners: Selections from the Fifth International Conference on Penal Abolition* (Vancouver: Collective Press, 1993), p. 592.

62. Ines Hernandez-Avila, In praise of insubordination, or what makes a good woman go bad?, In Emilie Buchwald, Pamela R. Fletcher, and Martha Roth (eds.), *Transforming a rape culture* (Minneapolis: Milkweed, 1993), pp. 388–389.

T H I R T Y - N I N E

◆◆◆

On Becoming Anti-Rapist

Haki R. Madhubuti

There are mobs & strangers in us who scream of the women we wanted and will get as if the women are ours for the taking.

. . . Male acculturation (or a better description would be males' "seasoning") is antifemale, antiwomanist/ feminist, and antireason when it comes to women's equal measure and place in society. This flawed socialization of men is not confined to the West but permeates most, if not all, cultures in the modern world. Most men have been taught to treat, respond, listen, and react to women from a male's point of view. Black men are not an exception here; we, too, are imprisoned with an intellectual/spiritual/sexual understanding of women based upon antiquated male culture and sexist orientation—or should I say mis-education. For example, sex or sexuality is hardly ever discussed, debated, or taught to black men in a nonthreatening or nonembarrassing family or community setting.

Men's view of women, specifically black women outside of the immediate family, is often one of "bitch," "my woman," "ho," or any number of designations that demean and characterize black women as less than whole and productive persons. Our missteps toward an understanding of women are compounded by the cultural environments where much of the talk of women takes place: street corners, locker rooms, male clubs, sporting events, bars, military service, business trips, playgrounds, workplaces, basketball courts, etc. Generally, women are not discussed on street corners or in bars as intellectual or culturally compatible partners. Rather the discussion focuses on what is the best way to "screw" or control them.

These are, indeed, learning environments that traditionally are not kind to women. The point of view that is affirmed all too often is the ownership of women. We are taught to see women as commodities and/or objects for men's sexual releases and sexual fantasies; also, most women are considered "inferiors" to men and thus are not to be respected or trusted. Such thinking is encouraged and legitimized by our culture and transmitted via institutional structures (churches, workplaces), mass media (*Playboy* and *Penthouse*), misogynist music (rap and mainstream), and R-rated and horror films that use exploitative images of women. And of course there are the ever-present, tall, trim, "Barbie-doll" women featured in advertising for everything from condoms to the latest diet "cures." Few men have been taught, really taught, from birth—to the heart, to the gut—to respect, value, or even, on occasion, to honor women. Only until very recently has it been confirmed in Western culture that rape (unwelcomed/ uninvited sex) is criminal, evil, and antihuman. . . .

Human proximity defines relationships. Exceptions should be noted, but in most cultures and most certainly within the black/African worldview, family and extended family ties are honored and respected. One's sexual personhood in a healthy culture is nurtured, respected, and protected. In trying to get a personal fix here, that is, an understanding of the natural prohibitions against rape, think of one's own personhood being violated. Think of one's own family subjected to this act. Think of the enslavement of African people; it was common to have breeding houses on most plantations where one's great-great-grandmothers were forced to open their insides for the sick satisfaction of white slave owners, overseers, and enslaved black men. This forced sexual penetration of African women led to the creation of mixed-race people here and around the world. There is a saying in South Africa that the colored race did not exist until nine months after white men arrived. This demeaning of black women and other women is amplified in today's culture, where it is not uncommon for young men to proclaim that "pussy is a penny a pound." However, we are told that such a statement is not meant for one's own mother, grandmother, sister, daughter, aunt, niece, close relative, or extended family. Yet the point must be made rather emphatically that incest (family rape) is on the rise in this country. Incest between adults and children is often not revealed until the children are adults. At that point their lives are so confused and damaged that many continue incestuous acts. . . .

Part of the answer is found in the question: Is it possible or realistic to view all women as precious persons? Selective memory plays an important role here. Most men who rape are seriously ill and improperly educated. They do not view women outside of their "protected zone" as precious blood, do not see them as extended family, and do not see them as individuals or independent persons to be respected as most men respect other men. Mental illness or brain mismanagement blocks out reality, shattering and negating respect for self and others, especially the others of which one wishes to take advantage. Power always lurks behind rape. Rape is an act of aggression that asserts power by defaming and defiling. Most men have been taught—either directly or indirectly—to solve problems with force. Such force may be verbal or physical. Violence is the answer that is promoted in media everywhere, from Saturday morning cartoons to everyday television to R-rated films. Popular culture has a way of trivializing reality and confusing human expectations, especially with regard to relationships between men and women. For too many black people, the popular has been internalized. In many instances, the media define us, including our relationships to each other. . . .

The brutality of everyday life continues to confirm the necessity for caring men and women to confront inhuman acts that cloud and prevent wholesome development. Much of what is defined as sexual "pleasure" today comes at the terrible expense of girls and often boys. To walk Times Square or any number of big-city playgrounds after dark is to view how loudly the popular, throwaway culture has trapped, corrupted, and sexually abused too many of our children. In the United States the sexual abuse of runaway children, and children sentenced to foster care and poorly supervised orphanages, is nothing less than scandalous. The proliferation of battered women's shelters and the most recent revelation of the sexual abuse of women incarcerated in the nation's prisons only underscores the prevailing view of women by a substantial number of men, as sex objects for whatever sick acts that enter their minds.

Such abuse of children is not confined to the United States. Ron O'Grady, coordinator of the International Campaign to End Child Prostitution in Asiatic Tourism, fights an uphill battle to highlight the physical and economic maltreatment of children. Murray Kempton reminds us in his essay "A New Colonialism" (*New York Review of Books,* November 19, 1992) of Thailand's "supermarkets for the purchases of small and disposable bodies." He goes on to state that

tourism is central to Thailand's developmental efforts; and the attractions of its ancient culture compare but meagerly to the compelling pull its brothels exercise upon foreign visitors. The government does its duty to the economy by encouraging houses of prostitution and pays its debt to propriety with its insistence that no more than 10,000 children work there. Private observers concerned with larger matters than the good name of public officials estimate the real total of child prostitutes in Thailand at 200,000.

The hunters . . . of children find no border closed. They have ranged into South China carrying television sets to swap one per child. The peasants who cursed the day a useless girl was born know better now: they can sell her for consumers overseas and be consumers themselves. Traffickers less adventurous stay at home and contrive travel agencies that offer cheap trips to Kuala Lumpur that end up with sexual enslavement in Japan or Malaysia.

That this state of affairs is not better known speaks loudly and clearly to the devaluation of female children. The war in Sarajevo, Bosnia, and Herzegovina again highlights the status of women internationally. In the rush toward ethnic cleansing and narrow and exclusive nationalism, Serbian soldiers have been indicted for murder and other war crimes. The story of one such soldier, Borislav Herak, is instructive. According to an article by John F. Burnes in the *New York Times* (November 27, 1992) entitled "A Serbian Fighter's Trial of Brutality," Mr. Herak and other soldiers were given the go-ahead to rape and kill Muslim women:

> The indictment lists 29 individual murders between June and October, including eight rape-murders of Muslim women held prisoner in an abandoned motel and cafe outside Vogosca, seven miles north of Sarajevo, where, Mr. Herak said, he and other Serbian fighters were encouraged to rape women and then take them away to kill them in hilltops and other deserted places.
>
> The indictment also covers the killings of at least 220 other Muslim civilians in which Mr. Herak has confessed to being a witness or taking part, many of them women and children. (Also see the January 4, 1993, issue of *Newsweek*.)

Much in the lives of women is not music or melody but is their dancing to the beat of the unhealthy and often killing drums of men and male teenagers. Rape is not the fault of women; however, in a male-dominated world, the victims are often put on the defensive and forced to rationalize their gender and their personhood.

> *Rape is not a reward for warriors*
> *it is war itself*
> *a deep, deep tearing, a dislocating of*
> *the core of the womanself.*
> *rape rips heartlessly*
> *soul from spirit,*
> *obliterating colors from beauty and body*
> *replacing melody and music with*
> *rat venom noise and uninterrupted intrusion and*
> *   beatings.*

The brutality of rape is universal. Most modern cultures—European, American, African, Asian, religious, and secular—grapple with this crime. Rarely is there discussion, and, more often than not, women are discouraged from being a part of the debates and edicts. Rape is cross-cultural. I have not visited, heard of, or read about any rape-free societies. The war against women is international. Daily, around the world, women fight for a little dignity and their earned place in the world. . . .

As a man of Afrikan descent, I would like to think that Afrikans have some special insight, enlightened hearts, or love in us that calms us in such times of madness. But my romanticism is shattered every day as I observe black communities across this land. The number of rapes reported and unreported in our communities is only the latest and most painful example of how far we have drifted from beauty. However, it is seldom that I have hurt more than when I learned about the "night of terror" that occurred in Meru, Kenya, on July 13, 1991, at the St. Kizito boarding school. A high school protest initiated by the boys, in which the girls refused to join, resulted in a night of death, rapes, and beatings unparalleled in modern Kenya, in Africa or in the world. . . .

A growing part of the answer is that we men, as difficult as it may seem, must view all women (no matter who they are—race, culture, religion, or nationality aside) as extended family. The question is, and I know that I am stretching: Would we rape our mothers, grandmothers, sisters, or other female relatives, or even give such acts a thought? Can we extend this attitude to all women? Therefore we must:

1. Teach our sons that it is their responsibility to be anti-rapist; that is, they must be counter-rapist in thought, conversations, raps, organizations, and actions.

2. Teach our daughters how to defend themselves and maintain an uncompromising stance toward men and boys.

3. Understand that being a counter-rapist is honorable, manly, and necessary for a just society.

4. Understand that anti-rapist actions are part of the black tradition; being an anti-rapist is in keeping with the best Afrikan culture and with Afrikan family and extended family configurations. Even in times of war we were known to

honor and respect the personhood of children and women.

5. Be glowing examples of men who are fighting to treat women as equals and to be fair and just in associations with women. This means at the core that families as now defined and constructed must continually be reassessed. In today's economy most women, married and unmarried, must work. We men must encourage them in their work and must be intimately involved in rearing children and doing housework.

6. Understand that just as men are different from one another, women also differ; therefore we must try not to stereotype women into the limiting and often debilitating expectations of men. We must encourage and support them in their searching and development.

7. Be unafraid of independent, intelligent, and self-reliant women. And by extension, understand that intelligent women think for themselves and may not want to have sex with a particular man. This is a woman's prerogative and is not a comment on anything else other than the fact that she does not want to have sex.

8. Be bold and strong enough to stop other men (friends or strangers) from raping and to intervene in a rape in process with the fury and destruction of a hurricane against the rapist.

9. Listen to women. Listen to women, especially to womanist/feminist/Pan-Africanist philosophies of life. Also, study the writings of women, especially black women.

10. Act responsibly in response to the listening and studying. Be a part of and support anti-rape groups for boys and men. Introduce anti-rape discussion into men's groups and organizations.

11. Never stop growing, and understand that growth is limited and limiting without the input of intelligent women.

12. Learn to love. Study love. Even if one is at war, love and respect, respect and love must conquer, if there is to be a sane and livable world. Rape is anti-love, anti-respect. Love is not easy. One does not fall in love but *grows* into love.

We can put to rest the rape problem in one generation if its eradication is as important to us as our cars, jobs, careers, sport-games, beer, and quest for power. However, the women who put rape on the front burners must continue to challenge us and their own cultural training, and position themselves so that they and their messages are not compromised or ignored.

A significant few of their
fathers, brothers, husbands, sons
and growing strangers
are willing to unleash harm onto the earth
and spill blood in the eyes
of
maggots in running shoes
who do not know the sounds of birth
or respect the privacy of the human form

If we are to be just in our internal rebuilding, we must challenge tradition and cultural ways of life that relegate women to inferior status in the home, church/mosque/temple, workplace, political life, and education. Men are not born rapists; we are taught very subtly, often in unspoken ways, that women are ours for the taking. Generally, such teachings begin with the family. Enlightenment demands fairness, impartiality, and vision; it demands confrontation of outdated definitions and acceptance of fair and just resolutions. One's sex, race, social class, or wealth should not determine entitlements or justice. If we are honest, men must be in the forefront of eradicating sex stereotypes in all facets of private and public life. I think that being honest, as difficult and as self-incriminating as it may be, is the only way that we can truly liberate ourselves. If men can liberate themselves (with the help of women) from the negative aspects of the culture that produced them, maybe a just, fair, good, and liberated society is possible in our lifetime.

The liberation of the male psyche from preoccupation with domination, power hunger, control, and absolute rightness requires an honest and fair assessment of patriarchal culture. This requires commitment to deep study, combined with a willingness for painful, uncomfortable, and often shocking change. We are not where we should be. That is why rape exists; why families are so easily formed and just as easily dissolved; why children are confused and abused; why our elderly are discarded, abused, and exploited; and why teenage boys create substitute families (gangs) that terrorize their own communities.

I remain an optimistic realist, primarily because I love life and most of what it has to offer. I often look at my children and tears come to my eyes because I realize how blessed I am to be their father. My wife and the other women in my life are special because they know that they are special and have taken it upon themselves, at great cost, to actualize their dreams, making what was considered for many of them unthinkable a few years ago a reality today. If we men, of all races, cultures, and continents would just examine the inequalities of power in our own families, businesses, and political and spiritual institutions, and decide today to reassess and reconfigure them in consultation with the women in our lives, we would all be doing the most fundamental corrective act of a counter-rapist. . . .

◆◆◆

My Vagina Was My Village

Eve Ensler

My vagina was green, water soft pink fields, cow mooing sun resting sweet boyfriend touching lightly with soft piece of blond straw.

There is something between my legs. I do not know what it is. I do not know where it is. I do not touch. Not now. Not anymore. Not since.

My vagina was chatty, can't wait, so much, so much saying, words talking, can't quit trying, can't quit saying, oh yes, oh yes.

Not since I dream there's a dead animal sewn in down there with thick black fishing line. And the bad dead animal smell cannot be removed. And its throat is slit and it bleeds through all my summer dresses.

My vagina singing all girl songs, all goat bells ringing songs, all wild autumn field songs, vagina songs, vagina home songs.

Not since the soldiers put a long thick rifle inside me. So cold, the steel rod canceling my heart. Don't know whether they're going to fire it or shove it through my spinning brain. Six of them, monstrous doctors with black masks shoving bottles up me too. There were sticks, and the end of a broom.

My vagina swimming river water, clean spilling water over sun-baked stones over stone clit, clit stones over and over.

Not since I heard the skin tear and made lemon screeching sounds, not since a piece of my vagina came off in my hand, a part of the lip, now one side of the lip is completely gone.

My vagina. A live wet water village. My vagina my hometown.

Not since they took turns for seven days smelling like feces and smoked meat, they left their dirty sperm inside me. I became a river of poison and pus and all the crops died, and the fish.

> My vagina a live wet water village.
> They invaded it. Butchered it and burned it
>   down.
> I do not touch now.
> Do not visit.
> I live someplace else now.
> I don't know where that is.

7

♦♦♦

Relationships, Families, and Households

Losing a close friend, asking for support from family and friends at difficult times, falling in love, moving in with a roommate or partner, holding your newborn baby for the first time, breaking up with a partner of many years, struggling to understand a teenage son or daughter, and helping your mother to die with dignity and in peace are commonplace life events. These ties between us, as human beings, define the very texture of our personal lives. They are a source of much happiness, affirmation, and personal growth as well as frustration, misunderstanding, anxiety, and, sometimes, misery. This chapter looks at personal relationships—between women and men, women and women, parents and children—and the ways in which an idealized notion of family masks the reality of family life for many people in the United States. We argue that families—however they are defined—need to be able to care for their members and that specific forms are much less important than the quality of the relationships between people.

Defining Ourselves Through Connections with Others

As suggested in Chapter 2, personal and family relationships are central to individual development, the definition of self, and the ongoing development of our identities. This happens across cultures, though it may not take the same form or have the same meaning in all cultural settings. It involves relying on others when we are very young and later negotiating with them for material care, nurturance, and security; defining our own voice, space, independence, and sense of closeness to others; and learning about ourselves, our family and cultural heritage, ideas of right and wrong, practical aspects of life, and how to negotiate the world outside the home. In the family we learn about socially defined **gender roles:** what it means to be a daughter, brother, wife, or father, and what is expected of us. Family resources, including material possessions, emotional bonds, cultural connections and language, and status in the wider community, are also important for the experiences and opportunities they offer children.

How we are treated by parents and siblings and our observations of adult relationships during childhood provide the early foundation for our own adult relationships. Friends and family members may offer rules for dating etiquette. Magazine features and advice columns coach us in how to catch a man (or woman, in the case of lesbian magazines) and how to keep him or her happy once we have. Jaclyn Geller (2001, p. 10), who teaches writing and literature, cites a "plethora of dating books" published in the 1980s and '90s by women for a mass women's readership. A sampling of titles over the past fifteen years includes *How to Get a Man to Make a Commitment or Know When He Never Will* (Barnes and Clarke 1986), *If I'm So Wonderful Why Am I Still Single? Ten Strategies That Will Change Your Love Life Forever* (Page 1988), *The Best Places to Meet Good Men* (Lederman 1991), *The Savvy Woman's Success Bible: How to Find the Right Job, the Right Man, and the Right Life* (Santi-Flaherty 1997), *How to Get Married After Thirty-five: The Game Plan for Love* (Rosenberg 1988), *He's Not All That! How to Attract the Good Guys* (Carle 2000), and *Date Like a Man: What Men Know about Dating and Are Afraid You'll Find Out* (Moore and Gould 2001). The ups and downs of personal relationships are the material of countless magazines, TV talk shows, movies, sit-coms, novels, and pop music. Many women value themselves in terms of whether they can attract and hold a partner. Whole sections of bookstores are given over to books and manuals that analyze relationship problems and teach "relationship skills"; counselors and therapists make a living helping us sort out our personal lives. Fairy tales and romantic stories may end with the characters living happily ever after, but the reality of personal relationships is often very different. Regardless of sexual orientation, we are all socialized in a heterosexual and heterosexist world, as argued by Adrienne Rich (1986a).

Marriage, Domestic Partnerships, and Personal Relationships

Young people in the United States currently face fundamental contradictions concerning marriage and family life. Marriage is highly romanticized: The partners marry for love and are expected to live happily ever after. Love marriages are a relatively recent phenomenon. Although most families in the United States no longer arrange a daughter's marriage, they usually have clear expectations of the kind of man they want her to fall in love with. The ideal of marriage as a committed partnership seems to hold across sexual orientation, with women looking for Mr. or Ms. Right. Marriage and motherhood are often thought to be an essential part of a woman's life, the status to strive for, even if she chooses to keep her own name or rarely uses the coveted title Mrs. People may not refer to unmarried women as "old maids" or "on the shelf" as much as in the past, but there is often still a stigma attached to being single in many cultural groups if a woman is still unmarried after a certain age.

Women marry for many reasons, following cultural and religious precepts. They may believe that marriage will make their relationship more secure or provide a stronger foundation for their children. There are material benefits in terms of taxes, health insurance, pension rights, ease of inheritance, and immigration status. It is the conventional and respected way of publicly affirming one's commitment to a partner and being supported in this commitment by family and friends, as well as societal institutions. However, under the excitement and romance of the wedding and despite the fact that many partnerships are thriving, marriage as an institution is taking a buffeting, mainly because of changes in the economy and changing ideas of women's role in society (Coontz 1997; Risman 1998; Skolnick 1991).

Contradictions Surrounding the Institution of Marriage

As marriage has become less necessary for women, the wedding industry has grown enormously (Geller 2001; Ingraham 1999). Weddings are a mainstay of popular culture. A very small sampling of successful wedding films includes *Four Weddings and a Funeral, Monsoon Wedding, My Big Fat Greek Wedding, The Wedding Banquet,* and *The Wedding Singer.* TV shows also include weddings, especially as the climax of a series. Weddings of movie stars, public figures, and royalty are featured in media photo spreads that make use of the "fairy tale formula familiar to many—especially women—since early childhood"

(Ingraham 1999, p. 127). Magazines like *Bride's*, wedding experts and managers, bridal-gown designers, florists, jewelers, photographers, and stationery specialists are all part of a highly profitable wedding industry. The average couple in the United States spends $19,000 on their wedding (Ingraham 1999, p. 4). Note that this current emphasis on weddings comes at a time when the institution of heterosexuality is under pressure from feminists and the lesbian, gay, bisexual, and transgender movement. Recent writings on marriage by heterosexual women reflect these contradictions, and also affirm the authors' decisions to marry (Cohen 2001; Corral and Miya-Jervis 2001; Nissinen 2000).

Compared with their mothers or grandmothers, fewer U.S. women are marrying, and many of those who do are marrying later, though they may be involved in committed relationships that last longer than many marriages. In 1998, 46 percent of women between the ages of 15 and 39 had never married (U.S. Bureau of the Census 1998). From 1970 to 2000, the proportion of women who never married doubled for women aged 20 to 24 (from 36 percent to 73 percent) and tripled for those aged 30 to 34 (from 6 percent to 22 percent) (U.S. Department of Commerce News 2001). Though some research suggests that the vast majority of young people want to marry, a growing number of them see marriage as financially unattainable for a couple who might have to depend on the income of a man without a college degree. Others oppose marriage as the institutionalization of social and economic inequalities between men and women. As Naomi Wolf notes in Reading 23, under English and subsequently U.S. law, a husband and wife were one person in law; married women and children were literally the property of their husbands and fathers. Not for nothing was it called wed*lock*. In Reading 42, Jaclyn Geller gives a detailed history of marriage as a patriarchal institution between fundamentally unequal partners. She views marriage as the paradigmatic institution that makes heterosexuality appear natural and "normal," and as a heterosexual woman, she vehemently opposes it. Sociologist Pepper Schwartz (1994) advocates peer marriage—a marriage of equal companions who collaborate to produce "profound intimacy and mutual respect" (p. 2), a model that many young women embrace. Yet, Geller argues, at root, marriage is still a legal contract, though intertwined with social, economic, religious,

and emotional aspects. Only a representative of the state can legally marry heterosexual couples, for example. In 1993 rape in marriage became a crime in all fifty states. In seventeen states and the District of Columbia, there are no exemptions for husbands from rape prosecution, while thirty-three states recognize marital rape only under certain circumstances (National Clearinghouse on Marital and Date Rape 1998), as mentioned in Chapter 6.

Personal Relationships: Living in Different Worlds?

Other commentators and theorists assume a basic inequality between men and women in personal relationships, though they do not critique the institution of heterosexuality. Therapist John Gray, the author of several best-sellers, including *Men Are from Mars, Women Are from Venus* (1992) argues that men and women are socialized differently and have different styles of communication (1994). He assumes that women as a group are naturally giving and caring and that men as a group are "wired up" to be providers, an assumption we reject, favoring a social constructionist view of gender as something learned rather than innate (see Chapter 1). Sociolinguist Deborah Tannen (1990) bases her work on the premise that boys and girls grow up in essentially different cultures. She analyzes everyday conversations between men and women to make sense of the "seemingly senseless misunderstandings that haunt our relationships" (p. 13). She argues that, for men, conversations are negotiations about independence; for women they are about connection and closeness. Partners in heterosexual relationships, she notes, are "living with asymmetry," and each can benefit from learning the other's conversational styles and needs (p. 287).

Sexuality is one of the few recognized ways in this society for people to make intimate connections, especially for men, who are not socialized to express emotions easily. In her groundbreaking research into men's and women's attitudes to sexuality and love, Shere Hite (1994) found that for her male respondents, dating and marriage are primarily about sex and that they often shop around for varied sexual experiences. For Hite's women respondents, expressing emotion through sexual intimacy and setting up a home were usually much more important than

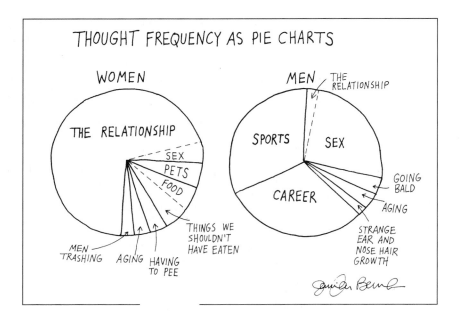

they were for men. Hite attributes much of the frustration in personal relationships to these very different approaches. She argues that many women give up on their hope for an emotionally satisfying relationship and settle for companionability with a male partner, while devoting much of their emotional energy elsewhere: to their children, work, or other interests. At the same time, she sees women as "revolutionary agents of change" in relationships, working with men to renegotiate this intimate part of their lives. Naomi Wolf's discussion of radical heterosexuality (Chapter 4) is also relevant here.

Personal relationships, whether between women and men or between women and women, always include an element of power, though in more **egalitarian** relationships this shifts back and forth. Social psychologist Hilary Lips (1991) describes this power imbalance in terms of "the principle of least interest" (p. 57), a concept taken from social exchange theory. The person who has the least interest in a relationship—in a heterosexual relationship, often the man—has the most power in it. The least-interested person's moods, wants, and needs will tend to be dominant. This principle is also applicable at the macro level. As a group, women learn that it is our job to catch a man, as mentioned at the beginning of this chapter. In dating relationships we often work on the principle of greatest interest, the place of least

power. This approach is also useful in thinking about gay and lesbian relationships.

Gay Marriage and Domestic Partnership

Through concerted lobbying and major national demonstrations, lesbians and gay men have emphasized the validity of their families. More gay and lesbian couples are celebrating their relationships in commitment ceremonies, and the *New York Times*, for example, publishes these announcements together with wedding announcements. Demands for gay marriage in the interests of equal treatment for lesbians, gay men, and heterosexual couples provide an interesting counterweight to feminist critiques of marriage as inherently patriarchal. Efforts to recognize same-sex marriages in Alaska and Hawai'i were defeated in state ballot measures. To date, thirty-six states have passed laws banning same-sex marriage (Human Rights Campaign Foundation 2002). In 1996 the U.S. Congress also passed an anti–gay marriage bill, the Defense of Marriage Act, that excludes same-sex couples from receiving federal protections and rights of marriage. Even if states allowed gay marriage, the Defense of Marriage Act would block gay partners from receiving federal benefits. Not all lesbians or gay men want to marry, understanding that "legalizing gay and lesbian marriage will not 'dismantle the legal structure of gender in every marriage'" (Polikoff 1993; also Gomez 2001).

Lesbians and gay men, together with heterosexual couples who have chosen not to marry, have campaigned for the benefits of "domestic partnership"—to be covered by a partner's health insurance, for example, or to be able to draw the partner's pension if he or she dies. As of July 11, 2002, 145 of the Fortune 500 companies offered domestic-partnership health benefits for same-sex partners, including AT&T, Chase Manhattan Bank, Chevron, Costco Wholesale, Mobil, Microsoft, Viacom, and Wells Fargo (American Civil Liberties Union [ACLU] 2002a). The list of state and local governments and academic institutions offering domestic-partnership benefits continues to grow. In a landmark decision on December 20, 1999, the Vermont Supreme Court ruled in *Baker v. Vermont* that lesbian and gay couples are entitled to all of the same "common benefits and protections" that the law gives to married couples (ACLU 1999).

College-educated women in their twenties, thirties, and forties have grown up with much more public discussion of women's rights than did their mothers and with expanded opportunities for education and professional work. Those who work in corporate or professional positions have more financial security in their own right than did middle-class housewives of the 1950s, for example, and are less interested in what sociologist Judith Stacey (1996) calls "the patriarchal bargain." Older women, born in the 1920s and brought up during the Great Depression of the 1930s, often valued material security with a man who would be a good provider above emotional closeness or sexual satisfaction. Nowadays, many women expect much more intimacy in personal relationships than did their mothers.

As we grow as individuals, our personal relationships may also develop in ways that continue to sustain us. Sometimes they cannot support our changing needs and concerns, and we may have to make the difficult decision to leave. Making a marriage or committed relationship "work" involves some combination of loving care, responsibility, communication, patience, humor, and luck. Material circumstances may have a significant impact, especially over the longer term. Having money, food, personal security, a home, reliable and affordable child care, and additional care for elderly relatives; being willing and able to move for a job or a chance to study; and having good health are examples of favorable circumstances. Negative factors that especially affect young African American women and Latinas are the high unemployment rates for men of color and the fact that roughly 30 percent of young African American and Latino men between 18 and 25 are caught up in the criminal justice system.

The couple may look to each other as friends, partners, and lovers and expect that together they can provide for each other's material and emotional needs and fulfill their dreams. In addition to experiencing the joy and satisfaction of sharing life on a daily basis, the partnership may also bear the brunt of work pressures, money worries, changing gender roles, or stress from a violent community, as well as difficulties due to personal misunderstandings, different priorities, or differing views of what it means to be a husband or a wife.

Half of U.S. marriages end in divorce, usually initiated by women, for reasons of incompatibility, infidelity, mistreatment, economic problems, or sexual problems (Kurz 1995). Many women experience the breakup with a mixture of fear, excitement, relief, and a sense of failure. Most divorced or widowed men marry within a year of the end of their previous relationship, often marrying women younger than themselves. Women wait longer to remarry, and fewer do. The majority of older men are married, while the majority of older women are widows. Being old and alone is something that women often fear, though some older women feel good about their relative autonomy, especially if they are comfortable financially and have support from family members or friends.

Motherhood and Parenting

Because women are daughters, we all have some perspective on motherhood through the experience of our own mothers or other women who mothered us. Many people regard motherhood as the ultimate female experience and disapprove of women who do not want to be mothers, especially if they are married. Magazines and advertising images show happy, smiling mothers who dote on their children and buy them their favorite foods, cute clothes, toys, videos, CDs, and so forth.

Like marriage, motherhood is also undergoing change. Generally, women in more affluent families have fewer children, across all racial groups. Roughly a third of all babies born in the United States are to unmarried women. Percentages vary considerably by race. Far fewer Chinese American and Japanese American mothers are unmarried (6.5 percent and 10 percent, respectively), compared to Native American and Puerto Rican women (58 and 61 percent) (Ventura et al. 1999, pp. 38–39). More African American and Native American women are likely to have a child die in infancy, compared to White women, Latinas, and Asian Americans. Sharon Olds, María Hinojosa, Carol Gill and Larry Voss, and Ann Filemyr describe varied experiences of parenting (Readings 41, 43, 45, 46, respectively; also see Reading 50 in Chapter 8). Rachel Aber Schlesinger (Reading 44) writes about the geographical and cultural contexts that shaped the lives of Jewish grandmothers who migrated to North America and about their role in the transmission of culture to their grandchildren, who live in a very different time and place.

More and more women are choosing not to have children or are having them later. In 1960, 80 percent of women between 25 and 29 years old had children. In 1996, this figure had dropped to 57 percent, and in the next age group (30 to 34 years) 26 percent of women had not birthed a child (U.S. Bureau of the Census 1998). Most of these women are childless on purpose, despite the idea, popularized in the media, that women are controlled by a "biological clock," ticking away the years when conception is possible. Many of these women describe themselves as child-free rather than childless, highlighting that this is a positive choice for them (Bartlett 1994; Ireland 1993; Morrell 1994; Reti 1992; Safe 1996). They challenge the idea that women must have children to be fulfilled; they prefer instead to focus on intimate relationships, friendships, work, travel, community involvements, and connections with other people's children.

Rearing children is hard work, often tedious and repetitive, requiring humor and patience. Many women experience contradictory emotions, including fear, resentment, inadequacy, and anger about motherhood despite societal idealization of it and their own hopes or expectations that they will find it fulfilling.

The Social Construction of Motherhood

Adrienne Rich (1986b) has argued that it is not motherhood itself that is oppressive to women, but the way our society constructs motherhood. A con- temporary media image of a young mother—usually White and middle-class—with immaculate hair and makeup, wearing a chic business suit, briefcase in one hand and toddler in the other, may define an ideal for many young women. But it also sets a standard that is virtually unattainable without causing the mother to come apart at the seams—that is, in the absence of a generous budget for convenience foods, restaurant meals, work clothes, dry cleaning, hairdressing, and good-quality child care. Despite contradictions and challenges, many women are finding joy and affirmation in motherhood (Abbey and O'Reilly 1998; Blakely 1994; Gore and Lavendar 2001; Hays 1996; Jetter, Orleck, and Taylor 1997; Kline 1997; Meyers 2001).

Motherhood has been defined differently at different times. During World War II, for example, when women were needed to work in munitions factories and shipyards in place of men drafted overseas, companies often provided housing, canteens, and child care to support these working women (Hayden 1981). After the war women were no longer needed in these jobs, and such facilities were largely discontinued. Psychologists began to talk about the central importance of a mother's care for the healthy physical and emotional development of children (Bowlby 1963). Invoking the notion of maternal instinct, some asserted that a mother's care is qualitatively different from that of others and that only a mother's love will do. Mothers who are not sufficiently "present" can be blamed for their children's problems. Ironically, mothers who are too present, said to be overidentified with their children and a source of negative pressure, are also blamed.

Blame It on the Mother

Mothers have been blamed for damaging their children psychologically, for bringing up children in poverty, for being lesbians, for marrying the wrong men, for divorce, for having children too young, for working outside the home, and for not working outside the home (Ladd-Taylor and Umansky 1998). In 1999, 10 million preschoolers had mothers in the paid workforce. But, according to syndicated columnist Ellen Goodman (1999), "the cultural consensus still says that professional mothers should be home with the kids while welfare mothers should be out working." Psychologist Elizabeth Harvey's (1999) research on children aged 3 to 12 showed that those whose mothers were in the paid workforce during the first three years were *not* significantly different in terms of behavior, cognitive development, self-esteem, and academic achievement compared with those whose mothers were at home. Any slight differences disappeared by the time the children were of school age.

Despite the fact that there are more mothers of young children in the paid workforce today than ever before, working mothers, especially women of color, risk being called unfit and perhaps losing their children to foster homes or state agencies if they cannot maintain some conventionally approved standard of family life. Throughout the 1990s, a series of news reports describing low-quality child-care facilities, including some cases in which children were said to have been sexually abused, contributed to the anxiety of working mothers. Cultural ideas about who makes a bad mother are most germane to custody cases. In 1994, for example, a full-time Michigan university student lost custody of her child because the judge decided that she would not be sufficiently available to care for the child properly. The father was awarded custody, even though his mother would be the one to take care of the child because he worked full time. This decision was overturned on appeal. But in a 1996 case involving a lesbian mother, a Florida appeals court judge ruled that the father—who had served eight years in prison for murdering his first wife—would make a better parent than the mother (Navarro 1996).

Motherhood has been a persistent rationale for the unequal treatment of women in terms of access to education and well-paid, professional work, though it has not impeded the employment of African American women, for example, as domestics and nannies in White people's homes or of White working-class women in factories. Not all of today's older women were able to choose whether or not to stay out of the paid workforce when their children were young, despite the popular and scholarly rhetoric advocating full-time motherhood. We take up the issue of juggling home and paid work in the next chapter.

Most women spend seventeen years of their lives, on average, taking care of children and eighteen years looking after their elderly parents or their husband's parents (Gould 1997). In reality these periods overlap, usually when the children are in their teens. An additional factor complicating daily life is the high divorce rate, which means that parents and stepparents are involved in ongoing negotiations over shared child-care arrangements—often a source of hostility and stress. Women always suffer a serious drop in their standard of living immediately after divorce—hence the saying, "Poverty is only a divorce away"—whereas men's standard of living goes up (Peterson 1996). Usually mothers retain custody of the children even though fathers may see them on weekends or during school vacations. Roughly 50 percent of divorced fathers pay child support. Those who do not pay are often unemployed or in low-wage jobs. Researchers Marcia Boumil and Joel Friedman (1996) estimate that "complete and regular child support payments are received in less than 50 percent of the cases where there is court-ordered child support" (p. 108). Children are usually affected emotionally and educationally by the ups and downs of parents' marital difficulties. Though a divorce may bring some resolution, children may have to adjust to a new home, school, neighborhood, a lowered standard of living, or a whole new family set-up complete with stepparent, and stepbrothers or sisters. Most children suffer emotionally as a result of divorce but recover their equilibrium within eighteen months (Stewart et al. 1997), and the large majority of children of divorced parents grow up socially and psychologically well-adjusted (Hetherington and Clingempeel 1992; Hetherington and Kelly 2002).

The Ideal Nuclear Family

The family is a key social institution in which children are nurtured and socialized. In much public debate and political rhetoric, the family is touted as the centerpiece of American life. This idealized family, immortalized in the 1950s TV show *Leave It to Beaver,* consists of a heterosexual couple, married for life, with two or three children. The father is the provider while the wife/mother spends her days running the home. This is the family that is regularly portrayed in ads for such things as food, cars, cleaning products, or life insurance, which rely on our recognizing—if not identifying with—this symbol of togetherness and care. It is also invoked by conservative politicians who hearken back to so-called traditional family values. The copious academic and popular literature on the family emphasizes change— some say breakdown—in family life (Coontz 1992, 1997; Mintz and Kellogg 1988; Risman 1998; Skolnick

Family Violence

- Up to 50 percent of all homeless women and children in this country are fleeing domestic violence. Approximately 1 out of every 25 elder persons is victimized annually. Of those who experience domestic elder abuse, 37 percent are neglected and 26 percent are physically abused. Of those who perpetrate the abuse, 30 percent are adult children of the abused person.

- As violence against women becomes more severe and more frequent in the home, children experience a 300 percent increase in physical violence by the male batterer.

- Sixty-two percent of sons over the age of 14 were injured when they attempted to protect their mothers from attacks by abusive male partners. Women are 10 times more likely than men to be victims of violent crime in intimate relationships.

Source: National Coalition Against Domestic Violence.

1991). Conservative politicians and religious leaders attribute many social problems to "broken homes," so-called dysfunctional families, and moral decline, citing divorce rates, teen pregnancy rates, numbers of single-parent families, large numbers of mothers in the paid workforce, a lack of Christian values, and violence. In a *New York Times* article on single mothers, the steady increase in the rate of births to unmarried women since 1952 was called "a predictable metaphor for the fraying of America's collective moral fiber" (Usdansky 1996). Note that this formulation blames women for several macro- and global-level processes. These include economic changes that have caused manufacturing jobs to be automated or moved overseas, a lack of adequate support for people in poverty, changing stresses on personal and family relationships, increased levels of incarceration, and so forth.

Although this mythic family makes up only a small proportion of U.S. families, much of the liter-ature on U.S. families assumes homogeneity. The prevalence of this ideal family image has a strong ideological impact, and it serves to both mask and delegitimize the real diversity of family forms. It gives no hint of the range of family forms, the incidence of family violence, or conflicts between work and caring for children. Sociologist Stephanie Coontz (1997) argues that the nostalgia for the so-called traditional family is based on myths. Specifically, the post–World War II White, middle-class family was the product of a particular set of circumstances that were short-lived:

> Fewer women remained childless during the 1950s than in any decade since the late nineteenth century. The timing and spacing of children became far more compressed, so that young mothers were likely to have two more children in diapers at once. . . . At the same time, again for the first time in 100 years, the educational gap between middle-class women and men increased, while job segregation for working men and women seems to have peaked. . . . The result was that family life and gender roles became much more predictable, orderly, and settled in the 1950s than they were either twenty years earlier or would be twenty years later. *(p. 36)*

Coontz (1997) argues that holding onto these nostalgic ideas creates problems for contemporary families. "The *lag* in adjusting values, behaviors, and institutions to new realities" can make for marital dissatisfaction and divorce, as well as inappropriate policy decisions (p. 109).

U.S. Families: Cultural and Historical Variations

The idealized family is assumed to provide a secure home for its members, what historian Christopher Lasch (1977) has called "a haven in a heartless world." For some this is generally true. Yet many marriages end in divorce, and a significant number are characterized by violence and abuse. For many women and children—in heterosexual and lesbian families—home is not a safe place but one where they experience emotional or physical violence through beatings, threats, or sexual abuse, as discussed in the previous chapter.

The ideal family, with its rigid gender-based division of labor, has always applied more to White families than to families of color. As cultural critic, teacher, and writer bell hooks (1984a) argues, many women of color and working-class White women have always had to work outside the home. Children are raised in multigenerational families, by divorced parents who have remarried, by adoptive parents, single parents (usually mothers), or grandparents. Eleanor Palo Stoller and Rose Campbell Gibson (1994) note that "when children are orphaned, when parents are ill or at work, or biological mothers are too young to care for their children alone other women take on childcare, sometimes temporarily, sometimes permanently" (p. 162). Sociologist Barbara Omolade (1986) describes strong female-centered networks linking African American families and households, in which single mothers support one another in creating stable homes for their children. She challenges official characterization of this kind of family as "dysfunctional." Anthropologist Leith Mullings (1997) notes that women-headed households are an international phenomenon, shaped by global as well as local processes like the movement of jobs from industrialized to developing nations. In some families, one or both parents may have a disability, as described by Carol Gill and Larry Voss (Reading 45). Other families are split between countries through work, immigration, and war.

Single women (not all of whom are lesbians) have children through alternative insemination. Lesbians and gay men have established networks of friends who function like family. Some have children from earlier, heterosexual relationships; other gay and lesbian couples are fostering or adopting children (Drucker 1998; Goss and Strongheart 1997; Howey and Samuels 2000; Moraga 1997; Wells 2000). According to the Family Pride Coalition, an umbrella organization for gay and lesbian family support groups, at least 2 million gay and lesbian parents in the United States are raising between 3 million and 5 million children, most of them children of heterosexual marriages. The National Adoption Information Clearinghouse, a federal agency, puts the figures much higher—between 2.5 million and 8 million gay and lesbian parents, and 6 million to 14 million children (Lowy 1999). In Reading 36, journalist, teacher, and poet Ann Filemyr describes "loving across the boundary," as a White woman in partnership with

Pam and Lisa Liberty-Bibbens with McKenzie and Brennan

Essie, a woman of color, and comments that "by sharing our lives, our daily survival, our dreams and aspirations, I have been widened and deepened." Their family includes Essie's son and her grandmother. Filemyr makes insightful connections between their personal experiences, other people's reactions to their multiracial household, and the impact of racism and heterosexism on their lives.

Besides providing for the care and socialization of children, families in the United States historically were also productive units. Before the onset of industrialization, work and home were not separated, as happened under the factory system, and women were not housewives but workers. Housework was directly productive in a home-based economy. In addition, women produced goods for sale—dyed cloth, finished garments, lace, netting, rope, furniture, and homemade remedies. Enslaved African women were involved in such production for their owners and sometimes also for their own families. Native American women were similarly involved in productive work for their family and community. Under such a family system both parents could integrate child care with their daily tasks, tasks in which children also participated. Indeed, childhood was a different phenomenon, with an emphasis on learning skills and responsibilities as part of a community, rather than on play or schooling.

Many shopkeeping and restaurant-owning families today—some of them recent immigrants, others the children or grandchildren of immigrants—continue to blend work and home.

Immigration and the Family

Chinese immigrant life in the United States was very different from these earlier family experiences. At first only Chinese men were allowed to enter the United States—to build roads and railroads, for example—creating a community of bachelors. Later, Chinese women were also permitted entry, and the Chinatowns of several major cities began to echo with children's voices for the first time.

Since 1952, U.S. immigration law and policy have allowed family members to join relatives in this country. This can be a lengthy process, and many families are split between the United States and their native countries. Men and women who migrate to this country often leave their children back home until they have gained a foothold here. Others send their children, especially teenagers, to the "old country" to keep them from the problems of life in the United States. Some recent Chinese immigrant women, who work long hours for low pay in New York garment factories, are sending their infants back to China to be cared for by family members (Sengupta 1999). They lack affordable child care and the support of an extended family. The children are U.S. citizens by birth and are expected to return to this country when they are school age.

Women who are recent immigrants may be more affected by the customs of their home country, though younger immigrant women see coming to the United States partly in terms of greater personal freedom, as do many young women born here to immigrant parents. Differing aspirations and expectations for careers, marriage, and family life between mothers and daughters may lead to tensions between the generations, as exemplified in Amy Tan's novel *The Joy Luck Club* (1989), and by Surina Khan (Reading 26). According to Stoller and Gibson (1994), many older Asian American women suffer both economic hardship and cultural isolation in this country. Recent elderly immigrants are also affected by cultural isolation, especially if they do not know English and their children and grandchildren are keen to become acculturated. First-generation immigrants who hold traditional views of family obligations, for example, may be disappointed by the treatment they receive from their Americanized children and grandchildren.

Feminist Perspectives on Marriage, Motherhood, and the Family

Marriage and family life are so much a part of our everyday lives, that many of us rarely stop to think much about them. Feminists often challenge commonplace beliefs about these bedrock social institutions that people may not even know they hold.

Challenging the Private/Public Dichotomy

A core idea in much U.S. political thought is that there is a dichotomy between the private and personal (dating, marriage, sexual habits, who does the housework, relationships between parents and children) and the public (religion, law, business). According to this view, these two spheres affect each other but are governed by different rules, attitudes, and behavior. The family, for example, is the place where love, caring, and sensitivity are assumed to come first. How a man treats his wife or children, then, is a private matter. A key aspect of much feminist theorizing and activism has been to challenge this public versus private dichotomy and to explain the family as a site of patriarchal power summed up in the saying "The working man's home is his castle." Every man may not be the most powerful person in the family, yet this is a culturally accepted idea. Such power may operate in relatively trivial ways—as, for example, when Mom and the kids cater to Dad's preferences in food or TV shows as a way of avoiding a confrontation. Usually, as the main wage earner and "head" of the family, men command loyalty, respect, and obedience. Some resort to violence or sexual abuse, as mentioned earlier. White, middle-class feminists like Betty Friedan (1963), who wrote about her dissatisfactions with suburban life and the boredom of being a full-time homemaker, which she described as "the problem which has no name," identify motherhood as a major obstacle to women's fulfillment. By contrast, working-class women—White women and women of color—name a lack of well-paying jobs, a lack of skills or education, and racism, not motherhood, as obstacles to their liberation.

Given the lower status of women in society, Jaclyn Geller points to marriage as a legal contract between unequal parties (Reading 42). As political scientist Susan Moller Okin (1989) notes, the much-repeated slogan "the personal is the political" is "the central message of feminist critiques of the public/private dichotomy" (p. 124). She lists four ways in which the family is a political entity:

1. Power is always an element of family relationships.

2. This domestic sphere is governed by external rules—for example, those concerning marriage and divorce, marital rape, or child custody.

3. It is in the family that much of our early socialization takes place and that we learn gender roles.

4. The division of labor within the family raises practical and psychological barriers against women in all other spheres of life.

(pp. 128–33)

Mothering and Maternal Thinking

In the late 1970s and early 1980s, feminist writing about motherhood increased enormously with an emphasis on the daily experience of mothering (Lazarre 1976; Rich 1976) and the symbolic meaning of motherhood (Chodorow 1978; Dinnerstein 1976). Adrienne Rich (1986b) advocated thinking of pregnancy and childbirth, a short-term condition, quite separately from child rearing, a much-longer-term responsibility. Psychologists Nancy Chodorow and Dorothy Dinnerstein both advocated shared parenting as essential to undermining rigid gender roles, under which many men are cut off, practically and emotionally, from the organic and emotional concerns of children and dissociated from life processes. Two decades later, sociologists Pepper Schwartz (1994) and Barbara Risman (1998) made similar arguments.

Historian Laurie Umansky (1996) notes that maternalist rhetoric and imagery were central to much 1980s ecofeminism and women's peace activism. Examples include the Unity Statement of the Women's Pentagon Action (Reading 65, Chapter 11). Philosopher Sara Ruddick (1989) argued, further, that the experience and the work of mothering (whether by women or men) has the potential to generate principles of "maternal thinking" based on the desire to preserve life and foster growth. Such principles could serve as a blueprint for human interaction that would involve genuine peace and security. Respon-

sible mothering has also led women to organize for better working conditions, improvements in welfare programs, and environmental justice (Jetter, Orleck, and Taylor 1997). Anthropologist Leith Mullings (1997) describes the transformative work of African American women she interviewed in New York in raising children and sustaining their households and communities as single parents. Sociologist Nancy Naples (1998, p. 113) uses the term "activist mothering" to explain the ways women community workers blend mothering, paid and unpaid labor, and political activism.

The Family and the Economic System

Other feminist theorists see the family as part of the economic system and emphasize its role in the **reproduction of labor** (Benston 1969; Dalla Costa and James 1972; Mitchell 1971; Zaretsky 1976). In this highly unsentimental view, marriage is compared to prostitution, whereby women trade sex for economic and social support. The family is deemed important for society because it is responsible for producing, nurturing, and socializing the next generation of workers and citizens, the place where children first learn to be "social animals." This includes basic skills like language and potty training and social skills like cooperation and negotiation with others or abiding by rules. Women's unpaid domestic work and child care, though not considered productive work, directly benefit the state and employers by turning out functioning members of society. The family also cares for its adult members by providing meals and clean clothes, as well as rest, relaxation, love, and sexual intimacy, so that they are ready to face another working day—another aspect of the reproduction of labor. Similarly, it cares for people who are not in the workforce, those with disabilities, the elderly, or the chronically ill. Still other theorists explain the family in terms of patriarchal power linked to a capitalist system of economic relations, with much discussion of exactly how these two systems are connected and how the gendered division of labor within the family first came about (Hartmann 1981; Jaggar 1983; Young 1980).

Policy Implications and Implementation

Many feminist scholars, policy makers, and activists have followed through on their analyses of women's roles in the family by taking steps to implement the policies they advocate. They have set up crisis lines and shelters for battered women and children across the country and made family violence and childhood sexual abuse public issues, as discussed in the previous chapter. They have argued for shared parental responsibility for child care, payment of child support, and redrawing the terms of divorce such that both postdivorce households would have the same standard of living. Above all, feminists have campaigned for good-quality child care subsidized by government and employers, on site at big workplaces, and they have organized community child-care facilities and informal networks of parents who share child care. Although some of these efforts have been successful, there is still a great deal to be accomplished if women are not to be penalized for having children, an issue we discuss in Chapter 8.

Although policy makers and politicians often declare that children are the nation's future and greatest resource, parents are given little practical help in caring for them. Susan Moller Okin (1989) notes that so few U.S. politicians have raised children that it seems almost a qualification for political office not to have done so. The editors of *Mothering* magazine pulled no punches when they asked:

> Why is the United States the only industrial democracy in the world that provides no universal pre- or postnatal care, no universal health coverage; . . . has no national standards for child care; makes no provision to encourage at-home care in the early years of life; . . . has no explicit family policies such as child allowances and housing subsidies for all families; and has not signed the United Nations Convention on the Rights of the Child—a dubious distinction shared with Iraq, Libya, and Cambodia?
>
> *(Brennan, Winklepleck, and MacNee 1994, p. 424)*

At the same time, former first lady Hillary Rodham Clinton (1996), adopting an African proverb, argued that "it takes a village to raise a child." Most European countries have instituted family policies with provisions for health care, child allowances, child care, prenatal care, parental leave, and services for the elderly. In the United States, family policy is an unfamiliar term and the few policies that support families, like welfare, unemployment assistance, and tax relief, are inadequate and uncoordinated (Al-

belda and Tilly 1997; Mason, Skolnick, and Sugarman 1998).

Toward a Redefinition of Family Values

Elevating the ideal of the nuclear, two-parent family is a major contradiction in contemporary U.S. society, as we argue earlier. Regardless of its form, the family should

> care for family members, emotionally and materially;
>
> promote egalitarian relationships among the adults, who should not abuse their power over children;
>
> share parenting between men and women so that it is not the province of either gender;
>
> do away with a gendered division of labor;
>
> teach children nonsexist, antiracist, anticlassist attitudes and behavior and the values of caring and connectedness to others;
>
> pass on cultural heritage; and
>
> influence the wider community.

For personal relationships to be more egalitarian, as far as possible the partners should have shared values or compatible nonnegotiables, have some compatible sense of why they are together, and share power in the relationship. They also need to be committed to a clear communication process and be willing to work through difficulties with honesty and openness. If the relationship is to last, it must be flexible and able to change over time so that both partners can grow individually as well as together. Few of us have much experience to guide us. Indeed, most people have experienced and observed unequal relationships—at home, in school, and in the wider community. Carol Gill and Larry Voss (Reading 45) discuss their experiences of egalitarian relationships and shared parenting and the importance of teaching children nonsexist, antiracist, anticlassist attitudes.

Susan Moller Okin (1989) argues that for society to be just, all social institutions must be just, including the family. We argue that the family must be a source of security for its members, an element in constructing a secure and sustainable future. A sustainable future means that we, in the present generation, must consider how our actions will affect people of future generations. A useful reference here is the Native American "seventh generation" principle: The community is responsible for those not yet born, and because of this, whatever actions are taken in the present must not jeopardize the possibility of well-being seven generations to come. How would we have to restructure our relationships as well as other social institutions in order to honor that principle?

Questions for Reflection

In reading and discussing this chapter, consider these questions:

1. What do you expect/hope for in an intimate relationship?

2. Are you in love now? How can you tell?

3. How does power manifest itself in your relationships with family members, friends, dates, or lovers?

4. Do you think intimate relationships should be monogamous? Why or why not?

5. Do you have friends or dates with people from a racial/ethnic/cultural group different from your own? If so, how did you meet? How have your differences been a factor in your friendship or relationship?

6. How do you define family? Whom do you consider family in your own life?

7. How do macro-level institutions—in particular the government, media, and organized religion—shape people's relationships and family lives?

8. Should there be gay marriage? Where do you stand on this issue?

9. If women are to have more equal treatment within the family, what kinds of changes in male attitudes and behavior will be needed also? How might this happen?

10. What changes are necessary to involve men in parenting? Look at the micro, meso, macro, and global levels of analysis.

Finding Out More on the Web

1. Visit the following Web sites for more information:

   Indiebride: **www.indiebride.com**

   Alternatives to Marriage Project: **www.unmarried.org**

   Amy Benfer, "I do—kind of," *Salon,* Aug. 15, 2001.

   http://dir.salon.com/mwt/feature/2001/8/15/i_do/index.html

2. Find out more about the Defense of Marriage Act (1996). What assumptions about marriage and the institution of heterosexuality is it based on?

3. Find out about family policies in western European countries (especially Denmark, Germany, the Netherlands, and Sweden). Why do these countries provide better supports for families than the United States?

Taking Action

1. Talk with your peers—women and men—about your nonnegotiables in a personal relationship. What are you willing to compromise on?

2. Talk with your mother or grandmother (or women their age) about their experiences of marriage, motherhood, and family. What choices have they made in their lives in this regard? What options did they have?

3. Look critically at the way women are portrayed in relationships and the family in magazines, ads, movies, and TV shows.

F O R T Y - O N E

35/10

Sharon Olds

Brushing out my daughter's dark
silken hair before the mirror
I see the grey gleaming on my head,
the silver-haired servant behind her. Why is it
just as we begin to go
they begin to arrive, the fold in my neck
clarifying as the fine bones of her
hips sharpen? As my skin shows
its dry pitting, she opens like a small
pale flower on the tip of a cactus;
as my last chances to bear a child
are falling through my body, the duds among
 them,
her full purse of eggs, round and
firm as hard-boiled yolks, is about
to snap its clasp. I brush her tangled
fragrant hair at bedtime. It's an old
story—the oldest we have on our planet—
the story of replacement.

F O R T Y - T W O

The Marriage Mystique

Jaclyn Geller

The late historian John Boswell has written that the most salient feature of the modern West's psychological landscape is its widespread obsession with romance and its assumption that amorous love should be the basis for marriage. . . .[1]

The belief in erotic love as the wellspring of personal happiness and the equation of long-term amorous relationships with maturity and mental health are ideas that now saturate every corner of American culture. But a cursory glance at popular advice literature reveals that these subjects are not assumed to be the equal obsession of men and women. Magazines, self-help books, and radio talk shows aimed at men cover issues ranging from health to consumer guidance to recreation to career management, but popular advice to contemporary American women is single-minded in its concern with obtaining and sustaining a monogamous sexual partnership. The dominant theme of virtually every current American woman's magazine is the romantic relationship. Other frequently discussed subjects in magazines such as *Cosmopolitan, Mirabella, Self, Marie Claire,* and *Glamour* are fashion, fitness, home management, and career strategies. It could be argued, however, that such topics are subsumed within or at least directly related to the culturally mandated quest for officialized love.

When a woman colors her hair, tones her body, re-designs her apartment, or even augments her résumé, she builds cultural capital that will recommend her on what relationship experts call "the dating scene," helping her to attract a male partner. Magazine articles, newspaper columns, how-to dating manuals, and call-in radio shows ready the female consumer for her hunt, instructing her to fortify herself physically, psychologically, and financially. . . . Televised daytime talk shows have become venues for husband-hunting advisors, and the popular psychology branch of the publishing industry panders increasingly to "single" women, offering a range of strategies for snagging a male partner.

Relationship experts focus on immediate romantic goals, appealing to the emotions rather than the intelligence of their female readers and urging women to use their analytical capacities solely as amorous strategists—operatives who secure male commitment through the clever deployment of tactical game plans. Self-scrutiny, and analysis of one's aspirations for an erotic relationship, the type of man one hopes to attract, and areas of compromise necessary to secure marital commitment are de rigueur in dating literature. But inquiry, through analysis and contextualization, of the institution of marriage itself, is taboo. Relationship pundits operate in an ahistorical void, a vacuum in which male-female partnership is a perpetual unassailable truth. Representatives of a media that provide easy ready-made solutions to female distress and assume such distress to always be personal, these advisors treat human relationships with a short-range approach that lacks the depth of historical perspective. . . .

What one scholar has described as a "present-minded" approach to reality[2] is necessary for these contemporary dating experts and essential to the cult of matrimony. Historical myopia on the part of both advisors and advice recipients is the fundamental requirement of today's marriage mania, a fetish for conjugality that demands each woman view herself as potentially or actually part of a marital unit—the female half of a couple—rather than a link between past and future generations of women. Viewing ourselves in a historical continuum of women who have been subordinate within male-dominated institutions such as wedlock would cloud the matrimonial mystique and problematize the all-important quest for conjugal commitment. Because marriage as an institution has been inextricably connected to the most potent forms of female oppression, its proponents cannot survey it from a detached perspective but must instead transform its inherently public, political nature into something magically personal, private, and inevitable. When a dating expert helps a female client determine whether her current beau is capable of "commitment," he assumes the permanent domestic contract to be a basic and universal female desire. He also naturalizes that desire. When a radio therapist advises a husband and wife to spend more private time away from the children—to reserve a part of each day solely for each other or to take romantic weekends away—she presumes the marital relationship to be sacrosanct and in need of unique kinds of maintenance. She also, perhaps without consciously intending to do so, projects romance-based marriage as a cultural idea.

Matrimony is not, however, a set of raw, untempered, universal experiences. It is a humanly shaped institution that has its origins in the inception of Western civilization itself. It is a political arrangement that merits a political critique rather than a personal impulse that deserves automatic complacent respect. When we remember the extent to which culture is cumulative, with each generation transferring economic conditions as well as social norms, precedents, laws, and interpretive metaphors to the next, we can begin to understand the fusion between contemporary women and the marriage ideal, a collaboration that has spawned and continues to sustain America's expanding relationship industry as well as its virtually recession-proof wedding industry. Marriage mania in modern American women did not arise sui generis. It is the result of millennia of law and social custom that have valued women solely in terms of their relationship to men, predicating female respectability on male stewardship. . . .

Simone de Beauvoir wrote famously in 1949 that women have no past and no history.[3] She was wrong. Women have a history, which, for the most part, appears unglamorous to modern female intellectuals, a history of private unpaid service within the family, a history in which marriage has been the central and defining act of most individual's lives, a history of absorption within an institution that has offered certain protections in exchange for the imposition of rigid restrictions. Wedlock has tended to offer women immediate social and psychological rewards while obstructing long-term female progress. Its traditional securities have come at a high price:

the containment of female sexuality and the limiting of female agency. Yet this contract has been central and desirable to most women in most times and places. As Olwen Hufton has written of private life in early modern Europe:

> Marriage was seen not merely as women's natural destiny but also as a metaphoric agent, transforming her into a different social being as part of a new household, the primary unit upon which all society was based. The husband's role was that of provider of shelter and sustenance . . . The role of the wife was that of helpmate and mother. At the highest levels of society, women became mistresses of houses with servants to organize, estates to manage with the help of stewards and agents, and hospitality to offer on their husband's behalf. The appearance and dignity of the wife confirmed the status of the husband.[4]

A helpmate, a domestic partner/subordinate/manager, and a visible index of male prestige, the wife traditionally received, and continues to garner, powerful social approbation. When we consider the primacy that the marital experience has had for Western women, the current female obsession with wedlock as reflected in popular culture becomes comprehensible as yet another historical chapter in which matrimony has been mandated as a natural and laudable female good.

Glancing back in time, though, we can perceive the facts of female subjugation in the West to be inseparable from the evolution of marriage law. In prehistory, inchoate attitudes, tribal customs, and legal dogma ossified over centuries in the process Gerda Lerner calls "the creation of patriarchy": a legitimized system of male dominance that culminated in the first Western law codes, the Hammurabic Law Codes of 1750 B.C.E. and the subsequent Middle Assyrian Law Codes of the fifteenth through the eleventh centuries B.C.E. These bodies of law institutionalized monogamous marriage arranged by men, with household assets transferred to male offspring—the custom that has, until very recently, dominated the West. Both corpi of law are based on assumptions that bear repetition. Ancient Near Eastern culture assumed the strength and superior rationality of men and the status of males as political citizens and women as contingent beings destined to exist outside of political life. While men through their rational faculties were equipped to order and interpret experience, women were intended to nurture and sustain life, overseeing the continuity of the species in a kind of perpetual service position. From the earliest marriage regulations on record, this role entailed male controls of female sexuality and reproductivity with no parallel female controls of male sexual and reproductive functions. It as well contained the belief in marriage as an asymmetrical partnership and the married couple as a unit whose stability was essential to the integrity of the public domain. The contractually united couple was, in Lerner's words, "the basic building block" of the healthy organism that was the state,[5] a belief echoed by marriage propagandists to this day. While historians disagree as to whether the ancient wife was a piece of property transferred from father to groom or a legally disenfranchised individual who garnered the symbolic gift of a bride price, it is clear that, from her beginnings as a historical entity, the wife occupied a subordinate position that was also, ironically, her sole option for respectability.

In ancient Greece marriage was, once again, a process of transfer by which a woman's *kyrios* ("lord" or "controller") gave her to another man for the purpose of procreating children. Normally the woman's father, but if he was deceased, her nearest male relative, the *kyrios* acted for her in all legal and economic transactions, as female judgment was thought to be impaired. A marriage in Athens was valid only if it began with a formal statement by the *kyrios* granting the bride-to-be to her husband.[6] In the Roman Republic matrimony was, again, "essentially the transfer of power over a woman, who had been under the control of her father (or brother, or uncle, or some adult male), to that of her new husband (or his father, if the husband was not head of his own household), who than stood in his role of her controller/protector."[7] Roman betrothal in fact entailed a ceremony between two men in which pledges were exchanged to cement the deal: the groom-to-be would ask his future father-in-law, "Do you promise to give your daughter to me to be my wedded wife?" "The gods bring luck! I betroth her!" the latter would reply.[8] While this concept of marriage, in which all persons in a household were subservient to a single adult male, changed in the later empire, imperial Roman marriage was by no means egalitarian. Roman law maintained mutual consent to be the basis of legal marriage, but the bride's consent was assumed unless she lodged an official protest, an objection taken seriously only if her fiancé was proven base or unworthy.[9] And although she was legally defined as an adult in her own right, the imperial wife was subject to the rampant sexual double standard prevalent throughout the ancient world. Her husband might well have married her for financial or dynastic reasons; this would not prevent his finding erotic fulfillment in concubines, slaves, and prostitutes with no fear of public recrimination, while, in order to ensure the "legitimacy" of his heirs, her chastity was requisite. "If your slave, your freedman, your woman, or your client dares answer you, get angry," wrote the Roman author Seneca.[10]

Early medieval marriage among the Barbarian tribes who migrated westward, penetrating and ultimately supplanting the waning Roman empire, was even more male dominated than Roman marriage had been, granting women few rights but imposing upon them many obligations. Betrothal was arranged by male relatives of the bride, whose consent was not required, and who, once married, could not seek divorce. It consisted of an agreement between two fathers sealed by a feast at which the groom-to-be's family paid a sum of money—a bride price—for her. Barbarian men commonly had concubines, but a Barbarian woman's adultery was, according to the Roman author Tacitus, punished immediately by her husband, who stripped her clothes off, cut her hair, ejected her from his home, and flogged her publicly throughout the village. Tacitus appreciated these firm measures to curtail female sexual autonomy. "No feature of their morality deserves higher praise," he wrote of Barbarian marriage.[11]

Medieval men were theoretically free to choose their marriage partners as soon as they attained majority—between the ages of twelve to fifteen according to various law codes. The Lombard Code, written down in the seventh century, enabled a woman's father or brother to choose for her without her consent, even after she had reached her twenties.[12] The ninth-century archbishop, Hincmar of Reims, who defined legal marriage as *mutually* consenting (with the exception that a woman must be given and financially endowed by her father) presents an unsavory picture of medieval marriage. His writings depict men using various stratagems to rid themselves of their wives, ploys that include murder as well as legal deception: "They seized any pretext to suspend conjugal relations after a few years of married life, took mistresses, slandered their spouses to the clergy,

forced them to tolerate concubines and to testify that their husbands were impotent or to pretend that they themselves longed to retire to a convent."[13]

Hincmar may have been exaggerating in order to justify his own reforms, but medieval marriage law, which operated from the premise that a woman's sexuality was not her own but her husband's, did give men overwhelming power over their wives. Anglo-Saxon legal codes in fact contained a scale of compensatory payments to husbands for the seduction of their wives. According to the eleventh-century laws of Cnut, a woman who committed adultery was a public disgrace, "and her lawful husband is to have all that she owns, and she is to lose her nose and ears."[14] According to feudal law in the high Middle Ages a wife could not plead in court without her husband's consent or make a will without his permission. His authority over her property was total; only when she reached widowhood did she acquire any degree of economic independence, and even then she was often subjected to powerful family pressures to remarry.[15]

Despite its brutal strictures marriage was, for medieval women, the universal objective. This was especially true for peasant women, to whom convents were closed.[16] Aristocratic women were pawns in the game of establishing dynastic households. According to the historian of marriage Georges Duby, the late medieval landholder did his best to marry off all available young women in order to distribute the blood of his ancestors, forging alliances that would last into the next generation.[17]

Medievalist Christopher N. L. Brooke writes, "The kings sought marriage above all to provide themselves with male heirs and for personal satisfaction; if the wife was unsatisfactory she was changed."[18] This changed in the twelfth century, when the Church took control of marriage, worked to stamp out concubinage, and imposed rules of permanence, and monogamy upon both women and men. Succumbing to Church pressure, heads of aristocratic households came to center their aspirations on inheritance, which necessitated monogamy and demanded the chastity of women.[19] Because it ensured the purity of blood lines and the orderly transmission of property from one generation of "legitimate" male heirs to the next, wifely fidelity was the bedrock on which the new family rested.

Embedded in both medieval and Renaissance notions of marriage was the belief that the sexes were unequal. The biblical story of Adam's creation in God's image and Eve's emergence as a secondary figure taken from his rib reinforced the notion of inherent, timeless gender inequality. Male and female were merged into one unit, but that unit contained a hierarchy. Woman, who had caused humanity's fall from grace and exile from edenic paradise, was naturally inferior,[20] a notion supported by Paul's letter to the Ephesians, which stated that the husband was head of the wife as Christ was head of the Church.[21] In 1439 marriage was officially proclaimed a sacrament of the Catholic Church. Renaissance marriage was arranged, as medieval marriage had been, with negotiations between families centering on the dowry contributed by the bride's side. Once the couple married, the husband assumed total control of both the dowry and all of his wife's effects. Renaissance wives were prohibited from acting for themselves in legal or commercial matters;[22] yet, as in previous centuries, they were socially mandated to desire and hopefully await their own legal subordination in wedlock. Those without husbands had no hope of obtaining a prestigious position in society. In Italy and elsewhere a favorite form of charity was the dowry fund, established by communities to help poor young girls attract husbands.[23]

Protestant reformers rejected the notion of marriage as a Christian sacrament as they likewise discarded the Catholic idea of clerical celibacy as a superior way of life. Martin Luther contended that marriage existed in order to satisfy the natural urge to procreate, effecting the salvation of souls by allowing men and women to act sinlessly in accordance with their physical natures. Sexuality, in this view, was the reason for marriage, and matrimony was thus the ideal state for all human beings. Subsequent theologians developed this idea, delineating the urgency of qualitative marital relations and, ultimately, allowing for divorce. (If individuals were compelled to marry by sexual drives, they must be permitted to separate and remarry when their unions failed.) The Protestant notion of holy matrimony, probably the distant wellspring of our own culture's obsession with the caliber and tenor of marital relations, was still absolutely patriarchal. Husbands were mandated to love and protect their wives; wives were expected to obey their husbands.[24]

The historian Lawrence Stone argued that the Protestant sanctification of marriage resulted in the further domination of wives.[25] With its emphasis on the couple, Protestant morality isolated the family from the larger kinship and community network, stressing the household as a moral center for the socialization of children in which "power flowed increasingly to the husband over the wife and to the father over the children"[26] and in which husbands were less hampered by interference from relatives, neighbors, and clergy. Early modernity also gave rise to the romance-based "companionate" marriage. In the seventeenth century the idea that two people could find fulfillment in a partnership based on unsupervised personal choice and mutual affection was still so radical that it was considered dangerously subversive. One century later marriage based on personal and erotic attraction had become a popular norm. A growing Protestant middle class re-envisioned wedlock as a complementary but unequal friendship. A stream of conduct books and novels—similar publications continue to the present day—suggested that women were naturally suited for this new model of wedlock, instructing them in the domestic arts and celebrating their wifely capacities.

These primers were, effectively, guidebooks on how to enjoy one's own subordination, since eighteenth-century domestic law incorporated previous gender biases. In his 1765 *Commentaries on the Laws of England,* the jurist William Blackstone codified preexisting regulations with the definition of coverture: "By marriage, the husband and wife are one person in law, that is, the very being or legal existence of the woman is suspended during the marriage, or at least incorporated and consolidated into that of her husband, under whose wing, protection, and cover, she performs everything.[27] As a *femme covert* a woman could not initiate independent lawsuits, and any income or property not protected by a prior marriage agreement was automatically her husband's. Family law dictated that children belonged exclusively to the husband; in the event of his death his widow had rights over them only if such rights were stipulated in his will. Wives who left their husbands could take neither children nor property and could be forced to return, regardless of the cause of the abandonment. In eighteenth-century England a husband who killed his wife was tried for murder (punishable by hanging), while a wife who killed her husband was tried for "petite treason," a crime punishable by drawing and burning alive.[28] In France things weren't much better. The 1804 Code Napoleon, influential throughout Europe, recapitulated the old terms of the marriage contract, proclaiming a husband head of his household and dictating the arrangement as one of male protection in return for female obedience. Under this code women were classified with children and mental defectives as legal incompetents. Again, a married woman's only possible source of legal protection lay in the marriage contract drawn up by her parents, but these contracts tended to subordinate wives to their husbands, making it impossible for women to manage their own assets without their husbands' consent.[29]

Bolstered by custom and law, the patriarchal family was the source of heated polemics in England throughout the nineteenth century. Supporters saw it as a sacrosanct institution, a tranquil haven in a rapidly changing world. Sanctified by the Victorian's brand of evangelical Protestantism, marriage was said to be an ethereal state in which men and women complemented each other by operating in separate spheres. The husband was protector and breadwinner to a domestic, submissive, and self-abnegating wife, whom one poet referred to as "the angel in the house."[30] Victorian culture seemed to have perfected the marital ideal set forth two centuries earlier by a Dorsetshire clergyman that "A good wife should be like a Mirrour which hath no image of its own, but receives its stamp from the face that looks in to it."[31] With its beatification of woman's role within marriage, the nineteenth century gave rise to the . . . big white wedding featuring elaborate pageantry and lavish displays of spending and sentiment. Victorians touted the components of the wedding—the gown and veil, the bridal procession, the throwing of rice, and the romantic honeymoon—as British traditions despite the fact that not one of these rites predated their own century. "The popularizing of the big white wedding as *the* British nuptial" was, according to scholar John Gillis, "an act of self-veneration by those seeking to legitimate and impose their own social standards."[32] Giving away a bride adorned in virginal white, hosting a family reception, and sending the couple off on an exclusive honeymoon enshrined the Victorian's romantic notions of female purity, conjugal love, and the nuclear family. This was the era in which marriage reached its apotheosis as an ideal. Despite the fact that it was, once again, legal subordination, with a husband controlling his wife's property and earnings,[33] wedlock continued to be the central aspiration of most women. ("Being married gives one one's position,

which nothing else can," wrote Queen Victoria to her daughter in 1858.[34]) . . .

Our own century has absorbed the Victorian's complex inheritance: a reformed legal model of marriage as well as the ideology of the private family based on the powerful belief that marriage is a relationship unlike any other—a sacrosanct bond that takes precedence over all other emotional ties. Matrimony now entails a more equal contract between men and women than has ever existed. It also has a sentimental luster that most of our ancestors would have found bizarre if not laughable. The obsessive romantic mystique surrounding wedlock creates other kinds of inequity. The state-sanctioned, monogamous heterosexual partnership is now touted as *the* pivotal adult relationship for most men and women—a liaison so momentous that it necessitates celebration via a costly extravaganza that no mere friendship would justify. Despite wedlock's sexist legacy, the American relationship industry encourages men and women, and women in particular, to strive for marital commitment in a way that they would never pursue same-sex friendships, intimacy with biological relatives, or closeness with colleagues, teachers, and mentors. Once married, women's loyalty to and love for their husbands is supposed to take precedence over obligations to all other partners.

Given wedlock's history, the sanctimoniousness with which self-help experts praise marriage and promote conjugal commitment, the doggedness with which "single" women pursue such commitment, and the enthusiasm with which engaged women plan and orchestrate their nuptial celebrations is deeply ironic. Certainly, the emotional reality of marriage has always been varied. Even in the most rigidly patriarchal settings there have always been women who stood on equal footing with or even dominated their husbands. But despite the daily realities that have moderated matrimony's sexist doctrines, the institution has always been powerfully biased against women. Marriage is not merely stained with the notion of gender inequality; it has been the West's central vehicle for enforcing that inequality, as it has simultaneously offered women their primary work and main source of identification. But given the degree to which it has dominated female experience for over three millennia, it is perhaps not surprising that matrimony remains the state to which the majority of contemporary women aspire. In every era, history has affirmed marriage as woman's natural state; in what are perhaps the two most influential ancient languages, Hebrew and Greek, the word for *woman* is also the word for *wife*. Western history records the names of male philosophers, generals, politicians, jurists, artists, and scientists. With few exceptions it has until recently recorded women only as wives of distinguished men or biological mothers, especially of prominent sons. With marriage as woman's chief occupation and sole honorable destination, the names of the great spinsters in Western history are unfortunately lost to us. Thousands of exceptional unmarried women must have made contributions to the culture of the West, but they have died anonymously, their achievements obscured by societal prescriptions for conjugal femininity.[35] With the weight of tradition mandating marriage as a woman's sole occupation, it is not surprising that American conduct literature written for females still traffics so heavily in the subject, especially by contrast with advice aimed at men. To be someone, to be like other important women, to prove oneself as a desirable person and mature adult, to maintain a very basic kind of social dignity, a woman must be a wife. American relationship experts capitalize on this assumption, and in so doing, perpetuate it. Despite their often frantic protestations to the contrary, such pundits presume that the healthy woman's deepest innate drive is toward wedlock and then toward motherhood. Their advice blends description with prescription, naturalizing conjugality as female destiny.

It would be easy to disregard matrimony's origins as those of a distant, primitive, and irrelevant past. American history and contemporary American politics, however, demonstrate irrefutably our society's powerful links to this past. Throughout much of the seventeenth century in Virginia and New England, adultery was technically punishable by execution. Defined as intercourse with a married or engaged woman, the colonial criminalization of extramarital sex perpetuated the old double standard and protected a husband's sexual control of his wife; a married man could not commit adultery with a "single" female.[36] Adultery is still a crime in many states, although the laws are rarely enacted and are considered "moribund." However, as recently as 1990 a twenty-six-year-old Wisconsin resident was charged with having an adulterous affair. (In order to avoid a trial, the defendant, Donna E. Carroll, agreed to forty hours of community service.)[37] Measures such as the 1872 Comstock Act prohibiting the use of mail to transport birth control, contraceptive information, or any other "indecent" or "immoral" material[38] may seem far away, but their premises are echoed in the 1996 Defense of Marriage Act invalidating same-sex partnership and protecting the traditional marital bond.[39] These measures attest to an ongoing societal interest in bolstering heterosexual partnership and controlling female sexuality. The 1998 feeding frenzy in which media analysts endlessly debated the state of the first marriage after President Clinton's sex life became public knowledge, vilifying the president's sexual partner, Monica Lewinsky, shows the degree to which marital fidelity and virtue are irrationally linked in the popular consciousness.[40]

The marriage mystique permeates American politics. The 2000 national conventions of both the Democratic and the Republican parties were not forums for policy discussion but prescriptions for heteronormativity in which male candidates vied for office by advertising their conjugal piety, and beaming political wives—both full-time homemakers who, in the words of one approving pollster, have "chosen to take on marriage, mortgage, and munchkins"[41]—gushed over their husbands, recounted their courtships, showed home movies chronicling their domestic lives, and smooched proudly with their consorts to demonstrate the health and happiness of their marriages. ("One's reserved, the other's outspoken, but Laura Bush and Tipper Gore have one thing in common: a commitment to family and their husbands' ambitions,"[42] a typically celebratory postconvention magazine headline proclaimed.) All indications point to our culture's enshrinement of the couple as well as the continued presence of the age-old, marriage-based sexual double standard validating female sexual activity solely within marriage and distinguishing sharply between respectable and nonrespectable women. When an elected official like Governor Frank Keating of Oklahoma appears on television as he did on June 24, 1999, and announces as part of his platform the goal of reducing the divorce rate by one-third by the year 2000,[43] it is clear that he, like most politicians, shares the timeless and traditional belief that families are best served by traditional sex roles, that women are best protected by the institution of marriage, and that conjugal households somehow strengthen the state.

This promarriage bias cuts across the public and private domains, shaping policy in areas as diverse as immigration, health care, personal finance, and employment. It is so pervasive as to be practically invisible. In her 1999 study, *White Weddings*, Chrys Ingraham provides a general list of state-controlled marital entitlements. Such privileges vary from region to region but tend to include automatic inheritance, automatic housing lease transfers, bereavement leave, burial determination, child custody, exemption of property tax upon either partner's death, immunity from testimony against one's spouse, crime victim recovery benefits, medical insurance privileges, sick leave to care for one's partner, reduced rate membership, visitation of one's partner in the hospital or in prison, and wrongful death benefits.[44] Because our culture celebrates only amorous love and distinguishes rigorously between romantic couples and all other species of relationship, no such privileges exist for platonic friends. In spite of escalating divorce statistics,[45] the widespread belief in wedlock and the state-sanctioned couple appears to be stronger than ever. . . .

"The historian of marriage will have to explain how a period that witnessed unprecedented divorce rates and a determined assault on the whole concept by many of the younger generation, and especially by the freed female slaves of our era, should yet have been presented at many levels and from many sources with an ideal of marriage unknown to most of our ancestors,"[46] remarks historian Christopher N. L. Brooke. The popular enshrinement of marriage, the growth of the wedding industry, and the various hymns of praise to domestic monogamy sung by media representatives are indeed ironic corollaries to the political gains that women have made during the past two centuries. Perhaps an institution so drenched in sexist cruelty demands the support of a strong sentimentalizing ideology. Or perhaps the current marriage craze is in part a reaction to both the conjugal impermanence of modern times and the critique of wedlock launched by a small but vocal feminist minority. Whatever the reason, it is clear that America's marital publicity machine is currently in high gear.

NOTES

1. John Boswell, *Same Sex Unions in Premodern Europe* (New York: Villard Books, 1994), xix. Boswell quotes Lou Phillips' 1959 hit, "Sea of Love" and Wayne Fontana's 1965 "The Game of Love."

2. Gerda Lerner, *Why History Matters: Life and Thought* (New York: Oxford University Press, 1997), 123.

3. Simone de Beauvoir, *The Second Sex,* trans. H. M. Parshley (New York: Bantam, 1970), xix.

4. Olwen Hufton, "Women, Work, and the Family," in *A History of Women in the West: Renaissance and Enlightenment Paradoxes,* ed. George Duby and Michelle Perrot (Cambridge: Harvard University Press, 1993), 29–30.

5. Gerda Lerner, *The Creation of Patriarchy* (New York: Oxford University Press), 121.

6. *The Oxford Companion to Classical Civilization,* ed. Simon Hornblower and Anthony Spawforth (Oxford: Oxford University Press, 1998). 446. Marilyn Yalom writes that Greek marriage was probably traumatic for the fourteen- and fifteen-year-old girls systematically obliged to leave their homes and take up residence with their husband's families, who might or might not treat them decently. *A History of the Wife* (New York: HarperCollins, 2001), 20–21.

7. Boswell, *Same Sex Unions,* 40.

8. Frances and Joseph Gies, *Marriage and the Family in the Middle Ages* (New York: Harper & Row Publishers: 1987), 23.

9. Ibid., 50.

10. Paul Veyne, "The Roman Empire," in *A History of Private Life: From Pagan Rome to Byzantium,* trans. Arthur Goldhammer, ed. Paul Veyne (Cambridge: Harvard University Press, 1987), 39.

11. Gies, *Marriage and the Family,* 33–34.

12. Ibid., 54.

13. Ibid., 91.

14. Ibid., 113–114.

15. C. Warren Hollister, *Medieval Europe: A Short History* (New York: John Wiley & Sons, 1964), 139. Georges Duby, *The Knight, the Lady, and the Priest: The Making of Marriage in Medieval France,* trans. Barbara Bray (New York: Pantheon, 1983), 90.

16. Gies, *Marriage and the Family,* 169.

17. Duby, *The Knight, the Lady,* 104–105.

18. Christopher N. L. Brooke, *The Medieval Idea of Marriage* (Oxford: Oxford University Press, 1989), 120.

19. Ibid., 263.

20. Duby, *The Knight, the Lady,* 24.

21. Brooke, *Medieval Idea of Marriage,* 50.

22. *Encyclopedia of the Renaissance,* Paul F. Grandler, Editor in Chief (New York: Charles Scribner's Sons, 1999), 51–52.

23. Elisja Schulte Van Kessel, "Virgins and Mothers Between Heaven and Earth," in *A History of Women in the West: Renaissance and Enlightenment Paradoxes,* trans. Arthur Goldhammer, ed. Paul Veyne (Cambridge: Harvard University Press, 1993), 149.

24. *The Oxford Encyclopedia of the Reformation,* Vol. 3, ed. Hans J. Hillerbrand (New York: Oxford University Press, 1996), 18–23. Yalom, *History of the Wife,* 99.

25. Lawrence Stone, *The Family, Sex, and Marriage in England: 1500–1800* (New York: Harper & Row, 1977), 109–145.

26. Ibid., 145.

27. James Trager, *A Woman's Chronology* (New York: Henry Holt, 1994), 190.

28. Kathleen Nulton Kemmerer, *"A neutral being between the sexes:" Samuel Johnson's Sexual Politics* (Lewisburg, Bucknell University Press, 1998), 32–33. Maureen Waller, *1700: Scenes from London Life* (New York: Four Walls Eight Windows, 2000), 31–32.

29. Bonnie S. Anderson and Judith P. Zinser, *A History of Their Own: Women in Europe from Prehistory to the Present,* Vol. II (New York: Harper & Row, 1988), 149.

30. The poet was Coventry Patmore. At a speech to the London National Society for Women's Service in January, 1931, Virginia Woolf spoke of the necessity of metaphorically killing the angel in the house as a necessary prelude to the act of writing, this speech became the basis of her famed essay "Professions for Women." Michele Barrett, ed., *Virginia Woolf: Women and Writing* (San Diego: Harcourt Brace & Company, 1942), 58–60.

31. Walter E. Houghton, *The Victorian Frame of Mind, 1830–1870* (New Haven: Yale University Press, 1957), 352.

32. John R. Gillis, *For Better, For Worse: British Marriages 1600 to the Present* (New York: Oxford University Press, 1985), 285–286.

33. Joan Perkin, *Victorian Women* (New York: New York University Press, 1993), 88.

34. Ibid., 75.

35. An important exception is the women who have distinguished themselves in religious life as mystics, itinerant preachers, and the leaders of devotional communities. See Gerda Lerner's *The Creation of Feminist Consciousness: From the Middle Ages to Eighteen Seventy* (New York: Oxford University Press, 1993), 46–115.

36. Carolyn B. Ramsey, "Sex and the Social Order: The Selective Enforcement of Colonial American Adultery Laws in the English Context," *Yale Journal of Law & the Humanities* 10:1 (Winter 1998), 191–228.

37. Phyllis Coleman, "Who's Been Sleeping in my Bed? You and Me and the State Makes Three," *Indiana Law Review* 24:1 (1991), 399–416.

38. Chrys Ingraham, *White Weddings : Romancing Heterosexuality in Popular Culture* (New York: Routledge, 1999), 167–168.

39. Ibid., 168–169.

40. For an excellent analysis of the plethora of damning media images of Ms. Lewinsky, see chapter 3 of Leora Tannenbaum's *SLUT: Growing Up Female With a Bad Reputation* (New York: Seven Stories Press, 1999), 95–99.

41. *People,* Oct. 2000:65.

42. Ibid., 64.

43. "Politically Incorrect," ABC, 24 June 1999.

44. Ingraham, *White Weddings,* 169–170.

45. Writing in 1997 the Americanist Gerda Lerner claimed "In 1980 the divorce rate was 3.5 percent of all marriages, today it is nearly 50 percent." [sic] *Why History Matters,* 97.

46. Brooke, *Medieval Ideas of Marriage,* 64.

FORTY-THREE

◆◆◆

Raising Kids como Los Americanos

María Hinojosa

Thank the santos for Annie LaMott's book *Operating Instructions.* I kept it near my bed at night and read it so that the author's baby and mine were growing up in the same time frame and I could compare notes. At least this way I felt as if there was someone else out there who wasn't a perfect mother. There were those moments when I did feel like things were smooth and sailing, but much of the time I felt simply inadequate. I saw all of these other mothers walking along Broadway, wheeling their babies around in groups of two and three, and wondered why I didn't have any other mom friends. And then I would see a newly arrived Mexicana immigrant around the corner from my house, walking with three young kids, managing a family and a new country and at least looking as if she had it under control. And then there was my son and me—all alone.

My notes in Raul Ariel's baby book continued as the weeks went by: "Constipation woes! First suppository—explosivo! First ah-goo. First time that you laugh and squeal in delight. You touched Mami's face deliberately for the first time. You love to stand on your legs and hold your head up. Your first shower. You loved it! First visit to a dim sum restaurant. First visit to church to say hello to your tocayo Jesús. First shots. Yikes! First day in your life that you feel warm air—it was seventy-four degrees today!"

That happened on April 12, the first fresh blue-sky day in what felt like months. That day I put Raul Ariel in the snuggly and went out to buy him his stroller. I was going to take him for his first-ever visit to the playground. I bought the stroller that the store owner recommended ("It's British," he said. "All Manhattan mothers buy this one!"), strapped my baby in, and walked his little Domini-Mex self to the park.

This was the new me. Mami the full-time mom. The newness of it reminded me of my first day as a working journalist—the day I walked into the NPR offices in Washington. I was excited and scared. And here I was feeling the same thing on my way to the playground.

At the park, it seemed like all the other mothers and nannies knew each other. I stayed to myself and placed Raul Ariel into a swing and we had a sweet fifteen minutes. But then he started pouting and I realized he needed to poo, so I lifted him up and held him upright. Moms were beginning to smile at me. I smiled back. This wasn't so bad after all.

Raul Ariel scrunched his face and pushed and I was laughing at him when all of a sudden the poo started slipping out of his diaper and onto his pants. I looked around, embarrassed. This had never happened before. I tried to keep him upright while I grabbed his bag from the stroller, and it was only then that I realized that I had forgotten his baby bag!

I had no wipes, no diaper, no change of clothes. Caca was everywhere. New stroller, new outfit, crying baby, and a long ten-block walk home.

Mala madre!

I never left the house again without a lifetime supply of baby needs.

It was just about that time that Gérman and I had one of our biggest fights ever. It was so bad that we stopped talking to each other for twenty-four hours—that had never happened before. And what did we fight about? Raul Ariel's naps!

Gérman wanted to play his music as loud as he usually did when he worked on his paintings. "The baby shouldn't change our lifestyle. He needs to integrate into our lives and not the other way around," he echoed what Dr. Mark had said to us.

"Yes, but Dr. Mark also said that the baby needs to take his naps and if the music is keeping him awake then it's not going to happen!"

Dr. Mark had become the invisible referee for our fights over babydom.

After twenty-four hours of noncommunication, we both broke down and compromised. The music would stay on but not full volume. And Raul Ariel would take naps in his room with the door closed.

Oh, the joys of co-parenting. Before, women ran the house and that was that. Now everything had to be debated and agreed on in conjunction and a mother's intuition had to be constantly explained to fathers.

It was hard enough just digging deep enough to find out what my mother's intuition was. I knew it had to be there. Somewhere. But now I had to give reasons for everything I did to my baby's father. Ay. More work.

What I did know was that I was in love with my son and every time I nursed him to sleep I would paint the picture of that moment in my mind and say to myself, "Never forget this moment. This is bliss." I would stare at his pursed lips as they sucked, marvel at his dark deer eyes and mile-long eyelashes. I would squeeze him tight and cover his face with besos. Te adoro, te quiero, te adoro, mi pequeño príncipe, I would whisper into his tiny ear.

And when he would wake from his nap I would turn on the music—maybe Juan Luis Guerra, maybe Ana Belem, maybe Tracy Chapman—and dance and sing with him. Mi muchachito is going to have rhythm, I would say to him as he stared at my curls, twirling through the air.

Sometimes I did think I was doing some things right.

On the phone, Bertha Elena gave me tips on stimulating him with colors and sounds. Mom told me not to carry him too much because "se me iba a embrasilar," he was going to get dependent on my arms for everything. Sandy told me to shower him with kisses, Ceci only asked me questions about her advancing pregnancy, Ro squeezed in my phone calls to her in between meetings, and Victor and Graci were busy traveling all over the world going to genetics conferences. But with all the talking on the phone, it wasn't like people were pouring into the house to visit. I got the feeling people didn't want to disturb us because life with a newborn was supposed to be so difficult or because they couldn't deal with us as parents. Nonetheless, I missed many of my friends.

Gérman was my rock. If I couldn't get Raul Ariel to go to sleep, Gérman would do it. If I couldn't get Raul Ariel's burp out, Gérman would do it. If I didn't get around to making dinner, Gérman would do it. Sometimes I thought Gérman was better at mothering than I was. I couldn't imagine doing this alone— as a single mom or doing it alone with a husband who worked all the time. Gérman and I were a team.

But with all my rap about accepting difference and how difference and diversity were good things,

I couldn't accept that the way I was mothering was okay, just different. I kept on comparing myself to all the moms I knew and coming up short. I wasn't like my cousins, I wasn't like the moms on TV, I wasn't like the moms in the magazines, I wasn't like my sister, or my mother, or even Ro. And I felt guilty about depending on Gérman so much. *A real mother sacrifices herself for her child*—the never-ending tape that played inside my head said. A real mother would wake up herself at three in the morning to feed the baby. A real mother wouldn't have a baby-sitter in the house. A real mother would have read all of the books about parenting and be an encyclopedia of information.

I wonder if the comparisons would ever end.

When Raul Ariel was five months old we took him to meet his future girlfriend in Chicago. Ceci had just had a little girl.

"Malu, I don't know what to do," Ceci said when we got together. She looked exhausted with dark rings under her eyes. Her usually flawless face looked gray and wrinkly. She seemed nervous. "My baby won't stop crying. She won't stop nursing. And she won't stay down for more than fifteen minutes at a time. I'm at my wit's end."

And just as my mother had done for me, I told Ceci that what she needed to do was to rest. So I took her daughter in one arm and Raul Ariel in the other and walked into the living room. I told Ceci to go to her bedroom and close the door.

"Sleep, Ceci," I said. "Just take a nap. I'll take care of both of them."

And while Raul Ariel napped, I held Ceci's baby. And when she started to cry, I thought of my mother when she had held Raul Ariel as a newborn. And I thought of how Mom had just exuded motherly know-how when she held him. And so I tried to do the same thing with Ceci's daughter. I told myself that I knew what I was doing, that I knew how to wrap and hold this newborn and make her go to sleep. All of a sudden I had become my mom. I knew how to do this. It was as if I stepped through some curtain and had made it to the other side. I knew how to mother, not only my own but someone else's. And I gave the gift of sleep to my querida amiga.

It really was a wonderful moment and I told Ceci all about it. She was feeling like I had felt not too long ago (more like days ago), like she was never going to get the hang of it, never going to be able to develop her own mother's intuition. So I decided to tell Ceci that beyond all of the romanticism of the moment and me proving to myself that I could mother two,

that there *was* one little practical thing I had done as well that had probably held Ceci's daughter finally sleep.

"Your baby had diaper rash, Ceci. So yeah, I have great motherly arms that can rock a crying newborn to sleep and all that, but the real secret is that I put Balmex on her colita!"

It was great to be back at my old apartment in Chicago with my family. Mom immediately started doing things with Raul Ariel that I would have never done. She got him in to a little high chair (But he can't even sit up yet! I said anxiously) and stuffed pillows all around him so that he was upright and then she gave him a hard roll to play with. "Ma, he doesn't even eat yet. How can you give him food? He's going to choke. Something is going to happen to him! He's too young to eat." And before I could finish listing my worries, Raul Ariel had grabbed the bread and was gnawing at it with gusto!

Then she pulled out a banana, "Un poquito, nada más, Malulis! Nothing is going to happen to him. This is what we use to do in México. We always started con un poquito de platanito."

"Mom, are you sure? Our doctor said he didn't have to eat solids for another month and he said to start him off with orange veggies, not fruit!"

Raul Ariel loved the banana.

And that night when I gave him his bath, Mom said, "Tu abuelita always said to let the baby taste a little of his bath water. It makes them talk sooner."

"Mami! No!"

But before I knew it Raul Ariel was smacking his lips and smiling in the tub. And a minute later he made a garbled attempt at a word.

Later, Mom and I talked as we cleaned up the kitchen. She had made her exquisite picadillo, Mexican-style ground beef with spices and raisins. I had eaten six tacos and was about to burst.

"I don't know how you did it, Mom. Four kids, in a new country, all alone, with Dad working all the time. Didn't you go through massive culture shock? Weren't you sad? Did you ever feel like you could never get things right? Like the mothers all around you knew more than you did?"

"You know what, mi'jita? I just did what I had to do. My feelings came last. And by the end of the day I was too tired to think about them. You women today suffer more. Pobrecitas! It was easier to be ignorant like I was."

"But Mom, you weren't ignorant. You were just young."

"Bueno, mi'jita. I'll never forget the time when my first American neighbor told me that I should go read some psychology books. She said she had never seen a mother as compulsive as me.

"I couldn't answer because I didn't even know what the word *psychology* meant," Mom said to me, laughing. She proceeded to tell me the story.

The year was 1958 and it was Dad's first sabbatical at the University of Chicago and their first time living in the United States. Every morning, Mami told me, she used to wake up and clean the entire apartment. She made the beds every day the way she was taught in Mexico. The sheets would all come off and be sacudidos out the window and then put on again. Changed and washed every week, Mami would iron them before putting them on the beds. My sister and brother would be dressed up in starched clean clothes every day—my four-year-old sister in petticoats and white patent-leather shoes; my brother, who was two, in crisp shirts and suspenders, his white shoelaces washed every night and hung on the banister to dry. This is how Mom would take them out to play in the backyard. But my sister, Bertha Elena, never played in the dirt. And my brother Raul had never been in a sandbox because sandboxes didn't exist in Mexico. And when it was time for meals, Mom spoon-fed them every meal, every day, every week—just as my tías did in Mexico.

The upstairs neighbor would see my mom doing all of this and, of course, thought she was manic and obsessive. Ruth, the mother of a three-year-old, was a graduate student in psychology. She was also a Jewish bohemian and decided she was going to be my mother's first teacher in America. They couldn't have possibly been more different.

Mami said she was open to this new experience sin prejuicios, without prejudice. She had to *learn* how to become a part of this strange place. And why not? This country was her new home. She was open and willing to learn. Maybe it was because she was a youngster herself, a mother of two and just twenty years old. Or maybe it was because it has always been my mother's character to be willing to try anything new. Or maybe it was because my mother was profoundly insecure about who she was and the new life she was leading in el Norte and she wanted to blend in as quickly as possible.

Ruth loaned my mom her child-psychology books. She talked to Mom about the importance of giving children their independence, of letting them experiment, how this helped build character. She explained that an apartment didn't need to be cleaned constantly. That the time she spent doing that might be better spent playing with my brother and sister, playing games that would stimulate their creative and intellectual development. She told Mom about how her kids should be put on a schedule because that's what Dr. Spock recommended. Mom went home and looked up the word schedule in the book Ruth had given her. All night she tried to understand how to pronounce it. *SSS-cheh-dool . . . sss-cheh-dool*, she repeated to herself. What did this word mean? *Sss-cheh-dool?* My father, whose English was just a bit better than Mom's, had no idea what word my mom was trying to say.

One night, Mom remembers, she put on a Cri Crí record, the Mexican singing grasshopper that sang children's songs, the same ones Mami listened to on the radio when she was a child growing up. In her small Chicago apartment, while everyone else was asleep, she sat next to the portable phonograph, listening to the scratchy Cri Crí rhymes and cried. She missed Mexico, she missed her mother, she missed the place where no one questioned her or called her words she didn't understand, like *obsessive*.

Ruth knew more about raising children than Mami, she thought. She would try doing things her way, the American way. She was alone, away from her family who only knew how to raise kids à la Mexicana. No one questioned how kids were raised back home—así se hace y punto. It was done that way and that was that, period. She decided there might be no better time to try something new. Maybe Ruth and this Dr. Spock were right.

So in no time, my brother was wearing sweatpants and playing in the mud. My sister discovered the sandbox, but she asked my mom to please let her wear petticoats and white shoes while she played there. They also started to eat by themselves and they liked it.

How gringo this all was. But Mom said she liked it, too. She felt like she was suddenly more sophisticated than her sisters back in Mexico. Así lo hacen los Americanos, she would say to them when she went back home and told them all she had learned. She would even take them a few jars of precooked Gerber food. My aunts would never think of feeding their babies this.

My father barely noticed this seismic shift in his newly Americanized household. He was busy at work with the microscope, developing his specialty of studying the inner ear. But when they went back to Mexico after spending the year in Chicago, there were many people who noticed and the criticisms were heaped on my mom fast and furious. How could she do this to her children? Let them eat on their own? Give them food out of a jar? Let them get dirty and not change their clothes? Estás muy rara, Berta, they would say. You are acting strange. Los Americanos are getting to you. But don't let them. Remember your traditions, remember that we have been raising our children like this for decades and we haven't changed and our children are fine.

Just as quickly as she had embraced the American ways of childrearing, Mom let them go soon after she had returned to Mexico. She had two more children and raised them à la Mexicana, Good-bye *sss-cheh-dools*, Dr. Spock, Gerber foods, and psychology. Back to "así se hace y punto." No more discussions with her sisters, no more accusations of becoming *agringada*, a gringa.

But then, four years later, la crisis occurred in Mexico and life changed forever.

When it happened Mom was the mother of four and happy with her life. The family had been struggling financially—there is no fortune to be made as a research medical doctor—but my father had been promised a job in the new hospital that was being built by the Mexican government. Finally, they would be able to make ends meet. Just as they were putting the finishing touches on the hospital construction, a new Mexican president was ushered in and the hospital was no longer on the new president's "to do" list and so it lay idle and my father was out of a job. Chicago was the one place where he knew he could continue his work.

He made arrangements with the hospital there and left before my mom to find a place to live. Three weeks later, we left Mexico to join him in our new home. . . .

One night during our visit to Chicago, after Raul Ariel had fallen to sleep, I stayed up looking through old boxes in what had been my room when I was growing up. As I picked through old pictures from grammar school and secret love notes from high school boyfriends, I thought about how my own experience growing up had been shaped by the very particular choices Mom had made for herself and for all of us. Just as Raul Ariel's experience would be shaped by my choices.

I opened up the boxes, laid out old dolls and photographs, and let my mind wander. I thought of friends, both old and new, and how important they were in my life. It was Mami who had been the one who taught me *how* to make friends, I realized.

It was the sixties when I was growing up and Chicago was a divided city but my mother was a woman of little prejudice and this she taught to us, not through lessons in a book or with words, but in the way she lived her life. Our parents seemed to be friends with everyone, and every weekend I looked forward to visiting someone else's house.

Like Peter and Pamela's, for instance.

"People we knew used to call Peter and Pamela white trash," Mami had once told me. "I didn't know what that meant back then, but I knew it wasn't anything good: I just kept those words to myself. But, when we would go visit Peter and Pamela, *they* in turn would say horrible things about Black people. And you know we had friends who were Black. I'll never forget the day Pamela said she wished all the Black people in the country would fall into a bucket of bleach. I told her that was a horrible thing to say but she just shushed me. I always felt as if we were in the middle, hearing people saying such nasty things. But all of these different people were our friends and yours, too."

I remembered that Pamela was twice as tall as Mami, with a head twice as long as mine and a smile that reminded me of the Joker from *Batman*. She wore black glasses that curled up in the corners and that had little pieces of crystal that made it look like there were stars on her face. Pamela taught Mom how to make fried chicken. They would spend most of their time in the kitchen. Sometimes I would see Pamela sitting hunched over the kitchen table, her shoulders shaking. Mami would stand next to her and rub her back. I didn't realize then that she was crying. I thought adults didn't cry since I had never seen Mom or Dad do it.

Peter was the manager at the gas station where Papi went every week to fill up the family car. He had a big belly and his hair always looked wet because of the gel he wore in it every day. At his house he would sit in front of the TV, smoking, talking to Dad about sports, and Dad would listen even though he didn't really care for baseball or football. But he would listen, mostly, because Peter didn't understand Dad too well because of his accent, and he would always ask one of us kids to tell him what

Dad was trying to say. So Dad just sat and listened while we played hide-and-seek with their six kids in the two-floor, two-bedroom, crooked white house.

I remember Peter and Pamela were the only friends of my parents who let us call them by their first names. I liked them a lot. But then one day they moved and didn't tell us where they were going. I cried because I missed Suzie, the girl my age who laughed like a seal. Only then did Mom explain to me that Suzie and her brother who died (he got run over by a car) were mentally retarded. Peter and Pamela moved away because the kids from their neighborhood used to tease Suzie too much and recently Suzie tried to run onto the same highway where her brother got killed, and it wasn't because she was running after a ball. It was because she was running away from kids who were calling her names. Peter and Pamela left to get away from that highway.

We didn't live near a highway, but there was a busy street on our route to school and there worked a crossing guard named Lorraine. She was short and round and dark, and we used to give her hugs and kisses on her soft face underneath her white crossing guard hat. One day Mami had to take my sister to the doctor for an emergency, and she had no one to leave my brothers and me with, so she asked Lorraine if we could stay with her at the corner until she came back. Lorraine offered to take us home and that was how our friendship began. After that day, Lorraine would always come to the house to take care of us, and she became like our second mother and all the kids at school thought it was strange that we would become friends with the school crossing guard.

Lorraine became my mother's best friend and a part of our family.

One Thanksgiving we spent with Lorraine in her apartment on the tenth floor of the Cabrini Green housing project. I remember the elevator was dirty and smelled and the windows had black grating over them so everything looked dark. We listened to Motown and Lorraine put on boxing gloves and started to teach my brother how to box. He had been beaten up in school a couple of times because he was a smart aleck and Lorraine told him he had to learn how to defend himself. My sister, who was by then a teenager, said that when she told her friends she was going to Lorraine's house in the projects, they all said she was going to come back with cooties.

All I knew was that I loved Lorraine and I knew Mami did as well and this was Lorraine's house and she had invited us here.

I always thought that what saved my mother from suffering in her new country was her ignorance and her naïveté. That what allowed her to be so open and accepting of so many people was the fact that she wasn't worldly enough to know prejudice. It wasn't her ignorance that kept her from being judgmental I realized. Her openness was part of her, part of her experience handed down to her by my own grandmother who was nicknamed la pata de perro, a dog's foot, because she was always taking her kids on one adventure or another, like a stray dog traveling the streets. Mami grew up traveling throughout Mexico, spending nights in pueblos, sharing buses and bedrooms with the peasants who lived in the countryside. I doubt that Mom grew up feeling superior to people. This was instilled in her as a child, by my abuelita.

The next morning in Chicago we all took a walk to the beach so that Raul Ariel could see Lake Michigan. Dad carried Raul Ariel in his arms the same way I had seen him carry me in the picture in our family photo album.

This trip home was all about memories.

We passed by the first apartment we lived in when we arrived here. I had an image in my head of when I was four years old. I am wearing pink-plastic high-heeled glittering slippers that Mami bought me at Woolworth's. I have a pair of pink nylon pajama pants on my head, my make-believe long locks of straight blond hair. I am wearing an old petticoat and skirt and twirling in circles in the kitchen, around the portable dishwasher, on the old rust-colored linoleum floor. I am singing, with a proper English accent, all of the lyrics of the Hollywood musicals that I love. My favorite was "I could have danced all night, I could have danced all night, and still have asked for more . . . !" I believe I am Eliza Doolittle, I am the Fair Lady, I am Audrey Hepburn. I *am* her. The next day I am Julie Andrews and my husband is the gorgeous Dick Van Dyke. I ride a pink horse that takes me down a cobblestone lane into a beautiful park where everything looks like it is made of candy. I can sing *supercalifragilistic-expialidocious*, repeating it faster and faster and faster because I can speak English. Yes, I can! I am Mary Poppins. I am that tall, graceful, sophisticated lady with the frilly umbrella. And as I get older I fall in love with Michael Jackson, Elton John, David Bowie. I dress up in high school on Saturday nights to go see *The Rocky Horror Picture Show.* I wear one of my mother's old black slips over a white T-shirt and paint my lips ruby red. Mami watches me as I become all of these things and she lets me be. She let me *be.*

I look at Raul Ariel and I think, if he ever wants to become a Power Ranger I will have a fit.

I'm already worrying about letting Raul Ariel watch Barney when he gets a little older. I want to keep him far away from the claws of popular, commercialized culture. I hide the Mickey Mouse doll a friend gave him and replace it with a Mayan one. Am I wrong? Am I crazy? How long am I going to do this for, I wonder?

I wish I could mother my son the way my mother mothered me. Just let things be.

But when I think about it, I find it hard to remember that Mom ever played with me. The message from all of the books and magazines is all about quality time with your children. About how important it is for you to just play with your kids.

And I realize that I don't often make time just to play with Raul Ariel. Our time together is often spent doing things—going shopping, cooking, cleaning up, bathing, nursing. I don't feel like it comes naturally to just sit and play with him for hours on end. Paty the babysitter does that. Maybe that's another reason why I feel like I'm an inadequate mother.

Back at home, I ask Mom if she ever made the time just to play with me.

"Pues, I didn't have that much time, mi reina. I was raising three other kids and running the entire household by myself," she says. "But I gave you other things, mi'jita," she says and gives me a hug. She takes my face in her hand and kisses me tenderly on the cheek.

"Yeah, Mom, you did," I said, and kissed her back.

It's true that I couldn't remember the times Mami played jacks with me, but I could remember specific moments of finding solace in her arms, her voice, her scent.

I remember that I loved to knead my small hands into the softness of her upper arms. I would squeeze her tight and she would squeeze back and cover my face with soft delicate kisses. Sometimes her kisses would be snuggly ones, hard and fast all over my neck and arms, ending up with my fingertips. Some nights when I was feeling especially needy for comfort I would call to Mami from my bed and tell her that my legs were hurting because I could feel them growing. She would bring in the alcohol that she bought in Mexico (made specifically for growing pains she would tell me), and then she would wet her hands in it and rub my legs from top to bottom. Up and down my legs, the cool alcohol lifting away my imaginary growing pains. Manos sobadoras, my mother has—like the hands of the medicine women in Mexico—las sobadoras.

"Sóbame aquí, Mami. Sóbame más, no pares," I would say to Mom. "Massage me here, Mom. Massage me more. Don't stop." And she wouldn't until I was fast asleep.

I remember that every night, Mom was there to tuck me in and bless me the way she had been taught by her mother. She would start by making a cross on my forehead, thumb and forefinger together. Then she would touch my lips with the same tender movement, and finally make another imaginary cross in front of my chest. She would whisper "Por la señal de la santa cruz, de nuestros enemigos, líbranos señor, Dios nuestro" so softly that it was only through sensing her breath that I knew she was talking. And then she would finish by blessing me in the name of the Father, the Son, and the Holy Ghost. "En el nombre del Padre, del Hijo, del Espíritu Santo." A kiss on her warm fingers and then Amén. We would always stare into each other's eyes for a long while after that and then she would come close to me and hug me again, another kiss on both cheeks, a long stroke with her hands through my hair. I would snuggle into bed and she would tuck the sheet tight across my body so I could barely move, immobilized under the covers, as if I was a newborn again and she was wrapping me papoose-style in a blanket. "Más apretado, Mami. Tighter, Mami. Make it tighter." And she would.

It is what I, without realizing until that very moment, give to my son already. Limitless closeness with hugs and kisses and my own manos sobadoras. My own long, luxurious stroking of his hair, my fingers sweeping down his eyes and nose until he is mesmerized into profound sleep. The interlocked eyes as he nurses. Giving him love the way I know how, the way I was taught. This I do know how to do. This I can give because it was given to me. This is my way of mothering and it is good and it is right, I say to myself.

◆◆◆

Personal Reflections on Being a Grandmother
L'Chol Dor Va Dor

Rachel Aber Schlesinger[1]

My Grandmother

My maternal grandmother lived with us. I learned from her that grandmothers have great power. They represent a relationship that, like a parent's, demands respect and provides love but is different. *Omamma* was a "queen," she kept religious standards high, passed on a sense of family history, and told wonderful stories. She helped give us a sense of who we were and what we stood for. Our family had religious and family traditions. We were a matriarchal family. The men were important and respected, but the names and the stories were those of the mothers.

The family stories began with my great-grandparents, the rabbi and *rebbitzin* of Luebeck. They had twelve children. My great-grandmother greeted the birth of each child, and indeed every family occasion with a poem, a *Tischlied*. In quiet moments she wrote a book of poetry for the young Jewish bride, stressing the family and religious roles of Jewish women. This book of poems was still given to my older cousin upon marriage. Before the Second World War, the lives of these women and the poems held commonly understood meanings.

My grandmother was the oldest of eight daughters. In her later years she wrote her memoirs. Even in this religious family the important items that she remembered were elegant balls, clothes, and meeting her husband. She lived in the age of romance, and saw her early years in these terms. She was also

[1]I was able to carry out this research with the help of a grant from Canada Multicultural Department and the Centre of Jewish Studies at York University. I want to thank Sarah Taieb Carlen for conducting some of the interviews with Sephardi women in French, and for her help with this project.

deeply religious and supervised the early religious teachings of her grandchildren.

Tragically, she was widowed as a young woman. Her life in Germany was devoted to social service activities; her home was filled with interesting people. Upon her death I found correspondence from Bertha Pappenheim dealing with rescue activities for Jewish women and children. Omamma spoke English well and came to America by way of Portugal in the 1940s. Once here, she divided her time between living with her two surviving children, my mother and my uncle. She did small jobs, was a companion to others, and baby-sat, yet this work never diminished her queenly status in her eyes or in the eyes of others.

My Mother as Grandmother

I was able to understand my mother in her role as a grandparent because of the influence of my grandmother. Both women were unique; daughters and wives of distinguished rabbis, they had a strong sense of self, of Jewish values, and of family *Yehus*.

Mutti's world changed with the Nazi era. My mother's stories were told not to her children who experienced the events she recounted, but to her grandchildren. Since I was the youngest of her children I didn't remember these experiences, but my children told me Mutti's stories. Here is one of the stories.

On *Krystallnacht* in November 1938, the synagogue in Bremen was destroyed and my father, the rabbi, was taken to a concentration camp. My mother, known by Jew and non-Jew in this middle-sized port city, worked for his release and that of the other men taken that night. Each day, as the story goes, she went with her three daughters to the Gestapo headquarters to ask when the men would be released. One day she was told that they would be sent home on a midnight train, but she did not know which night. Every night, at midnight, she walked to the railway station to see if my father would be coming on that train. Every night, she heard footsteps behind her as a Gestapo officer followed her through dingy parts of town. That did not deter her.

Weeks later, after this routine was followed each night, my father did indeed arrive on a train. Mutti turned around at the station. The footsteps behind

her had stopped. She looked up to see the Gestapo officer salute her and my father. He had been following her each night for her protection. That is the kind of devotion my beautiful mother inspired.

Mutti believed in the power of the individual, and the vital role of the woman in the family and in the community. She was a deeply committed Jew. Her religion, her vocation, and her belief system were holistic. I know that her grandchildren loved her, respected her, and understood her. My son told me, "Mutti was unusual. She really believed in what she believed in!"

My Own Experience

Now I am a grandmother. I am a living ancestor! My stories will be different, I live in another land, in another time. I wonder if any of us can transmit to our children's children the tastes, the smells, the environment, the understanding of the values that shaped us.

What do I want to pass on to my grandchildren? I find it easier to ask "how," than to pinpoint "what" it is I want to transmit. Like my grandmother I tell stories, sing songs, and recount family history. If my sisters and I have pictures, we put them on the walls. We use the ability to name to perpetuate memories and names. Those of us who were born in other countries speak in our mother tongue. We use language to recall roots. We model our religious practices and holiday observances. We convey our oral traditions in the kitchens of our homes. As our grandchildren get older, we share secrets often not told to our own children.

The bond between grandchild and grandparents may be the strongest, and of the longest duration, next to the parent bond. Can grandparents transmit values, or is this too difficult due to the age gap between the first and third generation, differences in life experiences, and competition from outside agents of socialization?

Immigrant Grandmothers

For the past few years I have been talking with Jewish grandmothers, asking them about their perceptions of being a grandparent and transmitting their own values to their grandchildren. Let me introduce some of the women who shared their thoughts on this question.

Sephardi Grandmothers

Sara comes from Morocco. There is a big difference between her world and that of her grandmother. Her grandmother was married at twelve years of age and was only fifteen when Sara's mother was born. The role of women in her community was important. Sara recounts that it was often the woman who urged the family to leave, either for Israel, France, or Canada. In Morocco, women lived in separate spheres, yet had valued roles. With the shift to a new country, their roles changed. The family changed from being a large, extended family living with each other to having members dispersed. Sara's family life is strongly linked to religious observance. "If you can't cook, you can't fulfill your religious obligations."

Leaving Morocco meant leaving cultural roles behind. "My grandmother's religious views and her ways will be acknowledged in her home, but maybe not in ours. This means that while we have memory, we may not have continuity of culture." In order for a culture to survive, it must be practiced. It is not good enough to talk of the "old days," if they are not followed today.

Lena, born in Morocco, adds: "Family traditions . . . are very important. They are mostly French traditions, like table manners, classical music, French literature. Yes, in my country, it was our way." She talks about a way of life that combines Jewish and secular culture, a civilized worldview, formed by Continental culture in an Arabic environment, far removed from her present North Toronto setting.

Pina says, "I want to give them an idea of the way we lived. My father taught me wisdom; my mother's family had been in Iraq for millennia, maybe since Abraham."

Nadia, who comes from Turkey adds: "I have to tell them about our life. . . . Here, there is no Turkish atmosphere, no Turkish synagogue, no Turkish bath, no Turkish schools . . . so I have to talk about our way of life, and it is not always possible to imagine. It's like a dream."

Values grow out of a culture. These Sephardi grandmothers want to pass on respect and obedience to elders, for "they know more than us, they have a whole life behind them. Respect, it's like breathing. It comes naturally; we are born with it" (Mrs. C).

Ashkenazi Grandmothers

While Jews from Eastern Europe also had close associations with their home countries, when they talk of bringing grandchildren "home" it is to teach them what can happen to Jewish communities. It is to put the Holocaust into personal terms. Or it is to put the Russian experience into perspective.

Ada is under five feet tall, and she is a survivor— of the Holocaust, of displaced-person camps, of migrations to several countries, before settling in Canada twenty years ago. She spoke in optimistic terms about her life.

For her, her grandchildren are a miracle, the remnants of a family that is once again extended. She feels the need to transmit memories, and has taken her five grandchildren to Poland, to see the *Camps,* to show them what she has survived. She tells them how she picked up her life after the war. She returned to Poland after the war, met her husband, lived in Israel, then came to Canada.

She wants to perpetuate language, not Polish but Hebrew, and speaks it with her grandchildren. Ada models her values, she still volunteers time as a nurse's aide, and together with her husband, remains active in the community. She lives within walking distance of her children.

She finds it difficult to convey her Jewish values. "One son-in-law does not speak Hebrew; he is a Canadian, and cannot even understand the feelings of being a survivor. He tells me I spoil the children."

Mrs. Z came to Canada seven years ago; she focuses on her Lithuanian experiences. Her grandchildren do not understand why she chose to remain in a Communist country. Indeed, she had a high position in the government. She was eventually able to connect with her grandchildren by telling them about her experiences in the underground during the Second World War. She still has difficulties, since her children in Canada became "very Jewish, and I don't understand this. It was not my way."

These women are survivors—of their generation, of the Holocaust, of war. They can no longer return for a visit with their grandchildren; their world died. Many return to visit the death camps, but some women do not want their grandchildren to associate the Jewish life of their own youth only with death and destruction.

Domestic Religion, Food, and Practice

In our families we model our beliefs, talk about them, emphasize what's important. Religious observance is an area we articulate, often in loud, judgmental terms. The grandmothers speak of learning, religious rituals, and observance.

Religion is often viewed from the perspective of the kitchen. Cooking for holidays, talking in the kitchen, passing on *kashrut* by doing, not by reading; these are all examples of transmitting values. Recipes are handed over from generation to generation; they are part of the .oral tradition. This too is religious commentary.

In terms of religious observances and even foods, the Sephardi feel a degree of cognitive dissonance. The foods they ate at home are not common in Canada. Ashkenaza families can find familiar kosher or kosher-style foods in supermarkets; the Sephardi cannot.

Mrs. W. had been unable to follow her religion in her home country. "In Latvia I couldn't be religious. Here I want to be, but my husband is still afraid. My granddaughter helps me."

Grandmothers feel that they have contributions to make to the family in terms of ideas, responsibilities, child care, and even financial assistance. Many of them hope that they are role models, as indeed their grandparents had been to them. It is important to them to be seen as representing the old culture, providing continuity of family traditions, while still being close to their grandchildren. They articulate the values of a Jewish education, family closeness and the concept of *Shalom Bayit*. They feel a sense of responsibility to ensure this for the next generation.

These grandmothers reflected a wistfulness for times past. Singing together reminds them of their own childhood. The first contacts with a new grandchild are often through singing songs in grandmother's mother tongue. They hope their grandchildren will respect them as older persons, by means of their behavior, such as good manners. They report that their grandchildren do respect their views and opinions, often coming to them before going to parents to ask for advice.

Roadblocks

Some fear they do not have a place in their grandchildren's lives now, but hope this will develop with time. Factors that impede communication and closeness include physical location, distance, family mobility, and family fragmentation.

Grandparents often have less formal education than their children or grandchildren, and some feel that this educational gap creates barriers. Others report feeling "inferior," "not modern enough." They feel inadequate because they can only transmit what is most common to their own life and experience, for example the customs, traditions, and history of their country of origin. Yet their children and grandchildren may not have a frame of reference for the information grandmothers wish to impart. So much is lost, replaced by strange new ways. Grandparents try to fit their culture into a new setting, and that is often a difficult task.

Even the words we use have changed. In Jewish tradition an older person was a *zakena*, a person of wisdom. In modern Hebrew, the terms *Saba* and *Safta* are used to denote grandparents, the father of my father; what has happened to the concept of wisdom?

Some Reflections

Some of the grandmothers felt frustrated, partly because the changes that have taken place during their lifetimes make it difficult to transmit a sense of what was. Their own world has been transformed through transitions.

Family roles have changed and older women see their status as lower in Canada than it might have been in the old society. The pattern of immigration itself has weakened family links. The new buzz-word of "individualization" undermines the sense of family and of community as well as woman's and grandmother's role in the family. Grandmothers no longer occupy the same physical space as their children and grandchildren, and they fear that their domestic religion is out of their hands. Today's grandmother may really have little influence in conveying her concept of Jewish culture. A way of life has altered in a short span of time.

The grandmothers I interviewed examined the concepts of societal changes and ideological shifts. The Sephardi women spoke of open community life; some of the Eastern Europeans had belonged to the *Bund* and grown up on socialism. One needs to question if it is possible to have cultural transmission when the culture and politics have changed so drastically.

Are Jewish grandmothers different? Perhaps. This generation of women gives great importance to perpetuating the Jewish people. Older grandparents today are a generation who experienced migrations, displacements, and the Holocaust. We cherish the ability to have given birth, to survive as a people. We worry about the Jewishness of our children and grandchildren. We do have values to pass on—from generation to generation.

Can I transmit a sense of family to my grandchildren? Hopefully, yes. I can provide the smells of *hallah* baking; I can surround them with pictures of family members, of places and events. I can record voices for them to listen to; I can even use videos to pinpoint places and people. Modern technology helps, but being there, talking, being willing to listen, trying to explain our perspective, and respecting our own children and grandchildren may be the keys to future communications and continuity. Our grandchildren are not mind readers; contact, open communication, and understanding are also necessary ingredients in a relationship.

It is harder to impart religious values for eventually we each must find our own path and follow it for a time. We too change and may change our perspectives. That is what we can try to pass on—the ability to see and judge for oneself.

What do I want to communicate? I want healthy, thoughtful, creative, and caring family members—the rest is commentary.

L'chol Dor Va Dor, from generation to generation. My grandmother once told me, "listen carefully to what I will tell you . . . then you will tell this story to your children, and they will tell it to their grandchildren.

But will the story lose its meaning? My grandmother's and mother's stories were unique, coming from urgent times and far away places. I am part of the quiet generation. While I was born in Germany and raised by European parents, I grew up in North America. I need to add my own stories to those of the women in my family.

We are links in a long chain—which of the stories will our great-grandchildren repeat?

FORTY-FIVE

◆◆◆

Shattering Two Molds
Feminist Parents with Disabilities

Carol J. Gill and Larry A. Voss

We are two persons with extensive physical disabilities who have raised a nondisabled son. Countering the stereotype of people with disabilities as childlike, fragile, and suffering, we have nurtured and, we believe, nurtured powerfully. With wonder and relief, we have watched our child's development into a generous, emotionally open, strong, and socially responsible adult. It was not a snap. All three of us waged a long struggle against society's devaluation of human difference to get to this place.

Our war against ableist beliefs began in childhood when we acquired our disabilities in the 1950 polio epidemic. We used braces and wheelchairs and would have had little problem attending our neighborhood school if not for architecture and its real foundation: attitudes. In those days before the disability rights movement, we were barred from mainstream life. No ramps or elevators were installed to ensure our access. Instead, we were bussed miles each day to a "special" school with similarly displaced children.

Undoubtedly, these experiences laid the groundwork for our acceptance of a feminist perspective. We acquired a deep suspicion of unequal treatment and stereotyping in any form. In high school, we identified with the civil rights struggle. In college, our rejection of sexism took definite shape. For Carol, the conscious decision to participate in the women's movement grew from classroom discussion of the work of Greer, Friedan, and Steinem. For Larry, it grew out of heated ideological debates between men and women in radical student collectives during the antiwar movement.

When Larry married a woman from this movement (his first marriage), he found daily life to be a mixture of new and traditional gender roles. During most of the marriage, his partner, who was not disabled, worked as an intensive care nurse while Larry completed his education. Although they shared household duties according to preferences as well as Larry's disability limitations, it was expected that his partner would cook and perform "housewife" chores after coming home from her job.

The decision to have a baby, on the other hand, was planned to be as joint a venture as possible. Larry remained by his wife's side during her prenatal exams and, long before it was accepted practice, he participated in the birth of his son in the hospital delivery room. He remembers this experience as ecstasy and agony—the incomparable joy of watching his child's birth and his sense of helpless horror as the emerging head made an audible tear in his wife's tissues. That painful moment registered clearly in Larry's consciousness—a factor, perhaps, in his later diligence in shouldering childcare duties.

Larry, in fact, became the primary parent. As is true of most children of disabled parents, Brian had little trouble adapting to his father's wheelchair and unconventional strategies for accomplishing daily tasks. When Larry's marriage foundered, he had no intention of parting with his son, then a toddler. Although it was rare for men to get custody of children in divorces, and even rarer for disabled persons, Larry fought to keep Brian with him and won.

Single parenthood was a rich and difficult time for them. Although Larry's sister and mother helped baby-sit, he experienced the loneliness and weight of responsibility that many single parents face. Additionally, there were unique physical and social difficulties. Unemployed and without child support, Larry could afford neither personal assistance nor adequate accessible housing. Consequently, errands such as grocery shopping became all-day feats of endurance. After driving home from the store, he would be forced to leave his wheelchair at the top of the stairs, crawl down the steps several times to his basement apartment and up again, hauling each bag of groceries followed by the baby, and then drag his wheelchair down the steps so he could get back into it and put groceries away!

Even more exhausting were the social hurdles. Strangers as well as family members challenged Larry's decision to keep his child, citing both gender- and disability-based concerns. Brian's first teachers suggested he was being shortchanged by not having a mother or nondisabled parent. (Brian's biological mother moved out of state and maintained very limited contact with him.) Neighborhood children teased or grilled him about his "wheelchair father" and asked why he had no mother. People who knew nothing about Larry's parenting skills would cluck over Brian's misfortune and tell him that having a "crippled daddy" was his cross to bear.

Although we—Carol and Larry—knew each other superficially while attending the same "special" high school, our paths did not cross again until a mutual friend brought us together at the time of Larry's divorce. After several years of intense and romantic friendship, we married.

At first, Brian was thrilled about Carol joining the family. Even before the wedding, which took place when he was seven, he insisted on calling her "Mom." But once it was official, he was ambivalent. Due both to her disability and her feminism, Brian's "new mother" was anything but the traditional nurturing figure people had told him he needed. She was physically incapable of performing many of the cooking and household chores mothers were supposed to do. She was not conventionally pretty. She was unexpectedly strong in communicating her ideas and affecting household decisions. She was even unwilling to change her name when she got married.

Not that Brian had been raised to be sexist. He had a father who baked cookies, cared for a home, brushed his lover's hair, and became an elementary school teacher. He also knew Larry's fondness for baseball, tools, and macho action movies. Father and son openly shared hugs and kisses between bouts of arm wrestling. Larry's philosophy of child-rearing, like his philosophy of education, stressed openness. He had always been pleased that Brian's early years were fairly non-sex-typed. He had let the toddler's strawberry blond hair grow to shoulder length undaunted by family predictions of gender confusion. He admired Brian's eclectic taste in toy trucks and stuffed animals as well as his drawings of kittens, nudes, Army tanks, Spiderman and posies.

But despite Larry's efforts to raise a child liberated from all the "isms," Brian was exposed to and affected by the sexism and ableism (not to mention racism, ethnocentrism, and heterosexism) of the surrounding culture. Dealing with this in addition to the typical tensions of stepparenting introduced a great deal of struggle into our family life.

It is hard for us to separate where our parenting was guided by feminism or by our experience and values as disabled persons. We believe in both notions of a women's culture and a disabled people's culture. Further, we believe the overlap of cultural values in the two communities is significant. Both feminist analysis and the disability independent living philosophy embrace values of interdependence, cooperative problem-solving, flexibility/adaptability, and the importance of relationships in contrast to traditional male values of autonomy, performance, competition, dominance, and acquisition.

By necessity, a guiding principle of our partnership has always been unfettered cooperation. There has been no "women's work" or "men's work." From the start, we negotiated most tasks of life by deciding who could do it, who was good at it, who wanted to do it, who had time, who needed help, etc. Larry's arm strength meant he had kitchen duty. Carol's greater physical limitations meant she organized the lists and schedules. In our professional jobs, we alternated being the major breadwinner. Everything from lovemaking to getting out of the car was an exercise in cooperation and respect—an orchestration of timing, assistance, and down-to-earth tolerance.

Our parenting was similarly orchestrated. As the only one who could drive, Larry did the car-pooling. Carol's math acuity made her the homework authority. Larry did more of the "hands-on" parenting jobs: cuddling, restraining, washing, roughhousing. Carol nurtured by storytelling, instructing, reprimanding, discussing, and watching endlessly ("Mom, watch this!").

We both did an enormous amount of talking. Larry explained and lectured. Carol questioned motivations and articulated feelings. We even entered family counseling during several difficult times to talk some more. Reflecting back on it, we realize one of the central themes of all this talking was nurturance: caring for and being responsible for people, animals, plants, and the environment. Larry encouraged empathy in Brian through questions like "How do you think you would feel if that happened to you?" Carol nudged Brian to write notes and make gifts for family members. We gave him regular chores

to do for the family and engaged him in many rescues of abandoned and injured stray animals.

Another major theme was prejudice and unfairness. Disability rights and women's rights were frequent topics in our household. Carol often directed Brian's attention to surrounding events, attitudes, and images that contributed to women's oppression, e.g., *Playboy,* sadistic images in rock videos, crude jokes. Most of the time, Brian would roll his eyes and protest that Carol could find sexism in anything. Larry usually backed her up but sometimes he lightened the tension by joining Brian in teasing Carol about her unwillingness to take her menfolk's last name. This was a family joke that ironically conveyed both affection and respect for Carol and got everyone to smile.

We also did a lot of the standard things most people do to raise a nonsexist son, from respecting his need to cry, to encouraging his interests and talents regardless of their traditional "gender appropriateness." Again, this lent a certain eclecticism to Brian's activities, which included sports, cooking, ceramics, drawing, music, reading, swimming and surfing, collecting, etc. On both feminist and pacifist grounds, we tried to avoid the most destructive "macho" stuff. For example, at his request, we enrolled Brian in a karate class. But when we discovered the instructor tested each boy's mettle by getting the class to take turns punching him in the stomach, Larry pronounced it barbaric and encouraged Brian to drop out, which he did. We also kept Brian out of formal team sports run by zealous competitive coaches and pressured him not to join the military when the gung-ho recruiters tried to nab him in high school.

Although we often held little hope that our battle against the "isms" was making an impact, like other parents, we now see that children do pay attention. Brian is now 22 and spontaneously uses words like "sexism" when critiquing the world. He is also our only relative who consistently uses Carol's proper name in introductions and addressing mail. He is comfortable in the friendship of both men and women. He loves sports and still hugs his childhood stuffed dog when he's sick. He has argued for the rights of women, people with disabilities, and other minorities.

Brian has shared his life for four years with a woman who also has strong goals and opinions. They have found a way to support each other, argue, and give space as needed. Like us, they are lover, companion, and family—equals. Seeing them interact is the great payoff to all our years of struggle. We enjoy watching our son laundering his partner's delicate sweaters or lovingly constructing her sandwiches. We listen to him express the depth of his feelings and respect for her. (Yes, he is a talker like his parents!) They have negotiated their course with cooperation, nurturance, and concern about unfairness. They want to have a family, they want to protect the earth.

When we told Brian about writing this piece, we asked his permission to tell the story of our family.

He was enthusiastic and helped us reminisce about the past. One of his recollections confirmed how much he had been affected by the equity in his parents' relationship. He told us that sometimes as a child when he would answer the family telephone, callers would ask to speak to the "head of the house." Brian remembers his natural response to this request was to ask "Which one?" Then he and the caller would have a confusing discussion about which parent was needed on the phone. He said it was always simpler when only one of us was home because then the choice was clear: he would just summon whichever "head of the house" happened to be present!

Loving Across the Boundary

Ann Filemyr

Nubian, our puppy, scratches and whines at the bedroom door. Essie sits bolt upright in bed crying out: "What time is it?" Groggy, I squint at the clock, "Almost seven—"

"Granny was supposed to wake us up at six!"

"Maybe she forgot—" I hustle into my bathrobe at the insistent scratching on the door, "I've got to let Nubi out—"

"Granny never forgets to wake us," Essie mutters under her breath as she scrambles out of the tangled sheets.

I race down the stairs, "Granny! GRANNY!"

I find her body on the cold kitchen floor, but she is gone. I can feel her spirit lifting up and out into the golden morning light filtering through the grand old maples that surround the farmhouse. Despite the utter peace in the room, I panic.

"Essie! Essie Carol!" I scream up the stairs to my partner.

Granny's breath is gone, but her body remains. A line from the book *Daughters of Copper Woman* circles through my mind, *"And she left her bag of bones on the beach. . . ."* Sun crowds the kitchen and the golden maple leaves gleam in October light. Essie flies barefoot across cold linoleum, cradling Granny in her arms, the first sob rising in our throats. . . .

Granny had made her bed that morning. She was dressed and ready for her Monday morning

walk. But instead of the familiar stroll, Granny had traveled where we could not follow. We shared a long, sad look. Essie's face crumpled in pain. . . .

In the hospital emergency room we wept, our heads bent over Granny's body. Stroking back her wavy black hair (even at 79 her hair had not turned white) we sighed and pleaded. Two years earlier in ICU the doctors had told us she was gone. Her heart would not hold a steady beat. They pointed to the monitor above her unconscious body to show us the erratic yellow line, the uneven blip across the screen. Only the machines kept her breathing. We said no. It was her second heart failure in three months that winter of 1991, but we had plans for our shared lives—Granny, Essie and me. We were anticipating spring. . . .

Granny regained her strength that time. But that was March 1991 and this was October 1993. The doctor nodded to us and spoke with her strong Pakistani accent, "She looks happy. She had a long life. She would die one day." Then she left us alone, but the nurse on duty asked us a million questions about "the body"—about funeral arrangements—about donating organs—about contacting "the family"—we could not respond.

We *are* the family—an elder with her two granddaughters. This is our story of love, though now we are the body of women weeping. Granny was ours to care for, we had taken her into our daily lives because we loved her, and now she is sleeping, and we cannot wake her.

Skin color marked Essie as the one who belonged to Granny. The nurse nodded and smiled at me, "It's so nice of you to stand by your friend at a time like this."

Where else would I be? Granny was my grandmother, too. She loved me like no one else in my life: she loved me fiercely. She knew I had stepped across the line in North America which is drawn across the center of our faces to keep us separate—to keep the great grandchildren of slavekeepers from the great grandchildren of slaves. When she met me as Essie's "friend" twelve years earlier, she had watched me closely, but then she accepted me into her household and into her family. As the elder, her acceptance meant acceptance. She recognized my love for her granddaughter and would say to me, "People talk, but you hold your head up. You walk tall. The Lord sees what you're doing for my granddaughter, how you help her with her son. He sees how you stick together and help each other out." As far as Granny was concerned it was the *quality of our caring* not our sexuality that mattered. In this she was far wiser than most.

For the past three years we had lived together in Yellow Springs, sharing meals and dishes. She would sometimes pull out her old photo albums and tell her stories, laughing at memories of wild times out dancing with her friends in the juke joint or riding horses with her cousin on her father's ranch or traveling cross country in the rig with her husband and his magical black cat when he worked as a truckdriver. Rich, warm memories, and I would sip my coffee and imagine her days and nights. What sustained her? Love—no doubt. Love and greens and cornbread—good food. That's what she craved. And the kitchen was her favorite room next to her bedroom.

She had been raised in the fields and farms of the south. When I was deciding whether or not to take the job in Ohio, Granny was part of the decision-making process. Moving back to the country after four decades in the city felt like coming full circle to her. She said she wanted to come with us. And it was here in Ohio that Granny and I had the luxury of time together to make our own relationship to each other. She would talk to me about "the things white folks do—" how they tend to "put themselves first like they better than other folks—" how foolish they

looked on the TV talk shows "tellin' all their business—" or how much she had enjoyed some of the white friends she and her husband once had.

She spoke her mind without embarrassment or apology. I listened. She had survived the jim crow laws of the south. She had survived segregation and desegregation. She kept a gun under her pillow she called "Ole Betsy" in case someone would try to break in or "mess with her." Granny paid attention to details as a matter of survival. She prided herself on the subtle things she observed in watching how people acted and how they treated one another. She would interpret everything: tone of voice, a simple gesture, the hunch of someone's shoulders. She always knew when someone felt sad or tired. You didn't have to say anything. She comforted. She sympathized. She was extremely skilled at making others feel loved, feel noticed, feel good about themselves. But if Essie had not been in my life it is doubtful that I would have ever known this remarkable woman, her namesake, Essie (Granny) Hall.

When I moved in with Essie in 1982, my nomadic tendencies were pulling at me, urging me to convince Essie that it was a perfect time for us to relocate to another city. I had lived in Milwaukee for two and a half years, for me that was long enough. I'd found a new love, an important someone in my life. It seemed like the perfect time to move on with my new partner. But Essie's life was described and defined by different currents. She had roots. She had family. She told me, "I will be here as long as Granny needs me." I was shocked. My feet carried me freely; I fought against family attachments. Was this difference cultural? Personal? Both? But now I have grown to respect and appreciate this way of being, this way of belonging. Is it a middle-class white cultural tendency to break free, to move on, to move up, to move out? Certainly the bonds of family and of commitment were far stronger for Essie than for me. One of the greatest gifts in my life has been that she shared her son and grandmother with me.

I wanted to tell the emergency room nurse all of this. I held Essie Carol in my arms as she cried. I wanted to scream, "Here we are, can't you see us? Lovers and partners holding each other in a time of crisis—What do you need for proof?" . . .

Sunday mornings Granny listened to gospel preachers on her old radio, rocking and clapping to the music. When we weren't home, she'd get up and dance through the rooms of the house, tears flowing freely as she sang outloud. We'd catch her and tease her. Once Granny hung a plastic Jesus in the bathroom; he had his hands folded in prayer and flowing blonde locks thrown back over his shoulders. Essie groaned, "A white man on the bathroom wall!" She took it down and tried to explain to Granny everybody did not worship the same way she did.

We were not only a multiracial household, but one that held different spiritual beliefs. Essie followed a path she had first been introduced to by Granny's mother, her great-grandmother, Caroline Kelly Wright, affectionately known as Ma. Ma wore her hair in long braids and had been called "the little Indian" most of her life. She had married a freed African slave, but she herself was Blackfoot. Ma smoked a pipe and prayed to the sun. Essie remembered as a child the whole family would gather in Ma's bedroom facing East. The dawn's pale light would begin to appear through the open window only a few city blocks from the enormous freshwater ocean called Lake Michigan. Everyone listened as Ma prayed aloud over the family, telling all secrets, opening up all stories, praying to Creator to provide answers, to help guide them to find their purpose in life and hold to it, to be strong. Everything was said on these Sunday mornings and tears fell as Ma blew her smoke toward the light of the rising sun.

Ma had delivered Essie during a wild January blizzard. Ma was a midwife, herbalist, neighborhood dream interpreter, the community sage and soothsayer. If the term had been as popular then as it is now, Ma would have been honored as a shaman. Essie remembers the Baptist preacher visiting their house and saying to Ma, "I'll pray for you, Miz Caroline," and Ma responding, "You can't pray for me, but I can pray for you."

At the age of eight after a preacher had singled her out to stand up and read the Bible as a punishment for something she hadn't even done, Essie told her great-grandmother that she did not want to attend church anymore. Ma agreed. So Essie had little patience for Granny's Christianity. She was especially offended by refrains such as the "Good Master" and would try to point out to Granny how Black Christian faith was a result of slavery, the product of an enforced cultural genocide. Essie would try to "educate" Granny about the ways slaves were punished for trying to hold on to older beliefs, such as

the care and worship of the ancestors or relating to land and nature as an expression of the Sacred. Of course this didn't work, and I would try to negotiate peace settlements between the two generations, between the two Essies, between the centuries, between the ancestors and the youth. Neither one of them really listened to me. I would take the younger Essie aside and tell her, "Leave Granny alone. You're not going to change her." And the younger Essie would retort, "But she's trying to change me!" . . .

[A]t the funeral the man in the black suit did his best. He tried to save us. He opened the doors of the church and urged us to enter. He forgot about the corpse in the casket behind him, and he called the stray flock home. White men and Black men held each other in the back row. White women held Black women in the front row. And in between were all shades of brown and pink, young and old, from four-week-old Jade, the last baby Granny had blessed, to Mrs. Cooper, Granny's phone buddy. They had spoken every day on the phone for a year. Granny adored "Cooper" as she called her, though they had never met in person. Here we sat in rows before an open casket: all colors, ages, sexualities, brought together by a mutual love for an exceptional person. As some of Essie's family members called out urgently, encouraging the preacher with *Amen* and *Yes, Lord* others ignored the eulogy, attending to their own prayers.

At the funeral we sat side by side in the front row in dark blue dresses. Essie's sister and son sat on the other side of her. We wept and held each other's hands. If Granny loved us for who we were, then we weren't going to hide our feelings here. Certainly there were disapproving glances from some family members, but not all. During the decade we lived in Milwaukee, we had shared childcare and holidays, made it through illnesses and the deaths of other beloved family members—what else qualifies someone as family? Yet despite this, I knew there were those who despised my presence for what I represented was the alien. I was the lesbian, and I was white. For some my presence was an inexcusable reminder of Essie's betrayal. She had chosen to be different, and I was the visible reminder of her difference. For some this was a mockery of all they valued, but she did not belong to them so they could control her identity. Granny knew this, and Granny loved her because she had the strength to be herself.

My family is liberal Democrat, yet my mother once said to me that my choice to love other women would make my life more difficult. She wanted to discourage me from considering it. She said, *I would tell you the same thing if you told me you loved a Black man.* I was then nineteen. It struck me as curious that to love someone of the same sex was to violate the same taboo as to love someone across the color line. In the end I chose to do both. Does this make me a rebel? Certainly if my attraction was based initially on the outlaw quality of it, that thrill would not have been enough to sustain the trauma of crossing the color line in order to share love. The rebellious young woman that I may have been could not make sense of the other story, the story of her darker-skinned sister, without a willingness to question everything I had been raised to accept as "normal," without an active analysis of the politics of racial subjugation and institutionalized white male supremacy. And without personal determination, courage, a refusal to be shamed, a sheer stubbornness based on our assumption that our lives held unquestionable worth as women, as women together, as women of different colors together, despite the position of the dominant culture—and even at times the position of the women's community—to diminish and deny us, we would not have been able to make a life together.

I have participated in and been witness to a side of American life that I would never have glimpsed if Essie had not been my partner. The peculiar and systematic practice of racial division in this country has been brought into sharp focus through many painful but revealing experiences. By sharing our lives, our daily survival, our dreams and aspirations, I have been widened and deepened. It has made me much more conscious of the privileges of being white in a society rigidly structured by the artificiality of "race."

One of the first awakenings came near the beginning of our relationship when her son came home with a note from the school librarian that said, "Your overdue books will cost 45 cents in fines. Irresponsible handling of school property can lead to problems later including prison." I was shocked—threatening a nine-year-old boy with prison because of overdue books? I couldn't imagine what that librarian was thinking. Did she send these letters home with little white boys and girls? I wanted to call the school and confront her. Essie stopped me by telling me a number of equally horrifying stories about this school so we agreed to take Michael out.

We decided that Michael, who had been staying with Granny and Daddy Son and attending the school near their home during the week, should move in full-time with us. Essie worked first shift at the hospital, and I was a graduate student at the university. She left for work at 6 A.M., and I caught the North Avenue bus at 9:30. I would be able to help Michael get to school before I left for the day. We decided to enroll Michael in our neighborhood school.

The neighborhood we lived in was one of the few mixed neighborhoods in the city. It formed a border between the rundown urban center and the suburbs on the west side. The neighborhood school was across an invisible boundary, a line I did not see but would grow to understand. Somewhere between our house and this building, a distance of approximately six blocks, was a color line. A whites-only-no-Blacks-need-apply distinctly drawn and doggedly patrolled. We scheduled a visit with the principal, and when both of us appeared the next morning, we observed a curious reaction. Though polite, she was absolutely flustered. She could not determine who to direct her comments to. She looked from Essie's closely cropped black hair to my long loose wavy hair, from cream skin to chocolate skin, and stammered, "Who—who is the mother?"

"I am," said Essie.

"I'm sorry," was the reply. "We have already reached our quota of Black students in this school."

"Quota? We live in this neighborhood," I replied. "This is not a question of bussing a child in. He lives here."

She peered at the form we had filled out with our address on it. Then responded coldly, "We are full."

"That's ridiculous," I objected.

"Are you telling me that my child is not welcome to attend the fourth grade in your school?" Essie asked icily.

"We simply don't have room."

Essie stood up and walked out of the room without another word. I wanted to scream. I wanted to force the principal to change her mind, her politics, her preoccupation with the boundaries defined by color. I sat there staring at her. She refused to meet my eyes. I said slowly, "This will be reported to the Superintendent and to the school board," and walked out following Essie to the car.

We scheduled a meeting at the school administration to register a formal complaint and find Michael another school. I was furious. We were taxpayers. These are public schools. How can he be refused entrance? How can a child be denied because of some quota determined by an administrator somewhere? I was naive in matters of race.

I would have to say all white people are naive about the persistence of the color line. We prefer naiveté—in fact we insist on it. If we, as white people, actually faced the entrenched injustice of our socioeconomic system and our cultural arrogance, we might suffer tears, we might suffer the enormous weight of history, we might face the iceberg of guilt which is the underside of privilege. We might begin to glimpse our losses, our estrangement from others, our intense fear as the result of a social system that places us in the precarious position of the top. We might be moved to call out and protest the cruelty that passes for normal behavior in our daily lives, in our cities, and on our streets. . . .

Nothing in my life, my education, my reading, my upbringing, prepared me to straddle the color-line with Essie under the Reagan years in Milwaukee, a post-industrial city suffering economic decline and social collapse. The rigidly entrenched division of social power by race and the enormously draining limitations we faced on a daily basis began to tear at the fabric of our daily survival. I began to experience a kind of rage that left me feeling as sharp as broken glass. I was in this inner state when we finally arrived in the long quiet corridors of the central administration of Milwaukee Public Schools.

We were ushered into an office with a man in a suit sitting behind a desk. He could have been an insurance salesman, a loan officer, or any other briefcase-carrying decision-making tall white man in a position of power and control. We were two women of small build and modest dress, but we were carrying the larger presence—righteous anger. We sat down. I leaned across his desk and challenged him to explain to us why Michael had been refused admittance into the school of our choice. He back-pedaled. He avoided. He dodged. Essie suddenly said, "I am finished. I am taking my child out of school," and stood up.

I snapped my notebook closed, signaling the end of the conversation. The man had never asked me who I was. Did he assume I was a social worker? a family member? a friend? a lawyer? a journalist? Had it even crossed his mind that he was looking at a pair of lovers, at a family, at the two acting parents of this child? For the first time he looked worried, "I am sure we can find an appropriate school for your son. Tell me his interests. We'll place him in one of our specialty schools."

We hesitated.

"I'll personally handle his registration," he seemed to be pleading with us. He looked from Essie to me wondering who his appeal would reach first.

We settled on a school with a square of wild prairie, the environmental science specialty school. It was a half hour bus ride from our home. Michael liked the school, but we did not feel completely victorious. How could we? Though we had challenged the system, these policies and practices which place undue emphasis on the color of a child's skin had not been changed. The school system simply accommodated us, perhaps fearing our potential to cause widespread dissent by giving voice to the intense dissatisfaction of the African American community with the public school system. We compromised—perhaps exhausted by the constant fight against feeling invisible and powerless. It was not just that Michael was Black. It was also that his family consisted of a white woman and a Black woman, and regardless of our commitment to him, we were not perceived as a valid family unit though we functioned as a family. . . .

It is heartbreaking to raise an African American boy in the U.S. From an early age he is taught that others fear him. He is taught that he is less than. He is taught that his future is defined by certain streets in certain neighborhoods, or that the only way out is through musical or athletic achievement. Michael played basketball and football. He wrote raps and performed them to the punctuated beat of electronic keyboards and drum machines. When it was fashionable, he would breakdance on the living-room floor. He had a few good years in school, but by and large school did not satisfy his quest for knowledge, nor did it provide him with creative avenues for self-expression. . . .

There were so many things I could not do for Michael. I could not clothe him in transparent skin to prevent him from being prejudged by color-conscious teachers who would label him inferior. I could not surround him with safety on the street corner where he waited for his school bus. One grisly morning in November he came home shaking. He and a small boy had been shot at while waiting on a familiar corner two blocks from the house. It was 7:30 A.M. While he was preparing to attend school, boys his age were shooting guns out of car windows hoping to kill somebody in order to get into a gang so they could make money.

On that gray morning, the capitalist notion of success as the acquisition of material wealth appeared for what it is: an absolute perversion of human dignity. Yet white American culture persists in holding material affluence as the highest symbol of achievement. The way this plays out in the lives of people of color and those who love them can be summed up in one word: cruelty. We suffer for a lack of basic resources because of the hoarding, the feverish consumerism, and the complete lack of concern by people who have more than they will ever possibly need. Fashion crimes, ganking [gang violence targeting rival gang members or other young people], children beating and killing other children to acquire the stingy symbols of status in a society devoid of real meaning—this is what happens on the city streets of the richest nation in the world.

I could not keep Michael from the bullets. I could not move him out into the suburbs where another kind of violence would confront him daily, those who would question his presence and limit his right to move freely from one house to the next. I could not close his eyes to the terror he would see in his friends when death visited among them. I could not hold him against the rage he held inside. A rage that thundered through the house pulverizing everything in its path, terrifying me, tearing at his mother.

What could we say to him about how to live on the mean streets of a bully nation? We did not live on those same streets even though we lived in the same neighborhood. His experience, my experience, his mother's experience—we walked out of the front door into three separate worlds. Worlds we did not define or control except in how we would respond to them. Michael watched the hours I spent typing, writing, scratching out, rewriting. He watched the transformations his mother carried out with color on canvas, making lumps of cold clay into warm red altar bowls with her naked hands. He saw that we took our pain and rage, our grinding frustration and radiant hope, and made something out of it that gave us strength. Michael is still writing, making music, performing in his own music videos. He sees himself as an artist as we see ourselves; this is the thing that has carried us through.

The Westside where we bought a home had always been a working class neighborhood where people invested in their sturdy brick and wood frame houses planting roses in their green squares of grass. The neighborhood had been built in the teens and twenties by German immigrants who took a certain pride in quality. These homes had fireplaces and stained-glass windows, beautifully crafted built-in bookshelves and beveled mirrors. Only a few generations earlier, there was safety and prosperity here. Waves of immigrants—Greek, Polish, Hasidic Jews, African Americans coming North to work in the factories, shared these streets. I can remember walking into the corner bakery and the Greek woman behind the counter asked Essie and I if we were sisters. It was possible there at that time. Blood was shared. Love between the races happened. We laughed and nodded, "Yes—yes, we're sisters." In these moments we utterly and joyfully belonged together.

My friends who lived on the Eastside of the city rarely came to visit after I moved in with Essie. It was as if I had moved to the other side of the moon. . . . I trusted white women less and less as friends because they could not be counted on when things got tough. They tended to retreat. Race issues are ugly and hard, but if white women who want to fight male supremacy can't stand up to their own fears around the issue of color and simultaneously fight white supremacy, how can they really undertake the work of women's liberation? Certainly without an analysis and willingness to deal with race, there is no depth to the commitment. It is simply a get-ahead strategy for a particular middle class white female minority. Today I feel there is a greater commitment to address issues of racism within the feminist movement, but most of the voices I hear are still women of color. . . .

White women are conditioned to stay put, even rebellious daughters who love other women rarely cross the road that divides the races. Any woman who engages in a serious relationship—as friend or family, as lover, or mother to daughter—with a woman of a different shade of skin will find this relationship demanding a deeper vulnerability than any other as long as race relationships continue to be fraught with tension. But if we settle for a divided nation, we settle for social rigidity and police brutality, we settle for ignorance and stereotypes, we settle for emptiness and fear.

I am still learning how to confront racism when I see it, how to educate my friends without alienating them, how to ask for what I need in terms of support. It has been a rare occurrence, but a joyful one, for us to find other mixed-race lesbian couples. When we begin to talk about how difficult it is, we discover certain patterns and find solace that we are not alone. But why should we suffer for being ourselves and finding ourselves in the borderless culture between races, in the undefined space where wakefulness is necessary for survival, where honest communication and self-reflection must replace the simple recipes of romance. . . .

Few of us born in the Americas can trace our bloodline with impunity. So many of our ancestors have been erased or invented as need be. I know very few family names that have not gone without at least one attempt at revision—to anglicize it—simplify it—discard the ethnic or cultural baggage of a *ski* or *stein* or other markers of race/ethnic identity. One who is raised as part of an unwanted people will shift the identity to become acceptable. Note the number of Chippewa and Menominee people in Wisconsin with French last names. One Chippewa man explained to me how in every neighborhood his family adopted another identity: Mexican when living on the Southside, French on the Eastside. Only back up on the reservation could they say aloud their true names. . . .

How many of us are of African descent? Slavery was challenged in part because of the enormous outcry against the "white slave children." Children of enslaved African women who were the result of forced sex with slavemasters ended up on the auction block. Some of these children looked just like the "free" children of "free" European-American mothers. Obviously there was a tremendous outcry resulting from the confusion that the rationale for chattel slavery was based on a strict hierarchy of skin color as the basis of privilege. How could they justify selling these children that by all appearances looked white even if the mother was a light-skinned African American slave? White men in the South parented children on both sides of the yard: women they took as wives, and women who worked the fields. The brown and pale children were half-brothers

and half-sisters related by blood through the father. This simple truth was denied, and these children were taught to never consider themselves as one family. There is no doubt that many of us have relatives we never considered before. Part of my work has been beginning to claim these unnamed Ancestors as family.

The day after I wrote that paragraph, I visited my parents. It was a week before Christmas, and I was planning to spend the day with my two grandmothers and my parents for Mimi's birthday. While in my parent's home, I asked about an old photo album that I remembered from childhood. My mother commented that it had recently surfaced from the jumble of daily life and brought it into the kitchen. Tintypes and daguerreotypes, family photographs spanning 1850–1900. Fifty years of Walkers, my mother's father's family.

That night, back in the city, stretched across the guest bed at a friend's house, I slowly turned the pages. There are my Ancestors, among the first generation here from the British Isles. Aunt Mary and Uncle Tom Walker. By pulling the photographs out and inspecting the little leather and brass book, I discovered they settled in Clinton and Seaforth, Ontario. I knew these relatives had lived in Canada, but hadn't known they lived between Lakes Huron, Erie and Ontario! All of the faces were unfamiliar, stiff, caught in frozen poses over a century ago. A few of the photographs I remembered from my childhood, especially the sad-faced child in the unusual robe with straight cropped black hair and Asian eyes. For the first time it occurred to me that this could be the face of a native child—not European at all! Who is this child? Then a particularly striking face caught my attention. A young woman gazed confidently, intently, at what? Her hair hung around her wide face and high cheekbones in thick black ringlets, her full lips barely open, her strong chin—this is a woman of African descent. Who is she to me? She wore a gold hoop earring and a checkered bow over a satin dress. With one arm resting against an upholstered pillow, she posed proudly. Why had I never heard of her before? . . .

No one in my family seems to know much about these faces, these people, these lives, and how they relate to us. . . . If I am supposed to be a proud daughter of the colonizing English and the migrating Irish, why can't I also be a proud daughter of the Anishinabeg or Haudenausaunee, two of the indigenous peoples of this Great Lakes region, as well as a proud daughter of the African Diaspora? In America the idea of Europe was created, as if my English Ancestors weren't trying to dominate my Irish Ancestors. Why can't we talk about our truly diverse heritages? Nothing has been passed down in my family of these darker-skinned faces in my family's picture album. Is the refusal to see ourselves as something other than Northern European based in a fearful grasping after shreds of white-skinned privilege? What do we lose if we acknowledge our connection? What do we gain?

Granny kept a photo album. The pictures were important. Some were tattered and worn out, but they mattered. They held the faces of relatives— cousins, aunts, sisters—men in fine hats and women in silk dresses looking into the camera, into the future. In the album is a small square black and white snapshot of two plump white babies seated outdoors on a stuffed armchair. The Kelly boys. Irish. Part of the family. Essie remembers her great-grandmother telling her children, grandchildren and great-grand-children, "These are your cousins." I bet those white boys don't show the dark faces of their cousins to their kin. . . .

The tight little boxes of identity defined by our society keep the building blocks of political and economic power in place. How can we gender-bend, race-cross, nature-bond, and love ourselves in our plurality enough to rebel against the deadening crush of conformity? Is it a crisis of the imagination which prevents us from extending compassion be-yond the boundaries of limited personal experience to listen *and be moved to action* by stories of injustice others suffer. How can we extend the boundaries of our own identities so that they include "the other"? If we have any hope for the future of life, how can we expand our sense of self to include other people as well as beings in nature? The structure of our society is articulated by separation and difference. How do we challenge this by living according to a sense of connection not alienation?

For us, for Essie and I, the greatest challenge has been inventing ourselves as we went along for we could not find a path to follow. Where are our fore-mothers? Light and Dark women who held each other's hands through childbirth and child-raising? Who stood side by side and loved each other refus-ing to budge despite everybody's objections? Who pooled their measly resources together to make sure there was food and heat and light enough for every-one's needs? I want to know them. I want to hear their stories. I'll tell them mine. . . .

Despite the absence of role models, we share specific Ancestors, disembodied presences gliding through our lives like a sudden breeze teasing the candle flame on the altar; secret-keepers who come under guard of moonlight, carrying apple baskets full of fresh fruit which they drop into our sleeping; we wake up before dawn with the sweet taste on our lips of good dreams and lucky numbers. We have our shared Ancestors to thank, and we are fortunate to count Granny among them.

ON STRIKE
AGAINST AMERICAN AIRLINES
US
ON
FOR YOU
ROM: AA Flight
Customers

8

♦♦♦

Work, Wages, and Welfare

Virtually all women in the world work. They are farmers, artists, craft workers, factory workers, businesswomen, maids, baby-sitters, engineers, secretaries, soldiers, teachers, nurses, sex workers, journalists, bus drivers, lawyers, therapists, waitpersons, prison guards, doctors, cashiers, airline pilots, executives, sales staff, professors, carpenters, dishwashers, filmmakers, mail carriers, dancers, homemakers, mothers, and wives. Many find satisfaction and challenge, even enjoyment, in their work; for others it is a necessary drudgery. This chapter looks at women's experiences of work in the United States, women's wages, and income supports for women without paid work. We argue that economic security is fundamental to women's well-being and the security of our families and communities.

Defining Women's Work

According to dictionary definitions, the English word *economy* comes from two Greek words: *oikos*, meaning "house," and *nemo*, meaning "to manage." Thus,

economy can be understood as managing the affairs of the household, and beyond the household, of the wider society. Modern-day professional economists make a distinction between "productive" and "unproductive" work, however, which is not implied in this original definition. So-called productive work is done for money; work not done for money is defined as unproductive. This distinction is central to the bind that many women experience in juggling their daily lives. By this analysis, a woman who spends her day making meals for her family, doing laundry, finding the schoolbooks and football shoes, packing school lunches, making beds, washing the kitchen floor, remembering her mother-in-law's birthday, changing diapers, waiting in for the TV repair person, taking the toddler to the park, walking the dog, meeting the older children after school, going to the doctor's office with her mother, making calls about an upcoming PTA meeting, changing the cat litter, paying bills, and balancing her checkbook is not involved in productive work (Waring 1988). A United Nations study released in Nairobi, Kenya, in 1985 at the end of the International Decade on Women

(1975–85) stated that women do 75 percent of the world's work; they earn 10 percent of the world's wages and own 1 percent of the world's property (Pharr 1988, p. 9). Worldwide, most of women's work is unpaid and officially unproductive.

Anthropologist Leith Mullings (1997) distinguishes four kinds of women's work: paid work in the formal sector; reproductive work, including housework and raising children as well as paid work taking care of children, the elderly, and the sick; work in the informal sector, which may be paid under the table or in favors returned; and transformational work, volunteering in community organizations, professional groups, and clubs of all kinds. As we discussed in Chapter 7, one effect of the gendered division of labor in the home has been a similar distinction between women's work and men's work in the paid workforce.

Although in recent years some women have broken into professions and jobs that were once the preserve of men, most paid jobs in the United States are divided along gender lines, and women are greatly overrepresented in low-paying jobs. Most women in the workforce do "women's work" in service and administrative support jobs, as secretaries, waitresses, and health aides. They work in day-care centers, elder-care facilities, garment factories, food processing, retail stores, restaurants, laundries, and other women's homes. In addition to earning low wages, such workers are often treated as expendable by employers, as Hattie Gossett points out in Reading 47. Women in professional jobs tend to be elementary school teachers, social workers, nurses, and health-care workers. There is an emphasis on caring for and serving others in many of these jobs; some may also require being on display and meeting dominant beauty standards. As syndicated columnist Cynthia Tucker (1996) remarked, "You do not have to look to Venus or Mars to find the difference in men and women. Just look at their paychecks" (p. 3).

In the idealized nuclear family described in Chapter 7, middle-class White women were not expected to be wage earners. Despite the fact that they were responsible for all the tasks involved in maintaining a home and taking care of a family, many said of themselves, "I don't work; I'm just a housewife." By contrast, women on welfare are thought lazy or work-shy if they concentrate on looking after their children and do not participate in the paid workforce.

Women in the U.S. Workforce

Before wage labor developed, several economic systems coexisted in this country. Economist Teresa Amott (1993) identifies

> family farming, the *hacienda* system of large ranches in the Southwest, plantation slavery in the South, the economies of the different Native American nations, and the early capitalist industrial enterprises.   *(p. 15)*

She notes that race and ethnicity were central in determining who was assigned to each of these labor systems; gender and class determined what work people performed. Amott and Matthaei present a detailed account of long-term trends in women's work, noting that the U.S. labor market is still structured hierarchically (Reading 48). Significant inequalities in women's work opportunities may mask economic interconnections among women:

> In a very real sense, the lives of any one group of women have been dependent upon the lives of others. . . . Unfortunately the ties which have joined us have rarely been mutual, equal, or cooperative; instead, our interdependence has been characterized by domination and exploitation. American Indian women's lost lands were the basis for European immigrant wealth. The domestic work of African American and poor European immigrant women, along with the labors of their husbands, sons, and daughters in factories, underwrote the lavish lifestyles of upper-class European American women. The riches enjoyed by the wives and children of Mexican American *hacienda* owners were created by the poverty of displaced and landless Indians and Chicanas. And U.S. political and economic domination of the Philippines and Puerto Rico allowed U.S. women to maintain higher standards of living, and encouraged the migration of impoverished Filipina and Puerto Rican women to U.S. shores.   *(Amott and Matthaei 1996, p. 3)*

The economy of the United States has changed fundamentally because of automation in manufacturing and office work and the movement of jobs overseas. Many U.S. companies have laid off workers, sometimes by the thousands, as they scramble to downsize their operations as a way to cut costs and maintain, or even increase, profits. Innovations such as ATMs, voice mail, salad bars, and self-service gas stations, to name a few everyday examples, all mean fewer jobs. One result has been a growing inequality in earnings between people in professional and technical positions and those without college educations who are working low-income jobs. Despite the influx of relatively inexpensive consumer goods into the United States, especially clothing and electronic items from "global factories" around the world, it has become much harder for many families to make ends meet. Several factors have made it imperative that more and more women are income earners. Rents and housing payments, health insurance, and the cost of college tuition, for example, have increased. Much manufacturing, such as car assembly and related engineering work, which was relatively well paid and largely done by men, has been automated or moved out of the United States. Divorce rates are high, and many fathers pay little or no child support.

According to the Bureau of Labor Statistics (2002b), nearly 60 percent of U.S. women worked full-time, year-round, in 2001, and women made up nearly half (46.5 percent) of all workers in that year. Most women work full-time, but 27 percent held part-time jobs. More than two-thirds of all part-time workers (70 percent) are women. Withorn (1999) notes that this is often a "devil's bargain," because wages are low and there are no benefits, but women take these jobs because they need flexibility in their lives to look after children or aging parents. The labor market is structured so that the best positions are reserved

> for those adults who have someone on call to handle the life needs of an always-available worker. Economist Randy Albelda calls these positions "jobs with wives."
>
> *(Withorn 1999, p. 9)*

Seventy-one percent of U.S. women with children under 18 are in paid employment. Black mothers are more likely to be in the paid workforce than White or Latina mothers. Although 26 percent of families with children under age 18 were maintained solely by women in 2000, there is a wide disparity based on race. Forty-seven percent of Black families, 24 percent of Latino families, and 14 percent of White families were maintained by women.

Economic Inequalities

- In 1999 the wealth held by the world's 475 billionaires was greater than the combined income of the poorest half of all the people in the world (Bigelow and Peterson 2002, p. 16).

- The average amount Enron paid each of its 140 top executives in 2001: $5,300,000 (Harper's Index, October 2002).

- The average CEO in the United States makes about 149 times the average factory worker's pay.

- In 2000, 31 million people, or 11.3 percent of the population, lived at or below the official poverty level (Bureau of Labor Statistics 2002a).

- Every day in the United States, 2,019 babies are born into poverty (Children's Defense Fund 2002).

- Nike CEO Philip Knight's stock in the company is estimated at $4.5 billion; Michael Jordan has a $20 million endorsement deal; a pair of Air Jordans retails generally around $135. The approximate cost of making one pair of Nike running shoes is $5. Women workers in Indonesia who make Nikes earn $1.10 per day (Bigelow and Peterson 2002, p. 151).

- The richest 20 percent of the world's population consumes 86 percent of the world's resources (Bigelow and Peterson 2002, p. 107).

Women's Wages: The Effects of Gender, Race, Class, Disability, and Education

The best-paid jobs for women are as lawyers, physicians, pharmacists, engineers, computer analysts, and scientists, but many more women earn the minimum wage. Ida Castro, acting director of the Women's Bureau of the U.S. Department of Labor, commented that "society needs to really look critically at the value given to work performed predominantly by women," and cites child-care workers, home-care attendants, and nursing-home workers as persons who earn the minimum wage but do the vitally important work of looking after children and older people (Angwin 1996; see also Folbre 2001). In 2001 women on average earned seventy-five cents for every dollar that men earned on average. This gap has slowly narrowed in the past two decades, partly because women's wages have improved but also because men's wages have fallen. The average salary of a Black woman college graduate in full-time work is less than that of a White male with a high school diploma. At the managerial level, women's salary levels are lower than men's and decreased for several industries from 1995 to 2000. In communications, for example, women managers' salaries were 86 percent of men's in 1995, but fell to 73 percent in 2000. In entertainment there was a drop from 83 percent to 62 percent; in retail trade from 69 percent to 65 percent; and in finance, insurance, and real estate from 76 percent to 68 percent. Women managers' salaries rose a modest amount in public administration, educational services, and hospital and medical services (General Accounting Office 2002).

According to the U.S. Bureau of the Census (2002) average annual earnings for full-time workers (aged 25 and over) in 2001 were as follows:

All women	$30,446
White women	30,815
Black women	27,335
Latinas	22,180
All men	40,796
White men	41,317
Black men	32,180
Latinos	26,483

Investigative journalist Barbara Ehrenreich (2001) called attention to the daily grind experienced by many working women in her firsthand account of low-wage women's work. She worked as a waitress and motel housekeeper in Florida, a cleaning woman and nursing-home aide in Maine, and a Wal-Mart sales clerk in Minnesota. She undertook this project as an experiment to see if she could subsist on her own as a full-time employee, paying for rent and food, while working these kinds of jobs. She admires many of the women she worked with and can readily understand that they are too overwhelmed by everyday existence to be able to improve their

prospects. For a woman to go back to school or to find a union job with better pay and benefits she needs access to information, transportation, and the time and "headspace" to explore alternatives. Ehrenreich's coworkers did not have any of these. Her absorbing and insightful account, published by a mainstream publisher and widely reviewed, has brought home the everyday experiences of many working women to middle-class readers.

Working wives contribute significantly to household income. According to the U.S. Bureau of the Census (2000), the average income of married couples with both partners in the paid workforce was $69,463. In families where the wife was not earning, the average income was $39,735. On divorce, the income of a mother and her children usually drops drastically from its predivorce level. More than 75 percent of divorced mothers with custody of their children are employed. Many fathers (more than 50 percent by some estimates) pay little or no child support. The average annual income of families maintained by women was $25,794 in 2000. White single mothers earn more than Black and Latina single mothers, on average. Bear in mind that averages always conceal extremes. Many women and men earn less than the average figures cited above and less than the official **poverty level,** which in 2002 was $15,020 for a family of three (Poverty Guidelines 2002). The federal poverty guideline does not take into account regional differences in the cost of living, and it does not include many basic needs such as housing, transportation, child care, and health care. Some advocates have campaigned for a "living wage" that more adequately reflects the cost of living. Others use a "self-sufficiency standard" that varies from state to state and "provides a measure of income needed to live at a basic level . . . without public or private assistance" (Women's Foundation 2002).

The more education a woman has the more likely she is to be employed. The close relationship between a woman's level of educational attainment and higher wage levels is expected to continue in many jobs, often linked to developments in computer technology. Workers need to keep skills up-to-date, which requires access to opportunities to keep learning and a willingness to do so. A lack of educational qualifications is a key obstacle for women on welfare who need greater educational opportunity if they are to acquire meaningful work.

Even with a college education, however, and equivalent work experience and skills, women are far less likely than men to get to the top of their professions or corporations. They are halted by unseen barriers, such as men's negative attitudes to senior women and low perceptions of their abilities, motivation, training, and skills. This barrier has been called a **glass ceiling.** Women can see what the senior positions in their company or their field look like, but few women reach them (Franklin and Sweeney 1988; Morrison et al. 1992). The Federal Glass Ceiling Commission, appointed by President George Bush, reported in 1995 that in the top Fortune 1000 industrial and 500 service companies 95 percent of senior-level managers were men and, of this number, 97 percent were White (Redwood 1996, p. 2). In 2002 women held 6 percent of corporate executive officer (CEO) positions among Fortune 500 companies and 11 percent among Fortune 1000 companies (Catalyst 2002). Women of color held 1.6 percent of positions with corporate-wide responsibility at the 429 companies reporting these data (Hua 2002).

Discrimination Against Working Women: Sexual Harassment, Age, and Disability

The segmented labor market is reproduced through micro-, meso-, and macro-level factors. These include unequitable educational opportunities for women, especially women of color; social attitudes and assumptions regarding women's skills, abilities, ambitions, and family responsibilities; and discriminatory practices—many of them subtle—in decisions about hiring, firing, and promotion, as well as the day-to-day organization of work. Reading 49 refers to different assumptions about women workers compared with men workers.

Sexual Harassment Sexual harassment is a serious problem for many working women. It is defined by the federal Equal Opportunity Commission guidelines as

unwelcome sexual advances, requests for sexual favors and other verbal or physical conduct of a sexual nature when

1. submission to such conduct is made either explicitly or implicitly a term or condition of employment;

2. submission to or rejection of such conduct by an individual is used as the basis for employment decisions affecting such individual; or

3. such conduct has the purpose or effect of unreasonably interfering with an individual's work performance or creating an intimidating, hostile or offensive working environment.

Sexual harassment at work can include verbal abuse, visual abuse, physical abuse, and rape and is against the law. In 1986 the first case concerning sexual harassment (*Meritor Savings Bank v. Vinson*) reached the Supreme Court and established that sexual harassment includes the creation of a hostile or abusive work environment. The Court also held that the appropriate question is not whether the victim tolerated the harassment "voluntarily" but whether it was "unwelcome." The testimony of Anita Hill in November 1991 before a Senate Judiciary Committee considering the confirmation of Clarence Thomas to the Supreme Court made this issue a lead story for virtually every TV talk show, magazine, and newspaper in the country (Morrison 1992). As women talked about their experiences of sexual harassment, its very widespread nature was publicly acknowledged. Employers hastily set up workshops and seminars for their staffs, mindful of the costs of losing sexual harassment lawsuits. Public figures who were sued for sexual harassment in the mid-1990s included President Bill Clinton and Senator Bob Packwood, who was forced by his Republican colleagues to resign his Senate seat. It is important to note that the federal law against sexual harassment applies only to behavior in the workplace or in schools, not to sexual intimidation and abuse in other situations. Daphne Patai (1998) goes so far as to claim that "the mere allegation of 'sexual harassment' now provides women with an extraordinarily effective weapon to wield against men." However, the Supreme Court strengthened protections against sexual harassment in 1998 (Mason 1998), and many women acknowledge the serious difficulties involved in making such allegations.

Age Discrimination The wage gap between women and men increases with age. One effect of corporate downsizing and layoffs is that a growing number of older, experienced workers are unemployed. They are too young to retire but often considered too old or too expensive to hire. For women over 40, age complicates the job search. It takes longer for such women to find new work than it does men, and their new jobs usually pay less than they were earning before or are part time. There are several myths about older women in the workforce: it is not cost-effective to hire an older woman; she will be hard to train and is likely to have difficulty with new technology; her insurance costs will be higher than for a younger person; and she will not have a strong commitment to work. According to the American Association of Retired Persons (n.d.), none of these myths are borne out by research findings.

Discrimination Against Women with Disabilities
Women with disabilities also have difficulty getting work. They are generally stereotyped as dependent, passive, and incompetent, qualities that are also often attributed to women in general. More African American women and Latinas report a work disability, a disabling condition that makes them unable to work outside the home, than do White women. Work disabilities are more prevalent among older women. At the same time, many women with disabilities that keep them out of the paid workforce do their own cooking, laundry, and housekeeping. Increasing numbers of students with disabilities are going to college. They tend to be older, married, financially independent, and/or veterans. In 2000, 9 percent of first-year college students reported having some kind of disability (University of Minnesota 2001).

Women with disabilities generally have much lower educational attainment than nondisabled women, which bars them from entering higher-paying professional work. They may have missed a lot of school as children or may not have been provided with relevant special education programs. Vocational schools and rehabilitation programs for women who suffer a disability after completing their education also tend to channel them into dependent roles within the family or to low-paying "women's work" in the labor force. Added to these limitations are the prejudices and ignorance of employers and coworkers and the ableist attitudes of this culture. Women with disabilities may also have to make "significant and sometimes costly special arrangements" (Mudrick 1988, p. 246) to maintain their employment, such as transportation or extra help at home.

Balancing Home and Work

In general, U.S. workplaces are still structured on the assumption that men are the breadwinners and women are the homemakers, despite the fact that more U.S. women are in the paid workforce than ever before, including 70 percent of mothers. Juggling the conflicting demands of paid work and family responsibilities is a defining life experience for many women (Reading 50; also Barnett and Rivers 1996; Crittenden 2001; Folbre 2001; Goule 1997; Hochschild 1989, 1997; Peters 1997; Williams 2000).

Flextime, Part-Time Work, Home Working, and the Mommy Track   Mothers may try to find a job with hours that are compatible with children's school schedules. This might mean working jobs that allow some flexible scheduling, seeking part-time work, or working at home—whether sewing, minding children, or "telecommuting." Thanks to innovations like fax-modems, electronic mail, and pagers, home working is currently touted for professional and corporate workers as a way to work flexible hours with greater personal freedom and no stressful commute. This may alleviate the problem of child care for some professional families and greatly help the commuter marriage, but for garment workers and child-care providers, who account for the majority of home workers, the pay is poor and there are no benefits. Garment workers on piecework rates put in long hours, often working into the night. They are also isolated from one another, which makes it much more difficult to improve their pay through collective bargaining.

Another solution to the problem for professional women, put forward in the late 1980s, was that firms adopt a "mommy track." Professional women who wanted career advancement comparable to that of men either would not have children or would somehow manage their lives so as to combine having children with working long hours, attending out-of-town meetings, taking little vacation time, and doing whatever the job demanded. Otherwise, they could "opt" for the mommy track and be recompensed accordingly. Law professor and legal scholar Joan Williams (2000) argues that professional women knew full well that this would mean being marginalized in their careers, and all but a few avoided the mommy track like the plague. Rather, she advocates "deconstructing the ideal-worker norm" and completely rethinking the divide between unpaid caring work and work in the paid workforce.

Child Care   Child care is a family's fourth highest expense, after housing, food, and taxes. For some women who want to work, the cost of child care is prohibitive, even if they can find suitable child-care providers. Federal and state governments, employers, and labor unions offer some assistance to child-care providers and parents in the form of tax credits, grants to child-care programs, on-site care, provisions for child care as part of a benefits package, flextime, and leave for family emergencies, such as sickness. Taken overall, these provisions are woefully inadequate. It is particularly difficult to obtain child care for the hours before and after school and during school vacations. Head Start programs, for example, which offer preschool education to low-income children, are usually available only for a half day and only one in seven children eligible for federal child-care assistance gets help (Children's Defense Fund 2002, p. 53). The Family and Medical Leave Act of 1993 provides for leave in family emergencies like the birth of a child or illness of a family member, but it covers only firms with fifty or more workers, and the leave is unpaid. By 1999 an estimated 20 million workers had used the law to take time off for family needs, but there was no information concerning how many low- to moderate-income families had been forced to forgo such leave because they could not afford to lose a paycheck. The Family Leave Commission reported that nearly 10 percent of workers who take family or medical leave are forced onto public assistance during that time (Gardner 1999).

Another aspect of this issue is the working conditions for child-care workers, the vast majority of whom are women who work in their own homes or at child-care centers and preschool programs. Although parents often struggle to afford child care, child-care workers are poorly paid and have no health insurance or retirement plans. Child-care workers, on average, earn less than animal caretakers, parking-lot attendants, and garbage collectors. Low pay and difficult working conditions mean that turnover among these workers is high. This situation says a lot about how our society values caring for children (Folbre 2001).

The Second Shift   Women employed outside the home still carry the main responsibility for housework and raising children and have very little time for themselves. Although this is particularly acute for single parents, many women living with men also do more housework and child care than their partners (Mainardi 1992; Bianchi et al. 2002). Undoubtedly, this pattern varies among couples and perhaps also at different stages in their lives. Sociologist Arlie Hochschild (1989) estimated that women in the labor force work a **second shift** of at least 15 hours a week more than men, or an extra month of 24-hour days over a year, and argues that men need to do more in the home. Suzanne Bianchi et al. (2002) report significant changes in the gender division of household labor since the 1960s, with men taking on more responsibilities as a result of wives devoting more time to waged work and "changed attitudes about

Pro-family Policies for the United States

- Provide financial support for full-time child care.
- Create more jobs and stop assuming job-holders have a wife at home.
- Raise wages to a "living wage" level. Mandate equal pay for comparable work.
- Provide financial support to cover housing and health costs—the two major "family budget busters."
- Expand the safety net—through unemployment insurance, temporary disability insurance, or welfare payments.
- Provide affordable and accessible education and training for all.
- Promote community-based economic development.
- Introduce a fairer tax structure that benefits people in the lower tax brackets.

Source: Albelda and Tilly 1997, pp. 147–64.

what is expected, reasonable and fair for men to contribute to the maintenance of their home" (p. 184). Nowadays, much less housework is done. Families rely more on the service economy, for example, for take-out meals, and they do less cleaning and far less ironing. In households where men are present, housework is often still divided along gendered lines. Husbands and fathers take care of the car, do yard work and household repairs, and take out the trash. Women usually have major responsibility for food shopping, meals, laundry, and child care. These tasks have to be done every day and take more time and emotional energy than "men's" tasks. Upper-middle-class households hire help in the home—cleaners, nannies, maids, and caregivers for the elderly—which helps to free such women from the time crunch and stress of balancing home and work. These domestic workers are usually paid low wages without benefits. In seeking greater freedom for themselves, upper-middle-class women thus find

themselves perpetuating poor working conditions for poorer women.

Organized Labor and Collective Action

Historically, the male-dominated labor movement has been weak in pressing for changes that would benefit women workers, and women have not been taken seriously as labor leaders. Some male workers were hostile to women in the workforce, fearing for their own jobs and their authority as breadwinners. In support of women in unions, the Coalition of Labor Union Women (CLUW) has four main goals: to organize the unorganized, to promote affirmative action in the workplace, to stimulate political action and legislation on women's issues, and to increase the participation of women in their unions. The coalition emphasizes such issues as equal pay, child care, universal access to health care, and reproductive freedom. It aims to educate working women about their rights, to provide training in dealing with management, and to prepare women for union leadership positions.

Workers usually make significant gains in wage levels and working conditions when they are members of a labor union. In 2001 women union members earned 30 percent more than nonunion women, and the differential is slightly higher for women of color (Bureau of Labor Statistics 2002c). Union workers are also more likely to have health and pension benefits. Women are now joining unions at a faster rate than men, particularly the hotel workers (HERE), service employees (SEIU), garment workers (UNITE), public employees (AFSCME), and communications workers (CWA).

The majority of women in the U.S. workforce are not union members. This is partly due to the decline of unions nationally in recent decades. Also, many women work in jobs that are hard to unionize, such as retailing or the fast-food business, where they are scattered at many separate locations. Seven women are plaintiffs in the biggest discrimination suit in U.S. labor history, *Dukes v. Wal-Mart*, "charging that Wal-Mart Stores Inc., the nations's largest private employer, has a pervasive and conscious pattern of discrimination against women" (Cox 2001a). The suit was filed in June 2001 and is expected to be a long-drawn-out legal battle. It is currently limited to California plaintiffs, but if the application for a class-action suit is successful, it could include more than

700,000 women (Featherstone 2002). The United Farm Workers of America (UFW), founded by Cesar Chavez and Dolores Huerta, has pressured growers to sign union contracts to improve the pay and working conditions of its members—women and men—many of whom are migrant workers and immigrants to the United States whose health is continually compromised by chemical pesticides. (Ferriss and Sandoval 1997). In Reading 52, Miriam Ching Yoon Louie describes immigrant women's labor organizing.

The Working Poor Organized labor also calls attention to low wages, a contributory factor in the raise in the minimum wage in 1996. More than 6 million working people were living in poverty in 2000, and 60 percent of them worked full-time, year-round (Bureau of Labor Statistics 2002a). More women than men make up the working poor, and women of color are more than twice as likely to be poor compared with White women. Twenty percent of children under the age of six are living in poverty. Ten percent of people with significant disabilities working full-time fell below the poverty line. In public debate, poor people are usually assumed to be on welfare, masking the reality of life for the many working poor. This includes legal immigrants, who often start off at the bottom of the employment hierarchy. Some people with very low incomes are working minimum-wage jobs, and others work part-time or seasonally. They may be involved in the informal economy as maids, baby-sitters, or gardeners, for example, doing home work for the garment trade, fixing cars, carrying and selling small amounts of drugs, getting money for sex, selling roses at off-ramps.

Others work in sweatshops, discussed in the next chapter, which are also unregulated in terms of wages, hours, and conditions of work. These are on the rise in many major U.S. cities and often employ undocumented workers. In the mid-1990s there were several media exposés of clothing companies whose subcontractors operate sweatshops, including The Gap, Macy's, and Mervyn's. The Union of Needletrades, Industrial and Textile Employees (UNITE) has organized demonstrations outside department stores to encourage shoppers to boycott brands that use sweatshop labor. In 1996 Asian Immigrant Women Advocates, after a three-year campaign, won a significant agreement from garment manufacturer Jessica McClintock to improve labor practices.

Affirmative Action Labor unions, as well as many women's organizations and civil rights organizations, also support affirmative action in employment, introduced as part of the Civil Rights Act of 1964 to improve job possibilities for White women and people of color, whose opportunities in education, job training, and hiring are not equal to those of White men. Affirmative action is not a quota system, as is often claimed; it is not reverse discrimination; and it is not a system for hiring unqualified people. The need for and desirability of affirmative action policies—which have benefited White women more than any other group—were called into question increasingly in the 1990s and were the subject of public campaigns. The affirmative action policy for state agencies in California was overturned in a ballot initiative in 1996, and in 1998 the University of California banned affirmative action in student admissions. Also in 1998, Washington State voters supported a ban on all state affirmative action programs for all women and men of color in education, contracting, and employment. In 2002 the Association of American Colleges and Universities affirmed its commitment to affirmative action "as the major strategy for achieving equal opportunity" (AACU 2002). Also in 2002, Ward Connerly, a regent of the University of California and opponent of affirmative action, started the Racial Privacy Initiative campaign in California that seeks to prohibit the state from collecting information and classifying "any individual by race, ethnicity, color or national origin in the operation of public education, public contracting or public employment" (Mallik 2002). This is now on the statewide ballot for the March 2004 elections.

Challenges of the Global Economy A great challenge for organized labor is the continued impact of the globalization of the economy on the availability of work, wage rates, working conditions in the United States, and continued pressure for immigration into this country, as discussed in Chapter 9. As capital becomes increasingly international in its movements, labor will need to become increasingly international in its strategies. This country has a vital tradition of labor organizing, including actions in support of workers in other countries. Although circumstances have changed, there is much to be learned from this history that can be applied today (Cobble 1993; Louie 2001; Milkman 1985, 2000; O'Farrell and Kornbluh 1996).

Pensions, Disability Payments, and Welfare

For women who cannot work because of illness, age, or disability, for those who are made redundant or who cannot leave their children, there is a complex patchwork of income-support measures and means-tested allowances provided by federal and state governments and private pension plans. Community organizations, particularly religious organizations, also provide much-needed informal support to poor people. Before the Great Depression of the 1930s, when the economy collapsed and many thousands were suddenly destitute, there was a commonly held belief that poverty was due to laziness and that there was plenty of work available for those willing to roll up their sleeves and get on with it. But the severity of the collapse, which put so many people on bread lines, desperate to feed their families, called for government intervention in the labor market to protect people from the worst effects of the booms and slumps inherent in the economy. This provided the impetus and the political justification for the establishment of Social Security and Medicare programs under the Social Security Act of 1935.

These programs are based on people's relationship to work and are rooted in the principle of the work ethic. Older people can claim pensions because they have already done their share and paid into the Social Security fund during their working lives; people with disabilities may be excused if they are not able to work as long or as vigorously as nondisabled people; those who are laid off because of plant closures or other company changes can usually claim unemployment benefits for a few months while they look for other jobs. Such people are considered "deserving" in contrast to the "undeserving," meaning those who are young and able-bodied but who "simply don't want to work," as is often said nowadays, no less than in the 1930s. This distinction underlies two kinds of benefits: one is based on the concept of social insurance, which allows individuals to draw from an insurance fund to which they have contributed during their working lives; the other is based on the concept of public assistance, under which the needy are given "means-tested" allowances.

Significantly for women today, this Social Security legislation was designed to assist the ideal nuclear family, where the male head of the household was in regular, full-time, paid employment until his death or retirement, and his wife was a full-time homemaker. Nearly seventy years later most U.S. families are not of this type, and most women's benefits are adversely affected because their employment histories, upon which payments are calculated, are not the same as men's.

Pensions and Disability Payments

Retirement pensions are a crucial source of income for older people, but women generally receive significantly lower pension payments than men (Cox 2001b). Pensions are based on wage levels while the person was working and on the number of years in employment. This assumes that only paid work is productive work, so no amount of housekeeping or caring for children and elderly relatives will count. As mentioned earlier, women generally earn lower wages than men and are more likely to work part-time and to move in and out of the workforce as they balance paid work with raising children and family responsibilities. Currently, few part-time jobs provide health insurance or a pension plan. When women retire, many have to rely on a Social Security pension that will be lower than that for most men, because women were not able to contribute as much to it during their working lives. Only 31 percent of retired women aged 65 or over have a private-sector pension; the average benefit for women who do have pensions is 50 percent of the average amount received by men (Social Security Administration 2001). For divorced women this is particularly serious. Many have not planned independently for retirement (Uchitelle 2001). Financial concerns for older women are further aggravated by the fact that women tend to live longer than men, so their retirement assets must be spread over a longer period of time.

Because work and retirement are defined according to the labor market experiences of White middle-class men, this penalizes not only many women but also men of color and people with disabilities. Poor women and men of color often have to piece together an income, depending on seasonal or part-time work, sometimes working informally for cash or favors returned. These factors make them less able to retire completely from paid work when they are older.

A new stereotype of affluent older people in ads for cruises, cars, vitamins, health insurance, and hear-

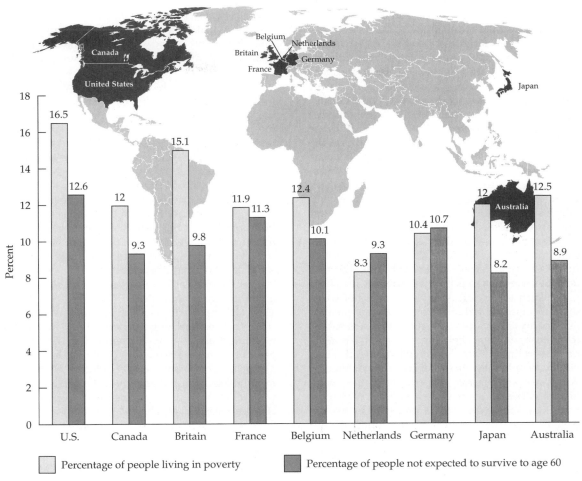

Figure 8.1 Poverty and Life Expectancy in Industrialized Countries. (*Source:* from *Human Development Report 1999* by United Nations Development Programme, copyright © 1999 by the United Nations Development Programme. Used by Permission of Oxford University Press, Inc.)

ing aids suggests that older people are physically fit and enjoying their retirement. This is a welcome change from negative images of elderly people, but it deflects attention from those who are poor. The poverty rate for elderly women was 13 percent, compared to 7 percent among men. For unmarried elderly women it was 19 percent (Social Security Administration 2001). For elderly African Americans living alone the poverty rate increases to 60 percent. Elderly Native Americans as a group have the lowest incomes and the worst housing in the country. At the same time, many older people provide valuable services for themselves and others: participat-

ing in community organizations, helping family and friends, looking after children, maintaining and repairing their homes, and doing daily cooking, cleaning, and other housework. Eleanor Palo Stoller and Rose Campbell Gibson (1994) point out that the advantages of a job with good pay and benefits, a comfortable home, and stimulating opportunities tend to accumulate across the life course. Similarly, disadvantages may also accumulate, producing large differences in economic resources, and often also in health, in old age (p. 107).

The country's elderly population will rise dramatically in the next two decades as baby boomers now in their middle years reach retirement age. There is concern over the future of the Social Security system, as a larger number of people will be drawing pensions than will be paying into it. Some, claiming that Social Security will become bankrupt, with nothing left for those who are now young, have gone so far as to call for its privatization. Others argue that Social Security can be fixed with relatively modest increases in contributions in the short term, rather than by wholesale privatization (Frank 2001; Lieberman 1997). Sixty percent of Social Security beneficiaries are women, and Social Security is the major source of retirement income for the majority of them. Social Security benefits are guaranteed for life, which is important because of women's longer life span (Institute for Women's Policy Research 1998).

Women with disabilities also receive less from public income support than do men with disabilities. As a result, fewer women with disabilities are able to claim Social Security Disability Insurance (DI), which was designed with the needs of working men in mind, and must rely on the Supplemental Security Income program (SSI), which is subject to a means test for eligibility and greater bureaucratic scrutiny, often demeaning. Some disabled elderly people may choose disability benefits over Social Security pensions, depending on their work histories. The future of income support for people with disabilities is likely to be influenced by two opposing trends: the growing political clout of the disability rights movement and the desire of many politicians to cut government spending.

Welfare

The issue of government support for poor families became especially controversial in the mid-1990s. In 1996, Aid to Families with Dependent Children (AFDC) was replaced by block grants for Temporary Assistance for Needy Families (TANF), as Title I of the Personal Responsibility and Work Opportunity Reconciliation Act (Albelda and Withorn 2002; Blau 1999; Goldberg and Collins 1999). This was signed into law by President Clinton against opposition from many welfare rights organizations and advocates for poor women and children, such as the National Welfare Rights Union, the Children's Defense Fund, and local campaigns like Survivors Inc. (Roxbury, Mass.) and the Coalition for Basic Human Needs (Cambridge, Mass.). Gwendolyn Mink (1998)

roundly criticizes feminist organizations and feminist policy makers for not opposing welfare reform more forcefully. The new law ended federal entitlement to assistance dating back to the Social Security Act of 1935.

TANF is a work-based temporary assistance program. States are required by the federal government to set the following conditions for TANF payments: time limits of two years or less, a five-year life-time limit on benefits, and a work requirement whereby welfare recipients have to spend at least thirty hours a week in "work experience." This does not include basic education, college classes, or training not related to a specific job. States have flexibility to provide other benefits, such as health care, transportation, or child-care subsidies to cushion the transition from welfare to work. Former welfare recipients are pitted against other low-paid workers, some of whom have been displaced by "workfare 'trainees' working off their welfare grant at less than minimum-wage equivalents" (Cooper 1997, p. 12). They also need affordable child care, a major obstacle for most working mothers. The advantage of workfare trainees to employers is that TANF—in place of wages—is paid out of state funds.

Welfare rolls dropped by roughly 50 percent from 1994 to 1999, and government officials claimed welfare reform a great success. In Wisconsin, early efforts to establish what had happened to former welfare recipients found that 38 percent were unemployed (*Los Angeles Times* 1999, p. A21). Studies from 21 states found that those who got jobs did not leave poverty in most cases (Associated Press, May 12, 1999); all jobs obtained by former welfare recipients were low-paying, and many were short-term (Havemann 1999). Critics of welfare reform argued that the changes had reduced the numbers on welfare but had done nothing to end poverty.

Myths about welfare recipients are central to the public discourse on this issue, stigmatizing those who need to rely on assistance and serving to erode the possibility of empathy by those who are better-off for those who are poor. The mass media give prominence to stories about welfare "cheats." The prevailing image of a welfare mother is a Black woman with a large family. Proponents of welfare reform justified cuts in welfare programs on the grounds that this would help to reduce the federal budget deficit. Welfare payments accounted for only approximately 1 percent of the federal budget and 2 to 3 percent of states' budgets. Congress is scheduled to vote on welfare reauthorization in 2003 and will likely include additional provisions for states to urge women on welfare to marry, ostensibly as a way of getting out of poverty. Gwendolyn Mink critiques this reasoning (Reading 51) and argues that "rethinking welfare as an income owed to caregivers would mitigate severe material vulnerabilities endured by poor single mothers." Several welfare-rights organizations advocate this position, including the Women's Committee of One Hundred, Every Mother Is a Working Mother Network, Quality Homecare Coalition (Los Angeles), and Welfare Warriors (Wisconsin). On December 31, 2002, thousands of poor families will reach their five-year lifetime limit for TANF. In the San Francisco Bay Area those affected are disproportionately people of color, many with limited proficiency in English. In Alameda County, in northern California, 72 percent of the adults affected are working for pay, but earning so little that they qualify for welfare. Sixty-seven percent of these working adults earn less than $1,000 per month, substantially below the official poverty line (Gustafson 2002).

It is important to note here that many people in this society receive some kind of government support, be it through income-tax deductions for homeowners, medical benefits for those in the military, tax breaks for corporations, agricultural subsidies to farmers, government bailouts to savings and loans companies, or government funding for high-tech military-related research conducted by universities and private firms. This is often not mentioned in discussions of welfare, but it should be.

Feminist Approaches to Women's Work and Income

Comparable Worth

Feminist researchers and policy analysts have been concerned with women's overall working conditions and women's labor history (Amott 1993; Amott and Matthaei 1996; Bergmann 1986; Jones 1985; Kessler-Harris 1990, 2001; Zavella 1987). They have questioned why the job market is segregated along gender lines and have challenged traditional inequities in pay between women and men. These may be partly explained by differences in education, qualifications, and work experience, but part of this

wage gap is simply attributabie to gender. This has led to detailed discussion of the **comparable worth** of women's jobs when considered next to men's jobs requiring comparable levels of skill and knowledge. Why is it, for example, that secretaries or child-care workers, who are virtually all women, earn so much less than truck drivers or mail carriers, who are mainly men? What do wage rates say about the importance of a job to the wider society? What is being rewarded? Advocates for comparable worth have urged employers to evaluate employees without regard to gender, race, or class, but in terms of knowledge and skills needed to perform the job, mental demands or decision making involved in the job, accountability or the degree of supervision involved, and working conditions, such as how physically safe the job is. Such calculations reveal many discrepancies in current rates of pay between women's work and men's work. Indeed, if pursued, this line of argument opens up the thorny question of how to justify wage differentials at all.

Feminization of Poverty

Feminist researchers have also pointed to the **feminization of poverty** (Abramovitz 1996; Dujon and Withorn 1996; Sidel 1996). The two poorest groups in the United States are women raising children alone and women over sixty-five living alone. *Poverty* is a complex term with economic, emotional, and cultural dimensions. One may be materially well-off but emotionally impoverished, for example, and vice versa. Poverty also needs to be thought about in the context of costs—for housing, food, transportation, health care, child care, and clothes needed to go to work—hence the value of a self-sufficiency standard. Poverty is also linked to social expectations of this materialist culture. Many poor children in the United States clamor for Nikes, for example, in response to high-pressure advertising campaigns.

Impact of Class

A key concept in any discussion of work, income, and wealth is class. In the United States today, most people describe themselves as "middle class," a term that includes a very wide range of incomes, occupations, levels of security, and life situations. Indicators of class include income, occupation, education, culture and language, neighborhood, clothes, cars, and, particularly important, unearned wealth. As noted in Chapter 2, some people raised in a working-class community may have a middle-class education and occupation later in life and a somewhat mixed class identity as a result. A woman's class position is usually linked to that of her father and husband. For Marxists, a person's class is defined in relation to the process of economic production—whether she or he has to work for a living. There is currently no politically accepted way for most people to make a livelihood except by working for it, and in this society work, in addition to being an economic necessity, carries strong moral overtones. Note that this same principle is not applied to those among the very rich who live on trust funds or corporate profits.

In much public debate in the United States, class is more of a psychological concept—what we think and feel about our class position—than an economic one. Poverty is often explained as resulting from individual low self-esteem, laziness, or dysfunctional families, as we pointed out in Chapter 1. In public discourse on inequality, race is invariably emphasized at the expense of class. Government census data, for example, are analyzed for racial differences much more than for class differences, which gives the impression that race is the most salient disparity among people. In practice race and class overlap, but greater attention to class differences would show different patterns of inequality. It would also show more similarities and more of a basis for alliances between people of color and White people who are economically disadvantaged. As mentioned in the previous chapter, feminist theorists who emphasize the crucial importance of class work within a Marxist or socialist tradition (Dalla Costa and James 1972; Hartmann 1981; Jaggar 1983). Scholar and activist Johanna Brenner (2001) argues that working-class women need to organize themselves against sexism and class exploitation—as the immigrant women interviewed by Miriam Ching Yoon Louie are doing, building on experiences of earlier radical labor organizing and community movements (Reading 52).

Policy Implications and Activist Projects

Feminists have tackled the issue of women and work from many angles. In addition to advocating for comparable worth in wage rates, they have encouraged women to return to school to improve their educational qualifications, opposed sexual harassment on the job, campaigned for decent, affordable child-care arrangements, exposed the dangers of occupational injury and the health hazards of toxic work environments, and advocated for women in senior positions in all fields, and that math, science, and computer education be more available and effective for girls. Examples of such organizations include the Institute for Women's Policy Research (Washington, D.C.), the National Organization for Women (Washington, D.C.), 9 to 5 National Organization of Working Women (with chapters in several states) and the Women's Economic Agenda Project (Oakland, Calif.) The "Take Our Daughters to Work Day" initiated by the Ms. Foundation, for example, exposes girls to jobs they may know little about and provides role models for them, which can have a powerful impact. Several organizations have worked to open up opportunities for women to enter well-paying trades such as carpentry and construction, including Hard Hatted Women (Cleveland, Ohio), Women in the Building Trades (Jamaica Plain, Mass.), Minnesota Women in the Trades, and Northern New England Tradeswomen (Essex Junction, Vt.). Many local groups help women to start small businesses, utilizing existing skills. The Women's Bean Project (Denver), Tierra Wools (Los Ojos, N. Mex.), and the Navaho Weaving Project (Kykotsmovi, Ariz.) are group projects that promote self-sufficiency. TeamX is a worker-owned and unionized garment factory in Los Angeles producing "SweatX Clothes with a Conscience." Funded by the Hot Fudge Social Venture Fund (controlled by directors of Ben and Jerry's Ice Cream), TeamX comprises 26 production workers who are paid between $8.50 and $14 an hour, plus benefits (www.sweatx.net).

Promoting Greater Economic Security for Women

A lack of jobs, low wages, low educational attainment, having children, and divorce all work against women's economic security and keep many women in poverty, dependent on men, or both. As we concluded in Chapter 7, an aspect of security and sustainability for family relationships involves equal opportunities and responsibilities for parenting, which in turn means a redefinition of work. Yet if current trends continue, many young people in the United States—especially young people of color—will never be in regular, full-time employment in their lives. Politicians and businesses promote almost any venture—building convention centers, ballparks, jails, and prisons and maintaining obsolete military bases—on the argument that it will create jobs. Changes in the economy force us to confront some fundamental contradictions that affect women's work and the way work is thought about generally:

What should count as work?

Does the distinction between "productive" and "unproductive" work make sense?

How should work be rewarded?

How should those without paid work, many of them women, be supported?

How can the current inequalities between haves and have-nots be justified?

Is the work ethic useful? Should it be redefined?

Is materialism the mark of success?

Years ago, pushed by the impact of the Great Depression of the 1930s, social commentators saw great potential for human development promised by (then) new technologies like telephones, Dictaphones, and washing machines, by means of which people could provide for their needs in a relatively short time each week. The British philosopher Bertrand Russell (1935), for example, favored such "idleness" as an opportunity to become more fully human, to develop oneself in many dimensions of life. Recognizing that this could not happen if material living standards had to keep rising, he put forth a modest notion of what people "need." He also understood that these kinds of changes would require political imagination and will.

◆◆◆

Questions for Reflection

As you read and discuss this chapter, think about these questions:

1. What are your experiences of work?

2. What have you learned through working? About yourself? About other people's lives? About the wider society? How did you learn it? Who were your teachers?

3. What have you wanted to change in your work situations? What would it take to make these changes? What recourse do you have as a worker to improve your conditions of work?

4. How might pension policies be changed to reflect the range of productivity of women across the life course?

◆◆◆

Finding Out More on the Web

1. Consult these Web sites for more information on the wage gap, poverty levels, and welfare reform:

   9 to 5 National Association of Working Women: **www.9to5.org**

   Children's Defense Fund: **www.childrensdefense.org**

   Coalition of Labor Union Women: **www.cluw.org**

   Institute for Women's Policy Research: **www.iwpr.org**

   National Jobs for All Coalition: **www.njfac.org/jobnews.html**

   Welfare Information Network: **www.financeprojectinfo.org-win**

2. Compare the very low amounts the government spends on welfare with other federal expenditures. See:

   National Priorities Project: **www.nationalpriorities.org**

   War Resisters League: **www.warresisters.org/piechart.htm**

Taking Action

1. Draw up a detailed budget of your needs, expenses, income, and savings.

2. Discuss work experiences with your mother or grandmother (or women of their ages). What opportunities did they have? What choices did they make? What similarities and differences do you notice between your own life and theirs at the same age?

3. Analyze representations of women workers in ads, news reports, TV shows, and movies.

FORTY-SEVEN

the cleaning woman/labor relations #4

Hattie Gossett

the doctors knew.

the lab people knew.

the secretaries knew.

the volunteers knew.

the patients knew.

the clinic was moving to a new spot and would be closed for a while and everybody knew ahead of time.

everybody except the cleaning woman.

she only found out on closing day.

i dont know why no one thought to tell you before this the woman doctor said to the cleaning woman over the phone annoyance all up in her voice at being asked by the cleaning woman why they hadnt given her an earlier notice.

i dont know why no one thought to tell you. anyway i have patients now and have no time for you.

it was the cleaning womans dime so she went for broke. but i am dependent on the salary you pay me and now suddenly it wont be there she protested. wouldnt it be fair to give me some kind of severance pay?

severance pay! shrieked the woman doctor. look she snapped you havent been with us that long. only a few weeks. besides i have help at home you know and i . . .

its like this the cleaning woman interrupted not wanting to hear about the doctors help at home (at least not what the doctor was going to say) when you work for a salary you need some kind of reasonable notice when its going to be discontinued so you can prepare yourself. how would you like it if you were in my place?

the woman doctor then tried to offer the cleaning woman a job in the new clinic plus a job in her own new private office but neither of these jobs would start for some weeks. she never did say how she would feel being in the cleaning womans place. the cleaning woman realized she was dealing with people who really didnt care about her. as far as they were concerned she could starve for those few weeks. she wondered how long you would have to work for these people before it was long enough for them to tell you at least 2weeks ahead of time that they were closing. how long is long enough?

forget it the cleaning woman told the woman doctor. she was pissed. she didnt like knowing that she was being shafted and that there wasnt anything she could do. when do you want me to bring back your keys? because she cleaned at night or very early in the morning she had keys to the clinic.

as soon as the woman doctor said anytime in a somewhat startled voice the cleaning woman hung up. she didnt slam down the phone. she put it down gently. but she didnt say goodbye or have a nice day.

damn the cleaning woman said to herself after she had hung up. here these people are supposed to be progressive and look at how they act. here they are running an alternative clinic for lesbians and gays and straights and yet they treat their help just as bad as the american medical association fools treat theirs. are they really an alternative she asked herself.

sure they treat their help bad herself answered laughingly.

the cleaning woman looked up a little surprised because she hadnt heard herself come in. now herself sat down and started eating some of the cleaning womans freshly sliced pineapple.

what do you mean girlfriend the cleaning woman asked herself.

have you forgotten that every sister aint a sister and every brother aint a brother herself began. where did you get this pineapple? its really sweet and fresh.

come on now. dont play games. tell me what you mean the cleaning woman said.

look herself said. some of these sisters and brothers aint nothing but secondhand reprints out of the bidness as usual catalogue in spite of all their tongue flapping to the contrary. and these secondhand reprints can be worse than the originals. like they have to prove that they know how to abuse people even more cold-heartedly than the originals do. its getting harder and harder to tell the real alternatives from the rank rapscallions. of course everybody else on the staff knew that the gig was moving but you. in their book you aint nothing no way.

what could the cleaning woman say?

herself was right once again and the cleaning woman tried to tell herself this but that girl didnt hear anything cuz she had already tipped on out taking the last piece of pineapple with her.

so the cleaning woman laughed for a minute. then she stopped brooding over those fools at the clinic.

she got on the phone and started lining up some more work.

later she sat down and wrote this story which she put in the envelope with the clinic keys. she wrote the woman doctors name on the front of the envelope cuz she wanted to be sure the woman doctor would be able to share the story. at the bottom of the story the cleaning woman put not to be copied or reproduced by any means without written permission from the author.

cuz one monkey sho nuff dont stop no show.

F O R T Y - E I G H T

◆◆◆

The Transformation of Women's Wage Work

Teresa Amott and Julie Matthaei

Over the last two centuries, the paid work performed by women has changed dramatically. This [essay] focuses on the transformation of women's occupations over the course of the twentieth century and on the changes in the racial-ethnic, gender, and class hierarchies within paid work. . . .

The Growth and Decline of Women's Paid Domestic Work

Along with agricultural work, domestic service was one of the first major occupations for women in all racial-ethnic groups. Although early domestic work was unpaid, performed by indentured servants, slaves, or apprentices, the job gradually came to be compensated in wages (although live-in servants still receive a substantial proportion of their pay in the form of room and board). Over the course of the twentieth century, employment in domestic service declined dramatically, moving much of women's paid employment out of the home sphere. At the same time, much of the work once assigned to women domestic servants is now performed by women employed by profit-motivated firms.

Homemaking was an arduous task from early colonial times through much of the nineteenth century, involving not simply child care and housework, but also the production of many household goods. Families of means employed others to do most of this work, and very wealthy families had large staffs of servants of both sexes, from maids and butlers to coachmen and cooks. In 1870, over half of all wage-earning women were found in domestic service, either as servants, laundresses, or boarding and lodging housekeepers—and 89 percent of all domestic servants were women.[1]

Regional differences in the racial-ethnic nature of the employer-servant relationship produced distinct differences in women's work experiences. In the South, Southwest, and West, domestic service usually involved a woman of color laboring for a white woman or family, and thus the work both reflected and reinforced racial domination. As slavery took hold in the South, domestic service there became a Black occupation. African American intellectual W. E. B. Du Bois noted, "Blacks . . . became associated with servitude generally . . . wherever Blacks served, domestic service was labeled 'nigger's work.'"[2] After the Civil War, domestic service continued to be seen in the East as an occupation dominated by Black women. In the Southwest and West, domestic service was also racially typed and devalued, and Mexicans, American Indians, and Asians predominated. On the West Coast, Asian men were often employed in domestic service since there was a shortage of women of all racial-ethnic groups.

Live-in servants in the North and Midwest generally enjoyed better treatment than those in the South and the West, particularly from the Revolution to about 1850, since servants and employers usually belonged to the same racial-ethnic group. During that period, most northern and midwestern servants were U.S.-born whites who worked under

relatively egalitarian conditions—indeed, they were often referred to as "help," not servants. The North's egalitarian view of domestic help began to change in the nineteenth century as U.S.-born servants were replaced by immigrants, especially Irish women. The combination of ethnic, religious, and class difference opened up a vast social distance between white, U.S.-born employers and their immigrant servants. However, this process took decades; as late as 1900, there were still twice as many U.S.-born white women employed as private household workers as there were foreign-born white women.[3]

During the nineteenth century, domestic service coincided with and promoted the cult of domesticity. Domestic servants were essential to wealthy women's aspirations toward ideal womanhood. Servants freed the homemaker from the drudgery of housework so that she could attend to the "higher" functions of homemaking: mothering, socializing, and for some, the volunteer work that was a form of social homemaking. At the same time, a large pool of women willing to work as domestic servants for low wages was guaranteed by the lack of other jobs for poor, racially subordinated, and immigrant women. Roughly half of African American and European immigrant women were in domestic service, compared to only 28 percent of U.S.-born white women. A substantial share of African and Asian men were also so employed. On the other hand, less than 1 percent of European American men performed domestic work.

Through the early twentieth century, most domestic servants lived in their employers' homes. Single women were far more likely to live in than married women, since living in provided a roof over their heads. Most worked for married, middle- and upper-class white homemakers in what was seen as helpful training for their servants' futures as homemakers. Hence, domestic service often involved a generational relationship (as well as one between classes and racial-ethnic groups) in which an older, married woman used her husband's income to pay a younger, single woman—and where the servant's pay was then often transferred to her parents.

However, taking on another woman's domestic work did not always involve living in the employer's home. Married women servants, who were disproportionately Black, preferred day work to live-in service whenever they could obtain it. Large numbers of married Black women took in laundry in their own homes in order to escape the direct supervision

Table 1   Share of Employed Women Working in Private Household Service,
by Racial-Ethnic Group, 1900–1990

	1900	1930	1960	1980	1990
American Indian	13.4	22.5	16.8	1.4	1.0
Chicana	n.a.	33.1	11.5	2.4	2.6
European American	29.8	12.0	4.4	0.8	0.6
African American	43.5	53.5	39.3	5.0	2.2
Chinese American	35.6	12.1	1.7	0.8	0.6
Japanese American	28.6	29.9	8.2	1.4	0.6
Filipina American	n.a.	34.4	3.7	0.9	0.6
Island Puerto Rican	78.4	27.5	13.7	1.4	1.4
U.S. Puerto Rican	n.a.	n.a.	1.2	0.7	0.7

Notes: Asian American data include Hawaii for all years; 1980 and 1990 data for American Indians include Eskimo and Aleut peoples; for 1900–1960, African American and European American include Latinas.

of a white mistress. On the West Coast, the Chinese, especially men, did laundry work. Caring for other women's children—the precursors of today's daycare centers—was another form of domestic service which could be performed in one's own home.

In urban areas, taking in boarders and lodgers provided yet another path to escape from domestic service in another woman's home, allowing married women and their daughters to contribute cash income to their families through cooking, cleaning, and laundering for their clients; this was especially common in immigrant communities. Boarding services were also in high demand by adult men in communities where women were scarce, such as among Asian plantation workers in Hawaii. Unlike domestic service, boarding and lodging appears rarely to have involved racial inequality. Boarding and lodging was, instead, an exchange between persons of the same class and racial-ethnic group who were of different ages and phases in their working lives.

Although domestic service was the single most important occupation for women in 1900, its significance declined dramatically in the course of the twentieth century. Between 1900 and 1990, although the population tripled and per capita output more than quadrupled, the total number of private household workers fell from about two million to under one-half million. The share of women employed in private household service fell from 35 percent to less than 1 percent.[4]

Both supply and demand factors contributed to the decline in women's paid domestic work. Many family needs formerly filled by women's domestic work—such as health care, child care and education, and meal preparation—are now serviced by hospitals, convalescent homes, medical and health professionals, schools, daycare centers, and hotels and restaurants, lowering the economy's overall demand for domestic workers. In addition, new commodities that reduce the amount of physical work necessary to fill family needs have become available and affordable: hot and cold running water, electricity and telephones; durable goods such as refrigerators, washing machines, and vacuum cleaners; and processed foods. All these changes have reduced the need for domestic servants, laundresses, and women who take in boarders and lodgers. At the same time, the growing availability of other jobs for women—many of them in the service sector, as well as in manufacturing and clerical work—has decreased the supply of women available for domestic work, and consequently increased the wages of domestic servants.

The movement out of domestic service has, however, been uneven across racial-ethnic groups, as shown in Table 1. African American women have remained the most likely to work as domestic servants. Since the overwhelming majority of the families employing domestics have been white, through the first third of the twentieth century, the majority of

African American women's working experiences entailed housework, child care, and laundry for white women and their families. This direct, personal, and continuing experience of racial subordination has been central to the lives of contemporary Black women's mothers and grandmothers.[5] On the other extreme, white and Asian American women were able to leave domestic service most rapidly. By 1990, no more than three in a hundred women worked in domestic service in any racial-ethnic group; the share for Blacks and Chicanas, however, remained much greater than that for other groups.

Thus, women left employment in the homes of other women for jobs in new settings, such as factories, offices, schools, nursing homes, and restaurants. In this process, they exchanged the direct supervision of a mistress or master for a more complicated and bureaucratic hierarchy of supervision. In some cases, this meant that supervision became less personal, and it often meant that the supervisor was no longer another woman.

The New Service Work

. . . Employment in service occupations grew rapidly between 1900 and 1990, from about 2 to 15 million workers, nearly 9 million of them women. Today, service occupations outside the private household include food preparation and service (waiters and waitresses, cooks, counter workers, and kitchen workers), health service (dental assistants, nurse's aides, orderlies, and attendants), cleaning and building service (maids, janitors, and elevator operators), personal service (barbers, hairdressers, guides, and child-care workers), and protective service (police officers, firefighters, and guards).

The expansion of service occupations in the twentieth century drew in large numbers of women workers. Service occupations employed 17 percent of women workers in 1990, compared to less than 3 percent of women workers in 1900. As shown in Table 2, the representation of women in these new service jobs varied across racial-ethnic groups. American Indian, Chicana, and African American women were more likely than other women to hold new service jobs in 1990, just as they were more likely to be domestic servants.

Women are overconcentrated in service jobs other than protective service: although they make up less than half of the workforce, women are two-thirds of

these service workers. Many service jobs involve traditionally female tasks, such as cooking, cleaning, and caring for the sick, the aged, and the very young. However, service work is not simply or only a women's job. First, there are racial-ethnic hierarchies within female-dominated service jobs. For instance, according to the 1980 Census, white and Asian women were about 50 percent more likely than other women to be supervisors. Black women were three times as likely as white and Asian American women to be janitors and cleaners, while American Indian and Latina women were about twice as likely.[6] (Unfortunately, detailed occupational data for these racial breakdowns are not available in the published reports of the 1990 Census, but there is no reason to believe that the relative positions have changed dramatically between 1980 and 1990.) Racial-ethnic typing is even more severe when we look within a region or within a place of work. In many northeastern and midwestern cities, all of the nurse's aides and cleaning-service workers are women of color; in most restaurants, waitresses are all of the same racial-ethnic group.

Second, just as men of color were significantly represented in domestic service jobs during the nineteenth and early twentieth centuries, so also a significant share are employed in non-protective service work today. Indeed, certain service jobs are dominated by poor or immigrant white men and men of color, such as janitors, bellhops, and elevator operators.

Another exception to women's dominance in service work occurs in the elite service jobs known as protective service, consisting predominantly of police officers and firefighters. Protective service was monopolized by white men for decades. In 1900, white men accounted for only 72 percent of the labor force, but made up 97 percent of all policemen, firemen, and watchmen. Men of color, in contrast, were seriously underrepresented, and women's shares were insignificant. Over the course of the century, struggles by white women and people of color, especially in the 1960s and 1970s, have brought them a greater share of these jobs. By 1990, men of color's share had grown from 3 percent to almost 20 percent, while their share of all jobs increased from 10 to 12 percent. Women of all racial-ethnic groups other than Chinese Americans have also increased their relative concentrations in protective service, with American Indian, Black, and Puerto Rican women making the greatest gains. Despite these inroads, white men are still overrepresented.[7]

Table 2 **Share of Employed Women Working in Service Occupations (Other than Private Household Service), by Racial-Ethnic Group, 1900–1990**

	1900	1930	1960	1980	1990
American Indian	12.1	2.9	25.8	23.9	22.4
Chicana	n.a.	3.8	16.5	20.4	21.1
European American	3.8	8.1	13.2	15.3	14.5
African American	7.9	7.5	23.0	24.2	22.9
Chinese American	8.7	8.8	9.2	13.0	13.0
Japanese American	3.8	10.1	12.9	15.8	13.1
Filipina American	n.a.	4.1	16.6	15.8	13.1
Island Puerto Rican	n.a.	1.3	12.2	14.8	12.9
U.S. Puerto Rican	n.a.	n.a.	7.3	14.4	16.7

Notes: Asian American data include Hawaii for all years; 1980 and 1990 data for American Indians include Eskimo and Aleut peoples; for 1900–1960, African American and European American include Latinas.

Were women's working conditions improved by moving out of domestic service into new service jobs? Certainly, most women have seen these jobs as an improvement over live-in domestic service, involving as they do more limited hours and the ability to live in one's own home and with one's children. Furthermore, earnings are higher, on the average: with median weekly earnings of $256 for full-time, full-year women workers in 1994, service occupations offered better pay than private household and agriculture ($177 and $234, respectively). However, women working in service occupations continued to earn considerably less than those in manufacturing, sales, or clerical jobs. In addition, 50 percent of women's new service jobs are part-time (compared to about 35 percent of all women's jobs), and 45 percent of service jobs involve work on weekends.[8]

New unionizing efforts promise to bring new service workers some measure of justice and dignity on the job. By using a variety of creative organizing tactics (modeled on the approaches of the National Welfare Rights Organization, the United Farm Workers, and community-based groups), unions have increased organizing among workers, such as home healthcare aides. By 1995, over 70,000 home healthcare aides had organized, reaching out to form client-worker coalitions that made the case for higher pay for aides as a way of increasing the quality of services delivered to clients. The Service Employees International Union has built a major campaign to raise wages for office building cleaners, most of whom are recent immigrants and people of color, by organizing 200,000 workers, one-fifth of the janitorial workforce.[9]

Out of the Fields

Through 1870, the majority of workers in the United States worked in agriculture. However, agriculture meant very different things to different people: for some, self-employment and a chance at earning wealth; for others, slavery, extreme exploitation as a migrant or plantation worker, or the perpetual debt of sharecropping or tenant farming.

The types and conditions of agricultural work depended in great measure on race-ethnicity, which to a large extent determined access to land. European immigrants, especially before the late 1800s, were able to homestead on lands stolen from Native Americans; thus, they were most likely to be self-employed farmers or ranchers. However, an elite of white farmers and ranchers held large parcels of land, squeezing smaller farmers; in the South, many poor whites were forced into tenant farming and sharecropping. During slavery, most African Americans worked in agriculture. Once freed, most were kept by Jim Crow racist practices from acquiring land of their own, and continued to labor for whites as sharecroppers or tenant farmers. The colonization of the Mexican Southwest stripped land from the indigenous peoples and concentrated ownership among a wealthy few. The remaining American Indians and Mexicans were reduced to the status of landless peasants or subsistence farmers. After the U.S. takeover, Anglos acquired most of the Mexican lands, leaving Chicanas/os to work as tenant farmers, sharecroppers, or migrant workers. American Indians, forced onto smaller, less fertile land areas, tried to continue the self-sufficient farming and ranching in which most had been occupied before the European invasion. Island Puerto Ricans also suffered from the concentration of lands in the hands of a few, with many small family farmers driven gradually into agricultural wage labor for wealthy farmers. Chinese, Japanese, and Filipinas/os were brought to the United States and Hawaii as plantation laborers and migrant workers, and prohibited by law from acquiring land in the United States. Nonetheless, some were able to escape this landless status into family farming and gardening.

The degree to which women participated in agricultural work varied greatly among these groups, depending both upon the overall importance of agricultural work for the racial-ethnic group as a whole and on the share of the work allocated to women. Census data on women's agricultural employment are unreliable, since they probably undercount women's participation; nevertheless, they may be useful for comparative purposes.

In 1900 over half of all American Indian, African American, Chicana/o, Puerto Rican, and Japanese workers were employed in agriculture, compared to only one-third of all whites and less than one-fourth of Chinese. This is due to a number of different reasons, including the rural nature of American Indian life, the importation of African and Asian workers to the United States specifically to perform agricultural work, the Great Driving Out of Chinese in the late 1800s, and the exclusion of people of color, especially Blacks, from non-agricultural employment. In general, however, a higher share of people of color remained in agriculture in 1900 than that of whites.

The share of agricultural work done by women within each racial-ethnic group was also higher among women of color in 1900 (except among Asians, whose population was still mostly male). Among American Indians, this stemmed from a cultural tradition involving women in farming. African American women's participation can be traced both to African traditions and to slaveowners' practice of

employing women in the fields. Among Puerto Ricans, farming was traditionally men's work. On the other hand, these data may understate the share of agricultural work performed by European American and Puerto Rican women, especially on family farms, where women usually contributed to cash crop production through harvesting, dairying, gardening, and cooking and cleaning for hired hands.

In the course of the twentieth century, agricultural productivity increased greatly as a result of labor-saving technological changes, especially mechanization. Consequently, agricultural employment fell from over 10 million to less than 3 million, and vast numbers of people left rural areas for the cities. In 1900, agriculture employed more than one in three workers; in 1990, the share had fallen to fewer than one in forty. Table 3 shows the changing shares of women workers employed in agriculture from 1900 through 1990. Through the first third of the twentieth century, substantial shares of American Indian, African, Chicana, and Japanese women continued to work in agriculture; however, by 1990, no more than 3 percent of women in any racial-ethnic group were so employed.

For those women, disproportionately Chicanas, who remain in agricultural wage labor, conditions have barely improved since the early twentieth century. Wages continue to be extremely low, as the presence of substantial numbers of undocumented workers allows super-exploitation by growers and foremen. The recent employers' offensive against unions has also taken its toll on farm worker organizing, although the 1995 victory at the Sainte Michelle winery has given new hope to the United Farm Workers.

Women family farmers have also suffered reversals in the past two decades. As farm indebtedness and bankruptcy soared in the 1980s, huge corporate firms increasingly came to dominate the agricultural landscape, absorbing family farms and turning farm owners into farm managers and tenants. Black farm ownership has fallen disproportionately, and farm women of all racial-ethnic groups have taken on a triple day: work on the farm, a second job in town, and continued responsibility for child care and other family work.[10] Despite this punishing schedule, women throughout the Midwest and South have organized to fight foreclosures, lobbied for aid to farmers, and developed farmer cooperatives. Many of these groups draw on old Pop-

**Table 3   Share of Employed Women Working in Agriculture,
by Racial-Ethnic Group, 1900–1990**

	1900	1930	1960	1980	1990
American Indian	47.2	26.1	10.5	1.2	1.1
Chicana	n.a.	21.2	4.3	2.9	2.5
European American	9.8	4.1	1.5	1.0	0.9
African American	44.2	24.7	3.7	0.5	0.3
Chinese American	7.3	2.5	0.7	0.3	0.2
Japanese American	58.1	22.9	6.7	1.3	0.8
Filipina American	n.a.	27.5	4.3	1.2	0.8
Island Puerto Rican	3.9	9.5	1.6	0.3	0.3
U.S. Puerto Rican	n.a.	n.a.	0.3	0.4	0.4

Notes: Asian American data include Hawaii for all years; 1980 and 1990 data for American Indians include Eskimo and Aleut peoples; for 1900–1960, African American and European American include Latinas.

ulist traditions, exhorting farmers to raise "less corn and more hell."[11]

Manufacturing Inequality

As capitalism developed in the United States, labor shifted out of agriculture and domestic service into manufacturing. Manufacturing itself gradually changed from predominantly skilled craft and artisan work to unskilled and semi-skilled factory work.

By 1900, manufacturing made up approximately one-fourth of total employment. There was great variation in the proportions of women and men workers of the different racial-ethnic groups who were employed in manufacturing occupations. Among women, more than one-fourth of European American, American Indian, and Chinese American women held manufacturing jobs, while for Japanese American, island Puerto Rican, and African American women the share in manufacturing was much lower, as shown in Table 4. Among men, only European Americans held more than their labor market share of manufacturing jobs; men of color remained relatively concentrated in agriculture. Thus, in 1900, manufacturing jobs still represented a white preserve from which most men and women of color were excluded.

Particular manufacturing occupations were typed by gender and/or by race-ethnicity. For example, skilled garment making—performed by dressmakers, seamstresses, shirt, collar, and cuff makers, tailors and tailoresses—was a job undertaken by women of all racial-ethnic groups, often in their own homes. Women made up 78 percent of these workers in 1900, and only African American women had less than their labor market share. European American women had five times their share (with immigrant women more likely to be so employed than U.S.-born), American Indian women four times, and Japanese and Chinese at least twice.[12] Needlework jobs were also important for Puerto Rican and Chicana women.

In contrast, in 1900, textile mill operatives were almost exclusively white, and about half men and half women. White men held less than their labor market share of these jobs (since they could find more lucrative jobs), while white women held more than three times their labor market share. Within the mills, jobs were typed according to sex and ethnicity. European immigrants, especially Irish, Italian, English, and Welsh, had higher relative concentrations in mill jobs than did U.S.-born whites. On the other hand, no group of men or women of color had achieved more than one-twentieth of their labor market share of textile mill jobs, which paid considerably more than the agricultural and domestic service jobs into which they were crowded.

A third set of jobs was monopolized by white males: traditional, masculine crafts, such as carpentry, masonry, plumbing, blacksmithing, cabinetmaking, and machine-making (machinists). In all of these jobs, European American men maintained a

**Table 4   Share of Employed Women Working in Manufacturing,
by Racial-Ethnic Group, 1900–1990**

	1900	1930	1960	1980	1990
American Indian	24.9	37.6	18.1	17.0	14.2
Chicana	n.a.	24.7	29.1	26.0	20.0
European American	32.6	21.2	18.5	12.6	9.4
African American	2.6	8.4	15.5	18.4	14.5
Chinese American	41.1	20.8	24.0	20.8	16.2
Japanese American	7.7	12.2	19.0	12.5	8.4
Filipina American	n.a.	15.3	17.4	13.8	8.4
Island Puerto Rican	14.6	52.4	31.3	22.0	17.5
U.S. Puerto Rican	n.a.	n.a.	69.3	29.1	16.1

Notes: Asian American data include Hawaii for all years; 1980 and 1990 data for American Indians include Eskimo and Aleut peoples; for 1900–1960, African American and European American include Latinas.

near monopoly. Many slave men, trained in these crafts, were prevented by white men from practicing their trades after Emancipation. However, this exclusion worked unevenly: in 1900, African American men held about their labor market share of masonry and plastering jobs, a little less than half their share of carpentry and blacksmithing, and only about one-tenth their share of plumbing and machinist jobs. No other group of men held even half its labor market share, although Chinese, Japanese, and American Indian men had a significant part of their shares in carpentry and blacksmithing. Women of all racial-ethnic groups were the most excluded from the crafts, with none receiving more than 6 percent of their labor market share.[13] Exclusion was costly since the crafts were generally much higher-paid than other manufacturing jobs.

Between 1900 and 1980, as the economy grew and changed, the number of manufacturing jobs quadrupled and manufacturing's share of total employment increased. Women's manufacturing employment also quadrupled, but women's total employment grew even faster, so the share of women in manufacturing fell. However, the decline in women's manufacturing employment was very uneven across racial-ethnic groups. Only among white women was there a smooth decline, as white women found better-paid jobs as sales, clerical, and professional and managerial workers. Not until the mid-twentieth century did Black women gain entry to manufacturing as a result

of organizing, wartime labor shortages, and white women's exodus. Very high percentages of Puerto Rican women have been employed in manufacturing, both in Puerto Rico and in the United States, at rates which have fluctuated widely with the movement of firms in and out of Puerto Rico or New York.

If we look at the overall pattern, an interesting change is clear. In 1900, when manufacturing represented a relatively good job, white women's share was greater than that of most women of color. In contrast, in 1980, most women of color, other than Japanese, had higher participation in manufacturing than white women. This signifies not a reversal of the racial-ethnic hierarchy, but the movement of white women into higher-paid, higher-status jobs such as clerical and professional work.

Since 1980, overall U.S. employment in manufacturing (excluding construction) has fallen in absolute terms as a result of a combination of factors, including productivity increases, the transfer of plants abroad, and competition from foreign producers. Ironically, the share of women workers in manufacturing actually rose between 1970 and 1990. In research on heavy manufacturing jobs such as steelworking, European American sociologist Joan Smith found that white men were likely to be replaced by workers of color and/or white women in sectors where profits were slipping and firms were not investing in new equipment. In those sectors, the strategy to boost profits was to employ lower-wage workers.[14]

Thus, even though factory jobs were in decline, employers have increasingly relied on two forms of manufacturing work common in the nineteenth and early twentieth century, sweatshops and industrial homework. Now, as then, these jobs employ a disproportionate number of immigrant women. Many Southeast Asian refugee women, undocumented Mexican immigrant women, and recent Chinese immigrant women are finding employment in the newly resurgent sweatshops. Industrial homework—manufacturing work contracted out to workers in their own homes—has also been on the rise. For employers, homework offers freedom from unionization, government regulations, and overhead costs. Women, on the other hand, turn to homework in the hopes of combining work and family, or because no other work is available. Under the Reagan administration, regulations prohibiting homework were dismantled. As a result, capitalists are opting to locate more work in workers' homes and have expanded the range of manufacturing jobs contracted out to homeworkers to include electronic component assembly as well as the traditional garment work.[15]

Today, as in the past, women of different racial-ethnic groups are unevenly represented within different manufacturing jobs. Garment work—both by dressmakers and by sewing-machine operators—continues to be female-dominated. However, Black women are no longer excluded, and in 1980 they held more than twice their labor market share of these jobs; Asian American and Latina women each occupied five to six times their labor market share, while white women held twice theirs. (1990 data are not available at this level of racial and occupational detail.)

Although women continue to be overrepresented in garment work, there has been progress in more lucrative areas of manufacturing as a result of the anti-discrimination struggles of the past 20 years. The most significant improvement has been for men of color, who were overrepresented in the crafts in 1990. In contrast, women of all racial-ethnic groups held less than one-third of their labor market share; these crafts, then, shifted from white-male-dominated to male-dominated. Women of color were doing better than white women at gaining representation in the crafts: in 1990, Chicana, American Indian, Asian, and U.S. Puerto Rican women had the highest relative concentrations in craft work, ranging from 33 to

26 percent respectively, with white women at 19 percent. Since craft work offers relatively high-paying and secure employment to people who cannot afford higher education, it is not surprising that women of color, who continue to have less access to higher education than white women, choose this route to economic security.

The Rise of Office Work

One of the most important occupational changes for women in the twentieth century has been the growth of clerical work. Women's clerical employment grew from 320,000 in 1900 to over 2 million in 1930 and nearly 15 million in 1990. Clerical work provides an interesting example of the transformation and reproduction of gender and racial-ethnic hierarchies. In the nineteenth century, a clerk was typically an

**Table 5   Share of Employed Women Working in Clerical Occupations,
by Racial-Ethnic Group, 1900–1990**

	1900	1930	1960	1980	1990
American Indian	0.1	3.3	14.2	27.4	24.9
Chicana	n.a.	2.8	21.8	26.2	24.7
European American	6.9	25.3	34.5	32.3	28.2
African American	0.1	0.6	8.0	25.8	25.8
Chinese American	0.5	11.7	32.1	24.7	20.7
Japanese American	0.1	3.7	30.5	31.6	28.0
Filipina American	n.a.	1.6	24.3	28.2	28.0
Island Puerto Rican	1.2	2.3	16.9	26.9	26.6
U.S. Puerto Rican	n.a.	n.a.	13.9	31.9	31.0

Notes: Asian American data include Hawaii for all years; 1980 and 1990 data for American Indians include Eskimo and Aleut peoples; for 1900–1960, African American and European American include Latinas.

educated white man who worked in an office as training for managerial work. When the typewriter was introduced, young European American middle-class women were hired to operate the machine, and the job was feminized: the clerical worker's career path to management was eliminated, and clerical workers found themselves acting as low-level assistants to male managers and treated as office wives.

The feminization of the office, as this process is called by European American sociologist Margery Davies, was at first a European American phenomenon. White immigrant women other than the English were kept out of offices, and women of color's access to clerical occupations was severely restricted through World War II. In 1900, as shown in Table 5, only among white women were a significant share employed in clerical work; a smaller share of Japanese and Chinese women were able to find clerical jobs in firms serving their communities. Black women and American Indian women were almost totally excluded from this new, relatively high-status job. Indeed, the relative concentration of white men among stenographers and typists (about one-third of their labor market share) was eight times higher than that of Black women.[16]

Clerical employment grew by over 1.5 million jobs between 1900 and 1930. Most of these new jobs were taken by European women, although women of color made small gains. Black women continued to face the greatest obstacles. However, as clerical jobs continued to multiply in the post–World War II era, racial barriers eventually broke down as a result of both the persistence of women of color and the economy's burgeoning demand for workers. Education and urbanization have also provided opportunities for women of color to gain access to clerical work. At the same time, the two groups most highly represented in clerical work in 1960—European and Chinese American women—reduced their share in the subsequent 20 years, as educated women in these groups took advantage of new opportunities in professional and managerial fields. As a result of all these changes, the differences between women of various racial-ethnic groups were greatly reduced: in 1990, from one-fourth to almost one-third of each group's employed women worked as clericals. Since women's clerical jobs pay substantially more than their jobs in services, manufacturing, and sales (with 1994 weekly earnings of $374, compared to $257, $293, and $324, respectively), and since many women prefer office working conditions to those in the factory or in service work, this movement has represented a genuine step forward for women of color.[17]

While clerical work is no longer reserved for white women, racial-ethnic and gender segregation persists. For instance, in 1980, 31 percent of white women were secretaries, compared to 18 percent of African American women. In contrast, women of color were more likely to be typists, data entry keyers, and file clerks—all occupations that were lower in pay and status than those dominated by white women. (As mentioned above, 1990 data are not available at this level of detail.) Furthermore, automation threatens to displace many lower-skilled clerical jobs, and it is likely that women of color, whose hold on clerical work is more tenuous, will be more affected by a retrenchment in this sector than white women. While women of color were concentrated in lower-level clerical jobs, the men in clerical work were concentrated in supervisory work in 1980, where they made up 41 percent of all workers, compared to only 2 percent of secretaries, stenographers, typists, and receptionists.[18]

Union organizing among clerical workers is succeeding in raising wages, much of it through the strategy of comparable worth (which demands equal pay for jobs of comparable skill, responsibility, and working conditions, regardless of the gender of the worker or the sex-typing of the job). Pressure from women of color has extended the concept of comparable worth to ensure equity between whites and people of color along with equity between men and women. Some of today's women office workers have also successfully fought to remove from their job descriptions such "wifely" tasks as preparing the office coffee and shopping for their bosses' anniversary gifts. However, many clerical workers continue to perform these tasks, receiving little recognition and low wages in return. Worse, office workers, like other women workers, continue to experience sexual harassment by male supervisors and co-workers.

Career Women: Women in Professional Jobs

Managerial and professional jobs offer women the highest wages and status. Like other jobs, they have been typed by gender and race-ethnicity, with white men at the top, although white women and people of color have made progress recently into some jobs which once were dominated by white men.

In 1900, over one-tenth of European American women were employed in managerial or professional jobs, compared to less than one in fifty workers among women of color. European American women were largely confined to a small set of managerial and professional jobs, including teaching, library science, and social work, all jobs which extended and professionalized woman's nurturing and caring roles. Indeed,

educated white women played a major role in the fight to develop and feminize these professions, which they saw as outgrowths of social homemaking.

Before the Civil War, most teachers were white men; during the war, white women were hired to replace them, and after the war, they remained, arguing that teaching was, after all, a form of mothering. For Black women, teaching played a special role as a means to elevate and emancipate their people.[19] In 1900, white women had five times their labor market share of elementary and secondary school teaching jobs. The only other group of men or women to have at least their labor market share was Native American women. Next came Black women with 78 percent of their labor market share, Chinese women with 64 percent, and white men with 33 percent. Just as schools were racially segregated, so teachers of color were assigned to teach children of their own racial-ethnic group; however, given the underrepresentation of men and women of color in teaching, white women also commonly taught students of color.

By 1900, women, mostly but not entirely white, had begun to professionalize nursing, elevating it from a form of domestic service to a skilled job which required professional education. As a broad occupational category, it was women's work; women of color had three times their labor market share of these jobs, and white women over five times, while men of color and white men each had less than one-tenth their labor market share. Within nursing, however, as within teaching, jobs were racially typed according to clientele, and access to nursing schools was limited for women of color.[20]

Other professions—physicians and surgeons, lawyers, and engineers, among others—became the province of white men. These jobs typically offered higher pay than white women's professions, called for more formal training, and involved control over, rather than service of, others. Indeed, they often required assistance by women, as nurses, receptionists, or legal secretaries. In 1900, no group other than white men held even half its labor market share of these elite professions, although a few individuals had gained admittance. Chinese men, American Indian men, and white women had made the most progress in medicine; American Indian men, Black men, and white women in law.[21] Women of color were almost totally excluded. The greatest relative concentration for women of color in white men's professions was that

Table 6   Share of Employed Women Working in Professional and Technical Occupations, by Racial-Ethnic Group, 1900–1990

	1900	1930	1960	1980	1990
American Indian	1.9	4.6	9.1	14.5	15.7
Chicana	n.a.	2.7	5.9	8.4	10.8
European American	10.2	16.2	14.6	18.0	21.4
African American	1.2	3.4	7.8	15.2	17.0
Chinese American	1.4	22.0	17.9	20.4	17.0
Japanese American	0.3	6.6	12.3	17.8	23.5
Filipina American	n.a.	6.0	26.4	27.1	19.3
Island Puerto Rican	0.7	4.5	15.5	21.1	21.9
U.S. Puerto Rican	n.a.	n.a.	4.0	10.9	12.2

Notes: Asian American data include Hawaii for all years; 1980 and 1990 data for American Indians include Eskimo and Aleut peoples; for 1900–1960, African American and European American include Latinas.

of Black women in law, at one-twentieth their labor market share; in most of the white men's professions, no Chinese, Japanese, or American Indian women were even recorded in 1900.[22]

Over the course of the twentieth century, professional and managerial employment has increased by a factor of nine, and the share of these jobs in total employment has risen from one-tenth to over one-quarter. Although men continue to make up the majority of workers, women's share of managerial and professional jobs has more than doubled, from 20 to 48 percent.

Central to women's entrance into professional and managerial jobs have been their successful struggles for access to higher education, which constitute an important part of African American, Chinese American, and Japanese American economic history, as well as of that of whites. Not surprisingly, the share of women in professional and managerial occupations by racial-ethnic group is highly correlated with the share of college graduates.[23] Because educational opportunity has such an important effect on labor market opportunities for women, lower educational attainment is also related to lower labor force participation rates, and may be both a cause and a result of Chicanas' and U.S. Puerto Rican women's relatively low labor force participation rates.[24]

While women's representation in professional work increased for all racial-ethnic groups between 1900 and 1990, levels and rates of growth differ (see Table 6). The share in the professions increased most dramatically for women of color, who had been almost entirely excluded from such jobs in 1900. By 1990, Japanese American and island Puerto Rican women were more likely to hold professional and technical jobs than European American women. However, in 1990, American Indian, Chicana, and U.S. Puerto Rican women were still less likely to hold professional and technical jobs than European American women had been in 1930.

Much of the growth in women's professional employment occurred in jobs that have historically been dominated by women: pre-kindergarten, kindergarten, and elementary school teacher; nurse; librarian; dietitian; and social worker. In 1994, these professions (each of which was at least 69 percent female) employed 48 percent of women professionals. Women made up 94 percent of all registered nurses and 86 percent of all elementary school teachers.[25]

The racial-ethnic composition of women's professions has also changed as the near-monopoly of white women has been challenged. Between 1900 and 1990, white women's relative concentration in teaching fell from 525 to 178, while that of women of color rose. In 1990, all racial-ethnic groups of women, except Chinese women and Filipinas, were overrepresented in elementary and secondary teaching, and even those two underrepresented groups had a higher relative concentration than any racial-ethnic group of men. Nursing has continued to be dominated by women, and women in all racial-ethnic groups except Chicanas and American Indians hold more than their employment share of nursing jobs.[26]

In 1990, despite increased representation of other groups, white men continued to make up the majority of such professions as engineering and medicine. In fact, between 1900 and 1990, white men's share of all jobs fell much more rapidly than their share of these professions, increasing their relative concentrations. However, all previously excluded groups (especially Asian American women and men) have made significant progress, increasing both their share of these jobs and their relative concentrations between 1900 and 1990 in almost all cases.[27] Among engineers, Filipinas and all three groups of Asian American men had equal or higher relative concentrations than white men—approximately two and three times their labor market shares, respectively. However, most groups of color continued to be underrepresented relative to their share of all jobs. For instance, African American men held less than half their employment share of physicians' jobs, and African American women held only one-fifth their share. Chicanas/os and American Indians were even more seriously underrepresented.

Although the increasing presence of people of color and white women in previously restricted occupations is a victory, racial-ethnic and gender hierarchies persist *within* the professions (and indeed, within all occupations) in the form of different job assignments, different treatment, and unequal pay for equal work. For example, women lawyers in corporations tend to work for smaller firms, where they earn lower pay and have fewer opportunities for advancement. Data on law school faculties show that women are more likely to be working in non-tenure-track jobs or to have achieved tenure at lower-status law schools. According to one study, women of color constituted less than 10 percent of women law faculty in 1986, and only 2 percent of all faculty.[28]

The Persistence of Racial-Ethnic, Gender, and Class Hierarchies in the Labor Market

This survey of occupations reveals a mixed picture: racial-ethnic and gender hierarchies have been reproduced and maintained in some ways at the same time

as they have broken down in others. Asian Americans have surpassed European Americans according to many average indicators, and small shares of previously marginalized groups have broken into the elite jobs from which they were once excluded. Yet men still earn much more than women, on average, as do whites compared to non-Asian people of color.

NOTES

1. Julie Matthaei, *An Economic History of Women in America: Women's Work, the Sexual Division of Labor, and the Development of Capitalism* (New York: Schocken Books, 1982), 284; *1870 Census of the United States*, Population and Social Statistics, Table XXIX.

2. Quoted in Judith Rollins, *Between Women: Domestics and Their Employers* (Philadelphia: Temple University Press, 1985), 51.

3. Ibid., 50–53; 1900 Census.

4. Constant dollar per GNP increased from $1,011 in 1900 to $3,555 in 1970, and has risen 45 percent since then. U.S. Bureau of the Census, *Historical Statistics of the United States, Colonial Time to 1970*, vol. 1 (Washington, D.C.: 1970); U.S. Bureau of the Census, *Statistical Abstract of the United States 1994*, 451; U.S. Census, 1900 and 1990.

5. bell hooks, presentation at New Words Bookstore, 5 March 1989, Cambridge, MA, on the occasion of the publication of *Talking Back: Talking Feminist, Talking Black* (Boston: South End Press, 1989).

6. Calculated from 1980 Census, provisional volume, U.S. Summary, Table 278.

7. Relative concentration can rise for all groups. White men's share of protective service jobs only dropped by 13 percentage points, while white men's share of all jobs dropped by 24 percentage points (as a result of women's movement into the labor force); thus, the relative concentration of white men in protective service rose. The 1980 data include police officers and firefighters.

8. *Employment and Earnings* (January 1995), 195 and 209–13; *Employment and Earnings* (March 1980), 35.

9. Michael Ybarra, "Janitors' Union Uses Pressure and Theatrics to Expand Its Ranks," *Wall Street Journal*, 21 March 1994, A1–6.

10. Blacks fell from 14.5 percent of all farm operators in 1910 to only 3.8 percent of the total in 1969, and only 2.1 percent in 1980. *Black Population*, 81, and 1980 Census.

11. One such group is the Rural Women's Leadership Development Project of Prairiefire Rural Action, which organizes an annual conference, "Harvesting Our Potential," and publishes a journal entitled "Women of the Land." Their address is 550 11th St., Des Moines, Iowa 50309.

12. The 1900 Census data presented here include only workers within the continental United States, and hence

excludes island Puerto Ricans. The numbers for Chinese women are very low, and data for Chicanas are not available.

13. Calculated from 1900 Census.

14. Joan Smith, "Impact of the Reagan Years: Race, Gender, and the Economic Restructuring," First Annual Women's Policy Research Conference Proceedings (Washington, D.C.: Institute for Women's Policy Research, 1989), 20.

15. An excellent set of essays on homework can be found in Eileen Boris and Cynthia R. Daniels, eds., *Homework: Historical and Contemporary Perspectives on Paid Labor at Home* (Urbana: University of Illinois Press, 1989).

16. Calculated from 1900 Census.

17. *Employment and Earnings* (January 1995), 210–13.

18. U.S. Department of Labor, Women's Bureau, *Women and Office Automation: Issues for the Decade Ahead* (Washington, D.C.: GPO, 1985), 20–22; *Statistical Abstract of the United States, 1988,* 376–77.

19. See Matthaei, 178–82.

20. Susan Reverby, *Ordered to Care: The Dilemma of American Nursing, 1850–1945* (New York: Cambridge University Press, 1987).

21. In medicine, Chinese men, American Indian men, and white women held 61, 44, and 40 percent of their labor market shares, respectively, with Black men and women at 13 and 3 percent. In law, American Indian men held 33 percent, Black men 7 percent, and white women 6 percent of their labor market shares. Calculated from 1900 Census.

22. Calculated from the 1900 Census. For a study of white and Black women's struggles to enter medicine, and white men's organizing to keep them out, see Gloria Mol-

dow, *Women Doctors in Gilded-Age Washington: Race, Gender, and Professionalization* (Chicago: University of Illinois Press, 1987).

23. The shares of women with a college education are as follows: Filipina (41.2 percent), Chinese American (29.5 percent), Japanese American (19.7 percent), island Puerto Rican (18.3 percent), European American (13.5 percent), African American (8.3 percent), American Indian (6.4 percent), U.S. Puerto Rican (4.8 percent), and Chicana (3.7 percent). See U.S. Census, 1980, Tables 160 and 166, and Junta de Planificación de Puerto Rico, *Indicadores Socio-Económicos de la Mujer en Puerto Rico* (San Juan, Puerto Rico; La Junta, March 1987), A-3.

24. Elizabeth Almquist, *Minorities, Gender and Work* (Lexington, MA: D. C. Heath, 1972), 149–52.

25. *Employment and Earnings* (January 1995), 175–76.

26. Calculated from the 1900 and 1990 Censuses. In 1990, the job category for nursing is "health assessment and treating." Filipinas are especially overrepresented in nursing, with a relative concentration over 600.

27. 1900 data for Latinas/os were not available. The two exceptions to rising relative concentrations are Chinese men, who experienced a decrease in their relative concentration in physicians' and surgeons' jobs, and white women, whose relative concentration held steady. Calculated from 1900 and 1990 Censuses.

28. Susan Erlich Martin and Nancy C. Jurik, *Doing Justice, Doing Gender: Women in Law and Criminal Justice Occupations* (Thousand Oaks, CA: Sage Publications, 1996), 115–27.

FORTY-NINE

◆◆◆

He Works, She Works,
but What Different Impressions They Make

Have you ever found yourself up against the old double standard at work? Then you know how annoying it can be and how alone you can feel. Supervisors and coworkers still judge us by old stereotypes that say women are emotional, disorganized, and inefficient. Here are some of the most glaring examples of the typical office double standard.

The family picture is on HIS desk:
Ah, a solid, responsible family man.

The family picture is on HER desk:
Hmm, her family will come before her career.

HIS desk is cluttered:
He's obviously a hard worker and busy man.

HER desk is cluttered:
She's obviously a disorganized scatterbrain.

HE'S talking with coworkers:
He must be discussing the latest deal.

SHE'S talking with coworkers:
She must be gossiping.

HE'S not at his desk:
He must be at a meeting.

SHE'S not at her desk:
She must be in the ladies' room.

HE'S having lunch with the boss:
He's on his way up.

SHE'S having lunch with the boss:
They must be having an affair.

HE'S getting married.
He'll get more settled.

SHE'S getting married:
She'll get pregnant and leave.

HE'S having a baby:
He'll need a raise.

SHE'S having a baby:
She'll cost the company money in maternity benefits.

HE'S leaving for a better job:
He recognizes a good opportunity.

SHE'S leaving for a better job:
Women are undependable.

HE'S aggressive.

SHE'S pushy.

HE'S careful.

SHE'S picky.

HE loses his temper.

SHE'S bitchy.

HE'S depressed.

SHE'S moody.

HE follows through.

SHE doesn't know when to quit.

HE'S firm.

SHE'S stubborn.

HE makes wise judgments.

SHE reveals her prejudices.

HE is a man of the world.

SHE'S been around.

HE isn't afraid to say what he thinks.

SHE'S opinionated.

HE exercises authority.

SHE'S tyrannical.

HE'S discreet.

SHE'S secretive.

HE'S a stern taskmaster.

SHE'S difficult to work for.

FIFTY

Reflections of a Feminist Mom

Jeannine Ouellette Howitz

I am seven months pregnant, slithering along my kitchen floor. The ruler I clutch is for retrieving small objects lost in the dust jungle beneath my refrigerator. After several swipes I come up with a pile of dirt and a petrified saltine, so I get serious and press my cheek against the floor, positioning my left eye just inches from the target zone. I spot it—the letter "G," a red plastic refrigerator magnet. "Here it is!" I cry, hoisting myself up to offer this hard-won prize to Sophie, my momentarily maniacal toddler. Her face collapses into a sob as she shrieks, "NOT THAT ONE!"

Sophie is 22 months old, and in the final stages of potty training, which I remember as I feel a gush of warm and wet on my outstretched leg. Wet clothes bring more tears (hers, not mine), and I quickly strip off her clothes, then pull off my own with one hand while I slice and peel an apple with the other. I might have barely enough time while she eats to run upstairs, grab dry clothes, and toss the dirty ones into the basket before I'm urgently missed.

That was how I came to be standing in the middle of my kitchen with the magnificence of my naked abdomen hanging low and wide on a clammy June afternoon. The sweat of my exertion had just begun trickling between my breasts when the phone rang. It was an old friend with whom I'd been out of touch for a while. I panted hello, eyeing Sophie as she climbed up and out of her booster chair to totter precariously on the table top. "What are you doing home?" my friend wanted to know. "Don't you work at all anymore?"

Don't you work at all anymore? Again and again since entering the life phase which positioned my work in the home, I have encountered the judgments, however unconscious, of those whose definition of work excludes most of what I do. The same system that discounts my labor scoffs at its rewards, which, like my productivity, are impossible to measure by conventional standards. By limiting our view to one which allows only for paid employment, usu-

ally only that located outside the home, to be included in the understood meaning of the word "work," we support the process through which all that we do and all that we are as women is ultimately devalued and despised.

Like most labels applied to women's roles, "working mother" is extremely inaccurate and defeating, because it foolishly implies that there is another type of mother: the non-working variety. Being a mother is work. On the other hand, it is equally absurd to call mothers who are not employed outside the home "full-time mothers," as this unfairly suggests that employed mothers are only mothers part-time. Ridiculous as they are, these labels go largely unchallenged, even by many feminists. They are a sinister trap, imprisoning women in feelings of inadequacy about whatever roles we have chosen or been required to perform.

The same process that forces a woman to say "I don't work" when she performs 12 to 16 hours of unpaid labor every single day at home ultimately transforms most female-dominated professions into mere chores that women and men alike come to consider less desirable and important than other types of work. Once stamped with the kiss of death "women's work," we can forget entitlement to the same respect and fair wages a man would get for equivalent labor.

Before motherhood, I sold advertising at a newspaper, with hopes of working my way into editorial. However, my sales performance exceeded standards, and I was quickly promoted to a well-paying position in management which required me to build a classified department from the ground up. I forged ahead until my daughter was born, when, after reexamining our options, my husband and I decided one of us should stay home with her. Although he was happily working in his chosen field, John's income as a schoolteacher was half that of mine, which rendered him the financially logical choice for at-home parenthood. But it was I who jumped at the chance, albeit scary, to shift the gears of my career and of my life.

When my maternity leave was up, I told the publishers that I wouldn't be returning to the office. Surprisingly, they offered me the chance to bring my daughter to work with me. I was thrilled; those long days at home with an infant weren't exactly what I had imagined. I discovered that although I didn't always enjoy my job, I did enjoy the recognition it provided me—something I found was not a part of the package for home-working moms. While my sister spoke with unveiled envy about all the reading and writing I would now be accomplishing, in reality I was lucky if I brushed my teeth. So I took the deal.

Seven weeks old on her first day at work, Sophie fascinated the staff as only a newborn can. A two-minute trip to the copier often turned into a half-hour social ordeal as one person after the next stopped to exclaim over her. She was a great diversion for a young and predominantly single staff. I had no idea, as a new mother, how fortunate I was to have an extroverted baby. It was my own introverted nature that suffered from the constant sensory bombardment. I was uncomfortably aware of my special status, and fighting a losing battle to hide how much time it actually took to care for Sophie on the job.

In a culture where women feel guilty to call in sick to work when a child is sick, it was tremendously difficult to be in an office setting, drawing a full salary, and to say, "Sophie's crying now—this phone call, this meeting, this project, whatever it is, will have to wait." In a society that expects workers to give 150 percent dedication to the job, and considers motherhood a terrible detriment to productivity, it was incredibly stressful and even painful at times to experience such a personal conflict in a very public setting when the two worlds collided.

For six months, I toted a baby, a briefcase, and a diaper bag back and forth from home to my office, which at first housed the crib and swing, after which came the walker, the play gym, and the toy box— not to mention the breast pump equipment and mini-diaper pail. I could hardly see my desk, let alone get to it. Not that it mattered, because by that time I wasn't doing any work that required a desk. It had gotten crazy, and I knew it. The circles under my eyes and my continued weight loss told me it was time for a change.

I explored every alternative I could think of, from researching and visiting daycares to negotiating with my employers for a part-time or home-based position, or a combination of the two. However, my key position on the management team required a full-time presence in the office.

Offering my resignation was an extremely difficult decision, particularly in light of my gratitude for the progressive opportunity to have my daughter on-site. My employers and I finally agreed to view my departure as the beginning of an indefinite unpaid leave that left the door open for my possible return at some unpredictable future date.

A two-month notice allowed me to finish up the last big sales project of the quarter, while my daughter was cared for by a neighbor. I got an unforgettable taste of the superwoman syndrome, rising at 5 A.M. and dashing out the door by 6 to drop Sophie off and commute an hour to the office for a grueling nine-hour day. This was followed by a long drive in Minnesota winter rush-hour traffic to pick my daughter up and go home, and was topped off with a couple of frantic hours that my husband and I spent getting everyone fed and Sophie bathed and to bed so that we could start all over again after what felt like a quick catnap. Relief overcame me as my last day at the office arrived, and I packed my diaper bags for good.

Our plans had always included my return to full-time paid employment upon our children's entry to school, which meant that, for the benefit of our financial solvency, we should have another baby quickly if at all. We chose "quickly," and shortly after our daughter's first birthday I was pregnant again.

I started stringing for our local newspaper, rushing out to city council and school board meetings as soon as my husband dragged himself through the door at seven o'clock. I got paid a measly 25 dollars a story, but since the meetings were at night and I could write the stories at home, I didn't have to pay for childcare. Moreover, it was the first time I saw my writing published; it signaled a turning point for me as I finally made the leap from advertising to editorial.

Since then, I've stuck to what I'm passionate about as I navigate the uncertain waters of these transitional years. I've redefined my priorities, and am using this time to lay the groundwork for a career that is going to work for me long after my children are grown. Like the many women who grow home businesses while growing young ones, I've discovered meaning in my personal work that was previously absent.

These days, since I do perform paid work from home, I could have an easy answer to "Don't you work at all anymore?" I could say that I am a freelance writer working at home. It's true, and since I know, based upon my own research, that it gains me a great deal more respect in the eyes of the asker than saying that I'm home with the kids, I'm tempted to offer it up. But I won't because every time I do, I'm perpetuating a system that defines work only in terms of what men have traditionally been paid to do, and discounts most of what women have traditionally done for centuries.

I have to make perfectly clear when I say that I work at home, I'm talking about the childcare and the home maintenance activities which utilize my talents as a manager, nurturer, healer, wise woman, acrobat . . . and retriever of small objects lost in the dust jungle beneath my refrigerator. Otherwise, people automatically dismiss these activities and conjure up a false image of an orderly day spent at the computer doing paid work. This strain toward clarity requires a lot more effort than calling myself a full-time mom, or proclaiming that I'm taking time off to be with my kids (motherhood is not a vacation), or worst of all, concurring that no, "I really don't work at all anymore." It demands concentration and patience, but it can be done.

We must find new words, or new combinations of and meanings for old words that more accurately reflect our reality. When we don't—when we resign ourselves to the old words that apportion us less worth than we deserve because it's less awkward and just plain easier—we are validating a description of ourselves that we know to be false. This danger is like that of looking into a fun house mirror, without challenging the falsehood of the contorted stranger staring back at you. Eventually, you're going to believe what you see is you, and that twisted version of yourself becomes the only truth you know.

FIFTY-ONE

◆◆◆

Violating Women
Rights Abuses in the Welfare Police State

Gwendolyn Mink

When the 1996 Personal Responsibility and Work Opportunity Reconciliation Act (PRWORA) replaced the old welfare system, it set up a harsh new system that subordinates recipients to a series of requirements, sanctions, and stacked incentives aimed at rectifying their personal choices and family practices. The Temporary Assistance for Needy Families (TANF) program, the welfare system established in 1996, disciplines recipients by either stealing or impairing their basic civil rights. In exchange for welfare, TANF recipients must surrender vocational freedom, sexual privacy, and reproductive choice, as well as the right to make intimate decisions about how to be and raise a family. Ordinarily, these rights are strongly guarded by constitutional doctrine, as they form the core of the Supreme Court's jurisprudence of (heterosexual) personhood and family. Not so for a mother who needs welfare.

The most talked-about aspect of TANF is its dramaturgy of work (cf. Piven and Cloward 1993, 346, 381, 395), but TANF's foremost objective is to restore the patriarchal family. Accordingly, numerous TANF provisions promote marriage and paternal headship while frustrating childbearing and child-raising rights outside of marriage. TANF's impositions on poor mothers' right to form and sustain their own families—as well as to avoid or exit untenable relationships with men—proceed from stiff paternity establishment and child support enforcement rules. According to the *2000 Green Book*, TANF's "exceptionally strong paternity establishment requirements" compose its most direct attack on nonmarital child-bearing, while mandatory maternal cooperation in establishing and enforcing child support orders impairs nonmarital child raising (U.S. House 2000c, 1530). If mothers do not obey these rules, they lose part or all of their families' benefits.

TANF's patriarchal solutions to welfare mothers' poverty have enjoyed bipartisan support. Democrats and Republicans did fight over some of the meaner provisions of the 1996 TANF legislation, but both agreed that poor women with children should at least be financially tied to their children's biological fathers or, better yet, be married to them. Endangering poor single women's independent childbearing decisions by condemning their decision to raise children independently, both parties agreed that poverty policy should make father-mother family formation its cardinal principle.

The 1996 PRWORA, which created TANF, spelled out policymakers' belief in the social importance of father-mother families in a preamble that recited correlations between single-mother families and such dangers as crime, poor school performance, and intergenerational single motherhood. Declaring that "marriage is the foundation of a successful society," the act went on to establish that the purpose of welfare must be not only to provide assistance to needy families but also to "end the dependence of needy parents on government benefits by promoting job preparation, work, and marriage," "prevent and reduce the incidence of out-of-wedlock pregnancies," and "encourage the formation and maintenance of two-parent families" (U.S. Public Law 104-193, Title I). Subsequent legislation and administrative regulations have strengthened TANF's founding goals through fatherhood programs that "strengthen [fathers'] ability to support a family" and that promote marriage (U.S. House 2000a).[1]

The TANF welfare regime backs up these interventions into poor single mothers' intimate relationships by sanctioning mothers with mandatory work outside the home if they remain single. Mothers who are married do not have to work outside the home, even though they receive welfare, for labor market work by only one parent in a two-parent family satisfies TANF's work requirement (U.S. Public Law 104-193, Title I, sec. 407(c)(1)(B); U.S. House 2000c, 357).[2]

Notwithstanding a decade of rhetoric about moving from welfare to work, the TANF regime treats wage work as the alternative to marriage, not to welfare—as punishment for mothers' independence.

Far from ending dependency, the TANF regime actually fosters poor mothers' dependency on individual men. Provisions that mandate father-mother family relations assume that fathers are the best substitute for welfare. The TANF regime's refusal to invest in mothers' employment opportunities and earning power enforces this assumption, for the combination of skills hierarchies and discrimination in the labor market keeps poor mothers too poor to sustain their families unassisted (see, for example, Acs et al. 1998; Moffitt and Roff 2000; Wider Opportunities for Women 2000). Moreover, the TANF regime's inattention to social supports such as transportation and child care ensures that single mothers' full-time employment will be an unaffordably expensive proposition indeed.

More than a cruel punishment for their persistent independence, the TANF work requirement is an injury to poor mothers' liberty as both mothers and workers. Obliging recipients to work outside the home 30 hours each week, the work requirement forecloses TANF mothers' choice to work as caregivers for their own children. It also interferes with their independent caregiving decisions, as absences due to lack of child care, for example, can lead to loss of employment—a failure to satisfy the work requirement. Further, the work requirement constrains TANF mothers' choices as labor market workers, such as the choice to prepare for the labor market through education or the choice to leave a hostile workplace (for key provisions see U.S. Public Law 104-193, Title I, sec. 407(a)(1), 407(c)(2)(B), 407(e)(1).

These injuries of welfare reform are born of poverty but lived through race. About two-thirds of recipients today are African American, Asian American, Latina, and Native American. From the 1960s to the present day, 35 to 40 percent of recipients have been African American; in 1998, 37.1 percent of TANF recipients were black. Latina and Asian American participation has increased over this period, and the Latino and Asian American populations as a whole have increased. Latina participation in 1998 was 20 percent, Asian American participation was 4.6 percent, and Native American participation was

1.6 percent (U.S. Department of Health and Human Services [DHHS] 1999, tab. 12; U.S. House 2000c, 438).

Steeper racial disparities in welfare participation may be in store, as white recipients are leaving the rolls more rapidly than are women of color or are not entering the rolls at all. In New York City, for example, the number of whites on welfare declined by 57 percent between 1995 and 1998, while the number of blacks declined by 30 percent and the number of Latinas by only 7 percent (DeParle 1998). Nationwide, whites' welfare participation has declined by 25 percent, while African Americans' participation has declined by 17 percent and Latinas' by 9 percent. As a result, women of color have increased as a percentage of TANF adults. In 24 states, women of color compose more than two-thirds of adult TANF enrollments; in 18 of those states, they compose three-quarters or more of enrollments (U.S. House 2000c, 439, tab. 7-29).

This racial distribution of welfare is the logical consequence of the racial distribution of poverty. Women of color have been and still are poorer than everyone else, single mothers of color even more so. In 1999, when 25.4 percent of (non-Hispanic) white single-mother families lived below the poverty line, 46.1 percent of African American and 46.6 percent of Latina single-mother families did so (U.S. Census Bureau 2000, tab. B-3). The racial distribution of poverty is enforced by racism and discrimination in most walks of life. In the labor market, for example, African American women who are employed full-time earn only 64 cents to the white male dollar and 84 cents to a white woman's. The wage gap for Latinas is even larger: 55 cents and 72 cents, respectively (U.S. Bureau of Labor Statistics 2000, chart 2, 3).

If the TANF regime's assault on poor mothers' rights wields an unmistakably disparate racial impact, it does so by imposing unmistakable constraints on poor mothers' gender practices. TANF's paternity establishment, child support enforcement, and work requirements primarily or exclusively target mothers who are not married—because they are not married.

Although the total number of nonmarital births is highest among white women, the number of nonmarital births per 1,000 unmarried women has been highest among women of color: 73.4 for non-Hispanic black women and 91.4 for Latinas, as compared to 27 for non-Hispanic white women (U.S. House 2000c, 1238, 1521). Further, although the total number of single-parent families is highest among whites, the percentage of single-parent families among black families (62.3 percent) is more than twice that among whites (26.6 percent). Moreover, the percentage of black families sustained by never-married mothers (36.5 percent) is exponentially greater than the percentage of white families (6.6 percent) (U.S. House 2000c, 1239, tab. G-4). Finally, according to the *2000 Green Book*, the poverty rate is highest among "independent families" (57.7 percent) and "cohabiting families" (58 percent) sustained by never-married mothers, among whom women of color figure disproportionately (U.S. House 2000c, 1246, tab. G-11).

Given the racial distribution of poverty, the presence of nonmarital mothers of color on TANF rolls is disproportionately high. TANF's gendered provisions are therefore racialized in their effects. These effects are not unplanned, for sounding the alarm against "fatherless childrearing," the TANF regime stakes itself to "the perspicacity of Moynihan's vision" that "black Americans [are] held back economically and socially in large part because their family structure [is] deteriorating" (U.S. House 2000c, 1519). And so the TANF regime exploits women-of-color poverty to suffocate single mothers' independence.

Women's Rights Under TANF

The rights imperiled by TANF policies range from basic expectations of autonomy and privacy among civilized and respectful people to liberty guarantees that have been deemed fundamental to constitutional citizenship. Diminishing liberty guarantees or withholding them from poor single mothers who receive welfare, the TANF regime creates a welfare caste to whom constitutional principles do not apply.

One of the engines behind the 1996 welfare reform legislation was the idea that constitutional protections won by recipients during the 1960s and early 1970s had undermined recipients' responsibility and increased their dependency. The 1996 law accordingly aimed to substitute welfare discipline for welfare rights. This involved inventing or refining program requirements to minimize participants' decisional autonomy, personal privacy, and independent personhood. Program rules not only require states to injure recipients' rights but also require recipients to explicitly acquiesce to injury in personal responsibility contracts that they must sign either to apply for or to participate in TANF (State Policy Documentation Project 1999b).

The most visible rights abuse of the TANF regime is its impairment of recipients' vocational liberty. Mandatory work requirements obligate recipients to perform labor-market work even if they are not paid for that work. Work requirements compel recipients entering the paid labor force to take the first job they are offered, even if they will not be paid a fair wage or supplied with tolerable working conditions. Moreover, work requirements prohibit recipients from performing family work except after hours, while these requirements permit them to perform the same work (that is, child care) for other people's families. By requiring a particular kind and location of work, TANF indentures recipients to the dramaturgy of work and so dictates their vocational choices (Mink 1998, chap. 4).

Family freedom is another right impaired by TANF program requirements, incentives, and preferences. TANF provisions tell recipients who gets to be part of their families. Paternity establishment and child support rules require mothers to associate at least financially with biological fathers. States may excuse a mother from complying for "good cause," if it is "in the best interest of the child" (U.S. House 2000c, 470). In general, however, a mother must reveal the identity of her child's father and must pursue a child support order against him, whether or not she wants him financially involved in her family's life. Seventeen states require mothers to cooperate with paternity establishment and child support enforcement while their TANF applications are pending—before they receive even a dime in cash assistance (State Policy Documentation Project 1999a). Once a mother receives TANF benefits, her failure to cooperate results in an automatic 25 percent reduction in cash assistance to her family; states are permitted to terminate welfare eligibility altogether (U.S. Public Law 104-193, Title I, sec. 408(a)(2).

In addition to requiring mothers to associate financially with fathers through child support, if not through marriage, TANF pressures mothers to yield parental rights to biological fathers. Access and visitation provisions authorize states to require moth-

ers to open their families to biological fathers. Until 1996, the federal government historically had separated fathers' rights from their obligations, treating visitation and child support as legally separate issues. Under TANF, however, these issues are explicitly connected because policymakers believe that it [is] more likely for noncustodial parents to make payments of child support if they [have] either joint custody or visitation rights" (U.S. House 2000c, 469).

As TANF's implementing agency at the federal level, the U.S. Department of Health and Human Services (DHHS) not only enforces TANF provisions but enhances enforcement with additional regulations and programs. One program, the Clinton administration's Fatherhood Initiative, aggressively works to improve paternity establishment rates. It claims to have contributed to the tripling of established paternities from 512,000 in fiscal year 1992 to 1.5 million in fiscal year 1998 (U.S. DHHS 2000c).

The DHHS administers TANF's provisions for access and visitation programs for fathers through a $10 million annual block grant to states to promote such programs. States may use their funds for mandatory mediation services, visitation enforcement, and to develop guidelines for alternative custody arrangements (U.S. DHHS 2000c). Access and visitation funds may also be used for programs to encourage or require separating or divorcing parents to reconsider their decision, such as Iowa's mandatory education program on the impact of divorce on children (Bernard 1998, 9–10).

To further promote fathers' involvement in families, Clinton's DHHS awarded grants and waivers to states in support of governmental, faith-based, and nonprofit initiatives such as Parents' Fair Share and Partners for Fragile Families, which aim to engage fathers in the legal, emotional, and financial aspects of parenthood (U.S. DHHS 2000b). DHHS complements its strategy toward fathers with suggestions about how TANF funds can be used to promote marriage among mothers. Department guidelines point out that TANF block grants are "extraordinarily flexible: and allow states to *change eligibility rules to provide incentives for single parents to marry or for two-parent families to stay together*" (U.S. DHHS 2000d, 3, 19; italics added). Eligibility rules for parents who need TANF—mostly single mothers—can include mandatory enrollment in marriage classes and couples counseling; incentives can include cash payments to TANF mothers who marry.

Asserting an inexorable connection between family structure, economic well-being, and child welfare, these sorts of initiatives override mothers' judgment of their own and their children's best interests. A condition of receiving welfare, these initiatives force poor single mothers to compromise their independence and even to put their rights to their children at risk.

TANF's insistence on biological fathers' responsibility for welfare mothers' children also invades recipients' sexual privacy. Although only consensual heterosexual sex between adults is shielded by privacy under reigning jurisprudence, even that partial right is withheld from unmarried mothers who seek welfare. Mandatory paternity establishment and child support provisions require a mother to identify her child's biological father in order to be eligible for welfare. These provisions single out nonmarital mothers for scrutiny and punishment, as paternity is automatically established at birth if a mother is married. A mother who is not married, who does not know who her child's biological father is, or who does not want anything to do with him must nevertheless provide welfare officials with information about him.

Even under TANF's predecessor, the Aid to Families with Dependent Children program, paternity establishment rules compromised recipients' privacy. To get the needed information, welfare officials and courts have required independent mothers to answer such questions as, "How many sexual partners have you had? . . . Whom did you have sex with before you got pregnant? . . . How often did you have sex? . . . Where did you have sex? . . . When did you have sex?" (Kelly 1994, 303–4). TANF encourages more aggressive and systematic intrusion into recipients' sex lives because states are required to punish noncooperating mothers with benefits cuts, because mothers must sign child support income over to the state as a condition of receiving welfare, and because the federal government offers states incentives and services to boost paternity establishment rates.

Sexual privacy is an aspect of reproductive freedom. TANF injures other reproductive rights when it interferes in women's childbearing decisions. For example, the TANF regime let stand state-level policies withholding benefits from children born to mothers who are already receiving welfare. Beginning in the early 1990s, many states had promulgated these "family cap" policies after securing waivers from federal welfare standards from the Bush (Sr.) and Clinton administrations. The family cap impairs reproductive rights because it punishes a recipient for choosing to complete a pregnancy.

TANF further injures reproductive rights through something called "illegitimacy bonuses" (U.S. Public Law 104-193, Title I, sec. 403(a)(2)). The bonus is paid to the five states that most successfully reduce the number of nonmarital births without raising the abortion rate. This gives states incentive to discourage conception by unmarried women—by offering cash awards to women who use Norplant, for example.

Sending a further message against having children outside marriage, the TANF regime funds states that offer abstinence education programs. The abstinence education program is required to teach women not to have sex, let alone babies, until they are "economically self-sufficient." States may devolve these programs to private grantees, including church-based groups that teach that abstinence is a matter of "values" and "sexual morality" (Toussaint n.d.). As a corollary to abstinence education, TANF calls for invigorated statutory rape prosecutions—underscoring the abstinence message with the threat of criminal sanctions when teenagers are involved (U.S. Public Law 104-193, Title I, sec. 402(a)(1)(v)). As a poor minor woman's nonmarital pregnancy is proof of sex before economic self-sufficiency, the threatened prosecution of nonmarital sex involving welfare recipients is another intrusion on poor single mothers' independence, including their reproductive autonomy. When threats fail in their desired effect of preventing sex and pregnancy, TANF's prohibition on assistance to unmarried teenage mothers delivers unambiguous punishment.

The TANF regime's various injuries to recipients' reproductive rights ultimately assail poor single women's right to be mothers. The final blow is delivered by the speed and ease with which child welfare and adoption provisions terminate poor mothers' right to custody of their children. Although the TANF legislation repealed the income entitlement that had belonged to poor mothers and their children, it maintained legislation for children to be removed from unfit parents and placed in foster care.

I have no quarrel with children's entitlement to protective services. However, the discretion delegated to child welfare workers permits them to deploy children's entitlement to foster care as a weapon of welfare discipline against their mothers. A mother who does not comply with work requirements might be deemed an unfit provider, for example. A mother who leaves her child alone to go to a job interview because she cannot find child care might be deemed an unfit caregiver. If she is sanctioned off welfare, has to take a low-wage job, or exhausts her eligibility, a mother may not be able to pay the rent or feed her children. These kinds of circumstances can lead to a finding that she is neglectful. A "neglectful" mother may lose custody of her child, or she may come under intensive supervision by government.

Indeed, TANF guidelines specifically encourage states to sustain scrutiny of sanctioned recipients for possible unfit parenting. The TANF regime mandates sanctions against recipients who do not meet work requirements, do not cooperate in establishing paternity, or do not cooperate in enforcing child support orders. Sanction penalties vary among states and range from a reduction in an individual mother's benefit the first time she fails to meet her work requirement, to the federally mandated reduction in a family's benefit when a mother fails to cooperate with paternity establishment and child support enforcement, to termination of a family's TANF assistance altogether (see State Policy Documentation Project 1999c). As a practical matter, sanctioned families frequently also lose their Medicaid, even though they remain entitled to receive it. Accordingly, TANF penalties not only breed material vulnerability but also medically endanger families (Dion and Pavetti 2000, 15–17).

DHHS guidelines stipulate that welfare monies may be used to "screen families who have been sanctioned under TANF" to determine whether children are at risk of child abuse or neglect. Mothers who do not want child support, or who do not want to identify biological fathers, or who cannot meet the 30-hour-weekly work requirement thus come under suspicion as abusive or neglectful parents. Mothers who exercise their rights and independent judgment are held to account for the consequences of TANF's brutal rules. If a mother's children are found to be at risk due to sanctions, TANF funds may be used to provide "case management services" to "cure" the mother's noncompliance with TANF rules (U.S. DHHS 2000d, 19).

TANF mothers who lose their benefits, like employed single mothers whose wages are too low to cover housing, food, or medical costs, may surrender their children to foster care. Occasionally, a mother might do so voluntarily until she can get back on her feet. Alternatively, child welfare workers might pressure a mother to do so. The 1997 Adoption and Safe Families Act threatens mothers who have lost their children to foster care with the permanent termination of their parental rights. Designed to accelerate and increase foster care adoptions, the act requires child welfare workers to consider terminating parental rights if a child has been in foster care for 15 out of the previous 22 months (U.S. House 1997; U.S. Public Law 105-89). In the four years since enactment of the adoption law, adoptions have increased significantly. According to the DHHS, adoptions rose from 28,000 in 1996 to 46,000 in 1999 (U.S. DHHS 2000a). We do not yet have hard evidence directly linking the rise in adoptions with recipients' loss of children. However, with a time limit on parental rights shorter even than the federal time limit on welfare, the adoption law hovers within the TANF regime as the regime's final solution to independent motherhood.

Ensuring Independence

Time limited and disciplinary, the terms of cash assistance enforce poor single mothers' inequality. One measure of this inequality is the persistence of poverty even among mothers who have left welfare for the labor market. Three years after leaving welfare, the median income among employed former welfare recipients was only $10,924 in 1999—well below the poverty line of $14,150 for a family of three. In many former TANF families, income is so low or so tenuous that families must skip meals, go hungry, use food pantries, or apply for emergency food assistance (Women of Color Resource Center 2000; Study Group on Work, Poverty and Welfare 1999). The main reasons for the persistence of poverty among former TANF recipients are that they are moving primarily into low-wage and contingent jobs without benefits, losing access to food stamps and Medicaid, and surrendering as much as 25 percent of their paychecks to child care.

Recognizing that ending welfare did not end single mothers' poverty, many policymakers are eager to pursue a next step in welfare reform. Already under way, this next step has taken legislative form in bipartisan initiatives to promote marriage and to enhance paternal wages and the paternal role. Such proposals have been espoused in various ideological quarters: by both Al Gore and George W. Bush during the 2000 presidential campaign; by Republican congresswoman Nancy Johnson (Conn.) and Democratic senator Evan Bayh (Ind.); by the Heritage Foundation's Robert Rector and by House Democrat Jesse Jackson Jr. (Ill.). They reveal a consensus that what poor single mothers need is a father's income. A related consensus is that if welfare reform has fallen short it is because too few recipients have gotten married.[3]

The most extreme calls for marriage promotion and fatherhood enhancement come, not surprisingly, from Robert Rector and others at the Heritage Foundation and from Wade Horn, a founder of the National Fatherhood Initiative whom the second George Bush picked to become assistant secretary of DHHS for welfare and related issues. In the Heritage Foundation's *Priorities for the President,* published to greet the new Bush (II) presidency in January 2001, Rector proposed substituting the current financial incentives to states that increase their marriage rates with financial punishments to states that fail to do so. In addition, he urged policymakers to set aside $1 billion in TANF funds annually for marriage promotion activities; to offer incentives and rewards to parents who marry; and to create an affirmative action program in public housing for married couples.

Many of Wade Horn's proposals closely track Rector's. In fact, he has endorsed Rector's suggestion that women "at high risk of bearing a child out of wedlock" be paid $1,000 annually for five years if they bear their first child within marriage and stay married (Horn 2001). In addition, Horn would further ratchet up the pressure on poor mothers to marry by limiting social programs—such as Head Start, public housing, and welfare—to married parents, allowing participation by single mothers only if funds are left over (Bush and Horn 1997).

Although the most strident calls to condition social benefits on poor mothers' family formation decisions come from conservatives, the idea that social policy should encourage marriage and promote fatherhood enjoys favor in both political parties. Some Democrats and liberal policy wonks—Evan Bayh and Wendell Primus, for example—have argued for Wade Horn's confirmation (Pear 2001). Meanwhile, four bipartisan fatherhood bills had been introduced into the 107th Congress by May 2001 (H.R. 1300; H.R. 1471; S. 653; S. 685).

The first major fatherhood bill to surface in Congress was the Father's Count Act, which sailed through the House of Representatives in fall 1999. During the final months of the 106th Congress in 2000, Representative Nancy Johnson shepherded similar fatherhood legislation through the House. Part of the Child Support Distribution Act of 2000, Johnson's bill included a $140 million matching-grant program for local projects that promote marital family formation among poor single mothers and a $5 million award to a national fatherhood organization with "extensive experience in *using married couples* to deliver their program in the inner city" (U.S. House 2000a, Title V, Subtitle B, sec. 511 (c)(2)(c); italics added). The committee report accompanying the bill explained that "increasing the number and percentage of American children living in two-parent families is vital if the nation is to make serious and permanent progress against poverty" (U.S. House 2000d, 17).

Measures like the Johnson bill explicitly give fathers incentives to enter poor mothers' families. For example, the Johnson bill offered funds to projects that teach fathers about their visitation and access rights (U.S. House 2000d, 42); promoted forgiveness of child support arrearages owed by men who become residential fathers; enhanced fathers' earning power through job training and "career-advancing education"; and tracked nonmarital fathers into various social services that encourage marriage (U.S. House 2000a, Title V, Subtitle A, sec. 501(a) and 501(b)). These incentives to fathers impose substantial pressures on mothers, for it is mothers, not fathers, who must obey TANF rules and suffer the consequences of time limits. Fathers get the "carrots," to borrow from Charles Murray, while mothers get the "sticks."

Jesse Jackson Jr.'s Responsible Fatherhood bill duplicated the Johnson bill in many respects. Perhaps more astounding, much of the race-coded, anti-single-mother rhetoric that introduced the Republicans' 1996 PRWORA was repeated in the preamble to the Jackson bill. For example, Jackson's bill asserted that "violent criminals are overwhelmingly males who grew up without fathers, and the best predictor of crime in a community is the percentage of absent-father households." The preamble concluded, "States should be encouraged, not restricted, from implementing programs that provide support for responsible fatherhood, promote marriage, and increase the incidence of marriage" (U.S. House 2000b).

Bipartisan marriage and fatherhood initiatives assume that poor mothers' intimate decisions about family forms and relationships cause their poverty. They also assume that it is appropriate for government to interfere in the intimate associational life of poor mothers. Even as government scales back its affirmative role in mitigating poverty, it is intensifying its coercive reach into the lives of the poor. Now squarely at the center of poverty policy, marriage promotion and fatherhood initiatives seek to compel mothers to follow the government's moral prescriptions and to accept economic dependence on men.

It is true that a family with a male income generally is better off than a family without one. While some moralistic welfare strategists believe that married fatherhood per se is an important governmental objective, more pragmatic policy strategists reason syllogistically that if men's families are better off economically than women's, then poverty can be cured by the presence of a male income in families. This kind of thinking short-circuits equality, foreclosing the question of improving women's own income. If we look at the various measures of women's and mothers' poverty—women's income as compared to men's, for example—it is clear that single mothers are poor because women's work is not valued. This is true of women's labor-market work, where a racialized gender gap in wages reflects the devaluation of the work women do. And it is true of women's nonmarket caregiving work, which garners no income at all.

The interconnectedness of poverty, caregiving, and inequality never has received wide or focused attention in the United States. While there have been policies that have provided income assistance to family caregivers, either those policies have been stingy and marginal or their beneficiaries have been rela-

tively few. In addition, to the extent that welfare and other policies have assisted family caregivers, they have done so primarily to protect children's interests rather than to compensate mothers' work or to promote mothers' equality.

Most U.S. feminists have been leery of taking up the cause of women's caregiving work, preferring to promote women's equality as labor market workers than to risk a return to compulsory domesticity. In response to the TANF regime, however, some feminists have begun not only to resist welfare's moral discipline but also to reconceive welfare as caregivers' income (Women's Committee of One Hundred 2000). The idea is that what caregivers—usually mothers—do for their families is work. Moreover, it is work that is indispensable not only to a mother's own family but to her community, the economy, and the polity as well.

Far from a sign of dependence on government, a caregivers' income would provide mothers with economic means in their own right. This would promote equality in father-mother relations both because it would unmask the economic value of mothers' side of the sexual division of labor and because it would enable mothers to exit unhappy, subordinating, or violent relations with the fathers of their children. It also would nurture equality among citizens by establishing that it is not only market work that should command a living wage but also the caring work upon which the market depends for workers. In turn, a caregivers' income would promote equality among women—between middle-class married caregivers who enjoy social and political support when they choose to work in the home raising children and poor unmarried caregivers whom welfare policy now compels to choose wages over children.

Improved economic rewards and social supports for women's work outside the home are necessary companions to a social wage for their work inside the home. Women must not be pressured into giving care by the low returns of their labor market participation. Just as important, they must not be pressured to forsake care work by the threat of destitution. In combination with labor market reforms, a caregivers' income would indemnify women's—and even men's—vocational choices. "Making work pay" both in the home and in the labor market would combat persistent poverty among single-mother families without pinning family security to fathers' responsibility.

Rethinking welfare as an income owed to caregivers would mitigate severe material vulnerabilities endured by single mothers. Further, it would exhume the rights suffocated by both poverty and the current welfare system. Once it is understood that welfare mothers are poor because their family caregiving work is unremunerated, not because they do not work or are not married, the focus of welfare prescriptions can shift from how to reform poor caregivers to how to ensure their economic and constitutional equality.

NOTES

1. The 1999 welfare-to-work amendments loosened rules governing noncustodial parents' eligibility for services. Noncustodial fathers of children enrolled in TANF are eligible for welfare-to-work services if, for example, they are unemployed, underemployed, or having difficulty fulfilling child support obligations. Eligibility for welfare-to-work services is not an entitlement—that is, it is not guaranteed to all who meet the program's criteria. Hence, fathers' increased access to services takes services away from mothers on the brink of reaching welfare time limits. (U.S. Department of Labor 1999).

2. A two-parent family is required to work 35 hours weekly (as compared to the 30-hour-per-week requirement for single parents), unless the family receives federally funded child care. A two-parent family that sends its child or children to federally funded child care must perform 55 hours of labor market work weekly, which permits married mothers to work part-time.

3. Only 0.4 percent of TANF cases closed between October 1997 and September 1998 were closed due to marriage (U.S. DHHS 1999, tab. 31).

REFERENCES

Acs, Gregory, Norma Coe, Keith Watson, and Robert I. Lerman. 1998. *Does Work Pay? An Analysis of the Work Incentives Under TANF.* Washington, DC: Urban Institute.

Bernard, Stanley. 1998. Responsible Fatherhood and Welfare: How States Can Use the New Law to Help Children. In *Children and Welfare Reform.* Issue Brief no. 4. New York: Columbia University, National Center for Children in Poverty.

Bush, Andrew and Wade Horn. 1997. Fathers, Marriage and Welfare Reform. Available at www.welfarereformer.org/articles/father.htm.

DeParle, Jason. 1998. Shrinking Welfare Rolls Leave Record High Share of Minorities. *New York Times,* 24 July.

Dion, Robin M. and LaDonna Pavetti. 2000. *Access to and Participation in Medicaid and the Food Stamp Program.* Washington, DC: Mathmatica Policy Research.

Heritage Foundation. 2001. *Priorities for the President* Alexandria, VA: Heritage Foundation.

Horn, Wade. 2001. Wedding Bell Blues: Marriage and Welfare Reform. *Brookings Review* 19(3):39–42.

Kelly, Lisa. 1994. If Anybody Asks Who I Am: An Outsider's Story of the Duty to Establish Paternity. *Yale Journal of Law and Feminism* 6:303–4.

Mink, Gwendolyn. 1998. *Welfare's End.* Ithaca, NY: Cornell University Press.

Moffitt, Robert and Jennifer Roff. 2000. The Diversity of Welfare Leavers: A Three-City Study. Working Paper 00–01. Johns Hopkins University, Baltimore, MD.

Pear, Robert. 2001. Nominee's Focus on Married Fatherhood Draws Both Praise and Fire. *New York Times,* 7 June.

Piven, Frances Fox and Richard Cloward. 1993. *Regulating the Poor.* Updated ed. New York: Vintage.

State Policy Documentation Project. 1999a. Pending Application Requirements. Available at www.spdp.org/tanf/applications. Accessed May 1999.

——. 1999b. Personal Responsibility Contracts: Obligations. Available at www.spdp.org/tanf/applications/appsumm. htm.Accessed June 1999.

——. 1999c. Sanctions for Noncompliance with Work Activities. Available at www.spdp.org/tanf/sanctions/sanctions_finding.htm. Accessed June 1999.

Study Group on Work, Poverty and Welfare. 1999. *Assessing Work First: What Happens After Welfare?* New Jersey: Study Group on Work, Poverty and Welfare. Cited in Women of Color Resource Center 2000.

Toussaint, Pierre. N.d. Empowering the Vision: Abstinence Education Grant Proposal to the Florida State Human Services Division. Duplicated.

U.S. Bureau of Labor Statistics. 2000. *Highlights of Women's Earnings in 1999.* Report 943. Washington, DC.

U.S. Census Bureau, 2000. *Poverty in the United States, 1999.* Washington, DC.

U.S. Department of Health and Human Services. 1999. Administration for Children and Families. *Characteristics and Financial Circumstances of TANF Recipients, Fiscal Year 1998.* Washington, DC.

——. 2000a. HHS Awards Adoption Bonuses and Grants. *HHS News,* 20 Sept.

——. 2000b. *HHS Fatherhood Initiative: Improving Opportunities for Low-income Fathers.* Washington, DC.

——. 2000c. *HHS's Fatherhood Initiative: Fact Sheet.* Washington, DC.

——. 2000d. Administration for Children and Families. Office of Family Assistance. *Helping Families Achieve Self-Sufficiency: Guide for Funding Services for Children and Families Through the TANF Program.* Available at www.acf.dhhs.gov/programs/ofa/funds2.htm.

U.S. Department of Labor. 1999. The 1999 Welfare to Work Amendments. Available at wtw.doleta.gov/laws-regs/99amedsum.htm.

U.S. House of Representatives. 1997. Adoption Promotion Act of 1997. 105th Cong., 1st sess., H.R. 867.

———. 2000a. *Child Support Distribution Act of 2000.* 106th Cong., 2nd sess., H.R. 4678.

———. 2000b. *The Responsible Fatherhood Act of 2000.* 106th Cong., 2nd sess., H.R. 4671, Jesse Jackson, Jr., sponsor.

———. 2000c. Committee on Ways and Means. *2000 Green Book: Overview of Entitlement Programs.* 106th Cong., 2nd sess.

———. 2000d. Committee on Ways and Means. *Child Support Distribution Act of 2000: Report to Accompany H.R. 4678.* 106th Cong., 2nd sess.

U.S. Public Law 104-193. 104th Cong., 22 Aug. 1996. *Personal Responsibility and Work Opportunity Reconciliation Act.*

U.S. Public Law 105-89. 105th Cong., 19 Nov. 1997. *Adoption and Safe Families Act.*

Wider Opportunities for Women. 2000. *Job Retention and Advancement Issues.* Washington, DC.

Women of Color Resource Center. 2000. *Working Hard, Staying Poor: Women and Children in the Wake of Welfare "Reform."* Berkeley, CA.

Women's Committee of One Hundred/Project 2002. 2000. *An Immodest Proposal: Rewarding Women's Work to End Poverty.* Available at www.welfare2002.org. Accessed 23 Mar. 2000.

FIFTY-TWO

◆◆◆

Movement Roots[1]

Miriam Ching Yoon Louie

This article will touch on how immigrant women workers' ethnic- and gender-based labor organizing is rooted in the history of prior movements, especially how the five workers' centers featured here are rooted in particular sections of sweatshop industry workers' struggles and in earlier stages of the Mexican/Chicano, Chinese, and Korean radical labor and community movements.

Earlier Stages of Immigrant Organizing

Today's workers' centers are being built on the foundation of the two prominent periods in 20th-century U.S. social change organizing—the '30s and the '60s—as well as the preceding labor history. Before immigration from Europe was restricted in the 1920s, many Jewish, Italian, German, Irish, and other European immigrant workers organized themselves along ethnic lines. Immigrant workers' organizations often fused radical political traditions from home with new organizing currents in the United States. Anti-racism was not necessarily one of those traditions and some of the craft-oriented, European immigrant-based

unions attacked workers of color whom they saw as competitors, for example spearheading campaigns to exclude Chinese immigrant and newly emancipated Black workers.[2]

Most mainstream labor organizations mirrored the American Federation of Labor's (AFL) racist exclusion of immigrants of color and African Americans. Left to fend for themselves, these workers formed ethnic-based organizations such as the Mexican *mutualistas*, the Chinese Seamen's Union formed in 1911, and the Chinese Hand Laundry Alliance formed in the '30s. In order to revive business and reduce widespread unemployment stemming from the Depression, the Roosevelt administration enacted legislation that guaranteed workers the right to organize, join unions of their own choosing, and bargain collectively with employers, leading to a wave of labor organizing.[3] The creation of the Congress of Industrial Organizations (CIO) in 1935 ushered in another wave of rank-and-file organizing that began to break with the practice of racist exclusion.

Unskilled first- and second-generation immigrants from southern and eastern Europe, as well as Mexicans and Asians in the Southwest and West, and Blacks in the South became the core of industrial unionism in the 1930s. Second-generation children of immigrants predominated among CIO activists.[4] Many Black workers during this period were racialized internal migrants, joining the Great Migration to urban centers within the South and to the North spurred by the increased demand for labor and grinding conditions in Southern agriculture during the World Wars.[5] Puerto Rican and Cuban immigrant cigar rolling workers in New York organized their own unions, as did other Latin American, Asian-American, and African-American workers.[6] By 1945 unionized labor had reached a high of 35.5 percent of all U.S. workers.[7]

Labor organizing during the 1930s and 1940s looked different among Latina/o and Asian workers depending on the gender composition of the particular wave of immigrant workers at the time. For example, given the focused recruitment of Chinese male laborers, the Chinese Exclusion Act, and skewed composition of male to female ratios, Chinese worker organizations consisted of immigrant men fighting for their rights practically alone within a racially segregated environment.[8] Once immigration policy changed to permit the immigration of women workers, a multi-generational community grew to reinforce the workers' organizations.

In contrast, given the higher proportion of women within the Mexican-American communities, that period also saw struggles by Mexican and Chicana women food packing workers, and *extended family support* for the struggles of Mexicano workers. According to historian Zaragosa Vargas, Tejana worker leaders like Manuela Solis Sager, Minnie Rendon, Juana Sanchez, and Emma Tenayuca played leading roles in Depression Era organizing in San Antonio. At the time, young and single Tejanas made up 79 percent of that city's low-waged garment, cigar, and pecan-shelling workers. Tenayuca emerged as the leader of the 1938 pecan-shellers' strike, which included over 10,000 strikers, and was the largest labor strike in San Antonio's history and biggest community-based labor struggle among the nation's Mexican population during the 1930s.[9] Mexicanas and Chicanas, the wives of male strikers, played a pivotal role in the strike by 1400 members (90 percent Mexican) of Local 890 of the International Union of Mine, Mill, and Smelter Workers against Empire Zinc in Grant County, New Mexico between October 1950 to January 1952—the longest strike in

New Mexico's history.[10] This struggle inspired the production of *Salt of the Earth,* the internationally known film that was banned in the United States but can still brings tears to the eyes of those who borrow it from their local Chicano or Labor Studies library.

Social unionism[11] severely threatened big capital, but during the McCarthy era the government and right-wing elites smashed the center-left alliance and purged leftists from the labor movement. A tamed labor and a chastened capital both endorsed a social pact promising ongoing raises in some workers' standard of living in exchange for worker compliance. Under the new "business unionism," workers exhibited more passivity toward bosses and supported the government's chauvinistic foreign policy. This period coincided with an extended interval of U.S. economic growth following the country's rise to superpower status during World War II.

"Young, Gifted, and Brown"

Since the 1960s, three demographic explosions rocked the U.S. workforce: massive Asian and Latina/o migration after the removal of racially discriminatory quotas; growing paid labor force participation of women of all races, including women with children; and the reverberations of the civil rights revolution through employment and education practices.

The workers' centers featured in this article all have linkages back to sections of the Asian and Latina/o radical movements that erupted in the United States and internationally in the late 1960s and early 1970s. In those adrenaline-filled days, many young folks of color (the equivalent of singer Nina Simone's "young, gifted, and Black") connected with first generation immigrant workers and other grassroots community people to develop "serve the people"[12] programs and organizing drives within the key racial, national, class and gender justice battles of the period. The struggles of immigrant farm, garment, and restaurant workers inspired and galvanized that generation of Latina/o and Asian-American sweatshop industry labor organizers. For example, the Filipino Independent Agricultural Workers Organizing Committee kicked off the 1965 Delano, California, grape strike and teamed up with the Mexican National Farm Workers Association (NFWA) to form the United Farm Workers Organizing Committee.[13] Some organizers who emerged in these movements later joined AFL-CIO unions, while others co-founded workers' centers and other grassroots community organizations.[14] Many of the workers and youth active in these struggles, including those who got jobs working in unions and community organizations, eventually returned to "civilian life" after both winning some victories and getting trounced by the reactionary backlash during the Reagan/Bush administrations. The mustered out troops continued to use their movement-acquired consciousness and skills at work and school, and in their families and communities.

Battered by the rupture of the social pact and economic decline of the '70s, and the subsequent deindustrialization, economic restructuring, and globalization, the proportion of unionized workers shrank to a mere 13.5 percent of the U.S. workforce by 2000.[15] *Today some 86 percent of U.S. workers are not unionized.* During the mid-1970s the neoliberal assault on workers, the poor, people of color, immigrants, women, lesbians, and gays shifted into high gear leading to the founding of workers' centers. Many movement organizations dissolved and those that continued were forced to adjust to a harsh new political climate.

Today's workers' centers emerged in response to this vacuum. By the 1990s, in grappling with an economy and workforce transformed by immigrant workers and globalization, some sections of the broader labor movement had begun to raise many similar questions and experiment with new approaches. In the late 19th and early 20th centuries, new organizing initiatives among immigrant workers from Asia, Latin America, and Europe flagged major shifts in the U.S. economy and new stages in the development of the broader labor movement. In the late 20th and early 21st centuries, independent, ethnic-based organizing among immigrant sweatshop industry workers provided an early warning signal both of the deleterious effects of global economic restructuring on the most vulnerable workers and of the means through which these workers can organize to defend themselves.

Below are brief "work visa" snapshots of the five workers' centers, in terms of their initial origins;

worker and intergenerational ethnic community base and ties; and victories and accomplishments. The centers are listed by order of their founding year.

Chinese Staff and Workers Association: Organizing Sewing Women and Kitchen Men

CSWA was born in 1979 "when a group of Chinese restaurant workers met at a hamburger joint in Chinatown and discussed their desire for rights and dignity in the workplace."[16] Some of CSWA's founding members had accumulated experience in various mass struggles including the marches of tens of thousands of Chinatown residents in 1974 and 1975 voicing support for low-income tenants' rights; the campaign to break racist hiring practices in the construction industry; and campaigns against police brutality, for quality health care and nutrition programs, and for normalization of U.S. relations with China.[17] CSWA reflects the radical perspectives and methods of workers and youth from across the Chinese diaspora.

Chinese immigrant men in New York have tended to take low-waged jobs in the restaurant industry. In 1980, after being spurned by the Hotel and Restaurant Employees and Bartenders Union, Local 69, former workers from the Silver Palace Restaurant formed their own union with the support of CSWA. They named it the 318 Restaurant Workers' Union, in honor of the day, March 18, on which they had been fired for protesting against the restaurant's management.

In the '70s and after, Chinese immigrant women followed a well-beaten path to garment sweatshops, revitalizing New York's then sagging rag trade, and yielding profits and start-up capital for Chinese and other entrepreneurs and real estate developers. The majority of Chinese garment workers became members of the International Ladies Garment Workers Union (ILGWU), Local 23-25, after the union reached agreements with the manufacturers and contractors top-down in 1974. Chinese immigrant women hit the streets 20,000 strong to defend their contract against the machinations of the Chinatown bosses in 1982. When ILGWU (and later the Union of Needletrades, Industrial and Textile Employees—UNITE) failed to harness their energy or adequately support their interests, many turned to CSWA.[18]

CSWA has won many precedent-setting victories. They successfully brought shorter working hours to many New York City Chinatown restaurants and garment factories. They've forced government and social institutions to allocate more space and support for childcare programs critical to Chinatown's working women. In 1985, CSWA led the Concerned Committee of the Chung Park Project to call for community space, including a daycare center. That year it also began organizing the first group of Chinese homesteaders on the Lower East Side, who won a building that houses 12 low-income co-op units, the Latino Workers' Center (originally a CSWA project), and the Committee Against Anti-Asian Violence (CAAAV). In 1989 CSWA helped Chinese workers at the Chinatown Planning Council (CPC) and African-American construction workers protest underpayment of workers under a federally funded CPC training program. These workers finally won a $2.15 million settlement in 1994. CSWA helped workers send employers to prison when they failed to pay. They have organized injured workers and fought for safer working conditions, and for workers to have more control over their time and lives.[19]

La Mujer Obrera:
¡La Unidad Nos Hara Fuertes!
[Unity Will Make Us Strong!]

A "handful of women, tempered by the painful experience" with the Amalgamated Clothing and Textile Workers' Union (ACTWU) and the Farah strike founded La Mujer Obrera in 1981. Nine years earlier some 4,000 workers had walked out on strike at Farah demanding to be represented by the ACTWU.[20]

In those days [The Farah workers] sought out the tool best known to them in order to defend themselves: the labor union. After many months of struggle they learned that the union, especially when it was governed by laws which favored big business and which allowed it to be controlled by corrupt leaders, was not the solution for all their problems. Then they

sought to preserve their struggle through a workers' center, an independent organization where they could not only defend themselves against the bosses, but also defend their right to be organized, a right which the "union" continued to deny them. This right to be organized was even more important for a sector which suffered a great deal of discrimination: the women who made up 80 percent of the garment labor force.[21]

Additionally some of the founding members of La Mujer Obrera had worked in the Rio Grande Valley in South Texas, which served as a focal of point for organizing by the Texas Farm Workers Union; in community struggles against racism, police, INS, and Border Patrol assaults; and for decent housing, public utilities, sanitation, education, and health care. With the birth of the modern Chicana/o movement, Tejana/o activists organized in border cities across the region. La Raza Unida Party registered and rallied voters, electrified the Chicano movement, and "pissed off red necks," when it swept the Board of Education and Crystal City and county elections in 1970.[22]

Given the special bi-national character of the border region, Mexican and Chicana/o activists have created "sister movements" and organized against the negative impacts of neoliberalism. The army and death squads' massacre of students in Mexico City's Tlatelolco Plaza on October 2, 1968, ten days before the opening of the Olympics, shocked and radicalized Mexicans on both sides of the border. Organizing spread among the urban and rural poor, indigenous peoples, and within the church, via liberation theology. La Mujer Obrera taps into these Chicana/Tejana/Mexicana radical labor, community, and indigenous movement roots.

Over its 20-year history, La Mujer Obrera has enabled immigrant workers to organize themselves to both win many disputes and develop programs to meet their basic needs in the face of massive deindustrialization. In 1990 LMO members chained themselves to their sewing machines and staged a hunger strike, outing the underground sweatshop system and flight of large companies. In 1991 the organization unionized three factories and one laundry (Sonia, DCB, H&R, and Apparel Conditioners Corp.), helping workers win collective bargaining agreements, including pay, vacation, and minimal health package increases. The nine-month strike, which included a hunger strike during which a 60-year-old garment worker fasted for 23 days, won broad support from labor, community, and church groups, as well as elected officials. It also prompted all five of El Paso's state legislators to immediately draft, lobby for, and win a bill that established criminal penalties including imprisonment, for non-payment of wages. LMO's efforts also convinced Texas' Attorney General to prosecute various sub-contractors, efforts which eventually recouped over $200,000 in back wages owed to women garment workers.[23] La Mujer persuaded the El Paso government to invest $367,000 in expanding child-care services and economic opportunities for low-income women workers. It also took part in local, state, national, and tri-national mobilizations against NAFTA [the North American Free Trade Agreement] and organized workers facing impending plant closures to fight for severance pay, benefits, and job retraining. In 1997 with the help of LMO, NAFTA-displaced workers won a $3 million extension in government funded training for laid-off workers in addition to the original $4.2 million allocated. In addition to running its own Popular School and women's organizing projects, LMO has generated independent organizations, including the Asociación de Trabajadores Fronterizos. Another spin-off, El Puente [the Bridge], focuses on development projects that create an economic base for the community, such as the Rayito del Sol Daycare Center, Café Mayapan Restaurant, and other low-cost housing and job training and creation projects.[24]

Asian Immigrant Women Advocates: Community Transformational and Organizing Strategy

In 1983, Asian Immigrant Women Advocates (AIWA) emerged in Oakland, California, from discussions between Korean hotel room cleaners; first and second generation Korean-American activists Young Shin and Elaine Kim of the Korean Community Center of the East Bay (KCCEB), a Korean community-oriented social service organization; and Chinese-American Local 2 union organizer Patricia Lee. KCCEB, AIWA's

co-founder, was the local Korean version of the "serve the people" programs that young progressives co-founded with immigrant elders to deal with pressing language, social, and economic needs of their emerging communities. As in other ethnic communities, women played a central role in these community service organizations, as part of their "triple *jornada*" [triple shift], of labor on the job, in the family, and in the community.

In the 1970s and '80s, San Francisco's hotel industry was undergoing a tremendous change, with growing numbers of "back of the house" Asian and Latino immigrant workers and "front of the house" college-educated waitresses, waiters, and receptionists. Despite this influx of non-English speakers, the Hotel and Restaurant Employees and Bartenders Union (HERE) Local 2, employed no organizers fluent in the Korean language. Thus, Korean hotel workers at the exclusive Fairmont Hotel atop Nob Hill in San Francisco, although members of the union, could neither understand the union contract nor participate in union activities.

After unseating the local's 35-year entrenched leadership, hotel workers went on strike in 1980 for better wages and improved working conditions. Local 2 emerged as San Francisco's largest union and a hotbed of radical organizing, with Filipina and Latina hotel maids comprising some 95 percent of strike picketers.[25]

As AIWA began organizing Asian garment workers in Oakland and Korean hotel room cleaners in San Francisco, the Asian Law Caucus argued the cases of garment workers and worked with Reverend Norman Fong of Cameron House and the Presbyterian Church in Chinatown to develop a San Francisco garment workers center that, like AIWA, offered English classes, information on labor, housing, and immigration law to workers, and social activities for the women and their families.[26] Many of the young people active in immigrant worker organizing, including at AIWA, had also been politicized and influenced by the 1968 strikes for ethnic studies programs at San Francisco State College and the University of California at Berkeley; the fight to defend the International Hotel, which had housed many low-income residents of San Francisco's Manilatown/Chinatown before they were brutally evicted on August 4, 1977;[27] the activities of the Chinatown Workers Sewing Coop, housed in the

I-Hotel storefront of the Asian Community Center (ACC);[28] the struggles of Jung Sai garment workers and Lee Mah electronics workers who worked under ILGWU and Teamster contracts for Esprit and Faranon respectively;[29] and the Filipino farm workers who invited young Filipina/os and other Asians to join them in the United Farm Workers Organizing Committee fight against the growers.

In October 1990, AIWA also launched a project targeting a new set of sweatshop industry workers—electronics assemblers in Santa Clara County's Silicon Valley. Tens of thousands of immigrant women from Asia and Latin America worked in shops, ranging from large factories to small fly-by-night shops set up in garages by subcontractors. The women often worked up to 14-hour days handling hazardous chemicals and inhaling toxic fumes as they assembled, cleaned, and tested printed circuit boards for "everything from watches to warheads."[30]

AIWA is strongly committed to developing grassroots women's leadership. The group's many accomplishments include providing workplace literacy and citizenship classes for immigrant women workers in Oakland's Chinatown and in Silicon Valley; organizing worker-led leadership development institutes and peer trainings around workers' rights; and leadership and organizing training for the children of garment and electronics workers.[31] In 1990, AIWA initiated an environmental health and safety project for Silicon Valley electronics workers, to help workers protect themselves from toxic chemicals and other industry hazards. In 1992, they launched the Garment Workers Justice Campaign, which resulted in an unprecedented settlement holding manufacturers accountable to their women workers and community. In 1997, AIWA pressured three more manufacturers to establish multilingual, confidential, and toll-free hotlines for garment workers to report violations of women's rights in the workplace. In 2000, AIWA co-sponsored the Asian Immigrant Women Workers Clinic to address the health needs of electronics workers.

Their work has developed concrete strategies for advancing immigrant women workers' leadership in the struggles for economic and social justice, and has catapulted women workers into various networks of workers' centers and grassroots organizations fighting for environmental and economic justice.[32]

Fuerza Unida: *La Mujer Luchando*

Fuerza Unida was founded in 1990 by "early victims of NAFTA," non-unionized workers laid off by Levi Strauss and Co.'s plant in San Antonio, Texas, on January 16. The laid-off workers first met at Our Lady of Angels Church on January 30, then launched the organization on February 6. Within a month the organization began negotiating for the workers. By May 1990, Fuerza Unida had elaborated a detailed list of 15 demands ranging from a statewide study about the feasibility of re-opening the plant to transferring ownership of the facility to laid-off workers, providing a specific severance package, and offering retraining programs. Marta Martínez, one of the laid-off workers recalled back in 1991

> First we organized 15 women, then 30, and then each month it's been getting larger. After 18 months we now have 650 members. They have regular meetings, committees taking up different responsibilities, a general council where decisions are made and a small coordinating committee. It doesn't work perfectly, and we're learning a lot about democracy as we go along.[33]

Fuerza Unida launched a national boycott of Levi's labels and carried out hunger strikes and pickets. The group filed two lawsuits against the company, one alleging pension fund violations, work injury claims, especially for carpal tunnel syndrome, and the other, racially discriminatory layoff practices towards the primarily Latina women workers. The work injury suit was denied by the right-to-work state of Texas and the discrimination suit by the federal district court, which discouraged many of the workers.

Many Latina/o and some white labor, community, church, and legal advocates offered initial support to the laid-off workers. When Levi's first announced the layoffs, the Southwest Public Workers Union (SPWU) demonstrated at the factory and met with workers. SPWU represents custodians and school cafeteria, hotel, and restaurant workers. SPWU's founding members Rubén Solís and Chavel López had been involved in the Centro de Acción Social Autonoma-Hermandad General de Trabajadores (CASA-HGT), a mass-based undocumented workers' rights organization active during the 1970s.[34] CASA-HGT served as basic training camp for many labor, immigrant, and civil rights leaders and organizers. During the 1980s at the height of U.S. intervention in Central America, ex-CASA and other Tejana/o activists worked in Chicanos Against Intervention in Latin America (CAMILA), an organization that fused the Chicana/o support for national liberation struggles with a critique of the racial blind spots of the white-dominated, anti-intervention movement.[35] During the 1990s, much of the energy of the anti-intervention movement shifted from military issues to the exploitation of women inside proliferating maquiladoras in Mexico and Central America and the impending passage of NAFTA. Tejana/o anti-interventionist activists introduced Fuerza Unida to women workers networks in those regions, with whom the women shared language, cultural, religious, and class commonalities.

Fuerza Unida enjoyed support from the Esperanza Peace and Justice Center, the American Friends Service Committee, the Southwest Network for Environmental and Economic Justice, and the [Chicana/o student organization] MEChA, many of whose members had organized against U.S. intervention in Central America. Each of these organizations in turn is rooted in different sections of the Mexican, Chicana/o, and Latina/o women's, lesbian, cultural, anti-intervention, solidarity, environmental justice, and student movements. Organizations like Mexican American Legal Education and Defense Fund, the League of United Latin American Citizens, and elected officials like Henry B. Gonzáles and Ciro Rodríguez also endorsed Fuerza Unida's campaign, then became the object of intense lobbying by the corporation seeking to dampen their support for the women.

The women of Fuerza Unida are recognized as early grassroots leaders of the national campaign for justice in the garment industry and against NAFTA and corporate globalization. Their organizing has scored impressive victories including the creation of a women workers' resource center for low-income residents of San Antonio's South and Westside barrios. They've developed women workers' leadership through a Promotora Leadership Development Campaign and peer group trainings. In 1996, they

worked with other local organizations to force the city council to adopt pro-worker legislation and legislation that requires companies to support and pay taxes for job training and other programs.[36] Fuerza's voice has been heard worldwide through their success in improving settlement packages for laid-off workers in the United States, Canada, Belgium, and France. While the group was born fighting against the world's largest garment corporation, Puerto Rican feminist activist Luz Guerra says that the group "is now engaged in what may be their biggest battle yet: to establish themselves as a community-based organization dedicated to supporting and empowering the poor and working-class women of San Antonio, on their own terms."[37] Reflecting on how the refusal of the Amalgamated Clothing and Textile Workers Union (ACTWU) to help the laid-off Levi's workers may have been a blessing in disguise, Fuerza Unida's Petra Mata explained,

> We have to be independent to be happy. We don't want people to tell us what to do and what not to do. Through Fuerza Unida we can speak out and say whatever we want, whatever is in our hearts. A lot of people go where the money and power is. Yes, money helps. But money is not everything. It depends on your vision and what you have in your mind. We have learned to be strong and we know how to struggle.[38]

Korean Immigrant Workers Advocates: Organizing *Minjung* Diaspora

Founded in 1992, one month before the Rodney King civil unrest, Korean Immigrant Workers Advocates (KIWA) in Los Angeles, California, organizes restaurant, janitorial, construction, garment, and other low-waged Korean and Latino immigrants who work for Korean employers.

KIWA grew out of the Korean progressive community that had spawned, a decade earlier, such Korean-American organizing as the intergenerational community campaign to free Chol Soo Lee,[39] and the initiatives launched by first-generation immigrant youth shaped by the Kwangju Uprising, such as Young Koreans United.[40] The legacy of these early efforts of the Korean progressive community include an ongoing identification with the history of progressive organizing in South Korea, support for peaceful reunification with North Korea, and opposition to U.S. neocolonial policies on the Korean peninsula. KIWA also received early support from former members of the Korean Labor Association in Los Angeles, which had previously organized in support of immigrant garment workers' wage claims and against the South Korean military regime.

KIWA had inside experience with the strengths and weaknesses of different AFL-CIO unions' approaches to the rights of immigrants, women, and people of color. KIWA founders Roy Hong and Danny Park had organized Korean janitors at the San Francisco airport, and Hong had worked as an organizer for Service Employees International Union (SEIU), at both the local and international levels. SEIU launched its innovative Justice for Janitors campaign in Los Angeles in 1988.[41] Hong and Park had also assisted HERE Local 11 in Los Angeles when Korean owners bought the Hilton Hotel and tried to fire its worker leaders. After an 11-month campaign, workers succeeded in keeping their jobs and winning a collective bargaining agreement.

Los Angeles has been repeatedly rocked and resegregated through race and class conflicts, making KIWA's cross-race organizing all the more important and noteworthy. The 1965 Watts rebellion was followed by deindustrialization and massive labor migration from Latin America and Asia. Ongoing racial and class tensions were manifested in the 1992 Rodney King civil unrest, the first "multiracial riot." Through its many victories, KIWA has served as a cutting-edge example of cross-racial worker organizing, building coalitions between Korean workers and other communities of color, including fighting to raise the state minimum wage, lower bus rates for the poor, maintain the state's affirmative action programs, and in solidarity with hotel workers and janitors fighting for jobs and dignity.

KIWA is also known for its role in co-organizing a campaign in defense of 78 Thai and 55 Latino workers from the El Monte "slave shop" where workers won a $4 million settlement with retailers. One of its first successes was in organizing 45 workers displaced by the April 1992 civil unrest, demanding inclusion of workers in relief fund distribution and winning $109,000 from conservative business owners. KIWA pressured the Korean Restaurant Owners Association members to join the California Workers Compensation Fund and participate in creating a community mediation-arbitration board to resolve workers disputes with employers. KIWA also raised over $30,000 for North Korean famine relief; supported the independent workers' movements in South Korea and Mexico; and organized Korean immigrant voters to collaborate with other communities of color to impact electoral politics.

In sum, the women's struggles and workers' centers are rooted both in resistance to sweatshop industry exploitation and in the accumulated experience of prior labor and community movements. The workers' centers represent a fusion of the different generations of workers and their expanded family members. The women in this article described how they were often compelled by the sheer force of anger and crisis to join or help create such organizations and take on leadership roles with the help of extended family members, often the descendants of prior generations of immigrant workers. In these positions, they took on powerful, well-entrenched institutions, and developed skills they never dreamed they could. They have won thousands of dollars in back wages, slowed the pace of layoffs, secured better settlement packages, strengthened legislation demanding greater corporate accountability to workers and their communities, increased visibility about industry abuses, and offered programmatic alternatives to employer greed. By example, the women showed their peers and communities that change is possible and worth fighting for. Although largely unsung heroines, these risk-takers and their organizations constitute the bleeding edge of anti-corporate movements in the age of globalization. Their perspectives and experiences constitute a treasure trove of lessons on how to organize the most disenfranchised sectors of their communities and create a more just society.

NOTES

1. This article first appeared in *Sweatshop Warriors: Immigrant Women Workers Take on the Global Factory.* Cambridge: South End Press, 2001. Chapter 5.

2. Saxton, 1971 and Douglass, 1892 (1962 revised edition).

3. Gómez-Quiñones, 1994:105

4. In terms of European ethnic immigrant workers see Cohen, 1990:324–25 and Friendlander, 1975, both cited in Milkman, 2000:4–5. For more on Mexican, Asian, and Black workers organizing linked to CIO unions, see Gómez-Quiñones, 1994; Ruíz, Vicki L., 1987; Vargas, 1997; Acuña, 1988; Yu, Renqiu, 1992: Kwong, Peter, 1979, Scharlin and Villanueva, 1994; Yoneda, 1983; and Kelley, 1990 and 1994.

5. Kelley, 1990 and 1994. Kelley analyzes CIO and left-related organizing among Black sharecroppers and steel-workers.

6. Vega, 1984; Yoneda, 1983; Scharlin and Villanueva, 1994; and Kelley, 1990 and 1994.

7. Gómez-Quiñones, 1994:333.

8. Yu, Renqiu, 1992:51–52. . . .

9. Vargas, 1997:553–80. See also Ruíz, Vicki L., 1987; and Calderón and Zamora, 1990.

10. Acuña, 1988:278–79.

11. Social unionism addresses both the connections between workers and their broader communities, and the process of labor organizing as part of the broader fight for social and economic justice. In contrast, business unions often engage in winnable fights to improve the terms of the deal workers get from bosses, build up the financial assets of the union, and lobby, finance, and influence politicians and other institutions, without regard to the interests of their mass members, unorganized workers, and the broader community. . . .

12. The concept of "serve the people" was advocated by revolutionaries in China. Young radicals of color identified with Third World national liberation movements in the 1960s and '70s, such as the Black Panther Party, Young Lords, I Wor Kuen, Wei Min Sei, Katipunan Ng Demokratic, and others developed U.S. inner-city versions of serve-the-people-style free breakfast, health clinics, low-cost housing, and other programs. For example, see Louie, Steve, et al., 2001.

13. Gómez-Quiñones, 1994:47–59; Yu, Renqiu, 1992; Kwong, Peter, 1979:116–30; Scharlin and Villanueva, 1992:27–42; and Acuña, 1988.

14. I hope that more Asian and Latina/o AFL-CIO union organizers will document the history in that section of the labor movement, including the stories of low-waged immigrant union members.

15. Bureau of Labor Statistics, 2000, cited in Moberg, 2001.

16. Chinese Staff and Workers Association, 1999a:1.

17. Kwong, Peter, 1987:137–73; Ho, Fred, 2000; and Louie, Steve, et al. 2001.

18. Kwong, Peter, 1987:137–59.

19. Chinese Staff and Workers Association, 1999a.

20. La Mujer Obrera, 1996:3.

21. La Mujer Obrera, 1996:2–3.

22. Acuña, 1988:339 and 387, Gutiérrez, 1998.

23. La Mujer Obrera, 1991:1 and 7; and Márquez, 1995: 68–78.

24. La Mujer Obrera, 1996; author interviews with María Antonia Flores and Cindy Arnold, December 9, 1997, and Guillermo Domínguez Glenn, May 5, 2000; presentation by Jena Camp and Yrene Espinoza, June 4, 2000; White Polk, 2000; La Mujer Obrera, 2001.

25. Interview with Lora Jo Foo, April 11, 1997. Wells, 2000:109–29.

26. Interview with Lora Jo Foo, April 11, 1997.

27. Toribio, Helen, 2000; and Habal, Stella, 2000.

28. Interview with Bea Tam and Harvey Dong, May 4, 1997. Ironically, the Coop's first contract was with garment manufacturer Jessica McClintock; in English classes, Coop members practiced how to say, "You're too cheap!" during negotiations over piece rates.

29. Interview with Bea Tam and Harvey Dong, May 4, 1997.

30. Asian Immigrant Women Advocates, 1993.

31. Shin, 1995:48–50; and Louie, Miriam, 1992.

32. AIWA, 1998:5–6, see also Shin, 1997.

33. *Canadian Tribune,* 1991.

34. . . . CASA combined two demographic pools: immigrant workers and young Chicana/o radical students, activists, and professionals who used their newly acquired skills to manage the organization's service programs. CASA was particularly strong in California, Texas, Illinois, and Washington, i.e., states with large Mexican immigrant worker populations during that period. See García, Mario, 1994:286–320. Interviews with Arnoldo García, April 21, 1997, and May 6, 1997; and Rubén Solís, October 8, 1997. See also Ruíz, 1998:99–126 about Chicanas' roles in the movement and struggles against sexism, particularly within CASA and La Raza Unida Party.

35. Interview with Antonio Díaz, December 7, 1999. See also Guerra, 1990.

36. Fuerza Unida, 1998:5–6.

37. Guerra, Luz. 1997:2.

38. Interview with Petra Mata, March 20, 2001.

39. Chol Soo Lee was on San Quentin's death row, convicted of a Chinatown murder he did not commit, and a killing while in prison. With the help of Korean community elders lawyer Jay Kun Yoo and newspaper man Kyung Won Lee, his case served as a rallying point for the Korean-American community during the late 1970s and early '80s. See Jay Kun Yoo's story in Kim and Yu, 1996:282–93.

40. Sim, 2000.

41. Acuña, 1996:184–88; and Fisk, Mitchell, and Erickson, 2000.

BIBLIOGRAPHY

Acuña, Rodolfo F. 1988. *Occupied America: A History of Chicanos.* New York: Harper & Row.

———. 1996. *Anything But Mexican: Chicanos in Contemporary Los Angeles*. London: Verso.

Asian Immigrant Women Advocates. 1993. *Environmental Safety and Health Proposal*. Oakland: AIWA.

———. 1998. *Building On Our Past, Rising Up in Unity Toward Our Future: Celebrating Asian Immigrant Women Workers*. Oakland: AIWA.

Calderón, Roberto R. and Emilio Zamora. 1990. "Manuela Solis Sager & Emma Tenayuca: A Tribute," In Córdova, et al., *Chicana Voices*.

Chinese Staff and Workers Association. 1999. "CSWA's First 20 Years: Workers Fighting Sweatshops Here." *CSWA News* 7:1 (Summer), pp. 1–10. New York: CSWA.

Cohen, Lizabeth. 1990. *Making a New Deal: Industrial Workers in Chicago, 1919–1939*. New York: Cambridge UP.

Córdova, Teresa, Norma Cantú, Gilberto Cardenas, Juan García, and Christina M. Sierra (eds.) for National Association for Chicano Studies. 1990. *Chicana Voices: Intersections of Class, Race, and Gender*. Albuquerque: UNM Press.

Douglass, Frederick. 1962. *Life and Times of Frederick Douglass: His Early Life As a Slave, His Escape from Bondage, and His Complete History*. Reprinted from the revised edition of 1892. London: Collier-MacMillan Ltd.

Fisk, Catherine L., Daniel J. B. Mitchell, and Christopher L. Erickson. 2000. "Union Representation of Immigrant Janitors in Southern California: Economic and Legal Challenges." In Milkman, *Organizing Immigrants*.

Friendlander, Peter. 1975. *The Emergence of a UAW Local, 1936–1939*. Pittsburgh: UP Press.

Fuerza Unida. 1998. *Hilo de La Justica/Thread of Justice* 1:1 (Spring).

García, Mario T. 1994. *Memories of Chicano History: The Life and Times of Bert Corona*. Los Angeles: UC Press.

Gómez-Quiñones, Juan. 1994. *Mexican American Labor, 1790–1990*. Albuquerque: UNM Press.

Guerra, Luz. 1990. "Witness for Peace and Comprehensive Inclusion: A Microcosm of Struggle within the Central America Movement." In Chicago Religious Task Force on Central America, "Challenge to the Central America Movement."

———. 1997. "Las Nuevas Revolucionarias." *AFSC-Texas-Arkansas-Oklahoma* 10:3, pp. 1–2. Austin: American Friends Service Committee.

Gutiérrez, José Angel. 1998. *The Making of a Chicano Militant: Lessons from Cristal*. Madison: UW Press.

Habal, Stella, 2000. "How I Became a Revolutionary." In Ho, *Legacy to Liberation*.

Ho, Fred (ed.). 2000. *Legacy to Liberation: Politics and Culture of Revolutionary Asian Pacific America*. San Francisco: AK Press & Big Red Media.

Kelley, Robin D. G. 1990. *Hammer and Hoe: Alabama Communists during the Great Depression*. Chapel Hill: UNC Press.

———. 1994. *Race Rebels: Culture, Politics, and the Black Working Class*. New York: Free Press.

Kim, Elaine H., and Eui-Young Yu. 1996. *East to America: Korean American Life Stories*. New York: New Press.

Kwong, Peter. 1979. *Chinatown, N.Y.: Labor & Politics, 1930–1950*. New York: Monthly Review.

———. 1987. *The New Chinatown*. New York: Noonday Press.

———. 1992. "Immigrant Asian Women in Bay Area Garment Sweatshops: 'After sewing, laundry, cleaning and cooking, I have no breath left to sing.'" *Amerasia Journal* 18:1 (Winter), pp. 1–27.

La Mujer Obrera. 1991. "The Strike for a Just Future Continues" and "Chronology of the Strike." *Unidad y Fuerza* 1:5 (July), pp. 1 & 7.

———. 1996. *XV Aniversario Mujer Obrera: ¡Felicidades!* El Paso: LMO.

———. 2001. "The Opening of Café Mayapan," *Voz de Mujer* (Feb.), p. 4.

Louie, Steve, Glenn Omatsu, and Mary Uyematsu Kao (eds.), 2001. *Asian Americans: The Movement and the Moment*. Los Angeles: UCLA Asian American Studies Center Press.

Márquez, Benjamin. 1995. "Organizing Mexican-American Women in the Garment Industry: La Mujer Obrera." *Women & Politics* 15:1, pp. 65–87.

Milkman, Ruth (ed.). 2000. *Organizing Immigrants: The Challenge for Unions in Contemporary California*. Ithaca: ILR press and Cornell UP.

Moberg, David. 2001. "Labor's Critical Condition." *In These Times* 25 (March 5), p. 7.

Ruíz, Vicki L. 1987. *Cannery Women/Cannery Lives: Mexican Women, Unionization, and the California Food Processing Industry, 1930–1950*. Albuquerque: UNM Press.

———. 1998. *From Out of the Shadows: Mexican Women in Twentieth-Century America*. New York & Oxford: Oxford UP.

Saxton, Alexander. 1971. *The Indispensable Enemy: Labor and the Anti-Chinese Movement in California*. Los Angeles: UC Press.

Scharlin, Craig and Lilia V. Villanueva. 1992. *Philip Vera Cruz: A Personal History of Filipino Immigrants and the Farmworkers Movement*. Los Angeles: UCLA Labor Center, Institute of Industrial Relations and UCLA Asian American Studies Center.

Shin, Young Hai. 1995. "Young Hai Shin" (interviewed by Miriam Ching Louie). In Sen, Rinku (ed.), *We Are the Ones We Are Waiting For: Women of Color Organizing for Transformation*, pp. 48–50. Durham: U.S. Urban-Rural Mission of the World Council of Churches.

———. 1997. "Build Your Own Base." Guest editorial, *Third Force* 5:3 (July–Aug.). Oakland: Center for Third World Organizing.

Sim, Inbo. 2000. "5.18 and Korean American Movements." Paper delivered at "Kwangju After Two Decades" Conference, April 20–22, University of Southern California and University of California Los Angeles.

Toribio, Helen. 2000. "Dare to Struggle: The KDP and Filipino American Politics." In Ho, *Legacy to Liberation*.

Vargas, Zaragosa. 1997. "Tejana radical: Emma Tenayuca and the San Antonio labor movement during the Great Depression." *Pacific Historical Review* 66:4 (Nov.), pp. 553–80.

Vega, Bernardo. 1984. *Memoirs of Bernardo Vega: A Contribution to the History of the Puerto Rican Community in New York*. Cesar Andreu (ed.). New York: Monthly Review.

Wells, Miriam J. 2000. "Immigration and Unionization in the San Francisco Hotel Industry." In Milkman, *Organizing Immigrants*.

White Polk, Wendy. 2000. "¡Que Mujer Obrera!: María Antonia Flores: La Mujer in Charge." *El Paso Inc.*, 6:14 (December 10–16).

Yoneda, Karl G. 1983. *Ganbatte: Sixty-Year Struggle of a Kibei Worker*. Los Angeles: Asian American Studies Center.

Yu, Renqiu. 1992. *To Save China, to Save Ourselves: The Chinese Hand Laundry Alliance of New York*. Philadelphia: Temple UP.

9

♦♦♦

Living in a Global Economy

In September 1995 more than thirty thousand women from virtually every country in the world gathered in Huairou, China, to discuss the many issues and problems faced by women and girls around the world and to work together for change (see Reading 82, Chapter 13). This was the forum for nongovernmental organizations (NGOs) and was the largest meeting of women in history. A two-hour bus ride away, at the official United Nations Fourth World Conference on Women in Beijing, some five thousand delegates discussed what their governments are doing to improve women's lives and negotiated an official U.N. document, the *Platform for Action* (Wong 1995).

There were nearly five thousand workshops listed in the NGO Forum schedule. Among the discussions about literacy and the education of women and girls, nutrition and health care for infants and adults, the need for clean water in many rural areas of the world, the need for jobs or guaranteed livelihood, the plight of millions of refugees, disability rights, violence against women, sexual freedom, solar stoves, and prostitution, to take just a few ex-

amples, one theme was repeated again and again: the effects on women and girls of the globalization of the economy, and the inequality between the rich countries of the world, often located in the Northern Hemisphere, and the poorer countries of the Southern. This seemingly abstract issue affects everyone and underlies many other problems.

To understand the situations and experiences of women in the United States, it is important to know something of women's lives and working conditions worldwide and the ways we all participate in, and are affected by, the global economy. This chapter takes this wider angle of view, with nation as an additional analytical category together with gender, race, and class. The films *The Global Assembly Line* (distributed by New Day Films, www.newday.com) and *Life and Debt* (distributed by New Yorker Films, www.newyorkerfilms.com) are excellent introductions to the topic, and readers are urged to see them, if possible, in conjunction with reading this chapter. Note the significance of gender in the international division of labor, and that this is reinforced by inequalities based on race, ethnicity, and nationality.

Workers in a Reebok factory in China

The Global Factory

In the past thirty-five years or so, electronic communications and air transport have made it increasingly possible for corporations to operate across national boundaries. Now a company based in the United States, such as Nike, Playtex, IBM, or General Motors, can have much of its manufacturing work done overseas—in, for example, Indonesia, China, Mexico, the Philippines, Guatemala, or Europe—by workers who are paid much lower wages than U.S. workers, as shown in the accompanying box (Enloe 1989; Fuentes and Ehrenreich 1983; Greider 1997; Kamel 1990; Kamel and Hoffman 1999; Ross 1997). This organization of work results in inexpensive consumer goods for the U.S. market, particularly clothing, toys, household appliances, and electronic equipment. Thus, our lives are dependent on the labor of a myriad of people in a vast global network.

Roughly 90 percent of the workers in this **offshore production** are young women in their late teens and early twenties. Some countries, like the Philippines and China, have established Export Pro-

cessing Zones (EPZs), where transnational corporations (TNCs) set up factories making products for export to Europe, the U.S., Canada, and Japan. In Mexico this is done through *maquiladoras*—factories that make goods on contract to a "parent" company, as described by María Patricia Fernández-Kelly in Reading 53.

Even in countries like Mexico, with protective labor and environmental legislation, these regulations are often not enforced in relation to the operations of transnational corporations. Thus, workers experience oppressive working conditions and suffer health problems such as stress from trying to make the assigned quotas; illnesses from exposure to glues, solvents, and other toxic chemicals; and lint and dust in textile factories; or poor eyesight from hours spent at microscopes. In addition, women are often subject to sexual harassment by male supervisors. Mexican women workers in *maquiladoras* have been required to undergo a pregnancy test as a condition of employment and have been denied work if they are pregnant (Human Rights Watch 1999b). Company doctors "routinely administer pregnancy tests and distribute birth control pills" (Tooher 1999,

Hourly Labor Costs in the Apparel Industry—by Country
(25 Largest Apparel Exporters)

REGION/COUNTRY	HOURLY APPAREL LABOR COSTS (WAGES AND FRINGE BENEFITS) U.S.$, 1998	REGION/COUNTRY	HOURLY APPAREL LABOR COSTS (WAGES AND FRINGE BENEFITS) U.S.$, 1998
North America		*South Asia (continued)*	
United States	10.12	Sri Lanka	0.44
Mexico	1.51	Pakistan	0.24
Northeast Asia		*Central and Eastern Europe*	
China	0.43	Turkey	1.84
Hong Kong	5.20	Poland	2.77
South Korea	2.69	Romania	1.04
Taiwan	4.68	Hungary	2.12
Southeast Asia		Czech Republic	1.85
Indonesia	0.16	*Africa*	
Thailand	0.78	Tunisia	0.98
Malaysia	1.30	Mauritius	1.03
Philippines	0.76	Morocco	1.36
Vietnam	0.22	*Caribbean Basin*	
South Asia		Dominican Republic	1.48
India	0.39	Costa Rica	2.52
Bangladesh	0.30		

Source: Werner International, Inc. Cited in Gary Gereffi, "Prospects for International Upgrading by Developing Countries in the Global Apparel Commodity Chain," in *International Journal of Business and Society*, Vol. 3, No. 1, 2002.

p. 39). Levimex, for example, a Tijuana *maquiladora* owned by the Leviton Manufacturing Co., gave contracts to workers for a month, three months, or one year. Each time the contract was renewed, women had to take a pregnancy test. When workers complain and organize to protest such dire conditions, they are often threatened that the plants will close and move elsewhere; indeed, this has sometimes happened. For example, Nike has moved some of its production from South Korea, where women have campaigned for better wages and working conditions, to Indonesia and the southern part of China, thereby pitting workers in one country against those in another.

Many thousands of U.S. workers have been laid off through automation or the movement of jobs overseas. Fewer and fewer products are made in the United States. With a lack of manufacturing jobs, the job market in the United States is becoming increasingly polarized between professional jobs and low-paying service work—flipping burgers at McDonald's, for example—that offers few, if any, benefits or job security. Rising unemployment, or underemployment—where people are overqualified for the jobs available—has had devastating social and economic effects across the country.

Public attention in the United States is increasingly focused on the poor working conditions of

Skirt Markup
Total price of skirt $157

Profit to the retailer: $78

The largest member of the food chain;
large retail chains set the prices and
the styles of garments.

Profit to the manufacturer: $33

Retailers purchase clothing from
manufacturers, which design and register
product lines and purchase the fabric.
They then contract out the actual
clothing production.

Profit to the contractor: $13

Receives orders from manufacturers, then
often subcontracts the work out. Cutting,
dyeing, and sewing clothing can be performed
by different contractors.

Cost to the contractor: $33
Material: $20, Misc. Labor: $10, Seamstress: $3

Garment workers cut, stitch, and dye the
clothing that consumers buy at the retail stores.

The skirt sells for $157.

You get paid $3.

Who gets the difference, and how do they spend it?

Source: Los Angeles Herald Examiner garment industry investigation.

those who make many of the things we buy, especially the role of sweatshops. The U.S. General Accounting Office defines sweatshops as employers
that violate more than one federal or state labor law.
Pharis Harvey, executive director of the International
Labor Rights Fund, defines a sweatshop as "any
workplace where the wages are inadequate, the
hours too long, and the working conditions endanger safety or health—whether or not any laws are violated" (Facts on the Global Sweatshop 1997, p. 16).
Sweatshops are common in the garment industry
and toy manufacturing (Louie 2001; Ross 1997). They
exist in many countries, including the United States.
The U.S. Department of Labor estimates that more

than half the country's 22,000 sewing shops violate
minimum wage and overtime laws. Many of these
workers are employed in cramped factories, often
with blocked fire exits, unsanitary bathrooms, and
poor ventilation. According to Sarah Wood (1997),
"The terms 'sweatshop' and 'sweating' were first used
in the nineteenth century to describe a subcontract-
ing system where the middlemen earned their profit
from the margin between the amount they received
from a contract and the amount they paid their workers. This margin was 'sweated' from the workers,"
who received minimal wages for excessive hours
worked under poor conditions. Nowadays, too, the
garment industry is organized in such a way that big-
name retailers like Gap, for example, and brand-
name manufacturers like Jessica McClintock contract
with sewing shops that hire workers to make the finished product, although they do not directly control
workers' wages and working conditions. The retailers and manufacturers, in effect, determine wages
for garment workers by controlling the price to the
contractor.

Despite serious risks to their jobs, workers are organizing for better pay and working conditions. The
National Mobilization Against Sweatshops, for example, was formed by the Chinese Staff and Workers' Association and works with women garment
workers in New York's Chinatown. Miriam Ching
Yoon Louie discusses other examples in Reading 52
(Chapter 8). Increased consumer awareness in the
United States and other industrialized countries has
brought about some changes in wages and working conditions for overseas workers, as consumers
have attempted to hold corporations accountable for
exploitative conditions. A major campaign against
Nike starting in 1997, for example, protested inhu-
mane working conditions in plants making Nike
shoes in Vietnam and China (Bourbeau 1998; Greenhouse 1997; Sanders and Kaptur 1997; Saporito
1998; Stewart 1997). In February 1997, North Olm-
stead, Ohio, a working-class suburb of Cleveland,
became the first U.S. city to ban municipal purchases
of sweatshop-made products (Facts on the Global
Sweatshop 1997, p. 16). In 1999 Duke University students staged a sit-in in the university president's office to ensure that clothing bearing Duke's name is
not made in sweatshops. Students from over 100 colleges called on their institutions to honor a strict code
of conduct for overseas factories that make goods
bearing college names. In response to this public out-

cry, the U.S. Department of Labor mounted a media campaign focusing on industry "trendsetters," and President Clinton created a task force of industry, labor, and human rights organizations, the Apparel Industry Partnership (Press 1997). The Partnership agreed on a workplace code of conduct, including health and safety measures, no forced labor or child labor (except in certain countries), nondiscriminatory practices, and limited protections for collective bargaining. The agreement, which is voluntary, also includes a sixty-hour work week and minimum wage (rather than living wage) standards (Ross 1997, pp. 293–94). The anti-sweatshop movement won another victory in 2002 when twenty-six major apparel companies (including Gap and Gymboree) settled a lawsuit in favor of workers on the island of Saipan in the western Pacific (Collier 2002). These companies agreed to establish a $20 million fund to pay back wages. The suit was brought by several groups including the Asian Law Caucus, Global Exchange, and Sweatshop Watch. These activists noted that one problem with winning such a suit is that it may propel manufacturers to move to areas where they can pay even lower wages, such as China.

The existence of sweatshops and the polarization of the U.S. job market are not random or isolated, however, but an integral part of the global economic system. The driving force is the accumulation of wealth by corporations and individuals. Their **capital**—money and property—is invested in manufacturing, communications, or agriculture, for example. By producing goods, services, and crops, workers earn wages and also increase the wealth of their employers. **Capitalism,** also called the **free market system,** is an economic, political, and cultural system in which the major means of production and distribution are privately held and operated for profit. Labor and nature are seen as resources. In practice there is no "pure" capitalism; rather, the system is a mixture of corporate and government decisions that provide the foundation for business operations. Governments levy taxes that may be used to alleviate poor social conditions. Government and corporate elites share assumptions about what makes the economy successful. In extreme circumstances, governments may sanction the use of police or military force against workers who strike for better pay and working conditions. Governments of some small countries may have operating budgets smaller than those of transnational corporations, a situation that makes control of the corporations difficult. For instance, according to activist and writer Charles Gray (1999) the top three companies in the world—Exxon-Mobil, General Motors, and Ford—each have higher revenues than the national budgets of all but seven countries (United States, Germany, Japan, China, Italy, United Kingdom, and France). Some companies have more revenue than the budgets of their home governments (e.g., Shell/Netherlands and Daewoo/South Korea). It is important to understand the underlying principles of this economic system outlined below.

The Profit Motive

Companies compete with one another to sell their services and products, and they stay in business only as long as it is profitable or while governments are willing to subsidize them, as happens, for example, with agriculture and defense industries in the United States. If enough people can afford to buy gold faucets or to change their cars every six months, these things will be produced regardless of whether ordinary people have an adequate diet or somewhere to live. Women in Malaysia or the Philippines, for example, spend their working lives producing more and more goods for the U.S. market even if their own daily survival needs are barely met.

Consumerism, Expansionism, and Waste

To expand, companies have to produce more products, develop new products, and find new markets and new needs to supply. The concept of "need" is a tricky one. Many of the things we think we need are not absolute necessities but contrived needs generated by advertising or social pressure. Some needs are also context specific. It is doubtful whether every household in an urban area in the United States with extensive public transportation needs a car, but a car is probably required in a rural area for basic necessities like getting to work, as there is unlikely to be adequate, if any, public transportation. This economic system is intrinsically wasteful. Companies have little or no responsibility to workers left stranded, or for polluted land and water they leave behind when, for example, car assembly plants close down in Detroit or Mattel moves its Barbie doll factory to Malaysia.

The Village

If we could shrink the earth's population to a village of precisely 100 people, with all the existing human ratios remaining the same, it would look like the following. There would be

    57 Asians

    21 Europeans

    14 from the Western Hemisphere, both north and south

    8 Africans

    52 would be female

    48 would be male

    70 would be non-white

    30 would be white

    70 would be non-Christian

    30 would be Christian

    89 would be heterosexual

    11 would be homosexual

    6 people would possess 59 percent of the entire world's wealth and all 6 would be from the United States

    80 would live in substandard housing

    70 would be unable to read

    50 would suffer from malnutrition

    1 would be near death; 1 would be near birth

    1 (yes, only 1) would have a college education

    1 would own a computer

_____

Source: E-mail widely circulated in 2000.

The Myth of Progress

There is an assumption that economic growth is the same as "progress"—a much more complex concept with economic, intellectual, social, moral, and spiri-

tual dimensions. This equation often leads people in a highly material society like the United States to value themselves primarily in terms of the money they make and the things they own. At a national level, too, it leads to an emphasis on material success and material security, with support for government policies that facilitate profit making regardless of social costs.

Emphasis on Immediate Costs

The business definition of costs—the immediate costs of raw materials, plant, payroll, and other operating expenses—is a narrow one. It does not take into account longer-term considerations like the effects of production on the environment or workers' well-being. Government regulation of pollution, for example, is frequently resisted by corporations on the grounds that it will increase costs and drive them out of business. In the nineteenth century, European and U. S. factory owners said the same thing about proposals to abolish child labor and reduce working hours to an eight-hour day, both of which were implemented through legislation.

The Global Economy

Complex Inequalities

Our economic system generates profound inequalities within countries—of wealth, material comfort, safety, opportunities, education, social standing, and so on. Members of wealthy elites in Brazil, Saudi Arabia, Indonesia, Turkey, Germany, South Africa, and the United States, to take a few random examples, often have more in common with one another than they do with many of their fellow citizens. Poor people living in Oakland, Detroit, or the south Bronx have rates of illiteracy and infant mortality as high as poor people in parts of Africa, Latin America, and the Caribbean. This has led some commentators to talk of "the Third World within the First World" as a way of emphasizing inequalties within countries and drawing connections among poor people worldwide, overwhelmingly people of color.

These inequalities are enhanced in a global economy, which produces inequalities between rich and

What's in a Name?

The various overlapping terms used in the discourse on the global economy offer a convenient shorthand but often obscure as much as they explain.

First World, Second World, Third World

These terms refer to countries that can be roughly grouped together according to their political alliances and economic status. The "First World" refers to North America, Western Europe, Australia, New Zealand, and Japan. The "Second World" includes Russia and countries of Eastern Europe. The "Third World" includes most of Asia, Latin America, Africa, and the Caribbean. There is an assumption of a hierarchy built into this terminology, with First World countries superior to the rest. Some Native Americans and indigenous peoples in Canada, Latin America, Australia, and New Zealand use the term "First Nations" to emphasize the fact that their ancestral lands were colonized and settled by Europeans. Some environmentalists use the term "Fourth World" to refer to a scattered collection of small-scale, environmentally sound projects, suggesting an alternative economic and political model. Some commentators use the term "Two-Thirds World" to draw attention to the fact that the majority of the world's population (approximately 68 percent) lives in Asia, Latin America, Africa, and the Caribbean.

Developed, Undeveloped, Underdeveloped, Developing, Maldevelopment

These terms refer to economic development, assuming that all countries will become industrialized like North America and Western Europe. Ranging these terms on a continuum from "undeveloped" to "developed" suggests that this process is linear and the best way for a nation to progress. Indeed, economic growth is often assumed to be synonymous with progress. This continuum masks the fact that so-called developing countries have thousands of years of traditional knowledge, and that much of the wealth of developed countries comes from developing countries and is a key reason for their lack of economic development. Vandana Shiva (1988), researcher, writer, and activist on issues of development and environment from India, emphasizes this connection by using the term "devastated" instead of "underdeveloped" economies. Other commentators speak of "maldevelopment" to refer to exploitation of undeveloped countries by developed ones.

East/West; North/South

The division between East and West refers to a political and military division between North America and Western Europe—the West—countries which, despite differences, have stood together against the East—the former Soviet Union and Eastern Europe. Clearly this notion of East and West excludes many countries in the Western and Eastern Hemispheres. This distinction also obscures the similarities between these blocs, which are both highly industrialized with massive military programs. Some writers use the terms North/South to distinguish between rich and poor countries. Rich countries may have their own material wealth and also colonial relationships (currently or in the past) whereby they could extort wealth from others. So-called poor countries often have land, forests, mineral wealth, and people's skills, creativity, knowledge, and hard work. These countries are poor because they do not have control over their resources.

poor nations. The richest 20 percent of the world's population receives 80 percent of the world's income. The richest 20 percent of the world's population in northern industrial countries uses 86 percent of the world's resources (Bigelow and Peterson 2002).

Workers in one country are pitted against those in another in the corporations' scramble for profits, as mentioned in the articles that follow, and this generally erodes their bargaining power. The internationalization and mobility of capital calls for an

International Economic Institutions and Trade Agreements

Several groups of countries have joined together, forming trading blocs such as the Economic Community of West African States (ECOWAS) and the European Union (EU), and agreements such as the North American Free Trade Agreement (NAFTA) between Canada, Mexico, and the United States. The goal of these regional institutions is to strengthen the economies of the member countries, although the various countries may not all have the same economic power or influence in the group.

The World Bank

Headquartered in Washington, D.C., the World Bank was set up in 1944 to provide loans for reconstruction after the devastation of World War II and to promote development in countries of the South, where the bank's emphasis has been on major, capital-intensive projects such as roads, dams, hydroelectric schemes, irrigation systems, and the development of large-scale, chemical-dependent, cash-crop production. The bank's investors are the governments of rich countries who make money on the interest on these loans. Because the World Bank assigns voting power in proportion to the capital provided by its shareholders, its decisions are dominated by the governments of the North, and its policies are in line with their concerns.

International Monetary Fund (IMF)

Also based in Washington, the IMF is an international body with 184 member countries. It was founded at the same time as the World Bank to promote international trade and monetary cooperation. It makes loans to governments for development projects and in times of severe budget deficits. France, Germany, Japan, Britain, and the United States have over 50 percent of the votes, which are allocated according to financial contribution to the fund. If member countries borrow from the fund, they must accept a range of conditions, such as structural adjustment programs, and must put export earnings above any other goal for the country's economy.

General Agreement on Tariffs and Trade (GATT)

This trade agreement was started after World War II to regulate international trade. Since its inception, over a hundred nations, responsible for four-fifths of world trade, have participated in the agreement. The latest round of GATT negotiations, which began in 1986, significantly changed the agreement in response to transnational corporations' demand for a reduction of import tariffs, in what consumer activist Ralph Nader (1993) described as "an unprecedented corporate power grab" (p. 1). The changed agreement was adopted by the United States in 1994. Transnational corporations will pay fewer tariffs on the goods they move around the world—data, components, partly finished products, and goods ready for sale. The World Trade Organization (WTO) is the GATT ruling body, established in 1995 in the "Uruguay Round" of GATT negotiations.

North American Free Trade Agreement (NAFTA) and Free Trade Agreement of the Americas (FTAA)

This agreement among the United States, Canada, and Mexico, established in 1994, allows for greater freedom of movement of jobs and products among the three countries. Its proponents argued that these countries needed to collaborate to remain as competitive internationally as the economi-

international labor movement to standardize wages and working conditions. The fact that standards of living and wage rates differ from country to country means that this process of moving work and factories around the world is likely to continue and to become increasingly complex. In addition to U.S.-based corporations, Western European, Japanese, Taiwanese, and South Korean firms also operate in other countries, seeking lower wages, better tax breaks, and other financial incentives.

cally powerful European Union and Pacific Rim trading groups. Like GATT, NAFTA was discussed in terms of a liberalization of trade but is in effect a liberalization of capital expansion, serving the interests of transnational corporations against opposition in all three countries from labor, environmentalists, and consumers. The Clinton administration admitted that 75,000 U.S. jobs were lost because of NAFTA. Workers in the Mexico-U.S. border region have suffered a sharp drop in their standard of living, "speed-ups" in the labor process, and opposition to labor rights and union organizing (Comité Fronterizo de Obreras—American Friends Service Committee 1999). In all three NAFTA countries, increases in real wages have lagged behind increases in productivity (Anderson, Cavanagh, and Ranney 1999).

The current plan is to expand NAFTA to cover the entire Western Hemisphere in a Free Trade Area of the Americas (FTAA). In July 2002 the House of Representatives narrowly approved "fast track" trade negotiating authority for President Bush. This gives the president full authority to negotiate trade agreements without needing to consult Congress. Proponents of the FTAA contend that increased free trade will result in increased prosperity. Opponents argue that workers are likely to lose jobs, and that legislation protecting workers and the environment is likely to be set aside or ruled to be an unlawful limitation on the operations of corporations. Workers, environmentalists, and human rights activists in Brazil, Peru, Paraguay, and Bolivia have organized massive protests against the FTAA, as have "fair trade" activists in the United States (Global Exchange 2002).

World Trade Organization (WTO)

This is an unelected international body over which member nations and their peoples have no dem-ocratic control. The WTO allows national governments to challenge each others' laws and regulations as violations of WTO rules against restraints to trade. Cases are decided by a panel of three trade experts. WTO tribunals are secret, binding on member states, and provide no outside appeal or review. Once a WTO ruling is issued, losing countries have a set time to change their law to conform to WTO requirements, pay compensation to the winning country, or face non-negotiated trade sanctions (Working Group on the WTO 1999, p. 5).

In September 1997, a WTO panel ruled that the European Union (EU) was giving preferential access to bananas produced by former colonies in the Caribbean. The United States brought this case against the EU on behalf of the U.S.-based Chiquita Corporation, formerly known as United Fruit. Chiquita produces bananas in Latin America on huge plantations that are notorious for exploiting cheap farm labor and using environmentally damaging techniques. In the Caribbean, banana producers tend to be small-scale farmers who own and work their own small farms, often incurring higher production costs. This was a very divisive case within the WTO because of its economic, social justice, and environmental dimensions. At one point the United States began implementing a threat to impose sanctions on more than $500 million of EU exports, nearly setting off a trade war. The EU eventually said that it would comply with the ruling, but it is still negotiating with the United States over the settlement terms (Rethinking Schools 2002). In the shrimp-turtle case, India, Malaysia, Pakistan, and Thailand challenged the U.S. Endangered Species Act that requires domestic and foreign shrimp fishers to catch shrimp by methods that do not kill endangered sea turtles. In 1998 the WTO determined that this law violates WTO rules.

Legacies of Colonialism

Current inequalities between countries are often based on older inequalities resulting from colonization. British colonies included India, Ghana, Kenya, Nigeria, Pakistan, and Hong Kong. France had colonial possessions in Algeria, Senegal, Togo, and Vietnam. Although the details varied from place to place and from one colonial power to another, several factors were central to this process:

- the imposition of legal and political institutions;
- cultural devastation and replacement of language;
- psychological dimensions such as internalized racism; and
- distortions of the economy with dependence on a few agricultural products or raw materials for export.

Colonial powers extracted raw materials—timber, minerals, and cash crops—which were processed into manufactured goods in the colonial centers for consumption there and for export. During the second half of the twentieth century, virtually all former colonies gained political independence, but they remain linked to their colonizers—politically through organizations like the British Commonwealth and economically through the activities of established firms in operation since colonial times, from the more recent activities of transnational corporations, and by loans from governments and banks of countries of the North (that is, the rich countries of the developed world). Many members of the new political and business elites were educated at prestigious universities in colonial capitals. Whether the handover of political power was relatively smooth or accompanied by turmoil and bloodshed, newly independent governments have been under pressure to improve living conditions for their populations and have borrowed capital to finance economic development. This combination of circumstances has led many commentators to characterize the continuing economic inequalities between rich and poor countries as **neocolonialism.** The United States is part

of this picture because of its colonial relationships with the Philippines, Hawaii (now a state), and Puerto Rico (a commonwealth); the strength of U.S. corporations worldwide; the dominance of U.S. news media and popular culture; the strength of the dollar as an international currency; and the relatively high U.S. shareholding in key international institutions like the World Bank and the International Monetary Fund. They both have their headquarters in the United States and are heavily influenced by U.S. investments and policies.

External Debt

All countries are involved in international trade, buying and selling goods and services. Currently many countries pay more for imports than they earn in exports, leading to external debt, or a balance of payments deficit. For many poor countries in Africa and Latin America, the burden of external debt is catastrophic. The external debt of developing countries rose by about $110 billion, or 6.4 percent, in 1996, reaching over $1.8 trillion, mostly owed to the World Bank and the International Monetary Fund (Group of 77, 1997). In 1999, Latin American and Caribbean countries had an estimated $700 billion in foreign debt (Lama 1999). The United States, too, has had an enormous budget deficit, dropping from $290 billion in 1992 to $164 billion in 1995 because of major budget cuts (Sivard 1996), but rising again to a total of $2.5 trillion in 2002 (Greider 2002).

Repayment of Loans Partly because countries of western Europe and North America have serious balance-of-payments problems themselves, they have pressured other debtor countries to repay loans. Like a person who acquires a second credit card to cover the debt on the first, a country may take out additional loans to cover interest repayments on earlier ones, thus compounding its debt. This situation is complicated by the fact that loans usually have to be repaid in hard currency that can be exchanged on world currency markets: U.S. dollars, Japanese yen, British pounds, French francs, Swiss francs, German marks, and now the euro. To repay the loans, debtor nations have to sell goods and services that richer countries want to buy or that can earn hard currency from poorer countries. These include raw materials (hardwoods, oil, copper, gold, diamonds), cash crops (sugar, tobacco, coffee, tea, tropical fruits and flowers), illegal drugs and drug-producing crops (coca, marijuana, opium poppies), and weapons. Debtor countries may also earn foreign exchange by encouraging their people to work abroad as construction workers or maids or to become mail-order brides. They may lease land for foreign military bases or trash dumps that take toxic waste from industrialized countries, or they may develop their tourist assets—sunny beaches, beautiful landscapes, and "exotic" young women and children who are recruited into sex tourism. Many heavily indebted countries make annual debt repayments that are between 20 percent and 45 percent of their budgets, and from two to five times their spending on basic social services (Bigelow and Peterson 2002).

Structural Adjustment Programs In addition to selling goods and services to offset their external debt, debtor nations have also been under pressure from the World Bank and the IMF to make stringent changes in their economies to qualify for new loans. The aim of such structural adjustment programs is to increase the profitability of the economy. Required measures include

- cutting back government spending on health, education, child care, and social welfare provisions;
- cutting government subsidies and abolishing price controls, particularly on food, fuel, and public transportation;
- adding new taxes, especially on consumer goods, and increasing existing taxes and interest rates;

- selling nationalized industries, or at least a majority of the shares, to private corporations, often from outside the country;
- reducing the number of civil servants on the government payroll;
- improving profitability for corporations through wage controls, tax breaks, loans, and credit, or providing infrastructure by building ports, better roads, or rail transportation;
- devaluing local currency to discourage imports and encourage exports; and
- increasing the output of cash crops, by increasing yields and/or increasing the amount of land in cash crop production.

Though not required to do so by the World Bank, the Reagan, Bush, and Clinton administrations all adopted similar policies for use in the United States, and this has continued under George W. Bush. Such policies are in line with global economic restructuring with the goal of increasing corporate profitability. Examples include the deregulation of air transport and the privatization of public utilities and aspects of the prison industry. In addition, these administrations restructured government spending by making reductions in the government workforce and cuts in, for example, Medicaid, Medicare, and welfare programs.

Implications of the Debt Crisis for Women Despite women's increased opportunities for paid work in urban areas and export-processing zones in Asia, Latin America, and the Caribbean, the external debt crisis and structural adjustment programs have had a severe impact on women's lives and livelihoods. Addressing the U.N. Commission on the Status of Women in March 1998, Rini Soerojo, the assistant minister of the Ministry of State for the Role of Women, Indonesia, spoke on behalf of 132 developing countries. She emphasized that "the full and effective enjoyment of human rights by women could never be achieved in the absence of sustainable economic growth and a supportive social and international order" (Deen 1998, p. 2). Cuts in social services and health care, often already woefully inadequate, have increased women's responsibilities for child care, health, and family welfare. Cuts in government subsidies for food and other basic items and devaluation of local currencies have reduced women's wages and raised prices, thus doubly reducing their buying power. The emphasis on cash crops at the expense of subsistence crops has devastating environmental consequences and makes subsistence agriculture—very often the responsibility of women—much more difficult. Growing cash crops on the flatter land, for instance, pushes subsistence farmers to use steep hillsides for food crops, which is harder work and often less productive and which increases soil erosion. Clearing forests to plant cash crops or raise cattle, as McDonald's did in parts of Central and Latin America, for example, increased soil erosion and reduced the supply of fuel wood, which has further added to women's daily burden of work (Dankelman and Davidson 1988; Sen and Grown 1987; Shiva 1988).

Other consequences of the debt crisis include an increase in the number of people seeking work overseas as temporary migrant workers or permanent immigrants; increasing unemployment and underemployment, with growth in the exploitative and unregulated informal sector of the economy (such as sweatshops and low-paid work in homes); an increase in the number of students who have to drop out of school and college because of financial pressures; and a general increase in poverty and hardship. Grace Chang shows how structural adjustment in the Philippines economy has affected Filipina workers, thousands of whom go abroad each year for work—particularly to Canada, western Europe, the Middle East, and the United States (Reading 54).

Debt Cancellation Between 1982 and 1990, $160 billion was transferred from Latin America to the developed world in debt repayments (O'Reilly 1991), but this was only the interest on 50 percent of their loans (George 1988). In 1982 Mexico announced that it could not repay its debt, and other countries suspended their repayments throughout the 1980s. This led to much political and financial debate concerning the legitimacy of debts owed by countries of the South to the North. According to Oxfam International (1998):

> In Ethiopia over 100,000 children die annually from easily preventable diseases, but debt payments are four times more than public spending on health care.
>
> In Tanzania, where 40 percent of people die before the age of 35, debt payments are six times as much as spending on health care.

In Africa as a whole, where one out of every two children doesn't go to school, governments transfer four times more to northern creditors in debt payments than they spend on the health and education of their citizens.

Many activist organizations worldwide support debt cancellation. They argue that much of the money borrowed has benefited only upper-class and professional elites or has gone into armaments, nuclear power plants, or luxuries such as prestige buildings, especially in urban areas. As summed up in the lyrics to *Ode to the International Debt:* "Guns you can't eat/And buildings you can't live/And trinkets you can't wear/It is a debt not owed by the people" (Reagon 1987). In some countries, large sums of money borrowed by governments were kept by corrupt politicians and businesspeople and then reinvested in the lender countries. Political economist Susan George (1988) claims that debt "cancellation would turn recipient countries into financial pariahs" who would not be able to borrow further loans. She argues that the goals of a debt campaign "should be to get money and the political power that goes with it directly into the hands of the poor majorities, bypassing the elites, and insofar as possible, the State; and to ensure much greater popular control over the development process" (p. 20).

It is an inescapable fact that the world's poorest countries are getting poorer and will never be able to pay their international debts. Although this debt is not the only cause of their poverty, the debt burden makes their situation significantly worse. With the agreement of the leading industrialized nations, the governing boards of the IMF and World Bank adopted a debt-relief proposal in 1996 for the most heavily indebted countries, mostly in Africa. A few countries benefited under this scheme, but progress has been very slow. During the 1990s, people in rich and poor countries took part in major protests against world economic priorities. In June 1999, a worldwide alliance of NGOs and religious groups known as the Jubilee 2000 Coalition presented the leaders of the G-8 (Group of Eight) nations (United States, Japan, Britain, France, Germany, Italy, Canada, and Russia) with a petition signed by 17 million people from rich nations urging debt cancellation (Francis 1999). The G-8 proposed an expansion of the World Bank/IMF debt-relief initiative, and three years later, at its annual meeting in Washington, D.C., in September 2002, the IMF promised that it will announce a dramatic new approach for countries in debt crisis in April 2003. The idea is to allow nations with "unmanageable debt to declare bankruptcy and force creditors to negotiate more lenient repayment terms" (Blustein 2002, p. A1). This proposal can be expected to face stiff opposition from large banks in industrialized countries, including the United States. However, several industrialized countries, including Britain, Canada, France, Italy, and Spain, have written off some of the debts owed them by very poor African countries.

Implications of Global Economic Inequalities

Addressing a vast crowd in Havana at the end of a visit to Cuba in January 1996, Pope John Paul II criticized unsustainable economic programs imposed by rich countries on the poor and "the resurgence of a certain capitalist neoliberalism that subordinates the human person to blind market forces"; he also deplored the fact that "a small number of countries [are] growing exceedingly rich at the cost of the increasing impoverishment of a great number of other countries" (News Services 1998, p. A1).

In principle, inequality is unjust. Some people's freedom and comfort cannot be bought at the expense of other people's oppression, degradation, and poverty. More pragmatically, inequality is a continual source of violence and conflict. On an international level it is one of the main causes of war; on a community level it can lead to alienation, anger, violence, theft, and vandalism.

Connections to U.S. Policy Issues

Two issues of national importance in the United States that are greatly affected by global inequalities are immigration and drugs. Vast differences in living standards between the United States and many other countries are a source of continuing pressure for immigration into this country. These same inequalities also drive the international drug trade, a lucrative earner of hard currency for producer countries as well as for those who procure and sell illegal drugs or launder drug money (Lusane 1991). It is important to understand the global economic forces driving the drug trade and pressures for immigration and to recognize the inadequacy of control measures that do not address underlying causes.

Discussion of the drug trade is beyond the scope of this book, but we consider the issue of immigration here, building on the brief history of immigration law and policy included in Chapter 2. The 1990s saw controversial and acrimonious debate in the United States over immigration, along with a range of new legislation, like the 1996 Illegal Immigration Reform and Immigrant Responsibility Act, which aims to control it. Anti-immigration politicians and countless media reports invoked the specter of "alien hordes" poised on the borders, ready to overrun the country, take jobs away from the native born, and drain the welfare system. Wendy Young (1997), director of government relations, Women's Commission for Refugee Women and Children, counters this perception, arguing that undocumented people "typically fill service-sector jobs and are ineligible for most benefits, even though they pay taxes and social security contributions. Moreover, 85% of immigrants come to the United States through legal channels" (p. 9).

At the heart of much of this debate are racism and xenophobia. White people particularly see the country changing demographically with the arrival of more people from Asia, Mexico, and Central and South America. This poses a threat to the dominance of "the Anglo-Saxon part of America's culture" (Holmes 1995b). Such fears have provided leverage for a greatly increased Immigration and Naturalization Service budget and tighter border control, especially along the long land border with Mexico, which has been strongly fortified (Ayres 1994), as described by Leslie Marmon Silko (Reading 55) and Pat Mora (Reading 56). Congress cut government funding for virtually all agencies except the military in the mid-1990s, but the INS budget has more than tripled from $1.4 billion in fiscal year 1992 to $4.8 billion in fiscal year 2001 (American Immigration Lawyers Association 2001).

The distinction between legal and illegal immigrants has been drawn more sharply. The 1986 Immigration Act introduced sanctions against employers, making it illegal to knowingly hire undocumented workers, with fines for those who violate the law. This controversial program was intended to eliminate the "pull" factor of jobs attracting undocumented migrants into the country. Illegal immigrants are hired at low wages by agricultural growers, construction firms, landscaping and cleaning businesses, and the garment industry, for example, as well as by private individuals as maids and baby-sitters.

Evidence indicates that employer sanctions have been ineffective; employers are not always prosecuted, and if they are, they tend to consider the relatively small fines as a hazard of doing business. However, as Wendy Young (1997) observed, "Numerous studies have shown that employer sanctions have caused employment discrimination against U.S. citizens and permanent residents who look or sound 'foreign.' Some employers will avoid hiring such individuals rather than risk being subjected to sanctions and fines" (p. 8).

Increasing numbers of undocumented workers were deported during the early 1990s (Holmes 1995a), and legal immigrants applied for citizenship in record numbers in response to growing controversy over immigration and moves to deny legal immigrants access to government supports. Anti-immigrant rhetoric took on a very different quality after the attacks on the World Trade Center and the Pentagon on September 11, 2001, and the Bush administration's declaration of a long-term "war on terrorism." Distrust and suspicion of foreigners, especially Arabs, South Asians, and "people who look like Muslims," was deployed in support of government policies, as discussed in Chapter 10. Migration policy will continue to be a contentious issue in the United States, particularly in states like California, Florida, New York, and Texas, which have large proportions of immigrants.

International Alliances Among Women

Women's organizations worldwide are concerned with economic issues, including economic development, loans to start small businesses, and other job opportunities for women, as well as the lack of government spending on health care, child care, or care for the elderly. At international feminist meetings and conferences, such as the NGO Forum in September 1995, these global inequalities are central to many discussions. Women from countries of the South invariably challenge those from the North to take up the issue of external debt and structural adjustment with our governments and banks.

Some U.S. feminist organizations focus their work on women's rights in this country, which is understandable, as earlier gains are being eroded. But the separation of domestic and foreign policy masks crucial connections and continuities and can lead to an insularity and parochialism on the part of women

in the United States, an important aspect of the ignorance that comes with national privilege. In the context of trade agreements like GATT and NAFTA, Mary McGinn, the North American coordinator for Transnationals Information Exchange, commented, "Unfortunately, most U.S. women's advocacy groups took no position on GATT. But clearly, all women have a lot to lose: expanded freedom for multinational corporations jeopardizes social justice everywhere" (1995, p. 15).

In order to build more effective international campaigns and alliances, women in the North need to learn much more about the effects of corporate and government policies on women in Asia, Africa, Latin America, and the Caribbean, and to understand the connections between these women's situations and our own.

Many women in the United States who attended the NGO Forum spoke to public meetings, religious organizations, women's groups, and school and college classes about their impressions and brought back a heightened understanding of global linkages to their ongoing efforts. The Women of Color Resource Center (Berkeley, Calif.), for instance, decided to give priority to the globalization of the economy in its organizing and educational work: "Global economics was at the top of the Beijing agenda; it is now at the top of ours as well" (1996, p. 2; 2000). A campaign titled Women's Eyes on the World Bank-U.S., based at Oxfam America (Washington, D.C.), began "to monitor Bank progress toward bringing its lending operations in line with the Beijing Platform" (Williams 1997, p. 1). This is the importance of international gatherings like the NGO Forum at Huairou or the U.N. *Platform for Action,* which

> criticizes structural adjustment programs; advises cuts in military spending in favor of social spending; urges women's participation at all peace talks and in all decision-making affecting development and environment; confronts violence against women; calls for measuring women's unpaid work; and refers to "the family" in all its various forms.
>
> *(Morgan 1996, p. 20)*

United Nations documents have to be ratified by the governments of individual countries to be accepted as national policy. Even if governments do not ratify them—and the U.S. on several occasions has not—they are still useful for activists in their attempts to hold governments accountable and to show what others have pledged to do for women and girls. Wangari Maathai, coordinator of the Kenyan Women's Green Belt, comments:

> It's very hard to push governments on issues that affect all aspects of society, let alone those that affect women. But the U.N. document has given us a tool with which to work. Now it's up to the women to push their issues into the boardrooms where political and economic decisions are made by those who did not even bother to come to Beijing.
>
> *(Quoted in Morgan 1996, p. 18)*

The Women's Environment and Development Organization evaluated governments' progress since the 1995 U.N. Conference in Beijing (WEDO 1998) and reported that "over 70 percent of the world's 187 countries have drawn up national action plans or drafts as required by the Beijing Platform" (WEDO press release, March 1, 1998). Sixty-six governments set up national offices for women's affairs, thirty-four of them with the power to initiate legislation. Fifty-eight countries adopted new legislation or policies to address women's rights, particularly concerning violence against women (Latin American and Caribbean countries, China, and New Zealand), female genital mutilation (Egypt), and the trafficking of women and children (Thailand). However, economic restructuring and negative effects of globalization have severely affected the realization of the Beijing commitments and reduced women's access to jobs, health care, and equal opportunity in most countries.

The global economic situation has generated new alliances and organizations working across national borders. Examples include STITCH (Support Team International for Textileras), a network of women organizers in the United States and Guatemala, and Comité Fronterizo de Obreras (CFO), or Border Committee of Women Workers, a Mexican worker-controlled organization that works closely with the American Friends Service Committee, a social justice organization. They have won several significant victories, such as winning wages that have been withheld illegally; pressuring companies to implement laws requiring safety equipment and protective clothing; challenging illegal layoffs and dismissals and winning legally mandated severance pay; curbing pollution in communities and factories; teach-

ing workers practical exercises to alleviate repetitive strain injuries; testifying at shareholder meetings to give details of how companies treat their workers; and building the confidence of women workers so that they can stand up for their rights (www.afsc.org/border/maquila.htm).

Diverse Women for Diversity are an international network with a secretariat in India. They oppose the corporate assault on biological and cultural diversity as argued in the statement they prepared for the WTO's Third Ministerial Conference, in Seattle, November 1999 (Reading 57). Thousands of people, including environmentalists, union members, indigenous people, feminists, and people of many faiths, came from all continents to participate in alternative workshops on economic and environmental issues, as well as to protest the WTO. This coordinated opposition was successful in stalling the "Seattle round" of talks aimed at further opening up global trade.

Since then, this growing anti-globalization movement has organized mass international protests at the IMF and World Bank meetings (Washington, D.C., April 2000, and September 2001; Prague, Czech Republic, September 2000), the Summit of the Americas (Quebec City, Canada, April 2001), the G-8 meeting (Genoa, Italy, July 2001), and innumerable demonstrations of support all over the world (Prokosch and Raymond 2002; Starhawk 2002b). Activists from all continents have participated in the World Social Forum (Porto Alegre, Brazil), which started in 2001 when 20,000 people from 117 countries came together to think and organize in favor of genuine human development, rather than globalization. Another international initiative is organized by the International Wages for Housework Campaign and Women's International Network for Wages for Caring Work. Starting in 2000, these groups have organized an annual Global Women's Strike on March 8, International Women's Day, involving women in over 80 countries. The strike draws attention to the fact that virtually all women are workers, though much of the work we do is unwaged.

The Seeds of a New Global Economy

In Latin America, the Caribbean, Africa, and Asia, thousands of workers' organizations, environmentalists, feminists, and religious groups are campaigning for better pay and working conditions and for economic development that is environmentally sound (Braidotti et al. 1994; De Oliveira et al. 1991; Leonard 1989), and they are protesting the poverty caused by external debt. Similarly, social and economic justice organizations and networks in countries of the North advocate that we in the United States learn more about the global economy and the impact of global inequalities on people's lives and livelihoods (Benjamin and Freedman 1989). They also urge us to live more simply: to recycle materials, wear secondhand clothing, barter for things we need, establish collectives and cooperatives, engage in socially responsible shopping and investing, and buy directly from farmers and craftspeople. A number of nonprofit organizations are involved in supporting fair trade between producers and craftspeople in the South and consumers in the North, including Equal Exchange (Cambridge, Mass.), Global Exchange (San Francisco Bay Area), Pueblo to People (Houston, Tex.), and Ten Thousand Villages (Akron, Pa.). Fair trade criteria include paying a fair wage in the local context; providing equal opportunities, especially for the most disadvantaged; engaging in environmentally sustainable practices; providing healthy and safe working conditions; and being open to public accountability. Other projects include dialogue projects linking workers of the North and South, such as North-South Dialogue of the American Friends Service Committee's Latin American/Caribbean Program; campaigns urging a debt amnesty for countries of the South, like Jubilee 2000; campaigns to get institutions to stop buying World Bank bonds; Third World study tours; and direct support through work brigades such as those in Cuba and Nicaragua.

In the 1960s and 1970s, those active in U.S. movements for liberation and civil rights made theoretical and practical connections with anticolonial struggles in such countries as South Africa, Vietnam, Cuba, Angola, and Mozambique. In the twenty-first century, these international linkages are crucial, not merely, as scholar and activist Angela Davis (1997) remarked, "as a matter of inspiration or identification, but as a matter of necessity," because of the impact of the globalization of the economy.

Activists and writers Mary Zepernick (1998a, 1998b) and Virginia Rasmussen (1998) both argue that corporate dominance is not inevitable. In the eighteenth and nineteenth centuries, U.S. city and state governments watched corporations closely and revoked or amended their charters if they harmed the

general welfare or exceeded the powers granted them by government. In 1843, for example, the Pennsylvania Legislature declared: "A corporation in law is just what the incorporation act makes it. It is the creature of the law and may be moulded to any shape or for any purpose the Legislature may deem most conducive for the common good" (quoted in Grossman 1998a, p. 1). In 1890 the highest court in New York revoked the charter of the North River Sugar Refining Corporation in a unanimous decision (*People v. North River Sugar Refining Corp.*, 24 N.E. 834.1890). In its judgment, the court noted:

> The judgment sought against the defendant is one of corporate death. The state which created, asks us to destroy, [sic] and the penalty invoked represents the extreme rigor of the law. The life of a corporation, is, indeed, less than that of the humblest citizen. . . . Corporations may, and often do, exceed their authority only where private rights are affected. When these are adjusted all mischief ends and all harm is averted. But where the transgression has a wider scope, and threatens the welfare of the people, they may summon the offender to answer for the abuse of its franchise and the violation of corporate duty. . . . The abstract idea of a corporation, the legal entity . . . is itself a fiction. . . . The state permits in many ways an aggression of capital, but, mindful of the possible dangers to the people, overbalancing the benefits, keeps upon it a restraining hand, and maintains over it prudent supervision.
>
> *(Quoted in Grossman 1998a, p. 2)*

Corporate owners worked hard to change the law and were successful over time. In an 1886 decision, the U.S. Supreme Court declared corporations legal persons. Gradually they were given a long list of civil and political rights, such as free speech, property rights, and the right to define and control investment, production, and the organization of work (Grossman 1998b). They became entitled to the Fourteenth Amendment protection that was added to the Constitution in 1870 to provide due process to freed African Americans (Zepernick 1998b). This resulted in a gradual reversal of the sovereignty of the people over corporations—originally mere legal entities—and an undermining of democracy, for people who are subordinate to corporations are not citizens. Zepernick and Rasmussen note that corporations are *things;* they cannot care or be responsible. The Program on Corporations, Law and Democracy (POCLAD) promotes public discussion of this fundamental contradiction between democracy and corporate control (Ritz 2001). It advocates that city governments, for example, create policies and programs to ensure control over corporations conducting business with the city, as a step toward reclaiming people's power over corporate entities.

This chapter raises key questions about our global economic system. In what ways is this a "free market"? Who pays and at what costs? Who should governments be responsible to? What is needed for this to be a secure and sustainable system?

Questions for Reflection

In thinking about the issues raised in this chapter, consider these questions:

1. Why does the impact of the globalization of the economy matter to people living in the United States? What does it tell us about structural privilege (which we may not know we have and may not want)? If some of this material is new to you, why do you think you have not learned it before?

2. How does global inequality reinforce sexism, racial prejudice, and institutionalized racism in the United States?

3. How do you define wealth, aside from material possessions? List all the ways you are enriched.

4. Does wealth equal political power? Are rich people always in the **power elite**—the group that influences political and economic decisions in the country? Who makes up the power elite in the United States?

5. How do people in elite positions justify the perpetuation of inequalities to others? To themselves? How are the ideologies of nationalism, racial superiority, male superiority, and class superiority useful here?

Finding Out More on the Web

1. Visit the following Web sites to find out more about organizations that are campaigning against sweatshops and urging Codes of Conduct for corporations:

   Community Aid Abroad: **www.caa.org.au/campaigns/nike/sweating.html**

   CorpWatch: **www.corpwatch.org**

   Sweatshop Watch: **www.sweatshopwatch.org**

2. The following Web sites have information about alternatives to globalization, including fair trade and debt relief:

   Global Exchange: **www.globalexchange.org**

   Global Women's Strike: **http://womenstrike8m.server101.com**

   Jubilee USA Network   **www.j2000usa.org/debt/edpac/debt.html**

   World Social Forum: **www.wsfindia.org**

◆◆◆

Taking Action

1. Look at the labels in your clothes and on all products you buy. Where were they made? Look up these countries on a map if you don't know where they are.

2. Do you need all you currently own? List everything you need to sustain life. Which items do you need to buy? Which might you make yourself, share, or barter with others?

3. Find out who manufactures the clothing that bears your college's name, and whether there are sweatshops in your region.

4. Get involved with a campaign that is tackling the issue of sweatshop production or debt relief.

FIFTY-THREE

◆◆◆

Maquiladoras

The View from Inside

María Patricia Fernández-Kelly

What is it like to be female, single and eager to find employment at a maquiladora? Shortly after arriving in Ciudad Juárez and after finding stable lodging, I began looking through the pages of newspapers hoping to find a "wanted" ad. My intent was to merge with the clearly visible mass of women who roam the streets of industrial parks of Ciudad Juárez searching for jobs. They are, beyond doubt, a distinctive feature of the city, an effervescent expression of the conditions that prevail in the local job market.

My objectives were straightforward: I was to spend from four to six weeks applying for jobs and obtaining direct experience about the employment policies, recruitment strategies and screening mechanisms used by companies in the process of hiring assembly workers. Special emphasis would be given to the average investment of time and money expended by individual workers in trying to gain access to jobs. In addition, I was to spend an equal amount of time working at a plant, preferably at one involved in the manufacture of apparel.

_____

As part of the fieldwork for her study of the *maquiladora* industry in Mexico, anthropologist María Patricia Fernández-Kelly worked in a textile factory in Ciudad Juárez.

With this I expected to learn more about working conditions, production quotas and wages at a particular plant. In general, both research stages were planned as exploratory devices that would elicit questions relevant to the research project from the perspective of workers themselves.

In retrospect, it seems odd that the doubt as to whether these goals were feasible or not never entered my design. However, finding a job at a maquiladora is not a self-evident proposition. For many women, actual workers, the task is not an easy one. This is due primarily to the large number of women they must compete with. Especially for those who are older than twenty-five years of age the probability of getting work in a maquiladora is low. At every step of their constant peregrination, women are confronted by a familiar sign at the plants, "No applications available," or by the negative response of a guard or a secretary at the entrance of the factories. But such is the arrogance of the uninformed researcher. I went about the business of looking for a job as if the social milieu had to comply with the intents of my research rather than the reverse. Moreover, I was pressed for time. It was indispensable that I get a job as quickly as possible.

By using newspapers as a source of information for jobs available, I was departing from the common strategy of potential workers in that environment. As my own research would show, the majority of these workers avail themselves of information by word of mouth. They are part of informal networks which include relatives, friends and an occasional acquaintance in the personnel management sector. Most potential workers believe that a personal recommendation from someone already employed at a maquiladora can ease their difficult path.

This belief is well founded. At many plants, managers prefer to hire applicants by direct recommendation of employees who have proven to be dependable and hard-working. For example, at Electro Componentes de Mexico, the subsidiary of General Electric and one of the most stable maquiladoras in Juárez, it is established policy not to hire "outsiders." Only those who are introduced personally to the manager are considered to fill up vacancies.

Such a policy is not whimsical. It is the result of evaluations performed on a daily basis during the interactions between company personnel and workers. By resorting to the personal linkage, managers attenuate the dangers of having their factories infiltrated by unreliable workers, independent organizers and "troublemakers." . . .

On the other hand, the resemblance of a personal interest in the individual worker at the moment of hiring enables management to establish a bond often heavily colored by paternalism. From the point of view of workers this is a two-faceted proposition. Some complain of the not unusual practice of superintendents and managers who are prone to demand special services, for example, overtime, in exchange for personal favors: a loan, an exemption from work on a busy day when the presence of the worker at home is required by her children, and so on. As in other similar cases, personal linkages at the workplace can and will be used as subtle mechanisms to exert control.

Workers, in turn, acknowledge a personal debt to the individual who has hired them. In the majority of cases, commitment to the firm is not distinct from the commitment to a particular individual through whom access to employment presumably has been achieved. A job becomes a personal favor granted through the kindness of the personnel manager or the superintendent of a factory. . . .

Only those who are not part of tightly woven informal networks must rely on impersonal ways to find a job. In this situation are recently arrived migrants and older women with children, for whom the attempt to find maquiladora employment may be a new experience after many years spent caring for children and the home. In objective terms my own situation as a newcomer in Ciudad Juárez was not markedly different from that of the former. Both types of women are likely to be found in larger numbers in the apparel manufacturing sector.

This is not a random occurrence. One of the basic propositions in the present work is that differences in manufacturing activity are related to variations in the volume of capital investments. In turn this combined variable determines recruitment strategies. Therefore different types of persons are predominately employed in different manufacturing sectors. Ciudad Juárez electronics maquiladoras, for example, tend to employ very young, single women. This is, in effect, a preferred category of potential workers from the point of view of industry.

Workers, on their part, also prefer the electronics sector, which is characterized by the existence of large stable plants, regular wages and certain additional benefits. In contrast, the apparel manufacturing sector is frequently characterized by smaller, less stable shops where working conditions are particularly strenuous. Because of their low levels of capital investment, many of these shops tend to hire personnel on a more or less temporary basis. The lack of even the smallest of commitments to their employees and the need to maintain an elastic work force to survive as capitalist enterprises in a fluctuating international market forces management to observe crude and often ruthless personnel recruitment policies.

One of such firms was Maquiladoras Internacionales. . . .

Attached to the tent-like factory where women work from 7:30 A.M. to 5:00 P.M. from Monday to Friday there is a tiny office. I entered that office wondering whether my appearance or accent would elicit the suspicion of my potential employers. The personnel manager looked me over sternly and told me to fill out a form. I was to return the following morning at seven to take a dexterity test.

I tried to respond to the thirty-five questions contained in the application in an acceptable manner. Most of the items were straightforward: name, age, marital status, place of birth, length of residence in Ciudad Juárez, property assets, previous jobs and income, number of pregnancies, general state of health, and so on. One, however, was unexpected: What is your major aspiration in life? I pondered briefly upon the superfluous character of that inquiry given the general features of the job sought. . . .

The following morning I was scheduled to take an on-the-job test. I assumed that this would consist of a short evaluation of my skills as a seamstress. I was to be proven wrong. At 7 A.M. I knocked at the door of the personnel office where I had filled out the application the day before. But no one was there yet. I peeked into the entrance of the factory in a state of moderate confusion. A dark-haired woman wearing false eyelashes ordered me to go in and promptly led me to my place. Her name was Margarita and she was the supervisor.

I had never been behind an industrial sewing machine of the kind I confronted at this time. That it was old was plain to see; how it worked was difficult to judge. An assortment of diversely cut denim parts was placed on my left side while I listened intently to Margarita's instructions. I was expected to sew patch-pockets on what were to become blue jeans. Obediently, I started to sew. The particulars of "unskilled" labor unfolded before my eyes.

The procedure involved in this operation required perfect coordination of hands, eyes and legs. The left hand was used to select the larger part of material from the batch next to the worker. Upon it, the pocket (swiftly grabbed by the right hand) had to be attached. There were no markers to guide the placement of the pocket on its proper place. This was achieved by experienced workers on a purely visual basis. Once the patch-pocket had been put on its correct position, the two parts had to be directed under a double needle while applying pressure on the machine's pedal with the right foot.

Because the pockets were sewed on with thread of a contrasting color, it was of peak importance to maintain the edge of the pocket perfectly aligned with the needles so as to produce a regular seam and an attractive design. Due to the diamond-like shape of the pocket, it was also indispensable to slightly rotate the materials three times while adjusting pressure on the pedal. Too much pressure inevitably broke the thread or resulted in seams longer than the edge of the pocket. Even the slightest deviation from the needles produced lopsided designs which had to be unsewed and gone over as many times as necessary to achieve an acceptable product. According to the instructions of the supervisor, once trained, I would be expected to sew a pocket every nine to ten

seconds. That is, between 360 and 396 pockets every hour, between 2,880 and 3,168 every shift.

For this, velocity was a central consideration. The vast majority of apparel manufacturing maquiladoras operate through a combination of the minimum wage and piecework. At the moment of being hired, workers receive the minimum wage. During 1978 this amounted to 125 pesos a day (approximately $5.00). However, they are responsible for a production quota arrived at by time-clock calculations. Workers receive slight bonus payments when they are able to fulfill their production quotas on a sustained basis throughout the week. In any case they are not allowed to produce less than 80% of their assigned quota without being admonished. And a worker seriously endangers her job when unable to improve her level of productivity.

At Maquiladoras Internacionales a small blackboard indicated the type of weekly bonus received by those able to produce certain percentages of the quota. These fluctuated between 50.00 pesos (approximately $2.20) for those who completed 80% to 100.00 pesos (about $4.40) for those who accomplished 100%. Managers call this combination of steep production quotas, minimum wages and modest bonuses, "incentive programs."

I started my test at 7:30 A.M. with a sense of embarrassment about my limited skills and disbelief at the speed with which the women in the factory worked. As I continued sewing, the bundle of material on my left was renewed and grew in size, although slowly. I had to repeat the operation many times before the product was considered acceptable. But that is precisely what was troubling about the "test." I was being treated as a new worker while presumably being tested. I had not been issued a contract and, therefore, was not yet incorporated into the Instituto Mexicano del Seguro Social (the National Security System). Nor had I been instructed as to working hours, benefits and system of payment.

I explained to the supervisor that I had recently arrived in the city, alone, and with very little money. Would I be hired? What was the current wage? When would I be given a contract? Margarita listened patiently while helping me unsew one of many defective pockets, and then said, "You are too curious. Don't worry about it. Do your job and things will be all right." I continued to sew aware of the fact that every pocket attached during the "test" was becoming part of the plant's total production.

At 12:30 during the thirty-minute lunch break, I had a chance to better see the factory. Its improvised aura was underscored by the metal folding chairs behind the sewing machines. I had been sitting in one of them during the whole morning, but not until then did I notice that most of them had the well-known emblem of Coca-Cola painted on their backs. I had seen this kind of chair many times in casual parties both in Mexico and in the United States. Had they been bought or were they being rented from the local concessionary? In any event they were not designed in accordance to the strenuous requirements of a factory job, especially one needing the complex bodily movements of sewing. It was therefore necessary for women to bring their own colorful pillows to ameliorate the stress on their buttocks and spines. Later on I was to discover that chronic lumbago was, and is, a frequent condition among factory seamstresses.

My curiosity did not decrease during the next hours, nor were any of my questions answered. At 5 P.M. a bell rang signaling the end of the shift and workers quickly prepared to leave. I marched to the personnel office with the intent of getting more information about a confusing day. But this time my inquiry was less than welcome. Despite my over-shy approach to the personnel manager, his reaction was hostile. Even before he was able to turn the disapproving expression on his face into words, Margarita intervened with energy. She was angry. To the manager she said, "This woman has too many questions: Will she be hired? Is she going to be insured?" And then to me, "I told you already we do piecework here; if you do your job you get a wage, otherwise you don't. That's clear, isn't it? What else do you want? You should be grateful! This plant is giving you a chance to work! What else do you want? Come back tomorrow and be punctual."

This was only the first in a number of application procedures that I underwent. Walking about the industrial parks while following other job-seekers was especially informative. Most women do not engage in this task alone. Rather, they do it in the company of friends or relatives. Small groups of two or three women looking for work may be commonly seen in the circumvicinity of the factories. Also frequent is the experience of very young women, ages between sixteen and seventeen, seen in the company of their mothers. . . .

At the times when shifts begin or end, the industrial parks of Juárez form a powerful visual image as thousands of women arrive in buses, taxi-cabs and *ruteras* while many others exit the factories. During working hours only those seeking jobs may be seen wandering about. Many, but not the majority, are "older women." They confront special difficulties due both to their age and to the fact that they often support their own children. These are women who, in most cases, enter the labor force after many years dedicated to domestic chores and child-care. The precipitant factor that determines their entry into the labor force is often the desertion by their male companions. The bind they are placed in at that time is well illustrated by the experience of a thirty-one-year-old woman, the mother of six children: "I have been looking for work since my husband left me two months ago. But I haven't had any luck. It must be my age and the fact that I have so many children. Maybe I should lie and say I've only one. But then the rest wouldn't be entitled to medical care once I got the job." Women often look for jobs in order to support their children. But being a mother is frequently the determining factor that prevents them from getting jobs.

In early June, 1978, Camisas de Juárez, a recently formed maquiladora, was starting a second (evening) shift. Until then it had hired approximately 110 workers operating in the morning hours. As it expanded production, a new contingent of workers had to be recruited. Advertisements to that effect appeared in the daily newspapers. I responded to them. So did dozens of other women.

Camisas de Juárez is located in the modern Parque Industrial Bermúdez. On the morning that I arrived with the intent of applying for a job, thirty-seven women had preceded me. Some had arrived as early as 6 A.M. At 10 the door which separated the front lawn from the entrance to the factory had not yet been opened. A guard appeared once in a while to peek at the growing contingent of applicants, but these were given no encouragement to stay on, nor was the door unlocked.

At 10:30 the guard finally opened the door and informed us that only those having personal recommendation letters would be permitted to walk inside. This was the first in a series of formal and informal screening procedures used to reduce the number of potential workers. It was an effective screening device: Thirteen women left immediately, as they did not have the letter of recommendation alluded to by the guard. Others tried to convince him that although they had no personal recommendation, they "knew" someone already employed at the factory. It was through the recommendation of these acquaintances that they had come to apply for a job.

One of them, Xochitl, lacked both a written or verbal recommendation but she insisted. She had with her a diploma issued by a sewing academy. She was hopeful that this would work in her favor. "It is better to have proof that you are qualified to do the job than to have a letter for recommendation, right?" I wondered whether the personnel manager would agree.

Indeed her diploma gave Xochitl claim to a particular skill. But academies such as the one she had attended abound in Ciudad Juárez. For a relatively small sum of money they offer technical and vocational courses which presumably qualify young men and women for skilled work. However, in an environment lacking in employment opportunities, their value is in question. In many cases, maquiladora managers prefer to hire women who have had direct experience on a job or those who are young and inexperienced but who can be trained to suit the needs of a particular firm. As one manager put it to me, "We prefer to hire women who are unspoiled, that is, those who come to us without preconceptions about what industrial work is. Women such as these are easier to shape to our own requirements." . . .

We waited upon the benevolence of the guard who seemed unperturbed by the fluctuating number of women standing by the door. To many of us he was the main obstacle lying between unemployment and getting a job from someone inside the factory in a decision-making position. If only we could get our foot in, maybe there was a chance. . . . The young man dressed in uniform appeared to the expectant women as an arrogant and insensitive figure. I asked him how long he had worked there. With the air of one who feels he has gained mastery over his own fate he answered, "Uy! I've been working here for a very long time, I assure you: almost two years."

To me his words sounded a bit pathetic. But Beatríz and Teresa, two sisters of twenty-three and nineteen years of age, respectively, were not pleased by his attitude. Their patience had been exhausted and their alternating comments were belligerent: "Why must these miserable guards always act this way? It would seem that they've never had to look for a job. Maybe this one thinks he's more important than the owner of the factory. What a bastard!" But

their dialogue failed to elicit any response. Guards are accustomed to similar outbursts.

Teresa wanted to know whether I had any sewing experience. "Not much," I told her, "but I used to sew for a lady in my hometown." "Well, then you're very lucky," she said, "because they aren't hiring anyone without experience." The conversation having begun, I proceeded to ask a similar question, "How about you, have you worked before?"

Yes, both my sister and I used to work in a small shop on Altamirano Street in downtown Juárez. There were about seventy women like us sewing in a very tiny space, about twenty square meters. We sewed pants for the minimum wage, but we had no insurance.

The boss used to bring precut fabric from the United States for us to sew and then he sold the finished products in El Paso. When he was unable to get fabric we were laid-off; sent to rest without pay! Later on he wanted to hire us again but he still didn't want to insure us even though we had worked at the shop for three years.

When I was sixteen I used to cut thread at the shop. Afterwards one of the seamstresses taught me how to operate a small machine and I started doing serious work. Beatríz, my sister, used to sew the pockets on the pants. It's been three months since we left the shop. Right now we are living from the little that my father earns. We are two of nine brothers and sisters (there were twelve of us in total but three died when they were young). My father does what he can but he doesn't have a steady job. Sometimes he does construction work; sometimes he's hired to help paint a house or sells toys at the stadium. You know, odd jobs. He doesn't earn enough to support us.

I am single, thanks be to God, and I do not want to get married. There are enough problems in my life as it is! But my sister married an engineer when she was only fifteen. Now she is unmarried and she has three children to support. They live with us too. Beatríz and I are the oldest in the family, you see, that's why we really have to find a job. . . .

At that point Beatríz intervened. I asked whether her husband helped support the children. Her answer was unwavering: "No, and I don't want him to

Herri/Mujeres en Acción

You don't understand; the "econo-me" grew, not the "econo-you."

give me anything, not a cent, because I don't want him to have any claim or rights over my babies. As long as I can support them, he won't have to interfere." I replied, "But aren't there better jobs outside of maquiladoras? I understand you can make more money working at a *cantina*. Is that true?"

Both of them looked at me suspiciously. Cantinas are an ever present reminder of overt or concealed prostitution. Teresa said,

> That is probably true, but what would our parents think? You can't stop people from gossiping, and many of those cantinas are whorehouses. Of course, when you have great need you can't be choosy, right? For some time I worked as a waitress but that didn't last. The supervisor was always chasing me. First he wanted to see me after work. I told him I had a boyfriend, but he insisted. He said I was too young to have a steady boyfriend. Then, when he learned I had some typing skills, he wanted me to be his secretary. I'm not stupid! I knew what he really wanted; he was always staring at my legs. So I had to leave that job too. I told him I had been rehired at the shop although it wasn't true. He wasn't bad looking, but he was married and had children. . . . Why must men fool around?

At last the guard announced that only those with previous experience would be allowed to fill out applications. Twenty women went into the narrow lobby of Camisas de Juárez, while the rest left in small quiet groups. For those of us who stayed a second waiting period began. One by one we were shown into the office of the personnel manager where we were to take a manual dexterity test. The point was to fit fifty variously colored pegs into fifty similarly colored perforations on a wooden board. This had to be accomplished in the shortest possible time. Clock in hand, the personnel manager told each woman when to begin and when to stop. Some were asked to adjust the pegs by hand, others were given small pliers to do so. Most were unable to complete the test in the allotted time. One by one they came out of the office looking weary and expressing their conviction that they wouldn't be hired.

Later on we were given the familiar application form. Again, I had to ponder what my greatest aspiration in life was. But this time I was curious to know what Xochitl had answered. "Well," she said, "I don't know if my answer is right. Maybe it is wrong. But I tried to be truthful. My greatest aspiration in life is to improve myself and to progress." . . .

After completing the application at Camisas de Juárez there was still another test to take. This one consisted of demonstrating sewing skills on an industrial machine. Again many women expressed doubts and concern after returning to the lobby where other expectant women awaited their turn. In the hours that had been spent together a lively dialogue had ensued. Evidently there was a sense that all of us were united by the common experience of job seeking and by the gnawing anxiety that potential failure entails. Women compared notes and exchanged opinions about the nature and difficulty of their respective tests. They did not offer each other overt reassurance or support, but they made sympathetic comments and hoped that there would be work for all.

At 3:30 P.M., that is, seven hours after the majority of us had arrived at the plant, we were dismissed. We were given no indication that any of us would be hired. Rather, we were told that a telegram would be sent to each address as soon as a decision was made. Most women left disappointed and certain that they would probably not be hired.

Two weeks later, when I had almost given up all hope, the telegram arrived. I was to come to the plant as soon as possible to receive further instructions. Upon my arrival I was given the address of a small clinic in downtown Ciudad Juárez. I was to bring two pictures to the clinic and take a medical examination. Its explicit purpose was to evaluate the physical fitness of potential workers. In reality it was a simple pregnancy test. Maquiladoras do not hire pregnant women, although very often these are among the ones with greater need for employment. . . .

Having been examined at the clinic, I returned to the factory with a sealed envelope containing certification of my physical capacity to work. I was then told to return the following Monday at 3:30 P.M. in order to start work. After what seemed an unduly long and complicated procedure, I was finally being hired as an assembly worker. For the next six weeks I shared the experience of approximately eighty women who had also been recruited to work the evening shift at Camisas de Juárez. Xochitl, Beatríz and Teresa had been hired too.

On weekdays work started at 3:45 P.M. and it ended at 11:30 P.M. At 7:30 P.M. a bell signaled the beginning of a half-hour break during which workers could eat their dinner. Some brought homemade sandwiches, but many bought their food at the factory. Meals generally consisted of a dish of *flautas* or *tostadas* and carbonated drinks. The persistence of inadequate diets causes assembly workers numer-

ous gastric problems. On Saturdays the shift started at 11:30 A.M. and it ended at 9:30 P.M. with a half-hour break. We worked in total forty-eight hours every week and earned the minimum wage, that is, 875 pesos per week; 125 pesos per day; an hourly rate of approximately $0.60. . . .

From the perspective of workers, medical insurance is as important as a decorous wage. This is particularly true in the case of women who have children in their care. Thus, it was not surprising to find out that some new workers at Camisas de Juárez were there mainly because of the *seguro*. María Luisa, a twenty-nine-year-old woman, told me, "I don't have a lot of money, but neither do I have great need to work. My husband owns a small restaurant and we have a fairly good income. But I have four children and one of them is chronically sick. Without insurance medical fees will render us poor. That's the main reason why I am working."

As do the majority of garment maquiladoras, Camisas de Juárez operates by a combination of piecework and the minimum wage. Upon being hired by the plant every worker earns a fixed wage. However, all workers are expected to fulfill production quotas. On the first day at the job I was trained to perform a particular operation. My task was to sew narrow biases around the cuff-openings of men's shirts. As with other operations I had performed before, this one entailed coordination and speed. . . .

As for the production quota, I was expected to complete 162 pairs of sleeves every hour, that is, one every 2.7 seconds, more than 1,200 pairs per shift. It seemed to me that to achieve such a goal would require unworldly skill and velocity. In six weeks as a direct production operator I was to fall short of this goal by almost 50%. But I was a very inexperienced worker. Sandra, who sat next to me during this period, assured me that it could be done. It wasn't easy, but certainly it could be done. . . .

The factory environment was all-embracing, its demands overwhelmed me. Young supervisors walked about the aisles asking for higher productivity and encouraging us to work at greater speed. Periodically their voices could be heard throughout the workplace: "Faster! Faster! Come on, girls, let us hear the sound of those machines!" They were personally responsible before management for the efficiency of the workers under their command.

Esther, who oversaw my labor, had been a nurse prior to her employment in the factory. I was intrigued by her polite manner and her change of jobs. She dressed prettily, seeming a bit out of place amidst the heated humdrum of the sewing machines, the lint and the dispersed fabric that cluttered the plant. She told me it was more profitable to work at a maquiladora than at a clinic or a hospital.

Esther saw her true vocation as that of a nurse, but she had to support an ill and aging father. Her mother had died three years earlier, and although her home was nice and fully owned, she was solely responsible for the family debts. Working at a factory entailed less prestige than working as a nurse, but it offered a better wage. She was now earning almost one thousand pesos a week. As a nurse she had earned only a bit more than half that amount. From her I also learned, for the first time, about the dubious advantages of being a maquiladora supervisor.

As with the others in similar positions, Esther had to stay at the plant long after the shift ended and the workers left. Very often the hours ran until one in the morning. During that time she verified quotas, sorted out production, tried to detect errors and, not seldom, personally unseamed defective garments. With the others she was also responsible for the preparation of shipments and the selection of material for the following day's production. In other words, her supervisory capacities included quality control and some administrative functions.

When productivity levels are not met, when workers fail to arrive punctually or are absent, or when there is trouble in the line, it is the supervisor who is first admonished by management. Thus, supervisors occupy an intermediary position between the firm and the workers, which is to say that they often find themselves between the devil and the deep blue sea.

As with the factory guard, supervisors and group leaders are frequently seen by workers as solely responsible for their plight at the workplace. Perceived abuses, unfair treatment and excessive demands are thought to be the result of supervisors' whims rather than the creature of a particular system of production. That explains, in part, why workers' grievances are often couched in complaints about the performance of supervisors.

But while supervisors may be seen by workers as close allies of the firms, they stand at the bottom of the administrative hierarchy. They are also the receivers of middle and upper management's dissatisfaction, but they have considerably less power and

their sphere of action is very limited. Many line supervisors agree that the complications they face in their jobs are hardly worth the differences in pay. . . .

The Organization of Labor in the Factory

The pressures exerted by supervisors at Camisas de Juárez were hard to ignore. Esther was considerate and encouraging: "You're doing much better now. Soon enough you'll be sewing as fast as the others." But I had doubts, as she was constantly asking me to repair my own defective work, a task which entailed an infinite sense of frustration. I began to skip dinner breaks in order to continue sewing in a feeble attempt to improve my productivity level. I was not alone. Some workers fearful of permanent dismissal also stayed at their sewing machines during the break while the rest went outside to eat and rest. I could understand their behavior; their jobs were at stake. But presumably my situation was different. I had nothing to lose by inefficiency, and yet I felt compelled to do my best. I started pondering upon the subtle mechanisms that dominate will at the workplace and about the shame that overwhelms those who fall short of the goals assigned to them.

The fact is that as the days passed it became increasingly difficult to think of factory work as a stage in a research project. My identity became that of the worker; my immediate objectives those determined by the organization of labor at the plant. Academic research became an ethereal fiction. Reality was work, as much for me as for the others who labored under the same roof.

These feelings were reinforced by my personal interactions during working hours. I was one link in a rigidly structured chain. My failure to produce speedily had numerous consequences for others operating in the same line and in the factory as a whole. For example, Lucha, my nineteen-year-old companion, was in charge of cutting remnant thread and separating the sleeves five other seamstresses and I sewed. She also made it her business to return to me all those parts which she felt would not meet Esther's approval. According to her she did this in order to spare me further embarrassment. But it was in her interest that I sewed quickly and well; the catch in this matter was that she was unable to meet her quota unless the six seamstresses she assisted met theirs.

Therefore, a careless and slow worker could stand between Lucha and her possibility to get a weekly bonus. The more a seamstress sewed, the more a thread cutter became indispensable. As a consequence, Lucha was extremely interested in seeing improvements in my level of productivity and in the quality of my work. Sometimes her attitude and exhortations verged on the hostile. As far as I was concerned, the accusatory expression on her face was the best work incentive yet devised by the factory. It was not difficult to discern impinging tension. I was not surprised to find out during the weeks spent at Camisas de Juárez that the germ of enmity had bloomed between some seamstresses and their respective thread cutters over matters of work.

Although the relationships between seamstresses and thread cutters were especially delicate, all workers were affected by each other's level of efficiency. Cuffless sleeves could not be attached to shirts. Sleeves could not be sewed to shirts without collars or pockets. Holes and buttons had to be fixed at the end. Unfinished garments could not be cleaned of lint or labeled. In sum, each minute step required a series of preceding operations effectively completed. Delay of one stage inevitably slowed up the whole process.

From the perspective of the workers, labor appeared as the interconnection of efficiently performed individual activities rather than as a structured imposition from above. Managers are nearly invisible, but the flaws of fellow workers are always apparent. Bonuses exist as seemingly impersonal rewards whose access can be made difficult by a neighbor's laziness or incompetence. As a result, complaints are frequently directed against other workers and supervisors. The organization of labor at any particular plant does not immediately lead to feelings of solidarity.

On the other hand, common experiences at the workplace provide the basis for dialogue and elicit a particular kind of humor. In this there is frequently expressed a longing for relief from the tediousness of industrial work. One of Sandra's favorite topics of conversation was to reflect upon the possibility of marriage. She did so with a witty and self-deprecatory attitude.

She thought that if she could only find a nice man who would be willing to support her, everything in her life would be all right. She didn't mind if he was not young or good-looking, as long as he had plenty of money. Were there men like that left in the world? Of course, with the children it was difficult, not to say impossible, to find such a godsend. Then again, no one kept you from trying. But not at the maquiladora. All of us were female. Not even a lonely engineer was to be found at Camisas de Juárez. One could die of boredom there.

However, the fact that there weren't men around at the plant had its advantages according to Sandra. At many factories men generally occupied supervisory and middle- and upper-management positions. Sandra knew many women who had been seduced and then deserted by engineers and technicians. In other cases, women felt they had to comply with the sexual demands of fellow workers because they believed otherwise they would lose their jobs. Some were just plain stupid. Things were especially difficult for very young women at large plants like RCA. They needed guidance and information to stay out of trouble, but there was no one to advise them. Their families had too many problems to care. . . .

Fortunately, there were the bars and the discotheques. Did I like to go out dancing? She didn't think so; I didn't look like the kind who would. But it was great fun; we should go out together sometime (eventually we did). The Malibú, a popular dancing hall, had good shows. But it was tacky and full of kids. It was better to go to the Max Fim, and especially the Cosmos. The latter was always crowded because everyone liked it so much. Even people from the other side (the United States) came to Juárez just to visit Cosmos. Its décor was inspired by outerspace movies like *Star Wars*. It was full of color and movement and shifting lights. They played the best American disco music. If you were lucky you could meet a U.S. citizen. Maybe he would even want to get married and you could go and live in El Paso. Things like that happen at discotheques. Once a Jordanian soldier in service at Fort Bliss had asked her to marry him the first time they met at Cosmos. But he wanted to return to his country, and she had said no. Cosmos was definitely the best discotheque in Juárez, and Sandra could be found dancing there amidst the deafening sound of music every Saturday evening.

The inexhaustible level of energy of women working at the maquiladoras never ceased to impress me. How could anyone be in the mood for all-night dancing on Saturdays after forty-eight weekly hours of industrial work? I had seen many of these women stretching their muscles late at night, trying to soothe the pain they felt at the waist. After the incessant noise of the sewing machines, how could anyone long for even higher levels of sound? But as

Sandra explained to me, life is too short. If you don't go out and have fun, you will come to the end of your days having done nothing but sleep, eat and work. And she didn't call that living. . . .

◆◆◆

The Global Trade in Filipina Workers

Grace Chang

Since the 1980s, the World Bank, the International Monetary Fund, and other international lending institutions based in the North have routinely prescribed structural adjustment policies (SAPs) to the governments of indebted countries of the South as pre-conditions for loans. These prescriptions have included cutting government expenditures on social programs, slashing wages, liberalizing imports, opening markets to foreign investment, expanding exports, devaluing local currency, and privatizing state enterprises. While SAPs are ostensibly intended to promote efficiency and sustained economic growth in the "adjusting" country, in reality they function to open up developing nations' economies and peoples to imperialist exploitation.

SAPs strike women in these nations the hardest and render them most vulnerable to exploitation both at home and in the global labor market. When wages and food subsidies are cut, wives and mothers must adjust household budgets, often at the expense of their own and their children's nutrition. As public healthcare and education vanishes, women suffer from a lack of prenatal care and become nurses to ill family members at home, while girls are the first to be kept from school to help at home or go to work. When export-oriented agriculture is encouraged, indeed coerced, peasant families are evicted from their lands to make room for corporate farms, and women become seasonal workers in the fields or in processing areas. Many women are forced to find work in the service industry, in manufacturing, or in home work, producing garments for export.[1]

When women take on these extra burdens and are still unable to sustain their families, many have no other viable option but to leave their families and migrate in search of work. Asian women migrate by the millions each year to work as servants, service workers, and sex workers in the United States,

Canada, Europe, the Middle East, and Japan. Not coincidentally, the demand for service workers, and especially for private household caregivers and domestic workers, is exploding in wealthy nations of the First World undergoing their own versions of adjustment.

For example, in the United States, domestic forms of structural adjustment, including cutbacks in healthcare and the continued lack of subsidized childcare, contribute to an expanded demand among dual-career, middle-class households for workers in childcare, eldercare, and housekeeping. The slashing of benefits and social services under "welfare reform" helps to guarantee that this demand is met by eager migrant women workers. The dismantling of public supports in the United States in general, and the denial of benefits and services to immigrants in particular, act in tandem with structural adjustment abroad to force migrant women into low-wage labor in the United States. Migrant women workers from indebted nations are kept pliable not only by the dependence of their home countries and families on remittances, but also by stringent restrictions on immigrant access to almost all forms of assistance in the United States. Their vulnerability is further reinforced by U.S. immigration policies, designed to recruit migrant women as contract laborers or temporary workers who are ineligible for the protections and rights afforded to citizens.[2]

Both in their indebted home countries and abroad, women suffer the most from the dismantling of social programs under structural adjustment. In the Third World, women absorb the costs of cuts in food subsidies and healthcare by going hungry and foregoing proper medical care. Ironically, these same women continue to take up the slack for vanishing social supports in the First World, by nursing the elderly parents and young children of their employers for extremely low wages. Thus, there is a transfer of costs from the governments of both sending and receiving countries to migrant women workers from indebted nations. In both their home and "host" countries, and for both their own and their employers' families, these women pay most dearly for "adjustment."

Testimonies of Women Living Under SAPs

At the 1995 Women's NGO Forum in China, women from the Third World gave first-hand testimony on the impact of SAPs on their daily lives and struggles for survival. The phenomenon consistently reported is that overall standards of living, and conditions for women and girls in particular, have deteriorated dramatically since the onset of SAPs. Often this has occurred after periods of marked improvement in women's employment, health, education, and nutrition following national independence movements prior to the institution of SAPs.

In a workshop on the impact of SAPs on women, an organizer from rural India spoke of the particular hardships women face, as those most affected by cuts in social programs and those first displaced from their farm lands. She reported that lands in India formerly used to produce rice have been rapidly converted to shrimp farms and orange orchards. While rice has always been a staple for local consumption, shrimp are purely cash crops for export to Japan, and the oranges are for export to the United States for orange juice. In her community, peasant women ran in front of bulldozers to try to prevent these lands from being taken over, but to no avail.[3]

Women from many other Third World countries reported similar conditions. An organizer from Malaysia observed, "We are adjusting with no limits to capital mobilizing everywhere. Malaysia has used all of the SAP principles, including privatization of services and deregulation of land acquisition." This woman reported that in Malaysia, land once held by small farmers has also been shifted to shrimp cultivation, while in Sri Lanka, peasants see their lands being taken up to cultivate strawberries for export to other countries.[4] Similarly, peasant women from the Philippines testified that, under SAPs, they have had to relinquish all the profits of their labor to landlords, and that lands once used to grow rice,

corn, and coffee have been converted to growing orchids and "other exotic flowers that you can't eat" for export.[5]

In each of these countries, women bear the brunt of SAP-induced poverty daily through lack of healthcare, housing, and food.[6] Filipina rural women have reported going without power for four to eight hours each day and coping with little or no water.[7] Urban women from the Philippines reported working an average of 18 hours a day doing domestic work, laundry work outside their homes, and begging, while men face increasing unemployment. Their children are most often on the street rather than in school, and many families are becoming homeless with the high price of housing and the demolition of houses under development. Families may eat only once or twice a day because they can't afford more, and most go without any healthcare as the public hospitals demand payment up front and prescription medicines become prohibitively expensive.[8] Similarly, one rural organizer from India reported that prices for essential medicines have gone up 600 percent since the onset of SAPs, severely reducing Indian women's access to proper healthcare.[9]

Consistently, women from around the Third World testified that, as women have been displaced from their lands and homes under structural adjustment, women who were once small farmers have been forced to do home work, to migrate to the cities to work in manufacturing and the electronic industry, or to migrate overseas to do nursing, domestic work, sex work, and "entertainment."[10] The women's testimony demonstrates their clear recognition that they bear the brunt of hardships under structural adjustment, while their nations' governments and elites reap fat rewards in the form of women's cheap or unpaid labor and remittances from migrant women workers abroad. Commentary of women organizing in countries affected by SAPs reflects an acute awareness of the ways in which the governments and economic elites of their countries and First World countries profit at the expense of women's labor conditions, education, nutrition, health, and safety. As one labor organizer from India remarked:

> Our governments are surrendering to these multinational corporations and Western agencies. These magnate[s] and mafias, in the name of globalization, want to exploit our workers and resources. Our real concerns are food, water, clean sanitary conditions, health, shelter,

and no exploitation. These are the human rights we want. All these governments are telling us to talk about human rights. What are they doing?[11]

Exporting Women: The "New Heroes"

Each day, thousands of Filipinas leave their homes and families in search of work abroad. The Philippine government estimates that more than 4 percent of the country's total population are contract workers overseas. About 700,000 Filipinas/os were deployed through a government agency, the Philippine Overseas Employment Administration (POEA), in each of the past two years.[12] In 1991, women constituted a larger proportion of the country's overseas workforce (41 percent) than its domestic workforce (36 percent). Of those overseas, approximately 70 percent are women working as domestic servants in middle- and upper-class homes in the United States, Britain, Europe, Japan, and the Middle East. Many of the others work as nurses, sex workers, and entertainers.[13] Such massive migrations of women have led to public charges that the Philippines government is selling or trafficking in women.

Indeed, this massive migration is no mere coincidence of individual women's choices to leave the Philippines. The Philippine government receives huge sums of remittances from its overseas workers each year. "Host" country governments and private employers welcome the migrant women workers for the cheap labor they provide. These governments and employers save money not only by paying abominably low wages, but by failing to provide public benefits or social services to these temporary workers. Finally, recruiting agencies and other entrepreneurs on each end of the trade route reap tremendous profits for providing employers in "host" countries with ready and willing service workers and caregivers of all kinds.

In 1994, the Central Bank of the Philippines recorded the receipt of USD $2.9 billion in remittances by overseas workers. Remittances through informal channels have been estimated at six to seven billion U.S. dollars each year. These remittances are the country's largest source of foreign exchange—surpassing income from either sugar or minerals—and provide currency for payments towards the country's USD $46 billion debt. In 1993, overseas contract workers' remittances were estimated at 3.4 percent of the gross domestic product, which is the equivalent of 30 percent of the trade deficit or of the entire sum of interest payments on the country's foreign debt. These estimates are based on official figures alone and do not include moneys that enter through informal channels. As the Freedom from Debt Coalition (FDC), an organization working to counter SAPs, has put it: "What the country cannot achieve through export of goods, it compensates for through the export of human resources."[14]

Of less importance to the Philippine government but certainly significant in explaining the continued massive migration of women workers are estimates that approximately 30 to 50 percent of the entire Filipino population are dependent on migrant worker remittances.[15] Furthermore, it has been found that women migrant workers send home a larger proportion of their wages than their male counterparts do, even though they tend to earn less than men.[16] Such contributions led one ambassador from the Philippines to Canada to proclaim: "The migrant workers are our heroes because they sustain our economy."[17]

"Host" countries are eager to receive these female mercenaries, as they bolster their economies, too. As many countries of the North undergo downsizing and the dismantling of public supports, migrant women workers offer the perfect solution. The steady flow of migrant women provides an ideal source of cheap, highly exploitable labor. These women are channeled directly into the service sector, where they do every form of care work for a pittance and no benefits. Ironically, immigrant domestic workers, nannies, in-home caregivers, and nurses pick up the slack for cuts in government services and supports that pervade the North as well as the South. Overseas, they provide care for the ill, elderly, and children, while their own families forego this care because of the economic restructuring that drives them overseas.

Filipina Nurses and Homecare Workers

Currently, there are 100,000 registered nurses in the Philippines, but almost none actually reside in the country. Similarly, 90 percent of all Filipino/a medical school graduates do not live in the Philippines. Since the 1970s, the United States has imported women from the Philippines to work as nurses, ostensibly in response to domestic shortages in trained nurses. This importation system became institutionalized with the H-1 nursing visa, which enables a hospital or nursing home to sponsor or bring a nurse with a professional license from abroad to work in the United States for two years.

Under the [earlier] H-1 program, a migrant woman must take the U.S. nurses' licensing exam. If she passes, she can gain permanent residency after two years. During those two years, she is almost captive to her original sponsoring employer. If she fails the exams she loses her sponsorship, and technically she must leave the country. More often, such women go underground until they can take the exam again. Sometimes, they work in nursing homes where they are underpaid at five dollars an hour. Others buy green-card marriages.

In 1988, the Filipina Nurses Organization fought for the Nursing Relief Act, which has provided some rights and stability to H-1 nurses in the last decade. The law grants nurses permanent residency after five years of living in the United States and working in the nursing profession. Prior to this act's passage, H-1 nurses had to go home after five years and could return after one year's residence in their home countries. Only after this period of absence could they apply to have their H-1 visas renewed. This system kept nurses in low-wage, temporary positions, forcing them to begin again and again at entry level with no seniority or benefits. The Immigration and Naturalization Service routinely conducted raids at hospitals to ensure that this turnover of temporary workers occurred.

Mayee Crispin, a Filipina nurse, organizes foreign nurse graduates (FNGs) at St. Bernard's Hospital on the south side of Chicago. At St. Bernard's, 80 percent of the nurses are single Filipina women on H-1. The starting wage at St. Bernard's is $14 an hour, in contrast to $16 an hour at other hospitals, and the ratio of patients to nurses is high. But many of the FNGs are reluctant to organize, fearful of losing their jobs or their employers' immigration sponsorship if they are identified as being pro-union. Many are sending remittances to their families at home and struggling to pay off their debts from migration.

Crispin proposes that importing nurses from the Philippines is a money-making venture for hospitals and the nursing recruiters they contract. According to Crispin, a hospital typically gets workers from overseas by making an official certification that they cannot find U.S. workers to fill its nursing positions. (This is usually because the hospital offers wages that no U.S. worker is willing to accept.) The hospital is then free to contract a recruiter to go to the Philippines in search of nurses. An FNG must pay, on average, between USD $7,000 and $9,000 to the recruiter. Ostensibly, a portion of this fee goes to the recruiter's salary, and a portion goes to a lawyer to arrange the woman's visa. Often both are employed by the hospital, which also gets a cut of the fee. Since most women cannot afford this fee, they agree to have it deducted from their wages. After paying off such fees and sending roughly 25 to 30 percent of their wages to their families at home, their monthly wages quickly disappear. In essence, most of these women live in a situation much like indentured servitude or debt bondage for at least two years. Crispin says that hospitals, by hiring FNGs, not only get cheap labor, they also get a workforce that is extremely vulnerable, fearful, uninformed of their rights, and thus likely to resist unionization.

Ninotchka Rosca of Gabriela Network USA observes the ironic history of Filipina nurses in the United States. In the 1980s, the nursing profession was extremely low-paying, with salaries at about $20,000 a year in the United States, so the country experienced a drastic shortage of nurses. With few U.S. citizens going into the field or willing to do nursing at such low wages, many Jamaican and Filipina women migrated here to do this work. With the downsizing in healthcare, many of the migrant nurses who have been here for over a decade are now finding themselves just as vulnerable as new migrants. Hospitals are attempting to reduce costs by firing their most experienced, and thus highest-paid, nurses. Rosca suggests that U.S. hospitals and the healthcare industry would collapse without Filipina nurses. "We take care of everybody else's weaker members of society, while we let our own society go to hell."[18]

Homecare Workers

Home healthcare is another industry in which immigrant women are highly concentrated and fall prey to both profit-seeking agencies and the cost-cutting U.S. government. Many homecare workers are employees of the state, under a state-funded program called "in-home support services" (IHSS). Some of these women are registered nurses, while others are not trained as nurses at all. The program provides no training, no regulations, and no monitoring of the work, which includes everything from performing medical procedures, preparing meals, and cleaning to helping elderly, frail, or ill clients go to the toilet, bathe, and move about. To keep costs down, the state pays workers a minimum wage of $4.50 an hour and provides no benefits, including no sick leave, family leave, overtime pay, compensation for injuries on the job, or reimbursement for bus fares or gasoline used to run errands for patients or to take them to the doctor.[19] In California, there are 170,000 of these workers statewide, of which approximately 80 percent are women, 60 to 70 percent are people of color, and 40 percent are immigrants.

Josie Camacho is an organizer with Service Employees International Union. Camacho points out that, particularly with the restructuring of hospitals under the ongoing privatization of healthcare, patients are being sent home too early and thus homecare workers are having to provide what should be trained nursing care, often without any formal training. For example, routine duties can include giving enemas and insulin shots, changing bandages, and hooking up dialysis machines.[20] In addition to the grueling work and low pay, immigrant workers in particular frequently report sexual harassment and other forms of abuse from their clients, including threats of deportation and general treatment as slaves. One worker was ordered to clean the bathroom with a toothbrush.[21]

The union is demanding the workers' rights to dignity and respect, to proper training in health and safety procedures, and to better wages. Camacho explains that these demands are aimed not only at improving the standard of living and rights for the workers, but at improving the quality of care provided to clients. Patients are typically Supplementary Security Income (SSI) recipients and must have assets under $2,000 to qualify for care under the state program. Thus, the government is relying on the weak positions of both impoverished patients, who have no control over the quality of care offered them, and low-wage workers, who have little recourse to fight these low wages and highly exploitative conditions.

Employing an IHSS worker saves taxpayers approximately $30,000 a year, the difference between the cost of keeping a patient in a nursing home and the typical salary of $7,000 a year earned by an IHSS worker who works 30 hours a week. This savings is reaped by the state, county, and (through Medicaid) federal governments, which all share the program's annual cost. Robert Barton, manager of the adult services branch of the California Department of Social Services overseeing the program, commented: "It's a good deal for the government." The union's director of organizing in Washington, D.C., David Snapp, retorts: "It's a scam."[22] The IHSS program provides perhaps the best illustration available of the tremendous savings to local, state, and federal governments through the low-wage labor of migrant care workers. Other savings to the state and employers have not been measured, such as those reaped from not providing public benefits, services, and protections to these workers.

In the private sector, the situation is no better. Agencies and companies turn a profit from placing these workers, just as the state saves money by underpaying workers. Homecare agencies, just like hospitals, make huge profits from recruiting and placing homecare workers. For example, an agency will typically contract out a live-in caregiver to a client for $120 to $200 a day, while the worker herself receives only $80 of that daily rate.

Domestic Workers and Nannies

The majority of migrant Filipina workers are domestic workers and nannies. Many of them work in Canada, which has had a "live-in caregiver program" since 1992 to facilitate the importation of these migrants. Through this program, a Canadian employer (either an individual or employment agency) may apply through the Canadian Employment Office for a prospective employee. The employer must show that it has first tried to find a Canadian to do the job. The prospective employee must have six months of formal training or 12 months' experience in caregiving work and be in good health. If approved, the employee can gain temporary employment authorization for one year, and this can be extended for an additional year. A nanny must undergo a personal interview with Canadian consular officials and obtain security clearance. Once matched with an employer, she must notify the Ministry of Citizenship and Immigration if she wishes to change employers. After two years of live-in work, a nanny can apply for landed-immigrant status. She can then sponsor immediate family members to join her if they can prove they have a source of steady income. Three years after applying for landed-immigrant status, she can become a Canadian citizen.[23]

The film *Brown Women, Blonde Babies,* produced by Marie Boti, documents the conditions for Filipina migrant women working as domestics and nannies in Canada. Typically, women work around the clock, from 7 A.M. to 10 P.M. and beyond, and are always considered on call. They earn an average of $130 a month after taxes. Women who wish to leave their employers must persuade an immigration officer to let them. In response to one woman's pleas for release from an employer, one immigration officer coldly responded, "You didn't come here to be happy."

In stark contrast to the conditions revealed in this documentary, employers of domestic workers and nannies in Canada romanticize the work and the "opportunities" they offer to immigrant women. For example, *The Globe and Mail,* a Toronto newspaper, boasted that Canada is the first-choice destination for Filipina migrant workers, claiming:

> For the women themselves, improving their economic status helps them challenge the Philippines' traditional stereotype of women as submissive homemakers who need to rely on their husbands, fathers, or brothers to survive. The huge exodus of female contract workers from the country in the past decade has created a generation of women who are more confident and independent about their role in a society that has now been forced to ask some hard questions about many of its traditional paternalistic attitudes.[24]

Clearly, if Filipina women's roles in their society are subservient, as this statement implies, then those roles are not overturned but reinforced when migrant women are forced to serve as low-wage workers overseas instead of homemakers. The only difference is that they provide domestic services to employers in the North instead of their own families, while servicing their government's foreign debt at the same time.

According to the Kanlungan Foundation Centre, an advocacy group for Filipina migrant workers,

> We do not migrate as totally free and independent individuals. At times, we have no choice but to migrate, to brave the odds. . . . Even from the very start, we are already victims of illegal recruitment, victims of our government's active marketing of our cheap labor, . . . and suffering the backlash of states that fail to provide adequate support for childcare services, we enter first world countries that seek to preserve patriarchal ideology.[25]

This statement reflects migrant women workers' clear understanding that they are being used to maintain patriarchy in the First World, as governments in these wealthy nations cut social supports.

Just as employers try to justify exploiting servants by romanticizing the "opportunities" they provide these women, the Philippine government attempts to rationalize the trade in women by glorifying its migrant women exports: In 1988, on a state visit to Hong Kong, President Aquino declared migrant women the new heroes of the Philippine economy.[26] Since then, many officials have taken this up as the party line in justifying the trade in women. In response, the FDC states: "Because of their economic contributions, migrant workers are hailed by the administration as the new heroes, and labor export is elevated into a national policy, the appalling social costs and the prevalence of abuses notwithstanding."[27]

Women's Resistance

In July of 1994, Sarah Balagaban, a 15-year-old Filipina working as a maid in the United Arab Emirates (UAE), was raped at knifepoint by her employer. In self-defense, Balagaban stabbed and killed her rapist/employer and was sentenced to seven years in prison. In response to protests, Balagaban was retried, but was then sentenced to death. In outrage, many overseas Filipinas joined protests staged by Gabriela Network USA in front of the UAE mission and the Philippine government consulate in the United States. Again, Balagaban's sentence was revised. This time, she was sentenced to one year in prison and 100 lashes, and ordered to pay her deceased employer's family 150,000 dirhams, the equivalent of USD $41,995. Gabriela's Ninotchka Rosca speculates that the main reason the UAE government rescinded the death sentence was for fear of a walkout by the approximately 75,000 Filipina/os working in the UAE—a walkout that would paralyze the country.

Protests continued after this last sentence, with objections that 100 lashes could actually kill Balagaban. The Philippine government agreed to the final sentence over these protests, reinforcing outrage that the Philippine government refuses to protect its overseas workers and is clearly willing to sacrifice women's lives to maintain good relations with its chief trade partners. Many Filipinas working in the UAE have collected a scholarship fund for Balagaban to complete her education once she finishes her prison sentence. She had quit school in order to work in the UAE to support her parents and to help pay for her brother's education. Balagaban has since become a symbol for overseas Filipinas fighting for their rights.[28]

Teresita Tristan is a widow who left two children behind in the Philippines for a job in Britain as a domestic worker. Before leaving, she had been promised a salary of $400 a month, but when she arrived, her employers took her passport and informed her she would be paid $108 a month. On her first day in the country, she was taken for a medical exam, given medicine to clean her stomach, and was instructed to take a bath and not to touch the dishes with her bare hands until five days had passed. Her daily work consisted of cleaning the entire house, taking the children to school, and preparing the family's meals, while she ate leftovers. She was not allowed to eat from plates or glasses or to use the toilet inside the house. When her employer kept making sexual advances and asking her to go to the guest house with him, she asked to be released so she could return home. Instead, she was transferred to her employers' daughter's home, where she was likewise treated badly.[29]

One day Tristan went to the park and met an Englishwoman who took her phone number and called the police for her. The Commission for Filipina Migrant Workers helped her to leave her employer's home and find shelter. For many weeks, she feared that her employer would come to find her. Now, Tristan belongs to an organization of unauthorized workers fighting for migrant worker rights.

Tristan's story is typical of that of migrant workers, according to Kalayaan, an organization working for justice for overseas domestic workers in Britain. Between January 1992 and December 1994, Kalayaan interviewed 755 migrant domestic workers who had left their employers. The results of these interviews revealed widespread abuses of migrant domestic

workers from the Philippines, Sri Lanka, India, Ghana, Nigeria, Colombia, and Brazil. Eighty-eight percent had experienced psychological abuse, including name-calling, threats, and insults, and 38 percent had endured physical abuse of some form. Eleven percent had experienced attempted, threatened, or actual sexual assault or rape. A full 60 percent had received no regular meals, 42 percent had no bed, and 51 percent had no bedroom and were forced to sleep in a hallway, kitchen, bathroom, or storeroom. Thirty-one percent reported being imprisoned or not being allowed to leave the house. Ninety-one percent reported working for an average of 17 hours a day with no time off. Fifty-five percent were not paid regularly, and 81 percent were paid less than was agreed upon in their contracts, with an average monthly wage of USD $105.

A spokeswoman from Kalayaan says that these widespread abuses are made possible by British immigration law. In 1979, the British government abolished work permits for overseas domestic workers but continued to allow overseas employers and returning British residents to bring domestic workers into the country. This concession was granted to wealthy people returning from traveling abroad with employees. As Maria Gonzalez of the Commission on Filipina Overseas Domestic Workers puts it: "In the United Kingdom, migrant women are brought into the country like the baggage of their employers."[30] Migrant women enter with their employers' names stamped on their passports, and they cannot change employers after entering. Even in the rare case that a woman negotiates a contract with her employer, she has no bargaining power or legal recourse if the employer violates it.

Migrant workers have mobilized worldwide to expose these abuses and to fight for protection of their rights. Women in many "host" countries, including Canada, Japan, Britain, and the United States, have organized grassroots organizations to offer support and legal advocacy, and to lobby for the protection of Filipina and other migrant workers abroad. Kalayaan lobbies to change British law to allow migrant workers to receive permits directly, to change employers freely, and to stay and work in the country while pursuing legal action against former employers.

INTERCEDE is a similar organization, based in Toronto, that conducts research and advocacy for Filipina and Caribbean migrant domestic worker rights.

It provides direct services, such as individual counseling on labor and immigration rights and educational meetings and social activities to aid settlement, and lobbies the Canadian government. In 1981, INTERCEDE succeeded in convincing the Canadian Parliament to grant the rights of Canadian citizens under labor laws to foreign domestic workers on temporary visas.[31] Currently, INTERCEDE is pressuring the government to recognize domestic work as an occupation, to do away with the live-in requirement, and to allow immigrants to gain "landed-immigrant" status immediately upon entering Canada, instead of having to wait two years.

In the United States, healthcare workers (many of whom are migrant women) are the fastest-growing service workers. As some of the most exploited and, until recently, least organized workers, they are a prime target for labor organizers.[32] A recent victory by SEIU against the California government represents the fruits of a five-year struggle by the union on behalf of over 50,000 homecare workers in the state. In the summer of 1990, the California legislature and Governor Pete Wilson failed to reach an agreement on a budget, and the state stopped issuing paychecks. IHSS homecare workers were the first to feel the impact of the budget crisis—some workers' paychecks were delayed up to two months. During the budget impasse of 1992, workers suffered the same series of events.

SEIU brought a class-action suit against the State of California on behalf of more than 10,000 IHSS workers. SEIU argued that the workers suffered extreme hardship because of the delayed payments, including having electricity turned off in their homes and not having enough money for food, among other necessities. A U.S. District Court judge ruled on March 17, 1994, that the delayed payments violated the Fair Labor Standards Act. A settlement reached in May 1995 awarded damages of four million dollars, to be divided among the approximately 50,000 workers who joined the action.[33] This SEIU struggle represents a dramatic victory.

Josie Camacho points to the ongoing challenges of organizing homecare workers: First, there is no central workplace, with workers scattered among as many as 6,000 different worksites in a county. Second, some immigrant workers feel indebted to their employers and are reluctant to join the union. They are afraid and don't know their rights. This has challenged the union to recruit organizers who are multilingual and able to inform workers of their rights. Third, no party is willing to admit responsibility for, or can be held accountable for, the rights and protection of these workers. All parties, including both the sending and receiving countries' governments, employers, and employment agencies, evade or completely deny responsibility. Yet all benefit immensely from these workers' labor, extracting foreign currency, profits, savings, and care services.

Groups such as Kalayaan, INTERCEDE, and SEIU focus on organizing migrant workers and providing direct services to them in "host" countries while lobbying these "host" governments to change oppressive immigration and labor policies. Other organizations have a different emphasis, putting pressure on the Philippine government to recognize the impact of SAPs on poor women of the Third World at home and abroad. They aim to expose how the Philippine government facilitates the exportation of women migrant workers, sacrificing women in the futile effort to keep up with debt payments. Finally, they pressure the Philippine government to redirect expenditures away from debt servicing, to institute protections for migrant workers abroad, and to stop the export of women from the Philippines and other impoverished countries.

While many organizations focus on fighting for protections for migrant workers overseas, others propose that ultimately the global trafficking in women must stop. Gabriela Network has led the fight against the trade in Filipina and other migrant women. Gabriela accused the Philippine government of feeding young Filipinas into the sex industry in Japan after the Philippine government's policy prohibiting women under 23 years old from migrating to Japan to work as entertainers was found to have been violated 35 times within a four-month period. Gabriela found that the government made exceptions to the policy for four "favored" recruitment agencies.[34] Gabriela has called for the government to stop labor exportation as its chief economic strategy. The Philippine government denies that it participates in such a trade.[35]

Mainstream U.S. feminist responses to the trade in women have been lukewarm at best. When Gabriela called on women's organizations around the world to put the issue of global trafficking of women on their agendas, the National Organization for Women (NOW) declined to do so, stating that it does not deal with international issues.[36] The real issue may be that privileged women of the First World, even self-avowed feminists, are some of the primary consumers and beneficiaries in this trade. Middle- and upper-class professional women generally have not joined efforts to improve wages or conditions for care workers in the United States, since they have historically relied on the "affordability" of women of color and migrant women working in their homes, daycare centers, and nursing homes. . . .

Even among grassroots organizations fighting for justice for migrant women workers, it may prove difficult to develop a unified position or strategy. The effectiveness and viability of one strategy, imposing a ban on recruitment of Filipinas for migrant work, has been debated since such a ban was imposed by the Aquino administration in 1988. A coalition of 22 migrant worker groups in Hong Kong formed to press the Aquino government to repeal the ban, arguing that it hindered Filipinas' ability to secure employment, actually debilitating rather than protecting them.[37]

Almost ten years later, debate over the efficacy of the ban continues. Felicita Villasin, executive director of INTERCEDE and executive board member of the National Action Committee on the Status of Women (NAC) in Canada, says that a ban on migrant workers will only drive women to face greater danger and abuses as illegal migrants. Instead, she calls for structural changes in the Philippine economy that will make migration a choice and not a necessity. At least on this last point, Villasin asserts, there seems to be consensus among the women's groups involved in Filipina migrant worker struggles.

Asian/Pacific Islander and other women of color feminists in the First World would do well to take the lead from groups like INTERCEDE and many of our Third World sisters who have been mobilizing around the issues of SAPs and the traffic in women for years now. At the NGO Forum, many First World women remarked that they were the least well-informed or organized on global economic issues. Many First World feminists of color came home from the Forum resolved to undertake or redouble efforts to understand and expose the links between economic restructuring in the First World, SAPs in the Third World, and the global trade in women. . . .

In the United States, Miriam Ching Louie and Linda Burnham of the Women of Color Resource Center, returned from the NGO Forum committed to designing a popular education project, Women's

Education in the Global Economy (WEdGE). The project includes a curriculum and set of trainings focused on a broad range of global economic issues and trends affecting women: the global assembly-line; SAPs; women's unpaid, contingent, and informal work; welfare; environmental justice; women's human rights, sex trafficking, and migration; and organizing around these issues.[38]

SAPs and other economic restructuring policies affect Third World women in similar ways the world over, making survival more precarious, making women's unpaid labor burdens heavier, and exacerbating women's exploitation as low-wage workers both at home and abroad. First World variations of structural adjustment bring consequences that are less well-known but no less insidious. Walden Bello describes the effects of "welfare reform" as the domestic version of SAPs in the United States: In 1992, [with] the Republicans' assault on social welfare programs, the living standards of many Americans had deteriorated to Third World levels. Approximately 20 million U.S. residents lived in hunger, and infant mortality rates among African Americans reached rates higher than those of countries such as Jamaica, Trinidad, and Cuba.[39]

Bello says that the original intentions of SAPs were: first, to resubordinate the Third World—particularly those nations threatening to become developed—by crippling the authority of their governments and, second, to repress labor globally in order to free corporate capital from any hindrances to maximum profits. Clearly SAPs in the Philippines have been an uncontested success by these measures. The Philippine government has been unable to protect its own female citizens abroad and apparently has given up any intention of doing so. The trade in women from the Philippines has proven immensely profitable to the Philippine government and entrepreneurs, and highly "economical" to the governments that recruit them and the elites who employ them. Yet the struggles and triumphs of women like Balagaban and Tristan, and groups such as Kalayaan, INTERCEDE, Gabriela, and SEIU stand as testament to the ability of women to resist this global assault on Third World women workers.

NOTES

This article is extracted from a chapter in my forthcoming book, *Gatekeeping and Housekeeping*. I would like to thank Luisa Blue, Josie Camacho, Mayee Crispin,

Ninotchka Rosca, Carole Salmon, and Felicita Villasin for sharing their great insights, expertise, and time in interviews. I am also indebted to Miriam Ching Louie and Linda Burnham for bravely leading the Women of Color Resource Center delegation to Huairou, and for their pioneering work on Women's Education in the Global Economy. I am grateful to Nathaniel Silva for his insights and comments in developing this piece.

1. Sparr, Pamela. *Mortgaging Women's Lives: Feminist Critiques of Structural Adjustment.* London: Zed Books, 1994.

2. Chang, Grace. "Disposable Nannies: Women's Work and the Politics of Latina Immigration." *Radical America* 26. 2 (October 1996): 5–20.

3. Testimony of Fatima. Workshop on the impact of SAPs, NGO Forum, September 2, 1995.

4. Testimony of Eileen Fernandez. Workshop on the impact of SAPs, NGO Forum, September 2, 1995.

5. Gabriela Workshop, NGO forum, September 3, 1995.

6. The "official" figures corroborate these first-hand testimonies of women in countries under structural adjustment: Between 1969 and 1985, per capita food production declined in 51 out of 94 developing countries. Simultaneously, access to food has been severely limited by increased food prices with the devaluation of local currencies under SAPs. Expenditures on education in all poor developing countries except India and China declined from 21 percent of national budgets in 1972 to 9 percent in 1988. Healthcare expenditures were also reduced from 5.5 percent to 2.8 percent of national budgets during this period. See UNICEF report cited by Peter Lurie, Percy Hintzen, and Robert A. Lowe, "Socioeconomic Obstacles to HIV Prevention and Treatment in Developing Countries: The Roles of the International Monetary Fund and the World Bank." *AIDS* 9(6): 542–543.

7. Testimony of Merceditas Cruz. Workshop on Migration and the Globalizing Economy, NGO Forum, September 6, 1995.

8. Testimony of Carmen. Organization of Free & United Women under Gabriela, NGO Forum.

9. Workshop on the Impacts of SAPs, NGO Forum, September 2, 1995.

10. Testimony of representative from International Organization of Prostitutes. Gabriela Workshop, NGO Forum, September 3, 1995.

11. Plenary on Globalization, NGO Forum, September 3, 1995.

12. This number does not include women who are trafficked or illegally recruited, those who migrate for marriage, students, or tourists who eventually become undocumented workers. Compiled by Kanlungan Center Foundation from Philippine Overseas Employment Administration (POEA) and Department of Labor and Employment (DOLE) statistics.

13. Vincent, Isabel. "Canada Beckons Cream of Nannies: Much-sought Filipinas Prefer Work Conditions." *The Globe and Mail.* 20 January 1996: A1, A6. Other authors address more extensively trafficking in women for the sex work, entertainment, and mail-order bride industries. See Rosca, Ninotchka. "The Philippines' Shameful Export." *The Nation.* 17 April 1995: 523–525; Kim, Elaine. "Sex Tourism in Asia: A Reflection of Political and Economic Equality." *Critical Perspectives of Third World America* 2.1 (Fall 1984): 215–231; *Sisters and Daughters Betrayed: The Trafficking of Women and Girls and the Fight to End It.* Video. Prod. Chela Blitt. Global Fund for Women.

14. "Flor Contemplación: Victim of Mismanaged Economy." Editorial. *PAID! (People Against Immoral Debt).* Newsletter of Freedom from Debt Coalition, April 1995: 7.

15. Kanlungan Center Foundation, Inc. fact sheet prepared for the 1995 UN Conference on Women.

16. Freedom from Debt Coalition, based on DOLE figures.

17. *Brown Women, Blonde Babies.* Film. Prod. Marie Boti. Multimonde Productions.

18. Rosca, Ninotchka. Personal interview. 29 April 1996.

19. Kilborn, Peter T. "Union Gets the Lowly to Sign Up: Home Care Aides Are Fresh Target." *New York Times.* 21 November 1995.

20. Ibid.

21. Camacho, Josie. Personal interview. 18 April 1996.

22. Kilborn, op cit.

23. Ms. Greenhill of the Canadian Consulate in Los Angeles, CA. Personal interview. December 1993; Vincent A1.

24. Vincent A6.

25. *A Framework on Women and Migration.* Kanlungan Center Foundation; prepared for the NGO Forum of 1995.

26. Rosca, Ninotchka. Personal interview. 29 April 1996.

27. Freedom from Debt Coalition, statement prepared for NGO Forum, 1995.

28. *Kapihan Sa Kanlungan: A Quarterly Digest of Migration News,* newsletter produced by Kanlungan Center Foundation. April–June 1995; Rosca, Ninotchka. Personal interview. 29 April 1996; Vincent A6.

29. Testimony, Workshop on Violence and Migration, NGO Forum, 1995.

30. Ibid.

31. Enloe, Cynthia. *Bananas, Beaches and Bases: Making Feminist Sense of International Politics.* Berkeley: University of California Press, 1989. 190.

32. Kilborn, op cit.

33. "Delayed Payment Case for Home Care Workers Settled with State for $4 Million." SEIU press release. May 30, 1995.

34. Press conference. National Press Club in Manila, Philippines, March 1994; "Gabriela Accuses Philippine

Government of Pimping." *Gabriela International Update.* August 1995.

35. Rosca, Ninotchka. Personal interview. 29 April 1996.

36. Ibid.

37. Enloe 188. Slowly, the Aquino government exempted one government after another from its requirements, and by 1989, 22 countries enjoyed exemption from the ban.

38. For information, contact: Women of Color Resource Center, 1611 Telegraph Ave., Suite 303, Oakland, CA 94612.

39. Bello, Walden, Shea Cunningham, and Bill Rau. *Dark Victory: The United States, Structural Adjustment and Global Poverty.* London: Pluto Press and Food First and Transnational Institute, 1994.

FIFTY-FIVE

The Border Patrol State

Leslie Marmon Silko

I used to travel the highways of New Mexico and Arizona with a wonderful sensation of absolute freedom as I cruised down the open road and across the vast desert plateaus. On the Laguna Pueblo reservation, where I was raised, the people were patriotic despite the way the U.S. government had treated Native Americans. As proud citizens, we grew up believing the freedom to travel was our inalienable right, a right that some Native Americans had been denied in the early twentieth century. Our cousin, old Bill Pratt, used to ride his horse 300 miles overland from Laguna, New Mexico, to Prescott, Arizona, every summer to work as a fire lookout.

In school in the 1950s, we were taught that our right to travel from state to state without special papers or threat of detainment was a right that citizens under communist and totalitarian governments did not possess. That wide open highway told us we were U.S. citizens; we were free. . . .

Not so long ago, my companion Gus and I were driving south from Albuquerque, returning to Tucson after a book promotion for the paperback edition of my novel *Almanac of the Dead.* I had settled back and gone to sleep while Gus drove, but I was awakened when I felt the car slowing to a stop. It was nearly midnight on New Mexico State Road 26, a dark, lonely stretch of two-lane highway between Hatch and Deming. When I sat up, I saw the headlights and emergency flashers of six vehicles—Border Patrol cars and a van were blocking both lanes of the highway. Gus stopped the car and rolled down the window to ask what was wrong. But the closest Border Patrolman and his companion did not reply; instead,

the first agent ordered us to "step out of the car." Gus asked why, but his question seemed to set them off. Two more Border Patrol agents immediately approached our car, and one of them snapped, "Are you looking for trouble?" as if he would relish it.

I will never forget that night beside the highway. There was an awful feeling of menace and violence straining to break loose. It was clear that the uniformed men would be only too happy to drag us out of the car if we did not speedily comply with their request (asking a question is tantamount to resistance, it seems). So we stepped out of the car and they motioned for us to stand on the shoulder of the road. The night was very dark, and no other traffic had come down the road since we had been stopped. All I could think about was a book I had read—*Nunca Más*—the official report of a human rights commission that investigated and certified more than 12,000 "disappearances" during Argentina's "dirty war" in the late 1970s.

The weird anger of these Border Patrolmen made me think about descriptions in the report of Argentine police and military officers who became addicted to interrogation, torture and the murder that followed. When the military and police ran out of political suspects to torture and kill, they resorted to the random abduction of citizens off the streets. I thought how easy it would be for the Border Patrol to shoot us and leave our bodies and car beside the highway, like so many bodies found in these parts and ascribed to "drug runners."

Two other Border Patrolmen stood by the white van. The one who had asked if we were looking for trouble ordered his partner to "get the dog," and from the back of the van another patrolman brought a small female German shepherd on a leash. The dog apparently did not heel well enough to suit him, and the handler jerked the leash. They opened the doors of our car and pulled the dog's head into it, but I saw immediately from the expression in her eyes that the dog hated them, and that she would not serve them. When she showed no interest in the inside of our car, they brought her around back to the trunk, near where we were standing. They half-dragged her up into the trunk, but still she did not indicate any stowed-away human beings or illegal drugs.

Their mood got uglier; the officers seemed outraged that the dog could not find any contraband, and they dragged her over to us and commanded her to sniff our legs and feet. To my relief, the strange violence the Border Patrol agents had focused on us now seemed shifted to the dog. I no longer felt so strongly that we would be murdered. We exchanged looks—the dog and I. She was afraid of what they might do, just as I was. The dog's handler jerked the leash sharply as she sniffed us, as if to make her perform better, but the dog refused to accuse us: She had an innate dignity that did not permit her to serve the murderous impulses of those men. I can't forget the expression in the dog's eyes; it was as if she were embarrassed to be associated with them. I had a small amount of medicinal marijuana in my purse that night, but she refused to expose me. I am not partial to dogs, but I will always remember the small German shepherd that night.

Unfortunately, what happened to me is an everyday occurrence here now. Since the 1980s, on top of greatly expanding border checkpoints, the Immigration and Naturalization Service and the Border Patrol have implemented policies that interfere with the rights of U.S. citizens to travel freely within our borders. I.N.S. agents now patrol all interstate highways and roads that lead to or from the U.S.-Mexico border in Texas, New Mexico, Arizona and California. Now, when you drive east from Tucson on Interstate 10 toward El Paso, you encounter an I.N.S. check station outside Las Cruces, New Mexico. When you drive north from Las Cruces up Interstate 25, two miles north of the town of Truth or Consequences, the highway is blocked with orange emergency barriers, and all traffic is diverted into a two-lane Border Patrol checkpoint—ninety-five miles north of the U.S.-Mexico border.

I was detained once at Truth or Consequences, despite my and my companion's Arizona driver's licenses. Two men, both Chicanos, were detained at the same time, despite the fact that they too presented ID and spoke English without the thick Texas accents of the Border Patrol agents. While we were stopped, we watched as other vehicles whose occupants were white—were waved through the checkpoint. White people traveling with brown people, however, can expect to be stopped on suspicion they work with the sanctuary movement, which shelters refugees. White people who appear to be clergy, those who wear ethnic clothing or jewelry and women with very long hair or very short hair (they could be nuns) are also frequently detained; white men with beards or men with long hair are more likely to be detained, too, because Border Patrol agents have "profiles" of "those sorts" of white people who may help political refugees. (Most of the political refugees from Guatemala and El Salvador are Native American or mestizo because the indigenous people of the Americas have continued to resist efforts by invaders to displace them from their ancestral lands.) Alleged increases in illegal immigration by people of Asian ancestry means that the Border Patrol now routinely detains anyone who appears to be Asian or part Asian, as well.

Once your car is diverted from the Interstate Highway into the checkpoint area, you are under the control of the Border Patrol, which in practical terms exercises a power that no highway patrol or city patrolman possesses: They are willing to detain anyone, for no apparent reason. Other law-enforcement officers need a shred of probable cause in order to detain someone. On the books, so does the Border Patrol; but on the road, it's another matter. They'll order you to stop your car and step out; then they'll ask you to open the trunk. If you ask why or request a search warrant, you'll be told that they'll have to have a dog sniff the car before they can request a search warrant, and the dog might not get there for two or three hours. The search warrant might require an hour or two past that. They make it clear that if you force them to obtain a search warrant for the car, they will make you submit to a strip search as well.

Traveling in the open, though, the sense of violation can be even worse. Never mind high-profile cases like that of former Border Patrol agent Michael

Elmer, acquitted of murder by claiming self-defense, despite admitting that as an officer he shot an "illegal" immigrant in the back and then hid the body, which remained undiscovered until another Border Patrolman reported the event. (Last month, Elmer was convicted of reckless endangerment in a separate incident, for shooting at least ten rounds from his M-16 too close to a group of immigrants as they were crossing illegally into Nogales in March 1992.) Or that in El Paso, a high school football coach driving a vanload of his players in full uniform was pulled over on the freeway and a Border Patrol agent put a cocked revolver to his head. (The football coach was Mexican-American, as were most of the players in his van; the incident eventually caused a federal judge to issue a restraining order against the Border Patrol.) We've a mountain of personal experiences like that which never make the newspapers. A history professor at U.C.L.A. told me she had been traveling by train from Los Angeles to Albuquerque twice a month doing research. On each of her trips, she had noticed that the Border Patrol agents were at the station in Albuquerque scrutinizing the passengers. Since she is six feet tall and of Irish and German ancestry, she was not particularly concerned. Then one day when she stepped off the train in Albuquerque, two Border Patrolmen accosted her, wanting to know what she was doing, and why she was traveling between Los Angeles and Albuquerque twice a month. She presented identification and an explanation deemed "suitable" by the agents, and was allowed to go about her business.

Just the other day, I mentioned to a friend that I was writing this article and he told me about his 73-year-old father, who is half Chinese and had set out alone by car from Tucson to Albuquerque the week before. His father had become confused by road construction and missed a turnoff from Interstate 10 to Interstate 25; when he turned around and circled back, he missed the turnoff a second time. But when he looped back for yet another try, Border Patrol agents stopped him and forced him to open his trunk. After they satisfied themselves that he was not smuggling Chinese immigrants, they sent him on his way. He was so rattled by the event that he had to be driven home by his daughter.

This is the police state that has developed in the southwestern United States since the 1980s. No person, no citizen, is free to travel without the scrutiny of the Border Patrol. In the city of South Tucson, where 80 percent of the respondents were Chicano or Mexicano, a joint research project by the University of Wisconsin and the University of Arizona recently concluded that one out of every five people there had been detained, mistreated verbally or nonverbally, or questioned by I.N.S. agents in the past two years.

Manifest Destiny may lack its old grandeur of theft and blood—"lock the door" is what it means now, with racism a trump card to be played again and again, shamelessly, by both major political parties. "Immigration," like "street crime" and "welfare fraud," is a political euphemism that refers to people of color. Politicians and media people talk about "illegal aliens" to dehumanize and demonize undocumented immigrants, who are for the most part people of color. Even in the days of Spanish and Mexican rule, no attempts were made to interfere with the flow of people and goods from south to north and north to south. It is the U.S. government that has continually attempted to sever contact between the tribal people north of the border and those to the south.* . . .

It is no use; borders haven't worked, and they won't work, not now, as the indigenous people of the Americas reassert their kinship and solidarity with one another. A mass migration is already under way; its roots are not simply economic. The Uto-Aztecan languages are spoken as far north as Taos Pueblo near the Colorado border, all the way south to Mexico City. Before the arrival of the Europeans, the indigenous communities throughout this region not only conducted commerce, the people shared cosmologies, and oral narratives about the Maize Mother, the Twin Brothers and their Grandmother, Spider Woman, as well as Quetzalcoatl the benevolent snake. The great human migration within the Americas cannot be stopped; human beings are nat-

*The Treaty of Guadalupe Hidalgo, signed in 1848, recognizes the right of the Tohano O'Odom (Papago) people to move freely across the U.S.-Mexican border without documents. A treaty with Canada guarantees similar rights to those of the Iroquois nation in traversing the U.S.-Canadian border.

ural forces of the Earth, just as rivers and winds are natural forces.

Deep down the issue is simple: The so-called "Indian Wars" from the days of Sitting Bull and Red Cloud have never really ended in the Americas. The Indian people of southern Mexico, of Guatemala and those left in El Salvador, too, are still fighting for their lives and for their land against the "cavalry" patrols sent out by the governments of those lands. The Americas are Indian country, and the "Indian problem" is not about to go away.

One evening at sundown, we were stopped in traffic at a railroad crossing in downtown Tucson while a freight train passed us, slowly gaining speed as it headed north to Phoenix. In the twilight I saw the most amazing sight: Dozens of human beings, mostly young men, were riding the train; everywhere, on flat cars, inside open boxcars, perched on top of boxcars, hanging off ladders on tank cars and between boxcars. I couldn't count fast enough, but I saw fifty or sixty people headed north. They were dark young men, Indian and mestizo; they were smiling and a few of them waved at us in our cars. I was reminded of the ancient story of Aztlán, told by the Aztecs but known in other Uto-Aztecan communities as well. Aztlán is the beautiful land to the north, the origin place of the Aztec people. I don't remember how or why the people left Aztlán to journey farther south, but the old story says that one day, they will return.

◆◆◆

La Migra

Pat Mora

I
Let's play *La Migra*
I'll be the Border Patrol.
You be the Mexican maid.
I get the badge and sunglasses.
You can hide and run,
but you can't get away
because I have a jeep.
I can take you wherever
I want, but don't ask
questions because
I don't speak Spanish.
I can touch you wherever
I want but don't complain
too much because I've got
boots and kick—if I have to,
and I have handcuffs.
Oh, and a gun.
Get ready, get set, run.

II
Let's play *La Migra*
You be the Border Patrol.
I'll be the Mexican woman.
Your jeep has a flat,
and you have been spotted
by the sun.
All you have is heavy: hat,
glasses, badge, shoes, gun.
I know this desert,
where to rest,
where to drink.
Oh, I am not alone.
You hear us singing
and laughing with the wind,
Agua dulce brota aquí,
aquí, aquí, but since you
can't speak Spanish,
you do not understand.
Get ready.

La migra: term along the border for Border Patrol agents

Agua dulce brota aquí, aquí, aquí: sweet water gushes here, here, here

FIFTY-SEVEN

Seattle Declaration

Diverse Women for Diversity

We, Diverse Women for Diversity, diverse in culture, race, religion, socio-economic conditions, have one common goal: biological and cultural diversity as the foundation of life on earth. Therefore we stand for self-sufficiency, self-reliance and solidarity, locally and globally.

For this reason we have gathered in Seattle in November 1999 to struggle against the WTO.

The WTO was created to further and stabilize the freedom of trade and profit on behalf of a few multinationals. Going far beyond this goal, however, it acts as a new World Government.

The WTO is a non-elected institution, based on secrecy and non-representation. It erodes the substance of democracy in our countries. Through its rules it imposes economic policies in favor of gigantic global corporate interests.

The WTO promises to create growth and wealth for all, equality, jobs, ecological sustainability through a "free globalized market."

The reality, however, is that the free market mechanism has led to increased poverty, to more unemployment, to more ecological destruction, and more violence against women, children and [subordinated peoples].

Our food and agricultural system has been brought under corporate control of global grain merchants like Cargill and ADM through WTO Agreements on Agriculture. This has robbed women and peasant producers of their livelihood and has denied consumers worldwide access to sufficient, safe and healthy food.

The WTO rejects precautionary principle and thus allows corporations like Monsanto (USA), Novartis (Switzerland), DuPont (USA), Astrazeneca (UK/Netherlands) and Aventis (Germany) to spread genetically modified seeds and foods without people's knowledge and consent, thus creating unprecedented ecological and health hazards. These corporations are a danger to life on earth.

For thousands of years, indigenous people, women and men have protected, nurtured and sustained the Biodiversity of food, crops and medicinal plants. This rich Biodiversity is now being stolen by monopolistic "life science" corporations, under the legal protection of the Agreement on Trade Related Intellectual Property Rights (TRIPs). TRIPs forces countries to introduce patents on life and promotes the piracy of millennia of innovation and creativity by millions of women and peasants through the privatization of traditional knowledge.

After the Multilateral Agreement on Investment was defeated by worldwide citizens' resistance in December 1998, the same proponents of unlimited free markets are now pushing for a new round of negotiation on the same issue in WTO. They also include new areas for liberalization, namely, TRIMs Services [Trade Related Investment Measures], Investment, Public Procurement and Competition. All these areas, if further liberalized, will have further negative effect, particularly on women.

In summary, this so called "free market" system is indeed a global war system, based on violence against nature, humanity, especially women and children.

Together with the thousands of children, women and men gathered here in Seattle, we, Diverse Women for Diversity, reject this global war system and the WTO. We pledge to build an economy and a society where nature and human beings can live and prosper in peace and happiness.

Seattle, 1st December 1999

10

◆◆◆

Women, Crime, and Criminalization

In the mid-1990s, movie audiences were entertained by a new Hollywood depiction of women
as violent criminals. *Thelma and Louise* (two White
women run from the police after one kills the man
who tried to rape the other), *Set It Off* (four young
Black women in dire straits go on a spree of bank
robberies), and *Bound* (two White lesbians try to steal
$2 million from the Mob), among others, introduced
images of women—Black and White, heterosexual
and lesbian, working class and middle class—seeking revenge, money, fun, a sense of being in charge,
adventure, and even "liberation" through criminal
activity. Many moviegoers reacted with approval

and excitement to these images of women breaking
out of stereotypical roles, no longer the moll, sister,
mother, or wife of the main character, a criminal
man. In reality, the life stories of women in the United
States who commit crimes and who are caught up
in the criminal justice system are very different. Some
steal from stores, bounce checks, use stolen credit
cards, and use illegal drugs; some are pickpockets
and small-scale drug dealers; some are simply in
the wrong place at the wrong time. They are disproportionately Latina and African American, and most
are poor.

The National Context: "Get Tough on Crime"

The number of people imprisoned in the United
States has been growing for the past thirty years. Ap-
proximately 330,000 people were in prison in 1972.
The incarceration rate increased rapidly during the

This chapter was originally written by Barbara Bloom,
MSW, Ph.D., a criminal justice consultant and researcher
specializing in the development and evaluation of programs serving girls and women under criminal justice
supervision; it has been edited, adapted, and updated by
Gwyn Kirk and Margo Okazawa-Rey.

1990s. At the end of 1998 there were 461 people in jails and prisons per 100,000 population. By 2000 this had grown to 699 prisoners per 100,000, the highest rate in the world (The Sentencing Project 2001). Indeed, according to organizer and writer Anannya Bhattacharjee (2002), "The entire apparatus of law enforcement in the United States has expanded dramatically, becoming more punitive, highly integrated, heavily funded, and technologically sophisticated" (p. 1). The criminalization of women must be understood in this pro-punishment context. In the 1988 presidential election, the Republican candidate George Bush used the case of Willie Horton, a Black inmate from a Massachusetts prison who committed murder while out of prison on the state's furlough program, to establish street crime—burglary, auto theft, mugging, murder, and rape committed by strangers—as one of the most important national issues. This tactic implied that Black people, especially men, were the ones to fear most. Since then, politicians and the media have reinforced that view by promoting and reporting on legislation such as the "three-strikes-you're-out" law, which requires a life sentence without parole for three-time felons, and by continually publicizing crime stories, particularly high-profile cases such as those involving murder and abduction of children. This trend continues although national and many local crime statistics show a decline in crime rates. According to the U.S. Department of Justice (2002), both violent crimes and property crimes are at their lowest since 1973.

This "get tough on crime" rhetoric taps into people's sense of futility and fear—especially White people's fear of people of color. People are led to believe that no one is safe from street crime anywhere, but especially around African American and Latino men, and that everyone labeled "criminal" is an incorrigible street tough or "gangsta." Contrary to this rhetoric, the facts show that women are least safe in their own homes or with male friends (as we argued in Chapter 6) and that the greatest economic losses from crime do not happen on the street. According to Alexander Lichtenstein and Michael Kroll (1996), "Society's losses from 'white collar crime' far exceed the economic impact of all burglaries, robberies, larcenies, and auto thefts combined" (p. 20). Nonetheless, high-income criminals who commit such crimes as fraud and embezzlement are not only less likely to be incarcerated but also less likely even to be considered hardened criminals; rather, they may be re-

garded as people who used bad judgment or went "off track" (Sherrill 1997). The year 2002 saw an unprecedented number of corporate scandals, most notably Enron, but also including Adelphia Communications, Rite Aid, and Martha Stewart. Dozens of corporate executives, financial analysts, regulators, and politicians were accused of greed, fraud, conflict of interest, or indifference; several were charged and others are under investigation.

According to Human Rights Watch (1999a), "get tough" anticrime policies, which have enjoyed significant public support, have become the vehicle for abusive policies and constitutional rights violations, documented by international human rights monitors. Although the United States regards itself highly in the area of human rights, "Both federal and state governments have nonetheless resisted applying to the U.S. the standards that, rightly, the U.S. applies elsewhere" (Human Rights Watch 1999a, p. 1). Since the attacks on the World Trade Center and the Pentagon on September 11, 2001, Congress has passed two far-reaching pieces of legislation with regard to civil rights. The Uniting and Strengthening America by Providing Appropriate Tools Required to Intercept and Obstruct Terrorism Act (USA PATRIOT Act) became law on October 26, 2001, and greatly increases the government's powers. It includes measures that

- allow for indefinite detention of noncitizens who are not terrorists on minor visa violations.
- minimize judicial supervision of federal telephone and Internet surveillance by authorities.
- expand the government's powers to conduct secret searches.
- give the attorney general and the secretary of state the power to designate domestic groups as terrorist organizations and deport any noncitizens who belong to them.
- give the FBI access to business records about individuals without having to show evidence of a crime.
- lead to large-scale investigation of U.S. citizens for "intelligence" purposes. (American Civil Liberties Union 2002b)

The Homeland Security Act, signed into law on November 25, 20002, involves the creation of a new Department of Homeland Security. Among its sweeping provisions, the Act authorizes the collection of data on individuals and groups, including databases that combine personal, governmental and corporate records, including e-mails and Web sites viewed. It also allows more latitude for government advisory committees to meet in secret, if deemed "national-security related" (Chaddock 2002).

Women in the Criminal Justice System

I stood with my forehead pressed as close as possible to the dark, tinted window of my jail cell. The window was long and narrow, the foot-deep wall that framed it made it impossible to stand close. The thick glass blurred everything outside. I squinted and focused, and I concentrated all my attention on the area where my mother said the family would stand and wave. . . . It would be good to see my grandparents and my mother, but it was my daughter I really wanted to see. My daughter who would be two years old in two months.

A couple of minutes passed, and in that small space of time, I rethought my entire life and how it had come to this absurd moment, when I became a twenty-one-year-old girl in jail on a drug charge, a mother who had to wait for someone to bring my own daughter to glimpse me. I could not rub my hands across her fat, brown cheeks, or plait her curly hair the way I like it. *(Gaines 1994, p. 1)*

In 1998 over 140,000 women were incarcerated in jails—where people are held before trial and when convicted of a misdemeanor with a sentence of less than one year—and prisons—where people convicted of felony charges and serving more than a one-year sentence are held. Another 800,000 were on probation or parole, being "supervised" in the community (Bureau of Justice Statistics 2000).

Historically, women offenders were ignored by researchers and media reports because their numbers were small in comparison with those of men. During the 1990s, however, the rate of growth in women's imprisonment far outstripped that of men's. Between 1990 and 1997, there was a 49 percent increase among men and a 71 percent increase among women. In 1980 there were roughly 12,000 women in state and federal prisons compared with approx-

imately 84,000 in 1998 (Bureau of Justice Statistics 1999a), an increase of 88 percent between 1990 and 1998. In 1998 women were 16 percent of the total number involved in the criminal justice system (Bureau of Justice Statistics 2000). There are ten times more incarcerated women in the United States than in Western Europe. Indeed, the United States leads the world in women's incarceration, but, according to criminologist Meda Chesney-Lind (2000), it is

> not alone in the mania to imprison. . . . Women's cell space in Canada has tripled since 1992; in Great Britain, the number of women in prison jumped nineteen percent between 1996 and 1997; and in New Zealand, the same two-year period showed a twenty percent increase. Essentially, it appears that around the world there is an increased willingness to incarcerate women. *(p. 7)*

In 1998 almost 1 million women were involved with the criminal justice system, or 1 woman for every 109 women in the U.S. population—nearly 1 percent of adult women (Bureau of Justice Statistics 2000). See Richie (1996), Rierden (1997), Ross (1993), Serna (1992), Stein (1991), and Watterson (1996) for firsthand accounts of women's experiences of incarceration. Shannon Murray (Reading 58) and Nancy Kurshan (Reading 59) describe prison life.

This dramatic increase in the imprisonment of women has been driven primarily by "the war on drugs" and mandatory sentencing for drug offenses (Scully 2002). The majority of female arrests are for drug offenses, such as possession and dealing, and crimes committed to support a drug habit, particularly theft and prostitution, sometimes referred to as drug-related crimes. About half of the women confined in state prisons had been using drugs, alcohol, or both at the time of the offense for which they were incarcerated (Bureau of Justice Statistics 2000). Between 1990 and 1997, the number of women serving time in state prisons doubled. This increase is also related to declining release rates and increasing time served. Almost 34 percent of women in state prisons and 72 percent in federal prisons have been convicted of drug-related offenses. Criminologist Stephanie Bush-Baksette (1999, p. 223) argues that the war on drugs targeted women intentionally. The sentencing guidelines, mandatory nature of the imprisonment laws, focus on first-time offenders, and mandatory minimums (prison sentences) for persons with prior felony convictions all brought more women into the criminal justice system and led to a tremendous increase in the number of incarcerated women.

Under current punishment philosophies and practices, women are also increasingly subject to criminalization of noncriminal actions and behaviors. For example, poor and homeless women—many of them mothers—are subject to criminalization as many cities pass ordinances prohibiting begging and sleeping in public places. Another disturbing trend has been the criminalization of HIV-positive women and pregnant drug-addicted women. For example, in 1992, a woman in North Carolina, allegedly HIV-positive, became entangled in the criminal justice system when she went to a public health facility for a pregnancy test. The test was positive, and she was arrested and prosecuted for "failure to follow public health warning." Her crimes were not advising her sexual partners of her HIV status and not using condoms whenever she had sexual intercourse (Cooper 1992; Seigel 1997). Although this may seem an extreme example, it is part of a growing trend, as discussed by legal scholar Dorothy Roberts in Reading 60. Pregnant women using illegal drugs are characterized as "evil women" and "bad mothers" who are willing to endanger the health of their unborn children in pursuit of drug-induced highs. There also has been a trend to arrest and prosecute these women for "the 'delivery' of controlled substances to their newborns; their alleged mode of 'delivery' to the newborn is through the umbilical cord between birth and the time the cord is cut" (Cooper 1992, p. 11).

Characteristics of Incarcerated Women

Women prisoners have a host of medical, psychological, and financial problems and needs. Substance abuse, compounded by poverty, unemployment, physical and mental illness, homelessness, and a history of sexual abuse, often propels women into a revolving cycle of life inside and outside jails and prisons. They are predominantly single heads of households, with at least two children under the age of 18. The majority of jailed and imprisoned women are high school graduates, but 60 percent of women in state prisons were not working full-time at the time of their arrest. About 37 percent of women had an income of less than $600 per month prior to arrest, and nearly 30 percent received welfare assistance. They frequently have histories of physical and sex-

ual abuse as children, adults, or both. Nearly 60 percent of women in state prisons report having been physically or sexually abused at least once at some time in their lives prior to incarceration (Bureau of Justice Statistics 2000).

The median age of women in prison is approximately 35; jailed women are a little younger, with an average age of 31. Nearly half of all women involved with the criminal justice system have never married. Approximately 70 percent have children under age 18. It is estimated that about 200,000 children under 18 are affected by the incarceration of their mothers (Bureau of Justice Statistics 2000). The majority of those children live with relatives, primarily grandparents, and approximately 10 percent of them are in foster care, a group home, or other social service agency. About 6 percent of women are pregnant when they are incarcerated. Most women in state prisons have a history of prior convictions (65 percent), and 19 percent had been convicted as juveniles (Bureau of Justice Statistics 2000).

Incarcerated women use more serious drugs and use them somewhat more frequently than do incarcerated men (Bureau of Justice Statistics 2000). The rate of HIV infection is higher for women prisoners than for men prisoners according to the Bureau of Justice Statistics (2000). An estimated 3.5 percent of the women report being HIV-positive, compared with 2.2 percent of the men. Nineteen percent of women in New York State prisons are HIV-positive (Lydersen 2001).

Offenses Committed by Women and Patterns of Arrest

Studies have consistently shown that women generally commit fewer crimes than men and that their offenses tend to be less serious, primarily nonviolent property offenses such as fraud, forgery, and theft, as well as drug offenses (Bloom, Chesney-Lind, and Owen 1994; Gilfus 1992; Pollack 1994). Notwithstanding movie images of violent female criminals, violent offenses committed by women continue to decline. When women do commit acts of violence, these are usually in self-defense against abusive spouses or partners. Forty-four percent of women who have committed murder have killed their abusive partners (Bureau of Justice Statistics 1999a).

Although it is commonly assumed that women addicts engage in prostitution to support their drug

Daily Life of Incarcerated Women

- Women prisoners spend on average 17 hours a day in their cells with 1 hour outside for exercise. By contrast, men prisoners spend on average 15 hours a day in their cells with 1.5 hours outside.

- Mothers in prison are less likely to be visited by their children than are fathers because women are sent away to other counties or remote areas of a state more often than men.

- A survey conducted in 38 states revealed that 58 percent of the prisons or jails serve exactly the same diet to pregnant prisoners as to others, and in most cases these meals do not meet the minimum recommended allowances for pregnancy.

- Many women come to prison pregnant; some become pregnant in prison. Few receive prenatal care and many pregnant prisoners suffer a high rate of miscarriage as a result. Congress has banned the use of federal funds for abortion in prison; women who can pay for an abortion themselves may be able to get one at a clinic, but will need to convince prison authorities to get them there. Women who carry their pregnancies to term are often treated inhumanely, denied prompt medical attention, and may be forced to undergo labor and childbirth in shackles (Siegal 1998).

- Health care for prisoners is totally inadequate. It is common practice for prisoners to be denied medical examinations and treatments outright. Incarcerated HIV-infected women have no access to experimental drug trials or the use of new drug protocols. The incidence and spread of HIV/AIDS, hepatitis C, tuberculosis, and other serious communicable diseases is reaching epidemic proportions in many prisons (Lydersen 2001).

- Menstruating women are given small quantities of sanitary products and have to buy more from the commissaries at grossly inflated prices (Lydersen 2001).

- Incarcerated women have specific needs stemming, in part, from the fact that they are responsible for children and that many have experienced sexual or physical violence. They are more likely to be addicted to drugs and to have mental illnesses than incarcerated men. In a National Institute of Justice study of correctional administrators, those in 17 states could name no women's programs that were effective or promising within their jurisdictions. Many of those who could point to existing education or health programs cited the need for more drug-treatment programs and mental health services (National Institute of Justice 1998).

- Sexual abuse of women inmates by male staff is common. This includes insults, harassment, rape, voyeurism in showers and during physical exams, and touching women's breasts and genitals during pat-downs and strip searches (Amnesty International USA 2000).

- It costs more to send a person to prison for a year than to an Ivy League university for a year.

Source: Prison Activist Resource Center 2003 (www.prisonactivist.org/women/), unless otherwise noted.

habits, their involvement in property crimes is even more common. In a sample of 197 female crack cocaine users in Miami, James Inciardi, Dorothy Lockwood, and Anne Pottieger (1993) found that in the women's last ninety days on the street, 76 percent had engaged in drug-related offenses, 77 percent had committed minor property crimes, and 51 percent had engaged in prostitution (p. 120). M. Douglas Anglin and Yih-Ing Hser (1987) found that the women in their sample supported their habits with a variety of crimes. Felony conviction data illustrate that women accounted for 41 percent of those convicted of forgery, fraud, and embezzlement in 1996 and for 17 percent of those convicted of drug offenses (Bureau of Justice Statistics 2000).

Sentence Length and Time Served

The Bureau of Justice Statistics (2000) provides some information on the length of women's sentences and the time they actually served. The average time served for those released in 1996 was 12 months. Violent offenders served an average of 20 months, property offenders 11 months, and drug offenders around 12 months. As found for sentencing, the average length of incarceration for women was less than that for men for every type of offense (Bureau of Justice Statistics 2000).

Because female prisoners tend to receive shorter sentences than men overall, it has been assumed by some researchers that women benefit from chivalrous treatment (a so-called chivalry factor) by sentencing judges. Although the chivalry factor does have some statistical support, there is more evidence that women may receive harsher sentences for some crimes or that women who do not fit traditional female stereotypes—such as butch lesbians—may receive more punitive sentences than men (Chesney-Lind 1987; Erez 1992). When women receive shorter sentences, this is due to gender differences in the offenses for which they are incarcerated, their criminal histories, whether they used violence, and the roles they played in the crime, such as whether they were accessories to men or were the "masterminds," and whether they acted alone.

Race and Class Disparities

Most women in the U.S. criminal justice system are marginalized by race and class. Poor women are pushed into the "underground economies" of drugs, prostitution, and theft as a way of supporting themselves and their children. African American women constitute 44 percent of women in jails, 48 percent in state prisons, and 35 percent in federal prisons; Latinas 15 percent of women in jails, 15 percent in state prisons, and 32 percent in federal prisons; White women 36 percent in jails, 33 percent in state prisons, and 29 percent in federal prisons (Bureau of Justice Statistics 2000). According to the Bureau of Justice Statistics (1998), young African American women

and Latinas have experienced the greatest rates of incarceration of all demographic groups studied. Women of color make up 21 percent of the general female population but 67 percent of the state prison population (Bureau of Justice Statistics 2000). According to writers and organizers Jael Stillman and Anannya Bhattacharjee (2002), "For the same offense, Black and Latina women are respectively eight and four times more likely to be incarcerated than white women" (p. xv).

Many crimes committed on Native American reservations are classified as federal offenses, and lawbreakers are held in federal prisons, usually in remote places long distances away from home and hard to get to by public transportation, two factors that increase the isolation of such prisoners.

Racial bias is a factor in arrests, pretrial treatment, and differential sentencing of women offenders. Professor of criminal justice Coramae Richey Mann (1995) documents disparity in prison sentences by comparing arrest rates with sentencing rates of women offenders in California, Florida, and New York. She found that, in all three states, women of color, particularly African Americans, were disproportionately arrested. The few studies that report race-specific differences indicate more punitive treatment of women of color. In their study of one Missouri institution over a sixteen-year period, Foley and Rasche (1979) found that, in general, African American women received longer sentences (55.1 months) than White women (52.5 months). They also discovered differences based on race in sentencing for the same offense. For example, White women imprisoned for murder served one-third less time than African American women for the same offense. In a study of gender differences in felony court processing in California in 1988, Farnsworth and Teske (1995) found that White women defendants were more likely to have charges of assault changed to nonassault than were women of color. In 1996 the issue of differential sentencing for cocaine use surfaced as a public issue. Currently the sentences for possession and use of crack cocaine, mainly used by poor people of color, are much higher than sentences for the possession of powdered cocaine, mainly used by middle- and upper-middle-class White people.

The "war on drugs," initiated by the Reagan administration in the 1980s, has been aggressively pursued in poor urban neighborhoods, especially poor

African American and Latino communities, and in Third World countries, despite the fact that White people make up the majority of drug users and traffickers. Proponents have justified massive government intervention as necessary to quell the drug epidemic, gang violence, and "narco-terrorism." However, critics charged that "Blacks, Latinos, and third world people are suffering the worst excesses of a program that violates . . . civil rights, human rights, and national sovereignty" (Lusane 1991, p. 4).

The declared intention to get rid of drugs and drug-related crime has resulted in the allocation of federal and state funding for more police officers on the streets, more federal law-enforcement officers, and more jails and prisons, rather than for prevention, rehabilitation, and education. Poor women of color have become the main victims of these efforts in two ways: They are trying to hold their families and communities together while so many men of color are incarcerated, and they are increasingly incarcerated themselves. As author, activist, and scholar Clarence Lusane (1991) observes, "The get-tough, mandatory-sentencing laws are forcing judges to send to prison first-time offenders who a short time ago would have gotten only probation or a fine. . . . It is inevitable that women caught selling the smallest amount of drugs will do time" (p. 56). As argued in Chapter 9, the international drug trade must be understood at the global level, as one way producer countries earn hard currency to repay foreign debt. Mandatory minimum prison sentences have had negligible effects on the drug trade in this country (Siegal 1998).

Girls in the Criminal Justice System

When people think of juvenile crime they often think of boys, but roughly two-thirds of incarcerated women were first arrested as juveniles, and about half of them spent time in detention when they were minors (Siegal 1995). Girls are likely to be held in detention for lesser offenses than boys, and a higher percentage of girls are in detention for offenses such as shoplifting, violations of probation and parole, minor public order disturbances, and driving without a license. African American girls are much more likely to be held in detention than White girls or Latinas. There are fewer options for girls as compared with boys in terms of rehabilitation and housing, so

girls spend more time in detention awaiting placement. The great majority of girls in the criminal justice system have been physically or sexually abused; many have learning disorders; many use drugs and alcohol (Chesney-Lind 1997). According to journalist Nina Siegal (1995), "Probation officers, counselors, and placement staffers prefer to work with boys because they say girls' problems are more complex and more difficult to address" (p. 16). Girls express more emotional needs than boys. "Middle-class girls with the same problems might end up in therapy, treatment programs, boarding schools, or private hospitals. But girls in Juvenile Hall have fallen through the system's proverbial safety net" (p. 17).

Dating from the 1890s, the early juvenile justice system held to the principle of rehabilitation, but the "get tough on crime" attitude has meant that many states have changed their approach. California, for example, has reduced the age at which minors can be tried as adults from 16 to 14 for 24 different crimes. The state has also changed the law on confidentiality so that the names of juvenile offenders can become public knowledge.

Women Political Prisoners

The International Tribunal on Human Rights Violations of Political Prisoners and Prisoners of War in the United States, held in New York City, December 1990, defined a political prisoner as "a person incarcerated for actions carried out in support of legitimate struggles for self-determination or for opposing illegal policies of the United States government" (Bin Wahad 1996, p. 277). A small but significant group of women in federal prisons is there as a result of such political activities, including members of the Puerto Rican Socialist Party, supporters of Native American sovereignty movements, and participants in Black revolutionary movements in the United States and abroad. Silvia Baraldini, who was given a forty-year sentence, is an Italian citizen, arrested on conspiracy charges arising out of militant political activities in solidarity with national liberation movements, including assisting in the escape of Black activist Assata Shakur. She was active in the women's movement and the anti–Vietnam War movement, and was a supporter of the national liberation movement in Zimbabwe. Laura Whitehorn and Marilyn Buck were charged with a number of bombings claimed by the Armed Resistance Unit and the Red Guerrilla Resistance (Browne 1996). Susan Rosenberg was involved in the student movement, the anti–Vietnam War movement, and the women's movement. According to Elihu Rosenblatt (1996), coordinator at the Prison Activist Resource Center, "She was targeted by the FBI for her support of the liberation of Assata Shakur from prison, and her support of the Black Liberation Army. After going underground in the 1980s she was arrested . . . in 1984, convicted of weapons possession, and sentenced to 58 years" (p. 355). From 1986 to 1988, Silvia Baraldini and Susan Rosenberg were held in the "High Security Unit" (HSU), a specially built underground prison for political prisoners in Lexington, Kentucky. Although this sixteen-bed prison housed no more than six women at a time, it became the center of intense scrutiny by national and international human rights organizations, including Amnesty International, and "became direct proof that political prisoners not only exist in the United States but are the targets of a well-organized counter-insurgency campaign" (O'Melveny 1996, p. 322). As a result of ongoing political pressure from activists and the Italian government, Silvia Baraldini was released to Italian authorities in 1999 so that she could return to Italy due to serious complications associated with cancer. Laura Whitehorn was released to a halfway house in 1999 having served a fourteen-year sentence.

Since about the mid-1950s, the federal government has operated "counter-insurgency programs," complete with special police forces and lockup facilities, to track, undermine, and destroy left-wing political organizations it deemed radical and militant and to imprison or kill activists. The Federal Bureau of Investigation (FBI) in its Counter Intelligence Programs (COINTELPRO) launched campaigns against the Communist Party in 1954 and, subsequently, against the Socialist Workers Party, the Puerto Rican independence movement, the Black Power Movement, particularly the Black Panther Party, and the American Indian Movement (AIM) in the 1960s and 1970s (Churchill 1992). Mumia Abu-Jamal, Leonard Peltier, and Geronimo Pratt were all convicted of murder, although they all claim to have been framed by the FBI. Geronimo Pratt was freed in 1997 after over twenty-five years in prison. A judge ruled that the evidence used to convict him had in-

deed been tampered with, as both Pratt and prison rights activists had been arguing all along (Booth 1997). Angela Davis, an internationally known scholar and activist, was imprisoned for two years on murder, conspiracy, and kidnapping charges but later acquitted.

Women jailed in the early 1900s for opposition to government policy were suffragists, whose crime was peacefully picketing the White House in their campaign for votes for women. In 1917, for example, hundreds of suffragists, mainly White, middle-class women, organized pickets around the clock. At first they were ignored by the police. By June they began to be arrested, and in August they received thirty-day and sixty-day sentences for obstructing traffic. A number of those who were jailed went on hunger strikes; they were forcibly fed and threatened with transfer to an insane asylum. They were released the following year by order of President Wilson, and the Washington, D.C., Court of Appeals ruled that their arrests, convictions, and imprisonment were illegal (Gluck 1976). This kind of political action was very different from that of revolutionary organizations committed to self-defense and armed struggle if necessary. But, like the sentences of political women prisoners active in the 1970s and '80s, suffragists also received disproportionately long sentences and harsh treatment, clearly intended to discourage this kind of sustained opposition to government policy. Activist and writer Julie Browne (1996) notes: "A Ku Klux Klansman, charged with violations of the Neutrality Act and with possessing a boatload of explosives and weapons to be used in an invasion of the Caribbean island of Dominica, received eight years. Yet Linda Evans [charged with bombings claimed by militant left-wing groups], convicted of purchasing four weapons with false ID, was sentenced to 40 years—the longest sentence ever imposed for this offense" (p. 285).

Another example of politically motivated incarceration was the internment of thousands of Japanese Americans in remote camps following the bombing of Pearl Harbor by Japanese troops during World War II, as described by Rita Takahashi in Reading 61. Most of these people were U.S. citizens, living in West Coast states. They were forced to leave their homes and property, and were kept in the camps for the duration of the war. In a similar move, authorities arrested some 1,500 men, mostly Arabs, after the attacks of September 11, 2001. Their names have not been released and their families do not know where they are. In addition, private citizens and various officials have committed acts of violence and harassment against Arab Americans, South Asians, and "people who look like Muslims." Reading 62 describes the case of Samar Kaukab, a U.S. woman of Pakistani descent, who was detained at Chicago's O'Hare International Airport in November 2001 and subjected to an unjustified, illegal, and degrading search by airport security personnel.

Theories of Women and Crime

There has been a lack of research specifically on women in conflict with the law in the United States. This is partly because until the 1980s far fewer women than men were caught up in the criminal justice system and also because it is difficult for researchers to obtain access to women in prison. Official data collected by the Bureau of Justice are limited and often date back several years by the time they are published, a limitation of the data cited in this chapter.

Theories of female criminality have been developed primarily from two strands of thought. The first approach is taken by those who attempt to explain female criminality in individual terms. These theories often apply assumptions and stereotypes about the "female psyche" that are blatantly sexist and without much evidence to support their claims. They include biological arguments—for example, that women commit crimes as a result of premenstrual syndrome (PMS)—and psychological notions—that "hysterical" women behave criminally, or that women are conniving and manipulative, and so resort to using poison rather than a gun to kill a person.

The second approach applies traditional theories of crime, developed to explain male criminality, to women. These include theories of *social learning* (crime is learned), *social process* (individuals are affected by institutions such as the family, school, and peers), and *social structure* (individuals are shaped by structural inequalities), and *conflict theory*, a specific social structure theory, which generally claims that the law is a weapon of social control used by the powerful against the less powerful (Turk 1995).

An apparent increase in female crime in the 1960s and '70s prompted new theories attributing female criminality to the women's liberation movement. The female offender was identified as its "dark side" (Chesney-Lind 1986). The phenomenon of girls in gangs has also been blamed on the women's movement (Chesney-Lind and Shelden 1992). Sociologist Freda Adler (1975), for example, proposed that women were committing an increasing number of violent crimes because the women's movement had created a liberated, tougher class of women, a view that became known as the "masculinity thesis." Similarly, criminologist Rita Simon (1975) argued that a rise in women's involvement in property crimes, such as theft, embezzlement, and fraud, was due to women entering previously male occupations, such as banking and business, and to their consequent exposure to opportunities for crime that were previously the preserve of men. This theory is called the "opportunity thesis." Neither of these theses is supported by much empirical evidence.

A third theory of female criminality, the "economic marginalization thesis," posits that it is the absence, rather than the availability, of employment opportunity for women that appears to lead to increases in female crime (Giordano, Kerbel, and Dudley 1981; Naffine 1987). According to this view, most crime committed by women is petty property crime, such as theft, a rational response to poverty and economic insecurity. The increasing numbers of single women supporting dependent children mean that more women may risk the benefits of criminal activity as supplements or alternatives to employment (Rafter 1990). Noting that the majority of female offenders are low-income women who committed nonemployment-related crimes, rather than middle- and upper-middle-class professional women who committed employment-related crimes, proponents of economic marginalization theory argue that the feminization of poverty, not women's liberation, is the social trend most relevant to female criminality.

Feminist scholars have attempted to explain crime, gender differences in crime rates, and the exploitation of female victims from different perspectives. Some view the cause of female crime as originating in male supremacy, which subordinates women through male domination and aggression, and in men's efforts to control women sexually. Such scholars attempt to show how physical and sexual victimization of girls and women can be underlying causes of criminal behavior (Chesney-Lind 1995;

Owen and Bloom 1995). They argue that the exploitation of women and girls causes some to run away or to begin abusing drugs at an early age, which often leads to criminal activity.

Other feminists view gender inequality as stemming from the unequal power of women and men in a capitalist society (Connell 1990; Messerschmidt 1986). They trace the origins of gender differences to the development of private property and male domination over the laws of inheritance, asserting that within the current economic system, men control women economically as well as socially. Such theorists argue that women commit fewer crimes than men because women are isolated in the family and have fewer opportunities to engage in white-collar crimes or street crimes. Because capitalism renders women relatively powerless both in the home and in the economic arena, any crimes they commit are less serious, nonviolent, self-destructive crimes such as drug possession and prostitution. Moreover, women's powerlessness also increases the likelihood that they will be the target of violent acts, usually by men.

Yet other feminist scholars foreground racism in explaining the disproportionately high incarceration rates for people of color and "assaults and searches by police, the Immigration and Naturalization Service (INS), and border patrol forces [which are] daily occurrences in communities of color" (Silliman and Bhattacharjee 2002, p. x). They focus on community experiences of state violence, including the incarceration of people of color, police brutality, and women's struggles to keep their families and communities intact in the face of arrests, harassment, and raids by the police or INS, now the Department of Homeland Security.

"Equality with a Vengeance": Is Equal Treatment Fair Treatment?

Feminist legal scholars have been very concerned about women's treatment in the criminal justice system. Pollack (1994) asks, Are women receiving more equal treatment today? If equal treatment relates to equal incarceration, then the answer appears to be a resounding yes. More women offenders are likely to be incarcerated than at any other time in U.S. history. There is a continuing debate among feminist legal scholars about whether equality under the law is

necessarily good for women (Chesney-Lind 1995; K. Daly 1994). On the one hand, some argue that the only way to eliminate the discriminatory treatment and oppression that women have experienced in the past is to push for continued equalization under the law. Though equal treatment may hurt women in the short run, in the long run it is the only way to guarantee that women will be treated as equal partners economically and socially. For example, legal scholar and professor of law Catharine MacKinnon (1987) states, "For women to affirm difference, when difference means dominance, as it does with gender, means to affirm the qualities and characteristics of powerlessness" (pp. 38–39). Even legal scholars who do not view women as an oppressed group conclude that women will be victimized by laws created out of "concern and affection" and designed to protect them.

In practice, gender-neutral sentencing reforms have aimed to reduce disparities in sentencing by punishing like crimes in the same way. Through this emphasis on parity and the utilization of a male standard, more women are being imprisoned (K. Daly 1994). New prison beds for women take the place of alternatives to prison, and gender-blind mandatory sentencing statutes, particularly for drug-law violations, have contributed to the rising numbers of women in prison. A Phoenix, Arizona, sheriff proudly boasted, "I don't believe in discrimination," after he established the first female chain gang in the United States, where women, whose work boots are chained together, pick up trash in downtown Phoenix (In Phoenix chain gangs for women 1996). This is what Lahey (1985) has called "equality with a vengeance."

Another effect of the equalization approach has been in the types of facilities women are sentenced to. For example, boot camps have become popular with prison authorities as an alternative to prison for juvenile and adult offenders. New York, for instance, operates a boot camp for women that is modeled on those for men. This includes uniforms, shorn hair, humiliation for behaviors considered to be disrespectful of staff, and other militaristic approaches.

Criminologist Pat Carlen (1989) argues that equality with men in the criminal justice system means more punitive measures applied to women. Instead, she advocates the supervision of women in noncustodial settings in their communities, where they can remain connected with their children and families, and calls for reducing the number of prison beds for women and using nonprison alternatives for all but the most dangerous offenders. She bases her argument on the fact that most women commit nonviolent crimes and are themselves victims of physical, sexual, and emotional abuse. Therefore, she claims, programs that acknowledge women's victimization and support their emotional needs are more appropriate than punitive measures.

The "Prison Industrial Complex"

Public policy, however, is going in the other direction, with an emphasis on incarceration. Currently there are more than 2 million people—women and men—in U.S. jails and prisons. Government funding for the building and operation of new jails and prisons has increased while funding for social services, education, welfare, and housing has been cut.

Some critics of the criminal justice system argue that this trend has created what they term the "prison industrial complex" (Browne 1996; Davis 1997; Walker 1996). Borrowing from the term "military industrial complex," coined by President Dwight Eisenhower in 1960, the phrase "prison industrial complex" refers to the increasingly interconnected relationship between private corporations, the public prison system, and public interests. The Corrections Corporation of America manages many prisons in this country. The construction and servicing of prisons and jails have become big business—indeed, the big growth industry of the 1990s (Walker 1996). Profits are being generated not only by architecture firms designing prisons, security companies supplying equipment, and food distribution companies providing food service but also, in part, by the direct and indirect exploitation of prisoners. For example, TWA and Best Western (the international motel chain) use prisoners to take calls from customers during times when there is an overflow, such as before holidays and certain vacation periods. Microsoft, Victoria's Secret, and Boeing are also using low-cost prison labor (Parenti 1999), as well as Starbucks and Nintendo (Barnett 2002). The prison industry employs some 500,000 people, more than any Fortune 500 corporation except General Motors transportation (Light 1999). This is being done for a number of reasons: It is difficult to attract regular workers for seasonal employment, prisoners do not have to be paid minimum wage or be covered by workers' compensation (a tax employers must pay for regular employees), and they cannot unionize (Lichtenstein and Kroll 1996). Telephone companies also profit because people outside jails and prisons are not allowed to call prisoners directly; prisoners are allowed only to call collect, which is one of the most expensive ways of making telephone calls. Telecommunications industry officials estimate that the corrections communications market generates about $1 billion annually, and it is expected to grow in the future (Walker 1996).

Inside/Outside Connections

The issue of crime and criminality is an important one for women because of the massive increase in the number of women who are serving time in U.S. jails and prisons and because the criminalization of women is one of the most dramatic ways in which gender, race, and class position shape women's lives. Many in this society are shielded from this reality because incarcerated women are literally locked away, behind bars, and out of sight. In many cases, they are considered disposable.

The societal assumptions that justify and reinforce this separation between "inside" and "outside" are that these are bad women, perhaps foolishly involved with criminal men, a little crazy from drink, drugs, or the pain of their lives, but that they must have done something *terrible* to end up in jail. Criminal and noncriminal women often share the same life situations. Many have experienced physical, sexual, and emotional abuse, racism, sexism, classism, and other forms of exploitation. Most women who commit crimes are economically marginalized, involved in drug and alcohol abuse, and single heads of households. The crimes they commit reflect their marginalization in our society and generally are a result of being poor, women of color, or both.

Women who have never been incarcerated can be allies to incarcerated and formerly incarcerated women by getting involved in advocacy organizations or by attending activities involving former prisoners and activists. Examples of organizations that support women in prison include Aid to Inmate Mothers (Montgomery, Ala.); California Coalition for Women Prisoners (San Francisco); Chicago Legal Advocacy for Incarcerated Mothers; Let's Start (St. Louis, Mo.); and the National Women's Law Center, Women in Prison project (Washington, D.C.). Women on the outside are working with women prisoners in literacy classes, creative writing projects, and theater projects (Fraden 2001; Troustine 2001) such as the Medea Project: Theater for Incarcerated Women (San Francisco) and the Women's Prison Book Project (Minneapolis), or supporting self-help groups run by prisoners, such as Convicted Women against Violence at the California Institution for Women. AIDS awareness programs for people in prison are sponsored by the ACLU National Prison Project (Washington, D.C.) and the AIDS in Prison Project (New York). Women in a maximum-security prison have organized HIV peer education (Members of the AIDS Counseling and Education Program of the Bedford Hills Correctional Facility 1998). Films by and about women who killed abusive partners include *Defending Our Lives* (Cambridge Documentary Films), which tells the story of Battered Women Fighting Back! a group of inmates at a prison in Framingham, Massachusetts. *From One Prison . . .* (Michigan Battered Women's Clemency Project) was produced in collaboration with women at a Michigan prison who are serving life or long-term sentences for killing their batterers.

Advocates for incarcerated women critique the inadequate provision of health care, drug treatment, and educational, therapeutic, and life-skills programs for incarcerated women. They also critique funding priorities of successive administrations that give a higher priority to building more jails and prisons than to education, social services, and welfare; they urge a fundamental redirection of these resources. The Rocky Mountain Peace and Justice Center's Prison Moratorium Project (Boulder, Colo.) challenges the idea that prisons can solve social problems based on poverty and inequality. It seeks to halt prison expansion and redirect resources toward the development of alternative sentencing, prevention, and treatment programs.

There is an enormous gap between organizations working on behalf of women in the criminal justice system and the wider women's movement. As mentioned in Chapter 6, there is a fundamental contradiction in seeking state solutions to the issue of domestic violence, when the state itself perpetrates violence, especially in communities of color. Andy Smith describes community-based approaches to domestic violence, rather than calling for stronger legal penalties against men who beat their partners (Reading 38). Anannya Bhattacharjee (2002) argues that "over time, the efforts of anti-violence organizations to develop working relationships with law enforcement agencies, coupled with their reliance on government funding, have restricted their ability to challenge a repressive state agenda" (p. 14). She notes that women of color have understood that "they cannot demand protection from law enforcement on the one hand and organize around police brutality on the other hand, as if dealing with separate entities" (p. 17). These very different assumptions about the role of the state have limited the formation of stronger coalition efforts to ensure safety and well-being for women and their communities.

◆◆◆

Questions for Reflection

As you read and discuss this chapter, consider these questions:

1. Why is there such attention by politicians and the media to street crimes?

2. Why are women so afraid of street crimes when they are least safe in the company of men they know?

3. Where is the prison nearest to where you live? Are men, women, or both incarcerated there? Who are they in terms of class, race, and age?

4. What do you know about prison conditions for women?

5. What conditions "outside" would compel a woman to think that a jail or prison is the best place for her to be?

Finding Out More on the Web

1. Research the work of organizations cited in this chapter. How are they working to support women in the criminal justice system? Try to find organizations that are active in your state.

2. Use your search engine to find out the financial and human costs each year of white-collar crime in the United States.

Taking Action

1. Analyze the way the news media reports crime, or analyze the portrayal of criminals in movies and TV shows. How are women who have committed crimes portrayed? Pay particular attention to issues of race and class.

2. Find out about the daily conditions for women in the jail or prison nearest to you.

3. Find out about activist groups in your area that support incarcerated women. What can you do on behalf of women in prison?

4. The USA PATRIOT Act allows law enforcement agencies access to information on students and to student records. Find out what steps your college or university has taken to provide information under the terms of this act.

FIFTY-EIGHT

Shannon's Story

Shannon Murray

I was born in Detroit Lakes, Minnesota, on September 21, 1969. I grew up in the Old Colony projects in South Boston. The neighborhoods in them days were quiet. The parents kept to themselves and the children were well behaved. We would play games like kick ball or Red Rover. There was a huge park across the street from the complex with a playground so there was always something to do.

My family consisted of my mother, my stepfather, my older sister Janine, and my younger brother Robbie. We were a close family that showed a lot of affection for each other. My parents were alcoholics so it was a struggle. We made the best of what we had. We weren't any worse off than other families; in some ways we had more. Somehow my parents managed to send me and my younger brother to Catholic school. In this way I felt more fortunate than others.

My sister and I are American Indians. My mother, stepfather, and brother are Irish. It was hard because my sister and I were often singled out. I've always felt different from everyone else at home and at school.

I first started smoking pot and drinking at the age of 12. By this time, I was more aware of the drug abuse in my neighborhood. The older teens would hang in the hallways smoking pot and drinking. I started to "use" to fit in. It also helped me to escape the feelings I had surrounding my parents' alcoholism.

My first arrest was at the age of 16 for drinking in public. Over the next four years I was able to avoid the arms of the law. I was put into Protective Custody a few times for disorderly conduct. By this time I was drinking and drugging daily. My disease had taken over. I supported my habits by baby-sitting and selling pot. I dropped out of school in the tenth grade because it was getting in the way of me partying the way I wanted to. I had a few jobs here and there but was unable to hold one because they also got in the way of my using.

After I had my daughter Jaquelin at the age of 18, I started smoking coke more and more often. I had used before that but I stopped during my pregnancy, only smoking pot because I was more afraid of the effects coke could have on my baby than the effect of pot.

The cocaine caused me to lose custody of my daughter to my parents and eventually my apartment. I couldn't deal with the pain of losing my daughter so I turned to heroin. This led to many arrests for shoplifting and possession. My first incarceration was at the age of 25. I was to do three months with probation upon my release.

I was scared because of the stories I had heard about jail. I just felt alone and cut off from reality. I kept to myself and didn't get involved with any of the programs except going to the AA meetings for my good time. I was released with the intention of never coming back.

About nine months later I was incarcerated again, this time for a year. I kind of welcomed the incarceration. This time I am taking advantage of the time I have here to learn more about myself. Being here has given me the chance to take a good look at my life-

style and what I need to change. I am in the Recovery Program here and I have taken classes like Peace at Home, HIV Prevention, Voices Within, Graphic Arts, and I tutor for pre-GED.

It is hard being locked up in a man's prison. I feel there are prejudices against women here at the Suffolk County House of Corrections. We don't have yard privileges except for a caged-in area that we are only allowed access to during the summer months. We aren't allowed to work in the kitchen or anywhere else in the prison except for the two floors which hold female inmates. We are only allowed to go to the other parts of the prison during the night for things like the library or computers.

I think poverty has a lot to do with people being incarcerated. Where there is poverty there is a lot of drug abuse and less access to structured programs. I think prejudice has a lot to do with being incarcerated because there aren't many jobs for minorities and people have to resort to crime to get things they need that you aren't able to at low-paying jobs.

I have learned that I want a better way of life and that I really don't want to come back here. I know I need to lead an honest life if I truly want to stay out of prison. I hope to become a productive person in society by taking on my responsibilities. I am afraid of failing but I know if I pick up by first dealing with my addictions then I won't have to resort to criminal behavior.

◆◆◆

FIFTY-NINE

Behind the Walls

The History and Current Reality of Women's Imprisonment

Nancy Kurshan

Prisons serve the same purpose for women as they do for men; they are instruments of social control. However, the imprisonment of women, as well as all the other aspects of our lives, takes place against a backdrop of patriarchal relationships. . . . Therefore, the imprisonment of women in the United States has always been a different phenomenon than that for men; the proportion of women in prison has always differed from that of men; women have traditionally been sent to prison for different reasons; and once in prison, they endure different conditions of

incarceration. Women's "crimes" have often had a sexual definition and been rooted in the patriarchal double standard. Furthermore, the nature of women's imprisonment reflects the position of women in society. . . .

As long as there has been crime and punishment, patriarchal and gender-based realities and assumptions have been central determinants of the response of society to female "offenders." In the late Middle Ages, reports reveal differential treatment of men and women. A woman might commonly be able to receive lenient punishment if she were to "plead her belly," that is, a pregnant woman could plead leniency on the basis of her pregnancy. On the other hand, women were burned at the stake for adultery or murdering a spouse, while men would most often not be punished for such actions. Such differential treatment reflected ideological assumptions as well as women's subordinate positions within the family, church, and other aspects of society. Although systematic imprisonment arose with industrialization, for centuries prior to that time unwanted daughters and wives were forced into convents, nunneries, and monasteries. In those cloisters were found political prisoners, illegitimate daughters, the disinherited, the physically deformed, and the mentally "defective."

A more general campaign of violence against women was unleashed in the witch-hunts of sixteenth- and seventeenth-century Europe, as society tried to exert control over women by labeling them as witches. This resulted in the death by execution of at least tens of thousands and possibly millions of people. Conservative estimates indicate that over 80 percent of all the people killed were women. Here in the United States, the witchcraft trials were a dramatic chapter in the social control of women long before systematic imprisonment. Although the colonies were settled relatively late in the history of European witch-hunts, they proved fertile ground for this misogynist campaign. The context was a new colonial society, changing and wrought with conflicts. . . .

Hundreds were accused of witchcraft during the New England witchcraft trials of the late 1600s, and at least 36 were executed. The primary determinant of who was designated a witch was gender; overwhelmingly, it was women who were the objects of witch fear. More women were charged with witchcraft, and women were more likely than men to be convicted and executed. In fact, men who confessed were likely to be scoffed at as liars. But age, too, was an important factor. Women over 40 were most likely to be accused of witchcraft and fared much worse than younger women when they were charged. Women over 60 were especially at high risk. Women who were alone, not attached to men as mothers, sisters, or wives were also represented disproportionately among the witches. Puritan society was very hierarchal, and the family was an essential aspect of that hierarchy. According to Carol Karlsen, the Puritan definition of woman as procreator and "helpmate" of man could not be ensured except through force. Most of the witches had expressed dissatisfaction with their lot, if only indirectly. Some were not sufficiently submissive in that they filed petitions and court suits, and sometimes sought divorces. Others were midwives and had influence over the well-being of others, often to the chagrin of their male competitors, medical doctors. Still others exhibited a female pride and assertiveness, refusing to defer to their male neighbors.

Karlsen goes on to offer one of the most powerful explanations of the New England witchcraft trials. She argues that at the heart of the hysteria was an underlying anxiety about inheritance. The inheritance system was designed to keep property in the hands of men. When there were no legitimate male heirs, women inheritors became aberrations who threatened the orderly transmission of property from one male generation to the next. Many of the witches were potential inheritors. Some of them were already widowed and without sons. Others were married but older, beyond their childbearing years, and therefore no longer likely to produce male heirs. They were also "disposable" since they were no longer performing the "essential" functions of a woman, as reproducer and, in some cases, helpmate. Many of the witches were charged just shortly after the death of the male family member, and their witchcraft convictions meant that their lands could easily be seized. Seen in this light, persecution of "witches" was an attempt to maintain the patriarchal social structure and prevent women from becoming economically independent. These early examples of the use of criminal charges in the social control of women may be seen as precursors to the punitive institutions of the 1800s. Up until this time, there were few carceral institutions in society. However, with the rise of capitalism and urbanization come the burgeoning of prisons in the United States. It is to those initial days of systematic imprisonment that we now turn.

The Emergence of Prisons for Women

The relatively few women who were imprisoned at the beginning of the nineteenth century were confined in separate quarters or wings of men's prisons. Like the men, women suffered from filthy conditions, overcrowding, and harsh treatment. In 1838 in the

New York City Jail (the "Tombs"), for instance, there were 42 one-person cells for 70 women. In the 1920s at Auburn Penitentiary in New York, there were no separate cells for the 25 or so women serving sentences up to 14 years. They were all lodged together in a one-room attic, the windows sealed to prevent communication with men. But women had to endure even more. Primary among these additional negative aspects was sexual abuse, which was reportedly a common occurrence. In 1826, Rachel Welch became pregnant while serving in solitary confinement as a punishment and shortly after childbirth she died as a result of flogging by a prison official. Such sexual abuse was apparently so acceptable that the Indiana state prison actually ran a prostitution service for male guards, using female prisoners.

Women received the short end of even the prison stick. Rather than spend the money to hire a matron, women were often left completely on their own, vulnerable to attack by guards. Women had less access to the physician and chaplain and did not go to workshops, mess halls, or exercise yards as men did. Food and needlework were brought to their quarters, and they remained in that area for the full term of their sentence.

Criminal conviction and imprisonment of women soared during and after the Civil War. In the North, this is commonly attributed to a multitude of factors, including men's absence during wartime and the rise of industrialization, as well as the impact of the dominant sexual ideology of nineteenth-century Victorianism. The double standard of Victorian morality supported the criminalization of certain behaviors for women but not for men. In New York in the 1850s and 1860s, female "crimes against persons" tripled while "crimes against property" rose 10 times faster than the male rate.

Black people, both women and men, have always been disproportionately incarcerated at all times and all places. This was true in the Northeast and Midwest prisons before the Civil War. It was also the case in the budding prison system in the western states, where Blacks outstripped their very small percentage of the population at large. The only exception was in the South, where slavery, not imprisonment, was the preferred form of control of African-American people. Yet while the South had the lowest Black imprisonment rate before the Civil War, this changed dramatically after the slaves were freed. This change took place for African-American women as well as men. After the Civil War, as part of the re-entrenchment of Euro-American control and the continuing subjugation of Black people, the post-war southern states passed infamous Jim Crow laws that made newly freed Blacks vulnerable to incarceration for the most minor crimes. For example, stealing a couple of chickens brought three to ten years in North Carolina. It is fair to say that many Blacks stepped from slavery into imprisonment. As a result, southern prison populations became predominately Black overnight. Between 1874 and 1877, the Black imprisonment rate went up 300 percent in Mississippi and Georgia. In some states, previously all-white prisons could not contain the influx of African-Americans sentenced to hard labor for petty offenses.

These spiraling rates in both the North and South meant that by mid-century there were enough women prisoners, both in the North and South, to necessitate the emergence of separate women's quarters. This practical necessity opened the door to changes in the nature of the imprisonment of women. In 1869, Sarah Smith and Rhoda Coffin, two Indiana Quakers, led a campaign to end the sexual abuse of women in that state's prison, and in 1874 the first completely separate women's prison was constructed. By 1940, 23 states had separate women's prisons. . . .

On the one hand, there were custodial institutions that corresponded by and large to men's prisons. The purpose of custodial prisons, as the name implies, was to warehouse prisoners. There was no pretense of rehabilitation. On the other hand, there were reformatories that, as the name implies, were intended to be more benevolent institutions that "uplifted" or "improved" the character of the women held there. These reformatories had no male counterparts. Almost every state had a custodial women's prison, but in the Northeast and Midwest the majority of incarcerated women were in reformatories. In the South, the few reformatories that existed were exclusively white. However, these differences are not, in essence, geographical; they are racial. The women in the custodial institutions were Black whether in the North or the South, and had to undergo the most degrading conditions, while it was mainly white women who were sent to the reformatories, institutions that had the ostensible philosophy of benevolence and sisterly and therapeutic ideals.

The Evolution of Separate Custodial Prisons for Women

In the South after 1870, prison camps emerged as penal servitude and were essentially substituted for slavery. The overwhelming majority of women in the prison camps were Black; the few white women who were there had been imprisoned for much more serious offenses, yet experienced better conditions of confinement. For instance, at Bowden Farm in Texas, the majority of women were Black, were there for property offenses, and worked in the field. The few white women who were there had been convicted of homicide and served as domestics. As the techniques of slavery were applied to the penal system, some states forced women to work on the state-owned penal plantations but also leased women to local farms, mines, and railroads. Treatment on the infamous chain gangs was brutal and degrading. For example, women were whipped on the buttocks in the presence of men. They were also forced to defecate right where they worked, in front of men.

An 1880 census indicated that in Alabama, Louisiana, Mississippi, North Carolina, Tennessee, and Texas, 37 percent of the 220 Black women were leased out whereas only 1 of the 40 white women was leased. Testimony in an 1870 Georgia investigation revealed that in one instance "There were no white women there. One started there, and I heard Mr. Alexander (the lessee) say he turned her loose. He was talking to the guard; I was working in the cut. He said his wife was a white woman, and he could not stand it to see a white woman worked in such places." Eventually, as central penitentiaries were built or rebuilt, many women were shipped there from prison farms because they were considered "dead hands" as compared with the men. At first, the most common form of custodial confinement was attachment to male prisons; eventually, independent women's prisons evolved out of these male institutions. These separate women's prisons were established largely for administrative convenience, not reform. Female matrons worked there, but they took their orders from men.

Like the prison camps, custodial women's prisons were overwhelmingly Black, regardless of their location. Although they have always been imprisoned in smaller numbers than African-American or Euro-American men, Black women often constituted larger percentages within female prisons than Black

men did within men's prisons. For instance, between 1797 and 1801, 44 percent of the women sent to New York state prisons were African-Americans as compared to 20 percent of the men. In the Tennessee state prison in 1868, 100 percent of the women were Black, whereas 60 percent of the men were of African descent. The women incarcerated in the custodial prisons tended to be 21 years of age or older. Forty percent were unmarried, and many of them had worked in the past.

Women in custodial prisons were frequently convicted of felony charges; most commonly for "crimes" against property, often petty theft. Only about a third of female felons were serving time for violent crimes. The rates for both property crimes and violent crimes were much higher than for the women at the reformatories. On the other hand, there were relatively fewer women incarcerated in custodial prisons for public order offenses (fornication, adultery, drunkenness, etc.), which were the most common in the reformatories. This was especially true in the South, where these so-called morality offenses by Blacks were generally ignored, and where authorities were reluctant to imprison white women at all. Data from the Auburn, New York, prison on homicide statistics between 1909 and 1933 reveal the special nature of the women's "violent" crimes. Most of the victims of murder by women were adult men. Of 149 victims, two-thirds were male; 29 percent were husbands, 2 percent were lovers, and the rest were listed as "man" or "boy" (a similar distribution exists today). Another form of violent crime resulting in the imprisonment of women was performing "illegal" abortions.

Tennessee Supreme Court records offer additional anecdotal information about the nature of women's violent crimes. Eighteen-year-old Sally Griffin killed her fifty-year-old husband after a fight in which, according to Sally, he knocked her through a window, hit her with a hammer, and threatened to "knock her brains out." A doctor testified that in previous months her husband had seriously injured her ovaries when he knocked her out of bed because she refused to have sex during her period. Sally's conviction stood because an eye-witness said she hadn't been threatened with a hammer. A second similar case was also turned down for retrial.

Southern states were especially reluctant to send white women to prison, so they were deliberately screened out by the judicial process. When white women were sent to prison, it was for homicide or sometimes arson; almost never did larceny result in incarceration. In the Tennessee prison, many of the African-American property offenders had committed less serious offenses than the whites, although they were incarcerated in far greater numbers. Frances Kellor, a renowned prison reformer, remarked of this screening process that the Black female offender "is first a Negro and then a woman—in the whites' estimation." A 1922 North Carolina report describes one institution as being "so horrible that the judge refuses to send white women to this jail, but Negro women are sometimes sent." Hundreds of such instances combined to create institutions overwhelmingly made up of African-American women.

The conditions of these custodial prisons were horrendous, as they were in prisons for men. The southern prisons were by far the worst. They were generally unsanitary, lacking adequate toilet and bathing facilities. Medical attention was rarely available. Women were either left totally idle or forced into hard labor. Women with mental problems were locked in solitary confinement and ignored. . . .

Generally speaking, the higher the proportion of women of color in the prison population, the worse the conditions. Therefore, it is not surprising that the physical conditions of incarceration for women in the custodial prisons were abysmal compared to the reformatories (as the following section indicates). Even in mainly Black penal institutions, Euro-American women were treated better than African-American women.*

Early Twentieth Century: Female Reformatories

Reformatories for women developed alongside custodial prisons. These were parallel, but distinct, developments. By the turn of the century, industrialization was in full swing, bringing fundamental changes in social relations: shifts from a rural society to an urban one, from a family to market economy; increased geographic mobility; increased disruption of lives; more life outside the church, family, and community. More production, even for women, was outside the home. By 1910, a record high of at least 27 percent of all women in New York state were "gainfully" employed. Thousands of women worked in the New York sweatshops under abominable conditions.

There was a huge influx of immigration from Southern and Eastern Europe; many of these were Jewish women who had come straight from Czarist Russia and brought with them a tradition of resistance and struggle. The division between social classes was clearly widening and erupted in dynamic labor struggles. For example, in 1909, 20,000 shirt-waist makers, four-fifths of whom were women, went on strike in New York. Racism and national chauvinism were rampant in the United States at the turn of the century in response to the waves of immigrants from Europe and Black people from the South. The Women's Prison Association of New York, which was active in the social purity movement, declared in 1906 that

> if promiscuous immigration is to continue, it devolves upon the enlightened, industrious, and moral citizens, from selfish as well as from philanthropic motives, to instruct the morally defective to conform to our ways and exact from them our own high standard of morality and legitimate industry. . . . Do you want immoral women to walk our streets, pollute society, endanger your households, menace the morals of your sons and daughters . . . ? Do you think the women here described fit to become mothers of American citizens? Shall foreign powers generate criminals and dump them on our shores?*

Also at the turn of the century various currents of social concern converged to create a new reform effort, the Progressive movement, that swept the country, particularly the Northeast and Midwest, for several decades. It was in this context that reformatories for women proliferated. Reformatories were actually begun by an earlier generation of female reformers who appeared between 1840 and 1900, but

---

*Estelle B. Freedman, *Their Sisters' Keepers: Women's Prison Reform in America, 1830–1930* (Ann Arbor: University of Michigan Press, 1981). Ch. 4, note 44.

*Nicole Hahn Rafter, *Partial Justice: Women in State Prisons 1800–1935* (Boston: New England University Press, 1985), pp. 93–94.

their proliferation took place during this Progressive Era as an alternative to the penitentiary's harsh conditions of enforced silence and hard labor. The reformatories came into being as a result of the work of prison reformers who were ostensibly motivated to improve penal treatment for women. They believed that the mixed prisons afforded women no privacy and left them vulnerable to debilitating humiliations.

Indeed, the reformatories were more humane and conditions were better than at the women's penitentiaries (custodial institutions). They did eliminate much male abuse and the fear of attack. They also resulted in more freedom of movement and opened up a variety of opportunities for "men's" work in the operation of the prison. Children of prisoners up to two years old could stay in most institutions. At least some of the reformatories were staffed and administered by women. They usually had cottages, flower gardens, and no fences. They offered discussions on the law, academics, and training, and women were often paroled more readily than in custodial institutions. However, a closer look at who the women prisoners were, the nature of their offenses, and the program to which they were subjected reveals the seamier side of these ostensibly noble institutions.

It is important to emphasize that reformatories existed for women only. No such parallel development took place within men's prisons. There were no institutions devoted to "correcting" men for so-called moral offenses. In fact, such activities were not considered crimes when men engaged in them and therefore men were not as a result imprisoned. A glance at these "crimes" for women only suggests the extent to which society was bent on repressing women's sexuality. Despite the hue and cry about prostitution, only 8.5 percent of the women at the reformatories were actually convicted of prostitution. More than half, however, were imprisoned because of "sexual misconduct." Women were incarcerated in reformatories primarily for various public order offenses or so-called "moral" offenses: lewd and lascivious carriage, stubbornness, idle and disorderly conduct, drunkenness, fornication, serial premarital pregnancies, keeping bad company, adultery, venereal disease, and vagrancy. A woman might face charges simply because a relative disapproved of her behavior and reported her, or because she had

been sexually abused and was being punished for it. Most were rebels of some sort.

Jennie B., for instance, was sent to Albion reformatory for five years for having "had unlawful sexual intercourse with young men and remain[ing] at hotels with young men all night, particularly on July 4, 1893." Lilian R. quit school and ran off for one week with a soldier, contracting a venereal disease. She was hospitalized, then sentenced to the reformatory. Other women were convicted of offenses related to exploitation and/or abuse by men. Ann B. became pregnant twice from older men, one of whom was her father, who was sentenced to prison for rape. She was convicted of "running around" when she was seven months pregnant. One woman who claimed to have miscarried and disposed of the fetus had been convicted of murdering her illegitimate child. There was also the increasing practice of abortion that accounted for at least some of the rise in "crime against persons."

As with all prisons, the women in the reformatories were of the working class. Many of them worked outside the home. At New York State's Albion Reformatory, for instance, 80 percent had, in the past, worked for wages. Reformatories were also overwhelmingly institutions for white women. Government statistics indicate that in 1921, for instance, 12 percent of the women in reformatories were Black while 88 percent were white.

Record keeping at the Albion Reformatory in New York demonstrates how unusual it was for Black women to be incarcerated there. The registries left spaces for entries of a large number of variables, such as family history of insanity and epilepsy. Nowhere was there a space for recording race. When African Americans were admitted, the clerk penciled "colored" at the top of the page. African-American women were much less likely to be arrested for such public order offenses. Rafter suggests that Black women were not expected to act like "ladies" in the first place and therefore were reportedly not deemed worthy of such rehabilitation.

The program of these institutions, as well as the offenses, was based on patriarchal assumptions. Reformatory training centered on fostering ladylike behavior and perfecting housewifely skills. In this way it encouraged dependency and women's subjugation. Additionally, one aspect of the retraining of these women was to isolate them, to strip them of environmental influences in order to instill them with new values. To this end, family ties were obstructed, which is somewhat ironic since the family is at the center of the traditional role of women. Letters might come every two months and were censored. Visits were allowed four times a year for those who were on the approved list. The reformatories were geographically remote, making it very difficult for loved ones to visit. Another thorn in the rosy picture of the reformatory was the fact that sentencing was often open-ended. This was an outgrowth of the rehabilitative ideology. The incarceration was not of fixed length because the notion was that a woman would stay for as long as it took to accomplish the task of reforming her.

Parole was also used as a patriarchal weapon. Ever since the Civil War, there was a scarcity of white working-class women for domestic service. At the same time, the "need for good help" was increasing because more people could afford to hire help. It was not an accident that women were frequently paroled into domestic jobs, the only ones for which they had been trained. In this way, vocational regulation went hand-in-hand with social control, leading always backwards to home and hearth, and away from self-sufficiency and independence. Additionally, independent behavior was punished by revoking parole for "sauciness," obscenity, or failure to work hard enough. One woman was cited for a parole violation for running away from a domestic position to join a theater troupe; another for going on car rides with men; still others for becoming pregnant, going around with a disreputable married man, or associating with the father of her child. And finally, some very unrepentant women were ultimately transferred indefinitely to asylums for the "feeble-minded."

Prison reform movements have been common; a reform movement also existed for men. However, all these institutions were inexorably returned to the role of institutions of social control. Understanding this early history can prepare us to understand recent developments in women's imprisonment and indeed imprisonment in general. Although the reformatories rejected the more traditional authoritarian penal regimes, they were nonetheless concerned with social control. Feminist criminologists claim that in their very inception, reformatories were institutions of patriarchy. They were part of a broad attack on young working-class women who were attempting to lead somewhat more autonomous lives. Women's sexual independence was being curbed in the context of "social purity" campaigns. As more and more white working-class women left home for the labor force, they took up smoking, frequenting dance halls, and having sexual relationships. Prostitution had long been a source of income for poor women, but despite the fact that prostitution had actually begun to wane about 1900, there was a major morality crusade at the turn of the century that attacked prostitution as well as all kinds of small deviations from the standard of "proper" female propriety.

Even when the prisons were run by women, they were, of course, still doing the work of a male supremacist prison system and society. We have seen how white working-class women were punished for "immoral behavior" when men were not. We have seen how they were indoctrinated with a program of "ladylike" behavior. According to feminist criminologists such as Nicole Hahn Rafter and Estelle Freedman, reformatories essentially punished those who did not conform to bourgeois definitions of femininity and prescribed gender roles. The prisoners were to embrace the social values, although, of course, never to occupy the social station of a "lady." It is relevant to note that the social stigma of imprisonment was even greater for women than men because women were supposedly denying their own "pure nature." This stigma plus the nature of the conditions of incarceration served as a warning to all such women to stay within the proper female sphere.

These observations shed some light on the role of "treatment" within penal practice. Reformatories were an early attempt at "treatment," that is, the uplifting and improvement of the women, as opposed to mere punishment or retribution. However, these reforms were also an example of the subservience of "treatment" to social control. They demonstrate that the underlying function of control continually reasserts itself when attempts to "improve" people take place within a coercive framework. The reformatories are an illustration of how sincere efforts at reform may only serve to broaden the net and extend the state's power of social control. In fact, hundreds and hundreds of women were incarcerated for public order offenses who previously would not have been vulnerable to the punishment of confinement in a state institution were it not for the existence of reformatories.

By 1935, the custodial prisons for women and the reformatories had basically merged. In the 1930s, the United States experienced the repression of radicalism, the decline of the progressive and feminist movements, and the Great Depression. Along with these changes came the demise of the reformatories. The prison reform movement had achieved one of its earliest central aims, separate prisons for women. The reformatory buildings still stood and were filled with prisoners. However, these institutions were reformatories in name only. Some were administered by women, but they were women who did not even have the progressive pretenses of their predecessors. The conditions of incarceration had deteriorated miserably, suffering from cutbacks and lack of funding.

Meanwhile, there had been a slow but steady transformation of the inmate population. Increasingly, the white women convicted of misdemeanors were given probation, paroled, or sent back to local jails. As Euro-American women left the reformatories, the buildings themselves were transformed into custodial prisons, institutions that repeated the terrible conditions of the past. As custodial prison buildings were physically closed down for various reasons, felons were transferred to the buildings that had housed the reformatories. Most of the women were not only poor but also were Black. African-American women were increasingly incarcerated there with the growth of the Black migration north after World War I. These custodial institutions now included some added negative dimensions as the legacy of the reformatories, such as the strict reinforcement of gender roles and the infantilization of women. In the end, the reformatories were certainly not a triumph for the women's liberation. Rather, they can be viewed as one of many instances in which U.S. institutions are able to absorb an apparent reform and use it for continuing efforts at social control.

Women and Prison Today

. . . There are a wide range of institutions that incarcerate women and conditions vary. Some women's prisons look like "small college campuses," remnants of the historical legacy of the reformatory movement. Bedford Hills state prison in New York is one such institution; Alderson Federal Prison in West Virginia is another. Appearances, however, are deceptive. For instance, Russell Dobash describes the "underlying atmosphere [of such a prison] as one of intense hostility, frustration, and anger."

Many institutions have no pretenses and are notoriously overcrowded and inadequate. The California Institution for Women at Frontera houses 2,500 women in a facility built for 1,011. Overcrowding sometimes means that women who are being held for trivial offenses are incarcerated in maximum-security institutions for lack of other facilities. Women's prisons are often particularly ill-equipped and poorly financed. They have fewer medical, educational, and vocational facilities than men's prisons. Medical treatment is often unavailable, inappropriate, and inconsistent. Job training is also largely unavailable; when opportunities exist, they are usually traditional female occupations. Courses concentrate on homemaking and low-paid skills like beautician and launderer. Other barriers exist as well. In an Alabama women's prison, there is a cosmetology program, but those convicted of felonies are prohibited by state law from obtaining such licenses.

In most prisons, guards have total authority, and the women can never take care of their basic intimate needs in a secure atmosphere free from intrusion. In the ostensible name of security, male guards can take down or look over a curtain, walk into a bathroom, or observe a woman showering or changing her clothes. In Michigan, for instance, male guards are employed at all women's prisons. At Huron Valley, about half the guards are men. At Crane prison, approximately 80 percent of the staff is male and there are open dormitories divided into cubicles. In one section the cubicle walls are only four feet high and there are no doors or curtains on any cubicles anywhere at Crane. The officers' desks are right next to the bathroom and the bathroom doors must be left open at all times. Male guards are also allowed to do body shakedowns where they run their hands all over the women's bodies.

Incarceration has severe and particular ramifications for women. Eighty percent of women entering state prisons are mothers. By contrast 60 percent of men in state prisons are fathers and less than half of them have custodial responsibility. These mothers have to undergo the intense pain of forced separation from their children. They are often the sole caretakers of their children and were the primary source of financial and emotional support. Their children are twice as likely to end up in foster care than the children of male prisoners. Whereas when a man goes to prison, his wife or lover most often assumes or continues to assume responsibilities for the children, the reverse is not true. Women often have no one else to turn to and are in danger of permanently losing custody of their children. For all imprisoned mothers the separation from their children is one of the greatest punishments of incarceration, and engenders despondency and feelings of guilt and anxiety about their children's welfare.

Visiting with children often is extremely difficult or impossible. At county jails where women are awaiting trial, prisoners are often denied contact visits and are required to visit behind glass partitions or through telephones. Prisons are usually built far away from the urban centers where most of the prisoners and their families and friends live. Where children are able to visit, they have to undergo frightening experiences like pat-downs under awkward and generally anti-human conditions. When women get out of prison, many states are supposed to provide reunification services, but in fact most do not. Although even departments of corrections admit that family contact is the one factor that most greatly enhances parole success, the prison system actively works to obstruct such contact.

Reproductive rights are nonexistent for the 10 percent of the women in prison who are pregnant. . . . All the essentials for a healthy pregnancy are missing in prison: nutritious food, fresh air, exercise, sanitary conditions, extra vitamins, and prenatal care. . . . Women frequently undergo bumpy bus rides, and are shackled and watched throughout their delivery. It is no wonder then that a 1985 California Department of Health study indicated that a third of all prison pregnancies end in late-term miscarriage, twice the outside rate. In fact, only 20 percent have live births. For those women who are lucky enough to have healthy deliveries, forced separation from the infant usually comes within 24 to 72 hours after birth.

Many commentators argue that, at their best, women's prisons are shot through with a viciously destructive paternalistic mentality. According to Rafter, "Women in prison are perpetually infantilized by routines and paternalistic attitudes." Assata Shakur describes it as a "pseudo-motherly attitude . . . a deception which all too often successfully reverts women to children." Guards call prisoners by their first names and admonish them to "grow up," "be good girls," and "behave." They threaten the women

with a "good spanking." Kathryn Burkhart refers to this as a "mass infancy treatment." Powerlessness, helplessness, and dependency are systematically heightened in prison while what would be most therapeutic for women is the opposite—for women to feel their own power and to take control of their lives. Friendship among women is discouraged, and the homophobia of the prison system is exemplified by rules in many prisons that prohibit any type of physical contact between women prisoners. A woman can be punished for hugging a friend who has just learned that her mother died. There is a general prohibition against physical affection, but it is most seriously enforced against known Lesbians. One Lesbian received a disciplinary ticket for lending a sweater and was told she didn't know the difference between compassion and passion. Lesbians may be confronted with extra surveillance or may be "treated like a man." Some Lesbians receive incident reports simply because they are gay.

Many prison administrators generally agree that community-based alternatives would be better and cheaper than imprisonment. However, there is very little public pressure in that direction. While imprisonment rates for women continue to rise, the public outcry is deafening in its silence. Ruth Ann Jones of the Division of Massachusetts Parole Board says her agency receives no outside pressure to develop programs for women. However, around the country small groups of dedicated people are working to introduce progressive reforms into the prisons. In Michigan, there is a program that buses family and friends to visit at prisons. In New York, at Bedford Hills, there is a program geared towards enhancing and encouraging visits with children. Chicago Legal Aid for Imprisoned Mothers (CLAIM), Atlanta's Aid to Imprisoned Mothers, and Madison, Wisconsin's Women's Jail Project are just some of the groups that have tirelessly and persistently fought for reforms as well as provided critical services for women and children.

The best programs are the ones that can concretely improve the situation of the women inside. However, many programs that begin with reform-minded intentions become institutionalized in such a way that they are disadvantageous to the population they are supposedly helping. Psychological counselors may have good intentions, but they work for the departments of corrections and often offer no confidentiality. And of course, even the best of them tend to focus on individual pathology rather than exposing systematic oppression. Less restrictive alternatives like halfway houses often get turned around so that they become halfway in, not halfway out. . . .

Prison Resistance

One topic that has not been adequately researched is the rebellion and resistance of women in prison. It is only with great difficulty that any information was found. We do not believe that is because resistance does not occur, but rather because those in charge of documenting history have a stake in burying this herstory. Such a herstory would challenge the patriarchal ideology that insists that women are, by nature, passive and docile. What we do know is that as far back as 1943 there was a riot in Sing Sing Prison in New York, which was the first woman's prison. It took place in response to overcrowding and inadequate facilities.

During the Civil War, Georgia's prison was burned down, allegedly torched by women trying to escape. It was again burned down in 1900. In 1888, similar activity took place at Framingham, Massachusetts, although reports refer to it as merely "fun." Women rebelled at New York's Hudson House of Refuge in response to excessive punishment. They forced the closing of "the dungeon," basement cells and a diet of bread and water. Within a year, similar cells were reinstituted. The story of Bedford Hills is a particularly interesting one. From 1915 to 1920 there were a series of rebellions against cruelty to inmates. The administration had refused to segregate Black and white women up until 1916, and reports of the time attribute these occurrences to the "unfortunate attachments formed by white women for the Negroes." A 1931 study indicated that "colored girls" revolted against discrimination at the New Jersey State Reformatory.

Around the time of the historic prison rebellion at Attica Prison in New York State, rebellions also took place at women's prisons. In 1971, there was a work stoppage at Alderson simultaneous with the rebellion at Attica. In June of 1975, the women at the North Carolina Correctional Center for Women staged a five-day demonstration "against oppressive working atmospheres, inaccessible and inadequate medical facilities and treatment, and racial discrimination, and many other conditions at the prison." Unprotected, unarmed women were attacked by male guards armed with riot gear. The women sustained physical injuries and miscarriages as well as punitive punishment in lockup and in segregation, and illegal transfers to the Mattawan State Hospital for the Criminally Insane. . . .

This short exposition of the rebellions in women's prisons is clearly inadequate. Feminist criminologists and others should look towards the need for a detailed herstory of this thread of the women's experience in America.

Conclusion

We began this research in an attempt to understand the ways that patriarchy and white supremacy interact in the imprisonment of women. We looked at the history of the imprisonment of women in the United States and found that it has always been different for white women and African-American women. This was most dramatically true in the social control of white women, geared toward turning them into "ladies." This was a more physically benign prison track than the custodial prisons that contained Black women or men. But it was insidiously patriarchal, both in this character and in the fact that similar institutions did not exist to control men's behavior in those areas. We also saw that historically the more "Black" the penal institution, the worse the conditions. It is difficult to understand how this plays out within the walls of prisons today since there are more sophisticated forms of tracking. That is, within a given prison there are levels of privileges that offer a better or worse quality of life. Research is necessary to determine how this operates in terms of white and African-American female prisoners. However, we can hypothesize that as women's prisons become increasingly Black institutions, conditions will, as in the past, come more and more to resemble the punitive conditions of men's prisons. . . .

Although the percentage of women in prison is still very low compared to men, the rates are rapidly rising. And when we examine the conditions of incarceration, it does appear as if the imprisonment of women is coming more and more to resemble that of men in the sense that there is no separate, more benign, track for women. Now more than ever, women are being subjected to more maximum-security, control units, shock incarceration; in short, everything negative that men receive. We thus may be looking at the beginning of a new era in the imprisonment of women. One observation that is consistent with these findings is that the purpose of prisons for women may not be to function primarily as institutions of patriarchal control. That is, their mission as instruments of social control of people of color generally may be the overriding purpose. Turning women into "ladies" or "feminizing" women is not the essence of the mission of prisons. Warehousing and punishment are now enough, for women as well as men.

This is not to suggest that the imprisonment of women is not replete with sexist ideology and practices. It is a thoroughly patriarchal society that sends women to prison; that is, the rules and regulations, the definition of crimes are defined by the patriarchy. This would include situations in which it is "okay" for a husband to beat up his wife, but that very same wife cannot defend herself against his violence; in which women are forced to act as accessories to crimes committed by men; in which abortion is becoming more and more criminalized. Once in prison, patriarchal assumptions and male dominance continue to play an essential role in the

treatment of women. As discussed previously, women have to deal with a whole set of factors that men do not, from intrusion by male guards to the denial of reproductive rights. Modern day women's imprisonment has taken on the worst aspects of the imprisonment of men. But it is also left with the sexist legacy of the reformatories and the contemporary structures of the patriarchy. Infantilization and the reinforcement of passivity and dependency are woven into the very fabric of the incarceration of women.

The imprisonment of women of color can be characterized by the enforcement of patriarchy in the service of the social control of people of color as a whole. This raises larger questions about the enormous attacks aimed at family life in communities of color, in which imprisonment of men, women, and children plays a significant role. However, since this area of inquiry concerns the most disenfranchised elements of our society, it is no wonder that so little attention is paid to dealing with this desperate situation. More research in this area is needed as there are certainly unanswered questions. But we must not wait for this research before we begin to unleash our energies to dismantle a prison system that grinds up our sisters.

SIXTY

◆◆◆

Punishing Drug Addicts Who Have Babies
Women of Color, Equality, and the Right of Privacy

Dorothy E. Roberts

In July 1989, Jennifer Clarise Johnson, a twenty-three-year-old crack addict, became the first woman in the United States to be criminally convicted for exposing her baby to drugs while pregnant.[1] Florida law enforcement officials charged Johnson with two counts of delivering a controlled substance to a minor after her two children tested positive for cocaine at birth. Because the relevant Florida drug law did not apply to fetuses, the prosecution invented a novel interpretation of the statute. The prosecution obtained Johnson's conviction for passing a cocaine metabolite from her body to her newborn infants

during the sixty-second period after birth and before the umbilical cord was cut.

A growing number of women across the country have been charged with criminal offenses after giving birth to babies who test positive for drugs. The majority of these women, like Jennifer Johnson, are poor and Black.[2] Most are addicted to crack cocaine. The prosecution of drug-addicted mothers is part of an alarming trend toward greater state intervention into the lives of pregnant women under the rationale of protecting the fetus from harm. Such government intrusion is particularly harsh for poor women of color. They are the least likely to obtain adequate prenatal care, the most vulnerable to government monitoring, and the least able to conform to the white middle-class standard of motherhood. They are therefore the primary targets of government control.

The prosecution of drug-addicted mothers implicates two fundamental tensions. First, punishing a woman for using drugs during pregnancy pits the state's interest in protecting the future health of a child against the mother's interest in autonomy over her reproductive life—interests that until recently had not been thought to be in conflict. Second, such prosecutions represent one of two possible responses to the problem of drug-exposed babies. The government may choose either to help women have healthy pregnancies or to punish women for their prenatal conduct. Although it might seem that the state could pursue both of these avenues at once, the two responses are ultimately irreconcilable. Far from deterring injurious drug use, prosecution of drug-addicted mothers in fact deters pregnant women from using available health and counseling services because it causes women to fear that, if they seek help, they could be reported to government authorities and charged with a crime. Moreover, prosecution blinds the public to the possibility of nonpunitive solutions and to the inadequacy of the nonpunitive solutions that are currently available.

The debate between those who favor protecting the rights of the fetus and those who favor protecting the rights of the mother has been extensively waged in the literature.[3] This [essay] seeks to illuminate the current debate by examining the experiences of the class of women who are primarily affected—poor Black women.

Providing the perspective of poor Black women offers two advantages. First, examining legal issues from the viewpoint of those they affect most helps to uncover the real reasons for state action and to explain the real harms it causes. It exposes the way the prosecutions deny poor Black women a facet of their humanity by punishing their reproductive choices. The government's choice of a punitive response perpetuates the historical devaluation of Black women as mothers. Viewing the legal issues from the experiential standpoint of the defendants enhances our understanding of the constitutional dimensions of the state's conduct.

Second, examining the constraints on poor Black women's reproductive choices expands our understanding of reproductive freedom in particular and the right of privacy in general. Much of the literature discussing reproductive freedom has adopted a white middle-class perspective, which focuses narrowly on abortion rights. The feminist critique of privacy doctrine has also neglected many of the concerns of poor women of color.

My analysis presumes that Black women experience various forms of oppression simultaneously, as a complex interaction of race, gender, and class that is more than the sum of its parts. It is impossible to isolate any one of the components of this oppression or to separate the experiences that are attributable to one component from experiences attributable to the others. The prosecution of drug-addicted mothers cannot be explained as simply an issue of gender inequality. Poor Black women have been selected for punishment as a result of an inseparable combination of their gender, race, and economic status. Their devaluation as mothers, which underlies the prosecutions, has its roots in the unique experience of slavery and has been perpetuated by complex social forces. . . .

Background: The State's Punitive Response to Drug-Addicted Mothers

The Crack Epidemic and the State's Response

Crack cocaine appeared in America in the early 1980s, and its abuse has grown to epidemic proportions. Crack is especially popular among inner-city women.[4] Most crack-addicted women are of child-bearing age, and many are pregnant.[5] This phenomenon has contributed to an explosion in the number of newborns affected by maternal drug use. Some experts estimate that as many as 375,000 drug-exposed infants are born every year.[6]

Babies born to drug-addicted mothers may suffer a variety of medical, developmental, and behavioral problems, depending on the nature of their mother's substance abuse. Data on the extent and potential severity of the adverse effects of maternal cocaine use are controversial.[7] The interpretation of studies of cocaine-exposed infants is often clouded by the presence of other fetal risk factors, such as the mother's use of additional drugs, cigarettes, and alcohol and her socioeconomic status.

The response of state prosecutors, legislators, and judges to the problem of drug-exposed babies has been punitive. They have punished women who use drugs during pregnancy by depriving these mothers of custody of their children, by jailing them during their pregnancy, and by prosecuting them after their babies are born.

The Disproportionate Impact on Poor Black Women

Poor Black women bear the brunt of prosecutors' punitive approach. These women are the primary targets of prosecutors, not because they are more likely to be guilty of fetal abuse, but because they are Black and poor. Poor women, who are disproportionately Black,[8] are in closer contact with government agencies, and their drug use is therefore more likely to be detected. Black women are also more likely to be reported to government authorities, in part because of the racist attitudes of health care professionals. Finally, their failure to meet society's image of the ideal mother makes their prosecution more acceptable.

It is also significant that, out of the universe of maternal conduct that can injure a fetus, prosecutors have focused on crack use. The selection of crack addiction for punishment can be justified by neither the number of addicts nor the extent of the harm to the fetus. Excessive alcohol consumption during pregnancy, for example, can cause severe fetal injury, and marijuana use may also adversely affect the unborn.[9] The incidence of both these types of substance abuse is high as well. In addition, prosecutors do not always base their claims on actual harm to the child, but on the mere delivery of crack by the mother.

Focusing on Black crack addicts rather than on other perpetrators of fetal harms serves two broader social purposes. First, prosecution of these pregnant women serves to degrade women whom society views as undeserving to be mothers and to discourage them from having children. If prosecutors had instead chosen to prosecute affluent women addicted to alcohol or prescription medication, the policy of criminalizing prenatal conduct very likely would have suffered a hasty demise. Society is much more willing to condone the punishment of poor women of color who fail to meet the middle-class ideal of motherhood.

In addition to legitimizing fetal rights enforcement, the prosecution of crack-addicted mothers diverts public attention from social ills such as poverty, racism, and a misguided national health policy and implies instead that shamefully high Black infant death rates[10] are caused by the bad acts of individual mothers. Poor Black mothers thus become the scapegoats for the causes of the Black community's ill health.

Punishing Black Mothers and the Perpetuation of Racial Hierarchy

The legal analysis of the prosecutions implicates two constitutional protections: the equal protection clause of the Fourteenth Amendment and the right of privacy. These two constitutional challenges appeal to different but related values. A basic premise of equality doctrine is that certain fundamental aspects of the human personality, including decisional autonomy, must be respected in all persons. Theories of racial equality and privacy can be used as related means to achieve a common end of eliminating the legacy of racial discrimination that has devalued Black motherhood. Both aim to create a society in which Black women's reproductive choices, including the decision to bear children, are given full respect and protection.

The equal protection clause[11] embodies the Constitution's ideal of racial equality. State action that violates this ideal by creating classifications based on race must be subjected to strict judicial scrutiny. The equal protection clause, however, does not explicitly define the meaning of equality or delineate the nature of prohibited government conduct. As a result, equal protection analyses generally have divided into two visions of equality: one that is informed by an antidiscrimination principle, the other by an antisubordination principle.[12]

The antidiscrimination approach identifies the primary threat to equality as the government's "failure to treat Black people as individuals without regard to race."[13] The goal of the antidiscrimination principle is to ensure that all members of society are treated in a color-blind or race-neutral fashion. The Supreme Court's current understanding of the

equal protection clause is based on a narrow interpretation of the antidiscrimination principle.[14] The
Court has confined discrimination prohibited by
the Constitution to state conduct performed with a
discriminatory intent. State conduct that disproportionately affects Blacks violates the Constitution only
if it is accompanied by a purposeful desire to produce this outcome.

Black women prosecuted for drug use during
pregnancy may be able to make out a prima facie
case of discriminatory purpose.[15] The Court has recognized that a selection process characterized by
broad government discretion that produces unex-
plained racial disparities may support the presumption of discriminatory purpose.[16]

A Black mother arrested in Pinellas County,
Florida, could make out a prima facie case of unconstitutional racial discrimination by showing that
a disproportionate number of those chosen for prosecution for exposing newborns to drugs are Black.
In particular, she could point out the disparity between the percentage of defendants who are Black
and the percentage of pregnant substance abusers
who are Black. A *New England Journal of Medicine* study
of pregnant women in Pinellas County found that
only about 26 percent of those who used drugs were
Black.[17] Yet over 90 percent of Florida prosecutions
for drug abuse during pregnancy have been brought
against Black women. The defendant could buttress
her case with the study's finding that, despite similar rates of substance abuse, Black women were ten
times more likely than white women to be reported
to public health authorities for substance abuse during pregnancy. In addition, the defendant could
show that both health care professionals and prosecutors wield a great deal of discretion in selecting
women to be subjected to the criminal justice system. The burden would then shift to the state "to dis-
pel the inference of intentional discrimination" by
justifying the racial discrepancy in its prosecutions.

The antisubordination approach to equality would
not require Black defendants to prove that the prosecutions are motivated by racial bias. Rather than
requiring victims to prove distinct instances of discriminating behavior in the administrative process,
the antisubordination approach considers the concrete effects of government policy on the substantive
condition of the disadvantaged. Under this conception of equality, the function of the equal protection
clause is to dismantle racial hierarchy by eliminat-

ing state action or inaction that effectively preserves
Black subordination.

The prosecution of drug-addicted mothers demonstrates the inadequacy of antidiscrimination analysis
and the superiority of the antisubordination approach. First, the antidiscrimination approach may
not adequately protect Black women from prosecutions' infringement of equality, because it is difficult
to identify individual guilty actors. Who are the government officials motivated by racial bias to punish
Black women? The hospital staff who test and report mothers to child welfare agencies? The prosecutors who develop and implement policies to charge
women who use drugs during pregnancy? Legislators who enact laws protecting the unborn?

It is unlikely that any of these individual actors intentionally singled out Black women for punishment based on a conscious devaluation of their
motherhood. The disproportionate impact of the
prosecutions on poor Black women does not result
from such isolated, individualized decisions. Rather,
it is a result of two centuries of systematic exclusion
of Black women from tangible and intangible benefits enjoyed by white society. Their exclusion is reflected in Black women's reliance on public hospitals
and public drug treatment centers, in their failure
to obtain adequate prenatal care, in the more frequent reporting of Black drug users by health care
professionals, and in society's acquiescence in the
government's punitive response to the problem of
crack-addicted babies.

In contrast to the antidiscrimination approach,
antisubordination theory mandates that equal protection law concern itself with the concrete ways
government policy perpetuates the inferior status of
Black women. From this perspective, the prosecutions of crack-addicted mothers are unconstitutional
because they reinforce the myth of the undeserving
Black mother by singling out—whether intentionally or not—Black women for punishment. The government's punitive policy reflects a long history of
denigration of Black mothers dating back to slavery,
and it serves to perpetuate that legacy of unequal
respect. The prosecutions should therefore be upheld only if the state can demonstrate that they serve
a compelling interest that could not be achieved
through less discriminatory means. A public commitment to providing adequate prenatal care for
poor women and drug treatment programs that
meet the needs of pregnant addicts would be a more

effective means for the state to address the problem of drug-exposed babies.

Claiming the Right of Privacy for Women of Color

Identifying the Constitutional Issue

In deciding which of the competing interests involved in the prosecution of drug-addicted mothers prevails—the state's interest in protecting the health of the fetus or the woman's interest in preventing state intervention—we must identify the precise nature of the woman's constitutional right at stake. In the *Johnson* case, the prosecutor framed the constitutional issue as follows: "What constitutionally protected freedom did Jennifer engage in when she smoked cocaine?" That was the wrong question. Johnson was not convicted of using drugs. Her "constitutional right" to smoke cocaine was never at issue. Johnson was prosecuted because she chose to carry her pregnancy to term while she was addicted to crack. Had she smoked cocaine during her pregnancy and then had an abortion, she would not have been charged with such a serious crime. The proper question, then, is "What constitutionally protected freedom did Jennifer engage in when she decided to have a baby, even though she was a drug addict?"

Understanding the prosecution of drug-addicted mothers as punishment for having babies clarifies the constitutional right at stake. The woman's right at issue is not the right to abuse drugs or to cause the fetus to be born with defects. It is the right to choose to be a mother that is burdened by the criminalization of conduct during pregnancy. This view of the constitutional issue reveals the relevance of race to the resolution of the competing interests. Race has historically determined the value society places on an individual's right to choose motherhood. Because of the devaluation of Black motherhood, protecting the right of Black women to choose to bear a child has unique significance.

Overview of Privacy Arguments

Prosecutions of drug-addicted mothers infringe on two aspects of the right to individual choice in reproductive decision making. First, they infringe on the freedom to continue a pregnancy that is essential to an individual's personhood and autonomy. This freedom implies that state control of the decision to carry a pregnancy to term can be as pernicious as state control of the decision to terminate a pregnancy. Second, the prosecutions infringe on choice by imposing an invidious government standard for the entitlement to procreate. Such imposition of a government standard for childbearing is one way society denies the humanity of those who are different. The first approach emphasizes a woman's right to autonomy over her reproductive life; the second highlights a woman's right to be valued equally as a human being.

Toward a New Privacy Jurisprudence

In this section, I will suggest two approaches that I believe are necessary in order for privacy theory to contribute to the eradication of racial hierarchy. First, we need to develop a positive view of the right of privacy. Second, the law must recognize the connection between the right of privacy and racial equality.

The definition of privacy as a purely negative right serves to exempt the state from any obligation to ensure the social conditions and resources necessary for self-determination and autonomous decision making. Based on this narrow view of liberty, the Supreme Court has denied a variety of claims to government aid.[18] Laurence Tribe has suggested an alternative view of the relationship between the government's negative and affirmative responsibilities in guaranteeing the rights of personhood: "Ultimately, the affirmative duties of government cannot be severed from its obligations to refrain from certain forms of control; both must respond to a substantive vision of the needs of human personality."[19]

Thus, the reason legislatures should reject laws that punish Black women's reproductive choices is not an absolute and isolated notion of individual autonomy. Rather, legislatures should reject these laws as a critical step toward eradicating a racial hierarchy that has historically demeaned Black motherhood. Respecting Black women's decision to bear children is a necessary ingredient of a community that affirms the personhood of all its members.

Our understanding of the prosecutions of drug-addicted mothers must include the perspective of the women who are most directly affected. The prosecutions arise in a particular historical and political context that has constrained reproductive choice for poor women of color. The state's decision to punish drug-addicted mothers rather than help them stems from the poverty and race of the defendants and society's denial of their full dignity as human beings.

A policy that attempts to protect fetuses by denying the humanity of their mothers will inevitably fail. The tragedy of crack babies is initially a tragedy of crack-addicted mothers. Both are part of a larger tragedy of a community that is suffering a host of indignities, including, significantly, the denial of equal respect for its women's reproductive decisions.

It is only by affirming the personhood and equality of poor women of color that we will ensure the survival of their future generation. The first principle of the government's response to the crisis of drug-exposed babies should be the recognition of their mothers' worth and entitlement to autonomy over their reproductive lives. A commitment to guaranteeing these fundamental rights of poor women of color, rather than punishing them, is the true solution to the problem of unhealthy babies.

NOTES

1. *See* State v. Johnson, No. E89-890-CFA, slip op. at 1 (Fla. Cir. Ct. July 13, 1989), *aff'd*, 578 So. 2d 419 (Fla. Dist. Ct. App. 1991), *rev'd*, 602 So. 2d 1288 (Fla. 1992).

2. According to a memorandum prepared by the ACLU Reproductive Freedom Project, of the fifty-two defendants, thirty-five are African American, fourteen are white, two are Latina, and one is Native American. *See* Lynn Paltrow and Suzanne Shende, State by State Case Summary of Criminal Prosecutions against Pregnant Women (Oct. 29, 1990). In Florida, where two women have been convicted for distributing drugs to a minor, ten out of eleven criminal cases were brought against Black women. *Id.* at 3–5.

3. For arguments supporting the mother's right to autonomy, see, e.g., Goldberg, *Medical Choices during Pregnancy: Whose Decision Is It Anyway?* 41 Rutgers L. Rev. 591 (1989). For arguments advocating protection of the fetus, see, e.g., Walker and Puzder, *State Protection of the Unborn after Roe v. Wade: A Legislative Proposal*, 13 Stetson L. Rev. 237, 253–63 (1984).

4. Approximately half of the nation's crack addicts are women. *See* Alters, *Women and Crack: Equal Addiction, Unequal Care*, Boston Globe, Nov. 1, 1989, at 1. The highest concentrations of crack addicts are found in inner-city neighbor-

hoods. *See* Malcolm, *Crack, Bane of Inner City, Is Now Gripping Suburbs*, N.Y. Times, Oct. 1, 1989, at 1.

5. Many crack-addicted women become pregnant as a result of trading sex for crack or turning to prostitution to support their habit. *See* Alters, *supra* note 4, at 1.

6. *See* Besharov, *Crack Babies: The Worst Threat Is Mom Herself*. Wash. Post, Aug. 6, 1989, at B1.

7. *See* Koren et al., *Bias against the Null Hypothesis: The Reproductive Hazards of Cocaine*, Lancet, Dec. 16, 1989, at 1440.

8. Black women are five times more likely to live in poverty, five times more likely to be on welfare, and three times more likely to be unemployed than are white women. *See* United States Comm'n on Civil Rights, The Economic Status of Black Women 1 (1990).

9. *See, e.g.*, Fried et al., *Marijuana Use during Pregnancy and Decreased Length of Gestation*, 150 Am. J. Obstetrics & Gyn. 23 (1984).

10. In 1987, the mortality rate for Black infants was 17.9 deaths per 1,000, compared to a rate of 8.6 deaths per 1,000 for white infants. *See* U.S. Dept. of Commerce, Bureau of Census, Statistical Abstract of the United States 77 (table 110) (1990).

11. The Fourteenth Amendment provides, in relevant part, that "[n]o State shall make or enforce any law which shall . . . deny to any person within its jurisdiction the equal protection of the laws." U.S. Const. amend. XIV, § 1.

12. These competing views of equal protection law have been variously characterized by commentators. *See, e.g.*, L. Tribe, American Constitutional Law §§ 16–21, at 1514–21 (2d ed. 1988).

13. Dimond, *The Anti-Caste Principle: Toward a Constitutional Standard for Review of Race Cases*, 30 Wayne L. Rev. 1, 1 (1983).

14. *See* Strauss, *Discriminatory Intent and the Taming of Brown*, 56 U. Chi. L. Rev. 935, 953–54 (1989).

15. For a discussion of equal protection challenges to racially selective prosecutions, see *Developments in the Law: Race and the Criminal Process*, 101 Harv. L. Rev. 1472, 1532–49 (1988).

16. *See* Kennedy, McCleskey v. Kemp: *Race, Capital Punishment and the Supreme Court*, 101 Harv. L. Rev. 1388, 1425–27 (1988).

17. *See* Chasnoff et al., *The Prevalence of Illicit Drug or Alcohol Use during Pregnancy and Discrepancies in Mandatory Reporting in Pinellas County, Florida*, 322 New Eng. J. Med. 1202, 1204 (table 2) (1990).

18. *See, e.g.*, DeShaney v. Winnebago County Dept. of Social Servs., 489 U.S. 189, 196 (1989) ("[O]ur cases have recognized that the Due Process Clauses generally confer no affirmative right to governmental aid, even where such aid may be necessary to secure life, liberty, or property interests of which the government itself may not deprive the individual").

19. Tribe, *supra* note 12, § 15–2, at 1305.

◆◆◆

SIXTY-ONE

U.S. Concentration Camps and Exclusion Policies
Impact on Japanese American Women
Rita Takahashi

During World War II, most women of Japanese ancestry residing in the United States received the same sentence from their government. Under Executive Order 9066, signed by President Franklin Delano Roosevelt on 19 February 1942, people of Japanese ancestry living on the West Coast were excluded from their communities and incarcerated in concentration camps. The government justified its actions on grounds of "military necessity," although more than two-thirds of the incarcerated people were U.S.-born citizens. The camps were initially established and temporarily operated by the U.S. Army, under the name of the Wartime Civil Control Administration (WCCA). Later, jurisdiction was transferred to a newly-created civilian federal agency, the War Relocation Authority (WRA).

U.S. Incarceration Policy for People of Japanese Ancestry

A documented 120,313 persons of Japanese ancestry fell under the jurisdiction of the WRA. Of this number, 112,603 people were forced to leave their homes and enter U.S. concentration camps in seven states—Arizona, Arkansas, California, Colorado, Idaho, Utah, and Wyoming. A third of those incarcerated were classified as resident "aliens," despite the fact that they lived in the United States for many years prior to World War II. Less than one-third of one percent of all evacuated persons of Japanese ancestry (native and foreign-born) had been living in the U.S. for less than ten years.

"Aliens" of Japanese ancestry were "non-citizens" because of discriminatory laws that made them ineligible for naturalized citizenship. At the time of incarceration, 30,619 (80.2 percent) of the first generation "aliens" (known as *Isseis*) had resided in the United States for 23 or more years. Almost all *Isseis*

had been residents for more than fifteen years, since the 1924 Immigration Act excluded Japan from further immigration to the United States. Only 345 alien Japanese had resided in the U.S. for less than ten years.

Banished individuals had the choice of moving "voluntarily" to inland states (they had about a three-week period to do so), and approximately 9,000 people did this, to avoid being sent to concentration camps. Approximately 4,000 of these "voluntary resettlers" moved to the eastern half of California. This group was subsequently forced to move again when the Government announced that the entire state of California, not just the western half, was off limits to people of Japanese ancestry. Some 4,889 persons "voluntarily" moved to states outside of California (1,963 to Colorado; 1,519 to Utah; 305 to Idaho; 208 to eastern Washington; 115 to eastern Oregon; and the remainder scattered throughout the United States).

This incarceration policy was consistent with previous discriminatory local, state, and federal policies affecting Asian Americans in the United States. Japanese Americans were targeted, in part because of the economic competition they posed in various states, particularly on the West Coast (California, Oregon, and Washington). Many government officials saw World War II as the perfect opportunity to get rid of Japanese Americans from their states, once and for all. For the U.S. government, under President Roosevelt, the war was a good opportunity to institute its assimilation policy and "Americanization" plan: to disperse persons of Japanese ancestry throughout the U.S., in a deliberate plan to break up the "Little Tokyos" and "Japantowns."

The U.S. Constitution calls for equal protection under the law and prohibits deprivation of life, liberty, or property without "due process of law." These "protective" guarantees were suspended in this case, and the Government was able to implement this massive program with few questions asked. Congress sanctioned the plan and the U.S. Supreme Court failed to challenge its constitutionality. Few dared to oppose such a plan, presented as an urgent necessity to secure a nation under what was rhetorically stated as a dire military threat.

Intelligence Reports Dispute "Military Necessity"

Although military necessity and national security were the stated reason and goal for mass incarceration, decision-making elites knew that there was no threat to U.S. security from Japanese Americans. Top officials had access to years of intelligence reports from a variety of sources, including the Department of State, Department of Justice (through the Federal Bureau of Investigation), Navy Intelligence, and Army Intelligence. In October 1941, Jim Marshall reported:

> For five years or more there has been a constant check on both Issei [first generation immigrants from Japan] and Nisei [second generation, U.S.-born persons of Japanese ancestry]—the consensus among intelligent people is that an overwhelming majority is loyal. The few who are suspect are carefully watched. In event of war, they would be behind bars at once. In case of war, there would be some demand in California for concentration camps into which Japanese and Japanese-Americans would be herded for the duration. Army, Navy or FBI never have suggested officially that such a step would be necessary. . . . Their opinion, based on intensive and continuous investigation, is that the situation is not dangerous and that, whatever happens, there is not likely to be any trouble— with this opinion west coast newspapermen, in touch with the problem for years, agree most unanimously.[1]

In an intelligence report submitted in November 1941 (only three months before President Roosevelt signed Executive Order 9066), Curtis Munson, a Special Representative to the State Department, said that:

> As interview after interview piles up, those bringing in results began to call it the same old

tune. . . . There is no Japanese "problem" on the Coast. There will be no armed uprising of Japanese. . . .[2]

Just two days before President Roosevelt signed Executive Order 9066, the Head of the Justice Department, Francis Biddle, encouraged Roosevelt to say something in defense of persons of Japanese ancestry, and wrote, "My last advice from the War Department is that there is no evidence of planned sabotage."[3]

Despite the evidence presented to President Roosevelt—all confirming that there was no threat that warranted *en masse* incarceration—he proceeded with the incarceration policy. He also maintained a consistent pattern of not "setting the record straight" based on intelligence facts.

Experiences of Japanese American Women

All Japanese American women felt the impact of World War II, and the exclusion policy caused major disruptions and upheavals in their lives. It affected their professional careers, impinged on the ways in which they viewed the world, and changed the course and direction of their lives.

Although the exclusion orders affected all women of Japanese ancestry, their specific experiences varied broadly due to many factors, including residence at the time of the exclusion order, age at the time of incarceration (adult or child), the camp that one went into, the job that one was able to get (inside and outside of camp), the college one was admitted to, the degree of co-operation one exhibited toward the concentration camp administrators, and one's status and socio-economic class.

From 1991 to 1997 this author conducted over 300 interviews with Japanese Americans, all of whom were affected by the U.S. Government's policy to banish, exclude, and incarcerate this population, *en masse*, because of their Japanese heritage. This author discovered that, although the same policies were directed at the entire group, the personal experiences were as diverse as the individuals themselves.

The following discussion represents a sampling of five Japanese American women's experiences during

World War II derived from interviews conducted by this writer.[4]

Meriko Hoshiyama Mori

A Teenager Left to Fend for Herself After FBI Picked Up Both Parents

Meriko Hoshiyama Mori, born in Hollywood, California, is the only child of Suematsu Hoshiyama (of Niigata-ken, Japan) and Fuki Noguchi Hoshiyama (of Tochig-ken, Japan). Her parents owned a nursery/gardening business in West Los Angeles until World War II. Her mother, who taught at a Japanese language school before the war, was picked up and detained by the Federal Bureau of Investigation (FBI) on 22 February 1942. Fuki Noguchi Hoshiyama was among the few women who were picked up by the FBI (she was later released and sent to Santa Anita Assembly Center, a converted race track). She had the presence of mind to collect the personal thoughts of detainees—other Japanese women who were also picked up by the FBI. These quotations, collected at the time of internment, are hand-written in Japanese.

A few weeks later, in March 1942, Meriko Mori's father, who was the Japanese Language School treasurer, was also picked up by the FBI. Consequently, Meriko Mori was left, by herself, to take care of all the family and business matters. She was only nineteen years of age when both parents were picked up.

As a teenager desperate for help, Meriko Mori went to the social welfare office to get aid. According to Mori, they told her that they could do nothing for her because there were no rules or regulations for cases like hers. Therefore, Mori got no assistance from them. Reflecting back on this experience in a letter dated 10 February 1997, Mori wrote:

> When I was left alone, it was a shock, but perhaps not as great as it might have been because by the time my father was picked up, the FBI had come several times, and did not find him at home, because he was at work. I recall the FBI sitting in the car waiting for him to come home. . . . Although I had said I would be all alone, I recall following them [FBI] to

Mr. Hayashida's home a block away where he was picked up. Even now as I write this, tears come to my eyes. It is very difficult to recall unpleasant memories.

> My Caucasian neighbors expressed concern and wrote to me in camp. My Japanese neighbors were so concerned [about] their own families and situation of packing, moving, etc. they expressed concern but did not have the time to be involved in my predicament. If my Aunt Maki and Uncle Iwamatsu Hoshiyama did not offer to include me in their family (they had 3 girls and 2 boys), I don't know what I could have done when the welfare department didn't know what to do. To say the least, I was very fortunate and am forever grateful to Maki and Iwamatsu Hoshiyama.

When the U.S. entered World War II, Meriko Mori was a sophomore at the University of California at Los Angeles. She was surprised that she was treated like an enemy alien, and angered by her exclusion. In the words of her letter (1997):

> I was angry at the U.S. Government for its treatment of a U.S. citizen, and felt forsaken by my country and lost faith in the U.S. . . . We had lost our freedoms on which the country was founded.

Her studies were disrupted when she had to leave for Manzanar Camp, where she was watched and controlled by the U.S. Army's armed guards. In 1997, she thought about her camp experience, and said, "My memories of Manzanar are [that it was a] very hot or cold desert. I recall many sand storms and walking against the wind backwards." This camp, originally established under the U.S. Army's WCCA, later became a WRA camp. While at Manzanar, Mori earned the top salary of $19 a month for her work as a school teacher. Fifty-five years later, in her 1997 letter, Mori addressed the impact of her experiences:

> These experiences have taught me to be self-reliant, independent, resourceful, and aware of how injustices can be perpetrated on innocent victims who are weak and have no voice. We need to be constantly vigilant.

Kiyo Sato-Viacrucis

A Student Who Left Camp for a Midwest School and Who Returned to Stolen Property

Kiyo Sato-Viacrucis was born in Sacramento, California, the eldest of nine children born to Shinji "John" Sato (from Chiba-ken, Japan) and Tomomi "Mary" Watanabe Sato (from Aizuwakamatsu, Fukushima-ken). When World War II broke out, the Sato family was farming in the Sacramento area. Having graduated from Sacramento High School in Spring 1941, Kiyo Sato-Viacrucis was attending Sacramento Junior City College at the time of the incarceration orders.

In May 1942, the Sato family was ordered to go to Pinedale Assembly Center, a WCCA facility set up and run by the U.S. Army. Ironically, while her family was sent to a concentration camp, under armed Army guard, her brother was serving in the U.S. Army. He had volunteered after Pearl Harbor was bombed by Japan, and ended up serving for the duration of the war. When Kiyo Sato-Viacrucis volunteered her services to the military, and when she attempted to gain admission into institutions of higher education, she was rejected. Later she wrote to the institutions, saying: "My brother and others are fighting to uphold democratic principles. I cannot understand that an institution of your standing would have such a policy." She was eventually accepted by Western Reserve University in 1945.

After four and one half months at Pinedale, she and her family were shipped, via train and open army truck, to Poston (Arizona) Camp, which was operated by the newly-established civil federal agency, the WRA. Upon her family's arrival in July 1942, the temperature was 127 degrees Fahrenheit. Viewing all the sage brush and experiencing the heat, Kiyo Sato-Viacrucis literally passed out.

Sato-Viacrucis did what she could to leave Poston quickly. After three and one half months, she managed to depart for Hillsdale College in Michigan. Since the college was located in an inland state, she was released only if she would agree to attend this private Baptist college.

After the West Coast was opened to Japanese Americans, Kiyo Sato-Viacrucis was one of the early returnees to Sacramento in 1945. She found that her family's home had been occupied by unknown and unauthorized persons, and that all their stored goods had been stolen. Further, she saw that the Mayhew Japanese Baptist Church (in Sacramento), which had stored the incarcerated Japanese Americans' belongings, had been burned to the ground the night before her return.

The incarceration experience had continuous and long-term impact on excludees. Reflecting on the implications for her and other women, Sato-Viacrucis said, "Partly because of our background, we *nisei* women retreated from a hostile world into our shells like turtles. Even after fifty years, we are afraid to come out and tell what happened." Reminiscing in 1997, fifty-five years after the exclusionary policies and programs, she said:

> *Nisei* [U.S.-born and second generation Japanese American] men were able to go to war and be recognized for their heroic efforts, but we *nisei* women were "war casualties" on two fronts. Not only were we not of the right color for the Navy or Air Force, but we were not acceptable by many institutions of higher learning "due to policy." It was certainly devastating to be rejected by the Navy because of my color, and then by Yale, Johns Hopkins, Western Reserve University schools of nursing, again because of their "policy." It is hard to believe that even our country's most prestigious institutions of higher learning succumbed to social pressure. That is scary. It happened so easily; will it happen again?

Yoshiye Togasaki

A Medical Doctor Who Took Her Practice to the Concentration Camps

Yoshiye Togasaki was born in an upstairs room of the Geary Theater, located in San Francisco. She was the fifth of six children born to Kikumatsu Togasaki (from Ibaraki-ken, Japan) and Shige Kushida Togasaki (from Tokyo). In 1892, her mother had been sent to the United States as an activist in the Women's Christian Temperance Union. This Japanese immigrant woman was a most unique person who did not shy away from publicly expressing her opinions and speaking her mind. She had stood out on the streets of San Francisco, preaching Christian doctrine.

When World War II broke out, Yoshiye Togasaki was already established in her profession as a medical doctor. In those days, women doctors—especially women of color—were a small minority. After her December 1921 graduation from Lowell High School in San Francisco, Togasaki attended the University of California, Berkeley, where she received a bachelor's degree in public health in 1929. With her medical doctor's degree from Johns Hopkins University in June 1935, she took an internship at the Los Angeles General Hospital.

In 1938, Togasaki became chief resident for communicable diseases at the L.A. General Hospital. She remained in this position until just six months before the U.S. entered World War II. At the time of the Pearl Harbor bombing, Togasaki was an assistant to the City of Los Angeles's epidemiologist. Because she knew she would be terminated when the war broke out, she resigned.

Togasaki spent time trying to correct public perceptions about Japanese Americans. Because the President of the Council on Churches harangued persons of Japanese ancestry, Togasaki went directly to him to try to change his belief that Japanese Americans were "untrustworthy." According to Togasaki, his mind was rigidly set.

After the incarceration orders were announced, and when it became clear that Manzanar, California, would be one of the WCCA Assembly Centers, Togasaki volunteered to help set it up. She arrived at the camp on 21 March 1942, and remained there until October 1942. Open trenches and hygienic problems were prevalent throughout the camp. According to Togasaki, she worked sixteen hours a day, dealing with public health and medical matters. For her services, she earned a salary of $16 per month. She managed to get scarce medical supplies, such as vaccines, from friends or associates outside the camp.

Due to overwork, Togasaki became ill, so she went to Tule Lake Camp (also in California) to join her two sisters. Because there were few resources to diagnose and care for her illness, she went to San Francisco's Children's Hospital for diagnosis. This was a rare event, since Japanese Americans were supposed to be excluded from the area. After five or six days at Children's Hospital, Togasaki stayed at the home of a doctor friend in San Francisco. In Togasaki's words, "No one complained that a Japanese American was there."

Togasaki worked as a pediatric doctor at Tule Lake, where she worked with Dr. Pedicord, a retired doctor from the Kentucky mountains who had failed to keep abreast of the latest developments in medicine. He stirred up a lot of antagonism around Tule Lake because of his attitude toward Japanese Americans, whom he viewed as inferior, foreign, and un-American. Considered whistle blowers and antagonists, Togasaki and her two sisters, Kazue (an obstetrician) and Chiye, were transferred to Manzanar in April 1943. Yoshiye Togasaki remained at Manzanar a few months before she left, in July 1943, for a pediatric position at New York's Bellevue Hospital.

Masako Takahashi Hamada

An Excludee Who "Voluntarily" Moved Inland to Idaho

Masako Takahashi Hamada was born in Seattle, Washington, the sixth of seven children born to Kumato Takahashi and Toshi Kato Takahashi, both of Niigata-ken, Japan. After graduating from Garfield High School, she was studying in Seattle when World War II broke out.

During a three-week period in March 1942, Japanese Americans were given the option to "voluntarily" leave their homes in the military exclusion zones (the entire West Coast of the U.S. mainland) and to resettle in an inland state outside the military zones, or be sent to a concentration camp. Masako Takahashi, her mother, and five siblings decided to move and join their oldest brother and his wife in Idaho, where his wife's family [Tamura] resided. Leaving most of their valuable possessions behind, they moved to avoid going into concentration camps. They were among the 305 "voluntary movers" who entered Idaho from the restricted military zones. Another older brother, who was living in Washington at the time of the exclusion, did not move because he was originally unaware of the orders. Consequently, he was incarcerated in a concentration camp.

In the Southern Idaho area where she settled, travel was restricted in certain areas, and "NO JAPS

ALLOWED" signs were posted in various businesses, alerting the public that "Japs" would not be served. Of course, it did not matter whether one was a citizen or not; service was denied, regardless. This discriminatory behavior was matched by the Idaho governor's attitude toward Japanese Americans. Governor Chase Clark openly expressed his aversion to any Japanese American migration into the state of Idaho.

Masako Takahashi and her family faced very tough times in the new area. They struggled to make enough money to live, as they encountered new work environments and life situations. They worked for the E. H. Dewey family, who are related to Colonel W. H. Dewey of Silver City, Idaho. Although her goal, at that time, was to be a dress designer, she spent her days working in the fields, hoeing, weeding, and toiling in the hot sun for minimal rewards.

She and her sister (Yuki) went to Chicago to further their education. After the war, she married an Idaho-born Japanese American veteran of World War II, who served with the 442nd Regimental Combat Team, whose motto was "Go for Broke." She remained in Idaho, where she served as a nurse for twenty-five years and where she volunteers her services in Mountain Home, Idaho.

Reflecting upon her experiences in a 3 February 1997 letter, Hamada said, "I hope that such a sad [and] shocking experience will never be repeated again in history. . . . Let us hope that each and every one of us [will] live in peace and harmony."

Tsuru Fukui Takenaka

A Businesswoman Outside the Military Zone Who Faced Government Restrictions

Tsuru Fukui Takenaka was born on 26 August 1900, in Wakayama-ken, Japan. In 1920, after marrying Sennosuke Takenaka in Japan, she came to the United States with her husband who had been working in the U.S. prior to marriage. Upon her arrival in San Francisco, she was detained and quarantined a week by the U.S. immigration authorities at Angel Island. In her words, her immigration detention was "just like jail."

In 1930, she and her husband went to Lovelock, Nevada, and took over the Up-to-Date Laundry from the Nakamuras. They owned and worked in this hand laundry throughout World War II, and they maintained the business for years thereafter. In fact, Tsuru Takenaka continued to work in the laundry until 1990, when she was 90 years of age. During the years at the laundry, she strenuously worked long hours.

The Takenakas did not have to leave their home and go into concentration camps because they were situated in a non-military exclusion zone. Therefore, the family continued to run the laundry business throughout the war. Although some established customers did not return after the start of World War II, the Takenakas remained busy enough to keep their business going. But the military restrictions, imposed during World War II, affected the Takenakas' free movement. They were restricted to a fifty-mile radius and could not go to the closest large town, Reno. Further, according to Tsuru Takenaka, the Reno mayor was known to harbor anti-Japanese sentiments.

Until after World War II, the Takenaka family was the only Japanese American family in Lovelock, and they did experience some discriminatory treatment. Takenaka's daughter, for example, was not allowed to board a train, and her husband, Sennosuke, was subjected to harassment and "bad" talk when he went to the Persian Hotel and Restaurant in downtown Lovelock.

Final Comments

The World War II experiences of Japanese American women are as varied as the number of people involved. In this paper, only five examples are presented, to illustrate the variety in experience. While some women were already established in their profession (e.g., Togasaki), others were just beginning their careers (e.g., Sato-Viacrucis). Some women owned their own businesses in the non-exclusion areas (e.g., Takenaka), while others were employees. All were affected by their residential location. Some living in the military exclusion zones were subjected to FBI raids (e.g., Mori), and most were forced, *en masse*, to go into concentration camps (Mori, Sato-Viacrucis, and Togasaki). With mandatory removal imminent, some chose to move from military exclusion zones prior to being incarcerated in concentration camps (Takahashi Hamada).

Nearly 40 years after this incarceration policy was instituted, the U.S. Commission on Wartime Relocation and Internment of Civilians (CWRIC) was established, in 1980, to "review the facts and circumstances surrounding Executive Order Number 9066 . . . and the impact of such Executive Order on American citizens and permanent resident aliens." The Commission concluded that these policy decisions were shaped by "race prejudice, war hysteria and a failure of political leadership." In summary, "a grave personal injustice was done." Furthermore,

The excluded people suffered enormous damages and losses, both material and intangible. To the disastrous loss of farms, businesses and homes must be added the disruption for many years of careers and professional lives, as well as the long-term loss of income and opportunity. . . .

Following these findings, there were years of debate in the U.S. House of Representatives and in the U.S. Senate concerning compensation to those who had suffered this injustice. After many Congressional sessions, compromises, and legislative drafts, the U.S. House of Representatives passed the Civil Liberties Act on 17 September 1987, by a vote of 243 to 141. The U.S. Senate passed a similar bill on 20 April 1988, also after lengthy discussion, by a vote of 69 to 27. To bring the two congressional versions together, a conference bill was worked out between the U.S. House and U.S. Senate leaders. This conference bill passed in the Senate on 17 July 1988 and in the House on 4 August 1988. President Ronald Reagan signed the Civil Liberties Act of 1988 into law on 10 August 1988.

Because the new law was an authorization bill, there was no provision for actual appropriations of $20,000 payments to each eligible individual. In November 1989, President George Bush signed an authorization bill into law, entitling the U.S. Government to pay up to $500 million each fiscal year, up to a total of $1.25 billion. With this entitlement in place, the Government was able to begin payments in October 1990.

The redress policy included provisions for a U.S. Government apology for discriminatory wrongs it committed and for individual monetary compensation. The following letter, signed by President George Bush, accompanied each individual redress check:

A monetary sum and words alone cannot restore lost years or erase painful memories; neither can they fully convey our Nation's resolve to rectify injustice and to uphold the rights of individuals. We can never fully right the wrongs of the past. But we can take a clear stand for justice and recognize that serious injustices were done to Japanese Americans during World War II.

In enacting a law calling for restitution and offering a sincere apology, your fellow Americans have, in a very real sense, renewed their traditional commitment to the ideals of freedom, equality, and justice. You and your family have our best wishes for the future.

NOTES

1. Carey McWilliams. *Prejudice: Japanese-Americans: Symbol of Racial Intolerance.* Hamden, CT: Shoe String Press (Reprint), 1971. P. 114.

2. Curtis B. Munson. "Japanese on the West Coast," reprinted in *Hearings before the Joint Committee on the Investigation of the Pearl Harbor Attack* (79th Congress, 1st Session, Part 6). Washington, D.C.: Government Printing Office, January, 1946. P. 2686.

3. Bill Hosokawa. *Nisei: The Quiet American.* New York: William Morrow and Company, Inc., 1969. P. 277.

4. Quotes from the five women were taken from interviews conducted by Rita Takahashi or from their letters to her.

Lawyers for the ACLU of Illinois noted that the search of Ms. Kaukab fits an emerging pattern in which security personnel at airports target Muslims and persons of Middle Eastern descent. Recent media reports indicate that many Muslims have been subjected to unnecessary harassment and searches because of their ethnicity or religious affiliation. One such incident involves security personnel surrounding a 17-year-old Muslim high school student from Virginia, and intimidating her into removing her hijab in public. . . .

A legal complaint in the case is available online at http://archive.aclu.org/court/kaukab.pdf.

11

◆◆◆

Women and the Military,
War, and Peace

In the United States most people grow up with pride in this country, its wealth, its power, and its superior position in the world. We learn the Pledge of Allegiance, a sense of patriotism, and that our way of life is worth fighting and perhaps dying for. Most families have at least one member who has served in the military. The United States is number one in the world in terms of military technology, military bases, training of foreign forces, and military aid to foreign countries (Children's Defense Fund 2000). It also spends the most. The U.S. military budget is six times larger than that of Russia, the second biggest spender. It is more than twenty-six times as large as the combined spending of the seven countries traditionally identified by the Pentagon as the most likely adversaries (Cuba, Iran, Iraq, Libya, North Korea, Sudan, and Syria) (Center for Defense Information 2002). The largest proportion of our federal budget, $876 billion for fiscal year 2003 or 46 percent, supports current and past military operations,

including the upkeep of over four hundred bases and installations at home and over two thousand of those abroad, the development and maintenance of weapons systems, pensions for retired military personnel, veterans benefits, and interest on the national debt attributable to military spending (War Resisters League 2002). Major companies with household names like Westinghouse, Boeing, and General Electric research and develop weapons systems and military aircraft. War movies are a film industry staple, portraying images of manly heroes. Many bestselling video games involve violent scenarios. G.I. Joe has a female colleague, a helicopter pilot, dressed in a jumpsuit and helmet and armed with a 9mm Beretta. Even Barbie is in uniform.

The military shapes our notions of patriotism, heroism, honor, duty, and citizenship. President Clinton's avoidance of military service as a young man was heavily criticized by his detractors in the 1992 and 1996 election campaigns, the suggestion being that this was unpatriotic and not fitting for a president of the United States, who is also the commander in chief of the armed forces. Politically, economically, and culturally, the military is a central U.S. institution. This is more explicit since the attacks on the World Trade Center and Pentagon on September 11, 2001, and the Bush administration's declaration of a long-term "war on terrorism." Under the banner of patriotism, young people decided to enlist in the military and parents were encouraged to support them. The Bush administration called on the Hollywood film industry to make more pro-war movies. The Walt Disney Corporation distributed a State Department ad nationwide, "Can you trust your neighbor?," that urged people to report any "suspicious" activity to the police. Political scientist Cynthia Enloe shows that many aspects of U.S. culture have become militarized and notes specific ways that culture is deployed in the service of militarism (Reading 68). In Reading 69, media analysts David Croteau and William Hoynes note the ideological role of the mainstream media in promoting and reinforcing beliefs and values. They argue that 1980s Vietnam War movies, exemplified by *Rambo* and *Missing in Action,* contributed to "a political culture that created the conditions for the popular 1989 invasion of Panama and the even more popular 1991 war in the Persian Gulf."

The Need for Women in the Military

Although the vast majority of U.S. military personnel have always been male, the military has needed and continues to need women's support and participation in many capacities (D'Amico and Weinstein 1999; Enloe 1983; Isakson 1988; Weinstein and White 1997). It needs mothers to believe in the concept of patriotic duty and to encourage their sons, and more recently their daughters, to enlist or at least to support their desire to do so. It needs women nurses to heal the wounded and the traumatized. It needs wives and girlfriends back home, the prize waiting at the end of war or a period of duty overseas, who live with veterans' trauma or who mourn loved ones killed in action. During World War II, White women and women of color symbolized by Rosie the Riveter, were needed for the war effort working in shipyards and munitions factories while men

were drafted for active service overseas (Denman and Inniss 1999).

Currently the military needs women to work in electronics and many other industries producing weapons components, machine parts, tools, uniforms, household supplies, and foodstuffs for military contracts. It needs women working in nightclubs, bars, and massage parlors near foreign bases and ports providing R and R, rest and relaxation, for military personnel, or, as it is sometimes called, I and I, intoxication and intercourse (Enloe 1993a, 2000; Sturdevant and Stoltzfus 1992). And the military needs women on active duty, increasingly trained for combat as well as performing more traditional roles in administration, communications, intelligence, or medicine.

Having women in the military to the extent that they are today is a relatively new phenomenon. In 1972 women were only 1.2 percent of military personnel. The following year, after much debate, Congress ended the draft for men, though young men are still required to register for the draft when they turn 18. Many left the services as soon as they could, causing a manpower shortfall that has been made up by recruiting women, especially women of color. In 2001 women were 15 percent of all military personnel (in the Army, Air Force, Navy, Marine Corps, and Coast Guard). Almost half the women in the Army's enlisted ranks were Black (46 percent), compared to 31 percent in the Navy and 28 percent in the Air Force. African American women, Asian American women, Native American women, and Latinas made up 63 percent of enlisted women in the Army, 52 percent in the Navy, and 40 percent in the Air Force. By contrast, 64 percent of women officers in the Army are White, 75 percent of the women officers in the Navy are White, and 76 percent of women officers in the Air Force are White (Women's Research and Education Institute 2002).

The Military as Employer

For many of these women, the military offers much better opportunities than the wider society: jobs with better pay, health care, pensions, and other benefits, as well as the chance for education, travel, and escape from crisis-torn inner cities in the United States. It enhances women's self-esteem and confers the status of first-class citizenship attributed to those who serve their country. Military recruiters emphasize security, professionalism, empowerment, adventure, patriotism, and pride. In noting the benefits of army life in the early 1950s, Jean Grossholtz (Reading 64) includes medical services, expanded opportunities, a ready-made community of women, and a sense of self-worth and accomplishment. Margarethe Cammermeyer served as a military nurse for twenty-six years, in the Army, the Army Reserves, and the National Guard; she was the highest-ranking officer to challenge military policy on homosexuality before being discharged in 1992 on the basis of sexual orientation. Her autobiography emphasizes the professionalism, structure, and discipline she experienced in military life and her keen sense of patriotism and duty (Cammermeyer 1994).

As we argued in Chapter 8, the U.S. labor market has changed markedly over the past three decades or so through automation and the movement of jobs overseas. In addition to a loss of jobs, there are few sources of funding for working-class women's (and men's) education. Government funding for education and many welfare programs was cut back during the 1980s and '90s, but despite the end of the cold war, enormous changes in the former Soviet Union, and cuts in U.S. bases and personnel, the U.S. military budget has been maintained at high levels. Women who enter the military are thus going where the money is. Their very presence, however, exposes serious dilemmas and contradictions for the institution, which we explore in the next section. Another contradiction of this situation is the fact that massive government spending on the military diverts funds that could otherwise be invested in civilian job programs and inner-city communities.

Limitations to Women's Equal Participation in the Military

Support for women's equality within the military is based on a belief in women's right to equal access to education, jobs, promotion, and authority in all aspects of society, and to the benefits of first-class citizenship. Women's rights organizations, such as the National Organization for Women, have campaigned for women to have equal opportunity with men in the military, as have women military person-

nel, military women's organizations like the Minerva Center (Pasadena, Md.) and the Pallas Athena Network (New Market, Va.), and key members of Congress like former representative Pat Schroeder, who was on the Armed Services Committee for many years. In 2001, in the military, as in the civilian job market, most enlisted women were doing "women's work," including support and administration (34 percent), health care (15 percent), service and supply (10 percent), and communications and intelligence (10 percent). Among officers this was also true: 41 percent worked in health care, 12 percent as administrators, and 10 percent in supply and logistics (Women's Research and Education Institute 2002).

After years of pressure, women who served in Vietnam were honored with a memorial in Washington, D.C. This advocacy and recognition, together with women's changing position in society, have also affected social attitudes. In 1991, in the Persian Gulf War, for example, military women were featured in headline news stories around the country. Saying good-bye to their families as they prepared to go overseas, they were portrayed as professional soldiers as well as mothers.

Women's equal participation in the military is limited in several ways, however, including limits on combat roles; limited access to some military academies; the effects of a general culture of racism, sexism and sexual harassment; and the ban on being openly lesbian.

Women in Combat Roles

Women served in the U.S. military during World War II, the Korean War, and the Vietnam War. They were generally designated as auxiliary, according to political scientist Mary Katzenstein (1993), despite the fact that they performed a wider range of tasks than is usually recognized—as transport pilots (Cole 1992), mechanics, drivers, underground reconnaissance, nurses (Camp 1997), and administrators. The influx of women into the military since the mid-1970s and the question of whether to train women for combat have exposed a range of stereotypical attitudes toward women on the part of military commanders, Pentagon planners, and members of Congress, depending on the degree to which they believe that combat is male. From the late 1980s well into the '90s, countless news reports, magazine articles, editorials, and letters to the editor took up this issue.

War-making is increasingly a high-tech, push-button affair, as exemplified in the bombing missions of the 1991 Gulf War and the bombing of Kosovo in 1999, of Afghanistan in 2001, and of Iraq in 2003. But old attitudes die hard. Combat roles are dangerous and demanding. Many argue that women are not physically strong enough, are too emotional, and lack discipline or stamina. They will be bad for men's morale, it is said, and will disrupt fighting units because men will be distracted if a woman buddy is hurt or captured. The country is not ready for women coming home in body bags.

Women in the military perform their jobs well. Military planners face a dilemma. They need women to make up the shortfall in personnel; at the same time, they hold sexist or condescending notions about women. Political scientists Francine D'Amico and Laurie Weinstein (1999) comment that the "military must camouflage its reliance on *woman*power in order to maintain its self-image as a quintessentially *masculine* institution" (p. 6). It does this by marginalizing women through sexual harassment, professional disparagement, and distinctions between combatant and noncombatant. What counts as combat in modern warfare is not as simple as it might seem, however, and definitions of "the front" and "the rear" change with developments in military technology. Communications and supply, defined as noncombat areas where women work, are both likely targets of attack.

Media attention on women's participation in the Persian Gulf War showed that many performed combat roles similar to those of men, and this led to changes in laws and regulations that had previously kept women out of combat assignments (Muir 1993; Peach 1997; Sadler 1997; Skaine 1998). In 1993 the rule barring women from dangerous jobs was changed, though some exceptions were preserved. Women can work on combat ships and jet planes, but not in submarines or in direct offensive combat on the ground. Restricting women from combat roles has been a way of limiting their career advancement, as senior positions often require combat experience (Francke 1997; Stiehm 1989). By 1997 women filled only 815 of the 47,544 combat-related jobs that were opened to women in 1993 and 1994 (Study shows few women in combat jobs 1997). In fiscal year 2001, there were 114 active-duty female

fighter and bomber pilots, 366 women pilots for other aircraft, and 653 women helicopter pilots. As of October 2002, no women had been involved in "the military aspect of the war on terrorism," as the Special Forces units that had carried out almost all the action were all male (D'Agostino 2002). This situation had changed by March 2003 and women fought in the war against Iraq, with women among those servicemembers killed or taken prisoner.

Officer Training: Storming the Citadel

In 1975 Congress mandated that the three military academies were to admit women. Researching the experiences of the first women to enter the U.S. Military Academy at West Point, Janice Yoder (1989) noted the severe pressure on these women to do well. They were a highly visible, very small minority, tokens in what had been constructed as an exclusively male institution. They faced tough physical tests designed for men; they were out of the loop in many informal settings and were routinely subjected to sexist notions and behavior by male cadets who did not accept them as peers (Campbell with D'Amico 1999). As a result, for the first four years at least, the dropout rate for women was significantly higher than it was for men, a fact that could be used by policy makers to justify exclusionary practices. Yoder concluded, however, that these women were not competing on equal terms with men, and she argued for changes in evaluation criteria and the overwhelmingly male culture of the Academy, an increase in the number of women entering the Academy, and greater commitment to women's full participation at an institutional level. Since then, women have entered other private military academies like the Citadel and the Virginia Military Institute with similarly mixed success. In January 1997, two of the first four women at the Citadel withdrew because of intolerable harassment (Applebome 1997). The other two became the first female cadets to graduate from the Citadel in 1999. Two women also completed their training at the VMI in the same year. In 2002 the first class of Black women graduated from the Citadel.

Sexism and Misogyny

Added to this chilly climate for women are overt sexual harassment and sexual abuse. Melinda Smith-

Wells notes her experience of sexual harassment in the Air Force (Reading 63), even though the Department of Defense has had a "specific policy prohibiting sexual harassment of military personnel for over fifteen years," summed up as "zero-tolerance" (Guenter-Schlesinger 1999, p. 195). A 1995 Department of Defense survey reported that 4 percent of all female soldiers said they had been the victim of a completed or attempted rape during their military service, and 61 percent said that they had been sexually harassed in the Army (High 1997). Ninety percent of women in a Veterans Administration study reported harassment, and a third said they had been raped by military personnel (*STAMP Newsletter* 1998/99). Paula Coughlin, a helicopter pilot, went public with her experiences of sexual assault at the 1991 Tailhook naval aviators' convention at the Las Vegas Hilton, where women were subjected to sexual harassment, indecent assault, and indecent exposure. She testified that she endured relentless harassment from colleagues afterward and had since resigned her commission as a Navy lieutenant (Noble 1994). More than eighty other women also filed complaints, and a few also filed civil lawsuits.

After hearing testimony from servicewomen in 1992, a Senate Committee estimated that as many as 60,000 women had been sexually assaulted or raped while serving in the U.S. armed forces. Senator Dennis DeConcini commented, "American women serving in the Gulf were in greater danger of being sexually assaulted by our own troops than by the enemy" (Walker 1992, p. 6). In the fall of 1996 this issue surfaced publicly again, when women at the Aberdeen Proving Grounds Ordnance Center in Maryland complained of being sexually harassed and raped by drill sergeants during training. As part of its investigations into these allegations, the Army set up a toll-free hotline, which took four thousand calls in the first week relating to harassment at many military facilities (McKenna 1996/1997). *Time* magazine reporter Elizabeth Gleick (1996) described this issue as an abuse of power by superiors, threatening "to undermine the thing that many in the military hold sacred: the chain of command" (p. 28). Interviewed for the ABC weekly news program *20/20*, Alan Cranston, former U.S. senator from California, suggested three reasons for the intensity of sexual abuse in the military: men feeling threatened by women coworkers, the general "macho" military culture, and the fact that many military personnel

have easy access to guns (Walters and Downs 1996). As the investigation spread, military commanders did their best to attribute any misconduct to "a few bad apples." Brigadier General Robert Courter, for example, commander of the 37th Training Wing at Lackland Air Force Base, was quoted as saying, "There are going to be incidents, but where we have those cases, we take action. . . . I feel certain the American people can be confident that their sons and daughters are going to be safe in the Air Force" (Military sex scandal 1996, p. A15).

In the past several years, more women have undertaken scholarly research on sexism as ingrained in military culture (D'Amico 1998; Guenter-Schlesinger 1999; Morris 1999), initiated internal proceedings or lawsuits concerning sexual abuse (Woodman 1997), opened up these issues to a wider audience by writing about their personal experiences (e.g., Dean 1997), and organized to change military protocols, regulations, practices, and culture. Survivors Take Action Against Abuse by Military Personnel (STAMP, Fairborne, Ohio), for example, grew out of women's anger and frustration with the lack of accountability for sexual harassment and abuse of women in the armed forces by their colleagues and superiors. Despite the existence of policies against sexual harassment, and an increase in sensitivity training for military personnel, entrenched military culture blocks the systematic implementation of such policies (Guenter-Schlesinger 1999).

Racism

Although the armed services were officially integrated in 1948, decades before desegregation in the southern states, racism, like sexism, is still a common occurrence in the military between individuals and at an institutional level. The preponderance of women of color in the enlisted ranks also demonstrates the institutionalized racism of the wider society (Hall 1999; Moore 1996). In 1994 a House Armed Services Committee investigation uncovered serious problems with institutionalized racism throughout the armed forces and warned about skinhead and other extremist activity on four military bases visited by investigators. In December 1995, for example, two African American civilians were random victims, shot and killed by three White servicemen, described in press reports as right-wing extremists, from the Army's 82nd Airborne Division at Fort Bragg, North

Carolina (Citizen Soldier 1996). In December 1996, two African American airmen at Kelly Air Force Base (Texas) talked to the media about a racist incident in which they were taunted by men wearing pillowcases resembling Ku Klux Klan hoods and said that they were dissatisfied with the Air Force's response to their complaints (2 Black airmen 1996). In 1995 the *New York Times* reported discrimination against African American military personnel in promotion decisions (Military is found 1995). Military statistics generally include Black women as part of the general category of "women in the military," whereas Black service personnel are assumed to be Black males. Official data do not take account of the intersectionality of race and gender. Hall (1999) notes that a 1994 U.S. House Armed Services Committee report found that service members of color perceived racial discrimination in opportunities for career-enhancing assignments or training. This information was not broken down by gender, making it impossible to track discrimination fully. Such limitations in reporting continue.

Sexual Orientation

A final area of limitation for women—and men—in the military concerns sexual orientation. The Pentagon considers homosexuality incompatible with military service, and a series of regulations have precluded lesbians and gay men from serving openly, despite their continuing presence as officers and enlisted personnel (Scott and Stanley 1994; Webber 1993). In Reading 64 Jean Grossholtz pinpoints the contradiction implicit in this policy: The military is based on male bonding, yet homosexuality is banned. Thousands of gay men and lesbians have been discharged over the years in what she refers to as "purges." Margarethe Cammermeyer (1994) notes that in June 1992 the General Accounting Office reported that 1,400 military personnel who had been trained for military service were discharged each year between 1980 and 1991, at an estimated cost of $494 million, not including the cost of investigations (p. 293). During his first presidential election campaign, Bill Clinton promised to lift the ban on gays in the military when he came into office in 1992. Concerted opposition from the Pentagon and many politicians made this impossible, however, and some argue that current policy, summed up as "Don't Ask,

Don't Tell, Don't Pursue," is not much different than before. "Homosexual conduct," defined as homosexual activity, trying to marry someone of the same sex, or acknowledging one's homosexuality, is grounds for discharge. A number of lesbians and gay men have challenged this policy in court. Gay rights organizations, like the National Gay and Lesbian Task Force and Gay, Lesbian, and Bisexual Vets of America, continue to raise this issue as an example of lesbians' and gay men's second-class citizenship.

Reports of anti-gay harassment—including verbal abuse, beatings, death threats, and apparent killings—more than doubled in the late 1990s, increasing from 182 violations documented in 1997 to 400 in 1998 (Servicemembers Legal Defense Network 1999). Military policy expressly forbids such harassment, but in April 1998, five years after the "Don't Ask, Don't Tell, Don't Pursue" policy was introduced, the Pentagon acknowledged that the service branches had not instructed commanders on how to investigate those who make anti-gay threats. The Department of Defense discharged 1,250 service members in 2001 for being lesbian, gay, or bisexual, the largest number of gay discharges in more than a decade (Servicemembers Legal Defense Network 2002). Women were 30 percent of those discharged, though they make up only 14 percent of active duty personnel. In August 1999, the Department of Defense issued its updated policy on gays in the military requiring mandatory training on anti-harassment guidelines for all troops, beginning in boot camp. In March 2000, Pentagon officials conceded that there is a "disturbing" level of gay harassment in the military (Richter 2000) and this continues. The Servicemembers Legal Defense Network (2002) urges Pentagon officials and service members to uphold the Anti-Harassment Action Plan published in 2000, and argues that "forcing lesbian, gay and bisexual service members to hide, lie, evade and deceive their commanders, subordinates, peers, families and friends breaks the bonds of trust among service members essential to unit cohesion" (p. 6).

Military Wives

Military wives have been the subject of a number of studies in the past decade or so (D'Amico and Weinstein 1999; Enloe 1988, 2000; Weinstein and White

1997). The model military wife is a staunch supporter of her husband's career. She learns to manage the moves from base to base, the disruption of family life, and interruptions in her own work (and, increasingly, she may be in the military herself). Wives and children of military families also suffer abuse at the hands of servicemen husbands and fathers. Researchers attribute this to a combination of factors: the stress of military jobs, family responsibilities, relatively low pay, uncertainty about job security, training for combat, and relative powerlessness at work. Reports of spousal abuse of wives associated with the military rose from 18.6 per thousand in 1990 to 25.6 per thousand in 1996 (U.S. Department of Defense 1996). As is the case for the estimate of domestic violence in civilian families, this is inevitably a conservative estimate. Rates of domestic violence among military personnel are considerably higher than civilian rates ("The War at Home," *60 Minutes*, Jan. 17, 1999). Women abused by military personnel are often fearful of reporting incidents because of a combination of lack of confidentiality and privacy; limited victim services; lack of training and assistance on the part of military commanders; and disruption caused by moving from base to base.

According to official policy, violence against women and children is not to be condoned or tolerated. However, the message has not been clear and consistent throughout command leadership (Miles Foundation 1999). "The War at Home," which first aired on *60 Minutes* in January 1999 and again in September 2002, helped to make this issue more public and to support victims of military violence. The Miles Foundation (Waterbury, Conn.) and Survivors in Service United have taken up the issue of violence within military families (Hansen 2001). In 2000, President Clinton appointed a Defense Task Force on Domestic Violence, comprising twelve high-ranking military members and twelve civilian members (domestic violence experts and legal practitioners), to assist in improving the military's response to domestic violence. In November 2001, Deputy Secretary of Defense Paul Wolfowitz issued an official memorandum stating that domestic violence will not be tolerated in the military and calling on all commanders to update and standardize education and training programs, to increase protection for victims, to improve coordination between military and civilian agencies that respond to incidents of domestic violence, and

to provide information to personnel on local services and resources. Meanwhile, this issue hit the headlines in the summer of 2002 when, within six weeks, the wives of four soldiers who had served in Afghanistan were killed at Fort Bragg (N.C.), allegedly by their husbands. Two of the soldiers killed themselves as well. Three of the four men were in the Special Forces, considered the toughest and most aggressive unit in the Army. The Special Operation command said it would study the stress wartime deployments may be adding to already-shaky marriages. The military announced that soldiers would be screened for psychological problems before they leave Afghanistan and commanders will watch out for symptoms of depression and anxiety among their troops. Also in 2002, a bipartisan effort by elected officials and activists was successful in getting increased funding for domestic violence services in the Defense Appropriation Act for Fiscal Year 2003. Moreover, the Armed Forces Security Act, which became law on December 2, 2002, provides for the enforcement of civilian court protective orders.

The Impact of the U.S. Military on Women Overseas

The worldwide superiority of the United States—in political, economic, and military terms—is sustained by a wide network of U.S. bases, troops, ships, submarines, and aircraft in Europe, Asia, Latin America, the Caribbean, the Pacific, and the Middle East. Since the Bush administration declared war on terrorism after the attacks of September 11, 2001, U.S. bases have been established at thirteen locations in nine countries around Afghanistan, and U.S. troops have returned to the Philippines. This U.S. presence relies on agreements with each particular government. In return the military may pay rent for the land it occupies. Some local people may be employed directly on the bases; many others work in nearby businesses patronized by U.S. military personnel. We consider four ways that U.S. military policies and bases abroad affect women: through militarized prostitution, through their responsibility for mixed-race children fathered by U.S. service personnel, through crimes of violence committed by U.S. troops, and through the harmful environmental effects of war and preparations for war.

Militarized Prostitution

As a way of keeping up the morale of their troops, military commanders have long tolerated, and sometimes actively encouraged, women to live outside military camps to support and sexually service the men. With U.S. bases positioned strategically around the globe, especially since World War II, militarized prostitution has required explicit arrangements between the U.S. government and the governments of the Philippines, Japan (Okinawa), Thailand, and South Korea, for example, where many women work in bars and massage parlors, "entertaining" U.S. troops (Enloe 1990, 1993a; 2000; Sturdevant and Stoltzfus 1992). As a way of protecting the men's health, women who work in bars must have regular medical exams, on the assumption that they are the source of sexually transmitted infections (Moon 1997). If the bar women fail such tests, they are quarantined until they pass. They usually earn better money than they can make in other ways, though this may be harder as they grow older. By creating a class of women who are available for sexual servicing, the governments attempt to limit the sexual demands of U.S. military personnel to specific women and specific locations.

Despite the low opinion many local people have of bar women, their work is the linchpin of the subeconomy of the "G.I. towns" adjoining the bases, and many people, including store owners, salespeople, bar owners, restaurateurs, cooks, pimps, procurers, cab drivers, and security men, are in business as a result of their work. Some of the bar women are able to send money to their aging parents or younger siblings, an important part of being a good daughter, especially in countries with few social services or welfare supports. Occupational dangers for the women include psychological violence, rape, and beatings from some of their customers; health risks from contraceptive devices, especially IUDs; abortions; AIDS and other sexually transmitted infections; drug use; and a general lack of respect associated with this stigmatized work. Currently, many women working in bars around U.S. bases in South Korea are recruited from the Philippines, part of the export of Filipino women workers described by Grace Chang (Reading 54, Chapter 9). In March 2002, the *Philippine Daily Inquirer* reported that Filipino women were being recruited in large numbers as sex workers to service U.S. troops recently stationed in various parts of the Philippines. Another noticeable group are Russian women, displaced due to the collapse of the Russian economy in the transition to a capitalist system and working in bars around U.S. bases overseas.

Mixed-Race Children Fathered by U.S. Troops

Many bar women and former bar women in Okinawa (Japan), South Korea, the Philippines, and Vietnam have Amerasian children, an often-neglected group. Some of them, born during the Korean War or Vietnam War, are now in their forties and fifties; others are young children born to women recently involved with U.S. troops stationed in South Korea or Okinawa. Most of them have been raised in poverty, further stigmatized by their mothers' occupation and their own mixed heritage. According to Margo Okazawa-Rey (1997), many of the mothers of Amerasian children in South Korea had serious relationships with the children's fathers. Although some marriages take place each year between Korean women and U.S. military personnel in South Korea, most of the men simply leave. They may turn out to be already married in the United States—a fact they had not thought necessary to mention—or they just disappear. Many of the children of these unions have not had much schooling as a result of poverty and intimidation and harassment from their peers. In South Korea, Amerasians whose fathers are African American are more stigmatized than those with White fathers. They may gain some acceptance by doing well in stereotypically Black spheres like sports and music. Some of the girls become bar women like their mothers. A relatively small number of such children are adopted by U.S. families, but this is expensive and not possible for children whose births have not been registered.

Crimes of Violence Against Women

The behavior of U.S. troops in other countries is governed by agreements between the U.S. government and the host government, called Status of Forces Agreements (SOFAs). Usually U.S. military personnel who commit crimes against civilians are dealt with, if at all, through military channels rather than the local courts. In many cases, U.S. troops are not held responsible for crimes they commit. Sometimes they are simply moved to another posting. This is a highly contentious issue, especially for those who do not support the U.S. military presence in their countries. In South Korea, for example, the National Campaign for Eradication of Crime by U.S. Troops in Korea was founded in 1993, growing out of a coalition of women, students, labor activists, religious people, and human rights activists that formed to protest the brutal murder of a young woman, Yoon Kum E, the previous year. The campaign collects information about crimes committed against Korean civilians by U.S. military personnel and cites a South Korean Assembly report that estimated 39,542 such crimes between 1967 and 1987, including murders, brutal rapes, and sexual abuse; incidents of arson, theft, smuggling, fraud, and traffic offenses; an outflow of P.X. (on-base department store) merchandise; and a black market in U.S. goods (Ahn 1996). This situation is not known by many in the United States and is rarely publicized here. This customary silence, however, was broken in the fall of 1995 when a 12-year-old Okinawan girl was abducted and raped by three U.S. military personnel. This incident is one of many; its brutality and the victim's age were important factors in generating renewed outrage at the presence of U.S. bases by many Okinawans (Okazawa-Rey and Kirk 1996; Takazato 2000).

Health Effects of Environmental Contamination

Militaries create more pollution than other institutions, but unlike industry, military pollution is governed by fewer regulations, monitoring programs, and controls (Seager 1993). Routine military operations involve the use of highly carcinogenic materials, including fuels, oils, solvents, and heavy metals, that are regularly released, affecting the land, water, air, and ocean, as well as the health of people living around U.S. bases overseas. Experience in the Philippines, for example, suggests that the U.S. military had not followed its own, admittedly weak, guidelines for the storage and disposal of contaminants. In the mid-1990s, after the U.S. military had evacuated long-term bases in the Philippines, Filipino families were housed at the former Clarke Air Force Base where their only water supply was a contaminated well. By 1999, eight women had been diagnosed with breast cancer and nineteen had suffered reproductive problems including miscarriages and

stillbirths. Twenty-five children suffer rare diseases such as leukemia, congenital heart disease, disorders of the central nervous system, and speech impairments. Some have already died from these effects of military contamination; others are only now beginning to show symptoms (Zamora-Olib 2000). Another example concerns the effects of sustained noise experienced by people living near bases where planes are constantly taking off and landing. Women living around Kadena Air Force Base in Okinawa (Japan), for example, have more low-birth-weight babies than are born in any other part of Japan, attributable to stress caused by noise (Okinawa Prefecture 1998).

The U.S. nuclear weapons industry has also caused long-term environmental devastation in this country and overseas (Birks and Erlich 1989; Lindsay-Poland and Morgan 1998; Seager 1993; Shulman 1990). In the 1950s and early 1960s the United States military, as well as those of Britain and France, undertook a series of atomic tests in the Pacific that irradiated whole islands and contaminated soil and water for generations to come. The U.S. military conducted tests in Micronesia, which it administered as a United Nations Strategic Trust Territory, supposedly as a step toward the political independence of the islanders. Many Micronesian women have since given birth to children with severe illnesses or disabilities caused by radiation, including some "jellyfish babies" without skeletons who live only a few hours (de Ishtar 1994; Dibblin 1989). Pacific Island women and men have contracted several kinds of cancer as a result of their exposure to high levels of radioactive fallout. Given the long-lasting effects of atomic material in the food chain and people's reproductive systems, these disabilities and illnesses are likely to last for many generations. Film footage of the U.S. tests, included in newsreels for U.S. audiences, described the islanders as simple people, indeed, as happy savages (O'Rourke 1985). In 1969, some years after the partial Test Ban Treaty (1963), which banned atomic tests in the atmosphere, the United States ended its trusteeship of Micronesia. Henry Kissinger, then secretary of state, was highly dismissive of the indigenous people in his comment "There's only 90,000 people out there, who gives a damn?" (Women Working for a Nuclear-Free and Independent Pacific 1987).

Many in Pacific Island nations see these atomic—and later nuclear—tests, which France continued until 1996, as imperialist and racist. Various activist organizations are campaigning for a nuclear-free and independent Pacific and see U.S. military bases in Hawaii and Guam, for example, and the activities of the U.S. Pacific fleet as a serious limitation on their sovereignty and self-determination (Trask 1999). Meanwhile, Pacific-island women take the lead in trying to keep their families and devastated communities together.

Women's Opposition to the Military

Early Peace Organizations in the United States

Activist organizations oppose the presence and impact of U.S. military bases in many countries, including those mentioned earlier. This opposition is sometimes based on nationalism, sometimes on arguments for greater self-determination, local control of land and resources, with more sustainable economic development. Women often play a key role in these organizations.

In the United States, too, although many women have supported and continue to support the military in various ways, there is a history of women's opposition to militarism and war with roots in Quakerism and the nineteenth-century suffrage and temperance movements (Alonso 1993; Washburn 1993). Julia Ward Howe, for example, remembered as the author of the Civil War song "The Battle Hymn of the Republic," was involved in the suffrage movement as a way of organizing women for peace. In 1873 she initiated Mothers' Day for Peace on June 2, a day to honor mothers, who, she felt, best understood the suffering caused by war. Women's peace festivals were organized in several U.S. cities, mainly in the Northeast and Midwest, with women speakers who opposed war and military training in schools. The Philadelphia Peace Society was still organizing in this way as late as 1909 (Alonso 1993). During the 1890s many women's organizations had peace committees that were active in the years before U.S. entry into World War I. In 1914 the Women's Peace Party was formed under the leadership of Carrie Chapman Catt and Jane Addams.

Despite difficulties of obtaining passports and wartime travel, over one thousand women from twelve countries, "cutting across national enmities," participated in a Congress of Women in the Hague, Holland, in 1915, calling for an end to the war. The congress sent delegations to meet with heads of state in fourteen countries and influenced press and public opinion (Foster 1989). A second congress at the end of the war proposed an ongoing international organization: the Women's International League for Peace and Freedom (WILPF), which is active in thirty-seven countries today and maintains international offices at the United Nations and in Geneva, Switzerland. Among the participants at the second congress were Mary Church Terrell, a Black labor leader from the United States, and Jeanette Rankin, the first U.S. congresswoman and the only member of Congress to vote against U.S. involvement in both world wars. In the 1950s and again in the 1960s, more U.S. women than men opposed the Korean War and Vietnam War. Women Strike for Peace, founded in 1961 and still active through the 1980s, was initially concerned with the nuclear arms race, as well as the Vietnam War (Swerdlow 1993). These organizations attracted members who were overwhelmingly White and middle class, though many women of color have an antimilitarist perspective, as exemplified by the Women of Color Resource Center statement on the "war on terrorism" (Reading 66).

Feminist Antimilitarist Perspectives

Women's opposition to militarism draws on a range of theoretical perspectives, which we discuss briefly below. In any particular organization several of these perspectives may provide the basis for activism, but it is useful to look at them separately here to clarify different and sometimes contradictory positions.

Women's Peaceful Nature   Although some women— and men—believe that women are "naturally" more peaceful than men, there is no conclusive evidence for this. Differences in socialization, however, from infancy onward, lead to important differences in attitudes, behavior, and responsibilities in caring for others. In U.S. electoral politics since 1980, these differences have been described as creating a "gender gap," under which more women than men oppose high military budgets and environmental destruction and support socially useful government

Human and Financial Costs of War

- Since 1900 there have been more than 250 wars. The civilian casualty rate in World War I was 5 percent, compared to 90 percent of war casualties in 1990, most of whom were women and children. This change is due in part to "deliberate and systematic violence against whole populations" (Swiss and Giller 1993, p. 612).

- There are approximately 50 million uprooted people around the world due to war— refugees who have sought safety in another country and people displaced within their own country. Between 75 and 80 percent of them are women and children who have lost their homes, farms, and sources of livelihood (UN High Commission for Refugees 2002).

- World military expenditure has been increasing since 1998, after an eleven-year period of reductions (1987–98). In 2001 it amounted to an estimated $839 billion, not including supplementary spending as a result of the September 11 attacks on the United States and the subsequent war on terrorism (Stockholm International Peace Research Institute 2002).

- The cost of the war against Iraq has been estimated at $50–140 billion, depending on the length of the war, and $25–100 billion for postwar reconstruction (Nordhaus 2002).

- Women are subjected to widespread sexual abuse in wartime. In the 1990s in Bosnia and Rwanda, rape was a deliberate weapon of war.

- More than 300,000 young people, many of them female refugees, are currently serving as child soldiers around the world (UN High Commission for Refugees 2002).

- The U.S. military budget of $369 billion for fiscal year 2003 is more than $1 billion per day. It could provide day care for 124,069 toddlers in urban areas (Billich 2001), or modernize 455 schools (American Society of Civil Engineers 1999), or provide annual tuition for 266,383 students at four-year public universities for 2002–2003 (College Board, n.d.).

- The cost of one Stealth bomber—$2.2 billion—could supply family planning services to 120 million women (Sivard 1996).

- The cost of one multiple launcher rocket system loaded with ballistic missiles (a long-range self-propelled artillery weapon widely used in the 1991 Persian Gulf War), at $29 million, could have supplied one year's basic rural water and sanitation services for 2 million people in developing countries (Sivard 1996).

- In Cambodia, where one of every 236 people is an amputee; there are as many land mines planted as there are people (estimated 10 million mines and 9.9 million people) (Sivard 1996).

spending (Abzug 1984; Gallagher 1993). Many who oppose the military see the current division of labor in society between men's and women's roles as a fundamental aspect of military systems, whereby men (and now a few women) "protect" women, children, and older people. They ask: Can we afford this dichotomy? Where does it lead? Those who support women's equal access to social institutions argue that everyone should have the opportunity to join the military and take on roles formerly reserved for men. Opponents argue that the abolition of war is dependent on changing this division of labor, with men taking on traditional women's roles and caring for infants and small children, the elderly, and the sick (Dinnerstein 1989; Ruddick 1989).

Maternalism Some women see their opposition to war mainly in terms of their responsibility to protect and nurture their children; they want to save the lives of both their own children and the children of "enemy" mothers. In the early 1980s, for example, when the U.S. and Soviet militaries were deploying nuclear weapons in Europe, Susan Lamb, who lived near USAF Greenham Common in England, a nuclear base, put it this way:

> I've got two young children, and I've taken responsibility for their passage into adulthood. Everyone tells me they are my responsibility. The government tells me this. It is my responsibility to create a world fit for them to grow up in. I can't say I'm responsible for my children not catching whooping cough and not responsible for doing anything about the threat of annihilation that hangs over them every minute of the day.
>
> *(Quoted in Cook and Kirk 1983, p. 27)*

Although this approach can sentimentalize motherhood, it is also powerful because mothers are behaving according to their roles and it is difficult for the state to suppress them. They expose contradictions: that the state, through militarism, does not let them get on with their job of mothering.

Diversion of Military Budgets to Socially Useful Programs   Another argument put forward by peace activists—women and men—concerns government spending. Organizations like Women's Action for New Directions (WAND, Arlington, Mass.) and the Women's International League for Peace and Freedom (U.S. Section, Philadelphia) argue for reductions in military expenditures and redistribution of those funds to provide for social programs that benefit women and their families. Cuts in funding for nuclear weapons, chemical and biological weapons, and U.S. troops, ships, and aircraft carriers around the world, they argue, could fund job-training programs, public housing, education, urban development, environmental cleanup, and AIDS research, for example. They would enable cuts in Medicaid, food stamps, and child nutrition programs to be restored.

Women's Action for New Directions is organizing nationwide on the issue of the bloated military budget. When tax dollars are diverted from civilian programs like education and health care, where many women are employed, military spending is also at the expense of women's jobs (Anderson 1999). A 1991 research report, *Converting the American Economy* (Anderson, Bischak, and Oden 1991), showed the economic effects of cutting the military budget by $70 billion per year and transferring these funds into health

care, Head Start, education, job training, mass transit, and the environment. This would have created 460,000 additional jobs for women. Economist and director of Employment Research Associates Marion Anderson (1999) notes that "every $1 billion transferred from the Pentagon to these civilian expenditures generates a net gain of about 6,800 women's jobs" (p. 248).

The Military as a Sexist and Racist Institution   Opposition to the military also turns on the argument that, by its very nature, the military is profoundly antifeminist and racist and is fundamental to political systems that oppress women and peoples of color. Its ultimate effectiveness depends on people's ability to see reality in oppositional categories: us and them, friends and enemies, kill or be killed (Reardon 1985). To this end it is organized on rigidly hierarchical lines, demanding unquestioning obedience to superiors. Although the military uses women's labor in many ways, as mentioned earlier, it does so strictly on its own terms. The military environment also fosters violence against women. The higher incidence of domestic violence in military families than in nonmilitary families and crimes of violence against women committed near military bases in the United States and overseas are not coincidences but integral aspects of military life and training (Morris 1999). Moreover, rape is used as a weapon of war (Peterson and Runyan 1993; Rayner 1997; Tétreault 1997), as mentioned in Chapter 6 (and Reading 40).

This opposition focuses not only on how the military operates but also on militarism as an underlying system and worldview based on the objectification of "others" as enemies, a culture that celebrates war and killing (Reardon 1985). The Women's Pentagon Action, for example, identified militarism as a cornerstone of the oppression of women and the destruction of the nonhuman world. Thousands of women surrounded the Pentagon in November 1980 and again in 1981. They protested massive military budgets; the fact that militaries cause more ecological destruction than any other institutions; the widespread, everyday culture of violence manifested in war toys, films, and video games; the connection between violence and sexuality in pornography, rape, battering, and incest; and the connections between militarism and racism. This was no routine demonstration but a highly creative action organized in four stages: mourning, rage, empowerment, and defiance, culminating in the arrest of many women who chose to blockade the doors of the Pentagon (King 1983). The Unity Statement of the Women's Pentagon Action is included as Reading 65.

At an Okinawan rally on violence and human rights violations against girls and women in September 1995, a women's declaration pointed to military training as a systematic process of dehumanization that turns "soldiers into war machines who inflict violence on the Okinawan community, only a chain-link fence away" (Okinawa Women Act against Military Violence 1996, p. 7). These activists see crucial connections between personal violence and international violence, both based on the objectification of others. Political scientist Cynthia Enloe's (1990, 1993b) concept of a constructed militarized masculinity fits in here. Citing the sexual assault of women at the Tailhook meeting of Navy aviators in 1991, the general incidence of sexual assault on military women, men's resistance to women in combat, and fears about openly gay men and lesbians in the military, she argues that the U.S. military is based on very specific notions of "militarized masculinity" (Enloe 1993b). Thus, women in combat roles threaten the manliness of war and the very nature of militarism as male.

Women who oppose militarism have very different perspectives from those who enter the military. They may also have different class positions and more opportunities for education and work. Liberal feminists have criticized feminist peace activists for being classist and racist in their condemnation of the military as an employer when working women, especially women of color, have few employment options. The Unity Statement of the Women's Pentagon Action, for example, argues for equality between men and women but against participation in the military for either sex. Peace activists also argue that the military is no place for gay men and lesbians. Jean Grossholtz (Reading 64) writes that, ironically, it was her involvement in the military, seeing casualties of the Korean War, that changed her views and led her to become a peace activist later in life. Professor of sociology and activist Barbara Omolade (1989) notes the contradictions of militarism for people of color in the United States, many of whom support the military because it provides economic opportunities that are lacking in civilian society. Military personnel of color fight for the United States, a country where they are oppressed. Since World

DO YOU HAVE A FEMALE *ACTION FIGURE* THAT SPEAKS OUT AGAINST *DISCRIMINATION AND WAR!?*

War II, the people they have fought against and are trained to kill are other people of color in various parts of the world—Vietnam, Grenada, Libya, Panama, and Iraq—to take examples from the past several decades. Combatants of color are more likely to be killed than their White counterparts, as happened in Vietnam.

Redefining Security

Since the attacks of September 11, 2001, and the Bush administration's immediate decision to take military action, many people have questioned whether the military and militarism—as a system of values and operations—can provide human security, as opposed to national security. In Reading 67, Charlotte Bunch, director of the Center for Women's Global Leadership (Rutgers University, N.J.), argues for a redefinition of security based on human rights, for example. The Women of Color Resource Center (Oakland, Calif.) point out that gender is an issue in the "war on terrorism." American sympathy for the brutal treatment of Afghan women at the hands of the Taliban regime was used to build support for the bombing of Afghanistan. This group produced thousands of postcards in 2002 and 2003, giving ten reasons why women should oppose the "war on terrorism" (Reading 66).

This international crisis has given new impetus to feminist understandings of links between U.S. domestic and foreign policy. It generated new energy for established organizations like Women's International League for Peace and Freedom (Philadelphia), Women's Action for New Directions (WAND, Arlington, Mass.), Women in Black (New York and other cities), and Women Against Military Madness (Minneapolis). It has also generated many new groups and networks, including Mothers Acting Up (Boulder, Colo.), Gather the Women, the Lysistrata Project, Racial Justice 911, and Women United for Peace, all organizing in a decentralized way, often via the Internet. Student groups include Students Taking Action for New Directions (STAND, Atlanta). In November 2002, Code Pink: Women for Peace started a daily peace camp and vigil outside the White House in Washington, D.C., that culminated in a major rally and demonstration against war in Iraq on March 8, 2003, International Women's Day. Also on that day the International Wages for Housework Campaign organized a Global Women's Strike, under the slogan "Invest in Caring, Not Killing," with participating groups from over thirty countries.

A world that will sustain the lives of individuals, as well as wider communities, has four basic requirements:

- The environment in which we live must be able to sustain human and natural life.
- People's basic survival needs for food, clothing, shelter, health care, and education must be met.
- People's fundamental human dignity, agency, and cultural identities must be honored.
- People and the natural environment must be protected from avoidable harm.

This view includes security for the individual—a major reason why women in the United States are drawn to enlist in the military—but also involves security at the meso, macro, and global levels (Boulding 1990; Reardon 1993).

Questions for Reflection

As you read and discuss this chapter, think about these questions:

1. What purposes does the military serve in this society?
2. Who joins the military? Why?
3. Why has the issue of gays in the military surfaced as an issue of mainstream U.S. politics?
4. What is your idea of security?
5. What can you do to improve your sense of safety/security in different settings?
6. How do you understand the "war on terrorism"?

Finding Out More on the Web

1. Compare the proportion of the federal budget that is spent on education, social services, health, and foreign aid with that spent on the military. How much does your state contribute to the military budget? How much do you contribute? Use the following Web sites:

   Center for Defense Information: **www.cdi.org**

   National Priorities Project: **www.nationalpriorities.org**

   War Resisters League: **www.warresisters.org**

2. Find out more about the organizations mentioned in this chapter. What are their strategies and activities?

3. In Reading 67, Charlotte Bunch mentions the International Criminal Court and the U.N. World Conference Against Racism (2001). What is the significance of these international efforts for world peace and security?

Taking Action

1. Think about the ways you usually resolve conflicts or serious differences of opinion with your family, friends and peers, teachers, and employers. What are the dynamics involved in each case? Do you cave in without expressing your opinion? Do you insist that you are right? Does violence play a part in this process? If so, why?

2. List all the kinds of service you can imagine, as an alternative to military service, that would improve people's security.

3. Analyze the representation of armed conflict and war in the news media or popular culture.

4. Using the information about federal spending you found on the Web, make a budget to provide for genuine security.

SIXTY-THREE

The Women in Blue

Melinda Smith-Wells

The advertising slogan says: "The United States Air Force, a great way of life!" Is it really? I beg to differ.

In order to fuel the war-fighting machine, and advance its economic and political goals, our government—the government I provide "muscle" for—embarked on a media campaign to attract young, adventurous dreamers like me. It has enticed and entrapped many.

"I promise to defend, honor and protect my country and fellow countrymen with my life, until the day that I die." In the early morning hours six years ago, in South Carolina, I swore to uphold and defend the Constitution of the United States against all enemies, foreign and domestic. In making this promise, I relinquished a substantial portion of my liberty to ensure that others would be able to have and enjoy their own. I did not foresee what the future had in store for me on that fateful morning that seems so long ago. Unaware of the consequences, I jumped in feet first, hoping to be successful and to achieve something great. Unfortunately, I seem to have landed in something bad.

Recruiting? I didn't need that; my father was "in." I thought I was doing the right thing at the time—securing my future and giving myself the opportunity to advance and excel in life. I wanted the finer things that life has to offer: education, training, travel, money: things that many only dream of. I must admit that I have received these things, more or less, but not the quality I was promised, and at a cost I didn't think would be so high.

I am a twenty-five-year-old woman of Portuguese–Puerto Rican ancestry, struggling to juggle my studies to attain a Bachelor of Arts Degree in Business Administration while serving as an active duty military member. Currently, I am a Maintenance Scheduler. I schedule maintenance for the various aircraft and support equipment in the Air Force inventory. During my six-year military career I have been stationed at three different Air Force bases in the U.S.:

Homestead AFB, Florida; McCord AFB, Washington; and Beale AFB, California. I have had the opportunity to travel to South Korea and England on temporary duty.

The military has affected my personal life in two ways. First, I don't know my husband as well as I'd like to because I constantly go on temporary assignments to various locations. This can be very stressful on a relationship because it keeps us apart for six months at a time or longer. There are times when we need each other, but due to the circumstances we can't be together. We have been married for nearly four years, but have only spent 2.5 years together. Second, I don't have any "true" friends with whom to socialize. Once you get to the point where you consider someone a friend, either one of you may be moved to a different location. You have to get used to people leaving, and the transient nature of the "business."

The "trials and tribulations" of military life have definitely had an effect on me and many other women that I have worked with. Sexual harassment has been and always will be a sensitive issue in all organizations because of the narrow-minded, insecure individuals that exist in our world. In the military, sexual harassment—regardless of what the establishment says—is very much alive and well. In my experience, the military leadership tends to look the other way when it comes to this issue. I think they feel that "boys will be boys," and women should accept this because the military is a man's world.

Oh yes, when you see incidents like "Tailhook" or those involving the Army training instructors, those of you on the outside might say, "the military will get to the bottom of this and resolve these matters." Don't be naïve enough to think that happens. The military will resolve matters in the media but not in the various units around the military world. What the leadership does is to send out memorandums or have a 1–2 hour "crash training course" on sexual harassment as if this will eliminate the problem! Does that resolve the matter? What do you think? It's just another piece of training for people to brush aside.

If you should go so far as to file a sexual harassment complaint, you may put your career in jeopardy. These matters are supposed to be confidential but they eventually get out. When they do, you walk around with a stigma attached to you. You become labeled a "bitch or whore" who wanted it to happen and couldn't handle it when it did. "You brought it upon yourself because you shouldn't walk around here looking and smelling nice." That's a great environment to live and work in, huh!

Although my overall experiences in the Air Force have been livable, I do not wish to endure them again for the simple fact that my military experience has not met my expectations. Budget cuts have had an intense impact on the quality of military life. Yes, the military offers educational benefits to its members if you can fit the classes into your hectic work schedule. Medical benefits have become nothing more than medical insurance, and the quality of care we receive is adequate at best. Then there are ongoing senseless changes, and the ongoing conversations and actions regarding sexual harassment.

Some of the "intangible benefits" of the military are achieving self-discipline and maturity. You must have both of these to keep from losing your composure, and maybe cursing someone out. It is very tough to do. Many military members judge your intelligence and ability by how many stripes you have on your sleeve instead of looking at you as an individual, and what you demonstrate through your work and conversation.

A disadvantage of the military is that military members are not compensated for the work we do. Can you actually put a price on someone's life and liberty? No, you can't, but you can show them through the compensation they receive that they are a respected, valuable, and integral part of this nation. The military robs a person of their dignity and individuality. Your thoughts and actions are not your own. You have to focus on the mission and not on your own personal agenda. There are times when you are given an assignment and told how to do it, but the instructions you've been given are wrong. You can't deviate because the person who gave you the assignment has more stripes than you. The worst part is that when it comes out in the wash that the job was done wrong, who gets blamed—you. You are manipulated like a puppet on a string in a never-ending play.

I will not continue pursuing the military as a career after my enlistment ends, nor would I recommend it to other adventurous women because it's not what you are led to believe it is. I recommend that young women take the time to assess their lives and determine what they truly want for themselves and their future. There are other options out there, and you should weigh them all before you make a decision that can have a lasting effect on the rest of your life.

In the military there is a gap between perception and reality that can be compared to the myth of "The Great American Dream": something that never really existed, or not the reality of your own experience. If it sounds too good to be true, then it probably is.

SIXTY-FOUR

◆◆◆

The Search for Peace and Justice

Notes Toward an Autobiography

Jean Grossholtz

I was standing in the sunlight on Pennsylvania Avenue watching the passing gays and lesbians, relishing the color, the noise, and the excitement. I saw them coming around the corner, men and women many in uniform carrying signs, "I'm gay and I served." I watched them as they passed, the pride in their faces, the confidence in their step. And suddenly there I was marching, tears streaming down my face, holding the hand of another woman beside me. Here I was, a 65-year-old dedicated peace activist, who had put my body on the line in such out of the way places as the Seneca Army Base, Greenham Common, and Diablo Canyon. I, who had courted federal prison and spent time in many jails for peace, was marching with the military for the rights of gays to serve in an institution I found distasteful in the extreme. But it was an institution in which I served for four years, nine months, and five days through the Korean War. It was an institution that had meant my personal survival, had honed my political passions to a fine level of anger, had given me a deep and everlasting commitment to end war.

Confused, conflicted, and still a strong lesbian political activist, I walked beside my newfound friend as we traded stories of the purges, the fears, the betrayals by our own and others as we had sought to survive in a hostile environment. I remembered sitting paralyzed in the mess hall while noncommissioned officers who outranked me discussed the dangers of getting too close to the "troops." I knew this was aimed at me. I had just returned from a weekend of love and lust with one of my "troops."

It did not matter that I knew some of them were guilty of the same infractions. I was in danger and they were warning me.

It took some time to understand those warnings before I began to hear them. The Lieutenant who made fun of me for walking with my arm around my friend. "Childish," she called it, "high school," not the behavior of a grown woman and a noncommissioned officer. The Captain who mentioned a missing light bulb as a means of casually warning me there was to be a surprise bed check. There were many such warnings as we all did our best to be decent people in an atmosphere of constant betrayal. This way surely madness lies, this occupation of a totally alien space where what one was and wanted to be was denied and hidden and yet ever present.

So there I was marching in the Gay Pride March for a Simple Matter of Justice, reliving those old fears and betrayals, the times I denied, the times I turned my back as others felt the wrath of the Army's purging. This was an important moment. Did I really want to honor the right to serve in this institution? Was I marching for the right of women, of lesbians to join this killing machine?

I had grown up committed to the organization of the working class. I grew up believing in freedom and justice. I read about the strikes of the women textile workers in Lawrence in 1912, and shed real tears when I read of the awful things that happened to strikers. I read of the Pullman Company and their private police and the murdered men at Haymarket in Chicago in 1894. I read of the government's and businessmen's fears of anarchism and the scapegoating of two foreign-born working men, Sacco and Vanzetti. Account after account of those martyred for justice made me understand that capitalism grew in this country at great cost to ordinary people, to the workers whose labor made it all possible. And I dreamed of playing that role, of being the one burnt at the stake or beheaded. Overhearing my father talking with his friends, I learned of the Industrial Workers of the World and their dream of one big union for all the working class. I fell in love with the words of these men and women. Elizabeth Gurley Flynn and Joe Hill and Big Bill Haywood of the Industrial Workers of the World. Nicknamed the Wobblies by some Chinese workers unable to pronounce the "W," these organizers moved around the country lending their skills to local leadership, integrating grassroots groups, trying to build one big union. Throughout middle school and high school I chased after stories of these grand ideas of equality and justice.

I joined the Army, as did most of the women I met in the Women's Army Corps, to get out of what looked to me a dead-end street. I was 17 years old and going nowhere, with nothing but drinking and living from one shit-level job to the next in my future. I had read enough war novels to know that the men in the Army were not all establishment puppets. I knew some of the people in the Army were the same people who walked the picket lines outside of factories. I did not make the connection between the Army, the state, and the destruction of the IWW. I only knew I had to get somewhere, go somewhere where I would be able to read, to think about these people and their ideas, to find people who used these words this way.

And I had another, deeper, darker secret for leaving my home town, I was a freak. I lusted after women. I did not like boys, could not relate to them except as friends, did not want to marry, or be what the women around me seemed to want. In the small town where I went to high school I was driven crazy by my inability to fit in, to even try, make an attempt. I did not know the words dyke, lesbian. I learned of homosexual and I heard people referring to sick people they called "queer" and I knew that was me. I had hopes and hints there were others like me. When I finally met one such, she was already going into the Army and she convinced me there would be others like us there.

But the driving force was economic. With a high school education all I could do was waitress, wash dishes, work in the laundry, stand all day on an assembly line. I had spent much of my life in small towns or on a farm; I was unused to being cooped up, unused to routine. I drifted from one job to another, failing as a waitress, having a brief happy fling for some months as a short order cook when the male cook got sick. Mostly it was jobs that were killing me, that I could not keep because my anger and despair led me to outraged rebellion. The middle-aged women who stood all day on an assembly line repeating the same movement endlessly hour after hour, having to ask permission to go to the toilet, tried to comfort me. They understood only that we had no choice, that the world offered only this to poor and uneducated people. When I raged they gave me cookies, when I spoke of strikes they laughed. My heart hurting, my body aching, my mind numbed, I would eventually explode at the foreman, the factory superintendent, the product we were making. And I would be fired and move to another factory to repeat the experience.

The Army saved me. Although it led me to some heavy drinking for a time, it also led me to reject that life full force and to see some hope in moving beyond this past to something new. For the first time we had medical care, good food, warm clothes. For many of us our first visit to the dentist. (I credit the Army for the fact that alone of all my siblings I still have real teeth at the age of 67.) I had the first medication for my chronic stomach ulcers that I never had a name for before. We laughed about our uniforms but it was for some of us the first time we were not in danger of being laughed at, criticized for what we wore and how we wore it. We had social services we never thought possible. The Army was the biggest welfare state in the world and it took great care of us. And in the end it gave me the GI Bill and a college education.

We complained and raged against the Army's peculiar ways of trying to break our spirit but all of us secretly gloried in our new wealth and were shamed into lying about our pasts, making up stories that were nowhere near true. We would tell Dick and Jane stories of loving fathers who wore suits and carried briefcases, of mothers smiling and young-looking, of little white houses with shutters and pets. And when one of us would tell the truth of the shopworn mother, the abusive father, the rape by a brother, the fights over money, we would sit together in silence, loving one another and knowing we were all afraid to speak out as she had done, afraid to make ourselves so vulnerable.

I learned that I could be somebody. That I could do all the things they asked of me, that I could stand up against the harshest, most angry of my peers and survive. A lieutenant, angry at me and humiliated because I knew more than she did about what was happening in the world, set me impossible tasks over and over until I was made into a zombie by tiredness and lack of sleep. And I still led my platoon and won good soldier awards. I was a good teacher, a popular leader. I began to see there was a way to have integrity, to be able to live as I really was. Not at first, at first I lied, I passed myself off as what I was not, indeed never wanted to be. I tried on different faces of myself searching for the one that fit. The Army allowed me that space, that time. As long as I did my duty. And that proved easy.

I learned how to act in concert with others. I learned the discipline that group activity required. Much of what the Army thrived on struck me as dumb and not worth paying attention to. The Army demanded total unquestioned obedience. They called it discipline, and punished infractions with idiotic penalties. For example, once, for arguing with an officer, I was sent to remove all the coal from the coal bin, scrub the bin, and put all the coal back. I found this ridiculous. If I thought someone was wrong I needed to say so. Sometimes this worked in my favor and allowed me to blossom, at other times it caused me grief and I paid for my inattention to the Army's rules.

Over time I realized that people liked me, that I was smart, that the Army appreciated me despite all my rebellions. I was sent to Leadership School and the entire unit showed me they thought this was a fine idea, that I was worthy of respect as a leader.

I was sent to Leadership School in Carlisle Barracks, Pennsylvania. There I met some wonderful historians who told us stories of the battles and generals of the Civil War. I fell in love with the history and with the ease which these men told the stories of Grant and Meade and Robert E. Lee and cavalry charges across peach orchids. And then I saw the pictures, the dead strewn across the battlefields. And I remembered Walt Whitman who had become the poet of my liberation, of my becoming.

I learned to teach everything from map-reading to first aid to current events. I grew daily more confident, less confused. I met women who had been to college and we talked of many things. I learned to read the *New York Times,* not knowing then how much it was misshaping and confusing my principled politics of the working class. I was sent to a detachment working with an engineering battalion in the woods of Wisconsin and I became a newspaper editor. Me, the farm girl, editing an Army newspaper. I found myself at the heart of some of the more important activities of the camp.

I learned about war. War had been something I'd read about, something that people became heroes in. And a hero I wanted to be. I did not like the killing. Felt instinctively it was wrong and that nothing would justify it or ever make me take a weapon against another human being. I had grown up with brothers and fathers hunting, hunting for meat for our food. I could not stand the smell of them when they returned—the smell of fresh blood and dead animals. I did not eat the meat they brought so proudly. I did not look at the carcasses as they carved them up and canned the results. Still I wanted to be a hero. I did not altogether reject the idea of armies in battle, of enemies.

After I had been in the Army for a few months, the United States began what they called "a police action" against North Koreans. This reaction started with a movement by North Koreans across the border with South Korea. But 1950 was the height of the Cold War frenzy. Washington was in turmoil over who had "lost" China to the Communists. The inside view in Washington was that the border crossings and troop movements in the North were a precursor of a massive, Soviet-backed invasion. This never happened. Instead the Americans, failing to stop at just policing the border, invaded North Korea and headed for Manchuria. In response, the People's Republic of China entered the war and drove the Americans from the North in a massive and bloody retreat.

A small peacetime army was suddenly increased. Thousands of new recruits were brought in, trained, and sent to Korea. Many died within days of landing at Inch'on. One young man I met from Kansas had lied about his age, entered the Army at 17, was dead on his eighteenth birthday.

As the U.S. Generals pushed to the border, proclaiming victory, the terrible retreats, the terrible killing fields of the North came to haunt us. Pictures of young men, their feet wrapped in blankets, their eyes hollow with horror. "They brought their dead out," the Generals crowed, as if that were a victory. I lay many nights in my cot listening to Taps and remembering the strong young men learning engineering skills in the woods of Wisconsin. I could no longer countenance war. I no longer wanted to be a hero. I wanted to stop war, this war, all wars.

I was transferred from Wisconsin to Fitzsimmons General Hospital in Denver and the wounded came flooding back. As editor of the hospital newspaper, my job was ostensibly to tout the patriotism of these young men. I had considerable freedom until I printed a story about the limited blood supply and then I was put under tighter rein.

As I haunted the wards talking with these men, I came to see what war was really about. I saw that the bravery I had identified with saving one's buddies was really the result of a foolish, meaningless slaughter. The broken bodies of the young men I met in those hospitals were the reverse image of the sweating healthy young men I had seen training in Wisconsin. I knew that I had to organize my life to destroy the idea that war and dying in war was glorious. This blatant disrespect for life was wrong.

The Army taught me that whatever else was true, war was never an answer to any political issue; that politicians and the Generals were not good judges of reality.

But the Army taught me also that I could not love my own kind. For many years I lived in fear and shame. Shame, because what I wanted was so far from what I was supposed to want. Shame, as I saw other WACs seeking private hideouts to live out their realities while maintaining a public posture rejecting that very reality. This option did not appeal to me, it demanded that I think of myself as less than what I was, what I wanted to be. Not being able to talk to each other honestly, not being able to be anything together, they turned to drink. I saw them drinking themselves into an oblivion where shame would be stilled and they could act on their feelings and for some brief moments forget the pain of their unacceptable existence. I could not do this. I felt confused, alienated from those who hated queers and those who would not admit to being queer except when drunk. I was unable to find a center for myself.

As confidence in my own abilities grew, confidence in who I was emerged and I came to understand that the Army's war on homosexuals was wrong, that there was nothing the matter with me that a little healthy acceptance wouldn't cure. I recognized an eerie similarity between the Army's relentless attack on homosexuality, the total rejection of love of your own sex, and the constant insistent bonding with your unit, your buddies. The Army runs on love for your buddies, the willingness to lay down your very life for the group.

The Army's internal war against homosexuality is a warning not to go too far, not to put your faith in individuals but in the unit. And the unit is the Army. Men must be willing to die for the Army, to see their manhood as coming out of the barrel of a gun and its use. It is our national idea of heroism. How many times have we seen U.S. Presidents (Ronald Reagan most especially) visiting caskets in an airplane hangar and declaring these were heroes. Sometimes men who only happened to be at the wrong end of the barracks when a "terrorist" ran his explosive-laden truck into the gate, or when an airplane crashed inadvertently. Heroes simply for being there. No one saw the heroism of the women left as single heads of family back home who still managed to raise their kids and keep them out of poverty in the face of terrible odds. If you put on a uniform you are a hero, you are somebody, you are your nation's finest. Even if you are treated like a pile of shit everywhere you go and are roughed up, discriminated against, called names, within the Army. Such a contradiction—love your buddy like your brother, do not love another man.

The Army's vicious, continuous, almost holy crusade against homosexuals, the periodic purges of the WAC detachments, and the continuous challenges to gay men were all means by which the Army kept its control. Gendered identities made men into soldiers willing to kill for their commanders, and women into either the girl back home or whores. There was no place for anyone who challenged these assumptions. A real man, a soldier, abjures homosexuals even as he learns to put his hope, trust and daily livelihood in his buddies, his unit, his commander. Study what happens to men in battle. Read the war novels by men from every war. They are driven nearly crazy with fear and grief before they can turn to help one another, to express their love physically. How can this clearly "men loving men" organization keep its militaristic pose without undercutting the very thing it is built on?

The Army's relentless pursuit of homosexuals is one way a gendered power structure is kept in place. If women can be competent, active public agents, and men can access that part of themselves which shares the softer, life-enhancing qualities of womanness, what will happen to the killingforce, to the automatic disciplined response to orders?

After I left the Army I watched the madness of the Korean War continue as the United States embarked upon a massive war economy, engaged in a worldwide contest with the "Evil Empire," the Soviet Union. I used the GI Bill to enter college and then went on to graduate school. I studied international relations and political economy. I became a specialist on Southeast Asian politics.

I came to know that the war machines were created not really to be used because that would be the end of the world, but to press the Soviets to spend their resources, to spend to bankruptcy. Meanwhile, American corporations feeding at the military trough developed technology to enter world markets at a great advantage, selling military equipment and technology developed at the taxpayers' expense. This military machine, now released by the fall of the Soviet Union, can be used to secure and guarantee the resources of a new global economic order. From Korea to Vietnam, Grenada, Afghanis-tan, and Kuwait, the American Army is used to keep imperialism solidly in place. Without the Soviet Army to oppose them, the U.S. military can freely intervene. The global success of the international capitalist economic system is ultimately guaranteed by that military force.

Years after I had left the Army, after I had earned a Ph.D. in Political Science, another American government entered into another war, reminiscent of the Korean War: Vietnam. An area of the world in struggle against colonial rule, a country also divided by international fiat into north and south. And again a U.S.-generated incident and a military response, and once again young men, barely out of basic training, sent to die and Generals chortling about how brave they were, how fine, counting up the numbers they killed as if at a football match.

And I now took to the streets and found myself many times on the opposite side of the Army. Standing holding hands with my colleagues staring into the faces of young men and women frightened by us and worried about their own self-esteem.

I began standing at the gates of Westover Air Base in Massachusetts with a remarkable woman named Frances Crowe. At first we were alone but in time others joined us. Other actions followed, lying in the streets to stop the buses taking the new draftees, blocking the doors of the New York Stock Exchange, surrounding the Pentagon, being dragged to police buses and jails. I learned remarkable strength as we faced our fears of what would happen, of how we would behave when threatened by the police. I sat through endless meetings processing and planning, and nights on church floors with hundreds of others, catching what little sleep we could before an action. I experienced wonderful togetherness in jail cells. And eventually there were the women's peace camps at Seneca and at Greenham Common. Public spaces where women met freely and as equals, seeking a new way of being, a new way of making decisions, a new way of resisting injustice. This it seemed to me was the real beginning of something new, something with hope for a different future.

I have seen women create community; create, without structured authority, large-scale actions and projects. These actions were not without problems and not, in the end, without being somewhat co-opted. But we did create and maintain organized effort, whether to bring attention to Cruise missiles stored at the Seneca Army Base or to keep constant attention on the delivery of Cruise missiles to Greenham. Communities formed, the discipline of consensus decision-making was accepted, and we learned to appreciate ourselves and each other as women. The Women's Peace Camps had their days of glory, of achievement, and to all who came there, something remains, the possibility, maybe only the hope, that another way of living, of making decisions, of sharing in a common life can happen. Those of us who experienced the camps changed our lives. We could hope for an alternative. Even if we had not found it altogether.

Later in New England I joined a wondrous group of women called the Women of Faith. We did monthly actions against the nuclear submarines and their D5 missiles being constructed at Electric Boat in Connecticut. We marched and demonstrated at each launching, sometimes getting arrested, sometimes simply doing guerrilla theater. But each month we did some action. Dancing at the gate one morning at 6:30, we shut down the missile business for 28 minutes and were inordinately proud of it. Another time we invaded their offices, several times we chained ourselves to gates or blockaded entrances.

We would think up our next action while we were waiting arraignment in the holding cell or sitting waiting as part of the support group in the courtroom. The night before the planned action we would meet to make signs, plan the press coverage, assign tasks. We would meet in a church or a private home near our action. For a couple of years we worked together without tension or friction, bringing new women into our group and learning how to talk to the media, handle the jail situation. What broke us up was some of the changes in the military situation and internal disruption caused by one new woman's inability to accept consensus. Until that time we had worked without a slip. Proving that it can be done.

I found some of the same camaraderie, the same sense of belonging to something bigger than one's self, the same willingness to accept others' decisions, as I found in the Army and this time aimed at peace, at justice, and at the creation of political community.

So why was I marching in a parade proclaiming the right of queers to serve in the military? What did I hope to accomplish by this? How did it fit with my peace activism?

I was marching along with hundreds of others to say "Yes, I was there. You can no longer deny my existence. Silencing me and all these others was useless because we know and you know what you are up to. Those of us in uniform are not just robots wound up and set out to kill and be killed at the bidding of the world economic order. We have lives that you do not approve of, we have thoughts and values that reject yours."

So I was marching for all of this, to challenge the Army's gendered system of power, to challenge its failure to honor the love of men and women for each other, to force them to change that reality. Because if they acknowledge the existence of queers in their ranks, in their leadership, and among those who make the decisions that vote them budgets, then they can no longer adhere to that male ideology of exclusion and machoism. Those qualities that have been assigned to women, the experiences and perceptions of women cannot so simply be dismissed. The Army as a male hierarchical institution is weakened.

And I was marching because I wanted to put the lie to all that we have been told was not possible, was dangerous. Contrary to what we are told, I have seen that this country can provide all the necessities of life, housing, food, clothing, health care, and education to hundreds of thousands of people in a very short time. An enormous army was assembled, housed, fed, and clothed in a very short time for the Korean War and again for the Vietnam War. Despite all we have heard of the dangers of the welfare programs and helping people out of trouble, the country did not go bankrupt, those people did not become lazy or valueless. Providing young people with all the necessities of life and good health made them strong and efficient.

Contrary to the claim that we only act out of individual self-interest, I have seen men and women put the good of the community above their own individual wishes. I have seen that men and women can think collectively about how to live together and get a job done. And I have seen them do this despite, not because of, the barbarous discipline.

Equality and justice, my lifelong dreams, are not to be found in fighting, in militarism. Killing people does not bring peace. There are other ways to create common commitments, a willingness to put one's body on the line, the courage to take risks.

It is here we must start to remake the world.

◆◆◆

SIXTY-FIVE

Unity Statement*

Women's Pentagon Action

We are gathering at the Pentagon on November 16 because we fear for our lives. We fear for the life of this planet, our Earth, and the life of the children who are our human future.

We are mostly women who come from the northeastern region of our United States. We are city women who know the wreckage and fear of city streets, we are country women who grieve the loss of the small farm and have lived on the poisoned earth. We are young and older, we are married, single, lesbian. We live in different kinds of households: In groups, families, alone, some are single parents.

We work at a variety of jobs. We are students, teachers, factory workers, office workers, lawyers, farmers, doctors, builders, waitresses, weavers, poets, engineers, homeworkers, electricians, artists, blacksmiths. We are all daughters and sisters.

We have come here to mourn and rage and defy the Pentagon because it is the workplace of the imperial power which threatens us all. Every day while we work, study, love, the colonels and generals who are planning our annihilation walk calmly in and out the doors of its five sides. They have accumulated over 30,000 nuclear bombs, at the rate of three to six bombs every day. They are determined to produce the billion-dollar MX missile. They are creating a technology called Stealth—the invisible, unperceivable arsenal. They have revised the cruel old killer, nerve gas. They have proclaimed Directive 59 which asks for "small nuclear wars, prolonged but limited." The Soviet Union works hard to keep up with the United States initiatives. We can destroy each other's cities, towns, schools and children many times over. The United States has sent "advisors," money and arms to El Salvador and Guatemala to enable those juntas to massacre their own people.

The very same men, the same legislative committees that offer trillions of dollars to the Pentagon have brutally cut day care, children's lunches, battered women's shelters. The same men have concocted the Family Protection Act which will mandate the strictly patriarchal family and thrust federal authority into our home life. They are preventing the passage of ERA's simple statement and supporting the Human Life Amendment which will deprive all women of choice and many women of life itself.

We are in the hands of men whose power and wealth have separated them from the reality of daily life and from the imagination. We are right to be afraid.

At the same time, our cities are in ruins, bankrupt; they suffer the devastation of war. Hospitals are closed, our schools deprived of books and teachers. Our Black and Latino youth are without decent work. They will be forced, drafted to become the cannon fodder for the very power that oppresses them. Whatever help the poor receive is cut or withdrawn to feed the Pentagon which needs about $500,000,000 a day for its murderous health. It extracted $157 billion dollars last year from our own tax money, $1,800 from a family of four.

With this wealth our scientists are corrupted; over 40 percent work in government and corporate laboratories that refine the methods for destroying or deforming life. The lands of the Native American people have been turned to radioactive rubble in order to enlarge the nuclear warehouse. The uranium of South Africa, necessary to the nuclear enterprise, enriches the white minority and encourages the vicious system of racist oppression and war.

The President has just decided to produce the neutron bomb, which kills people but leaves property (buildings like this one) intact. There is fear among the people, and that fear, created by the industrial militarists, is used as an excuse to accelerate the arms race. "We will protect you . . ." they say, but we have never been so endangered, so close to the end of human time.

We women are gathering because life on the precipice is intolerable. We want to know what anger in

---

*Statement from 1980.

these men, what fear, which can only be satisfied by destruction, what coldness of heart and ambition drives their days. We want to know because we do not want that dominance which is exploitative and murderous in international relations, and so dangerous to women and children at home—we do not want that sickness transferred by the violent society through the fathers to the sons.

What is it that we women need for our ordinary lives, that we want for ourselves and also for our sisters in new nations and old colonies who suffer the white man's exploitation and too often the oppression of their own countrymen?

We want enough good food, decent housing, communities with clean air and water, good care for our children while we work. We want work that is useful to a sensible society. There is a modest technology to minimize drudgery and restore joy to labor. We are determined to use skills and knowledge from which we have been excluded—like plumbing or engineering or physics or composing. We intend to form women's groups or unions that will demand safe workplaces, free of sexual harassment, equal pay for work of comparable value. We respect the work women have done in caring for the young, their own and others, in maintaining a physical and spiritual shelter against the greedy and militaristic society. In our old age we expect our experience, our skills, to be honored and used.

We want health care which respects and understands our bodies. Physically challenged sisters must have access to gatherings, actions, happy events, work.

For this, ramps must be added to stairs and we must become readers, signers, supporting arms. So close, so many, why have we allowed ourselves not to know them?

We want an education for children which tells the true story of our women's lives, which describes the earth as our home to be cherished, to be fed as well as harvested.

We want to be free from violence in our streets and in our houses. One in every three of us will be raped in her lifetime. The pervasive social power of the masculine ideal and the greed of the pornographer have come together to steal our freedom, so that whole neighborhoods and the life of the evening and night have been taken from us. For too many women the dark country road and the city alley have concealed the rapist. We want the night returned: the light of the moon, special in the cycle of our female lives, the stars and the gaiety of the city streets.

We want the right to have or not to have children—we do not want gangs of politicians and medical men to say we must be sterilized for the country's good. We know that this technique is the racists' method for controlling populations. Nor do we want to be prevented from having an abortion when we need one. We think this freedom should be available to poor women as it always has been to the rich. We want to be free to love whomever we choose. We will live with women or with men or we will live alone. We will not allow the oppression of lesbians. One sex or one sexual preference must not dominate another.

We do not want to be drafted into the army. We do not want our young brothers drafted. We want *them* equal with us.

We want to see the pathology of racism ended in our time. It has been the imperial arrogance of white male power that has separated us from the suffering and wisdom of our sisters in Asia, Africa, South America and in our own country. Many North American women look down on the minority nearest them: the Black, the Hispanic, the Jew, the Native American, the Asian, the immigrant. Racism has offered them privilege and convenience; they often fail to see that they themselves have bent to the unnatural authority and violence of men in government, at work, at home. Privilege does not increase knowledge or spirit or understanding. There can be no peace while one race dominates another, one people, one nation, one sex despises another.

We must not forget the tens of thousands of American women who live much of their lives in cages, away from family, lovers, all the growing-up years of their children. Most of them were born at the intersection of oppressions: people of color, female, poor. Women on the outside have been taught to fear those sisters. We refuse that separation. We need each other's knowledge and anger in our common struggle against the builders of jails and bombs.

We want the uranium left in the earth and the earth given back to the people who tilled it. We want a system of energy which is renewable, which does not take resources out of the earth without returning them. We want those systems to belong to the people and their communities, not to the giant corporations which invariably turn knowledge into weaponry. We want the sham of Atoms for Peace ended, all nuclear plants decommissioned and the construction of new plants stopped. That is another war against the people and the child to be born in fifty years.

We want an end to the arms race. No more bombs. No more amazing inventions for death.

We understand all is connectedness. We know the life and work of animals and plants in seeding, reseeding and in fact simply inhabiting this planet. Their exploitation and the organized destruction of never to be seen again species threatens and sorrows us. The earth nourishes us as we with our bodies will eventually feed it. Through us, our mothers connected the human past to the human future.

With that sense, that ecological right, we oppose the financial connections between the Pentagon and the multinational corporations and banks that the Pentagon serves. Those connections are made of gold and oil. We are made of blood and bone, we are made of the sweet and finite resource, water. We will not allow these violent games to continue. If we are here in our stubborn thousands today, we will certainly return in the hundreds of thousands in the months and years to come.

We know there is a healthy, sensible, loving way to live and we intend to live that way in our neighborhoods and our farms in these United States, and among our sisters and brothers in all the countries of the world.

S I X T Y - S I X

◆◆◆

Ten Reasons Why Women Should Oppose
the U.S. "War on Terrorism"

Women of Color Resource Center

1. War, no matter how high-tech, kills civilians. Women and children became "collateral damage."

2. War and militarism expose women and girls to rape and sexual violence; the culture of aggression encourages domestic violence against women.

3. Weapons of mass destruction, produced, used and sold by the U.S. worldwide, poison the environment, causing miscarriages, birth defects, and cancers.

4. Governments in Israel, Colombia, and the Philippines are using the U.S. "war on terrorism" as an excuse to strike out at political enemies, violating the human rights of women in war zones.

5. The "war on terrorism" is a cover for U.S. economic, political, and military domination, which increases women's poverty worldwide.

6. When Arab, Muslim, South Asian, and immigrant men are locked up without cause and without charges, women shoulder the burden of sustaining their families and communities.

7. Women's human rights are endangered when civil liberties are trampled.

8. U.S. war industries reap enormous profits, while programs that benefit women and girls—such as health care, education, welfare, and child care—face budget cuts.

9. Bush's war fuels racism worldwide, negatively impacting U.S. women of color and women of the Third World.

10. The oppression of Afghan women was used to justify the "war on terrorism," but the Pentagon cannot liberate Afghan women—or any other women.

S I X T Y - S E V E N

◆◆◆

Whose Security?

Charlotte Bunch

When I talk with feminists from other countries, whether from Europe or the Third World, I am repeatedly asked: "Where are the voices of the U.S. women's movement against what the Bush Administration is doing globally, using the excuse of 9/11?"

While I know that many U.S. feminists are concerned about these issues, it is clear that our voices are not being heard much—outside, or even inside, this country. The perception created by the Western media is that virtually all Americans support Bush's militaristic threats, his "you're with us or against us," evil-axis rhetoric, and his unilateralist positions against global treaties from the Kyoto Protocol on

the environment to the newly created International Criminal Court. When I mention activities like the weekly Women in Black vigils against U.S. policy in the Middle East held in New York and other cities, or feminists working to change the composition of the U.S. Congress, where only Barbara Lee spoke out against the Bush madness immediately after 9/11, they are somewhat relieved.

Yet it is clear that feminists in the United States do not have much impact on U.S. foreign policy, which is military- and corporate-driven. Even though Bush used Afghan women's rights to drum up support for his war, this did not lead to a sustained commitment to Afghan women. It is puzzling to many outside this country how a women's movement that has had such profound influence on U.S. culture and daily life could have so little effect on, or seemingly even concern for, U.S. foreign policy and its impact on women worldwide. The consequences of this failure are disastrous for women in many countries, and they threaten the advances that the global women's movement made in the 1990s.

Current U.S. foreign policy makes it harder to build women's international solidarity in a number of ways. The widespread sympathy that the world offered Americans at the time of 9/11 has given way to anti-Americanism and rage at what the U.S. government is doing in the name of that event. On the day of the attacks, I was still in South Africa following the U.N. World Conference Against Racism held in Durban the week before. People expressed intense concern about what had happened, especially when they learned that I lived in New York. And this was in spite of the great frustration that most felt about the inexcusable disdain for other countries the Bush Administration had just exhibited during the world conference. But now, resentment and anger at the United States is the overriding sentiment in many other nations. Even some feminist colleagues elsewhere tell me that they are now asked how they can really work with Americans, given how little opposition to Bush's foreign policies they see happening here.

This resentment stems in part from the fact that 9/11 is not seen as a defining moment for the rest of the world—at least not in terms of what happened that day. In many places, people have long lived with terrorism, violence, and death on a scale as great as or greater than 9/11. So, while they agree that this was a terrible and shocking event, they consider the U.S. obsession with it, including the assumption that it is the defining moment for everyone, to be self-indulgent and shortsighted.

Of course, September 11 has been a defining event within the United States. But how we understand it in a global context is important. First, we must recognize that our government's responses to it were not inevitable. This event could have taken the country in other directions, including toward greater empathy with what others have suffered, toward more concern for human security and the conditions that give rise to terrorism, and toward recognition of the importance of multilateral institutions in a globally linked world. But that would have required a very different national leadership. Instead, it has become the rationale for an escalation of the regressive Bush agenda domestically and internationally, including more unrestrained exercise of U.S. power and disregard for multilateralism. Other governments have also used the occasion to increase military spending and to erode support for human rights. In that sense, it has become a defining moment because of how it has been used. But the issues highlighted by 9/11 are not new and have been raised by many other events both before and after it.

Indeed, 9/11 has raised the profile of many of the issues feminists were already struggling with globally, such as

- growing global and national economic inequities produced by globalization, structural adjustment, privatization, etc.;

- the rise of extremist expressions of religious and/or nationalist "fundamentalisms" that threaten progress on women's rights around the world (including in the United States) in the name of various religions and cultures;

- the escalation of racist and sexist violence and terrorism in daily life and the growth of sexual and economic exploitation and trafficking of women across the globe;

- an increase in militarism, wars, internal conflicts, and terrorism, which are affecting or targeting civilians and involving more women and children in deadly ways.

Since 9/11 has been used to curtail human rights—including freedom of expression—in the name of "national security," it has added a greater sense of urgency to these concerns, but it has also made it more difficult to address them effectively from a feminist perspective.

Human vs. National Security

The call to redefine security in terms of human and ecological need instead of national sovereignty and borders was advancing pre-9/11 as an alternative to the state-centered concept of "national security," rooted in the military/security/defense domain and academically lodged in the field of international relations. For feminists this has meant raising questions about whose security "national security" defends, and addressing issues like the violence continuum that threatens women's security daily, during war as well as so-called peacetime.

The concept of human security had also advanced through the U.N.—first defined in the U.N. Development Program's 1994 Human Development Report and later taken up by Secretary General Kofi Annan in his Millennium Report in 2000, which spoke of security less as defending territory and more in terms of protecting people.

But efforts to promote the concept of human security—which emerged out of discussions in which women are active, from the peace movement and the debate over development—were set back by 9/11, with the subsequent resurgence of the masculine warrior discourse. The media have been dominated by male "authority" figures, providing a rude reminder that when it comes to issues of terrorism, war, defense, and national security, women, and especially feminists, are still not on the map.

Yet it is women who have been the major target of fundamentalist terrorism, from Algeria to the United States, over the past several decades. And it is mostly feminists who have led the critique of this growing global problem—focusing attention not only on Islamic fundamentalism but on Protestant fundamentalism in the United States, Catholic secret societies like Opus Dei in Latin America, Hindu right-wing fundamentalists in India, and so on.

The events of 9/11 should have generated attempts to address the very real threats to women's human rights posed by fundamentalism, terrorism, and armed conflict in many guises. Instead, the occasion was used to demonize the Islamic Other and to justify further militarization of society and curtailment of civil liberties. Growing militarization, often with U.S. support and arms, has brought an increase in military spending in many other regions, from India and Pakistan to Israel, Colombia, and the Philippines. Meanwhile, the Western donor countries' pledges to support economic development at the U.N. International Conference on Financing for Development in March 2002 fell far short of what would be needed to even begin to fulfill the mil-

lennium promises made in 2000 for advancing human security.

Thus, while human security is a promising concept, it is far from being embraced as a replacement for the national security paradigm to which governments remain attached and have made vast commitments.

September 11 and Human Rights

The excuse of 9/11 has been used not only to curtail human rights in the United States—which some here are challenging—but also around the world. The human rights system is in trouble when the U.S. government pulls out of global agreements like the ABM treaty, aggressively works to undermine new instruments like the International Criminal Court, and says it is not bound by international commitments made by previous administrations, such as the Beijing Women's Conference Platform—parts of which its delegation renounced at the U.N. Commission on the Status of Women in March 2002. All international treaties and human rights conventions depend on the assumption that a country is bound by previous agreements and cannot simply jettison them with every change of administration. This erosion of respect for human rights also appears in the U.S. media, where some mainstream journalists have defended, as a necessary part of the war on terrorism, the Bush Administration's defiance of international norms regarding political prisoners, and even suggested that the (selective) use of torture may be justified. These are the kinds of arguments put forward by governments that torture and abuse rights and are contrary to the most accepted tenets of human rights.

Indeed, the erosion of the U.S. commitment to human rights helps legitimize the abuses of governments that have never fully accepted or claimed these standards. For while the U.S. government has often been hypocritical in its human rights policies, open disregard for international standards goes a step further and thus strengthens fundamentalist governments and forces that seek to deny human rights in general, and the rights of women in particular.

Ironically, even as public discourse demonizes Islamic fundamentalists, the unholy alliance of the

Vatican, Islamic fundamentalists, and right-wing U.S. forces is still working together when it comes to trying to defeat women's human rights. Feminists encountered this alliance in full force at the International Conference on Population and Development in Cairo (1994) and at the World Conference on Women at Beijing (1995), as well as during the five-year reviews of those events in 1999 and 2000. One need only look at the allies of the Bush Administration at the U.N. children's summit in May 2002—such as the Holy See, Sudan, Libya, Iraq, and other gulf states—to understand that this alliance is still functioning globally. We need to closely track the connections among various antifeminist "fundamentalist" forces, not only at the U.N. but in other arenas as well, such as in the making of world health policies, or even in the passage of anti–women's rights national legislation in countries where outside forces have played a key role.

A high-profile example of how the Bush Administration is seeking to weaken the U.N.'s role in protecting human rights was its effort to ensure that the U.N. High Commissioner for Human Rights, Mary Robinson, would not get a second term. She was among the first to frame her response to 9/11 from the perspective of international law, by suggesting that these acts of terrorism be prosecuted internationally as crimes against humanity rather than used as a call to war, but she was quickly sidelined. Because of this, along with her efforts to make the World Conference Against Racism a success in spite of the U.S. contempt for it, the Bush Administration adamantly opposed her reappointment. This opposition dovetailed with that of a number of other governments unhappy with her attention to their human rights abuses. Robinson is only one of the U.N. officials the Bush Administration has targeted in its efforts to purge the institution of its critics and anyone else promoting policies not to its liking.

The Bush Administration's policies post-9/11 have provided cover for other governments, such as China, Pakistan, Russia, and Egypt, to jettison even a rhetorical commitment to certain human rights in the name of fighting terrorism or providing for national security, or for some countries even in Europe it has been an opportunity simply to label issues like racism and violence against women as lower-priority concerns. This has a particular impact on women because it reverses the broadening of the human rights paradigm, which had begun to encompass issues like violence against women and to focus more on socioeconomic rights in the 1980s and '90s.

Women's rights advocates are still seen as the new kids on the human rights block. Feminists only recently won the recognition of women's rights as human rights, and that is now jeopardized even before those rights have been fully accepted and mechanisms for their protection institutionalized. The need to articulate a feminist approach to global security that ensures human rights and human security, and recognizes their interrelationship, is therefore more urgent than ever.

Challenges Ahead for Global Feminism

Women have transformed many aspects of life over the past forty years, and we all live differently because of it. Looking at the world in 2002, however, we have to ask what went wrong: Why have feminists not had a greater impact on global issues? How can we more effectively address current challenges like an increasingly militarized daily life, the rise in the political use of fundamentalism in every religion and region, and the widening economic gap between the haves and have-nots?

Often what American feminists must do to help women elsewhere is not to focus on their governments but to work to change ours so that U.S. policies and corporate forces based here stop harming women elsewhere. To do this, we need to engage in more serious discussion that crosses both the local/global and the activist/academic divides. If we look at women's movements over the past thirty to forty years, their strength has been in very rooted and diverse local bases of action as well as in the development of highly specific research and theory. There has also been rich global dialogue and networking among women across national lines over the past two decades. But in the United States these discourses rarely intersect.

Because the local/national/domestic and the global/international are mostly seen as separate spheres, we often have trouble determining what local actions will have the greatest impact globally. Thus, for example, there has been little interest here in using international human rights treaties like the Convention on the Elimination of All Forms of Discrimination Against Women (CEDAW), to advance domestic issues. There is a tendency not to see the international arena as adding anything to causes at home. But just as women's global networking and international solidarity have helped sustain feminist activists who are isolated in their home countries, U.S. feminists can benefit from the support of women elsewhere, which we will need if we are to challenge what is now openly defended as the American Empire.

Women's activism in the United States must be both local and global to succeed. We must grapple with the dynamic tension between the universality and specificity of our work. Only through such a process can feminists address not only the needs of each situation but also the larger global structures creating many of these conflicts. Then we can move toward an affirmative vision of peace with human rights and human security at its core, rather than continue to clean up after the endless succession of male-determined crises and conflicts. This is our challenge.

S I X T Y - E I G H T

Sneak Attack
The Militarization of U.S. Culture

Cynthia Enloe

Things start to become militarized when their legitimacy depends on their associations with military goals. When something becomes militarized, it appears to rise in value. Militarization is seductive.

But it is really a process of loss. Even though something seems to gain value by adopting an association with military goals, it actually surrenders control and gives up the claim to its own worthiness.

Militarization is a sneaky sort of transformative process. Sometimes it is only in the pursuit of *de*-militarization that we become aware of just how far down the road of complete militarization we've gone. Representative Barbara Lee (D.-Calif.) pulled back the curtain in the aftermath of the September 11 attacks when she cast the lone vote against giving George W. Bush carte blanche to wage war. The loneliness of her vote suggested how far the militarization of Congress—and its voters back home—has advanced. In fact, since September 11, publicly criticizing militarization has been widely viewed as an act of disloyalty.

Whole cultures can be militarized. It is a militarized U.S. culture that has made it easier for Bush to wage war without most Americans finding it dangerous to democracy. Our cultural militarization makes war-waging seem like a comforting reconfirmation of our collective security, identity and pride.

Other sectors of U.S. culture have also been militarized:

- **Education.** School board members accept Jr. ROTC programs for their teenagers, and social studies teachers play it safe by avoiding discussions of past sexual misconduct by U.S. soldiers overseas. Many university scientists pursue lucrative Defense Department weapons research contracts.

- **Soldiers' girlfriends and wives.** They've been persuaded that they are "good citizens" if they keep silent about problems in their relationships with male soldiers for the sake of their fighting effectiveness.

- **Beauty.** This year, the Miss America Pageant organizers selected judges with military credentials, including a former Secretary of the Navy and an Air Force captain.

- **Cars.** The Humvee ranks among the more bovine vehicles to clog U.S. highways, yet civilians think they will be feared and admired if they drive them.

Then there is the conundrum of the flag. People who reject militarization may don a flag pin, unaware that doing so may convince those with a militarized view of the U.S. flag that their bias is universally shared, thus deepening the militarization of culture.

The events of post–September 11 have also shown that many Americans today may be militarizing non-U.S. women's lives. It was only after Bush declared "war on terrorists and those countries that harbor them" that the violation of Afghan women's human rights took center stage. Here's the test of whether Afghan women are being militarized: if their well-being is worthy of our concern only because their lack of well-being justifies the U.S.'s bombing of Afghanistan, then we are militarizing Afghan women—as well as our own compassion. We are thereby complicit in the notion that something has worth only if it allows militaries to achieve their missions.

It's important to remember that militarization has its rewards, such as new-found popular support for measures formerly contested. For example, will many Americans now be persuaded that drilling for oil in the Alaskan wilderness is acceptable because it will be framed in terms of "national security"? Will most U.S. citizens now accept government raids on the Social Security trust fund in the name of paying for the war on terrorism?

Women's rights in the U.S. and Afghanistan are in danger if they become mere by-products of some other cause. Militarization, in all its seductiveness and subtlety, deserves to be bedecked with flags wherever it thrives—fluorescent flags of warning.

SIXTY-NINE

◆◆◆

Media and Ideology (excerpt)

David Croteau and William Hoynes

Most media scholars believe that media texts articulate coherent, if shifting, ways of seeing the world. These texts help to define our world and provide models for appropriate behavior and attitudes. How, for example, do media products depict the "appropriate" roles of men and women, parents and children, or bosses and workers? What defines "success," and how it is achieved? What qualifies as "criminal activity," and what are the sources of crime and social disorder? What are the underlying messages in media content, and whose interests do these messages serve? These are, fundamentally, questions about media and ideology. . . .

What Is Ideology?

Ideology is a decidedly complicated term with different implications depending on the context in which it is used. In everyday language, it can be an insult to charge someone with being "ideological," since this label suggests rigidity in the face of overwhelming evidence contradicting one's beliefs. When Marxists speak of "ideology," they often mean belief systems that help justify the actions of those in power by distorting and misrepresenting reality. When we talk about ideology, then, we need to be careful to specify what we mean by the term.

When scholars examine media products to uncover their "ideology," they are interested in the underlying images of society they provide. In this context, an ideology is basically a system of meaning that helps define and explain the world and that makes value judgments about that world. Ideology is related to concepts such as "worldview," "belief system," and "values," but it is broader than those terms. It refers not only to the beliefs held about the world, but also to the basic ways in which the world is defined. Ideology, then, is not just about politics; it has a broader and more fundamental connotation.

When we examine the ideology of media, we are not so much interested in the specific activities depicted in a single newspaper, movie, or hit song as in the broader system of meaning of which these depictions are a part. For ideological analysis, the key is the fit between the images and words in a specific media text and ways of thinking about, even defining, social and cultural issues.

Media critics are interested in the images of women, or African Americans, or immigrants—and how these images may change over time—because they contribute to the ways we understand the roles of these groups in society. In this case, the question is not whether such media images are "realistic" depictions, because analysts of ideology generally perceive the definition of the "real" as, itself, an ideological construction. Which aspects of whose "reality" do we define as the most real? Those that are the most visible? The most common? The most powerful? Instead of assessing the images and making some judgment about levels of realness, ideological analysis asks what these images tell us about ourselves and our society.

Politicians have long perceived mass media, both news and entertainment forms, as sites for the dissemination of ideology. That is one reason why media are so frequently the subjects of political debate. For example, during just a few short weeks in the spring and summer of 1995, virtually every form of contemporary mass media was singled out for a scolding by prominent politicians. In the wake of the April 1995 bombing of the Oklahoma City federal building, President Clinton identified extremists on talk radio as purveyors of hatred, implying that these radio hosts were disseminating a worldview that condoned violence. Senate Majority Leader Robert Dole focused his attention on the entertainment industry, condemning what he defined as the rampant sex, violence, and general antifamily tone of popular television, movies, and music. Clinton responded with his own critique of violence on television and the worldview it sells to children. Former Secretary of Education William Bennett made a media splash with his attack on media giant Time Warner for its distribution of "gangsta" rap. Finally, various members of Congress identified the newly emerging cyberspace as a site where images of sex and obscenity were rampant and in need of legislative action.

Radio, television, movies, music, and computer networks all came under attack during this brief period by politicians from different political perspectives, all of whom had little doubt that the media are ideological, selling certain messages and worldviews. Given that these critiques of the media were generally well received, there is good reason to believe that large numbers of the public also perceive

the media as purveyors of ideology—even if they don't use the term. Media sell both products and ideas, both personalities and worldviews; the notion that mass media products and cultural values are fundamentally intertwined has gained broad public acceptance.

"Dominant Ideology" Versus Cultural Contradictions

Even though mass media texts can be understood in ideological terms, as forms of communication that privilege certain sets of ideas and neglect or undermine others, unambiguous descriptions of media ideology remain problematic. Research on the ideology of media has included a debate between those who argue that media promote the worldview of the powerful—the "dominant ideology"—and those who argue that mass media texts include more contradictory messages, both expressing the "dominant ideology" and at least partially challenging worldviews.

We prefer to think of media texts as sites where cultural contests over meaning are waged rather than as providers of some univocal articulation of ideology. In other words, different ideological perspectives, representing different interests with unequal power, engage in a kind of struggle within media texts. Some ideas will have the advantage because, for example, they are perceived as popular or build upon familiar media images—and others will be barely visible, lurking around the margins of media for discovery by those who look carefully. For those engaged in the promotion of particular ideas, including such diverse groups as politicians, corporate actors, citizen activists, and religious groups, media are among the primary contemporary battlegrounds.

Media, in fact, are the center of what James Davison Hunter (1991) has called the "culture wars" in contemporary American society, in which fundamental issues of morality are being fought. Hunter stresses the ways in which media—advertising, news, letters to the editor, and opinion commentary—provide the principal forms of public discourse by which cultural warfare is waged. The morality of abortion, homosexuality, or capital punishment is debated, often in very polarized terms, in the mass media, as cultural conservatives and cultural progressives alike use various media technologies to promote their positions.

But the media are not simply conduits for carrying competing messages; they are more than just the battlefield on which cultural warfare takes place. Much of the substance of the contemporary culture wars is about the acceptability of the images that the mass media disseminate. These struggles over morality and values often focus on the implications of our popular media images and the apparent lessons they teach about society. Among the more prominent examples are the struggles over the meaning of religion in films such as *Priest* and *The Last Temptation of Christ;* the controversy surrounding the pregnancy of the television character Murphy Brown, who became a single mother; the broadcast by PBS of the documentary "Tongues Untied," which explored the experience of black gay men; and the battles over the use of "obscene" language in rap and heavy-metal music. These media battles often become quite fierce, with some voices calling for outright censorship, others defending free speech, and still others worrying about the consequences of cultural struggles that seem to represent a war of absolutes, with no possibility of compromise.

One of the principal reasons why media images often become so controversial is that they are believed to promote ideas that are objectionable. In short, few critics are concerned about media texts that promote perspectives they support. Ideological analysis, then, often goes hand in hand with political advocacy, as critics use their detection of distorted messages to make their own ideological points. As a result, exploring the ideologies of mass media can be very tricky.

The most sophisticated ideological analysis examines the stories the media tell as well as the potential contradictions within media texts, that is, the places where alternative perspectives might reside or where ideological conflict is built into the text. Ideological analysis, therefore, is not simply reduced to political criticism, whereby the critic loudly denounces the "bad" ideas in the media. Nor, in our view, is analysis particularly useful if it focuses on the ideology of one specific media text without making links to broader sets of media images. It may be interesting to ruminate over the underlying ideol-

ogy of a popular movie like *Forrest Gump.* (Is it a nostalgic valorization of white men in the days before multiculturalism, or a populist story of the feats of an underdog?) However, this inquiry will move from party conversation to serious analysis only if we think more carefully about the *patterns* of images in media texts, rather than analyzing one film in isolation. At its best, ideological analysis provides a window onto the broader ideological debates going on in society. It allows us to see what kinds of ideas circulate through media texts, how they are constructed, how they change over time, and when they are being challenged.

Ideology as Normalization

What are the stakes in these battles over the ideology of media? From one standpoint, media texts can be seen as key sites where basic social norms are articulated. The media give us pictures of social interaction and social institutions that, by their sheer repetition on a daily basis, can play important roles in shaping broad social definitions. In essence, the accumulation of media images suggests what is "normal" and what is "deviant." This articulation is accomplished, in large part, by the fact that popular media, particularly television and mass advertising, have a tendency to display a remarkably narrow range of behaviors and lifestyles, marginalizing or neglecting people who are "different" from the mass-mediated norm. When such difference is highlighted by, for example, television talk shows that routinely include people who are otherwise invisible in the mass media—cross-dressers, squatters, or strippers—the media can become part of a spectacle of the bizarre.

Despite the likelihood of their having very different political stances, those who are concerned about media depictions of premarital sex have the same underlying concern as those who criticize the dominating images of the upper-middle-class family. In both cases, the fear is that media images *normalize* specific social relations, making certain ways of behaving seem unexceptional. If media texts can normalize behaviors, they can also set limits on the range of acceptable ideas. The ideological work lies in the *patterns* within media texts. Ideas and attitudes that are routinely included in media become part of the legitimate public debate about issues. Ideas that are excluded from the popular media or appear in the media only to be ridiculed have little legitimacy. They are outside the range of acceptable ideas. The ideological influence of media can be seen in the absences and exclusions just as much as in the content of the messages.

Media professionals generally have little patience with the argument that the media are purveyors of ideology. Instead of seeing media as places where behaviors are normalized and boundaries are created, those in the industry tend to argue that the images they produce and distribute simply reflect the norms and ideas of the public. This is not ideology but simply a mirror that reflects the basic consensus about how things are. Since mass media are commercially organized to attract audiences for profit, there is a good reason to believe that popularity will be more important to media producers than a commitment to any specific ideology. However, our investigation of the ideology of media does not mean that producers are consciously trying to sell certain ways of thinking and being. Ideology is not only produced by committed ideologues. We can find ideology in our everyday lives, in our definition of common sense, and in the construction of a consensus. . . .

Movies, the Military, and Masculinity

One of the difficulties of ideological analysis of media products is that there is no singular "mass media." The term *mass media*, we should reiterate, is plural, signifying the multiple organizations and technologies that make up our media environment. As a result, we have to be careful when we make generalizations about the ideological content of media, in large part because we are usually talking about a specific medium and perhaps even specific media texts. Another challenge for ideological analysis is that media texts are produced in specific historical contexts, responding to and helping frame the cultural currents of the day. Mass-mediated images are not static; they change in form and content in ways that are observable. Ideological analysis, therefore, needs to pay attention to the shifts in me-

dia images—sometimes subtle and sometimes quite dramatic—in order to allow for the dynamic nature of mass media.

If the study of media and ideology needs to be both historically specific and wary of overgeneralizing from single texts, what analytic strategies have proved useful? One of the most common approaches is to focus on specific types or "genres" of media, such as the television sit-com, the Hollywood horror film, or the romance novel. Because texts within the same genre adopt the same basic conventions, analysts can examine the underlying themes and ideas embedded within these conventional formats without worrying that any contradictions they might uncover are the result of the distinct modes of storytelling of different genres. The result is that most scholarly studies of media ideology are both quite specific about their subject matter and narrow in their claims, focusing on issues such as the messages about gender in the soap opera (Modleski, 1984) or the ideology of the American Dream in talk radio (Levin, 1987).

In addition, scholarly studies of media texts generally either focus on a specific historical period—for example, foreign policy news in the Reagan era (Herman and Chomsky, 1988)—or provide comparisons of one genre of media across several time periods—for example, best-selling books from the 1940s through the 1970s (Long, 1985). These analyses provide, on one hand, an understanding of how a specific medium displays a particular worldview or ideological conflict and, on the other hand, an understanding of how such stories about society change over time, in different historical contexts.

Two film genres, action-adventure and military/war films of the 1980s and early 1990s, are worth exploring for their underlying ideological orientation because of their popularity. With action-adventure movies such as *Raiders of the Lost Ark* and *Romancing the Stone* and military movies such as *Rambo* and *Top Gun* attracting large audiences—and inspiring sequels and seemingly endless imitators—scholars have used an ideological framework to understand the underlying messages in these films. What are these movies about, and why are they so attractive to American audiences? In other words, what are the ideologies of these films, and how do these ways of seeing the world fit within broader ideological currents? These questions help both to interpret the films and to locate their meaning in a social context.

Action-Adventure Films

Action-adventure films were among the most popular movies of the 1980s. The three Indiana Jones films, starring Harrison Ford, are the archetype of this genre, in which the male hero performs remarkable feats that require bravery and skill throughout a fast-paced 90-minute struggle with an evil villain. The hero ultimately emerges triumphant after several close calls, defeating the villain, saving the day, and usually winning the affection of the female lead. One version of this genre places the hero in faraway, exotic lands, making the villains and the action more unpredictable. But the basic story line can be found in films set in the United States, such as *Die Hard* and *Speed*. On one level, these kinds of movies can be thrilling, suspenseful (even though we know, deep down, that the hero will triumph), and even romantic as we watch the hero overcome new challenges and seemingly impossible odds on the road to an exciting and satisfying finish. However, if we dig below the surface of the action, we can explore the kinds of stories these movies tell and how the stories resonate with our contemporary social dilemmas.

Gina Marchetti (1989) has argued that the key to the ideology of the genre is the typical construction of the main characters, the hero and the villain, which leads to specific stories about the nature of good and evil, strength and weakness, and courage and cowardice. One underlying theme of the action-adventure genre is the drawing of rigid lines between "us" and "them," with the villain representing the dangers of difference. There are, of course, many different versions of the central determinant of the in-group and the out-group. Nationality and ethnicity are frequent boundary markers, with white Americans (Michael Douglas, Bruce Willis) defeating dangerous foreigners. In other versions, civilized people triumph over the "primitive" (*Indiana Jones and the Temple of Doom*), or representatives of law and order defeat the deranged (*Speed*).

Ultimately, the hero effectively eliminates the danger represented by "the other"—the difference embodied by the villain—usually by killing the villain in a sensational climatic scene. Metaphorically speaking, social order is restored by the reassertion of the boundaries between what is acceptable and what is not, with the unacceptable doomed to a well-deserved death. The films go beyond xenophobic demonization of difference, however, by demonstrating the terms on which people who are different can become part of mainstream society. The hero's local accomplices—such as Indiana Jones's child sidekick Short Round in *Temple of Doom*—demonstrate that it is possible to be incorporated into mainstream society. This is the flip side of the violent death of the villain: The difference represented by the friend or "buddy" can be tamed and made acceptable (Marchetti, 1989). Difference, then, must be either destroyed or domesticated by integrating the other into the hierarchical social relations of contemporary society, where the newly tamed other will likely reside near the bottom of the hierarchy. Ultimately, the action-adventure genre, with its focus on the personal triumph of the hero, is a tale about the power of the rugged male individual, a mythic figure in the ideology of the American Dream.

Vietnam Films

One particular 1980s version of the action-adventure genre was the "return to Vietnam" film, symbolized most clearly by the hit movie *Rambo*. In these films—which also include the *Missing in Action* trilogy and *Uncommon Valor*—the hero, a Vietnam veteran, returns to Vietnam a decade after the war to rescue American prisoners-of-war that the U.S. government has long since abandoned. In the process, the Vietnamese are demonized as brutal enemies who deserve the deaths that the heroes—most notably Sylvester Stallone and Chuck Norris—inflict upon the captors as they liberate the prisoners.

The ideological work of these films is not very subtle, and given that they were popular during Ronald Reagan's presidency their ideological resonance should not be surprising. In essence, these films provide a mass-mediated refighting of the war, in which Americans are both the good guys and the victors. The films serve as a kind of redemption for a country unable to accept defeat in Vietnam and still struggling with the shame of loss. If the United States did not win the Vietnam War on the battlefield, the movies allow its citizens to return in the world of film fantasy to alter the end of the story. In these stories, there is no longer shame or defeat but instead pride, triumph, and a reaffirmation of national strength. This outlook was, to be sure, part of the appeal of Ronald Reagan, whose campaign for President in 1980 called for a return to a sense of national pride, strength, and purpose that would move the nation beyond "the Vietnam Syndrome."

The back-to-Vietnam films are, perhaps most fundamentally, part of the ideological project to overcome the Vietnam syndrome by providing a substitute victory. Susan Jeffords (1989) has argued that these films are about more than our national pride and the reinterpretation of defeat in Vietnam. She makes a persuasive case that the return-to-Vietnam films are part of a larger process of "remasculinization" of American society, another key component of the ideology of the Reagan years, in which a masculinity defined by its toughness is reasserted in the face of the twin threats of defeat in Vietnam and the growth of feminism.

These Vietnam films are, to Jeffords, fundamentally about the definition of American "manhood" at a time when the traditional tough image had been challenged by the social movements of the 1960s and the defeat in Southeast Asia. The Sylvester Stallone and Chuck Norris characters—Rambo and Braddock—return to Vietnam in order to recapture their strength and power, all the while resisting and chastising the government for being too weak (read: "feminine") to undertake such a courageous mission. The "return" is as much about returning to a mythical past in which a strong America ruled the world and strong American men ruled their households as it is about rescuing POWs. Rambo and Braddock symbolize the desires of, and provide a mass-mediated and ideologically specific solution for, American men struggling with the changing social landscape of the 1980s.

Such popular media images are not simply innocent fantasies for our viewing entertainment. If we read these films in ideological terms, both the film texts themselves and their popularity tell us something about American culture and society in the 1980s. The masculine/military films of the time both reflected the fears and desires of American men and helped reproduce a new brand of toughness that became prevalent in the 1990s. The films were

part of a political culture that created the conditions for the popular 1989 invasion of Panama and the even more popular 1991 war in the Persian Gulf, where the TV news images did not differ much from those in the 1986 hit film *Top Gun*. Americans did overcome the "Vietnam syndrome" in the late 1980s, as symbolized by the willingness of the population to support military action in Panama and Iraq. Part of the ideological work necessary for that transformation was performed by popular Hollywood films. . . .

Conclusion

. . . Researchers who study the ideology of media are interested in the underlying stories about society that the media tell, the range of values that the media legitimize, and the kinds of behaviors that are deemed normal. Most popular media promote, often in subtle and even contradictory ways, perspectives that support our basic social arrangements and endorse the legitimacy of social institutions, marginalizing attitudes and behaviors that are considered to be out of the "mainstream."

Media images can and sometimes do challenge this mainstream, status quo–oriented ideology by providing a critique of contemporary social organization and norms, but commercialization makes it difficult for media to maintain a critical voice. The search for popularity, wider distribution, and profitability tends to dull the critical edges of media imagery, pushing media back toward more mainstream (and marketable) ideologies. There are, to be sure, media that consistently promote alternative ideological perspectives. Local weekly newspapers, journals of opinion, public access television, and independent films are often quite self-conscious about providing perspectives that differ from the dominant popular media. These alternatives, however, remain on the margins of the media scene, reaching small audiences and lacking the capital to mount a serious challenge to the dominant media.

REFERENCES

Herman, Edward, and Noam Chomsky. 1988. *Manufacturing consent.* New York: Pantheon.

Hunter, James Davison. 1991. *Culture wars.* New York: Basic Books.

Jeffords, Susan. 1989. *The remasculinization of America: Gender and the Vietnam War.* Bloomington: Indiana University Press.

Levin, Murray. 1987. *Talk radio and the American dream.* Lexington, Mass: Lexington Books.

Long, Elizabeth. 1985. *The American dream and the popular novel.* Boston: Routledge and Kegan Paul.

Marchetti, Gina. 1989. Action-adventure as ideology. In I. Angus and S. Jhally, eds., *Cultural politics in contemporary America.* New York: Routledge.

Modleski, Tania. 1984. *Loving with a vengeance.* New York: Methuen.

12

◆◆◆

Women and the Environment

Place is a fundamental element in our lives whether we live in a spacious suburb, a vibrant—maybe overcrowded—downtown area, an old-established inner-city neighborhood, on a farm, a ranch, or a reservation (Anderson 1991; Barnhill 1999; Williams 1992). Places change over time so that a formerly Polish American or Italian American community may now be home to African Americans or Vietnamese immigrants; a poorer neighborhood may become gentrified as middle-class people move in and push up property values. Neighborhood facilities—churches, temples, synagogues, schools, stores, restaurants, parks, community centers—reflect the interests and concerns of people who live there. The quality of some local services and the physical space also reflect the standing of a particular community in the wider society. In general, middle-class and upper-middle-class communities have better school buildings, more sports facilities, more doctors' offices, and a wider range of stores than poorer neighborhoods. They are also farther from factories, oil refineries, sawmills, stockyards, railway terminals, highways, garbage dumps, and other sources of pollution, bad smells, and noise.

Many people contribute to safeguarding our physical environment. Federal legislation like the Clean Air Act and regulatory agencies like the Environmental Protection Agency limit toxic emissions from factories, homes, and cars. Cities or counties provide services like potable water, garbage disposal, street cleaning and repair, snow clearance, stop signs and traffic lights, town parks, and recreation centers. National environmental organizations have lobbied for the preservation of wilderness areas as national parks, for the protection of endangered species, and for stronger environmental regulation of industry. Community organizations clear trash from highways and vacant lots, or work in community gardens. Individuals mow lawns, trim trees, sweep the sidewalk, recycle reusable materials, compost organic matter, and buy "green" or environmentally safe products like paper goods from recycled paper or biodegradable soaps and detergents. Important as they are, these efforts cannot keep up with the scale and pace of environmental degradation.

In the past thirty-five years or so, many people in the United States have become increasingly concerned with environmental issues. Hazardous industrial production processes have affected the health of workers and people who live near or downwind of industrial areas. Industrial pollutants, chemical pesticides and fertilizers, and wastes from nuclear power plants and uranium mines are seeping into the groundwater in many parts of the country as exemplified in feature films like *A Civil Action* and *Erin Brockovich*. Homes and schools have been built on land once used for toxic dumps (Gibbs 1995, 1998). Deforestation, global warming, and the disappearance of hundreds of species are also hallmarks of vast environmental destruction worldwide (Worldwatch Institute 2003). Given the enormous scale of the environmental crisis, the small steps mentioned earlier do not begin to touch the heart of the problem, though as we discuss later, there are many views as to what the heart of the problem is. United States environmental activists probably agree, however, that the greatest threat to environmental security worldwide comes from the waste-producing, industrialized, militarized countries of the North, especially the United States, Canada, Europe, and Japan.

This chapter is concerned with environmental effects on women particularly and with women's activism around environmental issues. It assumes that there is an ethical dimension to living in any location: that we care for the environment for our own sake and for the sake of future generations. As the world has become more integrated, place is a more amorphous concept. Our home places are deeply affected by corporate and governmental decisions often made many miles away. As with other topics in this book, environmental issues are experienced at the micro and meso levels, but also have macro- and global-level dimensions. The lenses of gender, race, class, and nation are also essential tools of analysis in this chapter.

In the United States the environmental crisis affects men as well as women, of course, but in terms of environmental health, women and children show the effects of toxic pollution earlier than men do, either because of low body weight or because women's bodies become what some have termed "unhealthy environments" for their babies (Nelson 1990; Steingraber 2001). A significant number of babies without brains have been born to women on both sides of the Rio Grande, a river polluted by U.S.-controlled *maquiladora* industries on the Mexican side (Kamel and Hoffman 1999). (Working conditions in these *maquiladoras*, or subassembly plants, are described in more detail in Chapter 9.) Contact with pesticides has led to poor health for many women farmworkers in the United States and to chronic illnesses or severe

disabilities for their children (Chavez 1993; Moses 1993). Several firms have tried to keep women of childbearing age out of the most noxious production processes—often the highest paid—or to insist that they be sterilized, lest women sue them later for fetal damage (Gottlieb 1993).

Children's health is also compromised by environmental factors such as lead in paints and gasoline, air pollution, traffic hazards, and violence that often involves the use of handguns, with significant differences between those living in inner cities and those in suburban neighborhoods (Hamilton 1993; Phoenix 1993). The Akwesasne Mothers' Milk project in upstate New York, founded by Katsi Cook, is a Native American research project that was started in response to women's concern that their breastmilk might be toxic and that breastfeeding, supposedly the best way to nurture infants, could expose them to pollutants from birth (LaDuke 1999).

Many more women than men are involved in campaigning on behalf of environmental issues at a grassroots level, though women are less active than men concerning environmental issues at the national level (Mohai 1997). We do not see women as somehow closer to nature than men, as is sometimes argued, or as having an essentially nurturing, caring nature. Rather, we see women's environmental activism as an extension of their roles as daughters, wives, and mothers, caring for families and communities. Because of the gendered division of labor between home and work, women have a long-standing history of involvement in community organizing: campaigning against poor housing conditions, high rents, unsafe streets, lead in gasoline, toxic dumps, and so on, described by sociologist Nancy Naples (1998) as "activist mothering." Ideally, taking care of children and other family members should be everyone's responsibility, as we argue in Chapter 7. We see organizing around environmental issues as part of this responsibility.

Theoretical and Activist Perspectives

Generally, theories grow out of and inform experience. Women who are concerned about environmental degradation draw on different theoretical and activist perspectives: deep ecology and bioregionalism, ecofeminism, and environmental justice. These are not unitary perspectives, though here we emphasize points of comparison between them rather than their internal variations.

Environmentalism

Over the past thirty-five years, successive U.S. Congresses have passed a number of fundamental environmental laws, for example, to improve air and water quality or to protect wilderness areas and endangered species. This is largely due to the work of dedicated environmentalists like Rachel Carson (1962; Dorsey and Thormodsgard 2003; Hynes 1989) and to concerted public education and lobbying by major environmental organizations such as the Sierra Club, the Natural Resources Defense Council, and the Environmental Defense Fund. Limitations of such efforts are that they are slow and invariably compromised by corporate interests. Currently, these hard-earned, crucial gains are being rolled back by President Bush's environmental policy that includes the weakening of existing environmental legislation, abandoning the international treaty on global warming (the Kyoto Treaty), and an energy plan based heavily on fossil fuels, including the proposal to drill for oil in the Alaska Arctic National Wildlife Refuge (Borenstein 2003).

Deep Ecology and Bioregionalism

Deep ecology is a term coined by Norwegian philosopher Arne Naess and taken up in the United States by ecological philosophers Bill Devall and George Sessions (1985). It is premised on two fundamental principles: self-realization for every being and a "biocentric" equality among species. Many environmental activists in the United States who are drawn to deep ecology are critical of the more mainstream environmental organizations mentioned above, which have a human-centered focus. Earth First! is an activist network that exemplifies principles of deep ecology in practice. It gained public recognition through direct action, particularly in opposition to the logging of old-growth forests in the Pacific Northwest and northern California (Davis 1991; Hill 2000; List 1993).

At its worst, deep ecology is sometimes reduced to a rather simplistic view of the world in which nature is "good" and people are "bad." Deep ecologists argue for reducing human population, reducing human interference in the biosphere, and reducing human standards of living. As its name implies, Earth First! has been more interested in saving the earth than in safeguarding the human population. This led to arguments that, for example, if AIDS didn't exist it would have had to be invented, or that starving people in Africa should be left to die so that the human population can be brought back into balance with the carrying capacity of the land (Thropy 1991). Deep ecologists value the preservation of nature in and of itself rather than for any benefit such preservation affords to humans. Nature is often seen in romantic terms: The virgin, feminized wilderness is vulnerable, innocent, and weak, and protecting "her" draws on old macho, militaristic iconography (King 1987). Wilderness is not thought of as the homeland of indigenous people but as a special place where people (at least athletic, nondisabled people) can get close to an "experience" of nature. Critics of U.S. deep ecology oppose its people vs. nature stance and argue, for example, that "if we believe that we are in essence bad for nature we are profoundly separated from the natural world" (Starhawk 2002a, p. 161). Nature is not something far away, to be encountered on weekend hikes or occasional camping trips. Everyone is connected to nature in the most mundane but profound way: through the air we breathe, the water we drink, and the food we eat, as embodied human beings in a continuum of life. Ecofeminist writer and activist Starhawk (2002a) also notes that a "humans-as-blight" view is self-defeating for organizing around environmental issues, as people "don't act effectively out of feeling bad, guilty, wrong, and inauthentic" (p. 161).

A significant development is the alliance between Earth First! and labor union members. In the 1980s and early '90s, people who tried to stop logging, for example, especially in old-growth forests of western states, often found themselves up against loggers who were dependent on timber companies for their livelihood. In urban areas, too, industrial jobs were often set against a cleaner environment. Corporations argued that they could not afford to clean up their operations or that cleaning up would be at the expense of jobs. An alliance between environmentalists and labor organizers is essential. People need a livelihood as well as good environmental conditions, and the two are not mutually exclusive (Goodstein 1999; Pulido 1996; Schwab 1994; Alliance for Sustainable Jobs and the Environment, Portland, Ore.).

A humans-as-nature view prevails within the bioregional movement, which emphasizes decentralization, small-scale projects, agricultural and economic self-sufficiency within bioregions, and a strongly developed attachment to place (Andruss et al. 1990; Berg 1993; Sale 1985). Indigenous people invariably emphasize the importance of connection to the land for their communities, as discussed by lawyer, legal scholar, and Hawaiian sovereignty activist Mililani Trask in the context of Hawai'i (Reading 73). This point is taken up by Starhawk (2002a) from the perspective of earth-centered spirituality. Vandana Shiva (2002), director of the Research Foundation on Science, Technology, and Ecology, focuses on "relocalization," as opposed to globalization, which places an enormous economic and environmental burden on countries of the South. She argues that "what can be grown and produced locally should be used locally" rather than exported, and, further, that "re-localization everywhere—in the South and in the North—would conserve resources, generate meaningful work, fulfill basic needs and strengthen democracy" (p. 249). Crucially important for ecofeminists and environmental justice activists is that these localized systems also include a commitment to anti-racist principles, women's liberation, and economic justice.

Ecofeminism

The term **ecofeminism** was first used by a group of French feminists who founded the Ecology-Feminism Center in 1974, and it was based on their analysis of connections between masculinist social institutions and the destruction of the physical environment (d'Eaubonne 1994). A few years later, groundbreaking work in the United States by poet and essayist Susan Griffin (1978) and environmental historian Carolyn Merchant (1980) articulated a central insight of ecofeminism, the connection between the domination of women and the domination of nature. These authors pointed to the ways in which Western thought and science from the time of Francis Bacon has seen nonhuman nature as wild and hostile, so much matter to be mastered and used:

> For you have to but follow and . . . hound nature in her wanderings, and you will be able when you like to lead and drive her afterward

to the same place again. . . . Neither ought a man make scruple of entering and penetrating into these holes and corners, when the inquisition of truth is his whole object.
>
> *(Quoted in Merchant 1980, p. 168)*

In Western thought, nature is often feminized and sexualized through imagery such as "virgin forest," "the rape of the earth," and "penetrating" the wilderness. Shiva (1988) notes that in the Western model of development, sources, living things that can reproduce life—whether forests, seeds, or women's bodies—are turned into resources to be objectified, controlled, and used. This makes them productive in economic terms. In this view, a forest that is not logged, a river that is not fished, or a hillside that is not mined, is unproductive (Waring 1988). A core point in ecofeminist analysis involves the concept of dualism, where various attributes are thought of in terms of oppositions: culture/nature; mind/body; male/female; civilized/primitive; sacred/profane; subject/object; self/other. Philosopher Val Plumwood (1993) argues that these dualisms are mutually reinforcing and should be thought of as an interlocking set. In each pair, one side is valued over the other. Culture, mind, male, civilized, for example, are valued over nature, body, female, primitive, which are thought of as "other" and inferior. Plumwood argues that dualism is the logic of hierarchical systems of thought—colonialism, racism, sexism, or militarism, for example, which rely on the idea of otherness, enemies, and inferiority to justify superiority and domination. Ecofeminism has the potential to link concerns with racism and economic exploitation to the domination of women and nature.

Such a broad approach is open to many interpretations and ideas for activism. The first ecofeminist conference in the United States, titled "Women for Life on Earth," was held in Amherst, Massachusetts, as a response to the near-meltdown at the Three Mile Island nuclear power plant in 1980, as discussed by ecofeminist writer Ynestra King (Reading 70). One outcome of the conference was the Women's Pentagon Action, a major demonstration against militarism in the early 1980s, mentioned in Chapter 11 (also see Reading 65). Currently, ecofeminism is explored and developed through newsletters and study groups, college courses, animal rights organizing, and long-term women's land projects.

Some ecofeminist writers and researchers work with local activist groups or contribute to national and international debates. Significant examples include the National Women's Health Network's research and organizing around industrial and environmental health (Nelson 1990), critiques of reproductive technology and genetic engineering by the Feminist Network of Resistance to Reproductive and Genetic Engineering (Mies and Shiva 1993), and the Committee on Women, Population, and the Environment, which has critiqued simplistic overpopulation arguments that focus only on countries of the South rather than also addressing the overconsumption of the North (Bandarage 1997; Hartmann 1995; Mello 1996; Silliman and King 1999). The Women's Environment and Development Organization (WEDO) coordinated a major international conference in 1991 to work out a women's agenda to take to the U.N. Conference on the Environment and Development in Rio de Janeiro in June 1992. This group was an active participant in the NGO Forum in China in 1995, as we noted in Chapter 9, and at the World Summit on Sustainable Development in Johannesburg, 2002 (WEDO 2002).

Ecofeminist writer Charlene Spretnak (1990) embraces the eclectic nature of U.S. ecofeminism and notes its varied roots in feminist theory, feminist spirituality, and social ecology. This diversity in ecofeminist approaches raises the question of whether there is a sufficiently consistent, intellectually coherent ecofeminist perspective, and many academics claim that there is not. Some women of color argue that, as with U.S. feminism in general, ecofeminism emphasizes gender over race and class; other women of color argue that it focuses on abstract ideas about women and nature rather than on practical issues with a material base (Davis 1998; Smith 1997; Taylor 1997). Left-wing radicals, some environmentalists, and many academics reject ecofeminism as synonymous with goddess worship or on the grounds that it assumes women are essentially closer to nature than men. Geographer Joni Seager (1993), for example, has developed a feminist understanding of environmental issues but does not use the term *ecofeminism* to describe her work. At present, U.S. ecofeminism is very much the preserve of writers and scholars, albeit those who are often on the margins of the academy in part-time or temporary positions. Although this may lead to an activism of scholarship—by no means insignificant, as suggested earlier—it does not often connect directly with the reality of life for many women organizing around environmental issues (also see Epstein 1993; Kirk 1997; Sachs 1996). We argue that an ecological feminism can, and should, integrate gender, race, class, and nation in its analyses and that its powerful theoretical insights can, and should, translate into activism.

Environmental Justice

The people most affected by poor physical environments in the United States are women and children, particularly women and children of color. Many women of color and poor White women are active in hundreds of local organizations campaigning for healthy living and working conditions in working-class communities, communities of color, and on Native American land, which are all disproportionately affected by pollution from incinerators, toxic dumps, pesticides, and hazardous working conditions in industry and agriculture (Bullard 1990, 1993; Hofrichter 1993; LaDuke 1999; Szasz 1994). Data show a strong correlation between the distribution of toxic wastes and race, which has been termed **environmental racism** (Lee 1987). The theory of environmental racism and the movement for **environmental justice** draw on concepts of civil rights, under which all citizens have a right to healthy living and working conditions. Organizationally, too, the environmental justice movement has roots in civil rights organizing, as well as in labor unions, Chicano land-grant movements, social justice organizations, and Native American rights organizations. Its tactics include demonstrations and rallies, public education, research and monitoring of toxic sites, preparing and presenting expert testimony to government agencies, reclaiming land through direct action, and maintaining and teaching traditional agricultural practices, crafts, and skills. Examples of local organizations include the Mothers of East Los Angeles (Pardo 1990), West Harlem Environmental Action (New York; see Miller 1993), the Asia Pacific Environmental Network (Oakland, Calif.), and the Southwest Network for Environmental and Economic Justice (Albuquerque, N.M., and Austin, Tex.; see Kirk 1998).

Local organizations embrace different issues depending on their memberships and geographic locations. Some are primarily concerned to stop the

location of toxic waste dumps or incinerators in their neighborhoods, an approach sometimes dubbed the Not-In-My-Back-Yard (NIMBY) syndrome. Most groups are quick to see that it is not enough to keep hazards out of their own neighborhoods if this means that dumps or incinerators will then be located in other poor communities. This has led to coordinated opposition on a local, regional, and national level. The First National People of Color Environmental Leadership Summit was held in Washington, D.C., in 1991. Over the next ten years, several major grassroots Networks were formed, such as the African American Environmental Justice Action Network, the Indigenous Environmental Network, and the Farmworkers Network for Economic and Environmental Justice, committed to building a multicultural, multiracial movement.

Besides opposing hazardous conditions, the environmental justice movement also has a powerful reconstructive dimension involving sustainable projects that intertwine ecological, economic, and cultural survival. Examples include Tierra Wools (northern New Mexico), where a workers' cooperative produces high-quality, handwoven rugs and clothing and organically fed lamb from its sheep (Pulido 1993); the Native American White Earth Land Recovery Project in Minnesota, which produces wild rice, maple sugar, berries, and birch bark (LaDuke 1993, 1999); and many inner-city community gardening projects

producing vegetables for local consumption (Bagby 1990; Hynes 1996; Warner 1987).

Although very few local environmental issues are exclusively the concern of women, women form the majority of local activists in opposing such hazards as toxic dumps. As noted, women have a history of community organizing. This activism may also be given special impetus if they have sick children or become ill themselves (see Reading 32, Chapter 5, concerning environmental factors and the incidence of breast cancer). Illnesses caused by toxics are sometimes difficult to diagnose and treat because they affect internal organs and the balance of body functioning, and symptoms can be mistaken for those of other conditions. Women have been persistent in raising questions and searching for plausible explanations for such illnesses, sometimes discovering that their communities have been built on contaminated land, as happened at Love Canal, New York, for example, or tracing probable sources of pollution affecting their neighborhoods (Reading 71; also Gibbs 1995, 1998; Kaplan 1997). They have publicized their findings and taken on governmental agencies and corporations responsible for contamination. In so doing they are often ridiculed as "hysterical housewives" by officials and reporters and their research trivialized as emotional and unscholarly. By contrast, others—Nelson (1990), for example—honor this work as kitchen table science. In October 1991, women were 60 percent of the participants at the First National People of Color Environmental Leadership Summit. The conference adopted a statement called "Principles of Environmental Justice," included here (Reading 72). Many urban gardeners in northern cities are elderly African American women (e.g., Bagby 1990). On the west coast, Latino and Asian immigrants continue the gardening traditions of their homelands. Cindy Chan Saelee describes her mother's garden in Richmond, California, in Reading 74. In rural areas, women work on family subsistence garden plots, planting, harvesting, and processing fruits and vegetables for home use (Sachs 1996). Some know the woods or backcountry areas in great detail, as ethnobotanists, because they go there at different seasons to gather herbs for medicinal purposes. Among Mexican Americans, for example, *curanderas*—traditional healers—continue to work with herbal remedies and acquire their knowledge from older women relatives (Perrone, Stockel, and Krueger 1989).

In 1989 the Citizens' Clearinghouse for Hazardous Wastes (now the Center for Health, Environment, and Justice, Falls Church, Va.) organized a conference to address women's experiences as environmental activists (Zeff, Love, and Stults 1989). Excerpts from the conference report are included in Reading 71. When women become involved with environmental justice organizing, they become politicized (Gibbs 1995, 1998; Krauss 1993; Zeff, Love, and Stults 1989). They are suddenly caught up in meetings, maybe traveling to other towns and cities and staying away overnight. They spend much more time, and money, on the phone than before. They are quoted in the local papers or on the TV news. They often face new challenges, balancing family responsibilities, perhaps struggling with their husbands' misgivings about their involvement, or facing the tensions of being strong women in male-dominated communities. As mentioned in our discussion of anti-militarist activism in the previous chapter, motherhood also provides a powerful stimulus for environmental justice activism (Glazer and Glazer 1998), as exemplified in Reading 71.

Women active in the environmental justice movement generally see themselves and their communities in terms of race and class and "have remained wary of a 'feminist' label" (Gottlieb 1993, p. 234). Indeed, most environmental justice organizations do not appear to draw on a gender analysis, even though many of their participants are women. By contrast, ecofeminists have tended to emphasize gender at the expense of race and class, and have failed to link theory and practice in a sustained way. Robert Gottlieb (1993), professor of urban and environmental policy, notes that the national environmental movement as a whole has been unable to respond to the question "What constitutes an agenda and organizing style that incorporates women's experiences?" (p. 234). Given the crucial importance of the environment in a more secure and sustainable world, there is a great need for a theoretical framework that integrates gender, race, class, nation, and environmental issues and that generates broad-based activist efforts.

Connectedness and Sustainability

The writers and activists mentioned in this chapter all work from their sense of relationship and responsibility to maintain or to remake connections between people and the natural world. Together such projects and movements draw on alternative visions and strategies for sustainable living, however small-scale and fragile they might be at present. At root this is about taking on the current economic system and the systems of power—personal and institutional—that sustain and benefit from it, working to transform relationships of exploitation and oppression.

The idea of sustainability is often invoked but means very different things to different people. For corporate economists, for example, it means sustained economic growth that will yield sustained profits; for ecologists it involves the maintenance of natural systems—wetlands, forests, wilderness, air and water quality; for environmentalists it means using only renewable resources and generating low or nonaccumulating levels of pollution (Pearce, Markandya, and Barbier 1990). Many concerned with environmental economics note the contradiction between the linear expansionism of capitalist economies and long-term sustainability (Daly and Cobb 1989; Henderson 1991; O'Connor 1994). Scholar and writer Maria Mies (1993) notes that for countries of the South to follow the development model of the industrial North there would need to be two more

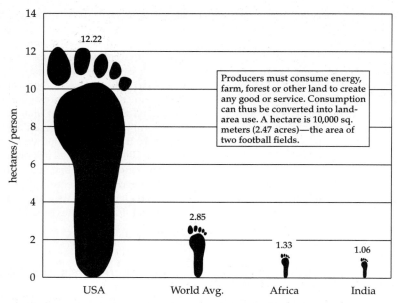

Figure 12.1 Comparative Consumption of Environmental Resources per Person, 2000 (in hectares). (*Source:* Bill Bigelow and Bob Peterson [eds.], *Rethinking Globalization* [Milwaukee, Wis.: Rethinking Schools Press, 2002.] Reprinted by permission of Rethinking Schools Press.)

worlds: one for the necessary natural resources and the other for the waste.

A more sustainable future for both North and South means rethinking current economic systems and priorities and emphasizing ecologically sound production to meet people's basic needs, as argued by scholar and writer H. Patricia Hynes (Reading 75). She uses the concept **ecological footprint** to refer to the amount of energy, land, water, minerals, and other natural resources required by varying lifestyles and levels of development (see Figure 12.1). A sustainable future implies local control over transnational corporations, reduction of poor countries' foreign debt, and making money available for development that is ecologically sound, as we suggested in Chapter 9. At a local level in the United States it implies support for community gardens, farmers' markets, credit unions, and small-scale worker-owned businesses and markets, as we suggested in Chapter 8. It means valuing women's unpaid domestic and caring work, a key aspect of sustaining home and community life (Mellor 1992; Waring 1988). So-

ciologist Mary Mellor notes that this work is geared to biological time. Children need feeding when they are hungry; sick people need care regardless of what time of day it is; gardens need planting in the right season. She argues that, given a gendered division of labor, "women's responsibility for biological time means that men have been able to create a public world that largely ignores it," a world "no longer rooted in the physical reality of human existence" (pp. 258–59). A sustainable future must be based in biological time and will require emotional as well as physical and intellectual labor. Novels provide an effective way of showing the possibilities—positive and negative—of particular philosophies and societal arrangements, and they can help us to imagine different futures (e.g., Butler 1993; Piercy 1976; Starhawk 1993).

To create such a future will also mean changing current definitions of wealth that emphasize materialism and consumerism. A broader notion of wealth includes everything that has the potential to enrich a person and a community, such as health, physical energy and strength, safety and security, time, skills, talents, wisdom, creativity, love, community support, a connection to one's history and cultural heritage, and a sense of belonging. This is not a philosophy of denial or a romanticization of poverty, though it does involve a fundamental **paradigm shift,** or change of worldview, in a country so dominated by material consumption and wealth. Writers included in this chapter all implicitly or explicitly argue for a profound change in attitudes, in which human life and the life of the natural world are valued, cared for, and sustained. Statements by Diverse Women for Diversity and the Women's Pentagon Action are also relevant here (Readings 57 and 65).

Questions for Reflection

As you read and discuss this chapter, ask yourself these questions:

1. What does it mean to be part of an interconnected chain of life?

2. What are the main environmental issues in your area?

3. Is there a farmers' market in your area? Are there community gardens in your area?

4. Do you have access to a compost pile or worm box?

5. What are the main illnesses in your area? Are they linked to environmental causes?

6. Think about the practical projects mentioned in the readings for this chapter. What resources were used by the people involved? What worldviews are implicit in their actions?

7. What is your vision of a sustainable future?

Finding Out More on the Web

1. Find out more about the organizations mentioned in this chapter. Evaluate their strategies and activities. The following are women's organizations or those where women are prominent.

   Center for Health, Environment, and Justice: **www.chej.org**

   Committee on Women, Population, and the Environment: **www.cwpe.org**

   Student Environmental Action Coalition: **www.seac.org**

   Tierra Wools: **www.tierrawools.com**

   White Earth Land Recovery Project: **www.welrp.org**

   Women's Environment and Development Organization: **www.wedo.org**

2. In Reading 70, Ynestra King gives data for nuclear warheads and toxic dumps. What are the current figures?

3. In reading 73, Mililani Trask refers to contamination and destruction of land by military operations at Kahoolawe Island and Johnston Island. What has happened at these places? Find out more about the environmental effects of military activities. A useful place to start is Global Green USA: **www.globalgreen.org.**

Taking Action

1. Find out about environmental organizations and environmental justice organizations in your area. What are their goals and perspectives? What projects are they currently working on? How could you participate in or support their work?

2. Find out about the people who used to live where you live now. What happened to the Native American people who used to live on this land? Are there other groups who used to live here? How did they support themselves? Why did they move? Where are they now? How are they living now?

3. How big is your ecological footprint? Work out how to make it smaller.

S E V E N T Y

The Ecofeminist Imperative

Ynestra King

In the one year since the Conference on Women and Life on Earth (held in Amherst, Massachusetts, in March 1980) our movement has burgeoned. The Conference grew out of hope and fear—out of a fear for life and the awesome powers of destruction arrayed against it and out of a hope—a hope for women's power to resist and create. We came together following the meltdown at Three Mile Island. We talked of our sisters we knew by name and reputation through the mythology of our own movement and of what together we might be, and we decided to call sisters to a conference on Women and Life on Earth.

We are both a beginning and a continuation. We are a beginning for this decade but we continue the work of the many brave and visionary women who have gone before us. There was Ellen Swallow, the founder of ecological science. There was Rachel Carson, who wrote *Silent Spring* [in 1962], sounding a warning about chemicals and pesticides which was not heeded until many years later. There were the women of the Women's Strike for Peace and the Ban the Bomb movements of the fifties, mailing their babies' teeth to Congressmen as a reminder of future generations. And there are the brave women scientists who have spoken out more recently, and the women who have been at the forefront of antinuclear struggles, peace movements, struggles against toxic wastes and for occupational health and safety.

There are those who have helped us to imagine the world as it could be: artists, poets, writers and dreamers who have given us new visions of culture, health, technology, community and politics. And there are our sisters the world over, with us in the creation of a planetary movement. We are shaking the world.

Over ten years ago this wave of the feminist movement began. We said then that "the personal is political," that the denial of our selfhood was systemic and political, that masculine society even had a name: "patriarchy."

Many more women now see their oppression as political, not individual. Over the past ten years women have begun to rediscover our history, and to name and work to end violence against women in all its forms, demand equal rights, the right of every woman to decide when and if to bear children, and to express her sexuality freely.

But as we have gained in consciousness and numbers the devastation of the planet has accelerated. Every day brings new disasters, some irrevocable. The story of Love Canal where a school and homes were built on a hazardous waste site is a warning of things to come. Three to six nuclear bombs are produced each day. The Pentagon nuclear arsenal now numbers over 30,000 warheads and it is growing. There are thousands of toxic waste dumps around the country that will not be discovered until observant women notice a common birth defect or sickness in their neighborhood. The coastlines are deteriorating, and the Amazon forest, the source of much of earth's oxygen, is being rapidly defoliated. Each day a whole species of life becomes extinct, never to be seen on this earth.

Eco-feminism is about connectedness and wholeness of theory and practice. It asserts the special strength and integrity of every living thing. For us, the snail darter is to be considered side by side with a community's need for water, the porpoise side by side with appetite for tuna, and the creatures it might fall on, over Skylab. We are a woman-identified movement, and we believe that we have special work to do in these imperilled times. We see the devastation of the earth and her beings by the corporate warriors, and the threat of nuclear annihilation by the military warriors, as feminist concerns. It is the same masculinist mentality which would deny us our right to our own bodies and our own sexuality, and which depends on multiple systems of dominance and state power to have its way.

At the same time as we have been making the connections between feminism, ecology, and militarism, *the New Right has been making those very same connections.* They are actively opposing women's reproductive freedom, attacking lesbians and gay men, undermining battered women's shelters and efforts to introduce anti-sexist and anti-racist curricula in schools. The Family Protection Act, now being introduced in Congress piecemeal, is explicit about its intention to shore up patriarchal authority in every aspect of our lives. They want to be sure that strong, angry women do not stand in their way, as the carnivorous appetite of the military gobbles up food stamps, Aid for Dependent Children, Medicaid, schools, legal aid and more. We are beginning to have an understanding of ourselves about how these concerns are intertwined and to act on them as we develop an imaginative, transformative women's movement.

Why women? Because our present patriarchy enshrines together the hatred of women and the hatred of nature. In defying this patriarchy we are loyal to future generations and to life and this planet itself. We have a deep and particular understanding of this both through our natures and through our life experience as women.

We have the wisdom to oppose experiments which could permanently alter the genetic materials of future generations. As feminists we believe that human reproduction should be controlled by women not by a male-dominated medical establishment. We insist on the absolute right of a woman to an abortion. We support the life-affirming right of women to choose when and if to bear children.

We oppose war and we recognize its terrible force when we see it, undeclared but all around us. For to us war is the violence against women in all its forms—rape, battering, economic exploitation and intimidation—and it is the racist violence against indigenous peoples here in the U.S. and around the world, and it is the violence against the earth.

We recognize and respect the beauty of cultural diversity as we abhor racism. Racism divides us from our sisters, it lines the pockets of the exploiters and underlies the decimation of whole peoples and their homelands. The imperialism of white, male, western culture has been more destructive to other peoples and cultures than any imperialist power in the history of the world, just as it has brought us to the brink of ecological catastrophe.

We believe that a culture against nature is a culture against women. We know we must get out from under the feet of men as they go about their projects of violence. In pursuing these projects, men deny and dominate both women and nature. It is time to reconstitute our culture in the name of that nature, and of peace and freedom, and it is women who can show the way. We have to be the voice of the invisible, of nature who cannot speak for herself in the political arenas of our society, of the children yet to be born and of the women who are forcibly silenced in our mental institutions and prisons. We have been the keepers of the home, the children and the community. We learn early to observe, attend and nurture. And whether or not we become biological mothers, we use these nurturant powers daily as we go about our ordinary work. No one pays us to do this. If the children are born deformed or go hungry, if the people in homes built on a dumping site or near a nuclear weapons factory have terrible sickness, we are the ones who care for them, take them to the doctor, console survivors and soothe the terrified. And it is women who have begun to confront government agencies, politicians and corporations. As the deadly sludge of our political system encroaches on every aspect of our most intimate lives, all of us know that life cannot go on this way. The political and the personal are joined: the activities of women as feminists and anti-militarists, and the activities of women struggling in our neighborhoods and communities for survival and dignity are the same struggle.

And with the same attentiveness we give consideration to the kinds of jobs people do. Many people in this society are compelled to accept jobs which contribute to the destruction of life. In the workplace women particularly are saddled with menial tasks and meaningless work. We oppose such "jobs" and propose instead that work must involve free self-expression and an execution which is playful, not drudgerous. Demands for full employment which ignore the ecological and social devastation daily wrought in the process of ordinary work are dangerously shortsighted. This technological society offers finally the possibility of a materially abundant society with meaningful work for everyone. It is this potential we must claim for ourselves—that these capacities be used for our needs and desires in an appropriately scaled, ecologically aware manner. To create such a web of life is a precondition for freedom. The creation of work that is not merely a job, or worse yet a perpetuation of the kind of machines which daily destroy both the biosphere and the worker must be a feminist priority. To this end we propose that women begin to use the powers of imagination and creativity we possess as builders, engineers, scientist-alchemists and artists to develop the ways of livelihood and life which fulfil this promise.

In all our workings, we believe in the philosophy of nonviolence—that no person should be make into an "other" to despise, dehumanize and exploit. As women we have been an "other" but we are refusing to be the "other" any longer and we will not make anyone else into an "other." Sexism, racism, class divisions, homophobia and the rape of nature depend on this process of objectification. Men's fear of female sexuality has led them to pile up institutions which limit women's options. These keep us obligated to man and unaware of alternatives to traditional women's roles and compulsory heterosexuality. It is in the interest of all women to support lesbian women. We oppose anything which presents women from loving each other freely in whatever way we choose.

We are building a feminist resistance movement in the tradition of the militant suffragists of the last wave of feminism, from whom Gandhi and Martin Luther King drew their inspiration. We believe in and practice direct action. By direct action we do not mean activity which is necessarily either legal or illegal, but intentional activity which does not even recognize these governmental sanctions. We mean the creation of a tradition which demands that we act directly, in all matters which concern us, that we do not recognize a higher authority whom we call upon to act for us. If we believe a parking lot should be a garden we might just dig it up and plant a garden. If we believe that there should be vigils of community women against militarism and violence . . . we go out and vigil. If we believe that there should be women's speakouts against violence in every community we will speak. If we believe that women should be safe walking the streets at night we will take back the night.

As ecofeminists the locus of our work is with women in our own communities, in small groups based on personal affinity, shared concerns and a sense of connectedness to our own landscape. But we are joining together regionally, nationally and internationally to confront systems of dominance that go beyond our communities and neighborhoods. Women all over the world are engaging in imaginative direct action to stop the war machine, and to assert our right to our own bodies and our own sexuality and to a poison-free, fruitful earth. Our feminist embrace must come to enfold all these women struggling in our respective communities.

We are the repository of a sensibility which can make a future possible. Feminists must exemplify this in our ideas, our relationships to each other, our culture, politics and actions. It is by necessity that we are feminist utopians. We look backwards to women-centered societies based on respect for life and life cycles. We look forward to new possibilities of reconstituting a culture which is non-hierarchical, which has not only the primitive respect for life and sense of interconnectedness but also those modern technologies which further peace and liberation. Peace is more than the absence of war, as freedom is more than the absence of coercion. They mean more than putting down the gun, taking off the shackles, or even just hearing and remembering. They are both ongoing processes which must be constantly attended to, criticized and expanded upon. Our movement is a process without end, much as life itself is a process without end.

◆◆◆

SEVENTY-ONE

Empowering Ourselves
Women and Toxics Organizing

Robbin Lee Zeff, Marsha Love, and Karen Stults

Health Effects

The environmental justice movement would not exist today were we not concerned about the devastating health effects on our families from exposure to toxic wastes. We got involved because we want justice for ourselves and others who have already been harmed. We're concerned about protecting families against future harm from incinerators, leaking landfills and other sources of hazardous waste contamination. Involuntary exposure to toxic substances is a form of persecution. We will no longer be victims to environmental persecution. . . .

Penny Newman

Penny Newman is a long-time veteran in the grassroots movement against toxics and . . . one of the first to work with Lois Gibbs at Love Canal, N.Y. . . .

"I Didn't Know the Danger."

We chose to move to our community because we thought it was the place to raise our kids. The small town atmosphere, the rural countryside, was the kind of place we wanted to be. I knew that when you go house hunting, you find out about the schools in the neighborhood. But I didn't know then that I had to ask whether the community had a toxic dump.

This community is near a Class 1 hazardous waste site. On the site there are volatile organics, TCE, DDT, the heavy metals. We have radiation. We have everything at Stringfellow. I didn't know it then.

When we moved there, I was three months pregnant. At 5 ½ months I miscarried. Eric was conceived just a few months after that. Eric was born 6 weeks premature. He had a lot of allergies from the very beginning and was always a fairly fragile child. It was routine not to sleep at night, because you lay there listening for his breathing. At any time you might have to rush him to the hospital for his injections.

"The Doctors Didn't Know What Was Wrong."

When Eric started school, instead of things getting better, like everybody told me he would, "he'd outgrow the asthma," he just got worse. We went through a year of really severe abdominal pains and the doctors just didn't know what was going on. Eric went through all kinds of tests. They finally said it was an epileptic stomach. It had to be a teacher who was putting pressure on Eric at school. That seemed really strange to me, because he had a very laid-back teacher.

One night he had to have emergency surgery. They thought it was appendicitis, but it wasn't. So they did exploratory surgery and took out Eric's gall bladder. They decided that's what it was. A six-year-old with a gall bladder problem! So unusual, they wrote articles in medical journals about him. On top of this, Eric was diagnosed as having a congenital defect which required being in braces. Eric also had no vision in one eye. They classified it as "lazy eye," but it wasn't quite that. So we went through a period of braces, glasses and an eye patch. He knocked out teeth, because he kept falling with his braces. He looked like a battered child. Every time we took him out, I'd have to say, "No, I really don't beat this kid." It was very embarrassing.

After the gall bladder surgery Eric seemed to do a little better. Every time the flu came around he wasn't drastically ill. Every time a cold came around he wouldn't be out of school for two weeks.

Shawn was always the healthy kid. I finally thought, "Aha, we've got one that is going to make it." Until he started school. The school is ¾ of a mile from the site. Shawn started with asthma, which he didn't have as a younger child. He seemed to develop it very quickly, as I did, because I had started working at the school. His skin would crack open and ooze. And he had ear infections, continuous ear infections.

"The Officials Didn't Tell Us."

In 1978, we had overflows from the site. They pumped 800,000 gallons of chemicals into the community. It flowed down the street and the flood canal, which goes directly behind the elementary school. It overflowed into the playground. The state officials didn't tell anyone they were doing this. They didn't want to panic the public.

The school district found out and decided they should do something. They didn't want to close the school, because they would lose state financing, based on the average daily attendance rates. So they set up an evacuation plan. They told the staff, "If you hear one bell, take the kids down to buses. If you hear two bells, it will be too late; the dam will be broken. Put the kids on the desks and hope for the best." The staff was instructed not to tell parents.

So we were sending our kids off to school every day, and the kids played in the puddles, as all kids do. They didn't know that they shouldn't be playing in that water; they thought it was rain water. We had foam in the community which they kept telling us was agricultural foam. The kids could actually make beards out of it. They put the foam on their faces.

"Doctors Ended Up Adding to the Problem."

After that, Shawn began having neurological symptoms—the blurred vision, the headaches. The headaches would get so bad he would just scream. It didn't do any good to put him in a dark room; it didn't do any good to give him aspirins. And then he'd start in with dizzy spells to the point of really being nauseous. And you'd actually have to hold on to him, so he could see he wasn't moving. He was in the fourth grade.

We went through two years of tests on him. It was probably the biggest nightmare I'd ever gone through. At that point I really began to hate doctors. They ended up adding to the problem rather than helping it, by telling a fourth grader that he had brain damage without giving him any explanation. By telling him later on that he was just doing it to

get attention. They said this to a young man in his formative years.

Shawn graduated into junior high school, which is out of that immediate area. Things began to subside a bit. He was put on phenobarbital. And we never figured out if it was the medication or just removing him from the area. But he seemed to improve a little bit. However, he never, from that fourth grade period on, never did well in school again, as he used to. And Shawn had been recommended for the gifted program. He was extremely bright and very well coordinated. But he wasn't any more. Clearly there was a change. He noticed it more than I did. He became very conscious of it, to the point that he didn't want to participate in sports any more because he couldn't do things that he used to be able to do. He has also told me he simply can't concentrate.

"The State Says There Are No Significant Health Effects."

In the last year we've started having testing done, as part of our lawsuit. And despite what the state has said in their epidemiological studies—and our community has been studied like a zoo by the state—they kept saying there were no significant health effects. But we got ahold of an internal memo, where they outlined health effects that included an increase in cancer, urinary tract infections, respiratory problems, ear infections, heart problems. But they considered this "no significant health impact." A young man with terrific potential. That potential is reduced. They'll never be able to give that back to him.

I look back now and think: How stupid could I have been? But I just never made the connection. And it wasn't until we got a list of all the chemicals and their health effects that I started reading and thinking, "My God, that's Eric's problem, that's Shawn's problem."

"People Were Scared."

My kids are not the sickest kids in our community. They are considered pretty healthy kids. For a long time people didn't even want to discuss what was going on, because they were scared. Some suspected, mainly because of skin problems. You could see the rashes; you could see the sores. Sores that didn't respond to treatment. And so people would talk about that. The things they wouldn't talk about were the suicide tendencies of their kids, or the really emotional state that some of the people were in. They didn't talk about the reproductive problems they were having. And a lot of it was that they didn't associate those problems with those chemicals.

It's frightening to have a doctor go through this whole list of things that are wrong. And knowing that there are not any doctors around us who are even going to acknowledge that it's happening, much less provide treatment. That's a real problem. What do you do with people by telling them they have these problems and not being able to offer them any help?

Luella Kenny

Luella Kenny joined the grassroots movement for environmental justice in 1978 when her son Jon died from chemical exposure at Love Canal. . . .

I was one of the original activists at Love Canal. And I'm ashamed to say that the only thing that got me involved was because my son died, because he was playing in his own backyard. Otherwise, I was just as complacent as the next person and didn't pay attention to what was going on.

Yet back in 1978 my 7-year-old son suddenly became ill. And I was too busy running back and forth from the hospital to pay attention. I knew that $\frac{1}{10}$ of a mile from my house there was a lot of ruckus going on. People were protesting.

Both my husband and I are in the sciences. We went to the medical library and started reading. Jon had a kidney disease, known as nephrosis. We found out that this disease could be triggered if you're exposed to chemicals. I was told not to worry about it.

But 4 months later this little 7-year-old boy died. The members of the Love Canal Home Owners Association were interested because the death occurred in the immediate neighborhood. And New York State said that they were going to investigate Jon's death. Ironically, I worked for the New York State Dept. of Health for 29 years. I was very trusting. I thought this was what we should do. We should investigate it.

"The Commissioner of Health Didn't Look Me in the Eye."

It's not very easy for a mother to have to read her son's autopsy report and to try and deal with the of-

ficials. I thought it was important to know what had happened, so I sat down with the Commissioner of Health of New York State and tried to go over this autopsy report. Typical of most officials, his head down, not looking me straight in the eye, he had the nerve to tell me that little boys have the tendency to pick their nose and therefore they get bloody noses, not because they are exposed to chemicals. Nothing happens to little boys' kidneys because they are exposed to chemicals; it's because they play football and they fall down and rupture them.

Children have a gland called the thymus gland. It is what determines immune response. It usually disappears when children are 14 years old. The autopsy report indicated that Jon's thymus was already shrunk. In the medical journals, all of the animal studies showed that a shrunken thymus is an indicator of exposure to dioxin. That's what was in our backyard. Dioxin.

Who would have thought that my other son who was 10, was anorexic because of the appetite-suppressing chemicals at the creek? Who would have thought that the hundreds and hundreds of warts that were all over his body which we constantly had to have removed, who would have thought it was due to chemical exposures?

"Don't Be Intimidated by Doctors."

I had worked in the scientific field, and yet I was given stupid answers. I was considered an hysterical housewife. But the officials didn't address the issues any better when I tried to approach them without emotion. Because they are not ready to accept it.

I want to make one last point. Don't be intimidated by doctors. They are not gods. And don't take what they say. You have to go out and search for what you know is true. Don't let them focus only on cancer and miscarriages, which are the obvious things. David Axelrod, the Health Commissioner, told me, "Collect yourself, go back home, start your life again." It's impossible. This is 9 years later. I've started my life again, but certainly not in the direction he told me to.

Patty Frase

Born and raised in Jacksonville, Arkansas, Patty first became involved in the toxics issue when she lost her parents to toxics-related illnesses. . . .

"Don't Trust Government and Industry Research Studies."

When I hear these stories I get so angry. I want to go out and grab these doctors and throw them in the pit. I want to take them out there and let them drink our water.

We have "independent" studies we're supposed to rely on. The majority of those studies are funded by the chemical companies. So they're going to have a study that says, "It's o.k. Don't worry about what's in your landfill. There is nothing wrong with your landfill."

"CDC: Center for Diffusing Citizen Concern."

The government studies are also bogus. We just have to start out knowing that the Centers for Disease Control, the EPA, or any of these regulatory agencies are not telling the truth. When they come your way, tell them to go away. Tell them, "We don't need your studies." You don't need their studies, because then you are countering more than you were before they got there. Because now they are reinforcing that you're crazy. But you're not crazy; there is nothing wrong with you.

Some of the things that go on with the CDC and the EPA are so incredible that it's hard to believe that we're the ignorant ones. The CDC and the EPA came to town and said, "We're going to do you a favor. You've been asking for all this stuff, so we're going to test 10 people that have died in your community. We're going to do liver samples. We're going to do brain samples. We're going to do intestinal samples. We're going to do it all."

My Congressman's office calls me two weeks later and says, "Patty, I don't think you want that. You're the control group for Times Beach, Missouri." So I called the CDC and I asked them if this was true. And I called the press, like crazy. The next day the study was cancelled. Thank goodness. We were supposed to be the control group. We were. Our contamination level was just as high, if not higher, in some parts of our community, than Times Beach. They evacuated Times Beach at the 1 part per billion (ppb) level. Some of our homes have 2.8 ppb, 3.7 ppb, 4.6 ppb.

Don't let any of them tell you anything, because it's all b.s. The CDC was supposed to test for 10 chemicals. There were no established background levels for these chemicals, so they compared the levels of these chemicals with DDT, DDE, etc. So that they can show you that you're crazy.

The CDC got up at a press conference with an autopsy report, and they say 508 ppb 3,5 dichlorophenyl, 2,4,5,T. This is the autopsy of a little baby. A baby that's never eaten anything. Been on canned formula. Canned formula. The CDC holds up the autopsy report and a can of moth balls and says, "These children are no more contaminated than if they ate these moth balls." They took the warning labels off the moth balls, and they held them up in front of us hysterical housewives to justify to us idiots that the children are no more contaminated than if they swallowed moth balls.

"They Don't Know How to Handle Us Hysterical Housewives."

They don't know how to handle us emotional people, which is wonderful. I thank God they don't, because otherwise we'd never win. I'm glad I'm hysterical. Now they're putting sociologists and psychologists in the field to come deal with us crazy people, us emotional people.

Health Effects: Obstacles and Solutions

Obstacles

Emotional Responses to Health Effects   Handling a serious illness in the family is difficult. Environmentally caused illnesses are all the more tragic and difficult for families because they are less understood, harder to treat, and caused by corporate carelessness. It is especially stressful for women since we are the primary caretakers of the ill family member. Whether we are dealing with illness or death, in ourselves or in others, we feel many emotions: denial, sadness, fear, and anger.

> **Denial:** You deny the death, hoping to cheer others up. You become a bit hard. You close off your feelings as you see someone dying. We are the strong ones. We have no one to break down with. We cannot show remorse, cry or be sad with our groups, whenever we feel like it. Most times, when it is time to cry,

we are the ones helping others to express their grief, enabling the process, rather than participating in it for ourselves. As organizers we are involved in the recovery, the moving on.

Sadness: Yet it's hard to keep being pumped up. You're losing still another person in your support group. We have delivered eulogies to beloved community leaders and have felt the loss of the entire community and have expressed that with sadness.

Death of children at a site is the most devastating. We have children ourselves and when we counsel others on the loss of a child, we are reminded of our own child's vulnerability. We own the problem twice.

Fear: It's terrifying. You wonder who's next.

Anger: I really had to work off my anger. My daughter was contaminated and had symptoms and I was contaminated and exposed to the chemicals. "I'm going to get these people," I thought, "they just can't do this to me and get away with it." I wanted to get them back.

Solutions

It's o.k. to be emotional. Warm and caring people feel emotions. In our work, we are reclaiming the role of women as healers and nurturers. Acknowledge your emotions and let your sadness, anger, and fear lead you to ACTION.

Obstacles

Physicians' Lack of Knowledge on Illnesses Due to Toxic Exposure   Your local family physician is not likely to know anything about toxic chemicals. Medical students receive only 4 hours of training on this subject in 4 years of medical school.

Solutions

It's our job to educate our doctors, so that they know what questions to ask us and how to treat our families when we become ill. Shortly after this conference CCHW began a newsletter called "Environmental Health Monthly" which is sent to doctors across the country to educate them about environmental health issues. Contact CCHW to get your local doctors on the mailing list.

Obstacles

Too Much Emphasis on Cancer   Scientists and government agencies who study our communities have not validated all the types of health effects that may occur. In their view there's only a problem if a population shows up with cancers and reproductive problems. They are not so quick to acknowledge or accept, for example, neurological damage or immune system dysfunction.

Solutions

Be persistent. Don't give up. Trust your instincts. We are being forced to be living experiments of chemical exposure. If you believe there's a real problem which they're not acknowledging, don't accept what they tell you. Contact CCHW for advice about what to do.

Obstacles

Experts   The environmental science field is not all that big. The same "experts" get called in to evaluate communities all over the country. Some of them do good work, but some of them do not. Many "experts" have bad reputations with environmental groups because they act more like "hired guns" than scientists and professionals.

Solutions

Let CCHW know of your experiences dealing with scientists and other experts. CCHW will keep a "Hit List" of names of people to avoid. If they are brought to your community, just say, "No thanks, we're not cooperating until this person is replaced." Try to check an expert's credentials and find out which other communities they have worked in. Call those communities to find out what kind of job they did. A national network of sympathetic doctors and industrial hygienists has also been created to help exposed workers and their families deal with work-related health problems. These professionals may be helpful to our local groups. Contact CCHW (now Center for Health, Environment, and Justice) for more information.*

---

*P.O. Box 6806, Falls Church, VA 22040 (703) 237-2249. www.chej.org.

Obstacles	Solutions

Intimidation of Scientific Language   Lots of scientific and medical terms are thrown at us by government agencies and scientists who study our communities. Learning the language they use and knowing how they operate can be confusing and difficult.

CCHW has a science department that can help you decipher technical reports and studies. There are books available for community groups that make science accessible to everyone. These books describe how epidemiological surveys are done and how to conduct your own health survey.

SEVENTY-TWO

Principles of Environmental Justice

The First National People of Color Environmental Leadership Summit

October 24–27, 1991
Washington, D.C.

Preamble

We, the people of color, gathered together at this multinational People of Color Environmental Leadership Summit, to begin to build a national and international movement of all peoples of color to fight the destruction and taking of our lands and communities, do hereby re-establish our spiritual interdependence to the sacredness of our Mother Earth; to respect and celebrate each of our cultures, languages and beliefs about the natural world and our roles in healing ourselves; to ensure environmental justice; to promote economic alternatives which would contribute to the development of environmentally safe livelihoods; and, to secure our political, economic and cultural liberation that has been denied for over 500 years of colonization and oppression, resulting in the poisoning of our communities and land and the genocide of our peoples, do affirm and adopt these Principles of Environmental Justice:

1. *Environmental justice* affirms the sacredness of Mother Earth, ecological unity and the interdependence of all species, and the right to be free from ecological destruction.

2. *Environmental justice* demands that public policy be based on mutual respect and justice for all peoples, free from any form of discrimination or bias.

3. *Environmental justice* mandates the right to ethical, balanced and responsible uses of land and renewable resources in the interest of a sustainable planet for humans and other living things.

4. *Environmental justice* calls for universal protection from nuclear testing, extraction, production and disposal of toxic/hazardous wastes and poisons and nuclear testing that threaten the fundamental right to clean air, land, water, and food.

5. *Environmental justice* affirms the fundamental right to political, economic, cultural and environmental self-determination of all peoples.

6. *Environmental justice* demands the cessation of the production of all toxins, hazardous wastes, and radioactive materials, and that all past and current producers be held strictly accountable to the people for detoxification and the containment at the point of production.

7. *Environmental justice* demands the right to participate as equal partners at every level of decision-making including needs assessment, planning, implementation, enforcement and evaluation.

8. *Environmental justice* affirms the right of all workers to a safe and healthy work environment, without being forced to choose between an unsafe livelihood and unemployment. It

also affirms the right of those who work at home to be free from environmental hazards.

9. *Environmental justice* protects the right of victims of environmental injustice to receive full compensation and reparations for damages as well as quality health care.

10. *Environmental justice* considers governmental acts of environmental injustice a violation of international law, the Universal Declaration on Human Rights, and the United Nations Convention on Genocide.

11. *Environmental justice* must recognize a special legal and natural relationship of Native Peoples to the U.S. government through treaties, agreements, compacts, and covenants affirming sovereignty and self-determination.

12. *Environmental justice* affirms the need for urban and rural ecological policies to clean up and rebuild our cities and rural areas in balance with nature, honoring the cultural integrity of all our communities, and providing fair access for all to the full range of resources.

13. *Environmental justice* calls for the strict enforcement of principles of informed consent, and a halt to the testing of experimental reproductive

and medical procedures and vaccinations on people of color.

14. *Environmental justice* opposes the destructive operations of multi-national corporations.

15. *Environmental justice* opposes military occupation, repression and exploitation of lands, peoples and cultures, and other life forms.

16. *Environmental justice* calls for the education of present and future generations which emphasizes social and environmental issues, based on our experience and an appreciation of our diverse cultural perspectives.

17. *Environmental justice* requires that we, as individuals, make personal and consumer choices to consume as little of Mother Earth's resources and to produce as little waste as possible; and make the conscious decision to challenge and reprioritize our lifestyles to ensure the health of the natural world for present and future generations.

Adopted, October 27, 1991
The First National People of Color
    Environmental Leadership Summit
Washington, D.C.

SEVENTY-THREE

◆◆◆

Native Hawaiian Historical and Cultural Perspectives on Environmental Justice

Mililani Trask

When you ask a Hawaiian who they are, their response is "Keiki hanau o ka aina, child that is borne up from the land." I am a Native Hawaiian attorney. I also have the great honor and distinction, and the great burden and responsibility, of being the first elected Kia'Aina of Ka Lahui Hawai'i, the sovereign

nation of the Native Hawaiian people, which we created ourselves in 1987.

It's a great pleasure and honor for me to be here to address a group such as yourselves, such a momentous occasion, the first time that the people of color will gather to consider the impacts on our common land base.

I thought I would begin by giving a little bit of history about Hawaii Nei because many people are not aware of the crisis there and the status of the Native Hawaiian people. As we approach the United Nations' celebration of the discoverers, we

This paper was presented at the First National People of Color Environmental Leadership Summit, October 24–27, 1991, Washington, D.C.

are celebrating not only the arrival of Columbus but also of Cortez and Captain Cook. In Hawaii Nei we are celebrating 500 years of resilient resistance to the coming of the "discoverers."

In 1778 Captain James Cook sailed into the Hawaiian archipelago. He found there a thriving Native community of 800,000 Native people, living in balance on their lands, completely economically self-sufficient, feeding and clothing themselves off of the resources of their own land base. Within one generation, 770,000 of our people were dead—dead from what is called "mai haole, the sickness of the white man," which Cook brought: venereal disease, flu, pox, the same tragic history that occurred on the American continent to Native American Indians and the Native people of Central and South America.

In 1893 the United States Marines dispatched a group of soldiers to the Island of Oahu for the purpose of overthrowing the lawful kingdom of Hawaii Nei. Prior to 1893, Hawaii was welcomed into the world family of nations and maintained over 20 international treaties, including treaties of friendship and peace with the United States. Despite those international laws, revolution was perpetrated against our government, and our lawful government overthrown. In two years we will mark the hundredth anniversary of when we had the right to be self-determining and self-governing.

In 1959, Hawaii was admitted into the Union of the United States of America. There were great debates that occurred in Washington, DC that focused on the fact that people were afraid to incorporate the Territory of Hawaii because it would become the first state in the union in which white people would be a minority of less than 25 percent. That was the reason for the concern when those debates were launched. In 1959, when Hawaii became a state, something happened that did not happen in any other state of the union. In all of the other states, when the U.S. admitted that state into the union, America set aside lands for the Native people of those states, as federal reserves. Today there is a policy that provides that Native Americans should be self-governing, should be allowed to maintain their nations, should be allowed to pass laws, environmental and otherwise, to protect their land base. That did not occur in the State of Hawaii. In the State of Hawaii in 1959, the federal government gave our lands to the state to be held in trust, and gave the Native Hawaiian people,

of which there are 200,000, the status of perpetual wardship. We are not allowed to form governments if we are Native Hawaiian; we are not allowed to control our land base. To this day our lands are controlled by state agencies and utilized extensively by the American military complex as part of a plan designed by Hawaii's Senator Daniel Inouye.

In 1987 we decided to exercise our inherent rights to be self-governing. The Hawaii Visitors Bureau declared 1987 the Year of the Hawaiian for a great tourist and media campaign. We took a look at our statistics: 22,000 families on lists waiting for land entitlements since 1920; 30,000 families dead waiting for their Hawaiian homelands awards; 22,000 currently waiting. We thought to ourselves, how are *we* going to celebrate 1987? And we decided that the time had come to convene a constitutional convention to resurrect our nation and to exert our basic and inherent rights, much to the dismay and consternation of the state and the federal government, and certainly to the shock of Senator Inouye.

We have passed a constitution that recognizes the right and the responsibility of Native people to protect their land base and to ensure water quality, because Western laws have been unable to protect the environment. We decided to lift up and resurrect our nation in 1987, passing our constitution, and we are proceeding now to come out, to announce that we are alive and well, and to network with other people.

I have come to announce that a state of emergency exists with regards to the natural environment of the archipelagic lands and waters of Hawaii, and also a state of emergency exists with regards to the survival of the Native people who live there and throughout the Pacific basin. We have many environmental injustices and issues that need to be addressed; most of them have dire global consequences. The expansion of the United States military complex presents substantial threats to our environment.

Right now on the Island of Hawaii and on the Island of Kauai, Senator Inouye is pressing for what he calls the "space-porting initiative," which we all know to be Star Wars. It will distribute large amounts of toxic gases, it will scorch the earth beyond repair and, most importantly and offensive to us, the lands that have been chosen are lands set aside by the Congress in 1920 for the homesteading of Hawaiian people. These are the lands that are pursued on the Island of Hawaii.

Our response to that is "kapu Ka'u." Ka'u is the district; kapu is the Hawaiian way for saying, "It is taboo." We cannot allow desecration of sacred lands, desecration of historic properties that are the cultural inheritance of our people to be converted for the military complex and for the designs of those who would further the interests of war against others. It is an inappropriate use of Native lands.

Other Threats

The United States Navy continues its relentless bombing of Kahoolawe Island. [This was discontinued in 1990, but the land was not returned to the State of Hawaii until 1994]. Not only have they denuded the upper one-third of that island, but as they have blasted away the lands, trees and shrubs, all that silt has come down to the channels between Kahoolawe and Maui Islands, the channels that are the spawning grounds of the whales that migrate every year to Hawaii Nei.

We now have information coming from Lualualie on the Island of Oahu that there is a very high incidence of leukemia and other cancers among the Hawaiian children who live there. We believe that this is due to electromagnetic contamination. In Lualualie the United States military is taking control of 2,000 acres of Hawaiian homelands, lands set aside by the Congress to homestead our people. These lands were taken over and converted for a nuclear and military storage facility. Ten years ago, in 1981, they issued a report saying that there's electromagnetic radiation there. After the report was issued all the military families were moved out of the base, but nobody told the Hawaiian community that lives in the surrounding area. We have taken it to the Western courts, we have been thrown out, because the court ruled that Native Hawaiians are wards of the state and the federal government. Therefore, Native Hawaiians are not allowed standing to sue in the federal courts to protect our trust land assets. We are the only class of Native Americans, and the only class of American citizens, that are not allowed access to the federal court system to seek redress of grievances relating to breach of trust.

Ka Lahui Hawai'i is pleased and proud to join all of the other Pacific Island nations in opposing the federal policy which is being perpetrated by Mr. Bush and Senator Inouye identifying the Pacific region as a national sacrifice area. What is a national sacrifice area? I did some legal research and I found out that national sacrifice areas usually occur on Indian reservations or in black communities. They are areas that the nation identifies primarily for the dumping of toxic wastes. As the Greens celebrate in Europe what they perceive to be an environmental victory in forcing America to remove its nuclear and military wastes from Europe, we in the Pacific region have been told that Johnston Island and other Pacific nations have been targeted for storage and dumping. We will not allow that and we will continue to speak out against it.

Tourist Evils

Tourism and its attendant evils continue to assault our island land base. Hundreds of thousands of tourists come to Hawaii every year. They are seeking a dream of paradise. They drink our water, they contaminate our environment. They are responsible for millions of tons of sewage every year, which is deposited into the Pacific Ocean. And, in addition, they are taking lands from our rural communities.

Tourism perpetuates certain Western concepts of exclusive rights to land. Tourists don't like to see other people on their beaches. Tourists don't like to allow Native people to go and fish in the traditional ways. And, because of toxification of the ocean due to release of sewage in Hawaii, there are many places where you can no longer find the reef fish. You cannot go there and take the opihi, the squid, or take the turtle, because they're gone now. So in the few remaining areas where there are fish, the state and federal governments have imposed public park restrictions to prevent Native people from going there to lay the net and take the fish. If the fish are taken out, what will the tourists see when they put on their snorkels? Native people are not allowed to fish so that tourists can view through their goggles what remains of the few species we have because their own tourist practices destroyed all the rest of the bounty of our fisheries.

Tourists need golf courses; golf courses need tons of pesticides, herbicides and millions of tons of water. Hawaii is an island ecology, we do not get fresh water from flowing streams. All the water that falls from the rain in Hawaii is percolated through the lava of the islands and comes to rest in a central basal lens underneath our island. As the rains percolate down they bring with them all the herbicides and pesticides that have been used for years by agribusiness: King Cane, Dole Pineapple, United States military. Already on the island of Oahu we have had to permanently close two of our drinking wells because of toxification. Nobody in the State of Hawaii or the Hawaii Visitors Bureau is going to tell you that at the present time there are 30 contaminants in the drinking water in the State of Hawaii.

The specter of geothermal development lays heavily upon our lands. For 25 years the United States and its allies have been developing geothermal energy in Hawaii. It is destroying the last Pacific tropical rain forest on the Island of Hawaii, Wao Kele o Puna Forest, sacred to the lands of Tutu Pele, our Grandmother Pele, who erupts and gives birth to the earth. This is her home, yet this is the place where they are developing geothermal. And as it proceeds, Native people are denied their basic right to worship there. We have taken this case to the United States Supreme Court. It was struck down along with the Native American freedom of religion cases because the court ruled that religious worship in America must be "site-specific." If you take the Akua, if you put God in the building, American courts will understand. But if you take God and say, "The earth is the Lord's and the fullness of it, the Black Hills of South Dakota, the lands and forests of Tutu Pele," American courts do not understand. . . .

International fishing practices, gill netting and drift netting, are genocide in the sea. As a result of these practices, the Native fisheries are diminished and depleted. In some areas our marine fisheries are depleted to the point that we can no longer harvest that resource.

What is the appropriate response to this environmental and human outrage? In Hawaii Nei we have undertaken to address these things through sovereignty and the basic exertion of the rights of Native people to govern and control their own land base. These are political issues, certainly. But they spring from a very ancient source, a source within our heart, a source that all Natives and people of color understand: our relationship in the global context. As Hawaiians say, "Keiki hanau o ka aina, child that is borne up from the land," understanding that there is an innate connection to the earth as

the Mother. We are called upon now as the guardians of our sacred lands to rise up in the defense of our Mother. You don't subdivide your Mother, you don't chop her body up, you don't drill, penetrate and pull out her lifeblood. You protect and nurture your Mother. And the Hawaiian value for that is aloha ai'na, love for the land, malama ai'na, care and nurturing for the land. It is reciprocal. It gives back to the Native people. Our people know that the Akua put us here on this earth to be guardians of these sacred lands. It is a God-given responsibility and trust that a sovereign nation must assume if it is to have any integrity. And so we in Ka Lahui have undertaken this struggle. Environmental racism is the enemy. The question is, What is our response? What really is environmental justice? I'll tell you one thing I learned in law school at Santa Clara. Do you know how they perceive and teach justice, the white schools of this country? A blind white woman with her eyes covered up by cloth, holding the scales of justice. And if you look at it, they're not balanced. The Native scale and the environmental scale are outweighed by other priorities.

Well, environmental justice is not a blindfolded white woman. When I saw the woman with the scales of justice in law school, I thought to myself, "You know, if you blindfold yourself the only thing you're going to do is walk into walls." You are not going to resolve anything. And that's where we are with Western law. I know that there are many attorneys here and others who are working on environmental cases. I support them. We have received a great deal of support from attorneys working in environmental law. But do not put your eggs in the basket of the blind white lady. We must try other approaches.

In closing, I would like to say in behalf of myself and the Hawaii delegation that we are very renewed in coming here, and that when we return to Hawaii in two or three days we will have good news to share with our people, that we have come ourselves these many thousands of miles, that we have looked in the faces of people of color, that we have seen there, in their hearts and in their eyes, a light shining, a light of commitment, a light that is filled with capacity and a light that is filled with love for the Mother Earth, a light that is the same that we have in our hearts.

I try to do one thing whenever I finish speaking. I try to leave the podium by telling people what the motto of Ka Lahui Hawaii is, the motto of our nation that we're forming now. I find it to be very applicable to the situations that we are in. We are facing a difficult struggle. Every bit of commitment and energy is needed to save our Mother Earth and to ensure the survival of our people and all of the species of the earth. It is a difficult row to hoe. There is going to be a great deal of strife and a great deal of pain. But we must proceed; we have no alternative. This is the same position that the native people of Hawaii Nei found themselves in 1987 when we committed to resurrecting our national government. And at the time that we passed that constitution we also adopted a motto. It is a motto that I think you might want to live by as we proceed in this environmental war that we are waging. That motto is: "A difficult birth does not make the baby any less beautiful."

SEVENTY-FOUR

◆◆◆

My Mom's Garden

Cindy Chan Saelee

My mom loves it when it rains—she always says that it's "a little help."

She says that her crops can't grow in our yard because there's not enough water to water the whole garden. The dirt is kind of like sand and it dries up quickly.

My mom had good experiences from the old days in Laos, working on the farm, growing rice, corn, cucumbers, long fat beans. . . . She never had to water the garden there, because the ground was rich, and it was always very moist in the mornings. Back in Thailand and Laos, mothers had to grow their own crops to feed the family. If they didn't, they'd all starve to death!

Now even though they can afford more things, and food, most Iu Mien mothers still like to have their own crops and gardens in their spare time. They love it when their gardens look nice, neat and healthy.

All they need to do is find a place they like, cut down the grass and trees, burn the area and let it dry for a few days before they plant the seeds. It's easy to plant fruits and vegetables—you have to put the seeds in soft dirt and then water it. It saves them a few bucks from having to buy the food.

My mom's garden is behind the garage. There's a small place for parsley, a big place for cucumbers, three different trees—peach and apples trees. It's all planted in a wooden box.

She gets all the seeds from my grandma or she goes and buys it at the store. Peppers, pumpkins, peaches, zucchini, tomatoes, mustard, etc. Some trees are short and some plants are tall.

My mom really likes her garden, especially her apple tree, because she doesn't have to water it as many times as the others. In her free time, she likes to just hang in her garden and water all the plants and vegetables. Every night, before bedtime, she goes back and checks her garden to water it and to make sure that no bugs are trying to eat her plants. If there are, she kills them all with salt.

For me, fun is going out and kicking it, but my mom likes her garden. She puts a lot of effort into making it look neat and good. It's not really easy at first, but you just pick it up and plant your crops. Corn, strawberries, apples, plums, peaches, green vegetables, cucumbers, etc. Imagine all those in a neat garden!

S E V E N T Y - F I V E

Consumption

North American Perspectives

H. Patricia Hynes

. . . The consumption of resources by individuals, by governments and ruling elites, by semi-autonomous and secretive institutions such as the military, and by macroeconomic systems is embedded within the matrix of political economy and cultural values [see Figure 1]. Yet consumption . . . has been reduced to a mere empirical, per capita phenomenon, as if it were detached from those structural and ideological forces that result in wealth-building for some and impoverishment and poor health for others. . . .

What, then, is the content of recent North American critiques of consumption and consumerism? What are their strengths and weaknesses? What core elements of a woman-centered analysis can we bring to them?

. . . A handful of analyses and practice-based responses have emerged to characterize, critique, and provide alternatives to consumption patterns and consumerist ideology in industrialized countries. Among the chief prototypes are three approaches: the "demographics of consumption," movements to simplify life and make consumer choices that are less environmentally damaging, and the computation of the ecological footprint.

Demographics of Consumption

Asking the question "How much is enough?" Worldwatch Institute researcher Alan Durning has amassed quite a stunning picture of the explosion in the consumption of consumer goods and services in the United States and worldwide.[1] He traces the origins of "consumer society" in the United States to the 1920s, with the emergence of name brands, the entrée of packaged and processed foods, the rise of the car as the popular symbol of American upward mobility, and the birth of mass marketing through advertising. Consumerism was stymied by the Depression and World War II, but it picked up enormous momentum in the United States after the war

and was rapidly disseminated worldwide, under the gospel of development and the democratization of consumerism, to gain markets for expanding U.S. industries. To cite a few supporting statistics on the radical change in post–World War II consumption: People in the United States own, on the average, "twice as many automobiles, drive two and a half times as far, use 21 times as much plastic, and cover 25 times as much distance by air as their parents did in 1950."[2]

Durning's data on the growth in household appliance ownership over time embody the triumph of the central message of mass marketing: Greater purchasing power and growing choice in the marketplace guarantee a better (and happier) life. Popular culture advertising underpins the macroeconomic maxim: An expanding economy—with rising per capita income and consumer spending—is a healthy economy.

Comparing global patterns of consumption leads Durning to a deeper inquiry into the qualitative differences in consumption among peoples in the world. He asks what kinds of resources people consume on a day-to-day basis and structures his answer around a comparison of consumption by diet, transport, and principal type of materials used. The result is three classes of consumption, the latter two being of much sounder environmental quality than the first, which has no sustainable characteristics.

The primary focus of this tripartite view of consumption in the world—emerging from Worldwatch Institute and a number of liberal environmental, economic, and alternative-lifestyle circles in the United States—is the plight of the consumer class in the United States. Economist Juliet Schor points out that people in the United States work more hours today in their jobs than they did two decades ago, even though we are twice as productive in goods and services as we were in 1948. Why, instead of working more and having less leisure, do we not work less and enjoy more leisure, she queries. Describing

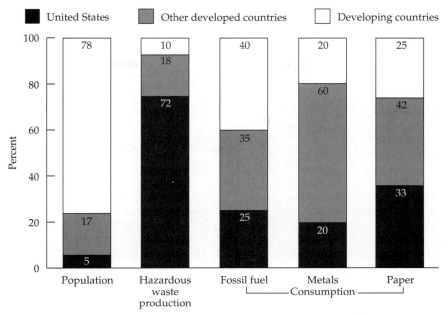

Figure 1 Share of Population, Hazardous Waste Production, and Natural Resource Consumption in the United States, Developing, and Developed Regions, 1990s. (*Source:* Natural Resources Defense Council, in Lori S. Ashford, *New Perspectives on Population: Lessons from Cairo. Population Bulletin* [Washington, D.C.: Population Reference Bureau, Inc.], Vol. 50, No. 1 [March 1995], 30.)

the pitfalls of consumerism and the manufacture of discontent that keep middle-class people locked into a work-and-spend cycle, she calls for overcoming consumerism, revaluing leisure, and rethinking the necessity of full-time jobs.[3]

Both Schor and Durning hinge a key part of their prescription—that people rethink and modify their consumerist work- and lifestyles—on the question of happiness. National polls conducted since the 1950s show no increase in the percentage of people who report being "very happy," despite the fact that people now purchase almost twice the number of consumer goods and services they did in the 1950s. Time spent enjoying two of the classic sources of happiness—social relations and leisure—has diminished as people work more to purchase more nondurable, packaged, rapidly obsolete, nonvital goods and services.

Durning advocates that the consumer class be wary of the estimated 3,000 advertising messages that bombard us per day cultivating consumer taste and

needs, and that we climb a few rungs down the consumption ladder by choosing durable goods, public transportation, and low-energy devices. In other words, he points to the consumption patterns of the 3.3 billion "middle consumer class" people in Table 1 as more sound and sustainable for the environment.

Voluntary Simplicity Movement

Arising from these same cultural observations, the voluntary simplicity, or new frugality, movement offers a new road map for those of the consumer class who wish to live better with less. Begun in Seattle and strong in the Northwest, this movement was given a high profile by the best-selling book *Your Money or Your Life,* a pragmatic self-help approach to living securely on less money in order to spend one's time in more meaningful social, personal, spiritual, and environmentally sustaining ways.[4]

Table 1. World Consumption Classes, 1992

CATEGORY OF CONSUMPTION	CONSUMERS (1.1 BILLION)	MIDDLE (3.3 BILLION)	POOR (1.1 BILLION)
Diet	meat, packaged food, soft drinks	grain, clean water	insufficient grain, unsafe water
Transport	private cars	bicycles, buses	walking
Materials	throwaways	durables	local biomass

Source: Alan Durning, *How Much Is Enough?* (New York: W. W. Norton, 1992), 27.

In this movement, people learn to assess their real financial needs (with generous distinctions made between "needs" and "wants"), how to budget and invest to achieve financial independence on a substantially reduced income, and how to calculate the impacts of their lifestyle on the environment through household audits of energy, products, and waste. More than 300,000 people have developed "new road maps" for their future lives, based on core values they have identified in the process of rethinking what ultimately matters to them. Most reduce their cost of living by 20 percent immediately and, eventually, by even more; many "retire" from careers and full-time jobs to pursue personal and social interests.

If It's Good for the Environment and Good for the Person, What's the Problem?

How can we fault the appeal to happiness and to core values that these critiques of the consumerist culture make? They result in people living "more softly" on the Earth. They reach deeper into a person's self than the green consumer movement, which redirects, but does not necessarily reduce or challenge, consumerism. How many green products are designed for durability and marketed as such? The majority of green product manufacturers employ mass marketing techniques, including the cultivation of "need," and use shallow appeals to feel-good environmentalism to sell their products. Green consumers get locked into seesaw debates over plastic versus paper, for example, never learning that the debate is a foil that deters deeper questions of product durability and necessity. At its best, says Durn-

ing, green consumerism outpaces legislation and uses market tactics to reform the market; at its worst, it is "a palliative for the conscience of the consumer class, allowing us to continue business as usual while feeling like we are doing our part."[5]

The primary shortcoming of the "consumer treadmill" critique is that it is socially and politically underdeveloped. Focusing on average per capita consumption, Durning and others make little distinction among the highly disparate economic classes of people within the United States. While our society as a whole is locked into meat, packaged food, soft drinks, and throwaways—with a McDonald's on every corner—the gap between the poorest fifth and richest fifth of the United States begs for an environmental policy that is based on "a hunger and thirst for justice" as well as national concern about global climate change and the decline of personal happiness. The prescriptions to live on less, to get out of the rat race and enjoy more leisure, to examine one's personal values and organize one's life by those values, may not necessarily result in a more equitable or humanistic society. Those who choose voluntary simplicity, durables, and bicycles may live happily and stress-free across town from the angry (or depressed) involuntary poor, with no more empathy, solidarity, or insight into undoing social injustice. (Alternatively, of course, by choosing to live on less, people may end up in less expensive mixed-income neighborhoods, join their neighborhood associations, and, in so doing, meet and collaborate with the involuntary poor on neighborhood betterment.)

The focus on the cultivation of need by mass marketing and the lack of personal fulfillment, when divorced from an inquiry into the patterns and structures that reward the well-off and punish the poor, creates islands of better-living and more personally

Table 2. The Ecological Footprint of the Average Canadian, in Hectares per Capita

	ENERGY	BUILT ENVIRONMENT	AGRICULTURAL LAND	FOREST	TOTAL
Food	0.4		0.9		**1.3**
Housing	0.5	0.1		0.4	**1.0**
Transport	1.0	0.1			**1.1**
Consumer Goods	0.6		0.2	0.2	**1.0**
Resources in Services	0.4				**0.4**
TOTAL	**2.9**	**0.2**	**1.1**	**0.6**	**4.8**

Source: Mathis Wackernagel, *How Big Is Our Ecological Footprint?* (Vancouver: University of British Columbia, 1993), 3.

satisfied people without necessarily generating a sense of a new social movement or new society. "Twelve-step" programs to break the consumer habit offer good techniques borrowed from self-fulfillment and self-control support-group settings, but they are no substitute for social responses to persistent poverty, to misogyny that sells women as sex to be consumed, to child labor and sweatshops, to the consumption engine of militarism and military spending that siphons the life force out of societies, and to all oppressions of "the other."

Social consciousness within the environmental movement on the other hand, speaks to people's civic and humanistic being, to their quest for a connectedness with others and the earth, to their desire to make the world more just and humane, as well as to the stressed, overworked, and seemingly optionless plight of individuals caught on the work-and-spend treadmill of late-twentieth-century industrial life. Taming consumption through a personal, spiritual quest is part of the answer, but not the whole one.

The Ecological Footprint

The intriguing epithet "ecological footprint" is shorthand for an analysis that more successfully integrates the calculation of consumer impact on the earth with the responsibilities of government, the right of every human to a fair and healthful share of the Earth's resources, and a deep concern for not overloading or degrading global ecosystems.[6] Here, too, the focus is primarily the North American consumer lifestyle

and an accounting of its impacts on the environment. However, the goal is to calculate the size of the Canadian and U.S. ecological footprint compared with that of others in lesser-industrialized and nonindustrialized countries and to determine how the oversized North American footprint can be reduced through better regional planning, more ecologically conscious consumption, and the restructuring of industrial technology and economics.

This ecological accounting tool, as geographer Ben Wisner points out so well, inverts "carrying capacity" to ask: Given nearly six billion people in the world, how should we live so as to enable all to live within the limits of the biosphere?[7] The premise of the ecological footprint is that although half the world lives in cities (and by 2020 an estimated two-thirds of people will), we live in a biosphere much larger than the physical boundaries of our cities and towns when we buy goods that are grown or made from resources outside our municipality or region and when we dispose of our wastes in the global atmosphere and marine environments. The ecological footprint is calculated by translating key categories of human consumption—food, housing, transport, consumer goods and services—into the amount of *productive land* needed to provide these goods and services and to assimilate their resultant waste.

Using assumptions about biomass substitutes for fossil fuels and so on, the authors of this method, Mathis Wackernagel and William Rees, calculate that the amount of land needed to support the average Canadian's present consumption, or ecological footprint, is 4.8 hectares [Table 2].

In their calculations of ecologically productive land, Wackernagel and Rees estimate that an average of 1.6 hectares of land per capita is available worldwide for goods and services. In other words, the average Canadian uses three times as much of the earth's capacity as is available to every person; in other words, the average Canadian's ecological footprint is three times the size it ought to be, since everyone deserves a fair share of the global commons. Correspondingly, the average Indian ecological footprint is 0.4 hectare per person.

The average per capita consumption in Canada, as in every country, is a composite of the consumption of the rich, poor, and middle consumption classes. Thus, Figure 2 compares the ecological footprints of various Canadian households in order to show where the extremes of consumption lie and whose consumer lifestyle inordinately appropriates the carrying capacity of the Earth.

Three aspects of this analysis are particularly laudable. First, its starting point is the assumption that every human being has the same claim on nature's productivity and utility. Thus, it is inequitable and undesirable for North Americans to appropriate others' share of the global commons. Second, it promotes an urban and regional planning strategy that would reduce North Americans' footprint on the global environment by reversing sprawl through integrating living, working, and shopping; promoting bike paths and public transportation; and favoring the local economy. Third, it calls for a massive reform of industrial society to free up the ecological space needed by the poor to raise their standard of living, while enabling the well-off to maintain their high material standards.[8] Wackernagel and Rees's recommendations for restructuring industrialism to achieve a smaller ecological footprint on the world include reforms that are simultaneously being advocated by radical environmental economists:

- Shift taxes from income to consumption and include the full costs of resources and pollution in consumer products through environmental taxes and fees. Including true environmental costs in the full cost of products will motivate industry to make cleaner products and consumers to buy them; it will favor reuse, repair, and reconditioning of products.

- Invest in research into energy- and material-efficient technologies to achieve the "four- to ten-fold reduction in material and energy intensity per unit of economic output" needed in industrial countries to reduce the ecological footprint to a sustainable size.

- Invest the anticipated economic gains from the enhanced efficiency in remediating and restoring critical ecosystems.[9]

Even with a more structural approach to macroeconomic systems and the socially conscious goal of commonweal, certain footprints, in this analysis, remain invisible. Women have much less stake in the global economy than men—by virtue of having little political and economic power, as well as by holding different economic priorities, in many instances, from men. Thus, women have a smaller individual and structural footprint than men and male institutions. The economic and political institution of the military, for example ([which has an] extreme impact on economies, cultures, and ecosystems), arises from patriarchal concepts of power and methods of conflict resolution.

What insights and efforts can a woman-centered analysis bring to the issue of consumption in order to further the goals of redistributing and humanizing our use of natural resources, consumer goods, and services, and of mitigating and reversing our pollution impacts on ecosystems?

Conclusion

. . . Why are more than a billion women and girls consigned to spending hours daily collecting wood and biomass and ingesting smoke when the dissemination of technologies such as more efficient cook stoves and solar cookers would ease their lives; save their health; and conserve woodlands, soil, water, and biomass in critical ecosystems? Authors Kammen and Dove have identified a bias in science against "research on mundane topics" in energy, agriculture, public health, and resource economics. . . .[10] Their analysis of the fallacies that underlie the inattention to labor-, time-, health- and environment-saving technologies is consonant with feminist critiques of science culture and science values.[11] According to the canon of science, the premier scientific work is basic research, uncontaminated by the needs of real people and characterized by objective and detached thought. The potential of "breakthrough discoveries" charges the rarefied atmosphere of science research and rele-

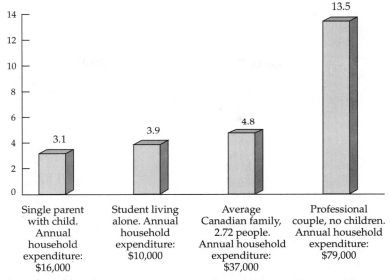

Figure 2 Examples of Ecological Footprints of Various Canadian Households, in Hectares per Capita. (*Source:* Mathis Wackernagel, *How Big Is Our Ecological Footprint?* (Vancouver: University of British Columbia, 1993), 3.)

gates revisiting old, unsolved, human-centered problems to second-tier science. In this first-order science, abstract theory, mathematical modeling, speed, distance, and scale are privileged over social benefits, qualitative methods, and the local and small-scale applications of "mundane" science. In other words, what might be seen as the subjectivizing, sociologizing, and feminizing of science popularizes and banalizes it. . . .

Social goodness and community health, as the "ecological footprint" analysis affirms, are requisites and indices of a sustainable community. In our effort to reduce overconsumption through distinguishing genuine needs and consumerist wants, we must confront the consumption of so-called goods and services that are based on the sexual exploitation of women and girls and are often a consequence of war and environmental degradation, such as prostitution, pornography, and mail-order brides. The impeccable logic of environmental justice—that poor communities of color have been systematically exploited by polluters and industry by reason of race, and suffer disproportionately from poor health— holds for women as well. Like racial justice, a sexual justice that seeks to eliminate the sexual exploitation of women is fundamental to environmental justice, to community health, and to social goodness.

NOTES

1. Alan Durning, *How Much Is Enough?* (New York: W. W. Norton, 1992).

2. Ibid., 30.

3. Juliet Schor, *The Overworked American: The Unexpected Decline of Leisure* (New York: Basic Books, 1991).

4. Joe Dominguez and Vicki Robin, *Your Money or Your Life* (New York: Viking, 1992).

5. Durning, *How Much Is Enough?* op. cit., 125.

6. Mathis Wackernagel and William Rees, *Our Ecological Footprint: Reducing Human Impact on the Earth* (Gabriola Island, British Columbia, and Philadelphia: New Society Publishers, 1996).

7. Ben Wisner, "The Limitations of 'Carrying Capacity,'" *Political Environments* (Winter–Spring 1996), 1, 3–4.

8. Wackernagel and Rees, *Our Ecological Footprint,* op. cit., 144.

9. Ibid., 144–45.

10. Daniel M. Kammen and Michael R. Dove, "The Virtues of Mundane Science," in *Environment,* Vol. 39, No. 6 (July/August 1997), 10–15, 38–41.

11. See Sue V. Rosser, *Female-Friendly Science* (New York: Teacher's College Press, 1990).

13

◆◆◆

Creating Change
Theory, Vision, and Action

In the last one hundred years, women in the United States have won the right to speak out on public issues, to vote, to own property in their own names, the right to divorce, and increased access to higher education and the professions. Developments in birth control have allowed women to have fewer babies, and family size is much smaller than it was in the early years of the twentieth century. Improved health care and better working conditions mean that women now live longer than ever before. Women's wage rates are inching closer to men's. Issues like domestic violence, rape, sexual harassment, and women's sexual freedom are public matters. As a group, women in the United States are more independent—economically and socially—than ever before.

Although women have broken free from many earlier limitations, this book also shows how much still needs to be done. As we argue in previous chapters, many aspects of women's lives are subject to debate and controversy as **contested terrains.** These controversial issues include women's sexuality, reproductive freedom, the nature of marriage and family relationships, the right to livelihood independent of men, and the right to affordable health care. Gains have been made and also eroded, as conservative pol-

iticians aided by conservative religious leaders and media personalities have attempted to turn the clock back.

It is easy to review the details of U.S. women's experiences of discrimination and to come away feeling angry, depressed, hopeless, and disempowered. The interlocking systems that keep women oppressed can seem monolithic and unchangeable. Major U.S. social movements of the past one hundred years—for the rights of working people; the civil rights of peoples of color; women's liberation; disability rights; gay, lesbian, bisexual, and transgender rights—have made significant gains and also seen those gains challenged and attacked.

In this final chapter we consider what is needed to tackle the problems for women that we have identified throughout the book. How can this be done in ways that address underlying causes as well as visible manifestations? More fundamentally, how can we—women and men—build relationships, systems of work, local communities, and a wider world based on sustainability and real security?

Each person needs to find meaning in his or her life. Knowing a lot of facts may be an effective way of doing well on tests and getting good grades, but this kind of knowledge does not necessarily provide meaning. Knowing what matters to you means that you can begin to take charge of your own life and begin to direct change. This process involves examining your own life, as suggested through the questions included in each chapter. Unless you do this, you will be absent from your own system of knowledge.

How Does Change Happen?

The process of creating change requires a combination of theoretical insights and understandings, visions of alternatives, and action. This involves using your head, heart, and hands in ways that reinforce one another. The readings in this chapter include a blend of these three aspects. This may involve a spiritual perspective (as in Reading 76 by Christina Leaño) or a conviction that women's lives can and should be changed for the better.

Using the Head: Theories for Social Change

As we pointed out in Chapter 1, doing something about an issue or a problem requires us to have a theory, an explanation, of what it is. The theory we create directly shapes what we think ought to be done. Thus *how* we theorize is a key first step in creating change. When people face difficult problems alone, they can draw only on their own insights. Although these are valuable, they are likely to be limited. In talking things over with others, we may discover that they can shed light on things we may have missed, or that they provide a completely different way to think about what we are dealing with. Similarly, if we examine only certain specifics of an issue, examine each issue separately, or use a limited analytical framework, we will end up with limited understandings of women's lives. For a fuller picture we need to analyze issues individually and together, looking for commonalities, recognizing differences, and using frameworks that illuminate as many parts as possible.

This principle has guided our choices in making the selections for this book. Our theoretical ideas, which run through the previous chapters—sometimes explicit, sometimes implicit—are summarized here:

- A social-constructionist perspective allows us to see how social and political forces shape our lives and our sense of ourselves. It encourages us to focus on the specificity of experience and also the diversity of experiences among people. It allows us to see that situations and structures are not fixed for all time but are changeable under the right circumstances.

- How an issue is defined and framed will affect how we think about the problem, where we look for probable causes, our ideas about what ought to be done about it, and who is likely to become involved.

- In analyzing social situations, it is necessary to look at them in terms of micro, meso, macro, and global levels and to understand how these levels affect one another. Strategies for change need to address all of these levels.

- Many women's activist organizations and projects are working on the issues discussed in this book.

- Efforts to create equal opportunities for women and equal access to current institutions have made a difference for many women, but by themselves they cannot achieve a genuinely secure and sustainable world because these are not the goals of most institutions.

Using the Heart: Visions for Social Change

Vision is the second necessary ingredient in creating social change—some idea of a different way of doing things, a different future for humankind, framed by explicit principles around which human relations ought to be organized. Otherwise, as the saying goes, "If you don't know where you're going, any road will get you there."

Visions are about values, drawing from inside ourselves everything we value and daring to think big. The many demands of our busy lives leave most people with little time or opportunity to envision alternatives. In school and college, for example, students are rarely asked to think seriously about their hopes and dreams for a more truly human world in which to live. Much of what we do is guided not by our own visions but in reaction to the expectations of others and outside pressures. Social issues, too, are framed in reactive and negative terms. People talk about "antiracism," for instance, not about what a truly multicultural society would be like.

Some people scorn this step as time-wasting and unrealistic. What matters, they say, is to come up with ideas that people feel comfortable with, that businesses will want to invest in, or that fit government programs and guidelines. Tackle something small and specific, something winnable. Don't waste time on grandiose ideas.

Because most of us are not encouraged to envision change, it may take a while to free ourselves from seemingly practical ideas. Our imaginations are often limited to what we know, and that makes it difficult to break out of our cramped daily routines and habits of thought. Envisioning something different also means putting on hold the voice inside your head that says: Are you *crazy?* This will never work! Who do you think you are? Where will you *ever* get the money? Better keep quiet on this one, people will think you're nuts. . . .

Go ahead. Envision the multicultural society, the women's health project, the community play/read/ care program for elders and children, the Internet information business run by inner-city teenagers, the women's taxi service, the intimate relationship of your dreams, your blossoming sexuality. Envision it in as much detail as you can. Think it, see it, taste it, smell it, sing it, draw it, and write it down. Share it with others who you think will be sympathetic to it and will engage with you. This is where you're headed. Now all you need is to create the road. The projects we mention throughout this book, like this book itself, all started this way, as somebody's dream.

Using the Hands: Action for Social Change

The third essential ingredient for change is action. Through action, theories and visions are tested, sharpened, and refined to create even more useful theories and more creative visions. In Chapter 1 we referred to philosopher Alan Rosenberg's (1988) distinction between *knowing* and *understanding*. Rosenberg further argues that understanding compels us to action, even though we may not initially want to change our habitual ways of thinking and being. When you understand something, you

> find that [your] world becomes a different world and that [you] must generate a new way to be in the new world. Since each person's way of being in the world is relatively fixed— and serves as protection against the anxieties of the unknown—integration is extremely hard. To give up a world in which one's life

makes sense means undergoing great loss. Yet without the readiness to risk that loss we cannot hope to pursue understanding.   *(p. 382)*

In previous chapters we mentioned many activist projects, which are all relevant to this discussion. In this chapter, readings by professor of education Cynthia Cohen (Reading 79) and Suzanne Pharr (Reading 81), address specific projects. Here we suggest a range of avenues for trying to implement your visions. Some will be more appropriate than others, depending on your goals and theoretical perspectives. Some of the activities we list below may be impossible for students, who need to concentrate on getting degrees, to participate in. Progressive social change is a long-term project; there will be plenty to do after you graduate (also see Naples and Bojar 2002).

- Think of yourself as someone with something valuable to say, who can take the initiative and start something you think is important. Think about what you want to do after college, how to live your values and ideals.

- Express your ideas: talk to others; write 'zines, poems, leaflets, speeches, letters to newspaper editors and politicians; put up flyers or posters; organize a film series; paint murals, dance, sing, or perform your ideas.

- Be a conscious shopper. Support fair-trade products; boycott products made in sweatshops, for example. Buy directly from farmers' markets or craft producers. Spend your money where it will support your values.

- Support women's organizations, environmental groups, antiracist organizations, or gay/ lesbian/bisexual/transgender groups by letting them know you appreciate their work, letting others know these groups exist, attending events, donating money or something the group needs, volunteering your time, proposing ideas for projects, working as an intern for college credit.

- Work for institutional change. Within your family you may want to stop others from telling sexist or racist jokes, create greater understanding between family members, or develop more egalitarian relationships. At school you may want to set up study groups to work

together, support teachers who help you, point out glaring gaps in the curriculum or college services to teachers and administrators, challenge racism or sexual harassment.

- Participate in direct action. This includes interrupting, keeping silent, organizing groups of women to walk together at night, defending clinics where abortions are performed, participating in demonstrations and rallies, boycotts, picketing, rent strikes, tax resistance. Whatever the setting, take back the Nike slogan. Just Do It!

- Get involved in grassroots organizing. Meet with others and decide what you can do together to tackle some issue of shared concern.

- Participate in coalitions. Consider joining with other groups on an issue of shared concern so as to be more visible and effective.

- Learn about local and national issues, and let your representatives at city, state, and national levels know your opinions. Urge them to pass appropriate laws and to speak out in public situations and to the media. Use your vote. Help to elect progressive candidates. Support them if they get into office, and hold them accountable to their election promises.

- Learn more about international networks and organizations working on issues that concern you. Consider participating in international meetings and bringing the knowledge you gain there to your organizing work back home.

A range of supports help us in taking action: a sense of hope and conviction that women's lives can be improved, anger at current inequalities and injustices, reliable allies, well-thought-out strategies, and help from parents, partners, neighbors, friends, children, or total strangers who make a crucial contribution by freeing us so that we can take action.

Overcoming Blocks to Effective Action

Political action does not always work; that is, a chosen course of action may not achieve our original goals. There are many possible reasons for this: inadequate theoretical understandings and analysis of the issues; choosing inappropriate or ineffective strategies; not following through on the course of action; not being able to get enough people involved for this particular strategy to be effective; wrong timing; the failure of the group to work together well enough; the failure of people whom you thought were allies to come through when needed; and so on. The other major reason, of course, is that the opposition—whether this is your sexist uncle, your boss, the university administration, the city school board, the opposing political party, or the U.S. Congress—was simply more powerful.

Feeling that an action has failed is disheartening and may lead people to give up, assuming that creating change is hopeless. But action *always* accomplishes something, and in this sense it always works. At the very least, activism that does not meet your goals teaches you something important. In hindsight, what may seem like mistakes are actually valuable ways to learn how to be more effective in the future. This is what we called "socially lived" theory in Chapter 1. Always evaluate what you did after some activity or event, personally and with the group. If it worked as you hoped, why did it work? What have you learned as a result? If it did not work, why? What will you do differently next time?

Personal blocks to activism may include practical factors like not having enough time or energy, or needing to focus on some other aspect of life. Emotional blocks include guilt—a paralyzing emotion that keeps us stuck—and cynicism—a frustrated idealism that has turned hopeless and bitter. Anger can be a very useful, high-octane fuel if you can channel it in a constructive direction. Overextending yourself is not a sign of your commitment to your ideals, and trying to do more than you can, under pressure, is one sure way to burn out quickly. Activism for progressive social change needs patience, humor, creativity, a wide range of skills and resources, an ability to talk to other people, a willingness to listen and to change, a willingness to be reflective, refining your ideas, holding onto your visions.

Theorists of social change usually see it as an interplay between actors or agents—individuals and groups—and the social and political structures that form the larger context of our lives and often restrict us. Some emphasize what English professor Ellen Messer-Davidow (1991) calls "agent-centered models of change" that represent powerful people and a passive system (p. 293). This is the view of much political opinion and rhetoric that characterize the U.S. political system as open and responsive to pressure from organized groups. "Social-system models of change represent powerful systems and passive people" (Messer-Davidow 1991, p. 294). This is the view of those who point to the central role money plays in determining who can run for office and, in many cases, who has access to them once they are in power. A third of all eligible voters appear to hold this view, as they are not registered to vote, even though many of these same people may be very active in community organizations, for example.

We see a key role for individuals, as change agents, working with others to envision alternatives and bring them into being through collective action: through identity-based politics, feminist movements, electoral politics, and broad-based coalitions and alliances.

Women and Political Activism

Politics involves the use of power. What is it? Who has it? How is it used? Who does it benefit and who is disadvantaged? Sociologists and political scientists define **power** as the ability to influence others. This may be by persuasion, charisma, law, political activism, or coercion (Andersen 2000). As we argue throughout this book, individuals and groups have power and influence based on a range of attributes (race, class, gender, age, education, etc.) that are valued in this society. Many people focus on the ways in which others exert power over us or on the fact that they have more power than we have. We generally pay less attention to the ways in which we have more power than others. This is true especially for members of oppressed groups, such as women and men of color in the United States, where some fundamental aspect of our existence, if not our identity, is predicated on being "the powerless" in many settings.

Poet and essayist Audre Lorde writes of women's personal power (Reading 28, Chapter 4), and several writers in this book refer to the importance of personal empowerment. People exercise power through institutions such as education, religion, corporations, the media, the law, the military, and all aspects of government. Sometimes this happens regardless of individual intent or knowledge of its existence (Baron 1970; Bulhan 1985). Power is also expressed in the values and practices of institutions that compel people to think and behave in specific ways. For example, the heterosexist values embedded in our culture and its institutions define the family as a heterosexual couple, legally bound by marriage, and their children. The value and legitimacy attached to this institution is a powerful influence on everyone and is in itself a pressure to marry. Higher education operates out of values that are overwhelmingly Eurocentric, middle class, and masculinist. These values uphold particular ways of learning, certain kinds of discourse, and the use of a specific language. To succeed in college, a student must subscribe to these values, at least in a minimal way.

Power operates at the community, macro, and global levels. Political scientists have focused on formal political organizations, especially the U.S. Congress, where there are relatively few women. As a result, past studies of women's political power have seriously underestimated it. Feminist researchers have pointed out that women's political participation includes active membership in a wide range of local, state, and national organizations including women's clubs and labor unions, working in support of candidates for political office, organizing fund-raising events, circulating petitions, participating in letter-writing and call-in campaigns, as well as voting (see West and Blumberg 1990; Naples 1997, 1998). Several articles in this collection give details of women's organizing: how they draw in participants; strategize about goals, priorities, and activities; and use their knowledge, personal connections, and links to institutions (e.g., Readings 30, 36, 37, 52, 54, 71, 79, 81).

Identity-Based Politics

Throughout this book many writers talk about identity and note significant changes in the way they think about themselves over time. Some mention the difficulties of coming to terms with who they are, the complexities of their contradictory positions, or breaking the silence surrounding taboo subjects, thoughts, and feelings. They also comment that coming to new understandings about themselves and being able to speak from a place of personal identity and self-knowledge is profoundly empowering.

Identity politics is a politics that puts identity at the center, based on, for example, age, race, ethnicity, or sexual orientation. It usually involves the assumption that this particular characteristic is the most important in the lives of group members and that the group is not differentiated according to other characteristics in any significant way. Identity politics is concerned with wider opportunities—maybe greater visibility and recognition in society, equality, justice, even liberation for ourselves and our group. Our authoritativeness comes from our experience of a shared identity, some common ground of experience that allows a group to say "we." This is the foundation for many student organizations, community groups, religious groups, national networks, and major social movements.

At the same time, identity politics has serious limitations, as mentioned by Suzanne Pharr, director of the Highlander Center (Tenn.), in Reading 81. Groups tend to remain separate, focused on their own issues and concerns, often competing with each other for recognition and resources. The language of identity politics gives voice to people's discrimination and oppression. It does not encourage us to think about identity in a more complex way, as a mix of privilege and disadvantage. In Chapter 2 we introduced the idea that most people occupy multiple positions and that salient aspects of identity may vary significantly depending on the context. An African American graduate student who is about to receive her Ph.D., for example, may be highly respected by her teachers and peers, regardless of their race or hers. A White man walking past her in the street may insult and curse her because she is Black.

Understanding this notion of multiple positionality helps us to see how our personal and group identities are political and how the various identity groups fit together in the wider society. The specific context is crucial. In the public discourse about immigration, for example, there is a fear on the part of White people—usually hinted at rather than stated directly—of being overrun by Asians. When the context shifts to a discussion of peoples of color in the United States, however, Asian immigrants and Asian Americans become the "model minority," the standard against which African Americans or Latinos are compared unfavorably. Understanding one's identity involves a recognition of the ways in which one is privileged as well as the ways in which one is disadvantaged, and the contradictions that this raises, as noted by Melanie Kaye/Kantrowitz in Reading 14. With this more nuanced perspective, one not only focuses on the circumstances and concerns of one's own group, but also can use the complexity of one's identity to make connections to other groups. Thus, a White, middle-class woman with a hearing disability can take all of these aspects of her identity and understand her social location in terms of privilege as well as disadvantage. This is important for building effective alliances with others, which we discuss in more detail later. We make a distinction between a narrower identity politics, discussed above, and **identity-based politics,** which has a strong identity component and also a broader view that allows people to make connections to other groups and issues. Melanie Kaye/Kantrowitz, Christina Leaño (Reading 76), and the Combahee River Collective (Reading 3) all exemplify this more connective, identity-based politics.

Feminist Movements

Feminist movements have accomplished enormous change in this country. At the beginning of the twentieth century, suffragists in the United States were nearing the end of a seventy-year-long campaign for women's right to vote, which was finally won in 1920. This campaign had its roots in the nineteenth-century movement for the abolition of slavery. Again in the 1960s, the struggle for racial equality was "midwife to a feminist movement" (Evans 1980, p. 24) as women in the civil rights movement began to look more closely at the ways they were oppressed as women. These two periods are sometimes referred to as feminism's "first wave" and "second wave," respectively.

Women's organizing since the 1960s has been a powerful force for change at micro, meso, and macro levels, and a transforming experience for those involved (Brenner 1996; Davis 1991; DuPlessis and Snitow 1998; Rosen 2000). Women identified sexism in every area of life, including their own personal relationships, traditional gender roles, language, children's play, and symbolic events like the Miss America pageant. They used their own life experience to theorize about patriarchal systems, and they envisioned women's liberation. Some challenged women's exclusion from well-paying jobs in blue-collar trades, higher education, the law, medicine, and the media, as well as seeking to increase pay and improve conditions for jobs based on women's traditional roles. Some organized alternative institutions for women like health centers, publishing projects, music events and recording companies, art, film, writing circles, poetry readings, dances, and women-owned land projects. Others campaigned to elect more women to political office at city, state, and federal levels, on the assumption that this would change law and policy to benefit women. Note that these different approaches were based on different theoretical positions, some women seeking equality with men within existing institutions, others wanting to change these structures to be more liberatory for women and men.

Feminist movements have centered on women's supposed shared identity as women. In emphasizing their oppression as women, White middle-class feminists of the 1960s and '70s generally glossed over inequalities based on race and class. This assumption of "sisterhood" ignored the experiences of women of color, working-class White women, and White women's racial privilege (Bunch and Myron 1974; Lorde 1984; Moraga and Anzaldúa 1981; Rich 1986c; Shah 1997; Smith 1983). By contrast, professor of sociology Barbara Omolade's feminist activism grew out of her involvement in the civil rights movement in the mid-1960s when she was just out of college (Reading 77). Her mentor and role model was Ella Baker, a courageous and vibrant African American leader, the executive secretary of the Southern Christian Leadership Conference. Omolade notes that Black nationalism provided a powerful liberatory vision for many young African American activists. Women worked hard alongside men, but became critical of and disillusioned with sexism in the civil rights movement and Black power organizations. In the 1970s and '80s, Omolade was involved in various campaigns, drawing on both the sisterhood of Black feminism and the militancy of nationalism.

By the 1990s, the most visible remnants of the 1970s women's movements were national organizations like the Fund for a Feminist Majority, the National Abortion Rights Action League (NARAL), the National Organization of Women (NOW), and the National Women's Political Caucus. They were founded by White, middle-class women who have been able

to attract the resources and the media coverage that have helped to maintain them over the years. But the women's movements were much wider, more diverse, more radical, and more challenging than these organizations (see Baxandall and Gordon 2000). Many women of color, and some White women, have tended to write off second-wave feminism as a White, middle-class movement that is irrelevant to them. In Reading 78, sociologist Becky Thompson gives a very different account of second-wave feminism from the point of view of women of color and White antiracist women that allows much stronger links between, for example, the Combahee River Collective Statement (Reading 3) and the contemporary feminism of Jee-Yeun Lee (Reading 6).

Movements call forth the energies, passions, and visions of many people, often in ways that are life-changing for participants. They generate groundbreaking projects and alternative institutions, as mentioned above. Over time they often generate arguments about strategy and political direction that can lead to more permanent splits. Some women created change through grassroots organizing, providing services and supports that did not exist before. They also provided powerful visions of women's *liberation*. Others focused on the need for laws and public policy to change women's lives, and set their sights on elected office.

Women in Electoral Politics

The main purpose for women going into electoral politics is to make a difference in people's lives, especially for women and children. Those who work hard to support women candidates for political office argue that a critical mass of women in elected office will be able to change public policy and legislation to provide for women's needs. This includes local offices like parent-teacher associations (PTAs), city council seats, statewide offices, and the U.S. Congress. Together with male allies in Congress, women officials and their staff have worked long and hard to pass legislation to ensure better opportunities for women, including, for example, Title IX of the 1972 Education Act, which requires schools and colleges that receive federal funding to provide equal opportunities for male and female students (see the box on page 529 for more details), the Family and Medical Leave Act, and the Violence Against Women Act. They have also worked for improvements in women's wages, the

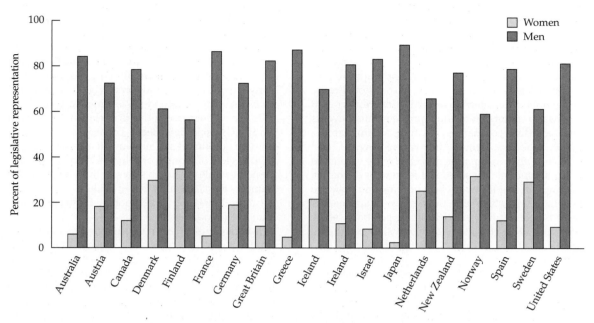

Figure 13.1 Women's and Men's Representations in National Legislatures. (*Source:* Andersen, M. 2000. *Thinking about Women: Sociological Perspectives on Sex and Gender,* 5th ed. Allyn & Bacon. Data from R. Darcy, Susan Welch, and Janet Clark. 1994. *Women, Elections, and Representation.* Lincoln: University of Nebraska Press, p. 78.)

availability of affordable child care, the opening of military combat roles to women, and so forth.

In 1990 women were 5.6 percent of congressional representatives. According to Susan Carroll of the Center for American Women and Politics at Rutgers University (New Jersey), that put the United States "about on a par with Iraq and Sri Lanka" (quoted in Davis 1991, p. 204). At that rate, it would be another fifty years before there was equality in state legislatures and at least another three hundred years before there were equal numbers of women and men in Congress. The proportion of women elected to political office has increased since then, though the United States has fewer women in office than many other countries, especially Denmark, Finland, Norway, and Sweden (see Figure 13.1). In 2003 women held 75 (14 percent) of the 535 seats in the U.S. Congress: 13 percent of the 100 seats in the Senate and 62 (14.25 percent) of the 435 seats in the House of Representatives. Of the 1,663 women state legislators nationwide, 16 percent were women of color (Center for American Women and Politics 2001). Sociologist Margaret Andersen (2000) notes the im-

pediments that limit women who want to run for political office: voter and media prejudice against women candidates, lack of support from party leaders, lack of access to extensive political networks, and lack of money. At the same time, women seeking office and organizations like Emily's List, the Fund for a Feminist Majority, and the National Women's Political Caucus are working to overcome these limitations (Burrell 1994; Ford 2002; Norris 1997; Thomas and Wilcox 1998; Woods 2000).

As elected officials and as voters, women are more likely than men to hold liberal views and to support the Democratic party. For example, more women than men support gun control, a national health-care system, social programs, tougher sentences for rapists and perpetrators of sexual assault and domestic violence, and workplace equality, as well as issues like women's right to abortion and gay/lesbian rights. This **gender gap** can be significant in two ways: getting more liberal candidates—women and men—elected and giving greater focus to liberal issues once such candidates are in office (Abzug 1984; Gallagher 1993; Norris 1997; Smeal 1984).

Title IX

Title IX ("title nine") of the 1972 Education Act is a landmark piece of civil rights legislation requiring educational institutions that receive federal funding to provide equal opportunities for male and female students in academics, athletics, financial assistance, and resources like student health and housing. Indeed, Title IX is a key reason that girls and women have made such gains in higher education, particularly in sports. In 1971, 294,015 girls participated in high school athletics compared to over 2.7 million girls in 2001—an 847 percent increase (U.S. Department of Education, quoted in Nelson 2002, p. 33), and there are now many more opportunities and facilities at the college level also.

A college must meet one of the following three standards to comply with the law. It must have roughly the same proportion of women among its varsity athletes as it has in its undergraduate student body; it must have a "history and continuing practice" of expanding opportunities for women; or it must demonstrate that it is "fully and effectively accommodating the interests and abilities" of its women students (Suggs 2002). Detractors argue that increased resources for women have resulted in fewer opportunities for men, and some athletics departments have achieved parity by cutting opportunities for male students rather than increasing those for women. A General Accounting Office report released in March 2001, however, found a net gain in men's teams from 1982 to 1999, and many more opportunities for men than for women (Nelson 2002). Denise Kiernan (2001) reported that "women receive only 38 percent of all athletic scholarship money, 27 percent of recruiting money and 23 percent of overall athletics budgets." Several Ivy League colleges and state universities have been forced to comply with the law, as women sued them for discrimination.

In 2001 the Department of Education appointed a Commission on Opportunity in Athletics to review the effects of Title IX. Its report, published in February 2003, includes the false assumption that opportunities for women in sports have resulted in fewer opportunities for men. The report recommends legal revisions "to ensure that new sports opportunities for girls and women do not come at the expense of boys' and men's teams" rather than suggesting ways to redirect resources to benefit all athletes (Schemo 2003, p. D1). These revisions are likely to have a significant impact on the number of places in sports programs available to women.

By the mid-1990s there were more women in elected positions than ever before. A growing bipartisan Congressional Women's Caucus served as a focus for women's concerns on Capitol Hill. Janet Reno was appointed as the first woman U.S. attorney general in the nation's history, and Madeleine Albright the first woman secretary of state. Bush administration "firsts" include the appointment of Condoleeza Rice as the first woman national security adviser. When the 108th Congress convened in January 2003, Nancy Pelosi, the new minority leader of the House, was the first woman to lead either political party and the highest-ranking woman in the 213-year history of Congress. More women also hold high office at the state level, whether as governors, attorneys general, state treasurers, chief educational officers, and so on. Whether or not elected women can make a significant difference in political institutions and public policy that is still overwhelmingly dominated by masculinist and corporate interests is the key question.

Many women are on committees concerned with health, education, and social services, and they bring their support for women and knowledge of women's experiences to their work. Those in high positions are doubtless constrained by political considerations. In the Clinton administration, Secretary of State Madeleine Albright, for example, was very vocal about women's oppression in Afghanistan, but, following U.S. government policy, she did not push for an end to economic sanctions against Iraq—a step that would have saved the lives of thousands of people, especially women and children.

In Reading 80, political scientist Michele Swers reviews data on the effects of women in public office.

She concludes that at the state and national levels women legislators do see women "as a distinct part of their constituency" and "do bring different policy priorities to the legislative agenda, particularly in the area of women's issues" (also see Carroll 2001). There are still too few women in elected office to be able to evaluate their effectiveness fully, and certainly no "critical mass" to change public policy and legislation significantly in favor of women.

In the second half of the nineteenth century, the activism of women, and their male allies, succeeded in winning the vote for women in 1920, and the strength of women's organizing in the 1980s and '90s made it possible for increasing numbers of women to become elected officials. Nevertheless, current public policy and budget priorities, together with a worsening economy, are having disastrous effects on women's lives. Restrictions on the availability of welfare, the erosion of *Roe v. Wade* and affirmative action policies, major tax cuts for the richest citizens, and increased military spending have all taken resources away from women. Women's organizations and elected officials who seek to improve women's lives currently face a hard road ahead, where a hallmark of success will be holding on to previous gains. This will require strategic thinking, clear focus, hard work, and acts of personal courage, such as that of Congresswoman Barbara Lee, who did not compromise her principles when she voted against authorizing military force in response to the attacks of September 11, in a historic 420-1 House vote on September 14, 2001.

Building Alliances for the Twenty-First Century

We emphasize the importance of alliances across lines of difference for two reasons. First, the many inequalities among women, mentioned throughout this book, often separate us and make it very difficult to work together effectively. Those with power over us know this and often exploit differences to pit one group against another. Second, progressive social change is a slow process that needs sustained action over the long haul. Effective alliances, based on a deepening knowledge of others and learning whom to trust over time, are necessary for long-term efforts, in contrast to coalition work, where the important thing is to stand together around a single issue, regardless of other differences. Alliances across lines of difference are both a means and an end. They provide both the process for moving toward, and some experience of, multicultural society. Melanie Kaye/Kantrowitz (Reading 14) offers insights for alliance building, especially across lines of race and class. Cynthia Cohen (Reading 79) describes a project that brings women together across significant differences.

Some Principles for Alliance Building

Alliances may be campus-wide, city-wide, national, or transnational in scope, as described by Kalima Rose, senior research associate at PolicyLink, in her account of the NGO (non-governmental organization) Forum of the United Nations Fourth World Conference on Women, held in Beijing in 1995 (Reading 82). Regardless of scale, some basic principles of alliance building include the following points:

- Know who you are, what is important to you, what are your nonnegotiables. Know your strengths and what you bring to a shared venture.

- Decide whether you want to be allies with a particular person or group. What are their values? What are they interested in doing in terms of creating social change? Are they open to the alliance? What is the purpose for coming together? Are you coming together as equals? In solidarity with another group?

- Check out the person or the group as the acquaintance grows. Are they who they say they are? Do you have reason to trust them to be there for you? Judge them by their track records and what actually happens, not by your fears, hopes, or expectations based on previous experiences.

- Commit yourself to communicate. Listen, talk, and listen more. Be committed to the process of communication rather than attached to a specific position. Communication may be through conversations, reading, films, events and meetings, or learning about one another's communities. Work together on projects and support one another's projects. Go into one another's settings as participants, observers, guests.

- Share your history. Talk about what has happened to you and to the people of your group.

- Be patient. Wanting to understand, to hear more, to stay connected requires patience from the inside. Allow one another room to explore ideas, make mistakes, be tentative. Hold judgment until you understand what's going on.

- Honesty is the most important thing. Be authentic and ask for authenticity from others. If this is not possible, what is the alliance worth?

- Keep the process "clean." Call one another on bad things if they happen—preferably with grace, teasing maybe, firmly but gently, so that the other person does not lose face. Don't try to disentangle difficulties when it is impossible to do so meaningfully, but don't use externals (too late, too tired, too busy, too many other items on the agenda) to avoid it.

- Be open to being called on your own mistakes, admitting when you're wrong, even if it is embarrassing or makes you feel vulnerable. Tell the other person when his or her opinions and experiences give you new insights and help you to see things differently.

- Do some people in the group take up a lot of time talking about their own concerns? Are they aware of it? How does privilege based on gender, race, class, nation, sexuality, disability, age, culture, or language play out in this relationship or alliance? Can you talk about it openly?

- What is the "culture" of your group or alliance? What kinds of meetings do you have? What is your decision-making style? If you eat together, what kind of food do you serve? What kind of music do you listen to? Where do you meet? What do you do when you are together? Does everyone in the group feel comfortable with these cultural aspects?

- Work out the boundaries of your responsibilities to one another. What do you want to do for yourself? What do you need others to help with? When? How?

- Look for the common ground. What are the perspectives, experiences, and insights we share?

Overcoming Impediments to Effective Alliances

Many sincere and committed attempts at building alliances have been thwarted, despite the best of intentions. Be aware of several common impediments to creating effective alliances, including the following beliefs and behaviors:

Internalized Oppression   This is a learned mindset of subservience and inferiority in oppressed peoples. It includes the acceptance of labels, characteristics, prejudices, and perceptions promoted by the dominant society. Specific behaviors include self-hatred and dislike, disrespect for and hatred of others of the same group.

Internalized Domination   This is a mindset of entitlement and superiority among members of the dominant group. Behaviors such as always speaking first in group discussions, being unconscious of the large amount of physical and social space one takes up, and automatically assuming leadership roles are some manifestations of internalized domination.

Operating from a Politics of Scarcity   This results from a deeply held, sometimes unconscious, belief that there is not enough of anything—material things as well as nonmaterial things like power, positive regard, popularity, friendship, time—and, more important, that however much there is, it will not be shared equally. In this view, inequality is simply a given that cannot be changed. It also justifies individualism and competition.

Subscribing to a Hierarchy of Oppression   This involves the placement of one oppressed group in relation to another so that one group's experiences of discrimination, prejudice, and disadvantage are deemed to be worse or better than another's.

Not Knowing One Another's History   Ignorance about other persons' backgrounds often results in drawing incorrect conclusions about their experiences. This prevents us from recognizing the complexity of women's experiences and can hide the ways our experiences are both different and similar.

Creating a Secure and Sustainable World

Central issues for women's movements in the United States have been diversity and inclusiveness. In Reading 6 (Chapter 1), JeeYeun Lee makes the point that diverse women bring assumptions, experiences, and understandings that should affect everyone's thinking. For example, women of color "call for recognition of the constructed racial nature of *all* experiences of gender"; lesbians and bisexual women have shown how heterosexist norms affect all our choices; and "ecofeminists challenge our fundamental ideas about living on and with the earth." Professor of Black studies Kimberly Springer (2002) speculates about "the possibilities for an inter-generational Black feminist theory." She opposes "a media-generated second-wave/third-wave fracture" and sees herself "as the bridge between my foremothers and future Black feminists" (p. 382).

Providing services to women and reforming existing institutions to make them more responsive to those who are excluded are crucially important in the overall work of progressive social change and have made a difference to generations of women. The challenge for the future is to continue to expand this work. Given the many insecurities of life for women and for men, and the growing threat to the planet itself from increasing industrialization, militarization, and ecological devastation, what sense does it make for women to seek an equal piece of what ecofeminist activist and writer Ynestra King (1993b, p. 76) has called this "rotten and carcinogenic" pie?

Women's movements are shared endeavors. They are many overlapping movements constructed around issues and identities, with links to other progressive movements such as the antiglobalization movement and the antimilitarist movement. Given that corporations control more and more of the world and that women's rights are under serious attack in this country, we need to work together to address interconnected issues: economic survival, reproductive rights, all forms of violence including state violence, criminalization, and incarceration, immigrant rights, and so on. These vibrant, broad-based efforts draw on our creativity, our emotions, our spirituality, and our sense of justice, strengthening connections between people and communities. There is great accumulated experience and insight about how to work on multi-issue politics, and also much to learn. Grace Lee Boggs, a long-time activist in Detroit, notes that this is both an exciting and a daunting time in human history. She urges: "For our own well-being, for the health and safety of our communities, our cities and our country, we need to accept the awesome responsibility of creating new ways of . . . living" (1994, p. 2).

This book is about U.S. women's lives and the kind of world we need to create for women's empowerment, development, and well-being. This world will be based on notions of genuine security and sustainability. The project of human development—for both women and men—is one that has been in process for a very long time. It is our challenge to take the next steps in this process. How can we settle for anything less?

> *Activism is not issue-specific*
> *It's a moral posture that, steady state,*
> *   propels you forward, from one hard*
> *   hour to the next.*
> *Believing that you can do something*
> *   to make things better, you do*
> *Something, rather than nothing.*
> *You assume responsibility for the*
> *   privilege of your abilities.*
> *You do whatever you can.*
> *You reach beyond yourself in your*
> *   imagination, and in your wish for*
> *Understanding, and for change.*
> *You admit the limitations of individual*
> *   perspectives.*
> *You trust somebody else.*
> *You do not turn away.*
>
> (June Jordan)

◆◆◆

Questions for Reflection

As you read and discuss this chapter, think about these questions:

1. What are your assumptions about how people and societies change? What do you think needs changing, if anything?

2. Have you ever been involved in a social-action project or electoral politics? What was your experience like? If you have not, why not?

3. Have you ever tried to establish and maintain an ongoing relationship, friendship, or working partnership with someone from a background very different from your own? What happened? What did you learn from that experience? What would you do differently, if anything?

4. If you have had such a relationship, why did you become involved in the first place? Was that a good enough reason? Why or why not? If you never have, why not?

5. What do you know about the history of the various groups you are a member of? What do you know about groups that are not your own? How does knowing this history help, and how does not knowing it hinder you in making alliances across lines of difference?

6. What is your vision of a secure and sustainable personal relationship? Community? Society? World?

Finding Out More on the Web

1. Research the work of organizations cited in this chapter. What are their strategies and visions? Who do they speak to? These are additional resources:

   Public Leadership Education Network (PLEN) is a consortium of women's colleges working together to prepare women for public leadership: **www.plen.org**

   Center for Women's Global Leadership (Rutgers University, N.J.) organizes sixteen days of international activism against gender violence: **www.cwgl.rutgers.edu**

   Guerilla Girls are a group of women intent on exposing patterns of sexism, racism, and censorship in the art world: **www.guerillagirls.com**

2. In Reading 76, Christina Leaño mentions FACES (Filipino/American Coalition for Environmental Solutions). Find out more about this group's strategies and activities.

3. In Reading 77, Barbara Omolade mentions the Women's Action Alliance, the Women's Survival Space in Brooklyn, and the Black Women's Health Project. Find out about recent developments of these projects.

4. In Reading 78, Becky Thompson mentions Hijas de Cuauhtemoc, Women of All Red Nations, and the National Black Feminist Organization. Find out more about their strategies, activities, and perspectives.

Taking Action

1. List all the ways you are an activist. Review the suggestions for taking action at the end of each chapter. Commit yourself to continuing to involve yourself in issues that matter to you.

2. Think about how aspects of your identity can help you to make alliances with others. Support campus or community groups that are working together on an issue of shared concern.

3. Where do your elected officials (at the city, state, and national levels) stand on issues that matter to you? What is their voting record on these issues? Write to thank them for

supporting issues you care about (if they do), or urge them to change their positions. Present them with information from your course materials or other sources to make a strong case.

4. Many of the issues we have discussed have implications at the global level. What can you do that will have an impact at that level?

SEVENTY-SIX

◆◆◆

Listening to the Voices of My Spiritual Self

Christina Leaño

We are not human beings on a spiritual journey, but spiritual beings on a human journey.

—Pierre Teilhard de Chardin, Jesuit priest and paleontologist (1881–1955)

My whole life has been driven by voices. Tiny, inner, voices that have emerged from some unknown depths and have guided me (during those times I was willing) to unexpected places. They have taunted me with questions like "What does it mean to be Filipina? Where is God in your life? Why are you doing this social justice work?" until the friction from their words was too uncomfortable to ignore.

During my junior year in college, I was in Kenya participating in a semester abroad program. I was amazed by the vibrancy of the people and the richness of Kenyan culture, yet something inside me was awry. The colorful markets, tropical forests, and reality of daily struggle were foreign and at the same time strangely familiar. I realized that Kenya reminded me of what I had seen in the Philippines during my only visit as a child. This revelation was nudged by one of those prodding voices: "Your experience in Kenya is beautiful. Can you imagine the richness if it were a culture of your own blood? You need not go any further than your own heritage to find cultural treasure. Go, explore that."

This voice spoke from a void within me—this disconnect between my culture and myself. For most of my twenty-one years I did not see myself as a Filipina. Growing up in a white, upper-middle-class suburb and attending a private college preparatory in Florida gave me little opportunity to claim my brownness. There were even times when my color (and my relatives' color) shamed me, as I tried to keep my white friends from seeing our darkness. I had always thought that I was just an average kid with a flat nose and shiny, black hair.

Yet, when that voice emerged within me, I was filled with fear. It was like waking up and realizing that the ground below me was but a mist I was about to slip through. How was it that I did not know my Filipino heritage? What is my history, my culture? Who are my ancestors? Where are my roots? This voice led me from fear toward a hunger that was waiting to be filled. And I realized that I would have to answer those questions before I could move on with my life. How else would I find the ground to walk upon? So I decided that my next destination after college would be the Philippines.

After graduating, I signed up with the Mennonite Central Committee for three years as a volunteer in the Philippines. I chose a Christian organization, because another emerging voice was calling me to explore my spirituality. It frightened the heck out of me, being a "missionary," as I knew the damage that missionaries had done in the Philippines in the past, first during Spanish colonization and then during the American occupation. But there were enough signs—a volunteer placement that fit my exact interests (with the People's Task Force for Bases Cleanup, which dealt with environmental justice issues, the subject of my college thesis) and with people who gave me the support I needed—to show me that my decisions were in line with the Universe's. All I had to do was take a deep breath and trust.

That decision led to a whirlwind of adventure, transformation, and growth. Being in the Philippines gave me an opportunity to learn Tagalog, to get to know tens of cousins, aunts, uncles, grandparents, and to embrace my Filipino-ness that I hardly knew existed. This seed sprouted and bloomed as soon as I swallowed my first drop of Philippine water. Qualities and values that had been passed on to me by my parents—the importance of smooth interpersonal relationships and the centrality of family, faith, and education—were revealed as legacies embedded within the culture. I was Filipina without even realizing it.

Most important, I realized that my identity as a Filipina American was self-defined. I worked in a campaign demanding U.S. responsibility for cleaning up toxic contamination left behind in their former military bases in the Philippines. Thus my passion and desire as a Filipina for justice for the communities around the bases, and my anger at what my government had left behind, provided an opportunity to bridge my two identities. I could use my Filipino heart and my American citizenship for social change in the Philippines that addressed the huge inequities in the hundred-year relationship between the two nations. There was no choosing. I am both.

After two-and-a-half years, I came back to the United States to work in Washington, D.C., as director of a newly launched organization, FACES (Filipino/American Coalition for Environmental Solutions), the U.S. counterpart of the Philippines clean-up campaign. Although there were times of incredible joy and growth, after a year I was overwhelmed with fatigue, sadness, and doubt. I was working too much (isn't 25 too young to burn out?), I was not taking care of my physical, emotional, and spiritual needs, and I was not quite sure why I was doing this social justice work. My good side wanted to assure me that it was because of the enormous injustice resulting from the negligence of the U.S. government. But then there was another side of me, the ego side, which was focused on me trying to make a difference.

Working at FACES, I was still supported by the Mennonite Central Committee and was surrounded by folks who were able to articulate their commitment to social and environmental justice in terms of their faith. They could pull out Bible verses this way and that, while me, with my Catholic non-Bible upbringing, had to tediously search the thin pages for the right lines. How I longed to be able to translate my Catholic faith into a justice-making language.

I also thought that most of my difficulties, such as relating to Congressional aides or public speaking, were rooted in the spiritual. I could not name it, but I sensed that if I was grounded in my faith, tapped into the power of God, I couldn't fail. Most of all, the fatigue and weight of the work I was experiencing felt so wrong. I was depending too much on myself instead of allowing the creative power of God to step in, but how could I let go? That, more than not knowing my ethnic identity, was frightening. But the weeks of crying and being so tired even when I got enough sleep broke me down. My spiritual director labeled my tears "grace," as they provided me an opening to listen to those voices asking me hard questions: "What does it mean to be a child of God? How can you truly ground your social justice work and activism in your faith?"

Next thing I knew, I was flying out to California to study at the Graduate Theological Union in Berkeley, which is where I am today. I thought I might be able to take a break from activism while studying, but I have learned that my activism is actually part of my "spiritual practice" and not a distraction from it. I became involved with the San Francisco Bay Area chapter of FACES as co-chair and the work has been non-stop. In the last year and a half, we have marched in rallies, filed a lawsuit against the U.S. military, hosted several cultural events, and given presentations to numerous colleges and organizations.

One of my greatest learnings from studying theology and engaging in movement work is realizing that the great divide between spirituality and activism, contemplation and action, is a false one. My spirituality and contemplation invite me further into my activism, and my activism further into my spirituality and contemplation. Meditation and prayer provide the space for me to get in touch with the suffering of others, to keep myself accountable to the Divine within and around me, and to be honest about my human limitations and needs. Activism allows me to transform the connectedness with others' suffering into action and to live out my beliefs through my relationships with others. Thus, spirituality and activism, contemplation and action are but two sides of the same coin of compassion and love.

It has been quite a journey, and I know there is more to come, thanks to the persistence of those voices. For a while I did not really name them. I now realize that they are the voices of my True Self, the God-self, urging me to follow the map imprinted in my heart, carved by the Life Source herself. To know myself is to peel back all the layers of identity that have been given to me on this earth—as a Filipina, as an American, as a woman, as a lover of justice and peace, and as a Christian—to get to my core as a child of the Universe, the Divine, God. Trusting this process, creating the space, and allowing myself to be led, I have found my true power and a sense of peace. Don't get me wrong, even amidst this happiness, I still seem to be wearing earplugs most of the time, listening to my own beat and rhythm. Thank goodness those voices are loud. May they continue to haunt me, until I claim them as my own.

◆◆◆

Ella's Daughters

Barbara Omolade

I worked with Ella Baker during the summer of 1964 at the Washington, D.C., office of the Mississippi Freedom Democratic Party (MFDP). She was already a legend in the Civil Rights Movement as the advisor to the radical and committed young activists in the organization she founded, the Student Nonviolent Coordinating Committee (SNCC).

Our Washington MFDP office staff included Ms. Baker, Walter Tillow, a white SNCC worker from New York, and myself, a recent college graduate who had been a part-time worker in the New York SNCC office. We were to gain support for seating the delegation from the MFDP instead of the regular Mississippi Democratic Party delegation at the National Democratic Party presidential convention in Atlantic City. We coordinated volunteers who lobbied Democrats on the Hill and raised funds to support MFDP activities.

Although a college graduate, I was so inept and anxious, most of my time was spent trying to deal with my newly discovered sexual freedom and autonomy—and marveling at Ms. Baker. She was everything I was not: self-assured and brilliant. Ms. Baker was able to easily communicate with and gain respect from "ordinary" people, young activists as well as powerful white men such as Attorney Joseph Rauh, a leading Democratic Party advisor. She immediately took command of every situation while I floundered and stumbled through the simplest chores.

In August, the bodies of three missing civil rights workers, Michael Schwerner, James Chaney, and Andy Goodman, were discovered. Andy had been my classmate at college and I had recruited him to participate in the Mississippi Freedom Summer Project. Because of his lynching and the gravity of the efforts in Mississippi, that summer my identity as a woman became intertwined with becoming like Ms. Baker, an effective and respected organizer. Fighting injustice and oppression, making sacrifices for social causes became, for me, the indicators of true womanhood or manhood. However, as the Civil Rights Movement waned I became absorbed in personal journeys and travels, and then in marriage and motherhood.

However, my interest in Ms. Baker and my quest to emulate her was reawakened by my relationship to the women's movement. I was thrust into the heart of second wave feminism, not by choice or politics—I was a staunch nationalist at the time—but because I worked for white feminist organizations. In the mid-'70s, I became the co-coordinator of Women's Survival Space, a 40-bed battered women's shelter located in Brooklyn, and then an administrator at the Women's Action Alliance, a national women's organization and resource center founded by Gloria Steinem and others.

The feminists around me constantly spoke about the roots of feminism being derived from books by Betty Friedan and Simone de Beauvoir, which raised women's consciousness and began a "second wave" of women's activism. Few acknowledged the contributions of white and Black women civil rights workers, or the critical role of the Civil Rights Movement, in general, to the material conditions which made the women's movement possible. The reality that much of Black and white feminist praxis and social theory came from the work and ideas of Ella Baker was ignored.

By the time Ella Baker founded SNCC, she had already been a full-time organizer for the NAACP in the Deep South from 1938 to 1946 and an executive secretary of the Southern Christian Leadership Conference. In 1943 she was named director of NAACP branches, in charge of establishing and maintaining the local chapters. At considerable risk to herself and her constituents, she traveled throughout the South enrolling southern Black people in the NAACP, an outlawed organization whose members were often harassed, tortured, killed, and run out of town. She helped community members identify local leaders and issues for struggle against segregation. This political work confronted the real possibility of torture and death because at the time the South was ruled by legalized apartheid. Not unlike police states and dictatorships worldwide, protesting Black southerners were "disappeared," their homes were bombed, or they were, at the very least, imprisoned. However, Ms. Baker was relentless and courageous in her determination to extend the mutual support and collectivity of Black communities to include active resistance to segregation.

In 1958, after living in New York for 12 years, Ms. Baker returned south at the age of 55 to become the executive secretary of the SCLC, founded by Martin Luther King, Jr. The conference was a network of Black ministers in southern cities who assumed local leadership of mass movements fighting segregation. One of Ms. Baker's assignments was to organize a meeting to mobilize the diverse and disparate groups of students who, during 1960, had "sat in" protesting segregated lunch counters and bus stations. Ms. Baker was outraged and walked out of a meeting where ministers mapped out plans to isolate students by region and pressure them to become part of an SCLC-dominated youth organization. Rejecting these high-handed pressure tactics, Ms. Baker held that "those who were under the heel were the ones to decide what action they were going to take to get from under their oppression." She encouraged the protesting students to establish their own organization, the Student Nonviolent Coordinating Committee (SNCC), and became its advisor, working part time for the Atlanta YWCA to support herself. She hired Jane Stembridge, a white student from Georgia, and Bob Moses, a Black high school teacher from New York, to become SNCC's first field secretaries.

SNCC became a racially mixed group of male and female field secretaries who from 1961 to 1966 organized voter registration and anti-segregation campaigns in Black communities throughout southwest Georgia, Alabama, and Mississippi. Its ambitious Mississippi Freedom Summer Project, organized with nominal support from the NAACP and SCLC, and in active partnership with CORE [Congress of Racial Equality], brought hundreds of northern students and volunteers into the state from 1963 to 1965 to organize Freedom Schools, medical and legal clinics, cultural programs and the MFDP.

Representing the fullest expression of Ella Baker's social praxis, SNCC and MFDP were more political collectives than organizations in the traditional sense. Ms. Baker's social theory and praxis is based upon face-to-face political work involving dialogue, where the organizer/initiator listens to the concerns of "local people," who articulate what they know, receive feedback about their ideas, and offer their own remedies, strategies, or solutions. From a series of dialogues held at people's homes or job sites, the organizer/initiator gathers together several people and calls a meeting—usually at a church. The meetings are usually accompanied by song and prayer, which continue earlier discussions, develop mutual courage, and enable members to resolve to execute an action to change some aspect of their political condition—a voting card, a traffic signal, a new policy. The activity must be decided upon by the consensus of those who will execute and be affected by the action.

The organizer is an "outsider" actively seeking anonymity and no personal rewards, while serving to facilitate the meetings and actions of local leaders and community members. The organizer without domestic or career ties is "called" to social action rather than employed by the civil rights organization.

Although many social theories and movements share Ms. Baker's approach to organizers and communities, hers is one of the few which emerged from an African American ethos of mutual aid and support. "Where we lived there was no sense of hierarchy, in terms of those who have, having the right to look down upon, or to evaluate as a lesser breed, those who didn't have" (Canterow, 60). An organizer's success depended upon "both your disposition and our capacity to sort of stimulate people—and how you carried yourself, in terms of not being above people" (Canterow, 71).

This ethos was expanded to include the collective power to challenge segregation and make social change in communities which were made up of "people from various and sundry other areas . . .

who had to learn each other . . . and begin to think in terms of a 'wider brotherhood'" (Canterow, 61). Class and gender, and even racial differences, were muted in this kind of organizing. White men and women SNCC workers became part of the community by rejecting their own racist backgrounds and communities in order to live and work among and *for* Black people.

Ms. Baker was not overtly ideological. She spouted no pre-packaged party line. She was not a Marxist, although she stood with the working class and the poor. She was not a professed nationalist, although she was deeply rooted in the African American ethos and community. Likewise, she was not a declared feminist but modeled for young Black and white women a powerful womanhood that was not tied to traditional domestic social roles. Ms. Baker was a "liberated" Black woman radical whose genius was her ability to develop democratic and activist political organizations and communities.

In giving students permission to organize on their own behalf and define their own role in the movement, Ella Baker transformed American politics. The organization she birthed, SNCC, took on a life of its own. Her philosophy affirming the right of Black poor people to organize gave rise to a political culture which is now commonplace. The idea of "grassroots" groups of ordinary people organizing to protest, petition, as well as develop their own agendas, was enlarged and expanded by Ella Baker to empower organizers to meet the needs of anti-segregation struggles in the Deep South. She developed a network and apparatus among alienated and disparate community leaders during her NAACP organizing years. She connected activist ministers during her SCLC years, concretizing King's vision and enabling him to be a leader among other ministers in the movement. She produced young student leaders who became the movement's "shock troops." Unencumbered by family or jobs, they could go into southern towns and give local people inspiration and technical assistance.

Bringing white and Black college students into SNCC enabled Ella Baker to influence and train leaders who became part of national movements promoting changes in the academy, including the free-speech movement, and protesting the Vietnam War. The white men she mothered brought the New Left Movement into being. The white women she moth-

ered in the movement inspired others, creating second-wave feminism.

Many white students attribute their political evolution and enlightenment to SNCC, not realizing that SNCC was Baker's creation. Bob Moses, Jim Forman, Ruby Doris Smith Robinson, Dorie Ladner, and other admired SNCC members worked closely with Ms. Baker in *their* formative years.

Her Black daughters combined and took from feminism, nationalism and the New Left, adding their own unique notions, to birth womanism. During the late 1970s and 1980s, a network of Black feminists or womanists in central Brooklyn emerged to carry on the traditions of Ella Baker. These daughters developed organizations and campaigns in spite of sexism and antifeminist sentiments within Black nationalism and the Black community.

During the 1970s most politically active women in Black communities were connected in some way to the building of nationalist institutions and groups. At the heart of many of these efforts was the construction of more explicitly "African" cultural forms. Outwardly signaled by African names, attire, music, and religions, cultural nationalism rejected the "White World" and its values. Many women were attracted to the ideals of nationalism which affirmed their "womanhood" and beauty. However, male nationalists attempted to confine "womanhood" to mating and motherhood. In spite of the significance of Assata Shakur and Angela Davis, most women found themselves restricted by the rather narrow definitions of their role in nationalist organizations.

Many nationalists believed "the struggle" should restore the traditional gender roles destroyed by slavery, colonialism and racism: strong patriarchal warriors with supportive wives who mothered their children. Although some nationalist men believed women should be co-warriors in restoring the Black nation, ultimately their place would be caring for the home and family. Nationalist men sought to restrict women from leadership roles, though they continued to need Black women's labor, creativity, and resourcefulness.

Nationalist women often saw themselves as "warriors" in their own right. Among themselves, sisters balked at being mere supporters and complained of male chauvinism—while maintaining a united front with men against white racism. Many didn't realize that Black women in the past, especially radical organizers such as Ella Baker and revolutionary women around the world, were battling the same two colonialisms: patriarchy and white supremacy.

Although Ms. Baker and other SNCC leaders understood that the struggle was really about creating a more equitable and just society, its immediate goals and forms were straightforward. The issues were there in Black and white: politically powerless Black people fought against the white power structure for the franchise, access to opportunity, and for equal treatment before the law. Such a movement required unity and sacrifice among a critical mass of people to show collective resistance for even a brief and defined period of time—the time it took for a demonstration, protest, or campaign. In this sense, the combination of Ms. Baker's work empowering local people (using students as their legs and arms), NAACP legal strategies, and King's spiritual and inspiring leadership was successful: Blacks have gained the franchise, and access to public facilities. But the movement unearthed other issues: free speech, sexism, peace. African Americans were radically changed because as the high points of the southern movement were ebbing, new forms of nationalist politics were being formed.

Both Ms. Baker and Martin Luther King became overshadowed by Malcolm X's post–civil rights message, which offered an alternate paradigm to citizenship for Blacks. His message of Black self-determination, anti-colonialism, and transformed identification forced Blacks to look at what kind of society they were struggling to become citizens of.

Inspired by the possibilities of nationalism, two of Ella's sons: Kwame Toure (aka Stokeley Carmichael) and Jamil Abdullah Al-Amin (aka H. Rap Brown) abandoned her grassroots, passive resistance strategies for a more militant and ideologically confrontational politics in the Black Panther Party. The Panthers' nationalist positions and radical rhetoric demonstrated their break with the methods of the southern struggle, although they grew out of the party of the same name in Lowndes County, one of SNCC's Alabama projects. Ella's sons rebelled against her model, her philosophy, and her name. The nationalism of organizations and groups founded by nationalist men did not allow women like Ella Baker to participate in their leadership.

In spite of the domination of men, Black women remained active in Black nationalist organizations.

Their sisterhood and connection to each other strengthened both their own commitment to all Black people and their definitions of nationalism. These organizations fought police brutality and racist schools while building alternative schools and cultural programs. They helped to foster "community" among those viewed as fragmented and brainwashed by white culture.

The East, founded in 1970 by Jitu Weusi, was the major nationalist institution in central Brooklyn. It began as an outgrowth of an alternative school for Black students expelled from a city high school after staging a tribute to Malcolm X; the protest had been viewed as anti-Semitic and militant by the school authorities. Uhuru Sasa, the East's Freedom School, soon drew hundreds of students supported by parents frustrated and angered at the racism in the public school system. It soon expanded into a cultural institution which included an annual street fair of Black merchants and craftsmen/women, musical concerts, and community forums.

"It is our belief that the most crucial work for this particular era of African existence is the building of Revolutionary Nationalist institutions. By 'institutions' we mean schools, political parties, cultural centers, military units, presses—all those programmatic structures that enable a people to see beyond survival; in short, the elemental ingredients of a viable nation" (*New Africa Education*). The East, at its height, was an internationally known model for this kind of vision.

Women such as Martha Bright, Abimbola, Atchuda Barkr, and Aminisha Weusi demonstrated that strong Black women continued to organize during the cultural nationalist era. Their hard work and strong women's circles enabled them to be effective in spite of male chauvinism. Ironically, most male leaders, needing skilled and loyal workers, expressed admiration and respect for "strong sisters." Some nationalists such as Kalamu ya Salaam and his wife Tayari attempted to address Black male chauvinism through a nonsexist practice involving study, seminars, and pamphlets. There were also some men in the East community who were struggling against their own sexism and its effect on the movement. In fact, during the late 1970s, Segun Shabaka encouraged me, a Black feminist and radical activist, by publishing my articles in the *Black News*, the East-sponsored journal he edited.

When I wrote those articles, I was a single mother of three children, working full time as an administrator at the Women's Action Alliance and part time as an adjunct in women's studies at a local college. As a result of my own search for an effective and hospitable political community, I threw myself into a flurry of activism. In addition to writing for *Black News*, I worked with white leftists, primarily in supporting normalized relationships between the United States and the People's Republic of China. I learned about Marxism and nationalist theory by attending meetings of many radical groups. In 1979, I was in a Black women's study group which included Susan McHenry, one of *Ms.* magazine's earliest Black woman editors, and Michele Wallace, when she first published *Black Macho and the Myth of the Superwoman*. I was also active in the Sisterhood of Black Single Mothers and the Women's Committee of the Black United Front. I demonstrated against and protested police brutality and South African apartheid. I spoke on feminism and activism to any group that asked me. I was trying very hard to be like Ms. Baker. Soon I kept meeting other activist Black women such as Daphne Busby, Safiya Bandele, Arlene Parker, Andree McLaughlin and others who could also claim to be Ella's daughters.

In 1972, Daphne Busby, a young single mother, founded the Sisterhood of Black Single Mothers, perhaps the first Black feminist grassroots group of the post–civil rights era not connected to any Black male organization. The Sisterhood always identified itself as a Black and female organization. By supporting Black single mothers and refusing to become embroiled in either feminist or nationalist ideological debates, the Sisterhood opened an entirely new arena for Black women's social activism. The Sisterhood was one of the first organizations to legitimate the connections between personal issues, such as sexuality and motherhood, and Black female consciousness.

Established to counteract the slandering of women who were regularly called "unwed mothers" of "broken homes" with "illegitimate" children, the Sisterhood defended and advocated for Black single mother families. Daphne Busby's pride in declaring herself the head of a "family that works" challenged critics to examine their own prejudices and sexist assumptions about Black single mothers.

The Sisterhood offered consciousness raising, social services, and social activities to diverse Black single mothers: professionals, welfare recipients, middle-age divorcees and teen mothers. As one of the first groups to work with these younger mothers and with Black single fathers, the organization pioneered in social policies and programs concerned with the Black family. While perfecting the white feminist movement's concern with connecting the personal to the political, which was merely a restating of Ella Baker's notion of dialogue, the Sisterhood deepened the Black community's traditions of self-help. Interestingly, the Sisterhood was able to simultaneously gain the respect of white feminists, Black nationalists, and Black single mothers, in part because of the timeless energy of Daphne Busby's outspoken and no-nonsense leadership, and in part for its tangible help for Black single mothers.

For nearly 20 years, the Sisterhood attracted scores of sisters like me who were searching for an authentic place to deal with our personal needs as mothers and women and who needed concrete help with our families. Safiya Bandele was one of the first women to answer Daphne Busby's call for interested Black single mothers to join her. Safiya worked steadfastly along with Daphne, and eventually became the Chair of the Sisterhood board.

By the mid 1970s, Safiya and I began to find ourselves at the same meetings of the Sisterhood, the Black United Front and other groups. She eventually became my closest *companera* because we both were searching for a sisterhood which had the feminism and supportiveness of the sisterhood of Black Single Mothers and the militancy and resistance politics of the Black United Front.

The Black United Front (BUF), founded in 1976 by Jitu Weusi and the Rev. Herbert Daughtry, was a multi-faceted political organization which mounted responses to police brutality and racial injustice, opposed apartheid, and supported radical international movements and human rights organizations.

The BUF women's committee was the largest and best fund-raiser of the dozen committees of the organization. The committee was composed of women from the church, from the general membership of BUF, and activists like myself. Together we organized buses to demonstrate in Washington D.C., protesting attacks against affirmative action. We sponsored programs for the general membership and developed strategies for reforming the public schools.

While I worked in the women's committee, Safiya was an officer on BUF's executive board. In spite of the respect given the work of the women's committee and Safiya's executive position, women's leadership in the organization was resisted. Frustrated and restless because of our marginal roles in BUF, both of us also worked with Daphne at the sisterhood and for a myriad of other causes, conferences, and campaigns.

During this period, Safiya and I learned a great deal about the patterns of male chauvinism and the subordinate position of women within nationalist organizations. Across the country, challenges to Black male chauvinism were increasingly made by Black women whose expertise and experience had been downplayed by dominant males. By the end of the 1970s virtually every Black organization or initiative seemed to break down over the appropriate place of Black women in its leadership. Some organizations, such as the National Black Independent Political Party (NBIPP), tried to create a formal approach by requiring that Black women co-lead with Black men in each of its chapters.

Safiya and I continued to straddle both the Sisterhood and BUF, striving to do work which would give sisters an authentic political voice while defending Black people against injustice. We encouraged each other, but grew increasingly dissatisfied, observing and noting male chauvinism while continuing to lend our labor power to the work of their organizations.

In 1981, I called together five Black women activist friends, including of course, Safiya, to develop a Black female response to the missing and murdered children in Atlanta, whose mothers were being maliciously attacked as "unfit" in the media, yet whose murderers were not being actively sought.

Since white men were reportedly implicated in the ritual murders of the children, many Black groups began rallying support for community patrols and more effective police activity. Newspaper accounts, however, repeatedly stated that the murdered Black boys were hanging in the streets late at night unsupervised because they came from "broken homes" with "unfit mothers"—meaning from families headed by Black women.

Some mothers of the missing and murdered children called press conferences and rallies to respond to these negative attacks on their families.

Our group in Brooklyn wanted to demonstrate solidarity with the mothers of Atlanta's missing and murdered children. We gathered more Black women together and formed the Coalition of Concerned Black

Women. We decided to have a Mother's Day march to highlight the plight of the children and their mothers. Over 300 people marched on Mother's Day, May 10, 1981, nearly two miles through Brooklyn in a demonstration supported by 54 organizations. It was one of the first political marches organized solely by Black women and featuring a significant number of Black women speakers on the program. Organized in 6 weeks, the march was a bold step in which Black women decided upon a goal to go forward and do something together and did it.

A year later, in 1982, I received a small grant from the Sisterhood to develop *The Rising Song*, a 13-week lecture series on Black women's history for the community. Held at the Restoration Corporation, a Brooklyn-based community development corporation, the lecture series attracted large audiences of community members. Week after week, noted Black women historians, activists, and poets provided information and vision about the historical accomplishments and achievements of Black women. The lecture series presented speakers such as Professor Myrna Bain speaking about the unremitting toil of African women's labor, the late Audre Lorde discussing sexuality, and poet Hattie Gossett showcasing Black women writers, singers, and "wild women."

While the lecture series occurred, protests were intensifying at nearby Medgar Evers College. Among faculty and student concerns were the competency of the college president and the lack of adequate support services and academic programs for the predominantly Black and female student body.

Medgar Evers College was founded in 1971 as a result of strong demands by the members of the Black community in Brooklyn that the City University of New York create "a new experimental and innovative institution which meets the needs of the community in which it is located and the needs of the City which it must serve." Once established, the college received little support and few resources from CUNY; its neglect and the lack of adequate leadership created a climate of discontent which erupted during the spring of 1982 into a four-month-long sit-in in the President's office, carried out by students and a few faculty members. The Student, Faculty, Community Coalition to save Medgar Evers College was founded to rid the college of its President and rebuild the college in the image of Medgar Evers, the man. The movement at MEC was eventually responsible for removing the President, for getting the Board to authorize new facilities and for establishing a woman's center. At the end of the four-month strike, a childcare center named in honor of Ella Baker and Charles Roman, a former professor at MEC, was started in the former President's quarters.

Embodying Ella's democratic notions of consensus, the sit-in's student, faculty, and community members argued, debated, and developed an agenda. The agenda presented the group's demands and set forth policies for governing the school. Because Black women students, faculty, staff, and community members performed support as well as leadership roles in all of its levels, the sit-in at MEC was perhaps the first political struggle in the post–civil rights era which connected an explicitly Black feminist praxis to a Black community struggle.

Unlike the students in the Civil Rights Movement, MEC students were workers and parents. The movement at MEC was sustained by women who were forced to strain the limits of their extended kin networks to get care for their children so they could be on the frontline. Some women brought their children with them, sleeping next to them on the floor and in chairs.

Four out of five officers of the Student government were women. The main security area in front of the President's office was staffed by a woman who at times literally put her body across the door. Women were prominent in maintaining a 24-hour watch down the halls and corridors from the office.

Inside another office, students ate together, slept together on the floor and shared resources and information. The domestic chores of cleaning, cooking, answering phones, which had been traditional roles for women in other political movements, were shared by all. Decisions were hammered out and executed democratically.

The militantly democratic nature of the protest, as well as its feminist and nationalist ideology, was ensured by the powerful experiences of its Black women faculty leaders: the student movement experience of Professor Andree McLaughlin, the political experience of Professor Zala Chandler, and the community and Black women's movement experience of Professor Safiya Bandele. Their role was matched by the dedication and power of women students such as Sharon Smith, Alice Turner and, Rhonda Vanzant. Students such as Trevor Belmosa, Norman Coward, and Vincent Manuel demonstrated

that Black men could work along with strong Black women. Not needing to dominate or cower, these men demonstrated the potency of a truly united effort among equals.

The Sisterhood, the Black United Front, Black Veterans for Social Justice, and other community organizations lent their support and expertise to the sit-in. I became a community representative to the Medgar Evers College Coalition which was created to support it. The MEC struggle brought many groups and individuals together in much the same way that the sit-ins and freedom rides had brought Black college students to SNCC decades before.

During the 1970s, the East and BUF were centers of male-dominated Black nationalist thought and practice. Black women were tentative in their search for an authentic place for their practice and ideas. After the struggle, Medgar Evers College became the center of explicit Black feminist concerns and womanist praxis.

A major issue of the sit-in at MEC had been the lack of support services, information, and scholarship which specifically addressed the needs of women students. Courageous women from the struggle demanded a women's center.

Directed by Safiya Bandele, the Center for Women's Development (CWD) opened its doors in April 1983. It has been one of the only women's centers in the country directed by a Black woman and established by Black women students. The center offers both individual and group counseling, especially for those who are depressed, battered and under stress. The CWD is also a referral service offering information about health, welfare, housing, and other support services. The CWD has sponsored and co-sponsored conferences, forums, and programs which reflect both the international and personal concerns of the student body. In 1985, the Center organized a delegation to attend the United Nations Decade for Women's Meeting in Kenya.

In 1985, Professor Andree McLaughlin, as coordinator of the Women's Studies, Research and Development, "piloted a Cross Cultural Black Women's Studies Curriculum" (Jackson, 2) which grew into a series of International Cross Cultural Black Women's Studies Summer Institutes. "Convening annually in different nations, the Institute is a world assembly of women activists, theorists, artists, writers, peasants, and workers who are concerned with learning about each other's realities to enable themselves to better control their destinies" (Jackson, 1).

Since its inception, the group has met in Zimbabwe, New Zealand, Berlin, and New York and discussed "Women and Communications," "Women and the Politics of Food," "Human Rights and Indigenous Peoples in the Information Age," and "Black People and the European Community." "This think tank for women and women's concerns has decided it is crucial to continue to address the legacies of colonialism and feudalism as well as the realities of patriarchy and imperialism which impact on their everyday existence in real ways . . ." (Jackson, 8–9). The Institutes, primarily led and developed by Andree McLaughlin, have created an international community of Black women which, like the anti-colonialist Pan African conferences at the beginning of the twentieth century, will undoubtedly have a major impact in global politics in the future.

In addition to the exciting potential of this international work, by the end of the 1980s Black women in Brooklyn had institutionalized many womanist-inspired programs and institutions. In 1989, the Sisterhood founded Kianga House, a residential program for homeless teen mothers, one of the first places to institutionalize Black feminist approaches to this issue. Martha Bright, formerly of the East, joined with Esmeralda Simmons and others to develop parenting groups and legal services at the Medgar Evers College Center for Law and Social Justice. Alice Turner, the heroic student leader of the MEC struggle, after receiving her MSW degree, returned to run the Center for Women's Development counseling unit, developing and expanding its program.

In 1985, the CWD sponsored a Black Women's Conference with over 500 participants. The conference planning committee, composed of lesbians and heterosexual sisters, had hoped it would heal wounds among Black women, and create a common and ongoing agenda. However, homophobic participants rejected lesbians who spoke openly about themselves and their issues. Although the conference failed to develop a true sisterhood, it encouraged CWD to do more intensive work on personal issues of sexuality and identity.

Gwen Braxton of the New York City Black Women's Health Project, a member of the conference planning committee, helped the CWD develop an agenda for its own members' health. The motto "if you are not working on yourself, you are not working" informed support groups and "internal work" among Center staff. The Center has implemented the self-help/support group/mutual-help model of the Black Women's Health Project, which emphasizes coming together to give and receive help, "*not as expert, social worker, psychologist, organizer, physician, teacher, paid helper, and needy paying client helpee*" (*NYC Black Women's Health Project*).

One of the women who helped the CWD institutionalize this approach is Arlene Parker, the first Black woman to receive a degree in Black women's studies from CUNY. Before working at the Center for Women's Development, Arlene worked at the Bedford Stuyvesant Restoration Community Development Corporation as Assistant to the President. Arlene brings a unique approach to her work by attending to the well-being of Black women. She affirms and connects women to each other by using the traditional approaches women have used to maintain kinship relationships: sending cards, phone calls, celebration of holidays, and birthdays. Arlene has fostered a sisterhood among the women at the Center for Women's Development.

The Center's special approach to Black women's self-help was consolidated in a series of workshops, "Healing Women Warriors," which grew out of an unpublished article I wrote with Andaye de la Cruz, a Latina activist and therapist. Both of us were recovering from our own "burnout" and overextension as activists, workers, and mothers. We looked around and saw that many of the women activists we worked with were themselves "sick" and overworked.

The "Healing Women Warriors" work enabled me to critically confront one of Ms. Baker's mottos: "She who believes in freedom cannot rest," a powerful yet dangerous message for overworked women activists. For more than a decade, I and other women were trying to work for the people and the sisters while we also worked for wages and raised families. Not only were we "burning out" and suffering from the same tragedies as other Black women—murder, rape, cancer, and depression—we were often neither effective, nor sisterly. Many of us realized that we could not remain wedded to a politics which tried to hold back the tide of diminishing political community, waning activism, and the avalanche of new and complicated social and personal issues, without strengthening and healing ourselves. Ella's daughters had to learn to rest and carve out time to recuperate. We also needed on-going support groups in order to be effective women and organizers.

Ms. Baker worked behind the scenes of major political organizations, doing the unrecognized toil of meetings and campaigns. Although she claimed not to want to "be in front," the tensions between the male authority in power and the authority she embodied were just below the surface of Ms. Baker's problems with SCLC and the NAACP. While Ella worked around gender issues in order to "contribute" to the Civil Rights Movement, today's Black women activists are compelled to focus on them—especially violence against women, women's development, homophobia, and challenges to male chauvinism.

Some of Ella's daughters have replicated her role as the "woman in front," the pioneer and initiator. The woman in front "puts her body into the movement." She, like Ella, is found working long hours, squeezing in family obligations and sacrificing personal pleasures. Policy, programs, and work evolves from and is most often initiated by her. Andree McLaughlin, founder and leader of the Cross Cultural Black Women's Institute, and Daphne Busby, founder and director of the Sisterhood of Black Single Mothers, are examples of the "woman in front" leadership model. In fact, because of the rise of such womanists in the Black community and in Black women's consciousness, more are daring to become "women in front."

Ella Baker's adherence to democratic collective work has inspired another womanist leadership model—the woman leader "in the circle." Groups of Black women work together on projects, campaigns, and programs and maintain friendships and personal relationships beyond their work. Safiya Bandele at the CWD has used this model in her work, empowering the women on staff to work on themselves as well as on the Center's tasks.

As Brooklyn's Black womanist community matures, it becomes clear that these two approaches— "woman in front" and "woman in the circle"—are not mutually exclusive. The "woman in front" leader often becomes "burned out," feels isolated, and truly needs to share her work and responsibilities with sisters in support groups and networks.

However, without the daring actions of these "women in front," women's circles can become overly concerned with raising the consciousness of their members. We, as Ella's daughters in central Brooklyn, have developed a praxis that uses and develops both kinds of Black women's leadership. Each woman in the group is encouraged to work on herself and her dreams, and somehow they all become part of the Center's mission and work.

Our Black womanist praxis is a process which utilizes the social distance between Black men and women to raise feminist consciousness. It enables women to see the social character of their personal and private oppression. It exposes male chauvinism and sexism as being detrimental to all Black life. It is a social movement concerned with the physical, emotional, political, and spiritual health of all members of the Black community. Our praxis attempts to bridge differences between lesbians and heterosexual women and tries to work and participate in an international sisterhood of Black women.

The Black Women's Health Project advocates resistance to all forms of oppression, and the complete elimination of oppression as essential to the Black Woman's struggle for and achievement of well-being. It considers violence a public health issue and seeks to eliminate the physical, institutional, psychological, and ideological violence perpetuated against Black women.

Furthermore, this social praxis is developing in the midst of a literary renaissance and an explosion of studies by and about Black women. More and more Black women who want to help their sisters and do something about the destitution and despair in the Black community are becoming leaders of unions and schools, owning their own businesses, and running for elected office.

There is also a transformation within the Christian Church because of the pro-woman praxis of Black women, laity and clergy. Not all Black women who sustain pro-active positions and commitments to social change consider themselves womanists. However, Black women activists and womanists alike rely on their personal relationship with God for guidance and determination. Like Ella Baker, they pray their feet be guided by God so their work will not be in vain. This faith informs and sustains their visions of social change.

Our praxis in the past has been to do anti-racist work with Black men, to do women's work with Black women within the Black community, and sometimes to do work on women's issues in coalition with white women and other women of color. The womanist praxis in Central Brooklyn has shown that when Black women develop their own power, consciousness, and skills, this resonates with Black people's overall survival, development, and peace. Andree McLaughlin challenges us to understand that our praxis must attempt to be nationalist, feminist, and socialist all at the same time, in opposition to the "multiple jeopardy which undermine the standard to all people's existence" (McLaughlin, 54).

Ella Baker believed, like many others, that a baton is passed from one generation to another to keep the struggle for social change alive. As the tireless "fundi" (a Swahili term for "the person in a community who passes on the crafts from one generation to another"), Ella Baker passed on her baton to me, a direct descendant of her praxis and her work. But I had to shape and redefine the baton to fit the requirements of my own time and needs. The power of her baton has grown to be shared with other women.

Our womanist praxis has been birthed, extended, and embraced by multiple circles of sisters, sometimes led by the "woman in front" and other times led by the "sister within the circle." While other children can afford the racial or gender privilege of ignoring or dropping the baton she offered them, Black womanists can never forget that Ella Baker was our mother and that, as her daughters, we owe it to her to continue to struggle in her name.

REFERENCES

Braxton, Gwen, *New York City Black Women's Health Project, Suggested 12 Step Program,* flyer.

Canterow, Ellen, with Susan Gushee O'Malley and Sharon Hartman Strom, "Moving the Mountain," *Women Working for Social Change,* Old Westbury, New York: Feminist Press, 1980: 52–93.

Jackson, Dr. Phyllis, *The International Cross Cultural Black Women Studies Seminar Institute Report (1987–1990).*

McLaughlin, Andree Nicola, "The International Nature of the Southern African Women's Struggle," *Network: A Pan African Women's Forum,* Harare, Zimbabwe, Vol. 1, No. 1, Winter, 1988: 49–56.

The Uhuru Sasa School Program, *Outline for New African Educational Institute,* Brooklyn, NY: Black Nation Education Series #7, 1971.

Ya Salaam, Kalamu, *Our Women Keep Our Skies From Falling,* New Orleans: Nkombo, 1980.

SEVENTY-EIGHT

◆◆◆

Multiracial Feminism

Recasting the Chronology of Second Wave Feminism

Becky Thompson

In the last several years, a number of histories have been published that chronicle the emergence and contributions of Second Wave feminism.[1] Although initially eager to read and teach from these histories, I have found myself increasingly concerned about the extent to which they provide a version of Second Wave history that Chela Sandoval refers to as "hegemonic feminism."[2] This feminism is white led, marginalizes the activism and world views of women of color, focuses mainly on the United States, and treats sexism as the ultimate oppression. Hegemonic feminism deemphasizes or ignores a class and race analysis, generally sees equality with men as the goal of feminism, and has an individual rights-based, rather than justice-based vision for social change.

Although rarely named as hegemonic feminism, this history typically resorts to an old litany of the women's movement that includes three or four branches of feminism: liberal, socialist, radical and sometimes cultural feminism.[3] The most significant problem with this litany is that it does not recognize the centrality of the feminism of women of color in Second Wave history. Missing too, from normative accounts is the story of white antiracist feminism which, from its emergence, has been intertwined with, and fueled by the development of, feminism among women of color.[4]

Telling the history of Second Wave feminism from the point of view of women of color and white antiracist women illuminates the rise of multiracial feminism—the liberation movement spearheaded by women of color in the United States in the 1970s that was characterized by its international perspective, its attention to interlocking oppressions, and its support of coalition politics.[5] Bernice Johnson Reagon's naming of "coalition politics"; Patricia Hill Collins's understanding of women of color as "outsiders within"; Barbara Smith's concept of "the simultaneity of oppressions"; Cherríe Moraga and Gloria Anzaldúa's "theory in the flesh"; Chandra Talpade Mohanty's critique of "imperialist feminism"; Paula Gunn Allen's "red roots of white feminism"; Adrienne Rich's "politics of location"; and Patricia Williams's analysis of "spirit murder" are all theoretical guideposts for multiracial feminism.[6] Tracing the rise of multiracial feminism raises many questions about common assumptions made in normative versions of Second Wave history. Constructing a multiracial feminist movement time line and juxtaposing it with the normative time line reveals competing visions of what constitutes liberation and illuminates schisms in feminist consciousness that are still with us today.

The Rise of Multiracial Feminism

Normative accounts of the Second Wave feminist movement often reach back to the publication of Betty Friedan's *The Feminine Mystique* in 1963, the founding of the National Organization for Women in 1966, and the emergence of women's consciousness-raising (CR) groups in the late 1960s. All signaled a rising number of white, middle-class women unwilling to be treated like second-class citizens in the boardroom, in education, or in bed. Many of the early protests waged by this sector of the feminist movement picked up on the courage and forthrightness of 1960s' struggles—a willingness to stop traffic, break existing laws to provide safe and accessible abortions, and contradict the older generation. For younger women, the leadership women had demonstrated in 1960s' activism belied the sex roles that had traditionally defined domestic, economic, and political relations and opened new possibilities for action.

This version of the origins of Second Wave history is not sufficient in telling the story of multiracial feminism. Although there were Black women involved with NOW from the outset and Black and Latina women who participated in CR groups, the feminist work of women of color also extended beyond women-only spaces. In fact, during the 1970s, women of color were involved on three fronts—working with white-dominated feminist groups forming women's caucuses in existing mixed-gender organizations; and developing autonomous Black, Latina, Native American, and Asian feminist organizations.[7]

This three-pronged approach contrasts sharply with the common notion that women of color feminists emerged in reaction to (and therefore later than) white feminism. In her critique of "model making" in Second Wave historiography, which has "all but ignored the feminist activism of women of color," Benita Roth "challenges the idea that Black feminist organizing was a later variant of so-called mainstream white feminism."[8] Roth's assertion—that the timing of Black feminist organizing is roughly equivalent to the timing of white feminist activism—is true about feminist activism by Latinas, Native Americans, and Asian Americans as well.

One of the earliest feminist organizations of the Second Wave was a Chicana group—Hijas de Cuauhtemoc (1971)—named after a Mexican women's underground newspaper that was published during the 1910 Mexican Revolution. Chicanas who formed this *femenista* group and published a newspaper named after the early-twentieth-century Mexican women's revolutionary group, were initially involved in the United Mexican American Student Organization which was part of the Chicano/a student movement.[9] Many of the founders of Hijas de Cuauhtemoc were later involved in launching the first national Chicana studies journal, *Encuentro Feminil.*

An early Asian American women's group, Asian Sisters, focused on drug abuse intervention for young women in Los Angeles. It emerged in 1971 out of the Asian American Political Alliance, a broad-based, grassroots organization largely fueled by the consciousness of first-generation Asian American college students. Networking between Asian American and other women during this period also included participation by a contingent of 150 Third World and white women from North America at the historic Vancouver Indochinese Women's Conference (1971) to work with Indochinese women against U.S. imperialism.[10] Asian American women provided services for battered women, worked as advocates for refugees and recent immigrants, produced events spotlighting Asian women's cultural and political diversity, and organized with other women of color.[11]

The best-known Native American women's organization of the 1970s was Women of All Red Nations (WARN). WARN was initiated in 1974 by women, many of whom were also members of the American Indian Movement which was founded in 1968 by Dennis Banks, George Mitchell, and Mary Jane Wilson, an Anishinabe activist.[12] WARN's activism included fighting sterilization in public health service hospitals, suing the U.S. government for attempts to sell Pine Ridge water in South Dakota to corporations, and networking with indigenous people in Guatemala and Nicaragua.[13] WARN reflected a whole generation of Native American women activists who had been leaders in the takeover of Wounded Knee in South Dakota in 1973, on the Pine Ridge reservation (1973–76), and elsewhere. WARN, like Asian Sisters and Hijas de Cuauhtemoc, grew out of— and often worked with—mixed-gender nationalist organizations.

The autonomous feminist organizations that Black, Latina, Asian, and Native American women were forming during the early 1970s drew on nationalist traditions through their recognition of the need for people of color-led, independent organizations.[14] At the same time, unlike earlier nationalist organizations that included women and men, these were organizations specifically for women.

Among Black women, one early Black feminist organization was the Third World Women's Alliance which emerged in 1968 out of the Student Nonviolent Coordinating Committee (SNCC) chapters on the East Coast and focused on racism, sexism, and imperialism.[15] The foremost autonomous feminist organization of the early 1970s was the National Black Feminist Organization (NBFO). Founded in 1973 by Florynce Kennedy, Margaret Sloan, and Doris Wright, it included many other well-known Black women including Faith Ringgold, Michelle Wallace, Alice Walker, and Barbara Smith. According to Deborah Gray White, NBFO, "more than any organization in the century . . . launched a frontal assault on sexism and racism."[16] Its first conference in New York was attended by 400 women from a range of class backgrounds.

Although the NBFO was a short-lived organization nationally (1973–75), chapters in major cities remained together for years, including one in Chicago that survived until 1981. The contents of the CR sessions were decidedly Black women's issues—stereotypes of Black women in the media, discrimination in the workplace, myths about Black women as matriarchs, Black women's beauty, and self-esteem.[17] The NBFO also helped to inspire the founding of the Com-

bahee River Collective in 1974, a Boston-based organization named after a river in South Carolina where Harriet Tubman led an insurgent action that freed 750 slaves. The Combahee River Collective not only led the way for crucial antiracist activism in Boston through the decade, but it also provided a blueprint for Black feminism that still stands a quarter of a century later.[18] From Combahee member Barbara Smith came a definition of feminism so expansive that it remains a model today. Smith writes that "feminism is the political theory and practice to free *all* women: women of color, working-class women, poor women, physically challenged women, lesbians, old women, as well as white economically privileged heterosexual women. Anything less than this is not feminism, but merely female self-aggrandizement."[19]

These and other groups in the early and mid-1970s provided the foundation for the most far-reaching and expansive organizing by women of color in U.S. history. These organizations also fueled a veritable explosion of writing by women of color, including Toni Cade's pioneering *The Black Woman: An Anthology* in 1970, Maxine Hong Kingston's *The Woman Warrior* in 1977, and in 1981 and 1983, respectively, the foundational *This Bridge Called My Back: Writings by Radical Women of Color* and *Home Girls: A Black Feminist Anthology.*[20] While chronicling the dynamism and complexity of a multidimensional vision for women of color, these books also traced for white women what is required to be allies to women of color.

By the late 1970s, the progress made possible by autonomous and independent Asian, Latina, and Black feminist organizations opened a space for women of color to work in coalition across organizations with each other. During this period, two cohorts of white women became involved in multiracial feminism. One group had, in the late 1960s and early 1970s, chosen to work in anti-imperialist, antiracist militant organizations in connection with Black Power groups—the Black Panther Party, the Black Liberation Army—and other solidarity and nationalist organizations associated with the American Indian, Puerto Rican Independence, and Chicano Movements of the late 1960s and early 1970s. These women chose to work with these solidarity organizations rather than work in overwhelmingly white feminist contexts. None of the white antiracist feminists I interviewed (for a social history of antiracism in the United States) who were politically active during the civil rights and Black Power movements had an interest in organizations that had a single focus on gender or that did not have antiracism at the center of their agendas.

Militant women of color and white women took stands against white supremacy and imperialism (both internal and external colonialism); envisioned revolution as a necessary outcome of political struggle; and saw armed propaganda (armed attacks against corporate and military targets along with public education about state crime) as a possible tactic in revolutionary struggle. Although some of these women avoided or rejected the term "feminist" because of its association with hegemonic feminism, these women still confronted sexism both within solidarity and nationalist organizations and within their own communities. In her autobiographical account of her late-1960s' politics, Black liberation movement leader Assata Shakur writes: "To me, the revolutionary struggle of Black people had to be against racism, classism, imperialism and sexism for real freedom under a socialist government."[21] During this period, Angela Davis was also linking anticapitalist struggle with the fight against race and gender oppression.[22] Similarly, white militant activist Marilyn Buck, who was among the first women to confront Students for a Democratic Society (SDS) around issues of sexism, also spoke up for women's rights as an ally of the Black Liberation Army.

Rarely, however, have their stories—and those of other militant antiracist women—been considered part of the Second Wave history. In her critique of this dominant narrative, historian Nancy MacLean writes: "Recent accounts of the rise of modern feminism depart little from the story line first advanced two decades ago and since enshrined as orthodoxy. That story stars white middle-class women triangulated between the pulls of liberal, radical/cultural, and socialist feminism. Working-class women and women of color assume walk-on parts late in the plot, after tendencies and allegiances are already in place. The problem with this script is not simply that it has grown stale from repeated retelling. It is not accurate . . ."[23]

The omission of militant white women and women of color from Second Wave history partly reflects a common notion that the women's movement followed and drew upon the early civil rights movement and the New Left, a trajectory that skips entirely the profound impact that the Black Power movement had

on many women's activism. Omitting militant women activists from historical reference also reflects a number of ideological assumptions made during the late 1960s and early 1970s—that "real" feminists were those who worked primarily or exclusively with other women; that "women's ways of knowing" were more collaborative, less hierarchical, and more peace loving than men's; and that women's liberation would come from women's deepening understanding that "sisterhood is powerful."

These politics were upheld both by liberal and radical white feminists. These politics did not, however, sit well with many militant women of color and white women who refused to consider sexism the primary, or most destructive, oppression and recognized the limits of gaining equality in a system that, as Malcolm X had explained, was already on fire. The women of color and white militant women who supported a race, class, and gender analysis in the late 1960s and 1970s often found themselves trying to explain their politics in mixed-gender settings (at home, at work, and in their activism), sometimes alienated from the men (and some women) who did not get it, while simultaneously alienated from white feminists whose politics they considered narrow at best and frivolous at worst.

By the late 1970s, the militant women who wanted little to do with white feminism of the late 1960s and 1970s became deeply involved in multiracial feminism. By that point, the decade of organizing among women of color in autonomous Black, Latina, and Asian feminist organizations led militant antiracist white women to immerse themselves in multiracial feminism. Meanwhile, a younger cohort of white women, who were first politicized in the late 1970s, saw feminism from a whole different vantage point than did the older, white, antiracist women. For the younger group, exposure to multiracial feminism led by women of color meant an early lesson that race, class, and gender were inextricably linked. They also gained vital experience in multiple organizations—battered women's shelters, conferences, and health organizations—where women were, with much struggle, attempting to uphold this politic.[24]

From this organizing came the emergence of a small but important group of white women determined to understand how white privilege had historically blocked cross-race alliances among women, and what they, as white women, needed to do to work closely with women of color. Not surprisingly,

Jewish women and lesbians often led the way among white women in articulating a politic that accounted for white women's position as both oppressed and oppressor—as both women and white.[25] Both groups knew what it meant to be marginalized from a women's movement that was, nevertheless, still homophobic and Christian biased. Both groups knew that "there is no place like home"—among other Jews and/or lesbians—and the limits of that home if for Jews it was male dominated or if for lesbians it was exclusively white. The paradoxes of "home" for these groups paralleled many of the situations experienced by women of color who, over and over again, found themselves to be the bridges that everyone assumed would be on their backs.

As the straight Black women interacted with the Black lesbians, the first-generation Chinese women talked with the Native American activists, and the Latina women talked with the Black and white women about the walls that go up when people cannot speak Spanish, white women attempting to understand race knew they had a lot of listening to do. They also had a lot of truth telling to reckon with, and a lot of networking to do, among other white women and with women of color as well.

Radicals, Heydays, and Hot Spots

The story of Second Wave feminism, if told from the vantage point of multiracial feminism, also encourages us to rethink key assumptions about periodization. Among these assumptions is the notion that the 1960s and early 1970s were the height of the radical feminist movement. For example, in her foreword to Alice Echols's *Daring to Be Bad: Radical Feminism in America, 1967–1975,* Ellen Willis asserts that by the mid-1970s, the best of feminism had already occurred.[26] In her history of the women's liberation movement, Barbara Ryan writes that the unity among women evident in the early 1970s declined dramatically by the late 1970s as a consequence of divisions within the movement.[27]

Looking at the history of feminism from the point of view of women of color and antiracist white women suggests quite a different picture. The fact that white women connected with the Black Power movement could rarely find workable space in the early feminist movement crystalized for many of them with the 1971 rebellion at Attica Prison in New York State

in response to human rights abuses.[28] For antiracist activist Naomi Jaffe, who was a member of SDS, the Weather Underground, and WITCH (Women's International Terrorist Conspiracy from Hell), attempts to be part of both early Second Wave feminism and an antiracist struggle were untenable. The Attica rebellion, which resulted in the massacre by state officials of thirty-one prisoners and nine guards, pushed Jaffe to decide between the two. She vividly remembers white feminists arguing that there was no room for remorse for the "male chauvinists" who had died at Attica. Jaffe disagreed vehemently, arguing that if white feminists could not understand Attica as a feminist issue, then she was not a feminist. At the time, Black activist and lawyer Florynce Kennedy had said: "We do not support Attica. We ARE Attica. We are Attica or we are nothing." Jaffe claimed: "That about summed up my feelings on the subject."[29] With this consciousness, and her increasing awareness of the violence of the state against Black Panthers, antiwar protesters, and liberation struggles around the world, Jaffe continued to work with the Weather Underground. She went underground from 1970 to 1978.

Naomi Jaffe, like other white women working with the Black Power movement, were turned off by a feminism that they considered both bourgeois and reductionist. They stepped out of what antiracist historian Sherna Berger Gluck has termed "the master historical narrative," and they have been written out of it by historians who have relied upon a telling of Second Wave feminism that focused solely on gender oppression. Although the late 1960s and early 1970s might have been the "heyday" for white "radical" feminists in CR groups, from the perspective of white antiracists, the early 1970s were a low point of feminism—a time when many women who were committed to an antiracist analysis had to put their feminism on the back burner in order to work with women and men of color and against racism.

Coinciding with the frequent assumption that 1969 to 1974 was the height of "radical feminism," many feminist historians consider 1972 to 1982 as the period of mass mobilization and 1983 to 1991 as a period of feminist abeyance.[30] Ironically, the years that sociologists Verta Taylor and Nancy Whittier consider the period of mass mobilization for feminists (1972–82) are the years that Chela Sandoval identifies as the period when "ideological differences divided and helped to dissipate the movement from within."[31] For antiracist women (both white and of color), the best days of feminism were yet to come when, as Barbara Smith explains, "Those issues that had divided many of the movement's constituencies—such as racism, anti-Semitism, ableism, ageism, and classism—were put on the table."[32]

Ironically, the very period that white feminist historians typically treat as a period of decline within the movement is the period of mass mobilization among antiracist women—both straight and lesbian. The very year that Taylor and Whittier consider the end of mass mobilization because the ERA failed to be ratified, 1982, is the year that Gluck rightfully cites as the beginning of a feminism far more expansive than had previously existed. She writes: "By 1982, on the heels of difficult political struggle waged by activist scholars of color, ground breaking essays and anthologies by and about women of color opened a new chapter in U.S. feminism. The future of the women's movement in the U.S. was reshaped irrevocably by the introduction of the expansive notion of feminisms."[33] Angela Davis concurs, citing 1981, with the publication of *This Bridge Called My Back,* as the year when women of color had developed as a "new political subject," due to substantial work done in multiple arenas.[34]

In fact, periodization of the women's movement from the point of view of multiracial feminism would treat the late 1960s and early 1970s as its origin and the mid-1970s, 1980s, and 1990s as a height. A time line of that period shows a flourishing multiracial feminist movement. In 1977, the Combahee River Collective Statement was first published; in 1979, *Conditions: Five,* the Black women's issue, was published, the First National Third World Lesbian Conference was held, and Assata Shakur escaped from prison in New Jersey with the help of prison activists.[35] In 1981, Byllye Avery founded the National Black Women's Health Project in Atlanta; Bernice Johnson Reagon gave her now-classic speech on coalition politics at the West Coast Women's Music Festival in Yosemite; and the National Women's Studies Association held its first conference to deal with racism as a central theme, in Storrs, Connecticut, where there were multiple animated interventions against racism and anti-Semitism in the women's movement and from which emerged Adrienne Rich's exquisite essay, "Disobedience and Women's Studies."[36] Then, 1984 was the year of the New York Women against Rape Conference, a multiracial, multiethnic conference that confronted multiple challenges facing women organizing against violence against women—by partners, police, social service agencies, and poverty. In 1985, the United Nations Decade for Women conference in Nairobi, Kenya, took place; that same year, Wilma Mankiller was named the first principal chief of the Cherokee Nation. In 1986, the National Women's Studies Association conference was held at Spelman College. The next year, 1987, the Supreme Court ruled that the Immigration and Naturalization Service must interpret the 1980s' Refugee Act more broadly to recognize refugees from Central America, a ruling that reflected the work on the part of thousands of activists, many of whom were feminists, to end U.S. intervention in Central America.

In 1991, Elsa Barkely Brown, Barbara Ransby, and Deborah King launched the campaign called African American Women in Defense of Ourselves, within minutes of Anita Hill's testimony regarding the nomination of Clarence Thomas to the Supreme Court. Their organizing included an advertisement in the *New York Times* and six Black newspapers which included the names of 1,603 Black women. The 1982 defeat of the ERA did not signal a period of abeyance for multiracial feminism. In fact, multiracial feminism flourished in the 1980s, despite the country's turn to the Right.

Understanding Second Wave feminism from the vantage point of the Black Power movement and multiracial feminism also shows the limit of the frequent assignment of the term "radical" only to the white antipatriarchal feminists of the late 1960s and early 1970s. Many feminist historians link the development of radical feminism to the creation of several antipatriarchy organizations—the Redstockings, Radicalesbians, WITCH, and other CR groups. How the term "radical" is used by feminist historians does not square, however, with how women of color and white antiracists used that term from the 1960s through the 1980s. What does it mean when feminist historians apply the term "radical" to white, antipatriarchy women but not to antiracist white women and women of color (including Angela Davis, Kathleen Cleaver, Marilyn Buck, Anna Mae Aquash, Susan Saxe, Vicki Gabriner, and Laura Whitehorn) of the same era whose "radicalism" included attention to race, gender, and imperialism and a belief that revolution might require literally laying their lives on the line? These radical women include political prisoners—Black, Puerto Rican, and white—some of whom are still in prison for their antiracist activism in the 1960s and 1970s. Many of these women openly identify as feminists and/or lesbians but are rarely included in histories of Second Wave feminism.

What does it mean when the term "radical" is only assigned to white, antipatriarchy women when the subtitle to Cherríe Moraga and Gloria Anzaldúa's foundational book, *This Bridge Called My Back,* was "Writings by *Radical* Women of Color"?[37] To my mind, a nuanced and accurate telling of Second Wave feminism is one that shows why and how the term "radical" was itself contested. Recognizing that there were different groups who used the term "radical" does not mean that we then need an overarching definition of "radical feminism" that includes all these approaches. It does mean understanding that white feminists of the "daring to be bad period" (from 1967 to 1975) do not have exclusive rights to the term.[38] An expansive history would emphasize that Second Wave feminism drew on the civil rights movement, the New Left, *and* the Black Power movement which, together, helped to produce three groups of "radical" women.

Principles of a Movement

Although analysis of the feminist movement that accounts for competing views of what it means to be "radical" is a step forward in developing a complex understanding of Second Wave history, what most interests me about comparing normative feminist history with multiracial feminism are the contestations in philosophy embedded in these coexisting frameworks. Both popular and scholarly interpretations of Second Wave feminism typically link two well-known principles to the movement—"Sisterhood Is Powerful" and the "Personal Is Political." From the point of view of multiracial feminism, both principles are a good start but, in themselves, are not enough.

Conversations and struggles between women of color and white women encouraged white women to think about the limits of the popular feminist slogan "Sisterhood Is Powerful." There were many reasons why the editors of *This Bridge Called My Back* titled one of the sections of the book, "And When You Leave, Take Your Pictures with You: Racism in the Women's Movement." Lorraine Bethel's poem, "What Chou Mean *We*, White Girl? or the Cullud Lesbian

Feminist Declaration of Independence" ("Dedicated to the proposition that all women are not equal, i.e., identical/ly oppressed"), clarifies that "we" between white and Black is provisional, at best.[39] Anthropologist Wendy Rose's critique of "white shamanism"—white people's attempt to become native in order to grow spiritually—applies as well to white feminists who treat Native American women as innately spiritual, as automatically their spiritual mothers.[40]

Cross-racial struggle made clear the work that white women needed to do in order for cross-racial sisterhood to *really* be powerful. Among the directives were the following: Don't expect women of color to be your educators, to do all the bridge work. White women need to be the bridge—a lot of the time. Do not lump African American, Latina, Asian American, and Native American women into one category. History, culture, imperialism, language, class, region, and sexuality make the concept of a monolithic "women of color" indefensible. Listen to women of color's anger. It is informed by centuries of struggle, erasure, and experience. White women, look to your own history for signs of heresy and rebellion. Do not take on the histories of Black, Latina, or American Indian women as your own. They are not and never were yours.

A second principle associated with liberal and radical feminism is captured in the slogan "The Personal Is Political," first used by civil rights and New Left activists and then articulated with more depth and consistency by feminist activists. The idea behind the slogan is that many issues that historically have been deemed "personal"—abortion, battery, unemployment, birth, death, and illness—are actually deeply political issues.

Multiracial feminism requires women to add another level of awareness—to stretch the adage from "The Personal Is Political" to, in the words of antiracist activist Anne Braden, "The Personal Is Political and the Political Is Personal."[41] Many issues that have been relegated to the private sphere are, in fact, deeply political. At the same time, many political issues need to be personally committed to—whether you have been victimized by those issues or not. In other words, you don't have to be part of a subordinated group to know an injustice is wrong and to stand against it. White women need not be victims of racism to recognize it is wrong and stand up against it. Unless that is done, white women will never understand how they support racism. If the only issues that feminists deem political are those they have experienced personally, their frame of reference is destined to be narrowly defined by their own lived experience.

The increasing number of antiracist white women who moved into mixed-gender, multi-issue organizations in the 1980s and 1990s after having helped to build women's cultural institutions in the 1970s and 1980s may be one of the best examples of an attempt to uphold this politic. Mab Segrest, perhaps the most prolific writer among lesbian antiracist organizers, provides the quintessential example of this transition in her move from working on the lesbian feminist journal, *Feminary,* in the late 1970s and early 1980s, to becoming the director of North Carolinians against Racist and Religious Violence in the 1980s. A self-reflective writer, Segrest herself notes this transition in the preface to her first book, *My Mama's Dead Squirrel: Lesbian Essays on Southern Culture.* Segrest writes: "In the first [essay] I wrote, 'I believe that the oppression of women is the first oppression.' Now I am not so sure. Later I wrote, 'Relationships between women matter to me more than anything else in my life.' Now what matters most is more abstract and totally specific: the closest word to it, justice. . . . During the early years the writing comes primarily out of work with other lesbians; later on, from work where I am the only lesbian."[42] The book opens with autobiographical essays about her family and women's writing, but the last essays chronicle the beginning of her organizing against the Klan—essays that became the backdrop of her second book, *Memoir of a Race Traitor.* In Segrest's view, by 1983, her work in building lesbian culture—through editing *Feminary* and her own writing—"no longer seemed enough, it seemed too literary." Segrest found herself both "inspired by and frustrated with the lesbian feminist movement." Segrest recalls that she

> had sat in many rooms and participated in many conversations between lesbians about painful differences in race and class, about anti-Semitism and ageism and ablebodiedism. They had been hard discussions, but they had given me some glimpse of the possibility of spinning a wider lesbian movement, a women's movement that truly incorporates diversity as its strength. But in all those discussions, difficult as they were,

we had never been out to kill each other. In the faces of Klan and Nazi men—and women—in North Carolina I saw people who would kill us all. I felt I needed to shift from perfecting consciousness to putting consciousness to the continual test of action. I wanted to answer a question that had resonated through the lesbian writing I had taken most to heart: "What will you undertake?"[43]

This, I believe, remains a dogged and crucial question before us and one that requires us to move beyond litanies ultimately based on only a narrow group's survival.

The tremendous strength of autonomous feminist institutions—the festivals, conferences, bookstores, women's studies departments, women's health centers—were the artistic, political, and social contributions activists helped to generate. All of these cultural institutions required women to ask of themselves and others a pivotal questions Audre Lorde had posited: Are you doing your work? And yet, by the mid-1980s, the resurgence of the radical Right in the United States that fueled a monumental backlash against gays and lesbians, people of color, and women across the races led multiracial feminists to ask again: Where and with whom are you doing your work? Many antiracist feminists who had helped to build the largely women-led cultural institutions that left a paper trail of multiracial feminism moved on, into mixed-gender, multiracial grassroots organizations, working against the Klan, in support of affirmative action and immigrant rights, and against police brutality and the prison industry. It is in these institutions that much of the hard work continues—in recognizing that "sisterhood is powerful" only when it is worked for and not assumed and that the "personal is political" only to the extent that one's politics go way beyond the confines of one's own individual experience.

Blueprints for Feminist Activism

There are multiple strategies for social justice embedded in multiracial feminism: a belief in building coalitions that are based on a respect for identity-based groups; attention to both process and product but little tolerance for "all-talk" groups; racial parity at every level of an organization (not added on later but initiated from the start); a recognition that race can not be seen in binary terms; a recognition that racism exists in your backyard as well as in the countries the United States is bombing or inhabiting economically; and a recognition of the limits of pacifism when people in struggle are up against the most powerful state in the world. Multiracial feminism is not just another brand of feminism that can be taught alongside liberal, radical, and socialist feminism. Multiracial feminism is the heart of an inclusive women's liberation struggle. The race-class-gender-sexuality-nationality framework through which multiracial feminism operates encompasses and goes way beyond liberal, radical, and socialist feminist priorities—and it always has. Teaching Second Wave feminist history requires chronicling how hegemonic feminism came to be written about as "the" feminism and the limits of that model. Teaching Second Wave history by chronicling the rise of multiracial feminism challenges limited categories because it puts social justice and antiracism a the center of attention. This does not mean that the work done within hegemonic feminism did not exist or was not useful. It does mean that it was limited in its goals and effectiveness.

Although the strategies for multiracial feminism were firmly established in the 1970s and 1980s, I contend that these principles remain a blueprint for progressive, feminist, antiracist struggle in this millennium. These are principles we will need in order to build on the momentum begun in Seattle (as activist energy shocked the World Trade Organization out of its complacency) while we refuse to reproduce the overwhelmingly white composition of most of the groups involved in that protest. We will need the principles introduced by multiracial feminism to sustain a critique of the punishment industry that accounts for the increasing number of women caught in the penal system. These are principles we will need to nurture what critical race theorist Mari Matsuda has named a "jurisprudence of antisubordination." Matsuda writes: "A jurisprudence of antisubordination is an attempt to bring home the lost ones, to make them part of the center, to end the soul-killing tyranny of inside/outside thinking. Accountability revisited. I want to bring home the women who hate their own bodies so much that they would let a surgeon's hand cut fat from it, or a man's batter and bruise it. I want to bring home the hungry ones eating from the trash bins; the angry ones who call me names; the little ones in foster care."[44] The principles of antisubordination embedded in multiracial femi-

nism, in antiracism feminism, are a crucial piece of this agenda.

Because written histories of social movements are typically one generation behind the movements themselves, it makes sense that the histories of the feminist movement are just now emerging. That timing means that now is the time to interrupt normative accounts before they begin to repeat themselves, each time, sounding more like "the truth" simply because of the repetition of the retelling. This interruption is necessary with regard to Second Wave feminism as well as earlier movements.

In her retrospective account of Black nationalism of the late 1960s and early 1970s, Angela Davis describes how broad-based nationalism has dropped almost completely out of the frame of reference in popular representations of the Black Power movement. This nationalism included alliances between Black and Chicano studies, in which students in San Diego were demanding the creation of a college called Lumumba-Zapata, and Huey Newton was calling for an end to "verbal gay bashing, urging an examination of black male sexuality, and calling for an alliance with the developing gay liberation movement." Davis writes: "I resent that the legacy I consider my own—one I also helped to construct—has been rendered invisible. Young people with 'nationalist' proclivities ought, at least, to have the opportunity to choose which tradition of nationalism they will embrace. How will they position themselves en masse in defense of women's rights, in defense of gay rights, if they are not aware of the historical precedents for such positionings?"[45]

In a parallel way, I want young women to know the rich, complicated, contentious, and visionary history of multiracial feminism and to know the nuanced controversies within Second Wave feminism. I want them to know that Shirley Chisholm ran for president in 1972; that Celestine Ware wrote a Black radical feminist text in the 1970s which offered an inspiring conception of revolution with a deep sense of humanity; that before Mab Segrest went to work for an organization against the Klan in North Carolina, she and others published an independent lesbian journal in the 1970s that included some of the most important and compelling race-conscious writing by white women and women of color to date.[46] I want people to know that there are antiracist feminist women currently in prison for their antiracist activism in the 1960s and since.[47] Among them is

Marilyn Buck, a poet, political prisoner and, in her words, "a feminist with a small 'f,'" who is serving an eighty-year sentence in California.[48] Her poems, including "To the Woman Standing Behind Me in Line Who Asks Me How Long This Black History Month Is Going to Last," eloquently capture why Buck must be included in tellings of multiracial feminism.[49] She writes:

> *the whole month*
> *even if it is the shortest month*
> *a good time in this prison life*
>
> you stare at me
> and ask why I think February is so damned fine
>
> I take a breath
> *prisoners fight for February*
> *African voices cross razor wire*
> *cut through the flim-flam*
> *of Amerikkan history*
> *call its cruelties out*
> *confirm the genius of survival*
> *creation and*
> *plain ole enduring*
>
> a celebration!
>
> ***
>
> The woman drops her gaze
> looks away and wishes
> she had not asked
> confused that white skin did not guarantee
> a conversation she wanted to have
>
> she hasn't spoken to me since
> I think I'll try to stand
> in line with her
> again

Marilyn Buck's poems and the work of other multiracial feminist activists help show that the struggle against racism is hardly linear, that the consolidation of white-biased feminism was clearly costly to early Second Wave feminism, and that we must dig deep to represent the feminist movement that does justice to an antiracist vision.

NOTES

The author would like to thank several people for their generous help on this article, especially Monisha Das Gupta, Diane Harriford, and two *Feminist Studies* anonymous reviewers.

1. For examples of histories that focus on white feminism, see Sheila Tobias, *Faces of Feminism: An Activist's Reflections on the Women's Movement* (Boulder: Westview Press, 1997); Barbara Ryan, *Feminism and the Women's Movement: Dynamics of Change in Social Movement Ideology and Activism* (New York: Routledge, 1992); Alice Echols, *Daring to Be Bad: Radical Feminism in America, 1967–1975* (Minneapolis: University of Minnesota Press, 1989).

2. Chela Sandoval, *Methodology of the Oppressed* (Minneapolis: University of Minnesota Press, 2000), 41–42.

3. Of these branches of feminism (liberal, socialist, and radical), socialist feminism, which treats sexism and classism as interrelated forms of oppression, may have made the most concerted effort to develop an antiracist agenda in the 1970s. For example, "The Combahee River Collective Statement" was first published in Zillah Eisenstein's *Capitalist Patriarchy and the Case for Socialist Feminism* (New York: Monthly Review Press, 1979), 362–72, before it was published in Barbara Smith's *Home Girls: A Black Feminist Anthology* (New York: Kitchen Table, Women of Color Press, 1983). *Radical America,* a journal founded in 1967 and whose contributors and editors include many social feminists, consistently published articles that examined the relationship between race, class, and gender. The 1970s' socialist feminist organization, the Chicago Women's Liberation Union, which considered quality public education, redistribution of wealth, and accessible childcare key to a feminist agenda, also made room for a race analysis by not privileging sexism over other forms of oppression. However, the fact that socialist feminist organizations were typically white dominated and were largely confined to academic and/or middle-class circles limited their effectiveness and visibility as an antiracist presence in early Second Wave feminism. For early socialist feminist documents, see Rosalyn Baxandall and Linda Gordon, eds., *Dear Sisters: Dispatches from the Women's Liberation Movement* (New York: Basic Books, 2000).

4. For an expanded discussion of the contributions and limitations of white antiracism from the 1950s to the present, see Becky Thompson, *A Promise and a Way of Life: White Antiracist Activism* (Minneapolis: University of Minnesota Press, 2001).

5. For a discussion of the term "multiracial feminism," see Maxine Baca Zinn and Bonnie Thornton Dill, "Theorizing Difference from Multiracial Feminism," *Feminist Studies* 22 (summer 1996): 321–31.

6. Bernice Johnson Reagon, "Coalition Politics: Turning the Century," in *Home Girls,* 356–69; Patricia Hill Collins, *Black Feminist Thought: Knowledge, Consciousness, and the Politics of Empowerment* (Boston: Unwin Hyman, 1990), 11; Barbara Smith, introduction, *Home Girls,* xxxii; Cherríe Moraga and Gloria Anzaldúa, eds., *This Bridge Called My Back: Writings by Radical Women of Color* (New York: Kitchen Table, Women of Color Press, 1981); Chandra Talpade Mohanty, "Under Western Eyes: Feminist Scholarship and Colonial

Discourses," in *Third World Women and the Politics of Feminism,* ed. Chandra Talpade Mohanty, Ann Russo, and Lourdes Torres (Bloomington: Indiana University Press, 1991), 51–80; Paula Gunn Allen, "Who Is Your Mother? Red Roots of White Feminism," in her *The Sacred Hoop: Recovering the Feminine in American Indian Traditions* (Boston: Beacon Press, 1986), 209–21; Adrienne Rich, *Blood, Bread, and Poetry* (New York: Norton 1986); Patricia Williams, *The Alchemy of Race and Rights* (Cambridge: Harvard University Press, 1991).

7. Here I am using the term "feminist" to describe collective action designed to confront interlocking race, class, gender, and sexual oppressions (and other systemic discrimination). Although many women in these organizations explicitly referred to themselves as "feminist" from their earliest political work, others have used such terms as "womanist," "radical women of color," "revolutionary," and "social activist." Hesitation among women of color about the use of the term "feminist" often signaled an unwillingness to be associated with white-led feminism, but this wariness did not mean they were not doing gender-conscious, justice work. The tendency not to include gender-conscious activism by women of color in dominant versions of Second Wave history unless the women used the term "feminist" fails to account for the multiple terms women of color have historically used to designate activism that keeps women at the center of analysis and attends to interlocking oppressions. Although the formation of a women's group—an Asian women's friendship group, a Black women's church group or a Native American women's arts council—is not inherently a feminist group, those organizations that confront gender, race, sexual, and class oppression, whether named as "feminist" or not, need to be considered as integral to multiracial feminism.

8. Benita Roth, "The Making of the Vanguard Center: Black Feminist Emergence in the 1960s and 1970s," in *Still Lifting, Still Climbing: African American Women's Contemporary Activism,* ed. Kimberly Springer (New York: New York University Press, 1999), 71.

9. Sherna Berger Gluck, "Whose Feminism, Whose History? Reflections on Excavating the History of (the) U.S. Women's Movement(s)," in *Community Activism and Feminist Politics: Organizing across Race, Class, and Gender,* ed. Nancy A. Naples (New York: Routledge, 1998), 38–39.

10. Miya Iwataki, "The Asian Women's Movement: A Retrospective," *East Wind* (spring/summer 1983): 35–41; Gluck, 39–41.

11. Sonia Shah, "Presenting the Blue Goddess: Toward a National Pan-Asian Feminist Agenda," in *The State of Asian America: Activism and Resistance in the 1990s,* ed. Karin Aguilar-San Juan (Boston: South End Press, 1994), 147–58.

12. M. Annette Jaimes with Theresa Halsey, "American Indian Women: At the Center of Indigenous Resistance in Contemporary North America," in *The State of Native America: Genocide, Colonization, and Resistance,* ed. M. Annette Jaimes (Boston: South End Press, 1992), 329.

13. Stephanie Autumn, ". . . This Air, This Land, This Water—If We Don't Start Organizing Now, We'll Lose It," *Big Mama Rag* 11 (April 1983): 4, 5.

14. For an insightful analysis of the multidimensionality of Black nationalism of the late 1960s and early 1970s, see Angela Davis, "Black Nationalism: The Sixties and the Nineties," in *The Angela Davis Reader,* ed. Joy James (Malden, Mass: Blackwell, 1998), 289–96.

15. Ibid., 15, 314.

16. Deborah Gray White, *Too Heavy a Load: Black Women in Defense of Themselves* (New York: Norton, 1999), 242.

17. Ibid., 242–53.

18. Combahee River Collective, "The Combahee River Collective Statement," in *Home Girls,* 272–82.

19. See Moraga and Anzaldúa.

20. Toni Cade, ed., *The Black Woman: An Anthology* (New York: Signet, 1970); Maxine Hong Kingston, *The Woman Warrior* (New York: Vintage Books, 1977); Moraga and Anzaldúa; Smith.

21. Assata Shakur, *Assata: An Autobiography* (Chicago: Lawrence Hill Books, 1987), 197.

22. Angela Davis, *Angela Davis: An Autobiography* (New York: Random House, 1974).

23. Nancy MacLean, "The Hidden History of Affirmative Action: Working Women's Struggles in the 1970s and the Gender of Class," *Feminist Studies* 25 (spring 1999): 47.

24. As a woman who was introduced to antiracist work through the feminist movement of the late 1970s—a movement shaped in large part by women of color who called themselves "womanists," "feminists," and "radical women of color"—I came to my interest in recasting the chronology of Second Wave feminism especially hoping to learn how white antiracist women positioned themselves vis-à-vis Second Wave feminism. I wanted to learn how sexism played itself out in the 1960s and how antiracist white women responded to Second Wave feminism. And I wanted to find our whether the antiracist baton carried in the 1960s was passed on or dropped by feminist activists.

One of the most compelling lessons I learned from white women who came of age politically before or during the civil rights and Black Power movements was how difficult it was for many of them to relate to or embrace feminism of the late 1960s and early 1970s. White antiracist women resisted sexism in SDS and in militant organizations. As they talked about the exclusions they faced in the 1960s' organizations and criticized early feminist organizing that considered gender oppression its main target, I realized how much different the feminist movement they saw in the early 1970s was from what I was introduced to in the late 1970s. By then, there was a critical mass of seasoned feminists who were keeping race at the center of the agenda. They were teaching younger feminists that race, class, gender, and sexuality are inextricably connected and that it is not possible to call oneself a feminist without dealing with race.

25. Several key Jewish feminist texts that addressed how to take racism and anti-Semitism seriously in feminist activism were published during this period and included Evelyn Torton Beck, ed., *Nice Jewish Girls: A Lesbian Anthology* (Trumansburg, N.Y.: Crossing Press, 1982); Melanie Kaye/Kantrowitz and Irena Klepfisz, eds., *The Tribe of Dina: A Jewish Women's Anthology* (Boston: Beacon Press, 1989), first published as a special issue of *Sinister Wisdom*, nos. 29/30 (1986); Melanie Kaye/Kantrowitz, *The Issue Is Power: Essays on Women, Jews, Violence, and Resistance* (San Francisco: Aunt Lute, 1992); Irena Klepfisz., *Periods of Stress* (Brooklyn, N.Y.: Out & Out Books, 1977), and *Keeper of Accounts* (Watertown, Mass: Persephone Press, 1982).

For key antiracist lesbian texts, see Adrienne Rich, *On Lies, Secrets, and Silence: Selected Prose, 1966–1978* (New York: Norton, 1979); Joan Gibbs and Sara Bennett, *Top Ranking: A Collection of Articles on Racism and Classism in the Lesbian Community* (New York: Come! Unity Press, 1980); Mab Segrest, *My Mama's Dead Squirrel: Lesbian Essays on Southern Culture* (Ithaca, N.Y.: Firebrand Books, 1985); Elly Bulkin, Minnie Bruce Pratt, and Barbara Smith, *Yours in Struggle: Three Feminist Perspectives on Anti-Semitism and Racism* (Brooklyn, N.Y.: Long Haul Press, 1984).

26. Ellen Willis, foreword to *Daring to Be Bad*, vii.

27. Barbara Ryan.

28. Howard Zinn, *A People's History of the United States* (New York: HarperPerennial, 1990), 504–13.

29. For a published version of Florynce Kennedy's position on Attica and Naomi Jaffe's perspective, see Barbara Smith, "'Feisty Characters' and 'Other People's Causes,'" in *The Feminist Memoir Project: Voices from Women's Liberation*, ed. Rachel Blau DuPlessis and Ann Snitow (New York: Three Rivers Press), 479–81.

30. Verta Taylor and Nancy Whittier, "The New Feminist Movement," in *Feminist Frontiers IV*, ed. Laurel Richardson, Verta Taylor, and Nancy Whittier (New York: McGraw-Hill, 1997), 544–45.

31. Chela Sandoval, "Feminism and Racism: A Report on the 1981 National Women's Studies Association Conference," in *Making Face, Making Soul: Haciendo Caras: Creative and Critical Perspectives by Women of Color*, ed. Gloria Anzaldúa (San Francisco: Aunt Lute, 1990), 55.

32. Smith, "'Feisty Characters,'" 470–80.

33. Gluck, 32.

34. James, 313.

35. Activists who helped Assata Shakur escape include political prisoners Marilyn Buck, Sylvia Baraldini, Susan Rosenberg, and Black male revolutionaries.

36. Adrienne Rich, "Disobedience and Women's Studies," *Blood, Bread, and Poetry* (New York: Norton, 1986), 76–84.

37. Moraga and Anzaldúa.

38. I am borrowing that phrase from Alice Echol's chronicling of white radical feminist history.

39. Lorraine Bethel, "What Chou Mean We, White Girl?" in *Conditions: Five* (1979): 86.

40. Wendy Rose, "The Great Pretenders: Further Reflections on Whiteshamanism," in *The State of Native America*, 403–23.

41. Thompson. See also Anne Braden, *The Wall Between* (Knoxville: University of Tennessee Press, 1999); Anne Braden, "A Second Open Letter to Southern White Women," *Southern Exposure* 6 (winter 1977): 50.

42. Segrest, *My Mama's Dead Squirrel*, 12.

43. Mab Segrest, "Fear to Joy: Fighting the Klan," *Sojourner: The Women's Forum* 13 (November 1987): 20.

44. Mari Matsuda, "Voices of America: Accent, Antidiscrimination Law, and a Jurisprudence for the Last Reconstruction," *Yale Law Journal* 100 (March 1991): 1405.

45. Davis, "Black Nationalism," 292.

46. See *Feminary: A Feminist Journal for the South Emphasizing Lesbian Visions*. Schlesinger Library at the Radcliffe Institute for Advanced Study at Harvard University has scattered issues of *Feminary*. Duke University Rare Book, Manuscript, and Special Collection Library has vols. 5–15 from 1974–1985. For analysis of the import of working on this journal on Mab Segrest's consciousness and activism, see Jean Hardisty, "Writer/Activist Mab Segrest Confronts Racism," *Sojourner: The Women's Forum* 19 (August 1994): 1–2; Segrest, *My Mama's Dead Squirrel*.

47. Marilyn Buck, Linda Evans, Laura Whitehorn, and Kathy Boudin are among the white political prisoners who are either currently in prison or, in the case of Laura Whitehorn and Linda Evans, recently released, serving sentences whose length and severity can only be understood as retaliation for their principled, antiracist politics.

48. Marilyn Buck is in a federal prison in Dublin, California, for alleged conspiracies to free political prisoners, to protest government policies through the use of violence, and to raise funds for Black liberation organizations.

49. Marilyn Buck's poem, "To the Woman Standing behind Me in Line Who Asks Me How Long This Black History Month Is Going to Last," is reprinted with written permission from the author.

Common Threads
Life Stories and the Arts in Educating for Social Change
Cynthia Cohen

Introduction

The Oral History Center for Education and Action, (OHC), a community organization currently located at the Center for Innovation in Urban Education at Northeastern University in Boston, uses oral history methods and the arts for the purpose of strengthening communities. Our work is informed by a strong multicultural and antiracist perspective; it is designed to facilitate the kinds of understanding needed to build alliances across differences.

The OHC's model is based on the idea that everyone has an important story to tell. It emphasizes an attentive quality of listening that can be transformative for both the listener and the teller. It also integrates the arts, in ways that nourish people's imagination, validate diverse cultures, and reach large audiences. The model evolved out of two projects I coordinated under the auspices of The Cambridge Arts Council, in 1980 through 1982: The Cambridge Women's Oral History Project (CWOHP) and the Cambridge Women's Quilt Project (CWQP). This article describes those two projects, as well as others the OHC sponsored during the years when I was its director, from 1982 through 1990.

The Cambridge Women's Oral History Project

In the CWOHP, high school students collected stories from their own and others' cultural communities. We chose the theme "transitions in women's lives" because the young women themselves were undergoing many transitions, and also because it

could embrace the experience of women from all groups in the city, including recent immigrants. The young women conducted interviews (mostly in English, but also in Haitian Creole, Portuguese and Spanish), indexed tapes, and created a visual exhibit incorporating photographic portraits, excerpts of oral narrative, and brief biographies. Working with the staff of the project, they created a slide-tape show "Let Life Be Yours: Voices of Cambridge Working Women," which focuses on the theme of work in women's lives. "Let Life Be Yours" asks a question: How have women's cultural and economic backgrounds affected their ability to make choices in their lives? Answers can be found in the women's stories.

> Antonia Cruz, a recent immigrant from Puerto Rico: "My father wanted to take me out of school, because it was too expensive, he said. They were poor, they took me out of school in the fifth grade."

> Addie Eskin, a Jewish woman born near Boston: "'What do you mean you have to go to high school, what do you have to go to high school for?' she said. 'Your father is very sick, what do you think, you're gonna go to school and hold your hand out?' And I said, 'Auntie, if I have to wear this middy blouse for the next four years, I'm going to graduate from high school.'"

> Henrietta Jackson, a black woman born in Cambridge: "One of the newspapers called Cambridge High and Latin School, and asked the office practice teacher if she had any good student who might want a few hours every day after school in the newspaper office. I was considered one of the fastest typists and I went with two other girls. I was rejected immediately. And she called them and she was practically told they weren't quite ready for a black

Records of the Oral History Center (1978–1998) are housed at Northeastern University: http://www.lib.neu.edu/archives/collect/findaids/m73find.htm.

person. She said that it will be a long time before there won't be this kind of unfair treatment of a person whose only fault is that she happens to have a black face."

Catherine Zirpolo, an Italian woman born in Boston: "1914. I was fortunate, I didn't have to go to work . . . being an only child. . . . When I became of age to go to high school, I wasn't a bit interested in high school. I wanted to be an actress even then. . . ."

When the older women who participated in the Cambridge Women's Oral History Project told stories about the obstacles they faced, they revealed inspiring spiritual strength. The project's political message (i.e., opposing oppression based on race, class and gender) is all the more powerful because their language is personal and accessible, devoid of rhetoric. In evaluation interviews at the end of the project, the young women involved reported that their participation in the project had changed their ideas about older people, about the study of history, and about working with women:

Books are dull, but this way I get enjoyment out of history. . . . Winona and I have had really different lives. She's black and I'm white; I have more opportunities with education, work, and money. She's religious. There's a strength about her, so it's nice to talk to her. She's the kind of inspiring person that makes us want to go out and read and read good books and take it in. She makes you see how somebody can be at peace with things. Part of this is kind of making up for what I couldn't find from my own grandmother.

The people changed my opinions a lot. . . . Older people are pretty active in the community; they have a lot to say, most of them. They are just older, not feeble or anything. I used to see them like stereotypes, as people who sat back and watched the world go by. But they have a big part while it goes by. I never realized that. I got a lot out of seeing women work together. It gives you a sense of self-respect, a sense that I'm a valuable person. You see women working together and taking each other seriously and you know it's there and you know it should be there all the time.

Since its completion in 1984, "Let Life Be Yours" has been translated into Portuguese, Haitian Creole and Spanish. It has been used as the basis for community education programs on women's history, multicultural issues, older people's lives, and oral history methods.

The Cambridge Women's Quilt Project

The Oral History Center's second major project involved sixty women and girls, ranging in age from eight to eighty, working in collaboration with two fabric artists to create images from their lives in fabric. The project was designed as a study of the historical, social and cultural factors that influenced changes in women's lives. Also we intended to reflect on quilt-making: its function in women's lives, and its relationship to oral tradition. Through the project, we were able to enact the very subjects we were studying. For instance, many women and girls found that their participation in the project was itself producing changes in their lives. As has been a part of the American quilting bee tradition historically, participants in the project shared medical and political information, reflected together on their relationships with boys and men, and gained perspective on the decisions they were facing. They felt themselves becoming part of a community.

The fabric artists supported each woman to create her own image of a story from her own life. One was about braiding a daughter's hair and another about a great-grandmother quilting. Others were about lighting Sabbath candles, dressing up to go to church, riding a donkey in Haiti, making wine in Italy, the dream of walking freely outside at night, hitchhiking throughout Europe and Africa, making life rafts during World War II, giving birth at home, reading alone in one's bedroom, reading to a group of neighborhood children, a childhood picking cotton in the South and a childhood dream of becoming a ballerina.

Our respect for each woman's expression was put to the test when one woman depicted in her quilt patch a child, pants rolled down, being spanked by his parent. When asked to document something important for history, this participant had chosen to represent "a time when parents cared enough about their children to set limits, to punish them when necessary." Other participants were upset by the expression of what they took to be violent: not only the spanking itself, but the humiliation of the child, with his bare bottom exposed. Through discussion, compromise was reached: the patch remained, but restitched with rolled-up pants.

In other ways too, the project created a congruence between the content and methods of our inquiry. For instance, women and girls depicted women weaving rugs, making lace and quilting, and here we were, making a quilt. Several patches honored women as bearers of traditional food ways: a Jamaican aunt carrying fruits home from market on her head, a Mennonite grandmother baking a cherry pie, and an Irish Nana heating tea. As we shared traditional foods and recipes at our potlucks, we were enacting as well as documenting this dimension of women's experience.

A total of 52 fabric images were sewn into two vibrant quilts. Some of the participants tape recorded interviews about the meaning of each patch; these oral narratives were edited into a catalog. Finally, a group of younger women worked with singer/songwriter Betsy Rose to compose a ballad, sung to a traditional Portuguese melody, based on the stories of the quilt patches. The ballad became the audio background for a slide-tape on the making of the quilts.

Informal conversations as well as the more formal sharing of stories in interviews were understood to be an important aspect of the projects. As one participant said,

> People who came were very shy and really, you couldn't see a visible importance about their lives. But once the little quilt square opened it was like they came alive. Everybody was so enthusiastic and one story led to another. . . . Maybe the most important thing about the quilt project was that the women who did it enjoyed each other and talked to each other. . . . There was no performance, and no being performed. Everybody is on stage. Everybody's the song. Everybody's the story teller.

Since their completion in 1982, the quilts have been exhibited in the neighborhoods of the city, at local festivals, and in libraries, stores, churches, schools and cultural and social service organizations. They have traveled to several other New England cities, and as far away as the International Women's Forum in Nairobi, Kenya, and to meetings of the Belize Rural Women's Association in Central America. In one of our most engaging exhibits, viewers of the quilts at the Boston Children's Museum could use nearby computer terminals to call up edited versions of the interview narratives according to a number of different categories.

Common Threads

As we watched women and girls from different ethnic communities interacting as they sewed the quilts, it became clear that fabric arts were familiar media in which many women felt comfortable expressing themselves. In fact, many of the participants in the quilt project were steeped in the skills and customs of rich fabric traditions such as Portuguese lace-making, Haitian embroidery, African-American appliqué quilting, as well as knitting, crocheting and sewing. Activities using fabric gave women and girls the chance to feel a sense of accomplishment for their skills (generally unacknowledged, even within their own communities), and to learn about one another's lives and cultures.

We used these insights to design Common Threads, an exhibit and series of events which highlighted the stories and work of ten traditional and contemporary fabric artists, each from a different local ethnic community. The exhibit, displayed at a branch of the local library and in the high school, consisted of samples of fabric art such as lace, embroidery, batik, appliqué and crochet, along with the life stories of the women who created the pieces. At several events, members of English-as-a-Second-Language classes and others in the community were invited to bring their own fabric work and other crafts, and to share stories about their lives and their work.

Following the exhibit, the OHC collaborated with several local organizations to sponsor a visit to Cambridge of two Chilean *arpilleristas*, women who use small burlap tapestries to depict the harsh realities of daily life under the dictatorship of Augusto Pinochet. One of the *arpilleristas*, for instance, used a series of her tapestries to document her ten-year search for her son, detained by the military police shortly after Pinochet came to power. Many of the community women who participated in Common Threads and the Cambridge Women's Quilt Project attended a workshop with the *arpilleristas,* making an immediate connection through their common interest in storytelling through fabric. The following year, the OHC built on this awareness by sponsoring our own Stories-in-Fabric workshop, and the resulting tapestries were taken to the International Women's Forum in Nairobi, Kenya.

Because the Common Threads exhibit was temporary, we created a slide-tape show, which explores the social, political, economic and artistic meanings of fabric art in the lives of women. The slide show has been used in educational programs with groups of older people, fabric artists and students of women's history.

Lifelines

In addition to conducting women's oral history projects in community settings, the OHC also collaborated with teachers to adapt its model to a classroom context. Lifelines was a curriculum development project, designed to support fifth through eighth grade and bilingual teachers to incorporate oral history into on-going Social Studies and Language Arts curricula. Two teachers, for example, worked with students on labor history projects. In one case, students created a visual exhibit combining excerpts of interviews with parents and older workers with statistical analyses of the shifting economic base of the city. In the other classroom, students interviewed six women who worked in Cambridge factories during the 1930s and 1940s, and produced an illustrated timeline, visual exhibit, and slide-tape show about the changing patterns of women's work in the Depression, World War II, and the post-war eras. Three Lifelines classes explored topics in family and ethnic studies.

The arts were especially important in a Lifelines project in a Haitian bilingual class. The project was designed specifically to enhance self-esteem. The Haitian students were at the bottom of the social hierarchy at their school. They were teased about their language, their body odor, the possibility of being carriers of AIDS. These assaults on their integrity were sustained while they were struggling to learn a new language, to adjust to separation from members of their families, and often while they were recovering from the political violence and the extreme poverty that had led their families to leave the island whose landscape and culture they still cherished.

Students who had been in the U.S. for just two or three years interviewed Haitian adults who worked in careers of interest to the children. As they began to hear the stories of the adults of their own community validated and celebrated in their classroom, there began an outpouring of expression from them: stories and especially pictures of their lives in Haiti and their bewildering encounters with an American city. With help from a student intern from Harvard, the students created a slide-tape show, "We Are Proud of Who We Are," in which they narrated the stories told them by adults. They also worked with a storyteller to prepare performances of their own narratives. The children's stories and artwork, exhibited in the school corridors, provided contexts for relationship-building between the teachers and administrators in the school's monolingual program and the Haitian children. In subsequent years, students created notecards embellished with their drawings of images from their lives, and sold the cards to raise funds for an eye clinic in Haiti. The entire school participated in that effort, and later a group traveled to Haiti to visit a sister school. Through this project, the students began to realize the possibilities inherent in their own expression, and to understand that they were not only documentors, but makers, of history.

A Passion for Life: Stories and Folk Arts of Palestinian Women

During the same years we were working in collaboration with the Cambridge Public School on Lifelines, one of the women drawn to our Stories-in-Fabric series became involved in the OHC. Her name was Feryal Abbasi Ghnaim, and she worked as a traditional Palestinian embroiderer. Her interests and skills helped define our next major oral history project, A Passion for Life: Stories and Folk Arts of Palestinian and Jewish Women. The project was designed to explore whether stories and folk arts could be used to facilitate communication not just across differences, but across the chasm created by long-standing political conflict and violence.

The project's final exhibition displayed the stories of eight Jewish and Palestinian women, along with objects of folk expression, such as baskets, embroidered dresses, family photographs and cooking utensils. Eighteen public events preceded and accompanied the exhibition; these ranged from sessions of sharing recipes, songs, dance and visual arts, to a theoretical discussion on the role of folk arts in communities in crisis and a workshop on challenging stereotypes of Arab and Jewish people. The members of the project's Directions Committee, which consisted of both Jewish and Palestinian women and others, wrote at the time that we were looking for modes of expression which would invite people in conflict to reach beneath their defenses and their fears, so they could come to recognize each other's humanity:

> In spite of our many differences, we believe there is wisdom in the perspectives of women, who are striving day to day, sometimes under harsh oppression, to create their lives and to recreate culture and community for their children. There is value in the stories of these regular common people who do the mundane but richly detailed work of sowing seeds and harvesting fruits, preparing foods and cleaning homes, fixing remedies and stitching cloth, selling goods and listening to the stories people share when they come together to celebrate, to grieve and to pass on traditions.
>
> The stories and works of art in our exhibition include descriptions of the tragedy of the Palestinian Diaspora and the oppression of Palestinian people under Israeli occupation. They speak to the terrible persecution which Jewish people have endured throughout history, most horrifyingly manifested in Europe during World War II.
>
> We bring these stories together in one exhibition not to suggest any simple parallels, but to create a vision broad enough to embrace them all. As we listen to stories from both Jewish and Palestinian women, we share feelings of sadness and anger, sometimes outrage. We believe that nothing excuses acts of inhumanity. Has the world not seen enough of families divided, homes and communities destroyed? Have there not been enough precious heirlooms confiscated, people imprisoned, children murdered? How can this fragile fabric of our lives, which we and our mothers and our grandmothers have stitched so carefully—note by note, spoonful by spoonful, caress by caress, story by story—be so brutally torn to shreds?
>
> We engage with this work out of a deep love for our own traditions and an appreciation for the richness of the others'.
>
> We recognize the deep-seated fears of both Palestinian and Jewish people. We are working towards a world in which we all are safe to preserve and develop our cultures. We are inspired by the passion for life which permeates these women's stories and their art: the impulse to create beauty, to nourish children, to take risks, to resist oppression, to celebrate community; and the determination to survive, both physically and spiritually, against forces of brutality and destruction.
>
> Take inspiration from these stories to reach out to each other with openness and respect. Let them motivate you to take a stand for justice and to work for peace.

A Passion for Life proved to be more difficult than we ever could have imagined at the outset. Sometimes it seemed to be little more than a snarl of ethical dilemmas, demanding relationships and intense emotions. At times, both Feryal and I, the project's co-directors, felt pressured by members of our families and communities to withdraw from the project. Key people from both communities chose not to participate, and in a couple of cases, backed out at the last minute. In retrospect, it seems like a miracle that we ever managed to bring the eight women's stories under one roof, even for just a couple of months.

Among the many conflicts we needed to resolve in the course of the project, the most contentious were misunderstandings about language, and our lack of awareness of the meanings and resonances of specific words for members of each other's communities. For many Palestinians, for instance, the word "peace," unless immediately followed by the word "justice," had come to signify a criticism of Palestinian resistance to the Israeli occupation. It was a kind of a code, understood by many Jewish people, who had themselves come to perceive the word "justice" as pro-Palestinian. The word "1948" also resonated very differently for members of each community. For Palestinians, 1948 is the year of the *nakba,* or disaster. It is the year of the dispersion, when many Palestinians were dispossessed of their land, the year when the fabric of their lives was permanently rent. Nineteen-forty-eight is the year of the massacre of the citizens of Deir Yessin, a Palestinian village plundered by members of two Jewish right-wing terrorist organizations. Thousands of Palestinians fled from their homes in fear of a repetition of Deir Yessin. For most Jewish people, on the other hand, 1948 marks the creation of the state of Israel, a time of rejoicing in the fulfillment of a dream of a homeland—a symbol that evokes images of security, justice, democracy, and the possibility of a post-holocaust renewal. It isn't just that one group views the history as victors and the other as a people defeated, but that each places the events of the year within a different frame of historical reference.

The most problematic and emotionally charged meanings were encoded in the phrase "the Holocaust." The emotional resonances which surround the memory of the holocaust, the politically motivated abuses of holocaust imagery by both sides, and the disparate meanings which are attached to the word may be among the central barriers to Palestinian-Jewish reconciliation. While most Palestinians and Jews understand each others' readings of the words "peace" and "justice," often they are unaware of the different resonances of references to the holocaust. For most Jews of Eastern European background, the holocaust is a sacred memory. Less than [sixty-five] years ago, a third of the Jewish people were killed, and this fact still defines communal reality.

What happened in Europe—the systematic obliteration of thousands of communities; the destruction of Yiddishkeit as a living culture; the challenge to Jewish understanding of God, and justice and faith; the magnitude of the suffering and the devastation underscoring the meaning of being homeless in the world—all of this is the context in which contemporary Jews of European heritage came to define their individual and collective identity.

From a Palestinian perspective, "the holocaust" is what they have repeatedly heard as an excuse for the inexcusable brutality and injustice to which they have been subjected. European and American guilt about it was a major factor in turning world opinion to support the Zionist claim to Israel. Palestinian people feel that they are being made to suffer for Europe's crimes, and that somehow the significance of their own suffering diminishes when it is compared to the holocaust. A Palestinian friend once said to me: "Don't put me beside a holocaust survivor; I feel like nothing. How can my suffering compare?"

While Jewish people feel a need to honor the memory of the holocaust by retelling the story and by bearing witness to the tragedy, many Palestinian people are weary of hearing the story. "Why do they have to tell us this story?" asked Feryal. "We are the ones who are suffering now." The documentaries and fictional renditions of the holocaust story on TV often culminate with hopeful references to the new state of Israel, accompanied by images which either demonize Arabs or render their true experience invisible. These are especially painful because of the media's relative silence about Palestinian history and culture, its muteness about Palestinian suffering and legitimate needs for security.

Throughout A Passion for Life, in spite of these misunderstandings of words, there were moments when Palestinian and Jewish people began to understand each other's point of view, to feel each other's suffering, to recognize themselves in each other's aspirations. This happened through hearing each other's stories, and seeing and appreciating each other's artistic work. After hearing the stories of Palestinian women who had become friends, one Jewish woman acknowledged for instance that she had never realized that Jewish people in Israel were living in the actual dwellings which had once belonged to Palestinian families. One Palestinian woman said that although she had known about the holocaust before, she had never truly felt the enormity of it. After seeing Feryal describe the symbols in her embroidery, an older Jewish man, a committed supporter of Israel, commented that he had never realized that Palestinian women were telling stories in their embroidery.

Often, A Passion for Life seemed like an enormous landscape, clouded by terror and confusion. It often seemed that what we were attempting was actually impossible. But, all along, there were moments when the terrain would shift, creating new contours of possibility. These openings, made possible by our caring for each other and by the power of stories and the arts, enlarged our imagination and deepened our yearning for reconciliation. These were the moments that sustained us in our work. Once after a particularly difficult phase of the project, Feryal and I spoke together at a gathering of people from both communities. She showed her beautiful tapestry of a Palestinian woman holding aloft a dove. In its beak is an envelope carrying this message:

Women of the world: Women love peace to raise their children in, so why don't you make peace your number one goal? I as a Palestinian know intimately that there are two kinds of peace. (1) Peace that is built on the bodies of those brutalized and murdered to silence their calls for their just rights; (2) peace which comes from understanding a people's suffering, sitting down with them to genuinely solve and resolve their problems, so that justice and equality can be the code of the land, not death and suffering.

Why don't we, women, raise our voices high and strong in the service of true peace to preserve our children, our future as human beings? I ask you to support my call for true peace for my people. We are not subhumans. We are people with history and civilization. We are mothers and fathers and children. We have had enough killing and Diaspora. I smuggled my dreams in my hidden wishes and crossed the ocean in hope for peace; for my Palestinian sisters who lost their children in wars and who have been widowed at an early age. I ask you for true peace for my people.

I followed Feryal by reading an excerpt from the extraordinary autobiography of Heda Margolius Ko-

valy, in which she recounts the events of her life in Prague from 1941 through 1968:

> Three forces carved the landscape of my life. Two of them crushed half the world. The third was very small and weak, and, actually, invisible. It was a shy little bird hidden in my rib cage an inch or two above my stomach. Sometimes in the most unexpected moments the bird would wake up, lift its head, and flutter its wings in rapture. Then I too would lift my head because, for that short moment, I would know for certain that love and hope are infinitely more powerful than hate and fury, and that, somewhere beyond the line of my horizon there was life indestructible, always triumphant.
>
> The first force was Adolf Hitler; the second was Iosif Stalin. They made my life a microcosm in which the history of a small country in the heart of Europe was condensed. The little bird, the third force, kept me alive to tell the story.

When I finished reading Kovaly's words, Feryal leaned over and pointed to the dove in her tapestry. "You see," she whispered, "it's the same bird."

EIGHTY

◆◆◆

Research on Women in Legislatures
What Have We Learned, Where Are We Going?

Michele Swers

Even before women secured the right to vote, members of Progressive Era women's groups demanded the appointment of women to public offices ranging from the school board to the labor bureau because they believed that female officeholders would consider the needs of children and the family and they would eliminate corruption in government (Baker 1984; Skocpol 1992). Similarly, the rise of feminism led to the creation of numerous political actions committees (PACs) that raise money to support women candidates who pledge support to specific issues including abortion

rights and the Equal Rights Amendment (Burrell 1994; Nelson 1994). These feminist groups believe that electing women will lead to a "feminization of politics" in which female legislators will make the interests of women, children, and families a central part of the national agenda and they will reform the very process by which public policy is made. To evaluate these long-held beliefs about women's impact on the political process, scholars of women in the state legislatures and Congress have focused their research on three broad areas: the experience of women as candidates, the policy impact of women as legislators, and the relationship of women to the institutions in which they serve. In this paper I review the major research findings in each of these three areas and I suggest directions for future research.

Women as Candidates

In the early years, particularly before World War II, the most common way for a woman to attain elective office was by inheriting the seat of her deceased husband (Gertzog 1995; Werner 1966). Despite the recent publicity dedicated to the Senate election of Jean Carnahan (D-MD), the widow of former governor and Senate candidate Mel Carnahan, the phenomenon of the congressional widow is largely a relic of the past as women, like men, compete as individuals for party nominations and political office.

The fact that women currently constitute only 13.6 percent of the House of Representatives, 13 percent of the Senate, and 22.3 percent of state legislatures raises the question of why more women are not elected to public office (Center for the American Woman and Politics 2000). Research reveals that the single greatest obstacle to the election of women is the "incumbency factor." Since incumbents are reelected at a rate of more than 90 percent, it is very difficult for challengers to gain legislative seats (Jacobson 1997; Palmer and Simon 2001). Studies comparing men and women in similar races, including open seat contestants, challengers, and incumbents, find that women win just as often as men (Darcy and Schramm 1977; Deber 1982; Darcy, Welch, and Clark 1994; Carroll 1994; Burrell 1994; Seltzer, Newman, and Voorhees Leighton 1997; Gaddie, Hoffman, and Palmer 2001). Additionally, research demonstrates that there is no gender gap in fundraising (Uhlaner and Schlozman 1986; Biersack and Hernson 1994; Burrell 1994, Darcy, Welch, and Clark 1994), although Herrick (1996) suggests that male challengers receive a larger benefit from each dollar raised than do female challengers.

Given the fact that women who run win, scholars must focus more attention on the stages before the campaign to understand why more women do not run for office. Does the paucity of women candidates reflect the underrepresentation of women in the occupations that lead to political careers (Nechemias 1987; Carroll 1994; Darcy, Welch, and Clark

1994; Duerst-Lahti 1998; McGlen and O'Connor 1998), the dearth of women in the local and state government positions that provide the necessary political experience to run for higher levels of office (Carroll and Strimling 1998; Darcy, Welch, and Clark 1994; Carroll 1994), the uneven distribution of and expectations concerning family responsibilities (Nechemias 1985; Dodson 1997; Duerst-Lahti 1998), or the recruitment patterns of political parties (Rule 1981; Bledsoe and Herring 1990; Carroll 1994; van Assendelft and O'Connor 1994; Niven 1998)?

While the studies of election outcomes indicate that men and women are equally successful in attracting votes, research on gender stereotypes demonstrates that voters view male and female candidates differently and these differences may impact their votes. Voter stereotypes generally fall into two categories, trait stereotypes and issue/belief stereotypes. With regard to personality traits, voters view women candidates as more compassionate and willing to compromise, while men are seen as more assertive and self-confident. On issues, voters view female candidates as more ideologically liberal than men and they favor women on such issues as education, health care, and welfare while they perceive men as more capable of handling the economy, military crises, and crime (Huddy and Terkildsen 1993a; 1993b; Burrell 1994; Alexander and Anderson 1993; Sapiro 1981–82; McDermott 1997).

Although numerous studies document the existence of voter stereotypes, scholars must illuminate more carefully the conditions in which these stereotypes affect actual votes. Since many of these studies are conducted as experiments in college classrooms (for example, Sapiro 1981–82; Huddy and Terkildsen 1993a, 1993b), it is not clear how much gender stereotypes influenced voters' decisions in the electoral arena. For instance, knowledge of the candidate's party affiliation may overshadow the use of gender stereotypes. Alternately, voters may only rely on gender stereotypes in "low-information" elections, when little is known about the candidates (Alexander and Anderson 1993; McDermott 1997). Thus, researchers should examine whether voters are more likely to rely on gender stereotypes in primary elections when party affiliation is held constant, rather than in the general election (King and Matland forthcoming). Similarly, voters may be more likely to utilize gender stereotypes in races that do not garner as much media attention, such as in a local election rather than a highly publicized U.S. Senate race (McDermott 1997) or for offices that draw on traditional male characteristics, such as attorney general, or female characteristics, such as superintendent of schools (Oxley and Fox 2000).

It is also possible that the damaging effects of gender stereotypes increase at higher levels of office. Dolan (1997) suggests that there is a glass ceiling, in which support for women candidates declines at higher levels of office, particularly among male voters. On the other hand, in the right electoral environment, voter stereotypes can favor women candidates. For example, analyses of the 1992 election indicate that the primary role of women's issues in the presidential and congressional campaigns and the media's combined focus on women's issues and the underrepresentation of women in office helped women candidates, particularly those who emphasized gender issues in their campaigns (Biersack and Hernson 1994; Jelen 1994; Schroedel and Snyder 1994; Chaney and Sinclair 1994; Wilcox 1994; Plutzer and Zipp 1996; Fox 1997; Dolan 2001).

Beyond analyses of voter choice, more research is needed on the experience of women in campaigns, particularly their treatment by their opponents, the political parties, and the media. For example, Fox (1997) found that women candidates in California ran a different kind of campaign than men, in which they used a more personal style of campaigning and were more likely to emphasize their credentials to compensate for the assumption that a woman is less qualified. Additionally, he found that male candidates running against women changed their strategies to place greater emphasis on women's issues than they would if they were running against a male opponent.

The role that political parties play in encouraging or discouraging the candidacies of women for state-level and national office is still unclear. Baer (1993) calls the political parties the missing variable in women and politics research. Research conducted in the 1970s and early 1980s highlighted the tendency of parties to run women as sacrificial lambs in contests the parties had little chance of winning (Gertzog and Simard 1981; Deber 1982). However, the increased attention to the gender gap since the early 1980s has led both the Republican and Democratic parties to create committees and structures within their national party institutions to facilitate efforts to recruit, train, and fund women candidates for Con-

gress (Jennings 1990; Burrell 1994). Studies that focus on the fundraising patterns of male and female candidates do not indicate any partisan bias against women candidates (Biersack and Hernson 1994; Burrell 1994; Herrick 1995).

While numerous scholars view the political parties as a positive force for increasing the presence of women in Congress and the state legislatures (Bernstein 1986; Bledsoe and Herring 1990; Burrell 1994; Carroll 1994; Darcy, Welch, and Clark 1994; Thomas 1994), a recent study by David Niven (1998) cautions against the assumption that the parties are no longer biased against women candidates. Surveying party chairs and female local legislators in four states, Niven found that male party chairs do discriminate against women in their recruitment patterns. He attributed this biased treatment to an outgroup effect in which party leaders relate positively to those potential candidates seen as being similar to themselves, while candidates viewed as dissimilar are thought to be part of a homogeneous and less valued group. Therefore, Niven concludes that the "old boys network" is still a powerful deterrent to women's candidacies, since a predominantly male party elite is less likely to recognize the merits of a potential female candidate.

While the political parties remain a significant force in legislative elections, the rise of the candidate-centered campaign highlights the importance of the media. The growing influence of the media in electoral campaigns requires a better understanding of the media's impact on women candidates and their campaigns. Kahn (1992, 1994a, 1994b, 1996) finds that the media does discriminate against women in the amount of coverage they receive in their Senate and gubernatorial races, in the quality of that coverage, and in the extent to which that coverage reflects the messages issued by the campaign. Other scholars maintain that the media portray women as less viable candidates than men and reporters focus a disproportionate amount of attention on their family situation, their appearance, and their position on women's issues (Witt, Piaget, and Matthews 1995; Braden 1996; Smith 1997; Vavrus 1998; Rausch, Rozell, and Wilson 1999; Kropf and Boiney 2001). This discriminatory coverage of female politicians continues once they reach elective office (Braden 1996; Carroll and Schreiber 1997; Niven and Zilber 2001). Future research must continue to investigate the differences in the ways men and women conduct their

campaigns and the ways in which the media and the electoral environment impact the success of women candidates.

The Policy Impact of Women in Congress and the State Legislatures

The overarching question facing those who study the policy impact of women in legislatures is whether descriptive representation, the election of women, leads to substantive representation—legislation on behalf of women's interests (Pitkin 1967). To answer this question, we first must demonstrate that women have distinct interests that require representation as members of a group and not just as individuals. Scholars focusing on representational theory assert that women do have distinct interests, which are based both on their private and public sphere responsibilities and the tension of integrating their private and public sphere roles (Sapiro 1981; Phillips 1991, 1995, 1998; Mansbridge 1999). Additionally, women's concerns are relatively new to the public agenda and have largely been ignored by politicians. Finally, since women as a group have historically been excluded from the political arena, women must be elected to provide role models for other women and to demonstrate that politics is not only a male domain (Shapiro 1981; Mansbridge 1999).

Evidence from the States

Scholars interested in delineating the policy impact of electing women originally focused their attention on the state legislatures because more women have served in the state legislatures than in Congress. Studies of women in state legislatures in the 1970s found differences in the attitudes of female legislators, but few differences in their policy priorities. For example, female state legislators expressed more liberal attitudes than men on feminist issues such as support for the ERA, public funding of day care, and the liberalization of abortion laws (Diamond 1977; Johnson et al. 1978). However, when asked to rank their policy priorities, these priorities were not significantly different from the legislative focus of their male colleagues (Mezey 1978; Thomas 1994). Thomas (1994) asserts that the slow acceptance of women into the political arena discouraged women from translating their more liberal policy attitudes into legislative priorities, since women were not willing to risk their standing in the legislature to pursue issues that were not viewed as legitimate by their male colleagues.

Additionally, women serving in the state legislatures in the 1970s were not fully integrated into the institutions in which they served. Women were disproportionately concentrated on committees that incorporate the traditional concerns of women, such as education, health, and welfare. Compared to their male colleagues, female legislators devoted more attention to constituency service and reported lower levels of activity in areas including speaking in committee and on the floor, working with colleagues, and bargaining with lobbyists (Kirkpatrick 1974; Diamond 1977; Thomas 1994). The focus on constituency service reflected women's background in community service, while women's lower rates of participation in the substance of legislative work was attributed to feelings of inefficacy that stemmed from the difficulty of adapting to the norms of a male-dominated institution (Kirkpatrick 1974; Diamond 1977; Thomas 1994).

As the number of women in state legislatures increased throughout the 1980s and the role of women in the public sphere became increasingly accepted, female state legislators became full participants in all legislative activities and began to pursue distinctive agendas. The evidence from studies since the 1980s demonstrates that women serving in the state legislatures exhibit unique policy priorities, particularly in the area of women's issues. In her comprehensive study of sex differences in legislative behavior across twelve legislatures, Thomas (1994) found that women held more liberal attitudes on policy issues than did their male colleagues. Additionally, women were more likely than their male counterparts to include legislation concerning women, children, and families among their top priorities and they were more successful in their efforts to pass these bills into law. These gender-related differences persisted across legislative bodies that differed by region of the country, political culture, and the proportion of women in the legislature.

In multi-state analyses and longitudinal studies of single legislatures, scholars have found that in comparison to men, female legislators are more liberal in their policy attitudes and they exhibit a greater commitment to the pursuit of feminist initiatives and legislation incorporating issues of traditional concern to women, including education, health, and welfare (Saint-Germain 1989; Dodson and Carroll 1991; Berkman and O'Connor 1993; Thomas 1994; Dolan and Ford 1995). Women are more likely to see their women's issue proposals passed into law (Saint-Germain 1989; Thomas 1994). In addition to differences in policy behavior, researchers found that women display a unique view of their representational role. Female legislators expressed a sense of responsibility to represent the interests of women,

and they were more likely than men to view women as a distinct part of their constituency (Reingold 1992; Thomas 1994, 1997). Some scholars maintain that women exhibit a distinctive way of thinking about policy problems; thus, in her analysis of crime policy, Kathlene (1995) notes that women favored rehabilitative initiatives while men preferred proposals concerning punishment.

By examining legislative behavior across time and in different states, scholars found that the sex differences in the policy priorities of members gained strength as the proportion of women in the legislature approached a "critical mass" (Saint-Germain 1989; Berkman and O'Connor 1993; Thomas 1994). Drawing on the theories of Rosabeth Moss Kanter (1977) concerning the impact of proportions on groups, these researchers noted that as women increase their numbers in the legislature, they feel more free to pursue policy preferences based on gender.[1] Additionally, Thomas (1994) and Saint-Germain (1989) maintain that the presence of a women's caucus provides women with additional resources beyond their numbers, thus reducing the negative effects of tokenism.

Congressional Research

The paucity of women in Congress before the 1992 Year of the Woman election made it difficult to evaluate the policy impact of electing women. Early works catalogued the backgrounds, committee assignments, and legislative priorities of individual congresswomen (Werner 1966; Leader 1977; Gertzog 1984). The first systematic efforts to delineate the policy impact of women in Congress focused on roll-call voting behavior (Gehlen 1977; Leader 1977; Frankovic 1977). Over time, studies that examine whether women are more liberal than their male colleagues have had mixed results (Leader 1977; Gehlen 1977; Frankovic 1977; Welch 1985; Burrell 1994; McCarty, Poole, and Rosenthal 1997). However, other research indicates that gender does exert a significant effect on voting for specific women's issues such as abortion (Tatalovich and Schier 1993) or a set of women's issues (Burrell 1994; Dolan 1997; Swers 1998).

Yet analyses of roll-call voting only scratch the surface of potential gender differences in legislative participation, since the position a legislator takes on a roll-call vote does not reveal the depth of the member's commitment to women's interests, nor does it indicate the process by which a bill advanced through the legislative process (Hall 1996; Swers 2000). Beginning in the early 1990s, scholarly efforts to examine women's influence on the entire legislative process demonstrate that, like their counterparts in the state legislatures, women in Congress have had a unique influence on the congressional policymaking process, particularly in the area of women's issues. Congresswomen are opening the national agenda to women's issues by sponsoring and cosponsoring more legislation concerning feminist issues and issues that reflect women's traditional role as caregiver than their male colleagues do (Tamerius 1995; Vega and Firestone 1995; Swers 2000, forthcoming; Wolbrecht forthcoming). Congresswomen utilize their committee positions to advocate for the incorporation of women's interests into committee legislation (Gertzog 1995; Dodson et al. 1995; Dodson 1998, forthcoming; Bratton and Haynie 1999; Norton forthcoming; Swers 2000, forthcoming). Female legislators also demonstrate higher rates of participation in floor debates on women's issues (Tamerius 1995; Swers 2000; Cramer Walsh forthcoming) and speak with a distinctive voice on these issues (Dodson et al. 1995; Swers 2000; Levy, Tien, and Aved 2001; Cramer Walsh forthcoming). Finally, Congresswomen do view women as a distinct portion of their constituency and they express a commitment to representing women's interests in their legislative activities (Margolies-Mezvinsky 1994; Boxer 1994; Dodson et al. 1995; Gertzog 1995; Foerstel and Foerstel 1996; Bingham 1997; Molinari 1998; Carroll forthcoming).

Clearly, the research on the policy impact of female officeholders at the state and national levels has revealed important differences in the legislative priorities of individual legislators. Additionally, the research on state legislatures highlights the influence of the proportion of women in the legislative body and the presence of a women's caucus on a legislator's ability to express unique preferences based on gender. However, scholars need to devote more attention to the ways in which the political and institutional contexts shape the decision calculus of legislators concerning what policies to pursue. A new frontier of women and politics research focuses on illuminating how institutional and political context factors, such as a member's position within the committee structure and the agenda of the majority party in the legislature, shape the range of choices available to members regardless of their abstract

policy preferences (for example, see Norton 1994; Dodson et al. 1995; Rosenthal 1998; Swers 2000).

The Relationship of Women to the Institution

The new institutional research illuminates the ways in which women are adapting to legislative norms as well as the ways in which the institutional and political contexts can inhibit legislators' efforts to advance their policy priorities. For example, Dodson (1995, 1998, forthcoming) demonstrates how Democratic and Republican women in the 103rd Congress used their positions on key committees and within the party leadership to ensure that legislation concerning violence against women, reproductive rights, and women's health gained a place on the national agenda and did not fall victim to issues of time and funding on their way to becoming law. By contrast, in her work on congressional action on reproductive issues, Norton (1994, 1995, 1999, forthcoming) reports that between 1969 and 1992, the members of key committees and subcommittees were able to impose their preferences on reproductive policy regardless of the will of the majority in Congress. The absence of women from these key committees inhibited their efforts to change policy regardless of their commitment to pro-choice initiatives. Similarly, Berkman and O'Connor (1993) maintain that state legislative committees with higher percentages of Democratic women were the most successful in blocking pro-life legislation. Demonstrating the importance of political context and majority vs. minority party status, Swers (2000, forthcoming) found that moderate Republican women changed their bill sponsorship patterns between the 103rd and 104th Congresses as they increased their sponsorship of social welfare bills and decreased their advocacy of more controversial feminist proposals in order to capitalize on their majority power and avoid antagonizing important party constituencies, particularly social conservatives. This new institutional research indicates that we must further investigate how the positions of members within the institution and changes in the external political environment alter the priorities of legislators regardless of their abstract policy preferences.

Beyond investigating the impact of institutional factors on the ability of members to pursue their policy priorities, scholars are also examining whether women are transforming the nature of the institutions in which they serve. These scholars start from the premise that institutions are gendered, meaning, "gender is present in the processes, practices, images, and ideologies, and distributions of power in the various sectors of social life" (Acker as quoted in Kenney 1996). Thus, male behavior is regarded as the norm in legislative institutions and women feel pressure to adapt to those expectations (Kenney 1996; Kelly and Duerst-Lahti 1995a, 1995b, Thomas 1997; Rosenthal 1998). Research on male-female differences in leadership style demonstrates that women exhibit an alternative method of leadership, which is challenging institutional norms. For example, Rosenthal (1997, 1998, 2000) finds that female committee chairs exhibited a more integrative leadership style than their male counterparts. As a result of gender role socialization and their distinctive paths to leadership, women's integrative style emphasizes consensual, cooperative, and inclusive decision-making rather than the transactional and competitive bargaining styles employed by their male colleagues. Similarly, in her analysis of crime legislation, Kathlene (1995) found that women focused more on community-based solutions such as prevention and rehabilitation proposals while men concentrated on abstract rights and expanding punishment.

Since women's integrative leadership style challenges established masculine legislative norms, women cannot easily incorporate this alternative style in all institutional settings. For example, Rosenthal (1998) found that integrative leadership behavior is less likely to occur in the more professionalized legislatures in which legislating is a full-time job and members have access to staff to develop policy expertise. She also notes that more states are trending toward the model of the professional legislature in which both male and female legislators eschew an inclusive, collaborative leadership style in favor of a more competitive model of leadership. Additionally, Kathlene (1989, 1994) reports that in committee hearings in the Colorado legislature, women entered the debate later, spoke less often than their male colleagues did, and interrupted witnesses less frequently than male legislators did. The aggressive behavior of men in committee hearings actually increased as the number of women in the committee room rose. This tension between the new methods of leadership in-

troduced by women and the established institutional norms demonstrates that political activists cannot assume that increasing the number of women in office will lead to reform of the political process.

Directions for Future Research

The existing research on women in Congress and the state legislatures has greatly expanded our understanding of the experience of women as candidates and legislators. However, significant gaps remain. Future scholarship on women as candidates must continue to investigate why more women do not run for office. This line of inquiry requires us to expand our perspective from the focus on candidates and voters to include psychological and sociological factors such as gender role socialization and occupational trends as well as a more careful examination of candidate recruitment patterns. Those scholars who study the impact of gender role stereotypes must illuminate the conditions in which voters utilize those stereotypes. Does voter reliance on stereotypes vary with the type of election or the prestige of the office? Do these stereotypes help women in certain races and hurt them in others? Do voter stereotypes affect Republican and Democratic women differently? For example, gender stereotypes may help Republican women draw independent voters, while hurting Democratic women who may be perceived as too liberal.

With regard to research on women as legislators, current research at the state and national levels demonstrates that female legislators do perceive women as a distinct part of their constituency, and they do bring different policy priorities to the legislative agenda, particularly in the area of women's issues. Future research must investigate the ways in which female legislators incorporate women's interests into the policy discussion on issues that are not obviously women's issues. Scholars should also examine whether the increasing presence of female officeholders is influencing the policy priorities of male representatives. Additionally, we must devote more attention to the intersections of race and gender (Barrett 1995; Darling 1998). How does being an African-American or Hispanic woman impact a legislator's policy priorities and her relationship with white female legislators, white male legislators, and male legislators of her own race?

Finally, scholars must devote more attention to the influence of the institutional and political contexts on the legislative activity of members. A focus on institutions allows us to move beyond the testimony of legislators concerning their policy interests to an understanding of how the positions members occupy within the institution shape their willingness to pursue policy preferences based on gender. Future research on institutions must also more carefully delineate the ways in which institutions are gendered and how these hidden norms influence the behavior of male and female legislators. Thus, more research is needed to expand our understanding of the ways in which gender considerations mediate the experience of women as candidates and officeholders.

NOTE

1. In her study of skewed groups, Kanter (1977) found that the more numerous "dominants" set organizational norms and treat members of the minority as "tokens" who represent their category as symbols rather than as individuals. Minorities do not escape the constraints of tokenism until the groups become "balanced" at approximately 35 percent.

REFERENCES

Alexander, Deborah, and Kristi Anderson. 1993. "Gender as a Factor in the Attribution of Leadership Traits." *Political Research Quarterly* 46: 527–545.

Baer, Denise. 1993. "Political Parties: The Missing Variable in Women and Politics Research." *Political Research Quarterly* 46: 547–576.

Baker, Paula. 1984. "The Domestication of Politics: Women and American Political Society, 1780–1920." *American Historical Review* 89: 620–647.

Barrett, Edith. 1995. "The Policy Priorities of African-American Women in State Legislatures." *Legislative Studies Quarterly* 20: 223–247.

Berkman, Michael B., and Robert E. O'Connor. 1993. "Do Women Legislators Matter? Female Legislators and State Abortion Policy." *American Politics Quarterly* 21: 102–124.

Bernstein, Robert. 1986. "Why Are There So Few Women in the House?" *Western Political Quarterly* 39: 155–163.

Biersack, Robert, and Paul S. Herrnson. 1994. "Political Parties and the Year of the Woman." In *The Year of the Woman: Myths and Realities*, eds. Elizabeth Adell Cook, Sue Thomas, and Clyde Wilcox. Boulder, CO: Westview Press.

Bingham, Clara. 1997. *Women on the Hill: Challenging the Culture of Congress*. New York: Time Books.

Bledsoe, Timothy, and Mary Herring. 1990. "Victims of Circumstances: Women in Pursuit of Political Office." *American Political Science Review* 84: 213–223.

Boxer, Barbara. 1994. *Strangers in the Senate*. Washington, DC: National Press Books.

Braden, Maria. 1996. *Women Politicians and the Media*. Lexington: University Press of Kentucky.

Bratton, Kathleen A., and Kerry L. Haynie. 1999. "Agenda Setting and Legislative Success in State Legislatures: The Effect of Gender and Race." *Journal of Politics* 61: 658–679.

Burrell, Barbara C. 1994. *A Woman's Place Is in the House: Campaigning for Congress in the Feminist Era*. Ann Arbor: University of Michigan Press.

Carroll, Susan J. Forthcoming. "Representing Women: Congresswomen's Perception of Their Representational Roles." In *Women Transforming Congress*, ed. Cindy Simon Rosenthal. Norman: University of Oklahoma Press.

Carroll, Susan J. 1994. *Women as Candidates in American Politics*. 2nd ed. Bloomington: Indiana University Press.

Carroll, Susan J., and Ronnee Schreiber. 1997. "Media Coverage of Women in the 103rd Congress." In *Women, Media, and Politics*, ed. Pippa Norris. New York: Oxford University Press.

Carroll, Susan, and Wendy S. Strimling. 1983. *Women's Routes to Elective Office: A Comparison with Men's*. New Brunswick: Center for the American Woman and Politics, Rutgers, The State University of New Jersey.

Center for the American Woman and Politics (CAWP). 2000. "Election 2000: Summary of Results for Women." New Brunswick: Center for the American Woman and Politics, Rutgers, The State University of New Jersey.

Chaney, Carole, and Barbara Sinclair. 1994. "Women and the 1992 House Elections." In *The Year of the Woman: Myths and Realities*, eds. Elizabeth Adell Cook, Sue Thomas, and Clyde Wilcox. Boulder, CO: Westview Press.

Cramer Walsh, Katherine. Forthcoming. "Resonating to Be Heard: Gendered Debate on the Floor of the House." In *Women Transforming Congress*, ed. Cindy Simon Rosenthal. Norman: University of Oklahoma Press.

Darcy, Robert, Susan Welch, and Janet Clark. 1994. *Women, Elections, and Representation*. 2nd ed. Lincoln: University of Nebraska Press.

Darcy, Robert, and Sarah Slavin Scramm. 1977. "When Women Run Against Men." *Public Opinion Quarterly* 41: 1–12.

Darling, Marsha L. 1998. "African-American Women in State Elective Office in the South." In *Women and Elective Office: Past, Present, and Future*, eds. Sue Thomas and Clyde Wilcox. New York: Oxford University Press.

Deber, Raisa. 1982. "The Fault Dear Brutus: Women as Congressional Candidates in Pennsylvania." *Journal of Politics* 44: 463–479.

Diamond, Irene. 1977. *Sex Roles in the State House.* New Haven: Yale University Press.

Dodson, Debra L. Forthcoming. "Representation, Gender and Reproductive Rights in the U.S. Congress." In *Women Transforming Congress,* ed. Cindy Simon Rosenthal. Norman: University of Oklahoma Press.

Dodson, Debra L. 1998. "Representing Women's Interests in the U.S. House of Representatives." In *Women and Elective Office: Past, Present, and Future,* eds. Sue Thomas and Clyde Wilcox. New York: Oxford University Press.

Dodson, Debra L. 1997. "Change and Continuity in the Relationship Between Private Responsibilities and Public Officeholding: The More Things Change, the More They Stay the Same." *Policy Studies Journal* 25: 569–584.

Dodson, Debra L., and Susan J. Carroll. 1991. *Reshaping the Agenda: Women in State Legislatures.* New Brunswick: Center for the American Woman and Politics, Rutgers, The State University of New Jersey.

Dodson, Debra L. et al. 1995. *Voices, Views, Votes: The Impact of Women in the 103rd Congress.* New Brunswick: Center for the American Woman and Politics, Rutgers, The State University of New Jersey.

Dolan, Julie. 1997. "Support for Women's Interests in the 103rd Congress: The Distinct Impact of Congressional Women." *Women & Politics* 18(4): 81–94.

Dolan, Kathleen. 2001. "Electoral Context, Issues, and Voting for Women in the 1990s." *Women & Politics* 23(1/2): 21–36.

Dolan, Kathleen. 1997. "Gender Differences in Support for Women Candidates: Is There a Glass Ceiling in American Politics?" *Women & Politics* 17(2): 27–41.

Dolan, Kathleen and Lynne Ford. 1995. "Women in the State Legislatures: Feminist Identity and Legislative Behaviors." *American Politics Quarterly* 23: 96–108.

Duerst-Lahti, Georgia. 1998. "The Bottleneck: Women Becoming Candidates." In *Women and Elective Office: Past, Present, and Future,* eds. Sue Thomas and Clyde Wilcox. New York: Oxford University Press

Duerst-Lahti, Georgia, and Rita Mae Kelly. 1995. "On Governance, Leadership, and Gender." In *Gender Power, Leadership, and Governance,* eds. Georgia Duerst-Lahti and Rita Mae Kelly. Ann Arbor: University of Michigan Press.

Foerstel, Karen, and Herbert Foerstel. 1996. *Climbing the Hill: Gender Conflict in Congress.* Westport, CT: Praeger.

Fox, Richard Logan. 1997. *Gender Dynamics in Congressional Elections.* Thousand Oaks, CA: Sage.

Frankovic, Kathleen A. 1977. "Sex and Voting in the U.S. House of Representatives 1961–1975." *American Politics Quarterly* 5: 315–330.

Gehlen, Freida. 1977. "Women Members of Congress: A Distinctive Role." In *A Portrait of Marginality: The Political Behavior of the American Woman,* eds. Marianne Githens and Jewell Prestage. New York: McKay.

Gertzog, Irwin. 1984. *Congressional Women: Their Recruitment, Integration, and Behavior.* Westport, CT: Praeger.

Gertzog, Irwin. 1995. *Congressional Women: Their Recruitment, Integration, and Behavior* 2nd ed. Westport, CT: Praeger.

Gertzog, Irwin, and M. Michele Simard. 1981. "Women and 'Hopeless' Congressional Candidacies: Nomination Frequency, 1916–1978." *American Politics Quarterly* 9:449–466.

Herrick, Rebecca. 1996. "Is There a Gender Gap in the Value of Campaign Resources?" *American Politics Quarterly* 24: 68–80.

Herrick, Rebecca. 1995. "A Reappraisal of the Quality of Women Candidates." *Women & Politics* 15(4): 25–38.

Hoffman, Kim U., Carrie Palmer, and Ronald Keith Gaddie. 2001. "Candidate Sex and Congressional Elections: Open Seats Before, During, and After the Year of the Woman." *Women & Politics* 23(1/2): 37–58.

Huddy, Leonie, and Nayda Terkildsen. 1993a. "Gender Stereotypes and the Perception of Male and Female Candidates." *American Journal of Political Science* 37: 119–147.

Huddy, Leonie, and Nayda Terkildsen. 1993b. "The Consequences of Gender Stereotypes for Women Candidates at Different Levels and Types of Offices." *Political Research Quarterly* 46: 502–525.

Jacobson, Gary C. 1997. *Politics of Congressional Elections.* 4th ed. New York: Longman.

Jelen, Ted G. 1994. "Carol Moseley-Braun: The Insider as Insurgent." In *The Year of the Woman: Myths and Realities,* eds. Elizabeth Adell Cook, Sue Thomas, and Clyde Wilcox. Boulder, CO: Westview.

Jennings, M. Kent. 1990. "Women in Party Politics." In *Women, Politics, and Change,* eds. Louise Tilly and Patricia Gurin. New York: Russell Sage Foundation.

Johnson, Marilyn, and Susan J. Carroll, with Kathy Stanwyck and Lynn Korenblit. 1978. *Profile of Women Holding Office II.* New Brunswick, NJ: Center for the American Woman and Politics.

Kahn, Kim Fridkin. 1996. *The Political Consequences of Being a Woman: How Stereotypes Influence the Conduct and Consequences of Political Campaigns.* New York: Columbia University Press.

Kahn, Kim Fridkin. 1994a. "The Distorted Mirror: Press Coverage of Women Candidates for Statewide Office." *Journal of Politics* 56: 154–173.

Kahn, Kim Fridkin. 1994b. "Does Gender Make a Difference? An Experimental Examination of Sex Stereotypes and Press Patterns in Statewide Campaigns." *American Journal of Political Science* 38: 162–195.

Kahn, Kim Fridkin. 1992. "Does Being Male Help? An Investigation of the Effects of Candidate Gender and Campaign Coverage on Evaluations of U.S. Senate Candidates." *Journal of Politics* 54: 497–517.

Kanter, Rosabeth Moss. 1977. "Some Effects of Proportions on Group Life: Skewed Sex Ratios and Responses to Token Women." *American Journal of Sociology* 82: 965–990.

Kathlene, Lyn. 1995. "Alternative Views of Crime: Legislative Policymaking in Gendered Terms." *Journal of Politics* 57: 696–723.

Kathlene, Lyn. 1994. "Power and Influence of State Legislative Policymaking: The Interaction of Gender and Position in Committee Hearing Debates." *American Political Science Review* 88: 560–576.

Kathlene, Lyn. 1989. "Uncovering the Political Impacts of Gender: An Exploratory Study." *Western Political Quarterly* 42: 397–421.

Kelly, Rita Mae, and Georgia Duerst-Lahti. 1995. "The Study of Gender Power and Its Link to Governance and Leadership." In *Gender Power, Leadership, and Governance*, eds. Georgia Duerst-Lahti and Rita Mae Kelly. Ann Arbor: University of Michigan Press.

Kenney, Sally. 1996. "New Research on Gendered Political Institutions." *Political Research Quarterly* 49: 445–466.

King, David C., and Richard E. Matland. Forthcoming. "Partisanship and the Impact of Candidate Gender in Congressional Elections: Results of an Experiment." In *Women Transforming Congress*, ed. Cindy Simon Rosenthal. Norman: University of Oklahoma Press.

Kirkpatrick, Jeane. 1974. *Political Woman*. New York: Basic Books.

Kropf, Martha E., and John Boiney. 2001. "The Electoral Glass Ceiling? Gender, Viability, and the News in U.S. Senate Campaigns." *Women & Politics* 23(1/2): 79–103.

Leader, Shelah Gilbert. 1977. "The Policy Impact of Elected Women Officials." In *The Impact of the Electoral Process*, eds. Joseph Cooper and Louis Maisel. Beverly Hills: Sage.

Levy, Dena, Charles Tien, and Rachelle Aved. 2001. "Do Differences Matter? Women Members of Congress and the Hyde Amendment." *Women & Politics* 23(1/2): 105–127.

Mansbridge, Jane. 1999. "Should Blacks Represent Blacks and Women Represent Women? A Contingent 'Yes.' " *Journal of Politics* 61: 628–657.

Margolies-Mezvinsky, Marjorie, with Barbara Feinman. 1994. *A Woman's Place . . . : The Freshmen Women Who Changed the Face of Congress*. New York: Crown Publishers.

McCarty, Nolan M., Keith T. Poole, and Howard Rosenthal. 1997. "Income Redistribution and National Politics." Monograph. Washington, DC: AEI Press.

McDermott, Monika L. 1997. "Voting Cues in Low-Information Elections: Candidate Gender as a Social Information Variable in Contemporary U.S. Elections." *American Journal of Political Science* 41: 270–283.

McGlen, Nancy, and Karen O'Connor. 1998. *Women, Politics, and American Society*. 2nd ed. Upper Saddle River, NJ: Prentice Hall.

Mezey, Susan Gluck. 1978. "Support for Women's Rights Policy: An Analysis of Local Politicians." *American Politics Quarterly* 6: 485–497.

Molinari, Susan, with Elinor Burkett. 1998. *Representative Mom: Balancing Budgets, Bill, and Baby in the U.S. Congress*. New York: Doubleday.

Nechemias, Carol. 1987. "Changes in the Election of Women to U.S. State Legislative Seats." *Legislative Studies Quarterly* 12: 125–142.

Nechemias, Carol. 1985. "Geographic Mobility and Women's Access to State Legislatures." *Western Political Quarterly* 38: 119–131.

Nelson, Candice. 1994. "Women's PACs and the Year of the Woman." In *The Year of the Woman: Myths and Realities*, eds. Elizabeth Adell Cook, Sue Thomas, and Clyde Wilcox. Boulder, CO: Westview Press.

Niven, David. 1998. *The Missing Majority: The Recruitment of Women as State Legislative Candidates*. Westport, CT: Praeger.

Niven, David, and Jeremy Zilber. 2001. " 'How Does She Have Time for Kids and Congress?' Views on Gender and Media Coverage from House Offices." *Women & Politics* 23(1/2): 147–165.

Norton, Noelle H. Forthcoming. "Transforming Congress from the Inside: Women in Committee." In *Women Transforming Congress*, ed. Cindy Simon Rosenthal. Norman: University of Oklahoma Press.

Norton, Noelle H. 1999. "Committee Influence Over Controversial Policy: The Reproductive Policy Case." *Policy Studies Journal* 27: 203–216.

Norton, Noelle H. 1995. "Women, It's Not Enough to Be Elected: Committee Position Makes a Difference." In *Gender Power, Leadership, and Governance*, eds. Georgia Duerst-Lahti and Rita Mae Kelly. Ann Arbor: University of Michigan Press.

Norton, Noelle H. 1994. "Congressional Committee Power: The Reproductive Policy Inner Circle, 1969–1992." Dissertation Manuscript.

Oxley, Zoe M., and Richard L. Fox. 2000. "Gender Stereotypes, Candidate Sex, and Success in Statewide Election." Presented at the annual meeting of the Midwest Political Science Association. Chicago, IL.

Palmer, Barbara, and Dennis Simon. 2001. "The Political Glass Ceiling: Gender, Strategy and Incumbency in U.S. House Elections, 1978–1998." *Women & Politics* 23(1/2): 59–78.

Phillips, Anne. 1998. "Democracy and Representation: Or, Why Should It Matter Who Our Representatives Are?" In *Feminism and Politics*, ed. Anne Phillips. New York: Oxford University Press.

Phillips, Anne. 1995. *The Politics of Presence*. Oxford: Oxford University Press.

Phillips, Anne. 1991. *Engendering Democracy*. University Park: Pennsylvania State University Press.

Pitkin, Hanna Fenichel. 1967. *The Concept of Representation*. University of California Press.

Plutzer, Eric, and John Zipp. 1996. "Identity Politics, Partisanship, and Voting for Women Candidates." *Public Opinion Quarterly* 60: 30–57.

Rausch, John David, Mark Rozell, and Harry L. Wilson. 1999. "When Women Lose: A Study of Media Coverage of Two Gubernatorial Campaigns." *Women & Politics* 20(4): 1–22.

Reingold, Beth. 1992. "Concepts of Representation Among Female and Male State Legislators." *Legislative Studies Quarterly* 17: 509–537.

Rosenthal, Cindy Simon. 2000. "Gender Styles in State Legislative Committees: Raising Their Voices in Resolving Conflict." *Women & Politics* 21(2): 21–45.

Rosenthal, Cindy Simon. 1998. *When Women Lead: Integrative Leadership in State Legislatures.* New York: Oxford University Press.

Rosenthal, Cindy Simon. 1997. "A View of Their Own: Women's Committee Leadership Styles and State Legislatures." *Policy Studies Journal* 25: 585–600.

Rule, Wilma. 1981. "Why Women Don't Run: The Critical Contextual Factors in Women's Legislative Recruitment." *Western Political Quarterly* 34: 60–77.

Saint-Germain, Michelle A. 1989. "Does Their Difference Make a Difference? The Impact of Women on Public Policy in the Arizona Legislature." *Social Science Quarterly* 70: 956–968.

Sapiro, Virginia. 1981. "Research Frontier Essay: When Are Interests Interesting? The Problem of Political Representation of Women." *American Political Science Review* 75: 701–716.

Sapiro, Virginia. 1981–82. "If U.S. Senator Baker Were a Woman: An Experimental Study of Candidate Images." *Political Psychology* 2: 61–83.

Schroedel, Jean, R., and Bruce Snyder. 1994. "Patty Murray: The Mom in Tennis Shoes Goes to the Senate." In *The Year of the Woman: Myths and Realities*, eds. Elizabeth Adell Cook, Sue Thomas, and Clyde Wilcox. Boulder, CO: Westview Press.

Seltzer, Richard, Jody Newman, and Melissa Voorhees Leighton. 1997. *Sex as a Political Variable: Women as Candidates and Voters in American Elections.* Boulder, CO: Lynne Rienner.

Skocpol, Theda. 1992. *Protecting Soldiers and Mothers: The Political Origins of Social Policy in the United States.* Cambridge, MA: Harvard University Press.

Smith, Kevin B. 1997. "When All's Fair: Signs of Parity in Media Coverage of Female Candidates." *Political Communication* 14: 71–82.

Swers, Michele L. Forthcoming. "Transforming the Agenda? Analyzing Gender Differences in Women's Issue Bill Sponsorship." In *Women Transforming Congress*, ed. Cindy Simon Rosenthal. Norman: University of Oklahoma Press.

Swers, Michele L. 2000. "From the Year of the Woman to the Republican Ascendancy: Evaluating the Policy Impact of Women in Congress." Dissertation, Harvard University, Political Sciences Department.

Swers, Michele L. 1998. "Are Congresswomen More Likely to Vote for Women's Issue Bills Than Their Male Colleagues?" *Legislative Studies Quarterly* 23: 435–448.

Tamerius, Karin L. 1995. "Sex, Gender, and Leadership in the Representation of Women." In *Gender Power, Leadership, and Governance*, eds. Georgia Duerst-Lahti and Rita Mae Kelly. Ann Arbor: University of Michigan Press.

Tatalovich, Raymond, and David Schier. 1993. "The Persistence of Ideological Cleavage in Voting on Abortion Legislation in the House of Representatives, 1973–1988." *American Politics Quarterly* 21: 125–139.

Thomas, Sue. 1997. "Why Gender Matters: The Perceptions of Women Officeholders." *Women & Politics* 17(1): 27–53.

Thomas, Sue. 1994. *How Women Legislate.* New York: Oxford University Press.

Thompson, Joan Hulse. 1980. "Role Perceptions of Women in the Ninety-fourth Congress, 1975–76." *Political Science Quarterly* 95: 71–81.

Uhlaner, Carole, and Kay Schlozman. 1986. "Candidate Gender and Congressional Campaign Receipts." *Journal of Politics* 48: 30–50.

van Assendelft, Laura, and Karen O'Connor. 1994. "Backgrounds, Motivations, and Interests: A Comparison of Male and Female Local Party Activists." *Women & Politics* 14(2): 77–92.

Vavrus, Mary. 1998. "Working the Senate from the Outside In: The Mediated Construction of a Feminist Political Campaign." *Critical Studies in Mass Communication* 15: 213–235.

Vega, Arturo, and Juanita M. Firestone. 1995. "The Effects of Gender on Congressional Behavior and the Substantive Representation of Women." *Legislative Studies Quarterly* 20: 213–222.

Welch, Susan. 1985. "Are Women More Liberal Than Men in the U.S. Congress?" *Legislative Studies Quarterly* 10: 125–134.

Werner, Emmy E. 1966. "Women in Congress 1917–1964." *Western Political Quarterly* 19: 16–30.

Wilcox, Clyde. 1994. "Why Was 1992 the 'Year of the Woman'?: Explaining Women's Gains in 1992." In *The Year of the Woman: Myths and Realities*, eds. Elizabeth Adell Cook, Sue Thomas, and Clyde Wilcox. Boulder, CO: Westview Press.

Witt, Linda, Karen Paget, and Glenna Matthews. 1995. *Running as a Woman: Gender and Power in American Politics.* New York: Free Press.

Wolbrecht, Christina. Forthcoming. "Female Legislators and the Women's Rights Agenda." In *Women Transforming Congress*, ed. Cindy Simon Rosenthal. Norman: University of Oklahoma Press.

EIGHTY-ONE

Multi-Issue Politics

Suzanne Pharr

At the National Gay and Lesbian Task Force's Creating Change Conference, I was asked to give a luncheon speech to the participants of the People of Color Institute and the Diversity Institute. Right off, I told them that I thought I was an odd choice for these groups because I don't really believe in either diversity or identity politics as they are currently practiced. Fortunately, people respectfully stayed to hear me explain myself.

First, diversity politics, as popularly practiced, seems to focus on the necessity for having everyone (across gender, race, class, age, religion, physical ability, etc.) present and treated well in any given setting or organization. An assumption is that everyone is oppressed, and all oppressions are equal. Since the publication of the report, "Workforce 2000," that predicted the U.S. workforce would be made up of 80 percent women and people of color by 2000, a veritable growth industry of "diversity consultants" has arisen to teach corporations how to "manage" diversity. With integration and productivity as goals, they focus on the issues of sensitivity and inclusion—a human relations approach—with acceptance and comfort as high priorities. Popular images of diversity politics present people holding hands around America, singing "We Are the World."

I have a lot of appreciation for the part of diversity work that concentrates on making sure everyone is included because the history of oppression is one of excluding, of silencing, of rendering people invisible. However, for me, our diversity work fails if it does not deal with the power dynamics of difference and go straight to the heart of shifting the balance of power among individuals and within institutions. A danger of diversity politics is becoming a tool of oppression by creating the illusion of participation when in fact there is no shared power. Having a presence within an organization or institution means very little if one does not have the power of decision-making, an adequate share of the resources, and participation in the development of the workplan or agenda. We as oppressed people must demand much more than acceptance. Toler-

ance, sympathy and understanding are not enough, though they soften the impact of oppression by making people feel better in the face of it. Our job is not just to soften blows but to make change, fundamental and far-reaching.

Identity politics, on the other hand, rather than trying to include everyone, brings together people who share a single common identity such as sexual orientation, gender, or race. Generally, it focuses on the elimination of a single oppression, the one that is based on the common identity, i.e., homophobia/heterosexism, sexism, racism. However, this can be a limited, hierarchical approach, reducing people of multiple identities to a single identity. Which identity should a lesbian of color choose as a priority—gender, race, or sexual orientation? And does choosing one necessitate leaving the other two at home? What do we say to bisexual or biracial people? Choose, damnit, choose??? Our multiple identities allow us to develop a politic that is broad in scope because it is grounded in a wide range of experiences.

There are positive aspects of organizing along identity lines: clarity of single focus in tactics and strategies, self-examination and education apart from the dominant culture, development of solidarity and group bonding, etc. Creating organizations based on identity allows us to have visibility and collective power, to advance concerns that otherwise would never be recognized because of our marginalization within the dominant society.

However, identity politics often suffers from failing to acknowledge that the same multiplicity of oppressions, a similar imbalance of power, exists within identity groups as within the larger society. People who group together on the basis of their sexual orientation still find within their groups sexism and racism that have to be dealt with—or if gathering on the basis of race, there is still sexism and homophobia to be confronted. Whole, not partial, people come to identity groups, carrying several identities. Some of the major barriers of our liberation movements to being able to mount a unified or cohesive strategy, I believe, come from our refusal to work directly on the oppressions—the fundamental issues of power—within our own groups. A successful liberation movement cannot be built on the effort to liberate only a few and only a piece of who we are.

Diversity and identity politics are responses to oppression. In confronting oppressions, we must remember that they are more than people just not being nice to one another: they are systemic, based in institutions and in general society, where one group of people is allowed to exert power and control over members of another group, denying them fundamental rights. Also, we must remember that oppressions are interconnected, operating in similar ways, and that many people experience more than one oppression.

I believe that all oppressions in this country turn on an economic wheel; they all, in the long run, serve to consolidate and keep wealth in the hands of the few, with the many fighting over crumbs. Oppressions are built in particular on the dynamic intersection of race and class. Without work against economic injustice, against the excesses of capitalism, there can be no deep and lasting work on oppression. Why? Because it is always in the best interest of the dominators, the greedy, to maintain and expand oppression—the feeding of economic and social injustice.

Unless we understand the interconnections of oppressions and the economic exploitation of oppressed groups, we have little hope of succeeding in a liberation movement. The religious Right has been successful in driving wedges between oppressed groups because there is little common understanding of the linkages of oppressions. Progressives, including lesbians and gay men, have contributed to these divisions because generally we have dealt with only single pieces of the fabric of injustice. We stand ready to be divided. If, for example, an organization has worked only on sexual identity issues and has not worked internally on issues of race and gender, then it is ripe for being divided on those issues.

The Right has had extraordinary success in using homosexuality as a wedge issue, dividing people on the issues clustered around the Right's two central organizing points: traditional family values and economics. An example is their success in using homosexuality as a way to organize people to oppose multicultural curricula, which particularly affects people of color and women; while acting to "save the family from homosexuals," women and people of color find themselves working against their own inclusion. If women's groups, people of color and lesbian and gay groups worked on gender, race and sexual identity issues internally, then perhaps we would recognize the need for a coalition and a common agenda for multicultural education.

An even more striking example is how the Right, in its "No Special Rights" campaign, successfully plays upon the social and economic fears of people, using homosexuality as the wedge issue, and as the *coup de grace*, pits the lesbian and gay community against the African-American community. Ingeniously, they blend race, class, gender and sexual identity issues into one campaign whose success has profound implications for the destruction of democracy.

In summary, the goal of the "No Special Rights" campaign is to change the way this nation thinks about civil rights so that the groundwork is laid for the gradual elimination of civil rights. This is not an easy idea to present to the general public in a straightforward manner. Therefore, the religious Right has chosen homosexuality and homophobia to open the door to thinking that is influenced by racial hatred and its correlatives, gender and class prejudice.

Depending upon the persuasion of racism, sexism and homophobia, the religious Right seeks these basic twisted and distorted changes in our thinking about civil rights:

1. **They suggest that** civil rights do not already exist in our Constitution and Bill of Rights; they are a special category for "minorities" such as people of color and women. The religious Right refers to these people as having "minority status," a term they have invented to keep us focused on the word **minority.** Most people think of minorities as people of color. Recently in Oregon, signs appeared that read, "End Minority Status." They did not specify gay and lesbian: the message was about **minorities** and what that so-called "status" brings them.

2. **Then they say that** basic civil rights are themselves "Special Rights" that can be given or taken away by the majority who has ordinary rights, not "special rights."

3. **They argue that** "Special Rights" should be given to people based on deserving behavior and hardship conditions (especially economic) that require special treatment. In their words, people who "qualify" for "minority status."

4. **Then they introduce the popular belief that** "Special Rights" given to people of color and women and people with disabilities have resulted in the loss of jobs for deserving, "qualified" people through affirmative action and quotas. This introduces the notion that rights for some has an economic cost for others; therefore the enhancement of civil rights for everyone is not a good thing.

5. **They argue that** lesbians and gay men have no hardship conditions that would require extending "Special Rights" to them. Further, homosexuals **disqualify** themselves from basic civil rights because, by the nature of who they are, they exhibit bad behavior. They do not, according to the Right's formula, "qualify" for "minority status."

6. **Then there is the pernicious connection:** There are other people who already have "Special Rights" who exhibit bad behavior and prove themselves undeserving as they use and deal drugs and commit crimes of violence and welfare fraud. The popular perception is that these are minorities. However, the Right also extends its description of the undeserving to those who bear children outside of two-parent married families, women who choose abortion, and even those who receive public assistance.

7. **And finally, their logical and dangerous conclusion:** Because giving "Special Rights" to undeserving groups is destroying our families, communities and jobs for good people, who deserves and does not deserve to be granted "Special Rights" should be put to the popular vote and good, ordinary citizens allowed to decide who gets them and who gets to keep them.

Clearly, the religious Right understands the interconnection among oppressions and in this campaign plays directly to that interweaving of racism, sexism, classism and homophobia that is virtually impossible to tease apart. To see this campaign as single issue, i.e., simply about lesbians and gay men, is to ensure defeat of our efforts in opposing it. It has to be responded to as the multi-issue campaign that it is. If the "No Special Rights" campaign is successful, everyone stands to lose.

The question, as ever, is what to do? I do not believe that either a diversity or identity politics approach will work unless they are changed to incorporate a multi-issue analysis and strategy that combine the politics of inclusion with shared power. But, you say, it will spread us too thin if we try to work on everyone's issue, and ours will fall by the wayside. In our external work (doing women's anti-violence work, working against police brutality in people-of-color communities, seeking government funding for AIDS research, etc.), we do not have to work on "everybody's issue" but how can we do true social change work unless we look at all within our constituency who are affected by our particular issue? People who are infected with the HIV virus are of every race, class, age, gender, geographic location, yet when research and services are sought, it is women, people of color, poor people, etc., who are usually overlooked. Yet today, the AIDS virus rages on because those in power think that the people who contract it are dispensable. Are we to be like those currently in power? To understand why police brutality is so much more extreme in people-of-color communities, we have to understand why, even within that community, it is so much greater against poor people of color, prostituted women and gay men and lesbians of color. To leave any group out leaves a hole for everyone's freedoms and rights to fall through. It becomes an issue of "acceptable" and "unacceptable" people, deserving and undeserving of rights.

Identity politics offers a strong, vital place for bonding, for developing political analysis, for understanding our relationship to a world that says on the one hand that we are no more than our identity, and on the other, that there is no real oppression based on the identity of race or gender or sexual identity. Our challenge is to learn how to use the experiences of our many identities to forge an inclusive social change politic. The question that faces us is how to do multi-issue coalition building from an identity base. The hope for a multi-racial, multi-issue movement rests in large part on the answer to this question.

Our linkages can create a movement, and our divisions can destroy us.

Internally, if our organizations are not committed to the inclusion and shared power of all those who share our issue, how can we with any integrity demand inclusion and shared power in society at large? If women, lesbians and gay men are treated as people undeserving of equality within civil rights organizations, how can those organizations demand equality? If women of color and poor women are marginalized in women's rights organizations, how can those organizations argue that women as a class should be moved into full participation in the mainstream? If lesbian and gay organizations are not antiracist and feminist in all their practices, what hope is there for the elimination of homophobia and heterosexism in a racist, sexist society?

When we grasp the value and interconnectedness of our liberation issues, then we will at last be able to make true coalition and begin building a common agenda that eliminates oppression and brings forth a vision of diversity that shares power and resources. In particular, I think there is great hope for this work among lesbians and gay men. First, we must reconceptualize who we are and see ourselves not as the wedge, not as the divisive, diversionary issue of the religious Right—but as the bridge that links the issues and people together. If we indeed represent everyone—cutting across all sectors of society, race, gender, age, ability, geographic location, religion—and if we develop a liberation politic that is transformational, that is, that eliminates the power and dominance of one group over another within our own organizations—we as old and young, people of color and white, rich and poor, rural and urban lesbians and gay men can provide the forum for bringing people and groups together to form a progressive, multi-issue, truly diverse liberation movement. Our success will be decided by the depth of our work on race, class and gender issues.

Instead of the flashpoint for division, we can be the flashpoint for developing common ground, a common agenda, a common humanity. We can be at the heart of hope for creating true inclusive, participatory democracy in this country.

E I G H T Y - T W O

◆◆◆

Taking On the Global Economy

Kalima Rose

The rain was with us every day, washing us, a metaphor for the tears of women from across the planet who came to share the pains and victories of their peoples. The earth turned to bog, wheelchairs became stranded and events were canceled. For some, the inconvenience of incessant rain symbolized the expected relegation of women to substandard facilities. For others, we felt the monsoon working on us, softening the definitions of land and boundaries of peoples, preparing the ground for the new seed that women carried here to share.

The distributed seeds held the kernels of analysis that women first brought to trial at the 1985 world women's conference in Nairobi. There, women from countries of the south were raising their analysis of the social disinvestment that was making women poorer in their countries. The disinvestment they experienced in '85 was a result of their countries' overdue foreign debts. The financial institutions that could help them out were dictating structural adjustment policies which compelled them to restructure their economies along free market principles to help exact the debt payments. Things like food, health, and other social infrastructure subsidies were jettisoned to meet these alignments. In 1985, this was news to women from the U.S., where, by the way, the financial institutions enforcing these policies are located.

A Tighter Analysis

At the Beijing conference in 1995, women from around the world, and particularly women of color, carried a further-developed version of this analysis. Structural adjustment policies were only one component of what women could now more specifically

---

Kalima Rose attended the NGO Forum of the United Nations Fourth World Conference on Women in Beijing, in 1995. She reports on theoretical perspectives discussed by participants, focusing on the globalization of the economy and its implications for women in the U.S.

Opening of the NGO Forum in Huairou, China

name as the detrimental aspects of the globalization of the economy. They brought criticism of the destructive nature of a world economic system that is driven by consumption and western industrial values. By 1995, women were much more unified in their understanding of the global deregulation that allows market capitalism to run more freely in its pursuit of "maximizing profits." From country after country, women reported disinvestment in social support programs, privatization, increasing domination by western media, and the "westernizing-down" of cultural integrity because of these influences. It was this discussion, about the effects of globalization on communities around the world, that marked a defining change in the world women's movement. World economic issues were now women's issues.

Winona LaDuke, an Anishinabe of the White Earth reservation in northern Minnesota, rejected any notion of gender equity within western, consumer, industrial development, which continually exploits the lands and natural resources of others. She noted the inherent difficulties of seeking gender equity within a system based on exploitation, that denies self-determination of peoples.

Vandana Shiva, a scientist from India associated with the international Women's Environment and Development Organization (WEDO), brought an understanding of how transnational corporations are using intellectual property rights, a particularly western notion of "owning" information, to privatize collective knowledge. For example, if a corporation names the genetics of a seed, or the chemical structure of a medicine, it can then copyright it and claim royalty rights. Farmers saving seed from crops they have grown can now be charged royalty payments, and medicines developed by women in communities as collective knowledge must be purchased.

Margaret Prescod, an African American member of the International Wages for Housework campaign, carried the analysis that economies are supposed to facilitate the exchange of goods and services necessary in caring for societies. But our contemporary economic system commodifies everything except caretaking work, which largely falls to and is carried out by women. Because it has no value, anyone performing that work is impoverished and anyone out working to earn a living can minister little caretaking. This campaign succeeded in persuading the official conference to adopt their position that governments should start quantifying and keeping account in national accounting systems of all the caretaking work that women do.

Regulating the Corporate Rampage

A common analysis that emerged from these women, is that we need ways of internationally and personally monitoring and regulating an out-of-control, profit-driven system. This has special meaning for women in the U.S., because while we are victims of this growing capitalism, we are also residents of its home territory. So while we can learn from women in other countries who deal with more extreme versions of increasing poverty, social dissolution, forced migration and homelessness, and share strategies to fight these trends, one of the key things we will learn from them is that we also need to rein in our own.

Consider, for example, that while the negative effects of the globalization of the economy was one of the largest issue areas raised at the conference, it got zero press coverage in the U.S. press. Human rights and violence against women got a lot more ink here, but the analysis of human rights is intimately linked to economic rights: women's experiences of violence are interwoven with economic insecurity and militarism. The western media drops its human rights coverage when women leaders challenge how the sacred tenets of capitalism feed human rights abuses.

While women at the NGO forum dealt significantly with this issue, and while the Platform for Action (the official document emerging from the UN forum) was supposed to address problems of poverty, the Clinton administration opposed including language advocating international regulation of transnational corporations, or investigation of the links between the structural adjustment policies of international financial institutions and the increasing poverty of people living under those policies. Our administration also opposed language that affirmed the importance of including environmental and labor protections in trade agreements. So you can see that the solutions that women presented from around the world to deal with the social disenfranchisement codified by a global economy are in direct opposition to the direction that our congress and our administration propose.

Though the Platform was supposed to address women's increasing poverty, solutions focus on improving women's access to credit and markets. This assumes that the problem is discrimination against women and not in how markets inherently work. Women from the Economic Justice Caucus (an international coalition of women's nongovernmental organizations that work on economic justice issues) tried to raise the issue that there are also inherent problems in the nature of the markets. This is a very important issue for women in the U.S. to continue to raise. Because, while the document specifically mentions providing adequate safety nets; doing macroeconomic analysis that includes a gender analysis; exploring how excess military spending, arms production, and trade contribute to women's poverty; and ensuring the full human rights of all migrants (not just the documented), the current federal government is actually undoing those things.

Strategies on the Homefront

What does this suggest that we should do here in the U.S.? First, we must develop an astute political and economic analysis of the global economy. We must not simply swallow the conservative rhetoric that decries the role of governments and characterizes regulations that protect the interests of citizens as bad. Every economy of every country on earth is undergoing dramatic changes that have to do with commodifying goods and services, specializing the products of each country, and using women as much of the labor force in this specialization, in low-paid and unpaid ways.

Second, we must analyze the kinds of democratic structures that can uphold community visions of what values we want our economy to serve. This means looking at policies that deal with both access and protection. While the U.S. signs international documents that endorse "access," it at the same time is actively undoing "access" regulations that we have in place (affirmative action). And current public rhetoric opposes regulating toxics, protecting workers or ecosystems, or targeting human rights abuses within our own borders.

Third, we should deeply question the idealized industrial model of development whose central tenet is profits dependent on increasing consumption throughout the world. Women from India sang a powerful song, "Coca cola, Pepsi cola, whatever cola, Why can I get any brand of cola, but when I turn on the tap, nothing comes out?" They boycotted the opening of Kentucky Fried Chicken in south India, and they clearly do not think that it is an improvement that western commercials can now be beamed into any hut in India, promoting Nikes, Reeboks, and Levis, along with the panoply of violent U.S. television shows.

Finally, we can strengthen our commitments to democracy, diversity, and human rights by building on the strengths of women. I believe these strengths include tremendous intelligence and the ability to carry cultural relevance and celebration from one generation to the next. Women from South Africa were a tremendous inspiration. They had just participated in drafting the most progressive constitution on earth, where gender rights were codified. The highest ranking member of the ANC [African National Congress] gave a rousing analysis of involving women in democratic participation, then she proceeded to embrace all the other women leaders who were on her panel, and later that night led the dance of women from South Africa in the cultural celebration. While that was an inspiring display of the rich gifts women leaders bring, our job is more challenging here at home. In the regional tents where cultural celebrations were rampant, the North American/Europe tent was anemic, to be generous. Factory clothes, no food, little art, no music. Our insipid cultural expression is closely linked with our consumerism.

So I close with an offering of the seeds passed to me in the rain of China. Like my sisters from other parts, I urge you to buck these trends. Educate yourself on these issues, educate other women, make friends and do organizing with people of other races, ages, abilities. It will expand your humanity. Bring celebrations to this work across difference, encourage art and music within it. Take a new track by looking deeply inside the negative values American "democracy" is pursuing. Do your best to change them. Forward yourself and encourage other women forward to take on these challenges. Because despite the power and inspiration of gatherings like this Fourth World Conference on Women, despite the important advances made in naming and overcoming the inequities faced by women around the world, we return home to an increasing military budget, decreasing investment in education and jobs, greater poverty and more obscene wealth, more goods and less natural beauty—and these decisions still made mostly by men.

Glossary

This glossary contains many of the key concepts found in this book. The first time the concept is used in the text it is shown in **bold.** Refer to the definitions here to refresh your memory when you come across the terms again later.

able-bodyism—Attitudes, actions, and institutional practices that subordinate people with disabilities.

adultism—Attitudes, actions, and institutional practices that subordinate young people on the basis of their age.

ageism—Attitudes, actions, and institutional practices that subordinate elderly persons on the basis of their age.

alliance—Working with others, as a result of a deepening understanding of one another's lives, experiences, and goals.

analytical framework—A perspective that allows one to analyze the causes and implications of a particular issue, rather than simply describing it.

anti-Semitism—Attitudes, actions, and institutional practices that subordinate Jewish people (the term *Semite* is used also to refer to some Arabs).

biological determinism—A general theory holding that a group's biological or genetic makeup shapes its social, political, and economic destiny. This view is used to justify women's subordination, or the subordination of peoples of color on the argument that they are biologically or genetically different from, and usually inferior to, men or White people.

capitalism—An economic system in which most of the **capital**—property, raw materials, and the means of production (including people's labor)—and goods produced are owned or controlled by individuals or groups—capitalists. The goal of all production is to maximize profit making. Also referred to as **free market system.**

classism—Attitudes, actions, and institutional practices that subordinate working-class and poor people on the basis of their economic condition.

coalition—Usually a short-term collaboration of organizations in which the strategy is to stand together to achieve a specific goal or set of goals around a particular issue, regardless of other differences among the organizations.

commodification—The process of turning people and intangible things into things, or commodities, for sale; an example is the commodification of women's bodies through advertising and media representations.

comparable worth—A method of evaluating jobs that are traditionally defined as men's work or women's work—in terms of the knowledge and skills required for a particular job; the mental demands or decision making involved; the accountability or degree of supervision involved; and working conditions, such as how physically safe the job is—so as to eliminate inequities in pay based on gender.

conscientization—A methodology for understanding reality, or gaining a "critical consciousness," through group dialogue, critical analysis and examination of people's experiences and conditions that face them, which leads to action to transform that reality (Freire 1989).

contested terrain—An area of debate or controversy, in which several individuals or groups attempt to impose their own views or meanings on a situation.

criminalization—The process of turning people's circumstances or behaviors into a crime, such as the criminalization of mothers with HIV/AIDS or homeless people.

cultural appropriation—Taking possession of specific aspects of another group's culture in a gratuitous, inauthentic way, as happens, for example, when White people wear their hair in "dreads" or when nonindigenous people use indigenous people's names and symbols or adopt indigenous people's spiritual practices without being taught by indigenous practitioners. A particularly egregious form of cultural appropriation involves using another group's culture to make money. This is routine in the tourist industry, and it also occurs in the "New Age" spirituality movement, for example.

cultural relativism—The view that all "authentic" experience is equally valid and cannot be challenged by others. For example, White-supremacist views of Ku Klux Klan members are seen to be equally as valid as those held by antiracist activists.

There are no external standards or principles by which to judge people's attitudes and behaviors.

culture—The values, symbols, means of expression, language, and interests of a group of people. The **dominant culture** includes the values, symbols, means of expression, language, and interests of people in power in this society.

discrimination—Differential treatment against less powerful groups (such as women, the elderly, or people of color) by those in positions of dominance.

ecofeminism—A philosophy that links the domination of women with the domination of nature.

ecological footprint—The amount of land and energy required by various lifestyles and levels of development; calculated by estimating the amount of productive land needed to provide food, housing, transport, and consumer goods and services, and to absorb the waste that results from these processes; expressed in hectares or acres.

environmental racism—The strong correlation between the distribution of environmental pollution, including toxic wastes, and race; the movement for **environmental justice** draws on concepts of civil rights, whereby all citizens have a right to healthy living and working conditions.

essentialism—The view that people have some inherent essence, or characteristics and qualities, that define them. Some people argue, for example, that women are essentially more caring and nurturing than men.

eugenics—The White-supremacist belief that the human race can be "improved" through selective breeding.

feminization of poverty—Women and children constitute the vast majority of poor people in the United States and throughout the world, a result of structural inequalities and discriminatory policies.

fertility rate—The number of children born to women between 15 and 54, considered by official census reports to be the childbearing years.

first-wave feminism—Organizations and projects undertaken by suffragists and women's rights advocates from the 1840s until 1920 when women in the United States won the vote. See **liberal feminism.**

free market system—An ideological term used to describe a capitalist economic system with an emphasis on transnational trade and freedom from government regulation. In reality, this system has both government regulation of and support for businesses.

gender bending—Adopting clothing, body language, or behavior that challenges and undermines conventional gender norms and expectations.

gendered division of labor—A division of duties between men and women under which women have the main responsibility for home and nurturing and men are mainly active in the public sphere. Also referred to as **gender roles.**

gender gap—A significant difference between the political attitudes and voting patterns of women and men.

gender socialization—The process of learning the attitudes and behaviors that are considered culturally appropriate for boys or girls.

glass ceiling—An unseen barrier to women's promotion to senior positions in the workplace. Women can see the senior positions in their company or field, but few women reach them because of negative attitudes toward senior women and low perceptions of their abilities and training.

global level of analysis—A term used to describe the connections among people and among issues as viewed from a worldwide perspective.

heterosexism—Attitudes, actions, and institutional practices that subordinate people on the basis of their gay, lesbian, bisexual, or transgender orientation.

imperialism—The process of domination of one nation over other nations that are deemed inferior and to have dependent status for the purpose of exploiting their human and natural resources, to consolidate its power and wealth. An empire is able to draw resources from many nations and to deploy those governments and territories in its interest. Examples include the Roman empire, the British empire, and the current U.S. empire.

identity politics—Activism and politics that put identity at the center. It usually involves the assumption that a particular characteristic, such as race, ethnicity, or sexual orientation, is the most important in the lives of group members and that the group is not differentiated according to other characteristics in any significant way.

identity-based politics—Activism and politics that have a strong identity component but also a broader view that allows people to make connections to other groups and issues.

ideology—Ideas, attitudes, and values that represent the interests of a group of people. The dominant ideology comprises the ideas, attitudes, and values that represent the interests of the dominant group(s). Thus, for example, the ideological role of the idealized nuclear family is to devalue other family forms.

internalized oppression—Attitudes and behavior of some oppressed people that reflect the negative, harmful, stereotypical beliefs of the dominant group directed at oppressed people. An example of internalized sexism is the view of some women that they and other women are inferior to men, which causes them to adopt oppressive attitudes and behaviors that reinforce the oppression of women.

intersectionality—An integrative perspective that emphasizes the intersection of several attributes, for example, gender, race, class, and nation.

liberal feminism—A philosophy that sees the oppression of women as a denial of equal rights, representation, and access to opportunities.

libertarianism—The belief in unrestricted liberty.

macro level of analysis—A term used to describe the relationships among issues, individuals, and groups as viewed from a national perspective.

marginality—The situation in which a person has a deep connection to more than one culture, community, or social group but is not completely able to identify with or be accepted by that group as an insider. For example, bisexual, mixed-race/mixed-culture, and immigrant peoples often find themselves caught between two or more social worlds.

marginalization—Attitudes and behaviors that relegate certain people to the social, political, and economic margins of society by branding them and their interests as inferior, unimportant, or both.

matrix of oppression and resistance—The interconnections among various forms of oppression based on gender, race, class, nation, and so on. These social attributes can be sources of disadvantage as well as privilege. Negative ascriptions and experiences may be the source of people's resistance of oppression.

medicalization—The process of turning life processes, like childbirth or menopause, into medical issues. Thus, menopause becomes an illness to be treated by medical professionals with formal educational qualifications and accreditation. By the same token, experienced midwives are considered unqualified because they lack these credentials.

meso level of analysis—A term used to describe the relationships among issues, individuals, and groups as viewed from a community, or local, perspective.

micro level of analysis—A term used to describe the connections among people and issues as seen from a personal or individual perspective.

militarism—A system and worldview based on the objectification of "others" as enemies, a culture that celebrates war and killing. This worldview operates through specific political, economic, and military institutions and actions.

militarized masculinity—A masculinity constructed to support militarism, with an emphasis on heroism, physical strength, lack of emotion, and appearance of invulnerability (Enloe 1990, 1993a).

misogyny—Woman-hating attitudes and behavior.

neocolonialism—Continuing economic inequalities between rich and poor countries that originated in colonial relationships.

objectification—Attitudes and behaviors by which people are treated as if they were "things." One example is the objectification of women through advertising images.

objectivity—A form of understanding in which knowledge and meaning are believed to come from outside oneself and are presumably not affected by personal opinion or bias.

offshore production—Factory work or office work performed outside the United States—for example, in Mexico, the Philippines, or Indonesia— that is done for U.S.-based companies.

oppression—Prejudice and discrimination directed toward whole socially recognized groups of people and promoted by the ideologies and practices of all social institutions. The critical elements differentiating oppression from simple prejudice and discrimination are that it is a group phenomenon and that institutional power and authority are used to support prejudices and enforce discriminatory behaviors in systematic ways. Everyone is socialized to participate in oppressive practices, either as direct and indirect perpetrators or passive beneficiaries, or—as with some oppressed peoples—by directing discriminatory behaviors at members of one's own group or another group deemed inferior. See **internalized oppression.**

paradigm shift—A complete change in one's view of the world.

patriarchy—A family, social group, or society in which men hold power and are dominant figures. Patriarchal power in the United States plays out in the family, the economy, the media, religion, law, and electoral politics.

peer marriage—An intentionally egalitarian marriage with an emphasis on partnership, cooperation, and shared roles that are not highly differentiated along gender lines.

postcolonial feminism—A perspective that critiques Western imperialism and imperialist tendencies of Western feminism, and emphasizes historically defined colonial power relations that provide a foundational context for women's lives and struggles for change.

postmodern feminism—A type of feminism that repudiates the broad-brush "universal" theorizing of liberalism, radical feminism, or socialism, and emphasizes the particularity of women's experiences in specific cultural and historical contexts.

poverty level—An income level for individuals and families that officially defines poverty.

power—The ability to influence others, whether through persuasion, charisma, law, political activism, or coercion. Power operates informally and through formal institutions and at all levels (micro, meso, macro, global).

power elite—A relatively small group—not always easily identifiable—of key politicians, senior corporate executives, the very rich, and opinion makers such as key media figures who influence political and economic decisions in the country. Although this group shifts over time, and according to the issue, it is relatively closed.

praxis—Reflection and action upon the world in order to transform it; a key part of socially lived theorizing.

prejudice—A closed-minded prejudging of a person or group as negative or inferior, even without personal knowledge of that person or group, and often contrary to reason or facts; unreasonable, unfair, and hostile attitudes toward people.

privilege—Benefits and power from institutional inequalities. Individuals and groups may be privileged without realizing, recognizing, or even wanting it.

public vs. private dichotomy—The view that distinguishes between the private and personal (dating, marriage, sexual habits, who does the housework, relationships between parents and children) and the public (religion, law, business). Although these two spheres affect each other, according to this view they are governed by different rules, attitudes, and behavior.

racism—Racial prejudice and discrimination that are supported by institutional power and authority. In the United States, racism is based on the ideology of White (European) superiority and is used to the advantage of White people and the disadvantage of peoples of color.

radical feminism—A philosophy that sees the oppression of women in terms of patriarchy, a system of male authority, especially manifested in sexuality, personal relationships, and the family, and carried into the male-dominated world of work, government, religion, media, and law.

reproduction of labor—Unpaid domestic work, usually performed by women, in producing, nurturing, and socializing the next generation of workers and citizens; caring for adult members by providing meals and clean clothes, as well as rest, relaxation, love, and sexual intimacy, so that they are ready to face another working day.

second shift—Responsibilities for household chores and child care after having already done a full day's work outside the home, mostly done by women.

second-wave feminism—Feminist projects and organizations from the late 1960s to the mid-1980s that campaigned for women's equality in all spheres of life and, in some cases, that argued for a complete transformation of patriarchal, capitalist structures. See **liberal feminism, radical feminism, socialist feminism.**

separatism—The process of creating a separate life-space, often for political purposes, such as White lesbian separatists in the 1970s who chose to live in community with other women, to work with women, and to support women's projects. Some people of color may also advocate separatism from White people, institutions, values, and culture, and decide to put their energies only in support of other people of color.

sexism—Attitudes, actions, and institutional practices that subordinate women because of their gender.

situated knowledge—Knowledge and ways of knowing that are specific to a particular historical and cultural context.

S/M or **sado-masochism**—A sexual encounter or relationship in which one partner plays a dominant role and the other a subordinate role. In sado-masochistic sexual relationships, this inequality is presumed to be consensual.

social constructionism—The view that concepts that appear to be immutable and often solely biological, such as gender, race, and sexual orientation, are defined by human beings and can vary, depending on cultural and historical contexts. On this view, for example, heterosexuality is something learned—socially constructed—not innate. The "normalcy" of heterosexuality is systematically transmitted, and appropriate attitudes and behaviors are learned through childhood socialization and life experiences.

social control—Attitudes, behaviors, and mechanisms that keep people in their place. Overt social controls include laws, fines, imprisonment, and violence. Subtle ones include ostracism and withdrawal of status, affection, and respect.

social institutions—Institutions such as the family, education, the media, organized religion, law, and government.

socialist—Someone who believes that work should be organized for the collective benefit of workers rather than the profit of managers and corporate owners, and that the state should prioritize human needs.

socialist feminism—A view that sees the oppression of women in terms of their subordinate position in a system defined as both patriarchal and capitalist.

social location—The social features of one's identity incorporating individual, community, societal, and global factors such as gender, class, ability, sexual orientation, age, and so on.

speciesism—Attitudes, actions, and institutional practices that subordinate nonhuman species; usually used in discussions of environmental and ecological issues.

standpoint theory—The view that different social and historical situations give rise to very different experiences and theories about those experiences. See **situated knowledge.**

state—Governmental institutions, authority, and control. This includes the machinery of electoral politics, lawmaking, government agencies that execute law and policy, law enforcement agencies, the prison system, and the military.

subjectivity—A form of understanding in which knowledge and meaning come from oneself and one's own experiences.

sustainability—The ability of an ecologically sound economy to sustain itself by using renewable resources and generating low or nonaccumulating levels of pollution. A more sustainable future means rethinking and radically changing current produc-

tion processes, as well as the materialism and consumerism that support excessive production.

theory—An explanation of how things are and why they are the way they are; a theory is based on a set of assumptions, has a perspective, and serves a purpose.

third-wave feminism—Feminist perspectives adopted in the 1990s often by younger women, with an emphasis on personal voice and multiple identities, ambiguity, and contradictions.

References

Abbey, S., and A. O'Reilly, eds. 1998. *Redefining motherhood: Changing identities and patterns.* Toronto: Second Story Press.

Abramovitz, M. 1996. *Regulating the lives of women.* Rev. ed. Boston: South End Press.

Abramovitz, M., and F. Newton. 1996. *Challenging AFDC Myths with the Facts.* Available from the Bertha Capen Reynolds Society, Columbus Circle Station, P.O. Box 20563, New York, NY 10023.

Abramson, W., E. Emanuel, V. Gaylord, and M. Hayden. 2000. *Impact: Special issue on violence against women with developmental or other disabilities* 13(3). Minneapolis: The Institute on Community Integration, University of Minnesota. Available online at http://ici.umn.edu/products/impact/133.

Abzug, B. 1984. *Gender gap: Bella Abzug's guide to political power for American women.* Boston: Houghton Mifflin.

Adler, F. 1975. *Sisters in crime: The rise of the new female criminal.* New York: McGraw-Hill.

Agarwal, B. 1992. The gender and environment debate: Lessons from India. *Feminist Review* 18(1): 119–57.

Ahn, I. S. 1996. Great army, great father. In *Great army, great father,* edited by T. H. Yu. Seoul, South Korea: Korean Church Women United.

Aisha. 1991. Changing my perception. *Aché: A Journal for Lesbians of African Descent* 3(3): 28–29.

Albelda, R., and C. Tilly. 1997. *Glass ceilings and bottomless pits: Women's work, women's poverty.* Boston: South End Press.

Albelda, R. and A. Withorn, eds. 2002. *Lost ground: Welfare, poverty, and beyond.* Cambridge, Mass.: South End Press.

Alcoff, L. 1988. Cultural feminism versus post-structuralism: The identity crisis in feminist theory. *Signs: Journal of Women in Culture and Society* 13(3): 405–36.

Alexander, J., and C. T. Mohanty, eds. 1997. *Feminist genealogies, colonial legacies, democratic futures.* New York: Routledge.

Allen, P. G. 1986. *The sacred hoop: Recovering the feminine in American Indian traditions.* Boston: Beacon Press.

Allison, D. 1992. *Bastard out of Carolina.* New York: Dutton.

Alonso, H. H. 1993. *Peace as a women's issue: A history of the U.S. movement for world peace and women's rights.* Syracuse, N.Y.: Syracuse University Press.

American Association of Retired Persons. N.d. *America's changing work force: Statistics in brief.* Washington, D.C.: American Association of Retired Persons.

American Civil Liberties Union. 1999. In stunning civil rights victory, VT court directs state to give same-sex couple marriage benefits. *ACLU News* [online], 20 December. Accessed online http://www.aclu.org/news/december99.html on 21 December 1999.

———. 2002a. *ACLU alert: Federal marriage amendment and domestic partner benefits.* Accessed online at http:// www.tgcrossroads.org/news/?aid-305 on 6 November 2002.

———. 2002b. *The USA Patriot Act.* Accessed online at http://www.aclu.org on 16 January 2003.

American Correctional Association. 1990. *The female offender: What does the future hold?* Washington, D.C.: St. Mary's Press.

American Federation of State, County, and Municipal Employees. 1988. *Stopping sexual harassment: An AFSCME guide.* Washington, D.C.: American Federation of State, County, and Municipal Employees.

American Friends Service Committee. 1989. *AFSC perspectives on the employer sanctions provisions of the Immigration Reform and Control Act of 1986.* Philadelphia: American Friends Service Committee.

American Heritage Dictionary. 1993. 3d ed. Boston: Houghton Mifflin.

American Immigration Lawyers Association. 2001. *Agency in meltdown: Major problems continue with INS benefits adjudications.* Posted on AILA InfoNet at Doc. No.39ip1001 7 May 2001. Accessed online at http://www.aila.org on 27 December 2002.

American Society of Civil Engineers. 1999. Data accessed online at http://www.asce.org/reportcard/index.cfm?reaction=factsheet&page=5 on 16 January 2003.

American Society of Plastic Surgeons. *National clearing-house of plastic surgery statistics, 1998.* Accessed online at http://www.plasticsurgery.org/mediactr/98avgsurgfees.htm on 6 January 2000.

———. 2002. Accessed online at http://www.plasticsurgery.org/mediactr on 5 October 2002.

Amnesty International USA. 1999. *"Not part of my sentence": Violations of human rights of women in custody.* New York: Amnesty International USA.

———. 2000. *United States of America: Breaking the chain. The human rights of women prisoners.* New York: Amnesty International USA.

Amott, T. 1993. *Caught in the crisis: Women and the U.S. economy today.* New York: Monthly Review Press.

Amott, T., and J. Matthaei. 1996. *Race, gender, and work: A multicultural economic history of women in the United States.* Rev. ed. Boston: South End Press.

Andersen, M. 2000. Women, power and politics. Pp. 290–322 in *Thinking about women: Sociological perspectives on sex and gender,* 5th ed. Boston: Allyn and Bacon.

Anderson, L., ed. 1991. *Sisters of the earth: Women's prose and poetry about nature.* New York: Vintage Books.

Anderson, M. 1999. A well-kept secret: How military spending costs women's jobs. Pp. 247–52 in *Gender camouflage,* edited by F. D'Amico and L. Weinstein. New York: New York University Press.

Anderson, M., G. Bischak, and M. Oden. 1991. *Converting the American economy.* East Lansing, Mich.: Employment Research Associates.

Anderson, M. L., and P. H. Collins, eds. 1995. *Race, class, and gender: An anthology.* 2d ed. Belmont, Calif.: Wadsworth.

Anderson, S., J. Cavanagh, and D. Ranney. 1999. NAFTA: Trinational fiasco. Pp. 104–7 in *The maquiladora reader: Cross-border organizing since NAFTA,* edited by R. Kamel and A. Hoffman. Philadelphia: American Friends Service Committee.

Andre, J. 1988. Stereotypes: Conceptual and normative considerations. In *Racism and sexism: An integrated study,* edited by P. S. Rothenberg. New York: St. Martin's Press.

Andruss, V., C. Plant, J. Plant, and S. Mills. 1990. *Home!: A bioregional reader.* Philadelphia: New Society.

Anglin, M., and Y. Hser. 1987. Addicted women and crime. *Criminology* 25: 359–94.

Angwin, J. 1996. Pounding on the glass ceiling. *San Francisco Chronicle,* 24 November, p. C3.

Anzaldúa, G. 1987. *Borderlands la frontera: The new mestiza.* San Francisco: Spinsters/Aunt Lute.

Applebome, P. 1997. Citadel's president insists coeducation will succeed. *New York Times,* 14 January, p. A1.

Arcana, J. 1994. Abortion is a motherhood issue. Pp. 159–63 in *Mother journeys: Feminists write about mothering,* edited by M. Reddy, M. Roth, and A. Sheldon. Minneapolis: Spinsters Ink.

Archibold, R. C. 1999. A chill at Stuyvesant High: Prudence, or paranoia, after sexual abuse by teacher? *New York Times,* 21 September, p. B1.

Arditti, R., R. D. Klein, and S. Minden, eds. 1984. *Test-tube women: What future for motherhood?* Boston: Pandora Press.

Associated Press. 1999. Most leaving welfare remain poor. *San Francisco Chronicle,* 12 May, p. A6.

———. 2002. Soldier kills wife, commits suicide. *Army Times,* 13 June, p. 1.

Association of American Colleges and Universities. 2002. *Statement of affirmative action, educational excellence, and higher education's civic mission.* Accessed online at http://www.aacu.org/About/affirmativeaction02.cfm on 21 December 2002.

Atkins, D., ed. 1998. *Looking queer: Body image and identity in lesbian, bisexual, gay, and transgender communities.* New York: Haworth Press.

Avery, B. 1990. Breathing life into ourselves: The evolution of the Black women's health project. Pp. 4–10 in *The Black women's health book,* edited by E. White. Seattle. Seal Press.

Ayres, B. D., Jr. 1994. U.S. crackdown at border stems illegal crossings. *New York Times,* 6 October, pp. A1, A14.

Baca Zinn, M. 1989. Family, race, and poverty in the eighties. *Signs* 14: 856–74.

Bagby, R. 1990. Daughter of growing things. Pp. 231–48 in *Reweaving the world: The emergence of ecofeminism,* edited by I. Diamond and G. Orenstein. San Francisco: Sierra Club.

Baird-Windle, P. and E. J. Bader. 2001. *Targets of hatred: Anti-abortion terrorism.* New York: Palgrave.

Baker, B. 1993. The women's convergence for national health care. *The Network News,* July/August, pp. 1, 3.

Bandarage, A. 1997. *Women, population and global crisis: A political-economic analysis.* London and New Jersey: Zed Books.

Baptists in Texas reject a call for wives to "submit" to husbands. 1999. *New York Times,* 10 November, p. A21.

Barnes, B. and T. Clarke. 1986. *How to get a man to make a commitment or know when he never will.* New York: St. Martin's Press.

Barnett, E. 2002. Prison coffee and games: Starbucks and Nintendo admit their contractor uses prison labor. *Prison Legal News* 13(3): 12–13.

Barnett, R., and C. Rivers. 1996. *She works, he works: How two-income families are happier, healthier, and better-off.* New York: HarperSanFrancsico.

Barnhill, D. L., ed. 1999. *At home on the earth: Becoming native to our place.* Berkeley: University of California Press.

Baron, H. M. 1970. The web of urban racism. In *Institutional racism in America,* edited by L. L. Knowles and K. Prewitt. Englewood Cliffs, N.J.: Prentice Hall.

Barry, K. 1995. *The prostitution of sexuality: The global exploitation of women.* New York: New York University Press.

Bart, P., and P. O'Brien. 1993. *Stopping rape: Successful survival strategies.* New York: Teachers College Press.

Bartlett, J. 1994. *Will you be a mother? Women who choose to say no.* London: Virago.

Bass, E., and L. Davis. 1988. *The courage to heal.* New York: Harper & Row.

Basu, A. 1995. *The challenge of local feminisms.* Boulder, Colo.: Westview Press.

Baumgardner, J., and A. Richards. 2000. *Manifesta: Young women, feminism, and the future.* New York: Farrar, Straus and Giroux.

Baxandall, R. 2001. Re-visioning the women's liberation movement's narrative: Early second-wave African American feminists. *Feminist Studies* 27(1): 225–45.

Baxandall, R. and L. Gordon, eds. 2002. *Dear sisters: Dispatches from the women's liberation movement.* New York: Basic Books.

Beasley, M., and D. Thomas. 1994. Violence as a human rights issue. Pp. 323–46 in *The public nature of private violence: The discovery of domestic abuse,* edited by M. A. Fineman and R. Mykitiuk. New York: Routledge.

Belenky, M. F., B. M. Clinchy, N. R. Goldberger, and J. M. Tarule. 1997. *Women's ways of knowing: The development of self, voice, and mind.* 10th anniversary ed. New York: Basic Books.

Bell, D. and R. Klein, eds. 1996. *Radically speaking: Feminism reclaimed.* North Melbourne, Australia: Spinifex Press.

Benard, C., and E. Schlaffer. 1997. "The man in the street": Why he harasses. Pp. 395–98 in *Feminist frontiers IV,* edited by L. Richardson, V. Taylor, and N. Whittier. New York: McGraw-Hill.

Benjamin, M., and A. Freedman. 1989. *Bridging the global gap: A handbook to linking citizens of the first and third worlds.* Cabin John, Md.: Seven Locks Press.

Bennett, K. 1992. Feminist bisexuality: A both/and option for an either/or world. Pp. 205–31 in *Closer to home: Bisexuality and feminism,* edited by E. R. Weise. Seattle, Wash.: Seal Press.

Bennett, M. and V. D. Dickerson. 2001. *Recovering the Black female body: Self-representations by African American women.* New Brunswick, N.J.: Rutgers University Press.

Benston, M. 1969. The political economy of women's liberation. *Monthly Review* 21(4): 13–27.

Berg, P. 1993. Growing a life-place politics. In *Radical environmentalism: Philosophy and tactics,* edited by J. List. Belmont, Calif.: Wadsworth.

Bergen, R. K. 1996. *Wife rape: Understanding the response of survivors and service providers.* Thousand Oaks, Calif.: Sage.

———. 1999. *Marital rape.* Department of Justice Online Resources. Accessed at http://www.vaw.umn.edu/vawmet/mrape.htm.

Bergmann, B. R. 1986. *The economic emergence of women.* New York: Basic Books.

Bernstein, R., and S. C. Silberman, eds. 1996. *Generation Q.* Los Angeles: Alyson.

Bhattacharjee, A. 1997. A slippery path: Organizing resistance to violence against women. Pp. 29–45 in *Dragon ladies: Asian American feminists breathe fire,* edited by S. Shah. Boston: South End Press.

———. 2002. Private fists: pubic force: Race, gender, and surveillance. Pp. 1–54 in *Policing the national body: Sex, race, and criminalization,* edited by J. Silliman and A. Bhattacharjee. Cambridge, Mass: South End Press.

Bianchi, S., M. Milkie, L. Sayer, and J. Robinson. 2002. Is anyone doing the housework? Trends in the gender division of household labor. Pp. 174–87 *Workplace/women's place,* 2d ed., edited by P. Dubeck and D. Dunn. Los Angeles: Roxbury Publishing.

Bigelow, B. and B. Peterson, eds. 2002. *Rethinking globalization: Teaching for justice in an unjust world.* Milwaukee, Wis.: Rethinking Schools.

Billich, K. 2001. *How much will child care cost?* Accessed online at http://www.americanbaby.com on 16 January 2003.

Bin Wahad, D. 1996. Speaking truth to power: Political prisoners in the United States. In *Criminal injustice: Confronting the prison crisis,* edited by E. Rosenblatt. Boston: South End Press.

Bird, C. 1995. *Lives of ours: Secrets of salty old women.* New York: Houghton Mifflin.

Bird, C., and S. W. Briller. 1969. *Born female: The high cost of keeping women down.* New York: Pocket Books.

Birks, J. and A. Erlich, eds. 1989. *Hidden dangers: The environmental consequences of preparing for war.* San Francisco: Sierra Club Books.

Black Women's Health Project. 1995. *Reproductive health and African American women. Issue brief.* Washington, D.C.: Black Women's Health Project.

Blakely, M. K. 1994. *American mom: Motherhood, politics, and humble pie.* Chapel Hill, N.C.: Algonquin Books.

Blank, H., ed. 2001. *Zaftig: Well-rounded erotica.* San Francisco: Cleis Press.

Blau, J. 1999. *Illusions of prosperity: America's working families in an age of economic insecurity.* New York: Oxford University Press.

Blauner, R. 1972. *Racial oppression in America.* New York: Harper & Row.

Blee, K. M. 1998. Radicalism. Pp. 500–501 in *The reader's companion to U.S. women's history,* edited by W. Mankiller, G. Mink, M. Navarro, B. Smith, and G. Steinem. Boston: Houghton Mifflin.

Bleier, R. 1984. *Science and gender: A critique of biology and its theories on women.* New York: Pergamon Press.

Bloom, B., M. Chesney-Lind, and B. Owen. 1994. *Women in California prisons: Hidden victims of the war on drugs.* San Francisco: Center on Juvenile and Criminal Justice.

Bloom, C., A. Gitter, S. Gutwill, L. Kogel, and L. Zaphiropoulos. 1994. *Eating problems: A feminist psychoanalytic treatment model.* New York: Basic Books.

Blustein, Paul. 2002. Bold IMF global debt relief plan. *San Francisco Chronicle,* 29 September, p. A1.

Boesing, M. 1994. Statement to the Court. Pp. 189–91 in *Mother journeys: Feminists write about mothering,* edited by M. Reddy, M. Roth, and A. Sheldon. Minneapolis: Spinsters Ink.

Boggs, G. L. 1994. Fifty years on the left. *The Witness,* May, 8–12.

Bohmer, C., and A. Parrot. 1993. *Sexual assault on campus: The problem and the solution.* New York: Lexington Books/Macmillan.

Booth, W. 1997. Ex-Black Panther freed. *Washington Post,* 11 June, p. A1.

Bordo, S. 1993. *Unbearable weight: Feminism, Western culture, and the body.* Berkeley: University of California Press.

Borenstein, S. 2003. A new environment: Bush alters policies, quietly and significantly. *San Jose Mercury News,* 18 January, p. 1A.

Borkovitz, D. K. 1995. Same-sex battering and the backlash. *NCADV Voice,* Summer, 4.

Bornstein, K. 1995. *Gender outlaw: On men, women, and the rest of us.* New York: Vintage/Random House.

———. 1998. *My gender workbook: How to become a real man, a real woman, the real you, or something else entirely.* New York: Routledge.

Boston Women's Health Book Collective. 1992. *The new our bodies, ourselves.* New York: Simon & Schuster.

———. 1994. *The new ourselves growing older.* New York: Simon & Schuster.

———. 1998. *Our bodies, ourselves for the new century: A book by and for women.* New York: Simon & Schuster.

Boswell, J. 1994. *Same-sex unions in premodern Europe.* New York: Villard Books.

Boumil, M., and J. Friedman. 1996. *Deadbeat dads: A national child support scandal.* Westport, Conn.: Praeger.

Boulding, E. 1990. *Building a civic culture: Education for an interdependent world.* Syracuse, N.Y.: Syracuse University Press.

Bourbeau, H. 1998. U.S. companies under fire for using Chinese sweatshops. *Financial Times,* 19 March, p. 8.

Bowlby, J. 1963. *Child care and the growth of love.* Baltimore: Penguin Books.

Boxer, M. 1998. *When women ask the questions: Creating women's studies in America.* Baltimore: Johns Hopkins University Press.

Braidotti, R., E. Charkiewicz, S. Häusler, and S. Wieringa. 1994. *Women, the environment and sustainable development: Towards a theoretical synthesis.* London: Zed Books.

Brant, B., ed. 1988. *A gathering of spirits: A collection by North American Indian women.* Ithaca, N.Y.: Firebrand.

Brennan, S., J. Winklepleck, and G. MacNee. 1994. *The resourceful woman.* Detroit: Visible Ink.

Brenner, J. 1996. The best of times, the worst of times: Feminism in the United States. Pp. 17–72 in *Mapping the women's movement,* edited by M. Threlfall. London: Verso Books.

———. 2001. *Women and the politics of class.* New York: Monthly Review Press.

Bright, S. 1994. *Herotica 3.* New York: Plume.

———, ed. 2000. *The best American erotica.* New York: Simon & Schuster.

Brody, J. 2001. Pregnancy prevention, the morning after. *New York Times,* 10 April, p. D8.

Brown, B. R. D. 1996. White North American political prisoners. In *Criminal injustice: Confronting the prison crisis,* edited by E. Rosenblatt. Boston: South End Press.

Browne, C. 1998. *Women, feminism, and aging.* New York: Springer.

Browne, J. 1996. The labor of doing time. In *Criminal injustice: Confronting the prison crisis,* edited by E. Rosenblatt. Boston: South End Press.

Brownmiller, S. 1975. *Against our will: Men, women, and rape.* New York: Simon & Schuster.

Bruce, C., ed. 2001. *Best bisexual women's erotica.* San Francisco: Cleis Press.

Brumberg, J. J. 1997. *The body project: An intimate history of American girls.* New York: Random House.

Buchwald, E., P. Fletcher, and M. Roth, eds. 1993. *Transforming a rape culture.* Minneapolis: Milkweed.

Bulhan, H. A. 1985. *Frantz Fanon and the psychology of oppression.* New York: Plenum Books.

Bullard, R. D. 1990. *Dumping in Dixie: Race, class, and environmental quality.* Boulder, Colo.: Westview Press.

———, ed. 1993. *Confronting environmental racism: Voices from the grassroots.* Boston: South End Press.

Bullough, V. L., and B. Bullough. 1993. *Cross dressing, sex, and gender.* Philadelphia: University of Pennsylvania Press.

Bunch, C. 1983. Not by degrees: Feminist theory and education. In *Learning our way: Essays in feminist education;* edited by C. Bunch and S. Pollack. Trumansburg, N.Y.: Crossing Press.

———. 1987. *Passionate politics: Essays 1968–1986.* New York: St. Martin's Press.

Bunch, C., and R. Carillo. 1991. *Gender violence: A human rights and development issue.* New Brunswick, N.J.: Center for Women's Global Leadership, Rutgers University.

Bunch, C., and N. Myron, eds. 1974. *Class and feminism: A collection of essays from the Furies.* Baltimore: Diana Press.

Bunch, C., and N. Reilly. 1994. *Demanding accountability: The global campaign and Vienna Tribunal for women's human rights.* New Jersey: Center for Women's Global Leadership, Rutgers University; New York: UNIFEM.

Bureau of Justice Statistics. 1991. *Special report: Women in prison in 1986.* Washington, D.C.: U.S. Department of Justice.

———. 1992. *Women in jail in 1989.* Washington, D.C.: U.S. Department of Justice.

———. 1994a. *Special report: Women in prison in 1991.* Washington, D.C.: U.S. Department of Justice.

———. 1994b. *National crime victimization survey, violence against women.* Washington, D.C.: U.S. Department of Justice.

———. 1995. *Violence against women: Estimates from the redesigned survey.* Washington, D.C.: U.S. Department of Justice.

———. 1998. *Criminal victimization 1997: Changes 1996–97 with trends 1993–97.* Washington, D.C.: U.S. Department of Justice.

———. 1999a, December. *Special report: Women offenders.* Washington, D.C.: U.S. Department of Justice.

———. 1999b, August. *Bulletin: Prisoners in 1998.* Washington, D.C.: U.S. Department of Justice.

———. 1999c. *Rates of HIV infection and AIDS-related deaths drop among the nation's prisoners.* Washington, D.C.: Bureau of Justice Statistics.

———. 2000.*Women offenders.* Washington, D.C.: U.S. Department of Justice.

———. 2002. *Crime and victim statistics.* Washington, D.C.: U.S. Department of Justice. Accessed online at http:// www.ojp.usdoj.gov/bjs/cvict.htm on 15 January 2003.

Bureau of Labor Statistics. 1998. *Employment and earnings.* Washington, D.C.: Bureau of Labor Statistics.

———. 2002a. *A profile of the working poor, 2000.* Washington, D.C.: U.S. Bureau of Labor. Accessed online at http://www.bls.gov/cps/cpswp2000.htm on 19 December 2002.

———. 2002b. *Work experience summary, Table 1.* Washington, D.C.: U.S. Bureau of Labor. Accessed online at http://www.bls.gov/news.release/work.t01.htm on 19 December 2002.

———. 2000c. *Employment and earnings. January.* Washington, D.C.: U.S. Bureau of Labor. Accessed online at http://www.aflcio.org/women/wwfacts.htm on 7 November 2002.

Burke, P. 1996. *Gender shock: Exploding the myths of male and female.* New York: Anchor Books.

Burrell, B. 1994. *A woman's place is in the House: Campaigning for Congress in the feminist era.* Ann Arbor: University of Michigan Press.

Burton, N. 1998. Resistance to prevention: Reconsidering feminist antiviolence rhetoric. Pp. 182–200 in *Violence against women: Philosophical perspectives,* edited by S. French, W. Teays, and L. Purdy. Ithaca, N.Y.: Cornell University Press.

Bury, J., V. Morrison, and S. McLauchlan, eds. 1992. *Working with women with AIDS.* New York: Routledge.

Bush-Baksette, S. R. 1999. The "war on drugs" a war against women? In *Harsh punishment: International experiences of women's imprisonment,* edited by S. Cook and S. Davies. Boston: Northeastern University Press.

Butler, J. 1990. *Gender trouble: Feminism and the subversion of identity.* New York: Routledge, Chapman, & Hall.

Butler, O. 1993. *The parable of the sower.* New York: Warner Books.

Calvo, J. 1996. Health care access for immigrant women. Pp. 161–81 in *Man-made medicine: Women's health, public policy, and reform,* edited by K. L. Moss. Durham, N.C.: Duke University Press.

Cammermeyer, M. 1994. *Serving in silence.* New York: Viking.

Camp, L. T. 1997. *Lingering fever: A World War II nurse's memoir.* Jefferson, N.C.: McFarland and Co.

Campbell, D., with F. D'Amico. 1999. Lessons on gender integration from the military academies. Pp. 67–79 in *Gender camouflage: Women and the U.S. military,* edited by F. D'Amico and L. Weinstein. New York: New York University Press.

Campbell, J. 1999, October. *Health insurance coverage 1998.* Washington, D.C.: U.S. Department of Commerce, Economics and Statistics Administration.

Candib, L. 1995. *Medicine and the family: A feminist perspective.* New York: Basic Books.

Caplan, P., ed. 1987. *The cultural construction of sexuality.* London: Tavistock Publications.

Caputi, J., and D. E. H. Russell. 1990. "Femicide": Speaking the unspeakable. *Ms.,* September/October, 34–37.

Carle, G. 2000. *He's not all that!: How to attract the good guys.* New York: Cliff Street Books/HarperCollins.

Carlen, P. 1989. Feminist jurisprudence, or womenwise penology. *Probation Journal* 36(3): 110–14.

Carroll, S. J., ed., 2001. *The impact of women in public office.* Bloomington: Indiana University Press.

Carson, R. 1962. *Silent spring.* Boston: Houghton Mifflin.

Catalyst. 2002. *Fact sheet: Women CEOs.* Accessed online at http://www.catalystwomen.org/press_room/factsheets/fact_women_ceos.htm on 21 December 2002.

Cavin, S. 1985. *Lesbian origins.* San Francisco: Ism Press.

Center for American Women and Politics. 1999. *Fact sheet: Women in the U.S. Congress 1999.* New Brunswick, N.J.: Center for American Women and Politics, Rutgers University.

Center for American Women and Politics. 2001. *Women state legislators: Past, present and future.* New Brunswick, N.J.: CAWP.

Center for Defense Information. 2002. *World military expenditures.* Accessed online at http://www.cdi.org/issues/wme on 14 January 2003.

Center for Reproductive Law and Policy. N.d. *The facts about contraceptive coverage in private and government insurance.* New York: Center for Reproductive Law and Policy.

Centers for Disease Control and Prevention. 1996. *Sexually transmitted disease surveillance.* Atlanta: U.S. Department of Health and Human Services.

———. 1999. *HIV/AIDS surveillance report* 11(1). Rockville, Md.: Centers for Disease Control and Prevention.

———. 2000. *Tracking the hidden epidemics: Trends in STDs in the United States 2000.* Accessed online at http://www.cdc.gov/nchstp/dstd/stats-Trends/Trends2000.pdf on 19 November 2002.

Chaddock, G. R., 2002. Security act to pervade daily lives. *Christian Science Monitor,* November 21. Accessed online at http://www.csmonitor.com/2002/1121/p01s03-usju.html on 17 January 2003.

Chalker, R. 1995. Sexual pleasure unscripted. *Ms.,* November/December, 49–52.

Chambers, V. 1995. Betrayal feminism. In *Listen up: Voices from the next feminist generation,* edited by B. Findlen. Seattle, Wash.: Seal Press.

Chapkis, W. 1986. *Beauty secrets: Women and the politics of appearance.* Boston: South End Press.

Chavez, C. 1993. Farm workers at risk. Pp. 163–170 in *Toxic struggles: The theory and practice of environmental justice,* edited by R. Hofrichter. Philadelphia and Gabriola Island, B.C.: New Society Publishers.

Chavkin, W. 1984. *Double exposure: Women's health hazards on the job and at home.* New York: Monthly Review Press.

Chernin, K. 1985. *The hungry self.* New York: Times Books.

Chesler, P. 1972. *Women and madness.* New York: Avon.

Chesney-Lind, M. 1986. Women and crime: A review of the literature on the female offender. *Signs: Journal of Women in Culture and Society* 12(1): 78–96.

———. 1987. Female offenders: Paternalism reexamined. In *Women, the courts and equality,* edited by L. Crites and W. Hepperle. Newbury Park, Calif.: Sage.

———. 1995. Rethinking women's imprisonment: A critical examination of trends in female incarceration. In *Women, Crime, and Criminal Justice,* edited by B. R. Price and N. Sokoloff. New York: McGraw-Hill.

———. 1997. *The female offender: Girls, women and crime.* Thousand Oaks, Calif.: Sage.

———. 2000, February. From bad to worse. Review of *Hard punishment: International experiences of women's imprisonment. Women's Review of Books* 17(5): 7.

Chesney-Lind, M., and R. G. Shelden. 1992. *Girls, delinquency and juvenile justice.* Pacific Grove, Calif.: Brooks/Cole.

Children's Defense Fund. 2000. Where America stands. In *The state of America's children yearbook.* Washington, D.C.: Children's Defense Fund.

———. 2002. *The state of children in America's union: A 2002 action guide to leave no child behind.* Washington, D.C.: Children's Defense Fund.

Chodorow, N. 1978. *Reproduction and mothering: Psychoanalysis and the sociology of gender.* Berkeley: University of California Press.

Chrichton, S. 1993. Sexual correctness: Has it gone too far? *Newsweek,* 25 October, 55.

Churchill, W. 1992. Introduction: The Third World at home. In *Cages of steel: The politics of imprisonment in the United States,* edited by W. Churchill and J. J. Vander Wall. Washington, D.C.: Maisonnueve Press.

Citizen Soldier. 1996. *Newsletter.* New York: Citizen Soldier.

Clare, E. 1999. *Exile and pride.* Cambridge, Mass.: South End Press.

Clinton, H. R. 1996. *It takes a village and other lessons children teach us.* New York: Simon & Schuster.

Cobble, D. S., ed. 1993. *Women and unions: Forging a partnership.* Ithaca, N.Y.: ILR Press.

Cohen, K. 2001. *A walk down the aisle: Notes on a modern wedding.* New York: W. W. Norton.

Cole, J. H. 1992. *Women pilots of World War II.* Salt Lake City: University of Utah Press.

College Board. N.d. *2002–2003 College costs: Keeping rising prices in perspective.* Accessed online at http://www.collegeboard.com/article/0,,6-29-0-4494,00.html?orig=sec on 16 January 2003.

Collier, R. 2002. For anti-sweatshop activists, recent settlement is only tip of iceberg. *San Francisco Chronicle,* 29 September, p. A14.

Collins, P. H. 1990. *Black feminist thought: Knowledge, consciousness, and the politics of empowerment.* Boston: Unwin Hyman.

Comité Fronterizo de Obreras-American Friends Service Committee. 1999. *Six years of NAFTA: A view from inside the maquiladoras.* Philadelphia: AFSC.

Commonwealth Fund. 1997. *The Commonwealth Fund Survey of the health of adolescent girls: Highlights and methodology.* New York: The Commonwealth Fund.

Connell, R. W. 1990. The state, gender, and sexual politics: Theory and appraisal. *Theory and Society* 19(4): 507–44.

Cook, A., and G. Kirk. 1983. *Greenham women everywhere: Dreams, ideas, and actions from the women's peace movement.* Boston: South End Press.

Coontz, S. 1992. *The way we never were: American families and the nostalgia trap.* New York: Basic Books.

———. 1997. *The way we really are: Coming to terms with America's changing families.* New York: Basic Books.

Cooper, E. 1992. When being ill is illegal: Women and the criminalization of HIV. *Health/PAC Bulletin,* Winter, 10–14.

Cooper, M. 1997. When push comes to shove: Who is welfare reform really helping? *The Nation,* 2 June, 11–15.

Corea, G. 1985. *The mother machine: Reproductive technologies from artificial insemination to artificial wombs.* New York: Harper & Row.

———. 1987. *Man-made women: How reproductive technologies affect women.* Bloomington: Indiana University Press.

Corral, J. and L. Miya-Jervis. 2001. *Young wives' tales: New adventures in love and partnership.* Seattle: Seal Press.

Cox, M. 2001a. Wal-martyrs: Women take aim at Wal-Mart's glass ceiling by filing the biggest discrimination suit in history. *Ms.,* October/November, 18–20.

———. 2001b. Zero balance: Watch out! Your retirement funds are in more trouble than you think. *Ms.,* February/March, 57–65.

Cox, T. 1999. *Hot sex: How to do it.* New York: Bantam Books.

Crenshaw, K. 1993. The marginalization of sexual violence against Black women. Speech to the National Coalition Against Sexual Assault, 1993 Conference, Chicago. Accessed online at http://www.ncasa.org/marginalization.html.

Crittenden, A. 2001. *The price of motherhood: Why the most important job in the world is still the least valued.* New York: Metropolitan Books.

Croteau, D., and W. Hoynes. 1997. *Media/society: Industries, images, and audiences.* Thousand Oaks, Calif.: Pine Forge Press.

D'Agostino, J. 2002. U.S. women may see fighting in Iraq. *Human Events,* 12 October. Accessed online at http://www.humaneventsonline.com/articles/10-12-02/dagostino.htm on 14 January 2003.

Dalla Costa, M., and S. James. 1972. *The power of women and the subversion of the community.* Bristol, England: Falling Wall Press.

Daly, F. 1994. Perspectives of Native American women on race and gender. In *Challenging racism: Alternatives to genetic explanations,* edited by E. Tobach and B. Risoff. New York: The Feminist Press.

Daly, H. E., and J. B. Cobb Jr. 1989. *For the common good: Redirecting the economy toward community, the environment, and a sustainable future.* Boston: Beacon Press.

Daly, K. 1994. *Gender, crime, and punishment.* New Haven, Conn.: Yale University Press.

Daly, M. 1976. *Gyn/ecology: The metaethics of radical feminism.* Boston: Beacon Press.

D'Amico, F. 1998. Feminist perspectives on women warriors. Pp. 119–25 in *The women and war reader,* edited by L. A. Lorentzen and J. Turpin. New York: New York University Press.

D'Amico, F., and L. Weinstein, eds. 1999. *Gender camouflage: Women and the U.S. military.* New York: New York University Press.

Danaher, K. N.d. *Seven arguments for reforming the world economy.* Accessed online at http://www.globalexchange.org/economy/econ101/sevenArguments.html.

Daniels, C. R. 1993. *At women's expense: State power and the politics of fetal rights.* Cambridge: Harvard University Press.

Dankelman, I., and J. Davidson. 1988. *Women and the environment in the Third World.* London: Earthscan.

Danquah, M. 1998. *Willow weep for me: A Black women's journey through depression.* New York: W. W. Norton.

Dargan, C. A. 1995. *Statistical record of health and medicine.* Detroit: Gale Research.

Darling, M., and J. Tyson. 1999. The state: Friend or foe? Distributive justice issues and African American women. Pp. 214–41 in *Dangerous intersections: Feminist perspectives on population, environment, and development,* edited by J. Silliman and Y. King. Cambridge, Mass.: South End Press.

das Dasgupta, S., and S. DasGupta. 1996. Public face, private space: Asian Indian women and sexuality. Pp. 226–43 in *"Bad girls"/"good girls": Women, sex, and power in the nineties,* edited by N. Bauer Maglin and D. Perry. New Brunswick, N.J.: Rutgers University Press.

Davis, A. Y. 1983a. Racism, birth control, and reproductive rights. In *Women, race, and class.* New York: Vintage Books.

———. 1983b. *Women, race, and class.* New York: Vintage Books.

———. 1997. A plenary address. Paper presented at conference, Frontline Feminisms: Women, War, and Resistance, 16 January, at University of California, Riverside.

———. 2001. The color of violence against women. *Sojourner: The Women's Forum,* October, 12–13.

Davis, F. 1991. *Moving the mountain: The women's movement in America since 1960.* New York: Simon & Schuster.

Davis, J., ed. 1991. *The Earth First! reader: Ten years of radical environmentalism.* Salt Lake City: Peregrine Smith Books.

Davis, M. 1998. Philosophy meets practice: A critique of ecofeminism through the voices of three Chicana activists. Pp. 201–31 in *Chicano culture, ecology, politics: Subversive kin,* edited by D. G. Peña. Tucson: University of Arizona Press.

Dean, D. 1997. *Warriors without weapons: The victimization of military women.* Pasadena, Md.: The Minerva Center.

d'Eaubonne, F. 1994. The time for ecofeminism. In *Ecology,* edited by C. Merchant. Atlantic Highlands, N.J.: Humanities Press.

de Beauvoir, S. 1973. *The second sex.* New York: Vintage Books.

Deen, T. 1998. Globalisation devastates women, say unions. *InterPress Service,* 4 March.

de Ishtar, Z. 1994. *Daughters of the Pacific.* Melbourne: Spinifex Press.

D'Emilio, J. 1984. Capitalism and gay identity. Pp. 100–13 in *Powers of desire: The politics of sexuality,* edited by A. Snitow et al. New York: Monthly Review Press.

D'Emilio, J., and E. Freedman. 1997. *Intimate matters: A history of sexuality in America.* 2d ed. Chicago: University of Chicago Press.

Denman, J. E., and L. B. Inniss. 1999. No war without women: Defense industries. Pp. 187–99 in *Gender camouflage: Women and the U.S. military,* edited by F. D'Amico and L. Weinstein. New York: New York University Press.

De Oliveira, O., T. De Barbieri, I. Arriagada, M. Valenzuela, C. Serrano, and G. Emeagwali. 1991. *Alternatives: The food, energy, and debt crises in relation to women.* Bangalore, India: DAWN.

DePalma, A. 1996. Why that Asian TV has a "Made in Mexico" label. *New York Times,* 23 May, p. D1.

Devall, B., and G. Sessions. 1985. *Deep ecology: Living as if nature mattered.* Salt Lake City: Smith Books.

Diamond, I., and G. F. Orenstein, eds. 1990. *Reweaving the world: The emergence of ecofeminism.* San Francisco: Sierra Club Books.

Diamond, S. 1995. *Roads to dominion: Right-wing movements and political power in the United States.* New York: Guilford Press.

Dibblin, J. 1989. *The day of two suns: U.S. nuclear testing and the Pacific Islands.* New York: New Amsterdam Books.

Dickersin, K., and L. Schnaper. 1996. Reinventing medical research. Pp. 57–76 in *Man-made medicine: Women's health, public policy, and reform,* edited by K. L. Moss. Durham, N.C.: Duke University Press.

Digby, T., ed. 1998. *Men doing feminism.* New York: Routledge.

Dinnerstein, D. 1976. *Sexual arrangements and the human malaise.* New York: Harper & Row.

———. 1989. Surviving on earth: Meaning of feminism. In *Healing the wounds,* edited by J. Plant. Philadelphia: New Society Publishers.

Disability Statistics Center. 1999. *How many Americans have a disability?* Accessed online at http://www.dsc.ucsf.edu/ on 1 August 2000.

Dittrich, L. 1997. Sociocultural factors that influence body image satisfaction in women. Doctoral dissertation, California Institute of Integral Studies, *Dissertation Abstracts International.*

DNA testing: A new military invasion. 1996. *Citizen Soldier.* Available from Citizen Soldier, 175 Fifth Ave., #2135, New York, NY 10010.

Donchin, A., and L. M. Purdy. 1999. *Embodying bioethics: Recent feminist advances.* Lanham, Md.: Rowman and Littlefield.

Doress, P. B., and D. L. Siegal. 1987. *Ourselves, growing older: Women aging with knowledge and power.* New York: Simon & Schuster.

Doress-Worters, P. and D. L. Siegal. 1994. *The new ourselves, growing older.* New York: Simon & Schuster.

Dorsey, E., and M. Thormodsgard. 2003. Rachel Carson warned us. *Ms.,* December 2002/January 2003, 43–45.

Douglas, M. 1966. *Purity and danger: An analysis of concepts of pollution and taboo.* London: Routledge and Kegan Paul.

Doyal, L. 1995. *What makes women sick: Gender and the political economy of health.* New Brunswick, N.J.: Rutgers University Press.

Drill, E., H. McDonald, and R. Odes. 1999. *Deal with it! A whole new approach to your body, brain and life as a gurl.* New York: Pocket Books.

Drucker, J. L. 1998. *Lesbian and gay families speak out: Understanding the joys and challenges of diverse family life.* Cambridge, Mass.: Perseus Publishing.

Duberman M. B., M. Vicinus, and G. Chauncey Jr. 1989. *Hidden from history: Reclaiming the gay and lesbian past.* New York: New American Library.

Duff, K. 1993. *The alchemy of illness.* New York: Pantheon.

Duggan, L., and N. Hunter. 1995. *Sex wars: Sexual dissent and political culture.* New York: Routledge.

Dujon, D., and A. Withorn, eds. 1996. *For crying out loud: Women's poverty in the United States.* Boston: South End Press.

Dula, A. 1994. The life and death of Miss Mildred: An elderly Black woman. *Clinics in Geriatric Medicine* 10(3): 419–30.

———. 1996. An African American perspective on reproductive freedoms. Panel on Reproduction, Race, and Class at the Third World Congress of Bioethics, Feminist Approaches to Bioethics, November, San Francisco.

DuPlessis, R. B., and A. Snitow, eds. 1998. *The Feminist Memoir Project: Voices from women's liberation.* New York: Three Rivers Press.

Duran, J. 1998. *Philosophies of science/feminist theories.* Boulder, Colo.: Westview Press.

Dworkin, A. 1987. *Intercourse.* New York: Free Press.

Dziemianowicz, J. 1992. How we make the stars so beautiful. *McCall's,* July, 105.

Echols, A. 1989. *Daring to be bad: Radical feminism in America 1967–1975.* Minneapolis: University of Minnesota Press.

Edison, L. T., and D. Notkin. 1994. *Women en large: Images of fat nudes.* San Francisco: Books in Focus.

Edut, O., ed. 2000. *Body outlaws: Young women write about body image and identity.* Seattle, Wash.: Seal Press.

Efon, S. 1997. Tsunami of eating disorders sweeps across Asia. *San Francisco Examiner,* 19 October, p. A27.

Ehrenreich, B. 2001. *Nickel and dimed: On (not) getting by in America*. New York: Henry Holt/Metropolitan Books.

Ehrenreich, B., and D. English. 1973. *Witches, midwives, and nurses: A history of women healers*. Old Westbury, N.Y.: Feminist Press.

———. 1978. *For her own good: 150 years of the experts' advice to women*. Garden City, N.Y.: Anchor/Doubleday.

Ehrenreich, B., E. Hess, and G. Jacobs. 1986. *Remaking love: The feminization of sex*. New York: Anchor/Doubleday.

Eisenstein, Z. R. 1979. *Capitalism, patriarchy, and the case for socialist feminism*. New York: Monthly Review Press.

———. 1981. *The radical future of liberal feminism*. New York: Longman.

———. 1988. *The female body and the law*. Berkeley: University of California Press.

———. 1998. Socialist feminism. Pp. 218–19 in *The reader's companion to U.S. women's history*, edited by W. Mankiller, G. Mink, M. Navarro, B. Smith, and G. Steinem. Boston: Houghton Mifflin.

Ekins, R. 1997. *Male femaling: A grounded theory approach to cross-dressing and sex-changing*. New York: Routledge.

Elliott, L. 1999. Britain ends Third World debt. *The Guardian*, 18 December, p. 1.

Eng, D. and A. Y. Hom, eds. 1998. *Q & A: Queer in Asian America*. Philadelphia: Temple University.

Enloe, C. 1983. *Does khaki become you? The militarization of women's lives*. Boston: South End Press.

———. 1990. *Bananas, beaches and bases: Making feminist sense of international politics*. Berkeley: University of California Press.

———. 1993a. *The morning after: Sexual politics at the end of the cold war*. Berkeley: University of California Press.

———. 1993b. The right to fight: A feminist Catch-22. *Ms.*, July/August, 84–87.

———. 2000. *Maneuvers: The international politics of militarizing women's lives*. Berkeley: University of California Press.

Ensler, E. 1998. *The vagina monologues*. New York: Villard/Random House.

Epstein, B. 1993. Ecofeminism and grassroots environmentalism in the United States. Pp. 144–52 in *Toxic struggles: The theory and practice of environmental justice*, edited by R. Hofrichter. Philadelphia and Gabriola Island, B.C.: New Society Publishers.

Erdman, C. 1995. *Nothing to lose: A guide to sane living in a larger body*. San Francisco: HarperSanFrancisco.

Erez, E. 1992. Dangerous men, evil women: Gender and parole decision making. *Justice Quarterly* 9(1): 105–27.

Eridani. 1992. Is sexual orientation a secondary sex characteristic? In *Closer to home: Bisexuality and feminism*, edited by E. R. Weise. Seattle, Wash.: Seal Press.

Evans, S. 1980. *Personal politics*. New York: Vintage Books.

Facts on the global sweatshop. 1997. *Rethinking Schools: An Urban Education Journal* 11(4): 16.

Faderman, L. 1981. *Surpassing the love of men: Romantic friendship and love between women from the Renaissance to the present*. New York: William Morrow.

Fallon, P., ed. 1994. *Consuming passions: Feminist perspectives on eating disorders*. New York: Guilford Press.

Faludi, S. 1991. *Backlash: The undeclared war against women*. New York: Crown.

Family Violence Prevention Fund. 1995. International peace begins at home. Pp. 2–3 in *News from the homefront*. San Francisco: FVPF.

———. 1998. *Domestic violence is a serious, widespread social problem in America: The facts*. Available from the Family Violence Prevention Fund, 383 Rhode Island Ave., San Francisco, CA 94103.

Fanon, F. 1967. *Black skin, white masks*. New York: Grove Press.

———. 1968. *The wretched of the earth*. New York: Grove Press.

Farnsworth, M., and R. Teske Jr. 1995. Gender differences in felony court processing: Three hypotheses of disparity. *Women and Criminal Justice* 6(2): 23–44.

Fausto-Sterling, A. 1993. The five sexes: Why male and female are not enough. *The Sciences*, March/April, 20–24.

Featherstone, L. 2002. Wal-Mart values: Selling women short. *The Nation*, 16 December, 11–14.

Federal Bureau of Investigation. 1992. *Uniform crime reports 1991*. Washington, D.C.: U.S. Department of Justice.

———. 1997. *Crime in the United States 1996*. Washington, D.C.: FBI, U.S. Department of Justice.

Federation of Feminist Health Centers. 1995. *A new view of a woman's body*. 2d ed. Los Angeles: Feminist Health Press.

Feinberg, L. 1993. *Stone butch blues*. Ithaca, N.Y.: Firebrand Books.

———. 1996. *Transgender warriors: Making history from Joan of Arc to RuPaul*. Boston: Beacon Press.

———. 1998. *Trans liberation: Beyond pink or blue*. Boston: Beacon Press.

Ferguson, A. 1989. *Blood at the root: Motherhood, sexuality, and male dominance*. London: Pandora.

Ferguson, M., and J. Wicke, eds. 1992. *Feminism and postmodernism*. Durham, N.C.: Duke University Press.

Ferree, M. M., and P. Y. Martin. 1995. *Feminist organizations: Harvest of the new women's movement*. Philadelphia: Temple University Press.

Ferreyra, S., and K. Hughes. 1991. *Table manners: A guide to the pelvic examination for disabled women and health care providers*. San Francisco: Sex Education for Disabled People and Planned Parenthood Alameda.

Ferriss, S., and R. Sandoval. 1997. *The fight in the fields: Cesar Chavez and the Farmworkers movement*. New York: Harcourt Brace.

Fiduccia, B. W., and M. Saxton. 1997. Disability feminism: A manifesto. *New Mobility: Disability Culture and Lifestyle* 8(49): 60–61.

Findlen, B., ed. 1995. *Listen up: Voices from the next feminist generation.* Seattle, Wash.: Seal Press.

Fineman, M. A., and R. Mykitiuk, eds. 1994. *The public nature of private violence: The discovery of domestic abuse.* New York: Routledge.

Finger, A. 1990. *Past due: A story of disability, pregnancy, and birth.* Seattle, Wash.: Seal Press.

Firestone, S. 1970. *The dialectics of sex: The case for feminist revolution.* New York: Morrow.

Flammang, J. A. 1997. *Women's political voice: How women are transforming the practice and study of politics.* Philadelphia: Temple University Press.

Flanders, L. 1997. *Real majority, media minority: The costs of sidelining women in reporting.* Monroe, Maine: Common Courage Press.

Folbre, N. 2001. *The invisible heart: Economics and family values.* New York: New Press.

Foley, L., and C. Rasche. 1979. The effect of race on sentence, actual time served and final disposition of female offenders. In *Theory and research in criminal justice,* edited by J. Conley. Cincinnati: Anderson.

Ford, L. E. 2002. *Women and politics: The pursuit of equality.* Boston: Houghton Mifflin.

Forrest, M. Silk. 1992. Groups: Powerful medicine for our deepest wounds. In *The Healing Woman: The Monthly Newsletter for Women Survivors of Childhood Sexual Abuse,* July, 1, 10–11.

Foster, C. 1989. *Women for all seasons: The story of W.I.L.P.F.* Athens, Ga.: University of Georgia Press.

Fox-Genovese, E. 1994. Beyond individualism: The new Puritanism, feminism, and women. *Salmagundi* 101(2): 79–95.

Fraden, R. 2001. *Imagining Medea: Rhodessa Jones and Theater for Incarcerated Women.* Chapel Hill: University of North Carolina Press.

Francis, D. 1999. Rich man's plan seen as stingy. *Christian Science Monitor,* 24 June, p. 6.

Francke, L. B. 1997. *The gender wars in the military.* New York: Simon & Schuster.

Frank, E. 2001. Social Security Q and A. *Dollars and Sense,* November/December, 18–21.

Frankenberg, R. 1993. *White women, race matters: The social construction of whiteness.* Minneapolis: University of Minnesota Press.

Franklin, D., and J. Sweeney. 1988. Women and corporate power. Pp. 48–65 in *Women, power and policy: Toward the year 2000,* 2d ed., edited by E. Boneparth and E. Stoper. New York: Pergamon Press.

Fraser, L. 1997. *Losing it: America's obsession with weight and the industry that feeds it.* New York: Dutton.

Freedberg, L. 1996. 1,000 more agents will be sent to the border. *San Francisco Chronicle,* 9 February, p. A3.

Free trade vs. fair trade. N.d. Available from Global Exchange, 2017 Mission St., Rm. 303, San Francisco, CA 94110.

Freire, P. 1989. *Pedagogy of the oppressed.* New York: Continuum.

Freudenheim, E. 1995. *Healthspeak: A complete dictionary of America's healthcare system.* New York: Facts on File.

Fried, M. G. 2002. Abortion in the United States: Barriers to access. Pp. 103–22 *Policing the national body: Race, gender, and criminalization,* edited by J. Silliman and A. Bhattacharjee. Cambridge, Mass: South End Press.

Friedan, B. 1963. *The feminine mystique.* New York: W. W. Norton.

Frye, M. 1983. Oppression. Pp. 1–16 in *The politics of reality: Essays in feminist theory.* Freedom, Calif.: The Crossing Press.

———. 1992. *Willful virgin: Essays in feminism 1976–1992.* Freedom, Calif.: The Crossing Press.

Fuchs, L. 1990. The reaction of Black Americans to immigration. In *Immigration reconsidered,* edited by V. Yans-McLaughlin. New York: Oxford University Press.

Fuentes, A., and B. Ehrenreich. 1983. *Women in the global factory.* Boston: South End Press.

Fund for a Feminist Majority. 1997. *Right-wing investment funds scare corporations away from RU 486 and contraceptive research.* Accessed online at http://www. feminist. org/rrights/rwfact1.html.

Furman, F. K. 1997. *Facing the mirror: Older women and beauty shop culture.* New York: Routledge.

Fuss, D., ed. 1991. *Inside out: Lesbian theories, gay theories.* New York: Routledge.

Gage, S., L. Richards, and H. Wilmot. 2002. *Queer.* New York: Thunder's Mouth Press.

Gaines, P. 1994. *Laughing in the dark: From colored girl to woman of color—a journey from prison to power.* New York: Anchor Books.

Gallagher, N. W. 1993. The gender gap in popular attitudes toward the use of force. Pp. 23–37 in *Women and the use of military force,* edited by R. Howes and M. Stevenson. Boulder, Colo.: Lynne Rienner Publishers.

Garber, M. 1992. *Vested interests: Cross-dressing and cultural anxiety.* New York: HarperPerennial.

Gardner, M. 1999. The family-leave law, and beyond. *Christian Science Monitor,* 4 August, p. 17.

Garner, D. M. 1997. The 1997 body image survey results. *Psychology Today,* January/February, 31–44, 75–84.

Geller, J. 2001. *Here comes the bride: Women, weddings, and the marriage mystique.* New York: Four Walls Eight Windows.

General Accounting Office. 2002. *Women in management: Analysis of current population survey data.* April 22. Report no. 02-648T. Washington, D.C. GAO p. 8.

George, S. 1988. Getting your own back: Solving the Third World debt crisis. *New Statesman & Society,* 15 July, 20.

Gibbs, L. 1995. *Dying from dioxin: A citizens' guide to reclaiming our health and rebuilding democracy.* Boston: South End Press.

———. 1998. *Love canal: The story continues.* Gabriola Island, B.C.: New Society Publishers.

Gilfus, M. 1992. From victims to survivors: Women's routes of entry and immersion into street crime. *Women and Criminal Justice* 4(1): 62–89.

Gill, C. 1996. Cultivating common ground: Women with disabilities. Pp. 183–93 in *Man-made medicine: Women's health, public policy, and reform,* edited by K. L. Moss. Durham, N.C.: Duke University Press.

Ginty, M. M. 2001. What you need to know about RU-486. *Ms.,* February/March, 72–29.

Giordano, P., S. Kerbel, and S. Dudley. 1981. The economics of female criminality. Pp. 15–82 in *Women and crime in America,* edited by L. Bowker. New York: Macmillan.

Girshick, L. B. 2002. *Women-to-women sexual violence.* Boston: Northeastern University Press.

Gladstar, R. 1993. *Herbal healing for women: Simple home remedies for women of all ages.* New York: Simon & Schuster.

Glazer, P. M., and M. P. Glazer. 1998. *The environmental crusaders: Confronting disaster and mobilizing community.* University Park: Pennsylvania State University Press.

Gleick, E. 1996. Scandal in the military. *Time,* 25 November, 28–31.

Global Exchange. 2002. Citizens across the Americas mobilize to fight the FTAA. *Global Exchange Quarterly Newsletter* 52: 3.

Glover, P. 1997. Ithaca HOURS makes social change pay: "Print money locally and make revolution globally." *Resist* 6(4): 3.

Gluck, S. 1976. *From parlor to prison: Five American suffragists talk about their lives.* New York: Vintage Books.

Gold, J., and S. Villari, eds. 2000. *Just sex: Students rewrite the rules on sex, violence, activism, and equality.* Lanham, Md.: Rowman and Littlefield.

Goldberg, G. S., and S. Collins. 1999. *Washington's new poor law: Welfare "reform" and the roads not taken, 1935–1998.* New York: Apex Press.

Goldstein, N., and J. L. Manlowe, eds. 1997. *The gender politics of HIV/AIDS in women.* New York: New York University Press.

Gomez, J. 2000. Otherwise engaged: Marriage is an offer I *can* refuse. *Ms.,* June/July, 67–70.

Goode, E. 2001. Study says 20% of girls report abuse by a date. *New York Times,* 1 August, p. A10.

Goodman, E. 1996. Predators and jailbait. *San Francisco Chronicle,* 21 February, p. A17.

———. 1999. Working moms do no harm. *San Francisco Chronicle,* 4 March, p. A23.

Goodstein, E. 1999. *The trade-off myth: Fact and fiction about jobs and the environment.* Washington, D.C.: Island Press.

Gordon, L. 1988. *Heroes of their own lives: The politics and history of family violence, Boston 1880–1960.* New York: Viking.

———. 1997. Killing in self-defense. *The Nation,* 24 March, 25–28.

Gore, A., and B. Lavendar. 2001. *Breeder: Real life stories from the new generation of mothers.* Seattle, Wash.: Seal Press.

Goss, R. and A. A. S. Strongheart, eds. 1997. *Our families, our values: Snapshots of queer kinship.* New York: Harrington Park Press.

Gottlieb, R. 1993. *Forcing the spring: The transformation of the American environmental movement.* Washington, D.C.: Island Press.

Gould, J. 1997. *Juggling: A memoir of work, family, and feminism.* New York: The Feminist Press.

Grady, D. 2000. Study backs hormone link to cancer for women. *New York Times,* 27 January, p. A17.

Grahn, J. 1984. *Another mother tongue: Gay words, gay worlds.* Boston: Beacon Press.

Gray, C. 1999. *Corporate cash: Few nations can top it.* Eugene, Oreg.: Author.

Gray, J. 1992. *Men are from Mars, women are from Venus: A practical guide for improving communication and getting what you want in your relationships.* New York: HarperCollins.

Greenfeld, L. A., et al. 1998, March. *Bureau of Justice Statistics factbook: Violence by intimates.* Washington, D.C.: Bureau of Justice.

Greenhouse, L. 1999. High court limits who is protected by disability law. *New York Times,* 23 June, p. A1.

Greenhouse, S. 1997. Nike shoe plant in Vietnam is called unsafe for workers. *New York Times,* 8 November, p. A1.

Greider, W. 1997. *One world ready or not: The manic logic of global capitalism.* New York: Simon & Schuster.

———. 2002. The end of empire. *The Nation,* 23 September, 13–15.

Griffin, S. 1971. Rape: The all-American crime. *Ramparts* 10(3): 26–35.

———. 1978. *Woman and nature: The roaring inside her.* San Francisco: Harper Colophon.

———. 1986. *Rape: The politics of consciousness.* 3d ed. San Francisco: Harper & Row.

———. 1999. *What her body thought: A journey into the shadows.* San Francisco: Harper San Francisco.

Grossholtz, J. 1983. Battered women's shelters and the political economy of sexual violence. Pp. 59–69 in *Families, politics, and public policy: A feminist dialogue on women and the state,* edited by I. Diamond. New York: Longman.

Grossman, R. 1998a. Can corporations be accountable? (Part 1). *Rachel's Environment and Health Weekly,* 30 July, 1–2.

———. 1998b. Can corporations be accountable? (Part 2). *Rachel's Environment and Health Weekly,* 6 August, 1–2.

Group of 77. 1997. Debt burden weighs heavily on developing nations, says G-77. *Journal of the Group of 77* 10 (9/10). Accessed online at http://www.g77.org/Journal/sepnov97/03.htm on 27 December 2002.

Grunwald, L. 1992. If women ran America. *Life Magazine,* June, 37–46.

Guenter-Schlesinger, S. 1999. Persistence of sexual harassment: The impact of military culture on policy implementation. Pp. 195–212 in *Beyond zero tolerance,* edited by M. Katzenstein and J. Reppy. Lanham, Md.: Rowman and Littlefield.

Gustafson, K. 2002. Five years isn't long enough. *Oakland Tribune,* 16 December, p. B9.

Haiken, E. 1997. *Venus envy: A history of cosmetic surgery.* Baltimore: Johns Hopkins University Press.

Hall, G. M. 1999. Intersectionality: A necessary consideration for women of color in the military? Pp. 143–61 in *Beyond zero tolerance,* edited by M. Katzenstein and J. Reppy. Lanham, Md.: Rowman and Littlefield.

Hamer, D., and B. Budge. 1994. *The good, the bad and the gorgeous: Popular culture's romance with lesbianism.* London: Pandora.

Hamilton, C. 1993. Coping with industrial exploitation. In *Confronting environmental racism: Voices from the grassroots,* edited by R. Bullard. Boston: South End Press.

Hammonds, E. 1995. Missing persons: African American women, AIDS, and the history of disease. Pp. 443–49 in *Words of fire: An anthology of African-American feminist thought,* edited by B. Guy-Sheftall. New York: New Press.

Hansen, C. 2001. A considerable service: An advocate's introduction to domestic violence and the military. *Domestic Violence Report* 6(4): 49, 50, 60–64.

Harman, B. 1996. Happy ending. Pp. 286–90 in *"Women in the trees": U.S. women's short stories about battering and resistance, 1839–1994,* edited by S. Koppelman. Boston: Beacon Press.

Harne, L., and E. Miller, eds. 1996. *All the rage: Reasserting radical lesbian feminism.* New York: Teachers College Press.

Harper's Index. October 2002.

Harris, J. and P. Johnson. 2001. *Tenderheaded: A comb-bending collection of hair stories.* New York: Pocket Books.

Hartmann, B. 1995. Dangerous intersections. *Political Environments,* no. 2 (summer): 1–7. Publication of the Committee on Women, Population and the Environment, Hampshire College, Amherst, Mass.

Hartmann, H. 1981. The unhappy marriage of Marxism and feminism: Towards a more progressive union. In *Women and revolution: A discussion of the unhappy marriage of Marxism and feminism,* edited by L. Sargent. Boston: South End Press.

Hartsock, N. 1983. *Money, sex, and power: Toward a feminist historical materialism.* New York: Longman.

Harvey, E. 1999. Short-term and long-term effects of early parental employment on children of the National Longitudinal Survey of Youth. *Developmental Psychology* 35(2): 445–459.

Havemann, J. 1999. Former welfare recipients got more jobs in past 3 years. *San Francisco Chronicle,* 27 May, p. A3.

Hayden, D. 1981. *The grand domestic revolution: A history of feminist designs for American homes, neighborhoods, and cities.* Cambridge, Mass.: MIT Press.

Hays, S. 1996. *The cultural contradictions of motherhood.* New Haven, Conn.: Yale University Press.

Healey, S. 1997. Confronting ageism: A MUST for mental health. Pp. 368–76 in *In our own words: Readings on the psychology of women and gender,* edited by M. Crawford and R. Unger. New York: McGraw-Hill.

Heise, L. 1989. Crimes of gender. *World Watch,* March/April, 12–21.

Heise, L., J. Pitanguy, and A. Germain. 1994. *Violence against women: The hidden health burden.* World Bank Discussion Papers #255. Washington, D.C.: The World Bank.

Hemmings, C. 2002. *Bisexual spaces: A geography of sexuality and gender.* New York: Routledge.

Henderson, H. 1991. *Paradigms in progress: Life beyond economics.* Indianapolis: Knowledge Systems.

Hennessy, R., and C. Ingraham, eds. 1997. *Materialist feminism: A reader in class, difference, and women's lives.* New York: Routledge.

Herman, J. 1981. *Father-daughter incest.* Cambridge, Mass.: Harvard University Press.

———. 1992. *Trauma and recovery.* New York: Basic Books.

Hesse-Biber, S. J. 1991. Women, weight, and eating disorders: A socio-cultural analysis. *Women's Studies International Forum* 14(3): 173–91.

———. 1996. *Am I thin enough yet?* New York: Oxford University Press.

Hetherington, E. M., and J. Kelly. 2002. *For better or for worse: Divorce reconsidered.* New York: W. W. Norton.

Hetherington, M., and G. Clingempeel. 1992. *Coping with marital transitions: A family systems perspective.* Chicago: Chicago University Press for the Society for Research in Child Development.

Heywood, L. 1998. *Bodymakers: A cultural anatomy of women's body building.* New Brunswick, N.J.: Rutgers University Press.

Heywood, L., and J. Drake. 1997. *Third wave agenda: Being feminist, doing feminism.* Minneapolis: University of Minnesota Press.

Hicks, G. 1994. *The comfort women.* New York: W. W. Norton.

High, G. 1997. Combating sexual harassment. *Soldiers* 52(2): 4–5.

Hill, J. 1993. Outrageous acts. Unpublished class assignment, Antioch College.

Hill, J. B. 2000. *The legacy of Luna: The story of a tree, and a woman, and the struggle to save the Redwoods.* San Francisco: Harper San Francisco.

Hinchman, H. 1997. *A trail through leaves: The journal as a path to place.* New York: W. W. Norton.

History Project. 1998. *Improper Bostonians: Lesbian and gay history from the Puritans to Playland.* Boston: Beacon Press.

Hite, S. 1994. *Women as revolutionary agents of change: The Hite Report and beyond.* Madison: University of Wisconsin Press.

———. 1995. *Hite Report on the family: Growing patriarchy.* New York: Grove Press.

Hochman, A. 1994. *Everyday acts and small subversions: Women reinventing family, community, and home.* Portland, Oreg.: Eighth Mountain Press.

Hochschild, A. R. 1989. *The second shift: Working parents and the revolution at home.* New York: Viking.

———. 1997. *The time bind: When work becomes home and home becomes work.* New York: Henry Holt.

Hofrichter, R., ed. 1993. *Toxic struggles: The theory and practice of environmental justice.* Philadelphia and Gabriola Island, B.C.: New Society Publishers.

Holmes, S. A. 1995a. Ousters of undocumented immigrants set a record. *San Francisco Chronicle,* 28 December, p. A13.

———. 1995b. The strange politics of immigration. *New York Times,* 31 December, p. E3.

hooks, b. 1984a. *Feminist theory: From margin to center.* Boston: South End Press.

———. 1984b. Feminist movement to end violence. Pp. 117–31 in *Feminist theory: From margin to center,* edited by b. hooks. Boston: South End Press.

———. 1993. *Sisters of the yam: Black women and self recovery.* Boston: South End Press.

———. 1994. Seduced by violence no more. Pp. 109–13 in *Outlaw culture: Resisting representations,* edited by b. hooks. New York: Routledge.

———. 2000. *Feminism is for everybody: Passionate politics.* Cambridge, Mass.: South End Press.

Howe, F., ed. 2000. *The politics of women's studies: Testimony from 30 founding mothers.* New York: The Feminist Press at the City University of New York.

Howey, N., and E. Samuels, eds. 2000. *Out of the ordinary: Essays on growing up with gay, lesbian, and transgender parents.* New York: St. Martin's Press.

Hua, V. 2002. Cracks widen in glass ceiling. *San Francisco Chronicle,* 19 November, p. B1.

Hubbard, R. 1989. Science, facts, and feminism. In *Feminism and science,* edited by N. Tuana. Bloomington: Indiana University Press.

———. 1990. *The politics of women's biology.* New Brunswick, N.J.: Rutgers University Press.

Human Rights Campaign. 1999. *State of the workplace report.* Washington, D.C.: HRC.

———. 2002. *States with and anti-gay marriage laws.* Washington, D.C.: HRC. Accessed online at http://www.hrc.org/familynet/chapter.asp?article=195 on 6 November 2002.

Human Rights Watch. 1999a. *World report 1999. United States: Human rights developments.* New York: Author.

———. 1999b. No guarantees: Sex discrimination in Mexico's maquiladora sector. Pp. 31–35 in *The maquiladora reader: Cross-border organizing since NAFTA,* edited by R. Kamel and A. Hoffman. Philadelphia: American Friends Service Committee.

Humm, A., ed. 1992. *Feminisms: A reader.* New York: Harvester Wheatsheaf.

Hurtado, A. 1996. *The color of privilege: Three blasphemies on race and feminism.* Ann Arbor: The University of Michigan Press.

Hutchins, L., and L. Kaahumanu. 1991. *Bi any other name: Bisexual people speak out.* Boston: Alyson.

Hynes, H. P. 1989. *The recurring silent spring.* New York: Pergamon Press.

Hynes, P. 1996. *A patch of Eden.* White River Junction, Vt.: Chelsea Green.

Inciardi, J., D. Lockwood, and A. Pottieger. 1993. *Women and crack cocaine.* New York: Macmillan.

Ingraham, C. 1999. *White weddings; Romancing heterosexuality in popular culture.* New York: Routledge.

In Phoenix chain gangs for women. 1996. *New York Times,* 28 August, p. C1.

Institute for Women's Policy Research. 1998. *Social Security reform and women: A factsheet.* Washington, D.C.: IWPR.

———. 2002. *Building a stronger child care workforce: A review of studies of the effectiveness of public compensation initiatives.* Washington, D.C.: IWPR.

Ireland, M. S. 1993. *Reconceiving women: Separating motherhood from female identity.* New York: Guilford Press.

Isakson, E., ed. 1988. *Women and the military system.* New York: St. Martin's Press.

Jacob, K. 2002. *Our choices, our lives: Unapologetic writings on abortion.* Minneapolis: Writers Advantage.

Jacobs, R. H. 1993. *Be an outrageous older woman.* 2d ed. Manchester, Conn.: Knowledge, Ideas & Trends.

Jaggar, A. M. 1983. *Feminist politics and human nature.* Totowa, N.J.: Rowman & Allanheld.

———, ed. 1994. *Living with contradictions: Controversies in feminist social ethics.* Boulder, Colo.: Westview Press.

Jaimes, A., and T. Halsey. 1986. American Indian women at the center of indigenous resistance in contemporary North America. Pp. 311–44 in *The state of Native America: Genocide, colonization, and resistance,* edited by A. Jaimes. Boston: South End Press.

Jetter, A., A. Orleck, and D. Taylor, eds. 1997. *The politics of motherhood: Activist voices from left to right.* Hanover, N.H.: University Press of New England.

Joffe, C. 1995. *Doctors of conscience: The struggle to provide abortion before and after* Roe v. Wade. Boston: Beacon Press.

Johnson, A. G. 1997. *The gender knot: Unraveling our patriarchal legacy.* Philadelphia: Temple University Press.

Johnson, M. L. 2002. *Jane sexes it up: True confessions of feminist desire.* New York: Four Walls, Eight Windows.

Jones, A. 1980. *Women who kill.* New York: Holt, Rinehart, and Winston.

———. 1994a. Is this power feminism? Living with guns, playing with fire. *Ms.,* June/July, 36–44.

———. 1994b. *Next time, she'll be dead: Battering and how to stop it.* Boston: Beacon Press.

Jones, J. 1985. *Labor of love, labor of sorrow: Black women, work, and the family, from slavery to present.* New York: Vintage Books.

Jong, E. 1998. Ally McBeal and *Time* magazine can't keep the good women down. *New York Observer,* 13 July, p. 19.

Kadi, J. 1996. *Thinking class: Sketches from a cultural worker.* Boston: South End Press.

Kamel, R. 1990. *The global factory: Analysis and action for a new economic era.* Philadelphia: American Friends Service Committee.

Kamel, R., and A. Hoffman, eds. 1999. *The maquiladora reader: Cross-border organizing since NAFTA.* Philadelphia: American Friends Service Committee.

Kaminer, W. 2000. Bad vibes in Alabama. *The American prospect* 11(25). Accessed online at http://www.prospect.org/print/V11/25/Kaminer-w.html on 1 December 2002.

Kaplan, L. 1995. *The story of Jane: The legendary underground feminist abortion service.* New York: Pantheon Books.

Kaplan, T. 1997. *Crazy for democracy: Women in grassroots movements.* New York: Routledge.

Katz, J. N. 1995. *The invention of heterosexuality.* New York: Plume.

Katzenstein, M. F. 1993. The right to fight. *Women's Review of Books* 11(2): 30–31.

Katzenstein, M. F., and J. Reppy, eds. 1999. *Beyond zero tolerance: Discrimination in military culture.* Lanham, Md.: Rowman and Littlefield.

Katz Rothman, B. 1986. *Tentative pregnancy: Prenatal diagnosis and the future of motherhood.* New York: Viking.

Kaye/Kantrowitz, M., and I. Klepfisz, eds. 1989. *The Tribe of Dina: A Jewish women's anthology.* Boston: Beacon Press.

Kaysen, S. 1994. *Girl interrupted.* New York: Vintage Books.

Kerr, J., ed. 1993. *Ours by right: Women's rights as human rights.* London: Zed Books.

Kessler-Harris, A. 1990. *A woman's wage: Historical meanings and social consequences.* Lexington: University Press of Kentucky.

———. 2001. *In pursuit of equity: Women, men, and the quest for economic citizenship in 20th-century America.* New York: Oxford University Press.

Kich, G. K. 1992. The developmental process of asserting a biracial, bicultural identity. Pp. 304–17 in *Racially mixed people in America,* edited by M. P. Root. Newbury Park, Calif.: Sage.

Kiernan, D. 2001. The little law that could. *Ms.,* February/March, 18–25.

Kilbourne, J. 1994. Still killing us softly: Advertising and the obsession with thinness. Pp. 395–418 in *Feminist perspectives on eating disorders,* edited by P. Fallon, M. K. Katzman, and S. C. Wooley. New York: Guilford Press.

———. 1999. *Deadly persuasion: Why women and girls must fight the addictive power of advertising.* New York: Free Press.

———. 2000. *Can't buy my love: How advertising changes the way we think and feel.* New York: Simon & Schuster.

Kim, E., L. V. Villanueva, and Asian Women United of California. 1989. *Making waves.* Boston: Beacon Press.

———. 1997. *Making more waves: New writing by Asian American women.* Boston: Beacon Press.

Kimmel, M. 1993. Clarence, William, Iron Mike, Tailhook, Senator Packwood, Spur Posse, Magic . . . and us. Pp. 119–38 in *Transforming a rape culture,* edited by E. Buchwald, R. Fletcher, and M. Roth. Minneapolis: Milkweed Editions.

———. 2000. *The gendered society.* New York: Oxford University Press.

Kimmel, M. and M. Messner. 1995. *Men's lives.* 3d ed. Boston: Allyn & Bacon.

———. 1998. *Men's lives.* 4th ed. Boston: Allyn & Bacon.

Kimmel, M. S., and T. Mosmiller, eds. 1992. *Against the tide: Pro-feminist men in the United States, 1776–1990.* Boston: Beacon Press.

King, Y. 1983. All is connectedness: Notes from the Women's Pentagon Action, USA. In *Keeping the peace,* edited by L. Jones. London: The Women's Press.

———. 1987. Letter to the editor. *The Nation,* 12 December, 702, 730–31.

———. 1988. Ecological feminism, *Z Magazine,* July/August, 124–27.

———. 1991. Reflection on the other body: Difference, disability and identity politics. Unpublished paper.

———. 1993a. The other body. *Ms.,* March/April, 72–75.

———. 1993b. Feminism and ecology. Pp. 76–84 in *Toxic struggles: The theory and practice of environmental justice,* edited by R. Hofrichter. Philadelphia and Gabriola Island, B.C.: New Society Publishers.

———. 1998. Ecofeminism. P. 207 in *The reader's companion to U.S. women's history*, edited by W. Mankiller, G. Mink, M. Navarro, B. Smith, and G. Steinem. Boston: Houghton Mifflin.

Kingston, M. H., 1976. *The woman warrior: Memoirs of a girlhood among ghosts.* New York: Knopf.

Kirk, G. 1997. Ecofeminism and environmental justice: Bridges across gender, race, and class. *Frontiers: A Journal of Women's Studies* 18(2): 2–20.

———. 1998. Ecofeminism and Chicano environmental struggles: Bridges across gender and race. Pp. 177–200 in *Chicano culture, ecology, politics: Subversive kin*, edited by D. G. Peña. Tucson: University of Arizona Press.

Klein, R., and L. J. Dumble. 1994. Disempowering midlife women: The science and politics of hormone replacement therapy (HRT). *Women's Studies International Forum* 17(4): 327–43.

Klepfisz, I. 1990. *Dreams of an insomniac: Jewish feminist essays, speeches and diatribes.* Portland, Oreg.: Eighth Mountain Press.

Kline, C. B., ed. 1997 *Child of mine: Writers talk about the first year of motherhood.* New York: Hyperion.

Koedt, A., E. Levine, and A. Rapone, eds. 1973. *Radical feminism.* New York: Quadrangle Books.

Kohl, H. 1992. *From archetype to zeitgeist: Powerful ideas for powerful thinking.* Boston: Little Brown.

Kohn, S. 1999, June. *The NGLTF domestic partnership organizing manual.* Washington, D.C.: National Gay and Lesbian Task Force.

Komesaroff, P., P. Rothfield, and J. Daly, eds. 1997. *Reinterpreting menopause: Cultural and philosophical issues.* New York: Routledge.

Koppelman, S., ed. 1996. *"Women in the trees:" U.S. women's short stories about battering and resistance, 1839–1994.* Boston: Beacon Press.

Koss, M. P. 1988. Hidden rape: Sexual aggression and victimization in a national sample of students in higher education. Pp. 3–25 in *Rape and sexual assault*, edited by A. W. Burgess. New York: Garland.

Koss, M. P., E. T. Dinero, and C. A. Seibel. 1988. Stranger and acquaintance rape: Are there differences in the victim's experience? *Psychology of Women Quarterly* 12: 1–24.

Koss, M. P., L. Goodman, A. Browne, L. Fitzgerald, G. P. Keita, and N. F. Russo. 1994. *No safe haven: Male violence against women at home, at work, and in the community.* Washington, D.C.: American Psychological Association.

Krauss, C. 1993. Blue-collar women and toxic-waste protests: The process of politicization. Pp. 107–17 in *Toxic struggles: The theory and practice of environmental justice*, edited by R. Hofrichter. Philadelphia and Gabriola Island, B.C.: New Society Publishers.

Krieger, L. 1998. RU-486 abortion pill is still not widely available in the U.S. *San Francisco Examiner*, 27 January, p. A1.

Krieger, N., and E. Fee. 1996. Man-made medicine and women's health: The biopolitics of sex/gender and race/ethnicity. Pp. 15–35 in *Man-made medicine: Women's health, public policy, and reform*, edited by K. L. Moss. Durham, N.C.: Duke University Press.

Krieger, N., and S. Sidney. 1996. Racial discrimination and blood pressure: The CARDIA study of young Black and White adults. *American Journal of Public Health* 86(10): 1370–78.

Kruttschnitt, C. 1980–81. Social status and sentences of female offenders. *Law and Society Review* 15(2): 247–65.

Kurz, D. 1995. *For richer, for poorer: Mothers confront divorce.* New York: Routledge.

Ladd-Taylor, M., and L. Umansky. 1998. *"Bad" mothers: The politics of blame in twentieth-century America.* New York: New York University Press.

LaDuke, W. 1993. A society based on conquest cannot be sustained: Native peoples and the environmental crisis. In *Toxic struggles: The theory and practice of environmental justice*, edited by R. Hofrichter. Philadelphia and Gabriola Island, B.C.: New Society Publishers.

———. 1999. *All our relations: Native struggles for land and life.* Cambridge, Mass.: South End Press.

LaFramboise, T., J. S. Berman, and B. Sohi. 1994. American Indian Women. In *Women of color: Integrating ethnic and gender identities in psychotherapy*, edited by L. Comas-Díaz and B. Greene. New York: Guilford Press.

Lahey, K. 1985. Until women themselves have told all they have to tell. *Osgoode Hall Law Journal* 23(3): 519–41.

Lakoff, R. T., and R. L. Scherr. 1984. *Face value.* Boston: Routledge & Kegan Paul.

Lama, A. 1999. *Queries on legality of external debt.* Washington, D.C.: Interpress Third World News Agency (IPS). Accessed online at http://www.aidc.org.za/j2000/documents/legality_ex_debt.html on 27 December 2002.

Lancaster, R. N., and M. di Leonardo, eds. 1997. *The gender/sexuality reader: Culture, history, political economy.* New York: Routledge.

Larkin, J., and K. Popaleni. 1997. Heterosexual courtship violence and sexual harassment: The private and public control of young women. Pp. 313–26 in *In our own words: Readings on the psychology of women and gender*, edited by M. Crawford and R. Unger. New York: McGraw-Hill.

Lasch, C. 1977. *Haven in a heartless world: The family besieged.* New York: Basic Books.

LaVigne, P. 1989. "Take a little off the sides": Baby boomers boost plastic surgery biz. *Utne Reader*, September/October, 12.

Lawe, C., and B. Lawe. 1980. The balancing act: Coping strategies for emerging family lifestyles. In *Dual career couples*, edited by F. Pepitone-Rickwell. Beverly Hills, Calif.: Sage.

Lazarre, J. 1976. *The mother knot.* New York: McGraw-Hill.

Lee, C. 1987. *Toxic wastes and race in the United States.* New York: New York Commission for Racial Justice United Church of Christ.

Lederman, E. 1991. *The best places to meet good men.* New York: Prima Publishing/Random House.

Lefkowitz, B. 1997. *Our guys: The Glen Ridge rape and the secret life of the perfect suburb.* Berkeley: University of California Press.

Lehrman, K. 1993. Off course. *Mother Jones,* September/October, 45–55.

Leidholdt, D., and J. Raymond. 1990. *The sexual liberals and the attack on feminism.* New York: Pergamon.

Leonard, A., ed. 1989. *SEEDS: Supporting women's work in the Third World.* New York: The Feminist Press.

Lerman, H. 1996. *Pigeonholing women's misery: A history and critical analysis of the psychodiagnosis of women in the twentieth century.* New York: Basic Books.

Lerner, S. 2001. GendeRx: What the medical field is learning about women's bodies, and why it will change your next doctor's visit. *Ms.,* February/March, 40–44.

Le Sueur, M. 1982. *Ripening: Selected work.* 2d ed. New York: Feminist Press at the City University of New York.

Lichtenstein, A. C., and M. A. Kroll. 1996. The fortress economy: The economic role of the U.S. prison system. In *Criminal injustice: Confronting the prison crisis,* edited by E. Rosenblatt. Boston: South End Press.

Lieberman, T. 1997. Social Security: The campaign to take the system private. *The Nation,* 27 January, 11–16, 18.

Light, J. 1996. Rape on the border. *The Progressive,* September, 24.

———. 1999, October. Prison industrial complex. *Corporate Watch.* San Francisco: Transnational Resource and Action Center.

Lindsay-Poland, J., and N. Morgan. 1998. Overseas Military Bases and Environment. *Foreign Policy in Focus* 3(15): 1–4. Interhemispheric Resource Center and Institute for Policy Studies.

Lips, H. 1991. *Women, men, and power.* Mountain View, Calif.: Mayfield.

Lipsky, S. 1977. Internalized oppression. *Black Reemergence,* Winter, 5–10.

List, P. C., ed. 1993. *Radical environmentalism: Philosophy and tactics.* Belmont, Calif.: Wadsworth.

Lobel, K., ed. 1984. *Naming the violence: Speaking out about lesbian battering.* Seattle, Wash.: Seal Press.

Lopez, A. S., ed. 1995. *Latina issues: Fragments of historia.* New York: Garland Press.

Lorber, J. 1994. *Paradoxes of gender.* New Haven, Conn.: Yale University Press.

Lord, S. A. 1993. *Social welfare and the feminization of poverty.* New York: Garland.

Lorde, A. 1984. *Sister outsider.* Freedom, Calif.: The Crossing Press.

———. 1996. *The cancer journals.* San Francisco: Aunt Lute Books.

Los Angeles Times. 1999. 38% of ex-welfare recipients jobless. 15 January, p. A21.

———. 2000. *Abortion: major proposals.* Accessed online at http://www.publicagenda.org/issues/major_proposals_detail.cfm?issue_type=abortion&list=2 on 6 December 2002.

Louie, M. C. Y. 2001. *Sweatshop warriors: Immigrant women workers take on the global factory.* Cambridge, Mass.: South End Press.

Louie, M. C. with L. Burnham. 2000. *Women's education in the global economy.* Oakland, Calif.: Women of Color Resource Center.

Lovejoy, M. 2001. Disturbances in the social body: Differences in body image and eating problems among African American and White women. *Gender and Society* 15(2): 239–61.

Lowy, J. 1999. Gay adoption backlash growing. *San Francisco Examiner,* 7 March, p. A20.

Lublin, N. 1998. *Pandora's box: Feminism confronts reproductive technology.* Lanham, Md.: Rowman and Littlefield.

Luebke, B. F., and M. E. Reilly. 1995. *Women's studies graduates: The first generation.* New York: Teachers College Press.

Luker, K. 1996. *Dubious conceptions: The politics of teenage pregnancy.* Cambridge, Mass.: Harvard University Press.

Lunneborg, P. 1992. *Abortion: A positive decision.* New York: Begin and Garvey.

Lusane, C. 1991. *Pipe dream blues: Racism and the war on drugs.* Boston: South End Press.

Lydersen, K. 2001. Bad medicine: For women in prison, health care is either defunct or dangerous. *In These Times* 25(3): 21–23.

Macdonald, B. 1983. *Look me in the eye: Old women, aging, and ageism.* San Francisco: Spinsters Ink.

MacKinnon, C. 1987. *Feminism unmodified: Discourse on life and law.* Cambridge, Mass.: Harvard University Press.

———. 1991. From practice to theory, or what is a white woman anyway? *Yale Journal of Law and Feminism* 4(13–22): 1281–1328.

———. 1993. Turning rape into pornography: Postmodern genocide. *Ms.,* June/July, 24–30.

———. 1998. Rape, genocide, and women's human rights. Pp. 43–54 in *Violence against women: Philosophical perspectives,* edited by S. French, W. Teays, and L. Purdy. Ithaca, N.Y.: Cornell University Press.

Maher, F. A., and M. K. T. Tétreault. 1994. *The feminist classroom.* New York: Basic Books.

Mahoney, M. 1994. Victimization or oppression? Women's lives, violence, and agency. Pp. 59–92 in *The public nature of private violence: The discovery of domestic abuse,* edited by M. A. Fineman and R. Mykitiuk. New York: Routledge.

Mainardi, P. 1992. The politics of housework. *Ms.*, May/June, 40–41.

Mainstream. 1997. 15(2): 14–16.

Mairs, N. 1990. Carnal acts. In *Carnal acts: Essays.* Boston: Beacon Press.

———. 1996. *Waist-high in the world: A life among the nondisabled.* Boston: Beacon Press.

Majaj, L. S. 1994. Boundaries: Arab/American. Pp. 65–86 in *Food for our grandmothers: Writings by Arab-American and Arab-Canadian feminists,* edited by J. Kadi. Boston: South End Press.

Males, M. 1999. *Framing youth: 10 myths about the next generation.* Monroe, Maine: Common Courage Press.

Mallik, A. 2002. Controversy over Racial Privacy Initiative. *Asian Week,* 19 July, 25.

Mann, C. R. 1995. Women of color and the criminal justice system. In *The criminal justice system and women,* edited by B. R. Price and N. J. Sokoloff. New York: McGraw-Hill.

Martin, G. 1986. *Socialist feminism: The first decade.* Seattle, Wash.: Freedom Socialist.

Martin, J. A., B. Hamilton, S. Ventura, F. Menacker, and M. Park. 2002. Births—final data for 2000. *National Vital Statistics Reports,* vol. 50, no. 6. Hyattsville, Md.: National Center for Health Statistics.

Martin, J. A., B. L. Smith, T. J. Mathews, and S. J. Ventura. 1999. Births and deaths: Preliminary data for 1998. *National Vital Statistics Reports,* vol. 47, no. 25. Hyattsville, Md.: National Center for Health Statistics.

Martinez, E. 1998. *De colores means all of us: Latina views for a multi-colored century.* Boston: South End Press.

Martinez, L. A. 1996. Women of color and reproductive health. In *Dangerous intersections: Feminist perspectives on population, immigration, and the environment,* edited by T. Reisz and A. Smith. Amherst, Mass.: Committee on Women, Population, and the Environment, Hampshire College.

Mason, M. 1998. *USA: Supreme Court strengthens sexual harassment law,* 30 June. Accessed online at http://www.igc.org/igc/wn/hl9806304896/hl1.html.

Mason, M. A., A. Skolnick, and S. Sugarman. 1998. *All our families: New policies for a new century.* New York: Oxford University Press.

Mauer, M., and T. Huling. 1995. *Young Black Americans and the criminal justice system five years later.* Washington, D.C.: The Sentencing Project.

McCarthy, C., and W. Crichlow, eds. 1993. *Race, identity, and representation in education.* New York: Routledge.

McGinn, M. 1995. How GATT puts hard-won victories at risk. *Ms.*, March/April, 15.

McIntosh, P. 1988. *White privilege and male privilege: A personal account of coming to see correspondences through work in women's studies.* Wellesley, Mass.: Center for Research on Women, Wellesley College.

McKenna, T. 1996/1997. Military culture breeds misogyny. *Women Against Military Madness,* December/January, 1.

Mello, F. V. 1996. Population and international security in the new world order. *Political Environments,* no. 3 (winter/spring): 25–26. Publication of the Committee on Women, Population and the Environment, Hampshire College, Amherst, Mass.

Mellor, M. 1992. *Breaking the boundaries: Towards a feminist green socialism.* London: Virago Press.

Members of the AIDS Counseling and Education Program of the Bedford Hills Correctional Facility. 1998. *Breaking the walls of silence: AIDS and women in a New York State maximum security prison.* Woodstock, N.Y.: Overlook Press.

Merchant, C. 1980. *The death of nature: Ecology and the scientific revolution.* San Francisco: Harper & Row.

Messer-Davidow, E. 1991. Know-how. Pp. 281–309 in *(En)gendering knowledge: Feminists in academe,* edited by J. E. Hartman and E. Messer-Davidow. Knoxville: University of Tennessee Press.

Messerschmidt, J. W. 1986. *Capitalism, patriarchy, and crime: Toward a socialist feminist criminology.* Totowa, N.J.: Rowman and Littlefield.

Messner, M. 1992. *Power at play: Sports and the problem of masculinity.* Boston: Beacon Press.

Meyers, D. T. 2001. The rush to motherhood—pronatalist discourse and women's autonomy. *Signs: Journal of Women in Culture and Society* 26(3): 735–73.

Mies, M. 1986. *Patriarchy and accumulation on a world scale: Women in the international division of labor.* London: Zed Books.

———. 1993. The need for a new vision: The subsistence perspective. In *Ecofeminism,* edited by M. Mies and V. Shiva. London: Zed Books.

Mies, M., and V. Shiva, eds. 1993. *Ecofeminism.* London: Zed Books.

Miles Foundation. 1999. E-mail communication from Christine Hansen, Miles Foundation, to Gwyn Kirk, 11 October 1999.

Military is found less likely to promote Blacks. 1995. *New York Times,* 22 November, p. A20.

Military sex scandal extends to Air Force base. 1996. *San Francisco Chronicle,* 15 November, p. A15.

Milkman, R., ed. 1985. *Women, work, and protest: A century of U.S. women's labor history.* London: Routledge & Kegan Paul.

Milkman, R., ed. 2000. *Organizing immigrants: The challenge for unions in contemporary California.* Ithaca, N.Y.: ILR Press.

Miller, P. 1993. *The worst of times: Illegal abortion—survivors, practitioners, coroners, cops, and children of women who died talk about its horrors.* New York: HarperCollins.

Miller, V. D. 1993. *Building on our past, planning our future: Communities of color and the quest for environmental justice.* Pp. 128–135 in *Toxic Struggles: The theory and practice of environmental justice,* edited by Richard Hofrichter, Philadelphia and Gabriola Is., B.C.: New Society Publishers.

Millett, Kate. 1990. *The loony bin trip.* New York: Simon & Schuster.

Mills, J. 1986. *The underground empire: Where crime and governments embrace.* New York: Doubleday.

Mills, R. 2000. *Health insurance coverage, 1999.* Washington, D.C.: U.S. Census Bureau.

Mink, G. 1998. Feminists, welfare reform, and welfare justice. *Social Justice* 25(1): 146–57.

Mintz, S., and S. Kellogg. 1988. *Domestic revolutions: A social history of American family life.* New York: Free Press.

Mitchell, J. 1971. *Woman's estate.* New York: Pantheon.

———. 1990. Women: The longest revolution. In *Women, class, and the feminist imagination,* edited by K. V. Hansen and I. J. Philipson. Philadelphia: Temple University Press.

Mohai, P. 1997. Men, women, and the environment: An examination of the gender gap in environmental concern and activism. Pp. 215–39 in *Women working in the environment,* edited by C. Sachs. New York: Taylor and Francis.

Mohanty, C., A. Russo, and L. Torres, eds. 1991. *Third World women and the politics of feminism.* Bloomington: Indiana University Press.

Moon, K. 1997. *Sex between allies: Military prostitution in U.S.-Korea relations.* New York: Columbia University Press.

Moore, B. 1996. From underrepresentation to overrepresentation: African American women. Pp. 115–35 in *It's our military too! Women and the U.S. military,* edited by J. H. Stiehm. Philadelphia: Temple University Press.

Moore, M., and J. Gould. 2001. *Date like a man: What men know about dating and are afraid you'll find out.* New York: Quill/HarperCollins.

Moraga, C. 1997. *Waiting in the wings: Portrait of a queer motherhood.* Ithaca, N.Y.: Firebrand.

Moraga, C., and G. Anzaldúa. 1981. *This bridge called my back: Writings by radical women of color.* New York: Kitchen Table/Women of Color Press.

Morgan, R. 1996. Dispatch from Beijing. *Ms.,* January/February, 12–15.

Morgen, S. 2002. *Into our own hands: The women's health movement in the United States, 1969–1990.* Piscataway, N.J.: Rutgers University Press.

Morell, C. M. 1994. *Unwomanly conduct: The challenge of intentional childlessness.* New York: Routledge.

Morris, M. 1999. In war and peace: Incidence and implications of rape by military personnel. Pp. 163–94 in *Beyond zero tolerance: Discrimination in military culture,* edited by M. F. Katzenstein and J. Reppy. Lanham, Md.: Rowman and Littlefield.

Morrison, A., R. White, E. Van Velsor, and the Center for Creative Leadership. 1992. *Breaking the glass ceiling: Can women reach the top of America's largest corporations?* Reading, Mass.: Addison-Wesley.

Morrison, T., ed. 1992. *Race-ing, justice, en-gendering power: Essays on Anita Hill, Clarence Thomas, and the construction of reality.* New York: Pantheon.

Morrow, D. 1999a. Maker of Norplant reaches settlement in suit over effects. *New York Times,* 27 August, p. A1.

———. 1999b. A moveable epidemic: Makers of AIDS drugs struggle to keep up with the market. *New York Times,* 9 September, p. C1.

Morrow, L. 1999. Folklore in a box. Pp. 22–26 in *Readings in mass communication: Media literacy and culture,* edited by K. B. Massey, Mountain View, Calif.: Mayfield.

Moses, M. 1993. Farmworkers and pesticides. Pp. 161–78 in *Confronting environmental racism: Voices from the grassroots,* edited by R. Bullard. Boston: South End Press.

Movement for a New Society. 1983. *Off their backs . . . and on our own two feet.* Philadelphia: New Society Publishers.

Mudrick, N. R. 1988. Disabled women and the public policies of income support. In *Women with disabilities: Essays in psychology, culture, and politics,* edited by M. Fine and A. Asch. Philadelphia: Temple University Press.

Muir, K. 1993. *Arms and the woman.* London: Hodder and Stoughton.

Mullings, L. 1997. *On our own: Race, class, and gender in the lives of African American women.* New York: Routledge.

Muscio, I. 1999. *Cunt: A declaration of independence.* Seattle, Wash.: Seal Press.

Musil, C. M., ed. 1992. *The courage to question: Women's studies and student learning.* Washington, D.C.: Association of American Colleges.

Myers, A., J. Taub, J. F. Morris, and E. D. Rothblun. 1998. Beauty mandates and the appearance obsession: Are lesbians any better off? Pp. 17–25 in *Looking queer: Body image and identity in lesbian, bisexual, gay, and transgender communities,* edited by D. Atkins. New York: Haworth Press.

Nadelson, C. C., and T. Nadelson. 1980. Dual-career marriages: Benefits and costs. In *Dual career couples,* edited by F. Pepitone-Rickwell. Beverly Hills, Calif.: Sage.

Nader, R. 1993. *The case against free trade.* San Francisco: Earth Island Press.

Naffine, N. 1987. *Female crime: The construction of women in criminology.* Boston: Allen & Unwin.

Naidus, B. 1993. *One size does not fit all.* Littleton, Colo.: Aigis Publications.

Naples, N., ed. 1997. *Community activism and feminist politics: Organizing across race, class, and gender.* New York: Routledge.

———. 1998. *Grassroots warriors: Activist mothering, community work, and the war on poverty.* New York: Routledge.

Naples, N., and K. Bojar, eds. 2002. *Teaching feminist activism: Strategies from the field.* New York: Routledge.

National Abortion Rights Action League. 2002. *Letter to NARAL supporters.* Washington, D.C.: NARAL.

National Cancer Institute. 1996. *SEER monograph: Racial/ ethnic patterns of cancer in the United States, 1988–1992.* Washington, D.C.: National Cancer Institute.

National Center for Chronic Disease Prevention and Health Promotion. 2002. *Abortion surveillance—United States 1998.* Accessed online at http://www.cdc.gov/ nccdphp/drh/surv-abort.htm on 7 December 2002.

National Center for Health Statistics. 1996a. *Health United States, 1995.* Hyattsville, Md.: Public Health Service.

———. 1996b. *Monthly vital statistics report on final mortality, 1994.* Hyattsville, Md.: National Center for Health Statistics.

———. 1999a. *Final data for 1997,* vol. 47, no. 19, p. 108. Hyattsville, Md.: National Center for Health Statistics.

———. 1999b. *Infant mortality statistics from the 1997 period linked birth/infant death data set,* vol. 47, no. 23, p. 24. Hyattsville, Md.: National Center for Health Statistics.

———. 2000. *Teen births.* Accessed online at http://www. cdc.gov/nchs/fastats/teenbrth.htm on 7 December 2002.

———. 2002a. *National vital statistics report,* vol. 50, no. 6. Hyattsville, Md.: National Center for Health Statistics.

———. 2002b. *National vital statistics report,* vol. 50, no. 16. Hyattsville, Md.: National Center for Health Statistics.

———. 2002c. *Trends in health insurance coverage by race/ ethnicity among persons under 5 years of age: United States, 1997–2001.* Hyattsville, Md.: National Center for Health Statistics. Accessed online at http://www. cdc.gov/nchs/products/pubs/pubd/hestats/ healthinsur.htm on 8 November 2002.

National Clearinghouse on Marital and Date Rape. 1998. Accessed online at http://members.aol.com/ncmdr/ index.html.

National Institute of Justice. 1998. *Women offenders: Programming needs and promising approaches.* Washington, D.C.: U.S. Department of Justice.

National Institute of Justice and Centers for Disease Control and Prevention. 1998. *Prevalence, incidence, and consequences of violence against women: Findings from the National Violence Against Women Survey.* Washington, D.C.: National Institute of Justice and Centers for Disease Control and Prevention.

National Victim Center. 1992. *Rape in America. A report to the nation.* Arlington, Va.: Author.

National Women's Studies Association. 1994. *NWSA directory of women's studies programs, women's centers, and women's research centers.* College Park, Md.: National Women's Studies Association.

Navarro, M. 1996. Lesbian loses court appeal for custody of daughter. *New York Times,* 31 August, p. A7.

Navarro, V. 1993. *Dangerous to your health: Capitalism in health care.* New York: Monthly Review Press.

Nechas, E., and D. Foley. 1994. *Unequal treatment: What you don't know about how women are mistreated by the medical community.* Philadelphia: Temple University Press.

Nelson, M. B. 2002. And now they tell us women don't really like sports? *Ms.,* December 2002/January 2003, 32–36.

Nelson, L. 1990. The place of women in polluted places. In *Reweaving the world: The emergence of ecofeminism,* edited by I. Diamond and G. Orenstein. San Francisco: Sierra Club Books.

Nestle, J., ed. 1992. *The persistent desire: A femme-butch reader.* Los Angeles: Alyson.

Neuborne, E. 1994. Cashing in on fear: The NRA targets women. *Ms.,* June/July, pp. 45–50.

Newman, L. 1991. *SomeBody to love: A guide to loving the body you have.* Chicago: Third Side Press.

News Services. 1998. Pope warns against dangers of capitalism. *St. Louis Dispatch,* 26 January, p. A1.

NiCarthy, G. 1986. *Getting free: You can end abuse and take back your life.* Seattle, Wash.: Seal Press.

———. 1987. *The ones who got away: Women who left abusive partners.* Seattle, Wash.: Seal Press.

Nicholson, L., ed. 1990. *Feminism/postmodernism.* New York: Routledge.

Nike: Just don't do it. 1997. Special report available from Global Exchange, 2017 Mission St., Rm. 303, San Francisco, CA 94110.

Nissinen, S. 2000. *The conscious bride: Women unveil their true feelings about getting hitched.* Oakland, Calif.: New Harbinger Publications.

Noble, K. 1994. Woman tells of retaliation for complaint on Tailhook. *New York Times,* 5 October, p. A10.

Nordhaus, W. D. 2002. Iraq: The economic consequences of war. *New York Review of Books,* 5 December, 9–12.

Norris, P., ed. 1997. *Women, media, and politics.* New York: Oxford University Press.

Norsigian, J. 1996. The women's health movement in the United States. Pp. 79–97 in *Man-made medicine: Women's health, public policy, and reform,* edited by K. L. Moss. Durham, N.C.: Duke University Press.

Norwood, R. 1986. *Women who love too much.* New York: Pocket Books.

NOW Legal Defense and Education Fund. 1999. *Violence against women legislative advocacy packet.* Accessed online at http://www.nowldef.org/html/policy/ violence.htm.

Nowrojee, S., and J. Silliman. 1997. Asian women's health: Organizing a movement. Pp. 73–89 in *Dragon ladies: Asian American feminists breathe fire,* edited by S. Shah. Boston: South End Press.

O'Connor, M., ed. 1994. *Is capitalism sustainable? Political economy and the politics of ecology.* New York: Guilford Press.

O'Connor, P. 1992. *Friendships between women: A critical review.* New York: Guilford Press.

Odubekun, L. 1992. A structural approach to differential gender sentencing. *Criminal Justice Abstracts* 24(2): 343–60.

O'Farrell, B., and J. Kornbluh. 1996. *Rocking the boat: Union women's voices, 1915–1975.* New Brunswick, N.J.: Rutgers University Press.

Ogur, B. 1996. Smothering in stereotypes: HIV-positive women. In *Talking gender: Public images, personal journeys, and political critiques,* edited by N. Hewitt, J. O'Barr, and N. Rosebaugh. Chapel Hill: University of North Carolina Press.

Okazawa-Rey, M. 1994. Racial identity development of mixed race persons: An overview. In *Diversity and human service education,* edited by J. Silver-Jones, S. Kerstein, and D. Osher. Council of Standards in Human Service Education Monograph Series, No. 4.

———. 1997. Amerasians in GI town: The legacy of U.S. militarism in South Korea. *Asian Journal of Women's Studies* 3: 1.

Okazawa-Rey, M., and G. Kirk. 1996. Military security: Confronting the oxymoron. *CrossRoads* 60: 4–7.

Okin, S. M. 1989. *Justice, gender, and the family.* New York: Basic Books.

Okinawa Prefecture. 1998. *Summary of the second interim report of the Field Study on Public Health around U.S. Bases in Okinawa.* Okinawa, Japan: Research Study Committee of Aircraft Noise Influence to Health.

Okinawa Women Act Against Military Violence. 1996. *An appeal for the recognition of women's human rights.* Naha, Okinawa: Author.

Okinawa women's America peace caravan. 1996. Unpublished program. February 3–17. Naha City, Okinawa: Okinawa Women Act Against Military Violence.

Oliker, S. J. 1989. *Best friends and marriage: Exchange among women.* Berkeley: University of California Press.

O'Melveny, M. 1996. Lexington Prison High Security Unit: U. S. political prison. In *Criminal injustice: Confronting the prison crisis,* edited by E. Rosenblatt. Boston: South End Press.

Omolade, B. 1986. *It's a family affair: The real lives of Black single mothers.* New York: Kitchen Table: Women of Color Press.

———. 1989. We speak for the planet. In *Rocking the ship of state: Toward a feminist peace politics,* edited by A. Harris and Y. King. Boulder, Colo.: Westview Press.

Ong, P., E. Bonacich, and L. Cheng. 1994. *The new Asian immigration in Los Angeles and global restructuring.* Philadelphia: Temple University Press.

O'Reilly, B. 1991. Cooling down the world debt bomb. *Fortune,* 20 May, 123.

Orlando, L. 1991. Loving whom we choose. Pp. 223–32 in *Bi any other name: Bisexual people speak out,* edited by L. Hutchins and L. Ka'ahumanu. Boston: Alyson Publications.

O'Rourke, D. 1985. *Half life: A parable for the nuclear age.* Video.

O'Shea, K. 1998. *Women and the death penalty in the United States, 1900–1998.* Westport, Conn.: Praeger.

O'Toole, L., and J. Schiffman. 1997. *Gender violence: Interdisciplinary perspectives.* New York: New York University Press.

Owen, B., and B. Bloom. 1995. Profiling women prisoners. *The Prison Journal* 75(2): 165–85.

Oxfam International. 1998. *Making debt relief work: A test of political will.* Accessed online at http://www.oxfamamerica.org/advocacy/Test_of_Political_Will.htm.

Page, S. 1988. *If I'm so wonderful, why am I still single? Ten strategies that will change your love life forever.* New York: Viking.

Paglia, C. 1990. *Sexual personae: Art and decadence from Nefertiti to Emily Dickinson.* New Haven, Conn.: Yale University Press.

———. 1992. *Sex, art, and American culture.* New York: Vintage Books.

———. 1994. *Vamps and tramps.* New York: Vintage Books.

Paley, G. 1998. The illegal days. Pp. 13–20 in *Just as I thought.* New York: Farrar, Straus, Giroux.

Pardo, M. 1990. Mexican American women grassroots community activists: "Mothers of East Los Angeles." *Frontiers: A Journal of Women's Studies* 11(1): 1–7.

Parenti, C. 1999, September. The prison industrial complex: Crisis and control. *Corporate Watch.* San Francisco: Transnational Resource and Action Center.

Parker, S., M. Nichter, C. S. Vuckovic, and C. Ritenbaugh. 1995. Body image and weight concerns among African-American and white adolescent females: Differences that make a difference. *Human Organization* 54: 103–14.

Patai, D. 1998. *Heterophobia: Sexual harassment and the future of feminism.* Lanham, Md.: Rowman and Littlefield.

Pateman, C. 1988. *The sexual contract.* Stanford, Calif.: Stanford University Press.

Peach, L. J. 1997. Behind the front lines: Feminist battles over combat. Pp. 99–135 in *Wives and warriors: Women and the military in the United States and Canada,* edited by L. Weinstein and C. White. Westport, Conn.: Bergin & Garvey.

Pear, R. 2001. Sex difference called key in medical studies. *New York Times,* 25 April, p. A14.

Pearce, D., A. Markandya, and E. B. Barbier. 1990. *Blueprint for a Green economy.* London: Earthscan.

Perrone, B., H. H. Stockel, and V. Krueger. 1989. *Medicine women, curanderas, and women doctors.* Norman: University of Oklahoma Press.

Petchesky, R. 1990. *Abortion and woman's choice: The state, sexuality, and reproductive freedom.* Rev. ed. Boston: Northeastern University Press.

———. 1997. Fetal images: The power of visual culture in the politics of reproduction. Pp. 134–50 in *The gender/sexuality reader,* edited by R. Lancaster and M. di Leonardo. New York: Routledge.

Peters, J. 1997. *When mothers work: Loving our children without sacrificing ourselves.* Reading, Mass.: Addison-Wesley.

Petersen, B. 1991. *Dancing with Daddy: A childhood lost and a life regained.* New York: Bantam Books.

Peterson, R. R. 1996. Re-evaluation of the economic consequences of divorce. *American Sociological Review* 61(3): 528–53.

Peterson, V. S., and A. S. Runyan. 1993. *Global gender issues.* Boulder, Colo.: Westview Press.

Pharr, S. 1988. *Homophobia: A weapon of sexism.* Inverness, Calif.: Chardon Press.

Pheterson, G. 1990. Alliances between women: Overcoming internalized oppression and internalized domination. In *Bridges of power,* edited by L. Albrecht and R. M. Brewer. Philadelphia and Gabriola Island, B.C.: New Society Publishers.

Phillips, L. 2000. *Flirting with danger: Young women reflect on sexuality and domination.* New York: New York University Press.

Phoenix, J. 1993. Getting the lead out of the community. In *Confronting environmental racism,* edited by R. D. Bullard. Boston: South End Press.

Physicians for a National Health Program. 2002. *Single payer fact sheet.* Chicago: PNHP.

Piercy, M. 1976. *Woman on the edge of time.* New York: Fawcett Crest.

Pitter, L., and A. Stilmayer. 1993. Will the world remember? Can the women forget? *Ms.,* March/April, 19–22.

Plant, C., and J. Plant, eds. 1992. *Putting power in its place: Create community control!* Philadelphia and Gabriola Island, B.C.: New Society Publishers.

Plath, S. 1971. *The bell jar.* New York: Harper and Row.

Plumwood, V. 1993. *Feminism and the mastery of nature.* New York: Routledge.

Polikoff, N. 1993. We will get what we ask for: Why legalizing gay and lesbian marriage will not "dismantle the legal structure of gender in every marriage." *Virginia Law Review* 79: 1535–50.

Pollack, J. 1994. The increasing incarceration rate of women offenders: Equality or justice? Paper presented at Prisons 2000 Conference, Leicester, England.

Pollitt, K. 1994. Subject to debate. *The Nation,* 11 July, 45.

Postman, N., and S. Powers. 1992. *How to watch TV news.* New York: Penguin Books.

Potts, B. 1988. *Witches heal: Lesbian herbal self-sufficiency.* 2d ed. Ann Arbor, Mich.: DuReve Publications.

Poverty guidelines. 2002. *Federal Register* 67(31): 6931–33.

Pratt, M. B. 1984. Identity: Skin blood heart. In Elly Bulkin, M. B. Pratt, and B. Smith, *Yours in Struggle: Three feminist perspectives on anti-semitism and racism.* Brooklyn, NY: Long Haul Press, pp. 9–63.

———. 1995. *S/he.* Ithaca, N.Y.: Firebrand Books.

Press, E. 1997. Breaking the sweats. *The Nation,* 28 April, 5–6.

Prison Activist Resource Center. 1997. *Women in prison.* Fact sheet prepared by Prison Activist Resource Center, Berkeley, Calif.

Prokosch, M., and L. Raymond, eds. 2002. *The global activist's manual: Local ways to change the world.* New York: Thunder's Mouth Press/Nation Books.

Pulido, L. 1993. Sustainable development at Ganados del Valle. In *Confronting environmental racism: Voices from the grassroots,* edited by R. Bullard. Boston: South End Press.

———. 1996. *Environmentalism and economic justice: Two Chicano struggles in the southwest.* Tucson: University of Arizona Press.

Quindlen, A. 1994. Feminism continues to grow and reach and affect us all. *Chicago Tribune,* 21 January, sec. 1, p. 21.

Rafter, N. 1990. *Partial justice: Women, prisons and social control.* New Brunswick, N.J.: Transaction.

Rape Abuse Incest National Network. 1999. RAINNews. Accessed online at http://www.rainn.org/news/stat.html.

Raphael, J., and R. Tolman. 1997. *Trapped in poverty, trapped by abuse: New evidence documenting the relationship between domestic violence and welfare.* Project for Research on Welfare, Work, and Domestic Violence. A collaboration between Taylor Institute and University of Michigan Development Center on Poverty, Risk, and Mental Health.

Rasmussen, V. 1998. Rethinking the corporation. *Food and Water Journal,* Fall, 17–21.

Raymond, J. G. 1986. *A passion for friends: Toward a philosophy of female affection.* Boston: Beacon Press.

———. 1994. *The transsexual empire: The making of the she-male.* 2d ed. New York: Teachers College Press.

Rayner, R. 1997. Women in the warrior culture. *New York Times Magazine,* 22 June, 24–29, 40, 49, 53, 55–56.

Reagon, B. J. 1987. *Ode to the international debt.* Boston: Songtalk.

Reardon, B. A. 1985. *Sexism and the war system.* New York: Teachers College Press.

———. 1993. *Women and peace: Feminist visions of global security.* Albany, N.Y.: SUNY Press.

———. 1998. Gender and global security: A feminist challenge to the United Nations and peace research. *Journal of International Co-operation Studies* 6(1): 29–56.

Redwood, R. 1996. The glass ceiling. *Motion Magazine.* Accessed online at http://www.inmotionmagazine.com/glass.html.

Rennison, C. M. 2001. *Intimate partner violence and age of victim, 1993–99.* Bureau of Justice Statistics, special report. Washington, D.C.: U.S. Department of Justice.

———. 2002. *Rape and sexual assault: Reporting to police and medical attention, 1992–2000.* Bureau of Justice Statistics, selected findings. Washington, D.C.: U.S. Department of Justice.

Renzetti, C. M. 1992. *Violent betrayal: Partner abuse in lesbian relationships.* Newbury Park, Calif.: Sage.

Rethinking schools. 2002. *The WTO in action: Case studies.* Accessed online at http://www.rethinkingschools.org/publication/rg/RGWto.shtml on 26 December 2002.

Reti, I., ed. 1992. *Childless by choice: A feminist anthology.* Santa Cruz, Calif.: Her Books.

Reynolds, M. 1992. *Erotica: Women's writing from Sappho to Margaret Atwood.* New York: Fawcett Columbine.

Rich, A. 1976. *Of woman born: Motherhood as experience and institution.* New York: W. W. Norton.

———. 1986a. Compulsory heterosexuality and lesbian existence. In *Blood, bread, and poetry.* New York: W. W. Norton.

———. 1986b. *Of woman born: Motherhood as experience and institution.* 10th anniversary ed. New York: W. W. Norton.

———. 1986c. Notes towards a politics of location. Pp. 210–31 in *Blood, bread, and poetry.* New York: W. W. Norton.

Richie, B. 1996. *Compelled to crime: The gender entrapment of battered Black women.* New York: Routledge.

Richter, P. 2000. Armed forces find "disturbing" level of gay harassment. *Los Angeles Times,* 25 March, p. A1.

Rierden, A. 1997. *The Farm: Inside a women's prison.* Amherst: University of Massachusetts Press.

Riley, D. 1988. *Am I that name? Feminism and the category of "women" in history.* Minneapolis: University of Minnesota Press.

Risman, B. J. 1998. *Gender vertigo: American families in transition.* New Haven, Conn.: Yale University Press.

Ritz, D., ed. 2001. *Defying corporations, defining democracy.* New York: Apex Press.

Roberts, D. 1997. *Killing the Black body: Race, reproduction, and the meaning of liberty.* New York: Pantheon.

Roberts, M. M., and T. Mizuta, eds. 1993. *The reformers: Socialist feminism.* London: Routledge/Thoemmes Press.

Roediger, D. R. 1991. *The wages of whiteness: Race and the making of the American working class.* New York: Verso.

Roiphe, K. 1993. *The morning after: Sex, fear, and feminism.* Boston: Little Brown.

Rooks, N. 1996. *Beauty, culture, and African American women.* New Brunswick, N.J.: Rutgers University Press.

Root, M. P. P., ed. 1996. *The multiracial experience: Racial borders as the new frontier.* Thousand Oaks, Calif.: Sage.

Rosen, R. 2000. *The world split open: How the modern women's movement changed America.* New York: Viking.

Rosenberg, A. 1988. The crisis in knowing and understanding the Holocaust. In *Echoes from the Holocaust: Philosophical reflections on a dark time,* edited by A. Rosenberg and G. E. Meyers. Philadelphia: Temple University Press.

Rosenberg, H. H. 1998. *How to get married after thirty-five: The game plan for love.* New York: HarperCollins.

Rosenblatt, E., ed. 1996. *Criminal injustice: Confronting the prison crisis.* Boston: South End Press.

Rosenblum, B. 1997. Living in an unstable body. Pp. 93–104 in *Staring back: The disability experiences from the inside out,* edited by K. Fries. New York: Penguin/Plume.

Ross, A., ed. 1997. *No sweat: Fashion, free trade, and the rights of garment workers.* New York: Verso.

Ross, L. 1993. Major concerns of imprisoned American Indian and White mothers. In *Gender: Multicultural perspectives,* edited by J. Gonzalez-Calvo. Dubuque, Iowa: Kendall Hunt.

Ross, L. J., S. L. Brownlee, D. D. Diallo, L. Rodriquez, and the SisterSong Women of Color Reproductive Health Project. 2002. Just choices: Women of Color, Reproductive Health and Human Rights. Pp. 147–74 in *Policing the national body: Race, gender, and criminalization,* edited by J. Silliman and A. Bhattacharjee. Cambridge, Mass.: South End Press.

Rubin, G. 1984. Thinking sex: Notes for a radical theory of the politics of sexuality. Pp. 267–319 in *Pleasure and danger: Exploring female sexuality,* edited by C. S. Vance. Boston: Routledge and Kegan Paul.

Ruddick, S. 1989. *Maternal thinking: Toward a politics of peace.* Boston: Beacon Press.

Russell, B. 1935. *In praise of idleness and other essays.* New York: W. W. Norton.

Russell, D. 1995. *Women, madness, and medicine.* Cambridge, England: Polity Press.

Russell, D. E. H. 1975. *The politics of rape: The victim's perspective.* New York: Stein and Day.

———. 1986. *The secret trauma: Incest in the lives of girls and women.* New York: Basic Books.

———. 1990. *Rape in marriage.* Rev. ed. Bloomington: Indiana University Press.

Russo, N. F., and M. A. Jansen. 1988. Women, work, and disability: Opportunities and challenges. In *Women with disabilities: Essays in psychology, culture, and politics,* edited by M. Fine and A. Asch. Philadelphia: Temple University Press.

Sachs, C. 1996. *Gendered fields: Rural women, agriculture, and environment.* Boulder, Colo.: Westview Press.

Sachs, S. 2000. Sexual abuse reported at an immigration center. *New York Times,* 5 October, p. A20.

Sadler, G. C. 1997. Women in combat: The U.S. military and the impact of the Persian Gulf War. Pp. 79–97 in *Wives and warriors*, edited by L. Weinstein and C. White.

Safe, J. 1996. *Beyond motherhood: Choosing a life without children*. New York: Pocket Books.

Sajor, I. L., ed. 1998. *Common grounds: Violence against women in war and armed conflict situations*. Quezon City, Philippines: Asian Center for Women's Human Rights.

Sale, K. 1985. *Dwellers in the land, the bioregional vision*. San Francisco: Sierra Club Books.

Sanday, P. 1990. *Fraternity gang rape: Sex, brotherhood, and privilege on campus*. New York: New York University Press.

Sanders, B., and M. Kaptur. 1997. Just do it, Nike. *The Nation*, 8 December, 6.

Santi-Flaherty, T. 1997. *The savvy woman's success bible: How to find the right job, the right man, and the right life*. New York: Perigee/Berkeley Publishing Group.

Saporito, B. 1998. Can Nike get unstuck? *Time*, 30 March, 47–53.

Schemo, D. J. 2003. Women's athletics: Title IX reformers keep men in mind. *New York Times*, 27 February, p. D1.

Scholinski, D. 1997. *The last time I wore a dress*. New York: Riverhead Books.

Schulman, K. A., J. Berlin, W. Harless, J. Kerner, S. Sistrunk, B. Gersh, R. Dubé, C. Talghani, J. Burke, S. Williams, J. Eisenberg, and J. Escarce. 1999. The effects of race and sex on physicians' recommendations for cardiac catheterization. *New England Journal of Medicine* 340(8): 618–26.

Schwab, J. 1994. *Deeper shades of green: The rise of blue-collar and minority environmentalism in America*. San Francisco: Sierra Club Books.

Schwartz, P. 1994. *Love between equals: How peer marriage really works*. New York: Free Press.

Scott, W. J., and S. C. Stanley. 1994. *Gays and lesbians in the military: Issues, concerns, and contrasts*. Hawthorne, N.Y.: Aldine de Gruyter.

Scully, J. A. M. 2002. Killing the Black community: A commentary on the United States war on drugs. Pp. 55–80 in *Policing the national body: Sex, race, and criminalization*, edited by J. Silliman and A. Bhattacharjee. Cambridge: Mass.: South End Press.

Seager, J. 1993. *Earth follies: Coming to feminist terms with the global environmental crisis*. New York: Routledge.

Sedgwick, E. K. 1990. *Epistemology of the closet*. Berkeley: University of California Press.

Segal, L. 1994. *Straight sex: Rethinking the politics of pleasure*. Berkeley: University of California Press.

Segell, M. 1996. The second coming of the Alpha male: A prescription for righteous masculinity at the millennium. *Esquire*, October, 74–82.

Segrest, M. 1994. *Memoir of a race traitor*. Boston: South End Press.

Seidman, S. 1992. *Embattled eros: Sexual politics and ethics in contemporary America*. New York: Routledge.

Seigel, L. 1997. The pregnancy police fight the war on drugs. Pp. 249–59 in *Crack in America: Demon drugs and social justice*, edited by C. Reinarman and H. G. Levine. Berkeley: University of California Press.

Sen, G., and C. Grown. 1987. *Development, crises, and alternative visions: Third World women's perspectives*. New York: Monthly Review Press.

Sengupta, S. 1999. Squeezed by debt and time, mothers ship babies to China. *New York Times*, 14 September, p. A1.

The Sentencing Project. 2001. *U.S. continues to be world leader in rate of incarceration*. Washington, D.C.: The Sentencing Project. Accessed online at www.sentencingproject.org on 16 January 2003.

Serna, I. 1992. *Locked down: A woman's life in prison*. Norwich, Vt.: New Victoria Publishers.

Servicemembers Legal Defense Network. 1999a. *Conduct unbecoming. Fifth annual report on "Don't ask, don't tell, don't pursue."* Accessed online at http://www.sldn.org/scripts/sldn.ixe?page?pr_03_15_99.

———. 1999b. Pentagon fires record number of gays. Accessed online at http://www.sldn.org/scripts/sldn.ixe?page=pr_01_22_99.

———. 2002. *Conduct unbecoming: The eighth annual report on "don't ask, don't tell, don't pursue, don't harass."* Washington, D.C.: SLDN.

Shah, S., ed. 1997. *Dragon ladies: Asian feminists breathe fire*. Boston: South End Press.

Sharf, J. 1997. Guess again: Sweatshop violations continue. *Jews for economic and racial justice*, Bulletin 33. Available from JREC, 64 Fulton St., #605, New York, NY 10038.

Sherrill, R. 1997. A year in corporate crime. *The Nation*, 7 April, 11–20.

Shields, K. 1994. *In the tiger's mouth: An empowerment guide for action*. Gabriola Island, B.C.: New Society Publishers.

Shin, A. 1999. Testing Title IX. *Ms.*, April/May, 32–33.

Shiva, V. 1988. *Staying alive: Women, ecology and development*. London: Zed Books.

———. 2002. Relocalization not globalization. Pp. 248–49 in *Rethinking globalization: Teaching for justice in an unjust world*, edited by B. Bigelow and B. Peterson. Milwaukee, Wis.: Rethinking Schools.

Showalter, E. 1987. *The female malady: Women, madness, and English culture, 1830–1980*. London: Virago.

Shugar, D. R. 1995. *Separatism and women's community*. Lincoln: University of Nebraska Press.

Shulman, S. 1990. Toxic travels: Inside the military's environmental nightmare. *Nuclear Times*, Autumn, 20–32.

Sidel, R. 1996. *Keeping women and children last: America's war on the poor*. New York: Penguin Books.

Siegal, N. 1995. Girl trouble. *San Francisco Bay Guardian,* 29 November, pp. 16–18.

———. 1998. Women in prison. *Ms.,* September/October, 64–73.

Sigler, H., S. Love, and J. Yood. 1999. *Hollis Sigler's breast cancer journal.* New York: Hudson Hills Press.

Silliman, J., and A. Bhattacharjee, eds. 2002. *Policing the national body: Sex, race, and criminalization.* Cambridge, Mass.: South End Press.

Silliman, J., and Y. King, eds. 1999. *Dangerous intersections: Feminist perspectives on population, environment, and development.* Cambridge, Mass.: South End Press.

Simon, R. 1975. *Women and crime.* Lexington, Mass.: Lexington Books.

Singh, G. K., and S. M. Yu. 1995. Infant mortality in the United States: Trends, differentials, and projections, 1950 through 2010. *American Journal of Public Health* 85(7): 957–64.

Sivard, R. L. 1995. *Women . . . a world survey.* 2d ed. Washington, D.C.: World Priorities.

———. 1996. *World military and social expenditures 1996.* 16th ed. Washington, D.C.: World Priorities.

Skaine, R. 1998. *Women at war: Gender issues of Americans in combat.* Jefferson, N.C.: McFarland and Co.

Skolnick, A. 1991. *Embattled paradise: The American family in an age of uncertainty.* New York: Basic Books.

Slater, L. 1998. *Prozac diary.* New York: Random House.

Slugocki, L. A. and E. C. Wilson. 2000. *The erotica project.* San Francisco: Cleis Press.

Smart, C. 1989. *Feminism and the power of law.* London: Routledge & Kegan Paul.

———. 1995. *Law, crime, and sexuality: Essays in feminism.* London: Sage.

Smeal, E. 1984. *Why and how women will elect the next president.* New York: Harper & Row.

Smelser, N. 1994. *Sociology.* Cambridge, Mass.: Blackwell.

Smith, A. 1991. To all those who were Indian in a former life. *Ms.,* November/December, 44–45.

———. 1997. Ecofeminism through an anti-colonial framework. Pp. 21–37 in *Ecofeminism: Women, culture, nature,* edited by K. Warren. Bloomington: Indiana University Press.

———. 2001. The color of violence: Violence against women of color. Conference report. *Meridians: Feminism, Race, Transnationalism* 1(2): 65–72.

———. 2002. Better dead than pregnant: The colonization of Native women's reproductive health. Pp. 123–46 in *Policing the national body: Race, gender, and criminalization,* edited by J. Silliman and A. Bhattacharjee. Cambridge, Mass.: South End Press.

Smith, B. 1998. *The truth that never hurts: Writings on race, gender, freedom.* New Brunswick, N.J.: Rutgers University Press.

Smith, B., ed. 1983. *Home girls: A Black feminist anthology.* New York: Kitchen Table: Women of Color Press.

Smith, M. 1997. When violence strikes home. *The Nation,* 30 June, 23–24.

Snitow, A., C. Stansell, and S. Thompson, eds. 1983. Powers of desire: *The politics of sexuality.* New York: Monthly Review Press.

Social Security Administration. 2001. *Women and retirement security.* Washington, D.C.: SSA. Accessed online at http://www.ssa.gov/policy/pubs/womenrs.html on 20 December 2002.

Solinger, R. 1994. *The abortionist: A woman against the law.* New York: Routledge.

Spelman, E. V. 1988. *Inessential woman: Problems of exclusion in feminist thought.* Boston: Beacon Press.

Spretnak, C. 1990. Ecofeminism: Our roots and flowering. In *Reweaving the world: The emergence of ecofeminism,* edited by I. Diamond & G. Orenstein. San Francisco: Sierra Club Books.

Springer, K. 2002. Being the bridge: A solitary Black woman's position in the women's studies classroom as a feminist student and professor. Pp. 381–89 in *This bridge we call home: Radical visions for transformation,* edited by G. Anzaldúa and A. Keating. New York: Routledge.

Stacey, Jackie. 1993. Untangling feminist theory. Pp. 49–73 in *Thinking feminist: Key concepts in women's studies,* edited by D. Richardson and V. Robinson. New York: Guilford Press.

Stacey, Judith. 1996. *In the name of the family: Rethinking values in the postmodern age.* Boston: Beacon Press.

———. 1999. The family values fable. Pp. 487–90 in *American families: A multicultural reader,* edited by S. Coontz with M. Parson and G. Raley. New York: Routledge.

Stanworth, M., ed. 1987. *Reproductive technologies.* Cambridge, England: Cambridge University Press.

Starhawk. 1987. *Truth or dare: Encounters with power, authority, and mystery.* San Francisco: Harper & Row.

———. 1993. *The fifth sacred thing.* New York: Bantam Books.

———. 2002a. Our place in nature. Pp. 160–68 in *Webs of power: Notes from the global uprising.* Gabriola Island, B.C.: New Society Publishers.

———. 2002b. *Webs of power: Notes from the global uprising.* Gabriola Island, B.C.: New Society Publishers.

State of the Workplace Report. 1999. Washington, D.C.: Human Rights Campaign.

Steedman, C. 1986. *Landscape for a good woman: A story of two lives.* New Brunswick, N.J.: Rutgers University Press.

Stefan, S. 1994. The protection racket: Rape trauma syndrome, psychiatric labeling, and law. In *Northwestern Law Review,* 88(4): 1271–1345.

Stein, A. 1997. Sisters and queers: The decentering of lesbian feminism. Pp. 378–91 in *The gender sexuality reader,* edited by R. Lancaster and M. di Leonardo. New York: Routledge.

Stein, D., ed. 1991. *From inside: An anthology of writing by incarcerated women.* Minneapolis: Honor Press.

Steinberg, J. 1989. At debt's door. *Ms.,* November, 78.

Steinem, G. 1983. *Outrageous acts and everyday rebellions.* New York: Holt, Rinehart, & Winston.

Steingraber, S. 2001. *Having faith: An ecologist's journey to motherhood.* Cambridge, Mass.: Perseus Publishing.

Stewart, A., A. Copeland, N. L. Chester, J. Malley, N. Barenbaum. 1997. *Separating together: How divorce transforms families.* New York: Guilford Press.

Stewart, I. 1997. Vietnam's fed-up workers striking for rights. *San Francisco Chronicle,* 23 June, p. A10.

Stiehm, J. H. 1989. *Arms and the enlisted woman.* Philadelphia: Temple University Press.

———, ed. 1996. *It's our military too! Women and the U.S. military.* Philadelphia: Temple University Press.

Stocker, M., ed. 1991. *Cancer as a women's issue: Scratching the surface.* Chicago: Third Side Press.

———. 1993. *Confronting cancer, constructing change: New perspectives on women and cancer.* Chicago: Third Side Press.

Stockholm International Peace Research Institute. 2002. Recent trends in military expenditure. *SIPRI Yearbook 2002.* Stockholm, Sweden: SIPRI.

Stoller, E. P., and R. C. Gibson, eds. 1994. *Worlds of difference: Inequality in the aging experience.* Thousand Oaks, Calif.: Pine Forge.

Stonequist, E. V. 1961. *The marginal man: A study in personality and cultural conflict.* New York: Scribner & Sons.

Storr, M., ed. 1999. *Bisexuality: A critical reader.* New York: Routledge.

St. Paige, E. 1999. *Zaftig: The case for curves.* Seattle, Wash.: Darling and Co.

Study shows few women in combat jobs. *San Francisco Chronicle,* 21 October 1997, p. A6.

Sturdevant, S., and B. Stoltzfus. 1992. *Let the good times roll: Prostitution and the U.S. military in Asia.* New York: New Press.

Suggs, W. 2002. Title IX at 30. *Chronicle of Higher Education,* 21 June, pp. A38–41.

Survivors take action against abuse by military personnel. 1999. *Newsletter 1998/99.* Fairborn, Ohio: Author.

Sward, S. 1997. S.F. police panel puts off FBI proposal. Feds want to team up to fight terrorism. *San Francisco Chronicle,* 16 January, p. A18.

Swerdlow, A. 1993. *Women strike for peace: Traditional motherhood and radical politics in the 1960s.* Chicago: University of Chicago Press.

Swiss, S., and J. Giller. 1993. Rape as a crime of war: A medical perspective. *Journal of the American Medical Association* (27): 612–15.

Szasz, A. 1994. *Ecopopulism, toxic waste and the movement for environmental justice.* Minneapolis: University of Minnesota Press.

Takaki, R. 1987. *Strangers from a different shore: Perspectives on race and ethnicity in America.* New York: Oxford University Press.

Takazato, S. 2000. Report from Okinawa: Long-term U.S. military presence and violence against women. *Canadian Women's Studies* 19(4): 42–47.

Tan, A. 1989. *The Joy Luck Club.* New York: G. P. Putnam's Sons.

Tan, C. I. 1997. Building shelter: Asian women and domestic violence. Pp. 108–17 in *Dragon ladies: Asian American feminists breathe fire,* edited by S. Shah. Boston: South End Press.

Tannen, D. 1990. *You just don't understand: Men and women in conversation.* New York: Morrow.

Taylor, A. J. 1999. High-tech, pop-a-pill culture: "New" forms of social control for Black women. Pp. 242–54 in *Dangerous intersections: Feminist perspectives on population, environment, and development,* edited by J. Silliman and Y. King. Cambridge, Mass.: South End Press.

Taueber, C. 1991. *Statistical handbook on women in America.* Phoenix: Oryx Press.

Tax, M. 1993. Five women who won't be silenced. *The Nation,* 10 May, 624–27.

Taylor, D. E. 1997. Women of color, environmental justice, and ecofeminism. Pp. 38–81 in *Ecofeminism: Women, culture, nature,* edited by K. Warren. Bloomington: Indiana University Press.

Teays, W., and L. Purdy. 2001. *Bioethics, justice, and health care.* Belmont, Calif.: Wadsworth.

Tenenbein, S. 1998. Power, beauty, and dykes. Pp. 155–60 in *Looking queer,* edited by D. Atkins. Binghampton, N.Y.: Harrington Park Press.

Tétreault, M. A. 1997. Accountability or justice? Rape as a war crime. Pp. 427–39 in *Feminist frontiers IV,* edited by L. Richardson, V. Taylor, and N. Whittier. New York: McGraw-Hill.

This Bud's for you. No, not you, her. 1991. *Business Week,* 4 November, 86.

Thomas, S., and C. Wilcox, eds. 1998. *Women and elective office: Past, present, and future.* New York: Oxford University Press.

Thompson, B. W. 1994. *A hunger so wide and so deep.* Minneapolis: University of Minnesota Press.

Thorne, B. 1997. *Gender play: Girls and boys in school.* New Brunswick, N.J.: Rutgers University Press.

Thornhill, R., and C. T. Palmer. 2000. *A natural history of rape: Biological bases of sexual coercion.* Cambridge: MIT Press.

Thropy, M. A. 1991. Overpopulation and industrialism. In *Earth First! reader,* edited by J. Davis. Salt Lake City: Peregrine Smith Books.

Tong, R. 1989. *Feminist thought: A comprehensive introduction.* Boulder, Colo.: Westview Press.

Tooher, N. L. 1999. For Mexican women, sexism is a daily battle. Pp. 38–40 in *The maquiladora reader: Cross-border organizing since NAFTA,* edited by R. Kamel and A. Hoffman. Philadelphia: American Friends Service Committee.

Torre, A. de la. 1993. Key issues in Latina health: Voicing Latina concerns in the health financing debate. In *Chicana critical issues,* edited by N. Alarcon, R. Castro, E. Perez, B. Pesquera, A. S. Riddell, and P. Zavella. Berkeley, Calif.: Third Woman Press.

Townsend, R., and A. Perkins. 1992. *Bitter fruit: Women's experiences of unplanned pregnancy, abortion, and adoption.* Alameda, Calif.: Hunter House.

Trask, H.-K. 1999. *From a native daughter: Colonialism and sovereignty in Hawai'i.* Rev. ed. Honolulu: University of Hawaii.

Troustine, J. 2001. *Shakespeare behind bars: The power of drama in a women's prison.* New York: St. Martin's Press.

Trujillo, C., ed. 1991. *Chicana lesbians: The girls our mothers warned us about.* Berkeley, Calif.: Third Women Press.

———. 1998. *Living Chicana theory.* Berkeley, Calif.: Third Women Press.

Tuana, N., ed. 1989. *Feminism and science.* Bloomington: Indiana University Press.

Tucker, C. 1996. Women's practical vote for Clinton. *Chicago Tribune,* 9 November, p. 3.

Turk, A. T. 1995. Transformation versus revolutionism and reformism: Policy implications of conflict theory. In *Crime and public policy: Putting theory to work,* edited by H. Barlow. Boulder, Colo.: Westview Press.

2 black airmen allege racial discrimination. 1996. *San Francisco Chronicle,* 4 December, p. A9.

Tyagi, S. 1996. Writing in search of a home: Geography, culture, and language in the creation of racial identity. In *Names we call home,* edited by B. Thompson and S. Tyagi. New York: Routledge.

Uchitelle, L. 2001. Lacking pensions, older divorced women remain at work. *New York Times,* 26 June, p. A1.

Umansky, L. 1996. *Motherhood reconceived: Feminism and the legacies of the sixties.* New York: New York University Press.

U.N. High Commissioner for Refugees. 2002. Refugee Women. Accessed online at http://www. worldrefugeeday.info/men2.html on 1 May 2003.

United Nations Development Program. 1999. *Human development report.* New York: Oxford University Press.

University of Minnesota. 2001. *Information about the Curriculum Transformation and Disability Project.* Accessed online at http://www.crk.umn.edu/people/services/ DisabilServ/CTAD.htm on 19 December 2002.

Unnecessary cesarean sections: Halting a national epidemic. 1992. *The Network News,* November/December, 7.

U.S. Bureau of the Census. 1996. *Statistical abstract of the United States: 1996.* 116th ed. Washington, D.C.: U.S. Bureau of the Census.

———. 1998. *Vital statistics of the United States.* Washington, D.C.: U.S. Bureau of the Census.

———. 1999a. *Health insurance coverage 1998.* Washington, D.C.: U.S. Bureau of the Census.

———. 1999b. *Current population reports. Series P-60.* Washington, D.C.: U.S. Bureau of the Census.

———. 2002. *Current population survey,* March 2002. Washington, D.C.: U.S. Bureau of the Census. Table PINC-03.

U.S. Department of Commerce News. 2001. *U.S. adults postponing marriage, Census Bureau reports.* Washington, D.C.: U.S. Department of Commerce. Accessed online at http://www.census.gov/Press-Release/ www/2001/cb01-113.html on 16 December 2002.

U.S. Department of Defense. 1992. *Department of Defense worldwide list of military installations (major, minor, and support).* Washington, D.C.: U.S. Department of Defense.

———. 1996. *FY 1990–96 spouse and child maltreatment.* Washington, D.C.: U.S. Department of Defense.

———. 2000. *Women in the military.* Washington, D.C.: U.S. Department of Defense.

U.S. Department of Health and Human Services. 1996. *Health, United States 1995. Chartbook: Women's health.* Washington, D.C.: U.S. Department of Health and Human Services.

U.S. Department of Justice. 1994. *Family violence.* Washington, D.C.: Bureau of Justice Statistics.

———. 1997. *Violence-related injuries treated in hospital emergency departments.* Michael R. Rand. Washington, D.C.: Bureau of Justice Statistics.

———. 1998. *Criminal victimization 1997: Changes 1996–97 with trends 1993–97.* Washington, D.C.: U.S. Department of Justice.

———. 2000. *Extent, nature, and consequences of intimate partner violence: Findings from the National Violence against Women Survey.* Washington, D.C.: U.S. Department of Justice.

———. 2002. *Nation's violent crime victimization rate falls 10 percent* (No. 202/307-0703). Washington, D.C.: U.S. Department of Justice. Accessed online at http:// www.ojp.usdoj.gov/bjs/pub/press/cv01pr.htm on 1 May 2003.

U.S. Department of Labor. 1993. *Facts on working women* (No. 93-2). Washington, D.C.: U.S. Department of Labor.

U.S. Department of Labor, Bureau of Labor Statistics. 1999. *Employment and earnings.* Washington, D.C.: U.S. Department of Labor.

U.S. Department of Labor, Women's Bureau. 1996. *Facts on working women. Domestic violence: A workplace issue.* Washington, D.C.: U.S. Department of Labor.

———. 1997. *First national working women's summit, June 5, 1997, Washington, D.C.* Accessed online at http://www. dol.gov/dol/wb/welcome.htm.

———. 1999. *Facts on working women.* Washington, D.C.: U.S. Department of Labor.

———. 2002. *How many people with disabilities are there in the United States?* Washington, D.C.: U.S. Department of Labor. Accessed online at http://www.dol.gov/odep/faqs/people.htm on 22 November 2002.

U.S. Immigration and Naturalization Service. 1996. *Immigration to the United States in fiscal year 1995.* Washington, D.C.: U.S. Immigration and Naturalization Service.

Usdansky, M. L. 1996. Single motherhood: Stereotypes vs. statistics. *New York Times,* 11 February, p. E4.

Ussher, J. 1991. *Women's madness.* Hemel Hempstead, England: Harvester Wheatsheaf.

Vance, C., ed. 1984. *Pleasure and danger: Exploring female sexuality.* Boston: Routledge and Kegan Paul.

Van Every, J. 1995. *Heterosexual women changing the family: Refusing to be a "wife"!* Bristol, Pa.: Taylor and Francis.

Ventura, S. J., J. A. Martin, S. C. Curtin, and T. J. Mathews. 1999. Births: Final data for 1997. *National Vital Statistics Reports,* vol. 47, no. 18. Hyattsville, Md.: National Center for Health Statistics.

Ventura, S. J., W. D. Mosher, S. C. Curtin, J. C. Abma, and S. Henshaw. 2000. Highlights of trends in pregnancies and pregnancy rates by outcome: Estimates for the United States, 1976–96. *National Vital Statistics Reports,* vol. 47, no. 29. Hyattsville, Md.: National Center for Health Statistics.

Wade-Gayles, G. 1993. *Pushed back to strength: A Black woman's journey home.* Boston: Beacon Press.

Waldman, A. 1997. Labor's new face: Women renegotiate their role. *The Nation,* 22 September, 11–15.

Walker, J. 1996. The prison industrial complex. *RESIST Newsletter* 5(9): 4–6.

Walker, L. 1979. *The battered woman.* New York: Harper & Row.

———. 1984. *The battered woman syndrome.* New York: Springer.

Walker, M. 1992. Sex attacks "rife" on U.S. servicewomen. *London Guardian,* 2 July, p. 6.

Walker, M. U. 1999. *Mother time: Women, aging and ethics.* Lanham, Md.: Rowman and Littlefield.

Walker, R. 1995. *To be real: Telling the truth and changing the face of feminism.* New York: Anchor/Doubleday.

———. 2001. *Black, white, and Jewish: Autobiography of a shifting self.* New York: Riverhead Books.

Walters, B., and H. Downs. 1996. *20/20,* November 15. New York: American Broadcasting Company.

Waring, M. 1988. *If women counted: A new feminist economics.* New York: Harper & Row.

Warner, S. B. 1987. *To dwell is to garden: A history of Boston's community gardens.* Boston: Northeastern University Press.

War Resisters League. 2002. *Where your income tax money really goes.* War Resisters League, 339 Lafayette St., New York, NY 10012.

———. 2001. *Where your income tax money really goes.* New York: War Resisters League.

Washburn, P. 1993. Women and the peace movement. Pp. 135–48 in *Women and the use of military force,* edited by R. Howes and M. Stevenson. Boulder, Colo.: Lynne Rienner Publishers.

Wasserman, C. 1992. FMS: The backlash against survivors. *Sojourner: The Women's Forum,* November, 18–20.

Watterson, K. 1996. *Women in prison.* Rev. ed. Boston: Northeastern University Press.

Webber, W. S. 1993. *Lesbians in the military speak out.* Northboro, Mass.: Madwoman Press.

Weedon, C. 1987. *Feminist practice and poststructuralist theory.* New York: Blackwell.

Weinstein, L., and C. White, eds. 1997. *Wives and warriors: Women and the military in the United States and Canada.* Westport, Conn.: Greenwood Press.

Weise, E. R., ed. 1992. *Closer to home: Bisexuality and feminism.* Seattle, Wash.: Seal Press.

Wells, J., ed. 2000. *Home fronts: Controversies in nontraditional parenting.* New York: Alyson Books.

Wendell, S. 1992. Toward a feminist theory of disability. Pp. 63–81 in *Feminist perspectives in medical ethics,* edited by H. B. Holmes and L. M. Purdy. Bloomington: Indiana University Press.

West, G., and R. L. Blumberg, eds. 1990. *Women and social protest.* New York: Oxford University Press.

White, E. 1991. Unhealthy appetites: Large is lovely, unless you're unhappy overeating and unable to lose weight. *Essence,* September, 28.

White, E. C. 1985. *Chain, chain, change: For Black women dealing with physical and emotional abuse.* Seattle, Wash.: Seal Press.

———, ed. 1990. *The Black women's health book: Speaking for ourselves.* Seattle, Wash.: Seal Press.

White, L. 1988. *The obsidian mirror: An adult healing from incest.* Seattle, Wash.: Seal Press.

Wider Opportunities for Women. 1989. *Women, work, and childcare.* Washington, D.C.: Wider Opportunities for Women.

Wilchins, R. A. 1997. *Read my lips: Sexual subversion and the end of gender.* Ithaca, N.Y.: Firebrand.

Williams, J. 2000. *Unbending gender: Why family and work conflict and what to do about it.* New York: Oxford University Press.

Williams, L., ed. 1997. *Gender equity and the World Bank group: A post-Beijing assessment.* Washington, D.C.: Women's Eyes on the World Bank-U.S.

Williams, T. T. 1992. *Refuge: An unnatural history of family and place.* New York: Vintage.

Wilson, M. 1993. *Crossing the boundary: Black women survive incest.* Seattle, Wash.: Seal Press.

Will the new corporations rule the new world order? 1992. *World Citizen News,* March, 9.

Wingspan Domestic Violence Project. 1998. *Abuse and violence in same-gender relationships: A resource for lesbian, gay, bi, and transgendered communities.* Tucson, Ariz.: Wingspan Domestic Violence Project.

Withorn, A. 1999. Temp work: "A devil's bargain" for women. *Sojourner: The Women's Forum,* October, 9.

Wittig, M. 1992. *The straight mind and other essays.* Boston: Beacon Press.

Wolf, N. 1991. *The beauty myth.* New York: Doubleday.

———. 1993. *Fire with fire: The new female power and how it will change the 21st century.* New York: Random House.

Women harassed at Naval Academy. 1990. *Rocky Mountain News,* 10 October, p. 35.

Women of Color Resource Center. 1996, December. Solicitation letter to donors. Berkeley, Calif.: Women of Color Resource Center.

Women's Environment and Development Organization (WEDO). 1998. *Mapping progress: Assessing implementation of the Beijing Platform.* New York: WEDO.

———. 2002. *Women's action agenda for a healthy and peaceful planet 2015.* New York: WEDO. Available online at http://www.wedo.org.

Women's Foundation. 2002. *Failing to make ends meet: The economic status of women in California.* San Francisco: The Women's Foundation.

Women's Research and Education Institute. 2002. *Women in the military.* Washington, D.C.: WREI. Accessed online at http://www.wrei.org/projects/wiu/wim/index.htm on 3 January 2003.

Women Working for a Nuclear Free and Independent Pacific, ed. 1987. *Pacific women speak.* Oxford, England: Green Line.

Wong, L. 1995. U.N. women's conference platform for action. *Sojourner,* October, 7.

Wood, S. 1997. Blood, sweat, and shears. *Corporate Watch Features,* 22 September. San Francisco: Corporate Watch.

Woodman, S. 1997. An officer and a . . . ? *Ms.,* March/April, 19–22.

Woods, H. 2000. *Stepping up to power: The political journey of American women.* Boulder, Colo.: Westview Press.

Working Group on the WTO. 1999. *A citizens' guide to the World Trade Organization.* New York: Apex Press.

World Health Organization. 2002. *The World Health Report 2002: Reducing risks, promoting healthy life.* New York: WHO.

World March of Women in the Year 2000. www.ffq.qc.ca/marche2000/.

Worldwatch Institute. 2003. *State of the world.* Washington, D.C.: Worldwatch Institute.

Yans-McLaughlin, V., ed. 1990. *Immigration reconsidered.* New York: Oxford University Press.

Yen, M. 1989. Refusal to jail immigrant who killed wife stirs outrage. *Washington Post,* 10 April, p. A3.

Yoder, J. 1989. Women at West Point: Lessons for token women in male-dominated occupations. In *Women: A feminist perspective,* edited by J. Freeman. Mountain View, Calif.: Mayfield.

Young, I. 1980. Socialist feminism and the limits of dual systems theory. *Socialist Review,* 10(2–3): 174.

Young, M. E., M. A. Nosek, C. A. Howland, G. Chanpong, and D. H. Rintala. 1997. Prevalence of abuse of women with physical disabilities. *Archives of Physical Medicine and Rehabilitation* 78: S34–S38.

Young, W. A. 1997. Women and immigration. Unpublished manuscript produced for Women's Commission for Refugee Women and Children, Washington, D.C.

Yu, B. N. 1990. Voices of hope and anger: Women speak out for sovereignty and self-determination. *Listen Real-Loud: News of Women's Liberation Worldwide* 10(1–2): 20. Philadelphia: Nationwide Women's Program, American Friends Service Committee.

Zambrano, M. Z. 1985. *Mejor sola que mal accompaña: For the Latina in an abusive relationship.* Seattle, Wash.: Seal Press.

Zamora-Olib, O. A., ed. 2000. *Inheritors of the earth: The human face of the U.S. military contamination at Clarke Air Base, Pampanga, Philippines.* Quezon City, Philippines: People's Task Force for Bases Cleanup.

Zaretsky, E. 1976. *Capitalism, the family, and personal life.* New York: Harper & Row.

Zavella, P. 1987. *Women's work and Chicano families: Cannery workers of the Santa Clara Valley.* Ithaca, N.Y.: Cornell University.

Zeff, R., M. Love, and K. Stults, eds. 1989. *Empowering ourselves: Women and toxics organizing.* Falls Church, Va.: Citizens Clearinghouse for Hazardous Wastes.

Zepernick, M. 1998a. The sovereign people are stirring. *The Cape Cod Times,* 27 November, p. A15.

———. 1998b. A lesson in democracy. *The Cape Cod Times,* 11 December, p. A15.

Zinn, H. 1995. *People's history of the United States: 1492–present.* Rev. and updated ed. New York: HarperPerennial.

Zita, J., ed. 1997. Special issue: Third wave feminisms. *Hypatia: A Journal of Feminist Philosophy,* vol. 12, no. 3 (summer).

Credits

Readings and Text Credits

ACLU OF ILLINOIS, "ACLU of Illinois Challenges Ethnic and Religious Bias in Strip Search of Muslim Woman at O'Hare International Airport," January 16, 2002. Reprinted by permission of ACLU.

DOROTHY ALLISON, "A Question of Class" from *Sisters, Sexperts, and Queers* by Arlene Stein, copyright © 1993 by Arlene Stein. Used by permission of Dutton Signet, a division of Penguin Putnam Inc.

TERESA AMOTT AND JULIE MATTHAEI, "The Transformation of Women's Wage Work" from *Race, Gender and Work*, pp. 317–354. Reprinted by permission of South End Press.

RITA ARDITTI AND TATIANA SCHREIBER, "Breast Cancer: The Environmental Connection—a 1998 Update" reprinted with permission from the *Resist Newsletter*, May/June 1992, published by Resist, Inc., 259 Elm St., Somerville, MA 02144. *Resist* has been funding social change since 1967. Copyright © 1998 Rita Arditti and Tatiana Schreiber.

GRACE CAROLINE BRIDGES, "Lisa's Ritual, Age 10" from *Resourceful Woman*, edited by Shawn Brennan, Julie Winklepleck, and G. MacNee. Copyright © 1994. Reprinted by permission of Visible Ink Press.

MARILYN BUCK, "To the Woman Standing Behind Me in Line Who Asks Me How Long This Black History Month Is Going to Last." Reprinted with permission from the author.

CHARLOTTE BUNCH, "Whose Security?" reprinted with permission from the September 23, 2002, issue of *The Nation*.

GRACE CHANG, "The Global Trade in Filipina Workers" from *Dragon Ladies*, pp. 132–151. Boston: South End Press. Reprinted by permission of the author.

ABRA FORTUNE CHERNIK, "The Body Politic" from *Listen Up: Voices from the Next Feminist Generation*, edited by Barbara Findlen and published by Seal Press, Seattle, WA. Copyright © 1995 by Barbara Findlen. Used with permission of the publisher.

SANDRA CISNEROS, "Guadalupe the Sex Goddess." Copyright © 1996 by Sandra Cisneros. From *Goddess of the Americas/La Diosa de Las Americas: Writings on the Virgin de Guadalupe*, edited by Ana Castillo. Copyright © 1996 by Ana Castillo. Riverhead Books, New York. Reprinted by permission of Susan Bergholz Literacy Services, New York. All rights reserved.

JUDITH ORTIZ COFER, "The Story of My Body" from *The Latin Deli: Prose and Poetry*. Copyright © 1993 by Judith Ortiz Cofer. Used by permission of University of Georgia Press.

CYNTHIA COHEN, "Common Threads: Life Stories and the Arts in Educating for Social Change" from *NWSA Journal*, Vol. 6, No. 2. Reprinted by permission of the author.

COMBAHEE RIVER COLLECTIVE, "A Black Feminist Statement" from *The Combahee River Collective Statement* in *Home Girls: A Black Feminist Anthology*. Copyright © 1983 by Barbara Smith. Reprinted by permission of the author and of Kitchen Table: Women of Color Press, P.O. Box 40-4920, Brooklyn, NY 11240-4920.

DAVID CROTEAU AND WILLIAM HOYNES, "Media and Ideology (excerpt)" from *Media/Society*, pp. 163–195. Copyright © 1997. Reprinted by permission of Pine Forge Press.

FREDERICA Y. DALY, "Perspectives of Native American Women on Race and Gender" from *Challenging Racism & Sexism: Alternatives to Genetic Explanations*, copyright © 1994 by Ethel Tobach and Betty Rosoff, by permission of the Feminist Press at the City University of New York, www.feministpress.org.

ANNETTE DULA, "The Life and Death of Miss Mildred: An Elderly Black Woman" from *Clinics in Geriatric Medicine*, Vol. 10, No. 3, pp. 419–430. Copyright © 1994. Reprinted by permission from Elsevier Science.

CYNTHIA ENLOE, "Sneak Attack: The Militarization of U.S. Culture" from *Ms. Magazine*, December/January 2002. Reprinted by permission of *Ms. Magazine*, © 2002.

EVE ENSLER, "My Vagina Was My Village" from *The Vagina Monologues*, copyright © 1998 by Eve Ensler; foreword copyright © 1998 by Gloria Steinem. Used by permission of Villard Books, a division of Random House, Inc.

LESLIE FEINBERG, "We Are All Works in Progress" from *Trans Liberation*. Copyright © 1998 by Leslie Feinberg. Reprinted by permission of Beacon Press, Boston.

ANGHARAD N. VALDIVIA, "A Latina in the Land of Hollywood: Transgressive Possibilities" from *A Latina in the Land of Hollywood: Essays on Media Culture,* edited by Angharad N. Valdivia, © 2000 The Arizona Board of Regents. Reprinted by permission of the University of Arizona Press.

CHERYL MARIE WADE, "I Am Not One of the" from *Radical Teacher,* No. 47, p. 30. First published in *Sinister Wisdom* in 1987. Reprinted by permission of the author. Ms. Wade is a playwright, poet, and activist residing in Berkeley, California.

DONNA WALTON, "What's a Leg Got to Do with It?" Used with permission of the author.

MARY C. WATERS, "Optional Ethnicities: For Whites Only?" from *Origins and Destinies: Immigration, Race and Ethnicity in America,* edited by Sylvia Pedraza and Ruben G. Rumbaut. Copyright © 1996. Reprinted with permission of Wadsworth, a division of Thomson Learning: www.thomsonrights.com, fax (800) 730-2215.

NAOMI WOLF, "Radical Heterosexuality." Used with permission of the author.

WOMEN OF COLOR RESOURCE CENTER, "Ten Reasons Why Women Should Oppose the U.S. 'War on Terrorism'." Reprinted by permission.

ROBBIN LEE ZEFF, MARSHA LOVE, AND KAREN STULTS, "Empowering Ourselves: Women and Toxics Organizing" from *Empowering Ourselves: Women and Toxics Organizing,* R. L. Zeff, M. Love, and K. Stults, eds. Reprinted by permission of CCHW, Center for Health, Environment, and Justice.

Photo and Cartoon Credits

Page xxiv © Digital Vision/Fotosearch

Page 5 Courtesy of Margo Okazawa-Rey

Page 6 By Kirk in *Ms. Magazine,* September/October 1993, p. 8. Copyright © 1991 by Kirk.

Page 8 Doug Menuez/PhotoDisc/Getty Images

Page 50 © Howard Jacqueline/Corbis Sygma

Page 58 upper left: © Rick Reinhard 2000; upper right: © Rick Reinhard 1992; lower right: © Rick Reinhard 1999; lower left: © Bob Gomel, Inc./CORBIS

Page 86 © Rick Reinhard/Impact Visuals 1996

Page 110 © Brenda Prager

Page 114 © Reuters NewMedia Inc./CORBIS

Page 142 top: © Tony Mott/S.I.N./Corbis; middle: © Underwood & Underwood/CORBIS; bottom: © Philippe Petit-Mars/CORBIS

Page 146 By R. Piccolo in *Ms. Magazine,* November/December 1997, p. 5

Page 150 © Jill Posener

Page 172 © Ronnie Farley

Page 184 © Reprinted by permission of Cameron Cardow

Page 220 © Joel Benjamin/HIV/AIDS Bureau, MA Department of Public Health

Page 224 © 1991 Rick Reinhard, Impact Visuals

Page 229 Reprinted by permission of Jacky Fleming

Page 268 Courtesy of Men Stopping Violence Against Women, Atlanta, GA

Page 272 © Dave Bartruff/Corbis

Page 276 Copyright © Jennifer Berman. Reprinted by permission.

Page 281 © Barbara Seyda

Page 300 © Walter Hodges/CORBIS

Page 316 © Rick Reinhard/Impact Visuals 1993

Page 323 Copyright by Nicole Hollander

Page 341 © Owen Seumptewa

Page 346 By Kirk in *Ms. Magazine,* May/June 1997, p. 5. Copyright © by Kirk.

Page 370 © Reuters NewMedia Inc./Corbis

Page 372 © Michael S. Yamashita/Corbis

Page 380 From CAFRA News, March–May 1990, p. 9. Reprinted by permission.

Page 393 Herri/Mujeres en Acción

Page 412 © Corbis

Page 450 © Charles Bennett/AP Photos/Wide World

Page 452 © Gary C. Knapp/AP Photos/Wide World

Page 465 Cartoons by bulbul. www.bulbul.com, P.O. Box 4100, Mountain View, CA 94040. Reprinted by permission.

Page 476 Courtesy of the War Resister's League

Page 490 © Peter Beck/Corbis

Page 496 © Jim Cummins/Corbis

Page 520 © Bettmann/Corbis

Page 524 Reprinted by permission of Jacky Fleming

Page 566 By Yang in *Ms. Magazine,* January/February 1993, p. 30

Page 578 © Attar Maher/Corbis Sygma

Page 581 From *Funny Girls* by Diane Atkinson, London: Penguin Books, 1997.

Name Index

Hansen, C., 459
Harman, B., 225
Harne, L., 14
Harris, J., 115
Hartmann, B., 495
Hartmann, H., 13, 283, 330
Hartsock, N., 17
Harvey, E., 278
Havemann, J., 328
Hayden, D., 278
Hays, S., 278
Healey, S., 182
Heise, L., 225, 226, 228, 238
Hemmings, C., 150
Henderson, H., 497
Hennessy, R., 13
Herman, J., 232, 234, 236
Hess, E., 144
Hesse-Biber, S. J., 118
Hetherington, E. M., 279
Heywood, L., 15
High, G., 457
Hill, J. B., 493
Hite, S., 145, 275
Hochschild, A. R., 322, 323
Hoffman, A., 372, 492
Hofrichter, R., 495
Holmes, S. A., 383, 384
Hom, A. Y., 150
hooks, b., 7, 14, 119, 144, 180, 227, 233, 234, 280
Howe, F., 2
Howey, N., 281
Hoynes, W., 18
Hser, Y., 417
Hua, V., 321
Hubbard, R., 11, 12, 178
Hunter, N., 148
Hutchins, L., 147
Hynes, H. P., 493
Hynes, P., 496

Inciardi, J., 417
Ingraham, C., 13, 274, 275
Inniss, L. B., 454
Ireland, M. S., 278
Isakson, E., 454

Jacob, K., 176
Jacobs, G., 144
Jacobs, R. H., 115
Jaffe, C., 175
Jaggar, A. M., 146, 148, 176, 283, 330
Jaimes, A., 177
James, S., 283, 330
Jetter, A., 278, 283
Johnson, A. G., 7, 113
Johnson, M. L., 150
Johnson, P., 115
Jones, A., 228, 236
Jones, J., 329

Jong, E., 4

Kaahumanu, L., 147
Kadi, J., 14
Kamel, R., 372, 492
Kaminer, W., 145
Kaplan, L., 175
Kaplan, T., 496
Katz, J. N., 147
Katzenstein, M. F., 455
Katz Rothman, B., 178
Kaysen, S., 182
Kellogg, S., 279
Kelly, J., 279
Kerbel, S., 421
Kerr, J., 12, 238
Kessler-Harris, A., 329
Kich, G. K., 62
Kiernan, D., 529
Kilbourne, J., 114
Kimmel, M., 7, 233
Kimmel, M. S., 7
King, Y., 15, 116, 465, 493, 495, 532
Kirk, G., 461, 464, 465
Klein, R., 14, 178
Klein, R. D., 178
Kline, C. B., 278
Koedt, A., 14
Kohl, H., 10
Komesaroff, P., 178
Koppelman, S., 225, 236
Kornbluh, J., 325
Koss, M. P., 230, 236
Krauss, C., 497
Krieger, N., 180, 185
Kroll, M. A., 414, 423
Krueger, V., 173, 497
Kurz, D., 277

Ladd-Taylor, M., 278
LaDuke, W., 492, 495, 496
Lahey, K., 422
Lakof, R. T., 112, 119
Lancaster, R. N., 143, 148, 149
Larkin, J., 229
Lasch, C., 280
Lavendar, B., 278
Lazarre, J., 283
Lee, C., 495
Lefkowitz, B., 233
Lehrman, K., 4
Leidholdt, D., 148
Leonard, A., 386
Lerman, H., 181
Lerner, S., 184
Le Sueur, M., 115
Levine, E., 14
Lichtenstein, A. C., 414, 423
Lieberman, T., 328
Light, J., 237, 423
Lindsay-Poland, J., 461

Lips, H., 276
List, P. C., 493
Lobel, K., 235
Lockwood, D., 417
Lopez, A. S., 177
Lorber, J., 147, 148
Lorde, A., 14, 178, 527
Louie, M. C. Y., 325, 374
Love, M., 497
Love, S., 178
Lovejoy, M., 115, 119, 180
Lowy, J., 281
Lublin, N., 178
Luebke, B. F., 1
Lunneborg, P., 174
Lusane, C., 383, 419
Lydersen, K., 416, 417

Macdonald, B., 115
MacKinnon, C., 15, 16, 237
MacNee, G., 284
Maher, F. A., 17
Mahoney, M., 234, 235
Mainardi, P., 323
Mairs, N., 113, 178
Males, M., 177
Mallik, A., 325
Manlowe, J. L., 180
Mann, C. R., 418
Markandya, A., 497
Martin, H., 179
Martinez, L. A., 237
Mason, M., 321
Mason, M. A., 284
Matthaei, J., 318, 329
McCarthy, C., 64
McDonald, H., 144
McGinn, M., 384
McIntosh, P., 3, 6
McKenna, T., 457
Mello, F. V., 495
Mellor, M., 498
Merchant, C., 494
Messer, M., 233
Messer-Davidow, E., 525
Messerschmidt, J. W., 422
Messner, M., 233
Meyers, D. T., 278
Mies, M., 495, 497
Milkman, R., 325
Miller, E., 14
Miller, P., 175
Miller, V. D., 495
Millett, K., 182
Minden, S., 178
Mink, G., 328
Mintz, S., 279
Mitchell, J., 283
Miya-Jervis, L., 275
Mizuta, T., 13
Mohai, P., 492

Index

About the Authors

Gwyn Kirk (left) has taught women's studies and sociology courses at a range of U.S. academic institutions, including Antioch College where she chaired the women's studies program (1992–95). She held the Jane Watson Irwin Chair in Women's Studies at Hamilton College (1999–2001), a joint appointment with Margo Okazawa-Rey. She received a Rockefeller Fellowship at the University of Hawai'i (2002) and was a Visiting Scholar at Mills College, 2002–2003. Gwyn Kirk is a long-time peace activist and divides her time between teaching, research, writing, and organizing. She is a founding member of the East Asia-US-Puerto Rico Women's Network Against Militarism, started in 1997 by an international group of academics and activists concerned about the negative effects of U.S. military bases, budgets, and operations on local communities, especially on women, children, and the environment. She co-authored *Greenham Women Everywhere: Dreams, Ideas and Actions from the Women's Peace Movement* with Alice Cook (South End Press, 1983). Gwyn Kirk holds a Ph.D. in political sociology from the London School of Economics.

Margo Okazawa-Rey (right) is currently director of the Women's Leadership Institute and Visiting Professor of Women's Studies at Mills College. Before going to Mills, she was professor of social work at San Francisco State University School of Social Work. She works in university, public school, and community settings to address issues related to the lives of women of color and their communities through activist scholarship, education, and political organizing. Current research and activism examine interconnections between militarism and globalization of the economy and their effects on women. Margo Okazawa-Rey was a Fulbright Scholar in Korea (1994), has served on editorial boards of several academic journals, and has worked with grassroots organizing groups in Boston and the San Francisco Bay Area. She has been a consultant to multicultural curricular revision and faculty development projects at colleges and universities around the country. She co-edited *The Encyclopedia of African American Education* with Faustine Jones-Wilson, Charles Asbury, D. Kamili Anderson, Sylvia Jacobs, and Michael Fultz (Greenwood, 1996), and *Beyond Heroes and Holidays: A Practical Guide to K–12 Anti-racist, Multicultural Education and Staff Development* with Enid Lee and Deborah Menkart (Teaching for Change, 1998). Margo Okazawa-Rey was one of the founding members of the Combahee River Collective and of the East Asia-US-Puerto Rico Women's Network Against Militarism. She holds an Ed.D. from Harvard Graduate School of Education.